W9-AEA-637

Soviet Union
a country study

Federal Research Division
Library of Congress
Edited by
Raymond E. Zickel
Research Completed
May 1989

On the cover: Spasskaia (Savior) Tower and the Kremlin Wall
with St. Basil Cathedral on the right and the Council of
Ministers building in the background

Second Edition, First Printing, 1991.

Library of Congress Cataloging-in-Publication Data

Soviet Union : a country study / Federal Research Division, Library
of Congress ; edited by Raymond E. Zickel. — 2nd ed.
    p.   cm. — (Area handbook series, ISSN 1057-5294)
(DA pam ; 550-95)
    "Supersedes the 1971 edition of Area handbook for the Soviet
Union written by Eugene K. Keefe, et al."—T.p. verso.
    "Research completed May 1989."
    Includes bibliographical references (pp. 895-977) and index.
    ISBN 0-8444-0727-5
    1. Soviet Union. I. Zickel, Raymond E., 1934- . II. Library
of Congress. Federal Research Division. III. Area handbook for
the Soviet Union. IV. Series. V. Series: DA pam ; 550-95.
DK17.S6396   1991   90-25756
947—dc20   CIP

Headquarters, Department of the Army
DA Pam 550-95

For sale by the Superintendent of Documents, U.S. Government Printing Office
Washington, D.C. 20402

Foreword

This volume is one in a continuing series of books prepared by the Federal Research Division of the Library of Congress under the Country Studies—Area Handbook Program sponsored by the Department of the Army. The last page of this book lists the other published studies.

Most books in the series deal with a particular foreign country, describing and analyzing its political, economic, social, and national security systems and institutions, and examining the interrelationships of those systems and the ways they are shaped by cultural factors. Each study is written by a multidisciplinary team of social scientists. The authors seek to provide a basic understanding of the observed society, striving for a dynamic rather than a static portrayal. Particular attention is devoted to the people who make up the society, their origins, dominant beliefs and values, their common interests and the issues on which they are divided, the nature and extent of their involvement with national institutions, and their attitudes toward each other and toward their social system and political order.

The books represent the analysis of the authors and should not be construed as an expression of an official United States government position, policy, or decision. The authors have sought to adhere to accepted standards of scholarly objectivity. Corrections, additions, and suggestions for changes from readers will be welcomed for use in future editions.

Louis R. Mortimer
Chief
Federal Research Division
Library of Congress
Washington, D.C. 20540

Acknowledgments

The authors wish to acknowledge the contributions that numerous persons made to the preparation of *Soviet Union: A Country Study*. Many past and present members of the Federal Research Division contributed to the preparation of the manuscript. Richard F. Nyrop furnished expert guidance on the composition and writing of the book and reviewed drafts of all the chapters. Sandra W. Meditz reviewed portions of the text and graphics and served as liaison with Ralph K. Benesch, who oversees the Country Studies—Area Handbook Program for the Department of the Army. Stephen R. Burant deserves special thanks because, after writing one chapter and coauthoring another, he provided substantive editing and rewriting of several other chapters. Special thanks are also due Helen R. Fedor, who reviewed bibliographies, regularized spellings, and prepared the Glossary, which was initially compiled by Pamela J. Perry and subsequently added to by Ihor Y. Gawdiak and Walter R. Iwaskiw. Ihor Y. Gawdiak revised Appendix C and, together with Glenn E. Curtis, revised Appendix B. Walter R. Iwaskiw prepared the map drafts with expert guidance from Carolina E. Forrester and Susan M. Lender and coordinated the subsequent work on the maps. The late Anthony S. Beliajeff prepared the Chronology. Sara C. Arason compiled the charts and tables from the authors' data and provided other assistance. Carol A. Corrigan and Rosette Konick helped select and organize the photographs and wrote captions for many of them and for the illustrations. Elizabeth A. Yates typed some of the chapters from handwritten manuscripts and assisted in many other details deserving of special thanks. Invaluable graphics support was provided by David P. Cabitto, who also prepared the final maps. He was assisted by Sandra K. Ferrell and Kimberly A. Lord; the latter artist drew the cover and chapter illustrations for the book. Helen C. Metz helped write the description of Islam contained in Chapter 4, and Stanley M. Sciora furnished detailed information on the uniforms and rank insignia of the Soviet armed forces. Finally, special thanks are given to Martha E. Hopkins and Marilyn L. Majeska, who managed the book's editing, and to Andrea T. Merrill, who managed production.

The following individuals are gratefully acknowledged as well: Mimi Cantwell, Sharon Costello, Barbara Dash, Deanna D'Errico, Vince Ercolano, Barbara Harrison, Martha E. Hopkins, Patricia Molella, Ruth Nieland, Evan Raynes, Gage Ricard, Sharon Schultz, and Mary Wild for editing the chapters; Beverly Wolpert for editing the Bibliography; Barbara Edgerton and Izella Watson for word processing; Angela L. Eveges for typing the Introduction; Andrea T. Merrill for performing the final prepublication editorial review; Joan C. Cook for preparing the index; and Malinda B. Neale of the Printing and Processing Section, Library of Congress, for phototypesetting, under the direction of Peggy Pixley.

The authors also wish to note the significant contributions of persons not on the staff of the Federal Research Division. Jimmy Pritchard furnished the vast majority of the photographs used in this volume, including some taken expressly for the study. David M. Goldfrank wrote the portion of Chapter 1 that deals with Russian history from 1855 to 1917 and reviewed all of Chapter 1 and Chapter 2. Paul Goble provided commentary on Soviet nationalities, and Graham Vernon reviewed Chapter 17 and Chapter 18.

Contents

	Page
Foreword	iii
Acknowledgments	v
Preface	xxiii
Country Profile	xlv
Introduction	lvii

Chapter 1. Historical Setting: Early History
to 1917 1
Zenon E. Kohut and David M. Goldfrank

EMERGENCE OF THE EAST SLAVS	4
The Peoples of the East European Plain	5
The East Slavs and the Varangians	5
The Golden Age of Kiev	6
The Rise of Regional Centers	8
The Mongol Invasion	9
MUSCOVY	10
The Rise of Muscovy	12
The Evolution of Russian Autocracy	12
Ivan IV	13
The Time of Troubles	14
The Romanovs	15
Expansion and Westernization	18
EARLY IMPERIAL RUSSIA	19
Peter the Great and the Formation of the Russian Empire	20
Era of Palace Revolutions	22
Imperial Expansion and Maturation: Catherine II	24
RULING THE EMPIRE	27
War and Peace, 1796–1825	27
Period of Reaction: Nicholas I, 1825–55	30
THE TRANSFORMATION OF IMPERIAL RUSSIA	32
Economic Developments	33
Reforms and Their Limits, 1855–92	33
Foreign Affairs after the Crimean War, 1856–93	36
The Age of Realism in Literature	38

The Rise of Revolutionary Populism and
  Russian Marxism, 1855–90 40
Serge Witte and Accelerated Industrialization,
  1891–1903 41
The Development of Radical Political Parties,
  1892–1904 42
Imperialism in Asia and the Russo-Japanese
  War, 1894–1905 44
THE LAST YEARS OF TSARDOM 45
The Revolution of 1905 and Counterrevolution,
  1905–07 45
The Tenuous Regimes of Stolypin and Kokovstev,
  1907–14 46
The Return to an Active Balkan Policy, 1906–13 48
Russia at War, 1914–16 49
The Strains of the War Effort and the Weakening
  of Tsarism 50

Chapter 2. Historical Setting: 1917 to 1982 53
Thomas Skallerup

REVOLUTIONS AND CIVIL WAR 56
The February Revolution 56
The Period of Dual Power 57
The Bolshevik Revolution 59
Civil War and War Communism 61
THE ERA OF THE NEW ECONOMIC POLICY 64
Lenin's Leadership 64
Stalin's Rise to Power 66
Foreign Policy, 1921–28 66
Society and Culture in the 1920s 67
TRANSFORMATION AND TERROR 68
Industrialization and Collectivization 68
The Period of the Purges 70
Mobilization of Society 71
Foreign Policy, 1928–39 72
WAR YEARS 73
Prelude to War 73
The Great Patriotic War 74
RECONSTRUCTION AND COLD WAR 77
Reconstruction Years 77
The Cold War 78
Death of Stalin 81
THE KHRUSHCHEV ERA 82
Collective Leadership and the Rise of Khrushchev ... 82
Foreign Policy under Khrushchev 85

Khrushchev's Reforms and Fall 87
THE BREZHNEV ERA 88
   Collective Leadership and the Rise of Brezhnev 88
   Foreign Policy of a Superpower 90
   The Economy 92
   Culture and the Arts 93
   Death of Brezhnev 94

Chapter 3. Physical Environment and Population

Chapter 3. Physical Environment and
Population 97

David E. McClave

PHYSICAL ENVIRONMENT 100
   Global Position and Boundaries 101
   Administrative-Political-Territorial Divisions 102
   Topography and Drainage 104
   Climate 109
   Natural Resources 112
   Environmental Concerns 113
POPULATION 115
   Vital Statistics 116
   Age and Sex Structure 119
   Mortality and Fertility 120
   Urbanization 121
   Migration 122
   Distribution and Density 124
   Marriage, Divorce, and the Family 125
   Population Problems and Policies 127

Chapter 4. Nationalities and Religions

Chapter 4. Nationalities and Religions 133

Ihor Y. Gawdiak

NATIONALITIES OF THE SOVIET UNION 137
   Slavic Nationalities 138
   Baltic Nationalities 146
   Nationalities of the Caucasus 152
   Central Asian Nationalities 159
   Other Major Nationalities 173
RELIGIOUS GROUPS IN THE SOVIET UNION 184
   Orthodox 184
   Armenian Apostolic 189
   Catholic 189
   Protestant 191
   Muslim 191
POLICY TOWARD NATIONALITIES AND RELIGIONS
   IN PRACTICE 195

MANIFESTATIONS OF NATIONAL
  ASSERTIVENESS 201
    Baltic Nationalities 201
    Armenians 202
    Ukrainians 202
    Central Asian Nationalities 204
    Russians 205
    Other Nationalities 205

Chapter 5. Social Structure 209
                    Kenneth E. Nyirady

FORMATION OF SOVIET SOCIETY 212
STRATIFICATION OF SOVIET SOCIETY 215
    Socio-Occupational Groupings 216
    Other Determinants of Social Position 217
    Benefits of Social Position 219
    Urban-Rural Cleavage 224
SOCIAL MOBILITY 227
SOCIAL ORGANIZATIONS 228
    Trade Unions 228
    Youth Organizations 229
    Sports Organizations 230
GENDER AND FAMILY ROLES 230
    Role of Women 230
    Male-Female Relationships 231
    The Soviet Family 234

Chapter 6. Education, Health, and Welfare 241
                    Irene M. Steckler

EDUCATION 244
    Philosophy and Aims 245
    Control and Administration 247
    Pedagogy and Planning 248
    Institutions of Learning 250
    Quality, Reform, and Funding 261
HEALTH CARE 262
    Provision of Medical Care 263
    Declining Health Care in the 1970s and 1980s 269
WELFARE 274
    Pension System 274
    Workers' Compensation 276
    Other Assistance 276

Chapter 7. The Communist Party 279
Stephen R. Burant

LENIN'S CONCEPTION OF THE PARTY 282
    Theoretical Underpinnings 283
    Democratic Centralism 284
PARTY LEGITIMACY 288
CENTRAL PARTY INSTITUTIONS 292
    Party Congress 293
    Party Conference 295
    Central Committee 296
    Central Auditing Commission 298
    Party Control Committee 298
    Politburo 298
    Secretariat 300
    Commissions 301
    General Secretary: Power and Authority 302
INTERMEDIATE-LEVEL PARTY ORGANIZATIONS 306
    Republic Party Organization 306
    Oblast-Level Organization 308
    District- and City-Level Organization 310
PRIMARY PARTY ORGANIZATION 312
NOMENKLATURA 313
    The Party's Appointment Authority 314
    Patron-Client Relations 315
PARTY MEMBERSHIP 316
    Selection Procedures 317
    Training 320
SOCIAL COMPOSITION OF THE PARTY 322

Chapter 8. Government Structure and Functions 327
Barry A. Zulauf, Stephen R. Burant, and James P. Nichol

CONSTITUTIONAL AUTHORITY OF
GOVERNMENT 331
    Early Soviet Constitutions 332
    The 1977 Constitution 333
CENTRAL GOVERNMENT 340
    Administrative Organs 341
    Congress of People's Deputies 346
    Supreme Soviet 350
    Control Organs 358

TERRITORIAL ADMINISTRATION 361
 Republic Level 362
 Provincial and District Levels 364
ELECTIONS 365

Chapter 9. Mass Media and the Arts 367
        Joshua Spero

POLITICIZATION OF THE MASS MEDIA AND
 THE ARTS 370
 Leninist Principles 371
 Socialist Realism 372
ADMINISTRATION OF THE MASS MEDIA AND
 THE ARTS 373
 The Party Role 373
 The Government Role 374
THE MASS MEDIA 377
 Newspapers 377
 Magazines and Journals 381
 Radio 382
 Television and Video Cassette Recorders 382
 Computers 384
THE ARTS 385
 Literature 388
 Cinema 390
 Theater 393
 Music 394
 Painting, Sculpture, and the Graphic Arts 396

Chapter 10. Foreign Policy 399
        James P. Nichol

IDEOLOGY AND OBJECTIVES 401
FOREIGN POLICY MAKING AND EXECUTION 403
 The Foreign Policy Makers 403
 Departments of the Central Committee 404
 Higher State and Government Organizations 407
 The Congress of People's Deputies and the
  Supreme Soviet 408
 The Council of Ministers and Its Presidium 408
 The Ministry of Foreign Affairs 409
INSTRUMENTS OF INFLUENCE 410
 Diplomatic Relations 410
 Party and State Visits Abroad 413
 Friendship and Cooperation Treaties 413
 Communist Parties Abroad 414

SOVIET-UNITED STATES RELATIONS 415
SOVIET-WEST EUROPEAN RELATIONS 419
    France 420
    West Germany 420
    Britain 421
    Spain and Portugal 422
    Scandinavia 422
SOVIET-EAST EUROPEAN RELATIONS 423
SINO-SOVIET RELATIONS 426
SOVIET-JAPANESE RELATIONS 427
THE SOVIET UNION AND THE THIRD WORLD 428
    Middle East and North Africa 430
    Asia 433
    Sub-Saharan Africa 438
    Central America and South America 440
THE SOVIET UNION AND NUCLEAR ARMS
    CONTROL 442
THE SOVIET UNION AND THE UNITED NATIONS 445

Chapter 11. Economic Structure and Policy 449
                               Becky Gates

ECONOMIC STRUCTURE 452
    Nature of the National Economy 452
    Labor 454
    Retail and Wholesale Distribution System 456
    Financial System 457
ECONOMIC PLANNING AND CONTROL 458
    Planning Process 458
    Reforming the Planning System 465
    Tools of Control 469
ECONOMIC POLICY 471
    Past Priorities 472
    The Twelfth Five-Year Plan, 1986–90 478

Chapter 12. Industry 483
                                Glenn E. Curtis

DEVELOPMENT OF SOVIET INDUSTRY 486
INDUSTRIAL RESOURCES 487
    Raw Materials 487
    Geographic Location Factors 488
    The Territorial Production Complexes and
        Geographic Expansion 488
    The Labor Force and Perestroika 490
INDUSTRIAL ORGANIZATION 491
    The Complexes and the Ministries 491

The Industrial Planning System 492
Structural Reform of Industry 492
The Military-Industrial Complex 493
Industrial Research and Design 494
MACHINE BUILDING AND METAL WORKING 495
The Structure and Status of the Machine-Building
and Metal-Working Complex 495
The Planning and Investment Process of the
Machine-Building and Metal-Working Complex ... 496
The Location of the Machine-Building Industry 497
The Automotive Industry 497
The Electronics Industry 499
METALLURGY 499
Role of Metallurgy 500
Metallurgy Planning and Problems 500
Metallurgical Combine Locations and Major
Producers 501
Nonferrous Metals 501
CHEMICALS 502
Plastics 502
Petrochemicals 502
Other Branches of the Chemical Industry 503
Chemical Planning Goals 503
FUELS 505
Fuel Resource Base 505
Oil 505
Natural Gas 507
Coal 508
Uranium 510
POWER ENGINEERING 510
Energy Planning Goals 510
The Balance among Energy Sources 511
Obstacles to Power Supply 512
Heat and Cogeneration 512
THE CONSUMER INDUSTRY 512
Consumer Supply in the 1980s 513
The Logic and Goals of Consumer Production 514
Textiles and Wood Pulp 514

Chapter 13. Agriculture 517
Ronald D. Bachman

POLICY AND ADMINISTRATION 520
Stalin's Legacy 520
Evolution of an Integrated Food Policy 522
LAND USE 525

PRODUCTION 529
    Grain 530
    Technical Crops 532
    Forage Crops 533
    Potatoes and Vegetables 533
    Other Crops 534
    Animal Husbandry 536
    Forestry 538
    Fishing 539
    The Twelfth Five-Year Plan, 1986–90 540

Chapter 14. Transportation and
Communications 543
Boris Hlynsky

RAILROADS 546
    Historical Background, 1913–39 546
    World War II 550
    The Postwar Period, 1946–60 552
    Organization and Equipment of the Railroads 554
    Passenger Operations 556
    The Baykal-Amur Main Line 557
    Other New Construction 558
    Metropolitan Railways 561
AUTOMOTIVE TRANSPORT 561
    Development of Automotive Transport 561
    Freight Transportation by Trucks 565
    Passenger Transportation 565
INLAND WATERWAYS 566
    Development of Waterways 566
    The Waterway System 567
    River Ports and Facilities 569
    Passenger Transportation 570
MERCHANT MARINE 570
    Initial Developments 571
    Fleet Operations 572
CIVIL AVIATION 576
    Postwar Evolution of Aeroflot 579
    Aeroflot Operations 579
PIPELINES 580
COMMUNICATIONS 582

Chapter 15. Foreign Trade 589
Malinda K. Goodrich

DEVELOPMENT OF THE STATE MONOPOLY ON
FOREIGN TRADE 593

STRUCTURE OF THE FOREIGN TRADE
   BUREAUCRACY 594
     Administration 594
     Operation 595
     Structural Reforms, 1986 to Mid-1988 597
TRADE WITH SOCIALIST COUNTRIES 601
     The Council for Mutual Economic
       Assistance 601
     Yugoslavia 603
     China 604
     Cambodia, Laos, and North Korea 605
TRADE WITH WESTERN INDUSTRIALIZED
   COUNTRIES 605
     The United States 607
     Western Europe 609
     Japan 610
     Finland 611
TRADE WITH THIRD WORLD COUNTRIES 612
     Balance of Trade 612
     Composition of Trade 613
     Africa, Asia, and Latin America 615
     Countries of Socialist Orientation 616
     Trade with the Organization of Petroleum
       Exporting Countries 616
GORBACHEV'S ECONOMIC REFORMS 618

Chapter 16. Science and Technology 621
               Cathleen A. Campbell

EARLY DEVELOPMENT 624
THE ADMINISTRATION OF SCIENCE AND
   TECHNOLOGY 628
     Policy Making 628
     Planning 629
     Financing 632
SCIENCE AND IDEOLOGY 633
RESEARCH, DEVELOPMENT, AND PRODUCTION
   ORGANIZATIONS 634
SOVIET INNOVATION: PROBLEMS AND
   SOLUTIONS 637
TECHNOLOGY AND INFORMATION
   TRANSFER 642
MILITARY RESEARCH AND DEVELOPMENT 646
TRAINING 648

Chapter 17. Military Doctrine and Strategic Concerns 651
Eugenia V. Osgood

MARXIST-LENINIST THEORY OF WAR 654
    War as a Continuation of Politics 655
    Laws of War 657
THE PARTY AND MILITARY DOCTRINE AND
POLICY 659
    Evolution of Military Doctrine 660
    Military Doctrine in the Late 1980s 662
    Doctrine and Weapons Programs 664
    Military Policy of the Communist Party of the
        Soviet Union 665
MILITARY SCIENCE 666
    Laws of Armed Conflict 668
    Principles of Military Art 668
    Military Art 668
STRATEGIC MISSIONS OF THE ARMED FORCES 675
    Threat Assessments and Force Requirements 676
    Offensive and Defensive Strategic Missions 676
GLOBAL STRATEGIC CONCERNS 681
    Force Projection on the Periphery 682
    Military Presence in the Third World 684
ARMS CONTROL AND MILITARY OBJECTIVES 685
    Strategic Arms Control 686
    Objectives in Space 688
    Intermediate-Range Nuclear Forces Arms
        Control 689
    Conventional Arms Control 691

Chapter 18. Armed Forces and Defense Organization 695
Karl Wheeler Soper

ORGANIZATIONAL DEVELOPMENT AND
COMBAT EXPERIENCE 697
STRATEGIC LEADERSHIP OF THE ARMED
FORCES 700
    Defense Council 700
    Main Military Council 701
    Ministry of Defense 701
    General Staff 702
THE ARMED SERVICES 703
    Strategic Rocket Forces 703

Ground Forces 705
Air Forces 710
Air Defense Forces 712
Naval Forces 716
Airborne Troops and Special Purpose Troops 719
Rear Services 720
Civil Defense 720
Specialized and Paramilitary Forces 722
TERRITORIAL ORGANIZATION OF THE ARMED
  FORCES 723
Military Districts 725
Fleets, Flotillas, and Squadrons 727
Groups of Forces Stationed Abroad 728
THE PARTY AND THE ARMED FORCES 728
Political-Military Relations 729
Military Representation in the Party 729
Party Control in the Armed Forces 730
MILITARY ECONOMICS 733
Defense Spending 733
Military Industries and Production 734
Military Technology 735
UNIFORMS AND RANK INSIGNIA 737
MILITARY MANPOWER 739
Premilitary Training 739
Conscripts 742
Officers 748
Reserves and Wartime Mobilization 750

Chapter 19. Internal Security 753
                              Amy W. Knight

PREDECESSORS OF THE COMMITTEE FOR STATE
  SECURITY AND THE MINISTRY OF INTERNAL
  AFFAIRS 756
The Tsarist Period 756
Soviet Predecessor Organizations, 1917–54 757
THE SECURITY APPARATUS AND KREMLIN
  POLITICS 760
Khrushchev Period 760
After Khrushchev 762
Gorbachev Era 763
ORGANIZATION OF THE COMMITTEE FOR
  STATE SECURITY 765
Structure 765
Functions and Internal Organization 766

Party Control 769
Personnel 770
DOMESTIC SECURITY AND THE COMMITTEE
FOR STATE SECURITY 771
Legal Prerogatives 771
Policy 772
Special Departments in the Armed Forces 775
THE FOREIGN INTELLIGENCE ROLE OF THE
COMMITTEE FOR STATE SECURITY 776
Organization 776
Intelligence and Counterintelligence 778
Active Measures 779
Influence on Foreign Policy 780
THE MINISTRY OF INTERNAL AFFAIRS 781
Functions and Organization 782
Leadership 783
Control by the Party 785
THE MINISTRY OF INTERNAL AFFAIRS, THE
JUDICIAL ORGANS, AND NONPOLITICAL CRIME .. 786
Socialist Legality 786
The Procuracy 787
Military Justice 787
The Judiciary and the Legal Profession 787
Legal Codes and Abuses of the System 788
Nonpolitical Crime and Punishment 790
INTERNAL SECURITY TROOPS 790
Border Troops of the Committee for State
Security 791
Security Troops of the Committee for State
Security 793
Internal Troops of the Ministry of Internal
Affairs 793

Appendix A. Tables 797

Appendix B. The Council for Mutual
Economic Assistance 853
Malinda K. Goodrich

MEMBERSHIP, STRUCTURE, NATURE, AND
SCOPE 854
Membership 854
Structure 856
Nature of Operation 858

EVOLUTION 858
   Early Years 858
   Rediscovery of Comecon after Stalin's Death 859
   Rapid Growth in Comecon Activity, 1956–63 860
   Inactivity and Subsequent Revitalization in the
      Late 1960s 861
   The 1971 Comprehensive Program 861
   The 1980s 862
COOPERATION UNDER THE 1971 COMPREHENSIVE
  PROGRAM 863
   Market Relations and Instruments 864
   Cooperation in Planning 866
POWER CONFIGURATIONS WITHIN COMECON 870
   The Soviet Union and Eastern Europe 870
   Mongolia, Cuba, and Vietnam 871
   Support for Developing Countries 872
TRENDS AND PROSPECTS 872

Appendix C. The Warsaw Pact 875
                 Karl Wheeler Soper

THE SOVIET ALLIANCE SYSTEM, 1943–55 875
THE FORMATION OF THE WARSAW PACT,
  1955–70 878
   The Polish October 880
   The Hungarian Revolution 880
   A Shift Toward Greater Cohesion 881
   The Prague Spring 882
ORGANIZATION AND STRATEGY OF THE
  WARSAW PACT 884
   Political Organization 884
   Military Organization 885
   Soviet Military Strategy and the Warsaw Pact 887
THE WEAKENING OF THE ALLIANCE'S COHESION,
  1970–85 888
   Détente 888
   The End of Détente 891
THE RENEWAL OF THE ALLIANCE, 1985–89 892

Bibliography 895

Glossary 979

Index 1009

List of Figures
 1 Administrative Divisions of the Soviet Union, 1989 lvi
 2 The Principalities of Kievan Rus', 1136 6

 3 Territorial Expansion of Muscovy and the Russian Empire,
   1550–1917 16
 4 Red Army Line, March 1920 62
 5 Military Operations Against Germany, 1941–45 76
 6 Topography and Drainage 106
 7 Major Mineral Deposits 114
 8 Population Distribution by Age and Sex, 1987 120
 9 Population Density, 1981 126
10 Nationalities and Nationality Groups, 1987 136
11 Structure of the Education System, 1987 252
12 Organization of the Communist Party of the Soviet
   Union, 1988 294
13 Central Apparatus of the Communist Party of the
   Soviet Union, 1988 302
14 Soviet Foreign Relations Worldwide, 1988 406
15 Automotive and Metallurgical Production Centers in
   the Western Soviet Union, 1988 498
16 Economic Regions, 1985 504
17 Land Use, 1982 528
18 Major Railroads, 1986 560
19 Major Roads, 1981 564
20 Major Inland Waterways, 1984 568
21 Major Maritime Ports, Airports, and Sea Routes, 1986 ... 574
22 Major Petroleum Deposits and Pipelines, 1982 584
23 Foreign Trade Bureaucracy, 1988 596
24 Organization of the Ministry of Foreign Trade, 1987 598
25 Composition of Foreign Trade, Selected Years, 1960–87 ... 602
26 Soviet Military-Political Concepts, 1989 656
27 Theaters of Military Operations, 1987 674
28 Organization of the Ministry of Defense, 1988 704
29 Typical Organization of an Armed Service, 1988 706
30 Military Districts and Fleets, 1988 724
31 Organization of a Typical Military District, 1988 726
32 Apparatus of the Communist Party of the Soviet Union
   in the Armed Services, 1988 732
33 Management of Defense Production, 1988 736
34 Ranks and Insignia of Strategic Rocket Forces and
   Ground Forces, 1989 740
35 Ranks and Insignia of Air Forces and Air Defense
   Forces, 1989 741
36 Ranks and Insignia of Naval Forces, 1989 744
37 Organization of the Committee for State Security
   (KGB), 1988 768
38 Organization of the Ministry of Internal Affairs
   (MVD), 1988 784

Preface

Soviet Union: A Country Study seeks to present factual descriptions and objective interpretations of a broad range of social, political, economic, and national security aspects of the Soviet Union in the late 1980s. The authors synthesized information from books, scholarly journals, official reports of governments and international organizations, foreign and domestic newspapers, and conference reports and proceedings.

This volume supersedes the *Area Handbook for the Soviet Union,* first published in 1971. Throughout the 1970s and early 1980s, the Soviet Union was politically, economically, and socially stagnant, according to many Western observers. After Mikhail S. Gorbachev came to power in March 1985, however, unprecedented events portending substantial change began to occur. To revitalize the critically ailing economy, Gorbachev introduced *perestroika;* to alter the political power structure, he introduced *demokratizatsiia;* and to provide information needed to implement both, he introduced *glasnost'*. These three slogans represented evolving concepts rather than formal programs with specific plans and time schedules. Information about events occurring in the late 1980s came in such volume that many observers were overwhelmed. The long-range impact of the events can be realistically assessed only after careful analysis of accurate and complete data and the perspective granted with the passage of time. Meanwhile, the basic elements of the Soviet Union, such as history, geography, and social, economic, and military structures, as described in this volume, can help readers understand the events as they occur.

This volume covers the salient features of the Soviet Union in nineteen chapters that attempt to provide balanced and straightforward descriptions and analyses of the subject matter. Readers wishing to obtain more information on subjects dealt with in each chapter can refer to the bibliographic essay at the end of the chapter. A complete Bibliography at the end of the book provides additional sources of information and complete citations. A Country Profile and a Chronology are also included as reference aids. The Glossary furnishes succinct definitions of many specialized terms used in the book. Measurements are given in the metric system; a conversion table is provided to assist readers unfamiliar with metric measurements (see table 1, Appendix A).

Because confusion often arises with respect to the use of the words *socialism* and *communism,* a note of caution is in order concerning their use in this book. The Soviet Union and other countries that people in the West generally refer to as *communist* usually describe themselves as *socialist,* making the claim that they are working toward communism, which Karl Marx described as a more advanced historical stage than socialism. In this book, *socialist* and *socialism* are generally used in the sense of Union of Soviet *Socialist* Republics. Soviet *socialism* has little resemblance to the democratic socialism of some West European countries. In this book, *communism* means a doctrine based on revolutionary Marxian socialism and Marxism-Leninism, which is the official ideology of the Soviet Union.

Readers specifically interested in information on the Russian nationality and the Russian Orthodox Church should note that information on these subjects is contained in a number of chapters. Hence, to avoid redundancy, the space devoted to these subjects in the chapter on nationalities and religions (Chapter 4) is proportionately less than that devoted to other nationalities and religions. Readers are especially referred to Chapter 1, which is primarily concerned with the history of the Russian nationality and frequently refers to the Russian Orthodox Church.

Statistics derived from Soviet sources, especially those dealing with the economy and transportation, have sometimes been disputed by Western authorities. Such statistics, occasionally containing unexplained discrepancies, have been used as the only available alternative and have been identified as of Soviet origin. Population statistics used in the book were based on the 1989 census. Because, however, complete results of that census had not been released or fully analyzed at the time the book was being written, some statistics were based on the 1979 census.

Transliteration of Russian names and terms generally follows the Library of Congress transliteration system, but geographic names follow the United States Board of Geographic Names romanization system. Exceptions were made, however, if the name or term was listed in *Webster's Ninth New Collegiate Dictionary.* For example, Leon Trotsky was used instead of Lev Trotskii and Moscow instead of Moskva. Most of the Russian terms used in the book were not in Webster's and were therefore transliterated and italicized as foreign words. Hence the term for one administrative subdivision *raion* was transliterated and italicized, but the term for another subdivision, oblast, listed in Webster's was not. For most organizational names, English translations—and if needed the acronym derived therefrom—were used. If a transliterated organizational name or its acronym was considered sufficiently well known, however, it was used. For example, most readers will know that the acronym KGB stands for the Soviet secret police and to use CSS (based on Committee for State Security—a translation of the name that is transliterated Komitet gosudarstvennoi bezopasnosti) made little sense.

Table A. Chronology of Important Events

Period	Description
NINTH CENTURY	
ca. 860	Rurik, a Varangian, according to earliest chronicle of Kievan Rus', rules Novgorod and founds Rurikid Dynasty.
ca. 880	Prince Oleg, a Varangian, first historically verified ruler of Kievan Rus'.
TENTH CENTURY	
911	Prince Oleg, after attacking Constantinople, concludes treaty with Byzantine Empire favorable to Kievan Rus'.
944	Prince Igor' compelled by Constantinople to sign treaty adverse to Kievan Rus'.
ca. 955	Princess Olga, while regent of Kievan Rus', converts to Christianity.
971	Prince Sviatoslav makes peace with Byzantine Empire.
988	Prince Vladimir converts Kievan Rus' to Christianity.
ELEVENTH CENTURY	
1015	Prince Vladimir's death leads Rurikid princes into fratricidal war that continues until 1036.
1019	Prince Iaroslav (the Wise) of Novgorod assumes throne of Kievan Rus'.
1036	Prince Iaroslav the Wise ends fratricidal war and later codifies laws of Kievan Rus' into *Ruska Pravda* (Rus' Justice).
1037	Prince Iaroslav the Wise defeats Pechenegs; construction begins on St. Sofia Cathedral in Kiev.
1051	Ilarion becomes first native metropolitan of Orthodox Church in Kievan Rus'.
TWELFTH CENTURY	
1113–25	Kievan Rus' experiences revival under Grand Prince Vladimir Monomakh.
1136	Republic of Novgorod gains independence from Kievan Rus'.
1147	Moscow first mentioned in chronicles.
1156	Novgorod acquires its own archbishop.

Table A.—Continued

Period	Description
1169	Armies of Prince Andrei Bogoliubskii of Vladimir-Suzdal' sack Kiev; Andrei assumes title "Grand Prince of Kiev and all Rus'" but chooses to reside in Suzdal'.
THIRTEENTH CENTURY 1219–41	Mongols invade: Kiev falls in 1240; Novgorod and Moscow submit to Mongol "yoke" without resisting.
1242	Aleksandr Nevskii successfully defends Novgorod against Teutonic attack.
1253	Prince Daniil of Galicia-Volhynia accepts royal crown of Kievan Rus' from pope.
FOURTEENTH CENTURY 1327	Ivan, prince of Moscow, nicknamed Kalita ("Money Bags"), affirmed as "Grand Prince of Vladimir" by Mongols; Moscow becomes seat of metropolitan of Russian Orthodox Church.
1380	Dmitrii Donskoi defeats Golden Horde at Battle of Kulikovo, but Mongol domination continues until 1480.
FIFTEENTH CENTURY 1462	Ivan III becomes grand prince of Muscovy and first Muscovite ruler to use titles of tsar and "Ruler of all Rus'."
1478	Muscovy defeats Novgorod.
1485	Muscovy conquers Tver'.
SIXTEENTH CENTURY 1505	Vasilii III becomes grand prince of Muscovy.
1510	Muscovy conquers Pskov.
1533	Grand Prince Ivan IV named ruler of Muscovy at age three.
1547	Ivan IV (the Terrible or the Dread) crowned tsar of Muscovy.
1552	Ivan IV conquers Kazan' Khanate.
1556	Ivan IV conquers Astrakhan' Khanate.
1565	*Oprichnina* of Ivan IV creates a state within the state.

Period	Description
1571	Tatars raid Moscow.
1581	Ermak begins conquest of Siberia.
1584	Fedor I crowned tsar.
1589	Patriarchate of Moscow established.
1596	Union of Brest establishes Uniate Church.
1598	Rurikid Dynasty ends with death of Fedor; Boris Godunov named tsar; Time of Troubles begins.

SEVENTEENTH CENTURY

Period	Description
1601	Three years of famine begin.
1605	Fedor II crowned tsar; First False Dmitrii subsequently named tsar after Fedor II's murder.
1606	Vasilii Shuiskii named tsar.
1606–07	Bolotnikov leads revolt.
1610	Second False Dmitrii proclaimed tsar.
1610–13	Poles occupy Moscow.
1611–12	Minin and Pozharskii organize counterattack against Poles.
1613	Mikhail Romanov crowned tsar, founding Romanov Dynasty.
1631	Metropolitan Mohila founds academy in Kiev.
1645	Alexis crowned tsar.
1648	Ukrainian Cossacks, led by Bohdan Khmel'-nyts'kyi, revolt against Polish landowners and gentry.
1649	Serfdom fully established by law.
1654	Treaty of Pereyaslavl' places Ukraine under tsarist rule.
1667	Church council in Moscow anathemizes Old Belief but removes Patriarch Nikon; Treaty of Andrusovo ends war with Poland.
1670–71	Stenka Razin leads revolt.
1676	Fedor III crowned tsar.

Period	Description
1682	Half brothers Ivan V and Peter I named co-tsars; Peter's half sister, Sofia, becomes regent.
1689	Peter I (the Great) forces Sofia to resign regency; Treaty of Nerchinsk ends period of conflict with China.
1696	Ivan V dies, leaving Peter the Great sole tsar; port of Azov captured from Ottoman Empire.
EIGHTEENTH CENTURY 1700	Calendar reformed; war with Sweden begins.
1703	St. Petersburg founded; becomes capital of Russia in 1713.
1705–11	Bashkirs revolt.
1708	First Russian newspaper published.
1709	Swedes defeated at Battle of Poltava.
1710	Cyrillic alphabet reformed.
1721	Treaty of Nystad ends Great Northern War with Sweden and establishes Russian presence on Baltic Sea; Peter the Great proclaims Muscovy the Russian Empire; Holy Synod replaces patriarchate.
1722	Table of Ranks established.
1723–32	Russia gains control of southern shore of Caspian Sea.
1725	Catherine I crowned empress of Russia.
1727	Peter II crowned emperor of Russia.
1730	Anna crowned empress of Russia.
1740	Ivan VI crowned emperor of Russia.
1741	Elizabeth crowned empress of Russia.
1762	Peter III crowned emperor of Russia; abolishes compulsory state service for the gentry; Catherine II (the Great) crowned empress of Russia.
1768–74	War with Ottoman Empire ends with Treaty of Kuchuk-Kainarji.

Period	Description
1772	Russia participates in first partition of Poland.
1773–74	Emelian Pugachev leads peasant revolt.
1785	Catherine II confirms nobility's privileges in Charter to the Nobility.
1787–92	War with Ottoman Empire ends with Treaty of Jassy; Ottomans recognize 1783 Russian annexation of Crimea.
1793 and 1795	Russia participates in second and third partitions of Poland.
1796	Paul crowned emperor of Russia; establishes new law of succession.
NINETEENTH CENTURY 1801	Alexander I crowned emperor; conquest of Caucasus region begins.
1809	Finland annexed from Sweden and awarded autonomous status.
1812	Napoleon's army occupies Moscow but is then driven out of Russia.
1817–19	Baltic peasants liberated from serfdom but given no land.
1825	"Decembrists' revolt" fails; Nicholas I crowned emperor.
1830	Polish uprising crushed.
1833	"Autocracy, Orthodoxy, and nationality" accepted as guiding principles by regime.
1837	First Russian railroad, from St. Petersburg to Tsarskoe Selo, opens; Aleksandr Pushkin, foremost Russian writer, dies in duel.
1840s and 1850s	Slavophiles debate Westernizers over Russia's future.
1849	Russia helps to put down anti-Habsburg Hungarian rebellion at Austria's request.
1853–56	Russia fights Britain, France, Sardinia, and Ottoman Empire in Crimean War; Russia forced to accept peace settlement dictated by its opponents.

Period	Description
1855	Alexander II crowned emperor.
1858	Treaty of Aigun signed with China; northern bank of Amur River ceded to Russia.
1860	Treaty of Beijing signed with China; Ussuri River region awarded to Russia.
1861	Alexander II emancipates serfs.
1863	Polish rebellion unsuccessful.
1864	Judicial system reformed; zemstvos created.
1869	*War and Peace* by Lev Tolstoy (1828–1910) published.
1873–74	Army reformed; Russian youths go "to the people."
1875	Kuril Islands yielded to Japan in exchange for southern Sakhalin.
1877–78	War with Ottoman Empire ends with Treaty of San Stefano; independent Bulgaria proclaimed.
1879	Revolutionary society Land and Liberty splits; People's Will and Black Repartition formed.
1879–80	*The Brothers Karamazov* by Fedor Dostoevskii (1821–81) published.
1881	Alexander II assassinated; Alexander III crowned emperor.
1894	Nicholas II crowned emperor.
1898	Russian Social Democratic Labor Party established and holds First Party Congress in March; Vladimir I. Lenin one of organizers of party.
TWENTIETH CENTURY 1903	Russian Social Democratic Labor Party splits into Bolshevik and Menshevik factions.
1904–05	Russo-Japanese War ends with Russian defeat; southern Sakhalin ceded to Japan.
1905	"Bloody Sunday" massacre in January begins Revolution of 1905, a year of labor and ethnic unrest; government issues so-called October Manifesto, calling for parliamentary elections.

Table A. —*Continued*

Period		Description
1906		First Duma (parliament) elected.
1911		Stolypin, chief minister since 1906, assassinated.
1914		World War I begins.
1916		Rasputin murdered.
1917	March	(February, according to Julian calendar) February Revolution, in which workers riot at Petrograd; Petrograd Soviet of Workers' and Soldiers' Deputies formed; Provisional Government formed; Emperor Nicholas II abdicates; Petrograd Soviet issues "Order No. 1."
	April	Demonstrations lead to Aleksandr Kerensky's assuming leadership in government; Lenin returns to Petrograd from Switzerland.
	July	Bolsheviks outlawed after attempt to topple government fails.
	September	Lavr Kornilov putsch attempt fails.
	November	(October, according to Julian calendar) Bolsheviks seize power from Provisional Government; Lenin, as leader of Bolsheviks, becomes head of state; Russian Soviet Federated Socialist Republic (Russian Republic) formed; Constituent Assembly elected.
	December	Vecheka (secret police) created; Finns and Moldavians declare independence from Russia; Japanese occupy Vladivostok.
1918	January	Constituent Assembly dissolved; Ukraine declares its independence, followed, in subsequent months, by Armenia, Azerbaydzhan, Belorussia, Estonia, Georgia, Latvia, and Lithuania.
	February	Basmachi Rebellion begins in Central Asia; calendar changed from Julian to Gregorian.
	March	Treaty of Brest-Litovsk signed with Germany; Russia loses Poland, Finland, Baltic lands, Ukraine, and other areas; Russian Social Democratic Labor Party becomes Russian Communist Party (Bolshevik).
	April	Civil War begins.

Table A.—Continued

Period	Description
June	Concentration camps established.
July	Constitution of Russian Republic promulgated; imperial family murdered.
Summer	War communism established; intervention in Civil War by foreign expeditionary forces—including those of Britain, France, and United States—begins.
August	Attempt to assassinate Lenin fails; Red Terror begins.
November	Treaty of Brest-Litovsk repudiated by Soviet government after Germany defeated by Allied Powers.
1919 January	Belorussia established as theoretically independent Soviet republic.
March	Communist International (Comintern) formally founded at congress in Moscow; Ukraine established as Soviet republic.
1920 January	Blockade of Russian Republic lifted by Britain and other Allies.
February	Peace agreement signed with Estonia; agreements with Latvia and Lithuania follow.
April	War with Poland begins; Azerbaydzhan established as Soviet republic.
July	Trade agreement signed with Britain.
October	Truce reached with Poland.
November	Red Army defeats Wrangel's army in Crimea; Armenia established as Soviet republic.
1921 March	War with Poland ends with Treaty of Riga; Red Army crushes Kronshtadt naval mutiny; New Economic Policy proclaimed; Georgia established as Soviet republic.
Summer	Famine breaks out in Volga region.
August	Aleksandr Blok, foremost poet of Russian Silver Age, dies; large number of intellectuals exiled.
1922 March	Transcaucasian Soviet Federated Socialist Republic formed, uniting Armenian, Azerbaydzhan, and Georgian republics.

Table A.—Continued

Period		Description
	April	Joseph V. Stalin made general secretary of party; Treaty of Rapallo signed with Germany.
	May	Lenin suffers his first stroke.
	June	Socialist Revolutionary Party members put on trial by State Political Administration; Glavlit organized with censorship function.
	December	Union of Soviet Socialist Republics (Soviet Union) established, comprising Russian, Ukrainian, Belorussian, and Transcaucasian republics.
1924	January	Lenin dies; constitution of Soviet Union put into force.
	February	Britain recognizes Soviet Union; other European countries follow suit later in year.
	Fall	Regime begins to delimit territories of Central Asian nationalities; Turkmenia and Uzbekistan elevated to Soviet republic status.
1925	April	Nikolai I. Bukharin calls for peasants to enrich themselves.
	November	Poet Sergei Esenin commits suicide.
	December	Russian Communist Party (Bolshevik) becomes All-Union Communist Party (Bolshevik).
1926	April	Grigorii V. Zinov'ev ousted from Politburo.
	October	Leon Trotsky and Lev B. Kamenev ousted from Politburo.
1927	Fall	Peasants sell government less grain than demanded because of low prices; peasant discontent increases; grain crisis begins.
	December	Fifteenth Party Congress calls for large-scale collectivization of agriculture.
1928	January	Trotsky exiled to Alma-Ata.
	May	Shakhty trial begins; first executions for "economic crimes" follow.
	July	Sixth Congress of Comintern names socialist parties main enemy of communists.
	October	Implementation of First Five-Year Plan begins.

Table A.—Continued

Period	Description
1929 January	Trotsky forced to leave Soviet Union.
April	Law on religious associations requires registration of religious groups, authorizes church closings, and bans religious teaching.
Fall	Red Army skirmishes with Chinese forces in Manchuria.
October	Tadzhikistan splits from Uzbek Republic to form separate Soviet republic.
November	Bukharin ousted from Politburo.
December	Stalin formally declares end of New Economic Policy and calls for elimination of kulaks; forced industrialization intensifies, and collectivization begins.
1930 March	Collectivization slows temporarily.
April	Poet Vladimir Maiakovskii commits suicide.
November	"Industrial Party" put on trial.
1931 March	Mensheviks put on trial.
August	School system reformed.
1932 May	Five-year plan against religion declared.
December	Internal passports introduced for domestic travel; peasants not issued passports.
1932–33	Terror and forced famine rage in countryside, primarily in southeastern Ukrainian Republic and northern Caucasus.
1933 November	Diplomatic relations with United States established.
1934 August	Union of Writers holds its First Congress.
September	Soviet Union admitted to League of Nations.
December	Sergei Kirov assassinated in Leningrad; Great Terror begins, causing intense fear among general populace, and peaks in 1937 and 1938 before subsiding in latter year.
1935 February	Party cards exchanged; many members purged from party ranks.
May	Treaties signed with France and Czechoslovakia.

Table A. —Continued

Period	Description
Summer	Seventh Congress of Comintern calls for "united front" of political parties against fascism.
August	Stakhanovite movement to increase worker productivity begins.
September	New system of ranks issued for Red Army.
1936 June	Restrictive laws on family and marriage issued.
August	Zinov'ev, Kamenev, and other high-level officials put on trial for alleged political crimes.
September	Nikolai Ezhov replaces Genrikh Iagoda as head of NKVD (police); purge of party deepens.
October	Soviet Union begins support for antifascists in Spanish Civil War.
December	New constitution proclaimed; Kazakhstan and Kirgizia become Soviet republics; Transcaucasian Soviet Federated Socialist Republic splits into Armenian, Azerbaydzhan, and Georgian republics.
1937 January	Trial of "Anti-Soviet Trotskyite Center."
June	Marshal Mikhail N. Tukhachevskii and other military leaders executed.
1938 March	Russian language required in all schools in Soviet Union.
July	Soviet and Japanese forces fight at Lake Khasan.
December	Lavrenty Beria replaces Ezhov; Great Terror diminishes.
1939 May	Viacheslav Molotov replaces Maksim M. Litvinov as commissar of foreign affairs; armed conflict with Japan at Halhin Gol in Mongolia continues until August.
August	Nazi-Soviet Nonaggression Pact signed; pact includes secret protocol.
September	Stalin joins Adolf Hitler in partitioning Poland.
October	Soviet forces enter Estonia, Latvia, and Lithuania.
November	Remaining (western) portions of Ukraine and Belorussia incorporated into Soviet Union; Soviet forces invade Finland.

Table A.—Continued

Period		Description
	December	Soviet Union expelled from League of Nations.
1940	March	Finland sues for peace with Soviet Union.
	April	Polish officers massacred in Katyn Forest by NKVD.
	June	Northern Bukovina and Bessarabia seized from Romania and subsequently incorporated into Ukrainian Republic and newly created Moldavian Republic, respectively.
	August	Soviet Union annexes Estonia, Latvia, and Lithuania; Trotsky murdered in Mexico.
1941	April	Neutrality pact signed with Japan.
	May	Stalin becomes chairman of Council of People's Commissars.
	June	Nazi Germany attacks Soviet Union under Operation Barbarossa.
	August	Soviet and British troops enter Iran.
	November	Lend-Lease Law of United States applied to Soviet Union.
	December	Soviet counteroffensive against Germany begins.
1942	May	Red Army routed at Khar'kov; Germans halt Soviet offensive; treaty signed with Britain against Germany.
	July	Battle of Stalingrad begins.
	November	Red Army starts winter offensive.
1943	February	German army units surrender at Stalingrad; 91,000 prisoners taken.
	May	Comintern dissolved.
	July	Germans defeated in tank battle at Kursk.
	September	Stalin allows Russian Orthodox Church to appoint patriarch.
	November	Teheran Conference held.
1944	January	Siege of Leningrad ends after 870 days.
	May	Crimea liberated from German army.

Table A.—Continued

Period		Description
	June	Red Army begins summer offensive.
	October	Tuva incorporated into Soviet Union; armed struggle against Soviet rule breaks out in western Ukrainian, western Belorussian, Lithuanian, and Latvian republics and continues for several years.
1945	February	Stalin meets with Winston Churchill and Franklin D. Roosevelt at Yalta.
	April	Soviet Union renounces neutrality with Japan.
	May	Red Army captures Berlin.
	July–August	Potsdam Conference attended by Stalin, Harry S Truman, and Churchill, who is later replaced by Clement R. Attlee.
	August	Soviet Union declares war on Japan; Soviet forces enter Manchuria and Korea.
1946	March	Regime abolishes Ukrainian Catholic Church (Uniate); Council of People's Commissars becomes Council of Ministers.
	Summer	Beginning of "Zhdanovshchina," a campaign against Western culture.
1947		Famine in southern and central regions of European part of Soviet Union.
	September	Cominform established to replace Comintern.
1948	June	Blockade of Berlin by Soviet forces begins and lasts through May 1949.
	Summer	Trofim D. Lysenko begins his domination of fields of biology and genetics that continues until 1955.
1949	January	Council for Mutual Economic Assistance formed; campaign against "cosmopolitanism" launched.
	August	Soviet Union tests its first atomic bomb.
1952	October	All-Union Communist Party (Bolshevik) becomes Communist Party of the Soviet Union (CPSU); name of Polituro is changed to Presidium.
1953	January	Kremlin "doctors' plot" exposed, signifying political infighting.

Table A.—Continued

Period		Description
	March	Stalin dies; Georgii M. Malenkov, Beria, and Molotov form troika (triumvirate); title of party chief changes from general secretary to first secretary.
	April	"Doctors' plot" declared a provocation.
	June	Beria arrested and later shot; Malenkov, Molotov, and Nikita S. Khrushchev form troika.
	August	Soviet Union tests hydrogen bomb.
	September	Khrushchev chosen CPSU first secretary; rehabilitation of Stalin's victims begins.
1955	February	Nikolai A. Bulganin replaces Malenkov as prime minister.
	May	Warsaw Pact organized.
1956	February	Khrushchev's "secret speech" at Twentieth Party Congress exposes Stalin's crimes.
	September	Minimum wage established.
	November	Soviet forces crush Hungarian Revolution.
1957	July	"Anti-party group" excluded from CPSU leadership.
	August	First Soviet intercontinental ballistic missile tested successfully.
	October	World's first artificial satellite, Sputnik I, launched.
1958	March	Khrushchev named chairman of Council of Ministers.
	October	Nobel Prize for Literature awarded to Boris Pasternak; campaign mounted against Pasternak, who refuses to accept award.
1959	September	Khrushchev visits United States.
1960	May	Soviet air defense downs United States U–2 reconnaissance aircraft over Soviet Union.
1961	April	Cosmonaut Iurii Gagarin launched in world's first manned orbital space flight.
	July	Khrushchev meets with President John F. Kennedy in Vienna.
	August	Construction of Berlin Wall begins.

Table A.—Continued

Period		Description
	October	Stalin's remains removed from Lenin Mausoleum.
1962	June	Workers' riots break out in Novocherkassk.
	October	Cuban missile crisis begins, bringing United States and Soviet Union close to war.
	November	Aleksandr Solzhenitsyn's *One Day in the Life of Ivan Denisovich* published in Soviet journal.
1963	August	Limited Test Ban Treaty signed with United States and Britain.
1964	October	Khrushchev removed from power; Leonid I. Brezhnev becomes CPSU first secretary.
1965	August	Volga Germans rehabilitated.
1966	February	Dissident writers Andrei Siniavskii and Iulii Daniel tried and sentenced.
	April	Brezhnev's title changes from first secretary to general secretary; name of Presidium is changed back to Politburo.
1967	April	Stalin's daughter, Svetlana Allilueva, defects to West.
	September	Crimean Tatars rehabilitated but not allowed to return home.
1968	June	Andrei Sakharov's dissident writings published in samizdat.
	July	Treaty on the Nonproliferation of Nuclear Weapons signed by Soviet Union.
	August	Soviet-led Warsaw Pact armies invade Czechoslovakia.
1969	March	Soviet and Chinese forces skirmish on Ussuri River.
	May	Major General Petr Grigorenko, a dissident, arrested and incarcerated in psychiatric hospital.
1970	October	Solzhenitsyn awarded Nobel Prize for Literature.
	December	Jewish emigration to avoid persecution begins to increase substantially.
1972	May	Strategic Arms Limitation Talks (SALT) result in signing of Anti-Ballistic Missile Treaty

Table A. —*Continued*

Period	Description
	(ABM Treaty) and Interim Agreement on the Limitation of Strategic Offensive Arms; President Richard M. Nixon visits Moscow.
1973 June	Brezhnev visits Washington.
1974 February	Solzhenitsyn arrested and sent into foreign exile.
1975 July	Apollo-Soiuz space mission held jointly with United States.
August	Helsinki Accords signed, confirming East European borders and calling for enforcement of human rights.
December	Sakharov awarded Nobel Prize for Peace.
1976	Helsinki watch groups formed to monitor human rights safeguards.
1977 June	Brezhnev named chairman of Presidium of Supreme Soviet.
October	New constitution promulgated for Soviet Union.
1979 June	Second SALT agreement signed but not ratified by United States Senate.
December	Soviet armed forces invade Afghanistan.
1980 January	Sakharov exiled to Gor'kiy.
August	Summer Olympics held in Moscow and boycotted by United States.
1981 February	CPSU holds its Twenty-Sixth Party Congress.
1982 June	Strategic Arms Reduction Talks (START) begin.
November	Brezhnev dies; Iurii V. Andropov named general secretary.
1983 September	Soviet fighter aircraft downs South Korean civilian airliner KAL 007 near Sakhalin.
1984 February	Andropov dies; Konstantin U. Chernenko becomes general secretary.
1985 March	Chernenko dies; Mikhail S. Gorbachev becomes general secretary.
November	Gorbachev meets with President Ronald W. Reagan in Geneva.

Table A.—Continued

Period		Description
1986	February–March	CPSU holds its Twenty-Seventh Party Congress.
	April–May	Nuclear power plant disaster at Chernobyl' releases deadly radiation.
	October	Gorbachev and Reagan hold summit at Reykjavik.
	December	Ethnic riots break out in Alma-Ata.
1987	December	Soviet Union and United States sign Intermediate-Range Nuclear Forces Treaty (INF Treaty).
1988	Winter	Ethnic disturbances begin in Caucasus.
	May	Soviet authorities stop jamming Voice of America broadcasts.
	May–June	Reagan visits Moscow.
	June	Millennium of establishment of Christianity in Kievan Rus' celebrated in Moscow.
	June–July	CPSU's Nineteenth Party Conference tests limits of *glasnost'* and *perestroika* in unprecedented discussions.
	October	Gorbachev replaces Andrei Gromyko as chairman of Presidium of Supreme Soviet; Gromyko and others removed from Politburo.
	December	Earthquake registering 6.9 on Richter scale strikes Armenian Republic, destroying much of cities of Leninakan and Spitak and resulting in 25,000 deaths.
1989	February	Soviet combat forces complete withdrawal from Afghanistan.
	March–April	Initial and runoff elections held for the 2,250 seats in Congress of People's Deputies; some seats have more than one candidate running; about 87 percent of elected deputies CPSU members or candidate members.
	May	Congress of People's Deputies meets, openly criticizes past and present regimes before television audiences, and elects 542 members to serve in Supreme Soviet; Gorbachev elected by Congress of People's Deputies to new position of chairman of Supreme Soviet.

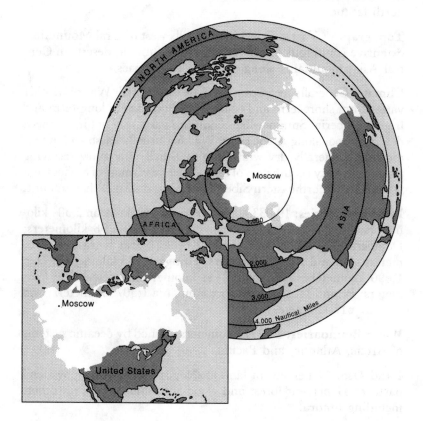

Country

Formal Name: Union of Soviet Socialist Republics; abbreviated: USSR; transliterated: Soiuz Sovetskikh Sotsialisticheskikh Respublik—SSSR.

Informal Name: Soviet Union.

Term for Citizens: Formally, Soviet people; informally, Soviets.

Capital: Moscow.

Geography

Size: Approximately 22,402,200 square kilometers (land area 22,272,000 square kilometers); slightly less than 2.5 times size of United States.

Location: Occupies eastern portion of European continent and northern portion of Asian continent. Most of country north of 50° north latitude.

Topography: Vast steppe with low hills west of Ural Mountains; extensive coniferous forest and tundra in Siberia; deserts in Central Asia; mountains along southern boundaries.

Climate: Generally temperate to Arctic continental. Wintry weather varies from short-term and cold along Black Sea to long-term and frigid in Siberia. Summer-like conditions vary from hot in southern deserts to cool along Arctic coast. Weather usually harsh and unpredictable. Generally dry with more than half of country receiving fewer than forty centimeters of rainfall per year, most of Soviet Central Asia and northeastern Siberia receiving only half that amount.

Land Boundaries: 19,933 kilometers total: Afghanistan 2,384 kilometers; China 7,520 kilometers; Czechoslovakia 98 kilometers; Democratic People's Republic of Korea (North Korea) 17 kilometers; Finland 1,313 kilometers; Hungary 135 kilometers; Iran 1,690 kilometers; Mongolia 3,441 kilometers; Norway 196 kilometers; Poland 1,215 kilometers; Romania 1,307 kilometers; and Turkey 617 kilometers.

Water Boundaries: 42,777 kilometers washed by oceanic systems of Arctic, Atlantic, and Pacific.

Land Use: 11 percent of land arable; 16 percent meadows and pasture; 41 percent forest and woodland; and 32 percent other, including tundra.

Natural Resources: Oil, natural gas, coal, iron ore, timber, gold, manganese, lead, zinc, nickel, mercury, potash, phosphates, and most strategic minerals.

Society

Population: 286,717,000 (January 1989 census). Average annual growth rate 0.9 percent. Density twelve persons per square kilometer; 75 percent of people lived in European portion.

Nationalities: About 51 percent of population Russian, 15 percent Ukrainian, 6 percent Uzbek, 3.5 percent Belorussian, and 24.5 percent about 100 other nationalities.

Religions: Religious worship authorized by Constitution, but Marxism-Leninism, the official ideology, militantly atheistic. Reliable statistics unavailable, but about 18 percent Russian Orthodox;

17 percent Muslim; and nearly 7 percent Roman Catholic, Protestant, Armenian Orthodox, Georgian Orthodox, and Jewish combined. Officially, most of remainder atheist.

Languages: Russian the official language. Over 200 other languages and dialects spoken, often as the primary tongue; 18 languages spoken by groups of more than 1 million each. About 75 percent of people spoke Slavic languages.

Education: Highly centralized school system with standardized curriculum. Compulsory attendance through eleventh grade. Strong emphasis on training for vocations selected by central authorities. Indoctrination in Marxist-Leninist ideology at all levels. Science and technology emphasized at secondary level and above. As of 1979 census, official literacy rate 99.8 percent for persons between nine and forty-nine years old. Over 5.3 million studied at universities and institutes, nearly 50 percent part time. All education free, and in many cases students received stipends.

Health and Welfare: Medical care by government health institutions; free but of poor quality for general public despite highest number of physicians and hospital beds per capita in world. Welfare and pension programs provided, albeit marginally, for substantial segments of population.

Politics and Government

Political Party: Communist Party of the Soviet Union (CPSU), only party permitted by Constitution, controlled government apparatus and decisions affecting economy and society. CPSU followed ideology of Marxism-Leninism and operated on principle of democratic centralism. Primary CPSU bodies: Politburo, highest decision-making organ; Secretariat, controller of party bureaucracy; and Central Committee, party's policy forum. CPSU membership more than 19 million (9.7 percent of adult population) in 1987, dominated by male Russian professionals. Party members occupied positions of authority in all officially recognized institutions throughout country.

Government: As authorized by 1977 Constitution, fourth since 1918, government executed decisions of CPSU pertaining primarily to economy but also to security affairs and social issues. Congress of People's Deputies created in 1988 by amendment to Constitution; highest organ of legislative and executive authority; consisted of 2,250 deputies, about 87 percent of whom CPSU members or candidate members and some of whom selected in first multicandidate (although not multiparty) elections since early Soviet period; slated to meet once a year for a few days; met for first time in May 1989; deputies openly discussed issues, elected a chairman, and selected 542 deputies from among its membership to constitute a reorganized, bicameral Supreme Soviet, a standing legislature slated to remain in session six to eight months annually. Prior to 1989, former Supreme Soviet was constitutionally highest organ of legislative and executive authority but met only a few days annually; its Presidium managed affairs throughout year. Council of Ministers administered party decisions, mainly regarding economic management, by delegating authority to its Presidium; chairman of Council of Ministers also sat on CPSU Politburo.

Judicial System: Supreme Court, highest judicial body, had little power, lacking authority to determine constitutionality of laws, to interpret laws, or to strike laws down.

Administrative Divisions: Country administratively divided into one soviet federated socialist republic (Russian) and fourteen soviet socialist republics (Armenian, Azerbaydazhan, Belorussian, Estonian, Georgian, Kazakh, Kirgiz, Latvian, Lithuanian, Moldavian, Tadzhik, Turkmen, Ukrainian, and Uzbek). Below republic level, administrative subdivisions complicated, varying with each republic and including following categories: autonomous oblast, autonomous *okrug,* autonomous republic, *krai,* oblast, and *raion.* Only Russian Republic had all categories.

Foreign Relations: Diplomatic relations with majority of world's nations. Main foreign policy objectives as determined by CPSU Politburo: enhance national security, maintain presence in Eastern Europe, continue ''peaceful coexistence'' with free world democracies, and seek increased influence in Third World.

International Agreements and Memberships: Dominant partner in Council for Mutual Economic Assistance (Comecon) and Warsaw Pact. Active participant in United Nations and its specialized agencies. Signatory to Final Act of Conference on Security and Cooperation in Europe (Helsinki Accords) and many other multilateral and bilateral agreements.

Economy

Salient Features: Centrally planned socialist economy. Government owned and operated all industries: banking, transportation, and communications systems; trade and public services; and most of agricultural sector. CPSU, guided by principles of Marxism-Leninism, controlled planning and decision-making processes; central planners determined investment, prices, distribution of goods and services, and allocation of material and human resources according to CPSU priorities. Defense and heavy industries emphasized over consumer and agricultural sectors. Availability and quality of food, clothing, housing, and services often inadequate for average citizen. Economy planned as being largely self-sufficient. Economic development and population centers primarily in European portion, but many raw material and energy resources in Asian areas, making access difficult and both exploration and transportation costly. Declining economic growth since mid-1970s. Beginning in 1985, regime attempted to implement economic reform.

Gross National Product (GNP): Estimated at US$2.4 trillion in 1986; US$8,375 per capita in 1986; real growth rate in 1988 about 1.5 percent, continuing deceleration begun in mid-1970s.

Revenue: Largest source of government funds taxation of enterprise profits and turnover taxes; personal income taxes provided less than 10 percent.

Industry: Diversified industrial base directed by complicated, centralized bureaucratic system. Highest priorities given to machine-building and metal-working industries and to military matériel manufacturing; consumer industries not allocated comparable human, financial, or material resources. Technological advances applied primarily to defense industries. Major industrial branches: manufacturing (including defense), chemicals, metallurgy, textiles, food processing, and construction. Employment in industry and construction 38 percent in 1988.

Energy: Self-sufficient in energy and a major energy exporter. World's largest producer of oil and natural gas and second largest coal producer. Enormous energy resources in Siberia, but cost of extraction and transportation over great distances to western industrial areas high. Main generators of electric power: thermoelectric (coal, oil, natural gas, and peat), nuclear power plants, and hydroelectric stations.

Agriculture: Collective farms and state farms supplied bulk of agricultural needs. Wheat and other grains, potatoes, sugar beets, cotton, sunflower seeds, and flax main crops. Private plots—small percentage of sown area—produced substantial quantities of meat, milk, eggs, and vegetables. Large amounts of grain and meat imported. Despite high investment, serious problems in agriculture persisted: insufficient fertilizer; inadequate refrigeration, storage, and transportation; wasteful processing; and unrealistic planning and management. More fundamental problems: only 1.3 percent of arable land receives optimal precipitation; widely fluctuating crop yields; and many fertile areas have insufficient growing seasons because of northern latitudes or moisture deficiency.

Fishing: World's largest oceangoing fishing fleet, accompanied by large, modern, fish-processing ships, operated in Atlantic and Pacific ocean systems. Inland seas and rivers accounted for less than 10 percent of catch.

Forestry: With a third of world's forested areas, country's production of logs and sawn timber exceeded that of all other countries, despite inefficient and wasteful processing. Inadequate processing capacity made production of pulp, paper cardboard, plywood, and other wood products low.

Foreign Trade: Government policies of self-sufficiency and strict control maintained trade in minor economic role. In 1985 exports and imports totaled US$185.9 billion, but each accounted for only 4 percent of GNP. Major trade partners included other communist countries, particularly those of Eastern Europe, which accounted for 67 percent of trade. Industrialized countries accounted for 22 percent and Third World countries for 11 percent. Major exports petroleum and petroleum products, natural gas, metals, wood, agricultural products, and manufactured goods, primarily machinery, arms, and military equipment. Major imports grain and other agricultural products, machinery and industrial equipment, steel products (especially large-diameter pipe), and consumer goods. Balance of trade favorable in mid-1980s. Trade with socialist countries conducted on bilateral basis with imports balancing exports. Value of exports to Third World countries, including arms and military equipment, exceeded hard-currency deficit caused by unfavorable trade balance with West. Merchant fleet consisted of about 2,500 oceangoing ships.

Exchange Rate: Officially, 0.61 ruble per US$1 (1988 average), but rubles had no official value outside of Soviet Union. Soviet authorities set exchange rates based on policy rather than market factors. Unofficial (black market) exchange rates offered considerably more rubles per United States dollar.

Fiscal Year: Calendar year.

Science and Technology: Marked by highly developed pure science and innovation at theoretical level, but interpretation and application fell short. Biology, chemistry, materials science, mathematics, and physics were fields in which Soviet citizens excelled. Science emphasized at all levels of education, and very large number of engineers graduated each year. Shortfall in science and technology could be attributed to centrally planned and controlled economy and to priority given to national security, all of which provided little incentive to design and create prototypes of products for mass market. Without orders from central government, no product design and prototype saw fruition or stimulated innovation of other products. Soviet regimes, in many cases, have chosen to adopt foreign technology rather than to invest money, talent, and time to develop Soviet Union's indigenous technological capacity.

Transportation and Communications

Railroads: In 1986 about 145,600 kilometers of track, of which 50,600 kilometers electrified, almost all wide gauge; 3.8 trillion ton-kilometers of freight and 4.3 billion passenger fares, of which 3.9 billion on suburban lines, transported in 1986.

Highways: 1,609,900 kilometers in 1987, of which 1,196,000 kilometers hard-surfaced (asphalt, concrete, stone block, asphalt-treated, gravel, or crushed stone) and 413,900 kilometers earth; 488.5 billion ton-kilometers of freight transported by trucks, primarily on short hauls for agricultural sector in 1986; 48.8 billion passengers boarded, primarily commuters transported by bus. Use of private automobiles limited.

Inland Waterways: 122,500 kilometers in 1987, exclusive of Caspian Sea; 255.6 billion ton-kilometers of freight transported by inland waterways in 1986.

Pipelines: 81,500 kilometers for oil and 185,000 kilometers for natural gas in 1986.

Ports: Over 100 major maritime and river ports, including Archangel, Astrakhan', Baku, Leningrad, Moscow, Murmansk, Odessa, Riga, Tallin, and Vladivostok. Many maritime ports on Arctic Ocean, northern Pacific Ocean, and Baltic Sea closed annually because of ice. Many river ports also closed for varying periods annually.

Civil Aviation: 4,500 major transport aircraft. Airfields: 4,530 usable; 1,050 with permanent surface runways; 30 with runways over 3,659 meters, 490 with runways 2,440 to 3,659 meters; and 660 with runways 1,220 to 2,439 meters.

Communications: Mass media controlled and directed by CPSU. More than 8,000 daily newspapers in about sixty languages with combined circulation of about 170 million. Nearly 5,500 weekly, monthly, and quarterly magazines and journals with combined circulation of about 160 million. About 83,500 books and brochures published in 1986 in 2.2 million copies. Radio broadcasting 1,400 hours of daily programs in seventy languages. Main programming emanated from Moscow's eight radio channels. 162 million radio sets. Television broadcasting, mainly from Moscow, by way of 350 stations and 1,400 relay facilities to 75 million households with television sets. Private telephones very limited.

National Security

Defense Establishment: Based on Marxist-Leninist theory of war, CPSU determined missions and directed management of world's largest military organization. Defense Council provided strategic leadership. Five armed services, numbering about 3,750,000 out of a total of nearly 6 million troops in uniform in 1989, and numerous logistical and support services. Of the 6 million, 75 percent conscripts, 5 percent career enlisted, and 20 percent officers, most of whom were Russian. Compulsory premilitary training; military conscription of males at age eighteen, with few exceptions.

Strategic Rocket Forces: Primary strategic offensive forces, numbering about 300,000 in 1989. Controlled all ground-based nuclear missiles and operations in space.

Ground Forces: Largest of services, with a force of about 2 million troops in 1989 and comprising 150 motorized rifle and 52 tank divisions, in three states of readiness, as well as rocket and artillery troops, air defense troops, and other combat and support troops.

Air Forces: In 1989 numbered about 450,000. Consisted of Strategic Air Armies, for long-range bombing; Frontal Aviation, for support of Ground Forces; and Military Transport Aviation, for strategic mobility of armed services.

Air Defense Forces: Numbered about 500,000 in 1989. Operated extensive air defense system, controlling surface-to-air missile launchers, air defense aircraft and missiles, and space defenses.

Naval Forces: In 1989 numbered about 500,000. Consisted of substantial numbers of surface combatants and support ships, missile and attack submarines, and naval aircraft. Organized into four fleets and several flotillas with shore-based support facilities in strategic locations.

Paramilitary Forces: Seven airborne divisions subordinate to Supreme High Command. Elite Special Purpose Forces subordinate to General Staff. Internal Troops and Border Troops organized, equipped, and trained as military forces but assigned to Ministry of Internal Affairs (Ministerstvo vnutrennykh del—MVD) and to Committee for State Security (Komitet gosudarstvennoi bezopasnosti—KGB), respectively.

Defense Spending: Estimated between 15 and 17 percent of gross national product (GNP) in 1989. Military matériel production, supervised by military, received best available managers, workers, technology, and materials.

Military Presence Overseas: Naval combatants in Mediterranean Sea and Indian Ocean with limited presence, mainly submarines, elsewhere. Ground Forces in Afghanistan numbered 115,000 until withdrawal in 1989; withdrawals announced in German Democratic Republic (East Germany) and elsewhere but, as of 1989, substantial forces remained in East Germany, and some forces remained in Czechoslovakia, Poland, Hungary, Mongolia, and Cuba. Military advisers in several Third World nations.

Security Police: Substantial political and regular police protected authoritarian CPSU from perceived internal and external threats and combated ordinary crimes. KGB maintained internal and external espionage and counterintelligence networks and controlled Border Troops and other specialized security troops. MVD investigated nonpolitical crime, operated labor camps for prisoners, and controlled militarized Internal Troops.

Introduction

IN MID-1991 THE SOVIET UNION remained in a state of turmoil after the weakening of the authority of the Communist Party of the Soviet Union (CPSU) had profoundly disturbed the socialist system and unleashed broad nationality unrest. Mikhail S. Gorbachev, the general secretary of the CPSU and president of the Soviet Union, had recognized that the development of socialism (see Glossary) was faltering and that the cooperation of the Soviet people was needed to revitalize the country's economy and society. He endeavored to reform both the party and the socialist system without radically altering either one. But Gorbachev's attempts at political reform and economic restructuring shook the centralized, authoritarian system that had been dominated and controlled by the party since the Bolshevik Revolution of 1917. The seriously flawed Soviet system could not readily adapt to extensive reform and restructuring.

The historical experience of the multinational Soviet Union is varied and complex and helps illuminate contemporary events and institutions. The histories of the predecessor states of the Soviet Union—Muscovy and the Russian Empire—demonstrate some long-term trends having applicability to the Soviet period: the predominant role of the East Slavs, particularly the Russians; the dominance of the state over the individual; territorial acquisition, which continued sporadically; nationality problems, which increased as diverse peoples became subjects of the state as a result of territorial expansion; a general xenophobia, coupled with admiration for Western ideas and technology and disruptive sporadic campaigns to adopt them; and cyclical periods of repression and reform.

The death knell of the Russian Empire came in March 1917, when the people of Petrograd (present-day Leningrad) rose up in an unplanned and unorganized protest against the tsarist regime and continued their efforts until Tsar Nicholas II abdicated. His government collapsed, leaving power in the hands of an elected Duma, which formed the Provisional Government. That government was in turn overthrown in November 1917 by the Bolsheviks, led by Vladimir I. Lenin. The Bolsheviks (who began calling themselves Communists in 1918) emerged victorious after a bitterly fought Civil War (1918–21). They secured their power and in December 1922 established the Union of Soviet Socialist Republics (Soviet Union), which included almost all the territory of the former Russian Empire. The new government prohibited other political organizations and inaugurated one-party rule, which exerted centralized control over the political, economic, social, and cultural lives of the people. Lenin, as head of the party, became the de facto ruler of the country.

After Lenin's death in 1924, Joseph V. Stalin gradually assumed supreme power in the party and the state by removing opponents from influential positions. Stalin ordered the construction of a socialist economy through the appropriation by the state of private industrial and agricultural properties. His ruthless policy of forced industrialization and collectivization of agriculture caused massive human suffering, as did his purge of party members. As the initiator of the Great Terror (see Glossary), Stalin also decimated the economic, social, military, cultural, and religious elites in the Russian Republic and in some of the non-Russian republics. Millions of citizens were executed, imprisoned, or starved. Nevertheless, the Soviet state succeeded in developing an industrial base of extraordinary dimensions, albeit skewed toward military and heavy industry rather than consumer needs. Stalin believed that the rapid development of heavy industry was necessary to ensure the Soviet Union's survival. His fear of attack led to the signing of the Nazi-Soviet Nonaggression Pact of 1939, enabling the Soviet Union to acquire the eastern portion of Poland (western Ukraine), the Baltic states, and Bessarabia but failing to forestall for long the Nazi invasion of the Soviet Union that began in June 1941. After several crushing military defeats, the Red Army finally gained the offensive in 1943, expelled the enemy, and, by 1945, had occupied most of Eastern Europe. Although more than 20 million Soviet citizens died as a result of the war, the world was forced to acknowledge the tremendous power of the Soviet military forces.

In the postwar period, the Soviet Union converted its military occupation of the countries of Eastern Europe into political and economic domination by installing regimes dependent on Moscow. It also pursued its goal of extending Soviet power abroad. The Western powers reacted to Soviet expansionism, and thus began the Cold War. Simultaneously, Stalin rebuilt the devastated Soviet economy while retaining central planning and the emphasis on heavy industry and military production rather than satisfying the needs of the citizens. Suppression of dissent and human rights continued unabated.

After Stalin's death in 1953, Nikita S. Khrushchev gradually became the dominant Soviet leader and, in a dramatic move, renounced his predecessor's use of terror and repression. He continued, however, a confrontational foreign policy toward the West. His attempts at domestic reform, particularly in agriculture, and his instigation of a missile crisis in Cuba, which almost launched a nuclear war, contributed to his ouster as party leader and head of state in 1964. After an extended period of collective leadership, Leonid I. Brezhnev assumed party and government power and initiated a foreign policy of détente with the West. He continued the traditional economic policy of emphasizing heavy industry and military production over civilian needs.

At the death of Brezhnev in 1982, the political, economic, and cultural life of the country was controlled by a conservative, entrenched, and aging bureaucracy. Brezhnev's successors, Iurii V. Andropov and Konstantin U. Chernenko, were in power too briefly before their deaths to effect lasting change, although Andropov attempted to initiate some reforms. When Gorbachev was selected general secretary of the CPSU and head of the Soviet state in 1985, the deterioration of the Soviet socialist system had nearly reached crisis proportions. Gorbachev announced that "revolutionary" change was required to revitalize the country, and he began his programs of *perestroika, glasnost'*, and *demokratizatsiia* (see Glossary).

Gorbachev's efforts at political and economic reform, however, unleashed a flood of events leading to a profound political crisis and broad nationality unrest while leaving fundamental economic problems unresolved. Several of the nationalities having union republic (see Glossary) status began to seek greater political and economic autonomy; indeed, some sought complete independence from the Soviet multinational federation. Longstanding rivalries and enmities among nationality groups that had been suppressed by successive Soviet regimes exploded in some areas of the country, causing loss of life and property. Thus, the authoritarian socialist system, although undergoing tentative restructuring, became less capable of effectively responding to societal disorder and of implementing necessary fundamental change rapidly. In the 1990s, Gorbachev's policy of *perestroika* offered the people little in substantive, near-term economic improvement, and his policies of *glasnost'* and *demokratizatsiia* resulted in rapidly raising their expectations while lessening the regime's controls over society. As a result, in mid-1991 the Soviet Union appeared to be a disintegrating federation with a collapsing economy and a despairing, confused society.

Internationally, the Soviet Union's affairs also appeared to be in a state of fundamental change. Beginning in late 1989, the Soviet Union's East European empire crumbled as citizens in Czechoslovakia, the German Democratic Republic (East Germany), and Romania overthrew their communist dictators with at least the tacit approval of Gorbachev. Earlier in the year, the people of Poland and Hungary had overthrown their communist systems. The actions of the peoples of Eastern Europe led to the dissolution, in May and June 1991, respectively, of the two Soviet-dominated, multinational organizations, the Warsaw Pact (see Appendix C) and the Council for Mutual Economic Assistance (Comecon; see Appendix B) that had helped bind Eastern Europe to the Soviet Union. In a collaborative effort with the United States, Gorbachev met with President George H.W. Bush at Malta in December 1989 and at Washington in May–June 1990 to effectively end the Cold War and to move toward a cooperative relationship. In August 1991, Bush and Gorbachev signed the Strategic Arms Reduction Treaty, which required the United States and the Soviet Union to cut their nuclear weapons within seven years so that each side would have only 4,900 ballistic missile nuclear warheads as part of a total of 6,000 "accountable" warheads. The two countries had been engaged in the Strategic Arms Reduction Talks (START) since 1982. In another collaborative effort, the Soviet Union voted with the United States and an international coalition of nations to oppose the invasion of Kuwait by Iraq, a nation that had been the recipient of substantial amounts of Soviet military advice, equipment, and weapons.

It was Gorbachev's "new thinking" (see Glossary) in foreign policy that produced the most dramatic and far-reaching results of his reform efforts. In addition to the significant developments just mentioned, these included the withdrawal of Soviet armed forces from Afghanistan; acceptance of national self-determination for the East European communist countries and a promised complete withdrawal of Soviet troops from those countries; agreement to a unified Germany remaining in the North Atlantic Treaty Organization (NATO); and the ending of support for Cuban military operations in Angola. The international community began to regard the Soviet Union as less menacing and acknowledged that the actions it had taken contributed substantially to the ending of the Cold War. Gorbachev was awarded the Nobel Prize for Peace in 1991 for his foreign policy initiatives and for their impact on world affairs. By no means, however, did the Soviet Union abandon its foreign policy goals. It continued its economic and military support of some longstanding allies, such as Afghanistan, Cuba, and Vietnam, as well as Third World client states, although it often chose to act covertly, in the hope of receiving economic aid from the West.

In 1991 the Soviet economy continued to be beset with serious problems that had brought the Soviet Union to the point of crisis. The problems included poor planning by government officials; inefficient production methods; lack of incentives to boost efficiency; lack of worker discipline; unemployment, underemployment, and strikes; shortages of food and consumer goods; theft of state property; wasteful use of resources; prices distorted by a lack of market mechanisms; and investments of scarce funds in projects of dubious value. The system of central planning and rigid control by Moscow bureaucrats was partially disrupted by economic problems and the regime's policy of *perestroika*. Nevertheless, almost all natural resources, agricultural and industrial enterprises (see Glossary), transportation and communications systems, and financial institutions remained in the hands of the party-controlled government. In addition, the vast majority of workers remained, effectively, salaried employees of the government. Although the 1977 Constitution, as amended and changed, provided for cooperative or collective ownership of property, it also stated that the "socialist ownership of the means of production" was the foundation of the economy, and socialist ownership remained the preferred form of ownership. The Gorbachev regime, however, sought to devise a restructuring program that would enable market forces rather than government planners to make many economic decisions. Thus, in the early 1990s the economic reform envisioned by Gorbachev in the late 1980s seemed to be shifting away from centralized planning to a market-oriented economy.

Indeed, in 1990 the Supreme Soviet debated several proposals for economic reform before it, in October of that year, approved one endorsed by Gorbachev called "Guidelines for the Stabilization of the Economy and Transition to a Market Economy." This program saw no alternative to shifting toward a market economy but provided neither a detailed plan nor a schedule for implementation. It did, however, establish four phases for the transition: first, stabilization of the economy and initiation of the privatization of state-owned enterprises; second, liberalization of prices, establishment of a safety net for people adversely affected, and exercise of fiscal restraints over government expenditures; third, adjustment of the pay scale for workers and institution of housing and financial reforms; and fourth, as markets stabilized, transformation of the ruble from being nonconvertible to convertible, so as to enable Soviet and foreign businesses to exchange currencies at international rates. Price reform, a key element of the transition to a market economy, was to be administered and monitored carefully by central authorities. This transition was estimated to require two years. An important, but not easily achieved, requirement for its success was the integrity of the union and its constituent republics.

In spite of its many economic and political problems, the Soviet Union had more of the natural and human resources essential for industrial production than any other country in the world. It had vast quantities of important minerals and abundant energy supplies. It also had a very large, technically qualified labor force and a higher percentage of people working in industry than most Western nations. Yet, industrial productivity regularly fell behind planned goals for several reasons. First, raw materials, including fuels, had become less readily available in the heavily industrialized and heavily populated European part of the Soviet Union, while the Asian part of the country, which contained abundant natural resources, continued to lack an industrial infrastructure and the stable, skilled labor force necessary to extract the needed materials. Second, the formidable, and perhaps impossible, task of uniting materials, energy, and skilled workers with appropriate industrial enterprises on a timely and cost-effective basis was the responsibility of the increasingly bureaucratic central planning agencies that responded to political, rather than economic, priorities. Third, industrial enterprises, particularly those engaged in exclusively nondefense production, were constrained by obsolescent machinery and a lack of innovation.

Producing and distributing food in sufficient quality, variety, and quantity had eluded the Gorbachev regime, as well as all the other regimes since the Bolshevik Revolution. Fresh fruits, vegetables, and meats were in chronically short supply in the stores owned and operated by the government, and imports of grain and meat were frequent and necessary. Nevertheless, possessing the world's most extensive cultivated area, a large agricultural labor force, considerable investment in machinery, chemical fertilizers, and irrigation, the Soviet Union had made itself the world's second largest grower of agricultural commodities and was first in many of them. The main reason for the anomaly between the high agricultural potential and the low food availability in the stores was the centralized administration of agriculture by bureaucratic planners who had little understanding of local conditions. Other reasons for the anomaly included the inadequacy of incentives, equipment, and modern techniques available to farm workers; the cold climate and uncertain moisture conditions; the failure of the transportation system to move harvested crops promptly; the lack of adequate storage facilities; and the paucity of refrigerated transportation. Massive amounts of foodstuffs simply rotted in the fields or in storage.

Bypassing the government system, peasant farmers, most of whom were women, raised about one-fourth of the country's food on their private plots and then sold their produce privately. The area thus farmed amounted to about 3 percent of the total cultivated area, most of which was on collective farms (see Glossary) and state farms (see Glossary).

The transportation system, owned and operated by the government, continued in 1991 to exhibit serious deficiencies, particularly with respect to its limited capacity, outdated technologies, and poor maintenance. The main purpose of transportation in the Soviet Union, as determined by successive regimes, was to fulfill national economic needs that the party decided on, rather than to serve the interests of private businesses or citizens. The structure of the subsidized Soviet transportation system was greatly affected by the large size, geographic features, and northern climate of the country. Also, the distribution of the population and industry (largely in the European part) and the natural resources (largely in the Asian part) helped determine the transportation system's structure. Railroads were the primary mode of transporting freight and passengers over long distances. Trucks were used mainly in urban and industrialized areas to transport raw materials from rail lines and manufactured products to them. Buses were the primary mode of conveyance for people in urban areas. For the vast majority of people, automobiles, which numbered only about 12 million, were not an important means of transportation. Without perceiving a need to move people or freight long distances on roads, successive Soviet regimes saw little economic reason to build a modern network of highways, even in the European part of the country. Roads outside of cities generally had gravel or dirt surfaces and were poor by Western standards. For intercity and long-distance travel where time was a factor, the government airline, Aeroflot, provided low-cost transportation but had few amenities, and it had a safety record that concerned many Western passengers.

Foreign trade, which might conceivably contribute to solving the Soviet Union's economic problems, traditionally played a minor role. The Soviet government preferred instead to strive for self-sufficiency in all areas of the economy. With extensive natural resources, including energy sources, decision makers saw foreign trade primarily as a device to serve international political interests. Thus, after World War II the Soviet Union's primary trading partners were the East European communist countries and other socialist and socialist-oriented countries. Trade with Third World countries was also conducted primarily for political rather than economic reasons and often involved the exchange of Soviet-made weapons and military equipment for raw materials. Trade with the West, particularly the United States, varied according to the political climate and the requirement for hard-currency (see Glossary) payments. The Soviet Union acquired hard currency by selling its minerals, fuels, and gold bullion on the world market, primarily to the West. In turn, the Soviet Union bought Western manufactures, especially high-technology items, and agricultural products, mainly grains. In the late 1980s, Soviet foreign indebtedness, principally to West European commercial banks, rose substantially, reaching US$54 billion in 1989, in part because the price of oil and natural gas, the main hard-currency exports, fell on the world market. Soviet exports to communist and other socialist countries consisted primarily of energy, manufactures, and consumer goods. In mid-1991 increasing hard-currency indebtedness, decreasing oil production, mounting domestic economic problems, and a requirement for advanced technology forced Gorbachev to seek increased participation in international economic organizations, trade with foreign countries, foreign economic assistance, and reduction of unprofitable trade with the Soviet Union's allies. Foreign trade and economic assistance were urgently needed to make the economy more efficient, as well as to help improve the standard of living.

The living conditions of the majority of the Soviet people were more comparable to some Third World countries than to those of an industrially developed superpower. Even Soviet sources acknowledged that about 55 million people (approximately 20 percent of the population) were living below the official poverty level, but some Western analysts considered that far more people were, in fact, impoverished. The availability and distribution of food, clothing, and shelter were controlled by the government, but the supply was inadequate and generally became worse as the Gorbachev regime attempted economic reforms.

The cost to Soviet consumers of many essential consumer items and services was remarkably low compared with the cost of similar items and services in the West. Soviet prices were set artificially low by the government, which subsidized the cost of selected items in an attempt to ensure accessibility by all citizens. The practical impact of the subsidies, however, was to distort the real production and distribution costs, reduce the availability of the items, and inflate the real cost of other items that were not subsidized. Another impact was to increase the resistance of citizens to price increases when the regime tried to adjust the prices of items and services to correspond more closely to the real costs of their production and distribution.

Many educational benefits were free and guaranteed to the citizens by the Constitution. Education, mandatory through the eleventh grade, provided excellent schooling in mathematics, foreign languages, and the physical sciences. Training in these fields was offered at universities, which were generally available to children of the elite, and at institutes, which were available to students without political connections. Universities and institutes were excellent by Western standards but tended to be very narrowly focused. The main purpose of education in the Soviet Union was to produce socially motivated and technically qualified people who were able to serve the state-run economy. In 1991 educators were developing reforms for the state-controlled system that included the privatization of schools.

Medical services were also guaranteed by the Constitution and enabled government officials to claim that the Soviet Union had the world's highest number of doctors and hospital beds per capita. Similar to the purpose of education, the main purpose of medical care was to ensure a healthy work force for the centrally controlled economy. Training of health care professionals, although not as advanced as that in the West, prepared the large numbers of doctors, the majority of whom were women, and medical assistants to attend to the basic medical needs of the people, millions of whom lived in rural or geographically remote areas. Medical care was free of charge, but to obtain specialized, or sometimes even routine, medicines or care, ordinary citizens used bribes or *blat* (see Glossary). Although hospital care was available without charge, it was comparable to some Third World countries because of the lack of modern medical equipment and some medicines and supplies, such as sterile syringes, and because of poor sanitation in general. Members of the elite, particularly high-level party, government, economic, and cultural officials and their families, were served by a much higher quality health care system than that available to average citizens.

Soviet society, although officially classless according to Marxism-Leninism, was divided into four socio-occupational groups by Western sociologists: peasants and agricultural specialists; blue-collar workers; white-collar workers; and the party and government elite and cultural and scientific intelligentsia. Social status was also affected by the level and field of education, place of residence, nationality, and party membership and party rank. High socio-occupational status was generally accompanied by above-average pay, but more important for the individual, it offered increased access to scarce consumer goods, and even foreign goods, as well as social prestige and other perquisites for the individual and his or her family. The pay of some skilled laborers exceeded that of many professionals, including teachers, doctors, and engineers, because Marxism-Leninism exalted manual work. Despite earning less money, however, professionals generally had higher social status than manual workers. The pay for many occupations was set low by government planners, requiring two incomes to maintain a family's living standard that often was at the poverty level. In contrast, the members of the elite of Soviet society not only received substantially higher salaries but also had access to special food and consumer goods stores, better housing and health care, and increased educational opportunities.

Women, although according to the Constitution the equal of men, were treated as if they were of a political, economic, and social status that was inferior to men. The vast majority of women worked because of economic necessity, but most often in low-paying positions. They endured the greater share of the burden of living in a country where the regime placed superpower military status above citizens' needs and desires for adequate housing, food, clothing, and other consumer goods. Crowded living quarters, often with shared bathrooms and kitchens that usually lacked modern kitchen appliances made life difficult. Waiting in long lines every day to purchase food and other essentials was another burden borne mostly by women, who received little assistance from their spouses and even less from the male-dominated society and the socialist regime. Although given some special benefits, including generous maternity and child care leave by the government, Soviet women were generally overburdened. As a consequence of the domestic stresses, the Soviet Union had high rates of abortion, alcoholism, and divorce, most evident among the Slavic nationalities.

The Soviet Union comprised more than 100 nationalities, twenty-two of which had populations of over 1 million. The Russian nationality made up only about 51 percent of the total population, according to the 1989 census, but the two other East Slavic nationalities—the Belorussians and the Ukrainians—together constituted about another 23 percent of the population. Some of the cultural and linguistic diversity of the Soviet nationalities could be seen when contrasting the North European heritage of the Estonians, Latvians, and Lithuanians with the Mongol, Persian, and Turkic roots of the Central Asian Kazakhs, Kirgiz, Tadzhiks, Turkmens, and Uzbeks. The cultures and languages of the three major nationalities of the Caucasus region—the Armenians, Azerbaydzhanis, and Georgians—were significantly different from each other as well as from the other nationalities. These fourteen nationalities, together with the Moldavians, each had union republic status. Many other nationalities were granted "autonomous" status in territorial and administrative subdivisions (i.e., autonomous republics, autonomous oblasts, and autonomous *okruga*—see Glossary). It should be noted, however, that despite the semblance of autonomy, real political and economic power was retained in Moscow, and the Russians remained, in mid-1991, the dominant nationality in the political and economic life of the Soviet

Union. It should also be noted that some nationalities were brought into the Soviet Union under duress, and others were annexed by force by its predecessor, the Russian Empire.

Several of the non-Russian nationalities formally objected to being part of the communist-controlled Soviet Union and had long viewed Russians as oppressors. In addition, many of the non-Russian peoples had had serious and longstanding disagreements and rivalries with neighboring peoples of other nationalities. Partly as a defense against criticism by non-Russian nationalities, Russians in some areas began to reassert their own nationality, but in other areas they felt compelled to leave their homes in some non-Russian republics because of anti-Russian sentiments. Successive Soviet regimes, including that of Gorbachev until the late 1980s, maintained that all peoples of the Soviet Union lived harmoniously and were content with their circumstances. When Gorbachev initiated reforms that relaxed the regime's system of constraints, the latent discontent erupted into disturbances and violence, resulting in hundreds of deaths.

Each nationality, having its own history, language, and culture, attempted to preserve its distinctive heritage and, in most cases, was permitted by the government to provide language instruction for children to that end. Nevertheless, instruction in Russian was also required, and Russian was the official language of the Soviet regime, although only a small percentage of non-Russians spoke and read Russian fluently. The religions of the various nationalities were almost universally repressed by the official antireligious policies of successive regimes. Although Gorbachev authorized the reopening of many churches in 1989 and 1990, most churches, mosques, and synagogues remained closed. Nevertheless, by mid-1991 religion was playing an increasingly significant role in the lives of some of the people.

An important domestic reform put forward by Gorbachev was *demokratizatsiia,* the attempt to introduce greater participation by citizens, including younger party members, in the political process. Having risen to leadership in the Soviet state through the party, Gorbachev attempted to use the party to implement his reform program. Since 1917 the party had held, in fact, the "leading and guiding role in Soviet society," but that role was formally abolished in March 1991 when the Supreme Soviet, as part of its program of *demokratizatsiia,* amended the Constitution and revised Article 6 to permit other parties to exist. The party thereby lost the legal basis for its authority over the government, economy, and society throughout the Soviet Union. In the late 1980s and early 1990s, even before the constitutional change, the CPSU's effectiveness in leading the Soviet Union appeared, to most observers, to have diminished markedly. The party had been unable to implement reform or make the Marxist-Leninist system function effectively on a continuing basis. This systemic failure, however, had not led to a complete renunciation of the underlying socialist ideology by mid-1991. This fact led many party members to resign in protest against the party's failure to promote genuine change, or in acknowledgment of the declining relevance of the party, or as a renunciation of Marxism-Leninism as a viable doctrine, or, perhaps, in recognition of the fact that continued membership could be detrimental to their future careers.

Among the many prominent party members who had resigned by mid-1991 were three former Politburo members: Boris N. Yeltsin, formerly also the Moscow party secretary; Eduard A. Shevardnadze, formerly also the minister of foreign affairs; and Aleksandr N. Iakovlev, formerly also a member of the CPSU Secretariat. The latter two were long-term, close advisers to Gorbachev. Yeltsin, however, was probably the most politically powerful of the former party members. He had been picked by Gorbachev for the Moscow post in 1985 but angered the party hierarchy with his outspoken criticism of the party and was dismissed from both that post and the Politburo in 1987. In a remarkable political comeback, however, Yeltsin was elected to the Congress of People's Deputies in 1989 and in 1990 was elected chairman of the supreme soviet of the Russian Republic, by far the largest and most important of the fifteen constituent republics of the Soviet Union. But his most significant victory came in June 1991, when he was elected to the newly created position of president of the Russian Republic by a majority of 57 percent of the voters in the Russian Republic in a direct, popular election. Meanwhile, the popularity of Gorbachev among Soviet citizens had fallen to less than 10 percent, according to a Soviet poll. Yeltsin's popularity among citizens of the Russian Republic was apparently based, in part, on his political agenda, which included establishing a market economy with private property rights and denationalizing government-owned enterprises; shifting more decision-making power from the central authorities to the republics; and reducing the power of the party, the size of the armed forces, and the influence of the Committee for State Security (Komitet gosudarstvennoi bezopasnosti—KGB). This ambitious agenda could not be accomplished quickly or easily under the best of circumstances, and some intellectuals and other Soviet citizens mistrusted Yeltsin as a leader.

Despite the CPSU's loss of many members—both prominent and rank-and-file members—and despite its loss of constitutional exclusivity and its failure to lead the country effectively, the party remained the Soviet Union's major political force and bastion of reaction in mid-1991. No longer the monolithic, disciplined power it had once been and often divided along nationality lines, the party retained as members, however, a large percentage of the male population over the age of thirty and having at least ten years of education, the segment of the population that had traditionally made the decisions and managed the affairs of the country. They and the party as a whole appeared to give Gorbachev their support. The party's de facto power appeared strong in the central government bureaucracy, in most city governments, in some republic governments, and in many administrative subdivisions but was weak in certain other republics and administrative subdivisions. Party members generally remained in charge of the Soviet government's controlled economy from the central planning organs and the military-industrial complex to the individual enterprises. And party members remained in positions of responsibility in the transportation, communications, agriculture, education, mass media, legal, and judicial systems. The party's power was weakest among the non-Russian nationalities, where some party leaders were prompted to advocate national sovereignty in an effort to maintain their positions. Significantly, the party was strongest among the leadership of the armed forces, the KGB, and the Ministry of Internal Affairs (Ministerstvo vnutrennykh del—MVD). These organs of party power—and their predecessor organizations—had been used to maintain the party's preeminence since the Bolshevik Revolution, and in mid-1991 the party continued to use them.

During the late 1980s, the popular elections that Gorbachev had instigated produced revitalized legislative bodies that could compete with the party for power at the all-union, republic, and lower levels of government. These elections spurred millions of ordinary citizens to become more politically involved than they had ever been and prompted many of their elected representatives to challenge party officials and other central authorities. Politically active individuals, including CPSU members, former prisoners in the Gulag (see Glossary), and citizens motivated by a variety of concerns created or joined disparate political action groups. For the most part, these groups represented liberal and democratic viewpoints, particularly in urban areas such as Moscow and Leningrad, or nationality interests in the non-Russian republics and administrative subdivisions. But conservative, reactionary, and pro-Russian groups also sprang up. The various liberal groups often opposed the CPSU and the central authorities but lacked positive, unifying goals and programs, as well as practical experience in democracy's way of coalition building, compromise, and the rule of law. They struggled to form political parties with broadened geographical and popular bases. But without the extraordinary financing, organization, communications, and material support retained by the CPSU, the emergent political groups found the competition especially difficult.

Political leaders in all fifteen republics asserted the precedence of their republics' laws over those of the central government and demanded control over their own natural resources, agricultural products, and industrial output. Leaders of several republics proclaimed complete independence, national sovereignty, and separation from the Soviet Union. Within many of the republics, however, officials of various minority nationalities in administrative subdivisions sometimes proclaimed their subdivision's independence from their republics or passed laws contradictory to the laws of higher legislative or executive bodies. Hence the Constitution, Gorbachev's decrees, and laws passed by the Supreme Soviet, by the supreme soviets of the republics, or by the soviets (see Glossary) of the various subdivisions were often disobeyed with impunity.

This so-called "war of laws" among the legislative and executive bodies at various levels contributed to the forging of an agreement between Gorbachev and the leaders of nine of the fifteen republics in April 1991. This agreement, which Yeltsin played a key role in formulating, promised that the central government would permit the republics to have more economic and political autonomy and that the republics would fulfill their economic and financial obligations to Moscow. At the time of the agreement, Gorbachev and Yeltsin and the eight other republic leaders endorsed, in principle, a revised draft of a new treaty, which would in effect reestablish the Soviet Union on a different basis from the original union treaty of 1922. The republics that did not sign the agreement were to be excluded from its provisions.

The six republics refusing to join the agreement between Gorbachev and the nine republics were the Armenian, Estonian, Georgian, Latvian, Lithuanian, and Moldavian republics. In these republics, the people had elected to their republic legislatures representatives who, for the most part, were not CPSU members but rather were advocates of the primacy of their nationality vis-à-vis the central regime in Moscow. The leaders of these republics indicated that they did not wish to be part of the Soviet Union and were attempting to sever their political ties with it and establish themselves as independent countries. The six republics together constituted about 1.4 percent of the territory and about 7.2 percent of the population of the Soviet Union.

Meanwhile, the Gorbachev regime continued its efforts to finalize a new union treaty that would replace the 1922 union treaty. During 1990 the Estonian, Latvian, and Lithuanian republics elected noncommunist governments. The elected representatives voted for independence from the Soviet Union and sought the same independent status that they had had before being absorbed into the Soviet Union in 1940. (It should be noted that the United States never recognized the incorporation of Estonia, Latvia, and Lithuania into the Soviet Union.) Gorbachev and the Supreme Soviet did not recognize the independence of the three Baltic states, and the Soviet armed forces were employed to disrupt their independence drives. It is likely that separation of the three republics was also hindered, in part, because their economies were closely intertwined with those of the other republics, particularly with that of the Russian Republic.

In March 1990, the regime created the office of the presidency in accordance with changes in the Constitution. The president and vice president were supposed to be elected by direct popular vote, but, by special exception, Gorbachev and Gennadii I. Ianaev were elected as the first president and vice president, respectively, by vote of the Congress of People's Deputies. The president, who could serve a maximum of two five-year terms, was authorized by the changes in the Constitution to appoint and remove high-level government officials; veto laws and suspend orders of the Council of Ministers; and declare martial law or a state of emergency, subject to approval by a two-thirds majority of the Supreme Soviet.

Also created in 1990 were two organizations designed to support the presidency. The new Presidential Council was given responsibility for implementing foreign and domestic policies and for ensuring the country's security. The new Council of the Federation, which was headed by the president of the Soviet Union and consisted also of the "supreme state official from each of the fifteen constituent republics," had duties that included developing ways to implement a nationalities policy, recommending to the Supreme Soviet solutions for interethnic problems, and ensuring that the union republics complied with international treaties. The creation of the presidency with its two supporting bodies was seen by some Western observers as helping Gorbachev to provide his regime with a renewed political power that was based on constitutionally established government organs rather than on the CPSU, the traditional source of political power.

In November 1990, Gorbachev proposed the establishment of several other new bodies (all directly subordinate to him) designed to strengthen the executive branch of the government. The new bodies included the Cabinet of Ministers (replacing the Council of Ministers), the Security Council, and the Coordinating Agency for the Supervision of Law and Order. The Presidential Council was dissolved, and its functions were given to the Council of the Federation, which was designated the chief policy-making organ in the country. These administrative changes appeared to some analysts to be an attempt by Gorbachev to recover the authority and control that his regime had lost during conflicts with several secessionist republics, as well as during disputes with radical and conservative opponents of his reforms. Gorbachev was, in the view of some analysts, also attempting to counter calls for his resignation for failing to initiate and implement measures that would cure the country's economic and political ills.

One of Gorbachev's main instruments in his attempt to improve the country's condition was his policy of *glasnost'*. Through this policy, he used the mass media to arouse the people who would help change the way the bureaucratic system functioned. He and all prior leaders of the Soviet Union had used the mass media and artistic expression to help govern the people and direct the society's course. Politicizing the mass media and the arts served not only to secure the regime's power but also furthered the role of the CPSU and the dominance of Marxism-Leninism (see Glossary) in the social, cultural, and economic life of the country. In the late 1980s, however, Soviet mass media and the arts became part of the revolution in information technologies that swept the globe and could not be sealed off from the Soviet Union. The regime needed those same technologies to compete with the West and to prevent falling further behind economically and technologically.

In the late 1980s, the Soviet regimes, first that of Andropov and then that of Gorbachev, relaxed their monopoly on the press and modern communications technology and eased the strictures of socialist realism (see Glossary), thus permitting open discussion of many themes previously prohibited. The implementation of the policy of *glasnost'* made much more information about government activities, past and present, accessible to ordinary citizens, who then criticized not only the government but also the CPSU and even Lenin, the founder of the Soviet state. Editors, journalists, and other writers transformed newspapers, journals, and television broadcasts into media for investigative reports and lively discussions of a wide variety of subjects that had been heavily censored before *glasnost'*. The works of previously banned writers, including Joseph Brodsky and Aleksandr Solzhenitsyn, both exiled winners of the Nobel Prize for Literature, and such exiled authors as Vasilii Aksionov and Vladimir Voinovich, were published in the Soviet

Union. Thus, the regime began to lose control of the policy of *glasnost'*, and the censors began to lose control of the mass media. In June 1990, the Supreme Soviet passed a law that purportedly sanctioned freedom of the press, but later that year the regime began again to restrict news reporting, particularly on radio and television. Still, in mid-1991 the mass media continued to offer interesting news and diverse viewpoints—although some less independent and revelatory than they had been in the late 1980s—that were eagerly followed by the people.

Another side effect of Gorbachev's policy of *glasnost'* was the exposure and public discussion of the severe degradation and official neglect of the environment that had been perpetuated by successive regimes in the drive to achieve industrial and national security goals at any price. As a consequence of this neglect, two of the twentieth century's worst man-made environmental disasters struck the Soviet Union: the Chernobyl' nuclear power plant accident, the consequence of an insufficient regard for safety to obtain increased energy; and the loss of huge amounts of water from the Aral Sea. Although the death toll from the Chernobyl' accident in 1986 was initially low, millions of people continued to live on radioactive land and raise and consume contaminated food. In addition to the human costs, cleaning up and repairing the after-effects of the accident, which continued to leak radioactive gases in 1991, were estimated to cost hundreds of billions of rubles (see Glossary) by the year 2000. The other major environmental disaster was the near destruction of the Aral Sea, whose main sources of water were diverted to irrigate arid land for the purpose of raising cotton and other crops beginning in 1960. Subsequently, the Aral Sea's coast receded sixty kilometers, in places, from its former location. Other environmental problems included the severe pollution of rivers, lakes, and the air resulting from the direct discharge of pollutants, particularly in the European part of the Soviet Union.

In the late 1980s, environmental concern spurred the formation of genuine grass-roots ecology groups that pressed the authorities to remedy the harmful conditions. Often these groups were supported by or were merged with nationality groups advocating increased self-determination or independence but nevertheless had little political power. Despite the efforts of the grass-roots groups, resolving the Soviet Union's many environmental problems, in the view of many Western specialists, will be costly and long-term. The Gorbachev regime as of mid-1991 had not redirected its economic policies regarding industrial and agricultural production, resource extraction, and consumption to provide adequate protection for the environment.

Another effect of *glasnost'* was the official acknowledgment of past civil and human rights abuses and the marked improvement in people's rights during Gorbachev's regime. The advancement of civil and human rights for the people of the Soviet Union was courageously sought by Andrei Sakharov, a winner of the Nobel Prize for Peace in 1975, who moved from internal exile in Gor'kiy to membership in the Congress of People's Deputies in Moscow before his death in December 1989. Freedom of speech and the press grew enormously after censorship was officially abolished. Freedom to assemble peacefully for political purposes, with or without government authorization, was tested frequently, generally without serious incident. (In January 1991, however, armed Soviet troops on two different occasions reportedly killed or wounded several dozen unarmed demonstrators occupying buildings in the Latvian and Lithuanian republics.) Political rights of individuals were enhanced when the Supreme Soviet approved legal authority for a multiparty system. But in 1991 the emerging political groups were too fragmented and weak to seriously challenge the power of the CPSU except in cities such as Leningrad and Moscow and in several of the republics' legislatures. In 1990 the regime expanded the right of citizens to emigrate. About 180,000 Jews departed for Israel, 150,000 Germans departed for a united Germany, and about 55,000 citizens emigrated to the United States. And, finally, independent trade unions were allowed to form, and strikes, made legal in 1989, were permitted by the regime, even one involving over 600,000 miners in several areas of the Soviet Union in 1990.

In the late 1980s, the Gorbachev regime released many prisoners of conscience (persons imprisoned for their political or religious beliefs) from imprisonment in the Gulag, from internal exile, and from psychiatric hospitals. Although authorities could still legally detain and arrest people without warrants, political killings, disappearances, or psychiatric hospitalizations for political or religious beliefs were rare. Nevertheless, human rights practices in the Soviet Union remained in transition in 1991.

Of major concern to successive Soviet regimes was the system of internal security, which in 1991 consisted primarily of the KGB and the MVD. They had been powerful tools for ferreting out and suppressing political and other internal threats to rule by the CPSU. The party always considered the KGB its most vital arm and maintained the closest supervision and control over it. The party controlled the KGB and MVD by approving personnel appointments through the *nomenklatura* (see Glossary) system and by exercising general oversight to ensure that party directives were followed. Party control was also exerted specifically and individually because all

KGB officers and the majority of MVD officers were members of the CPSU. Party membership subjected them to the norms of democratic centralism (see Glossary) and party discipline.

Internal security forces, particularly the KGB, had broad authority to employ severe and sometimes violent methods against the Soviet people while enforcing the regime's directives and thereby preserving the party's dominant role in the Soviet Union. In mid-1991 the KGB, under Vladimir A. Kriuchkov, and the MVD, under Boris K. Pugo beginning in October 1990, continued to give their loyalty and substantial support to the party. Thus, the internal security organs continued to oppose radical change and remained a significant, and perhaps immobilizing, threat to some citizens advocating substantial economic and political reform. At the same time, the internal security organs, particularly the KGB, continued to take advantage of the party's need for their vital support by exerting influence on the party's policies and the regime's decisions.

Like the KGB and MVD, the armed forces traditionally were loyal to the party and beneficiaries of the party's decisions. Control of the armed forces by the party was exercised primarily through the military leaders, the overwhelming majority of whom were loyal party members and followers of Marxism-Leninism. The armed forces were controlled by the party through networks of uniformed party representatives and covert informers who reported to the CPSU. Most of the middle and junior grade officers, although probably members of the CPSU or its youth affiliate, the Komsomol (see Glossary), were, in the view of some Western observers, less bound to party doctrine than were the senior military leaders. The vast majority of the military rank and file, however, were not affiliated with the party and resented the covert informers in their midst and the political indoctrination they endured.

The Soviet Union's military establishment was the justification for its international ranking as a superpower. With the world's largest military establishment—nearly 6 million people in uniform and a large arsenal of nuclear missiles—the Soviet Union's superpower status appeared justified on a military, if not on an economic, basis. The military establishment consisted not only of the armed forces but also of the internal security forces and an extensive military-industrial complex, all of which had priority use of human and economic resources. Decisions regarding the use of most human and material economic resources continued to be made by party members. The majority of the citizens, however, were dissatisfied with the party's decision-making role and were not in favor of Gorbachev's reform efforts. But the majority of the people were not allowed to choose alternative national leadership and appeared unwilling to exert their influence to radically change the course of events out of fear of the armed forces, and perhaps of civil war.

The armed forces consisted of the five armed services (Strategic Rocket Forces, Ground Forces, Air Forces, Air Defense Forces, and Naval Forces), extensive support and rear service organizations, and specialized and paramilitary forces, such as the Airborne Troops, the Internal Troops of the MVD, and the Border Troops of the KGB. The Internal Troops and the Border Troops had military equipment, organization, training, and missions. The most strategically significant of the five armed services were the Strategic Rocket Forces, whose main purpose was to attack an opponent's nuclear weapons, military facilities, and industry with nuclear missiles. The Ground Forces, the largest and most prestigious of the armed services, were also important, in part because the senior officers typically held high-level positions in the Ministry of Defense and the General Staff of the Armed Forces. Of the five armed services, the Strategic Rocket Forces in mid-1991 maintained the capability of destroying targets in the United States and elsewhere, and the Ground Forces continued to have the world's largest numbers of tanks, artillery pieces, and tactical nuclear weapons.

The armed forces were not without internal problems, however. The combat losses sustained in Afghanistan and the withdrawal without victory had a profound effect on the armed forces and tarnished their image in the eyes of the party and the society as a whole. The armed forces were also disturbed by mounting nationality problems, including the refusal of many non-Russian conscripts to report for induction, the continuing interethnic conflicts among conscripts, and the demographic trend in which non-Russians were likely to outnumber Russians in the biannual conscript inductions. The Soviet armed forces also lacked a well-trained, experienced, and stable noncommissioned officer corps, such as that forming the basis of many Western armies. Gorbachev's announcement in 1988 of a unilateral reduction of 500,000 officers and men from the armed forces and his announced cutbacks in the armed forces' share of the government budget were not received with enthusiasm by the military hierarchy.

The doctrine, structure, and mission of the Soviet armed forces were based on the theories of Marxism-Leninism. One of these theories rested on the principle, formulated by the nineteenth-century Prussian military theorist Carl von Clausewitz, that war is a continuation of politics and that an aim of war is the attainment of military victory. Marxism-Leninism added that military victory can accelerate the victory of the world socialist system (see Glossary).

Marxism-Leninism also provided the theoretical basis for Soviet military science and for the tactical operations of military units. In practice, Marxism-Leninism was interpreted and applied solely by the CPSU, which closely monitored military leaders' adherence to party policies and directives. Thus, when Gorbachev characterized Marxism-Leninism as an outdated dogma in July 1991 and called on the CPSU Central Committee to abandon it in favor of social democratic principles, military leaders probably were surprised and dismayed.

Under the direction of the party, the armed forces were organized and equipped mainly to accomplish offensive missions, the success of which were indispensable to victory in war. Although Soviet military doctrine was always defensive, according to Soviet leaders, Western specialists regarded it as offensive in emphasis because it stressed offensive strategy, weapons, and forces to achieve victory in war. As directed by Gorbachev, however, military leaders emphasized the defensive aspects of the doctrine. Gorbachev also directed that the military establishment adopt the doctrine of "reasonable sufficiency," new to the Soviet Union in the 1980s, to facilitate the conversion of portions of the military industrial complex to support civilian, consumer-oriented requirements.

With the apparent support of the armed forces, the internal security organs, and the governmental economic bureaucracies, the CPSU continued its efforts to control events in the country in mid-1991. Despite its problem-plagued economy and society and its altered international situation, the Soviet Union remained one of the two most powerful countries in the world. Its size and location, natural resources, industrial capacity, population, and military strength made it of continuing importance. Having large quantities of almost all the strategic minerals and large reserves of coal, iron ore, natural gas, oil, timber, gold, manganese, and other resources, the Soviet Union required little material support from beyond its borders. It was self-sufficient in coal, natural gas, and oil, the major fuels needed for its extensive industry. Industrial development had been a keystone of economic policies of all Soviet regimes beginning with the Bolshevik Revolution and had resulted in a higher percentage of Soviet citizens working in industry than in most Western nations. Soviet industrial development, however, always favored heavy industry, for reasons of national security and military production. Light industry, which mainly produced goods for consumers other than nonmilitary needs, such as agriculture, always had low priority. The emphasis on heavy industry produced some spectacular successes, particularly with regard to the production of large quantities of military equipment and weapons systems. As a result of this emphasis, however, the Soviet people had to settle for food, clothing, and housing of generally poor quality and insufficient quantity.

In mid-1991 the people gave the Gorbachev regime only minimal support and were beginning to reject the party's right to rule the Soviet Union. Gorbachev, however, continued to proclaim himself a Communist and to align himself with opponents of reform on some issues but with advocates of reform on other issues. He thus lost the support of almost all the democratic and market-oriented reformers and remained acceptable to the hard-line opponents of reform mainly because they lacked an alternative leader. Gorbachev apparently could not permanently join either the reformers or their opponents, but neither could he allow either group to gain continuing supremacy because his role as the arbiter of conflicting views would be unnecessary. His zigzags perhaps enabled him to remain in a position of power, but he continued to lose effectiveness as the director of major events in the country and therefore his relevance as a leader and reformer. His six years of historic political reform opened the Soviet Union to fundamental change. The reform effort, however, was not accompanied by significant changes in the party's ideology or the government's functions, and the irresolute and sporadic attempts to transform the centrally controlled economy into a market-based system had had little real success. Meanwhile, the country continued in its chaotic turmoil as the economy worsened, the regime became weaker, and several of the republics became more insistent on their national independence. The Soviet Union remained in flux and unpredictable.

August 16, 1991

* * *

Early in the morning of August 19, 1991, events began to occur that would have a greater historical impact than the Bolshevik Revolution of 1917, according to George F. Kennan, one of America's foremost specialists on the Soviet Union. The events began when Soviet radio and television broadcasts announced that Gorbachev, who was vacationing in Crimea, had been replaced by a committee of high-ranking party and government officials because "ill health" prevented him from performing his presidential duties at a time when the country faced "fatal dangers." The officials, who called themselves the State Committee for the State of Emergency, placed themselves in charge of the country and put Gorbachev under house arrest. The committee was headed by the vice president of the Soviet Union, Gennadii I. Ianaev, who was named acting president, and included the chairman of the KGB, Vladimir A. Kriuchkov; the minister of internal affairs, Boris K. Pugo; the minister of defense, Dmitrii T. Iazov; and the chairman of the Cabinet of Ministers, Valentin Pavlov. Anatolii I. Luk'ianov, the chairman of the Presidium of the Supreme Soviet, supported the committee, as did other CPSU leaders in the government, armed forces, internal security forces, and military-industrial complex. The committee issued several decrees that suspended democratic political organizations; promised housing improvements and the freezing or reduction of prices on some food items; banned publication of several newspapers and journals; forbade labor strikes and public gatherings; and declared martial law in Moscow. In an appeal to the people, Ianaev pledged to ensure the territorial integrity of the Soviet Union and indicated that the new union treaty, which was scheduled to be signed on August 20, would be reevaluated before final acceptance. In an appeal to foreign leaders, Ianaev stated that treaties and other international agreements signed by the Soviet Union would be upheld by the committee, but he warned against attempts by foreign governments to change Soviet boundaries.

The announcements by the leaders of the coup d'état brought immediate reactions, mostly negative. In Moscow crowds of people protested in the streets and eventually confronted tanks of the armed forces in defense of the building housing the Russian Republic's supreme soviet. Tens of thousands of people rallied around Yeltsin, who urged them to continue resisting the coup and asked the troops not to fire on fellow citizens. Masses of people in many other Soviet cities demonstrated against the coup, and leaders of most of the republics denounced the coup. On the second day of the coup, three people were killed attempting to defend the supreme soviet building against tanks. Soviet troops occupied radio and television facilities in the Estonian and Lithuanian republics, and the Estonian and Lithuanian legislatures declared immediate secession from the Soviet Union. President Bush and other foreign leaders voiced strong opposition to the coup, which they termed "illegal," and called for the organizers to restore Gorbachev to power.

Firm opposition from the Soviet people, Yeltsin and other republic leaders, and international figures was not the only problem facing the initiators of the coup. Some of the armed forces defected to the opposition, and some others—for example, General Evgenii Shaposhnikov, commander in chief of the Air Forces, and Lieutenant General Pavel Grachev, commander of the Airborne Troops—refused to obey the orders to deploy. Many other military leaders, as well as many senior members of the party, government, and media, apparently took no overt stand but waited to see if the coup was likely to succeed.

Early on the third day, the coup collapsed. The committee disbanded, and the Ministry of Defense directed all troops to leave Moscow. The Supreme Soviet of the Soviet Union formally reinstated Gorbachev as president, and he returned to Moscow from Crimea. Gorbachev returned to find that the political environment in Moscow and in many other places in the Soviet Union was radically different from the one that had existed before the coup attempt. At the urging of Yeltsin, Gorbachev, who had originally replaced coup members with their close subordinates, appointed persons more acceptable to the reformers. Shaposhnikov was appointed minister of defense, Vadim V. Bakatin the chairman of the KGB, and Viktor Barannikov the minister of internal affairs.

The failed coup and the events immediately following it represented a historic turning point for many reasons. The CPSU, which was a main bond linking the coup leaders, was thrown into further disarray, and it, together with the party-dominated central government, was seriously discredited. The position of conservative and reactionary leaders, who were mainly party members, was weakened relative to that of the advocates of substantial political and economic reform. In addition, Gorbachev, who had appointed or approved the appointment of the coup leaders and failed to forestall the coup, was diminished politically. Although he rejected collaborating with the coup leaders, Gorbachev fully advocated neither democracy nor a free-market economy and was viewed by many observers as a figure of mainly historical importance. Yeltsin, who had publicly defied the coup leaders, rallied the people to resist, and faced the tanks, used his position as the popularly elected president of the Russian Republic and his forceful personality to change the course of events. He altered Gorbachev's appointments, made economic and political agreements affecting the whole country, and revised the proposed new union treaty.

Although the precise roles that the armed forces, KGB, and MVD took during the coup were unclear, some people in these organs failed to respond to manipulation by the party apparatchiks (see Glossary). Some elements of the armed services, for example, opted not to support the coup. The vast majority of the armed forces, KGB, and MVD, however, were not actively involved in the coup and therefore did not attempt to influence the course of events. These organs traditionally had opposed change, and their considerable power remained available for commitment in a future struggle. The positions of the nationalities seeking independence, sovereignty, and secession was also strengthened as a result of the failure of the coup. Ten of the fifteen republics declared or reaffirmed their independence. The United States, as well as the European Community, recognized Estonia, Latvia, and Lithuania as separate and independent states. Finally, advocates of reform, in general, and democratic reform, in particular, were seen as ascendant by some Western observers, as a result of the coup. But perhaps equally as important, the advocates began to include not only members of the intelligentsia but also tens of thousands of ordinary citizens. Their activism helped defeat the coup, and it was possible they would be encouraged to participate in the democratic movement and thus help alter their political condition.

On August 24, 1991, the people received further encouragement when an evening television news program announced that Gorbachev had resigned as CPSU general secretary. Also announced was a plea from Gorbachev for the CPSU Central Committee to disband itself. On the same day, Gorbachev decreed that "soviets of people's deputies" should seize CPSU property and decide on its future use in accordance with Soviet law and the laws of the republics. In another decree, Gorbachev directed that political parties and political organizations must cease activities in the armed forces, MVD, KGB, and in the central government bureaucracy. Decrees limiting party activities had been issued earlier by Yeltsin for the Russian Republic and by some other republic leaders, but those decrees had generally not been carried out. Gorbachev did not quit the party, but although neither he nor Yeltsin outlawed it entirely, the people reacted as if the reign of the party had ended. They toppled numerous statues of Lenin and other party leaders, assaulted party members, and attempted to take over party buildings in several cities. The people's anger at the party erupted not only because of the coup attempt but because of the years of corruption, deceit, and tyranny that party members had inflicted on them in the exercise of near total power. Meanwhile, the Party Control Committee expelled the coup leaders from the party and claimed that the party as a whole should not be condemned for the illegal actions of a few "adventurers."

On September 5, 1991, perhaps the most significant aftereffect of the failed coup occurred: the Congress of People's Deputies, after being given an ultimatum by Gorbachev, dissolved both itself and the Union of Soviet Socialist Republics, after voting to transfer state power to a transitional government. The transitional government, which was largely controlled by the republics, was designed to rule until a new constitution and a new union treaty could be prepared and approved. It consisted of the State Council, a new bicameral Supreme Soviet, and the Interrepublican Economic Committee. The State Council, with Gorbachev as the head, had as members the leaders of the republics participating in the new "voluntary" union. The State Council acted as the collective executive, and its responsibilities included foreign affairs, national defense, and internal security. The Interrepublican Economic Committee, with members chosen by the republics, was responsible for coordinating the economic relations of the republics and the management of the national economy. Gorbachev chose the committee chairman with approval of the State Council. In one of its first acts, the State Council recognized the complete independence of the former Estonian, Latvian, and Lithuanian republics.

By successfully withstanding a coup and instituting a transitional government, Gorbachev once again displayed his masterful talent for tactical improvisation and political survival. Nevertheless, the political situation in the former Union of Soviet Socialist Republics was unstable, and the economy continued to worsen. Most of the people were apprehensive about their future.

September 7, 1991   Raymond E. Zickel

Chapter 1. Historical Setting: Early History to 1917

Icon, Mother of God (Georgian)

THE SOVIET UNION is inhabited by many nationalities with complex origins and different histories. Its historical roots, however, are chiefly those of the East Slavs, who evolved into the Russian, Ukrainian, and Belorussian peoples. The major pre-Soviet political formations of the East Slavs were, in order, medieval Kievan Rus', Muscovy, and the Russian Empire. Three other states—Poland, Lithuania, and the Mongol Empire—also played crucial roles in the historical development of the Soviet Union.

The first East Slavic state, Kievan Rus', emerged along the Dnepr River Valley, where it controlled the trade route between Scandinavia and the Byzantine Empire. By adopting Christianity from Constantinople, Kievan Rus' began a synthesis of Byzantine and Slavic cultures. Kievan Rus' was the collective possession of a princely family, a fact that led to armed struggles between princes and ultimately to the territorial disintegration of the state. Conquest by the Mongols was the final blow, and subsequently a number of states claimed to be heirs of Kievan Rus'. One of these was Muscovy, located on the northeastern periphery of Kievan Rus' and populated primarily by Russians. Muscovy gradually dominated neighboring territories and expanded into the Russian Empire.

The historical characteristics that emerged in Muscovy were to affect both Russia and the Soviet Union. One such characteristic was the state's dominance over the individual. Mongol, Byzantine, and native Russian roots all contributed to what was referred to as Russian autocracy: the idea that Russian rulers, or tsars, were unlimited in their power. All institutions, including the Russian Orthodox Church, were subordinated to the state and the autocrat. The idea of autocracy survived until the fall of the last tsar.

Continual territorial expansion was another characteristic of Russian history. Beginning with Muscovy's "gathering of the Russian lands," expansion soon went beyond ethnically Russian areas. As a result, Muscovy developed into the huge Russian Empire, eventually stretching from the border with Poland to the Pacific Ocean. Because of its size and military might, Russia became a major power, but acquisition of non-Russian lands and peoples posed continuing nationality problems.

Expansion westward forced Russia to face the perennial questions of its backwardness and its relationship to the West. Muscovy had grown in isolation from the West, but Russia had to adopt

3

Western technology to compete militarily in Europe. Thus, Peter the Great attempted to modernize the country, as did subsequent rulers who struggled, largely unsuccessfully, to raise Russia to European levels of technology and productivity. With the acquisition of technology came Western cultural and intellectual currents that disrupted the development of an independent Russian culture. Native and foreign cultural values were often in contention, and questions of Russia's relationship to the West became an enduring obsession of Russian intellectuals.

Russia's defeat in the Crimean War triggered another attempt at modernization, including the emancipation of the serfs—peasants bound to the land they tilled. Despite major reforms, agriculture remained inefficient, industrialization proceeded haltingly, and new problems emerged. In addition to masses of land-hungry peasants, a budding industrial proletariat and a small but important group of middle-class professionals were becoming dissatisfied. Non-Russians, resentful of Russification (see Glossary), struggled for autonomy. In response to these continuing problems, successive regimes vacillated between repression and reform. The tsars were unwilling to give up autocratic rule or to share power. They, their supporters, and government bureaucrats became more isolated from the rest of society. Intellectuals became more radical, and some became professional revolutionaries.

Despite its internal problems, Russia continued to play a major role in international politics. Its defeat in the Russo-Japanese War, however, sparked a revolution in 1905. Professionals, workers, peasants, non-Russians, and soldiers demanded fundamental reforms. Reluctantly, the last tsar granted a limited constitution, but for a decade he circumvented it and continued autocratic rule.

When World War I began, Russian patriotism at first compensated for the war's disruption and suffering. The government, however, proved incompetent in pursuing the war, and as war-weariness and revolutionary pressures increased, fewer and fewer defended autocracy.

Emergence of the East Slavs

Many ethnically diverse peoples migrated onto the East European Plain, but the East Slavs remained and gradually became dominant. Kievan Rus', the first East Slavic state, emerged in the late ninth century A.D. and developed a complex and frequently unstable political system. Nonetheless, Kievan Rus' flourished until the thirteenth century, when it rapidly declined. A Slavic variant of the Eastern Orthodox religion and a synthesis of Byzantine and Slavic cultures are among its lasting achievements. The disintegration of Kievan Rus' played a crucial role in the evolution of the East Slavs into the Russian, Ukrainian, and Belorussian peoples.

The Peoples of the East European Plain

Long before the appearance of Kievan Rus', Iranian and other peoples lived in the area of the present-day Ukrainian Republic. The most famous of these were the Scythians (ca. 600–200 B.C.), whose stylized animal jewelry can be seen in museums throughout the world. From A.D. 100 to 900, Goths and nomadic Huns, Avars, and Magyars passed though this region but left little of lasting import. More significant was the simultaneous spread of the Slavs, who were agriculturists and beekeepers, as well as hunters, fishers, herders, and trappers. The Slavs demographically dominated the region.

Little is known of the origins of the Slavs. Philologists and archaeologists have surmised that they settled very early in the Carpathian Mountains or in the area of the present-day Belorussian Republic. By A.D. 600, they had split linguistically into southern, western, and eastern branches. The East Slavs settled along the Dnepr River and its tributaries and then spread northward to Lake Ladoga and the Neva River Basin, northeastward to the northern Volga River region, and westward to the northern Dnestr and western Bug river basins. In the eighth and ninth centuries, many of the East Slavic tribes paid tribute to the Khazars, a Turkic-speaking people living in the southern Volga and Caucasus regions.

The East Slavs and the Varangians

By the ninth century, Scandinavian warriors and merchants, called Varangians, had penetrated the East Slavic regions. According to the earliest chronicle of Kievan Rus', a Varangian named Rurik first established himself in Novgorod ca. 860 before moving south and extending his authority to Kiev. The chronicle cited Rurik as the progenitor of the Rurikid Dynasty. This princely clan was to rule in eastern Europe until 1598. Another Varangian, named Oleg, moved south from Novgorod, expelled the Khazars from Kiev, and founded Kievan Rus' ca. 880. In a period of thirty-five years, he subdued the various East Slavic tribes. In 907 he led a campaign against Constantinople, and in 911 he signed a commercial treaty with the Byzantine Empire on the basis of equality. The new state prospered because it controlled the trade route stretching from the Baltic Sea to the Black Sea and because it had an abundant supply of furs, wax, honey, and slaves for export.

5

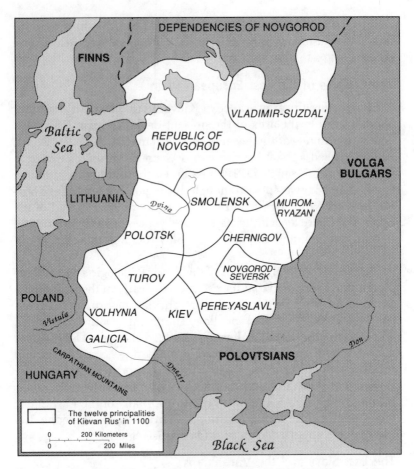

Source: Based on information from David MacKenzie and Michael W. Curran, *A History of Russia and the Soviet Union,* Chicago, 1987, 61.

Figure 2. The Principalities of Kievan Rus', 1136

Historians have debated the role of the Varangians in the establishment of Kievan Rus'. Most Russian—and particularly Soviet—historians have stressed the Slavic influence in the development of the state. Although Slavic tribes had formed their own regional entities by 860, the Varangians undoubtedly accelerated the crystallization of Kievan Rus'.

The Golden Age of Kiev

Kiev dominated Kievan Rus' for the next two centuries (see fig. 2). The grand prince controlled the lands around Kiev, while his theoretically subordinate relatives ruled in other cities and sent him tribute. The zenith of Kievan Rus' came during the reigns of Prince Vladimir (978–1015) and Prince Iaroslav the Wise (1019–54). Both rulers continued the steady expansion of Kievan Rus', begun under Prince Oleg. To enhance his power, Vladimir married the sister of the Byzantine emperor. Iaroslav arranged marriages for his sister and three daughters to the kings of Poland, France, Hungary, and Norway. Vladimir's greatest achievement was the Christianization of Kievan Rus', starting in 988, and he built the first great edifice of Kievan Rus', the Tithe Church in Kiev. Iaroslav promulgated the first East Slavic law code, *Ruska Pravda* (Rus' Justice); built the St. Sofia cathedrals in Kiev and Novgorod; patronized native clergy and monasticism; and is said to have founded a school system. Kiev's great Monastery of the Caves, which functioned in Kievan Rus' as an ecclesiastical academy, was developed under Iaroslav's sons.

Vladimir's choice of Eastern Orthodoxy reflected his close political ties with Constantinople, which dominated the Black Sea and hence the Dnepr River trade. His decision had long-range political, cultural, and religious consequences. The Eastern Orthodox Church had a liturgy written in Cyrillic (see Glossary) and a corpus of translations, which had been produced earlier for the South Slavs. This literature facilitated the conversion to Christianity and introduced East Slavs to rudimentary Greek philosophy, science, and historiography without their having to learn Greek. In contrast, educated people in medieval western and central Europe learned Latin. East Slavs learned neither Greek nor Latin and thus were isolated from Byzantine culture as well as from the culture of their European neighbors to the west.

Rurik's purported descendants organized Kievan Rus' as their shared possession. Princely succession devolved from elder to younger brother and from uncle to nephew, as well as from father to son. Junior members of the dynasty usually began their princely careers by ruling a minor district, then sought to obtain a more lucrative principality, and finally competed for the coveted golden throne of Kiev.

In the eleventh and twelfth centuries, the princes and their retinues—a mixture of Varangian and native Slavic elites plus small Finno-Ugric and Turkic elements—dominated the society of Kievan Rus'. Leading warriors and officials, who sometimes constituted an advisory council, or duma (see Glossary), received income or land from the princes in return for their services. The society of Kievan Rus' did not develop class institutions, the concept of legal reciprocity, or autonomous towns, all of which characterized Western feudalism. Nevertheless, urban merchants, artisans, and laborers sometimes exercised political influence through a popular assembly, or *veche*. In some cases, the *veche* either made agreements with princes or expelled them and invited others to take their places. At the bottom of society was a small stratum of slaves. More important were tribute-paying peasants, who gradually came under the influence of the Orthodox Church and landlords. As in the rest of eastern Europe, the peasants owed labor duty to the princes, but the widespread personal serfdom characteristic of western Europe did not exist in Kievan Rus'.

The Rise of Regional Centers

Kievan Rus' was not able to maintain its position as a powerful and prosperous state. Many factors contributed to its decline, among them its being an amalgamation of disparate lands held together by a ruling clan. As the descendants of Rurik multiplied, they identified themselves with regional interests rather than with a larger patrimony. The princes fought among themselves, frequently forming alliances with Polovtsians, Poles, Hungarians, and others. The decline of Kievan Rus' was further accelerated by a shift in European trade routes resulting from the Crusades. The sacking of Constantinople in 1204 by the Crusaders made the Dnepr trade route marginal. As it declined, Kievan Rus' splintered into many principalities and several large regional centers. The people inhabiting the regional centers evolved into several nationalities: Ukrainians in the southeast and southwest, Belorussians in the northwest, and Russians in the north and northeast.

In the north, Novgorod prospered because it controlled trade routes from the Volga River to the Baltic Sea. As Kievan Rus' declined, Novgorod became more independent. It was ruled by a town oligarchy, and major decisions, including the election or dismissal of a prince, were made at town meetings. In the twelfth century, Novgorod acquired its own archbishop—a sign of its importance and its political independence. In its political structure and mercantile activities, Novgorod, which became a republic in 1136, resembled the north European towns of the Hanseatic League more than the other principalities of Kievan Rus'.

In the northeast, the territory that eventually became Muscovy was colonized by East Slavs who intermingled with the Finno-Ugric tribes of the area. The city of Rostov was the oldest center of the northeast but was supplanted first by the city of Suzdal' and then by the city of Vladimir. By the twelfth century, the combined principality of Vladimir-Suzdal' had become a major power in Kievan Rus'. In 1169 Prince Andrei Bogoliubskii of Vladimir-Suzdal' dealt a severe blow to the waning power of the Kievan Rus' capital of

Kiev when his armies sacked the city. Prince Andrei installed his younger brother in Kiev and continued to rule his realm from the city of Suzdal'. Political power had shifted to the northeast. In 1299, in the wake of a Mongol invasion, the head of the Orthodox Church, the metropolitan of Kiev and all Rus', moved to the city of Vladimir. Thus Vladimir-Suzdal', with its increased political power and with the metropolitan in residence, acted as a continuator of Kievan Rus'.

The principality of Galicia-Volhynia, which had highly developed trade relations with its Polish, Hungarian, and Lithuanian neighbors, emerged as another successor to Kievan Rus' in the southwest. In the early thirteenth century, Prince Roman Mstislavich united the two previously separate principalities, conquered Kiev, and assumed the title of grand prince of Kievan Rus'. His son, Prince Daniil (1230–64), was the first ruler of Kievan Rus' to accept a crown from the Roman papacy, apparently without breaking with Orthodoxy. Early in the fourteenth century, the patriarch of the Orthodox Church in Constantinople granted the rulers of Galicia-Volhynia a metropolitan to compensate for the Kievan metropolitan's move to Vladimir.

A long and losing struggle against the Mongols, however, as well as internal opposition to the prince and foreign intervention, weakened Galicia-Volhynia. With the end of the Mstislavich Dynasty in the mid-fourteenth century, Galicia-Volhynia ceased to exist: Lithuania took Volhynia, and Poland annexed Galicia.

The Mongol Invasion

During its fragmentation, Kievan Rus' faced its greatest threat from invading Mongols. An army from Kievan Rus', together with the Turkic Polovtsians, met a Mongol raiding party in 1223 at the Kalka River. The army of Kievan Rus' and its Polovtsian allies were soundly defeated. A much larger Mongol force overran much of Kievan Rus' in the winter of 1237–38. In 1240 the city of Kiev was sacked, and the Mongols moved on to Poland and Hungary. Of the principalities of Kievan Rus', only the Republic of Novgorod escaped the invasion; it did, however, pay tribute to the Mongols. One branch of the Mongols withdrew to Sarai on the lower Volga River and established the Golden Horde (see Glossary). From Sarai the Golden Horde Mongols controlled Kievan Rus', ruling indirectly through its princes and tax collectors.

The impact of the Mongol invasion was uneven. Some centers, Kiev for example, never recovered from the devastation of the initial attack. The Republic of Novgorod continued to prosper unscathed, and a new entity, the city of Moscow, flourished under

9

the Mongols. Although a Russian army defeated the Golden Horde at Kulikovo in 1380, Mongol domination of territories inhabited by Russians, and demands for tribute from Russian princes, continued until about 1480. In the early fourteenth century, however, Lithuania pushed the Mongols from territories inhabited by Ukrainians and Belorussians and claimed these lands. The Lithuanians accepted the Ruthenian language (Ukrainian-Belorussian) as the state language and maintained the judicial and administrative practices of Kievan Rus'. The grand duke of Lithuania became a contender for the political and cultural heritage of Kievan Rus'. Ultimately, the traditions of Kievan Rus' were superseded by Polish influences in Lithuania.

Historians have debated the long-term impact of Mongol rule on Russian and Soviet society. The Mongols have been blamed for the destruction of Kievan Rus'; the breakup of an old "Russian" nationality into Ukrainian, Belorussian, and Russian components; and the introduction of "oriental despotism" to Russia. But most historians have agreed that Kievan Rus' was not a homogeneous political, cultural, or ethnic entity and that the Mongols merely accelerated its breakup, which had begun before the invasion. Nevertheless, modern historians have tended to credit the Mongol regime with a very important role in the development of Muscovy as a state. Muscovy, for example, adopted its postal road network, census, fiscal system, and military organization from the Mongols.

Kievan Rus' left a powerful legacy. Under the leadership of the Rurikid Dynasty, a large territory inhabited by East Slavs was united into an important, albeit unstable, state. After the acceptance of Eastern Orthodoxy, Kievan Rus' was united by a church structure and developed a Byzantine-Slavic synthesis in culture, the arts, and traditions. In the western part of this area, these traditions helped form the Ukrainian and Belorussian nationalities. On the northeastern periphery of Kievan Rus', these traditions were adapted to form the Russian autocratic state.

Muscovy

The development of the Russian state can be traced from Vladimir-Suzdal' through Muscovy to the Russian Empire. Muscovy drew people and wealth to the northeastern periphery of Kievan Rus'; established trade links to the Baltic, White, and Caspian seas and to Siberia; and created a highly centralized and autocratic political system. Muscovite political traditions, therefore, have exerted a powerful influence on Russian and Soviet society.

St. Sofia Cathedral
(completed in 1046),
Kiev, Ukrainian Republic
Courtesy Jimmy Pritchard

Cathedral of the Assumption
(completed in 1479)
in Moscow's Kremlin,
where coronations of tsars
took place, the last one for
Tsar Nicholas II in 1894
Courtesy Jimmy Pritchard

11

The Rise of Muscovy

When the Mongols invaded the lands of Kievan Rus', Moscow was an insignificant trading outpost in the principality of Vladimir-Suzdal'. Muscovy's remote, forested location offered some security from Mongol attack and occupation, while a number of rivers provided access to the Baltic and Black seas and to the Caucasus region. More important to Moscow's development in the state of Muscovy, however, was its rule by a series of princes who were ambitious, determined, and lucky. The first ruler of the principality of Muscovy, Daniil Aleksandrovich (d. 1303), secured the principality for his branch of the Rurikid Dynasty. His son, Ivan I (1325–40), known as Kalita ("Money Bags"), obtained the title of "Grand Prince of Vladimir" from his Mongol overlords. He closely cooperated with the Mongols and collected tribute from other Russian principalities on their behalf. This enabled him to gain regional ascendancy, particularly over Muscovy's rival, Tver'. In 1327 the Orthodox metropolitan transferred his residency from Vladimir to Moscow, further enhancing the prestige of the new principality.

The grand princes of Muscovy began gathering Russian lands to increase the population and wealth under their rule. The most successful "gatherer" was Ivan III (1462–1505), who in 1478 conquered Novgorod and in 1485 Tver' (see table 2, Appendix A). Through inheritance, Ivan obtained part of Ryazan', and the princes of Rostov and Yaroslavl' voluntarily subordinated themselves to him. Pskov, which remained independent, was conquered in 1510 by Ivan's son, Vasilii III (1505–33). By the beginning of the sixteenth century, Muscovy had united virtually all ethnically Russian lands.

Muscovy gained full sovereignty as Mongol power waned, and Mongol overlordship was officially terminated in 1480. Ivan III was the first Muscovite ruler to use the titles of tsar and "Ruler of all Rus'," laying claim not only to Russian areas but also to parts of the Ukrainian and Belorussian lands of Kievan Rus'. Lithuania, then a powerful state, included other parts of Belorussia and central Ukraine. Ivan III competed with Lithuania for control over some of the semi-independent former principalities of Kievan Rus' in the upper Dnepr and Donets river basins. Through defections of some princes, border skirmishes, and an inconclusive war with Lithuania, Ivan III was able to push westward, and Muscovy tripled in size under his rule.

The Evolution of Russian Autocracy

Outward expansion was accompanied by internal consolidation. By the fifteenth century, the rulers of Muscovy considered the entire territory their collective property. Various semi-independent princes still claimed specific territories, but Ivan forced the lesser princes to acknowledge the grand prince of Muscovy and his descendants as unquestioned rulers and having control over military, judicial, and foreign affairs.

Gradually, the Muscovite ruler emerged as a powerful, autocratic ruler, a "tsar." By assuming the title "tsar," the Muscovite prince underscored that he was a major ruler or emperor, much like the emperor of the Byzantine Empire or the Mongol khan. Indeed, Byzantine terms, rituals, emblems such as the double-headed eagle, and titles were adopted by the Muscovite court after Ivan III's marriage to Sophia Paleologue, the niece of the last Byzantine emperor. Ivan III was the first Russian prince to begin using the title "tsar and autocrat," mimicking the titles used by Christian emperors of Constantinople. At first, "autocrat" indicated merely that the tsar was an independent ruler, but in the reign of Ivan IV (1533–84) the concept was enlarged until it came to mean unlimited rule. Ivan IV was crowned tsar and was thus recognized, at least by the Orthodox Church, as emperor. An Orthodox monk had claimed that, with the fall of Constantinople to the Ottoman Empire in 1453, the Muscovite tsar was the only legitimate Orthodox ruler and that Moscow was the Third Rome because it was the final successor to Rome and Constantinople, the centers of Christianity in earlier eras.

Ivan IV

The development of the tsar's autocratic powers reached a culmination during the reign of Ivan IV. Ivan, who became known as "the Terrible" or "the Dread," strengthened the position of the tsar to an unprecedented degree, thus demonstrating the risks of unbridled power in the hands of an unbalanced individual. Although apparently intelligent and energetic, he suffered from bouts of paranoia and depression, and his rule was prone to extreme violence.

Ivan IV became grand prince of Muscovy in 1533 at the age of three. Various boyar (see Glossary) factions competed for control over the regency until Ivan assumed the throne in 1547. Reflecting Muscovy's new imperial claims, Ivan was crowned tsar in an elaborate ritual modeled after the coronation of the Byzantine emperors. Ivan continued to be assisted by a group of boyars, and his reign began a series of useful reforms. During the 1550s, a new law code was promulgated, the military was revamped, and local government was reorganized. These reforms were undoubtedly intended to strengthen Muscovy in the face of continuous warfare.

During the late 1550s, Ivan became angry with his advisers, the government, and the boyars. Historians have not determined whether his wrath was caused by policy differences, personal animosities, or mental imbalance. In any case, he divided Muscovy into two parts: his private domain and the public realm. For his private domain, Ivan chose some of the most prosperous and important districts in Muscovy. In these areas, Ivan's agents attacked boyars, merchants, and even common people, summarily executing them and confiscating their land and possessions. A decade of terror descended over Muscovy. As a result of the *oprichnina* (see Glossary), Ivan broke the economic and political power of the leading boyar families, thereby destroying precisely those persons who had built up Muscovy and were the most capable of running it. Trade was curtailed, and peasants, faced with mounting taxes and physical violence, began to leave central Muscovy. Efforts to curtail the mobility of the peasants brought Muscovy closer to legal serfdom. In 1572 Ivan finally abandoned the practices followed during the *oprichnina*.

Despite domestic turmoil, Muscovy continued to wage wars and to expand. Ivan defeated and annexed the Kazan' Khanate in 1552 and later the Astrakhan' Khanate. With these victories, Muscovy gained access to the entire Volga River littoral and Central Asia. Muscovy's expansion eastward encountered relatively little resistance. In 1581 the Stroganov merchant family, interested in the fur trade, hired a cossack (see Glossary) leader, Ermak, to lead an expedition into western Siberia. Ermak defeated the Siberian Khanate and claimed the territories west of the Ob' and Irtysh rivers for Muscovy (see fig. 3).

Expanding northwest toward the Baltic Sea proved to be much more difficult. In 1558 Ivan invaded Livonia, which eventually embroiled him in a twenty-five-year war against Poland, Lithuania, Sweden, and Denmark. Despite occasional successes, Ivan's army was pushed back, and Muscovy failed to secure a position on the Baltic Sea. The war drained Muscovy. Some historians believe that the *oprichnina* was initiated to mobilize resources for the war and to counter opposition to it. In any case, Ivan's domestic and foreign policies were devastating for Muscovy, and they led to a period of social struggle and civil war, the so-called Time of Troubles (1598–1613).

The Time of Troubles

Ivan IV was succeeded by his son Fedor, who was mentally deficient. Actual power was exercised by Fedor's brother-in-law, Boris Godunov, a boyar. Perhaps the most important event of Fedor's reign was the proclamation of the patriarchate of Moscow in 1589. The patriarchate culminated the evolution of a separate and totally independent Russian Orthodox Church.

In 1598 Fedor died without an heir, ending the Rurikid Dynasty. Boris Godunov called a *zemskii sobor* (see Glossary), which proclaimed him tsar, although various boyar factions refused to accept him. Widespread crop failures caused a famine between 1601 and 1603, and in the ensuing discontent, a leader emerged who claimed to be Dmitrii, a son of Ivan IV (the actual Dmitrii had died in 1591). This First False Dmitrii obtained military support in Poland and began a march toward Moscow. On his way, he was joined by dissatisfied elements ranging from peasants to boyars. Historians speculate that Godunov would have weathered the crisis, but he died in 1605, and, as a result, the pretender entered Moscow and was crowned tsar, following the murder of Fedor II, Boris Godunov's son.

Subsequently, Muscovy entered a period of continuous chaos. The Time of Troubles included a civil war in which a struggle over the throne was complicated by the machinations of rival boyar factions, the intervention of Poland and Sweden, and intense popular discontent. The First False Dmitrii and his Polish garrison were overthrown, and a boyar, Vasilii Shuiskii, was proclaimed tsar in 1606. In his attempt to retain the throne, Shuiskii allied himself with the Swedes. A Second False Dmitrii, allied with the Poles, appeared. In 1610 the Polish heir apparent was proclaimed tsar, and the Poles occupied Moscow. The Polish presence led to a patriotic revival among the Russians, and a new army—financed by northern merchants and blessed by the Orthodox Church—drove the Poles out of Moscow. In 1613 a *zemskii sobor* chose the boyar Mikhail Romanov as tsar, thus beginning 300 years of Romanov rule.

For over a decade, Muscovy was in chaos, but the institution of autocracy remained intact. Despite the tsar's persecution of the boyars, the dissatisfaction of the townspeople, and the gradual enserfment of the peasantry, efforts at restricting the tsar were only halfhearted. Finding no institutional alternative to autocracy, the discontented rallied behind various pretenders. During this period, politics consisted of gaining influence over an autocrat or placing one's candidate on the throne. The boyars fought among themselves, the lower classes revolted blindly, and foreign armies occupied the Kremlin in Moscow, prompting many to accept tsarist absolutism and autocracy as necessary to restore unity and order in Muscovy.

The Romanovs

The most immediate task of Romanov rule was to restore order. Fortunately for Muscovy, its major enemies, Poland and Sweden,

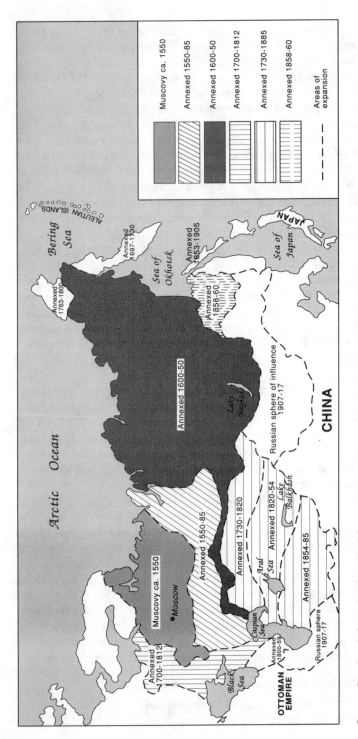

Source: Based on information from Basil Dmytryshyn, *A History of Russia*, Englewood Cliffs, New Jersey, 1977, 410.

Figure 3. Territorial Expansion of Muscovy and the Russian Empire, 1550–1917

were in bitter conflict with each other, and Muscovy obtained peace with Sweden in 1617 and a truce with Poland in 1619. After an unsuccessful attempt to regain Smolensk from Poland in 1632, Muscovy made peace with Poland in 1634. The Polish king, who had been elected tsar during the Time of Troubles, renounced all claims to the title.

Mikhail Romanov was a weak monarch, and state affairs were actually in the hands of his father, Filaret, who in 1619 became patriarch of the Orthodox Church. Similarly, Mikhail's son, Alexis (1645–76), relied on a boyar, Boris Morozov, to run the government. Morozov abused his position by exploiting the populace, and in 1648, after an uprising in Moscow, he was dismissed.

The autocracy survived the Time of Troubles and the rule of weak or corrupt tsars because of the strength of the government's central bureaucracy. Its functionaries continued to serve, regardless of the tsar's legitimacy or the boyar faction controlling the tsar. In the seventeenth century, this bureaucracy expanded dramatically. The number of government departments (*prikazi*) increased from twenty-two in 1613 to eighty by mid-century. Although the departments often had overlapping and conflicting jurisdictions, the central government, through provincial governors, controlled and regulated all social groups, trade, manufacturing, and even the Orthodox Church.

The extent of state control of Russian society was demonstrated by the comprehensive legal code introduced in 1649. By that time, the boyars had largely merged with the elite, who were obligatory servitors of the state, to form a new nobility (*dvorianstvo*). Both groups, whether old or new nobility, were required to serve the state, primarily in the military. In return, they received land and peasants. Peasants, whose right to move to another landlord had been gradually curtailed, were thereafter attached to their domicile. The state fully sanctioned serfdom, and runaway peasants became state fugitives. Landlords had complete power over their peasants and sold, traded, or mortgaged them. Peasants living on state-owned land, however, were not considered serfs. They were organized into communes, which were responsible for taxes and other obligations. Like serfs, however, state peasants were attached to the land they farmed. Burghers, who lived in urban areas and engaged in trade and handicrafts, were assessed taxes and were also prohibited from changing residences. All segments of the population were subject to military levies and special taxes. Flight was the most common escape from state-imposed burdens. By chaining much of Muscovite society to its domicile, the legal code of 1649 curtailed movement and subordinated the people to the interests of the state.

Increased state exactions and regulations exacerbated the social discontent that had been simmering since the Time of Troubles. A major uprising occurred in the Volga region in 1670 and 1671. Stenka Razin, a cossack from the Don River area, spearheaded a revolt that drew together dissatisfied cossacks, escaped serfs, and Turkic ethnic groups. The uprising swept the Volga River Valley and even threatened Moscow. Ultimately, tsarist troops defeated the rebels, and Stenka Razin was publicly tortured and executed.

Expansion and Westernization

Muscovy continued its territorial growth. In the southwest, it acquired eastern Ukraine, which had been under Polish rule. The Ukrainian Cossacks, warriors organized into military formations, lived in the frontier areas bordering Poland, the Tatar lands, and Muscovy. Although they had served the Polish king as mercenary troops, the Ukrainian Cossacks remained fiercely independent and staged a number of uprisings against the Poles. In 1648 the Ukrainian Cossacks revolted and were joined by most of Ukrainian society, which had suffered political, social, religious, and ethnic oppression under Polish rule. After the Ukrainians threw off Polish rule, they needed military help to sustain their gains. In 1654 the leader of the Ukrainian Cossacks, Bohdan Khmel'nyts'kyi, offered to place Ukraine under the protection of the Muscovite tsar rather than the Polish king. After some hesitation, the tsar accepted Khmel'nyts'kyi's offer, which led to a protracted war between Muscovy and Poland. The war was concluded by the Treaty of Andrusovo in 1667. Ukraine was split along the Dnepr River. The western bank was retained by Poland, and the eastern bank remained self-governing under the suzerainty of the tsar.

In the east, Muscovy had obtained western Siberia in the sixteenth century. From this base, merchants, traders, and explorers continued to push east from the Ob' River to the Yenisey River and then from the Yenisey River to the Lena River. By the middle of the seventeenth century, Muscovites had reached the Amur River and the outskirts of the Chinese Empire. After a period of conflict, Muscovy made peace with China in 1689. By the Treaty of Nerchinsk, Muscovy gave up claims to the Amur River Valley. By the middle of the seventeenth century, Muscovy extended eastward through Eurasia to the Pacific Ocean.

Muscovy's southwestern expansion, particularly its incorporation of eastern Ukraine, had unintended consequences. Most Ukrainians were Orthodox, but, having had to compete with the Polish Counter-Reformation, they combined Western intellectual currents with their religion. Through Kiev, Muscovy obtained links

to Polish and central European influences and to the wider Orthodox world. Historically, Ukrainians had been under the jurisdiction of the patriarch of Constantinople. Although the Ukrainian
link stimulated creativity, it also undermined traditional Russian
religious practices and culture. The Russian Orthodox Church discovered that because of its isolation from Constantinople, varia-
tions had crept into its liturgical books and practices. The Russian
Orthodox patriarch, Nikon, was determined to correct the texts
according to the Greek originals. Nikon, however, encountered
fierce opposition because many Russians viewed the corrections
as inspired by foreigners or the devil. The Orthodox Church forced
the reforms, which resulted in a schism in 1667. Those who did
not accept the reforms, the Old Believers, were pronounced heretics
and were persecuted by the church and the state. The chief opposition figure, Avvakum, was burned at the stake. The split subsequently became permanent, and many merchants and prosperous
peasants joined the Old Believers.

The impact of Ukraine and the West was also felt at the tsar's
court. Kiev, through its famed scholarly academy, founded by
Metropolitan Mohila in 1631, was a major transmitter of new ideas
and introduced the Muscovite elite to a central European variant
of the Western world. Among the results of this infusion of ideas
were baroque architecture, literature, and icon painting. Other
more direct channels to the West opened as international trade increased and more foreigners came to Muscovy. The tsar's court
was interested in the West's more advanced technology, particularly if its applications were military in nature. By the end of the
seventeenth century, Ukrainian, Polish, and West European penetration had undermined the Muscovite cultural synthesis—at least
among the elite—and had prepared the way for an even more radical transformation.

Early Imperial Russia

In the eighteenth century, Muscovy was transformed from a static,
somewhat isolated, traditional state into the more dynamic, partially
Westernized, and secularized Russian Empire. This transformation
was in no small measure a result of the vision, energy, and determination of Peter the Great (1682–1725). Historians disagree about
the extent to which Peter himself transformed Russia, but they generally concur that he laid the foundations that shaped the empire over
the next two centuries. The era he initiated signaled the advent of
Russia as a major European power. But although the Russian Empire would play a leading political role for the next century, its reten-
tion of serfdom precluded economic progress of any significant

degree. As west European economic growth accelerated during the Industrial Revolution, Russia began to lag ever further behind, creating new problems for the empire as a great power.

Peter the Great and the Formation of the Russian Empire

As a child of the second marriage of Tsar Alexis, Peter was at first relegated to the background of Russian politics as various court factions struggled for control of the throne. Tsar Alexis was succeeded by his son from his first marriage, Fedor III, a sickly boy who died in 1682. Peter was then made co-tsar with his half brother, Ivan V, but real power was held by Peter's half sister, Sofia. She ruled as regent while the young Peter was allowed to play war games with his friends and roam in Moscow's foreign quarters. These early experiences instilled in him an abiding interest in Western warfare and technology, particularly in military engineering, artillery, navigation, and shipbuilding. In 1689, using troops he had drilled during childhood games, Peter foiled a plot to have Sofia crowned. With the death of Ivan V in 1696, Peter became the sole tsar of Muscovy.

Much of Peter's reign was spent at war. At first he attempted to secure Muscovy's southern borders against the Tatars and the Ottoman Turks. His campaign against a fort on the Sea of Azov failed at first, but having created Russia's first navy, Peter was able to take the port of Azov in 1696. To continue the war with the Ottoman Empire, Peter began looking for allies in Europe. He traveled to Europe, the first tsar to do so, in a so-called Grand Embassy that included visits to Brandenburg, Holland, England, and the Holy Roman Empire. Peter learned a great deal and enlisted into his service hundreds of European technical specialists. The embassy was cut short by a revolt in Moscow that attempted to place Sofia on the throne. Peter's followers crushed the revolt. Peter had hundreds of the participants tortured and killed, and he publicly displayed their bodies as a lesson to others.

Although Peter was unsuccessful in forging an anti-Ottoman coalition in Europe, he found interest in waging war against Sweden during his travels. Seeing an opportunity to break through to the Baltic Sea, Peter made peace with the Ottoman Empire in 1700 and then attacked the Swedes at Narva. Sweden's young king, Charles XII, however, proved to be a military genius and crushed Peter's army. Fortunately for Peter, Charles did not follow his victory with a counteroffensive, but rather became embroiled in a series of wars over the Polish throne. The respite allowed Peter to build a new Western-style army. When the two met again in the town of Poltava in 1709, Peter defeated Charles. Charles escaped to

Column of Glory in Poltava, Ukrainian Republic. The bronze eagle at its top faces the battlefield where, in 1709, Peter the Great defeated King Charles XII of Sweden. Courtesy Jimmy Pritchard

Ottoman territories, and Russia subsequently became engaged in another war with the Ottoman Empire. Russia agreed to return the port of Azov to the Ottoman Empire in 1711. The Great Northern War, which in essence was settled at Poltava, dragged on until 1721, when Sweden agreed to the Treaty of Nystad. Muscovy retained what it had conquered: Livonia, Estonia, and Ingria on the Baltic Sea. Through his victories, Peter had acquired a direct link to western Europe. In celebration, Peter assumed the title of emperor as well as tsar, and Muscovy became the Russian Empire in 1721.

Muscovy's expansion into Europe and transformation into the Russian Empire had been accomplished by restructuring the military, streamlining the government, and mobilizing Russia's financial and human resources. Peter had established Russia's naval forces and reorganized the army along European lines. Soldiers, who served for life, were drafted from the taxed population. Officers were drawn from the nobility and were required to spend lifelong service in either the military or the civilian administration. In 1722 Peter introduced the Table of Ranks, which determined position and status on the basis of service to the tsar rather than on birth or seniority. Even commoners were ennobled automatically if they achieved a certain rank.

Peter also reorganized the governmental structure. The *prikazi* were replaced with colleges, or boards, and the newly created Senate coordinated government policy. Peter's reform of the local governmental system was less successful, but its operations were adequate for collecting taxes and maintaining order. As part of the governmental reform, the Orthodox Church was partially incorporated into the administrative structure of the country. The patriarchate was abolished and replaced by a collective body, the Holy Synod, which was headed by a lay government official.

Peter managed to triple the revenues coming into the state treasury. A major innovation was a capitation, or poll tax, levied on all males except clergy and nobles. A myriad of indirect taxes on alcohol, salt, and even beards added further income. To provide uniforms and weapons for the military, Peter developed a metallurgical and textile industry based on the labor of serfs.

Peter wanted Russia to have modern technologies, institutions, and ideas. He required Western-style education for all male nobles, introduced ''cipher'' schools to teach the alphabet and basic arithmetic, established a printing house, and funded the Academy of Sciences (see Glossary), established just before his death in 1725. He demanded that aristocrats acquire Western dress, tastes, and social customs. As a consequence, the cultural rift between the nobles and the mass of Russia people deepened. Peter's drive for Westernization, his break with past traditions, and his coercive methods were epitomized in the construction of the new, architecturally Western capital, St. Petersburg, situated on land newly conquered on the Gulf of Finland. St. Petersburg faced westward but was constructed by conscripted labor. Westernization by coercion could not arouse the individualistic creative spirit that was an important element of the Western ways Peter so much admired.

Peter's reign raised questions regarding Russia's backwardness, its relationship to the West, its coercive style of reform from above, and other fundamental problems that have confronted subsequent rulers. In the nineteenth century, Russians debated whether Peter correctly pointed Russia toward the West or violated its natural traditions. Historians' views of Peter's reign have tended to reveal their own political and ideological positions as to the essence of Russia's history and civilization.

Era of Palace Revolutions

Having killed his own son, Alexis, who had opposed his father's reforms and served as a rallying point for antireform groupings, Peter changed the rules of succession. A new law provided that the tsar would choose his own heir, but Peter failed to do so before his own death in 1725. The absence of clear rules of succession left the monarchy open to intrigues, plots, coups, and countercoups.

Henceforth, the crucial factor for obtaining the throne was the support of the elite palace guard stationed in St. Petersburg.

At first, Peter's wife, Catherine I, seized the throne. But she died in 1727, and Peter's grandson, Peter II, was crowned tsar. In 1730 Peter II succumbed to smallpox, and Anna, a daughter of the former co-tsar, Ivan V, ascended the throne. The clique of nobles that put Anna on the throne attempted to impose various conditions on her. Although initially accepting these "points," Anna repudiated them after becoming tsarina. Anna was supported by other nobles, who apparently feared oligarchic rule more than autocracy. Despite continuing chaotic struggles for the throne, the nobles did not question the principle of autocratic absolutism.

Anna died in 1740, and her infant grandnephew, Ivan VI, was proclaimed tsar. After a series of coups, however, he was replaced by Peter the Great's daughter Elizabeth (1741–62). During Elizabeth's reign, a Westernized yet Russian culture began to emerge, as witnessed by the founding of Moscow University (1755) and the Academy of Fine Arts (1757). In the same period, Russia also produced its first eminent scientist and scholar, Mikhail V. Lomonosov.

During the rule of Peter's successors, Russia increased its role in the European state system. From 1726 to 1761, Russia was allied with Austria against the Ottoman Empire, which, in turn, was usually supported by France. In the War of Polish Succession (1733–35), Russia and Austria blocked the French candidate to the Polish throne. In a costly war with the Ottoman Empire (1734–39), Russia reacquired the port of Azov. Russia's greatest reach into Europe was during the Seven Years' War (1756–63). Russia had continued its alliance with Austria, but in the "diplomatic revolution" of the period Austria allied itself with France against Prussia. In 1760 Russian forces were at the gates of Berlin. Fortunately for Prussia, Elizabeth died in 1762, and her successor, Peter III, was devoted to the Prussian emperor, Frederick the Great. Peter III allied Russia with Prussia.

Peter III had a very short and unpopular reign. Although a grandson of Peter the Great, he was the son of the duke of Holstein and was raised in a German Lutheran environment. He was therefore considered a foreigner. Making no secret of his contempt for all things Russian, Peter created deep resentment by foisting Prussian military drills on the Russian military, attacking the church, and creating a sudden alliance with Prussia, which deprived Russia of a military victory. Making use of the discontent and fearing for her own position, Peter III's wife, Catherine, deposed her husband in a coup. Peter III was subsequently murdered by Catherine's lover, Aleksei Orlov. Thus, in June 1762 a German princess, who had no legitimate claim to the Russian throne, became Tsarina Catherine II, empress of Russia.

Imperial Expansion and Maturation: Catherine II

Catherine II's reign was notable for imperial expansion and internal consolidation. The empire acquired huge new territories in the south and west. A war that broke out with the Ottoman Empire in 1768 was settled by the Treaty of Kuchuk-Kainarji in 1774. Russia acquired an outlet to the Black Sea, and the Crimean Tatars were made independent of the Ottomans. In 1783 Catherine annexed Crimea, helping to spark the next war with the Ottoman Empire in 1787. By the Treaty of Jassy in 1792, Russia acquired territory south to the Dnestr River. The terms of the treaty fell far short of the goals of Catherine's reputed "Greek project"—the expulsion of the Ottomans from Europe and the renewal of a Byzantine empire under Russian control. The Ottoman Empire, nevertheless, was no longer a serious threat to Russia and was forced to tolerate an increasing Russian influence over the Balkans.

Russia's westward expansion was the result of the partitioning of Poland. As Poland became increasingly weak in the eighteenth century, each of its neighbors—Russia, Prussia, and Austria—tried to place its own candidate on the Polish throne. In 1772 the three agreed on the first partition, by which Russia received parts of Belorussia and Livonia. After the partition, Poland initiated an extensive reform program, which in 1793 led to the second partition. This time Russia obtained most of Belorussia and Ukraine west of the Dnepr River. The partition led to an anti-Russian and anti-Prussian uprising in Poland, which ended with the third partition in 1795. The result was that Poland was wiped off the map.

Although the partitioning of Poland greatly added to Russia's territory and prestige, it also created new difficulties. Russia, having lost Poland as a buffer, had to share borders with both Prussia and Austria. In addition, the empire became more ethnically heterogeneous as it absorbed large numbers of Poles, Ukrainians, Belorussians, and Jews. The fate of the Ukrainians and Belorussians, who were primarily serfs, changed little at first under Russian rule. Roman Catholic Poles, however, resented their loss of independence and proved to be difficult to integrate. Jews, who had been barred from Russia in 1742, were viewed as an alien population, and a decree of January 3, 1792, formally initiated the Pale of Settlement (see Other Major Nationalities, ch. 4). The decree permitted Jews to live only in the western part of the empire, thereby setting the stage for anti-Jewish discrimination in later periods. At

Summer Palace of Peter the Great in Leningrad, Russian Republic. The palace, completed in 1712 in the Dutch style of architecture by the Italian Domenico Trezzini, was converted into a museum under the Soviet regime.
Courtesy Jimmy Pritchard

the same time, the autonomy of Ukraine east of the Dnepr, the Baltic states, and various cossack areas was abolished. With her emphasis on a uniformly administered empire, Catherine presaged the policy of Russification practiced by later tsars and by their successors.

Historians have debated Catherine's sincerity as an enlightened monarch, although few have doubted that she believed in government activism aimed at developing the empire's resources and making its administration more rational and effective. Initially, Catherine attempted to rationalize government procedures through law. In 1767 she created the Legislative Commission, drawn from nobles, townsmen, and others, to codify Russia's laws. Although no new law code was formulated, Catherine's Instruction to the Commission introduced some Russians to Western political and legal thinking.

During the 1768–74 war with the Ottoman Empire, Russia experienced a major social upheaval, the Pugachev Uprising. In 1773, a Don Cossack, Emelian Pugachev, announced that he was Peter III. He was joined in the rebellion by other cossacks, various Turkic tribes who felt the impingement of the Russian centralizing state,

25

and industrial workers in the Ural Mountains, as well as by peasants hoping to escape serfdom. Russia's preoccupation with the war enabled Pugachev to take control of a part of the Volga area, but the regular army crushed the rebellion in 1774.

The Pugachev Uprising bolstered Catherine's determination to reorganize Russia's provincial administration. In 1775 she divided Russia, strictly according to population statistics, into provinces and districts and gave each province an expanded administrative, police, and judicial apparatus. Nobles, who were no longer required to serve the central government, were given significant roles in administering provincial governments.

Catherine also attempted to organize society into well-defined social groups, or estates. In 1785 she issued charters to nobles and townsmen. The Charter to the Nobility confirmed the liberation of the nobles from compulsory service and gave them rights that not even the autocracy could infringe upon. The Charter to the Towns proved to be complicated and ultimately less successful than the one issued to the nobles. Failure to issue a similar charter to state peasants, or to ameliorate the conditions of serfdom, made Catherine's social reforms incomplete.

The intellectual Westernization of the elite continued during Catherine's reign. An increase in the number of books and periodicals also brought forth intellectual debates and social criticism. In 1790 Aleksandr Radishchev published his *Journey from St. Petersburg to Moscow,* a fierce attack on serfdom and the autocracy. Catherine, already frightened by the French Revolution, had Radishchev arrested and banished to Siberia. Radishchev was later recognized as "the father of Russian radicalism."

In many respects, Catherine brought the policies of Peter the Great to fruition and set the foundation for the nineteenth-century empire. Russia became a power capable of competing with its European neighbors on military, political, and diplomatic grounds. Russia's elite became culturally more like the elites of central and west European countries. The organization of society and the government system, from Peter the Great's central institutions to Catherine's provincial administration, remained basically unchanged until the emancipation of the serfs in 1861 and, in some respects, until the fall of the monarchy in 1917. Catherine's push to the south, with the founding of the city of Odessa on the Black Sea, provided the basis for Russia's nineteenth-century grain trade.

Despite such accomplishments, the empire built by Peter I and Catherine II was beset with fundamental problems. A small Europeanized elite, alienated from the mass of ordinary Russians, raised questions about the very essence of Russia's history, culture, and identity. Russia's military preeminence was achieved by reliance on coercion and a primitive command economy based on serfdom. Although economic development was almost sufficient for Russia's eighteenth-century needs, it was no match for those of the Western countries that were being transformed by the Industrial Revolution. Catherine's attempt at organizing society into corporate estates was already being challenged by the French Revolution, which emphasized individual citizenship. Russia's territorial expansion and the incorporation of an increasing number of non-Russians into the empire set the stage for the future nationalities problem. Finally, the first questioning of serfdom and autocracy on moral grounds foreshadowed the conflict between the state and the intelligentsia that was to become dominant in the nineteenth century.

Ruling the Empire

During the early nineteenth century, Russia's population, resources, international diplomacy, and military forces made it one of the most powerful states in the world. Its power enabled it to play an increasingly assertive role in the affairs of Europe. This role drew it into a series of wars against Napoleon, which had far-reaching consequences not only for Europe but also for Russia. After a period of enlightenment, Russia became an active opponent of liberalizing trends in central and western Europe. Internally, Russia's population had grown more diverse with each territorial acquisition. The population included Lutheran Finns, Baltic Germans, Estonians, and some Latvians; Roman Catholic Lithuanians, Poles, and some Latvians; Orthodox and Uniate (see Glossary) Belorussians and Ukrainians; Muslim peoples of various sects; Orthodox Greeks and Georgians; and Apostolic Armenians. As Western influence and opposition to Russian autocracy mounted, the regime reacted by curtailing the activities of persons advocating change, by creating a secret police, and by increasing censorship. The regime remained increasingly committed to its serf-based economy as the means of supporting the upper classes, the government, and the military forces. But Russia's backwardness and inherent weakness were revealed when several powers attacked a Russian fortress in Crimea and forced its surrender.

War and Peace, 1796-1825

Catherine II died in 1796 and was succeeded by her son Paul (1796–1801). Painfully aware that Catherine had planned to bypass him and name his son, Alexander, as tsar, Paul instituted primogeniture in the male line as the basis for succession. It was one

27

of the few lasting reforms of Paul's brief reign. He also chartered a Russian-American company, which led to Russia's acquisition of Alaska. Paul was haughty and unstable, and he frequently reversed his previous decisions, creating administrative chaos and accumulating enemies.

As a major European power, Russia could not escape the wars involving revolutionary and Napoleonic France. Paul became an adamant opponent of France, and Russia joined Britain and Austria in a war against France. Russian troops under one of Russia's most famous generals, Aleksandr Suvorov, performed brilliantly in Italy and Switzerland. Paul, however, reversed himself and abandoned his allies. This reversal, coupled with increasingly arbitrary domestic policies, sparked a coup, and in March 1801 Paul was assassinated.

The new tsar, Alexander I (1801-25), came to the throne as the result of the murder of his father, in which he was implicated. Groomed for the throne by Catherine II and raised in the spirit of enlightenment, Alexander also had an inclination toward romanticism and religious mysticism, particularly in the latter period of his reign. Alexander tinkered with changes in the central government, and he replaced the colleges set up by Peter the Great with ministries, but without a coordinating prime minister. The liberal statesman Mikhail Speranskii proposed a constitutional reform, but it was never implemented.

Alexander's primary focus was not on domestic policy but on foreign affairs, and particularly on Napoleon. Fearing Napoleon's expansionist ambitions and the growth of French power, Alexander joined Britain and Austria against Napoleon. The Russians and Austrians were defeated at Austerlitz in 1805, and the Russians were trounced at Friedland in 1807. Alexander was forced to sue for peace, and by the Treaty of Tilsit, signed in 1807, he became Napoleon's ally. Russia lost little territory under the treaty, and Alexander made use of his alliance with Napoleon for further expansion. He wrested the Grand Duchy of Finland from Sweden in 1809 and acquired Bessarabia from Turkey in 1812.

The Russo-French alliance gradually became strained. Napoleon was concerned about Russia's intentions in the Bosporous and Dardenelles straits. At the same time, Alexander viewed the Grand Duchy of Warsaw, the French-controlled reconstituted Polish state, with suspicion. The requirement of maintaining a continental blockade against Britain made trading difficult, and in 1810 Alexander repudiated the obligation. In June 1812, Napoleon invaded Russia with 600,000 troops—a force that was twice as large as the Russian regular army. Napoleon hoped to inflict a major defeat on the Russians and have Alexander sue for peace. As Napoleon pushed the Russian forces back, he became seriously overextended. Although Napoleon occupied a burning Moscow, the Russians refused to surrender, and Napoleon had to retreat. The harsh wintry weather, combined with continuous harassment by Russian forces, resulted in the destruction of Napoleon's Grand Army. Fewer than 30,000 troops returned from the Russian campaign.

As the French retreated, the Russians pursued them into central and western Europe, to the gates of Paris. After the defeat of Napoleon by the allies, Alexander became known as the "savior of Europe," and he played a prominent role in the redrawing of the map of Europe at the Congress of Vienna in 1815. In the same year, under the influence of religious mysticism, Alexander initiated the creation of the Holy Alliance, an agreement pledging the rulers of the nations involved to act according to Christian principles. More pragmatically, in order to prevent the resurgence of an expansionist France, the Quadruple Alliance had been formed by Russia, Britain, Austria, and Prussia in 1814. The allies created an international system to maintain the territorial status quo. This system, confirmed by a number of international conferences, ensured Russia's influence in Europe.

At the same time, Russia continued its expansion. The Congress of Vienna created the Russian Kingdom of Poland (Russian Poland), to which Alexander granted a constitution. Thus Alexander I became the constitutional monarch of Poland while remaining the autocratic tsar of Russia. He was also the limited monarch of Finland, which had been annexed in 1809 but awarded autonomous status. In 1813 Russia gained territory in the Baku area of the Caucasus at the expense of Iran. By the early nineteenth century, the empire also was firmly ensconced in Alaska.

Historians have generally agreed that a revolutionary movement was born during the reign of Alexander I. Young officers who had pursued Napoleon into western Europe came back to Russia with revolutionary ideas, including liberalism, representative government, and mass democracy. Whereas in the eighteenth century intellectual Westernization had been fostered by a paternalistic, autocratic state, in the nineteenth century Western ideas included opposition to autocracy, demands for representative government, calls for the abolition of serfdom, and, in some instances, advocacy of a revolutionary overthrow of the government. Officers were particularly incensed that Alexander had granted Poland a constitution while Russia remained without one. Several clandestine organizations were preparing for an uprising when Alexander died unexpectedly in 1825. Following his death, there was confusion as to who would succeed him because his heir, Constantine, had relinquished his right to the throne. A group of officers commanding about 3,000 men refused to swear allegiance to the new tsar, Nicholas I, and proclaimed their loyalty to "Constantine and Constitution." Because these events occurred in December 1825, the rebels were called Decembrists. Nicholas had them surrounded and, when they refused to disperse, ordered the army to fire on them. The revolt was soon over, and the Decembrists who remained alive were arrested. Many were exiled to Siberia.

To some extent, the Decembrists were in the tradition of a long line of palace revolutionaries who wanted to place their candidate on the throne. But because the Decembrists also wanted to implement a liberal political program, their revolt has been considered the beginning of a revolutionary movement. The "Decembrists' revolt" was the first open breach between the government and liberal elements—a breach that subsequently widened.

Period of Reaction: Nicholas I, 1825–55

Having experienced the trauma of the Decembrists' revolt, Nicholas I was determined to restrain Russian society. A secret police, the so-called Third Section, ran a huge network of spies and informers. Government censorship and controls were exercised over education, publishing, and all manifestations of public life. The minister of education, Sergei Uvarov, devised a program of "autocracy, Orthodoxy, and nationality" as the guiding principle of the regime. The people were asked to show loyalty to the unlimited authority of the tsar, the traditions of the Orthodox Church, and, in a vague way, to the Russian nation. These principles did not gain the support of the population but instead led to repression in general and to suppression of non-Russian nationalities and religions other than Russian Orthodoxy in particular. For example, the Uniate Church in Ukraine and Belorussia was suppressed in 1839.

The official emphasis on Russian nationalism to some extent contributed to a debate on Russia's place in the world, the meaning of Russian history, and the future of Russia. One group, the Westernizers, believed that Russia remained backward and primitive and could progress only through more thorough Europeanization. Another group, the Slavophiles, idealized the Russia that had existed before Peter the Great. The Slavophiles viewed old Russia as a source of wholeness and looked askance at Western rationalism and materialism. Some of them believed that the Russian peasant commune offered an attractive alternative to Western capitalism and could make Russia a potential social and moral savior

St. Nicholas Cathedral (completed in 1762), Leningrad, Russian Republic. This functioning church is an example of the Russian baroque style.
Courtesy Jimmy Pritchard

of mankind. The Slavophiles, therefore, represented a form of Russian messianism.

Despite the repressions of this period, Russia experienced a flowering of literature and the arts. Through the works of Aleksandr Pushkin, Nikolai Gogol, Ivan Turgenev, and numerous others, Russian literature gained international stature and recognition. After its importation from France, ballet took root in Russia, and classical music became firmly established with the compositions of Mikhail Glinka.

In foreign policy, Nicholas I acted as the protector of ruling legitimism and as the guardian against revolution. His offers to suppress revolution on the European continent, accepted in some instances, earned him the label of "gendarme of Europe." In 1830, after an uprising in France, the Poles in Russia revolted. Nicholas crushed the rebellion, abrogated the Polish constitution, and reduced Russian Poland to the status of a province. In 1848, when a series of revolutions convulsed Europe, Nicholas was in the forefront of reaction. In 1849 he intervened on behalf of the Habsburgs and helped suppress an uprising in Hungary, and he also urged Prussia not to accept a liberal constitution. Having helped conservative forces repel the specter of revolution, Nicholas I seemed to dominate Europe.

Russian dominance proved illusory, however. While Nicholas I was attempting to maintain the status quo in Europe, he adopted an aggressive policy toward the Ottoman Empire. Nicholas I was following the traditional Russian policy of resolving the "Eastern Question" by seeking to partition the Ottoman Empire and establish a protectorate over the Orthodox population of the Balkans. Russia fought a successful war with the Ottomans in 1828 and 1829. In 1833 Russia negotiated the Treaty of Unkiar-Skelessi with the Ottoman Empire. Western statesmen believed mistakenly that the treaty contained a secret clause granting Russia the right to send warships through the Bosporus and Dardanelles straits. As a result, the major European powers intervened and by the London Straits Convention of 1841 affirmed Ottoman control over the straits and forbade any power, including Russia, to send warships through the straits. Based on his role in suppressing the revolutions of 1848 and his mistaken belief that he had British diplomatic support, Nicholas moved against the Ottomans, who declared war in 1853. Thus the Crimean War began. But the European powers were frightened of Russia, and in 1854 Britain, France, and Sardinia joined the Ottoman Empire against Russia. Austria offered the Ottomans diplomatic support, while Prussia remained neutral. The European allies landed in Crimea and laid siege to a well-fortified base at Sevastopol'. After a year's siege the base fell, exposing Russia's inability to defend a major fortification on its own soil. Nicholas I died before the fall of Sevastopol', but even before then he had recognized the failure of his regime. Russia now had to initiate major reforms or cease to be a competitive major power.

The Transformation of Imperial Russia

The late nineteenth and early twentieth centuries were difficult for Russia. Not only did technology and industry continue to develop more rapidly in the West but also new, dynamic, competitive great powers appeared on the world scene: Otto von Bismarck's united Germany, the post-Civil War United States, and Meiji Restoration Japan. Although it was an expanding regional giant in Central Asia straddling the borders of the Ottoman, Iranian, British Indian, and Chinese empires, Russia could not generate enough capital to undergo rapid industrial development or to compete with advanced countries on a commercial basis. Russia's fundamental dilemma was that either it could attempt to accelerate domestic development and risk upheaval at home or it could progress slowly and risk becoming an economic colony of the more advanced world. The transformation of the economic and social structure of Russia was accompanied by political ferment, particularly among the intelligentsia, and also by impressive developments in literature, music, the fine arts, and the natural sciences.

Economic Developments

Throughout the last half of the nineteenth century, Russia's economy developed more slowly than did that of the major European nations to its west. The population of Russia was substantially larger than those of the more developed Western countries, but the vast majority of the people lived in rural communities and engaged in relatively primitive agriculture. Industry, in general, had greater state involvement than in western Europe, but in selected sectors it was developing with private initiative, some of it foreign. The population doubled between 1850 and 1900, but it remained chiefly rural well into the twentieth century. Russia's population growth rate from 1850 to 1910 was the fastest of all the major powers except for the United States (see table 3, Appendix A).

Agriculture, which was technologically underdeveloped, remained in the hands of former serfs and former state peasants, who together constituted about four-fifths of the population. Large estates of more than fifty square kilometers accounted for about 20 percent of all farmland, but for the most part they were not worked in efficient, large-scale units. Small-scale peasant farming and the growth of the rural population produced extensive agricultural development because land was used more for gardens and fields of grain and less for grazing meadows than it had been in the past (see table 4, Appendix A).

Industrial growth was significant, although unsteady, and in absolute terms it was not extensive. Russia's industrial regions included Moscow, the central regions of the country, St. Petersburg, the Baltic cities, Russian Poland, some areas along the lower Don and Dnepr rivers, and the Ural Mountains. By 1890 Russia had about 32,000 kilometers of railroads and 1.4 million factory workers, the majority of them in the textile industry. Between 1860 and 1890, coal production had grown about 1,200 percent to over 6.6 million tons, and iron and steel production had more than doubled to 2 million tons. The state budget, however, had more than doubled, and debt expenditures had quadrupled, constituting 28 percent of official expenditures in 1891. Foreign trade was inadequate to meet the empire's needs, and surpluses sufficient to cover the debts incurred to finance trade with the West were not realized until high industrial tariffs were introduced in the 1880s.

Reforms and Their Limits, 1855–92

Tsar Alexander II, who succeeded Nicholas I in 1855, was a conservative who nonetheless saw no alternative to change and who initiated substantial reforms in education, the government, the

33

judiciary, and the military, in addition to emancipating the serfs. His reforms were accelerated after Russia's military weakness and backwardness had become apparent during the Crimean War. Following Alexander's assassination in 1881, his son Alexander III reasserted government controls.

In 1861 Alexander II proclaimed the emancipation of about 20 million privately held serfs. Local commissions, which were dominated by landlords, effected emancipation by giving land and limited freedom to the serfs. The former serfs usually remained in the village commune, or mir (see Glossary), but were required to make redemption payments, which were stretched out over a period of almost fifty years, to the government. The government compensated former owners of serfs by issuing them bonds.

The regime had envisioned that the 50,000 landlords who possessed estates of over 110 hectares would thrive without serfs and would continue to provide loyal political and administrative leadership in the countryside. The government also had envisioned that peasants would produce sufficient crops for their own consumption and for export sales, thereby helping to finance most of the government's expenses, imports, and foreign debt. Neither of the government's visions was realistic, and both the former serfs and the former owners of serfs were dissatisfied with the outcome of emancipation. Because the lands given to serfs by local commissions were often poor and because Russian agricultural methods were inadequate, the new peasants soon fell behind in their payments to the government. The former owners of serfs, most of whom could neither farm nor manage estates without their former serfs, often had to sell their lands to remain solvent. In addition, the value of their government bonds fell as the peasants failed to make their redemption payments.

Reforms of the local governmental system closely followed emancipation. In 1864 most local government in the European part of Russia was organized into provincial zemstvos (see Glossary) and district zemstvos, which included representatives of all classes. In 1870 elected city councils, or dumas, were formed. Dominated by nobles and other property owners and constrained by provincial governors and the police, the zemstvos and city dumas were empowered to raise taxes and levy labor to develop, maintain, and operate local transportation, education, and public health care systems.

In 1864 the regime implemented judicial reforms. In major towns, it established Western-style courts with juries. In general, the judicial system functioned effectively, but sometimes juries sympathized with obvious criminals and refused to convict them. The government was unable, financially and culturally, to extend the court system to the villages, where traditional peasant justice continued to operate with minimal interference from provincial officials. In addition, judges were instructed to decide each case on its merits and not to use precedents, which would have enabled them to construct a body of law independent of state authority. Under the reform, the Senate, one of the highest government bodies, adopted more of the characteristics of a supreme court, with three major branches: civil, criminal, and administrative.

Other major reforms took place in the educational and cultural spheres. The accession of Alexander II brought a social restructuring that required a public discussion of issues. Accordingly, the regime lifted some manifestations of censorship, yet in 1863 it prohibited publishing in the Ukrainian language. In 1866, when an attempt was made to assassinate the tsar, censorship was reinstated, but pre-1855 levels of control were not restored. Universities, which were granted autonomy in 1861, were also restricted in 1866. The central government, attempting to act through the zemstvos but lacking effective resources, sought to establish uniform curricula for elementary schools and to control the schools by imposing conservative policies. Because many liberal teachers and school officials were only nominally subject to the reactionary Ministry of Education, the regime's educational achievements were mixed after 1866.

In the financial sphere, the State Bank was established in 1866, and Russia's currency was put on a firmer footing. The Ministry of Finance supported railroad development, facilitating vital exports, but it was cautious and moderate in its foreign ventures. The ministry also founded the Peasant Land Bank in 1882 to enable enterprising farmers to acquire more land. The Ministry of the Interior, however, countered this policy by establishing the Nobles' Land Bank in 1885 to forestall foreclosures of mortgages.

The regime also sought to reform the military. One of the chief reasons for the emancipation of the serfs was to facilitate the transition from a large standing army to a reserve army by instituting territorial levies and mobilization in times of need. Before emancipation, serfs could not be given military training and then returned to their owners. Bureaucratic inertia, however, obstructed military reform until the Franco-Prussian War (1870–71) demonstrated the necessity of building a modern army. The levy system introduced in 1874 gave the army a role in teaching many peasants to read and in pioneering medical education for women. But despite these military reforms, the army remained backward. Officers often preferred bayonets to bullets and feared that long-range sights on rifles would induce cowardice. In spite of some notable achievements, Russia did not keep pace with Western technological developments in the construction of rifles, machine guns, artillery, ships, and naval ordnance. Also, naval modernization in the 1860s failed to spur broad development of Russia's industrial base.

In 1881 revolutionaries assassinated Alexander II. His son Alexander III (1881–94) initiated a period of political reaction, which intensified a counterreform movement that had begun in 1866. He strengthened the security police, reorganized as the Okhrana (see Glossary), gave it extraordinary powers, and placed it under the Ministry of the Interior. Dmitrii Tolstoi, Alexander's minister of the interior, instituted the use of land captains, who were noble overseers of districts, and he restricted the power of the zemstvos and dumas. Alexander III assigned his former tutor, the reactionary Konstantin Pobedonostsev, to be the procurator (see Glossary) of the Holy Synod of the Orthodox Church and Ivan Delianov to be the minister of education. In their attempts to "save" Russia from "modernism," they revived religious censorship, persecuted the non-Orthodox and non-Russian population, fostered anti-Semitism, and suppressed the autonomy of the universities. Their attacks on liberal and non-Russian elements alienated large segments of the population. The nationalities, particularly Poles, Finns, Latvians, Lithuanians, and Ukrainians, reacted to the regime's efforts to Russify them by intensifying their own nationalism. Many Jews emigrated or joined radical movements. Secret organizations and political movements continued to develop despite the regime's efforts to quell them.

Foreign Affairs after the Crimean War, 1856–93

After the Crimean War, Russia pursued cautious and intelligent foreign policies until nationalist passions and another Balkan crisis almost caused a catastrophic war in the late 1870s. The 1856 Treaty of Paris concluded at the end of the Crimean War demilitarized the Black Sea and deprived Russia of southern Bessarabia and a narrow strip of land at the mouth of the Danube River. It also nullified the 1774 Treaty of Kuchuk-Kainarji by theoretically providing European protection of the Christians living in the Ottoman Empire. Russian statesmen viewed Britain and Austria (Austria-Hungary as of 1867) as opposed to revising the Treaty of Paris, and they sought good relations with France, Prussia, and the United States. Prussia (Germany as of 1871) replaced Britain as Russia's chief banker.

Following the Crimean War, the regime revived its expansionist policies. Russian troops first moved to quell the lingering revolts of Muslim tribesmen in the Caucasus. Once the revolts were crushed, the army resumed its expansion into Central Asia. Attempts were made to ensure that Britain would not be unduly alarmed by Russia's policy of leaving the territories directly bordering Afghanistan and Iran nominally independent. Russia also supported Iranian attempts to expand into Afghanistan—a move that strained the resources of British India. At the same time, Russia followed the United States, Britain, and France in establishing relations with Japan, and it, together with Britain and France, obtained concessions from China consequent to the Second Opium War (1856–60). By the Treaty of Aigun in 1858 and the Treaty of Beijing in 1860, China was forced to cede Russia extensive trading rights and regions adjacent to the Amur and Ussuri rivers, and it allowed Russia to begin building a port and naval base at Vladivostok. Meanwhile, in 1867 the logic of the balance of power and the cost of developing and defending the Amur-Ussuri region dictated that Russia sell Alaska to the United States in order to acquire much-needed funds.

As part of the regime's foreign policy goals in Europe, Russia gave guarded support to the anti-Austrian diplomacy of the French. A weak Franco-Russian entente soured, however, when France backed a Polish uprising against Russian rule in 1863. Russia then aligned itself more closely with Prussia and tolerated the unification of Germany in exchange for a revision of the Treaty of Paris and the remilitarization of the Black Sea. These diplomatic achievements came at a London conference in 1871, following Prussia's defeat of France. After 1871 Germany, united by Prussia, was the strongest continental power in Europe. It supported both Russia and Austria-Hungary, and in 1873 it formed the loosely knit League of the Three Emperors with those two powers to forestall them from forming an alliance with France.

Nevertheless, Austro-Hungarian and Russian ambitions clashed in the Balkans, where rival nationalities and anti-Ottoman sentiments seethed. In the 1870s, Russian nationalist opinion became a serious domestic factor, supportive of policies that advocated liberating Balkan Christians from Ottoman rule and making Bulgaria and Serbia quasi-protectorates of Russia. From 1875 to 1877, the Balkans crisis heated, with rebellions in Bosnia, Hercegovina, and Bulgaria, and with a Serbo-Ottoman war. Russia, however, promised not to exercise influence in the western Balkans.

In early 1877, Russia went to war with the Ottoman Empire, and by December its troops were nearing Constantinople. Russia's nationalist diplomats and generals persuaded Alexander II to force the Ottomans to sign the Treaty of San Stefano in March 1878. The treaty created an enlarged Bulgaria that stretched into the southwestern Balkans. This development alarmed Britain, which threatened war, and an exhausted Russia backed down. At the Congress of Berlin in July 1878, Russia agreed to the creation of a smaller Bulgaria. Russian nationalists were furious with Austria-Hungary and Germany, but the tsar accepted a revived and strengthened League of the Three Emperors as well as Austrian hegemony in the western Balkans.

Russian diplomatic and military interests subsequently turned to the East. Russian troops occupied Turkmen lands on the Iranian and Afghan borders, raising British concerns, but German support of Russian advances averted a possible Anglo-Russian war. The Bulgarians became angry with Russia's continuing interference in Bulgarian affairs and sought support from Austria. In turn, Germany, displaying firmness toward Russia, protected Austria from the tsar while mollifying him with a bilateral defensive alliance, the Reinsurance Treaty of 1887 between Germany and Russia. Within a year, Russo-German acrimony led to Bismarck's forbidding further Russian loans, and France replaced Germany as Russia's financier. In 1890 Kaiser Wilhelm II dismissed Bismarck, and the loose Russo-Prussian entente, which had held fast for more than twenty-five years, collapsed. The consequence of this development was that Russia allied itself with France in 1893 by entering into a joint military convention, which matched the German-Austrian dual alliance of 1879.

The Age of Realism in Literature

Russian literature in the last half of the nineteenth century provided a congenial and artistic medium for the discussion of political and social issues that could not be addressed directly because of government restrictions. The writers of this period shared important qualities: great attention to realistic, detailed descriptions of everyday Russian life; the lifting of the taboo on describing the vulgar, unsightly side of life; and a satirical attitude toward mediocrity and routine. Although varying widely in style, subject matter, and viewpoint, these writers stimulated government bureaucrats, nobles, and intellectuals to think about important social issues. This period of literature, which became known as the Age of Realism, lasted from about mid-century to 1905. The literature of the Age of Realism owed a great debt to three authors and to a literary critic of the preceding half-century: Aleksandr Pushkin, Mikhail Lermontov, Nikolai Gogol, and Vissarion Belinskii. These figures set a pattern for language, subject matter, and narrative techniques,

Grave of Russian novelist
Fedor Dostoevskii in the
Tikhvin Cemetery
of the Aleksandr Nevskii
Monastery, Leningrad,
Russian Republic
Courtesy Jimmy Pritchard

which before 1830 had been very poorly developed. The critic
Belinskii became the patron saint of the radical intelligentsia throughout the century.

The main outlet for literary opinion in the Age of Realism was
the "thick journal"—a combination of original literature, criticism,
and a wide variety of other material. These publications reached
a large portion of the intelligentsia. Most of the materials of the
major writers and critics of the period were featured in such journals, and published debates were common between journals of various viewpoints. Much of the prose literature of the period contained
sharply polemical messages, favoring either radical or reactionary
positions concerning the problems of Russian society. Ivan Turgenev
was perhaps the most successful at integrating social concerns with
true literary art. His *Hunter's Sketches* and *Fathers and Sons* portrayed
Russia's problems with great realism and with enough artistry that
these works have survived as classics. Many writers of the period
did not aim for social commentary, but the realism of their por-
trayals nevertheless drew comment from radical critics. Such writers
included the novelist Ivan Goncharov, whose *Oblomov* is a very negative portrayal of the provincial gentry, and the dramatist Aleksandr
Ostrovskii, whose plays uniformly condemned the bourgeoisie.

Above all the other writers stand two: Lev Tolstoy and Fedor
Dostoevskii, the greatest talents of the age. Their realistic style transcended immediate social issues and explored universal issues such

as morality and the nature of life itself. Although Dostoevskii was sometimes drawn into polemical satire, both writers kept the main body of their work above the dominant social and political preoccupations of the 1860s and 1870s. Tolstoy's *War and Peace* and *Anna Karenina* and Dostoevskii's *Crime and Punishment* and *The Brothers Karamazov* have endured as genuine classics because they drew the best from the Russian realistic heritage while focusing on broad human questions. Although Tolstoy continued to write into the twentieth century, he rejected his earlier style and never again reached the level of his greatest works.

The literary careers of Tolstoy, Dostoevskii, and Turgenev had ended by 1881. Anton Chekhov, the major literary figure in the last decade of the nineteenth century, contributed in two genres: short story and drama. Chekhov, a realist who examined not society as a whole but the foibles of individuals, produced a large volume of sometimes tragic, sometimes comic short stories and several outstanding plays, including *The Cherry Orchard,* a dramatic chronicling of the decay of a Russian aristocratic family.

The Rise of Revolutionary Populism and Russian Marxism, 1855–90

The reforms of Alexander II, particularly his lifting of state censorship, fostered the development of political and social thought. The regime relied on journals and newspapers to gain support for its domestic and foreign polices. But liberal, nationalist, and radical writers also helped mold opinion opposed to tsarism, private property, and the imperial state. Because many intellectuals, professionals, peasants, and workers shared these sentiments, the publications and the organizations that the radicals joined were perceived as dangerous to the regime. From the 1860s through the 1880s, Russian radicals, collectively known as "Populists" (Narodniki), focused chiefly on the peasantry, whom they identified as "the people" (*narod*).

Among the leaders of the Populist movement were radical writers, idealists, and advocates of terrorism. In the 1860s, Nikolai Chernyshevskii, the most important radical writer of the period, posited that Russia could bypass capitalism and move directly to socialism. His most influential work, *What Is to Be Done?* (1861), describes the role of an individual of a "superior nature" who guides a new, revolutionary generation. Other radicals such as the incendiary anarchist Mikhail Bakunin and his terrorist collaborator, Sergei Nechaev, urged direct action. The calmer Petr Tkachev argued against the advocates of Marxism (see Glossary), maintaining that a centralized revolutionary band had to seize power before socialism could fully develop. Disputing his views, the moralist and individualist Petr Lavrov made a call "to the people" that was heeded in 1873 and 1874 when hundreds of idealists left their schools for the countryside to try to generate a mass movement among the *narod*. The Populist campaign failed, however, when the peasants showed hostility to the urban idealists and the government more willingly began to consider nationalist opinion.

The radicals reconsidered their approach, and in 1876 they formed a propagandist organization called Land and Liberty (Zemlia i volia), which leaned toward terrorism. It became even more oriented toward terrorism three years later, renamed itself the People's Will (Narodnaia volia), and in 1881 was responsible for the assassination of Alexander II. In 1879 Georgii Plekhanov formed a propagandist faction of Land and Liberty called Black Repartition (Chernyi peredel), which advocated reassigning all land to the peasantry. This group studied Marxism, which, paradoxically, was principally concerned with urban industrial workers. The People's Will remained underground, but in 1887 a young member of the group, Aleksandr Ulianov, attempted to assassinate Alexander III and was arrested and executed. Another Ulianov, Vladimir, was greatly affected by his brother's execution. Influenced by Chernyshevskii's writings, he also joined the People's Will and later, under the influence of Plekhanov, converted to Marxism. The younger Ulianov later changed his name to Lenin.

Serge Witte and Accelerated Industrialization, 1891–1903

In the late 1800s, Russia's domestic backwardness and vulnerability in foreign affairs reached crisis proportions. A famine claiming a half-million lives in 1891 exemplified the domestic crisis, and activities by Japan and China near Russia's borders were perceived as threats from abroad. In reaction, the regime was forced to adopt the ambitious but costly economic programs of Sergei Witte, the country's strong-willed minister of finance. Witte championed a combination of foreign loans, conversion to the gold standard, heavy taxation of the peasantry, accelerated development of heavy industry, and a trans-Siberian railroad. These policies were designed to modernize the country, secure the Russian Far East, and give Russia a commanding position with which to exploit the resources of China's northern territories, Korea, and Siberia. This expansionist foreign policy was Russia's version of the imperialism so characteristic of the relations of advanced capitalist countries with weak and backward areas during the nineteenth century. The accession of the pliable Nicholas II in 1894 resulted in the domination of the government by Witte and other powerful ministers.

The results of Witte's policies were mixed. In spite of a severe depression at the end of the century, Russia's coal, iron, steel, and oil production tripled between 1890 and 1900. Railroad mileage almost doubled, giving Russia the most track of any nation other than the United States. Yet Russian grain production and exports failed to rise significantly, and imports grew faster than exports, although the latter subsequently rose. The state budget also more than doubled, absorbing some of the country's economic growth. Western historians have differed as to the merits of Witte's reforms, with some believing that many domestic industries that did not benefit from subsidies or contracts suffered a setback. Moreover, most analysts have agreed that the Trans-Siberian Railway and the ventures into Manchuria and Korea were economic losses for Russia and a drain on the treasury. Certainly the financial costs of his reforms contributed to Witte's dismissal as minister of finance in 1903.

The Development of Radical Political Parties, 1892–1904

During the 1890s, Russia's industrial development led to a significant increase in the size of the urban bourgeoisie and the working class, setting the stage for a more dynamic political atmosphere and the development of radical parties. Because much of Russia's industry was owned by the state or by foreigners, the working class was comparatively stronger and the bourgeoisie comparatively weaker than in the West. Because the nobility and the wealthy bourgeoisie were politically timid, the establishment of working-class and peasant parties preceded that of bourgeois parties. Thus, in the 1890s and early 1900s strikes and agrarian disorders prompted by abysmal living and working conditions, high taxes, and land hunger became more frequent. The bourgeoisie of various nationalities developed a host of different parties, both liberal and conservative.

Socialist parties were formed on the basis of the nationalities of their members. Russian Poles, who had suffered significant administrative and educational Russification, founded the nationalistic Polish Socialist Party in Paris in 1892. Its founders hoped that it would help reunite a divided Poland from territories held by Austria and Germany and by Russia. In 1897 the Bund was founded by Jewish workers in Russia, and it became popular in western Ukraine, Belorussia, Lithuania, and Russian Poland. In 1898 the Russian Social Democratic Labor Party was formed. The Finnish Social Democrats remained separate, but the Latvians and Georgians associated themselves with the Russian Social Democrats. Armenians were inspired by both Russian and Balkan revolutionary

On March 1, 1881, the building in the foreground was a cheese shop, from which members of the radical revolutionary group People's Will, posing as shop employees, assassinated Tsar Alexander II. Leningrad, Russian Republic. Courtesy Stephen Burant

traditions, and they operated in both Russia and the Ottoman Empire. Politically minded Muslims living in Russia tended to be attracted to the pan-Islamic and pan-Turkic movements that developed in Egypt and the Ottoman Empire. Russians who fused the ideas of the old Populists and urban socialists formed Russia's largest radical movement, the United Socialist Revolutionary Party, which combined the standard Populist ingredients of propaganda and terrorist activities.

Vladimir I. Ulianov was the most politically talented of the revolutionary socialists. In the 1890s, he labored to wean young radicals away from populism to Marxism. Exiled from 1895 to 1899 in Siberia, where he took the name Lenin, he was the master tactician among the organizers of the Russian Social Democratic Labor Party. In December 1900, he founded the newspaper *Iskra* (Spark). In his book *What Is to Be Done?* (1902), Lenin developed the theory that a newspaper published abroad could aid in organizing a centralized revolutionary party to direct the overthrow of an autocratic government. He then worked to establish a tightly organized, highly disciplined party to do so in Russia. At the Second Party Congress of the Russian Social Democratic Labor Party in 1903, he forced the Bund to walk out, and he induced a split between his majority Bolshevik faction and the minority Menshevik faction, which believed more in worker spontaneity than in strict organizational tactics. Lenin's concept of a revolutionary party and a worker-peasant alliance owed more to Tkachev and to the People's Will than to Karl Marx and Friedrich Engels, the developers of Marxism. Young Bolsheviks such as Joseph V. Stalin and Nikolai I. Bukharin looked to Lenin as their leader.

Imperialism in Asia and the Russo-Japanese War, 1894–1905

At the turn of the century, Russia gained maneuvering room in Asia because of its alliance with France and the growing rivalry between Britain and Germany. Tsar Nicholas failed to orchestrate a coherent Far Eastern policy because of ministerial conflicts. Russia's uncoordinated and aggressive moves in the region ultimately led to the Russo-Japanese War (1904–05).

By 1895 Germany was competing with France for Russia's favor, and British statesmen hoped to negotiate with the Russians to demarcate spheres of influence in Asia. This situation enabled Russia to intervene in northeastern Asia after Japan's victory over China in 1895. Japan was forced to make concessions in the Liaotung Peninsula and Port Arthur in southern Manchuria. The next year, Witte used French capital to establish the Russo-Chinese Bank. The goal of the bank was to finance the construction of a railroad across northern Manchuria and thus shorten the Trans-Siberian Railway. Within two years, Russia had acquired leases on the Liaotung Peninsula and Port Arthur and had begun building a trunk line from Harbin to Port Arthur.

In 1900 China reacted to foreign encroachments on its territory with an armed popular uprising, the Boxer Rebellion. Russian military contingents joined forces from Europe, Japan, and the United States in restoring order in northern China. A force of 180,000 Russian troops fought to pacify part of Manchuria and to secure its railroads. The Japanese, however, backed by Britain and the United States, insisted that Russia evacuate Manchuria. Witte and some Russian diplomats wanted to compromise with Japan and trade Manchuria for Korea, but a group of Witte's reactionary enemies, courtiers, and army and naval leaders refused to compromise. The tsar favored their viewpoint, and, disdaining Japan's threats—despite the latter's formal alliance with Britain—the Russian government equivocated until Japan declared war in early 1904.

Japan's location, technological superiority, and higher morale gave it command of the seas, and Russia's sluggishness and incompetent commanders were the cause of continuous setbacks on land. In January 1905, after an eight-month siege, Port Arthur surrendered, and in March the Japanese forced the Russians to withdraw north of Mukden. In May, at the Tsushima Straits, the

Japanese destroyed Russia's last hope in the war, a fleet assembled from the navy's Baltic and Mediterranean squadrons. Theoretically, Russian army reinforcements could have driven the Japanese from the Asian mainland, but revolution at home and diplomatic pressure forced the tsar to seek peace. Russia, accepting American mediation, ceded southern Sakhalin to Japan, and it acknowledged Japan's ascendancy in Korea and southern Manchuria.

The Last Years of Tsardom

The Russo-Japanese War was a turning point in Russian history. It led to a popular uprising against the government that forced the regime to respond with domestic economic and political reforms. Advocates of counterreform and groups serving parochial interests, however, actively sought control of the regime's policies. In foreign affairs, Russia again became an intrusive participant in Balkan affairs and in the international political intrigues of major European powers. As a consequence of its foreign policies, Russia was drawn into a world war that its domestic policies rendered it poorly prepared to wage. The regime, severely weakened by internal turmoil and a lack of strong leadership, was ultimately unable to surmount the traumatic events that would lead to the fall of tsarism and initiate a new era in Russian and world history.

The Revolution of 1905 and Counterrevolution, 1905–07

The Russo-Japanese War accelerated the rise of political movements among all classes and the major nationalities, including propertied Russians. By early 1904, Russian liberals active in assemblies of nobles, zemstvos, and the professions had formed an organization called the Union of Liberation. In the same year, they joined with Finns, Poles, Georgians, Armenians, and with Russian members of the Socialist Revolutionary Party to form an anti-autocratic alliance. They later promoted the broad, professional Union of Unions. In early 1905, Father Georgii Gapon, a Russian Orthodox priest who headed a police-sponsored workers' association, led a huge, peaceful march in St. Petersburg to present a petition to the tsar. Nervous troops responded with gunfire, killing several hundred people, and thus the Revolution of 1905 began. Called "Bloody Sunday," this event, along with the failures incurred in the war with Japan, prompted opposition groups to instigate more strikes, agrarian disorders, army mutinies, and terrorist acts and to form a workers' council, or soviet (see Glossary), in St. Petersburg. Armed uprisings occurred in Moscow, the Urals, Latvia, and parts of Poland. Activists from the zemstvos and the Union of Unions formed the Constitutional Democratic Party, whose members were known as Kadets.

Some upper-class and propertied activists were fearful of these disorders and were willing to compromise. In late 1905, Nicholas, under pressure from Witte, issued the so-called October Manifesto, giving Russia a constitution and proclaiming basic civil liberties for all citizens. The constitution envisioned a ministerial government responsible to the tsar, not to the proposed national Duma—a state assembly to be elected on a broad, but not wholly equitable, franchise. Those who accepted this arrangement formed a center-right political party, the Octobrists. The Kadets held out for a ministerial government and equal, universal suffrage. Because of their political principles and continued armed uprisings, Russia's leftist parties were in a quandary over whether or not to participate in the Duma elections. At the same time, rightists, who had been perpetrating anti-Jewish pogroms, actively opposed the reforms. Several monarchist and protofascist groups wishing to subvert the new order also arose. Nevertheless, the regime continued to function, eventually restoring order in the cities, the countryside, and the army. In the process, several thousand officials were murdered by terrorists, and an equal number of terrorists were executed by the government. Because the government was successful in restoring order and in securing a loan from France before the Duma met, Nicholas was in a strong position and therefore able to dismiss Witte, who had been serving as Russia's chief minister.

The First Duma, which was elected in 1906, was dominated by the Kadets and their allies, with the mainly nonparty radical leftists slightly weaker than the Octobrists and the nonparty center-rightists combined. The Kadets and the government were deadlocked over the adoption of a constitution and peasant reform, leading to the dissolution of the Duma and the scheduling of new elections. In spite of an upsurge of leftist terror, radical leftist parties participated in the election and, together with the nonparty left, gained a plurality of seats, followed by a loose coalition of Kadets and of Poles and other nationalities in the political center. The impasse continued, however, when the Second Duma met in 1907.

The Tenuous Regimes of Stolypin and Kokovstev, 1907–14

In 1907 Petr Stolypin, the new chief minister, instituted a series of major reforms. In June 1907, he dissolved the Second Duma and promulgated a new electoral law, which vastly reduced the electoral weight of lower class and non-Russian voters and increased the weight of the nobility. This political coup succeeded to the extent that the government restored order. New elections in the fall returned a more conservative Third Duma, which was dominated by Octobrists. Even this Duma, however, quarreled with the government over a variety of issues: the composition of the naval staff, the autonomous status of Finland, the introduction of zemstvos into the western provinces, the reform of the peasant court system, and the establishment of workers' insurance organizations under police supervision. In these disputes, the Duma, with the appointed aristocratic-bureaucratic upper house, was sometimes more conservative than the government, and at other times it was more legally or constitutionally minded. The Fourth Duma, elected in 1912, was similar in composition to the Third Duma, but a progressive faction of Octobrists split from the right and joined the political center.

Stolypin's boldest measure was his peasant reform program, which allowed, and sometimes forced, the breakup of communes as well as the establishment of full private property. Through the reform program, Stolypin hoped to create a class of conservative landowning farmers loyal to the tsar. Most peasants, however, did not want to lose the safety of the commune or to permit outsiders to buy village land. By 1914 only about 10 percent of all peasant communes had been dissolved. Nevertheless, the economy recovered and grew impressively from 1907 to 1914, not only quantitatively but also in terms of the formation of rural cooperatives and banks and the generation of domestic capital. By 1914 Russian steel production equaled that of France and Austria-Hungary, and Russia's economic growth rate was one of the highest in the world. Although Russia's external debt was very high, it was declining as a percentage of the gross national product (GNP—see Glossary), and the empire's overall trade balance was favorable.

In 1911 a double agent working for the Okhrana assassinated Stolypin. He was replaced by Vladimir N. Kokovtsev, Witte's successor as finance minister. Although very able and a supporter of the tsar, the cautious Kokovtsev could not compete with the powerful court factions that dominated the government.

Historians have debated whether or not Russia had the potential to develop a constitutional government between 1905 and 1914. At any rate, it failed to do so, in part because the tsar was not completely willing to give up autocratic rule or share power. By manipulating the franchise, the authorities obtained more conservative, but less representative, Dumas. Moreover, the regime sometimes bypassed the conservative Dumas and ruled by decree.

During this period, the government's policies were inconsistent—some reformist, others repressive. The bold reform plans of

Witte and Stolypin have led historians to speculate as to whether or not such reforms could have "saved" the Russian Empire. But the reforms were hampered by court politics, and both the tsar and the bureaucracy remained isolated from the rest of society. Suspensions of civil liberties and the rule of law continued in many places, and neither workers nor the Orthodox Church had the right to organize themselves as they chose. Discrimination against Poles, Jews, Ukrainians, and Old Believers was common. Domestic unrest was on the rise, while the empire's foreign policy was becoming more adventurous.

The Return to an Active Balkan Policy, 1906–13

The logic of Russia's earlier Far Eastern policy had required holding Balkan issues in abeyance—a strategy also followed by Austria-Hungary between 1897 and 1906. Japan's victory in 1905 forced Russia to make deals with the British and the Japanese. In 1907 Russia's new, more liberal foreign minister, Aleksandr P. Izvol'skii, concluded agreements with both nations. To maintain its sphere of influence in northern Manchuria and northern Iran, Russia agreed to Japanese ascendancy in southern Manchuria and Korea and to British ascendancy in southern Iran, Afghanistan, and Tibet. The logic of this policy demanded that Russia and Japan unite to prevent the United States from organizing a consortium to develop Chinese railroads and, after China's republican revolution of 1911, to recognize each other's spheres of influence in Outer Mongolia. In an extension of this logic, Russia traded recognition of German economic interests in the Ottoman Empire and Iran for German recognition of various Russian security interests in the region. Similarly, Russia's strategic and financial position required that it remain faithful to its alliance with France and that it bolster the Anglo-French and Anglo-Russian rapprochements with the informal Triple Entente of Britain, France, and Russia, but without antagonizing Germany or provoking a war.

Nevertheless, following the Russo-Japanese War, Russia and Austria-Hungary resumed their Balkan rivalry, focusing on the South Slavic Kingdom of Serbia and the provinces of Bosnia and Hercegovina. The two provinces had been occupied by Austria-Hungary since 1878. Only a handful of Russian and Austrian statesmen knew that in 1881 Russia secretly had agreed to Austria's future annexation of the provinces. But in 1908, Izvol'skii foolishly consented to their formal annexation in return for Austria's support for a revision of the international agreement that had insured the neutrality of the Bosporus and Dardanelles. This arrangement would have given Russia special navigational rights of passage.

When Britain blocked the revision, Austria nonetheless proceeded with the annexation and, backed by German threats of war, forced Russia to disavow support for Serbia—a pointed demonstration of Russian weakness.

After Austria's annexation of Bosnia and Hercegovina, Russian diplomacy increased tension and conflict in the Balkans. In 1912 Bulgaria, Serbia, Greece, and Montenegro defeated the Ottoman Empire but continued to quarrel among themselves. Then in 1913, the Bulgarians were defeated by the Serbians, Greeks, and Romanians. Austria became Bulgaria's patron, while Germany remained the Ottoman Empire's protector. Russia tied itself more closely to Serbia. When a Serbian terrorist assassinated the heir to the Austrian throne in late June 1914, Austria delivered an ultimatum to Serbia. Russia, fearing another humiliation in the Balkans, supported Serbia. The system of alliances began to operate automatically, with Germany supporting Austria and with France backing Russia. When Germany invaded France through Belgium, the conflict escalated into a world war.

Russia at War, 1914–16

Russia's large population enabled it to field a greater number of troops than Austria-Hungary and Germany combined, but its underdeveloped industrial base meant that its soldiers were as poorly armed as those of the Austrian army. Russian forces were inferior to Germany's in every respect except numbers. Generally, the larger Russian armies defeated the Austro-Hungarians but suffered reverses against German or combined German-Austrian forces unless the latter were overextended.

In the initial phase of the war, Russia's offensives into East Prussia drew enough German troops from the Western Front to allow the French, Belgians, and British to stabilize it. One of Russia's two invading armies was almost totally destroyed, however. Meanwhile, the Russians turned back an Austrian offensive and pushed into eastern Galicia. The Russians halted a combined German-Austrian winter counteroffensive into Russian Poland, and in early 1915 they pushed more deeply into Galicia. Then in the spring and summer of that year, a German-Austrian offensive drove the Russians out of Galicia and Poland and destroyed several Russian army corps. In 1916 the Germans planned to drive France out of the war with a large-scale attack in the Verdun area, but a new Russian offensive against Austria-Hungary once again drew German troops from the west. These actions left both major fronts stable and both Russia and Germany despairing of victory: Russia because of exhaustion, Germany because of its opponents' superior resources. Toward the end of 1916, Russia came to the rescue of Romania, which had just entered the war, and extended the Eastern Front south to the Black Sea. Russia had between 4 and 5 million casualties in World War I.

Wartime agreements among the Allies reflected the imperialist aims of the Triple Entente and the Russian Empire's relative weakness outside eastern Europe. Russia nonetheless expected impressive gains from a victory: territorial acquisitions in eastern Galicia from Austria, in East Prussia from Germany, and in Armenia from the Ottoman Empire; control of Constantinople and the Bosporus and Dardanelles straits; and territorial and political alteration of Austria-Hungary in the interests of Romania and the Slavic peoples of the region. Britain was to acquire the middle zone of Iran and share much of the Arab Middle East with France; Italy—not Russia's ally Serbia—was to acquire Dalmatia; Japan was to control more territory in China; and France was to regain Alsace-Lorraine and to have increased influence in western Germany.

The Strains of the War Effort and the Weakening of Tsarism

The onset of World War I had a drastic effect on domestic policies and a weak regime. A show of national unity had accompanied Russia's entrance into the war, but military reversals and the government's incompetence soon soured the attitude of much of the population. German control of the Baltic Sea and German-Ottoman control of the Black Sea severed Russia from most of its foreign supplies and potential markets. In addition, inept Russian preparations for war and ineffective economic policies hurt the country financially, logistically, and militarily. Inflation became a serious problem. Because of inadequate matériel support for military operations, the War Industries Committee was formed to ensure that necessary supplies reached the front. But army officers quarreled with civilian leaders, seized administrative control of front areas, and would not work with the committee. The central government disliked independent support activities organized by zemstvos and various cities. The Duma quarreled with the bureaucracy, and center and center-left deputies eventually formed the Progressive Bloc, which was aimed at forming a genuinely constitutional government.

After Russian military reversals in 1915, Nicholas II went to the front to assume nominal leadership of the army. His German-born wife, Aleksandra, and Rasputin, a debauched faith healer, who was able to stop the bleeding of the hemophiliac heir to the throne, tried to dictate policy and make ministerial appointments. Although their true influence has been debated, they undoubtedly decreased the regime's prestige and credibility.

While the central government was hampered by court intrigue, the strain of the war began to cause popular unrest. In 1916 high food prices and a lack of fuel caused strikes in some cities. Workers, who won for themselves separate representative sections of the War Industries Committee, used them as organs of political opposition. The countryside was becoming restive. Soldiers, mainly newly recruited peasants who had been used as cannon fodder in the inept conduct of the war, were increasingly insubordinate.

The situation continued to deteriorate. In an attempt to alleviate the morass at the tsar's court, a group of nobles murdered Rasputin in December 1916. But his death brought little change. In the winter of 1917, however, deteriorating rail transport caused acute food and fuel shortages, which resulted in riots and strikes. Troops were summoned to quell the disorders. Although troops had fired on demonstrators and saved tsarism in 1905, in 1917 the troops in Petrograd (the name of St. Petersburg after 1914) turned their guns over to the angry crowds. Support for the tsarist regime simply evaporated in 1917, ending three centuries of Romanov rule.

* * *

A good summary of Russian history is provided in *New Encyclopedia Britannica,* Macropaedia, "Russia and the Soviet Union, History of." Three excellent one-volume surveys of Russian history are Nicholas Riasanovsky's *A History of Russia,* David MacKenzie and Michael W. Curran's *A History of Russia and the Soviet Union,* and Robert Auty and Dmitry Obolensky's *An Introduction to Russian History.* The most useful thorough study of Russia before the nineteenth century is Vasily Kliuchevsky's five-volume collection, *Course of Russian History.* Good translations exist, however, only for the third volume, *The Seventeenth Century,* and part of the fourth volume, *Peter the Great.* For the 1800–1917 period, two excellent comprehensive works are the second volume of Michael T. Florinsky's *Russia: A History and Interpretation* and Hugh Seton-Watson's *The Russian Empire, 1801–1917.* The roots and nature of Russian autocracy are probed in Richard Pipes's controversial *Russia under the Old Regime.* A useful, if dated, translation of a Soviet interpretation of this subject is P.I. Liashchenko's *A History of the National Economy of Russia to the 1917 Revolution.* Social history is treated by Jerome Blum in *Lord and Peasant in Russia from the Ninth to the Nineteenth Century.* Cultural history is discussed in James H. Billington's *The Icon and the Axe* and Marc Raeff's *Russian Intellectual History.* (For further information and complete citations, see Bibliography.)

51

Chapter 2. Historical Setting: 1917 to 1982

Vladimir I. Lenin, founder of the Soviet state and the Russian Communist Party (Bolshevik)

THE UNION OF SOVIET SOCIALIST REPUBLICS (Soviet Union) was established in December 1922 by the leaders of the Russian Communist Party (Bolshevik) on territory generally corresponding to that of the old Russian Empire. A spontaneous popular uprising in Petrograd overthrew the imperial government in March 1917, leading to the formation of the Provisional Government, which intended to establish democracy in Russia. At the same time, to ensure the rights of the working class, workers' councils (soviets—see Glossary) sprang up across the country. The Bolsheviks (see Glossary), led by Vladimir I. Lenin, agitated for socialist revolution in the soviets and on the streets, and they seized power from the Provisional Government in November 1917. Only after the ensuing Civil War (1918–21) and foreign intervention was the new communist government secure.

From its first years, government in the Soviet Union was based on the one-party rule of the Communists, as the Bolsheviks called themselves beginning March 1918. After unsuccessfully attempting to centralize the economy during the Civil War, the Soviet government permitted some private enterprise to coexist with nationalized industry in the 1920s. Debate over the future of the economy provided the background for Soviet leaders to contend for power in the years after Lenin's death in 1924. By gradually consolidating influence and isolating his rivals within the party, Joseph V. Stalin became the sole leader of the Soviet Union by the end of the 1920s.

In 1928 Stalin introduced the First Five-Year Plan for building a socialist economy. In industry, the state assumed control over all existing enterprises and undertook an intensive program of industrialization; in agriculture, the state appropriated the peasants' property to establish collective farms. These sweeping economic innovations produced widespread misery, and millions of peasants perished during forced collectivization. Social upheaval continued in the mid-1930s when Stalin began a purge of the party; out of this purge grew a campaign of terror that led to the execution or imprisonment of untold millions of people from all walks of life. Yet despite this turmoil, the Soviet Union developed a powerful industrial economy in the years before World War II.

Stalin tried to avert war with Germany by concluding the Nazi-Soviet Nonaggression Pact with Adolf Hitler in 1939, but in 1941 Germany invaded the Soviet Union. The Red Army stopped the

Nazi offensive at the Battle of Stalingrad in 1943 and then over-ran much of eastern Europe before Germany surrendered in 1945. Although severely ravaged in the war, the Soviet Union emerged from the conflict as one of the world's great powers.

During the immediate postwar period, the Soviet Union first rebuilt and then expanded its economy. The Soviet Union consolidated its control over postwar Eastern Europe, supplied aid toward the victory of the communists in China, and sought to expand its influence elsewhere in the world. The active Soviet foreign policy helped bring about the Cold War, which turned its wartime allies, Britain and the United States, into foes. Within the Soviet Union, repressive measures continued in force; Stalin apparently was about to launch a new purge when he died in 1953.

In the absence of an acceptable successor, Stalin's closest associates opted to rule the Soviet Union jointly, although behind the public display of collective leadership a struggle for power took place. Nikita S. Khrushchev, who acquired the dominant position in the country in the mid-1950s, denounced Stalin's use of terror and effectively reduced repressive controls over party and society. Khrushchev's reforms in agriculture and administration, however, were generally unproductive, and foreign policy toward China and the United States suffered reverses. Khrushchev's colleagues in the leadership removed him from power in 1964.

Following the ouster of Khrushchev, another period of rule by collective leadership ensued, which lasted until Leonid I. Brezhnev established himself in the early 1970s as the preeminent figure in Soviet political life. Brezhnev presided over a period of détente with the West while at the same time building up Soviet military strength; the arms buildup contributed to the demise of détente in the late 1970s. Also contributing to the end of détente was the Soviet invasion of Afghanistan in December 1979.

After some experimentation with economic reforms in the mid-1960s, the Soviet leadership reverted to established means of economic management. Industry showed slow but steady gains during the 1970s, while agricultural development continued to lag. In contrast to the revolutionary spirit that accompanied the birth of the Soviet Union, the prevailing mood of the Soviet leadership at the time of Brezhnev's death in 1982 was one of cautious conservatism and aversion to change.

Revolutions and Civil War

The February Revolution

By early 1917, the existing order in Russia verged on collapse. The country's involvement in World War I had already cost millions

of lives and caused severe disruption in Russia's backward economy. In an effort to reverse the steadily worsening military situation, Emperor Nicholas II commanded Russian forces at the front,
abandoning the conduct of government in Petrograd (St. Petersburg before 1914; Leningrad after 1924) to his unpopular wife and
a series of incompetent ministers. As a consequence of these conditions, the morale of the people rapidly deteriorated.

The spark to the events that ended tsarist rule was ignited on
the streets of Petrograd in February 1917 (according to the old Julian
calendar [see Glossary] then in use in Russia). Provoked by shortages of food and fuel, crowds of hungry citizens and striking workers
began spontaneous rioting and demonstrations on March 7 (February 23, according to the Julian calendar). Local reserve troops,
called in to suppress the riots, refused to fire on the crowds, and
some soldiers joined the workers and other rioters. On March 12,
with tsarist authority in Petrograd rapidly disintegrating, two separate bodies emerged, each claiming to represent the Russian people. One was the Executive Committee of the Duma, which the
Duma (see Glossary) had established in defiance of the tsar's orders
of March 11. The other body was the Petrograd Soviet of Workers' and Soldiers' Deputies, founded on the model of the St. Petersburg Soviet of 1905. With the consent of the Petrograd Soviet, the
Executive Committee of the Duma organized the Provisional
Government on March 15. Delegates of the new government met
Nicholas that evening at Pskov, where rebellious railroad workers
had stopped the imperial train as the tsar attempted to return to
the capital. Advised by his generals that he lacked the support of
the country, Nicholas informed the delegates that he was abdicat-
ing in favor of his brother, Grand Duke Michael. When Michael
in turn refused the throne on March 16 (March 3), the rule of tsars
and emperors in Russia came to an end.

The Period of Dual Power

The collapse of the monarchy left two rival political institutions—
the Provisional Government and the Petrograd Soviet—to share administrative authority over the country. The Petrograd Soviet, drawing its membership from socialist deputies elected in factories and
regiments, coordinated the activities of other soviets that sprang up
across Russia at this time. The Petrograd Soviet was dominated by
moderate socialists of the Socialist Revolutionary Party and by the
Menshevik (see Glossary) faction of the Russian Social Democratic
Labor Party. The Bolshevik faction of the latter party provided the
opposition. While representing the interests of Russia's working
classes, the Petrograd Soviet at first did not seek to undermine the

Provisional Government's authority directly. Nevertheless, the Petrograd Soviet's "Order No. 1" of March 14 (March 1) instructed soldiers and sailors to obey their officers and the government only if their orders did not contradict the decrees of the Petrograd Soviet, thereby effectively limiting the Provisional Government's control over the armed forces.

The Provisional Government, in contrast to the socialist Petrograd Soviet, chiefly represented the propertied classes. Headed by ministers of a moderate or liberal bent, the new government pledged to convene a constituent assembly that would usher in a new era of bourgeois democracy. In the meantime, the government granted unprecedented rights—full freedom of speech, press, and religion, as well as legal equality—to all citizens. The government did not take up the matter of land redistribution, however, leaving it for the constituent assembly. Even more damaging, the ministers favored keeping Russia's military commitments to its allies, a position that became increasingly unpopular as the war dragged on. The government suffered its first crisis in the "April Days," when demonstrations against the government's annexationist war aims forced two ministers to resign, leading to the appointment of moderate socialist Aleksandr Kerensky as war minister. Kerensky, quickly assuming de facto leadership of the government, ordered the army to launch a major offensive in June, which, after early successes, turned into a full-scale retreat in July.

While the Provisional Government grappled with foreign foes, the Bolsheviks, who were opposed to bourgeois democracy, gained new strength. Lenin, the Bolshevik leader, returned to Petrograd in April 1917 from his wartime residence in Switzerland. Although he had been born into a noble family, from his youth Lenin espoused the cause of the common workers. A committed revolutionary and pragmatic Marxist thinker, Lenin astounded the Bolsheviks already in Petrograd by his *April Theses,* boldly calling for the overthrow of the Provisional Government, the transfer of "all power to the soviets," and the expropriation of factories by workers and of land belonging to the church, the nobility, and the gentry by peasants. Lenin's dynamic presence quickly won the other Bolshevik leaders to his position, and the radicalized orientation of the Bolshevik faction attracted new members. Inspired by Lenin's slogans, crowds of workers, soldiers, and sailors took to the streets of Petrograd in July to wrest power from the Provisional Government. But the spontaneity of the "July Days" caught the Bolshevik leaders by surprise, and the Petrograd Soviet, controlled by moderate Mensheviks, refused to take power or enforce Bolshevik demands. After the uprising died down, the Provisional Government outlawed the Bolsheviks and jailed Leon Trotsky (Lev Trotskii, originally Lev Bronstein), an active Bolshevik leader. Lenin fled to Finland.

In the aftermath of the "July Days," conservatives sought to reassert order in society. The army's commander in chief, General Lavr Kornilov, who protested the influence of the soviets on both the army and the government, appeared as a counterrevolutionary threat to Kerensky, now prime minister. Kerensky dismissed Kornilov from his command, but Kornilov, disobeying the order, launched an extemporaneous revolt on September 10 (August 28). To defend the capital, Kerensky sought help from all quarters and relaxed his ban on Bolshevik activities. Railroad workers sympathetic to the Bolsheviks halted Kornilov's troop trains, and Kornilov soon surrendered, ending the only serious challenge to the Provisional Government from the right.

The Bolshevik Revolution

Although the Provisional Government survived the Kornilov revolt, popular support for the government faded rapidly as the national mood swung to the left in the fall of 1917. Workers took control of their factories through elected committees; peasants expropriated lands belonging to the state, church, nobility, and gentry; and armies melted away as peasant soldiers deserted to take part in the land seizures. The Bolsheviks, skillfully exploiting these popular trends in their propaganda, dominated the Petrograd Soviet and the Moscow Soviet by September, with Trotsky, freed from prison after the Kornilov revolt, now chairman of the Petrograd Soviet.

Realizing that the time was ripe for seizing power by armed force, Lenin returned to Petrograd in October and convinced a majority of the Bolshevik Central Committee, which had hoped to take power legally, to accept armed uprising in principle. Trotsky won the Petrograd garrison over to Soviet authority, depriving the Provisional Government of its main military support in Petrograd.

The actual insurrection—the Bolshevik Revolution—began on the morning of November 6 (October 24) when Kerensky ordered the Bolshevik press closed. Interpreting this action as a counterrevolutionary move, the Bolsheviks called on their supporters to defend the Petrograd Soviet. By evening the Bolsheviks controlled utilities and most government buildings in Petrograd, allowing Lenin to proclaim the downfall of the Provisional Government on the morning of November 7 (October 25). The Bolsheviks captured the Provisional Government's cabinet at its Winter Palace headquarters that night with hardly a shot fired in the government's defense. Kerensky left Petrograd to organize resistance, but his countercoup failed and he fled Russia. Bolshevik uprisings soon took place elsewhere; the Bolsheviks gained control of Moscow by November 15 (November 2). The Second Congress of Soviets, meeting in Petrograd on November 7 (October 25), ratified the Bolshevik takeover after moderate deputies (mainly Mensheviks and right-wing members of the Socialist Revolutionary Party, or SRs) quit the session. The remaining Bolsheviks and left-wing SRs declared the soviets the governing bodies of Russia and named the Council of People's Commissars (Sovet narodnykh komissarov— Sovnarkom) to serve as the cabinet. Lenin became chairman of this council (see table 5, Appendix A). Trotsky took the post of commissar of foreign affairs; Stalin, a Georgian, became commissar of nationalities. By acting decisively while their opponents vacillated, the Bolsheviks succeeded in effecting their coup d'état.

On coming to power, the Bolsheviks issued a series of revolutionary decrees that ratified peasants' seizures of land and workers' control of industry; abolished legal class privileges; nationalized the banks; and set up revolutionary tribunals in place of the courts. At the same time, the revolutionaries now constituting the regime worked to secure power inside and outside the government. Deeming Western forms of parliamentary democracy irrelevant, Lenin argued for a dictatorship of the proletariat (see Glossary) based on one-party Bolshevik rule, although for a time left-wing SRs also participated in the Sovnarkom. The Soviet government created a secret police, the Vecheka (see Glossary) to persecute enemies of the state (including bourgeois liberals and moderate socialists) (see Predecessors of the Committee for State Security and the Ministry of Internal Affairs, ch. 19). Having convened the Constituent Assembly, which had been elected in November with the Bolsheviks winning only a quarter of the seats, the Soviet government dissolved the assembly in January after a one-day session, ending a short-lived experiment in parliamentary democracy in Russia.

In foreign affairs, the Soviet government, seeking to disengage Russia from the world war, called on the belligerent powers for an armistice and peace without annexations. The Allied Powers rejected this appeal, but Germany and its allies agreed to a ceasefire and began negotiations in December 1917. After dictating harsh terms that the Soviet government would not accept, however, Germany resumed its offensive in February 1918, meeting scant resistance from disintegrating Russian armies. Lenin, after bitter debate with leading Bolsheviks who favored prolonging the war in hopes of precipitating class warfare in Germany, persuaded a slim majority of the Bolshevik Central Committee that peace must be made at any cost. On March 3, Soviet government officials signed the Treaty of Brest-Litovsk, relinquishing Poland, the Baltic lands, Finland, and Ukraine to German control and giving up a portion of the Caucasus region to Turkey. With the new border dangerously close to Petrograd, the government was soon transferred to Moscow. An enormous part of the population and resources of the Russian Empire was lost by this treaty, but Lenin understood that no alternative could ensure the survival of the fledgling Soviet state.

Civil War and War Communism

Soon after buying peace with Germany, the Soviet state found itself under attack from other quarters. By the spring of 1918, elements dissatisfied with the Communists (as the Bolsheviks started calling themselves, conforming with the name change from Russian Social Democratic Labor Party to Russian Communist Party [Bolshevik] in March) established centers of resistance in southern and Siberian Russia against the Communist-controlled area (see fig. 4). Anti-Communists, often led by former officers of the tsarist army, clashed with the Red Army, founded and organized by Trotsky, now serving as commissar of war. A civil war to determine the future of Russia had begun.

The White armies (see Glossary) enjoyed, to varying degrees, the support of the Allied Powers. Desiring to defeat Germany in any way possible, Britain, France, and the United States landed troops in Russia and provided logistical support to the Whites, whom the Allies trusted to resume Russia's struggle against Germany after overthrowing the Communist regime. (Japan also sent troops, but with the intention of seizing territory in Siberia.) After the Allies defeated Germany in November 1918, they opted to continue their intervention in the Russian Civil War against the Communists in the interests of averting world socialist revolution.

During the Civil War, the Soviet regime also had to deal with struggles for independence in regions that it had given up under the Treaty of Brest-Litovsk (which the regime immediately repudiated after Germany's defeat by the Allies in November 1918). By force of arms, the Communists established Soviet republics in Belorussia (January 1919), Ukraine (March 1919), Azerbaydzhan (April 1920), Armenia (November 1920), and Georgia (March 1921), but they were unable to win back the Baltic region, where the independent states of Estonia, Latvia, and Lithuania had been founded shortly after the Bolshevik Revolution. In December 1917, during a civil war between Finnish Reds and Whites, the Soviet government recognized the independence of Finland but was disappointed

Source: Based on information from David MacKenzie and Michael W. Curran, *A History of Russia and the Soviet Union,* Chicago, 1987, 611.

Figure 4. Red Army Line, March 1920

when that country became a parliamentary republic in 1918. Poland, reborn after World War I, fought a successful war with Soviet Russia from April 1920 to March 1921 over the location of the frontier between the two states.

During its struggle for survival, the Soviet state placed great hope on revolution's breaking out in the industrialized countries. To coordinate the socialist movement under Soviet auspices, Lenin founded the Communist International (Comintern) in March 1919. Although no successful socialist revolutions occurred elsewhere immediately after the Bolshevik Revolution, the Comintern provided the Communist leadership with the means through which they later controlled foreign communist parties. By the end of 1920, the Communists had clearly triumphed in the Civil War. Although in 1919 Soviet Russia had shrunk to the size of sixteenth-century Muscovy, the Red Army had the advantage of defending the heartland with Moscow at its center. The White armies, divided geographically and without a clearly defined cause, went down in defeat one by one. The monarchical cause was effectively killed when Communists shot the imperial family in July 1918. The Allied governments, lacking support for intervention from their war-weary citizenry, withdrew most of their forces by 1920. The last foreign troops departed Siberia in 1922, leaving the Soviet state unchallenged from abroad.

During the Civil War, the Communist regime took increasingly repressive measures against its opponents within the country. The Soviet constitution of 1918 deprived members of the former "exploiting classes"—nobles, priests, and capitalists—of civil rights. Left-wing SRs, formerly partners of the Bolsheviks, became targets for persecution during the Red Terror that followed an attempt on Lenin's life in August 1918. In those desperate times, both Reds and Whites murdered and executed without trial large numbers of suspected enemies. The party also took measures to ensure greater discipline among its members by tightening its organization and creating specialized administrative organs.

In the economic life of the country, too, the Communist regime sought to exert control through a series of drastic measures that came to be known as war communism. To coordinate what remained of Russia's economic resources after years of war, in 1918 the government nationalized industry and subordinated it to central administrations in Moscow. Rejecting workers' control of factories as inefficient, the regime brought in expert managers to run the factories and organized and directed the factory workers as in a military mobilization. To feed the urban population, the Soviet government carried out mass requisitions of grain from the peasantry.

The results of war communism were unsatisfactory. Industrial production continued to fall. Workers received wages in kind because inflation had made the ruble practically worthless. In the countryside, peasants rebelled against payments in valueless money by curtailing or consuming their agricultural production. In late 1920, strikes broke out in the industrial centers, and peasant uprisings sprang up across the land as famine ravaged the countryside. To the Soviet government, however, the most disquieting manifestation of dissatisfaction with war communism was the rebellion in March 1921 of sailors at the naval base at Kronshtadt (near Petrograd), which had earlier won renown as a bastion of the Bolshevik Revolution. Although Trotsky and the Red Army succeeded in putting down the mutiny, the rebellion signaled to the party leadership that the austere policies of war communism had to be abolished. The harsh legacy of the Civil War period, however, would have a profound influence on the future development of the country.

The Era of the New Economic Policy
Lenin's Leadership

While the Kronshtadt base rebelled against the severe policies of war communism, the Tenth Party Congress of the Russian Communist Party (Bolshevik) met in March 1921 to hear Lenin argue for a new course in Soviet policy. Lenin realized that the radical approach to communism was unsuited to existing conditions and jeopardized the survival of his regime. Now the Soviet leader proposed a tactical retreat, convincing the congress to adopt a temporary compromise with capitalism under the program that came to be known as the New Economic Policy (NEP). Under NEP, market forces and the monetary system regained their importance. The state scrapped its policy of grain requisitioning in favor of taxation, permitting peasants to dispose of their produce as they pleased. NEP also denationalized service enterprises and much small-scale industry, leaving the "commanding heights" of the economy—large-scale industry, transportation, and foreign trade—under state control. Under the mixed economy of NEP, agriculture and industry staged recoveries, with most branches of the economy attaining prewar levels of production by the late 1920s. In general, standards of living improved during this time, and the "NEP man"—the independent private trader—became a symbol of the era.

About the time that the party sanctioned partial decentralization of the economy, it also approved a quasi-federal structure for the state. During the Civil War years, the non-Russian nationalities on the periphery of the former Russian Empire were theoretically independent, but in fact Moscow attempted to control them through the party and the Red Army. Some Communists favored a centralized Soviet state, while nationalists wanted autonomy for the borderlands. A compromise between the two positions was reached in December 1922 by the formation of the Union of Soviet Socialist Republics. The constituent republics of this Soviet Union (the Russian, Belorussian, Ukrainian, and Transcaucasian republics) exercised a degree of cultural and linguistic autonomy, while the Communist, predominantly Russian, leadership in Moscow retained political authority over the entire country.

The party consolidated its authority throughout the country, becoming a monolithic presence in state and society. Potential rivals outside the party, including prominent members of the abolished

Menshevik faction and the Socialist Revolutionary Party, were exiled. Within the party, Lenin denounced the formation of factions, particularly by radical-left party members. Central party organs subordinated local soviets under their authority. Purges of party members periodically removed the less committed from the rosters. The Politburo (see Glossary) created the new post of general secretary for supervising personnel matters and assigned Stalin to this office in April 1922. Stalin, a minor member of the Central Committee at the time of the Bolshevik Revolution, was thought to be a rather lackluster personality and therefore well suited to the routine work required of the general secretary.

From the time of the Bolshevik Revolution and into the early NEP years, the actual leader of the Soviet state was Lenin. Although a collective of prominent Communists nominally guided the party and the Soviet Union, Lenin commanded such prestige and authority that even such brilliant theoreticians as Trotsky and Nikolai I. Bukharin generally yielded to his will. But when Lenin became temporarily incapacitated after a stroke in May 1922, the unity of the Politburo fractured, and a troika (triumvirate) formed by Stalin, Lev B. Kamenev, and Grigorii V. Zinov'ev assumed leadership in opposition to Trotsky. Lenin recovered late in 1922 and found fault with the troika, and particularly with Stalin. Stalin, in Lenin's view, had used coercion to force non-Russian republics to join the Soviet Union; he was "rude"; and he was accumulating too much power through his office of general secretary. Although Lenin recommended that Stalin be removed from that position, the Politburo decided not to take action, and Stalin remained general secretary when Lenin died in January 1924.

As important as Lenin's activities were to the foundation of the Soviet Union, his legacy to the Soviet future was perhaps even more significant. By willingly changing his policies to suit new situations, Lenin had developed a pragmatic interpretation of Marxism (later called Marxism-Leninism—see Glossary) that implied that the party should follow any course that would ultimately lead to communism. His party, while still permitting intraorganizational debate, insisted that its members adhere to its decisions once they were adopted, in accordance with the principle of democratic centralism (see Glossary). Finally, because his party embodied the dictatorship of the proletariat, organized opposition could not be tolerated, and adversaries would be prosecuted (see Lenin's Conception of the Party, ch. 7). Thus, although the Soviet regime was not totalitarian when he died, Lenin had nonetheless laid the foundations upon which such a tyranny might later arise.

Stalin's Rise to Power

After Lenin's death, two conflicting schools of thought regarding the future of the Soviet Union arose in party debates. Left-wing Communists believed that world revolution was essential for the survival of socialism in the economically backward Soviet Union. Trotsky, one of the primary proponents of this position, called for Soviet support for permanent revolution (see Glossary) around the world. As for domestic policy, the left wing advocated the rapid development of the economy and the creation of a socialist society. In contrast with these militant Communists, the right wing of the party, recognizing that world revolution was unlikely in the immediate future, favored the gradual development of the Soviet Union through NEP programs. Yet even Bukharin, one of the major right-wing theoreticians, believed that socialism could not triumph in the Soviet Union without assistance from more economically advanced socialist countries.

Against this backdrop of contrasting perceptions of the Soviet future, the leading figures of the All-Union Communist Party (Bolshevik)—the new name of the Russian Communist Party (Bolshevik) as of December 1925—competed for influence. The Kamenev-Zinov'ev-Stalin troika, supporting the militant international program, successfully maneuvered against Trotsky and engineered his removal as commissar of war in 1925. In the meantime, Stalin gradually consolidated his power base and, when he had sufficient strength, broke with Kamenev and Zinov'ev. Belatedly recognizing Stalin's political power, Kamenev and Zinov'ev made amends with Trotsky to join against their former partner. But Stalin countered their attacks on his position with his well-timed formulation of the theory of "socialism in one country." This doctrine, calling for construction of a socialist society in the Soviet Union regardless of the international situation, distanced Stalin from the left and won support from Bukharin and the party's right wing. With this support, Stalin ousted the leaders of the "Left Opposition" from their positions in 1926 and 1927 and forced Trotsky into exile. By the end of the NEP era, free debate within the party thus became progressively limited as Stalin gradually eliminated his opponents.

Foreign Policy, 1921–28

In the 1920s, as the new Soviet state temporarily retreated from the revolutionary path to socialism, the party also adopted a less ideological approach in its relations with the rest of the world. Lenin, ever the practical leader, having become convinced that socialist revolution would not break out in other countries in the near future, realized that his government required normal relations with the Western world for it to survive. Not only were good relations important for national security, but the economy also required trade with the industrial countries. Blocking Soviet attainment of these desires were lingering suspicions of communism on the part of the Western powers and concern over the foreign debts incurred by the tsarist government that the Soviet government had unilaterally canceled. In April 1922, the Soviet commissar of foreign affairs, Georgii Chicherin, circumvented these difficulties by achieving an understanding with Germany, the other pariah state of Europe, at Rapallo, Italy. In the Treaty of Rapallo, Germany and Russia agreed on mutual recognition, cancellation of debt claims, normalization of trade relations, and secret cooperation in military development. After concluding the treaty, the Soviet Union soon obtained diplomatic recognition from other major powers, beginning with Britain in February 1924. Although the United States withheld recognition until 1933, private American firms began to extend technological assistance and develop commercial links beginning in the 1920s.

Toward the non-Western world, the Soviet leadership limited its policy to promoting opposition among the indigenous populations against imperialist exploitation. Moscow did pursue an active policy in China, aiding the rise of the Nationalist Party, a non-Marxist organization committed to reform and national sovereignty. After the triumph of the Nationalists, a debate developed among Soviet leaders concerning the future status of relations with China. Stalin wanted the Chinese Communist Party to join the Nationalists and infiltrate the government from within, while Trotsky proposed an armed communist uprising and forcible imposition of socialism in that country. Although Stalin's plan was finally accepted, it came to nought when in 1926 the Nationalist leader Chiang Kai-shek ordered the Chinese communists massacred and Soviet advisers expelled.

Society and Culture in the 1920s

In many respects, the NEP period was a time of relative freedom and experimentation for the social and cultural life of the Soviet Union. The government tolerated a variety of trends in these fields, provided they were not overtly hostile to the regime. In art and literature, numerous schools, some traditional and others radically experimental, proliferated. Communist writers Maksim Gorky and Vladimir Maiakovskii were active during this time, but other authors, many of whose works were later repressed, published work lacking socialist political content. Film, as a means of influencing a largely illiterate society, received encouragement from the state; much of cinematographer Sergei Eisenstein's best work dates from this period.

Education, under Commissar Anatolii Lunacharskii, entered a phase of experimentation based on progressive theories of learning. At the same time, the state expanded the primary and secondary school system and introduced night schools for working adults. The quality of higher education suffered, however, because admissions policies preferred entrants from the proletarian class over those of bourgeois backgrounds, regardless of the applicants' qualifications.

Under NEP the state eased its active persecution of religion begun during war communism but continued to agitate on behalf of atheism. The party supported the Living Church reform movement within the Russian Orthodox Church in hopes that it would undermine faith in the church, but the movement died out in the late 1920s.

In family life, attitudes generally became more permissive. The state legalized abortion, and it made divorce progressively easier to obtain. In general, traditional attitudes toward such institutions as marriage were subtly undermined by the party's promotion of revolutionary ideals.

Transformation and Terror
Industrialization and Collectivization

At the end of the 1920s, a dramatic new phase in economic development began when Stalin decided to carry out a program of intensive socialist construction. To some extent, Stalin chose to advocate accelerated economic development at this point as a political maneuver to eliminate rivals within the party. Because Bukharin and some other party members would not give up the gradualistic NEP in favor of radical development, Stalin branded them as "right-wing deviationists" and used the party organization to remove them from influential positions in 1929 and 1930. Yet Stalin's break with NEP also revealed that his doctrine of building "socialism in one country" paralleled the line that Trotsky had originally supported early in the 1920s. Marxism supplied no basis for Stalin's model of a planned economy, although the centralized economic controls of the war communism years seemingly furnished a Leninist precedent. Nonetheless, between 1927 and 1929 the State Planning Commission (Gosplan—see Glossary) worked out the First Five-Year Plan for intensive economic growth; Stalin began to implement this plan—his "revolution from above"—in 1928.

The First Five-Year Plan called for rapid industrialization of the economy, with particular growth in heavy industry. The economy was centralized: small-scale industry and services were nationalized, managers strove to fulfill Gosplan's output quotas, and the trade unions were converted into mechanisms for increasing worker productivity. But because Stalin insisted on unrealistic production targets, serious problems soon arose. With the greatest share of investment put into heavy industry, widespread shortages of consumer goods occurred, and inflation grew.

To satisfy the state's need for increased food supplies, the First Five-Year Plan called for the organization of the peasantry into collective units that the authorities could easily control. This collectivization program entailed compounding the peasants' lands and animals into collective farms (see Glossary) and state farms (see Glossary) and restricting the peasants' movements from these farms, thus in effect reintroducing a kind of serfdom into the countryside. Although the program was designed to affect all peasants, Stalin in particular sought to liquidate the wealthiest peasants, the kulaks. Generally speaking, the kulaks were only marginally better off than other peasants, but the party claimed that the kulaks ensnared the rest of the peasantry in capitalistic relationships. Yet collectivization met widespread resistance not only from kulaks but from poorer peasants as well, and a desperate struggle of the peasantry against the authorities ensued. Peasants slaughtered their cows and pigs rather than turn them over to the collective farms, with the result that livestock resources remained below the 1929 level for years afterward. The state in turn forcibly collectivized reluctant peasants and deported kulaks and active rebels to Siberia. Within the collective farms, the authorities in many instances exacted such high levels of procurements that starvation was widespread. In some places, famine was allowed to run its course; millions of peasants in the Ukrainian Republic starved to death when the state deliberately withheld food shipments.

By 1932 Stalin realized that both the economy and society were seriously overstrained. Although industry failed to meet its production targets and agriculture actually lost ground in comparison with 1928 yields, Stalin declared that the First Five-Year Plan had successfully met its goals in four years. He then proceeded to set more realistic goals. Under the Second Five-Year Plan (1933–37), the state devoted attention to consumer goods, and the factories built during the first plan helped increase industrial output in general. The Third Five-Year Plan, begun in 1938, produced poorer results because of a sudden shift of emphasis to armaments production in response to the worsening international climate. All in all, however, the Soviet economy had become industrialized by the end of the 1930s. Agriculture, which had been exploited to finance the industrialization drive, continued to show poor returns throughout the decade.

The Period of the Purges

The complete subjugation of the party to Stalin, its leader, paralleled the subordination of industry and agriculture to the state. After squelching Bukharin and the "right-wing deviationists" in 1929 and 1930, Stalin's position was assured. To secure his absolute control over the party, however, Stalin began to purge from party ranks those leaders and their followers whose loyalty he doubted.

The period of Stalin's purges began in December 1934 when Sergei Kirov, a popular Leningrad party chief who advocated a moderate policy toward the peasants, was assassinated. Although details remain murky, many Western historians believe that Stalin instigated the murder to rid himself of a potential opponent. In any event, in the resultant mass purge of the local Leningrad party, thousands were deported to camps in Siberia. Zinov'ev and Kamenev, Stalin's former political partners, received prison sentences for their alleged role in Kirov's murder. At the same time, the NKVD (see Glossary), the secret police, stepped up surveillance through its agents and informers and claimed to uncover anti-Soviet conspiracies among prominent long-term party members. At three publicized show trials held in Moscow between 1936 and 1938, dozens of these Old Bolsheviks, including Zinov'ev, Kamenev, and Bukharin, confessed to improbable crimes against the Soviet state and were executed. (The last of Stalin's old enemies, Trotsky, who had supposedly masterminded the conspiracies against Stalin from abroad, was murdered in Mexico in 1940, presumably by the NKVD.) Coincident with the show trials against the original leadership of the party, unpublicized purges swept through the ranks of younger leaders in party, government, industrial management, and cultural affairs. Party purges in the non-Russian republics were particularly severe. The Ezhovshchina ("era of Ezhov," named for NKVD chief Nikolai Ezhov) ravaged the military as well, leading to the execution or incarceration of about half the entire military officer corps. The secret police also terrorized the general populace, with untold numbers of common people punished for spurious crimes. By the time the purges subsided in 1938, millions of Soviet leaders, officials, and other citizens had been executed, imprisoned, or exiled.

The reasons for this period of widespread purges remain unclear. Western historians variously hypothesize that Stalin created the

terror out of a desire to goad the population to carry out his intensive modernization program, or to atomize society to preclude
dissent, or simply out of brutal paranoia. Whatever the causes,
the purges must be viewed as a counterproductive episode that
weakened the Soviet state and caused incalculable suffering.

In 1936, just as the purges were intensifying the Great Terror
(see Glossary), Stalin approved a new Soviet constitution to replace
that of 1924. Hailed as ''the most democratic constitution in the
world,'' the 1936 document stipulated free and secret elections based
on universal suffrage and guaranteed the citizenry a range of civil
and economic rights. But in practice the freedoms implied by these
rights were denied by provisions elsewhere in the constitution that
indicated that the basic structure of Soviet society could not be
changed and that the party retained all political power (see Early
Soviet Constitutions, ch. 8).

The power of the party, in turn, now was concentrated in the
persons of Stalin and his handpicked Politburo. Symbolic of the
lack of influence of the party rank and file, party congresses (see
Glossary) met less and less frequently. State power, far from
''withering away'' after the revolution as Karl Marx had predicted,
instead grew in strength. Stalin's personal dictatorship found reflec-
tion in the adulation that surrounded him; the reverence accorded
Stalin in Soviet society gradually eclipsed that given to Lenin.

Mobilization of Society

Concomitant with industrialization and collectivization, society
also experienced wide-ranging regimentation. Collective enterprises
replaced individualistic efforts across the board: not only did the
regime abolish private farms and businesses, but it collectivized
scientific and literary endeavors as well. As the 1930s progressed,
the revolutionary experimentation that had characterized many
facets of cultural and social life gave way to conservative norms.

Considerations of order and discipline dominated social policy,
which became an instrument for the modernization effort. Workers came under strict labor codes demanding punctuality and discipline, and labor unions served as extensions of the industrial
ministries. At the same time, higher pay and privileges accrued
to productive workers and labor brigades. To provide greater social stability, the state aimed to strengthen the family by restricting divorce and abolishing abortion.

Literature and the arts came under direct party control during
the 1930s as mandatory membership in unions of writers, musicians, and other artists entailed adherence to established standards.
After 1934, the party dictated that creative works had to express

71

socialistic spirit through traditional forms. This officially sanctioned doctrine, called socialist realism (see Glossary), applied to all fields of artistic endeavor. The state repressed works that were stylistically innovative or lacked appropriate content.

The party also subjected science and the liberal arts to its scrutiny. Development of scientific theory in a number of fields had to be based upon the party's understanding of the Marxist dialectic, which derailed serious research in certain disciplines. The party took a more active role in directing work in the social sciences. In the writing of history, the orthodox Marxist interpretation employed in the late 1920s was modified to include nationalistic themes and to stress the role of great leaders to foster legitimacy for Stalin's dictatorship.

Education returned to traditional forms as the party discarded the experimental programs of Lunacharskii after 1929. Admission procedures underwent modification: candidates for higher education now were selected by their academic records, rather than by class origins.

Religion suffered from a state policy of increased repression, starting with the closure of numerous churches in 1929. Persecution of clergy was particularly severe during the purges of the late 1930s, when many of the faithful went underground.

Foreign Policy, 1928–39

Soviet foreign policy underwent a series of changes during the first decade of Stalin's rule. Soon after assuming control of the party, Stalin oversaw a radicalization of Soviet foreign policy that complemented his strenuous domestic policies. To heighten the urgency of his demands for modernization, Stalin portrayed the Western powers, particularly France, as warmongers eager to attack the Soviet Union. The diplomatic isolation practiced by the Soviet Union in the early 1930s seemed ideologically justified by the Great Depression; world capitalism appeared destined for destruction. To aid the triumph of communism, Stalin resolved to weaken the moderate social democrats of Europe, the communists' rivals for working-class support. Conversely, the Comintern ordered the Communist Party of Germany to aid the anti-Soviet National Socialist German Workers' Party (the Nazi Party) in its bid for power in the hopes that a Nazi regime would exacerbate social tensions and produce conditions that would lead to a communist revolution in Germany. Stalin thus shares responsibility for Hitler's rise to power in 1933 and its tragic consequences for the Soviet Union and the rest of the world.

The dynamics of Soviet foreign relations changed drastically after Stalin recognized the danger posed by Nazi Germany. From 1934 through 1937, the Soviet Union tried to restrain German militarism by building coalitions hostile to fascism. In the international communist movement, the Comintern adopted the popular front (see Glossary) policy of cooperation with socialists and liberals against fascism, thus reversing its line of the early 1930s. In 1934 the Soviet Union joined the League of Nations, where Maksim M. Litvinov, the commissar of foreign affairs, advocated disarmament and collective security against fascist aggression. In 1935 the Soviet Union concluded defensive military alliances with France and Czechoslovakia, and from 1936 to 1939 it gave assistance to antifascists in the Spanish Civil War. The menace of fascist militarism to the Soviet Union increased when Germany and Japan (itself a threat to Soviet Far Eastern territory in the 1930s) signed the Anti-Comintern Pact in 1936. But the West proved unwilling to counter German provocative behavior, and after France and Britain acquiesced to Hitler's demands for Czechoslovak territory at Munich in 1938, Stalin abandoned his efforts to forge a collective security agreement with the West.

Convinced now that the West would not fight Hitler, Stalin decided to come to an understanding with Germany. Signaling a shift in foreign policy, Viacheslav Molotov, Stalin's loyal assistant, replaced Litvinov (who was Jewish) as commissar of foreign affairs in May 1939. Hitler, who had decided to attack Poland despite the guarantees of Britain and France to defend that country, soon responded to the changed Soviet stance. While Britain and France dilatorily attempted to induce the Soviet Union to join them in pledging to protect Poland, the Soviet Union and Germany engaged in intensive negotiations. The product of the talks between the former ideological foes—the Nazi-Soviet Nonaggression Pact of August 23, 1939—shocked the world. The open provisions of the agreement pledged absolute neutrality in the event one of the parties should become involved in war, while a secret protocol partitioned Poland between the parties and assigned Romanian territory as well as Estonia and Latvia (and later Lithuania) to the Soviet sphere of influence. With his eastern flank thus secured, Hitler began the German invasion of Poland on September 1, 1939; Britain and France declared war on Germany two days later. World War II had begun.

War Years

Prelude to War

When German troops invaded Poland, the Soviet Union was ill prepared to enter a major war. Although military expenditures had increased dramatically during the 1930s and the standing army was expanded in 1939, Soviet weaponry was inferior to that of the German army. More important, the purges had deprived the armed services of many capable leaders, resulting in diminished morale and effectiveness. The time gained through the pact with the Nazis was therefore critical to the development of Soviet defenses, particularly after Hitler's forces had overrun much of western Europe, against little resistance, by the summer of 1940.

To strengthen its western frontier, the Soviet Union quickly secured the territory located in its sphere of interest. Soviet forces seized eastern Poland in September 1939; entered Estonia, Latvia, and Lithuania (which were later converted into Soviet republics) in October 1939; and seized the Romanian territories of Bessarabia (later incorporated into the Moldavian Republic) and northern Bukovina (later added to the Ukrainian Republic) in June 1940. Only Finland resisted Stalin's program of expansion, first by refusing to cede territory and then by putting up a determined defense when the Red Army invaded in November 1939. Although the Soviet Union finally won its original demands in March 1940, the Soviet-Finnish War (also known as the Winter War) pointed out grave deficiencies in Soviet military capabilities, which Hitler undoubtedly noted.

As the European war continued and the theaters of the conflict widened, Hitler began to chafe under his pact with the Soviet Union. The German dictator refused to grant Stalin a free hand in the Balkans and instead moved the German forces deeper into eastern Europe and strengthened his ties with Finland. Hitler thus prepared for war against the Soviet Union under a plan that he officially approved in December 1940. Stalin, however, apparently believed that the Soviet Union could avert war by not offending Germany. The Soviet Union continued its regular shipments of resources to Germany and maintained its armed forces at a low stage of readiness. But despite Stalin's efforts to mollify Hitler, Germany declared war on the Soviet Union just as 180 German divisions swept across the border early on the morning of June 22, 1941.

The Great Patriotic War

The German blitzkrieg nearly succeeded in defeating the Soviet Union within the first months. The Soviet forces, caught unprepared, lost whole armies and vast quantities of equipment to the German onslaught in the first weeks of the war, By November the German army had seized the Ukrainian Republic, begun its siege of Leningrad, and threatened the security of Moscow itself (see fig. 5). The Great Patriotic War, as the Soviet Union calls the phase of World War II involving that country, thus began inauspiciously for the Soviet Union.

By the end of 1941, however, the German forces had lost their momentum. Harsh winter weather, attacks from bands of partisans, and difficulties in obtaining supplies over long distances restricted German movements. At the same time the Red Army, after recovering from the initial blow, launched its first counterattacks against the invaders in December. To ensure the army's ability to fight the war, the Soviet authorities evacuated thousands of factories and key personnel from the war zone to the interior of the country, where the plants began producing war matériel. Finally, the country was bolstered by the prospect of receiving assistance from Britain and the United States.

After a lull in active hostilities during the winter of 1941–42, the German army renewed its offensive, scoring a number of victories in the Ukrainian Republic, Crimea, and southern Russia in the first half of 1942. Then, in an effort to gain control of the lower Volga River region, the German forces attempted to capture the city of Stalingrad (present-day Volgograd) on the west bank of the river. Here, Soviet forces put up fierce resistance even after Hitler's determined actions to take the city had reduced it to rubble. Finally, Soviet forces led by General Georgii K. Zhukov surrounded the German attackers and forced their surrender in February 1943. The Soviet victory at Stalingrad proved decisive; after losing this battle the Germans lacked the strength to sustain their offensive operations against the Soviet Union.

After Stalingrad, the Soviet Union held the initiative for the rest of the war. By the end of 1943, the Red Army had broken through the German siege of Leningrad and recaptured much of the Ukrainian Republic. By the end of 1944, the front had moved beyond the 1939 Soviet frontiers into eastern Europe. With a decisive superiority in troops and weaponry, Soviet forces drove into eastern Germany, capturing Berlin in May 1945. The war with Germany thus ended triumphantly for the Soviet Union.

In gaining the victory, the Soviet government had to rely on the support of the people. To increase popular enthusiasm for the war, Stalin changed his domestic policies to heighten patriotic spirit. Nationalistic slogans replaced much of the communist rhetoric in official pronouncements and the mass media. Active persecution of religion ceased, and in 1943 Stalin allowed the Russian Orthodox Church to name a patriarch after the office had stood vacant for nearly two decades. In the countryside, authorities permitted greater freedom on the collective farms. Harsh German rule in the occupied territories also aided the Soviet cause. Nazi administrators of

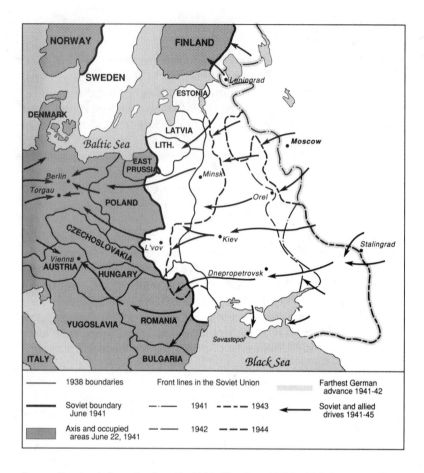

Source: Based on information from David MacKenzie and Michael W. Curran, *A History of Russia and the Soviet Union,* Chicago, 1987, 742.

Figure 5. Military Operations Against Germany, 1941–45

conquered Soviet territories made little attempt to exploit the population's dissatisfaction with Soviet political and economic policies. Instead, the Nazis preserved the collective-farm system, systematically carried out genocidal policies against Jews, and deported others (mainly Ukrainians) to work in Germany. Under these circumstances, the great majority of the Soviet people fought and worked on their country's behalf, thus ensuring the regime's survival.

The war with Germany also brought about a temporary alliance with the two greatest powers in the "imperialist camp," namely, Britain and the United States. Despite deep-seated mistrust between the Western democracies and the Soviet state, the demands of war made cooperation critical. The Soviet Union benefited from shipments of weaponry and equipment from the Western Allies; during the course of the war the United States alone furnished supplies worth over US$11 billion. At the same time, by engaging considerable German resources, the Soviet Union gave the United States and Britain time to prepare to invade German-occupied western Europe. Relations began to sour, however, when the war turned in the Allies' favor. The postponement of the European invasion to June 1944 became a source of irritation to Stalin, whose country meanwhile bore the brunt of the struggle with Germany. Then, as Soviet armies pushed into eastern Europe, the question of the postwar order increased the friction within the coalition. At the Yalta Conference in February 1945, Stalin clashed with President Franklin D. Roosevelt and Prime Minister Winston Churchill over his plans to extend Soviet influence to Poland after the war. At the same time, however, Stalin promised to join the war against Japan ninety days after Germany had been defeated. Breaking the neutrality pact that the Soviet Union had concluded with Japan in April 1941, the Red Army entered the war in East Asia several days before Japan surrendered in August 1945. Now, with all common enemies defeated, little remained to preserve the alliance between the Western democracies and the Soviet Union.

The end of World War II saw the Soviet Union emerge as one of the world's two great military powers. Its battle-tested forces occupied most of postwar Eastern Europe. The Soviet Union won island holdings from Japan and further concessions from Finland (which had joined in the German invasion in 1941) in addition to the territories the Soviet Union had seized as a consequence of the Nazi-Soviet Nonaggression Pact. But these achievements had been bought at a high cost. An estimated 20 million Soviet soldiers and civilians perished in the war, the heaviest loss of life of any of the combatant countries. The war also inflicted severe material losses throughout the vast territory that had been included in the war zone. The suffering and losses resulting from the war made a lasting impression on the Soviet people and leaders that cannot be overlooked.

Reconstruction and Cold War

Reconstruction Years

Although the Soviet Union was victorious in World War II, its economy had been devastated in the struggle. Roughly a quarter of the country's capital resources had been destroyed, and industrial and agricultural output in 1945 fell far short of prewar levels. To help rebuild the country, the Soviet government obtained limited credits from Britain and Sweden but refused economic assistance proposed by the United States under the Marshall Plan. Instead, the Soviet Union compelled Soviet-occupied Eastern Europe to supply machinery and raw materials. Germany and former Nazi satellites (including Finland) made reparations to the Soviet Union. The Soviet people bore much of the cost of rebuilding because the reconstruction program emphasized heavy industry while neglecting agriculture and consumer goods. By the time of Stalin's death in 1953, steel production was twice its 1940 level, but the production of many consumer goods and foodstuffs was lower than it had been in the late 1920s.

During the postwar reconstruction period, Stalin tightened domestic controls, justifying the repression by playing up the threat of war with the West. Many repatriated Soviet citizens who had lived abroad during the war, whether as prisoners of war, forced laborers, or defectors, were executed or sent to prison camps. The limited freedoms granted in wartime to the church and to collective farmers were revoked. The party tightened its admission standards and purged many who had become party members during the war.

In 1946 Andrei Zhdanov, a close associate of Stalin, helped launch an ideological campaign designed to demonstrate the superiority of socialism over capitalism in all fields. This campaign, colloquially known as the Zhdanovshchina (era of Zhdanov), attacked writers, composers, economists, historians, and scientists whose work allegedly manifested Western influence. Although Zhdanov died in 1948, the cultural purge continued for several years afterward, stifling Soviet intellectual development. Another campaign, related to the Zhdanovshchina, lauded the real or purported achievements of past and present Russian inventors and scientists. In this intellectual climate, the genetic theories of biologist Trofim D. Lysenko, which were supposedly derived from Marxist principles but lacked scientific bases, were imposed upon Soviet science to the detriment of research and agricultural development. The anticosmopolitan trends of these years adversely affected Jewish cultural and scientific figures in particular. In general, a pronounced sense of Russian nationalism, as opposed to socialist consciousness, pervaded Soviet society.

The Cold War

After World War II, the Soviet Union and its Western allies soon parted ways as mutual suspicions of the other's intentions and

Monument at Babi Yar, Kiev, Ukrainian Republic, in memory of the more than 100,000 Soviet citizens murdered by German troops during World War II Courtesy Jimmy Pritchard

actions flourished. Eager to consolidate influence over a number of countries near the Soviet Union, Stalin pursued aggressive policies after World War II that provoked strong Western reaction. The United States worked to contain Soviet expansion in this period of international relations that has come to be known as the Cold War.

Mindful of the numerous invasions of Russia and the Soviet Union from the West throughout history, Stalin sought to create a buffer zone of subservient East European countries, most of which the Red Army (known as the Soviet armed forces after 1946) had occupied in the course of the war. Taking advantage of its military occupation of these countries, the Soviet Union actively assisted local communist parties in coming to power. By 1948 seven East European countries had communist governments. The Soviet Union initially maintained control behind the ''iron curtain'' (to use Churchill's phrase) through troops, security police, and its diplomatic service. Unequal trade agreements with the East European countries permitted the Soviet Union access to valued resources.

Soviet actions in Eastern Europe helped produce Western hostility toward their former ally, but the Western powers could do nothing to halt consolidation of Soviet authority in that region short of going to war. However, the United States and its allies had greater success in halting Soviet expansion in areas where Soviet influence was more tenuous. British and American diplomatic support for Iran

79

forced the Soviet Union to withdraw its troops from the northeastern part of that country in 1946. Soviet efforts to acquire territory from Turkey and establish a communist government in Greece were stymied when the United States extended military and economic support to those countries under the Truman Doctrine in 1947. Later that year, the United States introduced the Marshall Plan for the economic recovery of other countries of Europe. The Soviet Union forbade the countries it dominated from taking part in the program, and the Marshall Plan contributed to reducing Soviet influence in the participating West European nations.

Tensions between the United States and the Soviet Union became especially strained over the issue of Germany. At the Potsdam Conference of July–August 1945, the Allied Powers confirmed their decision to divide Germany and the city of Berlin into zones of occupation (with the eastern sectors placed under Soviet administration) until such time as the Allies would permit Germany to establish a central government. Disagreements between the Soviet Union and the Western Allies soon arose over their respective occupation policies and the matter of reparations. In June 1948, the Soviet Union cut off the West's land access to the American, British, and French sectors of Berlin in retaliation for steps taken by the United States and Britain to unite Germany. Britain and the United States thereupon sponsored an airlift to keep the beleaguered sectors provisioned until the Soviet Union lifted the blockade in May 1949. Following the Berlin blockade, the West and the Soviet Union divided Germany into two countries, one oriented to the West, the other to the East. The crisis also provided the catalyst for the Western countries in 1949 to form the North Atlantic Treaty Organization (NATO), a collective security system designed to use conventional armies and nuclear weapons to offset Soviet forces.

While the Soviet Union gained a new satellite nation in the German Democratic Republic (East Germany), it lost its influence in Yugoslavia. The local communists in Yugoslavia had come into power without Soviet assistance, and their leader, Josip Broz Tito, refused to subordinate the country to Stalin's control. Tito's defiance led the Communist Information Bureau (Cominform—founded in 1947 to partially replace the Comintern, which had been abolished in 1943) to expel the Yugoslav party from the international communist movement in 1948. To guard against the rise of other independent leaders, Stalin purged many of the chief communists in other East European states.

In Asia, the Chinese Communists, headed by Mao Zedong and assisted by the Soviet Union, achieved victory over the Nationalists in 1949. Several months afterward, in 1950, China and the

Soviet Union concluded a mutual defense treaty against Japan and the United States. Hard negotiations over concessions and aid between the two communist countries served as an indication that China, with its independent party and enormous population, would not become a Soviet satellite, although for a time their relations appeared particularly close. Elsewhere in Asia, the Soviet Union pursued a vigorous policy of support for national liberation movements, especially in Malaya and Indochina, which were still colonies of Britain and France, respectively. Thinking that the West would not defend the Republic of Korea (South Korea), Stalin allowed or encouraged the Soviet-equipped forces of the Democratic People's Republic of Korea (North Korea) to invade South Korea in 1950. But forces from the United States and other members of the United Nations came to the aid of South Korea, leading China to intervene militarily on behalf of North Korea, probably on Soviet instigation. Although the Soviet Union avoided direct participation in the conflict (which would end in 1953), the Korean War inspired the United States to strengthen its military capability and to conclude a peace treaty and security pact with Japan. Chinese participation in the war also strengthened China's independent position in relation to the Soviet Union.

Death of Stalin

In the early 1950s, Stalin, now an old man, apparently permitted his subordinates in the Politburo (enlarged and called the Presidium by the Nineteenth Party Congress in October 1952) greater powers of action within their spheres. (Also at the Nineteenth Party Congress, the name of the party was changed from the All-Union Communist Party [Bolshevik] to the Communist Party of the Soviet Union—CPSU.) Indicative of the Soviet leader's waning strength, Secretary Georgii M. Malenkov delivered the political report to the Nineteenth Party Congress in place of Stalin (see Party Congress, ch. 7). Although the general secretary took a smaller part in the day-to-day administration of party affairs, he maintained his animosity toward potential enemies. In January 1953, the party newspaper announced that a group of predominantly Jewish doctors had murdered high Soviet officials, including Zhdanov. Western historians speculate that the disclosure of this "doctors' plot" may have been a prelude to an intended purge directed against Malenkov, Molotov, and secret police chief Lavrenty Beria. In any case, when Stalin died on March 5, 1953 (under circumstances that are still unclear), his inner circle, which had feared him for years, secretly rejoiced.

During his quarter-century of dictatorial control, Stalin had overseen impressive development in the Soviet Union. From a comparatively backward agricultural society, the country had been transformed into a powerful industrial state. But in the course of that transformation, millions of people had been killed, and Stalin's use of repressive controls had become an integral function of his regime. How Stalin's system would be maintained or altered would be a question of vital concern to Soviet leaders for years after him.

The Khrushchev Era

Collective Leadership and the Rise of Khrushchev

Stalin died without naming an heir, and none of his associates had the power to immediately claim supreme leadership. The deceased dictator's colleagues initially tried to rule jointly through a collective leadership, with Malenkov holding the top positions of prime minister (chairman of the Council of Ministers; the name changed from Council of People's Commissars in 1946) and general secretary (the latter office for only two weeks). The arrangement was first challenged in 1953 when Beria, the powerful head of the security forces, plotted a coup. Beria's associates in the Presidium, however, ordered Marshal Zhukov to arrest him, and he was secretly executed. With Beria's death came the end of the inordinate power of the secret police; the party has maintained strict control over the state security organs ever since.

After the elimination of Beria, the succession struggle became more subtle. Malenkov found a formidable rival in Nikita S. Khrushchev, whom the Presidium elected first secretary (Stalin's title of general secretary was abolished) in September. Of peasant background, Khrushchev had served as head of the Ukrainian party organization during and after World War II and was a member of the Soviet political elite during the Stalin period. The rivalry between Malenkov and Khrushchev surfaced publicly through Malenkov's support for increased production of consumer goods, while Khrushchev conservatively stood for development of heavy industry. After a poor showing by light industry and agriculture, Malenkov resigned as prime minister in February 1955. The new prime minister, Nikolai A. Bulganin, had little influence or real power; Khrushchev was now the most important figure within the collective leadership.

At the Twentieth Party Congress, held in February 1956, Khrushchev further advanced his position within the party by denouncing Stalin's crimes in a dramatic "secret speech." Khrushchev revealed

Statue "Motherland" on Mamayev Hill, Volgograd (formerly Stalingrad), Russian Republic. During the Battle of Stalingrad, some of the fiercest fighting took place here before the German troops surrendered in February 1943.
Courtesy Jimmy Pritchard

that Stalin had arbitrarily liquidated thousands of party members and military leaders (thereby contributing to the initial Soviet defeats in World War II) and had established a pernicious cult of personality (see Glossary). With this speech Khrushchev not only distanced himself from Stalin and from Stalin's close associates, Molotov, Malenkov, and Lazar M. Kaganovich, but also abjured the dictator's policies of terror. As a direct result of the "de-Stalinization" campaign launched by the speech, the release of political prisoners, which had begun in 1953, was stepped up, and some of Stalin's victims were posthumously rehabilitated (see Glossary). Khrushchev later intensified his campaign against Stalin at the Twenty-Second Party Congress in 1961, winning approval to remove Stalin's body from the Lenin Mausoleum, where it had originally been interred. De-Stalinization encouraged many in artistic and intellectual circles to speak out against the abuses of the former regime. Although Khrushchev's tolerance of critical creative works vacillated during his years of leadership, the new cultural period—known as the "thaw"—represented a clear break with the repression of the arts under Stalin.

After the Twentieth Party Congress, Khrushchev continued to expand his influence, although he still faced opposition. Khrushchev's rivals in the Presidium, spurred by reversals in Soviet foreign policy in Eastern Europe in 1956, potentially threatening economic reforms, and the de-Stalinization campaign, united to vote him out of office in June 1957. Khrushchev, however, demanded that the question be put to the Central Committee of the CPSU, where he enjoyed strong support. The Central Committee overturned the Presidium's decision and expelled Khrushchev's opponents (Malenkov, Molotov, and Kaganovich), whom Khrushchev labeled the "anti-party group." In a departure from Stalinist procedure, Khrushchev did not order the imprisonment or execution of his defeated rivals but instead placed them in relatively minor offices. Khrushchev moved to consolidate his power further in the ensuing months. In October he removed Marshal Zhukov (who had helped Khrushchev squelch the "anti-party group") from the office of defense minister, presumably because he feared Zhukov's influence in the armed forces. Khrushchev became prime minister in March 1958 when Bulganin resigned, thus formally confirming his predominant position in the state as well as in the party.

Despite his rank, Khrushchev never exercised the dictatorial authority of Stalin, nor did he ever completely control the party even at the peak of his power. His attacks on members of the "anti-party group" at the Twenty-First Party Congress in 1959 and the Twenty-Second Party Congress in 1961 suggest that his opponents

Room in the Livadia Palace where Stalin, Churchill, and Roosevelt met for the Yalta Conference in February 1945
Courtesy Jimmy Pritchard

still retained support within the party. Khrushchev's relative political insecurity probably accounted for some of his grandiose pronouncements (for example, his 1961 promise that the Soviet Union would attain communism by 1980). His desire to undermine opposition and mollify critics explained the nature of many of his domestic reforms and the vacillations in his foreign policy toward the West.

Foreign Policy under Khrushchev

Almost immediately after Stalin died, the collective leadership began altering the conduct of Soviet foreign policy to permit better relations with the West and new approaches to the nonaligned countries. Malenkov introduced a change in tone by speaking out against nuclear war as a threat to civilization. Khrushchev initially contradicted this position, saying capitalism alone would be destroyed in a nuclear war, but he adopted Malenkov's view after securing his preeminent position. In 1955, to ease tensions between East and West, Khrushchev recognized permanent neutrality for Austria. Meeting President Dwight D. Eisenhower in Geneva, Switzerland, later that year, Khrushchev confirmed Soviet commitment to "peaceful coexistence" with capitalism. Regarding the developing nations, Khrushchev tried to win the goodwill of their national leaders, instead of following the established Soviet policy of shunning the governments while supporting local communist parties. Soviet influence in the international alignments of India and Egypt, as well as of other Third World countries, began in the middle of the 1950s. Cuba's entry into the socialist camp in 1961 was a coup for the Soviet Union.

With the gains of the new diplomacy came reversals as well. By conceding the independence of Yugoslavia in 1955 as well as by his de-Stalinization campaign, Khrushchev provoked unrest in Eastern Europe, where the policies of the Stalin era weighed heavily. In Poland, riots brought about a change in communist party leadership, which the Soviet Union reluctantly recognized in October 1956. A popular uprising against Soviet control then broke out in Hungary, where the local communist leaders, headed by Imre Nagy, called for a multiparty political system and withdrawal from the Warsaw Pact, the defensive alliance founded by the Soviet Union and its East European satellites in 1955 (see Appendix C). The Soviet army crushed the revolt early in November 1956, causing numerous casualties. Although the Hungarian Revolution hurt Soviet standing in world opinion, it demonstrated that the Soviet Union would use force if necessary to maintain control over its satellite states in Eastern Europe.

Outside the Soviet sphere of control, China grew increasingly restive under Chinese Communist Party chairman Mao Zedong. Chinese discontent with the new Soviet leadership stemmed from low levels of Soviet aid, feeble Soviet support for China in its disputes with Taiwan and India, and the new Soviet doctrine of peaceful coexistence with the West (which Mao viewed as a betrayal of Marxism-Leninism). Against Khrushchev's wishes, China embarked on a nuclear arms program, declaring in 1960 that nuclear war could defeat imperialism. The dispute between militant China and the more moderate Soviet Union escalated into a schism in the world communist movement after 1960. Albania left the Soviet camp and became an ally of China, Romania distanced itself from the Soviet Union in international affairs, and communist parties around the world split over orientation to Moscow or Beijing. The monolithic bloc of world communism had shattered.

Soviet relations with the West, especially the United States, seesawed between moments of relative relaxation and periods of tension and crisis. For his part, Khrushchev wanted peaceful coexistence with the West, not only to avoid nuclear war but also to permit the Soviet Union to develop its economy. Khrushchev's meetings with President Eisenhower in 1955 and President John F. Kennedy in 1961 and his tour of the United States in 1959 demonstrated the Soviet leader's desire for fundamentally smooth relations between the West and the Soviet Union and its allies. Yet

Khrushchev also needed to demonstrate to Soviet conservatives and militant Chinese that the Soviet Union was a firm defender of the socialist camp. Thus in 1958 Khrushchev challenged the status of Berlin; when the West would not yield to his demands that the western sectors be incorporated into East Germany, he approved the erection of the Berlin Wall around those sectors in 1961. To maintain national prestige, Khrushchev canceled a summit meeting with Eisenhower in 1960 after Soviet air defense troops shot down a United States U–2 reconnaissance aircraft over Soviet territory. Finally, mistrust over military intentions hobbled East-West relations during this time. The West feared the Soviet lead in space technology and saw in the buildup of the Soviet military an emerging "missile gap" in the Soviet Union's favor. By contrast, the Soviet Union felt threatened by a rearmed Federal Republic of Germany (West Germany), by the United States alliance system encircling the Soviet Union, and by the West's superior strategic and economic strength. To offset the United States military advantage and thereby improve the Soviet negotiating position, Khrushchev in 1962 tried to install nuclear missiles in Cuba, but he agreed to withdraw them after Kennedy ordered a blockade around the island nation. After coming close to war in the Cuban missile crisis, the Soviet Union and the United States took steps to reduce the nuclear threat. In 1963 the two countries established the "hot line" between Washington and Moscow to reduce the likelihood of accidental nuclear war. In the same year, the United States, Britain, and the Soviet Union signed the Limited Test Ban Treaty, which forbade testing nuclear weapons in the atmosphere.

Khrushchev's Reforms and Fall

Throughout his years of leadership, Khrushchev attempted to carry out reform in a range of fields. The problems of Soviet agriculture, a major concern of Khrushchev, had earlier attracted the attention of the collective leadership, which introduced important innovations in this area of the Soviet economy. The state encouraged peasants to grow more on their private plots, increased payments for crops grown on the collective farms, and invested more heavily in agriculture. In his dramatic virgin land campaign (see Glossary) in the mid-1950s, Khrushchev opened to farming vast tracts of land in the northern part of the Kazakh Republic and neighboring areas of the Russian Republic. These new farmlands turned out to be susceptible to droughts, but in some years they produced excellent harvests. Later innovations by Khrushchev, however, proved counterproductive. His plans for growing maize and increasing meat and dairy production failed miserably, and his reorganization of collective farms into larger units produced confusion in the countryside.

Khrushchev's reforms in industry and administrative organization created even greater problems. In a politically motivated move to weaken the central state bureaucracy, in 1957 Khrushchev did away with the industrial ministries in Moscow and replaced them with regional economic councils. Although Khrushchev intended these economic councils to be more responsive to local needs, the decentralization of industry led to disruption and inefficiency. Connected with this decentralization was Khrushchev's decision in 1962 to reorganize party organizations along economic, rather than administrative, lines. The resulting bifurcation of the party apparatus into industrial and agricultural sectors at the oblast (see Glossary) level and below contributed to the disarray and alienated many party officials at all levels. Symptomatic of the country's economic difficulties was the abandonment in 1963 of Khrushchev's special seven-year economic plan (1959–65) two years short of its completion.

By 1964 Khrushchev's prestige had been injured in a number of areas. Industrial growth slowed, while agriculture showed no new progress. Abroad, the split with China, the Berlin crisis, and the Cuban fiasco hurt the Soviet Union's international stature, and Khrushchev's efforts to improve relations with the West antagonized many in the military. Lastly, the 1962 party reorganization caused turmoil throughout the Soviet political chain of command. In October 1964, while Khrushchev was vacationing in Crimea, the Presidium voted him out of office and refused to permit him to take his case to the Central Committee. Khrushchev retired as a private citizen after his successors denounced him for his "harebrained schemes, half-baked conclusions, and hasty decisions." Yet along with his failed policies, Khrushchev must also be remembered for his public disavowal of Stalinism and the cult of personality.

The Brezhnev Era

Collective Leadership and the Rise of Brezhnev

After removing Khrushchev from power, the leaders of the Politburo (as the Presidium was renamed in 1966 by the Twenty-Third Party Congress) and Secretariat again established a collective leadership. As was the case following Stalin's death, several individuals, including Aleksei N. Kosygin, Nikolai V. Podgornyi, and Leonid I. Brezhnev, contended for power behind a facade of unity. Kosygin accepted the position of prime minister, which he held until his retirement in 1980. Brezhnev, who took the post of first secretary, may have originally been viewed as an interim appointment by his fellows.

Born to a Russian worker's family in 1906, Brezhnev became a protégé of Khrushchev early in his career and through his influence rose to membership in the Presidium. As his own power grew, Brezhnev built up a coterie of followers whom he, as first secretary (the title reverted to general secretary after April 1966), gradually maneuvered into powerful positions. At the same time, Brezhnev slowly demoted or isolated possible contenders for his office. He succeeded in elevating Podgornyi to the ceremonial position of chairman of the Presidium of the Supreme Soviet, the highest legislative organization in the government, in December 1965, thus eliminating him as a rival. But Brezhnev's rise was very gradual; only in 1971, when Brezhnev succeeded in appointing four close associates to the Politburo, did it become clear that his was the most influential voice in the collective leadership. After several more personnel changes, Brezhnev assumed the chairmanship of the Presidium of the Supreme Soviet in 1977, confirming his primacy in both party and state.

The years after Khrushchev were notable for the stability of cadres (see Glossary) in the party and state apparatus. By introducing the slogan "Trust in Cadres" in 1965, Brezhnev won the support of many bureaucrats wary of the constant reorganizations of the Khrushchev era and eager for security in established hierarchies. As an example of the new stability, nearly half of the Central Committee members in 1981 were holdovers from fifteen years earlier. The corollary to this stability was the aging of Soviet leaders; the average age of Politburo members rose from fifty-five in 1966 to sixty-eight in 1982. The Soviet leadership (or the "gerontocracy," as it was referred to in the West) became increasingly conservative and ossified.

Conservative policies characterized the regime's agenda in the years after Khrushchev. Upon assuming power, the collective leadership not only reversed such policies of Khrushchev's as the bifurcation of the party but also halted de-Stalinization, and positive references to the dead dictator began to appear. The Soviet Constitution of 1977, although differing in certain respects from the 1936 Stalin document, retains the general thrust of the latter (see The 1977 Constitution, ch. 8). In contrast to the relative cultural freedom tolerated during the early Khrushchev years, Brezhnev and his colleagues continued the more restrictive line of the later Khrushchev era. The leadership was unwilling or unable to employ Stalinist means to control Soviet society; instead, it opted to exert repressive tactics against political dissidents even after the Soviet Union acceded to the Helsinki Accords (see Glossary) in 1975. Dissidents persecuted during this time included writers and activists in outlawed religious, nationalist, and human rights movements. In the latter part of the Brezhnev era, the regime tolerated popular expressions of anti-Semitism. Under conditions of "developed socialism" (the historical stage that the Soviet Union attained in 1977 according to the CPSU), the study of Marxism-Leninism served as a means to bolster the authority of the regime rather than as a tool for revolutionary action.

Foreign Policy of a Superpower

A major concern of Khrushchev's successors was to reestablish Soviet primacy in the community of communist states by undermining the influence of China. Although the new leaders originally approached China without hostility, Mao's condemnation of Soviet foreign policy as "revisionist" and his competition for influence in the Third World soon led to a worsening of relations between the two countries. Sino-Soviet relations reached a low point in 1969 when clashes broke out along the disputed Ussuri River in the Far East. Later the Chinese, intimidated by Soviet military strength, agreed not to patrol the border area claimed by the Soviet Union; but strained relations between the two countries continued into the early 1980s.

Under the collective leadership, the Soviet Union again used force in Eastern Europe, this time in Czechoslovakia. In 1968 reform-minded elements of the Communist Party of Czechoslovakia rapidly began to liberalize their rule, loosen censorship, and strengthen Western ties. In response, Soviet and other Warsaw Pact troops entered Czechoslovakia and installed a new regime. Out of these events arose the so-called Brezhnev Doctrine, which warned that the Soviet Union would act to maintain its hegemony in Eastern Europe (see Soviet-East European Relations, ch. 10). Soviet suppression of the reform movement reduced blatant gestures of defiance on the part of Romania and served as a threatening example to the Polish Solidarity trade union movement in 1980. But it also helped disillusion communist parties in Western Europe to the extent that by 1977 most of the leading parties embraced Eurocommunism, which freed them to pursue political programs independent of Moscow's dictates.

Soviet influence in the developing world expanded somewhat during this period. New communist or Marxist governments having close relations with the Soviet Union rose to power in several countries, including Vietnam, Ethiopia, and Nicaragua. In the Middle

Veterans of the Great Patriotic War (World War II) pose in Moscow.
Courtesy Irene Steckler

East, the Soviet Union vied for influence by backing the Arabs in their dispute with Israel. After the June 1967 War, the Soviet Union rebuilt the defeated Syrian and Egyptian armies, but it suffered a setback when Egypt expelled Soviet advisers from the country in 1972 and subsequently entered a closer relationship with the United States. The Soviet Union retained ties with Syria and supported Palestinian claims for their right to an independent state. But Soviet prestige among moderate Muslim states suffered in the 1980s as a result of Soviet military activities in Afghanistan. Attempting to shore up a communist government in that country, Brezhnev sent in Soviet armed forces in December 1979, but a large part of the Afghan population resisted both the occupiers and the Afghan regime. The resulting war in Afghanistan continued to be an unresolved problem for the Soviet Union at the time of Brezhnev's death in 1982.

Soviet relations with the West first improved, then deteriorated in the years after Khrushchev. The gradual winding down of the United States commitment to the war in Vietnam after 1968 opened the way for negotiations between the United States and the Soviet Union on the subject of nuclear arms. After the Treaty on the Nonproliferation of Nuclear Weapons was signed in July 1968, the two countries began the Strategic Arms Limitation Talks (SALT) in

1969. At the Moscow Summit of May 1972, Brezhnev and President Richard M. Nixon signed the Anti-Ballistic Missile Treaty and the Interim Agreement on the Limitation of Strategic Offensive Arms. Both agreements essentially froze the deployment of strategic defensive and offensive weapons. A period of détente, or relaxation of tensions, between the two superpowers emerged, with a further agreement concluded to establish ceilings on the number of offensive weapons on both sides in 1974. The crowning achievement of the era of détente was the signing in 1975 of the Helsinki Accords, which ratified the postwar status quo in Europe and bound the signatories to respect basic principles of human rights. But even during the period of détente, the Soviet Union increased weapons deployments, with the result that in the 1970s it achieved rough parity with the United States in strategic nuclear weaponry (see Arms Control and Military Objectives, ch. 17). The Soviet Union also heightened its condemnation of the NATO alliance in an attempt to weaken Western unity. Although a second SALT agreement was signed by Brezhnev and President Jimmy Carter in Vienna in 1979, after the Soviet invasion of Afghanistan the Carter administration withdrew the agreement from consideration by the United States Senate, and détente effectively came to an end. In reaction to the Soviet involvement in Afghanistan, the United States imposed a grain embargo on the Soviet Union and boycotted the Summer Olympics in Moscow in 1980. Tensions between the United States and the Soviet Union continued up to Brezhnev's death.

The Economy

Despite Khrushchev's tinkerings with economic planning, the economic system remained dependent on central plans drawn up with no reference to market mechanisms. Reformers, of whom the economist Evsei Liberman was most noteworthy, advocated greater freedom for individual enterprises (see Glossary) from outside controls and sought to turn the enterprises' economic objectives toward making a profit. Prime Minister Kosygin championed Liberman's proposals and succeeded in incorporating them into a general economic reform program approved in September 1965. This reform included scrapping Khrushchev's regional economic councils in favor of resurrecting the central industrial ministries of the Stalin era. Opposition from party conservatives and cautious managers, however, soon stalled the Liberman reforms, forcing the state to abandon them.

After this short-lived attempt at revamping the economic system, planners reverted to drafting comprehensive centralized plans of the type first developed under Stalin. In industry, plans stressed the heavy and defense-related branches, with the light consumer-goods branches slighted (see Economic Policy, ch. 11). As a developed industrial country, the Soviet Union by the 1970s found it increasingly difficult to maintain the high rates of growth in the industrial sector that it had sustained in earlier years. Increasingly large investment and labor inputs were required for growth, but these inputs were becoming more difficult to obtain. Although the planned goals of the five-year plans of the 1970s had been scaled down from previous plans, the targets remained largely unmet. The industrial shortfalls were felt most sharply in the sphere of consumer goods, where the public steadily demanded improved quality and increased quantity.

Agricultural development continued to lag in the Brezhnev years. Despite steadily higher investments in agriculture, growth under Brezhnev fell below that attained under Khrushchev. Droughts occurring irregularly throughout the 1970s forced the Soviet Union to import large quantities of grain from the West, including the United States. In the countryside, Brezhnev continued the trend toward converting collective farms into state farms and raised the incomes of all farm workers. Despite the wage raises, peasants still devoted much time and effort to their private plots, which provided the Soviet Union with an inordinate share of its agricultural goods (see Policy and Administration, ch. 13).

The standard of living in the Soviet Union presented a problem to the Brezhnev leadership after improvements made in the late 1960s gradually leveled off at a position well below that of many Western industrial (and some East European) countries. Although certain goods and appliances became more accessible during the 1960s and 1970s, improvements in housing and food supply were slight. Shortages of consumer goods abetted pilferage of government property and growth of the black market. Vodka, however, remained readily available, and alcoholism was an important factor in both the declining life expectancy and the rising infant mortality that the Soviet Union experienced in the later Brezhnev years.

Culture and the Arts

Progress in developing the education system was mixed during the Brezhnev years. In the 1960s and 1970s, the percentage of working-age people with secondary and higher education steadily increased. Yet at the same time, access to higher education grew more difficult. By 1980 the percentage of secondary school graduates admitted to universities had dropped to only two-thirds of the 1960 figure. Students accepted into the universities increasingly came from professional families rather than from worker or peasant households. This trend toward the perpetuation of the educated elite was not only a function of the superior cultural background of elite families but was also, in many cases, a result of their power to influence the admissions procedures.

Progress in science also enjoyed varied success under Brezhnev. In the most visible test of its ability—the race with the United States to put a man on the moon—the Soviet Union failed, but through persistence the Soviet space program continued to make headway in other areas. In general, despite leads in such fields as metallurgy and thermonuclear fusion, Soviet science lagged behind that of the West, hampered in part by the slow development of computer technology.

In literature and the arts, a greater variety of creative works became accessible to the public than had previously been available. True, the state continued to determine what could be legally published or performed, punishing persistent offenders with exile or prison. Nonetheless, greater experimentation in art forms became permissible in the 1970s, with the result that more sophisticated and subtly critical work began to be produced. The regime loosened the strictures of socialist realism; thus, for instance, many protagonists of the novels of author Iurii Trifonov concerned themselves with problems of daily life rather than with building socialism. In music, although the state continued to frown on such Western phenomena as jazz and rock, it began to permit Western musical ensembles specializing in these genres to make limited appearances. But the native balladeer Vladimir Vysotskii, widely popular in the Soviet Union, was denied official recognition because of his iconoclastic lyrics.

In the religious life of the Soviet Union, a resurgence in popular devotion to the major faiths became apparent in the late 1970s despite continued de facto disapproval on the part of the authorities. This revival may have been connected with the generally growing interest of Soviet citizens in their respective national traditions (see Manifestations of National Assertiveness, ch. 4).

Death of Brezhnev

Shortly after his cult of personality began to take root in the mid-1970s, Brezhnev began to experience periods of ill health. After Brezhnev's first stroke in 1975, Politburo members Mikhail A. Suslov and Andrei P. Kirilenko assumed some of Brezhnev's functions for a time. Then, after another bout of poor health in 1978, Brezhnev delegated more of his responsibilities to Konstantin U. Chernenko, a long-time associate who soon began to be regarded as the heir apparent. His prospects of succeeding Brezhnev, however, were hurt by problems plaguing the general secretary in the early 1980s. Not only had economic failures hurt Brezhnev's prestige, but scandals involving his family and political allies also damaged his stature. Meanwhile, Iurii V. Andropov, chief of the secret police, the Committee for State Security (Komitet gosudarstvennoi bezopasnosti—KGB), apparently also began a campaign to discredit Brezhnev. Andropov took over Suslov's functions after Suslov died in 1982, and he used his position to advance himself as the next CPSU general secretary. Brezhnev himself, despite ill health following another stroke in March, would not relinquish his office. Soon after reviewing the traditional Bolshevik Revolution parade in November 1982, Brezhnev died.

Ultimately, the Soviet Union paid a high price for the stability that prevailed during the years of the Brezhnev regime. By avoiding necessary political and economic change, the Brezhnev leadership ensured the economic and political decline that the country experienced during the 1980s. This deterioration of power and prestige stood in sharp contrast to the dynamism that marked the Soviet Union's revolutionary beginnings.

* * *

A number of comprehensive texts covering the history of the Soviet Union have recently appeared. Most worthy of recommendation to the nonspecialist is *A History of Russia and the Soviet Union* by David MacKenzie and Michael W. Curran. A thoughtful survey can be found in Geoffrey A. Hosking's *The First Socialist Society.* Other general works covering the Soviet period include Robert V. Daniels's *Russia: The Roots of Confrontation,* Donald W. Treadgold's *Twentieth Century Russia,* and Adam B. Ulam's *A History of Soviet Russia.* There are also a number of excellent books on the various phases of Soviet history. The recognized classic on the revolutionary and Civil War period is William H. Chamberlin's *The Russian Revolution, 1917-1921.* Recommended for the Stalin era is *Stalin* by Adam B. Ulam. For Khrushchev, the reader is referred to Carl A. Linden's *Khrushchev and the Soviet Leadership, 1957-1964.* Khrushchev's two-volume memoirs, *Krushchev Remembers,* are fascinating reading. Harry Gelman's *The Brezhnev Politburo and the Decline of Detente* treats the Brezhnev period in detail. (For further information and complete citations, see Bibliography.)

Chapter 3. Physical Environment
and Population

People of the Soviet Union against a backdrop of the Kremlin in Moscow and mountains in the Georgian Republic

CURVING AROUND THE North Pole and the Arctic Ocean like a huge arc, the Soviet Union spans almost half the globe from east to west and about 5,000 kilometers from north to south. It is the world's largest country, occupying the major portions of Europe and Asia and including one-sixth of the earth's inhabited land area. Its diverse terrain ranges from vast deserts to towering mountains, yielding huge stores of natural resources and enabling the country to satisfy almost all of its own essential natural resource needs. In terms of population, the Soviet Union ranks third after China and India. Its peoples, however, as its terrain, are as diverse as those of any continent.

The Ural Mountains extend more than 2,200 kilometers, forming the northern and central boundary separating Asia from Europe. The continental divide continues another 1,375 kilometers from the Ural Mountains through the Caspian Sea and along the Caucasus Mountains, splitting the Soviet Union into grossly unequal Asian and European parts. Roughly three-quarters of Soviet territory encompass a part of Asia far larger than China and India combined. Nevertheless, it is the western quarter, the European part, that is home to more than 70 percent of all Soviet citizens. Surveys of Soviet geography and population have long pointed out the acutely uneven distribution of human and natural resources throughout the country. Despite considerable attempts to settle people in Asian areas that are abundant in resources, this imbalance persists. Rapid depletion of water and fuel resources in the European part has continued to outstrip development in resource-rich Siberia, which is east of the Ural Mountains. From 1970 to 1989, the campaign to settle and exploit the inhospitable frontier region of western Siberia with its plentiful fuel and energy supplies was costly but successful.

Although the Soviet Union is richly endowed with resources, several factors severely restrict their availability and use. The extreme climate and the northern position of the country, plus the unfavorable location of major deposits, present formidable geographic impediments. Massive depopulation, firmly established patterns of settlement, and disparate birth rates have resulted in regional labor shortages and surpluses.

In the years since the Bolshevik Revolution of 1917, the inhabitants of the Soviet Union have suffered terrible hardships. Before the 1950s, in each decade the population experienced a cataclysmic demographic event in the form of epidemics, wars, or famines and in state-sanctioned mass killings. Only those persons born since World War II (62 percent of the population in 1987) have been spared the havoc that ravaged their grandparents' and parents' generations. The long-term effects of these disasters on the population can hardly be overstated. The opportunity to examine in relative tranquillity the national demographic situation is a postwar phenomenon. During this time, Soviet officials have become increasingly aware of the importance of demographic issues. The most visible signs of this are the policies aimed at influencing and directing demographic processes such as reproduction and migration for the benefit of society and the economy.

Encouraged by *glasnost'* (see Glossary), in the 1980s Soviet and foreign geographers and demographers engaged in spirited and open discussions. Probing articles and books began appearing on previously sensitive or taboo topics. Alcohol and drug abuse, high rates of infant and adult mortality, environmental degradation, the decline of the Soviet family, and the frequency of divorce were among them. Population problems stemming from sharp differences in the reproduction rates and migration patterns of the numerous Soviet nationalities were also openly debated.

Physical Environment

Any geographic description of the Soviet Union is replete with superlatives. Its inventory of land and water contains the world's largest and deepest lakes, the most expansive plain, and Europe's highest mountain and longest river. Desert scenes from Soviet Central Asia resemble the Australian outback. The Crimean coast on the Black Sea is the Soviet Riviera, and the mountains rimming the southern boundary are as imposing as the Swiss Alps. However, most of the topography and climate resembles that of the northernmost portion of the North American continent. The northern forests and the plains to the south find their closest counterparts in the Yukon Territory and in the wide swath of land extending across most of Canada. Similarities in terrain, climate, and settlement patterns between Siberia and Alaska and Canada are unmistakable.

After the Bolshevik Revolution and the ensuing Civil War (1918–21), Soviet regimes transformed, often radically, the country's physical environment. In the 1970s and 1980s, Soviet citizens, from the highest officials to ordinary factory workers and farmers, began to examine negative aspects of this transformation and to call for more prudent use of natural resources and greater concern for environmental protection.

Global Position and Boundaries

Located in the middle and northern latitudes of the Northern Hemisphere, the Soviet Union on the whole is much closer to the North Pole than to the equator. Individual country comparisons are of little value in gauging the enormous size (more than twice that of the United States) and diversity of the Soviet Union. A far better perspective comes by viewing the country as a truly continental-sized landmass only slightly smaller than North America and larger than South America in both area and population.

The country's 22.4 million square kilometers include one-sixth of the earth's inhabited land area. Its western portion, more than half of all Europe, makes up just 25 percent of the Soviet Union; this, however, is where the overwhelming majority (about 72 percent) of the people live and where most industrial and agricultural activities are concentrated. It was here, roughly between the Dnepr River and the Ural Mountains, that the Russian Empire took shape, following Muscovy's gradual expansion that reached the Pacific Ocean in the seventeenth century.

Although its historical, political, economic, and cultural ties bind it firmly to Europe, the Soviet Union is largely an Asian country because of Siberia. For centuries this land between the Urals and the Pacific was infamous as a place of exile, a land of endless expanses of snow and frigid temperatures. In the post-World War II period, however, Siberia has also become known as a new frontier because of its treasure of natural resources.

The Soviet Union measures some 10,000 kilometers from Kaliningrad on the Gulf of Danzig in the west to Ratmanova Island (Big Diomede Island) in the Bering Strait, or roughly equivalent to the distance from Edinburgh, Scotland, east to Nome, Alaska. From the tip of the Taymyr Peninsula on the Arctic Ocean to the Central Asian town of Kushka near the Afghan border extend almost 5,000 kilometers of mostly rugged, inhospitable terrain. The east-west expanse of the continental United States would easily fit between the northern and southern borders of the Soviet Union at their extremities.

Extending for over 60,000 kilometers, the Soviet border is not only one of the world's most closely guarded but also is by far the longest. Along the nearly 20,000-kilometer-long land frontier, the Soviet Union abuts twelve countries, six on each continent. In Asia, its neighbors are the Democratic People's Republic of Korea (North Korea), China, Mongolia, Afghanistan, Iran, and Turkey; in Europe, it borders Romania, Hungary, Czechoslovakia, Poland, Finland, and Norway. Except for the icy eighty-six kilometers of the Bering Strait, it would have a thirteenth neighbor—the United States (see fig. 1).

Approximately two-thirds of the frontier is bounded by water, forming the longest and, owing to its proximity to the North Pole, probably the most useless coastline of any country. Practically all of the lengthy northern coast is well above the Arctic Circle and, with the important exception of Murmansk, which receives the warm currents of the Gulf Stream, is locked in ice much of the year. A dozen seas, part of the water systems of three oceans—the Arctic, Atlantic, and Pacific—wash Soviet shores.

Administrative-Political-Territorial Divisions

Since 1956 the enormous territory of the Soviet Union has consisted of fifteen union republics—the largest administrative and political units—officially known as Soviet republics or union republics (see Glossary). Nationality (see Glossary), size of the population, and location are the determinants for republic status. By far the largest and most important of the union republics is the Russian Republic, containing about 51 percent of the population (see table 6, Appendix A). Largely because it encompasses Siberia, the Russian Republic alone accounts for 75 percent of Soviet territory and forms the heartland of both the European and the Asian portions of the Soviet Union. Although in 1989 Russians made up over 51 percent of the Soviet population and were in many ways the dominant nationality, they are just one of more than 100 nationality groups that make up Soviet society. Fourteen other major nationalities also have their own republics: in the European part are the Lithuanian, Latvian, Estonian, Belorussian, Ukrainian, and Moldavian republics; the Georgian, Azerbaydzhan, and Armenian republics occupy the Caucasus; and Soviet Central Asia is home to the Kazakh, Uzbek, Turkmen, Kirgiz, and Tadzhik republics (see Nationalities of the Soviet Union, ch. 4; table 13, Appendix A). The Soviet system also provides for territorial and administrative subdivisions called autonomous republics, autonomous oblasts, autonomous *okruga, kraia,* or most often oblasts (see Glossary). These subdivisions make the country easier to manage and at times serve to recognize additional nationalities. In terms of political and administrative authority, the more than 130 oblasts and autonomous oblasts resemble to a limited degree counties in the United States. Many oblasts, however, are about the size of states. For example, Tyumenskaya Oblast, the storehouse of Soviet fuels, is only slightly smaller than Alaska (see Fuels, ch. 12). A more appropriate comparison with counties, in terms of numbers and area,

Panoramic view from the Trans-Siberian Railway
Dnepr River in Kiev, Ukrainian Republic
Courtesy Jimmy Pritchard

can be made with the more than 3,200 *raiony* (see Glossary), the Soviet Union's smallest administrative and political subdivision.

Topography and Drainage

Most geographers divide the vast Soviet territory into five natural zones that generally extend from west to east: the tundra zone; the taiga or forest zone; the steppe or plains zone; the arid zone; and the mountain zone. Most of the Soviet Union consists of three plains (East European Plain, West Siberian Plain, and Turan Lowland), two plateaus (Central Siberian Plateau and Kazakh Upland), and a series of mountainous areas, concentrated for the most part in the extreme northeast or extending intermittently along the southern border. The West Siberian Plain, the world's largest, extends east from the Urals to the Yenisey River (see fig. 6). Because the terrain and vegetation are uniform in each of the natural zones, the Soviet Union, as a whole, presents an illusion of uniformity. Nevertheless, the Soviet territory contains all the major vegetation zones with the exception of tropical rain forest. Almost 10 percent of Soviet territory is tundra, that is, a treeless marshy plain. The tundra is the Soviet Union's northernmost zone of snow and ice, stretching from the Finnish border in the west to the Bering Strait in the east and then running south along the Pacific coast to the earthquake and volcanic region of northern Kamchatka Peninsula. It is the land made famous by herds of wild reindeer, by "white nights" (dusk at midnight, dawn shortly thereafter) in summer, and by days of total darkness in winter. The long harsh winters and lack of sunshine allow only mosses, lichens, and dwarf willows and shrubs to sprout low above the barren permafrost (see Glossary). Although the great Siberian rivers slowly traverse this zone in reaching the Arctic Ocean, drainage of the numerous lakes, ponds, and swamps is hampered by partial and intermittent thawing. Frost weathering is the most important physical process here, shaping a landscape modified by extensive glaciation in the last Ice Age. Less than 1 percent of the Soviet population lives in this zone. The fishing and port industries of the Kola Peninsula and the huge oil and gas fields of northwestern Siberia are the largest employers in the tundra. The frontier city of Noril'sk, for example, with a population of 181,000 in 1987, is one of the largest settlements above the Arctic Circle.

The northern forests of spruce, fir, cedar, and larch, collectively known as the taiga, make up the largest natural zone of the Soviet Union, an area about the size of the United States. Here too the winter is long and severe, as witnessed by the routine registering of the world's coldest temperatures for inhabited areas in the

Figure 6. Topography and Drainage

northeastern portion of this belt. The taiga zone extends in a broad band across the middle latitudes, stretching from the Finnish border in the west to the Verkhoyansk Range in northeastern Siberia and as far south as the southern shores of Lake Baykal. Isolated sections of taiga are found along mountain ranges, as in the southern part of the Urals, and in the Amur River Valley in the Far East. About 33 percent of the population lives in this zone, which, with the mixed forest zone, includes most of the European part of the Soviet Union and the ancestral lands of the earliest Slavic settlers.

Long associated with traditional images of Russian landscape and cossacks (see Glossary) on horseback are the steppes, which are treeless, grassy plains. Although they cover only 15 percent of Soviet territory, the steppes are home to roughly 44 percent of the population. They extend for 4,000 kilometers from the Carpathian Mountains in the western Ukrainian Republic across most of the northern portion of the Kazakh Republic in Soviet Central Asia, between the taiga and arid zones, occupying a relatively narrow band of plains whose chernozem (see Glossary) soils are some of the most fertile on earth. In a country of extremes, the steppe zone, with its moderate temperatures and normally adequate levels of sunshine and moisture, provides the most favorable conditions for human settlement and agriculture. Even here, however, agricultural yields are sometimes adversely affected by unpredictably low levels of precipitation and occasional catastrophic droughts (see Production, ch. 13).

Below the steppes, and merging at times with them, is the arid zone: the semideserts and deserts of Soviet Central Asia and, particularly, of the Kazakh Republic. Portions of this zone have become cotton- and rice-producing regions through intensive irrigation. For various reasons, including sparse settlement and a comparatively mild climate, the arid zone has become the most prominent center for Soviet space exploration.

One-quarter of the Soviet Union consists of mountains or mountainous terrain. With the significant exceptions of the Ural Mountains and the mountains of eastern Siberia, the mountains occupy the southern periphery of the Soviet Union. The Urals, because they have traditionally been considered the natural boundary between Europe and Asia and because they are valuable sources of minerals, are the most famous of the country's nine major ranges. In terms of elevation (comparable to the Appalachians) and vegetation, however, they are far from impressive, and they do not serve as a formidable natural barrier.

Truly alpine terrain is found in the southern mountain ranges. Between the Black and Caspian seas, for example, the Caucasus

Mountains rise to impressive heights, marking a continuation of the boundary separating Europe from Asia. One of the peaks, Mount El'brus, is the highest point in Europe at 5,642 meters. This range, extending to the northwest as the Crimean and Carpathian mountains and to the southeast as the Tien Shan and Pamirs, forms an imposing natural barrier between the Soviet Union and its neighbors to the south. The highest point in the Soviet Union, at 7,495 meters, is Mount Communism (Pik Kommunizma) in the Pamirs near the border with Afghanistan, Pakistan, and China. The Pamirs and the Tien Shan are offshoots of the tallest mountain chain in the world, the Himalayas. Eastern Siberia and the Soviet Far East are also mountainous regions, especially the volcanic peaks of the long Kamchatka Peninsula, which juts down into the Sea of Okhotsk. The Soviet Far East, the southern portion of Soviet Central Asia, and the Caucasus are the Soviet Union's centers of seismic activity. In 1887, for example, a severe earthquake destroyed the city of Vernyy (present-day Alma-Ata), and in December 1988 a massive quake demolished the Armenian city of Spitak and large sections of Kirovakan and Leninakan. The 1988 quake, one of the worst in Soviet history, claimed more than 25,000 lives.

The Soviet Union's water resources are both scarce and abundant. With about 3 million rivers and approximately 4 million inland bodies of water, the Soviet Union holds the largest fresh, surface-water resources of any country. Unfortunately, most of these resources (84 percent), as with so much of the Soviet resource base, are at a great distance from consumers; they flow through sparsely populated territory and into the Arctic and Pacific oceans. In contrast, areas with the highest concentrations of population, and therefore the highest demand for water supplies, tend to have the warmest climates and highest rates of evaporation. The result is barely adequate (or in some cases inadequate) water resources where they are needed most.

Nonetheless, as in many other countries, the earliest settlements sprang up on the rivers, and that is where the majority of the urban population prefers to live. The Volga, Europe's longest river, is by far the Soviet Union's most important commercial waterway. Three of the country's twenty-three cities with more than 1 million inhabitants are located on its banks: Gor'kiy, Kazan', and Kuybyshev.

The European part of the Soviet Union has extensive, highly developed, and heavily used water resources, among them the key hydrosystems of the Volga, Kama, Dnepr, Dnestr, and Don rivers. As is the case with fuels, however, the greatest water resources are found east of the Urals, deep in Siberia. Of the sixty-three rivers in the Soviet Union longer than 1,000 kilometers, forty are east of the Urals, including the four mighty rivers that drain Siberia

Siberian village in winter
Courtesy Jimmy Pritchard

as they flow northward to the Arctic Ocean: the Irtysh, Ob',
Yenisey, and Lena rivers. The Amur River forms part of the winding and sometimes tense boundary between the Soviet Union and
China. Taming and exploiting the hydroelectric potential of these
systems has been a monumental and highly publicized national
project. Some of the world's largest hydroelectric stations operate
on these rivers. Hundreds of smaller hydroelectric power plants
and associated reservoirs have also been constructed on the rivers.
Thousands of kilometers of canals link river and lake systems and
provide essential sources of irrigation for farmland.

The Soviet Union's 4 million inland bodies of water are chiefly
a legacy of extensive glaciation. Most prominent among them are
the Caspian Sea, the world's largest inland sea, and Lake Baykal,
the world's deepest and most capacious freshwater lake. Lake Baykal
alone holds 85 percent of the freshwater resources of the lakes in
the Soviet Union and 20 percent of the world's total. Other water
resources include swampland, a sizable portion of territory (10 percent), and glaciers in the northern areas.

Climate

Notorious cold and long winters have, understandably, been the
focus of discussions on the Soviet Union's weather and climate.

From the frozen depths of Siberia have come baby mammoths perfectly preserved, locked in ice for several thousand years. Millions of square kilometers experience half a year of subfreezing temperatures and snow cover over subsoil that is permanently frozen in places to depths of several hundred meters. In northeastern Siberia, not far from Yakutsk, hardy settlers cope with January temperatures that consistently average − 50°C. Transportation routes, including entire railroad lines, have been redirected in winter to traverse rock-solid waterways and lakes.

Howling Arctic winds that produce coastal wind chills as low as − 152°C and the *burany,* or blinding snowstorms of the steppe, are climatic manifestations of a relatively unfavorable position in the Northern Hemisphere. The dominance of winter in the Soviet Union is a result of the proximity to the North Pole—the southernmost point of the country is about on the same latitude as Oklahoma City, Oklahoma—and remoteness from oceans that tend to moderate the climate. As a result, cold, high-pressure systems in the east—the "Siberian high"—and wet, cold cyclonic systems in the west largely determine the overall weather patterns.

The prolonged period of cold weather has a profound impact on almost every aspect of life in the Soviet Union. It affects where and how long people live and work and what kinds of crops are grown and where they are grown (no part of the country has a year-round growing season). The length and severity of winterlike weather, along with the sharp fluctuations in the mean summer and winter temperatures, impose special requirements on many branches of the economy: in regions of permafrost, buildings must be constructed on pilings, and machinery must be made of specially tempered steel; transportation systems must be engineered to perform reliably in extremely low and high temperatures; the health care field and the textile industry are greatly affected by the ramifications of six to eight months of wintry weather; and energy demands are multiplied by extended periods of darkness and cold.

Despite its well-deserved reputation as a generally snowy, icy northern country, the Soviet Union includes other major climatic zones as well. According to Soviet geographers, most of their country is located in the temperate zone, which for them includes all of the European portion except the southern part of Crimea and the Caucasus, all of Siberia, the Soviet Far East, and the plains of Soviet Central Asia and the southern Kazakh Republic. Within this belt are the taiga, the steppes, and the deserts of Soviet Central Asia. In fact, the climate in much of this zone is anything but temperate; it varies from the moderate maritime climate of the Baltic republics, which is similar to the American Northwest, to the

Apartment house in Spitak, Armenian Republic, destroyed by an earthquake in December 1988 that registered 6.9 on the Richter scale. Such apartment houses were not designed, or built, to withstand seismic activity of that magnitude. The earthquake claimed 25,000 victims.
Courtesy United States Geological Survey

continental climate of the east and northeast, which is akin to that of the Yukon Territory. Leningrad and Yakutsk, although roughly on the same latitude, have average January temperatures of $-7°C$ and $-50°C$, respectively.

Two areas outside the temperate zone demonstrate the climatic diversity of the Soviet Union: the Soviet Far East, under the influence of the Pacific Ocean, with a monsoonal climate; and the subtropical band of territory extending along the southern coast of the Soviet Union's most popular resort area, Crimea, through the Caucasus and into Soviet Central Asia, where there are deserts and oases.

With most of the land so far removed from the oceans and the moisture they provide, levels of precipitation in the Soviet Union are low to moderate. More than half the country receives fewer than forty centimeters of rainfall each year, and most of Soviet Central Asia and northeastern Siberia can count on barely one-half that amount. The wettest parts are found in the small, lush subtropical region of the Caucasus and in the Soviet Far East along the Pacific coast.

Natural Resources

The Soviet Union is richly endowed with almost every major category of natural resource. Drawing upon its vast holdings, it has become the world leader in the production of oil, iron ore, manganese, and asbestos. It has the world's largest proven reserves of natural gas, and in 1984 it surpassed the United States in the production of this increasingly important fuel. It has enormous coal reserves and is in second place in coal production (see fig. 7).

Self-sufficiency has traditionally been a powerful stimulus for exploring and developing the country's huge, yet widely dispersed, resource base. It remains a source of national pride that the Soviet Union, alone among the industrialized countries of the world, can claim the ability to satisfy almost all the requirements of its economy using its own natural resources.

The abundance of fossil fuels supplies not only the Soviet Union's domestic needs; for many years, an ample surplus has been exported to consumers in Eastern Europe and Western Europe, where it earns most of the Soviet Union's convertible currency (see Raw Materials; Fuels, ch. 12).

However, as resource stocks have been depleted in the heavily populated European section, tapping the less accessible but vital riches east of the Urals has become a national priority. The best example of this process is fuels and energy. The depletion of readily accessible fuel resources west of the Urals has caused development and exploitation to shift to the inhospitable terrain of western Siberia, which in the 1970s and 1980s displaced the Volga-Ural and the southern European regions as the country's primary supplier of fuel and energy (see table 7, Appendix A). Fierce cold, permafrost, and persistent flooding have made this exploitation costly and difficult.

Environmental Concerns

In spite of a series of environmental laws and regulations passed in the 1970s, authentic environmental protection in the Soviet Union did not become a major concern until General Secretary Mikhail S. Gorbachev came to power in March 1985. Without an established regulatory agency and an environmental protection infrastructure, enforcement of existing laws was largely ignored. Only occasional and isolated references appeared on such issues as air and water pollution, soil erosion, and wasteful use of natural resources in the 1970s. This lack of concern was prompted by several factors. First, after collectivization in the 1930s, all of the land became state owned and managed. Thus, whenever air and water were polluted, the state was most often the agent of this pollution. Second, and this was true especially under Joseph V. Stalin's leadership, the resource base of the country was viewed as limitless and free. Third, in the rush to modernize and to develop heavy industry, concern for damage to the environment and related damage to the health of Soviet citizens would have been viewed as detrimental to progress. Fourth, pollution control and environmental protection itself is an expensive, high-technology industry, and even in the mid-1980s many of the Soviet Union's systems to control harmful emissions were inoperable or of foreign manufacture.

Under Gorbachev's leadership, the official attitude toward the environment changed. Various social and economic factors helped produce this change. To maintain economic growth through the 1980s, a period in which the labor force had been declining significantly, intensive and more prudent use of both natural and human resources was required. At the same time, *glasnost'* provided an outlet for widespread discussion of environmental issues, and a genuine grass-roots ecological movement arose to champion causes similar to the ecological concerns of the West. Public campaigns were mounted to protect Lake Baykal from industrial pollution and to halt the precipitous decline in the water levels of the Caspian Sea, the Sea of Azov, and, most urgently, the Aral Sea. A grandiose scheme to divert the northern rivers southward had been counted on to replenish these seas, but for both economic and environmental reasons, the project was canceled in 1986.

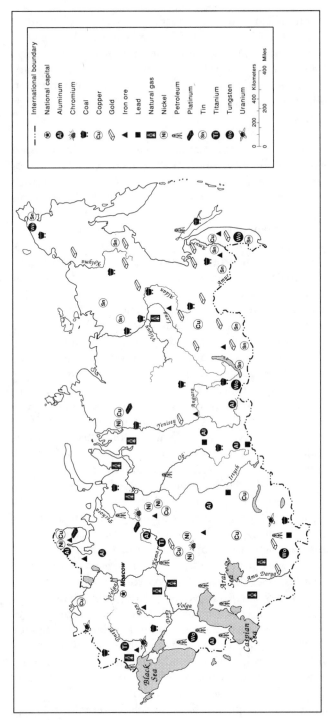

Source: Based on information from William Henry Parker, *The Soviet Union*, New York, 1983, 7.

Figure 7. Major Mineral Deposits

Without this diversion project, the Aral Sea, once a body of water larger than any of the Great Lakes except Lake Superior, seemed destined to become the world's largest salt flat as early as the year 2010. By 1987 so much water had been siphoned off for irrigation of cotton and rice fields south and east of the sea that all shipping and commercial fishing had ceased. Former seaports, active as late as 1973, were reported to be forty to sixty kilometers from the water's edge. Belatedly recognizing the gravity of the situation for the 3 million inhabitants of the Aral region, government officials declared it an ecological disaster area.

With respect to air pollution, mass demonstrations protesting unhealthful conditions were held in cities such as Yerevan in the Armenian Republic. Official reports confirmed that more than 100 of the largest Soviet cities registered air quality indexes ten times worse than permissible levels. In one of the most publicized cases, the inhabitants of Kirishi, a city not far from Leningrad, succeeded in closing a chemical plant whose toxic emissions were found to be harming—and in some cases killing—the city's residents. Finally, separate, highly publicized cases of man-made disasters, the most prominent of which was the Chernobyl' (see Glossary) nuclear power plant accident in 1986, highlighted the fragility of the man-production-nature relationship in the Soviet Union and forced a reconsideration of traditional attitudes and policies toward industrialization and development.

As part of the process of restructuring (*perestroika*—see Glossary), in the 1980s concrete steps were taken to strengthen environmental protection and to provide the country with an effective mechanism for implementing policy and ensuring compliance. Two specific indications of this were the inclusion of a new section devoted to environmental protection in the annual statistical yearbook and the establishment of the State Committee for the Protection of Nature (Gosudarstvennyi komitet po okhrane prirody—Goskompriroda) early in 1988.

Despite these measures, decades of environmental degradation caused by severe water and air pollution and land abuse were unlikely to be remedied soon or easily. Solving these critical problems will require not only a major redirection of capital and labor but also a fundamental change in the entire Soviet approach to industrial and agricultural production and resource exploitation and consumption.

Population

Seven official censuses have been taken in the Soviet Union (1920, 1926, 1939, 1959, 1970, 1979, and 1989). Both the quality and the

115

quantity of the data have varied: in 1972 seven volumes totaling 3,238 pages were published on the 1970 census. In contrast, the results of the 1979 census were published more than five years later in a single volume of 366 pages.

According to the census of 1989, on the day of the census, January 12, the population of the Soviet Union was estimated to be 286,717,000. This figure maintained the country's long-standing position as the world's third most populous country after China and India. In the intercensal period (1979–88), the population of the Soviet Union grew from 262.4 million to 286.7 million, a 9 percent increase.

During the 1970s and early 1980s, the Soviet Union experienced declining birth rates, increasing divorce rates, a trend toward smaller nuclear families, and increasing mobility and urbanization. Major problems associated with such factors as migration, tension among nationality groups, uneven fertility rates, and high infant and adult mortality became increasingly acute, and various social programs and incentives were introduced to deal with them.

Vital Statistics

In the period after World War II, annual population growth rates gradually declined from a high of 1.4 percent during the 1961–65 period to 0.9 percent, the rate throughout the 1970s and most of the 1980s. Such a rate of increase is typical for an industrialized urbanized society, and it closely matched the 1.0 percent growth rate recorded in the United States for the same period.

Between 1971 and 1986, average life expectancy fluctuated and actually decreased in some years before stabilizing at about seventy years (see table 8, Appendix A). The difference of eight to ten years between male and female life expectancy in favor of women was somewhat greater than in most Western countries. Life expectancy was longest (73.3 years in 1985–86) in the Armenian Republic and shortest (64.8 years) in the Turkmen Republic.

More than any other demographic index, infant mortality underscored most sharply the tremendous regional differences in the population and its health care. Beginning in the mid-1970s, reporting of infant mortality rates was discontinued; in October 1986, however, Soviet sources revealed that infant mortality rates had actually increased between 1970 and 1986, from 24.7 per 1,000 to 25.4 per 1,000 births. While the rate for the Russian Republic, which is generally better supplied with health facilities, declined by 19 percent, the rate increased for most Soviet Central Asian republics. In one case, the Uzbek Republic, the rate increased by almost 50 percent, to 46.2 per 1,000. In 1986 infant mortality was

Satellite imagery of the Aral Sea in 1987. A catastrophic loss of 60 percent of the sea's volume of water followed the near total diversion of inflow for agricultural irrigation south and east of the sea (see shaded areas). The dotted line shows the 1973 shoreline. The formerly active ports of Aral'sk and Muynak were stranded in a desert forty to sixty kilometers from the water in 1987.
Courtesy United States Air Force Defense Meterological Satellite Program and CIRES/National Snow and Ice Data Center

lowest (11.6 per 1,000) in the Lithuanian Republic and highest (58.2 per 1,000) in the Turkmen Republic.

Analysts proposed a number of reasons to explain what was viewed as an abnormally high rate of infant mortality for a developed country. Among the reasons given were excessive consumption of alcohol and heavy smoking among women; widespread use of abortion as a means of birth control, a procedure that could impair the health of the mother and of children carried to term; teenage pregnancy; unsanitary conditions; and a deteriorating health care system (see Health Care, ch. 6).

In the Soviet Union, virtually all national growth has been the result of natural increase because of traditionally rigid control over immigration and emigration. Growth, however, varies considerably from region to region and from nationality to nationality. In terms of population, there is a clear trend toward the Soviet Union's becoming more Asian and less European. Birth rates in parts of Soviet Central Asia are in some cases ten times higher than birth rates among Slavs. In the intercensal period 1970–78, population growth in the Asian part of the Soviet Union was almost triple the rate of growth in the European section, 16.8 percent versus 5.9 percent.

Although most facets of the population were dynamic, some demographic aspects remained constant: women have outnumbered men since the Bolshevik Revolution, and the overwhelming majority of the people have opted to live in the cities and on the collective farms (see Glossary) and state farms (see Glossary) of the European part of the country. In more than seven decades of Soviet power, the population has experienced periodic cataclysmic demographic events, some of them self-inflicted and some of them of external origin. These wars, famines, purges, and epidemics have left an enduring imprint on the society and on its ability to reproduce and renew itself. The magnitude of human loss in the Soviet Union can be shown by estimating the 1987 population as if it had grown at a relatively modest annual rate of 1 percent from 1917 to 1987. At that rate, the population would have reached approximately 325 million citizens by the seventieth anniversary of the Bolshevik Revolution. Instead, that figure is expected to be reached only in 2016, a delay of more than one generation. The difference between this estimate of 325 million and the actual population in 1987 of 281 million suggests that some 45 to 50 million lives were lost in wars, famines, forced collectivization, and purges.

The single most devastating event by far was World War II, commonly referred to in the Soviet Union as the Great Patriotic War (see The Great Patriotic War, ch. 2). Estimates vary, but an absolute population decline of some 20 to 25 million seems quite plausible. There were 194 million people reportedly living in the Soviet Union in 1940. Only 209 million were counted by the census of 1959 instead of the roughly 234 million that might have been expected, given a moderate rate of growth. Since the end of the war, the population has increased by more than 100 million.

Age and Sex Structure

The aspect of the population most affected by the cataclysmic demographic events was its age and sex structure. The consequences of World War II ensured that the existing surplus of women would persist for at least another generation; more than four decades after its conclusion, women, most of whom were born before the war, still outnumbered men by about 16 million (see table 9, Appendix A). This imbalance has had a profound impact on the economy, social structure, and population reproduction in the Soviet Union. Before the war, just under 40 percent of women were in the work force: since 1970 they have been a slight majority of all workers. The female component of the work force since the start of the war has become an indispensable feature of the Soviet economy, and the overwhelming majority of working-age women were employed in 1987.

Because a significant portion of an entire generation perished in the war, marriages and births were fewer for some time thereafter. The decline in the marriage and birth rates produced a population pyramid with bulges and contractions in specific age and sex groups and with significantly higher percentages of older women at the top of the pyramid (see fig. 8). Expressed another way, in 1987 for every one *dedushka* (grandfather), there were almost three *babushki* (grandmothers).

Because both the economic and the military might of a country largely depend upon its labor force, the able-bodied population (defined in the Soviet Union as males sixteen to fifty-nine years of age and females sixteen to fifty-four years of age) was for Soviet planners an increasing cause of concern. Additions to the working-age population peaked in the 1970s, with a growth of almost 23 million; projected increases in the 1980s were expected to be one-quarter that number, with a gradual improvement to one-half (11.6 million) in the 1990s. This slowed growth placed a strain on the economy in the late 1970s and early 1980s by requiring continuous boosts in productivity (see Labor, ch. 11).

In 1985 the sexes were in rough balance, with a slight male preponderance up to the population median age of 33.4 years. Beyond the median age, however, women outnumbered men in the

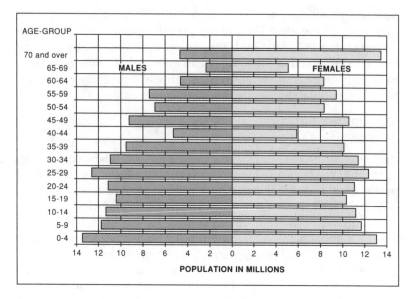

Source: Based on information from "Naselenie SSSR," *Vestnik statistiki* [Moscow], No. 12, December 1987, 44.

Figure 8. Population Distribution by Age and Sex, 1987

population and in the work force. In some professions and economic sectors (health care, trade, food services, social services, and physical education, for example), more than 80 percent of all workers were women.

Mortality and Fertility

Between 1970 and 1986, the mortality rate in the Soviet Union increased from 8.2 per 1,000 to 9.8 per 1,000. Some of this increase was attributable to the aging of the population, as the number of old-age (fifty-five for women, sixty for men) pensioners grew from 36.5 million to 47.4 million. Other factors, however, contributed to this upswing, one of the most disturbing of which was an increase in the mortality of infants and able-bodied men. The male mortality increase was highlighted by the almost ten-year differential in male and female life expectancies. Intense urbanization and the attendant pressures of living and working in an urban environment undoubtedly exacerbated the mortality rate. As in most developed countries, the leading causes of death in the Soviet Union were cardiovascular diseases, malignant tumors, and injuries and accidents. Suicide cases in 1987 were officially recorded at 54,105, or 19.1 per 100,000 population.

Under Gorbachev a concerted effort has been made to reduce mortality and improve productivity. The government initiated active campaigns to limit the number of deaths from accidents and chronic degenerative diseases by drastically curtailing the availability of alcohol and by attempting to persuade the more than 70 million (in 1986 about 25 percent of the population) smokers to renounce the habit. The overall health of the population, the state of Soviet health care, and the environment became recurrent topics of open discussion and debate. By 1986 these measures seemed to be having some effect: one year was added to average male life expectancy, and mortality started to decline. Some Soviet demographers stressed, however, that long-term improvements would only be ensured by focusing on four factors that they believed to be major determinants of the level of mortality: the quality of life, including working and living conditions, nutrition, and clothing; the quality of the environment; the quality and accessibility of health care; and the people's sanitary and hygienic habits.

In the 1970–78 intercensal period, overall fertility rates in the Soviet Union declined slightly. Regionally, however, there were sharp differences. In Soviet Central Asia, for example, women consistently expected to have at least twice as many children as their counterparts in the European part of the Russian Republic. The Caucasus region registered rates between these two extremes. The government addressed the issue of declining fertility by enacting a series of measures in the late 1970s and early 1980s aimed at making it easier for women to cope with the onerous burden of being mother, wife, and worker (see Population Problems and Policies, this ch.; Role of Women, ch. 5).

Urbanization

In a span of over seventy years, the Soviet Union has undergone a transition from a largely rural agricultural society to an urban industrial society. In 1917 only about 17 percent of the population lived in cities or urban settlements; in 1961 the urban and rural population was in balance; and by 1987 two of every three Soviet citizens were urban dwellers (see table 10, Appendix A).

The levels of urbanization in 1989 highlighted the uneven development of the regions and nationalities. The populations of the Estonian, Latvian, Lithuanian, and Russian republics were 70 percent urbanized, approximating levels found in Western Europe and the United States. Four of the five Central Asian republics (the Kirgiz, Tadzhik, Uzbek, and Turkmen republics), however, continued to have a majority of the population living in rural areas, and the Tadzhik Republic's 33 percent rate of urbanization was

121

only slightly higher than that of Albania. In the European part, the Moldavian Republic with a rural majority was an exception to the rule of higher rates of urbanization.

Until the early 1980s, the growth of large cities and the concentration of industry there went mostly unchecked. However, because of such problems as a chronic housing shortage, pollution, and a declining birth rate, authorities attempted to exercise greater control over migration to the major cities; among other things, the government encouraged greater development and growth in small and medium-sized cities. Nevertheless, the scope and tempo of big-city growth has continued. In 1970 ten cities had a population of 1 million or more, but in 1989 the number had risen to twenty-three (see table 11, Appendix A). Most of these cities, including the three largest—Moscow, Leningrad, and Kiev—were located west of the Urals. Only five of the largest cities were east of the Urals, and the largest city in the entire eastern half of the Soviet Union (beyond the Yenisey River) was Vladivostok (615,000 inhabitants in 1987).

Despite its size and the length of its coastline, the Soviet Union's global position and climate have restricted the number of seaports to fewer than a dozen key cities (Leningrad, Odessa, Murmansk, and Vladivostok, among them). Many of the largest cities, however, are located on water, primarily on rivers, that have long been powerful settlement-forming influences and key transportation arteries. The Volga and its tributaries remain the key geographic features toward which people and commerce continue to gravitate. Two of the youngest and fastest growing cities, Tol'yatti and Naberezhnyye Chelny, were boom towns that sprang up in the 1970s around giant automobile and truck plants on the Volga and Kama rivers, respectively.

Migration

Two aspects of the Soviet system tended to act as impediments to voluntary migration: state ownership of the land and, in theory at least, a rigid system of internal passports that regulated where people live and work. Despite these impediments, in the 1980s approximately 15 million citizens (5 percent of the total population), some with the state's approval and some without it, changed their place of residence each year. The overwhelming majority of the migrants were young males sixteen years of age and older. Many of these were students. Millions of pioneers arrived at or departed from newly explored territories in western Siberia or the Soviet Far East. Many of the migrants abandoned the hard work and simple life on state farms and collective farms for the better pay and amenities of the largest cities.

By far the largest percentage of migration (40 percent) has been from villages to cities: for example, between 1959 and 1979 the agricultural work force in the nonchernozem region of the Russian Republic declined by 40 percent as a result of movement to cities. Since the Bolshevik Revolution, the urban population grew by almost 85 million people as a result of in-migration from rural areas alone. Between 1970 and 1979, more than 3 million people left the countryside annually, and just 1.5 million moved in the opposite direction. A substantial proportion of migration (34 percent) took place from city to city.

The pervasive influence of the severe climate exerted pressure on migration patterns. In some parts of Siberia, the climate and working conditions were so harsh that shifts were set up, based on the recommendations of medical authorities, to return workers to more hospitable climes after a tour of two or three years. As an incentive to attract workers to sparsely settled areas such as western Siberia, the government established a system of bonuses and added credit toward retirement. Between 1970 and 1985, migration patterns began to adapt to the needs of the national economy, and the long-standing maldistribution of natural and human resources began to improve. The incentives helped to reverse, at least temporarily, the negative migration stream out of Siberia in the first part of the 1970s. Still, the age-sex structure of the newly exploited areas was one typical for frontiers. Disproportionate numbers of young males made the area far from conducive for establishing a stable population base and labor force.

In the 1980s, the government continued to find it difficult to stimulate migration out of the southern parts of the country and into the northern and eastern sections of the Soviet Union. Contrary to the desired migratory pattern, the areas with the greatest levels of mobility were generally those with the lowest birth rates, in particular the Estonian, Latvian, Lithuanian, Russian, Ukrainian, and Belorussian republics. In Soviet Central Asia, where birth rates were considerably higher, the levels of migration and population mobility were low. These demographic patterns were not seen by planners as contributing to the long-term solution of labor supply problems stemming from labor deficiencies in the central European region and labor surpluses in Soviet Central Asia.

Because the government continued to maintain tight control over migration into or out of the country, between 1970 and 1985 the population remained largely a "closed" one, in which increases or decreases as a result of immigration or emigration were insignificant.

According to figures released in 1989, some 140,000 persons emigrated from the Soviet Union in 1987 and 1988. Authorities expected the rate to stabilize at about 60,000 to 70,000 per year. Overall, observers estimated that as many as 500,000 émigrés, mostly Jews, Armenians, Germans, and Poles, were allowed to leave between 1960 and 1985.

Distribution and Density

Because so much of its territory is poorly suited for human habitation, the Soviet Union on the whole is a sparsely populated country. In 1987 it registered an average density of twelve inhabitants per square kilometer. The density varied greatly by region, however (see fig. 9). In the mid-1980s, the density of the European portion of the Soviet Union was thirty-four inhabitants per square kilometer, about the same as in the American South. The republics with the greatest population density were the Moldavian, Armenian, and Ukrainian republics (see table 12, Appendix A).

Moskovskaya Oblast, largely because of its historical, cultural, and political significance and the presence in it of the Moscow urban metropolitan area, was one of the country's most thickly settled oblasts. Despite attempts to limit the capital's growth, Moscow continued to attract numerous migrants each year. The entire region between the Volga and Oka rivers had a high concentration of settlements. The most sparsely populated regions of the country have persistently been in the Far North, which is considerably more sparsely settled than Alaska.

The "center of gravity" of the population is gradually moving in a southeasterly direction and in the mid-1980s was located west of the Urals just below the city of Kuybyshev. The main belt of settlement forms a wedge whose base is a line going from Leningrad to the Moldavian Republic. In the European part of the Soviet Union, its northern boundary runs through the cities of Cherepovets, Vologda, and Perm'; the southern arm passes through Kherson, Rostov-na-Donu, Volgograd, and Chelyabinsk. Significant concentrations of population outside this wedge were found in the Caucasus and in Central Asia. The roughly 10 percent of the population in Siberia was concentrated in a rather narrow belt surrounding the two major transportation arteries of the Trans-Siberian Railway (see Glossary) and the Baykal-Amur Main Line (BAM—see Glossary) and in the energy-producing region of western Siberia. Future population growth and settlement in Siberia and the Soviet Far East for the most part was expected to take place in the environs of the BAM.

The rural population was also concentrated in the southern and central sections of the European part. Densities of more than 100 persons per square kilometer were found in the Dnestr River Valley and in several parts of the Ukrainian Republic, the Soviet Union's traditional breadbasket. Rural population density tapered off in the taiga zone and sharply diminished in the tundra of the European north. The arid steppes and semideserts in the southeast European part were lightly settled.

Starting in the 1970s, an active campaign was mounted to reduce and consolidate the number of rural populated places in the Soviet Union. The number of rural places in the nonchernozem region of the Russian Republic alone declined from 180,000 to 118,000 between 1959 to 1979. Nationally, a reasonable estimate of the numbers of phased-out ("future-less settlements" in Russian) populated places, most with fewer than 200 inhabitants, was more than 100,000.

The ninth, tenth, and eleventh five-year plans (1971–85) provided for stimulating further economic development and settlement in Siberia and the Soviet Far East. Under Gorbachev, reports indicated a possible change in emphasis to stress modernization and intensification of production by using existing capacity in the European portion.

Marriage, Divorce, and the Family

As early as the mid-1970s, open acknowledgment and frank discussions of demographic problems in the Soviet Union began to take place. The family, as "the key social unit," was at the center of these discussions. For many years, population growth was taken for granted. In the 1970s, however, authorities became concerned about declining birth rates in the European part of the Soviet Union, especially among Russians. In addition to urbanization and industrialization, other factors affecting family size were rising divorce rates, an acute shortage of housing, and poor health care. Another factor was that Slavic women had the world's highest abortion rates.

The Twenty-Fifth Party Congress of the Communist Party of the Soviet Union (CPSU) in 1976 was the first to recognize that the Soviet Union had a demographic problem, and it proposed measures to deal with "the aggravation of the demographic situation." Two key areas pertaining to the family were mentioned as contributing to an intensification of population problems: the lowering of birth rates to levels below those necessary for replacement and for guaranteeing an adequate supply of labor; and continuing high rates of divorce. The Twenty-Sixth Party Congress (1981) and the Twenty-Seventh Party Congress (1986) established a pronatalist policy that probably accounted for a slight upswing in fertility as the decade progressed.

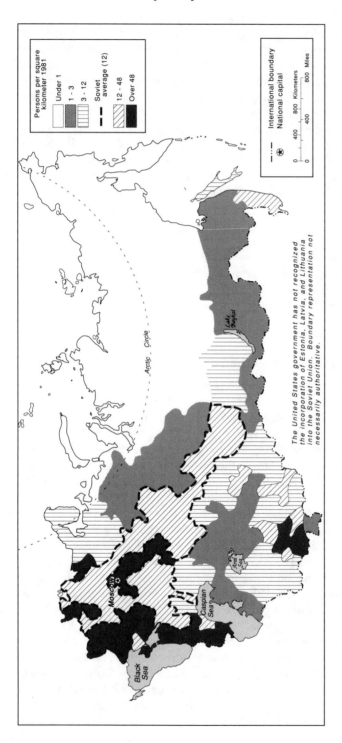

Source: Based on information from J.P. Cole, *Geography of the Soviet Union*, Cambridge, 1984, 244.

Figure 9. Population Density, 1981

In the 1970s and 1980s, some population problems were associated with a developmental trend that the socialist system had traditionally encouraged, i.e., urbanization and industrialization. The demographic price for this process is normally paid in declining birth rates and shrinking family sizes. An efficient modern economy ordinarily can adjust to a smaller work force. The Soviet economy, however, has remained relatively labor intensive in the key agricultural and industrial sectors, and as a result there were labor shortages in many of the larger cities.

The 1979 census registered more than 66 million families; by the mid-1980s there were about 70 million families. In 1979 the overwhelming majority (86.2 percent) of urban families consisted of two to four members. In the urban areas of the European part, in particular, the trend was to limit the number of children to two and in many cases to only one. In 1979 about 60 percent of the families with children under eighteen years of age had only one child; 33 percent had two children. The negative consequences of this trend, especially in the European part of the country, led the government to begin an active campaign to encourage families to have a third child.

Population Problems and Policies

Unless unfavorable trends can be reversed, the Soviet Union eventually will have to deal with the threat of depopulation in much of the European portion of the Russian Republic and in the Estonian, Latvian, Lithuanian, Belorussian, and Ukrainian republics, the very political, military, and economic base of the country. Persistently low birth rates and a sharp downward trend in family size among most Soviet Europeans has been the root cause. The pattern became more obvious, and the alarms became louder, in the late 1970s and 1980s.

The declining Russian representation in the multinational Soviet population has caused great concern. Such a trend has serious international and national political, economic, social, and military implications. For example, with fewer native speakers of Russian, it becomes progressively more difficult to maintain Russian as the national language. As the Russian language declines in importance, the challenge of both raising the national level of education and training a skilled labor force becomes more complicated and costly. The armed forces, as well, face the prospect of adding to their ranks a smaller percentage of Soviet Europeans and a greater share of Soviet Asians, who may not serve with the dedication of the Slavs and whose service imposes additional demands on the military in terms of special training to improve communications skills.

*Village in the Tadzhik Republic near Dushanbe at the foot of the Hissar
Mountains about 160 kilometers north of the Afghan frontier
Courtesy Jimmy Pritchard*

In the 1970s and 1980s, the government introduced some key initiatives that were intended to ameliorate demographic difficulties: occupations restricted to males for health and safety reasons were expanded; maternity leave was extended to one year after the birth (eight weeks fully paid), and the leave was counted as service time; lump-sum cash payments for each birth were provided, with higher premiums for the third and fourth child; child support payments to low-income families were increased; and families were to be given preferential treatment in the assignment of housing and other services.

At the same time, campaigns were introduced aimed at raising overall "demographic literacy" (developing a citizenry better informed about the national demographic situation) and improving public health. By far the most publicized and most controversial of these campaigns was the attack on alcoholism and public drunkenness. The sale of alcoholic beverages was sharply curtailed in the mid-1980s. Soviet authorities felt that the elimination of this traditional social ill would have an immediate and direct impact on demographic processes by eliminating a major cause of divorce and premature disability and death. In addition, promoting safe and healthful working and living conditions was one of the chief aims of the growing numbers of officials and citizens concerned with the environment.

The success of these government measures remained in doubt in 1989. Persuasive evidence supported the view that patterns of urbanization, extreme reluctance to migrate, and higher fertility rates in Soviet Central Asia have continued. These demographic patterns, together with the strengths and limitations of the physical environment, have affected such critical issues as the cohesion of the Soviet federation and its nationality representation, the acutely uneven distribution of natural and human resources, investment in industrial development, and the character and composition of the work force and the military.

* * *

By far the most important English-language source of current information on the geography and population of the Soviet Union is the monthly journal *Soviet Geography*. Much of the information in the chapter derives from the excellent articles in this journal, some of which were written by its founder and editor, Theodore Shabad, who was, until his death in 1987, the foremost expert on the subject in the United States. Some standard texts on the geography of the Soviet Union are Paul E. Lydolph's *Geography of the*

U.S.S.R; J.P. Cole's *Geography of the Soviet Union;* David Hooson's *The Soviet Union: People and Regions;* G. Melvyn Howe's *The Soviet Union: A Geographical Study;* and William Henry Parker's *The Soviet Union.* Pending publication of the final results of the 1989 all-union census, the most important source of data on the Soviet population has been the statistical handbook *Naselenie SSSR, 1987.* In recent years, more information has been made available to both Western and Soviet scholars on demographic developments in the Soviet Union. As of 1989, among the experts on the subject in the United States were Murray Feshbach, Stephen Rapawy, and W. Ward Kingkade. All three, especially Feshbach, have written extensively on various aspects of Soviet population (fertility, mortality, age and sex structure, and ethnicity). Particularly valuable was Kingkade's article ''Demographic Trends in the Soviet Union.'' (For further information and complete citations, see Bibliography.)

Chapter 4. Nationalities and Religions

People of various nationalities and religions

ON FEBRUARY 17, 1988, General Secretary Mikhail S. Gorbachev declared that the nationalities question in the Soviet Union was a "crucially important vital question" of the times. He went on to call for a "very thorough review" of Soviet nationalities policy, an acknowledgment of the failure of the past Soviet regimes' attempts to solve the problem of nationalities that was inherited from tsarist Russia. With remarkable candor, Gorbachev admitted that the problem not only still existed but that it was more acute than ever.

For close to seventy years, Soviet leaders had maintained that frictions among the many nationalities of the Soviet Union had been eliminated and that the Soviet Union consisted of a family of nations living harmoniously together, each national culture adding to and enriching the new Soviet culture and promoting the development of a single Soviet nationality. However, the national ferment that shook almost every corner of the Soviet Union in the late 1980s proved that seventy years of communist rule had failed to obliterate national and ethnic differences and that traditional cultures and religions would reemerge given the slightest opportunity. This unpleasant reality facing Gorbachev and his colleagues meant that, short of relying on the traditional use of force, they had to find alternative solutions in order to prevent the disintegration of the Soviet empire. Whether they succeed or fail in this task will, to a large degree, determine the future of the Soviet Union.

The extensive multinational empire that the Bolsheviks (see Glossary) inherited after their revolution was created by tsarist expansion over some four centuries. Some nationality groups came into the empire voluntarily, but most were brought in by force. Generally, the Russians and most of the non-Russian subjects of the empire shared little in common—culturally, religiously, or linguistically. More often than not, two or more diverse nationalities were collocated on the same territory. Therefore, national antagonisms built up over the years not only against the Russians but often among some of the subject nations as well.

Like its tsarist predecessor, the Soviet state has remained ethnically complex (see fig. 10). Indeed, the distinctions between the various nationalities of the Soviet Union have sharpened during the Soviet period. The concessions granted national cultures and the limited autonomy tolerated in the union republics (see Glossary) in the 1920s led to the development of national elites and a

135

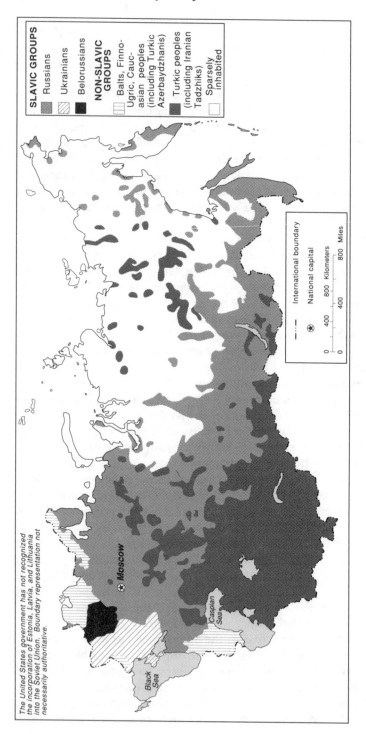

The United States government has not recognized the incorporation of Estonia, Latvia, and Lithuania into the Soviet Union. Boundary representation not necessarily authoritative.

SLAVIC GROUPS
Russians
Ukrainians
Belorussians

NON-SLAVIC GROUPS
Balts, Finno-Ugric, Cauc-asian peoples (including Turkic Azerbaydzhanis)
Turkic peoples (including Iranian Tadzhiks)
Sparsely inhabited

International boundary
National capital

0   400   800 Kilometers
0   400   800 Miles

Figure 10. Nationalities and Nationality Groups, 1987

heightened sense of national identity. Subsequent repression and Russianization (see Glossary) fostered resentment against domination by Moscow and promoted further growth of national consciousness. National feelings were also exacerbated in the Soviet multinational state by increased competition for resources, services, and jobs.

Nationalities of the Soviet Union

The official Soviet census of 1989 listed over 100 nationalities in the Soviet Union (see table 13, Appendix A). Each had its own history, culture, and language. Each possessed its own sense of national identity and national consciousness. The position of each nationality in the Soviet Union depended to a large degree on its size, the percentage of the people using the national language as their first language, the degree of its integration into the Soviet society, and its territorial-administrative status. This position was also dependent on each nationality's share of membership in the Communist Party of the Soviet Union (CPSU), the number of students in higher institutions, the number of scientific workers, and the degree of urbanization of each nationality.

The various nationalities differed greatly in size. On the one hand, the Russians, who constituted about 50.8 percent of the population, numbered about 145 million in 1989. On the other hand, half of the nationalities listed in the census together accounted for only 0.5 percent of the total population, most of them having fewer than 100,000 people. Twenty-two nationalities had more than 1 million people each. Fifteen of the major nationalities had their own union republics, which together comprised the federation known as the Soviet Union.

The nationalities having union republic status commanded more political and economic power than other nationalities and found it easier to maintain their own language and culture. In 1989 some nationalities formed an overwhelming majority within their own republics; one nationality (the Kazakhs), however, lacked even a majority. In addition to the fifteen nationalities having union republics, some others had their own territorial units, such as autonomous republics, autonomous oblasts, and autonomous *okruga* (see table 14, Appendix A). The remaining nationalities did not have territorial units of their own and in most cases only constituted minorities in the Russian Republic (see table 15, Appendix A).

The nationalities that have had a significant political and economic impact on the Soviet Union include the fifteen nationalities that have their own union republics and the non-union republic nationalities that numbered at least 1 million people in 1989. They are the Slavic nationalities, the Baltic nationalities, the nationalities of the Caucasus, the Central Asian nationalities, and a few other nationalities.

Slavic Nationalities

Since the establishment of the Soviet Union, the most dominant group of people numerically, politically, culturally, and economically have been the Slavs, particularly the East Slavs. Although little is known of the early history of the Slavs, they had by the seventh century A.D. divided into three distinguishable groups: the West Slavs, ancestors of the Poles, the Czechs, and the Slovaks; the South Slavs, ancestors of the Bulgarians, the Slovenes, the Serbs, and the Croatians; and the East Slavs, ancestors of the Russians, the Ukrainians, and the Belorussians. The East Slavic tribes settled along the Dnepr River in the present-day Ukrainian Republic in the first centuries after the birth of Christ and from there spread northward and eastward. In the ninth century, these tribes became part of the foundation of Kievan Rus', the medieval state of the East Slavs ruled by a Varangian dynasty (see The East Slavs and the Varangians, ch. 1).

The East Slavs enhanced their political union in the tenth century when they adopted Christianity as the state religion of Kievan Rus'. Nevertheless, tribal and regional differences persisted and became more marked as the realm of Kievan Rus' expanded. To the northwest, East Slavic tribes mixed with the local Baltic tribes, while in the north and northeast they mixed with the indigenous Finno-Ugric tribes. By the time Kievan Rus' began to disintegrate into a number of independent principalities in the twelfth century, the East Slavs were evolving into three separate people linguistically and culturally: Russians to the north and northeast of Kiev, Belorussians to the northwest of Kiev, and Ukrainians around Kiev itself and to the south and southwest of Kiev. This process of ethnic differentiation and consolidation was accelerated by the Mongol invasion of Kievan Rus' and its collapse as a political entity in the thirteenth century. For several centuries, the three East Slavic nationalities remained related culturally, linguistically, and to a great extent religiously. Nevertheless, each of them has been influenced by different political, economic, religious, and social developments, further separating them from each other (see The Rise of Regional Centers, ch. 1).

Russians

Russians have been the largest and most dominant nationality in both the Soviet Union and its predecessors, the Russian Empire and Muscovy. From the time of Muscovy's rise as the dominant principality in the northeast of the territory of Kievan Rus', a Russian state continually extended its territory and enabled Ivan III (1462–1505) to proclaim himself "Ruler of all Rus'." Peter the Great (1682–1725) established the Russian Empire, which by the end of the nineteenth century reached the Baltic Sea in the northwest and the Black Sea in the southwest, the Pacific Ocean in the east, and the Pamirs in the south (see fig. 3). The Romanov Dynasty, which promoted Russian administrative control over the disparate nationalities in its domain, ruled for three centuries until it was overthrown in February 1917 (according to the Julian calendar (see Glossary); March 1917 according to the Gregorian calendar). After the seizure of power by the Bolsheviks in October 1917 (November 1917), Russian domination of political, economic, and cultural life in the Soviet Union continued despite the rule of Joseph V. Stalin, who was Georgian by birth. Yet throughout their history, Russians themselves were subjected to oppressive rulers, whether tsarist or communist. Particularly devastating since the advent of communist rule in November 1917 were the Civil War (1918–21), forced collectivization and industrialization, the Great Terror (see Glossary), and World War II, each of which resulted in extreme hardship and loss of great numbers of Russian people.

According to the 1989 census, some 145 million Russians constituted just over half of the population of the Soviet Union, although their share of the total has been declining steadily. A low fertility rate among the Russians and a considerably higher fertility rate among the peoples of Soviet Central Asia may make Russians a minority nationality by the year 2000.

Most Russians lived in the Russian Soviet Federated Socialist Republic (Russian Republic), an immense area occupying three-fourths of the Soviet Union and stretching from Eastern Europe across the Ural Mountains and Siberia to the Kamchatka Peninsula in the Pacific Ocean. Many other nationalities lived in the Russian Republic. Sixteen of the twenty autonomous republics were located here, as well as five of the eight autonomous oblasts and all ten of the autonomous *okruga*. But Russians also constituted substantial minorities in the populations of most non-Russian union republics in the Soviet Union (see table 16, Appendix A). Only a small percentage of Russians claimed fluency in the languages of the non-Russian republics in which they resided.

In the late 1980s, Russians were the second most urban nationality in the Soviet Union (only Jews were proportionally more urbanized). Russians constituted about two-thirds of the entire urban population of the Soviet Union; all major cities in the Soviet

Union had a large Russian population. In addition, Moscow, the largest city and capital of the Soviet Union, served as the administrative center for the Russian Republic. The domination by Russians has been evident in almost every phase of Soviet life and has increased in the 1970s and 1980s. In 1972, 62.5 percent of the members of the Politburo, the highest organ of the CPSU, were Russians. In 1986 the percentage of Russians rose to 84.6 and then to 89 in 1989. Generally, Russians were the party second secretaries and the chiefs of the Committee for State Security (Komitet gosudarstvennoi bezopasnosti—KGB) in non-Russian republics. Russians also constituted a majority of CPSU membership, amounting to about 61 percent in the 1980s. Only Jews and Georgians have also had representation in the party that was higher than their proportion of the population. Russian dominance of the CPSU has also helped them dominate Soviet society.

Russians held a high percentage of the most important positions in government, industry, agriculture, education, science, and the arts, especially in the non-Russian republics. The number of Russians attending higher education institutions also was disproportionate to their share of the population. Only Jews, Armenians, and Georgians had a proportionally higher number of students at these institutions.

Russian language and culture has had special status throughout the Soviet Union. The Russian language has been the common language in government organizations as well as in most economic, social, and cultural institutions. Higher education in many fields has been provided almost exclusively in Russian, and mastery of that language has been an important criterion for admission to institutions of higher learning. Administrative and supervisory posts in non-Russian republics were often held by Russians having little knowledge of the native language. In 1986 Russian was the language used to publish 78 percent of the books by number of titles and 86 percent of the books by number of copies. The publication of magazines and newspapers printed in Russian and in the other indigenous languages has been equally disproportionate.

The homeland of about 119.8 million Russians and over 27 million non-Russian people, the Russian Republic also provided substantial industrial, agricultural, and natural resources to the Soviet Union. Nevertheless, in 1989 the Russian Republic, alone among the fifteen union republics, had no party apparatus separate from that of the CPSU. The functions performed in non-Russian republics by republic-level CPSU organizations were performed for the Russian Republic by the central agencies of the CPSU.

Ukrainians

Ukrainians trace their ancestry to the East Slavic tribes that inhabited the present-day Ukrainian Republic in the first centuries after the birth of Christ and were part of the state of Kievan Rus' formed in the ninth century. For a century after the breakup of Kievan Rus', the independent principalities of Galicia and Volhynia served as Ukrainian political and cultural centers. In the fourteenth century, Galicia was absorbed by Poland, and Volhynia, together with Kiev, became part of the Grand Duchy of Lithuania. In 1569 Volhynia and Kiev also came under Polish rule, an event that significantly affected Ukrainian society, culture, language, and religion. Ukrainian peasants, except for those who fled to join the cossacks (see Glossary) in the frontier regions southeast of Poland, were enserfed. Many Ukrainian nobles were Polonized.

The continuous oppression of the Ukrainian people by the Polish nobility led to a series of popular insurrections, culminating in 1648, when Ukrainian Cossacks joined in a national uprising. Intermittent wars with Poland forced the Ukrainian Cossacks to place Ukraine under the protection of the Muscovite tsar. A prolonged war between Muscovy and Poland followed, ending in 1667 with a treaty that split Ukraine along the Dnepr River. Ukrainian territory on the right (generally western) bank of the Dnepr remained under Poland, while Ukrainian territory on the left (generally eastern) bank was placed under the suzerainty of the Muscovite tsar. Although both segments of Ukraine were granted autonomous status, Muscovy and Poland followed policies to weaken Ukrainian autonomy. A number of uprisings by Ukrainian peasantry led to the crushing of the remainder of Ukrainian autonomy in Poland (see Expansion and Westernization, ch. 1). Ukrainian self-rule under the tsar ended after Mazepa, the Ukrainian hetman (leader), defected to the Swedish side during the war between Muscovy and Sweden at the beginning of the eighteenth century. In 1775 Catherine the Great dispersed the Ukrainian Cossacks and enserfed those Ukrainian peasants who had remained free. The partitions of Poland at the end of the eighteenth century placed most of the Ukrainian territory on the right bank of the Dnepr River under Russian rule. The westernmost part of Ukraine (known as western Ukraine) was incorporated into the Austrian Empire.

The resurgence of Ukrainian national consciousness in the nineteenth century was fostered by a renewed interest among intellectuals in Ukrainian history, culture, and language and the founding of many scholarly, cultural, and social societies. The Russian government responded by harassing, imprisoning, and exiling leading

Ukrainian intellectuals. Ukrainian academic and social societies were disbanded. Publications, plays, and concerts in Ukrainian were forbidden. Finally, the existence of a Ukrainian language and nationality was officially denied. Nevertheless, a Ukrainian national movement in the Russian Empire persisted, spurred partially by developments in western Ukraine, where Ukrainians in the more liberal Austrian Empire had far greater freedom to develop their culture and language.

After the collapse of the Russian Empire in 1917 and the Austro-Hungarian Empire in 1918, Ukrainians in both empires proclaimed their independence and established national republics. In 1919 the two republics united into one Ukrainian national state. This unification, however, could not withstand the aggression of both the Red and White Russian forces and the hostile Polish forces in western Ukraine. Ukraine again was partitioned, with western Ukraine incorporated into the new Polish state and the rest of Ukraine established as the Ukrainian Soviet Socialist Republic in March 1919, which was later incorporated into the Soviet Union when it was formed in December 1922.

In the decade of the 1920s, the Ukrainian Republic experienced a period of Ukrainization. Ukrainian communists enjoyed a great deal of autonomy in running the republic, and Ukrainian culture and language dominated. Stalin's rise to power, however, halted the process of Ukrainization. Consequently, Ukrainian intellectual and cultural elites were either executed or deported, and leading Ukrainian party leaders were replaced by non-Ukrainians. The peasantry was forcibly collectivized, leading to a mass famine in 1932–33 in which several million peasants starved to death. Pointing to the fact that grain was forcibly requisitioned from the peasantry despite the protests of the Soviet government in the Ukrainian Republic, some historians believe that Stalin knowingly brought about the famine to stop national ferment in the Ukrainian Republic and break the peasants' resistance to collectivization. When western Ukraine was incorporated into the Soviet Union following the Nazi-Soviet Nonaggression Pact of 1939, the population suffered terror and mass deportations.

When the Germans attacked the Soviet Union in 1941, Ukrainians anticipated establishing an independent Ukraine. As the Red Army retreated eastward, Ukrainian nationalists proclaimed an independent state, but the invading Germans arrested and interned its leaders. Ukrainian nationalist forces consequently began a resistance movement against both the occupying Germans and the Soviet partisans operating in the Ukrainian Republic. When the Red Army drove the Germans out of the Ukrainian Republic,

Russian children on the train to Krasnoyarsk, in Siberia, Russian Republic
Courtesy Jimmy Pritchard

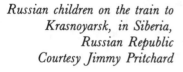

Armenian family celebrating the New Year at a fair in the central square, Yerevan, Armenian Republic
Courtesy Jimmy Pritchard

Ukrainian partisans turned their struggle (which continued until 1950) against the Soviet armed forces (the name Red Army was dropped just after the war) and Polish communist forces in western Ukraine. The Soviet regime deported Ukrainian intelligentsia to Siberia and imported Russians into the Ukrainian Republic as part of their pacification and Russification (see Glossary) efforts.

The vast majority of Ukrainians, the second largest nationality in the Soviet Union with about 44 million people in 1989, lived in the Ukrainian Republic. Substantial numbers of Ukrainians also lived in the Russian, Kazakh, and Moldavian republics. Many non-Ukrainians lived in the Ukrainian Republic, where the Russians, with over 11 million, constituted the largest group.

Ukrainians have a distinctive language, culture, and history. In 1989, despite strong Russifying influence, about 81.1 percent of Ukrainians residing in their own republic claimed Ukrainian as their first language.

By the 1980s, the majority of Ukrainians, once predominantly agrarian, lived in cities. The major Ukrainian cities in 1989 were Kiev, the capital of the Ukrainian Republic, with a population of 2.6 million, and Khar'kov, Dnepropetrovsk, Odessa, and Donetsk, all with over 1 million people.

Although Ukrainians constituted about 15 percent of the Soviet Union's population in 1989, their educational and employment opportunities appeared unequal to their share of the population. In the 1970s, they ranked only eleventh out of seventeen major nationalities (the nationalities corresponding to the fifteen union republics plus Jews and Tatars) in the number of students in secondary and higher education and ninth in the number of scientific workers in proportion to their share of the total population. Since the death of Stalin in 1953, the number of Ukrainians in the CPSU has steadily increased. Nevertheless, Ukrainians remained underrepresented in the party relative to their share of the population. This was particularly true in the Ukrainian Republic, where in the 1970s the Ukrainian proportion of party membership was substantially below their proportion of the population. The percentage of Russians in the CPSU in the Ukrainian Republic, however, was considerably higher than their share of the republic's population. Although in the past Ukrainians had held a disproportionately high percentage of seats on the CPSU Central Committee, since 1961 their share of membership in this body has steadily declined to 13 percent of the seats in 1986.

Belorussians

The ancestors of present-day Belorussians were among those East Slavic tribes that settled the northwestern part of Kievan Rus' territory, mixing with and assimilating the indigenous Baltic tribes. After the Mongol invasion in the thirteenth century and the collapse of Kievan Rus', Belorussian lands, together with the greater part of Ukraine, became part of the Grand Duchy of Lithuania. When in 1569 the Grand Duchy of Lithuania joined in dynastic union with Poland to form the Polish-Lithuanian Commonwealth, Belorussians shared with Poles and Lithuanians a common king and parliament. For the next two centuries, Polish influence in Belorussia was dominant. Belorussian nobles, seeking the same privileges as their Polish counterparts, became Polonized and converted from Orthodoxy to Catholicism. Only the peasants retained their Belorussian national culture and Orthodox religion.

With the partitions of Poland at the end of the eighteenth century, Belorussian lands passed to the Russian Empire. The tsarist government viewed Belorussians as simply backward, somewhat Polonized, Russians. It persecuted those Belorussians who had become Uniates in 1596 and forced them to reconvert to Orthodoxy (see Catholic, this ch.). Nevertheless, in the second half of the nineteenth century Belorussians experienced a national and political revival and developed a renewed awareness of their separateness from both the Poles and the Russians. The fledgling Belorussian political movement at the turn of the century reached its zenith during the February Revolution in 1917 and culminated in the establishment of the Belorussian Democratic Republic in March 1918. The newly created republic had its independence guaranteed by the German military. But when Germany collapsed, the new republic was unable to resist Belorussian Bolsheviks, who were supported by the Bolshevik government in Russia. On January 1, 1919, the Belorussian Soviet Socialist Republic was established and was subsequently incorporated into the Soviet Union. The western portion of Belorussia was ceded to Poland. At the end of World War II, that territory was incorporated into the Soviet Union.

Numerically the smallest of the three East Slavic nationalities, Belorussians in 1989 numbered about 10 million people and constituted about 3.5 percent of the Soviet Union's total population, making them the fourth largest nationality in the country. Although most of them lived in the Belorussian Republic, over 1.2 million Belorussians lived in the Russian Republic, with sizable Belorussian minorities in the Ukrainian, Kazakh, and Latvian republics. Belorussians, like Russians and Ukrainians, speak an East Slavic language. Prior to 1917, both Latin and Cyrillic (see Glossary) alphabets were used, but subsequently Cyrillic became the official alphabet. In 1989 about 71 percent of Belorussians in the Soviet

Union considered the Belorussian language their first language, while the remainder considered Russian their native tongue.

In the late 1980s, the Belorussian Republic was the third most urbanized in the Soviet Union, with 64 percent of the republic's population residing in urban areas in 1987—a jump of 33 percent from 1959. Of the Belorussian population in the Soviet Union, about half lived in urban areas. This apparent anomaly was caused chiefly by the large number of Russians residing in the republic's cities. The capital and largest city in the Belorussian Republic, Minsk, had a population of almost 1.6 million people in 1989. Other major cities were Gomel', Mogilev, Vitebsk, Grodno, and Brest, all of which had populations of fewer than 500,000.

Although Belorussians were the fourth most prevalent nationality in the Soviet Union, they ranked only fifteenth in the number of students in higher education institutions and tenth in the number of scientific workers in the Soviet Union. They have fared much better in terms of sharing political power, however. Between 1970 and 1989, Belorussian membership in the CPSU has been fairly representative of their share of the population. In the CPSU Central Committee, Belorussians have actually held a somewhat higher percentage of full-member seats than warranted by their share of population. Paradoxically, they have not fared so well in their own republic. Although Belorussians made up 78.7 percent of the population of the republic in 1989, they had only 70 percent of the party membership in the Belorussian Republic. Russians, however, with only 12 percent of the population of the republic, constituted about 19 percent of the party membership.

Other Slavs

Poles made up the largest of the West Slavic nationalities in the Soviet Union. Although their numbers have been declining, in 1989 over 1 million Poles remained. Most of them lived in the western republics—the Belorussian, Ukrainian, Lithuanian, and Latvian republics. Bulgarians, belonging to the South Slavic group, numbered nearly 379,000 in 1989. A majority of the Bulgarians lived in the Ukrainian Republic, with a large number residing also in the Moldavian Republic. In the 1980s, small numbers of Czechs and Slovaks (members of the West Slavic group) and Croatians and Serbs (members of the South Slavic group) also lived in the Soviet Union.

Baltic Nationalities

Although each is a separate and distinct nationality, the three Baltic peoples share many characteristics and experiences. Residing in the northwestern corner of the Soviet Union, the Baltic peoples have been the most Western oriented of all the Soviet nationalities. They have had a strong and highly developed national consciousness, primarily because of the historic German and Polish influences and the religious heritage of western Europe. They were the only non-Russian nationalities to have experienced significant periods of political independence after World War I. It should be noted that the United States government has not recognized the incorporation of Estonia, Latvia, and Lithuania into the Soviet Union. Although in 1989 the approximately 5.6 million members of the three Baltic nationalities made up only a small fraction of the Soviet population, they have achieved a higher level of economic and industrial development and social modernization than any other peoples in the Soviet Union.

Lithuanians

The ancestors of modern Lithuanians first settled in the present-day Belorussian Republic around 2000 B.C. Beginning in the fourth century A.D., Lithuanian tribes were steadily pushed northwest by Slavic tribes until they occupied the territory of the present-day Lithuanian Republic. United into a loose monarchy by King Mindaugas at the beginning of the thirteenth century, Lithuanians began to expand south and east. By the mid-fourteenth century, Lithuania had become one of the largest kingdoms in medieval Europe. With Vilnius as its capital, Lithuania encompassed much of what had been Kievan Rus', including the present-day Belorussian and Ukrainian republics.

The marriage of the Lithuanian king to the Polish queen in 1385 began a period of dynastic union that culminated in the creation of the Polish-Lithuanian Commonwealth in 1569. The union with Poland had a profound influence on Lithuanians. For example, Polonized Western culture was superimposed on native Lithuanian culture, Catholicism was established as the national religion, and Lithuanian nobility was almost completely Polonized.

By the end of the eighteenth century, most of Lithuania, along with parts of Poland, was incorporated into the Russian Empire. The remaining part of Lithuania, known as Lithuania Minor, became part of Prussia. After the Lithuanian national revival of the nineteenth century emerged in Lithuania Minor, it spread to the rest of Lithuania. When the Poles rose in an anti-tsarist, anti-Russian revolt in 1830, Lithuanians joined them. They did so again in 1863. And during the Revolution of 1905 in Russia, the Assembly of Vilnius raised the question of Lithuanian autonomy. By the time of the revolutions of 1917 and the Civil War that followed,

Lithuanians strove for nothing less than national independence. To reach that goal, they had to fight not only the Red Army but also the Germans and the Poles.

The independent Lithuanian state that emerged after the struggle was a democratic republic. It lasted until 1926, when it was toppled by rightist forces, which then established a form of benevolent dictatorship. That government lasted until 1940, when Lithuania was absorbed by the Soviet Union following the Nazi-Soviet Nonaggression Pact of 1939. Thousands of Lithuanians were deported eastward by the Soviet government, the country's economy was nationalized, the peasantry was collectivized, and Catholic believers and Lithuanian intellectuals were persecuted. Not surprisingly, Lithuanians, like other nationalities in the western regions of the Soviet Union, greeted the attacking German army in 1941 as liberators. When the Germans refused to recognize their independence, however, Lithuanian nationalists engaged in underground resistance and partisan activity against them. After the Red Army's recapture of Lithuania in 1944, nationalists turned against the Russians. Guerrilla warfare against Soviet occupation did not end until the late 1940s.

In 1989 an overwhelming majority of the approximately 3 million Lithuanians resided in the Lithuanian Republic, the largest of the three Baltic republics. Small communities of Lithuanians were also in other republics. Although Lithuanians have resisted emigration, they have not been able to prevent immigration of Russians and other nationalities into the Lithuanian Republic. Lithuanians constituted about 80 percent of the residents of the republic in 1989, while Russians and Poles made up most of the remainder.

Lithuanians speak an Indo-European language that is distinct from both the Germanic and the Slavic languages. In 1989 the vast majority of Lithuanians considered Lithuanian their first language.

In 1987 about half of all Lithuanians were urban residents. But because a large number of Russians in the Lithuanian Republic lived in the cities, about 67 percent of the population of the republic was urban. The largest city in Lithuania was Vilnius, the capital of the republic, with a population of about 582,000 in 1989. Four other cities had populations of over 100,000. Relative to their share of the Soviet population, Lithuanians ranked high in terms of education and technological advancement. Although Lithuanians were the twelfth most populous nationality in the Soviet Union, they ranked seventh in the 1970s in both the number of students in higher education institutions and the number of scientific workers. Lithuanian membership in the CPSU was not in equal ratio to Lithuanians' share of the population. Also, Lithuanian

Panoramic view of Riga, Latvian Republic
Courtesy Jonathan Tetzlaff

representation on the CPSU Central Committee has been less than their share of the population. Native Lithuanians, however, have in the past held the most important positions in the party in the Lithuanian Republic.

Latvians

Like the Lithuanians, Latvians are descended from the tribes that migrated into the Baltic area during the second millennium B.C. Subsequently, they mixed with the indigenous Finno-Ugric tribes and formed a loose defensive union of Latvian tribes. Until the end of the thirteenth century, these tribes were preoccupied with the constant threat of invasion and subjugation, first by the Vikings and the Slavs and later by the Germans. Early in the thirteenth century, the Germanic Order of the Brethren of the Sword forcibly began to convert the pagan Latvians to Christianity. They were finally subdued by the Livonian Order of the Teutonic Knights, which then established the Livonian Confederation, a state controlled by landowning German barons and Catholic clergy but with no strong central authority. The Latvian people were reduced to enserfed peasants. By the end of the sixteenth century, the power of the Teutonic Knights had weakened considerably, and Latvia was partitioned between Sweden and Poland, with only the Duchy

149

of Courland remaining autonomous under the Polish crown. Russia, desiring to reach the Baltic Sea, also wanted Latvian territory. These desires were realized in the reign of Peter the Great, when Sweden was forced to cede its Latvian territory to Russia. With the partitions of Poland in the late eighteenth century, the remainder of Latvia fell under Russian control. In the nineteenth century, Latvians experienced the same period of national reawakening as the other nations in European Russia.

When the Russian Empire collapsed in 1917, Latvians sought national autonomy. Overrun by the German army, and formally ceded to Germany by the Treaty of Brest-Litovsk in March 1918, Latvian nationalists overcame both German and Soviet Russian forces before they established an independent Latvian Republic later in 1918. Latvian independence lasted until 1940, when the Latvians, like the Lithuanians and Estonians, were forced first to allow Soviet troops to be stationed on their soil and then to accept a communist government. Shortly thereafter, Latvia was incorporated into the Soviet Union. Thousands of Latvians were killed or deported by the Soviet regime in 1940 and 1941 and again after the Red Army drove the Germans out of Latvia at the end of World War II. The Latvian peasantry was forcibly collectivized. Like the Lithuanians, Latvians carried on a guerrilla war against the Soviet occupation forces until 1948.

The vast majority of the almost 1.5 million Latvians in the Soviet Union in 1989 lived in the Latvian Republic, but they constituted a bare majority (52 percent) in their own republic. Russians made up almost 34 percent of the republic's population, with about twice as many Russians residing in the Latvian Republic as in the Estonian Republic or the Lithuanian Republic. The rest of the population consisted of considerable numbers of Belorussians, Ukrainians, and Poles.

The Latvian language is a distinct language, although it belongs to the same group of Indo-European languages as Lithuanian. The first books in Latvian appeared in the early seventeenth century, but literary Latvian was not fully established as a national language until the nineteenth century. In 1989 about 95 percent of all Latvians in the Soviet Union and 97.4 percent of those living in the Latvian Republic claimed Latvian as their first language.

The Latvian Republic was one of the most urbanized republics in the Soviet Union. In 1989 about 70 percent of its population resided in urban areas, which made it the third most urban republic. The most populous city was the capital, Riga, with about 915,000 people; two other cities had over 100,000 people each. Latvian cities have become very Russified, however, by the continuous influx of Russians. The Latvian Republic also has a highly educated population. In 1986 the republic ranked fourth in the proportion of people with higher or secondary education. The more urbanized Russians in the republic, however, reaped most of the benefits of higher education. In the early 1970s, Latvians ranked only twelfth in the number of students in higher and secondary education and sixth in the number of scientific workers compared with their share of the Soviet population.

In 1984 the percentage of Latvians in the CPSU in the Latvian Republic was well below the percentage of Latvians in the republic. In the past, non-Latvians or Russified Latvians, some of whom could no longer speak Latvian, have held the top posts in the party leadership of the republic.

Estonians

Although they have a shared history with the Lithuanians and Latvians, Estonians are ethnically related to the Finns. The Finno-Ugric tribes from which Estonians are descended migrated into the present-day Estonian Republic thousands of years ago. They maintained a separate existence and fought off invaders until the thirteenth century, when they were subdued by Germans and Danes. With the Danish presence in Estonia more nominal than real, German control of Estonia lasted into the sixteenth century. Estonian nobility was Germanized, and the peasantry was enserfed. Attempts by German clergy to Christianize the Estonian peasantry were firmly rebuffed, and it was not until the eighteenth century that most of the Estonian population was finally converted to Lutheranism.

During the sixteenth century, Russians, Swedes, and Poles fought for control of Estonia. Victorious Sweden held Estonia until the beginning of the eighteenth century, when it was forced to cede Estonia to Russia. By the beginning of the nineteenth century, Estonia, granted autonomy under its own nobility, abolished serfdom and enjoyed a period of national reawakening that lasted for most of the century. In 1880, when the Russian government introduced a Russification policy for Estonia, the national consciousness had progressed too far to accept it. In 1918 Estonian nationalists, after fighting both the Germans and the Russians, declared the independence of Estonia. With the exception of a four-year period of dictatorship, Estonia flourished as a democracy until 1940, when the Soviet Union absorbed it along with the other two Baltic states. The Estonians suffered the same fate as the Lithuanians and Latvians. The Estonian peasantry was collectivized, and the Estonian national elite was imprisoned, executed, or exiled.

151

Altogether about 10 percent of the Estonian population was deported eastward. The remaining population was subjected to a policy of Russification, made easier by the large influx of Russians into the republic.

In 1989 Estonians were numerically the smallest nationality to have their own republic. According to the 1989 census, just over 1 million Estonians lived in the Soviet Union, fewer than nationalities without their own republics, such as the Tatars, Germans, Jews, Chuvash, Bashkirs, and Poles. Almost 94 percent of the Estonians lived in the Estonian Republic, the smallest and northernmost of the three Baltic republics. In 1989 it had a population of almost 1.6 million, of which Estonians made up just over 61 percent. The largest national minority in the Estonian Republic was the Russians, constituting over 30 percent of the population. A small Estonian population resided in the Russian Republic.

Estonians, like Finns, speak a language that belongs to the Finno-Ugric group of languages. Like the other two Baltic nationalities, Estonians use the Latin alphabet. Of the three Baltic nationalities, Estonians have been the most tenacious in preserving their own language. In the 1989 census, 95.5 percent of the Estonians in the Soviet Union and 98.9 percent of those residing in the Estonian Republic considered Estonian their first language.

Estonians, the majority of whom live in cities and towns, ranked as one of the most urbanized peoples in the Soviet Union. In 1989 the Estonian Republic was the second most urbanized republic, with over 70 percent of its population residing in urban areas. However, only two cities in the Estonian Republic had a population of over 50,000: Tallin (482,000), the capital of the republic, and Tartu (115,000).

The Estonian Republic ranked sixth among the republics in the number of citizens with secondary and higher education per thousand people. Within the Estonian Republic, the percentage of Estonians among the educated elite was very high, particularly in cultural and educational fields. Estonians also ranked high in the number of scientific workers. Whereas Estonians have dominated the cultural fields in the republic, Russians have held political power out of proportion to their share of the republic's population. Only 52 percent of the party members in the Estonian Republic were Estonians. In the past, Russians have not held the top posts in the Estonian Republic's party leadership, but many of the top Estonian leaders in the party were highly Russified.

Nationalities of the Caucasus

A small mountainous region in the southwestern portion of the Soviet Union known as the Caucasus has been the home to three major nationalities—the Armenians, Georgians, and Azerbaydzhanis—and to twenty-four minor nationalities. The three major nationalities had their own union republics along the southern slopes of the Caucasus Mountains, sometimes known as the Transcaucasus. The other nationalities resided in their own autonomous republics or autonomous oblasts, mostly along the northern slopes of the Caucasus Mountains, or lived scattered within the boundaries of the three Caucasian republics or the Russian Republic. Over 15.7 million people, or 5.5 percent of the total population of the Soviet Union in 1989, lived in the Caucasus, a region not much larger than the territory of the three Baltic republics. Although they have shared historical experiences, the three major nationalities of the Caucasus have far greater differences than the three Baltic nationalities or the three East Slavic nationalities. The differences are particularly sharp between the Azerbaydzhanis and the Armenians and Georgians. The Turkic-speaking Azerbaydzhanis are Muslims. Culturally and historically linked to both Iran and Turkey, they have not experienced independent statehood except for a brief period after the fall of the tsarist government in 1917. Both Armenians and Georgians have been Christian since the fourth century, and their history of independent statehood dates back to classical antiquity.

Armenians

The first Armenians inhabited the territory of the present-day Armenian Republic as early as the seventh century B.C. The first Armenian state, however, came into existence in the second century B.C. At least part of Armenia was able to retain a degree of independence until the beginning of the seventeenth century, when it was divided between the Ottoman Empire and the Persian Savafid Empire. The fate of the Armenians was particularly harsh in the Ottoman Empire. Persecution of Armenians by the Ottoman Turks reached its peak in 1915, when the government forcibly deported Armenians to Syria and Mesopotamia. Estimates of Armenians who were killed or otherwise perished at that time range as high as 1.5 million people. Only a small number of Armenians—about 120,000—remained in Turkey in the 1970s.

The Armenian Republic encompasses the territory of Persian Armenia, which was conquered by Russia in 1828. Here, as elsewhere in the Russian Empire, cultural nationalism of the nineteenth century was an important factor in the development of Armenian national consciousness. With the coming of the Bolshevik Revolution, Armenian nationalists joined the Georgians and the Azerbaydzhanis to form the short-lived Transcaucasian Federated

Republic. By May 1918, the union of the three peoples broke up into three independent republics. Armenian independence lasted only until November 1920, when, with the help of the Red Army, the Armenian Soviet Socialist Republic was proclaimed. In March 1922, the republic joined again with Georgia and Azerbaydzhan to form the Transcaucasian Soviet Federated Socialist Republic, which—together with the Russian, Belorussian, and Ukrainian republics—joined to form the Soviet Union in December of that year. In December 1936, the Soviet government broke the federation into three separate union republics.

In the 1920s, the Soviet regime gave Armenians the same opportunity as it gave other nationalities to revitalize their culture and language. The onset of Stalin's rule at the end of the 1920s, however, brought dramatic changes. Together with forced collectivization of agriculture and rapid industrial development, the Soviet regime tightened political controls over the Armenian people and applied to them, as to others, its policy of Russification.

Two-thirds of the more than 4.6 million Armenians living in the Soviet Union resided in the Armenian Republic, the smallest and least populous of the three Caucasian republics. The Armenian Republic was the most ethnically homogeneous of all the Soviet republics. Over 93 percent of the population of the Armenian Republic in 1989 were Armenians. Only the Azerbaydzhanis formed a substantial national minority in Armenia. No other republic, however, had such a large percentage of its nationals living outside its borders. Large numbers of Armenians lived in the Azerbaydzhan, Georgian, and Russian republics.

Armenians speak a unique Indo-European language, which uses an equally unique alphabet. The vast majority of the Armenians living in the Soviet Union and over 99 percent of the Armenians in the Armenian Republic regarded Armenian as their first language.

The citizens of the Armenian Republic rank among the most highly educated people in the Soviet Union. In the 1970s, the republic ranked second among the republics in the number of individuals with higher and secondary education per thousand people. Armenians also ranked second among Soviet nationalities in the number of scientific workers per thousand people.

Armenians were the third most urbanized nationality in 1970s. Some 68 percent of the Armenian Republic's population resided in towns and cities. The major city in the Armenian Republic was Yerevan, the capital, with nearly 1.2 million people in 1989. Two other cities, Leninakan and Kirovakan, had populations of more than 100,000.

Armenian representation in the CPSU has been quite high relative to their share of the Soviet population. Armenians also dominated in the party apparatus of the Armenian Republic.

Georgians

Georgians possess perhaps the oldest culture among the major nationalities of the Soviet Union. The ancestral Georgian tribes appeared in the Caucasus probably during the second millennium B.C. These tribes began to unite into larger political entities in the first millennium B.C., and by the sixth century B.C. the first Georgian kingdom was established. From the first century A.D. until the early twelfth century, Georgians endured a succession of conquests by the Romans, Iranians, Arabs, and Seljuk Turks. After each conquest, Georgians were able to regain their independence, reaching a golden age during the late twelfth and early thirteenth centuries, when Georgian power extended to include other parts of the Caucasus. Between the thirteenth and fifteenth centuries, Georgia was invaded first by Chinggis Khan's and then by Tamerlane's hordes. The destruction wrought by these invasions and internal feuding between the Georgian rulers and their vassals led to the disintegration of Georgia at the end of the fifteenth century. Beginning in the sixteenth century, the Georgians faced two new powerful foes, Turkey and Iran. Unable to resist the threat of either, the Georgians sought the aid of their Russian neighbors and in 1783 signed a treaty of friendship with imperial Russia, which guaranteed Georgia's independence and territorial integrity. By the beginning of the nineteenth century, however, Russia began the process of annexation of Georgian lands, which was completed in the second half of the nineteenth century.

The nineteenth-century nationalist reawakening that swept the Russian Empire and aroused its nationalities had a much stronger socialist content in Georgia than in any other non-Russian part of the empire. From the beginning, it was closely identified with Marxism (see Glossary), particularly the Menshevik (see Glossary) branch of Russian Marxism. In 1918 Georgian Mensheviks, who were in control of the revolutionary ferment in Georgia, declared Georgian independence. In 1921 the Red Army invaded Georgia in support of a Bolshevik coup there and established it as a Soviet republic; in December 1922 the Georgian Republic entered the union of Soviet republics as part of the Transcaucasian Soviet Federated Socialist Republic. The Georgian Soviet Socialist Republic was established as a union republic of the Soviet Union in 1936.

According to the 1989 census, Georgians numbered almost 4 million, and 95 percent of them lived in the Georgian Republic.

Only the Baltic nationalities were as concentrated in their own republics. Within its borders were also two autonomous republics, the Abkhazian Autonomous Republic and the Adzhar Autonomous Republic, and one autonomous oblast, the South Ossetian Autonomous Oblast.

In 1989 over 5.4 million people lived in this densely populated republic, of whom about 69 percent were Georgians. Armenians, Russians, and Azerbaydzhanis were the largest national minorities in the republic. Since 1970 the number of Russians in the republic has steadily decreased.

Georgians speak an Ibero-Caucasian language that belongs to the Caucasian group of languages. Like the Armenian language, the Georgian language has a distinct alphabet. The overwhelming majority of Georgians living in the Soviet Union and 99.7 percent of Georgians in their own republic considered Georgian their native tongue in 1989.

Georgians constitute one of the most highly educated nationalities in the Soviet Union. In 1971 Jews were the only nationality having a greater percentage of students in higher education institutions, and Georgians had the third highest number of scientific workers relative to their share of the population. Yet the Georgian Republic was one of the least urbanized. In 1987 only 55 percent of Georgian residents lived in towns and cities, and as of 1970 only 44 percent of all Georgians in the Soviet Union lived in urban areas. Among the major cities in the Georgian Republic were Tbilisi, the capital with 1.3 million people, and Kutaisi with 230,000; three other cities had populations over 100,000.

Traditionally, Georgians have been very active participants in the CPSU. In 1983 Georgians ranked first, ahead of the Russians, in the size of party membership relative to their share of the total population. The most famous Georgian CPSU member was Joseph V. Stalin, whose surname was Dzhugashvili. Other prominent Georgians were the Bolshevik leader Sergo Ordzhonikidze and the longtime chief of the secret police, Lavrenty Beria. Eduard A. Shevardnadze, a full member of the Politburo and minister of foreign affairs in the 1980s, was also a Georgian.

Azerbaydzhanis

The early inhabitants of the present-day Azerbaydzhan Republic were a mix of different people, as the country had endured many invasions since the sixth century B.C. Until the ninth century A.D., however, the Iranians were dominant. The large migration of Turkic tribes into the area between the tenth and twelfth centuries, and their subsequent mixing with the indigenous population,

Residents of Tbilisi reading declarations at a "democracy wall" near the center of the Georgian capital
Courtesy Jimmy Pritchard

led to the formation of the Azerbaydzhan people. With time, the Turkic element became culturally dominant except in religion. Unlike most Turkic Muslims, who were Sunni, most Azerbaydzhanis became Shia Muslims akin to the Muslims of Iran. From the eleventh to the early nineteenth century, Azerbaydzhan was almost continuously under Iranian control. In 1724 Peter the Great annexed the Baku and Derbent regions of Azerbaydzhan, but Iran regained them a dozen years later. Russian presence became permanent in the first half of the nineteenth century, when Azerbaydzhan was divided between Iran and Russia.

At first, Russian control of Azerbaydzhan had little effect on the life of the people. In fact, the rise of Azerbaydzhan national consciousness in the late nineteenth century was influenced more by the changes within Turkey and Iran than by the political and social events in imperial Russia. Rapid development of the oil industry, the growth of such industrial centers as Baku, and the influx of Slavs into Azerbaydzhan at the turn of the century, however, drew Azerbaydzhanis closer to Russia. A secularized elite, modeled on the Young Turks, came into being. It soon split between a relatively urban Marxist faction and an Islamic faction closely tied to the rural areas of Azerbaydzhan. In 1918 the more rightist, Islamic

157

faction formed an independent republic with the help of the Turkish army. The short-lived independence of the Azerbaydzhanis came to an end in 1920 when the Red Army invaded and established a communist regime, which helped turn Azerbaydzhan into a Soviet republic.

Although Soviet rule was accompanied by repressive measures, tight political control, and collectivization, the Azerbaydzhan Republic grew industrially and economically. Another result of Soviet rule was the dramatic rise in literacy. In 1927 only 31.9 percent of the deputies in the Baku soviet were literate. By 1959 some 97 percent of the entire population of the Azerbaydzhan Republic was literate, according to Soviet statistics.

The most populous of the three major nationalities in the Caucasus region, the Azerbaydzhanis have important characteristics that distinguish them from the other two nationalities. Being Muslim and of Turkic origin, they differ ethnically and culturally from the Armenians and Georgians. Also, they are separated by a long international border from fellow Azerbaydzhanis in Iran with whom they share their origins, culture, language, and religion. Occupying the southernmost part of the European Soviet Union, the Azerbaydzhan Republic includes the Nakhichevan' Autonomous Republic, which is separated from the rest of the Azerbaydzhan Republic by the Armenian Republic, and the Nagorno-Karabakh Autonomous Oblast, which is populated mostly by Armenians.

Like other Muslim groups in the Soviet Union, the Azerbaydzhanis have demonstrated a remarkable population growth since the 1950s. In 1989 the Azerbaydzhanis numbered almost 6.8 million. Some 5.8 million of them lived in the Azerbaydzhan Republic, where they made up 83 percent of the population. The largest national minorities within the borders of the Azerbaydzhan Republic were Russians and Armenians, who together made up about 11 percent of the population. About 37 percent of the Armenians in Azerbaydzhan resided in the Nagorno-Karabakh Autonomous Oblast, where they constituted 77 percent of the population. The number of Russians living in the Azerbaydzhan Republic in 1989 was slightly larger than the number of Armenians.

Azerbaydzhanis speak a Turkic language that belongs to the southern branch of Altaic languages. Originally the language developed from a mixture of languages spoken by the Iranian and Turkic tribes living there. It became a literary language late in the nineteenth century when the Azerbaydzhan intelligentsia popularized literature written in their native language. In 1922 Soviet officials replaced the original Arabic alphabet, first with the Latin alphabet and then in 1937 with the Cyrillic alphabet. According to the 1989 census, about 97.6 percent of the Azerbaydzhanis in the Soviet Union regarded the Azerbaydzhan language as their native tongue.

In 1987 the Azerbaydzhan Republic was among the least urbanized republics, with only 54 percent of its population living in urban areas. Large cities included the capital, Baku, with a population of over 1.1 million, Kirovabad with 270,000, and Sumgait with 234,000.

The level of Azerbaydzhan education was high. Azerbaydzhanis ranked fifth among the nationalities in the number of students in institutions of higher education per thousand people, but they ranked eighth in their share of scientific workers. In 1979 Azerbaydzhanis were seventh in CPSU membership.

Other Nationalities of the Caucasus

In addition to the three major nationalities in the Caucasus region, about two dozen other nationalities and numerous subgroups resided there. Most of these nationalities lived in the Dagestan Autonomous Republic located northeast of the Caucasus Mountains in the Russian Republic. In 1989 the more than 2 million people of the Dagestan Autonomous Republic were among the most diverse populations, ethnically and linguistically, in the world. The nationalities ranged in size from almost half a million Avars to barely 12,000 Aguls and even smaller groups. The great majority of the Dagestan people were Sunni Muslims; but small numbers of Shia Muslims, Christians, and Jews were also present.

Central Asian Nationalities

Soviet Central Asia, a vast area of over 3.9 million square kilometers, is made up of the Kazakh, Kirgiz, Turkmen, Uzbek, and Tadzhik republics. In 1989 some 49 million people, or over 17 percent of the population of the Soviet Union, lived there. About 37 million people, or over 75 percent of the population of Soviet Central Asia, belonged to nationalities that were traditionally Islamic. In the 1980s, they, like Muslims in other parts of the Soviet Union, have been very resistant to the process of Russification. In 1989 some 98 percent of Soviet Central Asian Muslims spoke primarily their own languages, and their fluency in Russian was low in comparison with other Soviet nationalities.

The five nationalities of Soviet Central Asia shared a number of common characteristics. They had similar ethnic origins, experienced similar historical development, and, most important, were all part of an Islamic society. But regional and cultural differences were also present, especially between the Tadzhiks, who speak an

Iranian language, and the rest, who speak Turkic languages with various degrees of commonality. The life-styles of the five peoples also differed, from the Tadzhiks, who have an ancient urban tradition, to the Kazakhs, some of whom were still nomadic as late as the 1920s.

Uzbeks

The history of the Uzbeks and their homeland is closely tied to that of Turkestan, an ancient territory stretching from the Caspian Sea in the west and extending into China and Afghanistan in the east, encompassing most of the areas of the present-day Turkmen, Uzbek, Tadzhik, and Kirgiz republics and the southern portion of the Kazakh Republic. In the centuries before the birth of Christ, Turkestan was populated by people of Persian stock, and they endured successive waves of invaders. In the sixth century B.C., Turkestan for the most part belonged to the Persian Achaemenid Empire. Alexander the Great invaded Turkestan in the fourth century B.C., and the Huns overran the area in the fifth century A.D. Arabs conquered Turkestan in the seventh century A.D. and introduced the Islamic religion and culture. Another series of invasions by predominantly Turkic peoples began at the end of the tenth century and continued into the thirteenth century when the great Mongol invasion swept the area. The Mongol invaders were soon assimilated by the Turkic population and adopted their language, culture, and religion.

In the beginning of the sixteenth century, Turkestan was conquered by yet another wave of Turkic nomads, the Uzbeks. The Uzbeks, whose name derives from Uzbek Khan, the ruler of the Golden Horde (see Glossary) at the beginning of the fourteenth century, were a mixture of Turkic tribes within the Mongol Empire. The center of the Uzbek state became the city of Bukhara. Subsequently, the independent Uzbek khanates of Khiva and Kokand evolved. The khanates of Bukhara, Khiva, and Kokand inherited aspects of the Iranian, Turkic, and Arabic civilizations. Their populations were mostly Uzbek, but within their borders also lived considerable numbers of Tadzhiks, Turkmens, and Kirgiz. By the eighteenth century, the khans of Khiva, Bukhara, and Kokand had extended their control over the innumerable independent tribal kingdoms and ruled central Turkestan. But the process of consolidation was not complete, and many peripheral areas in Turkestan remained almost totally independent of or in rebellion against one or another of the three khanates. In the vast steppes and deserts in the north, the Kazakhs grazed their herds as they always had; the nomadic Turkmens roamed the wide stretches of

Kalyan Minaret (completed in 1127) and Kalyan Mosque (completed in 1514) in the old section of Bukhara, Uzbek Republic
Courtesy Jimmy Pritchard

pastureland to the west; the rebellious Kirgiz made their home in the mountainous valleys in the east; and the Iranian-speaking Tadzhiks maintained their traditional life-style in the southeast, in the highlands north of the Hindu Kush.

Although Peter the Great attempted the first Russian invasion of Turkestan in the beginning of the eighteenth century, systematic Russian penetration of Turkestan was undertaken only in the mid-nineteenth century. By the end of the nineteenth century, the khanates of Bukhara and Khiva, greatly reduced in size, had become vassal states of the Russian Empire. The rest of the territory and the entire territory of Kokand was incorporated into Russian Turkestan, created in 1867, which was divided into five provinces and presided over by a Russian governor general. Turkestan, together with the four provinces of Kazakhstan (see Glossary), constituted what came to be known as Russian Central Asia (subsequently Soviet Central Asia). In spite of tsarist toleration of the Muslim religion and customs, Russian conquest of Turkestan had an immediate impact on aspects of the indigenous culture and society. Early in the twentieth century, economic development came to Turkestan, new towns sprang up, cotton grew where once nomads grazed their herds, and railroads linked Turkestan with

161

markets in Russia. The nomadic Kirgiz, Kazakhs, and Turkmens were especially resentful of the evolving changes. In 1916, when the Russian government ended its exemption of Muslims from military service, much of Russian Central Asia rose in a general revolt against Russian rule.

In November 1917, the Bolsheviks established Soviet power in the city of Tashkent. In April 1918, they proclaimed the Turkestan Autonomous Republic. The great mass of the Muslim population, however, took no part in these events. Only after the Bolsheviks attacked the Muslim religion, intervened directly in native society and culture, and engaged in armed seizure of food did the indigenous population offer fierce resistance in a national and holy war against the Soviet regime, known as the Basmachi Rebellion (see Glossary).

The autonomous soviet republics of Khorzem (formerly Khiva) and Bukhara were established in 1920 and incorporated into the Soviet Union. In 1924 and 1925, the entire Soviet Central Asian territory was reorganized by an act known as the national delimitation process in Central Asia. The Turkestan Autonomous Republic was abolished and divided along ethnic and linguistic lines into the Uzbek and Turkmen union republics, the Tadzhik Autonomous Republic within the Uzbek Republic, and the Kirgiz Autonomous Republic and the Karakalpak Autonomous Oblast within the Russian Republic. At the same time, the Kazakh Autonomous Republic within the Russian Republic was also established. The Tadzhik Autonomous Republic became a union republic in 1929, and the Kirgiz Autonomous Republic became a union republic in 1936. The Karakalpak Autonomous Oblast became an autonomous republic in 1932 and was transferred to the Uzbek Republic in 1936. The same year, the Kazakh Autonomous Republic was transformed into a union republic.

In the 1980s, the Uzbeks were the most populous nationality in Soviet Central Asia. Of the nearly 16.7 million Uzbeks in the Soviet Union in 1989, most of them lived in the Uzbek Republic, which lies in the middle of Soviet Central Asia. Most of the remaining Uzbeks lived in the other four Central Asian republics. In the 1989 census, the population of the Uzbek Republic was slightly over 19.9 million, with Uzbeks making up almost 71 percent. The largest minority in the Uzbek Republic in 1989 was the Russians with over 1.6 million, or 8.3 percent of the total population, followed by the Tadzhiks (932,000), Kazakhs (808,000), and Tatars (468,000). In addition, there were 411,000 Karakalpaks, most of whom lived in the Karakalpak Autonomous Republic in the Uzbek Republic. The Karakalpaks constituted only 31 percent of their autonomous republic's total population and were the second largest nationality, after the Uzbeks.

Uzbek, the language of the Uzbeks, belongs to the Turkic family of languages and has both a variety of dialects and a mixed vocabulary of Arabic, Persian, and Russian loanwords. The original Arabic alphabet was replaced in the 1920s by the Soviet government with an alphabet based on Latin script and subsequently with an alphabet based on Cyrillic script. In 1989 about 98.3 percent of the Uzbeks regarded Uzbek as their first language.

Uzbeks were among the least urbanized people in the Soviet Union. In 1979 only about 25 percent of all Uzbeks lived in cities. Nevertheless, Tashkent, the capital of the Uzbek Republic, had a population of nearly 2.1 million people in 1989, and five other cities had populations over 200,000. The populations of these cities had a disproportionately high number of Russians and other non-Uzbeks, however.

Uzbeks were the third largest nationality in the Soviet Union but in 1971 ranked tenth in the number of students in institutions of higher education and fifteenth in the number of scientific workers per thousand. Uzbeks were also very underrepresented in the CPSU. In the early 1980s, Uzbeks ranked twelfth among Soviet nationalities in party membership. Although they made up about 4.8 percent of the total population of the Soviet Union in 1979, they held only 1.5 percent of the seats on the CPSU Central Committee. Uzbek membership in the Uzbek Republic's party organization was also below their share of the republic's population. Russians, in contrast, made up only about 8.3 percent of the population of the republic but held 21 percent of party membership. Russians also had a majority in the Central Committee of the CPSU in the Uzbek Republic and tended to occupy top party positions.

Kazakhs

The origins of the Kazakh people and their name itself are matters of historical debate. First emerging as an identifiable group in the fifteenth century, they were a mix of indigenous Turkic tribes, which had been in the area since the eighth century, and nomadic Mongols, who invaded the area in the thirteenth century. Originally they differed little from their Turkic neighbors—the Uzbeks, the Kirgiz, and the Karakalpaks—but political divisions and different economic development caused them to enter the nineteenth century as distinctly different from the other three peoples.

Russians had limited and intermittent contacts with the Kazakhs between the mid-sixteenth century and the beginning of the eighteenth century, when Russia began to exert control over them.

Harassed by their neighbors, particularly the Kalmyks, in 1731 the nomadic Kazakhs placed themselves under the protection of the much more powerful Russian state. Afterward, Russian penetration into Kazakhstan was unremitting and included building a network of forts and settling the land with Russian peasants. Despite a series of Kazakh rebellions against them, Russian expansion continued, and by the second half of the nineteenth century Kazakhstan was firmly under Russian control. The tsarist policy of ending Kazakh nomadism and of settling the land with Russians, Ukrainians, Germans, and Jews continued. The new settlers received huge portions of the most fertile land. An almost exclusively non-Kazakh class of workers began to appear, and a budding industry, operated by the new immigrants, began to grow. These developments threatened to destroy the traditional form of existence of the Kazakh pastoral nomads.

The indigenous population's resentment against the settlers, as well as against conscription of Muslims into the military, erupted as a major rebellion in 1916 and, although quickly suppressed, set the stage for the nationalist movement in Kazakhstan following the February Revolution of 1917. Kazakh nationalists established a national government and engaged in an armed struggle against both pro- and anti-Bolshevik Russian forces. By mid-1919, however, weakened by the struggle, Kazakh nationalists sought accommodation with the Bolsheviks. In August 1920, the Kirgiz Autonomous Republic was established for the Kazakhs (until the mid-1920s Soviet officials called them Kirgiz) within the Russian Republic. In 1925 it was renamed the Kazakh Autonomous Republic and became a union republic in 1936.

The Bolshevik Revolution and the Civil War that followed further disrupted the traditional life of the Kazakhs. Many Kazakhs left with their herds for China and Afghanistan. Almost a million died from starvation in the famine of 1921–22. The rest were soon faced with forced collectivization, and a continuous influx of Russians and other people gradually reduced the Kazakhs to a minority in their own land. Kazakh leaders, even Kazakh communists, who protested these policies were purged or executed, first in the late 1920s and then during the purges of the Great Terror in the 1930s.

In 1989 the 8.1 million Kazakhs constituted the fifth most populous nationality in the Soviet Union. Over 6.5 million, or 80 percent of the Kazakhs, lived in the Kazakh Republic, by far the largest of the five Soviet Central Asian republics. In fact, after the Russian Republic, it was the second largest republic and had a territory of over 2.7 million square kilometers. It was also the least homogeneous of all the union republics. No nationality constituted

Children in the old section of
Tashkent, Uzbek Republic
Courtesy Jimmy Pritchard

Young boy collecting firewood,
Dushanbe, Tadzhik Republic
Courtesy Jimmy Pritchard

a majority of the 16.5 million people in the Kazakh Republic. The Kazakhs, with nearly 40 percent of the population, were the most numerous nationality. Russians, with about 38 percent, were the second most populous nationality in the Kazakh Republic. From 1959 to 1989, however, the Kazakhs have shown a steady increase in their share of the republic's population. Simultaneously, the percentage of Russians in the total population has declined. Ukrainians and Germans, the next two largest national minorities, whose individual shares made up about 5 percent and 6 percent of the population, respectively, also declined from 1959 to 1989. More than 1.5 million Kazakhs lived in other parts of the Soviet Union, with the largest concentrations in the Uzbek and Russian republics.

The language of the Kazakhs belongs to the same family of Turkic languages as the languages of the Kirgiz, the Uzbeks, and the Turkmens. Kazakh, a unique language with Arabic and Tatar elements, became a literary language in the 1860s. Until 1926, Kazakh had an Arabic script; from 1926 until 1940, it had a Latin alphabet; and since 1940, it has had a Cyrillic alphabet. In spite of the significant numbers of Russians and other nationalities in the republic, the Kazakhs have retained very high usage of their own language. In 1989 about 98 percent of the Kazakhs living in the republic regarded Kazakh as their native tongue. Of the non-Kazakh residents of the Kazakh Republic, only 1 percent could converse fluently in the Kazakh language.

In 1987 the great majority of the Kazakhs lived in rural areas. Nevertheless, because of the large numbers of urban Russians and other nationalities, 58 percent of the Kazakh Republic's population was urban. Many large cities were scattered throughout the republic. The capital city of Alma-Ata, for example, had a population of over 1.1 million in 1989. Other large cities included Karaganda (about 650,000) and five others having populations over 300,000.

In the 1980s, the Kazakh Republic ranked ninth among the fifteen union republics in the educational level of its residents. But the educational achievements of Russians residing in the republic were considerably higher than those of the indigenous Kazakhs. In 1970 forty-two Russians for every thirty-one Kazakhs studied in institutions of higher learning; and in special secondary schools the ratio was eighty-six Russians to thirty-six Kazakhs. Kazakhs ranked sixth among all nationalities in the number of students in higher education institutions and thirteenth in the number of scientific workers per thousand.

Between 1969 and 1989, Kazakh membership in the CPSU was considerably below their share of the country's population. In the

Kazakh Republic, however, their membership in the party was somewhat higher than their share of the republic's population. Kazakhs also held a relatively high percentage of the leadership positions in the republic's party organization, with Russians or other Slavs generally acting as their deputies. Kazakh representation in the CPSU Central Committee nearly equaled their share of the population in the Soviet Union.

Kirgiz

The term *Kirgiz* was first used in the eighth century in reference to the tribes occupying the upper reaches of the Yenisey River. Historians disagree on the early history of the Kirgiz; but in the tenth century they apparently began migrating south searching for new pastures or driven by other people—particularly the Mongols in the thirteenth century—until they settled in the present-day Kirgiz Republic. By the early sixteenth century, they were the area's predominant people. Between the sixteenth and the nineteenth centuries, the Kirgiz people alternated between periods of tribal independence and foreign conquest. They were overrun by the Kalmyks late in the seventeenth century, the Manchus in the mid-eighteenth century, and the Kokand Khanate in the first half of the nineteenth century.

Russian conquest of the Kirgiz began in the mid-nineteenth century, and by 1876 they were absorbed into the Russian Empire. Kirgizia became a major area of Russian colonization, with Russians and other Slavs given the best land to settle, reducing considerably the grazing lands used by the Kirgiz nomads. Kirgiz resentment against Russian colonization policies and conscription for noncombatant duties in the army led to a major revolt throughout Russia's Central Asian territory, including Kirgizia. Casualties were high on both sides, and thousands of Kirgiz fled with their flocks to Afghanistan and China.

The tsarist government did not recognize the Kirgiz as a separate national entity or political unit. Kirgizia, along with other Turkic nations of Central Asia, was included in Russian Turkestan, created in 1867. At first the Bolshevik attitude toward the Kirgiz was equally unenlightened. Having defeated the nationalists, the White armies (see Glossary), and foreign interventionists in Kirgizia by 1919, the Bolsheviks included it in the newly established Turkestan Autonomous Republic. In 1924 the Kara-Kirgiz Autonomous Oblast was created (called Kara-Kirgiz to distinguish it from the Kazakh Autonomous Republic, which was named the Kirgiz Autonomous Republic). In 1925 it was renamed the Kirgiz Autonomous Oblast and in 1926 the Kirgiz Autonomous Republic. In 1936 it became a union republic.

In the first years of their rule, Soviet authorities continued the colonization policies of the tsarist regime. The Soviet government mitigated its policy, however, after the Basmachi Rebellion, a popular Turkic nationalist movement that swept former Turkestan from 1918 to 1924 and recurred periodically until 1931. In the mid-1920s, the Soviet government permitted traditional Kirgiz culture to flourish. It also promoted the creation of native leadership and slowed the influx of Slavs into the region. In the late 1920s and throughout the 1930s, these policies were replaced by Stalin's program of forced denomadization and collectivization and replacement of the Kirgiz intelligentsia and leadership with an ideologically acceptable Stalinist elite. Some Kirgiz protested by slaughtering their herds or driving them into China. Nevertheless, by 1933 about 67 percent of the nomads were collectivized. The Kirgiz intelligentsia was decimated. Many Kirgiz members of the CPSU in the republic were purged. Despite the turmoil, the Kirgiz subsequently achieved some industrialization, a higher standard of living, and substantial achievements in education.

According to the 1989 census, slightly more than 2.5 million Kirgiz lived in the Soviet Union, 88 percent of them in the Kirgiz Republic. About 175,000 Kirgiz also resided in the Uzbek Republic.

According to the 1989 census, the Kirgiz, with 52 percent of the population, for the first time in decades constituted a majority within their own republic. Russians, with almost 22 percent of the population, were second. Other large minorities included the Uzbeks, Ukrainians, Germans, and Tatars. Like other Muslim groups in the Soviet Union, the Kirgiz showed a phenomenal population growth between 1959 and 1979. While the population of the Soviet Union grew by 15.8 percent between 1959 and 1970, the Kirgiz increased by 49.8 percent. As a result, the proportion of the Kirgiz in the republic has been steadily increasing, while the Russian share of the population has been declining despite their continuous immigration into the republic.

The Kirgiz language, which belongs to the Turkic group of languages prevalent in Soviet Central Asia, has three regional dialects. A Kirgiz literary language was not fully developed until the Soviet period. It merges all three dialects and incorporates Iranian, Arabic, and Russian elements. Like other Turkic languages of Soviet Central Asia, the Kirgiz language first used an Arabic script, which later was replaced by a Latin script in 1928 and finally by a Cyrillic one in the early 1940s. According to the 1989 census, Kirgiz was spoken as a native language by about 97.8 percent of all Kirgiz in the Soviet Union and 99.5 percent of those living in the Kirgiz Republic.

The Kirgiz were the least urbanized major nationality in the Soviet Union. During the 1970s, only 14.5 percent of the Kirgiz lived in urban areas. In the Kirgiz Republic, they constituted less than one-fifth of the republic's urban population. Russians residing in the republic were the most urbanized segment of the population, with over half of them living in towns and cities. In 1989 the Kirgiz Republic was the second least urbanized republic in the Soviet Union, with 40 percent of its population residing in urban areas. Frunze, the capital and largest city, had a population of 616,000, and Osh had over 200,000; but only one other city had a population of more than 50,000.

In the 1970s, the Kirgiz were eighth among the seventeen major nationalities in number of students attending institutions of higher education and fourteenth in the number of scientific workers per thousand. In 1987 the Kirgiz Republic ranked eleventh among the fifteen union republics in number of individuals with higher or secondary education per thousand residents.

In the 1980s, the Kirgiz ranked eleventh in CPSU membership corresponding to their share of the population. The Kirgiz Republic ranked twelfth among Soviet republics in the percentage of its citizens belonging to the CPSU, but Russians residing in the republic were clearly overrepresented.

Tadzhiks

Unlike the other nationalities of Soviet Central Asia who are ethnically Turkic, the Tadzhiks trace their origins primarily to the Persians who settled the area as early as the sixth century B.C. and were part of the Persian Achaemenid Empire. From the seventh century A.D. until the fourteenth century, the Tadziks were overrun, as were the other people of Central Asia with whom the Tadzhiks developed a common civilization, first by the Arabs and then by other invaders. By the fourteenth century, the Tadzhiks were distinguished from the other peoples of Central Asia primarily by their language and the fact that they were sedentary, not nomadic like their neighbors. The name *Tadzhik* is derived from a word used to distinguish the Turkic people from Iranian subjects of the Arab Empire. By the sixteenth century, however, it had come to mean a trader from Central Asia or simply a sedentary person.

Beginning in the fifteenth century, the Tadzhiks were under Uzbek rule, and by the eighteenth century most of Tadzhik territory was under the khanate of Bukhara. The Afghan conquest of

Tadzhik territory from the south began in the mid-eighteenth century, and Russian expansion into Tadzhik lands from the north followed a century later. By the end of the nineteenth century, northern Tadzhikistan was under Russian rule, southern Tadzhikistan continued under the khanate of Bukhara, and the remaining Tadzhik territory was within Afghanistan.

Russian conquest of Tadzhikistan and subsequent immigration of Russian settlers had a minimal effect on traditional Tadzhik society. The revolutionary movement in Tadzhikistan was composed of Russians, not Tadzhiks. Therefore, Soviet power was established in 1918, and, with little resistance, northern Tadzhikistan was included in the newly created Turkestan Autonomous Republic. Nevertheless, when the Red Army invaded the khanate of Bukhara in 1921, it met with fierce resistance from the growing Basmachi movement. The movement continued until 1924 when the Tadzhik Autonomous Republic was created and incorporated into the Uzbek Soviet Socialist Republic. In 1929 the Tadzhik Autonomous Republic was made a union republic.

In 1989 the Tadzhiks numbered about 4.2 million, three-fourths of whom lived in the Tadzhik Republic. They were divided into the Tadzhiks proper (the Tadzhiks of the plain) and the Pamiris (the Tadzhiks of the mountains). Most of the Pamiris lived in the Gorno-Badakhshan Autonomous Oblast, located in the western Pamirs in the southeastern Tadzhik Republic. The Soviet census of 1989, however, did not distinguish between the two groups. Over 900,000 Tadzhiks also lived in the Uzbek Republic. In 1989 the Tadzhiks made up only about 62 percent of the Tadzhik Republic's population. The largest national minority living in the Tadzhik Republic was the Uzbeks, followed by the Russians.

The most distinguishing characteristic of the Tadzhiks is their language, which is closely related to Persian and belongs to the Southwest Iranian group of languages. The Tadzhik alphabet, like the alphabets of Turkic languages, was Arabic until 1930, Latin in the next decade, and finally Cyrillic in 1940. Almost 98 percent of the Tadzhiks regarded Tadzhik as their native language.

The Tadzhiks were among the least urbanized of all the nationalities in the Soviet Union. In 1989 about 67 percent of the Tadzhik Republic's population lived outside urban areas, making it the least urbanized republic. It was also the only republic to show a decline in the percentage of urban population between 1970 and 1987. The Tadzhik Republic had only two large cities in 1989, the capital, Dushanbe (595,000), and Leninabad (165,000).

The Tadzhiks rated very low in their level of education. Although they had officially achieved 99 percent literacy by 1971, the Tadzhiks ranked sixteenth among the seventeen major nationalities both in the number of students in institutions of higher learning and in the number of scientific workers per thousand.

In 1983 the Tadzhiks were the most underrepresented among the nationalities in their share of CPSU members and very underrepresented in the Central Committee of the party.

Turkmens

The Orguz Turks, forebears of the Soviet Turkmens, migrated into the territory of the present-day Turkmen Republic at the end of the tenth century and beginning of the eleventh century. Composed of many tribes, they began their migration from eastern Asia in the seventh century and moved slowly toward the Middle East and Central Asia. By the twelfth century, they had become the dominant group in the present-day Turkmen Republic, assimilating the original Iranian population as well as other invaders who preceded them into the area. By the end of the fourteenth century, the Orguz tribes had developed a common language and traditions, and by the fifteenth century they were recognizable as a single people. Although they often became subjects of a neighboring state, their military skills and pastoral culture enabled them to enjoy an independent existence. Forced into a cooperative and defensive alliance first by the Mongol invasion and then by the Uzbek conquest, the Turkmens nevertheless retained their strong tribal divisions and failed to establish a lasting state of their own.

The Turkmens opposed Russian expansion into Central Asia more vigorously than other nationalities. They defeated a Russian force in 1717, when Peter the Great first attempted the conquest of Central Asia. And, in the nineteenth century, when the Russians resumed their expansion into the area, Turkmen cavalry posed determined and prolonged opposition. The conquest of Turkmenia (also known as Turkmenistan) was not completed until 1885, and the territorial boundary of Russian Turkmenia was not set until a decade later by an Anglo-Russian border treaty. That treaty separated the Turkmens of Russia from the roughly equal number of their brethren in present-day Iran, Afghanistan, Iraq, and Turkey.

Turkmenia became part of Russian Turkestan and was treated by the tsarist government as a colonial territory where Russians and other Slavs were encouraged to settle. A railroad was built, and other features of modernity were introduced. Turkmens resented losing their grazing land and in 1916 joined a Muslim uprising throughout Russia's Central Asian territory.

After the February Revolution of 1917, several political forces competed for power in Turkmenia. The Turkmens were divided between Islamic traditionalists and the more progressive nation-alist intelligentsia. At this time, both Bolshevik and White armies sought the loyalty of Turkmenia's Russian population. A provisional government, established by Turkmen nationalists with support of the White forces and limited British assistance, was able to maintain itself against the Bolsheviks until mid-1919. Thereafter, Turkmen resistance against the Bolsheviks was part of the general Basmachi Rebellion, which reemerged sporadically until 1931. By 1920, however, the Red Army controlled the territory, and in 1924 the Turkmen Republic was established in accordance with the national delimitation process in Central Asia.

The Soviet policy of forced collectivization in the late 1920s and early 1930s was particularly abhorrent to the nomadic Turkmens. It led to enhanced national self-awareness and an opposition movement, which burst into an open rebellion in 1928–32. In response, Soviet authorities arrested scores of native communist leaders and broad segments of the Turkmen intelligentsia. Most perished in the Great Terror of the 1930s.

The great majority of the over 2.7 million Soviet Turkmens lived in the Turkmen Republic, the least populous of the Soviet Central Asian republics. Turkmens constituted nearly 72 percent of the republic's 3.5 million population. Russians and Uzbeks were the largest minorities.

The Turkmen language, which developed from several Turkic dialects and has adopted some Arabic, Persian, and Russian loanwords, belongs to the southern group of Turkic languages. In the 1989 census, about 98.5 percent of the Turkmens considered it their first language. Only slightly more than 25 percent of the Turkmens had fluency in Russian.

In 1987 Turkmens were more rural than urban, even though the population of the Turkmen Republic, which included a large number of highly urban Russians, was almost evenly divided between urban and rural residents. The Turkmen Republic had only a few large cities in 1989. Ashkhabad, the capital, had a population of 398,000; only Chardzhou and Tashauz also had populations over 100,000.

In 1971 Turkmens were fourteenth among the seventeen major nationalities in the number of students in higher education institutions and twelfth in the number of scientific workers per thousand. In 1986 the Turkmen Republic ranked tenth among the union republics in the number of students in higher education per thousand.

Turkmens were among the least represented nationalities in the CPSU. In 1984 they ranked thirteenth among the union republics.

Man in native costume,
Ashkhabad, Turkmen Republic
Courtesy Jimmy Pritchard

Other Major Nationalities

In addition to the nationalities just described, seven other nationalities numbered over 1 million people in the 1989 census: Moldavians, Tatars, Jews, Germans, Chuvash, Bashkirs, and Mordvins. None of these nationalities fit into the preceding groups of nationalities, yet each was a significant part of the complex fabric constituting the multinational Soviet state, either because of their large population or because of some other critical factor.

Moldavians

Although Moldavians have their own union republic, the existence of Moldavians as a separate nationality has been debatable. Soviet authorities consider Moldavians a distinct nationality. But most Moldavians see themselves as ethnic Romanians because they do not differ from the population of Romania linguistically or culturally. They believe that the creation of the Moldavian Republic and the "artificial" Moldavian nationality was, from its inception, an attempt to legitimize Soviet political claims to a portion of Romanian territory.

Ancient Moldavia, a territory that included portions of both present-day Romania and the Soviet Union's Moldavian Republic, was part of Scythia. Later, it fell under partial control of the Roman Empire. As the Roman Empire declined, Moldavia was

173

invaded by successive waves of barbarians moving into the empire. Between the tenth and twelfth centuries, part of Moldavia belonged to Kievan Rus' and later to the principality of Galicia. Between the thirteenth and fourteenth centuries, most of Moldavia was a vassal state of the Tatars. The first independent Moldavian state arose in the mid-fourteenth century and lasted until the beginning of the sixteenth century when Moldavia became a vassal state of Turkey. In the late eighteenth century, Russia attempted to secure control of Moldavia and finally succeeded in 1812, when the portion of Moldavia known as Bessarabia was ceded to Russia.

Despite tsarist efforts to Russify Bessarabia by settling large numbers of Russians, Ukrainians, and Jews there, at the time of the February Revolution of 1917 most of the inhabitants considered themselves Romanians. They established the Democratic Moldavian Republic soon after the onset of the revolution and then joined with Romania in April 1918.

In 1924 Soviet authorities created the Moldavian Autonomous Republic for the Romanian-speaking population remaining in the Soviet Union. But only about 30 percent of the inhabitants of the newly created autonomous republic were "Moldavians," or Romanian speaking. The majority of the residents of the republic were Ukrainians, Jews, or Russians. In 1940 the Soviet Union reincorporated Bessarabia and, together with the territory of the Moldavian Autonomous Republic that contained a mostly Romanian-speaking population, formed the Moldavian Republic. In 1944 Romania, under pressure from the Soviet Union, formally recognized the existence of the Moldavian Soviet Socialist Republic. According to the 1989 census, over 3.3 million Moldavians lived in the Soviet Union, of whom 83 percent resided in the Moldavian Republic. The republic, the second smallest of the union republics in area, had a population of over 4.3 million, of which nearly 2.8 million, or over 64 percent, were Moldavians. Ukrainians constituted 14 percent of the population, while Russians made up another 13 percent. Only the Ukrainian and Russian republics had sizable Romanian-speaking minorities in their territory.

According to 1989 statistics, 91.6 percent of Moldavians in the Soviet Union considered Moldavian their first language. Spoken Moldavian did not differ from the language spoken in Romania; however, Soviet authorities replaced the traditional Latin alphabet with the Cyrillic alphabet.

The Moldavians were one of the least urbanized nationalities, behind only the Kirgiz as the most rural people in the 1970s. In 1986 only 47 percent of the Moldavian Republic's population lived in urban areas. This represented an increase of 15 percent from

1970, when it was the least urbanized of all the union republics. The overwhelming majority of Moldavians lived in rural areas, while Russians in the republic resided mostly in the cities. The largest city in 1989 was the capital, Kishinev, with a population of 665,000. Two other cities had populations of over 100,000.

In the 1970s, Moldavians were last among the major nationalities in the number of students in higher education institutions and the number of scientific workers per thousand. The Moldavian Republic also consistently ranked last among the union republics in the number of students in higher education per thousand.

Moldavian representation in the CPSU as well as in its own republic party organization has been among the lowest of all the nationalities. In the 1980s, Moldavians were next to last among union republic nationalities in their share of total party membership. In the republic, Russians and Ukrainians held a disproportionate number of seats in the party. Of the nine Moldavian Republic's Central Committee members elected in 1971, five were Russian, three were Ukrainian, and one was Moldavian.

Tatars

Three major Tatar groups reside in the Soviet Union: Volga Tatars (the overwhelming majority of all Tatars in the Soviet Union), Crimean Tatars, and Siberian Tatars. Most are descended from the Turkic-speaking Bulgars who came into the Volga-Ural region in the seventh century and the Kipchak tribes who invaded the area as part of the Mongol Empire. From the thirteenth to the fifteenth century, they were part of the Golden Horde. In the fifteenth century, the Golden Horde broke up into the Kazan', Astrakhan', Crimean, and Siberian khanates. The Volga Tatars, the descendants of the Kazan' and Astrakhan' hordes (see Glossary), were conquered by Russia in the sixteenth century. The Siberian Tatars were incorporated into the Russian Empire later that century, and the Crimean Tatars were incorporated at the end of the eighteenth century.

After their conquest by Russia, the Volga Tatars were subjected to harsh political, economic, and religious policies. Only the Tatar nobles who had intermarried with Russians and, in many instances, gained positions of power and influence in the Russian state, escaped persecution. Thousands of Tatars were deported north to work in Russian shipyards. Russians confiscated Tatar property, destroyed their mosques and religious shrines, and pressured them to convert to Christianity. After a series of Tatar revolts in the seventeenth and eighteenth centuries, the tsarist government began to change its policies. In 1788 Islam was given official status in Russia,

175

and in 1792 Tatars were granted the right to trade with the Turkic populations of Turkestan, Iran, and China.

Repressive measures by the Russian government against Crimean Tatars and Slavic immigration into Crimea forced many Tatars to emigrate. Others were forcibly deported. During a century of Russian rule, the Tatar population in Crimea declined from about 500,000 at the end of the eighteenth century to fewer than 200,000 by the end of the nineteenth century.

Siberian Tatars—mainly hunters, trappers, and horse breeders scattered over a large territory—presented no threat to the Russian state and for a time continued to live unmolested. In the nineteenth century, many Siberian Tatars moved to the cities, seeking employment in the newly built sawmills and tanneries.

Despite renewed harassment in the second half of the nineteenth century, Tatars formed the intellectual and political elite of the Muslim population in Russia. Tatars were active in the Revolution of 1905 in Russia. They participated in the First Duma of 1906 and the Second Duma of 1907, and they were the leading proponents of the pan-Turkic movement that emphasized racial, religious and linguistic unity of all Turkic-speaking peoples.

After the February Revolution in 1917, the Volga Tatars tried to established an independent federation of Volga-Ural states. This dream proved impossible in the face of both Bolshevik and White Russian opposition. Instead, with the help of the Red Army, the Tatar Autonomous Republic was created in May 1920 as part of the Russian Republic.

The Crimean Tatars' attempts to create an independent state in 1917 were also thwarted by the Bolsheviks, and in October 1921 the Soviet leaders created the Crimean Autonomous Republic. Later, however, the Crimean Tatars were exiled from Crimea during World War II and scattered throughout Soviet Central Asia.

In the 1989 census, the Tatars, with over 6.6 million people, were the sixth largest nationality in the Soviet Union. Nevertheless, they did not have their own union republic. Over 1.7 million Tatars lived in the Tatar Autonomous Republic, one of sixteen autonomous republics in the Russian Republic, where they had a plurality of almost 48 percent of the population. About 1 million others lived in the Bashkir Autonomous Republic, also located in the Russian Republic, where they ranked second in population after the Russians and just ahead of the Bashkirs, a closely related Turkic nationality. Another 2.6 million Tatars lived scattered throughout the rest of the Russian Republic. Of these, about 500,000 were Siberian Tatars living in western Siberian towns and villages. Over 1 million Tatars—a majority of whom were probably exiled

Crimean Tatars—were also found in Soviet Central Asia—mostly in the Uzbek and Kazakh republics.

Each of the three Tatar groups speaks a distinct language, although all belong to the West Turkic-Kipchak group of languages. The language of the Crimean Tatars also contains a large number of Arabic and Persian loanwords. The Siberian Tatars have no written language of their own and use the literary language of the Volga Tatars.

In 1989 over 83 percent of all Tatars and 96.6 percent of those residing in the Tatar Autonomous Republic regarded Tatar as their native language. A high percentage of Tatars were also fluent in Russian. The educational level of Tatars in the Soviet Union varied. Tatars living in their own autonomous republic or elsewhere in the Russian Republic were not as well educated as the highly urbanized Crimean Tatars who lived in the Soviet Central Asian republics.

Tatar representation in the CPSU both in the Soviet Union and in the Tatar Autonomous Republic has been consistently low. In the 1980s, they were particularly underrepresented in the Central Committee of the CPSU.

Jews

Jews first appeared in eastern Europe several centuries before the birth of Christ. By the first century A.D., Jewish settlements existed along the northern shores of the Black Sea. In the eighth century, the descendants of these early Jewish settlers converted the nomadic Turkic Khazars to Judaism. Jewish communities existed in Kiev and other cities of Kievan Rus'. They were destroyed, however, during the Mongol invasion in the thirteenth century.

Persecuted in western Europe, Jews began migrating to Poland in the fourteenth century, and from there they moved to the present-day Lithuanian, Ukrainian, and Belorussian republics, where by the mid-seventeenth century they numbered in the hundreds of thousands. Although initially they were under royal protection and enjoyed communal autonomy, life for the great majority of Jews in Poland worsened, and they became as oppressed as Poland's Christian subjects. Forbidden to own land, many Jews served as estate managers and as middlemen between the Catholic Polish landowning nobility and the Orthodox Ukrainian and Belorussian enserfed peasants living on the nobles' estates. On the estates, they often collected taxes for the nobles, controlled the sale of salt and fish, ran the grain mills, and acted as overseers of peasant labor. Jews also owned the local village taverns. Particularly insidious was the Polish Catholic nobles' practice of making the Jews collect taxes on Orthodox churches. As a result, in addition to disliking them as foreigners and non-Christians, the peasants held Jews directly responsible for their oppressed and miserable lives. These early resentments were the seeds of primitive anti-Semitism in eastern Europe and later in the Russian Empire. When the Orthodox peasantry joined the Ukrainian Cossacks in the mid-seventeenth century in a revolt against the Poles and the Catholic Church, thousands of Jews were also killed. When Russian armies swept into Polish-Lithuanian territories following Muscovy's alliance with the Ukrainian Cossacks in 1654, they killed additional thousands of Jews, forcibly converting some to Christianity and driving others into exile. From 100,000 to 500,000 Jews perished, some 700 Jewish communities were destroyed, and untold thousands fled the war-ravaged areas.

Although Jews had been expelled from Russia in 1742, the subsequent incorporation of Polish territory as a result of the partitions of Poland meant that by the end of the eighteenth century Russia had the largest Jewish community in the world. The tsarist government prohibited Jews from living anywhere except in the area known as the Pale of Settlement, which included the Baltic provinces, most of Ukraine and Belorussia, and the northern shore of the Black Sea.

About 1.5 million Jews lived in the Russian Empire in the beginning of the nineteenth century. Confined within the Pale of Settlement, they were subjected to stringent anti-Jewish regulations. Although for the next century restrictions on Jews were periodically eased, they were reimposed or even made harsher during the frequent periods of reaction that followed. Nicholas I (1825–55) promoted forced induction of Jewish youth into military service, where they were often coerced into being converted to Christianity. Jewish rights to lease land and keep taverns were rescinded, and the Pale of Settlement was reduced in size. However, the reign of Alexander II (1855–81) brought a relaxation of the restrictions imposed on the Jewish population: some Jews were permitted to settle outside the Pale of Settlement, to attend universities, and to enter government service. After the assassination of Alexander II, however, the old restrictions were reimposed, and persecution of Jews continued until the February Revolution in 1917. Government-sanctioned pogroms against Jewish communities, during which Jews were beaten or killed and their personal property destroyed, were particularly brutal. The pogroms were led by the Black Hundreds, an officially sanctioned reactionary group composed largely of civil servants.

In spite of persecution, the Jewish population in the Russian Empire expanded rapidly during the nineteenth century. Later, on the eve of World War I, it was estimated at 5.2 million. Jewish culture flourished within the bounds imposed on their community. Jews became more active politically, and the more radical among them joined the spreading revolutionary movements.

For Jews, World War I and the Civil War that followed the revolutions in Russia were great calamities. The Pale of Settlement was the area where most of the prolonged military conflict took place, and Jews were killed indiscriminately by cossack armies, Russian White armies, Ukrainian nationalist forces, and anarchist peasant armies. In addition, the emergence of an independent Poland, Lithuania, and Latvia and the annexation of Bessarabia by Romania left large numbers of Jews outside the Soviet state borders. By 1922 the Jewish population in the Soviet Union was less than half of what it had been in the former Russian Empire.

The early years of the Soviet state provided unusual opportunities for Jews to mainstream into Soviet society. Although the majority of Jews had opposed the Bolsheviks during the Civil War, many supported the creation of the new, "non-national" state, which they expected would tolerate Jews. Hundreds of thousands of Jews were integrated into Soviet cultural and economic life, and many Jews occupied key positions in both areas. Jews were particularly numerous in higher education and in scientific institutions. Official anti-Semitism ceased, restrictions on Jewish settlement were banned, Jewish culture flourished, and Jewish sections of the CPSU were established. Many Jews, such as Leon Trotsky, Grigorii V. Zinov'ev, Lev B. Kamenev, Lazar M. Kaganovich, and Maksim M. Litvinov, occupied the most prominent positions in party leadership. The purges in the mid- to late 1930s, however, reduced considerably the Jewish intelligentsia's participation in political life, particularly in the party's top echelons.

The 1941 German invasion of the Soviet Union was particularly horrific for Soviet Jewry. About 2.5 million Jews were annihilated, often by collaborators among the native populations in the occupied territories who aided the Germans in killing Jews. Paradoxically, in Soviet territories that escaped German occupation, anti-Semitism also reemerged in the local population's resentment against the often better educated, wealthier Jews who were evacuated there before the advancing German armies.

Jews were the most dispersed nationality in the Soviet Union. In 1989 a majority of the 1.4 million Jews in the Soviet Union lived in the three Slavic republics. Approximately 536,000 lived in the Russian Republic, 486,000 in the Ukrainian Republic, and 112,000 in the Belorussian Republic. Large Jewish minorities also lived in the Uzbek and Moldavian republics, and smaller numbers of Jews lived in all the remaining republics.

Although the Jewish (Yevreyskaya) Autonomous Oblast in the Soviet Far East was designated as the homeland of the Soviet Jews, only 8,887 Jews lived there in 1989, just over 4 percent of the population of the oblast. Never high, the number of Jews in the Jewish Autonomous Oblast has been declining—14,269, or 8.8 percent, of the oblast's population in 1959 and 11,452, or 6.6 percent, in 1970.

Between 1959 and 1989, the Jewish population in the Soviet Union declined by about 900,000. The decline was attributed to several factors—low birth rate, intermarriage, concealment of Jewish identity, and emigration.

Although 83 percent of the Jews regarded Russian as their native language in 1979, Soviet authorities recognized Yiddish as the national language of Soviet Jewry. Small groups of Soviet Jews spoke other "Jewish" languages: in Soviet Central Asia some Jews spoke a Jewish dialect of Tadzhik, in the Caucasus area Jews spoke a form of Tat, while those in the Georgian Republic used their own dialect of the Georgian language.

Soviet Jews were overwhelmingly urban. In 1979 over 98 percent of all Jews in the Soviet Union lived in urban areas. Four cities in particular—Moscow, Leningrad, Kiev, and Odessa—had large concentrations of Jews. Along with being the most urbanized nationality, in the 1970s Jews also ranked first among all nationalities in educational level and in numbers of scientific workers per thousand.

Traditionally, Jews have been highly represented in the CPSU, and their membership exceeded considerably their proportion of the total population. Soviet statistics show that 5.2 percent of all CPSU members in 1922 were Jews; in 1927 the figure declined to 4.3 percent. In 1976 the figure was 1.9 percent, almost three times the percentage of Jews in the general population.

Chuvash

Descended from the Finno-Ugric tribes of the middle Volga area and the Bulgar tribes of the Kama and Volga rivers, the Chuvash were identifiable as a separate people by the tenth century A.D. Conquered by the Mongols in the thirteenth century, they became part of the Kazan' Horde. Since the mid-sixteenth century, they have been under Russian rule. After the revolutions of 1917 and the Civil War, the Soviet government established the Chuvash Autonomous Oblast within the Russian Republic. In 1925 the oblast became the Chuvash Autonomous Republic.

The Chuvash were originally Muslim but were forced to convert to Christianity by the Russians. Many reconverted to Islam in the nineteenth and early twentieth centuries. In the 1980s, some were Orthodox Christians, others Sunni Muslims.

In 1989 the Chuvash population was over 1.8 million. Slightly over half lived in the Chuvash Autonomous Republic, within the Russian Republic, where they constituted over 67 percent of the population. Large concentrations of Chuvash also resided in the Tatar Autonomous Republic, the Bashkir Autonomous Republic, and other parts of the Russian Republic.

The Chuvash speak a unique language that includes a large number of Finno-Ugric and Slavic loanwords but that belongs to the Bulgar group of Turkic languages. Because no written Chuvash language had existed before the Russian conquest, it is the only Turkic language in the Soviet Union to have always used a Cyrillic alphabet. In 1989 about 76.5 percent of the Chuvash considered Chuvash as their first language.

In the 1980s, the Chuvash remained overwhelmingly rural and agricultural. In 1987 Cheboksary, the administrative center of the Chuvash Autonomous Republic, was the only city in the autonomous republic with over 100,000 people.

Bashkirs

The Bashkir nationality developed from a mixture of Finno-Ugric tribes and a variety of Turkic tribes. They were recognized as a distinct people by the ninth century, when they settled an area between the Volga, Kama, Tobol, and Ural rivers, where most Bashkirs still live. Conquered by the Mongols of the Golden Horde in the thirteenth century, the Bashkirs were absorbed by different hordes after the breakup of the Golden Horde. Since the sixteenth century, they have been under Russian rule. Impoverished and dispossessed of their land by Russian settlers, the once-nomadic cattle breeders were forced to labor in the mines and new factories being built in eighteenth-century Russia. For two centuries prior to 1917, the Bashkirs had participated—together with the Chuvash, the Tatars, and other nationalities in the area—in the many violent outbreaks and popular uprisings that swept the Russian Empire. After the revolutions of 1917, a strong Bashkir nationalist and Muslim movement developed in the territory of the Bashkirs, where much of the Civil War was fought. In their quest for an autonomous state, the Bashkirs sought the support of both the Bolsheviks and the White forces. In the end, most joined with the Bolsheviks, and in February 1919 the Bashkir Autonomous Republic was established, the first autonomous republic within the Russian Republic.

The great majority of Bashkirs were Sunni Muslims. They had originally adopted Islam in the tenth century, but many were forced by the Russians between the sixteenth and eighteenth centuries to convert to Christianity. Most, however, reconverted to Islam in the nineteenth century.

In 1989 over 1.4 million Bashkirs lived in the Soviet Union. Nearly 864,000 of them resided in the Bashkir Autonomous Republic, where they made up about 22 percent of the population. The Bashkirs were only the third largest nationality in the Bashkir Autonomous Republic, behind the Russians and the Tatars.

The Bashkir language belongs to the West Turkic group of languages. Until the Soviet period, the Bashkirs did not have their own literary language, using at first the so-called Turki language and in the early twentieth century a Tatar language. Both languages used an Arabic script as their written language. In 1940 Soviet authorities gave the Bashkir language a Cyrillic script. In 1989 about 72 percent of the Bashkirs claimed Bashkir as their first language.

The Bashkirs remained predominantly rural and agricultural; less than 25 percent of them lived in urban areas in the 1980s. Although Ufa, the capital of the Bashkir Autonomous Republic, had over 1 million people in 1987, the overwhelming majority were Russians.

Mordvins

Like the Chuvash, the Mordvins were another nationality having their own autonomous republic along the middle reaches of the Volga River in the Russian Republic. The Mordvins, like the Chuvash and the Bashkirs, were Finno-Ugric and like the Chuvash had been a part of the Kazan' Horde prior to their incorporation into the Russian Empire in the sixteenth century. Soviet authorities established the Mordvinian Autonomous Oblast in 1930, which in 1934 became the Mordvinian Autonomous Republic.

The Mordvins, who numbered around 1.2 million people in 1989, were mostly scattered throughout the Russian Republic. Less than a third lived in the Mordvinian Autonomous Republic. Mordvins, who made up less than 32 percent of the population, were the second largest nationality in their autonomous republic, while Russians, with 61 percent, constituted a majority.

A predominantly agricultural people, the Mordvins speak their own language, which belongs to the Finno-Ugric group of languages. Their written language, which came into being under Soviet rule, uses a Cyrillic alphabet. In 1989 about 67 percent of the nationality claimed Mordvinian as their native tongue. Mordvin religious believers were mostly Orthodox Christians.

Germans

About 2 million Germans lived in the Soviet Union in 1989. The Kazakh Republic had the largest concentration of Germans (over 956,000), followed by the Russian Republic (841,000) and the Kirgiz Republic (101,000). Prior to World War II, many Germans lived in their own autonomous republic on the Volga River and were referred to as Volga Germans. Stalin ordered their dispersal into Soviet Central Asia and Siberia when Germany attacked the Soviet Union in 1941. Unrepatriated German prisoners of war further increased the German population in the Soviet Union. Since World War II, however, a considerable number of Germans have returned to German territory. In 1989 only 49 percent of the Germans claimed German as their first language.

Others

In addition to the nationalities discussed in the preceding pages, many other nationalities with populations of fewer than 1 million have been recognized by Soviet authorities. Several of the larger nationalities not previously mentioned had autonomous republics of their own: the Buryat, the Yakut, the Ossetian, the Komi, the Tuvinian, the Kalmyk, and the Karelian nationalities. Also, two pairs of nationalities, the Chechen-Ingush and the Kabardian-Balkar, each shared an autonomous republic. About eighteen nationalities lived either in autonomous oblasts or in autonomous *okruga*. All of these nationalities resided in the Russian Republic. In many cases, Russians had either a majority or a plurality of the population in these autonomous territorial units. Numerous other nationalities without an administrative territory of their own lived scattered throughout the Soviet Union, generally in the Russian Republic.

Religious Groups in the Soviet Union

Official figures on the number of religious believers in the Soviet Union were not available in 1989. But according to various Soviet and Western sources, over one-third of the people in the Soviet Union, an officially atheistic state, professed religious belief. Christianity and Islam had the most believers. Christians belonged to various churches: Orthodox, which had the largest number of followers; Catholic; and Baptist and various other Protestant sects. The majority of the Islamic faithful were Sunni. Judaism also had many followers. Other religions, which were practiced by a relatively small number of believers, included Buddhism, Lamaism, and shamanism, a religion based on primitive spiritualism.

The role of religion in the daily lives of Soviet citizens varied greatly. Because Islamic religious tenets and social values of Muslims are closely interrelated, religion appeared to have a greater influence on Muslims than on either Christians or other believers. Two-thirds of the Soviet population, however, had no religious beliefs. About half the people, including members of the CPSU and high-level government officials, professed atheism. For the majority of Soviet citizens, therefore, religion seemed irrelevant.

Orthodox

Orthodox Christians constituted a majority of believers in the Soviet Union. They hold that the Orthodox Church is the true, holy, and apostolic church and that it traces its origin directly to the church established by Jesus Christ. Orthodox beliefs are based on the Bible and holy tradition as defined by the seven ecumenical councils held between A.D. 325 and 787. Orthodox teachings include the doctrine of the Holy Trinity and the inseparable but distinguishable union of the two natures of Jesus Christ—one divine, one human. Mary is revered as the mother of God but is not regarded as free from original sin. Other saints are also highly revered. Persons become saints simply by being recognized over a long period of time by the whole church. No official canonization is required.

Orthodox believers recognize seven sacraments and punishment after death for sins committed but do not recognize the concept of purgatory. Baptism and the Eucharist are the two most important sacraments. After the ninth century, the sacrament of marriage became requisite for a valid marriage. Holy orders are conferred on both married and unmarried men, but only the latter are eligible to become bishops.

Worship is an essential part of Orthodoxy and is centered on the liturgical celebration every Sunday and holy day. Laity fully participate in the liturgy, responding in unison to the priest and singing hymns a cappella (organs and other musical instruments are not allowed). Church services are notable for their splendor, pageantry, profusion of candles, and bright colors. Priests' garments, as well as altars and church vestments, are ornate and colorful. Icons—pictures of Christ, Mary, and the saints, as well as representations of biblical events—adorn church walls. An ornate screen of icons, the iconostasis, separates the altar from the worshipers. Icons, often lit by candles, also adorn the homes of most Orthodox faithful. Icons are venerated but not worshiped. Worship is reserved for God alone.

In the late 1980s, three Orthodox churches claimed substantial memberships in the Soviet Union: the Russian Orthodox Church, the Georgian Orthodox Church, and the Ukrainian Autocephalous Orthodox Church. They, together with the much smaller Belorussian Autocephalous Orthodox Church, were members of the major confederation of Orthodox churches in the world, generally referred to as the Eastern Orthodox Church. The first two churches functioned openly and were tolerated by the regime. The Ukrainian and Belorussian autocephalous Orthodox churches were not permitted to function openly.

Orthodox churches that make up Eastern Orthodoxy are autonomous bodies, sometimes referred to as autocephalous or self-governing. The highest authority in each church is either a patriarch or an archbishop who governs in conjunction with the Holy Synod, an assembly of bishops, priests, monks, and laity. The Holy Synod elects the head of its church, the patriarch or archbishop, and in concert administers the church. Matters of faith or other matters of importance are decided by ecumenical councils in which all member churches of Eastern Orthodoxy participate. Decisions of the councils regarding faith are accepted by the followers as infallible.

185

Eastern Orthodoxy does not have a strict hierarchical order with one head, but the ecumenical patriarchate in Istanbul is generally recognized as the leading official. Individual churches, however, share the same doctrine and beliefs.

Russian Orthodox Church

The Russian Orthodox Church, which has the largest religious following in the Soviet Union, traces its origins to Kievan Rus' when in 988 Prince Vladimir made Byzantine Christianity the state religion. When Kievan Rus' disintegrated in the thirteenth century, the metropolitan of Kiev and all Rus' moved to Vladimir, one of the newly established principalities in the northeast. By the fourteenth century, the metropolitan's seat was permanently established in Moscow, the capital of Muscovy. Until the fall of the Byzantine Empire, the Russian church was subordinate to the Orthodox patriarch in Constantinople (present-day Istanbul). Afterward, the Russian Orthodox Church considered itself independent of the church in Constantinople, and in 1589 the title of patriarch was accorded to the metropolitan in Moscow (see The Golden Age of Kiev; The Time of Troubles, ch. 1).

The Russian Orthodox Church in Muscovy was closely tied to the state and was subservient to the throne, following a tradition established by the Byzantine Empire. That subservience was reinforced during Moscow's drive to acquire the lands of Kievan Rus', a drive that the Russian Orthodox Church supported. Another characteristic of the medieval Russian Orthodox Church was its emphasis on asceticism and the development of monasticism. Hundreds of monasteries dotted the forests and remote regions of medieval Russia. Monasteries not only served as the centers of religious and cultural life in Russia but also played important social and economic roles as they settled and developed their surrounding land.

Isolated from the West, the Russian Orthodox Church was largely unaffected by the Renaissance and Reformation and continued its essentially inward orientation. The introduction of Western-influenced doctrinal and liturgical reforms by Ukrainian clergy in the seventeenth century aroused deep resentment among Russian Orthodox believers and clergy and led to a split within the church (see Expansion and Westernization, ch. 1).

Peter the Great, while transforming Muscovy into the Russian Empire, further curtailed the minimal secular power the Russian Orthodox Church had held previously. In 1721 Peter abolished the patriarchate and established a governmental Holy Synod, an administrative organ, to control the church. From that time through

Church of the Epiphany (completed in 1845), Moscow. A functioning church, it is the seat of the patriarch of the Russian Orthodox Church.
Courtesy Jimmy Pritchard

the fall of the Russian monarchy in 1917, the Russian Orthodox Church remained directly under state control. Its spiritual and worldly power was further reduced after the Bolsheviks came to power (see Peter the Great and the Formation of the Russian Empire, ch. 1).

According to both Soviet and Western sources, in the late 1980s the Russian Orthodox Church had over 50 million believers but only about 7,000 registered active churches. Over 4,000 of the registered Orthodox churches were located in the Ukrainian Republic (almost half of that number in western Ukraine, where much of the population remained faithful to the banned Ukrainian Catholic Church). The distribution of the Russian Orthodox Church's six monasteries and ten convents was equally disproportionate. Only two of the monasteries were located in the Russian Republic. Another two were in the Ukrainian Republic and one each in the Belorussian and Lithuanian republics. Seven convents were located in the Ukrainian Republic and one each in the Moldavian, Estonian, and Latvian republics; none were located in the Russian Republic. Because most of the Orthodox believers in these western Soviet republics were not Russian, many resented the word *Russian* in the title of the Russian Orthodox Church. They viewed that church as a willing instrument of the Soviet government's Russianization policy, pointing out that only Russian is used in the liturgical services in most Russian Orthodox churches in Ukrainian and Belorussian republics and elsewhere.

Georgian Orthodox Church

The Georgian Orthodox Church, another autocephalous member of Eastern Orthodoxy, was headed by a Georgian patriarch. In the late 1980s, it had 15 bishops, 180 priests, 200 parishes, and an estimated 2.5 million followers.

The spread of Christianity in Georgia began in the fourth century. It became the state religion in the sixth century, and in 1057 the Georgian Orthodox Church became autocephalous. In 1811 the Georgian Orthodox Church was incorporated into the Russian Orthodox Church but regained its independence in 1917 after the fall of tsarism. Nevertheless, the Russian Orthodox Church did not officially recognize its independence until 1943.

Ukrainian Autocephalous Orthodox Church

When the metropolitan of Kiev and all Rus' moved to Moscow in the fourteenth century, Ukrainian Orthodox believers were left without an ecclesiastical leader. From the mid-fifteenth to the late seventeenth century, the see of Kiev was under the jurisdiction of the patriarch of Constantinople and had its own metropolitan. In 1686, however, the Russian government's pressure on Constantinople led to a transfer of the metropolitan see of Kiev to the jurisdiction of the patriarch of Moscow.

The Ukrainian Autocephalous Orthodox Church separated from the Russian Orthodox Church in 1919, and the short-lived Ukrainian state adopted a decree confirming autocephaly for the Ukrainian Orthodox Church. The church's independence was reaffirmed by the Bolshevik regime in the Ukrainian Republic, and by 1924 the church had 30 bishops, almost 1,500 priests, nearly 1,100 parishes, and between 3 and 6 million members.

From its inception, the church faced the hostility of the Russian Orthodox Church in the Ukrainian Republic. In the late 1920s, Soviet authorities accused the church of nationalist tendencies. In 1930 the government forced the church to reorganize as the "Ukrainian Orthodox Church," and few of its parishes survived until 1936. Nevertheless, the Ukrainian Autocephalous Orthodox Church continued to function outside the borders of the Soviet Union, and it was revived on Ukrainian territory under the German occupation during World War II. In the late 1980s, some of the Orthodox faithful in the Ukrainian Republic appealed to the Soviet government to reestablish the Ukrainian Autocephalous Orthodox Church.

Armenian Apostolic

The Armenian Apostolic religion is an independent Eastern Christian faith. It follows Orthodox Christian beliefs but differs from most other Christian religions in its refusal to accept the doctrine of Christ's two natures—divine and human—promulgated by the Council of Chalcedon in 451.

Armenians were converted to Christianity in the third century and became the first people in the world to adopt Christianity as a state religion. Despite seizing its property and subsequently persecuting and harassing its clergy and faithful, the Soviet government has allowed the Armenian Apostolic Church to continue as the national church of the Armenian Republic.

In the 1980s, the Armenian Apostolic Church had about 4 million faithful, or almost the entire Armenian population of the country. The church was permitted 6 bishops, between 50 and 100 priests, and between 20 and 30 churches, and it had one theological seminary and six monasteries.

Catholic

Catholics accounted for a substantial and active religious body in the Soviet Union. Their number increased dramatically with

189

the annexation of western Ukraine in 1939 and the Baltic republics in 1940. Catholics in the Soviet Union were divided between those belonging to the Roman Catholic Church, recognized by the government, and those remaining loyal to the Ukrainian Catholic Church, banned since 1946.

Roman Catholic Church

The majority of the 5.5 million Roman Catholics in the Soviet Union lived in the Lithuanian, Belorussian, and Latvian republics, with a sprinkling in the Moldavian, Ukrainian, and Russian republics. Since World War II, the most active Roman Catholic Church in the Soviet Union was in the Lithuanian Republic, where the majority of people are Catholics. The Roman Catholic Church there has been viewed as an institution that both fosters and defends Lithuanian national interests and values. Since 1972 a Catholic underground publication, *The Chronicle of the Catholic Church in Lithuania,* has spoken not only for Lithuanians' religious rights but also for their national rights.

Ukrainian Catholic Church

The Ukrainian Catholic Church was established in 1596, when a number of Ukrainian and Belorussian bishops, clergy, and faithful of the Orthodox Church recognized the supremacy of the Roman Catholic pope at the Union of Brest. Nevertheless, the Uniates (see Glossary) retained the administrative autonomy of their church and preserved most of their traditional rites and rituals, as well as the Old Church Slavonic (see Glossary) liturgical language. Belorussian Uniates were forced to reconvert to Orthodoxy after the partitions of Poland in the late eighteenth century when Belorussia became part of the Russian Empire. The Ukrainian Catholic Church, however, continued to function and grow in western Ukraine, which was ceded to the Austrian Empire in the partitions. By the twentieth century, it acquired standing as a national church in western Ukraine. Its close identity with the national aspirations of the Ukrainian people and the loyalty it commanded among its 4 million faithful aroused the hostility of the Soviet regime. In 1945 Soviet authorities arrested and deported the church's metropolitan and nine bishops, as well as hundreds of clergy and leading lay activists. A year later, the Ukrainian Catholic Church, which at that time had some 2,500 parishes, was declared illegal and forcibly united with the Russian Orthodox Church. Nonetheless, the Ukrainian Catholic Church continued to survive underground (see Policy Toward Nationalities and Religions in Practice, this ch.).

Taza Pir Mosque (completed in 1906), Baku, Azerbaydzhan Republic. An active mosque, it is the largest in the Caucasus. Courtesy Jimmy Pritchard

Protestant

Various Protestant religious groups, according to Western sources, collectively had as many as 5 million followers in the 1980s. Evangelical Christian Baptists constituted the largest Protestant group. Located throughout the Soviet Union, some congregations were registered with the government and functioned with official approval. Many other unregistered congregations carried on religious activity without such approval.

Lutherans, making up the second largest Protestant group, lived for the most part in the Latvian and Estonian republics. In the 1980s, Lutheran churches in these republics identified to some extent with nationality issues in the two republics. The regime's attitude toward Lutherans has been generally benign. A number of smaller congregations of Pentecostals, Seventh-Day Adventists, Mennonites, Jehovah's Witnesses, and other Christian groups carried on religious activities, with or without official sanction.

Muslim

In the late 1980s, Islam had the second largest number of believers in the Soviet Union, with between 45 and 50 million people identifying themselves as Muslims. But the Soviet Union had only about 500 working Islamic mosques, a fraction of the mosques in prerevolutionary Russia, and Soviet law forbade Islamic religious activity outside working mosques and Islamic schools. All working mosques, religious schools, and Islamic publications were supervised by four "spiritual directorates" established by Soviet authorities to provide governmental control. The Spiritual Directorate for Central Asia and Kazakhstan, the Spiritual Directorate for the European Soviet Union and Siberia, and the Spiritual Directorate for the Northern Caucasus and Dagestan oversaw the religious life of Sunni (see Glossary) Muslims. The Spiritual Directorate for Transcaucasia dealt with both Sunni and Shia (see Glossary) Muslims. The overwhelming majority of the Muslims were Sunnis; only about 10 percent, most of whom lived in the Azerbaydzhan Republic, were Shias.

Islam originated in the Arabian Peninsula in 610 when Muhammad (later known as the Prophet), a merchant in the Arabian town of Mecca, began to preach the first in a series of revelations granted him by God through the angel Gabriel. Muhammad's denunciation of the polytheism of his fellow Meccans earned him the bitter enmity of the leaders of Mecca, whose economy was based largely on the thriving business generated by pilgrimages to the pagan Kaabah shrine. In 622 Muhammad and a group of followers were invited to the town of Yathrib, which came to be known as Medina (meaning the city) because it was the center of Muhammad's activities. The move to Medina, called the hijra (hegira), marks the beginning of Islam as a force in history; it also marks the first year of the Muslim calendar. Subsequently, the Prophet converted the people of the Arabian Peninsula to Islam and consolidated both spiritual and temporal leadership of all Arabia in his person.

After Muhammad's death in 632, his followers compiled those of his words regarded as coming directly from God as the Quran, the holy scripture of Islam; others of his sayings and teachings and precedents of his personal behavior, recalled by those who had known him during his lifetime, became the hadith. Together they form the sunna, a comprehensive guide to the spiritual, ethical, and social life of orthodox Muslims. Muhammad's followers spread Islam to various parts of the world. Some oasis-dwelling people of Central Asia were first converted to Islam in the seventh century. The Tatars of the Golden Horde, who converted to Islam in the thirteenth and fourteenth centuries, spread Islam throughout Central Asia (see The Mongol Invasion, ch. 1). Most of the Kirgiz and Kazakh tribes of Central Asia, however, converted to Islam in the nineteenth century while they were under Russian rule. In the Caucasus region, Islam was introduced in the eighth century, but not until the seventeenth century was it firmly established there.

Islam means submission (to God), and one who submits is a Muslim. The *shahada* (testimony or creed) states the central belief of Islam: "There is no god but God [Allah], and Muhammad is his Prophet." Muhammad is considered the "seal of the prophets"; his revelation completes for all time the biblical revelations received by Jews and Christians.

The duties of Muslims form the five pillars of the faith. They are the recitation of the creed (*shahada*), daily prayer (*salat*), alms-giving (*zakat*), fasting (*sawm*), and pilgrimage (hajj) to Mecca. Believers pray while facing toward Mecca in a prescribed manner each day at dawn, midday, midafternoon, sunset, and nightfall. When possible, men pray in congregation at a mosque under a prayer leader; on Fridays they are obliged to do so. Women generally pray at home but may also attend public worship at a mosque, where they are segregated from the men. A special functionary, the muezzin, intones a call to prayer to the entire community at the appropriate hour.

Since the early days of Islam, religious authorities have imposed a tax (*zakat*) on personal property proportionate to one's wealth; this is distributed, along with free-will gifts, to the mosques and to the needy. The ninth month of the Muslim calendar is Ramadan, a period of obligatory fasting (*sawm*) during daylight hours for all but the sick, the weak, children, and others for whom fasting would be an unusual burden. Finally, all Muslims at least once in their lifetime should, if possible, make the hajj, or pilgrimage, to the holy city of Mecca to participate in special rites held there during the twelfth month of the calendar.

Ideally every Muslim is expected to practice all five pillars of the faith, but Islam accepts what is possible under the circumstances. This acceptance is particularly significant for Soviet Muslims, who can thus function both as Soviet citizens and as members of an Islamic community. Soviet Muslims, however, have had difficulty adhering to certain Islamic practices. For example, fasting during the month of Ramadan was infrequently observed because of the demands of meeting agricultural and factory work quotas. In the late 1980s, permission to make the hajj was given only to about twenty Soviet Muslims annually. A commonly observed practice, however, was circumcision of young Muslim boys at around the age of seven. Regardless of the degree of their adherence to all Islamic precepts, most Soviet citizens born to Muslim parents consider themselves Muslims.

A Muslim is in direct relationship with God; Islam has neither intermediaries nor clergy. Those who lead prayers, preach sermons, and interpret the law do so by virtue of their superior knowledge

193

and scholarship rather than by virtue of special powers or prerogatives conferred by ordination.

The differences between Sunnis and Shias were originally political. After Muhammad's death, the leaders of the Muslim community chose Abu Bakr, the Prophet's father-in-law, as caliph (from
the Arabic word *khalifa;* literally, successor). Some persons favored
Ali, the Prophet's cousin and husband of his favorite daughter,
but Ali and his supporters (the Shiat Ali, or Party of Ali) eventually recognized the community's choice. Ali became the fourth
caliph in 656. A great schism followed, splitting Islam between the
Sunnis, who supported an elected caliph, and the Shias, who supported Ali's line as well as a hereditary caliph who served as spiritual
and political leader. Over the centuries, the Sunnis have come to
be identified as the more orthodox of the two branches.

The differences between the Sunni and Shia interpretations
rapidly took on theological and metaphysical overtones. The Sunnis retained the doctrine of leadership by consensus, although Arabs
and members of the Quraysh, Muhammad's tribe, predominated
in the early years. Meanwhile, the Shia doctrine of rule by divine
right became more and more firmly established, and disagreements
over which of several pretenders had the truer claim to the mystical power of Ali precipitated further schisms. Some Shia groups
developed doctrines of divine leadership far removed from the strict
monotheism of early Islam, including belief in hidden but divinely
chosen leaders and in spiritual powers that equaled or surpassed
those of the Prophet himself.

Muslims in the Soviet Union are a disparate and varied group.
Although most of them reside in Central Asia, they can be found
on the western borders of the Soviet Union as well as in Siberia
and near the border with China. Ethnically they include Turkic
people like the Azerbaydzhanis, Uzbeks, Tatars, and Uygurs;
Iranian people like the Tadzhiks, Ossetians, Kurds, and Baluchi;
Caucasian people like the Avars, Lezgins, and Tabasarans; and
several other smaller groups.

Soviet Muslims also differ linguistically and culturally from each
other. Among them, they speak about fifteen Turkic languages,
ten Iranian languages, and thirty Caucasian languages. Hence,
communication between different Muslim groups has been difficult.
Although in 1989 Russian often served as a lingua franca among
some educated Muslims, the number of Muslims fluent in Russian
was low. Culturally, some Muslim groups had highly developed
urban traditions, whereas others were recently nomadic. Some lived
in industrialized environments; others resided in isolated mountainous regions. In sum, Muslims were not a homogeneous group

with a common national identity and heritage, although they shared the same religion and the same country.

In the late 1980s, unofficial Muslim congregations, meeting in tea houses and private homes with their own mullahs (see Glossary), greatly outnumbered those in the officially sanctioned mosques. The mullahs in unofficial Islam were either self-taught or were informally trained by other mullahs. In the late 1980s, unofficial Islam appeared to split into fundamentalist congregations and groups that emphasized Sufism (see Glossary).

Policy Toward Nationalities and Religions in Practice

Since coming to power in 1917, the Soviet regime has failed to develop and apply a consistent and lasting policy toward nationalities and religions. Official policies and practices have not only varied with time but also have differed in their application from one nationality to another and from one religion to another. Although all Soviet leaders had the same long-range goal of developing a cohesive Soviet people, they pursued different policies to achieve it. For the Soviet regime, the questions of nationality and religion were always closely linked. Not surprisingly, therefore, the attitude toward religion also varied from a total ban on some religions to official support of others.

The Soviet Constitution, in theory, describes the regime's position regarding nationalities and religions. It states that every citizen of the Soviet Union is also a member of a particular nationality, and a citizen's internal passport identifies that nationality. The Constitution grants a large degree of local autonomy, but this autonomy has always been subordinated to central authority. In addition, because local and central administrative structures are often not clearly divided, local autonomy is further weakened. Although under the Constitution all nationalities are equal, in practice they have not been. In 1989 only fifteen nationalities had union republic status, granting them, in principle, many rights, including the right to secede from the union. Twenty-two nationalities lived in autonomous republics with a degree of local self-government and representation in the Council of Nationalities in the Supreme Soviet. Eighteen additional nationalities had territorial enclaves (autonomous oblasts and autonomous *okruga*) but possessed very little power of self-government. The remaining nationalities had no right of self-management. Stalin's definition in 1913 that "A nation is a historically constituted and stable community of people formed on the basis of common language, territory, economic life, and psychological makeup revealed in a common culture" was retained by Soviet authorities through the 1980s. But, in granting nationalities a union republic status, three additional factors were considered: a population of at least 1 million, territorial compactness of the nationality, and location on the borders of the Soviet Union.

Although Vladimir I. Lenin believed that eventually all nationalities would merge into one, he insisted that the Soviet Union be established as a federation of formally equal nations. In the 1920s, genuine cultural concessions were granted to the nationalities. Communist elites of various nationalities were permitted to flourish and to have considerable self-government. National cultures, religions, and languages were not merely tolerated but in areas with Muslim populations were encouraged.

These policies toward the nationalities were reversed in the 1930s when Stalin achieved dictatorial control of the Soviet Union. Stalin's watchwords regarding nationalities were centralism and conformity. Although Georgian, Stalin pursued a policy of drawing other nationalities closer to the Russian nationality (*sblizhenie*—see Glossary). He looked toward Russian culture and language as the links that would bind different nations together, creating in the process a single Soviet people who would not only speak Russian but also for all intents and purposes be Russian. Native communist elites were purged and replaced with Russians or thoroughly Russified persons. Teaching the Russian language in all schools became mandatory. Centralized authority in Moscow was strengthened, and self-governing powers of the republics were curtailed. Nationalities were brutally suppressed by such means as the forced famine of 1932–33 in the Ukrainian Republic and the northern Caucasus and the wholesale deportations of nationalities during World War II, against their constitutional rights. The Great Terror and the policies following World War II were particularly effective in destroying the non-Russian elites. At the same time, the onset of World War II led Stalin to exploit Russian nationalism. Russian history was glorified, and Soviet power was identified with Russian national interests. In the post-World War II victory celebration, Stalin toasted exclusively the Russian people while many other nationalities were punished as traitors.

The death of Stalin and the rise of Nikita S. Khrushchev to power eliminated some of the harshest measures against nationalities. Among the non-Russian nationalities, interest in their culture, history, and literature revived. Khrushchev, however, pursued a policy of merger of nationalities (*sliianie*—see Glossary). In 1958 he implemented educational laws that furthered the favoring of the Russian language over native languages and aroused resentment among Soviet nationalities.

Although demographic changes in the 1960s and 1970s whittled down the Russian majority overall, they also led to two nationalities (the Kazaks and Kirgiz in the 1979 census) becoming minorities in their own republics and decreased considerably the majority of the titular nationalities in other republics. This situation led Leonid I. Brezhnev to declare at the Twenty-Fourth Party Congress in 1971 that the process of creating a unified Soviet people had been completed, and proposals were made to abolish the federative system and replace it with a single state. The regime's optimism was soon shattered, however. In the 1970s, a broad national dissent movement began to spread throughout the Soviet Union. Its manifestations were many and diverse. The Jews insisted on their right to emigrate to Israel; the Crimean Tatars demanded to be allowed to return to Crimea; the Lithuanians called for the restoration of the rights of the Catholic Church; and Helsinki watch groups (see Glossary) were established in the Georgian, Lithuanian, and Ukrainian republics. Petitions, samizdat (see Glossary) literature, and occasional public demonstrations voiced public demands for the rights of nationalities within the human rights context. By the end of the 1970s, however, massive and concerted efforts by the KGB had largely suppressed the national dissent movement. Nevertheless, Brezhnev had learned his lesson. Proposals to dismantle the federative system were abandoned, and a policy of further drawing of nationalities together (*sblizhenie*) was pursued.

Language has often been used as an important tool of the nationality policy. According to the Constitution, the Soviet Union has no official language, and all languages are equal and may be used in all circumstances. Citizens have the right to be educated in their own language or any language chosen by them or by their parents. Nevertheless, demography and Soviet policies have made Russian the dominant language. Under Brezhnev, Soviet officials emphasized in countless pronouncements that the Russian language has been "voluntarily adopted" by the Soviet people as the language of international communication, has promoted the "social, political, and ideological unity" of Soviet nationalities, has enriched the cultures of all other nationalities in the Soviet Union, and has given "each Soviet people access to the treasure of world civilization." Russian has been a compulsory subject in all elementary and secondary schools since 1938. In the schools of all the republics, where both a national language and Russian were used, science and technical courses have been mainly taught in Russian. Some higher education courses have been available only in Russian. Russian has been the common language of public administration in every republic. It has been used exclusively in the armed forces, in scientific research, and in high technology. Yet despite these measures to create a single Russian language in the Soviet Union, the great majority of non-Russians considered their own native language their first language. Fluency in Russian varies from one non-Russian nationality to another but is generally low, especially among the nationalities of Soviet Central Asia. A proposal in the 1978 Georgian Republic's constitution to give the Russian language equal status with the Georgian language provoked large demonstrations in Tbilisi and was quickly withdrawn.

Soviet policy toward religion has been based on the ideology of Marxism-Leninism (see Glossary), which has made atheism the official doctrine of the Soviet Union. Marxism-Leninism has consistently advocated the control, suppression, and, ultimately, the elimination of religious beliefs. In the 1920s and 1930s, such organizations as the League of the Militant Godless ridiculed all religions and harassed believers. Propagation of atheism in schools has been another consistent policy. The regime's efforts to eradicate religion in the Soviet Union, however, have varied over the years with respect to particular religions and have been affected by higher state interests.

Soviet officials closely identified religion with nationality. The implementation of policy toward a particular religion, therefore, has generally depended on the regime's perception of the bond between that religion and the nationality practicing it, the size of the religious community, the degree of allegiance of the religion to outside authority, and the nationality's willingness to subordinate itself to political authority. Thus the smaller the religious community and the closer it identified with a particular nationality, the more restrictive were the regime's policies, especially if in addition it recognized a foreign religious authority such as the pope.

As for the Russian Orthodox Church, Soviet authorities have sought to control it and, in times of national crisis, to exploit it for the regime's own purposes; but their ultimate goal has been to eliminate it. During the first five years of Soviet power, the Bolsheviks executed 28 Russian Orthodox bishops and over 1,200 Russian Orthodox priests. Many others were imprisoned or exiled. Believers were harassed and persecuted. Most seminaries were closed, and publication of most religious material was prohibited. By 1941 only 500 churches remained open out of about 54,000 in existence prior to World War I.

The German attack on the Soviet Union in 1941 forced Stalin to enlist the Russian Orthodox Church as an ally to arouse Russian patriotism against foreign aggression. Religious life revived within the Russian Orthodox Church. Thousands of churches were reopened and multiplied to 22,000 before Khrushchev came to power. The regime permitted religious publications, and church membership grew.

The regime's policy of cooperation with the Russian Orthodox Church was reversed by Khrushchev. Although the church remained officially sanctioned, in 1959 Khrushchev launched an anti-religions campaign that was continued in a less stringent manner by his successor. By 1975 the number of operating Russian Orthodox churches was reduced to 7,000. Some of the most prominent members of the Russian Orthodox hierarchy and activists were jailed or forced to leave the church. Their place was taken by a docile clergy who were obedient to the state and who were sometimes infiltrated by KGB agents, making the Russian Orthodox Church useful to the regime. The church has espoused and propagated Soviet foreign policy and has furthered the Russification of non-Russian believers, such as Orthodox Ukrainians and Belorussians.

The regime applied a different policy toward the Ukrainian Autocephalous Orthodox Church and the Belorussian Autocephalous Orthodox Church. Viewed by the government as very nationalistic, both churches were suppressed, first at the end of the 1920s and again in 1944 after they had renewed themselves under German occupation. The leadership of both churches was decimated; large numbers of priests—2,000 Belorussian priests alone—were shot or sent to labor camps, and the believers of these two churches were harassed and persecuted.

The policy toward the Georgian Orthodox Church has been somewhat different. That church has fared far worse than the Russian Orthodox Church under the Soviet regime. During World War II, however, the Georgian Orthodox Church was allowed greater autonomy in running its affairs in return for the church's call to its members to support the war effort. The church did not, however, achieve the kind of accommodation with the authorities that the Russian Orthodox Church had. The government reimposed tight control over it after the war. Out of some 2,100 churches in 1917, only 200 were still open in the 1980s, and the church was forbidden to serve its faithful outside the Georgian Republic. In many cases, the regime forced the church to conduct services in Old Church Slavonic instead of in the Georgian language.

The Soviet government's policies toward the Catholic Church were strongly influenced by Soviet Catholics' recognition of an outside authority as head of their church. Also, in the two republics where most of the Catholics lived, the Lithuanian Republic and the Ukrainian Republic, Catholicism and nationalism were closely linked. Although the Roman Catholic Church in the Lithuanian Republic was tolerated, large numbers of the clergy were imprisoned, many seminaries were closed, and police agents infiltrated the remainder. The anti-Catholic campaign in the Lithuanian Republic abated after Stalin's death, but harsh measures against the church were resumed in 1957 and continued through the Brezhnev era.

Soviet religious policy was particularly harsh toward the Ukrainian Catholic Church. Ukrainian Catholics fell under Soviet rule in 1939 when western Ukraine was incorporated into the Soviet Union as part of the Nazi-Soviet Nonaggression Pact. Although the Ukrainian Catholic Church was permitted to function, it was almost immediately subjected to intense harassment. Retreating before the German army in 1941, Soviet authorities arrested large numbers of Ukrainian Catholic priests, who were either killed or deported to Siberia. After the Red Army reoccupied western Ukraine in 1944, the Soviet regime liquidated the Ukrainian Catholic Church by arresting its metropolitan, all of its bishops, hundreds of clergy, and the more active faithful, killing some and sending the rest to labor camps, where, with few exceptions, they perished. At the same time, Soviet authorities forced some of the remaining clergy to abrogate the union with Rome and subordinate themselves to the Russian Orthodox Church.

Prior to World War II, the number of Protestants in the Soviet Union was low in comparison with other believers, but they have shown remarkable growth since then. In 1944 the Soviet government established the All-Union Council of Evangelical Christian Baptists to give the government some control over the various Protestant sects. Many congregations refused to join this body, however, and others that initially joined the council subsequently left. All found that the state, through the council, was interfering in church life.

The regime's policy toward the Islamic religion has been affected, on the one hand, by the large Muslim population, its close ties to national cultures, and its tendency to accept Soviet authority and, on the other hand, by its susceptibility to foreign influence. Since the early 1920s, the Soviet regime, fearful of a pan-Islamic movement, has sought to divide Soviet Muslims into smaller, separate entities. This separation was accomplished by creating six separate Muslim republics and by fostering the development of a separate culture and language in each of them. Although actively encouraging atheism, Soviet authorities have permitted some limited religious activity in all the Muslim republics. Mosques functioned in most large cities of the Central Asian republics and the Azerbaydzhan

Republic; however, their number had decreased from 25,000 in 1917 to 500 in the 1970s. In 1989, as part of the general relaxation of restrictions on religions, some additional Muslim religious associations were registered, and some of the mosques that had been closed by the government were returned to Muslim communities. The government also announced plans to permit training of limited numbers of Muslim religious leaders in courses of two- and five-year duration in Ufa and Baku, respectively.

Although Lenin found anti-Semitism abhorrent, the regime was hostile toward Judaism from the beginning. In 1919 Soviet authorities abolished Jewish community councils, which were traditionally responsible for maintaining synagogues. They created a special Jewish section of the party, whose tasks included propaganda against Jewish clergy and religion. Training of rabbis became impossible, and until the late 1980s only one Yiddish periodical was published. Hebrew, because of its identification with Zionism, was taught only in schools for diplomats. Most of the 5,000 synagogues functioning prior to the Bolshevik Revolution were closed under Stalin, and others were closed under Khrushchev. For all intents and purposes, the practice of Judaism became impossible, intensifying the desire of Jews to leave the Soviet Union.

Manifestations of National Assertiveness

Gorbachev's policy of *glasnost'* (see Glossary) exposed the official corruption, economic malaise, and general discontent that had permeated Soviet society for some time prior to his assumption of power. Gorbachev encouraged public discussion of sensitive issues, including the question of nationalities and religions in the Soviet Union. These policies led to a renewed ferment among the nationalities throughout the Soviet Union. By 1987 the Baltic nationalities, Armenians, Ukrainians, Soviet Muslims, Belorussians, Georgians, and others, including native Russians themselves, were expressing their national and religious grievances and calling on the regime to redress them.

Baltic Nationalities

In the 1980s, the most extensive movements among the Soviet nationalities, in terms of both participation and far-reaching demands, took place in the Baltic republics. In 1986 peaceful demonstrations began in Riga, the capital of the Latvian Republic, and from there quickly spread to the other two republics. Originally, the demonstrations were held to denounce Stalin's crimes and to demand that the Soviet government reveal the truth about the forced annexation of the Baltic states into the Soviet Union in 1940. In the late 1980s, public demonstrations of 100,000 people or more occurred in all three republics. The republics' parliaments declared their native languages as official and replaced the republics' flags with their pre-1940 national flags. All demanded sovereignty in managing their political and economic affairs, formed quasi-political popular fronts, and replaced their respective CPSU first secretaries with less conservative and more nationalistic party leaders. The Soviet regime made concessions to the Catholic Church in the Lithuanian Republic, permitting the pope to elevate one of the bishops to cardinal. Churches were reopened for worship in all three republics, and a more tolerant attitude toward religion was generally accepted.

Armenians

The complexity of the nationalities question and the potential danger it has raised for the Soviet regime were clearly demonstrated in the nationalist movements in the Armenian Republic in 1988. In the past, Armenians had been one of the nationalities most loyal to Moscow. Nevertheless, in February 1988 hundreds of thousands of Armenians staged a four-day demonstration in Yerevan, the republic's capital, demanding the return to the Armenian Republic of the Nagorno-Karabakh Autonomous Oblast, an autonomous region that had been under the administration of the Azerbaydzhan Republic since the early 1920s but was populated largely by Armenians. When Soviet authorities showed some sympathy for Armenian demands, infuriated Azerbaydzhan residents of the city of Sumgait, which had a considerable Armenian population, went on a rampage that left 32 dead and 197 wounded, according to official accounts. The regime recognized that altering nationality borders could provoke dire consequences and refused the Nagorno-Karabakh Autonomous Oblast's request to unite with the Armenian Republic. When the Nagorno-Karabakh soviet voted to secede from the Azerbaydzhan Republic, the regime declared the vote illegal, arrested and expelled the leader of the Nagorno-Karabakh Committee, which had been formed in the Armenian Republic, and sent armed troops into Yerevan, the capital of the Armenian Republic. Other members of the Nagorno-Karabakh Committee were arrested and taken to Moscow. But the aroused passions continued, and the Armenian national movement gathered momentum in September 1988, when 100,000 people demonstrated in Yerevan.

Ukrainians

National assertiveness was awakened much more slowly in the Ukrainian Republic. Although Gorbachev seemed willing to grant

*Nationalist demonstrators gather in 1989 in Baku's
central square, Azerbaydzhan Republic.
Young men in Yerevan, Armenian Republic, raise their
fists to protest service in the Soviet armed forces.
Courtesy Jimmy Pritchard*

extensive concessions to the small Baltic nationalities, he was much less inclined to allow them for the much more numerous Ukrainians, whose natural, agricultural, and industrial resources have been vital to the Soviet Union and whose size has contributed significantly to the country's large Slavic majority. Ukrainian nationalists were viewed by the regime as a severe threat, and Soviet authorities have used harsh measures against Ukrainian national and religious leaders. Nevertheless, a democratic national movement gained momentum in the late 1980s. It was particularly strong in the western regions of the Ukrainian Republic, where the population had not been exposed as long to a policy of Russification as had the people of the eastern regions of the Ukrainian Republic. A democratic front with a program similar to the Baltic popular fronts, a Ukrainian cultural club to preserve Ukrainian culture and history, and an ecological movement have been formed and have gained an increasing following. The crucial issue for Ukrainians in the late 1980s was the use of the Ukrainian language as the official language of the republic and as the language of instruction in the republic's schools. Ukrainians raised demands for transforming the Soviet Union into a voluntary confederation of free republics.

Another important development in the Ukrainian Republic was the revived activity of the Ukrainian Catholic Church. Several bishops and clergy and thousands of believers of the illegal church appealed to the Supreme Soviet in 1988 for the church's legalization. Also, clergy and thousands of faithful began to defy the authorities by holding open religious services.

Central Asian Nationalities

National discontent in Soviet Central Asia erupted during the mid-1980s. The discontent began over the removal for corruption of the native CPSU first secretaries in the Kirgiz, Tadzhik, and Turkmen republics. When the CPSU first secretary of the Kazakh Republic was also ousted and replaced with an ethnic Russian in December 1986, however, an unprecedented two days of rioting followed, with a large number of casualties. The riots demonstrated the local population's resentment against Russians' occupying the most prestigious jobs in the republic, a grievance that was shared by the native populations of the other Central Asian republics. Other commonly held grievances of Central Asian nationalities included resentment against the government's decision to drop the diversion of Siberian rivers, which would have brought badly needed water to the area, and the continuous distortion of their national history by pro-Russian historians.

Russians

The rise of Russian nationalism was another notable development during the first years of Gorbachev's rule. Begun as a movement for preservation and restoration of historic monuments and for a more balanced treatment of the tsarist past, it increasingly assumed a politically conservative character. The chauvinistic, anti-Semitic, and xenophobic group called Pamiat (Memory) won considerable public support among Russians and official toleration in Moscow and Leningrad. In a more positive manifestation of Russian nationalism, the government granted new visibility and prestige to the Russian Orthodox Church. The Russian Orthodox hierarchy was given favorable exposure in the Soviet media, and in 1988 the government sponsored celebrations in Moscow of the millennium of the adoption of Christianity in Kievan Rus'. The regime, in an unprecedented event, permitted the broadcast of a televised Easter Mass celebrated by the Russian Orthodox Church. It also handed over to the Russian Orthodox Church some of the most important shrines and hundreds of churches, many of which had previously belonged to Ukrainian religious denominations.

Other Nationalities

In the late 1980s, other nationalities, including the Belorussians, Moldavians, Georgians, and Jews, demanded that measures be taken to preserve their cultures and languages. Belorussians centered their demands primarily on recognition of the Belorussian language as the official language of the republic. Moldavians asked the government to allow them to use the Latin alphabet, as do other Romanian speakers, while Georgians appealed for greater religious concessions. Soviet officials, meanwhile, had changed their policy toward Jews and were allowing greater numbers to emigrate. The Soviet press was also giving increased and positive coverage to Jewish cultural activity, and Soviet authorities had promised to permit the teaching of Hebrew and to allow the opening of a kosher restaurant in Moscow, a Jewish museum, and a Jewish library.

* * *

English-language sources on nationalities in the Soviet Union are abundant. The *Handbook of Major Soviet Nationalities,* edited by Zev Katz, provides a very good overview of the fifteen nationalities that have their own union republics, as well as the Tatars and the Jews. Stephen Rapawy's ''Census Data on Nationality Composition and Language Characteristics of the Soviet Population: 1959, 1970, and

1979" and W. Ward Kingkade's "USSR: Estimates and Projections of the Population by Major Nationality, 1979 to 2050" give comprehensive statistical analyses of the nationalities listed in the Soviet census of 1979. The Soviet government's *Natsionalnyi sostav naseleniia, Chast' II* gives data on the 1989 census. Excellent essays on various aspects of the nationality question and on particular nationalities in the Soviet Union can be found in *The Last Empire,* edited by Robert Conquest; in *Soviet Nationality Policies and Practices,* edited by Jeremy R. Azrael; and in *Soviet Nationality Problems,* edited by Edward Allworth. The availability of English-language secondary sources on particular nationalities varies. The history, religion, culture, and demography of Soviet Muslims are covered in great detail in such recent works as Shirin Akiner's *Islamic Peoples of the Soviet Union* and Alexandre Bennigsen and S. Enders Wimbush's *Muslims of the Soviet Empire.* Equally comprehensive is the treatment of Estonians in Toivo U. Raun's *Estonia and the Estonians;* of Kazakhs in Martha Brill Olcott's *The Kazakhs;* and of Tatars in Azade-Ayse Rorlich's *The Volga Tatars* and in *Tatars of the Crimea,* edited by Edward Allworth. Nora Levin's two-volume *The Jews in the Soviet Union since 1917,* Benjamin Pinkus's *The Jews of the Soviet Union,* and Mordechai Altshuler's *Soviet Jewry since the Second World War* are some of the available sources on Soviet Jewry. Orest Subtelny's *Ukraine: A History* is an excellent general treatment of the relationship between Ukrainians and Russians, while Jaroslaw Bilocerkowycz's *Soviet Ukrainian Dissent* is particularly valuable for the period since the 1960s. Alexander R. Alexiev's *Dissent and Nationalism in the Soviet Baltic* sets the scene for the stormy events that took place in the Estonian, Latvian, and Lithuanian republics in the late 1980s. Few or no monographs are available in English on such major ethnic groups as Belorussians, Moldavians, Poles, and Germans or on the large number of smaller nationalities. Analyses of current developments regarding these and other Soviet nationalities are provided, however, by Radio Free Europe/Radio Liberty's weekly publication *Report on the USSR.*

The status of various religions in the Soviet Union and their relationship with the Soviet regime are treated extensively in such works as *Eastern Christianity and Politics in the Twentieth Century, Cross and Commissar,* and *Religion and Nationalism in Soviet and East European Politics,* all three edited by Pedro Ramet, as well as in *Christianity and Government in Russia and the Soviet Union* by Sergei Pushkarev, Vladimir Rusak, and Gleb Yakunin. John Anderson's *Religion and the Soviet State* deals primarily with religious repression in the 1980s and with Soviet authorities' varying treatment of the different religions. An analysis of the basis of Soviet atheism and a historical analysis of Soviet religious policy is provided in Dmitry V. Pospie-lovsky's *A History of Marxist-Leninist Atheism and Soviet Antireligious Policies* and *Soviet Antireligious Campaigns and Persecutions.* A detailed, extensive, and most readable account of Russian Orthodoxy can be found in Jane Ellis's *The Russian Orthodox Church,* while Bohdan R. Bociurkiw presents a clear and concise history of the Ukrainian Catholic Church and the Ukrainian Autocephalous Orthodox Church in his *Ukrainian Churches under Soviet Rule.* (For further information and complete citations, see Bibliography.)

Chapter 5. Social Structure

Statue commemorating an industrial worker and a collective farmer

SINCE 1917 THE SOVIET UNION has transformed itself from a predominantly agricultural, rural, and developing-capitalist society into an industrial, urban, socialist (see Glossary) society. Its social structure developed from the imposition of a centralist, Marxist state on a geographically, ethnically, and culturally diverse population.

Western sociologists generally categorized Soviet society into four major socio-occupational groupings: the political-governmental elite and cultural and scientific intelligentsia; white-collar workers; blue-collar workers; and peasants and other agricultural workers. Soviet ideology held that Soviet society consisted solely of two nonantagonistic classes—workers and peasants. Those engaged in nonmanual labor (from bookkeepers to party functionaries) formed strata in both classes.

Social position was determined not only by occupation but also by education, party membership, place of residence, and even nationality. Membership in the ruling group, the Communist Party of the Soviet Union (CPSU), aided career advancement. Those who worked full time for the party received political power, special privileges, and financial benefits. Social status increased the higher one was promoted in the party, but this power was derived from position and could neither be inherited from nor be bequeathed to relatives.

Unlike in the West, private property played no role in social stratification, and income generally was a consequence of social position, not its determinant. In general, the higher the social position, the greater the pay, benefits, access to scarce goods and services, and prestige. The Soviet regime glorified manual labor and often paid higher wages to certain types of skilled laborers than to many white-collar workers, including physicians, engineers, and teachers. These professionals, however, enjoyed higher social prestige than the better-paid laborers. Considerable differences existed among the country's various social and economic groups. Soviet statistics showed that the income for many occupations was not sufficient to support a family, even if both spouses worked. These statistics on income, however, did not take into account money or benefits derived from the unofficial economy, that is, the black market in goods and services.

The social structure of the Soviet Union has shown some signs of immobility and self-perpetuation. Children of the political elite, intelligentsia, and white-collar workers had a better chance to receive university educations than those of unskilled laborers and agricultural workers. Most children of agricultural workers began their careers without higher education and remained at the same socio-occupational level as their parents.

The largest official social organizations, such as the trade unions, youth organizations, and sports organizations, were tightly controlled by the state. Unofficial organizations, once banned, were becoming increasingly evident in the late 1980s.

Under the Soviet Constitution, women possessed equal rights with men and were granted special benefits, such as paid maternity leave for child-bearing. At the same time, women as a group were overrepresented in the lower-paid occupations and underrepresented in high positions in the economy, government, and the party. If married, they performed most of the homemaking chores in addition to their work outside the home. This overwork, coupled with crowded housing conditions, contributed to a high rate of divorce and abortion, which was higher in the European part of the country than in the Asian part.

Families in the southern and Islamic parts of the country were larger than those in the northern and non-Islamic sections. The increased size reflected the more traditional Islamic cultural norms and the inclusion of other relatives, particularly grandparents, in families.

Formation of Soviet Society

From 1861 to early 1917, the population of the Russian Empire officially consisted of six social categories: the nobility, clergy, distinguished citizens (professionals), merchants, townspeople (a catch-all term for city artisans, clerks, and workers not included in the other groups), and peasants. The intelligentsia, consisting of those who created and disseminated culture and often served as social critics, was not considered a separate class but rather, as one scholar put it, "a state of mind."

The upper level of the nobility and military officers were further hierarchically ordered according to the Table of Ranks issued by Peter the Great in 1722, which based rank on service to the tsar rather than on birth or seniority. This table continued in use, with some modifications, until abolished in 1917. The tsar was at the apex of this system, from which Jews, Muslims, and many of the smaller non-Russian nationalities were excluded.

The peasants, who were liberated in 1861 from serfdom and obligatory service on private or government lands, were at the bottom of the pre-1917 social pyramid. Before 1905 the government required peasants to obtain permission from the local peasant community—the mir (see Glossary)—before leaving the land. Although much of the peasant migration before the Bolshevik Revolution was seasonal, some permanent migration into the cities did occur, especially during the 1890s and after 1906, when the peasants were freed from obligations to the mir. The move from village to city was naturally accompanied by the move from farm to factory. Between 1895 and 1917, the factory labor force tripled to more than 3 million as Russia began to industrialize. The urban population of Russia increased from 9 percent in 1860 to 16 percent in 1910. Traditionally, urban life in Russia had been connected with government administration; but at the turn of the century, it began to be tied to industry.

The revolutions of 1917 overturned the old social order. In that year, the new Bolshevik (see Glossary) government nationalized private estates and church lands, and it abolished class distinctions and privileges. Workers' councils (soviets—see Glossary) took over the operation of factories and were given the right to set production goals and remuneration levels. Banking was declared a state monopoly. Thus, the economic foundations of the old social order crumbled. The new ruling elite, the Bolshevik-Marxist intelligentsia, drew its support from what it called the proletariat—workers, landless peasants, and employees—while the formerly privileged—the clergy, nobility, high-ranking civil servants, and merchants—found themselves stripped of their property and even hindered in obtaining housing, education, and jobs. The Bolsheviks lifted some of the restrictions a short while later when they realized that they needed the professional knowledge and skills of some former members of the elite to operate the government and the economy. Yet the children of the formerly privileged were barred from educational and career opportunities for nearly two decades after the Bolshevik Revolution.

Vladimir I. Lenin's nationalization of the land, factories, and financial institutions destroyed the prerevolutionary social system. In turn, Joseph V. Stalin's forced collectivization of agriculture, which began in 1929, annihilated the more prosperous peasantry during the early 1930s, while his industrialization program destroyed the new elite class that had developed as a result of Lenin's New Economic Policy (NEP—see Glossary). Seeking political scapegoats in the 1930s, the government directed widespread purges against the technical experts operating fledgling industries. In the late 1930s, Stalin's purges also destroyed much of the military and party elite.

During the 1930s, the social system adapted to the industrializing economy. Stalin ended the official leveling of incomes in 1931, when he announced that needed increases in production could be effected only by paying more to skilled workers and the intelligentsia. The new system provided incentives for workers and partly ended legal discrimination against some of the former privileged classes. Official discrimination against the former "exploiting classes" (nobles, priests, and capitalists) was abolished by the 1936 constitution.

Other events at that time reflected Stalin's move away from the egalitarian ideas that the regime had promoted during its first decade. In 1934 egalitarianism itself was repudiated, in 1935 military ranks were introduced, and in 1939 the Stalin Prize was created to reward favored artists. In 1940 school fees were reestablished for the final year of secondary school and for universities, and in 1943 and 1945 inheritance laws were made more favorable to inheritors.

From Stalin's death in 1953 to the late 1970s, an expanding Soviet economy continued to provide ample opportunity for career and social advancement. The state increased incomes of and benefits for the lowest-paid strata of society while providing more privileges for the elite. Beginning in the 1960s, however, access to higher education became increasingly restricted, thus impeding social advancement by this means. In the early 1980s, a stagnant economy reduced overall social mobility, a situation that highlighted differences among social groups.

In 1989 Marxism-Leninism, the official Soviet ideology, held that social classes have been historically defined by their relationship to the means of production, i.e., land and factories. The official view was that Soviet society represented "a new and distinctly different human community, free from traditional class antagonisms and contradictions." Soviet society supposedly consisted of two classes, workers and peasants, with those who engaged in non-manual or intellectual labor forming a stratum within both (see table 17, Appendix A). These two classes were considered to be nonantagonistic because neither exploited the other and because they jointly owned the means of production.

Stratification in the Soviet Union, according to Soviet officials, was based only on merit and not on the ownership of private property. Privilege proceeded from one's position in society and not the reverse. Soviet ideology held that this stratification would disappear in the future as Soviet society progressed from socialism to communism. In contrast, capitalist society, according to Soviet ideology, was torn by class conflict between the capitalists, or those who owned the means of production, and the workers. The capitalists ruthlessly exploited the workers, who had only their

Newlyweds at the Lenin Mausoleum, Moscow
Courtesy Jimmy Pritchard

labor to sell. This exploitation, Marxist-Leninists believed, created class antagonisms and inevitable conflict.

The official ideology ignored some very profound cleavages in Soviet society, and it created some that, in fact, had not existed. For example, despite overwhelming similarities in income, life-style, education, and other determinants of social position, only those employed in agricultural work on a collective farm (see Glossary) were considered to be peasants, while those employed in agriculture on a state farm (see Glossary) were called workers. Moreover, a bookkeeper on a collective farm, a schoolteacher, and an armed forces general, all of whom performed mental labor, were considered to belong to the nonmanual labor strata, often and imprecisely called the intelligentsia. This classification also failed to take into account the role political power and party membership played in social stratification within a one-party state. If under capitalism power flows from ownership, then under communism power confers the effect of ownership because political power in the Soviet Union determined who controlled collective property.

Stratification of Soviet Society

Western authorities on the Soviet Union divide Soviet society into various groupings or strata based primarily on occupation but also on education, pay and remuneration, place of residence, nationality, party membership, life-style, and, to a lesser extent, religion. Because the state owned virtually all property, private ownership played no role in social stratification. The influence of private enterprise was negligible because of its small-scale and often tenuous nature. Political decisions, not market forces, determined who had access to resources and therefore played the predominant role in social stratification.

Socio-Occupational Groupings

Western analysts have divided Soviet society into four broad socio-occupational groupings. At the apex of this social pyramid were the elite or intelligentsia, followed by white-collar workers, blue-collar workers, and, last, agricultural workers.

The Elite

The uppermost socio-occupational group, the elite, included leading party and state officials; high-ranking military, Committee for State Security (Komitet gosudarstvennoi bezopasnosti—KGB), and diplomatic personnel; directors of the largest enterprises (see Glossary) and of the largest educational, research, and medical establishments; and leading members of the cultural intelligentsia, e.g., academics, editors, writers, and artists. These groups received the most income and had access to goods and services that those lower in the social hierarchy found difficult or even impossible to obtain. Unlike Westerners, members of the Soviet elite were not allowed to amass great wealth and bequeath it to their offspring. When a member of the elite died, even luxury items such as a dacha (a country cottage) or an automobile could revert to the state.

White-Collar Workers

Soviet sociologists have grouped many of those who perform nonmanual labor into a category comparable to Western "white-collar workers." The approximately 25 million members of this group ranged from specialists who possessed high educational qualifications to administrators and clerks. The group included the majority of party and government bureaucrats, teachers, scientists, scholars, physicians, military and police officers, artists, writers, actors, and business managers. In the late 1980s, about 30 percent of white-collar workers belonged to the CPSU; the more prestigious occupations within this group had the highest percentage of CPSU members. White-collar workers on the average received higher wages and more privileges than the average Soviet worker, although physicians and schoolteachers who were just starting out earned less than the national average for all employees.

Blue-Collar Workers and Manual Laborers

The category of blue-collar workers included those who performed manual labor in industrial enterprises as well as those on collective farms and state farms engaged in transport, construction, and other nonfarming activities. In the late 1980s, blue-collar workers and their families made up about two-thirds of the country's population.

The CPSU has always loudly proclaimed blue-collar workers to be the backbone of the state and the most honored segment of society. Although newspaper accounts and photographs glorified their labor accomplishments, blue-collar workers were masters in name only. Only 7 percent belonged to the CPSU, the ruling group, and their pay and benefits were close to the national average and considerably less than those of the elite.

Agricultural Workers

Agricultural workers, on both state farms and collective farms, formed the bottom layer of the social structure in 1989. They were the least well paid and the least educated, and they were severely underrepresented in the CPSU. Most agricultural workers performed unspecialized labor. Where specialization existed, it did so only to the extent that raising poultry or livestock demanded greater skill than growing crops. In general, mechanized agriculture benefited men more than women because men tended to operate the tractors while women continued to perform manual work.

Although all farmers cultivated state-owned farmland, in 1989 farm workers were divided into two categories. State farmers were technically employees of the state. Working with government-owned machinery and seed, they received wages from the state for their labor. In contrast, collective farmers theoretically owned their machinery and seed and shared the proceeds from the produce sold.

Other Determinants of Social Position

Social position in the Soviet Union in 1989 was determined not only by occupation but also by level of education, party membership, place of residence (urban or rural), and nationality. Education level and party affiliation were by far the most important nonoccupational determinants.

Education

Education was the chief prerequisite for social mobility, playing an important role in determining one's occupation and hence

217

one's position in society. Few opportunities for advancement existed for individuals who lacked formal education. In general, the person who had an incomplete secondary education, that is, left school after eight years, received only a factory apprenticeship or an unskilled job. The person who completed secondary education, that is, finished school through the eleventh year, was placed in a skilled or perhaps a low-level white-collar position, depending on the type of secondary school attended (see Institutions of Learning, ch. 6). Professional and bureaucratic positions required an even higher level of education.

Access to higher education, however, was not equal for all social groups. In general, the higher the parents' status in the social hierarchy, the better were the children's chances of entering a university. This advantage was only partially attributable to the parents' better connections and influence. Children from these families also received better primary and secondary educations, which made it more likely that they would pass difficult university entrance examinations. In addition, their parents could more easily afford tutoring for these examinations if it were needed. They could also better afford the expense of school tuition in the absence of a stipend. Because of their better educational backgrounds, the children of white-collar workers and the elite were more likely to obtain higher positions in the social structure than the offspring of agricultural and blue-collar workers. Since education was the chief means of social advancement in the Soviet Union, this unequal opportunity greatly hindered upward social mobility and tended to perpetuate the intelligentsia and political elite.

Party Membership

Membership in the CPSU for both political and nonpolitical careers was absolutely essential for advancement above a certain level in society. All of the key positions of power in the Soviet Union were subject to the *nomenklatura* (see Glossary), the list of positions over which a given party committee had the right of confirmation. Power and authority increased the higher one rose in the party, as did monetary and nonmonetary benefits. Also, party membership often brought an opportunity denied to most Soviet citizens—the right to travel abroad.

Nationality

In 1989 Russians possessed an inherent social advantage in the Soviet Union. They, and to a lesser extent other Slavs, dominated the central government, party, economy, military, and security hierarchies. Possessing a higher educational level and a higher rate of party membership than most of the non-Russian nationalities, Russians also were overrepresented in skilled labor, white-collar, and elite positions. The Russian language was the official language of the state and the language of interethnic communication, which gave an advantage to Russians over non-Russians, who needed to master Russian as a second language for socioeconomic advancement. Non-Russians also generally possessed a lower rate of urbanization than Russians, who thus enjoyed better access to higher-paying employment and to education institutions.

Jews, as well, were overrepresented in certain areas of the arts, science, academe, and certain professions; but this predominance did not stem from an inherent advantage, as with the Russians, but rather from achievement. Unlike Russians, Jews were subject to discriminatory quotas for admission to academe and some professions and, according to one Western scholar, were excluded from foreign trade organizations.

Within the non-Russian republics and smaller administrative divisions, local ethnic hierarchies or "mafias" existed, especially in those regions where the clan system was still pervasive, such as the Caucasus and Central Asia. These patronage systems flourished during the era of Leonid I. Brezhnev, but Mikhail S. Gorbachev has attempted to weaken their economic and political power.

Intermarriage among nationalities has produced social mobility, particularly in the case of offspring, who legally must identify themselves by the nationality of either their mother or their father. In this case, upward mobility has occurred if the children have chosen the larger or more dominant nationality in the area, especially if it were Russian.

Benefits of Social Position

In the Soviet Union income and related benefits generally derived from one's social position and not the reverse. Ordinarily, the higher one's social position in the Soviet Union, the higher one's total benefits, which included not only better wages but also increased access to scarce goods and services. Access to goods and services more accurately reflected social status than cash income because social groups did not have equal access to them and because perpetual shortages of goods and services diminished the usefulness of cash earned. Other benefits, such as government subsidies for transportation, food, and housing, were not obtained by virtue of one's social status but were equally enjoyed by all. Occupational prestige appeared to be related to both income and occupation, although some professional positions, despite their higher prestige, were worth less in wages than certain jobs requiring skilled manual labor.

Monetary Compensation

Within the general pay hierarchy, the order, going from the highest to the lowest level of pay, was as follows: the upper crust of the political and artistic elites; the professional, intellectual, and artistic intelligentsia; the most highly skilled workers; white-collar workers and the more prosperous farmers; the average workers; and, at the bottom, the average agricultural laborers and workers with few skills. The policy of wage differentiation, put into practice in the 1930s, has continued into the late 1980s. Western scholars, however, have disagreed about the exact level of such differentiation. During the 1970s, the salary ratio of the highest 10 percent of all wage earners to the lowest 10 percent has been estimated as ranging from four to one to ten to one. A leading French expert on Soviet society, Basile Kerblay, has stated that within the same enterprise the salaries of senior executives ranged from ten to fifty times that of workers. Most industries had six grades of pay, and most workers had incomes near to but not at the bottom of the pay scale (see table 18, Appendix A).

As a group, leaders in the government, party, and military received the highest pay. In February 1989, the editor of a Soviet journal admitted to a Western reporter that the top marshals and generals in the Ministry of Defense earned the highest salaries, as much as 2,000 rubles (for value of the ruble—see Glossary) per month. Gorbachev, the head of the Soviet state and the CPSU, was said to receive 1,500 rubles a month, while other Politburo members earned 1,200 to 1,500 rubles a month. Another Soviet official has acknowledged that entertainers and other artists with nationwide recognition received about 1,000 rubles a month, as did seasonal construction workers, whose work sent them to various areas of the country. Western sources have estimated that the government leaders at the republic level earned 625 rubles a month. Those receiving high incomes often were awarded extra pay in the form of a "thirteenth month" or "holiday increment."

At the lower end of the pay scale were those workers employed in what one Western sociologist called the "traditionally neglected economic areas," which not only paid lower wages but also awarded smaller bonuses and fringe benefits. In the 1980s, an estimated 7 million people worked in low-paying industrial sectors, such as light industries (textiles, clothing, and footwear) and food processing. Another 30 million workers were employed in low-paying jobs involving retail trade, food service, state farming, education, public amenities, and health care. Those who performed unskilled supportive functions, the so-called "assistant workers" and "junior service personnel," such as janitors, watchmen, and messengers, also received low wages, as did office personnel in all sectors. And although the income of collective farmers had improved greatly since the 1960s, their average monthly income in 1986 was only 83 percent of the average wage of 195.6 rubles.

Not all individuals in positions requiring higher or specialized education were paid more than those requiring less education, even though they received greater prestige. Low-paid specialists included engineers, veterinarians, agronomists, accountants, legal advisers, translators, schoolteachers, librarians, organizers of clubs and cultural events, musicians, and even physicians. Women dominated these professions (see table 19, Appendix A). In 1988 the average monthly wage of medical personnel who had completed secondary or higher education was 160 rubles, or 82 percent of the average wage.

Lack of official statistics made it difficult to determine the number of Soviet citizens living in poverty. Until Gorbachev assumed power in 1985, Soviet officials claimed that poverty could not exist in their country, although they did admit to the problem of "underprovisioning" (*maloobespechennost'*). In the late 1980s, however, Soviet economists acknowledged that 20 percent of the population lived under the poverty threshold, which was estimated at 254 rubles a month for an urban family of four. Mervyn Matthews, a British expert on Soviet poverty, estimated that 40 percent of blue-collar workers and their dependents lived below the poverty threshold. Matthews calculated that in 1979 the poverty threshold was 95 percent of the average income of a family of four that had two parents working outside the home. Similar figures for the late 1980s were unavailable in the West. Many pensioners likewise appear to fall under the official poverty level. The 56.8 million pensioners in 1986 received an average of only 38 percent of the average wage, while pensioners from collective farms averaged only 25 percent (see Welfare, ch. 6).

The official statistics reflected income obtained from the state-controlled economy. They did not include income that was obtained legally or illegally outside of the official economy (see Nature of the National Economy, ch. 11). Unofficial income included earnings from such varied sources as private agricultural production, goods produced on official time with company resources and then sold privately, and profit realized from illegal currency exchanges. Western specialists had little information on the exact extent of this activity but acknowledged that it was widespread, especially in

Soviet Central Asia and the Caucasus. However, the extent to which income derived from unofficial sources raised the per capita income of the average Soviet citizen in 1989 was undetermined.

Noncash Benefits and Access to Goods and Services

Besides wages, citizens received two types of noncash benefits. The first, artificially low prices for food, transportation, and housing, amounted to approximately 42 percent of the average salary in 1986. These subsidies and other types of transfer payments were available to all and were not awarded according to status.

Other types of noncash benefits were allotted according to social position. For example, high-ranking party and government officials received such benefits as chauffeurs, domestic staff, living quarters (size and quality dependent on status), priority tickets for entertainment and travel, special waiting rooms at public places, and passes allowing them to jump lines to make purchases. As a rule, those receiving the least pay received the fewest noncash benefits. This group included unskilled workers, lower level white-collar and service workers, farm workers, many pensioners, and the temporarily unemployed. Farm workers, who generally received the lowest pay, were able to supplement their incomes with the proceeds from their private agricultural plots.

Social position also determined access to goods and services, an important benefit in a country where, as Matthews has written, "Deprivation is a recognized but unpublicized feature of . . . life." Those in the party, military, security, and cultural elites had the right to shop at special restricted stores that required either foreign currency or so-called certificate rubles. In such stores, imported goods or goods not available in the public markets could be purchased. The average citizen, in contrast, was obligated to stand in line for hours at public markets where many goods, including clothing and foodstuffs, were either in short supply or unavailable. Some occupations, however, bestowed privileges that were not officially recognized or that offered opportunities for *blat* (see Glossary). For example, managers of businesses and business activities had higher standards of living than their positions implied because they could demand special favors in exchange for the scarce goods and services they controlled. In turn, shop personnel possessed low occupational prestige but enjoyed high, albeit unofficial and sometimes illegal, fringe benefits. In addition, some blue-collar occupations could be put into this group.

Social position also played a significant role in the allocation of living space. The perennial shortage of urban housing meant that insufficient individual apartments existed for those who desired them. Income played only a small role in housing distribution because the state owned most of the housing and charged artificially low rents. (A small number of cooperative apartments were sold, but these were beyond the means of most people.) The elite received the most spacious and best quality housing, often as a job benefit. The elite also possessed more influential friends who could help them bypass the usually long waiting periods for apartments. The average family, in contrast, either shared an apartment with other families, using the bathroom and kitchen as common areas, or lived in a very small private apartment. A 1980 article in a prestigious Soviet journal on economics stated that about 20 percent of all urban families (53 percent in Leningrad) lived in shared apartments, although for the country as a whole this percentage was decreasing in the late 1980s. The housing situation for young unmarried, and often unskilled, workers was worse. They often could find living space only in a crowded hostel operated by the enterprise in which they worked or in the corner of a room in a shared apartment. Until they could find their own apartment, young married people often lived with one set of parents. Housing in rural areas was more spacious than that found in urban apartments, but it usually had few amenities.

Other forms of unequal access that favored those of higher social status included better holiday facilities, better medical care, and better education for children. The special schools that taught advanced languages, arts, and sciences were generally attended by the children of the privileged. Official state honors, both civilian and military, also brought benefits in the form of better travel, lodging, and holiday accommodations.

Occupational Prestige

In surveys questioning Soviet citizens about occupational prestige, professional and technical positions, especially those in science, medicine, and the arts, ranked high consistently; unskilled manual labor, agricultural labor, and sales and service jobs consistently ranked low. In general, Soviet citizens viewed the scientific professions as the most prestigious. While manual labor was glorified by the party and the press, it was not pursued and was even looked down upon. Nonmanual labor was considered cleaner, less tiring, and more prestigious. Agricultural jobs were considered less desirable than industrial jobs even in cases where the qualifications required for the job were equivalent. Urban work was considered more desirable than rural work, which was considered backbreaking, dirty, and offering few possibilities for advancement. The city

223

also offered more amenities than the countryside, where most of the underpaid, unskilled jobs were located.

Earnings and benefits seemed to play a key, although not exclusive, role in this social ranking. Generally, nonmanual workers received higher wages than manual laborers, but pay scales often overlapped, and many exceptions existed. For example, the low-prestige jobs, such as unskilled manual or nonmanual labor, were low paying, but not all of those in the high-prestige positions received high wages. Medical doctors, for instance, were highly esteemed, but their income was not high. Low prestige was attached to mid-level white-collar jobs because of their low pay and reduced benefits; coal miners, in contrast, had greater prestige because of good pay and benefits.

Urban-Rural Cleavage

The difference between urban and rural life in the Soviet Union has been called by Basile Kerblay "the most obvious gulf within Soviet society." This gulf remained despite the rapid urbanization that the society has undergone since the Bolshevik Revolution and the urbanization of rural life itself. Between 1917 and 1987, the urban population increased by 156.9 million; in contrast, the rural population decreased by 38.2 million. By 1968 the Soviet Union had become more urban than rural (see table 20, Appendix A). A Soviet village, officially defined as a community with fewer than 2,000 inhabitants, had, on the average, 225 inhabitants.

Differences in Life-Styles

Rural dwellers faced culture shock when moving from the countryside to the city. Until they were assimilated into their new way of life, they were marked by their dress, speech, and behavior. The rural existence they left behind was slower paced and socially and economically more homogeneous than life in the cities. They no longer received essential services, such as housing, medical care, job training, and entertainment, from their village communities but rather from their urban employers. Their new urban neighbors not only saved less of their wages each month but also spent an average of three times as much on leisure and culture.

The difference between urban and rural society was also reflected in housing conditions. Rural inhabitants traditionally lived in detached houses and had access to private garden plots. These rural gardens provided produce either for home consumption or for sale. City dwellers, in contrast, did not usually have this extra source of income. And although rural housing sometimes lacked indoor plumbing and other features of urban housing, it was roomier.

Ukrainian thatched-roof cottage at the Museum
of Folk Architecture, Kiev, Ukrainian Republic
Courtesy Jimmy Pritchard

One major legal difference between urban and rural dwellers disappeared in 1976, when collective farmers were issued internal passports (see Glossary) required for travel outside of their particular district. Before 1976 collective farmers were obliged to obtain the permission of employers before such travel was allowed.

Structure of Rural Society

Rural society reflected the predominance of agriculture as the major employer and the CPSU as the sole political organization. In 1989 the village community was controlled by an economic institution, the farm (collective or state), and an administrative one, the village soviet (*sel'sovet*). These organizations employed the elite of rural society, at the very top of which were the "heads" (*golovki*), who were either party members or party appointees. *Golovki* included the party secretary for the *raion* (see Glossary), the chairman of the collective farm or state farm (in the 1980s most were university-trained specialists, but a few were those who had learned on the job), the chairman of the *sel'sovet*, and the secretaries of the party cells in the state farm or collective farm. Men occupied most of the top positions on collective farms.

225

The rural nonpolitical elite consisted of agronomists, veterinary surgeons, engineers, and schoolteachers. Their life-style resembled that of urban dwellers. Among this group, rural society held schoolteachers in high esteem, in part because they played a role in selecting which of their students could continue their studies and thus have increased opportunity for upward social mobility. For rural women, regional teacher-training colleges offered the best chance to rise in the social hierarchy. Despite the relatively high esteem in which they were held, teachers were poorly paid and, in general, were forced to maintain private garden plots to support themselves.

An emerging group in the rural social structure consisted of agricultural machinery specialists. This group included truck drivers or other heavy machinery drivers and mechanics who had completed their secondary education and whose income was higher than many white-collar workers.

Workers who remained in the countryside had fewer avenues for upward mobility than did urban dwellers. Tractor drivers, for example, were more upwardly mobile than most rural laborers. Managers and white-collar workers employed in rural regions were generally brought in from urban areas.

Decreasing Social Differences

In the late 1980s, rural depopulation and modernization were eroding those aspects of rural society that distinguished it from its urban counterpart. Depopulation resulted from the migration of young people to the city to study and acquire a trade. This migration was especially apparent in the European part of the Russian Republic and in the Lithuanian, Latvian, and Estonian republics, where annually 2 to 3 percent of the rural population moved from the countryside to the city. (In Soviet Central Asia, the reverse was true; the rural population continued to increase because of high birthrates and a reluctance to move out of the countryside.) The loss of young people made rural society older, and because of the loss of males in World War II, the older age-groups were predominantly female (see fig. 8).

Concurrent with the increased flight from rural areas was the urbanization of members of the rural areas themselves. The government, for example, merged many villages to form urban-style centers for rural areas. Farming itself had become more professional, requiring a higher level of education or training obtainable only in cities. Additionally, in the late 1980s farming became more industrialized as rural processing industries were developed, as stock breeding become more industrialized, and as more agro-industrial organizations were formed. The modernization of rural areas developed unevenly, however; modernization was more evident in the Baltic area and the fertile northwest Caucasus and less evident in the southeast Caucasus and Central Asia. Rural areas also experienced a constant influx of urbanites: people who had moved to the cities but returned to visit, urban residents vacationing in the countryside, and seasonal workers and students mobilized for the harvest. During each harvest, the government organized about 900,000 city dwellers and 400,000 to 600,000 students to assist in gathering crops. All of these factors lessened the decreasing, although still profound, distinction between urban and rural society.

The reverse process—the "ruralization" of urban society—has not occurred in the Soviet Union, despite the rural origin of many unskilled urban laborers. The percentage of rural-born unskilled workers in the urban work force was declining in the 1980s as more urban-born workers reached working age. This process also was occurring in industry, where the percentage of urban workers with peasant backgrounds was greater among older workers. Workers in skilled industrial positions generally had urban backgrounds.

Social Mobility

Social mobility, or an individual's movement upward or downward through the strata of society, has been facilitated in the Soviet Union through changes in occupation, marriage, education, and political or even ethnic affiliation. Nepotism and cronyism have also played a significant role in social advancement. In addition, social mobility has stemmed from geographic mobility, such as the move of an agricultural worker to the city to work in industry. For non-Russians, social mobility has also involved learning the Russian language and culture.

Given the centralized and bureaucratic official structure of the Soviet Union in 1989, citizens could not legally become wealthy or achieve high social status outside official channels. Therefore, the paths for advancement remained fairly fixed, and an individual's upward progress was usually slow. In the past, political purges and an expanding economy had created positions for the ambitious. The faltering of the economy in the mid-1980s, however, restricted upward mobility, and as of 1989 Gorbachev's attempt to restructure the economy had not created new opportunities for social mobility.

In the 1980s, downward mobility was less of a problem than it had been during the Stalin era, when high-level government bureaucrats were demoted to menial jobs. However, even though elite positions had become more secure under Brezhnev, children

227

of the elite who lacked higher education did not necessarily retain their parents' social position.

In 1989 upward social mobility tended to be "inter-generational" (advancement to a social position higher than the one occupied by parents) rather than "intra-generational" (advancement to a higher social position during one's own adult life). Thus, social mobility had slowed down. Soviet studies from the 1960s to the mid-1980s also showed that children of manual laborers were less likely to obtain high-level educational qualifications than children of non-manual laborers. Nearly four-fifths of the children of unskilled manual laborers began their work careers at the same social level as their parents.

Social Organizations

Social organizations were strictly controlled by the party and government except for a small number of unofficial groups that continued to be tolerated by the authorities in the late 1980s. The largest social organizations in the country were the trade unions and DOSAAF (see Glossary); next in line were the youth and sports organizations.

Trade Unions

The trade union system consisted of thirty unions organized by occupational branch. Including about 732,000 locals and 135 million members in 1984, unions encompassed almost all Soviet employees with the exception of some 4 to 5 million collective farmers. Enterprises employing twenty-five or more people had locals, and membership was compulsory. Dues were about 1 percent of a person's salary. The All-Union Central Council of Trade Unions served as an umbrella organization for the thirty branch unions and was by far the largest public organization in the Soviet Union.

Like the CPSU, the trade unions operated on the principle of democratic centralism (see Glossary), and they consisted of hierarchies of elected bodies from the central governing level down to the factory and local committees. Union membership influenced union operations only at the local level, where an average of 60 percent of a union's central committee members were rank-and-file workers.

Unlike labor unions in the West, Soviet trade unions were, in fact, actually governmental organizations whose chief aim was not to represent workers but to further the goals of management, government, and the CPSU. As such, they were partners of management in attempting to promote labor discipline, worker morale, and productivity. Unions organized "socialist competitions" and

Pool players in Baku, Azerbaydzhan Republic
Courtesy Jimmy Pritchard

awarded prizes for fulfilling quotas. They also distributed welfare benefits, operated cultural and sports facilities, issued passes to health and vacation centers, oversaw factory and local housing construction, provided catering services, and awarded bonuses and prepaid vacations.

Although unions in the Soviet Union primarily promoted production interests, they had some input regarding production plans, capital improvements in factories, local housing construction, and remuneration agreements with management. Unions also were empowered to protect workers against bureaucratic and managerial arbitrariness, to ensure that management adhered to collective agreements, and to protest unsafe working conditions. After the Polish labor union movement, Solidarity, had achieved some success in Poland, Soviet labor unions became more vocal in protecting workers' interests.

Youth Organizations

To instill communist values into the younger generation, the CPSU employed a system of nationwide youth organizations: the Young Octobrists, the Pioneers, and the Komsomol (see Glossary). Of the three organizations, the Komsomol was, in the late 1980s, by far the largest and most active organization, with over 40 million members ranging in age from fourteen to twenty-eight. The Komsomol's structure mirrored the party's structure, from its primary units in schools and workplaces to its first secretary. The congress of the Komsomol met every five years and elected a central committee, which in turn elected a bureau and secretariat to direct the organization's day-to-day affairs between central committee meetings. Komsomol members were encouraged to take part in political activities of the CPSU and to assist in industrial projects and harvesting. Most important, its members received preference for entry into higher education, employment, and the CPSU.

The other two youth groups, the Young Octobrists and the Pioneers, were organizations devoted to the political indoctrination of children through age fifteen. The Young Octobrists prepared children ages six to nine for entry into the Pioneers, which in turn prepared them for entry into the Komsomol beginning at age fourteen.

Sports Organizations

In 1989 the Soviet Union had thirty-six sports societies, consisting of an urban and rural society for each of the fifteen union republics and six all-union (see Glossary) societies. All but two of these organizations were operated by the trade unions. The State Committee for Physical Culture and Sports served as the umbrella organization for these societies. Each society built its own sports facilities, secured equipment for its members, and hired a permanent staff of coaches and other personnel. Each held local and all-union championships for various sports, and each society's teams played against the teams of other societies. Although in theory the Soviet Union had no professional sports, each society supported athletes who played sports full time. Furthermore, the best, or "master sportsmen," received additional pay from the State Committee for Physical Culture and Sports.

Gender and Family Roles

In 1989 the Soviet Union resembled other modernized European societies in terms of divorce rates, roles of men and women in marriage, and family size, structure, and function. The twin pressures of urbanization and industrialization have radically changed gender and family relations in the Soviet Union since 1917. These changes, however, were less evident among the non-Russian populations of Soviet Central Asia and the Caucasus.

Role of Women

Article 35 of the Soviet Constitution clearly states that women and men "have equal rights" and possess equal access to education and training, employment, promotions, and remuneration and to participation in social, political, and cultural activity. Women also receive special medical and workplace protection, including incentives for mothers to work outside the home and legal and material support in their role as mothers; the latter support includes 112 days of maternity leave at full pay. At the conclusion of their maternity leave, women may take up to a year of leave without pay and return to the same job if they desire. Employers may not discriminate against pregnant or nursing women by reducing their pay or dismissing them, and mothers with small children have the right to work part time.

Nevertheless, both within society in general and within the family, the position of women in 1989 was not equal to that of men. Soviet authorities have often pointed to the high percentage of women in certain fields as proof of gender equality in the country. For example, in the 1980s women constituted just over half the country's work force, four-fifths of its health workers, more than two-thirds of its physicians and economists, and three-quarters of those employed in education. The authorities neglected to add, however, that the average pay for most women in these fields was below the country's average pay. Moreover, the higher the level in a profession, the smaller the percentage of women. For instance, in 1984 women constituted 83 percent of elementary school directors but only 42 percent of secondary school directors and 38 percent of middle school directors. In the early 1980s, 46 percent of all collective farm workers were women, but they constituted only 1.9 percent of collective farm chairpersons.

Women were also underrepresented in the CPSU and its leadership. In 1983 women constituted only 27.6 percent of the membership of the party and only 4.2 percent of the Central Committee; in 1986 they were totally absent from the Politburo (see Social Composition of the Party, ch. 7).

Male-Female Relationships

Male-female relationships in the Soviet Union reflected not only the stresses generally present in urban and industrial societies, plus those peculiar to communist societies, but also the influence of different cultural traditions. Predictably, the non-Russian Central Asian and Caucasian nationalities exhibited more traditional attitudes regarding marriage, divorce, and abortion than did the European population of the country.

Marriage

Unless specified otherwise by the laws of the individual republics, Soviet citizens may marry at age eighteen without parental permission. The Latvian, Estonian, Moldavian, Ukrainian, Armenian, Kazakh, and Kirgiz republics have lowered this age to seventeen years. In 1980 approximately 73 percent of the brides and 62 percent of the grooms were under twenty-five years of age. One-third of all marriages involved persons under twenty years of age, and in 20 percent of the marriages involving persons under that age the bride was pregnant.

In the larger cities, newly married couples often lived with either set of parents; often the honeymoon consisted of a short private stay in the parents' home. About 70 percent of childless young couples lived with parents during the first years of marriage because of low income or a shortage of housing.

Cultural compatibility played a larger role in the selection of a mate than did race, religion, occupation, or income. Soviet surveys also pointed to love, mutual attraction, and common interests as important reasons given for marriage. British sociologist David Lane has observed that "companionship" between spouses has been a more important notion in the West than in the Soviet Union, where couples have often taken separate vacations while the children were sent to camp.

Roles in Marriage

Most married women in the Soviet Union worked outside the home in addition to fulfilling their roles of wife, mother, and homemaker. As in other industrialized countries, women had difficulty reconciling the demands of career and home. At home, Soviet women spent more than twice as much time on housework as men—an average of twenty-eight hours a week as opposed to twelve—and women resented this. Before marriage, the average woman was said to have had forty-two hours a week of free time, but after marriage this number was cut in half. Not surprisingly, Soviet research has shown that marital happiness was directly connected to the extent a husband shared in domestic work. Husbands and wives from the elite tended to share decisions and housework to a greater extent than those from other social strata. In blue-collar and agricultural families, the husband was considered head of the household, although the wife held the purse strings.

Nationality appeared to be less of an influence on marital roles than social status and place of residence. By the mid-1970s, even most Muslim husbands were willing to share in some housework with their wives; the higher the socioeconomic status of the family, the more the husband shared the work. In Muslim families and in other nationality groups where the patriarchal system has remained strong, the husband was regarded as the head of the family and made most of the major family decisions. Among younger and better educated Muslims, however, and in the European part of the Soviet Union, the husband and wife shared in the decision making, a practice that may have resulted from the wife's increasing contribution to family income.

Divorce

With a rate of 3.4 divorces per 1,000 people, the Soviet Union was second only to the United States (4.8 divorces) among industrialized countries in 1986. David Lane has asserted, however, that the real family disintegration rate between these two countries was comparable because the legal difficulties and expense of a divorce in the Soviet Union encouraged "unofficial" divorces or separations.

The Soviet divorce rate varied according to region and population density. In Soviet Central Asia, it was two to three times lower than in European areas; the rate was also higher in cities and in newly developed regions. Divorce rates in rural areas averaged about 40 percent of those in cities.

Surveys have shown that couples divorced for a variety of reasons. Drunkenness, incompatibility, and infidelity were major causes; jealousy of the spouse, separation, and physical incompatibility were minor causes. In the Muslim areas of the country, conflict between the wife and the husband's parents was a major reason for divorce; however, Muslim women were less likely to initiate divorce than women in other regions of the Soviet Union. Stronger devotion to family life and the nature of marriage itself lowered acceptance of divorce in Muslim areas. Soviet surveys have shown that 87 percent of urban and 84 percent of rural Uzbeks opposed divorce for couples with children, whereas only 54 percent of urban Russians and 51 percent of urban Estonians held this view.

Housing problems and the lack of privacy contributed significantly to the high rate of divorce. One study showed that nearly 20 percent of divorces occurring during the first years of marriage were attributed to housing problems and about 18 percent to conflicts with parents. In 1973 in Leningrad, 31.7 percent of divorcing couples had lived with parents or in a hostel, 62.3 percent in a shared apartment, and only 5.1 percent in a separate apartment.

Divorces cost between 60 and 200 rubles depending on income and were granted more quickly if the couple had no children. In general, divorces were relatively simple to obtain, but the court always attempted to reconcile the couple first. Courts also generally awarded the mother custody of the children.

Sex and Contraception

Soviet society in general did not approve of unmarried couples living together but was somewhat more tolerant of occasional premarital sexual relations. The lack of suitable contraceptive devices, combined with rare public discussion about contraception, led to a large number of unwanted pregnancies. Studies in Leningrad have shown that 38 percent of all babies born in Leningrad in 1978 were conceived before marriage. A Soviet study revealed that the number of children born out of wedlock in the Soviet Union amounted to nearly 10 percent of all births, ranging from 22 percent in the Estonian Republic to 3 percent in the Azerbaydzhan Republic. Courts could order an unmarried father to pay child support if he lived with the child's mother; otherwise, the law was not firm, especially where proof of paternity was insufficient. No social stigma was attached to illegitimate children, and unmarried women received maternity benefits. Sex for sale—prostitution—however, was illegal and punishable by law. The Soviet penal code severely punished individuals running a brothel, pimping, or soliciting.

Although women were officially discouraged from having abortions, they were legal and were the chief form of birth control in the country. An estimated 8 million took place each year. Abortions were free for working women and cost 2 to 5 rubles for other women, depending on where they lived. Despite their availability, an estimated 15 percent of all abortions in the Soviet Union were illegally performed in private facilities. The approximate ratio of abortions to live births was nearly three to one.

In Muslim regions, the rate of abortion was much lower than in the European part of the country, although the higher her status or the more Russified the Muslim woman was, the more likely she was to have an abortion. Ironically, in European areas the situation was reversed; less educated couples were more likely to seek abortions than better educated couples, who were likely to use effective contraception.

The Soviet Family

The Soviet view of the family as the basic social unit in society has evolved from revolutionary to conservative; the government first attempted to weaken the family and then to strengthen it. According to a 1968 law, Principles of Legislation on Marriage and the Family of the USSR and the Union Republics, parents are "to raise their children in the spirit of the moral code of a builder of communism, to attend to their physical development and their instruction in and preparation for socially useful activity."

Evolution of the Soviet Family

The early Soviet state sought to remake the family, believing that although the economic emancipation of workers would deprive families of their economic function, it would not destroy them but rather base them exclusively on mutual affection. Religious marriage was replaced by civil marriage, divorce became easy to obtain, and unwed mothers received special protection. All children, whether legitimate or illegitimate, were given equal rights before the law, women were granted sexual equality under matrimonial law, inheritance of property was abolished, and abortion was legalized.

In the early 1920s, however, the weakening of family ties, combined with the devastation and dislocation caused by the Civil War (1918–21), produced a wave of nearly 7 million homeless children. This situation prompted senior party officials to conclude that a more stable family life was required to rebuild the country's economy and shattered social structure. By 1922 the government allowed some forms of inheritance, and after 1926 full inheritance rights were restored. By the late 1920s, adults had been made more responsible for the care of their children, and common-law marriage had been given equal legal status with civil marriage.

During Stalin's rule, the trend toward strengthening the family continued. In 1936 the government began to award payments to women with large families and made abortions and divorces more difficult to obtain. In 1942 it subjected single persons and childless married persons to additional taxes. In 1944 only registered marriages were recognized to be legal, and divorce became subject to the court's discretion. In the same year, the government began to award medals to women who gave birth to five or more children and took upon itself the support of illegitimate children.

After Stalin's death in 1953, the government rescinded some of its more restrictive social legislation. In 1955 it declared abortions for medical reasons legal, and in 1968 it declared all abortions legal. The state also liberalized divorce procedures in the mid-1960s but in 1968 introduced new limitations.

In 1974 the government began to subsidize poorer families whose average per capita income did not exceed 50 rubles per month (later raised to 75 rubles per month in some northern and eastern regions). The subsidy amounted to 12 rubles per month for each child below eight years of age. It was estimated that in 1974 about 3.5 million families (14 million people, or about 5 percent of the entire population) received this subsidy. With the increase in per capita income, however, the number of children requiring such assistance decreased.

235

In 1985 the government raised the age limit for assistance to twelve years and under. In 1981 the subsidy to an unwed mother with a child increased to 20 rubles per month; in early 1987 an estimated 1.5 million unwed mothers were receiving such assistance, or twice as many as during the late 1970s.

Family Size

Family size and composition depended mainly on the place of residence—urban or rural—and ethnic group. The size and composition of such families was also influenced by housing and income limitations, pensions, and female employment outside the home. The typical urban family consisted of a married couple, two children, and, in about 20 percent of the cases, one of the grandmothers, whose assistance in raising the children and in housekeeping was important in the large majority of families having two wage earners. Rural families generally had more children than urban families and often supported three generations under one roof. Families in Central Asia and the Caucasus tended to have more children than families elsewhere in the Soviet Union and included grandparents in the family structure. In general, the average family size has followed that of other industrialized countries, with higher income families having both fewer children and a lower rate of infant mortality. From the early 1960s to the late 1980s, the number of families with more than one child decreased by about 50 percent and in 1988 totaled 1.9 million. About 75 percent of the families with more than one child lived in the southern regions of the country, half of them in Central Asia. In the Russian, Ukrainian, Belorussian, Moldavian, Estonian, Latvian, and Lithuanian republics, families with one and two children constituted more than 90 percent of all families, whereas in Central Asia those with three or more children ranged from 14 percent in the Kirgiz Republic to 31 percent in the Tadzhik Republic. Surveys suggested that most parents would have had more children if they had had more living space.

Beginning in the mid-1980s, the government promoted family planning in order to slow the growth of the Central Asian indigenous populations. Local opposition to this policy surfaced especially in the Uzbek and Tadzhik republics. In general, however, the government continued publicly to honor mothers of large families. Women received the Motherhood Medal, Second Class, for their fifth live birth and the Heroine Mother medal for their tenth. Most of these awards went to women in Central Asia and the Caucasus (see table 21, Appendix A).

Children playing in Orel,
Russian Republic
Courtesy Jimmy Pritchard

Children playing on an ice slide
during winter holidays
in Khabarovsk, Soviet Far East
Courtesy Jimmy Pritchard

Family and Kinship Structures

The extended family was more prevalent in Central Asia and the Caucasus than in the other sections of the country and, generally, in rural areas more than in urban areas. Deference to parental wishes regarding marriage was particularly strong in these areas, even among the Russians residing there.

Extended families helped perpetuate traditional life-styles. The patriarchal values that accompany this life-style affected such issues as contraception, the distribution of family power, and the roles of individuals in marriage and the family. For example, traditional Uzbeks placed a higher value on their responsibilities as parents than on their own happiness as spouses and individuals. The younger and better educated Uzbeks and working women, however, were more likely to behave and think like their counterparts in the European areas of the Soviet Union, who tended to emphasize individual careers.

Extended families were not prevalent in the cities. Couples lived with parents during the first years of marriage only because of economics or the housing shortage. When children were born, the couple usually acquired a separate apartment.

Function of Family

The government has assumed many functions of the pre-Soviet family. Various public institutions, for example, have taken responsibility for supporting individuals during times of sickness, incapacity, old age, maternity, and industrial injury. State-run nurseries, preschools, schools, clubs, and youth organizations have taken over a great part of the family's role in socializing children. Their role in socialization has been limited, however, because preschools had places for only half of all Soviet children under seven. Despite government assumption of many responsibilities, spouses were still responsible for the material support of each other, minor children, and disabled adult children.

The transformation of the patriarchal, three-generation rural household to a modern, urban family of two adults and two children attests to the great changes that Soviet society has undergone since 1917. That transformation has not produced the originally envisioned egalitarianism, but it has forever changed the nature of what was once the Russian Empire.

*   *   *

Excellent monographs analyzing Soviet society include *Soviet Economy and Society* by David Lane and *Modern Soviet Society,* originally published in French, by Basile Kerblay. In *Poverty in the Soviet Union* and other articles and books, Mervyn Matthews discusses the problems of poverty and low wages in certain sectors of the Soviet economy. Providing a general overview of the Soviet Union, Vadim Medish's *The Soviet Union* contains useful insights into Soviet society, as does the *Cambridge Encyclopedia of Russia and the Soviet Union*. In their monograph *Modernization, Value Change, and Fertility in the Soviet Union,* Ellen Jones and Fred W. Grupp provide useful information on the position of women in Soviet society and on male and female roles. Genia K. Browning's *Women and Politics in the USSR* focuses on the position of Soviet women in society in general and Soviet feminism in particular. Gail Warshofsky Lapidus has written several informative books and articles on Soviet women. (For further information and complete citations, see Bibliography.)

Chapter 6. Education, Health, and Welfare

Newborn baby and nurse, young children, and pensioner

THE SOVIET CONSTITUTION GUARANTEES to Soviet citizens free, universal, and multilingual education; free, qualified medical care provided by state health institutions; provision for old age, sickness, and disability; and maternity allowances and subsidies to families with many children. In quantitative terms, Soviet regimes have made impressive strides in these areas since 1917. The quality of the education and care, however, often fell below standards achieved in the West.

Before the Bolshevik Revolution (see Glossary), education was available to only an elite minority, consisting largely of the aristocratic upper class; tsarist Russia's literacy rate was barely 25 percent. By the mid-1980s, more than 110 million students—about 40 percent of the population—were enrolled in the Soviet Union's government-controlled coeducational schools, universities, and institutes. The nation's literacy rate reached nearly 100 percent— proclaimed by Soviet officials as the highest in the world. Western authorities stressed, however, that the quality of Soviet education often lagged behind that of the West, in large measure because of the high degree of centralization and standardization of Soviet schools, the emphasis on political indoctrination, and the reliance on learning by rote and memorization.

On the eve of the Bolshevik Revolution, medical care was available to only a minority of the population, made up largely of aristocrats and upper-level civil servants. The annual death toll from epidemics and famine was in the millions. By the mid-1980s, the Soviet Union had the world's highest ratio of physicians and hospital beds per inhabitant, and basic medical care was available to the large majority of the Soviet population, although the quality of health care, in general, was considered low by Western standards.

Apart from limited assistance provided by private and church-run charitable organizations, no nationwide welfare programs provided for the needs of the old, disabled, and poor before the Soviet era began. In the 1980s, social security and welfare programs were providing modest support to over 56 million veterans and old-age pensioners, millions of invalids and disabled children and adults, expectant mothers, and multichildren families.

During the regimes of Joseph V. Stalin and Nikita S. Khrushchev, Soviet authorities established the underlying principles and basic organization of education, health care, and welfare programs. The common denominator linking these programs was the country's concern with establishing a technically skilled, well-indoctrinated, and healthy labor force. A hallmark of Soviet education was its primary political function, originally enunciated by Vladimir I. Lenin, as a tool for remaking society. Political indoctrination—the inculcation of Marxist-Leninist (see Glossary) ideals—thus remained a constant throughout the uneven, decades-long process of educational expansion and reform, and it set the Soviet system of schooling apart from contemporary Western models.

With the coming to power of General Secretary Mikhail S. Gorbachev in 1985 and the introduction of his policy of *glasnost'* (see Glossary), the achievements made in education, health, and welfare since 1917 were being increasingly overshadowed by open criticism and even growing alarm over serious failures in these spheres. By the mid-1980s, the Soviet leadership and public alike finally acknowledged what Western observers had been noting for some time, namely, that the decades-long emphasis on quantitative expansion had come at the expense of quality. Schools were failing to develop the technically skilled work force needed to achieve the goals of *perestroika* (see Glossary) and to create a modern and technologically developed economic system on a par with the advanced economies of the Western world.

The situation in Soviet health care was even more serious. In the 1970s and 1980s, significant increases in infant mortality and considerable declines in life expectancy accompanied an alarming deterioration in the quality of health care. Pension and welfare programs were also failing to provide adequate protection, as evidenced by the large segment of the population living at the poverty threshold. In the mid-1980s, Soviet leaders openly acknowledged these problems and introduced a number of reforms in an effort to rectify them.

Education

From its inception, Soviet education had Marxist-Leninist philosophical underpinnings, including the dual aim of educating youth and shaping their character. These aims were brought together, as well, in the notion of "polytechnical education," defined loosely as integrating education with life—ideally connecting formal schooling with practical training in all kinds of schools and at all levels of education—with the aim of providing a dedicated and skilled work force.

The government operated all schools, except for a handful of officially approved church-run seminaries, which had an enrollment of only several hundred people. Other characteristics were the leading role of the Communist Party of the Soviet Union

(CPSU) in all aspects of education; the centralized and hierarchically structured administrative organs; and an essentially conservative approach to pedagogy. The contemporary system also reflected some holdovers from tsarist schools, including the five-point grading scale, a formal and regimented classroom environment, and school uniforms—dark dresses with white collars (and white pinafores in the lower grades) for girls and dark pants and white shirts for boys—in the secondary schools.

Educational reforms in the 1980s called for increased funding and changes in curriculum, textbooks, and teaching methods to correct serious shortcomings in the schools and improve the quality of education nationwide. An important aim of the reforms was the creation of a "new school" that could meet fully the economic and social demands of the greatly modernized and technologically advanced nation the Soviet leadership wished to create as it led the country into the twenty-first century.

Philosophy and Aims

The philosophical underpinnings and ultimate goals of Soviet education were closely interwoven and could be expressed through two Russian words: *vospitanie* (upbringing or rearing) and *obrazovanie* (formal education). Marxist-Leninist ideology, the philosophical foundation of Soviet education, stressed the proper upbringing of youth to create the "new Soviet man" (see Glossary). To this end, the school system bore the lion's share of forming character by instilling and reinforcing Marxist-Leninist morals and ethics, beginning with preschool and kindergarten and continuing throughout the entire schooling process. Lenin stressed the moral goal of education, declaring after the Bolshevik Revolution: "The entire purpose of training, educating, and teaching the youth . . . should be to imbue them with communist ethics." The schools taught children key socialist (see Glossary) virtues, such as love of labor, the atheist (scientific-materialist) view of life, Soviet patriotism and devotion to the homeland, and the primacy of the collective, namely, the need to place the interests of society before those of the individual.

The extent to which Soviet education bore the responsibility for the rearing, or socialization, of youth set it apart from contemporary Western education systems and led many Western observers to see a similarity between modern Soviet schools and American parochial schools of the past. Another uniquely Soviet feature was the close integration of the schools with other major areas of society—cultural, political, economic, and mass media—all of which served to reinforce the political indoctrination process.

The role of the family in child-rearing was not ignored, however, and beginning in the 1980s Soviet leaders renewed emphasis on the family's central role in character formation. Parents were encouraged to create a nurturing and loving environment at home and to cooperate actively with the schools, which generally led the way, in fostering in their children the personal qualities considered essential to a socialist morality: "Soviet patriotism, devotion to socially useful labor, and a feeling of being part of a social group."

The task of molding the "builders of communism" was advanced as well through extracurricular activities centered on youth organizations that had close ties to the CPSU. Almost all schoolchildren belonged to these groups: the Young Octobrists, for ages six to nine, and the Pioneers, ages ten to fifteen. Most of the students in the upper classes of secondary school belonged to the Komsomol (see Glossary) for ages fourteen to twenty-eight, which was specifically tasked with providing active assistance to the CPSU in building a communist society. To this end, Komsomol members supervised and guided the two younger groups in a wide range of activities, including labor projects, sports and cultural events, field trips, summer camp programs, and parades and ceremonies commemorating national holidays (for example, May Day and Lenin's birthday), to develop in them proper socialist behavior and values and to attract them, even at these early stages, to "socially beneficial" work.

In addition to molding socialist morality, Soviet schools provided formal academic education, transmitting the knowledge and skills to provide the nation's economy with a qualified and highly skilled labor force needed to sustain the country in a modern technological age. The dual concept of rearing and educating was brought together as well in the notion of "polytechnical education," which stressed the inclusion of practical training at all levels of schooling. The polytechnical approach to education, which had waxed and waned since the era of Khrushchev, was receiving renewed emphasis in the late 1980s under Gorbachev. Polytechnical schooling had three key components: cognitive—gaining knowledge about production sectors and industrial processes and organization, production tools and machinery, and energy and power sources; moral—developing respect for, and dedication to, both intellectual and physical endeavor and eradicating the distinction between mental and manual labor; and practical—acquiring sound work habits through direct involvement in the production or creation of goods and services. A polytechnical approach was important not only to provide the dedicated, highly technically trained, and productive workers needed to realize Gorbachev's program of economic restructuring and modernization but also to adhere to a

246

central, publicly stated, aim of higher education, namely, the creation of a classless society.

Control and Administration

As was the case in every other major area of Soviet life in the late 1980s, the CPSU exercised ultimate control over the development and functioning of the nation's education system. Designated by the Constitution as "the leading core of all organizations of the working people, both public and state," the Central Committee of the CPSU made major policies and decisions regarding all aspects of education (see Central Committee, ch. 7). The party leadership accepted fully Lenin's dictum about the inseparability of politics and schooling/schools, and it appreciated the far-reaching power of education as a tool for refashioning the country's social fabric, "an instrument for the formation of a Communist society." Specifically, the Central Committee's Science and Education Institutions Department initiated education policies to ensure ideological conformity in all instruction. Together with the committee's Ideological Department, it issued laws and regulations governing all major spheres of education. The Council of Ministers and the Supreme Soviet, in turn, gave pro forma ratification to party directives and executed them (see Central Government, ch. 8). Administration of the school system was carried out by the government's education ministries under the direct authority of the Council of Ministers. In the late 1980s, the two chief administrative organs were the Ministry of Education, which administered primary and general secondary schools, and the Ministry of Higher and Specialized Secondary Education, which oversaw institutions of higher learning and specialized secondary schools. These central, union-republic ministries (see Glossary) operated through similarly named republic ministries, which were further broken down into province, district, and local school committees. The republic ministries and their administrative organs at the province, district, and local levels were responsible for implementing the laws, regulations, and directives concerning school curricula, methods of instruction, and textbooks, and they also supervised the allocation of funds at their respective levels.

Other main administrative organs (with counterpart agencies at lower governmental levels) were the Ministry of Culture, which operated special schools of art, ballet, and music, and the All-Union Central Council of Trade Unions, which oversaw vocational and technical schools. Management of higher education institutions involved administrative agencies from the various party organs and government ministries, such as those involved with health, agriculture, communications, and civil aviation. Not surprisingly, these numerous entities spawned a huge bureaucracy, one that represented a formidable obstacle to implementation of major school reforms introduced in the mid-1980s.

In the 1980s, overbureaucratization was openly criticized by the official press and by leading educators as a major cause of the serious lack of quality in education. For example, management of technical training, the most critical area for the success of economic reform, was excessive: seventy-four ministries and administrative departments oversaw institutions of higher learning, with thirty of these ministries directing only one or two institutes each. Another 200 administrative departments were in charge of specialized secondary schools.

Traditionally, the party apparatus had exercised control over not only the direction of educational development but also the implementation of policies and directives. The essentially parallel structure between party and government provided the main mechanism for this oversight. Furthermore, most administrators in central, republic, and local education posts were party members, as were the majority of school directors and many teachers, particularly at the higher levels (one-sixth of secondary school teachers belonged to the CPSU). The large body of Komsomol members in the upper grades of secondary schools and in institutions of higher learning also aided party oversight.

Pedagogy and Planning

Under the administrative oversight of the Academy of Sciences (see Glossary) and the Ministry of Education, the Academy of Pedagogical Sciences was responsible for conducting research and development in education. The Academy of Pedagogical Sciences had thirteen institutes, several experimental schools, and other facilities. Each institute focused on a specific area of research, such as curriculum and teaching methods, general and pedagogical psychology, visual teaching aids and school equipment, labor training, and professional orientation. The academy's research efforts also included special education (for the physically and mentally impaired), teacher training, testing methodology, and textbook preparation.

The academy brought together the country's leading researchers in the pedagogical sciences, prominent teachers, and a small number of foreign (mostly East European) education specialists. The efforts of these pedagogues and educators were guided by the academy's dual mission: first, developing a socialist mentality by inculcating a Marxist-Leninist worldview; and, second, providing highly qualified and committed workers for the nation's economy.

The first component—developing a Marxist-Leninist worldview and communist ethics—was geared to general character training as well, impressing upon youth basic ideas of good and bad, honesty, modesty, kindness, friendship, self-discipline, love of studies and conscientiousness, and "correct social behavior." Although the political content of school subjects had to be ideologically correct, the materials were not necessarily overwhelmingly politicized, as indicated by a Western study of reading topics in secondary schools that found less than one-third of them dealt with clear-cut sociopolitical themes.

The second chief concern of Soviet pedagogy was upgrading vocational education and labor training in the general secondary school. A related central goal was inculcating in youngsters a respect for blue-collar work. This remained a difficult if not insurmountable challenge because of Soviet society's traditional view of manual labor as intrinsically inferior to work that involved purely mental or intellectual effort.

The most important Soviet pedagogue historically was Anton S. Makarenko (1888–1939), whose theories on child-rearing and education, which rejected corporal punishment and stressed persuasion and example, served as the foundation of contemporary education and parenting. His methodology also emphasized development of good work habits, love of work, self-discipline, and collective cooperation. Makarenko's approach to discipline remained the norm in Soviet schools in the 1980s. Physical punishment was forbidden; disciplinary measures included oral reprimands by teachers, collective pressure (peer disapproval), bad marks in record books (demerits), consultations with parents, and, only as a last resort, expulsion from school.

Change in pedagogy's predominantly conservative approach came very slowly. Old-fashioned teaching methods, a regimented and formal classroom environment, and the rote method of learning—holdovers from tsarist Russia that became firmly entrenched in the Stalin era—were still the norm in the Soviet schools of the 1980s. But during the second half of the 1980s, theories and practices of a number of progressive educators were being advanced in conjunction with efforts to reform schooling. One of the important figures in this area was Leonid V. Zankov, an education theorist who had been influenced by the writings and philosophy of American educator John Dewey and who had advocated in the 1960s the elimination of the rote-learning approach. The leading figures in the 1980s among those striving to develop the philosophy and methodology for a "new school" were sociologist Vladimir N. Shubkin, mathematician Mikhail M. Postnikov, and innovative teacher M. Shchetinin.

The State Planning Committee (Gosudarstvennyi planovyi komitet—Gosplan; see Glossary), part of the Council of Ministers, played a major role in Soviet education by influencing the training and distribution of specialists in institutions of higher learning. Its task was to ensure graduation of sufficient numbers of people trained in certain specialties to meet the work force requirements of the nation's economy. By directing the higher schools to admit only a limited number of students in each specialty, Gosplan in effect established a quota for student admissions.

But despite extensive planning efforts, Gosplan consistently did more to cause than to alleviate the country's manpower problems, primarily because planning was based on immediate rather than long-term needs. The situation was particularly serious in the 1980s, when the push to modernize the economy with high technology and automation was seriously hampered by the lack of skilled engineering and technical workers. Although the schools graduated a large number of engineers, their training was often too theoretical, narrow in scope, and limited in practical experience. Broader training and multiple-skill capability were needed. The shortsightedness of the planning apparatus was exacerbated by a continuing contradiction between student preferences and economic and social demands, as well as by an inability to attract enough young people into lower level technical fields.

Institutions of Learning

To provide free, universal, and multilingual education to all citizens, the government operated a vast network of learning institutions, including preschools, general secondary schools, specialized secondary schools, vocational-technical schools, trade schools, and special education schools, as well as universities and other institutions of higher learning (see fig. 11). Completion of the secondary school program, roughly equivalent to American high school, became compulsory in 1970. By 1987 more than 120 million people, out of a population of nearly 282 million, had completed secondary and higher education; another 43.7 million had finished at least eight years of schooling.

The common threads linking all institutions of learning were the central aims of rearing and educating youth; thus, political indoctrination and the education and training of specialists and skilled workers remained of pivotal concern at all levels of schooling. Curricula, textbooks, and teaching methods were standardized nationwide. Except for a low enrollment fee for preschool, all tuition was free, and the majority of students in specialized secondary schools and institutions of higher learning received monthly stipends. Although the degree of standardization and centralization was very great, the school system was not totally monolithic, and it reflected the multiethnic diversity of the country's fifteen republics as well as considerable differences, particularly in quality, between urban and rural schools.

About 600 schools specialized in teacher training. Many university graduates also joined the ranks of secondary school teachers. In general, although salaries were not always commensurate with status, Soviet society had a great deal of respect for the teaching profession.

Preschool

In 1986 the Soviet Union operated approximately 142,700 preschool institutions on a year-round basis, with an enrollment of over 16.5 million; this represented 57 percent of all preschool-age children and was 1.6 million below demand. To eliminate this shortage, as well as to encourage women with infants or toddlers to return to the work force, the government planned to make available new preschool facilities for another 4.4 million youngsters during the Twelfth Five-Year Plan (1986–90).

Preschool institutions included nurseries (*iasli*) and kindergartens (*detskie sady*), often housed in the same buildings and located in urban and suburban neighborhoods, as well as at factory sites and on collective farms. Nurseries accepted children between the ages of six months and three years, but the percentage of youngsters under two years of age was typically low. Many mothers preferred to stay home with their infant children through the first year (working women were granted a full year of maternity leave), and frequently a grandmother or another family member or friend provided child care to toddlers. (In 1979, for example, 8 to 9 million preschool children were cared for by grandmothers.) The more common practice was to enroll children of about three years of age in preschool. The government subsidized 80 percent of preschool tuition, requiring parents to pay fairly low fees of 12 rubles (for value of the ruble—see Glossary) a month for nursery care and about 9 rubles a month for kindergarten; in certain cases—for example, for children from large families—enrollment was free. By freeing women for the work force, the preschool system was economically beneficial both to the state and to the family, which generally needed two incomes. Kindergarten combined extended day care (as a rule, from 8:00 A.M. to 6:00 P.M.) with some

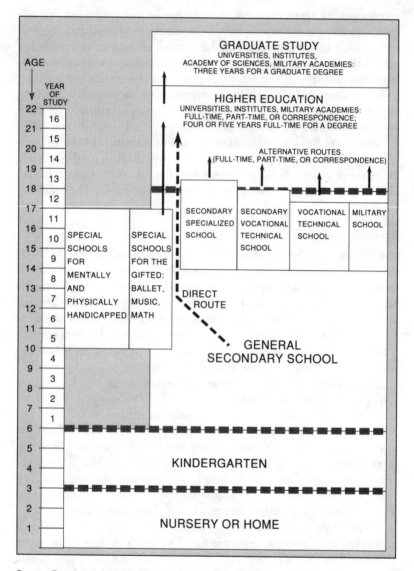

Source: Based on information from David Lane, *Soviet Economy and Society,* New York, 1985, 272; and Vadim Medish, *The Soviet Union,* Englewood Cliffs, New Jersey, 1987, 197.

Figure 11. Structure of the Education System, 1987

academic preparation for entry into the first grade (the starting age was gradually lowered to six years of age in the mid-1980s).

In addition to providing children with a head start for regular school, preschools began the important process of instilling societal values and molding socialist character. The children's daily activities, which included story-telling, drawing, music, games, and outdoor play, were highly structured and consistently conducted in groups, fostering a sense of belonging to the collective, the primacy of the needs of the group over those of the individual, and the preference for competition among groups rather than individuals. Political indoctrination at this level consisted of songs and slogans, celebration of national holidays, and stories about Lenin and other heroes of the Bolshevik Revolution. Preschoolers were also taught respect for authority, patriotism, obedience, discipline, and order. Children were provided hot meals and snacks, child-size beds for nap time, and basic health care.

Western visitors to Soviet preschools in the 1970s and early 1980s reported seeing children who were happy, healthy, and well cared for. But this positive image was sharply contradicted in 1988 with the publication in a Soviet newspaper of an article titled ''Attention: Children in Trouble!'' The article was endorsed by a group of specialists (including R. Bure, doctor of pedagogical sciences and head of the Academy of Pedagogical Sciences Preschool Scientific Research Laboratory) who participated in a seminar called ''Kindergarten in the Year 2000.'' According to the newspaper piece, a crisis in preschool education was emerging: the ratio of twenty-five children per teacher was far too high; teachers and other staff were poorly trained; and children's health was suffering because of inadequate medical care. Children were entering first grade unprepared intellectually and physically. More than 50 percent were ''neurotic,'' two-thirds suffered from allergies, 60 percent had poor posture, and 80 percent suffered from upper-respiratory infections. The large majority had not mastered the most basic norms of conduct and social interaction.

Secondary Education

In the late 1980s, the Soviet Union had in place a vast and complex network of secondary schools comprising general secondary schools (grades one through eleven), secondary vocational-technical schools, specialized secondary schools, special education schools, and extramural schools (part-time, evening, and correspondence programs). In 1970 compulsory secondary education was extended to ten years from eight. The 1984 reform of general secondary schools and secondary vocational-technical schools lowered the starting age for first grade from age seven to age six and increased compulsory schooling to eleven years.

In 1987 the Soviet Union operated 138,000 general secondary schools, with a total enrollment of 43.9 million students. There were roughly three phases to the general secondary program of study, reflecting differences in curriculum and total time in class: the primary grades, one through three; intermediate, four through eight; and upper secondary, nine and ten. The 1984 reform added a year at the beginning level, modifying these grade groupings as follows: one through four, five through nine, and ten and eleven. As a rule, secondary schools in urban areas combined all grades, but rural schools were small, with only four or eight grades in the same building.

The school year ran approximately from September 1 (the official Holiday of Learning) to June 1. Classes were held Monday through Saturday, and total class time ranged from about twenty-four hours a week in the primary grades to thirty-six at the upper levels (following the reform, the range of class time was reduced to twenty to thirty-four hours). At all levels, class periods lasted forty-five minutes, with ten-minute breaks and a half-hour for lunch.

The 1986–87 school year marked the wide-scale entry of six-year-olds into secondary schools; by September 1987, an estimated 42 percent of all six-year-olds were enrolled in first grade. In some republics, e.g., the Georgian, Lithuanian, and Belorussian, the transition was nearly completed; but because of lack of space and school equipment (a chronic problem), many schools had to operate on double and even triple shifts to accommodate the additional new entrants.

The primary curriculum emphasized reading, writing, and arithmetic. Children spent from ten to twelve periods a week learning to read and write in Russian or the native language and six periods a week on mathematics. The curriculum was rounded out with art and music classes, physical education, and vocational training. Children attending non-Russian schools—representing a total of forty-four different Soviet nationalities in 1987—began learning Russian, the lingua franca in the Soviet Union, in the second grade, resulting in an even heavier academic load for them (see Nationalities of the Soviet Union, ch. 4).

Foreign language study, with English the most popular, began in the fifth grade. The curriculum in the intermediate and upper classes included courses in literature, history, social studies, geography, mathematics, biology, physics, chemistry, and technical drawing. Consistent with the 1984 school reform's call for achieving computer literacy, the schools introduced computer training in the upper grades in the mid-1980s (see Computers, ch. 9). Vocational counseling was also introduced in the upper grades in an effort to direct more students to pursue training in technical areas

Typical classroom, Moscow
Courtesy Irene Steckler

requiring high-level skills. The new curriculum for grades ten and eleven included courses called "Ethics and Psychology of Family Life" and "Elementary Military Training." From one to four hours per week of "socially beneficial" labor was made compulsory for grades two through eleven.

General secondary schools emphasized mathematics and science; science courses were designed not only to teach the fundamentals but also to develop the official scientific-materialist worldview. Teaching of history and literature was particularly politicized and biased, through selection and interpretation, toward inculcation of communist values and ideology. As an outgrowth of the de-Stalinization effort under Gorbachev, the official Soviet press denounced elementary and secondary school history books as "lies," and, to the students' glee, school authorities canceled final history examinations in the spring of 1987.

On the whole, final examinations were rigorous and comprehensive, and they included both written and oral parts. Performance was graded on a number scale of one (failure) to five (outstanding). The general secondary school diploma was roughly equivalent to a high school diploma in the United States. Completion of this program offered the most direct route to entrance into an institution of higher learning.

255

After the eighth or ninth grade, students who chose not to finish the final two years of the general secondary school had several options. The most popular in the 1980s was enrollment in secondary vocational-technical schools or specialized secondary schools. In 1987 nearly 25 percent of students chose the former and almost 13 percent the latter route (more than 60 percent continued in the general secondary school).

The secondary vocational-technical school (*srednee professional'no-tekhnicheskoe uchilishche*—SPTU) combined a full secondary education with training for skilled and semiskilled jobs in industry, agriculture, and office work. In 1986 more than 7,000 such schools were in operation; the period of instruction was two or three years. Graduates received diplomas and could apply to institutions of higher education. An incomplete secondary education trade school variant, vocational-technical schools (*professional'no-tekhnicheskie uchilishcha*—PTU), numbering about 1,000 in the mid-1980s, provided training in skilled and semiskilled jobs.

At the beginning of the 1986–87 school year, 4,506 specialized secondary schools (*srednie spetsial'nye zavedeniia*), commonly called technicums (*tekhnikumy*), had an enrollment of nearly 4.5 million students (2.8 million in regular daytime programs and 1.7 million in evening or correspondence schools). The course of study lasted from three to four years and combined completion of the final two grades of general secondary schooling with training at a paraprofessional level. Technicums offered over 450 majors, most of them in engineering and technical areas, as well as paraprofessional-level training in health care, law, teaching, and the arts. Graduates received diplomas and could obtain jobs as preschool and primary school teachers, paramedics, and technicians; they could also apply to higher education institutions. A technicum education corresponded roughly to an associate degree or two years of study in an American junior college or community college.

In 1986 another school reform stressed the specialized secondary school system and higher education. The qualitative improvement of the technicums, which traditionally had served as an important source of technically trained workers, was a key component in providing skilled, technically qualified manpower required for the success of economic restructuring and modernization. To this end, the reform called for revamping both technicums and secondary vocational-technical schools to train specialists with diverse technical skills and hands-on experience with computer technology and automated production processes, as well as a more independent, creative, and responsible approach to their jobs.

Special Education

Special schools included those for physically and mentally handicapped children as well as those for intellectually and artistically gifted youth. They also included military schools for secondary-level cadet training.

In 1987 about 500,000 youngsters with mental and/or physical impairments were enrolled in 2,700 schools designed to meet their special needs. Schools for the mentally retarded strived to help children acquire as much of a general or vocational education as their abilities permitted and also encouraged them to become as self-reliant as possible. The blind and those with partial sight could complete the regular secondary program and/or vocational training in schools with a modified curriculum and special physical accommodations. There were also schools for deaf children, deaf-mutes, and the hearing impaired.

Universities operated a small number of advanced academic programs for exceptionally bright children who demonstrated outstanding abilities in the sciences and mathematics. Schools also specialized in a specific foreign language, for example, English or German. About 50 percent of all subjects were taught in the given language. These highly prestigious schools provided complete secondary schooling, and their graduates were guaranteed entrance into institutions of higher learning.

The Ministry of Culture operated a small network of schools for artistically gifted youngsters, which combined regular secondary education with intensive training in music, ballet, or the arts. These special schools were located primarily in Moscow, Leningrad, and other large Soviet cities.

First established during World War II, military boarding schools continued to provide free care and education to war orphans of military personnel and to train future officers of the armed forces. With enrollments of between 150 to 500 students, the eight Suvorov military schools and the Nakhimov Naval School offered a regular, general school curriculum supplemented by a heavy load of mathematics, political and military training, and physical education. Most graduates of these schools entered higher military institutions (see Officers, ch. 18).

Higher Education

In 1987 the Soviet Union had 896 institutions of higher learning (*vysshie uchebnye zavedeniia*—VUZy), of which only 69 were universities. The remainder included more than 400 pedagogical, medical, and social science institutes and art academies and conservatories of music; over 360 institutes of specialized engineering and natural sciences; and about 60 polytechnical institutes. VUZy were located in major cities, including the union republic and autonomous republic capitals, with the highest concentrations in Moscow, Leningrad, and Kiev. Enrollment was over 5 million students, with nearly 50 percent (2.4 million) attending part time. Women made up 56 percent of the student body. Forty-one percent of the students came from the working (blue-collar) class, 9 percent from the collective farm (see Glossary) sector, and 50 percent from families working in the services (white-collar) sector.

With nearly 587,000 students enrolled, universities offered a broad range of disciplines in the arts and sciences, while concentrating on the theoretical aspects of the given field. Institutes and polytechnics were more specialized and stressed specific applied disciplines, for example, engineering, education, and medicine. The approach to higher education traditionally focused on acquiring knowledge and comprehension rather than on developing skills of analysis and evaluation.

As the country's major scientific and cultural centers, universities produced the leading researchers and teachers in the natural and mathematical sciences, social and political sciences, and humanities, e.g., literature and languages. They also developed textbooks and study guides for disciplines in all institutions of higher learning and for university courses in the natural sciences and humanities.

On the whole, Soviet society considered universities the most prestigious of all institutions of higher learning. Applicants considerably exceeded openings, and competition for entrance was stiff. Officially, acceptance was based on academic merit. In addition to successful completion of secondary schooling, prospective entrants had to pass extremely competitive oral and written examinations, given only once a year, in their area of specialization, as well as in Russian and a foreign language. Students commonly employed private tutors to prepare for university entrance examinations. Beyond this generally accepted practice, other less honest methods were used widely and included drawing on personal connections of parents and even resorting to bribes. Party or Komsomol endorsement strengthened an applicant's chances for admission.

Moscow University, established in 1755, was the Soviet Union's largest, most prestigious, and second oldest institution of higher learning (the Ukrainian Republic's L'vov University was founded in 1661). It comprised seventeen colleges or schools (in Russian, *fakultety*—faculties), divided into 274 departments, each offering

Turkmen University, Ashkhabad, Turkmen Republic
Courtesy Jimmy Pritchard

a wide range of related subjects. A major research center, the state university had a library of over 6.5 million volumes. A teaching staff of about 7,000 full-time and part-time professors and instructors taught over 30,000 students (more than half attended on a part-time basis).

Full-time higher education took 4 to 5.5 years of study, depending on the area of specialization, for example, 5.5 years for medicine; 5 years for engineering; 4.5 years for agriculture; and 4 years for law, history, journalism, or art. The programs combined lectures, seminars, practicums, and research. At the final stage, students had to complete an approved thesis and defend their work before the State Examination Committee; they also had to pass extensive examinations in their field of specialization. Graduates were awarded diplomas; depending on the course of study and institution, the diploma fell roughly between a bachelor's degree and master's degree in the United States.

Tuition at all institutions of higher learning was free; in the 1986–87 school year, 78 percent of full-time students received monthly stipends ranging from 40 to 70 rubles. Students paid only minimum room and board because dormitories (albeit crowded and lacking most modern amenities) and cafeterias were subsidized by the government. The universities also provided basic medical care

259

at no cost, as well as free passes to rest and recreation homes and summer and winter resorts.

Graduates were expected to repay the government's generosity by devoting two or three years to a job assigned by the government. This practice was becoming an increasingly serious problem with respect to labor distribution in the 1980s. Among the major contributing factors were Gosplan's failure to forecast correctly the country's needs for specialized labor cadres (graduates frequently were assigned to jobs totally unrelated to their areas of specialization) and the often outright refusal by graduates to accept jobs in undesirable (remote or rural) parts of the country.

Graduate training could be pursued at all universities and selected institutes and polytechnics. Relative to the number of undergraduates, the number of Soviet graduate students was small, about 100,000 in the mid-1980s. Many pursued their studies on a part-time basis while continuing to work in their field.

Two advanced degrees, the candidate of science and the doctor of science (*kandidat nauk* and *doktor nauk*), were available. To be admitted to a course of study for the candidate degree, applicants had to pass competitive examinations in a foreign language, philosophy (primarily Marxism-Leninism), and the field of specialization. Completion of this degree required three years of course work, training and research, and a dissertation dealing with an original topic and representing a significant contribution to the given field. The thesis had to be defended publicly before an academic panel and was published. In the 1980s, about 500,000 specialists, primarily university and institute faculty staff and members of the scientific and research community, held candidate degrees. These degrees might be equated to the master's and doctor of philosophy degrees in the United States, depending on the specialization and the institution attended.

A much smaller group (fewer than 45,000) of scholars and scientists held a doctor of science degree, also commonly called a *doktorat*. It was conferred on a selective basis to well-established experts whose considerable research and publications represented original major contributions to their specialized areas. Doctoral work was generally part of the individual's professional or teaching activity. A one-year paid leave of absence was granted for the writing and defense of a doctoral thesis. The doctorate was also sometimes conferred for outstanding past achievements. According to Vadim Medish, holders of this advanced degree represented "the elite of the Soviet scientific establishment and academe."

Teacher Training

Soviet society generally held the teaching profession in high esteem, continuing the long prerevolutionary tradition, although teachers' salaries were not commensurate in this regard. With starting pay as low as 140 to 150 rubles per month (compared with the average worker's salary of 200 rubles), teachers' salaries, especially at the primary and secondary school levels, were on the lower rungs of the pay scale. The most common Western explanation for this disparity was the preponderance of women in the field. In 1987 nearly three-fourths of the more than 2.6 million secondary school teachers and school directors were women. Among secondary school teachers, 77.7 percent had completed higher education, 16.3 percent had completed secondary school teacher training, 3.5 percent had completed a portion of their higher education, and 2.5 percent had completed specialized or general secondary education.

In the 1986–87 school year, more than 2 million students were enrolled in teacher training programs in about 400 specialized secondary-school teachers' schools and more than 200 pedagogical institutes. Teacher training focused on the chosen specialty; a significant amount of time was devoted to the study of Marxism-Leninism, as well as courses in education and applied psychology. Because the university curriculum included courses in teaching methodology, university graduates also often taught upper-level secondary grades.

The salaries and prestige of teachers at universities, institutions of higher learning, and specialized secondary schools were considerably higher than those of general secondary-school teachers. About 750,000 professors and instructors, of whom only about one-third were women, belonged to this elite group of professionals.

Quality, Reform, and Funding

A "report card" for Soviet education in the 1980s based on comments from government leaders, educators, and rank-and-file teachers, as well as from the public at large, indicated the schools were failing in serious ways. The picture that emerged from articles published in the Soviet press revealed inadequate facilities, crowded classrooms, and schools operating on two- and even three-shift schedules. Shortages of school materials and equipment were serious. The quality of teaching was often low. These deficiencies were particularly acute in rural areas and in the Soviet Central Asian republics. Abuses, such as cheating by students and grade inflation by many teachers, were widespread as well. The schools were failing to meet the nation's labor needs: shortages of adequately skilled workers existed in almost every sector of the economy, and, although institutions of higher learning were graduating large numbers of engineers and specialists, their training was theoretical and narrow and lacked practical applicability. These limitations, together with excessive bureaucracy, led to poor performance (see The Administration of Science and Technology, ch. 16). Industrial accidents, most notably the Chernobyl' nuclear power plant accident, were openly attributed to inappropriate training and technical incompetence.

The schools were failing as well in the task of inculcating youth with Marxist-Leninist ideals and socialist morality. Young people were becoming increasingly cynical about official ideology; they were motivated more and more by the pursuits of material things, personal comforts, societal status, and privilege. Moreover, the school system's emphasis on uniformity and conformity, rote learning, and memorization quashed students' creativity and the development of critical thinking and individual responsibility.

The 1984 reform of the general and vocational schools together with the 1986 reform of higher and specialized secondary education aimed at fundamental *perestroika* (restructuring) and *demokratizatsiia* (democratization) of the education system. The Soviet leadership saw the role of teachers as central to this endeavor; in addition to increased wages, they promised that teachers would have greater autonomy and flexibility and that the ''command mentality, formalism, and overbureaucratization'' produced by the multilayered administrative bureaucracies would be eradicated. Articles in the official Soviet press called for the ''teacher-creator'' to take the ''path of freedom,'' with a ''freely searching mind . . . tied to no one and to no thing.''

Implementation of these reforms would require major increases in funding, which in the mid-1980s was about 12 billion rubles for general secondary schools. The state spent about 1,200 rubles per student for higher education and 780 rubles for secondary specialized study. Calling allocation of less than 8 percent of a nation's income to education a sign of societal degradation, Soviet education specialists expressed alarm that the country was currently allocating only about 4 percent of its national income to its schools. But the greater, and perhaps insurmountable, obstacle to genuine reform of education in the 1980s remained the overriding importance assigned to ideological purity in all aspects of schooling.

Health Care

The Soviet system of socialized medicine, introduced during the Stalin era, emphasized ''quantitative'' expansion. The system was driven by three basic underlying principles: provision by government health institutions of readily available and free, qualified medical care to all citizens; an emphasis on the prevention of illness; and the related goal of guaranteeing a healthy labor force for the nation's economy. Indeed, the individual citizen's health was viewed not only as a personal matter "but as part of the national wealth."

In the mid-1980s, the government operated a huge network of neighborhood and work site clinics to provide readily accessible primary care and large hospitals and polyclinic complexes for diagnosis and treatment of more complicated illnesses and for surgery. Health care facilities included numerous women's consultation centers and pediatric clinics, emergency ambulance services, and sanatoriums and rest homes for extended and short-term therapy and relaxation. Psychiatric care remained the most outdated and abuse-ridden area of the country's medical system.

The mid-1980s were marked by growing concern on the part of officials and the public over the serious decline in the country's health and the low quality of medical services available to the general populace. In addition to Gorbachev's war against alcoholism, which was seen as a principal contributing factor in increased male mortality rates, reforms in the 1980s called for eliminating overbureaucratization of medical services, improving medical training and salaries, expanding fee-for-service care, and significantly increasing funding to improve the quality of health care nationwide.

Provision of Medical Care

Having emphasized quantitative expansion of medical services, the Soviet Union, by the 1980s, took first place worldwide with respect to the number of hospital beds and physicians per 10,000 people and had in place a huge network of hospitals, polyclinics, consultation centers, and emergency first-aid stations throughout the country. As in the education system, administration and control of these numerous medical facilities was carried out by a centralized, hierarchically structured government apparatus. In cooperation and consultation with CPSU organs, the Ministry of Health set basic policies and plans for the entire nationwide health care system. These in turn were transmitted through the administrative chain of command, starting with the republic-level health ministries down through the territorial, regional, district, municipal, and local levels.

In coordination with Gosplan, the Ministry of Health developed nationwide annual programs for all aspects of health care services. The ministry's planning effort reflected an overwhelming concern "with numbers and complex formulas," such as setting norms, standards, and quotas with virtually no flexibility, spelling out the number of new 1,000-bed hospitals to be built, the number of patient visits and medical exams to be performed, and even the number of sutures per given type and size of laceration.

The numerous administrative entities and planning offices spawned a huge bureaucracy, with all the attendant problems of overbureaucratization, red tape, and paper deluge. Most affected and afflicted were physicians, who devoted 50 percent of their time to filling out medical forms and documentation.

A large portion of the Soviet annual health care budget (about 18 billion rubles) was allotted to construction of a vast and complex network of medical facilities, including polyclinics, consultation and dispensary centers, emergency first-aid stations and ambulance services, hospitals, and sanatoriums. In 1986 more than 40,000 polyclinics provided primary medical care on an outpatient basis. They ranged in size from huge urban complexes staffed by hundreds of physicians and responsible for the health care needs of up to 50,000 people, to small rural clinics consisting of several examination rooms and three or four doctors, whose training was often at the physician's assistant or paramedic (*fel'dsher*) level.

Generally, the first place turned to for medical assistance was the polyclinic. Individuals and families were assigned to a specific polyclinic, based on their place of residence, and could not choose their physician within the polyclinic system. Outpatient services stressed prevention and provided only the most basic medical treatment, including preliminary diagnosis and evaluation by a general practitioner or internist (*tevrapet*). If the patient's condition was determined to be a more serious or complicated one (hypertension, heart disease, or cancer, for example), the individual usually was referred to another specialist and/or was hospitalized for more extensive diagnosis and treatment. The polyclinic system was delivering 90 percent of the country's medical care in the 1980s.

An important facet of medical care was the provision of services at the place of work, reflecting the country's focus on maintaining a healthy labor force. Large production enterprises (see Glossary), factories, and plants, as well as many other institutions, such as research facilities and universities, had their own clinics or medical units. The railroad workers' union operated its own autonomous health care system, including rest homes and sanatoriums.

Consonant with the nation's concern with worker productivity and loss of valuable production time, workplace clinics allowed workers to get medical attention without leaving the work site. They also monitored and controlled worker absenteeism through issuance of sick leave certificates. In 1986 approximately 4 million workers (about 3 percent of the total work force) were on sick leave each

Schoolchildren in Vyborg, Russian Republic
Courtesy Jimmy Pritchard

day; about 700,000 of them, mostly women, stayed home to care for sick children.

Nationwide, in 1986 there were 23,500 hospitals with more than 3.6 million beds. In an effort to eliminate duplication of medical services by combining general and specialized hospital care, beginning in the mid-1970s the Ministry of Health began building large urban hospital complexes that provided specialized care in the hospital and on an outpatient basis. A 1,600-bed hospital was built in Novosibirsk; Rostov-na-Donu had a 1,700-bed hospital tower; huge multidepartment hospitals appeared in other cities as well.

Although the thrust of hospital care was to provide diagnosis and treatment of more complicated health problems and to provide facilities for surgery, people suffering from such minor illnesses as influenza or gastroenteritis were often hospitalized. This exacerbated the already serious crowding problem in hospitals despite the large number of hospital beds per capita. The situation stemmed in part from official specification of exact periods of hospitalization for each and every type of medical problem, for example, ten days for childbirth, appendectomy, or gallbladder surgery; two weeks for a hysterectomy; and eight weeks for a heart attack. These prescribed "recovery" periods were strictly adhered to, even when the patient clearly no longer needed further hospital care. In the early 1980s, one-quarter of the population was hospitalized each year. The average hospital stay was 15 days, with a nationwide average of 2.8 hospital days per person per year (the average hospital stay in the United States was 5 days, with 1.2 hospital days per person per year).

The propensity for medically unwarranted, extended hospitalizations reflected old-fashioned practice, the inefficiency of hospitals (for example, delays in diagnostic tests caused by excessive paperwork and shortages in medical equipment), and the difficulty for patients to recover at home because of crowded living conditions. In addition, patients tended to prefer hospitalization to curative treatment in the clinics because hospitals were generally better equipped and better staffed.

A pivotal concern of the public health system was the care and treatment of women and children. More than 28,000 women's consultation centers, children's polyclinics, and pediatric hospital facilities focused on prevention and cure of women's and children's health problems. A number of institutes of pediatrics, obstetrics, and gynecology conducted research to improve diagnosis and treatment of disease and contribute to overall health and well-being, especially of pregnant women, infants, and young children. All maternity services were free, and women were encouraged to obtain regular prenatal care; expectant mothers visited maternity clinics and consultation centers on an average of fourteen to sixteen times. About 5 percent of physicians specialized in obstetrics and gynecology. Women had ready access to free routine examinations, Pap smears, and prenatal care. Abortions were also available on demand but sometimes required a small fee.

The Ministry of Health operated an extensive network of emergency first-aid facilities. This ''rapid medical assistance'' (*skoraia meditsinskaia pomoshch'*) system consisted of more than 5,000 emergency first-aid stations and included 7,700 specialized ambulance teams. Dialing ''03'' on any telephone (pay telephones did not require the usual 2 kopek coin) called out an ambulance (*skoraia*, as it was popularly called). Most often ambulances were equipped with only the barest first-aid basics: stretcher, splints and fracture boards, oxygen equipment. But specialized antitrauma ambulances with portable equipment, such as an electrocardiograph, electric heart defibrillator, and anesthesia equipment were available for major emergencies. After administration of first aid, patients with major medical problems or severe trauma were taken to special emergency hospitals because most regular hospitals were not equipped with emergency rooms. In the early 1980s, the average ambulance arrival time was eight minutes in Moscow and eleven in Leningrad.

Rounding out the nation's health care system, and giving it a uniquely Soviet coloration, was the country's large network of sanatoriums, rest homes, and health resorts, which was both an integral part of Soviet health care and extremely popular among the people. Labor unions controlled about 80 percent of the sanatoriums; generally, a person's place of work granted the highly desirable *putevka* (ticket) to such facilities. Some sanatoriums were specialized, providing therapy for children, diabetics, or hypertensives; many health resorts offered mud baths, mineral springs, and herbal therapies; all of them offered a much-welcomed period of rest and recreation in pleasant natural surroundings along seacoasts and in forests with fresh air. Demand for such facilities, dubbed "functional equivalents of tranquilizers" by one Western observer, far exceeded availability. In 1986 over 15,800 sanatoriums and rest homes served more than 50.3 million people, less than 20 percent of the population.

The most outdated and abuse-ridden area of health protection was the system of psychiatric services. In the mid-1980s, psychiatric care continued to operate primarily on the outdated principles on which it was originally based in the 1950s: Pavlovian (conditioned-response) psychology, a black-and-white approach to diagnosis of mental illness, heavy reliance on psychotropic drug therapies, very little practice of individual or group counseling, and an emphasis on work as the best form of treatment and therapy. The average citizen avoided seeking psychiatric help, convinced it was "better to suffer" than have one's life ruined—an almost certain outcome of Soviet psychiatric clinics and services.

Among the corrupt practices (including bribery and blatant disregard of individual rights), the gravest and most infamous abuses in Soviet psychiatric medicine were political, namely, using mental hospitals as prisons for political dissenters. Along with schizophrenics and violent prisoners, dissenters were institutionalized in special psychiatric hospital-prisons operated by the Ministry of Internal Affairs (see The Ministry of Internal Affairs, ch. 19). Anyone who actively disagreed with the official Soviet ideology could be easily and swiftly declared "insane" by a committee of psychiatrists, locked up in a mental institution, and subjected to compulsory treatment with powerful, at times permanently damaging, psychotropic drugs. In the mid-1980s, estimates of the total number of political prisoners in Soviet psychiatric facilities numbered from 1,000 to several thousand.

A harbinger of possible reform of the psychiatric system came in January 1988 with the issuance of a decree by the Presidium of the Supreme Soviet transferring the special psychiatric hospitals from the Ministry of Internal Affairs to the Ministry of Health, which operated a system of regular psychiatric hospitals and polyclinics. A number of government-sponsored private psychiatric clinics offered slightly better levels of therapy and counseling, for a fee.

In 1985 Soviet officials began publishing limited statistics on the incidence of mental illness among the population, reporting 335 cases of schizophrenia per 100,000 people and over 1.3 million children suffering from mental retardation. A total of 335,200 hospital beds were devoted to psychiatric care in 1986, compared with 863,000 for general medicine, 526,900 for surgery, and 411,500 for pediatrics.

Between 1960 and 1986, the number of physicians and dentists increased from 400,000 to 1.2 million, and mid-level personnel increased from 1.4 to 3.2 million. Medical training for physicians (*vrachi*) required six or seven years. The emphasis was on practical training with little exposure to basic research or pure science (of ninety-two medical institutes, only nine were attached to universities). Beginning in the 1970s, specialization began early, in the third year, and became increasingly more narrow, resulting in a serious decline in the number and quality of general or family practitioners. The majority of doctors were women. As was the case in teaching and other social services areas, their salaries were low (in the mid-1980s, physicians earned about 180 to 200 rubles per month compared with 200 rubles per month for industrial workers).

Mid-level medical personnel included physician's assistants, or paramedics, midwives, and nurses. These categories required only two years of practical training and little or no scientific background. These mid-level health practitioners frequently served as physician surrogates in rural areas, where the shortage of trained physicians was serious.

Although the underlying principle of Soviet socialized medicine was equality of care and access, the reality was a multitiered, highly stratified system of care and facilities. The disparity between the services provided to the general populace and to special groups was great. The so-called "fourth department" of the Ministry of Health operated a separate network of clinics, hospitals, and sanatoriums exclusively for top party and government officials as well as for other elite groups, such as writers, musicians, artists, and actors. These special facilities were far superior to those found in ordinary health care networks. They provided the best care, were staffed by top-ranking physicians, and had the latest equipment, including Western-made modern diagnostic and treatment units. The medical care available in cities, which tended to have the better equipped hospitals and clinics, differed considerably from that available in rural areas, which often lacked specially constructed medical facilities.

Similarly, although in principle health care was free, citizens often paid money or gave bribes to receive better treatment. Moreover, hospital patients routinely paid for basic services, such as changes of bed linen and meals.

Declining Health Care in the 1970s and 1980s

After Evgenii Chazov became the minister of health in February 1987 and Gorbachev's policy of *glasnost'* was extended to the realm of health care, Soviet authorities finally acknowledged what Western observers had suspected for some time, namely, that major health indicators depicted a disturbing picture of the nation's health. Statistics for the 1970s and 1980s showed rising infant mortality rates, falling life expectancy (particularly among the male population), increases in infectious diseases, rises in sexually transmitted illnesses, and a high rate of new cases of tuberculosis among children and adolescents.

Statistics on the major causes of death were not published for the total population but were published for the working-age group (sixteen to fifty-nine for men and sixteen to fifty-four for women). In 1986 the greatest number of deaths among those of working age (the total number of deaths was 401 per 100,000) was caused by cardiovascular disease (120 per 100,000); accidents, poisoning, and traumas (109 per 100,000); cancer (94 per 100,000); and lung disease (20 per 100,000). On a population-wide basis, official Soviet sources ranked the major causes of death somewhat differently: cardiovascular diseases, malignant tumors, and accidents and injuries. Statistics on sex-specific death rates and cause of death by age-group have not been published since the early 1970s.

A key contributing factor in the major causes of death, particularly among the male population, was the high level of alcoholism—a long-standing problem, especially among the Slavic peoples (Russian, Ukrainian, and Belorussian). Alcoholism was often referred to as the "third disease," after cardiovascular illness and cancer. Soviet health organizations and police records put the total number of alcoholics at over 4.5 million, but Western experts contended that this number applied only to those at the most advanced stage of alcoholism and that in 1987 the real number of alcoholics was at least 20 million.

Soon after coming to power, Gorbachev launched the most massive antialcohol campaign in Soviet history and voiced his concern not only about the health problems stemming from alcohol abuse but also about the losses in labor productivity (up to 15 percent) and the increased divorce rate. The drive appeared to have an almost immediate effect on the incidence of diseases directly related to alcohol: for example, cirrhosis of the liver and alcohol poisoning decreased from 47.3 per 1,000 in 1984 to 23.3 per 1,000 in 1986. The biggest declines were in the Russian and Ukrainian republics, where the problem was the most widespread. Some attributed the modest rise in male life expectancy between 1985 and 1986 to success in the battle against the "green snake," a popular Russian term for vodka. But to counter the major cut in government production of alcohol, people distilled their own alcoholic beverages at home. One-third of illicit alcohol reportedly was produced using government agricultural facilities.

To succeed in the battle against alcoholism, Soviet health care had to expand significantly its alcohol-abuse treatment and education programs. Of particular concern was increased alcohol consumption and another major health problem—smoking—among women and teenagers. The rise in infant mortality, as well as other early childhood disease and abnormalities (8 to 10 percent of children reportedly suffered from congenital or infantile abnormalities), was linked to increased drinking and smoking among females in their childbearing years.

A Soviet statistical study (based on a 1987 survey of 62,000 families) indicated that about 70 million people smoked—nearly 70 percent of men and nearly 5 percent of women more than eighteen years of age. Although an antismoking campaign was also under way in the 1980s, it was on a much smaller scale than the campaign against alcohol, and the government did far less to decrease production of tobacco products. In fact, output reached 441 billion cigarettes in 1987, which was an increase of 23 percent over 1970 production.

In addition to increased infant mortality rates in the 1970s and 1980s, the Caucasian and Central Asian republics experienced a rise in infectious diseases, such as typhoid fever and other gastrointestinal illnesses, and viral hepatitis. Poor sanitation and contaminated water supplies were largely responsible for outbreaks of typhoid fever and other gastrointestinal infections; the lack of disposable syringes was blamed for the upsurge in hepatitis infections.

Deteriorating environmental factors, crowded living conditions, and poor nutrition were seen as principal contributors to negative health trends. But the low quality of health care available to the general populace was a major culprit and stemmed in large measure from the widespread lack of modern medical equipment, technology, and pharmaceuticals. For example, the low life expectancy, particularly for males, was linked in part to the lack of medical equipment needed to perform bypass surgery and angioplasty procedures in the treatment of heart disease. Indeed, deaths from cardiovascular diseases increased from 88 per 100,000 to 120 per 100,000 between 1970 and 1986.

With *glasnost'* came publication in Soviet newspapers of numerous articles and letters—written by physicians as well as by ordinary citizens—highlighting the crisis in the country's health care system. Frequently attacked was the severe shortage of modern medical equipment in medical facilities; for example, women's consultation centers had no fetal heart monitors, ultrasound units, or equipment for monitoring labor and delivery, resulting in thousands of additional infant deaths. Poor training of physicians was singled out as the cause of 600 to 700 deaths of women each year in childbirth and following abortions in the Russian Republic alone. The poor treatment and care of terminally ill cancer patients was openly decried; mentioned were the serious shortage of beds in cancer wards, lack of painkillers, blatant neglect, and absence of compassion from medical staff. The widespread and long-standing practice of exchanging bribes and gifts for slightly better medical care and attention was specifically attacked, as were over-bureaucratization and its major product, "paper fever," and the common practice of falsifying medical statistics to fulfill planned quantitative quotas. People also wrote to newspapers documenting personal tragedies involving the deaths of small children—deaths that need not have happened and that were caused by gross negligence on the part of hospital staff and physicians.

Glasnost' brought into the open other previously taboo subjects, as the press began to publish articles on drug abuse, venereal disease, and even acquired immune deficiency syndrome (AIDS). Drug abuse and venereal disease were reported to be on the rise in some regions of the country, most notably in the Georgian Republic. The number of drug addicts nationwide varied depending upon the official source: the Ministry of Health claimed 50,000; police records documented 130,000 addicts.

In early 1987, the Soviet press began publishing a number of articles about AIDS, referring to the deadly virus by the Russian acronym SPID (*sindrom priobretennogo immunodefitsita*). Although little concrete advice was being made available to the public regarding prevention and high-risk groups, by the summer of 1987 a number of AIDS testing centers had been opened, and a Moscow center reportedly was testing about 100 people each day. Claiming the infection was "imported," Soviet medical authorities required mandatory testing of all foreign students in the country; they also required compulsory testing of suspected Soviet carriers, namely, prostitutes and members of other high-risk groups. In August 1987, the Supreme Soviet passed the strictest anti-AIDS law in the world, making the knowing transmittal of an AIDS infection a criminal offense punishable by up to eight years in prison.

By the time the law was passed, 130 AIDS cases were officially registered; only 19 of these were said to be Soviet citizens. But numerous Soviet sources indicated the actual number of cases was in the thousands; this figure still represented a minuscule percentage of the population compared with AIDS incidence in the United States and other Western countries. Nevertheless, Soviet virology specialists foresaw serious spread of the infection, noting that domestic production of AIDS testing equipment had to be significantly increased. They claimed that the 1987 output of 2 million units was 8 million short of the required number and anticipated that 20 million test sets would be needed within two or three years. Public education about AIDS transmission and infection was hampered by general Soviet prudishness about sex, but of greater importance was the fact that the government ranked homosexual activity and prostitution as criminal offenses punishable by imprisonment, which meant that these high-risk groups were unlikely to cooperate in the battle against AIDS. The chronic shortage of condoms (which Soviet medical officials euphemistically called "Article Number 2") further increased the threat of the spread of AIDS among the Soviet population. But the widespread shortage of disposable hypodermic syringes in hospitals and clinics, which often led to the repeated use of unsterilized needles, posed the greatest danger to checking the spread of AIDS in the Soviet Union. This fact was shockingly demonstrated by the tragic case involving the infection with the AIDS virus of up to forty-one children and eight mothers in late 1988 at a children's hospital in the Kalmyk Autonomous Republic.

Major reforms of the health care system were announced in November 1987, underscoring the growing alarm over the nation's deteriorating health. The reforms reaffirmed the antialcohol and antismoking campaigns and called for improving personal hygiene and physical fitness training of the population in general and of schoolchildren in particular. The reforms stressed improving the quality of care, as opposed to the past practice of quantitative expansion alone, and advocated increasing the salaries and prestige of medical personnel. They called for shifting physician training from the narrow specialization of the past to family or general practice, as well as expansion and improvement in certification of medical school graduates and periodic recertification of practicing physicians. The central role of mid-level medical personnel—such as physician's assistants, nurses, and pharmacists—was reaffirmed, and improvements in the quality of their training were promised. The quality of medical teaching was to be raised by directly involving medical teachers in research and development in the country's leading medical research institutes. The reforms also stressed expansion of biotechnical and other advanced medical research and called for increasing domestic production of the most modern medical equipment, high-quality pharmaceuticals, and biotechnology products.

Special efforts were planned to rectify the low level of health care found in rural areas, where 80 percent of the 18,000 polyclinics and outpatient facilities did not have specially constructed medical buildings. A majority—65 percent—of regional hospitals in rural areas had no hot water supply; 27 percent were not equipped with sanitation systems; and 17 percent had no water supply at all. To correct these serious deficiencies, plans called for construction of more than 14,000 outpatient clinics equipped with pharmacies, as well as living quarters for medical and pharmaceutical personnel. Along with continued emphasis on providing outpatient polyclinic care, a significant expansion—a fivefold increase—of fee-for-services medical care was planned by the year 2000.

The country's need for maternity wards and pediatric facilities was to be met by 1995; the population's outpatient and hospital needs were to be met by the year 2000. To this end, the reforms called for a significant increase—between 100 and 150 percent—in capital expenditures for renovation, equipment, and construction of polyclinics and hospital complexes. A final goal was the establishment by the year 2000 of a "unified system of health care" for the entire population.

To achieve these ambitious goals and to ensure the full health of its population, the Soviet Union would have to increase substantially the level of funding allocated to its health care system. Since the 1960s, the percentage of the gross national product (GNP—see Glossary) spent on health had continuously eroded, dropping from a high of 6.6 percent of GNP in 1960 to about 4 percent in the mid-1980s. (In 1986 the United States spent 11.1 percent; the Federal Republic of Germany [West Germany], 8.1 percent; and Britain, 6.2 percent of GNP for medical services.) According to Minister of Health Chazov, more than 8 percent would be needed to meet fully the medical needs of the entire Soviet population.

273

Welfare

In the 1980s, the Soviet government maintained a comprehensive system of social security and social insurance that included old-age retirement and veterans pensions, disability benefits and sick leave compensation, maternity leave and allowances, and subsidies to multichildren and low-income families. Soviet workers did not contribute directly to their social security and insurance coverage; funding was provided by the government and from compulsory deductions from industrial and agricultural enterprises. Most welfare funds were spent on retirement pensions and disability benefits.

Pension System

In 1987 the Soviet Union had 56.8 million pensioners; of this number, 40.5 million were retired with full pensions on the basis of twenty years of service and age eligibility—sixty for men and fifty-five for women. Reduced pensions were paid to those who met the age eligibility requirement and had worked at least five years, three of them uninterrupted, just prior to retirement. Miners and those working under other arduous or hazardous conditions could retire five to ten years earlier. In 1987 Soviet authorities were reducing the retirement age for other groups as well.

Pensions, on the whole, were quite low. The average monthly pension in 1986 was 75.1 rubles, with considerable disparity between the average monthly pension of blue- and white-collar workers (averaging 81.2 rubles for the two categories of workers) and collective farm workers (48 rubles). In fact, the average pension was only slightly above the unofficial level of poverty—or "underprovisioning" (*maloobespechennost'*)—of 70 rubles per month per person. It was likely that millions of pensioners lived under or close to this poverty threshold. Indeed, pensioners made up the majority of the poor. According to figures published in an official Soviet newspaper, in 1985 a minimum of 13.7 million pensioners were receiving pensions far below 70 rubles per month. About 12 million old-age pensioners continued to work, many of them in extremely low-paying jobs, for example, as cloakroom attendants in restaurants and theaters or sweeping metro station interiors and street pavements. Retirees who lived with their children (a common situation, given the extreme housing shortage) obtained some financial relief and in return helped with housework, cooking, and care of small grandchildren. In 1988 about 1 million pensioners lived alone and were by far the worst off, living in almost total neglect and near destitution.

*Senior citizen resting
in a Moscow park
Courtesy Irene Steckler*

Not all pensions were this low, however. A special category of "personal pensions" could be awarded for outstanding political, cultural, scientific, or economic service to the state. In 1988 over 500,000 personal pensioners, including essentially all of the CPSU administrative elite, were receiving pensions of 250 rubles, and even up to 450 rubles, per month. A separate but similar retirement program, known as long-service pensions, was maintained for some groups of white-collar workers, including teachers, academic and medical personnel, and military retirees. Lowered retirement ages and/or pension augmentations were provided to disabled workers and mothers of large families.

The government operated a small network of homes for the elderly, invalids, and disabled children. In 1986 these "total-care" facilities accommodated 388,000 people, but another 90,000 were on waiting lists.

In 1988–89 the State Committee for Labor and Social Problems (Gosudarstvennyi komitet po trudu i sotsial'nym voprosam—Goskomtrud) was developing a new pension law to replace the outdated laws of 1956 and 1964. Although not expected to become fully effective before 1991, the new law envisioned a guaranteed subsistence wage, a higher ceiling on old-age pensions, and regular cost-of-living increases. Workers could also obtain supplemental pension coverage through a voluntary payroll deduction program introduced in January 1988 and administered by the Main Administration for State Insurance.

275

Workers' Compensation

In the 1980s, workers were covered by disability insurance. Individuals who were permanently disabled as a result of on-the-job injuries received a pension equal to 100 percent of their wages, irrespective of their length of service. Compensation for sickness or injury causing temporary incapacity to work but unrelated to employment required appropriate physician certification of the illness or injury. Benefits depended on length of service: 50 percent of full wages was paid for fewer than three years of uninterrupted work; 80 percent for three to five years; and 100 percent for more than eight years. Service in the armed forces, time spent in party or government posts, and maternity leave were not considered breaks in employment. Sick leave was also paid to workers (usually working mothers) who stayed home to care for ill family members. In 1987 the government extended the period of paid leave for the care of a sick child to fourteen days.

Maternity allowances were fairly generous. Expectant mothers were granted a total of 112 days of maternity leave, 56 days before and 56 days after the birth of a child, with payment of full wages, irrespective of length of employment. The postnatal leave period was extended to seventy days for women who had multiple or abnormal births. Mothers were entitled to unpaid leave up to the child's first birthday, without a break in their employment record and with the guarantee of returning to their original job.

Other Assistance

Since the mid-1940s, the government has provided financial subsidies to mothers with "many children," meaning two or more. This program had three facets: mothers received a lump-sum grant upon the birth of the third and each subsequent child; they received a monthly subsidy upon the birth of the fourth and each subsequent child; and, beginning with the Eleventh Five-Year-Plan (1981–85), one-time maternity grants (50 rubles for the first child and 100 for the second) were given to working women or female students on a leave-of-absence basis. In 1986 the government paid monthly subsidies to almost 2 million mothers having four or more children.

In addition to pensions and financial subsidies, veterans, invalids, and multichildren families received a number of nonmonetary benefits, such as top consideration for housing, telephones, and priority services in shops and restaurants. In 1985 and again in 1987, the Central Committee of the CPSU, the Council of Ministers, and the All-Union Central Council of Trade Unions issued resolutions to improve living conditions of the "underprovisioned," including pensioners, invalids, old people living alone, and single-parent families with three or more children under the age of eighteen and with an average monthly per capita income of 50 rubles (75 rubles in certain regions, for example, the Soviet Far East). This program provided free school, sports, and youth organization uniforms and free breakfasts for children up to the age of sixteen. The resolutions also called for child-support payments by the absent parent of at least 20 rubles per month per child up to the age of eighteen, as well as a government subsidy of 12 rubles per month for each child up to the age of eight. Underprovisioned families were provided free sanatorium and rest-home stays; the children were sent to summer youth camps, as well, at government expense.

Although no official calls for comprehensive restructuring of welfare programs were made, by 1987 and 1988 the policy of *glasnost'* embraced the topic of poverty in the Soviet Union. Numerous articles appeared in the press reflecting a growing concern—on the part of both Soviet officials and the general public—about the number of poor in the Soviet Union, estimated in 1988 to include 20 percent of the population.

The leadership under Gorbachev fully acknowledged the pressing need for improving the quality and availability of education, health care, and welfare services nationwide and seemed genuinely committed to achieving these objectives by the year 2000. But the obstacles to reforms in these spheres were numerous and formidable. The country had to significantly raise funding for these programs, and to do so would require a shift in spending priorities. Moreover, excessive centralization and overbureaucratization in the administration of social services had to be overcome. And the incompatibility of maintaining ideological purity in all aspects of education, on the one hand, and developing in youth the ability to think critically, comparatively, and creatively, on the other hand, had to be reconciled.

* * *

Inside Soviet Schools by Susan Jacoby, an American educator, offers a comprehensive view of the upbringing of Soviet youth from infancy through secondary school. Kitty D. Weaver's *Russia's Future* examines the role of the youth organizations (Young Octobrists, Pioneers, and Komsomol) in the education process. *The Making of the Soviet Citizen,* edited by George Avis, covers school reforms of the 1980s, the dual concept of character formation and formal

277

education, the role of political indoctrination, and vocational training. *Soviet Politics and Education* by Frank M. Sorrentino and Frances R. Curcio, includes several articles dealing with the role of ideology and political indoctrination in Soviet education. Vadim Medish's *The Soviet Union* provides an excellent chapter on the education system, from the nursery school level through the university level. *Inside Russian Medicine* by William A. Knaus, M.D., an American physician who observed Soviet health care first hand, covers polyclinic and hospital care, emergency services, and psychiatric treatment. *The Medical and Pharmaceutical Sectors of the Soviet Economy* by Christopher Davis discusses the organization and financing of medical care, the medical industry, pharmaceuticals, and foreign trade in medical products. *Economic Welfare in the Soviet Union* by Alastair McAuley discusses the historical background, organization, eligibility requirements, and payments provided by Soviet welfare programs. *Poverty in the Soviet Union* by Mervyn Matthews includes some recent information on old-age pensions and child support payment. Matthews also discusses these topics in his article ''Aspects of Poverty in the Soviet Union.'' (For further information and complete citations, see Bibliography.)

Chapter 7. The Communist Party

Clockwise from bottom: Gorbachev, Brezhnev, Khrushchev, and Stalin

THE COMMUNIST PARTY of the Soviet Union (CPSU) governs the Union of Soviet Socialist Republics (Soviet Union). In 1917 the party seized power in Russia as the vanguard of the working class, and it has continued throughout the Soviet period to rule in the name of the proletariat. The party seeks to lead the Soviet people to communism, defined by Karl Marx as a classless society that contains limitless possibilities for human achievement. Toward this end, the party has sought to effect a cultural revolution and create a "new Soviet man" bound by the strictures of a higher, socialist morality.

The party's goals require that it control all aspects of Soviet government and society in order to infuse political, economic, and social policies with the correct ideological content. Vladimir I. Lenin, the founder of the Bolshevik (see Glossary) party and the leader of the Bolshevik Revolution, justified these controls. Lenin formed a party of professional revolutionaries to effect a proletarian revolution in Russia. In the late 1980s, however, the party no longer sought to transform society and was apparently attempting to withdraw itself from day-to-day economic decisions. Nevertheless, it continued to exert control through professional management. Members of the party bureaucracy are full-time, paid officials. Other party members hold full-time positions in government, industry, education, the armed forces, and elsewhere. In addition, Lenin argued that the party alone possesses the correct understanding of Marxist ideology. Thus, state policies that lack an ideological foundation threaten to retard society's advance toward communism. Hence, only policies sanctioned by the party can contribute to this goal. Lenin's position justifies party jurisdiction over the state. The CPSU enforces its authority over state bodies from the all-union (see Glossary) level to that of the district and town. In the office, factory, and farm, the party has established its primary party organizations (PPOs) to carry out its directives.

The role of ideology in the political system and the party's efforts to enforce controls on society demonstrate the party leadership's continuing efforts to forge unity in the party as well as among the Soviet people. Democratic centralism, the method of intraparty decision making, directs lower party bodies unconditionally to execute the decisions of higher party bodies. Party forums from the town and district levels up to the Central Committee bring together party, government, trade union, and economic elites to create a desired consensus among policy makers. Party training, particularly for officials of the CPSU's permanent bureaucracy, shapes a common understanding of problems and apprises students of the party's current approaches to ideology, foreign affairs, and domestic policy. Party training efforts demand particular attention because of the varied national, class, and educational experiences of CPSU members.

The party exercises authority over the government and society in several ways. The CPSU has acquired legitimacy for its rule; that is, the people acknowledged the party's right to govern them. This legitimacy derives from the party's incorporation of elites from all parts of society into its ranks, the party's depiction of itself as the representative of the forces for progress in the world, and the party's postulated goal of creating a full communist society. Paradoxically, the party's legitimacy is enhanced by the inclusion of certain prerevolutionary Russian traditions into its political style, which provides a sense of continuity with the past. A different source of authority lies in the power of PPO secretaries to implement party policies on the lowest rungs of the Soviet economy. The CPSU obligates members participating in nonparty organizations to meet regularly and ensure that their organizations fulfill the directives the party has set for them. Finally, as part of the *nomenklatura* system, the party retains appointment power for influential positions at all levels of the government hierarchy (higher party bodies hold this power over lower party bodies as well). Taken together, the legitimacy accorded to it and the prerogatives it possesses enable the party to perform its leading role within the Soviet political system.

Lenin's Conception of the Party

The origins of the CPSU lie in the political thought and tactical conceptions of Lenin, who sought to apply Marxism to economically backward, politically autocratic Russia. Toward this end, Lenin sought to build a highly disciplined, monolithic party of professional revolutionaries that was to act as the general staff of the proletarian movement in Russia. Lenin argued that this underground party must subject all aspects of the movement to its control so that the actions of the movement might be guided by the party's understanding of Marxist theory rather than by spontaneous responses to economic and political oppression. Lenin envisaged democratic centralism as the method of internal party decision making best able to combine discipline with the decentralization necessary to allow lower party organs to adapt to local conditions. Democratic centralism calls for free discussion of alternatives, a vote on the matter at hand, and iron submission of the minority to the majority once a decision is taken. As time passed, however, centralism gained sway over democracy, allowing the leadership to assume dictatorial control over the party.

Theoretical Underpinnings

Lenin's ideas about the proletarian revolutionary party differed from the ideas of Marx. According to Marx, the working class, merely by following its own instincts, would gain rational insight into its plight as the downtrodden product of capitalism. Based on that insight, Marx held, the workers would bring about a revolution leading to their control over the means of production. Further, Marx predicted that the seizure by the proletariat of the means of production (land and factories) would lead to a tremendous increase in productive forces. Freedom from want, said Marx, would liberate men's minds. This liberation would usher in a cultural revolution and the formation of a new personality with unlimited creative possibilities.

As he surveyed the European milieu in the late 1890s, Lenin found several problems with the Marxism of his day. Contrary to what Marx had predicted, capitalism had strengthened itself over the last third of the nineteenth century. The working class in western Europe had not become impoverished; rather, its prosperity had risen. Hence, the workers and their unions, although continuing to press for better wages and working conditions, failed to develop the revolutionary class consciousness that Marx had expected. Lenin also argued that the division of labor in capitalist society prevented the emergence of proletarian class consciousness. Lenin wrote that because workers had to labor ten or twelve hours each workday in a factory, they had no time to learn the complexities of Marxist theory. Finally, in trying to effect revolution in autocratic Russia, Lenin also faced the problem of a regime that had outlawed almost all political activities. Although the autocracy could not enforce a ban on political ideas, until 1905—when the tsar agreed to the formation of a national duma (see Glossary)—the tsarist police suppressed all groups seeking political change, including those with a democratic program.

Based on his observations, Lenin shifted the engine of proletarian revolution from the working class to a tightly knit party of intellectuals. Lenin wrote in *What Is to Be Done* (1902) that the "history of all countries bears out the fact that through their own powers alone, the working class can develop only a trade-union consciousness." That is, history had demonstrated that the working class could engage in local, spontaneous rebellions to improve its position within the capitalist system but that it lacked the understanding of its interests necessary to overthrow that system. Pessimistic about the proletariat's ability to acquire class consciousness, Lenin argued that the bearers of this consciousness were déclassé intellectuals who made it their vocation to conspire against the capitalist system and prepare for the dictatorship of the proletariat. Lenin also held that because Marx's thought was set forth in a sophisticated body of philosophical, economic, and social analysis, a high level of intellectual training was required to comprehend it. Hence, for Lenin, those who would bring about the revolution must devote all their energies and resources to understanding the range of Marx's thought. They must be professional activists having no other duties that might interfere with their efforts to promote revolution.

Lenin's final alteration of Marx's thought arose in the course of his adaptation of Marxist ideology to the conditions of Russia's autocracy. Like other political organizations seeking change in Russia, Lenin's organization had to use conspiratorial methods and operate underground. Lenin argued for the necessity of confining membership in his organization to those who were professionally trained in the art of combating the secret police.

The ethos of Lenin's political thought was to subject first the party, then the working class, and finally the people to the politically conscious revolutionaries. Only actions informed by consciousness could promote revolution and the construction of socialism and communism in Russia.

The CPSU continues to regard itself as the institutionalization of Marxist-Leninist consciousness in the Soviet Union, and therein lies the justification for the controls it exercises over Soviet society. Article 6 of the 1977 Soviet Constitution refers to the party as the "leading and guiding force of Soviet society and the nucleus of its political system, of all state organizations and public organizations." The party, precisely because it is the bearer of Marxist-Leninist ideology, determines the general development of society, directs domestic and foreign policy, and "imparts a planned, systematic, and theoretically substantiated character" to the struggle of the Soviet people for the victory of communism.

Democratic Centralism

Democratic centralism involves several interrelated principles: the election of all leadership organs of the party from bottom to top; periodic accounting of party organs before their membership and before superior organs; strict party discipline and the subordination of the minority to the majority; unconditional obligation

Lenin Mausoleum, Red Square, Moscow
House where Lenin was born, Ulyanovsk
(formerly Simbirsk), Russian Republic
Courtesy Jimmy Pritchard

285

by lower party bodies to carry out decisions made by higher party bodies; a collective approach to the work of all organizations and leadership organs of the party; and the personal responsibility of all communists to implement party directives.

According to American specialist on Soviet affairs Alfred G. Meyer, democratic centralism is primarily centralism under a thin veil of democracy. Democratic centralism requires unanimity on the part of the membership. The concept requires full discussion of policy alternatives before the organization, as guided by the leadership, makes a decision. Once an alternative has been voted upon, however, the decision must be accepted by all. In principle, dissent is possible, but it is allowed only before a decision becomes party policy. After the party makes a decision, party norms discourage criticism of the manner of execution because such criticism might threaten the party's leading role in Soviet society.

The principles of democratic centralism contradict one another. One contradiction concerns the locus of decision making. Democratic centralism prescribes a collective approach to the work of all organizations, which connotes participation of all party members in decision making. Yet, democratic centralism also holds that criticism of agreed-upon policies is permissible only for the top leadership, not for rank-and-file party members. Hence, discussion of these policies can take place only after the leadership has decided to permit it. The leadership will not allow discussions of failed policies, for fear that such discussions will undermine its power and authority.

A second contradiction concerns the issue of accountability. Democratic centralism holds that lower party bodies elect higher party bodies and that the latter are accountable to the former. Nevertheless, democratic centralism also prescribes the unconditional subordination of lower party bodies to higher party bodies. In reality, superiors appoint those who nominally elect them to their positions and tell them what decisions to make (see Nomenklatura, this ch.).

Democratic centralism undermines intraparty democracy because the party has formally proscribed factions. The Tenth Party Congress in 1921 adopted a "temporary" ban on factions in response to the Kronshtadt Rebellion (see Revolutions and Civil War, ch. 2). In 1989 this ban remained in effect. Every party member has the right to express an opinion in the party organization to which he or she belongs. Before a decision is taken, however, party members cannot appeal to other members in support of a given position. Moreover, party members cannot engage in vote trading. In democratic systems, a party member holding a minority position

*Banner across a Moscow
street reflects the regime's
policies in 1989.
It reads, "PERESTROIKA,
DEMOKRATIZATSIIA,
GLASNOST'."
Courtesy Jonathan Tetzlaff*

*May Day banner
depicting Lenin,
Engels, and Marx,
Red Square, Moscow
Courtesy Jimmy Pritchard*

on an issue can exercise influence if allowed to organize people with similar views and if allowed the opportunity to persuade others. Without these opportunities, democratic procedures remain an empty formality.

Devoid of democratic content, the political and organizational logic of democratic centralism contributed to the emergence of dictatorship in the Soviet Union. Despite the formal ban, in the early 1920s factions emerged in the party because Lenin failed to work out orderly procedures for leadership succession (see The Era of the New Economic Policy, ch. 2). In the absence of these procedures, new leaders had to attempt to cloak their policies in the mantle of ideological orthodoxy. To prevent criticism from rivals, the new leader could label real and potential opponents a faction and, according to the *Party Rules* (see Glossary), which banned factions, take steps to remove them from the party. For example, Nikita S. Khrushchev took these steps against his opponents in 1957 (see Collective Leadership and the Rise of Khrushchev, ch. 2). The leader thus could eliminate real and potential rivals, but ultimately, however, only success in action could prove a leader's policies correct. Success in action required the commitment of the party, and commitment of the party demanded that ordinary party members perceive that the leader possessed infallible judgment. Democratic centralism provided a necessary condition for the leader's claim to infallibility because it prevented ordinary party members from criticizing the policies of the party elite.

Party Legitimacy

Western political scientists define legitimacy as the acceptance by the people of their government's right to rule. Legitimacy emerges from a broad range of sources. In democratic countries, the citizenry holds governments legitimate because citizens participate in the selection of their rulers, and these governments are subject to laws that the people or their representatives have made. Tradition also is a persuasive source of legitimation because it places the origins of institutions and political values in a distant and mythical past. Other governments may acquire legitimacy because they have proved themselves able to ensure the well-being of their people. Legitimacy also may emanate from an ideology (such as communism, fascism, religious orthodoxy, and nationalism) whose adherents portray it as the key to understanding human history and resolving all social problems. In reality, the legitimacy of any government emanates from a combination of these sources.

The legitimacy of the CPSU, too, derived from various sources. The party has managed to recruit a significant percentage of members having occupations carrying high status in Soviet society. In addition, the party has served as a vehicle of upward mobility for a significant share of the citizenry. By joining the party, members of the working class could ensure a secure future for themselves in the political apparatus and access for their children to a good education and high-status jobs. The party also justified its right to rule by claiming to embody the "science" of Marxism-Leninism and by its efforts to lead society to full communism. In addition, the CPSU appealed to the patriotism of the citizenry. In the more than seventy years of the party's rule, the Soviet Union has emerged as a superpower, and this international status is a source of pride for the Soviet people. Finally, tradition bolstered the legitimacy of the CPSU. The party located its roots in Russian history, and it has incorporated aspects of Russian tradition into its political style.

The CPSU is an elite body. In 1989 it comprised about 9.7 percent of the adult population of the Soviet Union. Among the "movers and shakers" of society, however, the percentage of party members was much higher. In the 1980s, approximately 27 percent of all citizens over thirty years of age and with at least ten years of education were members of the party. About 44 percent of all males over thirty with at least ten years of education belonged to the CPSU. Hence, in the words of American Soviet specialist Seweryn Bialer, males over thirty with at least an elementary education formed a "strong, politicized, and involved stratum which provides a buttress of the system's legitimacy within society."

Among certain occupations, party saturation (the percentage of party members among a given group of citizens) was even higher. In 1989 some occupations were restricted to party members. These positions included officers of youth organizations, senior military officers, and officials of government bodies such as the ministries, state committees, and administrative departments. Occupations with saturation rates ranging from 20 to 50 percent included positions as mid-level economic managers, scholars and academics, and hospital directors. Low saturation existed among jobs that carried low status and little prestige, such as industrial laborers, collective farmers, and teachers. Thus, the party could represent itself as a legitimate governing body because it commanded the talents of the most talented and ambitious citizens in society.

The CPSU derived some legitimacy from the fact that it acted as a vehicle for upward mobility in society. People who have entered the party apparatus since the 1930s have come from a working-class background. The party widely publicized the working-class origins of its membership, which led members of that class to believe they could enter the elite and be successful within it (see Social Composition of the Party, this ch.).

Another source of party legitimacy lay in Marxist-Leninist ideology, which both promises an absolute good—communism—as the goal of history and shrouds its understanding of the means to that goal with the aura of science. The party justified its rule as leading to the creation of a full communist society. Hence, the CPSU claimed that the purpose of its rule was the common good and not the enrichment of the rulers. The party also identified Marxism-Leninism and the policies that it developed on the basis of this ideology with the absolute truth of science. The CPSU maintained that the laws of this science hold with the same rigor in society as the laws of physics or chemistry in nature. In part, the party justified its rule by claiming that it alone could understand this science of society.

Soviet society has not reached full communism, and so the party has altered its ideology to ensure its continued legitimacy despite the inability to fulfill the promises contained in Marxism-Leninism. One modification has been the rejection of some of Marxism-Leninism's original ideological tenets. For example, in the early 1930s the party renounced an egalitarian wage structure. A second modification has been the indefinite postponement of goals that cannot be realized. Thus, the party continued to assure the populace that the achievement of economic abundance or the completion of proletarian revolutions in developed Western countries would take place, but it did not specify a date. A third modification has been the ritualization of some of the goals whose fulfillment the party has postponed. American scholar Barrington Moore has written that on party holidays CPSU leaders reaffirmed various ideals that no longer served as guides for policy. For example, in his first public address as general secretary in 1984, Konstantin U. Chernenko averred that concern for the development of the new Soviet man remained an essential part of the CPSU's program. In the late 1980s, few accorded that goal much practical import, but the reaffirmation of that objective probably reassured the party faithful that the new leadership would remain true to the CPSU's ideology and traditions.

The party attempted to strengthen its legitimacy with appeals to the pride Soviet citizens feel for their country. The party has led Soviet Russia from the devastation the country suffered in the Bolshevik Revolution and Civil War (1918–21) to victory in World War II over an ancient Russian enemy and then to superpower status. In 1989, moreover, the CPSU could still claim to lead a world communist movement (see Communist Parties

Abroad, ch. 10). Since World War II, Soviet influence has extended to Asia, Africa, and Latin America. A feeling of patriotic pride for these accomplishments united the Soviet elite, and it bound the elite to the masses.

The CPSU has incorporated aspects of traditional Russian culture into its political style. The party drew upon Russia's revolutionary tradition and represented itself as the culmination of a progressive and revolutionary movement that began with the "Decembrists' revolt" of 1825 (see War and Peace, 1796–1825, ch. 1). Most aspects of this revolutionary tradition centered on Lenin. The fact that the state preserved his remains in a mausoleum on Red Square echoed an old Russian Orthodox belief that the bodies of saints do not decay. In addition, the regime bestowed Lenin's name on the second largest city of the Soviet Union, a bust or picture of Lenin decorated all party offices, and quotations from his writings appeared on billboards throughout the country. All Soviet leaders since Lenin have tried to show that they follow Lenin's policies. The CPSU has sought to maintain and strengthen its legitimacy by drawing upon the legacy of this charismatic figure.

Another element of old Russian culture that has entered the CPSU's political style was the cult of the leader (also referred to as cult of personality—see Glossary). The Soviet cult of the leader appropriated a cultural form whose sources lay deep in the Russian past. Cults of saints, heroes, and the just tsar had long existed in Russia. In the 1920s, the cult of Lenin emerged as part of a deliberate policy to gain popular support for the regime. Joseph V. Stalin, who built the most extensive cult of the leader, was reported to have declared that the "Russian people is a tsarist people. It needs a tsar." Stalin assumed the title of generalissimo during World War II, and throughout his rule he was referred to by the title *vozhd'* (leader). Other titles appropriated by Stalin included Leader of the World Proletariat, Great Helmsman, Father of the Peoples, and Genius of Mankind.

Soviet leaders since Stalin have also encouraged the development of their own cults, although on a smaller scale than that of Stalin. These cults of the party leaders replicated that of the just tsar. Like the cult of the just tsar, who was depicted as having remained true to his faith of Russian Orthodoxy, the cults of party leaders such as Khrushchev and Leonid I. Brezhnev represented them as leaders who remained true to their faith in Marxism-Leninism. Like the just tsar, who was depicted as being close to the common people, these leaders represented themselves as having the interests of the common people at heart.

Central Party Institutions

In a political organization like the CPSU, which aims to be monolithic and centralized, central party institutions assume supreme importance. Central institutions in the CPSU included the party congress, the Central Committee, the Central Auditing Commission, the Party Control Committee, the Politburo (political bureau), the Secretariat, and the commissions. These organs made binding decisions for intermediate and local party bodies down to the PPO (see fig. 12).

According to the *Party Rules,* the party congress was the highest authority in the party. This body was too large and unwieldy to exert any influence, however, and its members were appointed either directly or indirectly by those whom it ostensibly elected to the Central Committee and Politburo. Moreover, the party congress met only once every five years. Another large party body of note was the party conference, which met infrequently upon the decision of the Central Committee. The Central Committee itself, which met every six months, theoretically ruled the party between congresses. Although more influential than the party congress and the party conference, the Central Committee wielded less power than the Politburo, Secretariat, and the party commissions.

The Politburo, the Secretariat, and the party commissions paralleled a set of central governmental institutions that included the Council of Ministers and the Presidium of the Supreme Soviet (see Central Government, ch. 8). The distinction between party and government institutions lay in the difference between policy formation and policy implementation. Stated briefly, the central party institutions made policy, and the government carried it out. The distinction between policy formation and policy implementation was often a narrow one, however, and party leaders frequently involved themselves in carrying out policies in the economic, domestic political, and foreign policy spheres. This problem, known in the Soviet Union as *podmena* (substitution), occurred throughout all party and government hierarchies (see Intermediate-Level Party Organizations, this ch.).

The distinction between policy formation and policy execution also characterized the differences between the Politburo, on the one hand, and the Secretariat and the commissions, on the other hand. The Politburo made policy for the party (as well as for the Soviet Union as a whole). The Secretariat and, apparently, the party commissions produced policy alternatives for the Politburo and, once the latter body made a decision, carried out the Politburo's directives. In fulfilling these roles, of course, the Secretariat often made policy decisions itself. The Secretariat and the commissions administered a party bureaucracy that numbered in the hundreds of thousands. Through this apparatus, the CPSU Secretariat and the party commissions radiated their influence throughout the middle and lower levels of the party and thereby throughout the government, economy, and society.

The general secretary, as a member of the Politburo and the leader of the Secretariat, was the most powerful official in the CPSU. The general secretary was the chief policymaker, enjoyed the greatest amount of authority in party appointments, and represented the Soviet Union in its dealings with other states. The absence of a set term of office and the general secretary's lack of statutory duties meant that candidates for this position had to compete for power and authority to attain it. Once having been elected to this position, the general secretary had to maintain and increase his power and authority in order to implement his program.

Party Congress

According to the *Party Rules,* the party congress was "the supreme organ" of the CPSU. The First Party Congress took place in 1898 in Minsk, with 9 delegates out of a party membership of about 1,000. In 1986 the Twenty-Seventh Party Congress had 5,000 delegates, or 1 for every 3,670 party members. Delegates were formally elected by republic party congresses or, in the case of the Russian Republic, by conferences of *kraia* (see Glossary), oblasts (see Glossary), and autonomous republics (see Glossary). Attendance at a party congress was largely honorific. Approximately half the delegates were luminaries in the party. The Twenty-Seventh Party Congress included 1,074 important party functionaries, 1,240 executive government officials, 147 distinguished scholars and scientists, 332 high-ranking military officers, and 279 writers and artists. The party reserved the remainder of delegate positions for rank-and-file party members. For the rank and file, attendance at a party congress was a reward for long years of service and loyalty.

Relative to other central party institutions, the size of the party congress was inversely proportional to its importance. Lack of debate and deliberation have been characteristic of party congresses since the Tenth Party Congress in 1921 (see Democratic Centralism, this ch.). Party congresses convened every year until 1925. Thereafter, they began to lose their importance as an authoritative party organ, and the intervals between congresses increased to three or four years. From 1939 to 1952, the party neglected to hold a congress. After Stalin's death in 1953, the party elite decided to convene congresses more frequently. Since the mid-1950s,

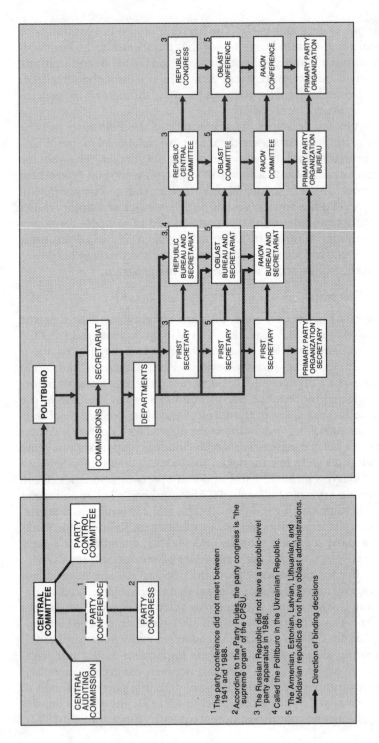

Figure 12. Organization of the Communist Party of the Soviet Union, 1988

the *Party Rules* have stipulated that congresses be held every five years.

Since 1925, however, some notable congresses have taken place. The Seventeenth Party Congress in 1934 praised collectivization and the successes of the First Five-Year Plan (1928–32), and it confirmed Stalin as head of the party and the country. In 1956, at the Twentieth Party Congress, Khrushchev criticized Stalin's cult of personality (see The Khrushchev Era, ch. 2). In 1986, at the Twenty-Seventh Party Congress, General Secretary Mikhail S. Gorbachev attempted to break with Stalin's legacy by enunciating policies calling for more openness (*glasnost'*—see Glossary) in Soviet life and for restructuring (*perestroika*—see Glossary).

The party congress normally met for about a week. The most important event occurred when the general secretary delivered the political report on the state of the party, reviewed Soviet economic and foreign policy over the preceding five years, cited achievements and problems of the world communist movement, and delivered a prospectus for the next five years. In another important speech, the chairman of the Council of Ministers presented the targets for the next five-year plan. These two speeches provided the setting for a number of shorter speeches that followed. Republic party secretaries, oblast committee (*oblast' komitet—obkom*) secretaries, and government officials offered very formalized comment on the policies enunciated by the general secretary. The central apparatus also selected a few rank-and-file members to give speeches praising party policies. Finally, the congress listened to brief reports given by secretaries of foreign communist and workers' parties friendly to Moscow. Some party congresses adopted a broad statement called the party program (see Glossary).

While in session, the party congress voted on several kinds of issues. All decisions were unanimous. The congress enacted a series of resolutions that stemmed from the general secretary's political report, and those resolutions became party policy until the next congress. In addition, the party leadership could offer changes in the *Party Rules* to the congress. Most important, the party congress formally elected the members of the Central Committee, which it charged to govern the party until the next congress.

Party Conference

Similar in size to the congress was the party conference, although unlike the congress it did not meet regularly. The Nineteenth Party Conference—the most recent—took place in 1988. (The Eighteenth Party Conference had been convened in 1941.) Officially, the conference ranked third in importance among party meetings, after the congress and the Central Committee plenum. Oblast and district party leaders handpicked most of the delegates to the Nineteenth Party Conference, as they had for party congresses in the past, despite Gorbachev's desire that supporters of reform serve as delegates. Nevertheless, public opinion managed in some instances to pressure the party apparatus into selecting delegates who pressed for reform.

The Nineteenth Party Conference made no personnel changes in the Central Committee, as some Western observers had expected. However, the conference passed a series of resolutions signaling policy departures in a number of areas. For example, the resolution "On the Democratization of Soviet Society and the Reform of the Political System" called for the creation of a new, powerful position of chairman of the Supreme Soviet, limited party officeholders to two five-year terms, and prescribed multicandidate elections to a new Congress of People's Deputies (see Congress of People's Deputies, ch. 8). The conference passed other resolutions on such topics as legal reform, interethnic relations, economic reform, *glasnost'*, and bureaucracy.

By convening the Nineteenth Party Conference approximately two years after initiating his reform program, Gorbachev hoped to further the democratization of the party, to withdraw the party from many aspects of economic management, and to reinvigorate government and state institutions. He also sought to rouse the party rank and file against the bureaucracy. In this vein, the conference was a success for Gorbachev because it reaffirmed his program of party-directed change from above.

Central Committee

The Central Committee met at least once every six months in plenary session. Between party congresses, the *Party Rules* required that the Central Committee "direct all the activities of the party and the local party organs, carry out the recruitment and the assignment of leading cadres, direct the work of the central governmental and social organizations of the workers, create various organs, institutions, and enterprises of the party and supervise their activities, name the editorial staff of central newspapers and journals working under its auspices, disburse funds of the party budget and verify their accounting." In fact, the Central Committee, which in 1989 numbered more than 300 members, was too large and cumbersome to perform these duties; therefore, it delegated its authority in these matters to the Politburo and Secretariat.

The history of the Central Committee dates to 1898, when the First Party Congress of the Russian Social Democratic Labor Party elected a three-person body to run its affairs. In May 1989, the Central Committee had 251 full members and 109 candidate members. (Candidate members do not have the right to vote.)

Western scholars know little about the selection processes for membership on the Central Committee. British Sovietologists Ronald J. Hill and Peter Frank have suggested that the party leadership drew up a list of candidates before the party congress. Party leaders then discussed the list and presented it to the congress for ratification. Both personal merit and institutional affiliation determined selection, with the majority of members selected because of the positions they held. Such positions included republic party first and second secretaries; *obkom* secretaries; chairmen of republic, provincial, and large urban governmental bodies; military leaders; important writers and artists; and academics.

During periods of policy change, turnover in the Central Committee occurred at a rapid rate. A new leadership, seeking to carry out new policies, attempted to replace officials who might attempt to block reform efforts with its own supporters. Thus, at the Twenty-Seventh Party Congress, the first for Gorbachev as general secretary, the rate of turnover for full members was 41 percent, as compared with 25 percent at the Twenty-Sixth Party Congress in 1981. In addition, of the 170 candidate members elected by the Twenty-Seventh Party Congress, 116 (or 68 percent) were new.

Gorbachev effected further changes at the April 25, 1989, Central Committee plenum. As a result of personnel turnover because of death, retirement, or loss of position since the Twenty-Seventh Party Congress, a significant percentage of the Central Committee had come to be classified as "dead souls," that is, people who no longer occupied the position that had originally gained them either full or candidate status in the Central Committee. At the April 25 plenum, seventy-four full members resigned their Central Committee positions. Twenty-four members received promotion to full-member status. (The *Party Rules* dictate that only the party congress can name new candidate members and that a plenum can only promote new full members from among the pool of candidate members.)

The changes signified a reduction of influence for both the party apparatus and the military. Party apparatchiks (see Glossary) declined from 44.5 percent to 33.9 percent of the full members. The military's representation fell from 8.5 percent to 4.4 percent among the full members.

Worker and peasant representation rose from 8.5 percent to 14.3 percent. But because members of these groups lacked an independent political base, they usually supported the general secretary.

Thus, the changes indicated a victory for Gorbachev. He eliminated many Central Committee members who lost power under his rule and were therefore considered opponents of reform. Gorbachev also increased the number of his own supporters in the Central Committee.

The Central Committee served significant functions for the party. The committee brought together the leaders of the most important institutions in Soviet society, individuals who had the same rank in the institutional-territorial hierarchy. The Central Committee thus provided a setting for these organizational and territorial interests to communicate with one another, articulate their concerns, and reconcile their positions on various issues. Membership in the Central Committee defined the political elite and reinforced their high status. This status lent the committee members the authority necessary to carry out policies in their respective institutions. Members also possessed a great deal of expertise in their respective fields and could be consulted by the Central Committee apparatus in preparing policy recommendations and resolutions for plenums, party conferences, and party congresses.

Central Auditing Commission

Every party congress elected a Central Auditing Commission, which reviewed the party's financial accounts and the financial activities of its institutions. The commission also investigated the treatment accorded to letters and complaints by the party's central institutions. The status of membership on the Central Auditing Commission appeared to fall just below that of candidate status on the Central Committee. In 1989 the commission had seventy members. The commission elected a bureau, which in May 1989 was headed by Deputy Chairman Alla A. Nizovtseva.

Party Control Committee

The Party Control Committee, which was attached to the Central Committee, investigated violations of party discipline and administered expulsions from the party. Because it examined the work of party members in responsible economic posts, this committee could involve itself in financial and economic management. The Party Control Committee also could redress grievances of party members who had been expelled by their PPO. In 1989 its chairman was Boris K. Pugo.

Politburo

Two weeks before the Bolshevik Revolution in 1917, the Bolshevik leadership formed the Politburo as a means to further centralize decision making and to permit effective adaptation of party policies to rapidly changing circumstances. Since the Bolshevik Revolution, the Politburo of the Central Committee of the CPSU has consisted of the highest party and government officials in the Soviet Union. Despite the importance of this body, only a small amount of space was devoted to it in the *Party Rules,* which noted only that the Central Committee chose the Politburo for "leadership of the work of the party between plenums of the Central Committee." The Politburo formed the highest decision-making body in the Soviet Union. Its full and candidate members served on the Politburo by virtue of their party or government positions.

The Politburo was a standing subcommittee of the Central Committee. Like the Central Committee, the Politburo was composed of full and candidate (nonvoting) members. The *Party Rules* neither specified the size of the Politburo nor mentioned candidate status.

Four general career patterns determined accession to membership in the Politburo. Officials of the central party apparatus could rise within that hierarchy to acquire a position that led to a seat on the Secretariat. In 1989 several secretaries of the Central Committee sat on the Politburo. Other officials, such as Mikhail A. Suslov (the party's leading ideologist under Brezhnev) and Aleksandr N. Iakovlev, who also made his career in ideology, attained membership in the Politburo because of their expertise. The technical or economic specialist was a third pattern. For example, Nikolai Sliun'kov probably was brought into the Politburo because of his expertise in economic administration. Finally, a successful career in the provinces often led to a call to Moscow and a career in the central apparatus. Volodymyr Shcherbyts'kyy exemplified this career pattern.

Several interlocking trends have characterized the Politburo since Stalin's death in 1953. Membership in the Politburo has become increasingly representative of important functional and territorial interests. Before 1953 the party leadership concentrated on building the economic, social, and political bases for a socialist society. In the post-Stalin period the leadership has sought instead to manage society and contain social change. Management of society required a division of labor within the Politburo and the admission of people with specialized expertise. Stalin kept the lines of responsibility ambiguous, and he tightly controlled the kinds of information his comrades on the Politburo received. Since 1953 Politburo members have had greater access to information and hence more opportunity to develop consistent policy positions. Because the party leadership eliminated violence as an instrument of elite politics and restrained the secret police after Stalin's death, Politburo members began advancing policy positions without fear of losing their seats on this body, or even their lives, if they found themselves on the wrong side of the policy debate.

Secretariat

Until September 1988, the Secretariat headed the CPSU's central apparatus and was solely responsible for the development and implementation of party policies. The Secretariat also carried political weight because many of its members sat on the Politburo (see fig. 13). In 1989 eight members of the Secretariat, including the general secretary of the Secretariat of the Central Committee of the CPSU, served as full members of the Politburo. One member, Georgii P. Razumovskii, was a candidate member of the Politburo. Those officials who sat on the Politburo, served in the Secretariat, and chaired a party commission were the most powerful in the Soviet Union.

After the formation of the party commissions in the fall of 1988, lines of authority over the central party bureaucracy became very unclear because the responsibilities of the secretaries and the responsibilities of the commissions considerably overlapped. Of the nine secretaries, excluding the general secretary, six chaired party commissions. One Western observer, Alexander Rahr, believed that this factor limited the power of the Secretariat because the influence of the secretaries who chaired the commissions was restricted to specific areas of competence as defined by their commission chairmanships. In addition, the secretaries became answerable to the commissions they chaired. Finally, in one case, a secretary served as a subordinate to another secretary in the latter's role as the chairman of a commission. Viktor P. Nikonov, a secretary responsible for agriculture, was deputy chairman of the Agrarian Policy Commission, which was chaired by Egor K. Ligachev, another party secretary.

Western specialists poorly understood lines of authority in the Secretariat. It was clear that the members of the Secretariat supervised the work of the Central Committee departments. Department chiefs, who normally sat on the Central Committee, were subordinate to the secretaries. For example, in 1989 Aleksandr S. Kapto, the chairman of the Ideological Department, answered to Vadim A. Medvedev, party secretary for ideology, and Valentin A. Falin, the head of the International Department, answered to Iakovlev, party secretary for international policy. Most department heads were assisted by a first deputy head (a first deputy administrator in the case of the Administration of Affairs Department) and from one to six deputy heads (deputy administrators in the case of the Administration of Affairs Department). However, the International Department had two deputy heads.

In 1989 a variety of departments made up the CPSU's central apparatus. Some departments were worthy of note. The Party Building and Cadre Work Department assigned party personnel in the *nomenklatura* system (see Nomenklatura, this ch.). The State and Legal Department supervised the armed forces, the Committee for State Security (Komitet gosudarstvennoi bezopasnosti—KGB), the Ministry of Internal Affairs, the trade unions, and the Procuracy.

Before 1989 the apparatus contained many more departments responsible for the economy. These departments included one for the economy as a whole, one for machine building, and one for the chemical industry, among others. The party abolished these departments in an effort to remove itself from the day-to-day management of the economy in favor of government bodies and a greater role for the market. In early 1989, Gorbachev suggested that the agrarian and defense industry departments might be disbanded as well as part of his ongoing reform efforts.

Commissions

At the September 30, 1988, plenum of the Central Committee, the CPSU announced that six new commissions would be formed to develop policy and oversee its implementation in a series of key areas. A resolution of the November 1988 plenum that actually established the commissions maintained that their purpose was to "facilitate the involvement of Central Committee members and candidate members in active work on major directions of domestic and foreign policy."

Several factors led to the formation of these new party bodies. First, Gorbachev probably sought to strengthen reformist influence at the top of the party hierarchy. Second, the move was designed to reduce the party's day-to-day involvement in the economy. Thus, only one of the six commissions was concerned with economic policy, while another dealt with agriculture. Finally, Gorbachev's desire to reduce the power of his conservative rival, Ligachev, also helped to explain the move. Prior to September 1988, Ligachev had been the party's second secretary, the official who usually chaired meetings of the Secretariat. By limiting the influence of the Secretariat and by placing Ligachev in charge of agriculture—the Achilles heel of the economy—Gorbachev eliminated Ligachev as a competitor for power.

As of May 1989, the actual work of the commissions belied the significance the party attached to them. In their first six months,

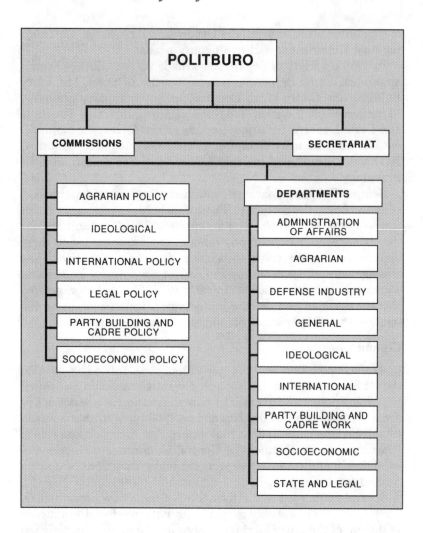

Figure 13. Central Apparatus of the Communist Party of the Soviet Union, 1988

none of the commissions had met more than once. All the communiqués reporting on their meetings have been devoid of substance.

General Secretary: Power and Authority

That certain policies throughout Soviet history have been so clearly identified with the general secretary of the CPSU demonstrated the importance of that position as well as of the stakes in

302

the succession struggle upon a general secretary's death or removal from office. As general secretary, Stalin determined the party's policies in the economy and foreign affairs and thus gave his name to a whole era in Soviet history. Khrushchev put his stamp on a variety of policies, including peaceful coexistence with the West and the virgin land campaign (see Khrushchev's Reforms and Fall, ch. 2). Soviet and Western observers identified Brezhnev with détente and the Soviet military buildup (see The Brezhnev Era, ch. 2). In the late 1980s, Gorbachev associated his name with the policies of openness, restructuring, and democratization.

The general secretary possessed many powers. As chairman of the Politburo, the general secretary decided the agenda and timing of its deliberations. The general secretary acted as chief executive of the party apparatus and thus supervised the *nomenklatura*. The general secretary also chaired the Defense Council, which managed the Soviet military-industrial complex (see Defense Council, ch. 18). Finally, through attendance at summit meetings with world heads of state, the general secretary acquired symbolic legitimation as the Soviet Union's top ruler.

Once selected for this position by other members of the Politburo and confirmed by the Central Committee, the general secretary had to proceed to build a base of power and strengthen his authority. Officials considered eligible for the position of general secretary held a great amount of power to begin with; they always occupied seats on the Politburo and Secretariat, and they developed a large number of clients throughout the party and government bureaucracies. The general secretary's efforts to extend this power base involved placing loyal clients in strategic positions throughout party and government hierarchies. One measure of the success of the general secretary's efforts in this regard was turnover in the Central Committee at the first party congress following the secretary's accession to the position (see Central Committee, this ch.). The general secretary used these clients to promote desired policies at all levels of the party and government bureaucracies and to ensure accurate transmission of information about policy problems up the hierarchy (see Nomenklatura, this ch.).

To secure his rule and advance his policies, the general secretary also had to increase his authority. American Sovietologist George Breslauer has written that efforts to build authority involved legitimation of the general secretary's policies and programs and demonstration of his competence or indispensability as a leader. The general secretary strove to show that his policies derived from Lenin's teachings and that these policies have led to successes in socialist construction. Moreover, the general secretary strove to demonstrate a unique insight into the teachings of Marx and Lenin and into the current stage of world development. The general secretary also emphasized personal ties to the people and a leadership motivated by the interests of the workers and peasants (see Party Legitimacy, this ch.). One further means to strengthen the legitimacy of the general secretary's power has been the acquisition of high government offices. Thus in October 1988, Gorbachev became chairman of the Presidium of the Supreme Soviet, which was the titular head of the Soviet state. He retained his position as head of state when in May 1989 the newly elected Congress of People's Deputies chose a new Supreme Soviet and elected Gorbachev to the just created position of chairman of the Supreme Soviet. In the past, the head of the Soviet state sometimes had been referred to as "president" in Soviet and Western media, although such a position was not identified in the Constitution.

Another means that Soviet general secretaries have used to ensure their authority is the cult of the leader. The cult of the leader has several intended audiences. For example, the general secretary used the cult of the leader to intimidate actual or potential rivals and thus force them to accept and follow his policies. In addition, the cult of the leader reassured those members of the party and government hierarchies whose careers depended upon the success of the general secretary's policies. The cult of the leader provided inspiration to those who wished to identify with a patriarchal figure.

Breslauer has written that Soviet general secretaries since Stalin have attempted to build their authority by creating a sense of national élan. For example, Iurii V. Andropov, general secretary from November 1982 to February 1984, sought to rouse Soviet society with his campaign against alcoholism and corruption. The general secretary has also sought to play the role of problem solver. For example, in the mid- and late 1980s, Gorbachev sought to reverse a decline in economic efficiency by promoting economic policies designed to curb the ministries' role in Soviet economic life and thereby encourage enterprise initiative (see Reforming the Planning System, ch. 11).

Since the death of Lenin, the party elite has been unable to institute regulations governing the transfer of office from one general secretary to the next. The Nineteenth Party Conference called for limiting party officeholders to two five-year terms. However, it was unclear whether this proviso would apply to the general secretary and other top leaders. The party leadership has yet to devise procedures by which the general secretary may relinquish the office. The powers of the office were not set; neither were its rights and duties. These factors combined to generate a high degree of unpredictability in selecting a new leader and a period of uncertainty while the new general secretary consolidates power.

Three stages have characterized the efforts of various general secretaries to consolidate their power and authority. The first stage begins while the incumbent leader is in power and lasts through his death or ouster. Potential successors seek to place themselves in more powerful positions relative to their rivals. For example, under Konstantin U. Chernenko (general secretary from February 1984 to March 1985) Gorbachev chaired Politburo meetings in the general secretary's absence and also assumed responsibilities for cadre policy. These responsibilities enabled Gorbachev to set the agenda for Politburo meetings and to place persons loyal to him in important positions throughout the regime. Gorbachev's unsuccessful rivals for power, Grigorii V. Romanov and Viktor V. Grishin, had fewer such opportunities to influence the outcome of the struggle to succeed Chernenko.

The second stage occurs with the transfer of authority to the new leader and both the accumulation of positions and the authority that goes with them. This stage can occur over a prolonged period of time and coincide with the next stage. For example, only in 1977 did Brezhnev, named general secretary in 1964, become chairman of the Presidium of the Supreme Soviet and thus de facto head of state. The third stage involves two steps: consolidation of the new leader's power through the removal of his predecessor's clients and those of his actual and potential rivals for power; and the installation of the new leader's clients in key positions. This stage probably lasts for the duration of the general secretary's tenure.

A succession struggle entails opportunities and problems for the new party leader and for the Soviet leadership as a whole. Transfer of office from one general secretary to another can improve the possibilities for change. Seweryn Bialer has written that "ambition, power, and the desire for innovation all meet in a succession struggle and so prepare the ground for change." Succession disrupts the normal pattern of business. Also, policy initiatives are a critical means of consolidating a new leader's position. Khrushchev's condemnation of Stalin represented an appeal to party officials dissatisfied with Stalinism and an effort to define and control a new program that would better meet the needs of the party and society. Similarly, in the late 1980s Gorbachev's initiatives appealed to officials and citizens who were dissatisfied with the inertia of the late Brezhnev period and who sought to modernize the Soviet economy.

Yet, a succession struggle can also occasion serious difficulties for the leadership. A succession struggle increases the probability for personal and policy conflicts. In turn, these conflicts can lead to political passivity as the rivals for power turn their attention to that struggle rather than to policy development and execution. When the general secretary lacks the influence necessary to promote desired policies, a sense of inertia can debilitate the political system at the intermediate and lower levels. This factor partially explains the resistance that Khrushchev and, in the late 1980s, Gorbachev met in their respective efforts to alter the policies of their predecessors.

Intermediate-Level Party Organizations

The intermediate-level party structure embraced the republic, oblast, *raion* (see Glossary), and city levels of the hierarchy. The organizational scheme of each of these levels resembled the others. In addition, at each of these levels the party organization corresponded to a similar layer in the government administration. According to the *Party Rules,* the authoritative body at each of these levels was the congress (republic level) or conference. These bodies elected a committee that, in turn, chose a bureau with several members (including a first secretary) and a secretariat. Conferences at one level elected delegates to the conference or congress at the next highest level. Thus, the rural or city conference designated delegates to the oblast conference or, in the case of the smaller republics, directly to the republic party congress. The oblast conference elected delegates to congresses of the larger republics. In May 1989, the Russian Republic had no party congress. Delegates from provinces (oblasts, *kraia,* and autonomous subdivisions) in that republic were elected directly to the all-union party congress. Of course, at each level of the hierarchy the term *election* generally was a euphemism. By the norms of democratic centralism, party leaders at each level approved the makeup of the party conference or congress that ostensibly elected them, as well as the composition of party bodies on the next lowest level.

Republic Party Organization

The republic party organization replicated the party structure on the all-union level except for the Russian Republic, which had no republic-level party organization in 1989. A congress, made up of delegates from the oblast or district and town organizations, elected a central committee to govern the republic in the five-year interval between party congresses. The central committee of the republic, which held a plenum once every four months, named a bureau (in the case of the Ukrainian Republic, this body was called a politburo) and a secretariat to run the affairs of the republic between plenums of the central committee.

Full and candidate (nonvoting) members of republic bureaus included officials who held seats on this body by virtue of their party or government positions. Party officials who sat on the republic party bureaus normally included the first secretary of the republic and the second secretary for party-organizational work, as well as others selected from among the following: the first secretary of the party organization in the capital city of the republic, the chairman of the republic party control committee, and the first secretary of an outlying city or province. Government officials who could serve on the republic bureau were elected from among the following: the chairman of the republic's council of ministers, the chairman of the presidium of the republic's supreme soviet, the first deputy chairman of the republic's council of ministers, the republic's KGB chairman, and the troop commander of the Soviet armed forces stationed in the republic.

In 1989 the secretariats of the fourteen republic party organizations included a second secretary for party-organizational work and a secretary for ideology. The number of departments has, however, shrunk as the party has attempted to limit its role in economic management. Some sources also indicated the formation of commissions similar to those of the central party apparatus. Thus, the republic first secretaries in the Kazakh, Latvian, Lithuanian, and Moldavian republics and the second secretaries in the Belorussian and Turkmen republics assumed the chairmanships of their republics' commissions on state and legal policy.

With the exception of the Kazakh Republic (where a Russian, Gennadii Kolbin, served as first secretary), the first secretaries of the republic party organizations in 1989 were all members of their republic's dominant nationality. However, in 1989 the officials responsible for party-organizational work—the second secretaries—were predominantly Russians. (The Kazakh party's second secretary was Sergei M. Titarenko, a Ukrainian; the second secretary in the Ukrainian Republic was a Ukrainian.) The second secretary supervised cadre policy in the republic and hence managed the republic's *nomenklatura* appointments. As an official whose primary loyalty was to Moscow, the second secretary acted as a vehicle for the influence of the CPSU's central apparatus on the affairs of the republic's party organization and as a watchdog to ensure the republic organization's adherence to Moscow's demands.

Oblast-Level Organization

Below the all-union organization in the Russian Republic (which sufficed for the Russian Republic's party organization in 1989) and the union republic party organizations in the Azerbaydzhan, Belorussian, Georgian, Kazakh, Kirgiz, Tadzhik, Turkmen, Ukrainian, and Uzbek republics stood the oblast party organization, 122 of which existed in the Soviet Union in 1989. (Six large, thinly populated regions in the Russian Republic have been designated by the term *krai;* these regions are treated herein as oblasts.) The Armenian, Estonian, Latvian, Lithuanian, and Moldavian republics had no oblasts. An oblast could embrace a large city or nationality unit. According to the *Party Rules,* the authoritative body in the province was the party conference, which met twice every five years and consisted of delegates elected by the district or city party conference. Between oblast party conferences, an oblast committee (*obkom*) comprising full and candidate members selected by the conference supervised the provincial party organization and, through it, the province as a whole. The oblast party committee met once every four months. That committee chose a bureau made up of voting and nonvoting members and a secretariat.

The bureau integrated officials from the most important sectors of the provincial party, economic, and governmental organizations into a unified political elite. Membership on the bureau enabled these officials to coordinate policies in their respective administrative spheres.

American Sovietologist Joel C. Moses found that as of the mid-1980s five different kinds of specialists served on the *obkom* bureau. The first category, composed of agricultural specialists, could be selected from among the *obkom* agricultural secretary, the agricultural administration of the oblast, or the *obkom* first secretary in predominantly rural regions. A second category of bureau membership consisted of industrial specialists, who were drawn from among the *obkom* industry secretary, the first secretary of the provincial capital (where most provincial industries were located), the provincial trade union council chairman, the first secretary of a large industrialized city district, or the *obkom* first secretary. Ideology specialists made up the third category. They were selected from the *obkom* secretary for ideology, the editor of the provincial party newspaper, or the first secretary of the Komsomol (see Glossary). A fourth category was the cadres specialist, who supervised *nomenklatura* appointments in the province. The cadres specialist on the provincial party bureau normally occupied one of the

Monument in a Moscow park honoring Pavlik Morozov (1918–32). During collectivization the Soviet youth was murdered by local villagers for informing authorities about the illegal activities of his kulak relatives.
Courtesy Jimmy Pritchard

following positions: *obkom* first secretary, head of the *obkom* party-organizational department, chairman of the provincial trade union council, or *obkom* cadres secretary. "Mixed generalists" made up the fifth category. These officials served on the *obkom* bureau to fulfill positions that required a broader background than those possessed by the functional specialists. A wide range of roles prepared the mixed generalists to carry out their tasks. Prior to serving on the provincial party bureau, these officials generally worked in industry, agriculture, party administration, or ideology.

Reform of the party's central apparatus, however, portended significant changes at the regional level. According to Georgii Kriuchkov, a senior official of the Central Committee, "the party is shedding the functions of dealing with day-to-day problems as they arise, because these problems are within the competence of the state, managerial, and public bodies." Hence, parts of the *obkom* bureau that paralleled government and managerial bodies—mainly in the area of economic management—were to be dismantled.

The first secretary of the party *obkom* was the most powerful official in the province. Paradoxically, much of that power stemmed from Soviet economic inefficiency. According to the norms of democratic centralism, the *obkom* secretary had to carry out decisions made by leaders at the all-union and republic levels of the party hierarchy. Nevertheless, the *obkom* secretary preserved some scope for independent political initiative on issues of national importance.

Initiative, perseverance, and ruthlessness were necessary characteristics of the successful *obkom* secretary, who had to aggregate scarce resources to meet economic targets and lobby central planners for low targets. Soviet émigré Alexander Yanov has argued that the interest of the *obkom* secretary, however, lay in preserving an inefficient provincial economy. Yanov has written that the *obkom* secretaries were "the fixers and chasers" after scarce resources who made the provincial economy work. If the economy were decentralized to allow greater initiative and if efforts were made to ensure greater agricultural productivity, one element of the *obkom* secretary's power—the ability to find resources to meet the plan—would diminish. For this reason, the *obkom* secretaries formed an important source of resistance to Khrushchev's efforts at economic reform (see Khrushchev's Reforms and Fall, ch. 2). Western observers held that these officials were an important source of opposition to Gorbachev's economic reforms because these reforms envisaged a greater role for the government and the market at the expense of the party.

District- and City-Level Organization

In 1988 more than 3,400 district (*raion*) organizations made up the position in the CPSU hierarchy below that of the oblast. Of these organizations, 2,860 were located in rural areas and 570 in wards of cities. In addition, this hierarchical level encompassed 800 city (*gorod*) organizations.

The structure of these organizations resembled that of organizations on the republic and oblast levels. In theory, the party conference, with delegates selected by the PPOs in each district or city, elected a committee composed of full and candidate members. In practice, the party leadership in the district or town chose the delegates to the party conference and determined the composition of the district or town committee. Party conferences took place twice every five years. In the interim, the district committee (*raion komitet—raikom*) or city committee (*gorodskoi komitet—gorkom*) was the most authoritative body in the territory. The committee consisted of party officials, state officials, local Komsomol and trade union officers, the chairmen of the most important collective farms, the managers of the largest industrial enterprises, some PPO secretaries, and a few rank-and-file party members.

The *raikom* or *gorkom* elected a bureau and a secretariat, which supervised the daily affairs of the jurisdiction. The bureau numbered between ten and twelve members, who included party officials, state officials, and directors of the most important economic enterprises (see Glossary) in the district or city. The composition of the bureau at this level varied with location. For example, the *gorkom* had no specialist for agriculture, and the rural *raikom* had no specialist for industry. The *raikom* and *gorkom* bureaus met two to three times per month to review the affairs of the district or city and to examine the reports of the PPOs.

The first secretary of the *raikom* or *gorkom* bureau headed the party organization at this level. As part of its *nomenklatura* authority, the oblast party organization made appointments to these positions. In 1987, however, reports of multicandidate elections for first secretary of a *raikom* appeared in the Soviet press. Two candidates competed for the position of *raikom* secretary in the Kemerovo and Vinnitsa districts. In the case of Kemerovo, *Pravda* reported that the oblast party secretary nominated the candidates, and the party conference at the district level settled the contest in a secret ballot. The Nineteenth Party Conference called for the institutionalization of multicandidate elections for these and other party positions.

The secretariat of a *raikom* and *gorkom* resembled that of the oblast party committee. In contrast to the party committee of the oblast level, however, the composition of this body varied with location. All had a department for agitation and propaganda; an organizational department, which staffed the positions for PPO secretaries and supervised the performance of the PPOs; and a general department, which coordinated the affairs of the district and city party organizations by circulating documents, administering party work, and preparing the agenda and materials for conferences, plenums, and bureau meetings. In 1988 the *raikom* or *gorkom* included a department for either agriculture or industry, which supervised those elements of the Soviet economy on the district level. In contrast to efforts to reduce the number of departments at higher levels of the party apparatus, no such reduction on the district level was planned as of early 1989.

As in the oblast, until the late 1980s the party organization in the district and city tended to involve itself in economic administration and production, which Gorbachev intended to place within the purview of the government. The CPSU judged its officials on their ability to meet and exceed the state economic plan. Party officials used their power as the representatives of the leading political institution in the country to engage themselves in economic administration. For fear of offending party officials and in the expectation that the party would solve their problems, until the late 1980s government and economic administrators were reluctant to exercise initiative and take responsibility in economic matters. The ability of *raikom* and *gorkom* secretaries to involve themselves in government activities formed one aspect of their power and influence within their respective jurisdictions. During the Khrushchev era, these officials resisted reforms that led to a diminution of their responsibilities (see Khrushchev's Reforms and Fall, ch. 2).

Primary Party Organization

In 1987 primary party organizations (PPOs) numbered 441,851. The PPO was the lowest rung on the party's organizational ladder. (PPOs were called party cells until 1934.) One PPO existed in every factory, office, collective farm, military unit, and education institution having more than three party members (see table 22, Appendix A). According to the *Party Rules,* the highest organ of the PPO was the party meeting, which comprised all party members in a given work unit. PPOs having more than fifty members could be divided into groups led by steering committees. Party meetings generally convened at least once a month, although the interim could be longer for PPOs having more than 300 members. The party meetings elected a bureau of two or three persons to supervise the affairs of the PPO. The secretary of the PPO, nominally elected by the party meeting but actually appointed by the next highest party organization, managed the work of the PPO and was a full-time, salaried member of the party.

The PPO performed many important tasks. It admitted new members into the party; apprised rank-and-file party members of their duties, obligations, and rights within the party; organized agitation and propaganda sessions to educate party members in the ideology of Marxism-Leninism; stimulated productivity in the enterprise; encouraged efficiency and effectiveness of production methods and innovation; and disciplined party members for dereliction of their duties. An enumeration of the activities of the PPO only begins to suggest the importance of this organization to the party. For several reasons, the PPO was an important factor underlying the party's control over society. The PPO possessed what was known as the right of verification (*pravo kontrolia*), checking how managers met the demands of their position and how faithfully they implemented the plan for their enterprise. This power led to the PPO secretary's involvement in the day-to-day affairs of the enterprise. Moreover, factory managers or chairmen of collective farms, as well as chiefs of the enterprise trade unions normally were party members; consequently, they were bound by democratic centralism to follow the orders and suggestions of their party leader, the PPO secretary. Thus, the PPO secretary and not the manager carried primary responsibility to the party for the work of the enterprise.

The PPO itself was also critical to the implementation of the economic plan. The state devised its economic plan on the basis of party requirements. The government implemented the party's plan, and therefore the norms of democratic centralism obligated the PPOs to enforce it. At the enterprise level, the principal activity of the PPO secretary and of all party members was to stimulate production. Party members had to set an example with their work and encourage nonmembers to fulfill their production quotas and improve their labor productivity.

The PPO not only conveyed party policies to nonmembers in the enterprise but also apprised the party hierarchy of the mood of the masses and prevented the formation of groups to promote grass-roots change. Rank-and-file party members were scattered throughout the Soviet Union. Party members had hands-on experience in their jobs and knew nonparty members personally. Because of this intimate knowledge of their surroundings, party members were in a position to inform their superiors about the concerns and problems of people in all walks of life. With this knowledge, the party could take steps to stem potential sources of unrest, to institute new methods of control, and, more generally, to tailor its policies toward the maintenance of the population's political quiescence.

Nomenklatura

The *nomenklatura* referred to the CPSU's authority to make appointments to key positions throughout the governmental system, as well as throughout the party's own hierarchy. Specifically, the *nomenklatura* consisted of two separate lists: one was for key positions, appointments to which were made by authorities within the party; the other was for persons who were potential candidates for appointment to those positions. The Politburo, as part of its *nomenklatura* authority, maintained a list of ministerial and ambassadorial positions that it had the power to fill as well as a separate list of potential candidates to occupy those positions.

Coextensive with the *nomenklatura* were patron-client relations. Officials who had the authority to appoint individuals to certain positions cultivated loyalties among those whom they appointed. The patron (the official making the appointment) promoted the interests of clients in return for their support. Powerful patrons, such as the members of the Politburo, had many clients. Moreover, an official could be both a client (in relation to a higher-level patron) and a patron (to other, lower-level officials).

Because a client was beholden to his patron for his position, the client was eager to please his patron by carrying out his policies.

The Soviet power structure essentially consisted of groups of vassals (clients) who had an overlord (the patron). The higher the patron, the more clients the patron had. Patrons protected their clients and tried to promote their careers. In return for the patron's efforts to promote their careers, the clients remained loyal to their patron. Thus, by promoting his clients' careers, the patron could advance his own power.

The Party's Appointment Authority

The *nomenklatura* system arose early in Soviet history. Lenin wrote that appointments were to take the following criteria into account: reliability, political attitude, qualifications, and administrative ability. Stalin, who was the first general secretary of the party, also was known as "Comrade File Cabinet" (Tovarishch Kartotekov) for his assiduous attention to the details of the party's appointments. Seeking to make appointments in a more systematic fashion, Stalin built the party's patronage system and used it to distribute his clients throughout the party bureaucracy (see Stalin's Rise to Power, ch. 2). Under Stalin's direction in 1922, the party created departments of the Central Committee and other organs at lower levels that were responsible for the registration and appointment of party officials. Known as *uchraspredy,* these organs supervised appointments to important party posts. According to American Sovietologist Seweryn Bialer, after Brezhnev's accession to power in October 1964, the party considerably expanded its appointment authority. However, in the late 1980s some official statements indicated that the party intended to reduce its appointment authority, particularly in the area of economic management, in line with Gorbachev's reform efforts.

At the all-union level, the Party Building and Cadre Work Department supervised party *nomenklatura* appointments. This department maintained records on party members throughout the country, made appointments to positions on the all-union level, and approved *nomenklatura* appointments on the lower levels of the hierarchy. The head of this department sometimes was a member of the Secretariat and was often a protégé of the general secretary.

Every party committee and party organizational department—from the all-union level in Moscow to the district and city levels—prepared two lists according to their needs. The basic (*osnovnaia*) list detailed positions in the political, administrative, economic, military, cultural, and educational bureaucracies that the committee and its department had responsibility for filling. The registered (*uchetnaia*) list enumerated the persons suitable for these positions.

Patron-Client Relations

An official in the party or government bureaucracy could not advance in the *nomenklatura* without the assistance of a patron. In return for this assistance in promoting his career, the client carried out the policies of the patron. Patron-client relations thus help to explain the ability of party leaders to generate support for their policies. The presence of patron-client relations between party officials and officials in other bureaucracies also helped to account for the control the party exercised over Soviet society. All of the 2 million members of the *nomenklatura* system understood that they held their positions as a result of a favor bestowed on them by a superior official in the party and that they could be replaced if they manifested disloyalty to their patron. Self-interest dictated that members of the *nomenklatura* submit to the control of their patrons in the party.

Clients sometimes could attempt to supplant their overlord. For example, Khrushchev, one of Lazar M. Kaganovich's former protégés, helped to oust the latter in 1957. Seven years later, Brezhnev, a client of Khrushchev, helped to remove his boss from power. The power of the general secretary was consolidated to the extent that he placed his clients in positions of power and influence (see General Secretary: Power and Authority, this ch.). The ideal for the general secretary, writes Soviet émigré observer Michael Voslensky, "is to be overlord of vassals selected by oneself."

Several factors explain the entrenchment of patron-client relations. First, in a centralized nondemocratic government system, promotion in the bureaucratic-political hierarchy was the only path to power. Second, the most important criterion for promotion in this hierarchy was not merit but approval from one's supervisors, who evaluated their subordinates on the basis of political criteria and their ability to contribute to the fulfillment of the economic plan. Third, political rivalries were present at all levels of the party and state bureaucracies but were especially prevalent at the top. Power and influence decided the outcomes of these struggles, and the number and positions of one's clients were critical components of that power and influence. Fourth, because fulfillment of the economic plan was decisive, systemic pressures led officials to conspire together and use their ties to achieve that goal.

The faction led by Brezhnev provides a good case study of patron-client relations in the Soviet system. Many members of the Brezhnev faction came from Dnepropetrovsk, where Brezhnev had served as first secretary of the provincial party organization. Andrei P. Kirilenko, a Politburo member and Central Committee secretary under Brezhnev, was first secretary of the regional committee of Dnepropetrovsk. Volodymyr Shcherbyts'kyy, named as first secretary of the Ukrainian apparatus under Brezhnev, succeeded Kirilenko in that position. Nikolai A. Tikhonov, appointed by Brezhnev as first deputy chairman of the Soviet Union's Council of Ministers, graduated from the Dnepropetrovsk College of Metallurgy and presided over the economic council of Dnepropetrovskaya Oblast. Finally, Nikolai A. Shchelokov, minister of internal affairs under Brezhnev, was a former chairman of the Dnepropetrovsk soviet.

Patron-client relations had implications for policy making in the party and government bureaucracies. Promotion of trusted subordinates into influential positions facilitated policy formation and policy execution. A network of clients helped to ensure that a patron's policies could be carried out. In addition, patrons relied on their clients to provide an accurate flow of information on events throughout the country. This information assisted policy makers in ensuring that their programs were being implemented.

Party Membership

The CPSU placed stringent requirements on its membership. Party members had to work indefatigably on the party's behalf, actively participate in the political life of the country, and set a moral and political example for those who were not members of the party. Despite these obligations, the benefits of membership compelled many to join the party. Membership in the CPSU was a requirement for career advancement. In addition, a career in the party could also serve as a means for upward mobility from the working class or peasantry into white-collar positions. Moreover, for those interested in political activities, the party was a vehicle for political participation.

Party members had a duty to increase their political knowledge and qualifications. Such efforts indicated a willingness to make a career of party work. The CPSU has set up a series of party schools whose courses range in difficulty from the elementary to the advanced. These schools were located at the local, intermediate, and all-union levels of the political system. Training in party schools strengthened the ideological, political, and administrative abilities of party members, especially officials of the CPSU apparatus. Although the stated purpose of party training was to better equip party members to perform their jobs, it acted as one additional means to promote a common outlook and ideological perspective among members of the party apparatus.

Honor boards, such as this one in Narva, Estonian Republic, recognized the work of CPSU members.
Courtesy Jonathan Tetzlaff

Selection Procedures

The standards for admission into the CPSU required that a person be at least eighteen years old, have a good personal record, and possess some knowledge of the principles of Marxism-Leninism. Those who wanted to become party members had to secure references from at least three party members of at least five years' standing. In the case of prospective members entering the party from the Komsomol, one of the references had to have been written by a member of the Komsomol city or district committee. These references attested to the candidate's moral, civic, and professional qualities.

Only the PPO general meeting could accept or reject an application for membership (see Primary Party Organization, this ch.). Before the general meeting, however, the PPO secretary reviewed that person's application, and the secretary's recommendations counted heavily in the selection process. The district or town party committee then confirmed the acceptance of the prospective member. Upon acceptance, the individual became a candidate (nonvoting) member of the party for one year. The new candidate paid an admission fee of 2 rubles (for value of the ruble—see Glossary)

317

and monthly dues that varied from 10 kopeks to 3 percent of salary, depending on the person's income.

During the candidate stage, the individual had to faithfully carry out responsibilities assigned by the party. Candidates had to demonstrate their ability to cope with the obligations of party membership, which included attendance at party meetings, improvements in labor productivity, and efforts to strengthen one's understanding of Marxism-Leninism. After one year, the candidate had to again solicit recommendations from three members of five years' standing and undergo a review by the PPO secretary. The PPO general meeting then voted on the candidate's application for full membership, and the district or city organization confirmed the acceptance of the full member.

The *Party Rules* defined many obligations for CPSU members. For example, the party member had to resolutely execute the general line and directives of the party, explain to the nonparty masses the foreign and domestic policies of the CPSU, and facilitate the strengthening of the party's bonds with the people. In addition, party members had to strive to increase productivity in their regular jobs, improve the quality of their work, and "inject into the economy the achievements of science and technology." The *Party Rules* required that members participate in party activities, broaden their political horizons, and struggle against any manifestation of bourgeois ideology and religious prejudices. Party members had to strictly observe the norms of communist morality, place social interests higher than personal interests, and exhibit modesty and orderliness. Party members also undertook criticism of other members and self-criticism in meetings. Criticism and self-criticism uncovered conflicts, mistakes, and shortcomings that resulted from personal or organizational inadequacies. Once flaws were uncovered, criticism and self-criticism generated peer pressure to remove the problem. Finally, party members had to consistently promote the foreign policy of the Soviet Union and work to strengthen the defense forces of the country.

In addition to their obligations, full members of the CPSU had certain rights. They participated in elections of candidates to party organs, and they could be chosen for positions in the hierarchy. At party meetings, conferences, meetings of party committees, and in the party press, party members could freely discuss issues connected with the policy and activities of the party. According to the *Party Rules,* party members could criticize any party organ and any other party member (including members of the leadership) at party meetings, plenums and conferences, and congresses at all levels of the party hierarchy. The norms of democratic centralism precluded such criticism, however. Any party member brave enough to make such criticism would have been subject to party discipline and possible exclusion from the CPSU. A party member had the right to participate in party meetings, bureau sessions, and committees when these bodies discussed that person's activities or behavior. In addition, a party member could submit questions, statements, and suggestions to any party body, including the Central Committee, and demand a reply.

The party could take several forms of disciplinary action against members who broke its rules. The lightest penalty was a reprimand, followed by a censure. Both of these measures were entered into the member's permanent party record. A harsher punishment was reduction to candidate status for one year. For severe rule infractions, a party member could be expelled. The stigma attached to expulsion from the party remained with the individual throughout his life and precluded career advancement, access to better housing facilities, and educational opportunities for the person's children. In some instances, expelled party members have lost high-status positions.

Another form of disciplinary action, which occurred on a wider scale, was the so-called ''exchange of party documents.'' This entailed a review of the party's membership and discussions between party members and their superiors, followed by replacement of old party cards. The exchange of party documents provided an occasion for the CPSU to rid itself of members who breached party discipline. Party sources reported that exchanges of party cards were not purges (see The Period of the Purges, ch. 2). Nevertheless, the Russian word *chistka,* which means purge, was the term the party used to describe these exchanges. The last exchange of party documents occurred in 1975.

Several reasons accounted for the desire of Soviet citizens to join the party, despite the stringent obligations it placed upon its members and the formal nature of their rights. The primary reason for joining the party was opportunity for career advancement and social mobility. Party membership was a prerequisite for promotion to managerial positions in Soviet society. In addition, party membership opened up the possibility for travel abroad, admission to special shops for consumer goods, access to Western media, and cash bonuses for work. Party membership also provided the chance for upward mobility from the working class or peasantry into professional, white-collar positions in the party apparatus. Children of lower-class parents tended to enter this ''political class'' in order to raise their status. Having become members of this class, these people could then ensure their offspring access to the amenities Soviet life has to offer.

Party membership had other, less tangible rewards. It enabled an individual to claim membership in an organization linked to Russian historical tradition, to the Bolshevik Revolution, and to the world-historical movement the CPSU claimed to lead. In addition, as the dominant political institution in society, the party offered the most important outlet for political participation. These benefits encouraged a feeling of in-group solidarity with other members of the CPSU and a sense of civic efficacy.

Training

The CPSU obligated its members constantly to improve their understanding of Marxism-Leninism and political qualifications. Toward these goals, the party operated a series of schools to train party members in Marxism-Leninism, to recruit rank-and-file members into its administration, and to communicate party principles and policies to the membership, particularly to officials in the apparatus.

Party schools operated at all levels of the hierarchy. The primary party schools formed the elementary level of the training system. These schools were informal; they could be as simple as a circle of workers who met after work to discuss the life of Lenin, political and economic affairs, or current party policies. Since the mid-1960s, enrollments in these schools have been declining because of the increased education level of the population. These courses were open to nonmembers, whose participation could be used to demonstrate a desire to join the party. Trade unions and the Komsomol administered schools with similar levels of instruction. Trade unions operated "people's universities" and "schools of communist labor." The former treated a variety of topics and enrolled students in a group that advanced as a class from level to level. Schools of communist labor were oriented to problems of production. Lectures often dealt with the correct attitude toward work.

The party had a variety of schools at the intermediate level. Schools of the Fundamentals of Marxism-Leninism, administered by district and city party committees, required some knowledge of Marxism-Leninism. Classes were small, which permitted individual attention to students and the examination of subject matter in detail. Courses in these schools reviewed the fundamentals of party doctrine and included subjects such as party history, political economy, and Marxist-Leninist philosophy. Since the mid-1970s, enrollment in these schools has grown. In 1981 the party formed the Schools for Young Communists. These institutions offered instruction to candidate members of the party and to people who had recently become full members.

The Schools of Scientific Communism offered more specialized instruction at the intermediate level. In 1989 topics included current events in domestic and international affairs. Schools for the party's economic specialists offered training in such areas as party direction of trade unions, economic policy, and the theory of developed socialism. Schools for ideological specialists included courses for PPO secretaries and group leaders, party lecturers, and media personnel. These schools offered courses on the principles of Marxism-Leninism and on the means and methods of the party's control over ideological affairs.

Party training at the intermediate level also encompassed seminars in Marxist-Leninist theory and methods. Members of the scientific intelligentsia and professors at institutions of higher education attended these seminars. Subjects included philosophical and social science topics: the scientific-technical revolution, economics, the theory of proletarian internationalism, communist morality, and socialist democracy.

Finally, the party offered courses for raising the qualifications of party and soviet officials at the provincial and republic levels. These courses involved supplementary training in a variety of subjects first treated in lower-level party schools. Party officials also could take correspondence courses offered either by the higher party school of their republic or under the auspices of the Academy of Social Sciences of the CPSU Central Committee.

At the all-union level, the Higher Party School and the Academy of Social Sciences in Moscow were staffed with instructors attached to the CPSU Central Committee departments (see Secretariat, this ch.). These schools trained officials to enter the party elite at the all-union level. The Higher Party School graduated about 300 students per year; the Academy of Social Sciences graduated approximately 100.

Training at party schools served a variety of purposes. Willingness to participate in party courses at the lowest level could indicate an aspiration to join the party or ensure advancement from candidate status to that of full member. Once in the party, participation in training courses demonstrated a desire to enter into full-time, salaried party work. Indeed, such coursework was a prerequisite for this kind of a career. Party training also created an in-group consciousness among those who attended courses, particularly at the intermediate and all-union levels. Various kinds of specialists from wide-ranging backgrounds took these courses;

321

hence, party schools integrated officials from all sectors of the party and government bureaucracies and inculcated a shared consciousness of their duties and status. Equally important, party schools, according to American Soviet specialists Frederick C. Barghoorn and Thomas F. Remington, underscored the CPSU's legitimacy by providing a theoretical basis for its policies. Courses in party schools examined current events and policy issues from the party's perspective. Thus, party training counteracted the insular viewpoints that could arise as a result of officials' attention to their narrow fields of specialization.

Social Composition of the Party

The Bolshevik organization began as a tightly knit group of revolutionaries whose leadership was dominated by members of the Russian, Jewish, and Polish intelligentsia but whose mass base consisted mainly of industrial workers from Russia's largest cities. By the late 1980s, for the most part the social characteristics of the party membership reflected the social and economic changes the Soviet Union had undergone over the more than seventy years of its existence. Consequently, professionals made up a percentage of party membership that exceeded their percentage of the population, and the number of party members with a secondary or higher education has constantly risen since the mid-1930s. Similarly, the party has recruited its members from all nationalities. As a result, the gap between the ethnic groups that dominated the party and other ethnic groups in the early years has narrowed. However, this gap has not disappeared completely. By contrast, the percentage of women in the party has continued to lag behind the percentage of women in the population. Altogether, the social characteristics of party members confirmed their status as an elite in the society. The social composition of the party reflected the decision made by Stalin in the 1930s and reaffirmed since that time both to make professional achievement and merit the primary criteria for admission into the party and to strive for the proportional representation of all groups within the party's ranks.

In 1987 the CPSU numbered more than 19 million members (see table 23, Appendix A). Party members constituted about 9.7 percent of the adult population. This figure represented an increase of 4 percent since 1956. Most of that increase, however, reflected the CPSU's rapid growth between 1956 and 1964 under the leadership of Khrushchev. Since 1971 the share of party membership in the adult population has risen only 0.3 percent.

In general, party members possessed a high occupational status in society, which belied the party's claims to be the vanguard of the working class. The party did not publish statistics on the social status of its membership. Nevertheless, the CPSU did publish statistics on its membership's "social position," which denoted the class affiliation of members at the time they joined the CPSU. Workers and peasants who joined the party often used their membership to advance into white-collar positions. Were statistics available on the social status of party members, they would reveal the disproportional representation of white-collar professionals in party ranks. Available figures on the social position of party members, however, also indicated the importance of professionals in the party (see table 24, Appendix A). In 1987 persons who were members of the white-collar professions when they joined the CPSU made up 43.1 percent of the party, while those who were members of the working class made up 45.3 percent and those who were peasants made up 11.6 percent. By contrast, in 1987 Soviet sources reported that 27.8 percent of the working population consisted of white-collar professionals, 62.7 were workers, and 9.5 percent were peasants. The high percentage of members who were professionals when they joined the party, together with the accelerated advancement into white-collar positions by members who were workers or peasants, suggested that the CPSU was not a proletarian party but rather one dominated by white-collar professionals.

Statistics on the percentage of party members with higher education replicated this pattern (see table 25, Appendix A). Between 1967 and 1987, the percentage of party members who had completed higher education almost doubled. In 1987 over 32 percent of the party membership had received a degree from an institution of higher education. By contrast, in that same year only 7.3 percent of the general population had received a similar degree. Again, the figures indicate that the CPSU was less the party of the working class than the party of the white-collar intelligentsia.

The ethnic composition of the party reflected further disproportions between the party and the population as a whole (see table 26, Appendix A). In 1922 the share of Russian members in the party exceeded their proportion of the population by 19 percent. Since that time, the gap between Russians and other nationalities has narrowed. In 1979 Russians constituted 52 percent of the Soviet population; however, they constituted 60 percent of the party in 1981. Moreover, the percentage of Russians in the party apparatus was probably even greater than their percentage in the party as a whole.

In the late 1970s and early 1980s, other major nationalities whose share of party membership exceeded their proportion of the population were the Belorussians, the Georgians, and the Jews (the percentage of Jews in the party was twice their percentage in the Soviet population as a whole). The proportion of Ukrainians and Armenians in the party equaled their share of the Soviet population. Armenians and Jews shared certain characteristics that help explain their relatively high proportion of party membership. Members of these nationalities tended to be more urbanized, educated, and geographically mobile than the norm. These characteristics correlated strongly with party membership. The Georgians, although not as urbanized as the Armenians or the Jews, tended to be highly educated. Other reasons explained the relatively high percentage of party membership among the Belorussians and Ukrainians. These two East Slavic nationalities are culturally close to the Russians. In addition, the central party apparatus has sought to demonstrate that political opportunities for Belorussians and Ukrainians equal those for Russians.

Those major nationalities having the lowest proportion of party members compared with their share of the population were the Tadzhiks, Uzbeks, Kirgiz, and Turkmens of Central Asia, and the Moldavians. The Central Asians resisted membership in an organization they perceived to be dominated by East Slavs in general and Russians in particular. Similar considerations applied to the Moldavians, whose territory the Soviet Union seized from Romania in World War II (see Other Major Nationalities, ch. 4).

The percentage of women in the party lagged far behind the proportion of women in the population (see table 27, Appendix A). In 1987 women comprised 29.3 percent of the party and 53 percent of the population. Several reasons explained women's lack of interest in joining the party. First, party work required a substantial commitment of time from each member (see Selection Procedures, this ch.). Approximately 80 percent of Soviet women held jobs and, in addition, spent long hours caring for children, shopping, and running households. Second, Muslim peoples, who constituted a high percentage of the Soviet population, discouraged female participation in politics. Third, Soviet women might not enter the CPSU because they perceived that the social mores of that organization restricted their ability to move up the hierarchy into positions of power. The 307 members elected to the CPSU Central Committee at the Twenty-Seventh Party Congress in 1986 included only 13 women. In the 1980s, women made up only about 33 percent of PPO secretaries, 20 percent of district party organization secretaries, and 3.2 percent of *obkom* bureau members. No woman has been a full member of the Politburo. Thus, the higher the level in the party hierarchy, the lower the percentage of women.

In his report to the CPSU Central Committee on January 27, 1987, General Secretary Gorbachev called for the promotion of more women and representatives of national minorities and ethnic groups into leading positions in the party. That policy, together with the pursuit of other policies that encourage greater urbanization, geographic mobility, and higher education levels, may lead to a greater proportion of women and national minorities in influential party positions. If women and national minorities perceive the opportunity to move up the hierarchy into positions of power, a greater number of these underrepresented groups might be willing to join the party and thus help to balance the sexual and ethnic composition of the CPSU with that of the population as a whole.

* * *

A plethora of works has been written on all aspects of the CPSU. The following general works on the Soviet Union contain chapters on the party: John A. Armstrong's *Ideology, Politics, and Government in the Soviet Union,* John N. Hazard's *The Soviet System of Government,* and Frederick C. Barghoorn and Thomas F. Remington's *Politics in the USSR.* The best general treatment of the CPSU is found in *The Soviet Communist Party* by Ronald J. Hill and Peter Frank. A number of specialized treatments of various aspects of the party also have been written. Alfred G. Meyer's *Leninism* remains a classic study of the thought, political program, and tactics of Lenin. Nina Tumarkin's *Lenin Lives!* examines the Lenin cult in the Soviet Union. George Breslauer's *Khrushchev and Brezhnev as Leaders* treats attempts by Khrushchev and Brezhnev to build authority in the political system. For thorough analyses of intermediate-level and local-level party organizations, works by Joel C. Moses are helpful. Scholars who have examined the *nomenklatura* and patron-client relations include John P. Willerton, Jr., Bohdan Harasymiw, and Gyula Jozsza. Michael Voslensky's *Nomenklatura* provides an insider's account of the ruling class. John H. Miller's "The Communist Party" treats the social characteristics of the CPSU's membership. (For further information and complete citations, see Bibliography.)

Chapter 8. Government Structure and Functions

Meeting of the Presidium of the Supreme Soviet

THE GOVERNMENT OF the Soviet Union administered the country's economy and society. It implemented decisions made by the leading political institution in the country, the Communist Party of the Soviet Union (CPSU).

In the late 1980s, the government appeared to have many characteristics in common with Western, democratic political systems. For instance, a constitution established all organs of government and granted to citizens a series of political and civic rights. A legislative body, the Congress of People's Deputies, and its standing legislature, the Supreme Soviet, represented the principle of popular sovereignty. The Supreme Soviet, which had an elected chairman who functioned as head of state, oversaw the Council of Ministers, which acted as the executive branch of the government. The chairman of the Council of Ministers, whose selection was approved by the legislative branch, functioned as head of government. A constitutionally based judicial branch of government included a court system, headed by the Supreme Court, that was responsible for overseeing the observance of Soviet law by government bodies. According to the Constitution of 1977, the government had a federal structure, permitting the republics some authority over policy implementation and offering the national minorities the appearance of participation in the management of their own affairs.

In practice, however, the government differed markedly from Western systems. In the late 1980s, the CPSU performed many functions that governments of other countries usually perform. For example, the party decided on the policy alternatives that the government ultimately implemented. The government merely ratified the party's decisions to lend them an aura of legitimacy. The CPSU used a variety of mechanisms to ensure that the government adhered to its policies. The party, using its *nomenklatura* (see Glossary) authority, placed its loyalists in leadership positions throughout the government, where they were subject to the norms of democratic centralism (see Glossary). Party bodies closely monitored the actions of government ministries, agencies, and legislative organs.

The content of the Soviet Constitution differed in many ways from typical Western constitutions. It generally described existing political relationships, as determined by the CPSU, rather than prescribing an ideal set of political relationships. The Constitution was long and detailed, giving technical specifications for individual organs of government. The Constitution included political statements, such as foreign policy goals, and provided a theoretical definition of the state within the ideological framework of Marxism-Leninism (see Glossary). The CPSU could radically change the constitution or remake it completely, as it has done several times in the past.

The Council of Ministers acted as the executive body of the government. Its most important duties lay in the administration of the economy. The council was thoroughly under the control of the CPSU, and its chairman—the prime minister—was always a member of the Politburo (see Politburo, ch. 7). The council, which in 1989 included more than 100 members, was too large and unwieldy to act as a unified executive body. The council's Presidium, made up of the leading economic administrators and led by the chairman, exercised dominant power within the Council of Ministers.

According to the Constitution, as amended in 1988, the highest legislative body in the Soviet Union was the Congress of People's Deputies, which convened for the first time in May 1989. The main tasks of the congress were the election of the standing legislature, the Supreme Soviet, and the election of the chairman of the Supreme Soviet, who acted as head of state. Theoretically, the Congress of People's Deputies and the Supreme Soviet wielded enormous legislative power. In practice, however, the Congress of People's Deputies met only a few days in 1989 to approve decisions made by the party, the Council of Ministers, and its own Supreme Soviet. The Supreme Soviet, the Presidium of the Supreme Soviet, the chairman of the Supreme Soviet, and the Council of Ministers had substantial authority to enact laws, decrees, resolutions, and orders binding on the population. The Congress of People's Deputies had the authority to ratify these decisions.

The government lacked an independent judiciary. The Supreme Court supervised the lower courts and applied the law, as established by the Constitution or as interpreted by the Supreme Soviet. The Constitutional Oversight Committee reviewed the constitutionality of laws and acts. The Soviet Union lacked an adversary court procedure. Under Soviet law, which derived from Roman law, a procurator (see Glossary) worked together with a judge and a defense attorney to ensure that civil and criminal trials uncovered the truth of the case, rather than protecting individual rights.

The Soviet Union was a federal state made up of fifteen republics joined together in a theoretically voluntary union. In turn, a series of territorial units made up the republics. The republics also contained jurisdictions intended to protect the interests of national minorities. The republics had their own constitutions, which, along with the all-union (see Glossary) Constitution, provide the theoretical division of power in the Soviet Union. In 1989, however, the CPSU and the central government retained all significant authority, setting policies that were executed by republic, provincial (oblast, *krai*—see Glossary, and autonomous subdivision), and district (*raion*—see Glossary) governments.

Constitutional Authority of Government

The political theory underlying the Soviet Constitution differed from the political theory underlying constitutions in the West. Democratic constitutions are fundamentally prescriptive; they define a set of political relations to which their governments and citizens aspire. By contrast, Soviet constitutions have purported to describe a set of political relationships already in existence. Thus, as changes have occurred in the socioeconomic and political systems, the government has adopted new constitutions that have conformed to the new sets of realities.

The 1977 Constitution was generally descriptive; it differed from past constitutions in containing a preamble and a section on foreign policy that were prescriptive in tone. The Soviet Union has had a series of four constitutions, ratified in 1918, 1924, 1936, and 1977, respectively. On the surface, the four constitutions have resembled many constitutions adopted in the West. The differences between Soviet and Western constitutions, however, overshadowed the similarities. Soviet constitutions appeared to guarantee certain political rights, such as freedom of speech, assembly, and religious belief. They also identified a series of economic and social rights, as well as a set of duties that obligated all citizens. Nevertheless, Soviet constitutions did not contain provisions guaranteeing the inalienable rights of the citizenry, and they lacked the machinery to protect individual rights contained in many democratic constitutions. Thus, the population enjoyed political rights only to the extent that these rights conformed to the interests of building socialism (see Glossary). The CPSU alone reserved the authority to determine what lay in the interests of socialism. Finally, Soviet constitutions specified the form and content of regime symbols, such as the arms, the flag, and the state anthem.

The four constitutions had provisions in common. These provisions expressed the theoretical sovereignty of the working class and the leading role of the CPSU in government and society. All the constitutions have upheld the forms of socialist property (see

Glossary). Each of the constitutions has called for a system of soviets, or councils, to exercise governmental authority.

Early Soviet Constitutions

In the *Civil War in France, 1848–1850,* Karl Marx maintained that constitutions ought to reflect existing class and political relationships, not prescribe the nature of such relations. Vladimir I. Lenin adopted Marx's understanding of the role of constitutions in a state. Of certain provisions in the first Soviet constitution, he wrote that they were embodied in it *"after* they were already in actual practice." Joseph V. Stalin rejected a prescriptive preamble for the 1936 constitution, stating that the constitution should "register" the gains of socialism rather than prescribe "future achievement." The four Soviet constitutions thus have reflected the changes that government and society have undergone over the course of Soviet history.

The 1918 Constitution

The first constitution, which governed the Russian Soviet Federated Socialist Republic, described the regime that assumed power in the Bolshevik Revolution of 1917 (see Revolutions and Civil War, ch. 2). This constitution formally recognized the Bolshevik (see Glossary) party organization as the ruler of Russia according to the principle of the dictatorship of the proletariat (see Glossary). The constitution also stated that under the leadership of the Bolsheviks the workers formed a political alliance with the peasants. This constitution gave broad guarantees of equal rights to workers and peasants. It denied, however, the right of social groups that opposed the new government or supported the White armies in the Civil War (1918–21) to participate in elections to the soviets or to hold political power.

Supreme power rested with the All-Russian Congress of Soviets, made up of deputies from local soviets across Russia. The steering committee of the Congress of Soviets—known as the Central Executive Committee—acted as the "supreme organ of power" between sessions of the congress and as the collective presidency of the state.

The congress recognized the Council of People's Commissars (Sovet narodnykh komissarov—Sovnarkom) as the administrative arm of the young government. (The Sovnarkom had exercised governmental authority from November 1917 until the adoption of the 1918 constitution.) The constitution made the Sovnarkom responsible to the Congress of Soviets for the "general administration of the affairs of the state." The constitution enabled the

Sovnarkom to issue decrees carrying the full force of law when the congress was not in session. The congress then routinely approved these decrees at its next session.

The 1924 Constitution

The 1924 constitution legitimated the December 1922 union of the Russian Soviet Federated Socialist Republic, the Ukrainian Republic, the Belorussian Republic, and the Transcaucasian Soviet Federated Socialist Republic to form the Union of Soviet Socialist Republics. This constitution also altered the structure of the central government. It eliminated the Congress of Soviets and established the Central Executive Committee as the supreme body of state authority. In turn, the constitution divided the Central Executive Committee into the Soviet of the Union, which would represent the constituent republics, and the Soviet of Nationalities, which would represent the interests of nationality groups. The Presidium of the Central Executive Committee served as the collective presidency. Between sessions of the Central Executive Committee, the Presidium supervised the government administration. The Central Executive Committee also elected the Sovnarkom, which served as the executive arm of the government.

The 1936 Constitution

The 1936 constitution, adopted on December 5, 1936, and also known as the "Stalin" constitution, redesigned the government. The constitution repealed restrictions on voting and added universal direct suffrage and the right to work to rights guaranteed by the previous constitution. The constitution also provided for the direct election of all government bodies and their reorganization into a single, uniform system.

The 1936 constitution changed the name of the Central Executive Committee to the Supreme Soviet of the Union of Soviet Socialist Republics. Like its predecessor, the Supreme Soviet contained two chambers: the Soviet of the Union and the Soviet of Nationalities. The constitution empowered the Supreme Soviet to elect commissions, which performed most of the Supreme Soviet's work. As under the former constitution, the Presidium exercised the full powers of the Supreme Soviet between sessions and had the right to interpret laws. The chairman of the Presidium became the titular head of state. The Sovnarkom (after 1946 known as the Council of Ministers) continued to act as the executive arm of the government.

The 1977 Constitution

On October 7, 1977, the Supreme Soviet unanimously adopted

333

the fourth constitution, also known as the "Brezhnev" Constitution, named after CPSU general secretary Leonid I. Brezhnev (see Supreme Soviet, this ch.). The preamble stated that "the aims of the dictatorship of the proletariat having been fulfilled, the Soviet state has become the state of the whole people." That is, according to the new Constitution, the government no longer represented the workers alone but expressed "the will and interests of the workers, peasants, and intelligentsia, the working people of all nations and nationalities in the country." Compared with previous constitutions, the Brezhnev Constitution extended the bounds of constitutional regulation of society. The first chapter defined the leading role of the CPSU and established principles for the management of the state and the government. Later chapters established principles for economic management and cultural relations.

The 1977 Constitution was long and detailed. It included twenty-eight more articles than the 1936 constitution. The Constitution explicitly defined the division of responsibilities between the central and republic governments. For example, the Constitution placed the regulation of boundaries and administrative divisions within the jurisdiction of the republics. However, provisions established the rules under which the republics could make such changes. Thus, the Constitution concentrated on the operation of the government system as a whole.

Amendments to the 1977 Constitution

In October 1988, draft amendments and additions to the 1977 Constitution were published in the Soviet media for public discussion. Following the public review process, the Supreme Soviet adopted the amendments and additions in December 1988. The amendments and additions substantially and fundamentally changed the electoral and political systems. Although Soviet officials touted the changes as a return to "Leninist" forms and functions, citing that the Congress of People's Deputies had antecedents in the Congress of Soviets, they were unprecedented in many respects (see Central Government, this ch.). The position of chairman of the Supreme Soviet was formally designated and given specific powers, particularly leadership over the legislative agenda, the ability to issue orders (*rasporiazheniia*), and formal power to conduct negotiations and sign treaties with foreign governments and international organizations. The Constitutional Oversight Committee, composed of people who were not in the Congress of People's Deputies, was established and given formal power to review the constitutionality of laws and normative acts of the central and republic governments and to suggest their suspension and repeal. The electoral process was constitutionally opened up to multiple candidacies, although not to multiple-party candidacies. A legislative body—the Supreme Soviet—was to convene for regular spring and fall sessions, each lasting three to four months. Unlike the old Supreme Soviet, however, the new Supreme Soviet was indirectly elected by the population, being elected from among the members of the Congress of People's Deputies.

Amendment Process

Adoption of the Constitution was a legislative act of the Supreme Soviet. Amendments to the Constitution were likewise adopted by legislative act of that body. Amendments required the approval of a two-thirds majority of the deputies of the Congress of People's Deputies and could be initiated by the congress itself; the Supreme Soviet, acting through its commissions and committees; the Presidium or chairman of the Supreme Soviet; the Constitutional Oversight Committee; the Council of Ministers; republic soviets; the Committee of People's Control; the Supreme Court; the Procuracy; and the chief state arbiter. In addition, the leading boards of official organizations and even the Academy of Sciences (see Glossary) could initiate amendments and other legislation.

Soviet constitutions have been frequently amended and have been changed more often than in the West. Nevertheless, the 1977 Constitution attempted to avoid frequent amendment by establishing regulations for government bodies in separate, but equally authoritative, enabling legislation, such as the Law on the Council of Ministers of July 5, 1978. Other enabling legislation has included a law on citizenship, a law on elections to the Supreme Soviet, a law on the status of Supreme Soviet deputies, regulations for the Supreme Soviet, a resolution on commissions, regulations on local government, and laws on the Supreme Court and the Procuracy. The enabling legislation provided the specific and changing operating rules for these government bodies.

Constitutional Rights

Like democratic constitutions, the Soviet Constitution included a series of civic and political rights. Among these were the rights to freedom of speech, press, and assembly and the right to religious belief and worship. In addition, the Constitution provided for freedom of artistic work, protection of the family, inviolability of the person and home, and the right to privacy. In line with the Marxist-Leninist ideology of the regime, the Constitution also granted certain social and economic rights. Among these were the rights

Panoramic view of Moscow, photographed from Moscow University
Courtesy Jimmy Pritchard

to work, rest and leisure, health protection, care in old age and sickness, housing, education, and cultural benefits.

Unlike democratic constitutions, however, the Soviet Constitution placed limitations on political rights. Article 6 effectively eliminated organized opposition to the regime by granting to the CPSU the power to lead and guide society. Article 39 enabled the government to prohibit any activities it considered detrimental by stating that "Enjoyment of the rights and freedoms of citizens must not be to the detriment of the interests of society or the state." Article 59 obliged citizens to obey the laws and comply with the standards of socialist society as determined by the party. The regime did not treat as inalienable those political and socioeconomic rights the Constitution granted to the people.

Citizens enjoyed rights only when the exercise of those rights did not interfere with the interests of socialism, and the CPSU alone had the power and authority to determine policies for the government and society (see Lenin's Conception of the Party, ch. 7). For example, the right to freedom of expression contained in Article 52 could be suspended if the exercise of that freedom failed to be in accord with party policies. Until the era of *glasnost'* (see Glossary), freedom of expression did not entail the right to criticize the regime. The government had the power to ban meetings by unsanctioned religious groups, and violations of the laws that allowed limited religious expression were severely punished under the republics' criminal codes.

The Constitution also failed to provide political and judicial mechanisms for the protection of rights. Thus, the Constitution lacked explicit guarantees protecting the rights of the people, contained in the first ten amendments to the United States Constitution. In fact, the Supreme Soviet has never introduced amendments specifically designed to protect individual rights. Neither did the people have a higher authority within the government to which to appeal when they believed their rights had been violated. The Supreme Court had no power to ensure that constitutional rights were observed by legislation or were respected by the rest of the government. Although the Soviet Union signed the Final Act of the Conference on Security and Cooperation in Europe (Helsinki Accords—see Glossary), which mandated that internationally recognized human rights be respected in the signatory countries, no authority outside the Soviet Union could ensure citizen rights and freedoms. The government generally has failed to observe the provisions of this act. In the late 1980s, however, realigning constitutional and domestic law with international commitments on human rights was publicly debated.

Role of the Citizen

Article 59 of the Constitution stated that citizens' exercise of their rights was inseparable from performance of their duties. Articles 60 through 69 defined these duties. Citizens were obliged to work and to observe labor discipline. The legal code labeled evasion of work as "parasitism" and provided severe punishment for this crime. The Constitution also obligated citizens to protect socialist property and oppose corruption. All citizens performed military service as a duty to safeguard and "enhance the power and prestige of the Soviet state." Violation of this duty was a betrayal of the motherland and the gravest of crimes. Finally, the Constitution obligated parents to train their children for socially useful work and to raise them as worthy members of socialist society.

The Constitution and other legislation protected and enforced Soviet citizenship. Legislation on citizenship granted equal rights of citizenship to naturalized citizens as well as to the native born. Laws also specified that citizens could not freely renounce their citizenship. Citizens were required to apply for permission to do so from the Presidium of the Supreme Soviet, which could reject the application if the applicant had not completed military service, had judicial duties, or was responsible for family dependents. In addition, the Presidium could refuse the application to protect national security. However, the Presidium could revoke citizenship for defamation of the Soviet Union or for acts damaging to national prestige or security.

State Symbols

The Constitution specified the state flag and the arms of the Soviet Union. The flag had a red field, the traditional color of proletarian revolution. On the flag was a gold hammer and sickle, which represented the workers and the peasants, respectively, and the red star, which symbolized Soviet power, bordered in gold to contrast with the red field. The arms had a hammer and a sickle superimposed on a globe, with rays of the sun radiating from below, surrounded by sheaves of wheat. The rays of the sun represented the dawn of a new world, and the sheaves of wheat symbolized the economic plenty that was to be created in Soviet society. The inscription "Proletarians of all countries, unite!"—from Karl Marx and Friedrich Engels's *The Communist Manifesto*—was written on a red banner wound around the sheaves of wheat. The arms and flags of the republics carried the same visual themes, underscoring the unity of all the republics in the federation.

The Constitution specified that the state anthem be selected and confirmed by the Presidium of the Supreme Soviet. In 1989 the anthem was the *Anthem of the Soviet Union,* which had been composed under Stalin and contained fulsome praise of the dictator. After Stalin's death, the Presidium removed the offensive lyrics.

Central Government

Soviet political and legal theorists defined their government as a parliamentary system because in principle all power in the government emanated from the Congress of People's Deputies. In addition, according to the Constitution the Supreme Soviet elected both its own leadership and that of the all-union administrative and judicial agencies, which were responsible to it. In fact, the congress was too large to effectively exercise power, and it met only for short periods every year. When in session, the congress ratified legislation already promulgated by the Council of Ministers, the ministries, and the Supreme Soviet or its Presidium, and it discussed domestic and foreign policy. It also set the agenda for activities of the Supreme Soviet.

The lines separating legislative from executive functions were rather blurred. Thus, in addition to administering the government and the economy, the Council of Ministers could promulgate both resolutions that had the force of law and binding administrative orders. (The Supreme Soviet, however, had the ability to repeal such resolutions and orders.) Individual ministries—the chief administrative organs of the government—had the power to make laws in their respective fields. Thus, the legislative authority in this system was highly dispersed. In the late 1980s, some officials criticized law making by organs other than the Supreme Soviet and called for further amendments to the Constitution to give the Supreme Soviet greater authority over law making.

The CPSU effectively exercised control over the government. Leaders of the government were always party members and served on such party bodies as the Politburo and the Central Committee (see Central Party Institutions, ch. 7). In their role as party leaders, government officials participated in the formation of political, social, and economic policies. In addition, these officials were subject to the norms of democratic centralism, which required that they carry out the orders of the CPSU or face party discipline (see Democratic Centralism, ch. 7). Equally important, as part of its *nomenklatura* authority, the party had appointment power for all important positions in the government hierarchy (see Nomenklatura, ch. 7). The party also exercised control through the commissions and committees of the Supreme Soviet, which were supervised by Central Committee departments and commissions in their respective fields (see Secretariat, ch. 7). Each ministry contained its own primary party organization (PPO), which ensured that the staff of the ministry daily adhered to party policies (see Primary Party Organization, ch. 7). In fact, the party, not the ministerial and legislative system, was the leading political institution in the Soviet Union (see table 28, Appendix A).

Administrative Organs

Article 128 of the Constitution named the Council of Ministers as the "highest executive and administrative body of state authority" in the Soviet Union. Although the members of the council were subject to ratification and change by the Supreme Soviet and the Congress of People's Deputies, in 1989 they were actually appointed by the party. However, the council was too large to act as an effective decision-making body. The Council of Ministers Presidium, made up of the most influential economic administrators in the government, had the power to act in the name of the full council when it was not in session. The chairman of the full Council of Ministers, the equivalent of a prime minister, acted as head of government and chief economic administrator. In 1989 the chairman of the Council of Ministers, Nikolai I. Ryzhkov, sat on the Politburo.

Below the central institutions stood the ministries, state committees, and other governmental organs, which carried out regime policies in their respective fields subject to strict party control. The ministries managed the economic, social, and political systems.

Council of Ministers

The Council of Ministers and its agencies carried out the following tasks of government: internal and external security of the state; economic development, management, and administration; and ideological instruction and education. The council enacted the decisions of the party and therefore administered, through its bureaucratic regulatory and management arms, every aspect of Soviet life. As its primary task, however, the council managed the economy.

The Supreme Soviet ratified council membership as submitted by the chairman of the Council of Ministers. However, the actual selection of council ministers was made by the party leadership as part of its *nomenklatura* authority and was only later confirmed by a vote of the Supreme Soviet. Until recently, the Supreme Soviet endorsed such decisions unanimously and without debate. In mid-1989, however, Ryzhkov was forced to withdraw some candidates for ministerial posts because some of the committees of the

Supreme Soviet objected that the candidates were unqualified, thus forcing him to submit alternative candidates.

The Council of Ministers had the power to issue decrees, which carried the same force of law as legislative acts of the Supreme Soviet. The Supreme Soviet or, indirectly, the Congress of People's Deputies, could annul a decree if it found the decree to be in violation of the Constitution or an existing statute (perhaps upon the recommendation of the Constitutional Oversight Committee). Orders of the Council of Ministers on administrative matters technically did not carry the force of law, but they were binding on the ministerial apparatus. Although some decrees were published, most remained secret.

In 1989 the Council of Ministers had more than 100 members, including the ministers, the heads of government bureaus and state committees, and the chairmen of the councils of ministers of the fifteen constituent republics. Soviet scholars maintained that the Council of Ministers met "regularly," but reports in the press indicated that full meetings occurred only quarterly to hear and ratify a plan or a report from the chairman. In reality, the Council of Ministers delegated most of its functions to its Presidium or to the individual ministries.

Chairman of the Council of Ministers

The Constitution placed the chairman of the Council of Ministers at the head of government. As such, the chairman acted as the prime minister and therefore was responsible for enacting party decisions and ensuring that their implementation conformed to the intentions of the party leadership. Three party leaders have served concurrently as the chairman of the Council of Ministers. Lenin chaired the Sovnarkom when he was the de facto head of the party. Stalin, who was the party's first general secretary, became chairman during World War II and remained in that position until his death in 1953. In March 1958, Nikita S. Khrushchev, who had been first secretary since 1953 (the title changed to first secretary after Stalin's death and reverted to general secretary in 1966), took over the position of chairman of the Council of Ministers also. After Khrushchev's ouster in 1964, in order to avoid too much concentration of power, the party established a policy that the positions of chairman of the Council of Ministers and first (general) secretary of the party had to be filled by two different persons.

Because of the heavy involvement of the government in economic administration, chairmen of the Council of Ministers since Khrushchev have been experienced industrial administrators rather than political decision makers. Although the chairman occupied a seat

Officials leave the Kremlin after a CPSU Central Committee plenum in September 1988. The Council of Ministers and the Presidium of the Supreme Soviet buildings are in the background.
Courtesy Jimmy Pritchard

on the Politburo and thus had a voice in decision making at the highest level, this official was obliged to defer to other leaders in matters not pertaining to the economy. Thus, the chairman of the Council of Ministers had less power than the general secretary and perhaps less power than party secretaries who were members of the Politburo (see Secretariat, ch. 7).

Council of Ministers Presidium

The Constitution stipulated that the Council of Ministers form a Presidium as the "standing body of the Council of Ministers" to coordinate its work. The Presidium had the power to act on questions and speak for the government when the council was not in session. Apart from a few references in the Soviet literature indicating that the Presidium provided top-level guidance and coordination for the economy, little was known about the Presidium. In the words of American Sovietologist Jerry F. Hough, it was "a most shadowy institution."

Members of the council's Presidium represented the government's major planning and production organizations. Although Soviet sources had differing opinions on its membership, they always pointed to the council's chairman, first deputy chairmen, and

343

deputy chairmen as members. Deputy chairmen and first deputy chairmen usually served as the head of the State Planning Committee (Gosudarstvennyi planovyi komitet—Gosplan); the chairmen of the state committees for science and technology, construction, and material and technical supply; and the permanent representative to the Council for Mutual Economic Assistance (Comecon—see Appendix B). Deputy chairmen could also act as high-level planners in the major sectors of the economy, known as industrial complexes (see The Complexes and the Ministries, ch. 12). These planners served as chairmen of the Council of Ministers' bureaus and commissions for foreign economic relations, the defense industry, machine building, energy, and social development. Some Soviet sources included the minister of finance, the chairman of the Committee of People's Control, and the CPSU general secretary as members of the Presidium of the Council of Ministers. Thus, the membership of the Presidium indicated that it functioned as the "economic bureau" of the full Council of Ministers.

Ministerial System

Ministers were the chief administrative officials of the government. While most ministers managed branches of the economy, others managed affairs of state, such as foreign policy, defense, justice, and finance. Unlike parliamentary systems in which ministers are members of the parliament, Soviet ministers were not necessarily members of the Supreme Soviet and did not have to be elected. Soviet ministers usually rose within a ministry; having begun work in one ministry, they could, however, be appointed to a similar position in another. Thus, by the time the party appointed an official to a ministerial position, that person was fully acquainted with the affairs of the ministry and was well trained in avoiding conflict with the party. Until the late 1980s, ministers enjoyed long tenures, commonly serving for decades and often dying in office.

Two types of ministries made up the ministerial system: all-union and union-republic. All-union ministries oversaw a particular activity for the entire country and were controlled by the all-union party apparatus and the government in Moscow. Republic governments had no corresponding ministry, although all-union ministries had branch offices in the republics. Union-republic ministries had a central ministry in Moscow, which coordinated the work of counterpart ministries in the republic governments. Republic party organizations also oversaw the work of the union-republic ministries in their domain.

The Constitution determined into which category certain ministries fell. The Ministry of Foreign Affairs was a union-republic ministry, reflecting the republics' constitutional right to foreign representation. Although the republics had foreign ministries, the central Ministry of Foreign Affairs in Moscow in fact conducted all diplomacy for the Soviet Union (see The Ministry of Foreign Affairs, ch. 10).

All-union ministries were more centralized, thus permitting greater control over vital functions. Union-republic ministries appeared to exercise limited autonomy in nonvital areas. In practice, the central government dominated the union-republic ministries, although in theory each level of government possessed equal authority over its affairs.

Union-republic ministries offered some practical economic advantages. Republic representatives in the union-republic ministries attempted to ensure that the interests of the republics were taken into account in policy formation. In addition, the arrangement permitted the central ministry to set guidelines that the republics could then adapt to their local conditions. The central ministry in Moscow also could delegate some responsibilities to the republic level.

The internal structures of both all-union and union-republic ministries were highly centralized. A central ministry had large functional departments and specialized directorates. Chief directorates carried out the most important specialized functions in larger ministries. Specialized functions included foreign contracts, planning, finance, construction, personnel, and staff services. The first department of any ministry, staffed by personnel from the Committee for State Security (Komitet gosudarstvennoi bezopasnosti—KGB), controlled security.

State committees and government agencies similarly were categorized as all-union and union-republic organizations. State committees oversaw technical matters that involved many aspects of government, such as standards, inventions and discoveries, labor and social issues, sports, prices, and statistics. Other agencies, such as the news agency TASS (see Glossary) and the Academy of Sciences, oversaw affairs under their purview.

Ministries and state committees not only managed the economy, government, and society but also could make laws. Most ministries and state committees issued orders and instructions that were binding only on their organizations. Some ministries, however, could issue orders within a legally specified area of responsibility that were binding on society as a whole. These orders carried the same force of law as acts of the Supreme Soviet. For example, the Ministry of Finance set the rules for any form of foreign exchange.

Party Control of the Ministerial Apparatus

The ministries and state committees operated without the appearance of party control. Nevertheless, the party ensured its authority over the government through several mechanisms designed to preserve its leading role in society.

Considerable overlap between the memberships of the Council of Ministers and leading party bodies facilitated both policy coordination between the two organizations and party control. The chairman of the Council of Ministers normally occupied a seat on the Politburo, which gave him additional authority to ensure the implementation of his decisions. In 1989 the first deputy chairman of the Council of Ministers, Iurii D. Masliukov, was promoted to full-member status on the Central Committee, and both he and deputy chairman Aleksandra P. Biriukova were candidate members of the Politburo. In early 1989, Viktor M. Chebrikov, the head of the KGB, and Eduard A. Shevardnadze, the minister of foreign affairs, were also Politburo members. In addition, most ministers and chairmen of state committees were either full or candidate members of the Central Committee (see Central Committee, ch. 7). Thus, the norms of democratic centralism obliged council members to adhere to party policies.

Within the Council of Ministers and the ministries, the party used its *nomenklatura* authority to place its people in influential positions. *Nomenklatura* refers both to the positions that the Central Committee apparatus of the party has the power to fill and to a list of people qualified to fill them. Approximately one-third of the administrative positions in the council bureaucracy, including the most important ones, were on the *nomenklatura* list. Occupants of these positions well understood that the party could remove them if they failed to adhere to its policies.

Finally, in what is known as dual subordination, the staff of each ministry was required to respond to orders and directions from its primary party organization (PPO), as well as to the ministries' hierarchy. Party members on the staff of the ministry were bound by the norms of democratic centralism to obey the orders of the secretary of the PPO, who represented the CPSU hierarchy in the ministry. The secretary of the PPO ensured that CPSU policies were carried out in the day-to-day activities of the ministries.

Congress of People's Deputies

In 1989 the Congress of People's Deputies stood at the apex of the system of soviets and was the highest legislative organ in the country. Created by amendment to the Constitution in December

1988, the Congress of People's Deputies theoretically represented the united authority of the congresses and soviets in the republics. In addition to its broad duties, it created and monitored all other government bodies having the authority to issue decrees. In 1989 the Congress of People's Deputies, however, was largely a ceremonial forum meeting only a few days a year to ratify and debate party and government decisions and to elect from its own membership the Supreme Soviet to carry out legislative functions between sittings of the congress. Other responsibilities of the Congress of People's Deputies included changing the Constitution, adopting decisions concerning state borders and the federal structure, ratifying government plans, electing the chairman and first deputy chairman of the Supreme Soviet, and electing members of the Constitutional Oversight Committee.

In the elections that took place under the 1988 law on electing deputies to the Congress of People's Deputies, several candidates were allowed to run for the same office for the first time since 1917. Nevertheless, no party except the CPSU was allowed to field candidates, and a large bloc of seats was reserved for CPSU members and members of other officially sanctioned organizations. In the Estonian, Latvian, and Lithuanian republics and to a far lesser degree in the Belorussian Republic, however, popular fronts, which were tantamount to political parties, fielded their own candidates. The regime maintained that these elections demonstrated that the Soviet people could freely choose their own government.

The Congress of People's Deputies that was elected in March through May 1989 consisted of 2,250 deputies—1,500 from the electoral districts and national-territorial electoral districts and 750 from officially sanctioned organizations, including the CPSU. In all, 5,074 individuals were registered as candidates. A main election was held in which 89.8 percent of the eligible voters, or 172.8 million people, participated. Following the main election, runoff elections were held in districts in which a candidate failed to obtain a majority of the votes cast in the main election. Runoff elections took place in 76 out of 1,500 electoral districts. Repeat elections were also held in 198 electoral districts where less than one-half of the eligible voters in the district voted. Official organizations also held elections in which 84.2 percent of the eligible voters, or 162 million people, participated. Five repeat elections were for organizations. Of the 2,250 deputies elected, 8.1 percent were newly elected to the legislature.

The CPSU has used several means to exercise control over the activities of the legislative system. Since 1964 the chairman of the Supreme Soviet's Presidium has been a member of the Politburo, and other members of the Presidium have sat on the party's Central Committee. In addition, since 1977 CPSU general secretaries have usually held the post of chairman of the Presidium of the Supreme Soviet, although Mikhail S. Gorbachev, at first, did not hold this post. Also, the party has had a large role in determining which of the elected deputies would serve as deputies in the Supreme Soviet. As part of their own *nomenklatura* authority, local party organizations have selected candidates to run in the elections. The commissions and committees, which had some power to oversee government policy, have accepted direction from the CPSU's Central Committee departments and their chairmen, and a large proportion of their memberships has consisted of CPSU members. In the Congress of People's Deputies elected in 1989, about 87 percent, or 1,957 deputies, were members or candidate members of the CPSU.

Elections to the Congress of People's Deputies

In 1989 three categories of deputies were selected to the Congress of People's Deputies: those representing the CPSU and officially recognized organizations; those representing the population as divided into residential electoral districts; and those representing the population as divided into national territories. In 1989 one-third (750) of the deputies were elected in each category. Quotas for deputies were assigned to the various official organizations, electoral districts, and national-territorial electoral districts. The largest organizational quotas were reserved for the CPSU, trade unions, collective farms (see Glossary), Komsomol (see Glossary), veterans, retired workers, and the Committee of Soviet Women. Minor but officially sanctioned groups such as stamp collectors, cinema fans, book lovers, and musicians were also represented. Because individual voters belonged to several different constituencies, they could vote in elections for several deputies.

In principle, voters in nationwide elections had the freedom to vote for the party-endorsed candidate or for other candidates on the ballot (if any), to write in the name of another candidate, or to refrain from voting. In the early 1989 elections, some of the candidates officially endorsed by the CPSU were rejected by the voters, including high-level party officials, such as Iurii Solov'ev, the party secretary of Leningrad.

The regime considered voting a duty rather than a right. Citizens age eighteen and older voted in soviet elections, and those age twenty-one and older were eligible to be elected to the Congress of People's Deputies. Persons holding governmental posts, however, could not be elected deputy to the soviet that appointed them. Citizens

Building housing the Supreme Soviet and the Council of Ministers
of the Tadzhik Republic in Dushanbe
Building housing the Presidium of the Supreme Soviet
of the Kirgiz Republic in Frunze
Courtesy Jimmy Pritchard

349

had the right to participate in election campaigns and the right to campaign for any candidate.

Deputies and Citizen Involvement

Deputies to the Congress of People's Deputies represented a cross section of the various economic and professional groups in the population. According to the official Credentials Commission report, in terms of occupation 24.8 percent of the deputies to the congress were "workers in industry, construction, transport, or communications," 18.9 percent were in agriculture, and of both these groups 23.7 percent were ordinary workers and peasants. Managers in industry and agriculture made up 6.8 percent and 8.5 percent of the deputies, respectively. Party secretaries at various levels made up 10.5 percent of the deputies. Military officers made up 3.6 percent of the deputies. In terms of age, 88.6 percent were under age sixty, while 8.3 percent were under age thirty. Regarding level of education, 75.7 percent possessed complete or incomplete higher education, and 6.2 percent were full or corresponding members of the central or republic academies of sciences. Nevertheless, selection procedures underrepresented some segments of society. Only 15.6 percent of the delegates were women, and just seven of the deputies (0.3 percent) were religious leaders.

Supreme Soviet

The Supreme Soviet served as the highest organ of state power between sittings of the Congress of People's Deputies. The Supreme Soviet formally appointed the chairman of the Council of Ministers, ratified or rejected his candidates for ministerial posts and supervised their work, and adopted economic plans and budgets and reported on their implementation. Through its chairman, the Supreme Soviet represented the country in formal diplomacy. It also had the authority to appoint the Defense Council, confer military and diplomatic ranks, declare war, ratify treaties, and repeal acts of the Presidium of the Supreme Soviet, the chairman of the Supreme Soviet, and the Council of Ministers.

The Supreme Soviet has traditionally delegated its powers to the government bodies it has elected and nominally supervised. The Supreme Soviet reserved the right to review and formally approve their actions, and in the past it always gave this approval. Actions of other government bodies elected by the Supreme Soviet became law with force equal to the Supreme Soviet's own decisions (see Administrative Organs, this ch.). The commissions and committees have played a minor role in ensuring that the language of legislation was uniform. In 1989 they took an active role in judging the qualifications of candidates for ministerial bodies and in questioning governmental operations.

Organs of the Supreme Soviet

The Supreme Soviet has functioned with the help of several secondary organs. The Presidium has acted as the steering committee of the Supreme Soviet while it was in session. In 1989 both chambers of the Supreme Soviet—the Soviet of the Union and the Soviet of Nationalities—met either individually or jointly in sessions planned to last six to eight months. Each chamber had commissions and committees that prepared legislation for passage, oversaw its implementation, and monitored the activities of other governmental bodies. In 1989 the Supreme Soviet also had fourteen joint committees, and each chamber had four commissions.

Presidium

In 1989 the Presidium, as designated by the Constitution, had forty-two members. The Presidium was made up of a chairman, a first vice chairman, fifteen vice chairmen (who represented the supreme soviets of the fifteen republics), the chairmen of the Soviet of the Union and the Soviet of Nationalities, the chairman of the Committee of People's Control, and the twenty-two chairmen of the commissions and committees of the Supreme Soviet. Only a few members regularly resided in Moscow, where the Presidium has always met. Before 1989 the Presidium membership served a symbolic function through the inclusion of twenty-one at-large members, made up of factory workers, peasants, scientists, professionals, and leaders of professional organizations. Valentina Tereshkova, the first woman in space, was the most prominent of these at-large members. The purpose of this broadened membership was to show that all strata of society participated in the state's leading organ. In addition, some high-level party figures who were not members of the government sat on the Presidium as a symbol of CPSU authority in the legislature. For instance, General Secretary Gorbachev sat on the Presidium as an at-large member from 1985 to 1988.

Prior to 1989, the Presidium was the leading legislative organ between sessions of the Supreme Soviet, which met only a few days a year and held formal sessions only once every two months. Announcements of Presidium decrees, however, appeared in the press nearly every day, which indicated that the Presidium's staff worked full time. Presidium decrees, issued over the signatures of the chairman and the secretary, merely certified and legitimated decisions made by the CPSU. Nevertheless, decrees issued in the Presidium's

351

name demonstrated wide-ranging powers to supervise the government bureaucracy.

The 1988 amendments and additions to the Constitution reduced
the powers of the Presidium by making it more of an agenda-setting
and administrative body (see The 1977 Constitution, this ch.). According to Article 119 of the Constitution, the Presidium was authorized to convene sessions of the Supreme Soviet and organize their
preparation, coordinate the activities of the commissions and committees of the Supreme Soviet, oversee conformity of all-union and
republic laws with the Constitution, confer military and diplomatic
ranks, appoint and recall diplomats, issue decrees and adopt resolutions, and declare war or mobilize troops in between sessions of
the Supreme Soviet, among other duties.

Chairman

The office of chairman of the Presidium of the Supreme Soviet
before 1989 was little more than a ceremonial and diplomatic con-
venience. The chairman had the formal authority to sign treaties
and to receive the credentials of diplomatic representatives. The
power of the person occupying the office stemmed from other positions that person may have held. In the past, CPSU general secretaries who also served as chairmen of the Presidium have given
priority to their party duties rather than to the ceremonial duties
of the chairmanship. Taking this consideration into account, the
1977 Constitution provided for the office of first deputy chairman
to relieve the chairman of most ceremonial duties. When the chairmanship has been vacant, the first deputy chairman has acted in
his place, as Vasilii Kuznetsov did after Brezhnev's death and before Iurii V. Andropov assumed the chairmanship. Gorbachev
assumed the office of chairman in October 1988. The 1988 amendments and additions to the Constitution retained the post of first
deputy chairman in recognition of its usefulness in relieving the
legislative burden on the person occupying the positions of general secretary of the party and chairman of the Supreme Soviet.

The 1988 amendments and additions to the Constitution substantially altered the status of the chairman of the Presidium of
the Supreme Soviet by making him also chairman of the Supreme
Soviet and having him elected by the Congress of People's Deputies.
By designating a formal chairman of the Supreme Soviet, the Constitution changed the status of the head of state from a collective
Presidium to a single chairman. Also, the Constitution for the first
time listed responsibilities of the chairman of the Supreme Soviet.
These responsibilities included the exercise of leadership over the

preparation of agendas of the Congress of People's Deputies and the Supreme Soviet, the signing of laws and treaties, the negotiation of treaties, the submission of reports on domestic and foreign policy, and the submission of candidates for first deputy chairman of the Supreme Soviet, members of the Constitutional Oversight Committee, chairman of the Council of Ministers, and other candidates for leading government posts. The Constitution also stipulated that the chairman of the Supreme Soviet head the Defense Council, a body that determined broad military policy and funding.

Soviet of the Union and Soviet of Nationalities

The two chambers that made up the Supreme Soviet—the Soviet of the Union and the Soviet of Nationalities—were selected from among the membership of the Congress of People's Deputies at the beginning of a convocation by a general vote of the deputies. The members of the Soviet of Nationalities were selected by each republic's delegation to the congress (in actuality by the republic's party officials) on the basis of eleven deputies from each union republic, four deputies from each autonomous republic (see Glossary), two deputies from each autonomous oblast (see Glossary), and one deputy from each autonomous *okrug* (see Glossary). The members of the Soviet of the Union were selected on the basis of the population of the union republics and regions. One-fifth of the membership of each chamber was changed each year from the pool of congress deputies.

The two-chamber system has attempted to balance the interests of the country as a whole with those of its constituent nationalities. The Soviet of the Union and the Soviet of Nationalities could meet either separately or jointly. Officials elected from each chamber could preside over the sessions. Either chamber could propose legislation. Legislation passed by majorities in each chamber did not need to be referred to joint session. If the two chambers met in joint session, the chairman of the Supreme Soviet presided. If the chairman was absent, the first deputy chairman presided. Disagreements between the two chambers, if they occurred, could be referred to a conciliation commission, then back to the chambers sitting in joint session. If still unresolved, the question would be decided by the Congress of People's Deputies.

The two chambers of the Supreme Soviet have exercised equal powers and have shared equal status, although they theoretically served different purposes. The Soviet of the Union, established in 1924, grew out of the system of workers' councils at the time of the Bolshevik Revolution (see Revolutions and Civil War, ch. 2). It has been the primary venue for discussion of issues on socioeconomic development of the country as a whole, the rights and duties of citizens, foreign policy, defense, and state security. The Soviet of Nationalities, also established in 1924, ostensibly represented the interests of the national minorities in the central government. Because of its limited power, however, its significance remained more symbolic than real. Its sphere of authority included only issues of national and ethnic rights and interethnic relations. Nevertheless, the regime has traditionally pointed to the existence of this body as proof that the country's nationalities had an equal voice in decision making and policy formation.

Sessions of the Supreme Soviet

Until 1989 the Supreme Soviet was convoked for five-year terms but met in session only for a few days twice a year. Thus, each five-year convocation had ten or more sessions. The Supreme Soviet elected to a five-year term in early 1989 was the twelfth convocation. According to the 1988 amendments and additions to the Constitution, the Supreme Soviet was slated to meet daily, holding two sessions a year, with each lasting three to four months.

Councils of elder members, meeting briefly before sessions, have traditionally helped organize the meetings of both chambers. The staff of the Presidium has assisted in the preparatory paperwork. At the twelfth convocation in 1989, the two councils of elders met in a joint session chaired by Gorbachev to discuss procedures for opening the session, the leadership of the chambers, the agendas, and the composition and functions of commissions and committees. The councils have scheduled meetings of the two chambers in separate session—one after the other—in the same semicircular amphitheater of the Presidium building in the Kremlin, although joint sessions of both chambers have taken place in the Great Hall of the Palace of Soviets. The oldest deputy has opened the sessions. The two chambers then have elected chairmen and two vice chairmen on the recommendations of the councils of elders. The chairmen have set speaker lists and ensured the observance of the established schedule. Until the next session, when they faced another election, the chairmen of the two chambers worked with the Presidium and the chairman of the Supreme Soviet.

The sessions have followed a standard sequence of events. The Supreme Soviet first approved changes in the Council of Ministers and changes in its own membership. It then heard regular reports on the actions taken by the Council of Ministers and by its own Presidium since the last session. Debate and approval of these actions followed. The two regular sessions of the Supreme Soviet in the spring and fall have served different purposes. The spring session traditionally has heard reports from government bodies and its own commissions. It then has passed legislation based on these reports. The second session has approved the budget for the following year. The fall sessions have also ratified the annual and five-year economic plans of the government.

Commissions and Committees

Commissions and committees, each made up of some thirty to fifty members, have been important because they have prepared and proposed legislation for formal approval by the Supreme Soviet and monitored activities of ministries and other government bodies. Each chamber of the Supreme Soviet had fourteen committees, which had jointly shared functions, and four commissions, which had unique functions. In 1989 the commissions and committees were tasked by the Congress of People's Deputies and the Supreme Soviet with examining myriad issues, among them ethnic strife, economic autonomy for the republics, the draft economic plan and budget, efficiency in agriculture, social policy, legal reform, and the conformity of various laws to the Constitution. The commissions and committees also evaluated decrees issued by the Presidium of the Supreme Soviet that had been rejected by the Supreme Soviet and sent to the commissions and committees for reworking.

In the 1984–89 convocation of the Supreme Soviet, 1,200 deputies served on the commissions (as the committees were called at that time), and 800 worked on the draft economic plan and the draft budget for the following year. In the 1989–94 convocation, 320 deputies served on the commissions and 616 served on the committees. About one-half of the deputies serving on the commissions and committees of the Supreme Soviet were deputies to the Congress of People's Deputies but were not members of the Supreme Soviet. One-fifth of their membership has usually been replaced each year by other deputies of the Supreme Soviet or the Congress of People's Deputies.

In making assignments to commissions and committees, the preferences and expertise of the deputies were taken into account; deputies have included party leaders, scientists, educators, agricultural specialists, and foreign policy experts. This variegated membership not only has obtained contributions of experts on legislation but also has permitted the party to communicate its policies to important segments of society. In 1989 the four commissions in each chamber that had functions unique to the chamber included, among others, planning, budgeting, and finance; labor, prices, and social policy; transportation, communications, and information sciences;

and nationalities policy and interethnic relations. The fourteen committees in each chamber that had jointly shared functions covered such areas as foreign affairs, ecology, women and family, veterans and invalids, youth, *glasnost'*, economic reform, agronomy, and construction, among others. In addition to drafting legislation, the commissions and committees monitored the activities of the ministries and other government bodies. Their oversight of the government included evaluating candidates for ministerial posts and questioning ministerial personnel while preparing legislation. In 1989 the committees of the Supreme Soviet rejected several candidates nominated by the chairman of the Council of Ministers, Ryzhkov, forcing him to submit other, more qualified candidates for the posts. Candidates approved by the committees were subject to questioning by deputies on the floor of the Supreme Soviet. To monitor compliance with existing law, the commissions and committees heard ministerial reports and requested materials and documents from the ministries and other government bodies. Government bodies were required to consider the recommendations on government operations of the commissions or committees and to report implementation measures to them.

Prior to 1989, the commissions of the Supreme Soviet had been instruments by which the CPSU controlled legislation and supervised the Supreme Soviet and the ministries. In 1989 the CPSU remained an important influence over the work of the commissions and committees because the vast majority of members were party members, and influential party leaders either chaired the commissions and committees or served as members. The departments of the party's Secretariat watched over commissions and committees that monitored work under their purview (see Secretariat, ch. 7). Although by law government officials were not permitted to serve on the commissions and committees, this ban did not apply to party officials, so that the membership on the commissions and committees was able to overlap with that of the party's departments. Through this overlap, party officials were thus able to ensure that the Supreme Soviet adhered to party decisions. For example, prior to 1989 the chairman of the Foreign Affairs Commission (present-day Foreign Affairs Committee) of the Soviet of the Union was usually the second-ranking member of the Politburo. The chairman of the Foreign Affairs Commission of the Soviet of Nationalities was normally the head of the CPSU International Department. The deputy chairmen and secretaries of the two commissions were also deputy heads of the party's International Department or the Liaison with Communist and Workers' Parties of Socialist Countries Department. Party leaders used these roles to

Government House, Lenin Square, Baku, Azerbaydzhan Republic
Courtesy Jimmy Pritchard

conduct diplomacy on behalf of the Soviet Union. Thus, during his 1984 visit to Britain, Gorbachev acted in his capacity as chairman of the Foreign Affairs Commission of the Soviet of the Union. As of 1989, the chairman of the Foreign Affairs Committee (formerly the Foreign Affairs Commission) of the Soviet of the Union was no longer a major party figure but was still a party official.

Legislative Process

The legislative process has worked in a very formalized manner. For example, the Ministry of Finance, Gosplan, and other institutions submitted economic planning documents to the Soviet of the Union's Planning, Budgeting, and Finance Commission and to other Supreme Soviet commissions and committees and to republic representatives. Deputies of the various commissions and committees of both chambers and other individuals met to review the documents, hear expert testimony, make amendments, and submit the economic plan to the Supreme Soviet. The minister of finance and the chairman of the Council of Ministers submitted their own reports as well.

The Supreme Soviet, after debate, traditionally disposed of the plan with a resolution and a law. The resolution noted reports on the plan delivered by the chairman of Gosplan and the minister

357

of finance. It evaluated the work of the Council of Ministers in fulfilling the previous year's plan and instructed the Council of Ministers to examine proposals prepared by the commissions and committees and those comments made by deputies in the debate and then to take appropriate action. The Law of the Plan formally ratified the plan, taking into account the work of the commissions and committees and setting out in detail budget and plan targets for the following year.

Party Controls

The CPSU has exercised control over the activities of the Supreme Soviet in a variety of ways. Most important has been the extent of party membership among the delegates. In the first eleven convocations of the Supreme Soviet, party membership averaged about 75 percent. Another 15 percent of the delegates were members of the Komsomol. At the twelfth convocation beginning in 1989, party membership in the Congress of People's Deputies amounted to 87 percent, and Komsomol membership amounted to 5.9 percent. The party caucus, which received its instructions directly from the CPSU's central apparatus, was led by party members and controlled legislative procedures.

Leadership positions in the Supreme Soviet were under the *nomenklatura* of the Politburo. Thus, members of the Presidium, all but one of whom were usually party members, abided by the decisions of the party leadership or risked losing their positions. Members of the Presidium, as well as rank-and-file party members who were elected delegates, were subject to the norms of democratic centralism.

The party controlled the selection process for ordinary deputies as well. Local party organs supervised nominations and elections. Party officials carefully selected delegates either to ensure the selection of party leaders and party stalwarts in the arts, literature, the military, and the scientific and scholarly communities, or to reward rank-and-file members for long years of service to the party and government. In the event that delegates proved uncompliant, the Constitution granted the party the power to initiate a recall election. Recalls have been rare, however. Out of 7,500 deputies elected between 1960 and 1985, only 12 have been recalled, mainly for serious personal failings.

Control Organs

The term *control* (*kontrol'*) referred to a system of government and public monitoring of every sphere of production, trade, and administration. Through the government's control organs, the party ensured that the government and society functioned in compliance with the interests of socialism. The Supreme Soviet nominally formed and directed the three kinds of control organs: the court system, the Procuracy, and the Committee of People's Control. These control organs administered a system of law that derived from the Russian Empire, whose system of law was in turn based on Roman law.

Court System

Article 151 of the Constitution and the Law on the Supreme Court specified the composition of the Supreme Court but assigned it few duties and little power. The Supreme Court lacked the authority to determine the constitutionality of legislation, to strike down laws, or to interpret the law. Unlike the United States Supreme Court, the Soviet court did not have the power to establish norms of law. The Supreme Court and the lower courts only applied legal principles established by the Constitution or interpreted by the Presidium of the Supreme Soviet.

The Supreme Court was at the apex of a pyramid of lower courts. Cases came to the Supreme Court on appeal from these lower courts. The lowest-level court, called the people's court (see Glossary), was presided over by a professional, elected judge and two people's assessors (lay judges) who were also elected. Provincial soviets and republic supreme soviets elected judges between the district level and the Supreme Court. The Supreme Court also has created a separate series of military tribunals. The Supreme Soviet supervised the application of the law in all these courts to ensure uniform standards.

Procuracy

The Procuracy (Prokuratura) functioned like a cross between a police investigative bureau and a public prosecutor's office. It investigated crimes, brought criminals to trial, and prosecuted them. The Procuracy also supervised courts and penal facilities within its jurisdiction (see The Procuracy, ch. 19).

The Supreme Soviet appointed the procurator general of the Soviet Union for a five-year term. Like other leading positions in the Soviet government, the position of the procurator general was on the *nomenklatura* of the central party apparatus. In turn, the procurator general appointed each officer of the Procuracy, known as a procurator (see Glossary), who served at the republic, provincial, district, or city level. Procurators at all levels theoretically answered to the Supreme Soviet for their actions. Moreover, they derived authority from the procurator general and thus exercised their authority independent of any regional or local government body.

The Procuracy, as well as the Supreme Court, ensured the strict and uniform observance of law by all government bodies, enterprises (see Glossary), and public institutions. The Procuracy also reviewed all court decisions in both civil and criminal cases. A procurator could appeal decisions considered flawed to higher courts. The Procuracy was therefore responsible for ensuring the uniform application of law in the courts.

The Procuracy supervised investigations conducted by other government agencies. A procurator could file protests in the court system when evidence indicated an agency acted illegally. In theory, these rights of supervision extended to the KGB and other security agencies. In practice, however, the KGB often operated outside the law.

Committees of People's Control

The 1979 Law on People's Control established the committees of people's control in each republic under the supervision of the central Committee of People's Control. These committees had the authority to audit government and economic administration records. Officials found guilty of illegalities could be publicly reprimanded, fined for damages, or referred to the procurator for prosecution. In the late 1980s, the committees of people's control had been an invaluable instrument in Gorbachev's efforts at reform and restructuring.

The committees of people's control extended throughout the Soviet Union. In 1989, of the more than 10 million citizens who served on these organs, 95 percent were volunteers. General meetings of work collectives at every enterprise and office elected the committees for tenures of two and one-half years. The chairman of the Committee of People's Control and a professional staff served for five years. The chairman sat on the Council of Ministers (see Administrative Organs, this ch.).

Law

Lacking a common-law tradition, Soviet law did not provide for an adversary system in which the plaintiff and the defendant argued before a neutral judge. Court proceedings included a judge, two people's assessors, a procurator, and a defense attorney and provided for free participation by the judge in the trial. The same courts heard both civil and criminal cases. Although most cases were open to the public, closed hearings were legal if the government deemed it necessary. Judges kept legal technicalities to a minimum because the court's stated purpose was to find the truth of a case rather than to protect legal rights.

Other aspects of Soviet law more closely resembled the Anglo-Saxon system. In theory, all citizens were equal before the law. Defendants could appeal convictions to higher courts if they believed the sentence was too harsh. Yet, the procurator could also appeal if the sentence was considered too lenient. The law also guaranteed defendants legal representation and the right to trial in their native language or to the use of an interpreter.

Territorial Administration

The central government in Moscow and the governments of the fifteen republics—consisting of fourteen soviet socialist republics (SSR—see Glossary) and the Russian Soviet Federated Socialist Republic—were joined in a theoretically voluntary union. The republic constitutions and the Soviet Constitution established the rules of the federal system.

The Constitution specified the relationship of the central government to the republics. Article 73 of the Constitution limited the central government to the administration of matters requiring central leadership of the country as a whole: national and internal security and the economy. In entering the union, the republics ceded these responsibilities to the central government bodies.

The governmental system below the central level appeared complicated because it was organized according to the two often contradictory principles of geography and nationality. The administrative subdivisions of a republic, oblast (roughly equivalent to a province), and *raion* (district) were based primarily on geography. The larger republics, such as the Russian and Ukrainian republics, were divided into oblasts. But smaller republics (the Latvian, Lithuanian, Estonian, Armenian, and Moldavian republics) did not have an oblast administration between the republic and the district levels. In addition, six large, thinly populated regions in the Russian Republic have been designated by the term *krai*. A *krai* could contain an autonomous oblast or an autonomous *okrug* inhabited by a national minority. About 300 large cities and approximately 3,000 rural and urban districts (*raiony*) made up the next lowest government level. In turn, the large cities were divided into urban districts, or *gorodskie raiony*. Approximately 40,000 village centers made up the rural districts.

The Russian Republic and some of the other republics also contained administrative subdivisions with boundaries drawn according to nationality or language. The three kinds of such subdivisions included twenty autonomous republics, eight autonomous oblasts, and ten autonomous *okruga*.

Republic Level

In theory, the fifteen republics entered into a free and voluntary union of sovereign states when they joined the Soviet Union. The Constitution granted the republics the right to secede; nonetheless, as of 1988 the republics had exercised very little sovereignty. In 1989, however, the Lithuanian, Estonian, Moldavian, and several other republics sought greater national autonomy (see Manifestations of National Assertiveness, ch. 4).

Legal Status

Long-standing practice has established three nonconstitutional requirements for republic status. First, as stated by Stalin in supervising the writing of the 1936 constitution, the republics had to border on territory outside the Soviet Union, enabling them to exercise their theoretical right to secede. All republics met this requirement. Second, the national minority that gave its name to the republic was supposed to make up a majority of its population and to number more than 1 million people. In 1989 the Kazakhs, however, did not constitute a majority of the Kazakh Republic's population, constituting about 40 percent of the republic's population of 16.5 million people. Third, republics were supposed to have the potential to be economically viable states, should they secede from the union.

Over the course of Soviet history, the Supreme Soviet has created new union republics within the territory of the Soviet Union. In 1922 the Soviet Union comprised four republics: the Russian Soviet Federated Socialist Republic, the Ukrainian Republic, the Belorussian Republic, and the Transcaucasian Soviet Federated Socialist Republic. The Soviet government elevated Turkmenia (also known as Turkmenistan) and Uzbekistan to republic status in 1924, and Tadzhikistan split from the Uzbek Republic in 1929 to form a separate republic. Kazakhstan and Kirgizia became republics in 1936. (Turkmenia, Uzbekistan, Kirgizia, and Kazakhstan had been part of the Russian Republic.) In 1936 the Transcaucasian Soviet Federated Socialist Republic split into the Armenian, Azerbaydzhan, and Georgian republics.

As the Soviet Union gained territory, the Supreme Soviet created new republics. Territory taken from Finland was joined in March 1940 with the Karelian Autonomous Republic to form the Karelo-Finnish Republic. (In 1956 this republic, which had never had a majority of the nationality whose name it bore, was demoted to

Building housing the Supreme Soviet of the Estonian Republic, Tallin. The flag on the adjacent tower is the national flag of Estonia.
Courtesy Jonathan Tetzlaff

the status of an autonomous republic and was renamed the Karelian Autonomous Republic.) Moreover, in 1940 Lithuania, Latvia, and Estonia were incorporated into the Soviet Union as republics. Finally, in 1940 Bessarabia, taken from Romania, was joined with the Romanian-speaking portion of the Moldavian Autonomous Republic in the Ukrainian Republic to form the Moldavian Soviet Socialist Republic.

Government

The union republics and the autonomous republics shared the same basic principles of government. As in the central government, in theory the republic congresses of people's deputies exercised authority. In practice, the congresses delegated their power to the presidiums of their supreme soviets and to the republic councils of ministers, and the first secretary of the republic party organization set policy for the republic as a whole (see Republic Party Organization, ch. 7). Between supreme soviet sessions, the presidium and its chairman exercised the legislative powers of the republic. By custom, the chairman was a member of the republic's dominant nationality, a practice that highlighted the theoretical sovereignty of the republics and the influence of their dominant nationality on policy making.

The council of ministers administered the government of the republic. The chairman of the council headed the republic but

363

deferred in all matters to the first secretary of the republic's party organization. The council of ministers included union-republic ministries and republic ministries (see Administrative Organs, this ch.). The latter, which had no counterpart in the central government, administered local public services and light industry. Both kinds of ministries functioned under dual subordination: they were responsible to the central party organization and government and to the republic's party organization and government.

Provincial and District Levels

Below the union-republic level of territorial administration, subdivisions were complex, varied with each republic, and included the following categories: autonomous oblast, autonomous *okrug,* autonomous republic, *krai,* oblast, and *raion.* Only the Russian Republic had all categories of subdivision. Western specialists often termed the administrations of the autonomous subdivisions, *kraia,* and oblasts generically as provincial and that of the *raion* as district. Provincial and district governments shared the same structure. For example, oblast and district soviets—single chambers elected for two and one-half years—exercised all legislative authority. These soviets met up to four times a year for one-day sessions. Between sessions, each soviet delegated its authority to an executive committee (*ispolnitel'nyi komitet—ispolkom*), which combined the functions of a council of ministers and a presidium. *Ispolkom* chairmen were the chief executives in the oblast and in the district. These officials normally sat on the party bureaus at these respective hierarchical levels (see Oblast-Level Organization; District- and City-Level Organization, ch. 7).

The *ispolkom* lacked decision-making authority. Although members of the *ispolkom* headed departments that managed oblast and district services such as education, health, and culture, the central government controlled the more important tasks of the administration of justice, the budget, and economic planning and heavy industry. In addition, a substantial number of other social services were controlled by industrial enterprises and were thus beyond the control of local governments. Finally, the party first secretaries exercised power at both the oblast and the district levels. These officials, not the *ispolkom* chairmen, were obliged to answer to the party for the economic performance of their domain of authority.

The approximately 52,500 soviets at the provincial and urban and rural district levels had little power. These soviets, however, were important as vehicles for large-scale citizen participation in the government. The size of these soviets ranged from 200 deputies in rural areas to more than 1,000 in large cities. Thus, more than

2.3 million people served on local soviets at any one time, and, given the high turnover rate, more than 5 million citizens served on the local soviets each decade.

Although sessions of the full soviets at the provincial and district levels were strictly ceremonial, their commissions had some influence. The constituencies of these commissions were small, enabling them to respond to the needs of the people. Practical expertise often determined assignment to these commissions. For example, a teacher could serve on an education commission. Deputies served as channels for criticism and suggestions from constituents, and the deputies' expertise could qualify them as problem solvers on issues that confronted the commission.

Elections

In theory, citizens selected the candidates for election to local soviets. In practice, at least before the June 1987 elections, these candidates had been selected by local CPSU, Komsomol, and trade union officials under the guidance of the district (*raion*) party organization. Elections took place after six weeks of campaigning, and the candidates, always unopposed until 1987, had usually received more than 99 percent of the vote.

Despite the party's historic control over local elections—from the nomination of candidates to their unopposed elections—the citizens used the elections to make public their concerns. They sometimes used the furnished paper ballots to write requests for particular public services. For example, the 1985 elections to an Omsk soviet included instructions to move the airfield farther from the city center, construct a new music center, and build parking facilities for invalids. Subsequently, the Omsk soviet took steps to provide these services, all of which had the approval of the relevant party authorities. Thus, citizen demands that coincided with the interests of the party apparatus have been met through election mandates.

In June 1987, under Moscow's guidance, multicandidate local elections took place experimentally in less than 5 percent of the districts. Presented with a paper ballot listing more candidates than positions, voters indicated their choices by crossing off enough names so that the number of candidates matched the number of positions. Although generally opposed by local administrators, who could no longer assume automatic election, this reform found strong support among the general public. In early 1989, steps to limit the power of official organizations over the nominating process also came under discussion.

Nevertheless, the outcome of efforts to democratize the local election process remained far from certain in 1989. On the one hand, public anger over the autocratic and sometimes arbitrary styles of local leaders, their perceived incompetence, and their inability to provide needed goods and services forced some reforms. On the other hand, opposition by government and party bureaucrats, combined with the lack of a political culture—that is, experience in self-government—obstructed and diluted reforms of the government's structure and functions, as advocated by Gorbachev in the late 1980s.

* * *

Several general works on Soviet politics contain much useful information on the government. Among these works are Darrell P. Hammer's *The USSR: The Politics of Oligarchy* and Jerry F. Hough and Merle Fainsod's *How the Soviet Union Is Governed*. Hough and Fainsod devote special attention to the relationship between the party and the government. Vadim Medish's *The Soviet Union* is a good reference work on the terminology of government. Other works contain more specialized information. Julian Towster's *Political Power in the USSR* provides material on the first three Soviet constitutions. Boris Toporin's *The New Constitution of the USSR* is widely viewed as one of the best English-language books available on the 1977 Constitution. Lev Tolkunov's *How the Supreme Soviet Functions* covers the legislature, as well as other organs of the central government, from a Soviet perspective. Everett M. Jacobs's *Soviet Local Government and Politics* is an invaluable source for this little-studied aspect of Soviet government. (For further information and complete citations, see Bibliography.)

Chapter 9. Mass Media and the Arts

Images from the media and the arts: ballet, television broadcasting, and the press

SINCE THE BOLSHEVIK REVOLUTION of 1917, the leadership of the Soviet Union has used the mass media and the arts to assist in its efforts at changing and regulating society. To propagate values encouraging the construction and stabilization of the new regime, Vladimir I. Lenin, the Bolshevik (see Glossary) leader, centralized political control over the mass media and the primary forms of artistic expression. He drew upon nineteenth-century Russian radical views that advocated politicizing literature and challenging tsarist government policy through artistic protest. Lenin's successors manipulated the mass media and the arts in ways that preserved and strengthened the regime and the party's supremacy.

Leaders of the Communist Party of the Soviet Union (CPSU) believed that strict control over mass media and the arts was essential for governing the country. "Socialist realism"—an aesthetic formula calling for the portrayal of Soviet society in a positive light to inspire its constant improvement along the lines of Marxist-Leninist ideology—was implemented under Joseph V. Stalin. The regime required the media, literature, and the arts to adhere to this formula. A vast bureaucracy, which included party and government censorship organs and official political, military, economic, and social unions and associations, together with self-censorship by writers and artists, ensured a thorough and systematic review of all information reaching the public. Under the leadership of general secretary of the CPSU Mikhail S. Gorbachev, however, Soviet mass media and the arts in the late 1980s were experiencing a loosening of the controls governing the dissemination of information. Nevertheless, the principle of party and government control over newspapers, journals, radio, television, and literature, which helped to ensure the regime's stability, remained firmly intact.

The technological revolution in the 1970s and 1980s, however, hindered rather than helped the regime's control of mass media and the arts. New technology disrupted party and government domination of mass media and the arts and enabled the population to gain greater access to unsanctioned, globally available information. But the regime needed to employ the same technological advances to maintain its influence and power. The mass media linked the leadership to the population, and the socialist (see Glossary) system required politicized media to endure. The regime's attempt to use this new technology while regulating the global flow of information

369

to Soviet citizens presented one of the most difficult challenges to the leadership, particularly in light of Gorbachev's campaigns for public discussion, democratization, and societal restructuring.

In the late 1980s, newspapers, journals, magazines, radio, television, films, literature, and music espoused poignant, sensitive, and often painful themes that had previously been taboo. The party deemed greater tolerance for criticism of the regime essential in order to placate the intelligentsia and encourage it to support efforts for change. Indeed, the censors eased their restrictions to the point where, in the late 1980s, penetrating historical analyses critical of previous Soviet leaders (including Lenin) and stories about the rehabilitation (see Glossary) of banned writers and artists filled the pages of newspapers, magazines, and journals. Previously proscribed information also appeared in television and radio broadcasts and in film and stage performances. Relaxation of restrictions was also apparent in classical music, jazz, rock and roll, and the plastic arts.

Politicization of the Mass Media and the Arts

The CPSU used the mass media and the arts to enhance its control over society. The justification for such controls was developed by nineteenth-century Russian revolutionary writers who sought to transform Russia through the politicization of literature. Literature and literary criticism were to provide means to challenge tsarist authority and awaken the political consciousness of the population. Specifically, radical writers and artists used ''critical realism'' (the critical assessment of society) in literature, theater, music, and other forms of creative expression to denounce the authoritarian system. Later, the early Soviet government integrated ''critical realism'' into its policies to serve as a foundation for the politicization of the media and literary worlds in the early Soviet government.

When Lenin and the other Bolshevik leaders governed the country, however, they employed the concept of critical realism to exercise political control over culture rather than to inspire writers and artists to question Bolshevik rule. In its early years, the government established political guidelines for media and the arts. In the late 1920s, the regime determined that its enforcement of stringent publication criteria would be executed by an organization formed by the government. The regime chose to use literature as its model for politicization of the media and the arts and in 1932 formed the Union of Writers to enforce the doctrine of socialist realism over all writing. All modes of creative thought and artistic expression required approval by the regime's authoritative bodies, rigidly structured after the Union of Writers, for every kind of mass media and form of art. Under Stalin's leadership, socialist realism dictated the content and form to which writers and artists had to adhere. Since Stalin's death in 1953, successive regimes had relaxed the restrictions of socialist realism. In the period after Leonid I. Brezhnev, hitherto prohibited articles and literary works passed CPSU regulations. In the late 1980s, socialist realism was more liberally interpreted; it still, however, retained the basic tenets instituted by the Bolshevik leadership.

Leninist Principles

Calls for the politicization of literature and art appeared in the works of several radical nineteenth-century Russian thinkers. The literary critic Vissarion Belinskii (1811–48) called upon literary figures to channel their creative energies toward changing the sociopolitical environment. He believed that writers could influence the masses by challenging the status quo through their works. Eventually, his philosophy of criticism galvanized other writers and other artists. Several of his disciples continued to advocate Belinskii's message after he died. Like Belinskii, both the journalist and author Nikolai Chernyshevskii (1828–89) and one of his followers, Nikolai Dobroliubov (1836–61), a literary critic, argued that progress could be achieved only if the individual human being were liberated and could espouse his or her own beliefs without feudal oppression. Both Chernyshevskii and Dobroliubov motivated writers and artists to contribute to this progress by criticizing society and presenting examples of human liberation in their works.

Following these radical ideas, the Bolsheviks, too, rejected the notion of art for art's sake. Like the nineteenth-century radical theorists, the Bolsheviks held that media and the arts were to serve political objectives. Unlike the critical realists, however, who called for protests against social injustice, the Bolsheviks used media and the arts to mobilize the population in support of the new sociopolitical system.

One of the initial means for controlling the population through the politicization of the media entailed closing newspapers deemed anti-Bolshevik. On November 9, 1917, the new Bolshevik regime declared in the Decree of the Press that all nonsocialist newspapers would be closed because they endangered the newly formed government. In the November 10, 1917, issue of *Pravda*—the newspaper of the Bolshevik Central Committee and the main voice of the new regime—the Bolshevik leadership stated that ''the press is one of the strongest weapons in the hands of the bourgeoisie'' and added that, given its capacity to incite rebellion among workers and peasants by distorting reality, the press ought to be strictly controlled.

On January 28, 1918, the Bolshevik leadership decreed that "revolutionary tribunals" would be used to prevent the bourgeois press from spreading "crimes and misdemeanors against the people." On April 5, 1918, Bolshevik censors instituted further controls by mandating that "decrees and ordinances of the organs of the Soviet power" had to be included in all newspapers. By the early 1920s, all non-Bolshevik newspapers had been outlawed, thus giving full control to the regime. Such controls continued in the late 1980s.

Socialist Realism

Similar principles of party control applied to the arts. During the early years of Bolshevik rule, the party leadership sought to enforce strict guidelines to ensure that literature conformed to Bolshevik policies and that dissent was stifled. With the implementation of the First Five-Year Plan in 1928, political controls over cultural activity increased. By 1932 the party and the government had decreed that all writing groups and associations were under the control of the Union of Writers. In the early 1930s, socialist realism became the official aesthetic doctrine prescribed for artists (see Mobilization of Society, ch. 2). According to this formula, artists, composers, architects, and sculptors had to define history in a realistic and truthful light based on its revolutionary evolution. Socialist realism demanded portrayal of society as if it had already been perfected according to Marxist-Leninist ideology. Under Stalin's leadership, writers served as the "engineers of human souls" and produced novels, short stories, articles, editorials, critiques, and satires within a restrictive framework in which they strove to glorify Soviet society and socialism.

Throughout Stalin's rule, socialist realism confined the arts to expressing a narrowly controlled party line, but when Nikita S. Khrushchev came to power in 1955, some guidelines were loosened. The short literary "thaw" in the late 1950s allowed artists more freedom and creativity. This literary thaw lasted only a few years, and with Khrushchev's ouster in 1964, artistic freedom suffered setbacks. Further controls prevented artists from expressing themselves outside the boundaries of socialist realism. Artists were imprisoned if they protested the party line.

Brezhnev's death in November 1982, however, initiated a very slow but gradual change in the Soviet mass media and the arts. Under the successive leadership of Iurii V. Andropov and Konstantin U. Chernenko, society experienced further loosening of party strictures on the media and the arts, albeit mostly during Andropov's rule. After Gorbachev assumed power in 1985, the system witnessed significant liberalization. Topics previously proscribed were discussed and analyzed by all the mass media, and the government allowed publication of previously banned materials. The regime, however, still maintained ultimate control over the ways of evaluating the state, criticizing the past, and transforming the system. Mass media and cultural events enhanced the image of a "new face" and "new thinking" in society. The persistence of an elaborate administrative censorship system, however, demonstrated that the leadership continued to hold sway over the information revealed publicly.

Administration of the Mass Media and the Arts

As of 1987, several party and government organizations exerted control over the media and the arts. Censorship extended from the central party departments and government ministries to their republic and regional counterparts. The CPSU Central Committee Secretariat contained various departments and committees that supervised distinct sectors in the media and the arts (see Secretariat, ch. 7). A government organization, the Main Administration for Safeguarding State Secrets in the Press (Glavnoe upravlenie po okhrane gosudarstvennykh tain v pechati—Glavlit; see Glossary), had to sanction any work published in more than nine copies. Government ministries responsible for large cultural institutions as well as state committees also concerned themselves with the regulation of state information (see Administrative Organs, ch. 8). The government news organs—the Telegraph Agency of the Soviet Union (Telegrafnoe agentstvo Sovetskogo Soiuza—TASS) and the News Press Agency (Agentstvo pechati novosti—Novosti)—limited information disseminated to domestic and foreign newspaper wire services. Ultimately, government institutions involved in censorship responded to CPSU directives. The party ensured that only approved information appeared publicly. Underground materials existed, but the Committee for State Security (Komitet gosudarstvennoi bezopasnosti—KGB) and the Ministry of Internal Affairs actively opposed the dissemination of any unsanctioned material. The party, government organizations, and security organs combined with the other official censorship controls to guarantee party domination over the mass media and the arts.

The Party Role

In the late 1980s, the secretary for ideology and the Central Committee's Ideological Department functioned mainly to mold popular opinion. The former not only regulated the media but also issued directives to republic and provincial (oblast, *kraia*—see Glossary, and autonomous division) leaders to administer the mass media and the arts through the various "letters" departments (the media control organs that oversee "letters to the editor" offices), the International Information Department (foreign affairs information overseer), and the Culture Department. Parallel departments dealing with ideology and propaganda operated at lower party levels throughout the country to centralize control over local publications (see Intermediate-Level Party Organizations, ch. 7). Both the central and the local ideology and propaganda departments supervised culture, education, and science. In addition, as part of the party's *nomenklatura* (see Glossary) authority, party leaders at all levels selected editors of newspapers, magazines, and journals within their domains (see Nomenklatura, ch. 7). According to Soviet émigrés surveyed in a 1982 Rand study, "The Media and Intra-Elite Communication in the USSR," the Propaganda Department (which was absorbed by the Ideological Department in 1988) wielded great power in selections of editors for the central press organs and publishing houses. In many instances, these high positions were filled by party members who had previously worked in some section of a propaganda department, whether at the all-union (see Glossary) or at the local level.

The Government Role

In the late 1980s, censorship authority was exercised by Glavlit, which employed some 70,000 censors to review information before it was disseminated by publishing houses, editorial offices, and broadcasting studios. Government censorship organs attended to all levels, in the forms of territorial, provincial, municipal, and district organs. No mass medium escaped Glavlit's control. All press agencies and radio and television stations had a Glavlit representative on their editorial staffs. Although Glavlit was attached to the Council of Ministers, many émigrés asserted that Glavlit answered not only to the Propaganda Department but also to the KGB.

Although the Ideological Department regulated ideological and political censorship, the KGB handled classified information and, by extension, controlled Glavlit's "administrative and staffing" responsibilities. Many Glavlit censors were former KGB members. The KGB and Glavlit worked together to implement a compendium of regulations contained in the *Censor's Index,* which contained classified information on "state secrets" that could not be revealed in the media. Apparently, the index contained between 300 and 1,000 pages, with periodically updated lists of military, technical, economic, statistical, and other data on various people and issues forbidden for dissemination. As a result, editors and writers rarely touched on proscribed material. If they published any unsanctioned information, the censors either instituted harsher publication restrictions or fired those who broke the rules.

The government also regulated information through the central and republic ministries of culture and similar all-union state committees and specialized state censors. The ministries of culture helped coordinate centralized censorship for Glavlit as well as execute other literary controls. Three distinct state committees implemented censorship policies throughout the country: the State Committee for Publishing Houses, Printing Plants, and the Book Trade (Gosudarstvennyi komitet po delam izdatel'stv, poligrafii, i knizhnoi torgovli—Goskomizdat); the State Committee for Television and Radio Broadcasting (Gosudarstvennyi komitet po televideniyu i radioveshchaniyu—Gostelradio); and the State Committee for Cinematography (Gosudarstvennyi komitet po kinematografii—Goskino). Furthermore, the dissemination of books on cultural, political, military, scientific, technical, economic, and social issues fell under the purview of separate government printing houses. These individual printing houses oversaw the numerical distributions of all titles, and they limited access to certain books deemed to be related to state security, even if the information was unclassified. The publishing houses also regulated the number of copies of foreign titles published internally and Soviet titles published for distribution abroad.

The government censorship hierarchy not only maintained comprehensive controls over information distributed by the news services worldwide but the official news organs—TASS and Novosti—regulated all news wire service information to ensure government control of information disseminated to the public. In 1988 TASS employed about 65,000 professional correspondents and journalists. Because TASS operated an extensive number of news agencies around the world, in the late 1980s its 2.5 million lines reached more than 20,000 subscribers daily. From 20 to 25 percent of its subscribers were media organizations that depended almost entirely on TASS for foreign and domestic reporting. Consequently, TASS officials, who were located in every republic's capital and in nearly all provincial cities, serviced many newspapers, some of which allotted nearly 50 percent of their news space to TASS-relayed information.

Created in 1961, Novosti supplemented TASS. Serving as the conduit for information that TASS could not accommodate, Novosti focused mainly on foreign reporting. By assuming responsibilities for feature stories, commentary, interviews, and other articles

375

featuring the best side of Soviet society, Novosti attempted to provide its domestic and foreign readership with human interest stories in ways TASS could not. Novosti's correspondents annually transmitted almost 50,000 articles. Together, TASS and Novosti served as the primary means for distributing Soviet viewpoints around the world.

Procedures for censorship of military and scientific information differed from those followed for other kinds of information. Before information relating to any aspect of the Soviet military was disseminated through the media, the material first had to have been approved by the military censor and then by Glavlit. This complex censorship process began with the first-level editor in Moscow, who censored the article and sent a letter detailing the author's background and sources used to a military censor. Once it reached the military censorship authorities of the General Staff, the material had to be sanctioned again before it reached the penultimate stage—review by the political-military and KGB editors. Whether the information was regional or all-union in scope, the Main Political Directorate of the Soviet Army and Navy and the military directorate of the KGB reportedly advised, if not instructed, the military censors, despite the military censors' official obligations to the General Staff. Once these military officers had read and approved the article, it went to the Glavlit censors for publication. If the military officers had any hesitation about a piece, they had the authority to request that the editor discuss with them any aspect of the article under question. Soviet sources also have revealed that once the Glavlit censors received the edited piece from the military officers, they never questioned the revisions and routinely distributed the article to the appropriate media.

Similar procedures applied to science censors within the Academy of Sciences (see Glossary), who targeted material related to ''national defense'' in the areas of science and technology. Censors specializing in various scientific disciplines concentrated on stripping any material that could be construed to reveal the regime's national security policies. For example, publications and broadcasts related to outer space events were examined by the Commission on Research and Exploitation of Cosmic Space, associated with the Presidium of the Academy of Sciences.

Other censors concentrated on such topics as radio electronics, chemistry, geology, and computer science. The atomic energy censors, located at the State Committee for the Utilization of Atomic Energy, oversaw materials concentrating on nuclear energy, even those that focused on science fiction. After approval by the specialized censors, the works were referred to Glavlit.

Man posting a copy of
Pravda, *the CPSU newspaper,*
at a sidewalk display in
Odessa, Ukrainian Republic
Courtesy Jimmy Pritchard

The Mass Media

The mass media acted as an instrument of the CPSU, not only to control society but also to mobilize it. Lenin and the Bolshevik leadership depended on the media to win support for the new regime. Indeed, without important communications links from the party to the people, the Bolsheviks' message would never have been broadly disseminated. During the early years, the leadership sought to galvanize the population by spreading the party line and encouraging the population to build a strong communist society, exhorting it through editorials, commentaries, and tributes in newspapers, journals, and radio. Over time, television, films, and computers became essential components of the CPSU's agitprop (see Glossary) efforts, as well as of its campaigns to spread Marxist-Leninist values among the people. The technological information revolution forced the party to reevaluate its efforts to control the masses because advances in technology also created the potential for communications links outside regime control. For example, with the spread of video cassette recorders (VCRs) in the late 1980s, the party leadership faced the problems created by the underground circulation of video tapes, in addition to the circulation of illegal periodicals.

Newspapers

In 1988 the regime published more than 8,000 daily newspapers in approximately sixty languages, with a combined circulation of about 170 million. Every all-union newspaper was circulated in its Russian-language version. Nearly 3,000 newspapers, however, reached the population in non-Russian languages. Minority-language newspapers constituted roughly 25 percent of the total circulation, although non-Russians made up almost 50 percent of the population (see Nationalities of the Soviet Union, ch. 4).

All newspaper reporters and editors belonged to the party-controlled Union of Journalists, composed of nearly 74,000 members. In 1988 some 80 percent of the union's reporters and editors were party members. Inevitably, assignments of editors had to be approved by the party. In the late 1980s, all the central editors in chief of major all-union newspapers belonged to the CPSU Central Committee. The party also sought to control journalists by combining higher education and higher party schools with schools of journalism (see Training, ch. 7). Reporters and editors thus were trained under the aegis of the professional party elite. For newspaper journalists and television and radio reporters, newspaper photographers, and literary editors, Moscow University's School of Journalism provided a main conduit to party positions concerned with the media. In the 1980s, some 2,500 graduate, undergraduate, evening school, and correspondence students annually graduated from the School of Journalism. Students were taught party strictures within the following eight departments: theory and practice of the party-Soviet press, history of the party-Soviet press, television and radio broadcasting, movie-making and editorial-publishing work, foreign press and literature, Russian journalism and literature, stylistics of the Russian language, and techniques of newspaper work and information media. By the late 1980s, Moscow University's School of Journalism had graduated approximately 100,000 journalists.

Party members supposedly read the all-union newspapers differently from their nonparty counterparts. Trained to scan certain sections of the paper, party members read with an eye toward instruction and guidance. In contrast to nonparty members, the loyal party elite apparently first read any article or editorial related to ideology, the *Party Rules* (see Glossary), or instructions. By contrast, most nonparty members reportedly read the international news first, followed by sports, science and culture, and economic events before they turned to political or ideological articles, if they read articles on these subjects at all.

In the late 1980s, newspapers gradually developed new formats and new issues. Under Andropov, *Pravda* began to print short reports of weekly Politburo meetings. Eventually, other major newspapers published accounts of these meetings as well.

Under Gorbachev, Politburo reports expanded to provide more details on the leadership's thinking about domestic and foreign affairs. Before Gorbachev's assumption of power, Western sources had identified a partial list of proscribed topics, which included crime, drugs, accidents, natural disasters, occupational injuries, official organs of censorship, security, intelligence, schedules of travel for the political leadership, arms sales abroad, crime or morale problems in the armed forces, hostile actions against Soviet citizens abroad, and special payments and education for athletes. After 1985 Gorbachev's policy of *glasnost'* (see Glossary) gave editors a freer hand to publish information on many of these subjects.

In the 1980s, regional newspapers differed in several ways from all-union newspapers. The distribution of regional newspapers varied from circulation at the republic level to circulation in a province, city, or district. The party allowed many regional newspapers to print most of their issues in the region's native language, which reflected the Stalinist policy of "national in form, socialist in content." Local newspaper circulation remained restricted to a region. These publications often focused on such issues as local heroes who contributed to the good of the community or significant problems (as expressed in letters to the editor) relating to crime or natural disasters. By contrast, after Gorbachev came to power, most all-union newspapers began to report on societal shortcomings. However, in the late 1980s regional papers continued to contain more personal advertisements and local merchant notices than the all-union newspapers, if the latter carried any at all.

Originally, Lenin argued that criticism should be channeled through letters to the editor and would assist in cleansing society of its problems. He believed that public discussion would facilitate the elimination of shortcomings and that open expression of problems would create a significant feedback mechanism for the leadership and for the country as a whole. Lenin's ideas in this regard were not carried out by Stalin and Khrushchev, who apparently believed the party needed no assistance from the people in identifying problems. But in 1981, Brezhnev created the Central Committee Letters Department, and later Andropov called for more letters to editors to expose corruption and mismanagement. Chernenko advocated that greater "media efficacy" be instituted so that newspapers, for example, would carry more in-depth and current analyses on pressing issues. Gorbachev expanded the flexibility allowed by giving newspapers leeway in publishing letters critical of society and even critical of the government.

Newspaper letters departments usually employed large staffs and handled extremely high volumes of letters daily. Not all letters were published because they often dealt with censored subjects or their numbers simply posed too great a burden for any one newspaper to handle. The letters departments, however, reportedly took their work very seriously and in the late 1980s were used by the press to encourage the population to improve society.

Letters to editors on a great number of previously forbidden topics also elicited responses from the population that could be manipulated by the Soviet newspapers to influence public opinion in the desired direction. Because party members made up the majority of active newspaper readers, according to polls conducted in the Soviet Union, they wrote most of the letters to the editor. Thus, their perspectives probably colored the newspapers' letters sections.

Of all the newspapers, *Pravda* (Truth), an organ of the CPSU Central Committee, was the most authoritative and, therefore, the most important. Frequently, it was the bellwether for important events, and readers often followed its news leads to detect changes in policies. With about 12 million copies circulated every day to over 20 million citizens, *Pravda* focused on party events and domestic and foreign news.

Other newspapers, however, also commanded wide circulation. *Izvestiia* (News), the second most authoritative paper, emanated from the Presidium of the Supreme Soviet and in the late 1980s circulated to between 8 and 10 million people daily. *Izvestiia* also contained official government information and general news and an expanded Sunday section composed of news analysis, feature stories, poetry, and cartoons. *Trud* (Labor), issued by the Soviet labor unions, circulated six days a week, reaching 8 to 9 million people. It emphasized labor and economic analyses and included other official decrees. *Komsomol'skaia pravda* (Komsomol Truth), published by the Komsomol (see Glossary), was distributed to between 9 and 10 million people. *Krasnaia zvezda* (Red Star), published by the Ministry of Defense, covered most daily military news and events and published military human interest stories and exposés. The literary bimonthly *Literaturnaia gazeta* (Literary Gazette) disseminated the views of the Union of Writers and contained authoritative statements and perspectives concerning literature, plays, cinema, and literary issues of popular interest. A publication of the Central Committee, *Sovetskaia Rossiia* (Soviet Russia), was the Russian Republic's most widely distributed newspaper, with a circulation of nearly 12 million. A weekly regional newspaper, *Moskovskie novosti* (Moscow News), appeared in both Russian and English editions and reported on domestic and international events.

It became very popular during the late 1980s, both in the Soviet Union and abroad. The weekly newspaper *Za rubezhom* (Abroad) devoted its pages exclusively to international affairs and foreign events. Finally, *Sotsialisticheskaia industriia* (Socialist Industry), a daily newspaper, concentrated on industrial and economic events, statistics, and human interest stories.

Magazines and Journals

In the late 1980s, weekly, monthly, and quarterly magazines and journals numbered almost 5,500 and had a circulation nearly equal to that of the daily newspapers. The same CPSU regulations and guidelines that applied to newspapers extended to magazines and journals. In the mid-1980s, under the regime's less-restrictive censorship policy, both magazines and journals published articles and stories to fill in historical "blank spots." These articles included works of past and contemporary authors once banned and new works that challenged the limits imposed on literary society by previous leaders. Assessments and criticisms of past leaderships exposed many historical atrocities, particularly those committed under Stalin. As a result, in the late 1980s the number of subscribers to periodicals climbed considerably, and magazines and journals frequently sold out at kiosks within minutes.

In the late 1980s, these magazines and journals created reverberations throughout society with their publication of controversial articles. *Krokodil* (Crocodile), one of the most popular magazines with a circulation of approximately 6 million, contained humor and satire and featured excellent artistic political cartoons and ideological messages. In 1987 *Krokodil* published a short excerpt from *In Search of Melancholy Baby* by Vasilii Aksionov, an émigré writer and poet living in the United States. The piece portrayed Moscow intellectuals' fascination with American fads during the 1950s and prompted many letters to the editor that both praised and criticized the excerpt. *Nedelia* (Week), another magazine, supplemented *Izvestiia* and appeared every Sunday, having a circulation of some 9 to 10 million.

Such journals as *Ogonek* (Little Fire), a weekly that became more popular in the late 1980s because of its insightful political exposés, human interest stories, serialized features, and pictorial sections, had an audience of over 2 million people. In 1986 it published excerpted works by the previously banned writer Nikolai S. Gumilev, who was shot in 1921 after being accused of writing a counterrevolutionary proclamation. In 1988 it also published excerpts of poetry from Iulii Daniel, imprisoned after a famous 1966 trial for publication of his work abroad. *Novyi mir* (New World), one of the most controversial and often original literary reviews, attracted widespread readership among the intelligentsia. The monthly publication reached nearly 2 million readers and concentrated on new prose, poetry, criticism, and commentary. Many previously banned works were published in its pages, most notably *Doctor Zhivago* by Boris Pasternak. (The publication of *Doctor Zhivago* in the West not only resulted in Pasternak's expulsion from the Union of Writers in 1956 but won him the 1958 Nobel Prize for Literature.) *Oktiabr'* (October), a journal resembling *Novyi mir* in content, circulation, and appeal, espoused more conservative viewpoints. Nevertheless, Anna Akhmatova's "Requiem," a poetic tribute to those who perished during Stalin's purges, appeared in its November 1987 issue. Finally, *Sovetskaia kul'tura* (Soviet Culture), a journal with broad appeal, published particularly biting indictments of collectivization, industrialization, and the purges of the 1930s. In 1988 the journal published articles indirectly criticizing Lenin for sanctioning the establishment of the system of forced labor and concentration camps.

Radio

Like other party-controlled media in the late 1980s, radio broadcasts attempted to instill in the population a sense of duty and loyalty to the party and state. Every day the government broadcast an estimated 1,400 hours of radio programming to all parts of the country, often in as many as 70 languages. The main programming emanated from Moscow, where eight radio channels broadcast 180 hours daily to audiences throughout the country. Government domination of radio broadcasts was, however, not complete. Since the onset of the post-World War II Cold War, government programs have competed with broadcasts originating in the West, which have been aimed across the country's borders with the intention of providing independent information to the population, particularly on topics that censors desperately tried to ban. The government, until 1988, routinely jammed radio broadcasts by American-sponsored Radio Free Europe/Radio Liberty, the Voice of America, the British Broadcasting Corporation, and Deutsche Welle, the broadcast of the Federal Republic of Germany (West Germany) Ministry of the Interior. An estimated 2 to 3 million citizens regularly listened to these foreign broadcasts when the authorities were not jamming them.

Television and Video Cassette Recorders

In the 1970s and 1980s, television became the preeminent mass medium. In 1988 approximately 75 million households owned

Television equipment vehicle in Riga, Latvian Republic
Courtesy Jonathan Tetzlaff

television sets, and an estimated 93 percent of the population watched television. Moscow, the base from which most of the television stations broadcast, transmitted some 90 percent of the country's programs, with the help of more than 350 stations and nearly 1,400 relay facilities. Moscow projected some fifty hours of news, commentaries, education, and entertainment every day from its four channels. About 20 percent of this programming consisted of news, the main program being "Vremia" (Time), a thirty-five- to forty-five-minute news program beginning at 9:00 P.M Moscow time. Between 80 and 90 percent of all families who owned televisions followed "Vremia" broadcasts. Normally, about two-thirds of reporting on each telecast consisted of domestic affairs, usually stories concentrating on the government, the economy, and important regional events. International news filled just under one-third of the format; three to four minutes were devoted to sports and two minutes to weather. Another news program, "Segodnia v mire" (Today in the World), which featured foreign affairs reports and short but in-depth news analyses, attracted from 60 to 90 million viewers every evening, particularly because it was broadcast both in the early evening and in the late evening.

Countless "firsts" were achieved on Soviet television, beginning under Andropov and continuing with Gorbachev. During

Andropov's rule, coverage was given to the downing of the South Korean airliner that strayed over Soviet territory in 1983, including a live broadcast featuring several high-level political and military leaders who answered questions from reporters without prior submission. With Gorbachev's accession, many live programs were broadcast via satellite television bridges (satellite electronic links) between the Soviet Union and the United States; footage and commentary were shown on the war in Afghanistan; the Chernobyl' nuclear reactor accident was explored in-depth; the Armenian earthquake was covered; and live interviews, speeches, and debates involving Gorbachev and other Politburo members were broadcast.

Almost every television program tried to include an ideological theme. Televised propaganda bombarded viewers in many forms; themes on the benefits of the economy were especially prevalent. Economic series, such as "Construction Sites of the Twelfth Five-Year Plan," "Winner in Socialist Emulation," and "How to Put Your Heart into Your Work," exhorted viewers to help to improve the economy. Patriotic films portrayed Soviet victories during World War II, and spy movies depicted the efforts of the country's security services to protect it from the "imperialist threat." Other programs featured lectures ranging from secondary school class instruction to party virtues, nonviolent cartoons for children, some game shows highlighting proper social values, and sports competitions. In an effort to create a larger viewer constituency, Gorbachev took advantage of television's popular appeal by being the first leader to use it to reach the population with his speeches and public relations campaigns.

With television, in contrast to radio, where the authorities had a difficult time controlling foreign broadcasts, censors could exercise greater control. Yet, with the dramatic increase in VCRs, unauthorized tapes circulated around the major ports and cities. This circulation complicated the regime's attempts to control the information revolution. In fact, Western specialists estimated that Soviet households contained approximately 300,000 VCRs. The problem of control became more acute in the mid-1980s as the policy of *glasnost'* led the younger generation to yearn for more information.

Computers

After Gorbachev's accession to power, the leadership promulgated a new series of telecommunications and computerization goals. Some of those efforts had already been incorporated into the Twelfth Five-Year Plan (1986–90). They included a universal implementation of computers and data bases throughout the economy and an all-union computer modernization and training program aimed at the younger generation. In 1988 Western estimates put the number of computers at 30,000 mainframes and 70,000 smaller computers. In 1985 a law requiring ninth and tenth graders to learn computer fundamentals was introduced. In the Twelfth Five-Year Plan, the leadership declared its goal to furnish high schools with at least 500,000 computers by 1990, representing 45 percent of national computer production. By the year 2000, the leadership projected that 5 million computers would be distributed throughout the schools. The Soviet Union developed a copy of the Apple II computer (called the Agat) and International Business Machines personal computer clones. In addition, the Soviet Union developed the Janus with Hungary and the MMS–16 with the German Democratic Republic (East Germany). All of these computer models, however, encountered production problems.

Achievements in computer technology may have benefited the national economy, especially industry and the military, but they also may have imperiled the leadership's ability to control access to information. The leadership's control of information was likely to be further reduced by a continuing rise in the number of VCRs, access to direct-broadcast satellite transmissions, and access to Western data networks that managers and scientists desired. Despite measures to suppress the dissemination of mass information, the regime faced a dilemma. It could not expect to compete with the West unless it modernized its technology and improved its computer facilities, yet it wanted to maintain strict controls over data networks and personal computer use.

The Arts

Throughout Soviet history, the arts have played an integral role in influencing the population. In particular, literature has served as the main political instrument through which the leadership has regulated cultural currents. As, by Stalin's definition, the "engineers of human souls," writers were required to bolster policies sanctioned by the leadership. All writers, whether or not members of the party-controlled Union of Writers, submitted their works for party approval. After Stalin's death, writers experienced a brief literary thaw when some party constraints lessened. Not until the late 1980s, however, did the regime loosen its previously confining strictures on literary form and content.

The regime exercised strict controls over other forms of art as well. The leadership's political line dictated the content and form of cinema, theater, music, the plastic arts such as painting and sculpture, and the graphic arts. The party used the cinema screen to portray its societal ideals. Directors had to produce films praising

Theater of Drama and Comedy, Leningrad
Courtesy Jimmy Pritchard

the regime and exhorting moral conduct. On the stage, playwrights and actors operated within the party's controlled framework under which themes had to be approved in advance of a performance. Musicians wrote and played only music sanctioned by the regime for public performances. Art galleries displayed works approved by party officials. In the 1980s, however, artists began to express harsh and painful themes in their works, sometimes cutting a fine line between permitted and forbidden subjects. In the post-Brezhnev period, the government vacillated between imposing more restrictive artistic controls and allowing greater freedom of expression. After 1985 the Soviet artistic world experienced a number of contentious debates about the liberties allowed to artists.

Literature

Since the 1930s, the regime has regulated literary expression through socialist realism. In spite of the brief literary thaw during the late 1950s, throughout the Brezhnev period writers endured a reemphasis of Stalinist constraints over their works. Traditional ways of thinking and of viewing history no longer applied to many parts of literature, however, once Gorbachev assumed power.

The ferment inspired a creativity not witnessed since Khrushchev's literary thaw. Books began to treat conflicts faced by real human beings and to portray critical and poignant topics theretofore banned. Poets such as Evgenii Evtushenko and Andrei Voznesenskii, who had receded into the background from the mid-1960s to the mid-1980s, were again able to express their desire for a more humane society, uncovering the truth about the past and seeking greater freedom for the arts. Previously banned themes began to appear for the first time since the 1920s. Conservative elements persisted in some literary circles, however, and in the late 1980s some bans on literary themes remained in effect.

A limited degree of freer expression on topics dealing with societal changes was permitted between Brezhnev's death and Gorbachev's rise to power. For example, in 1983 Andropov allowed the publication in book form of Chingiz Aitmatov's, *The Day Lasts More Than a Hundred Years*. In this novel, Aitmatov, a native of the Kirgiz Republic, confronts such historical themes as the brutal Stalinist period, social and moral turpitude, and nationality tensions in the Soviet Union. In the novel, he treats tensions between Russians and non-Russians from a Central Asian perspective. This book, however, stands alone.

Chernenko reintroduced strict bans on critical and innovative works. One example concerns Sergei Zalygin's (editor in chief of *Novyi mir*) novel *After the Storm*, which appeared shortly after

Chernenko's death. During Chernenko's rule, the second half of the novel had been withheld from publication without explanation.

Under Gorbachev, literary treatment of such topics as alcohol and drug addiction, juvenile delinquency, religious subjects (including references to God), historical reassessments of previous leaders, and even harsh criticisms of past leaders have been approved, provided they contained the prescribed amount of support for the regime. Yet in the late 1980s, editors continued to uphold the party creed to prevent works containing unsanctioned views from reaching the public. In 1988 books almost never contained material on or made reference to "anti-Soviet émigrés" or defectors, anticommunist foreign literature, pornographic topics, or "underground" works—referred to as samizdat (see Glossary) if self-published in the country or *tamizdat* if published abroad.

Gorbachev's policy of openness also contributed to more lively discussions among members of the Union of Writers. Controversy erupted at the Eighth Congress of the Union of Writers during the summer of 1986, where the majority of speeches centered on hotly disputed topics. Speeches by Voznesenskii and Evtushenko criticized the neglect shown by the regime toward some of the Soviet Union's most talented writers, and they advocated support for publication of their works. Thus, by 1988 the journal *Novyi mir* had published Pasternak's novel *Doctor Zhivago* in four installments. In addition, at Voznesenskii's behest, the Union of Writers approved the selection of such nondelegates as the famous poet Bella Akhmadulina, the writer and balladeer Bulat Okudzhava, and the firebrand writer Iurii Chernichenko to membership on the union's administrative board. Finally, the writers' congress witnessed the changing of the guard as Vladimir Karpov, a survivor of Stalinist labor camps, replaced the conservative Georgii Markov as first secretary of the Union of Writers.

At the congress, ethnic confrontations also arose between Russian and non-Russian authors; opposition was voiced against bureaucratic publishing roadblocks; and vehement demands were made favoring a reevaluation of Soviet history. Conservative views, however, also appeared. Sergei Mikhalkov, the first secretary of the Russian Republic's writers' union and a declared opponent of Gorbachev's openness policy, cautioned against "parasites" who lack a direct relation to literature and others who espouse overly liberal views. In addition, Nikolai Gribachev, a conservative writer, advocated a return to "classic Soviet writers," especially Maksim Gor'kiy, associated with "proletarian populism," and Aleksei N. Tolstoi, a supporter of "Russian nationalism." The conservatives highlighted the importance of nationalism and the legacy of socialist realism's emphasis on the "positive hero." Nationalistic defenses prompted another conservative writer, Aleksandr Prokhanov, to criticize the emergence of the "new social type" of individual in literature, an ideologically apathetic citizen overly sympathetic to the West.

Nevertheless, at the Eighth Congress of the Union of Writers, the liberals gained ground and secured a number of dramatic changes. After much lobbying by prominent writers and poets, including Evtushenko and Voznesenskii, the liberal and conservative elements of the writers' union reached agreement in mid-1988 to turn Peredelkino, Pasternak's former home, into an official museum. The Eighth Congress also served as a harbinger for loosening the censorship restrictions on the publication of several politically charged novels. Among these works were Anatolii Rybakov's penetrating *Children of the Arbat,* which offered insights into the origins of Stalinism, and Vasilii Grossman's *Life and Fate,* which drew historical comparison between Stalinism and Nazism. The late 1980s ushered in the way for poet Tat'iana Tolstaia, the granddaughter of the Soviet writer Aleksei Tolstoi (1882–1945), to publish. Known for her dramatic realism about death in ordinary people's lives, Tolstaia saw her publications appear in *Oktiabr'* and *Novyi mir* and won great acclaim, even though the Union of Writers continued to exclude her.

Cinema

A long tradition of classic and monumental films created by film makers such as Sergei Eisenstein served the regime's intent of portraying a strong socialist society (see Society and Culture in the 1920s, ch. 2). The party dictated the themes and issues that Soviet film makers would depict.

In the late 1980s, the film industry underwent dramatic changes as the CPSU allowed film makers to analyze social dilemmas and propose remedies. From 1986 to 1988, three important developments occurred within the film-making leadership. First, film makers banded together to remove conservative bureaucrats from the Union of Cinematographers and to replace them with younger, bolder, and more innovative directors. Second, these changes led to the formation of the Disputes Committee within the union headed by an important, more open-minded *Pravda* critic in order to examine approximately sixty films that had been "withheld" without any proper justification. Among these prohibited films were three directed by the new head of the Union of Cinematographers, Elem Klimov. Third, the official state organ controlling cinema, Goskino, was forced to yield to an ever-increasing number of union

*Home of poet and
novelist Boris Pasternak,
southwest of
Moscow in the
writers' colony at
Peredelkino
Courtesy Jimmy Pritchard*

demands for greater cinematic freedom. Previously, film makers who wanted to produce films were required to please Goskino and the censors. Box office success was unimportant. In the late 1980s, film makers won the right to have their films judged on their merits. As a result, success for film makers meant producing money-making ventures. They no longer required the full professional and financial support of Goskino.

The CPSU Central Committee also reduced the power and influence of the Ministry of Culture's Glavrepertkom (see Glossary), the official film-release control apparatus. By the end of 1986, many previously banned or withheld films were showing in movie theaters. Yet as of 1988, Glavrepertkom continued to wield substantial censorship influence, with its reach extending to theaters, circuses, concerts, phonograph records, and general musical productions.

One of the most adventuresome film makers was a seasoned film professional, Iulii Raizman. Born in 1903, Raizman survived many tribulations during the oppressive eras of Soviet film making. He poignantly explored such themes as family trauma, societal immorality, materialism and corruption, and economic deprivation. His *Private Life* (1982) explores the ordeals of a factory manager who, when forced into retirement, realizes that he has sacrificed time with his family. *A Time of Wishes* (1984) examines how women

391

endure their inferior lot in society. Raizman has gained such renown, particularly as head of Mosfilm studios in Moscow, that he has been able to initiate the production of progressive films and has supported efforts of younger, aspiring, and creative film makers to voice their concerns through their works.

The relaxation of controls over film making has also permitted the release of numerous films that had been restricted for many years. Four such prominent films released were Klimov's *Agoniia* and *Come and See*, Aleksei German's *My Friend Ivan Lapshin*, and Tengiz Abuladze's *Repentance*. Known in the West as *Rasputin*, Klimov's *Agoniia* presents a more balanced view of Tsar Nicholas II than that historically taught in the school systems, and it also contains religious overtones. The film maintains an unusual silence regarding the Bolshevik Revolution. Klimov completed *Agoniia* in 1975, but it was not released until 1985. In *Come and See*, Klimov captures the horrors of war from a typical Soviet perspective, that of destruction symbolized not only by the Nazi genocide but also by the premonition of nuclear holocaust.

The other two films deal with some of the horrors of the Stalin period. German's *My Friend Ivan Lapshin*, which required three years for approval after it had been completed, contains an investigation said to depict innocent people being persecuted during Stalin's reign of terror. Abuladze's *Repentance* created a stir throughout the Soviet Union as well as the outside world. Written in 1982, produced in 1984, and approved for public viewing in 1987, *Repentance* concentrates on the crimes of the Stalin era and the evil involved in the arrests of innocent people, some of whom were later executed. The dictator portrayed supposedly is based on a number of evil men in recent history, the most important of whom are Stalin and his secret police chief, Lavrenty Beria. Echoes of Adolf Hitler and Benito Mussolini are also evident in the dictator's appearance. Not only was the film viewed as an overt attack on Stalinism but it also was intended to shock Soviet citizens and raise their political consciousness to prevent a recurrence of these horrors. Evtushenko has likened the film to "the cultural event of Gorbachev's cultural thaw, just as Aleksandr Solzhenitsyn's *One Day in the Life of Ivan Denisovich* represented the spiritual acme of the Khrushchev era." As Gorbachev stressed in a speech on the seventieth anniversary of the Bolshevik Revolution in a 1987 Central Committee plenum, such films are more openly watched in a society encouraged to reassess itself and ensure that "no forgotten names and no blank pages . . . of the years of industrialization and collectivization" be left untouched.

Taganka Theater, Moscow. The Taganka was founded in 1964 by the director Iurii Liubimov; Vladimir Vysotskii performed here until his death in 1980.
Courtesy Jimmy Pritchard

Theater

Soviet citizens have a rich cultural heritage in theater. Two of the most internationally famous theaters, Moscow's Bolshoi Theater and Leningrad's Kirov Theater, attracted both domestic and foreign audiences with striking performances in huge, ornate, and festive halls. The performers who played to sold-out performances in these theaters and who adhered to the regime's acting and directing guidelines received special benefits such as worldwide travel, luxurious apartments, and the highest state honors for their artistic contributions. Those artists, however, who chose to portray views opposed to the regime's artistic standards experienced shame and denunciation, even though audiences often admired them.

Such an artist was Vladimir Vysotskii. In his short lifetime, Vysotskii attracted widespread popularity but railed against a system he opposed. Although he died in 1980 of a heart attack, apparently the result of alcoholism, Vysotskii's mass appeal became in many ways more pervasive after his death. His memory evolved into a veritable cult, with thousands of people mourning the anniversaries of his death by filing past his burial place. This balladeer and actor, who for years played such famous roles as Hamlet under the tutelage of Taganka Theater director Iurii Liubimov, raised the avant-garde theater to a cultural pinnacle in Moscow by attracting thousands of followers, even for unannounced or unpublicized programs that featured his protests, often against the leadership's failings. His poetry and music, once banned in the Soviet Union, have been disseminated throughout the country and depict bureaucratic corruption, elitism, poverty, war, and prison camp horror. In the late 1980s, Vysotskii's mentor, Liubimov, continued to leave an indelible mark on the theater, even after his forced exile by the authorities and the bans on his productions. He lived abroad and continued to produce masterpieces adapted from Gor'-kiy's novel *Mother,* Bertold Brecht's play *The Good Woman of Szechuan,* Mikhail Bulgakov's novel *The Master and Margarita,* and Fedor Dostoevskii's novel *Crime and Punishment,* making him the greatest Soviet theatrical director. The Taganka Theater performed without him, but the stage did not retain the same popularity. Under Gorbachev, Liubimov was allowed back to his homeland to direct his version of the opera *Boris Godunov,* banned in 1983 when he was forced to leave the Soviet Union. However, Liubimov remained only long enough to oversee the project's completion and left of his own accord, preferring to live abroad.

After 1985 a degree of liberalization similar to that permitted for literature and cinema prevailed for the stage. In 1985 and 1986, approximately 10 percent of the directors were replaced in favor of younger and more innovative directors, who, in turn, opened the door to more creative playwrights. In addition, theater groups (collectives) gained "full independence in the selection of plays," releasing them in some measure from the onus of the regime's authoritarian and arbitrary decisions. As a result of these changes, playwrights such as Mikhail Shatrov blossomed within the freer theater environment. In 1986 his "neo-Leninist" work *Dictatorship of Conscience,* which portrayed Stalin and Brezhnev as shady and sometimes unfaithful communists, played to receptive audiences. Shatrov's other prominent play from the 1987–88 period, . . . *Further . . . Further, and Further!,* offered a scathing indictment of the Stalin period, this time concentrating on Lenin's legacy and the way Stalin manipulated the other Bolshevik leaders during the 1920s in his successful effort to defeat them. Shatrov captured the characters of many early revolutionary leaders, using strong dialogue to depict vivid conflicts.

Music

The Soviet Union has produced some of the world's foremost

Grave of Vladimir Vysotskii
Courtesy Jimmy Pritchard

composers and musicians. The authorities, however, have sought to control their music as well as their performances. As a result, composers struggled to produce their works under strict limitations. Some artists emigrated, but their works endured and continued to attract large audiences when performed.

Restrictions on what musicians played and where they performed often caused artists to leave the country either of their own accord or through forced exile. Great composers and musicians such as Dmitrii Shostakovich, Mstislav Rostropovich, and Vladimir Fel'tsman were persecuted, and some ultimately emigrated. In 1986, however, Moscow and Leningrad audiences were privileged to hear several memorable performances by the brilliant pianist Vladimir Horowitz, who left the Soviet Union in 1925 and who previously had not been allowed to reenter the country. A composer who decided to remain in the Soviet Union was Alfred Schnittke, acclaimed as the best Soviet composer since Shostakovich and a formidable technician of surrealist expression. Although at times he was restricted by the authorities to presenting unoriginal and party-line works, Schnittke attracted both avant-garde and mainstream audiences because of his original, deeply spiritual, and often mystical compositions. When not confined by the regime to recording certain compositions, Schnittke created such masterpieces as (K)ein Sommernachtstraum, Concerto No. 4 for Violin and Orchestra,

Concerto Grosso No. 1, and Concerto Grosso No. 2, which appealed to audiences around the world.

In addition to classical music, jazz endured and survived the official denunciations the government had cast upon it over the years. The regime distrusted this form of music because it had originated in the United States and because its essence was improvisation. As a symbol of artistic freedom and individual expression, jazz was difficult to control. In the late 1960s and 1970s, jazz was one of the most popular forms of music in the Soviet Union. Such famous jazz artists as Vadim Mustafa-Zadek and Aleksei Kozlov became music idols to a generation of jazz lovers. In the late 1980s, however, the popularity of jazz declined because of the emergence of rock and roll.

The rhythms and sounds of rock and roll appealed mainly to the young. In the 1980s, the popularity of the once leading rock bands Winds of Change and The Time Machine faded in favor of younger groups. Leningrad rock groups such as Boris Grebenshchikov's band Aquarium and the group Avia, which incorporated slogans, speeches, loud sounds, unorthodox mixtures of instruments, and screams, provided an important outlet for youth. Some of their music supported themes along the lines of Gorbachev's policies, expressing a desire for change in society. Rock-and-roll lyrics sometimes exceeded the boundaries of the politically permissible. Yet, the leadership realized that this music could not be eliminated or even censored for long because it not only appealed to many citizens but also could help disseminate the leadership's policies.

For many youth, rock and roll served as a means to live out dreams and desires that might not be possible in daily life. Aspiring rock or popular musicians expressed themselves publicly in the more open political environment during the late 1980s. In that period, Moscow and Leningrad permitted performances of music by *punki* (punk fans) and *metallisti* (heavy metal fans), whose loud, raucous music appealed to alienated and rebellious youth. Most rock music, however, portrayed the artist as explorer and expressed the desire for new styles and forms.

Painting, Sculpture, and the Graphic Arts

Moscow and Leningrad housed the two most popular art museums in the Soviet Union, the Tret'iakov Gallery and the Hermitage Museum, respectively. The Tret'iakov contained medieval and modern Russian masterpieces; the Hermitage's collection of Impressionist painters was one of the best in the world.

Until the mid-1980s, avant-garde expression appeared not in state museums but within the confines of the basement galleries on Moscow's Malaia Gruzinskaia street. Displays of overtly religious, surrealist, or semiabstract works began in 1978. The artists who created such works became an integral part of the cultural life of Moscow, as their art directly contrasted with socialist realism. These "survivalists" withstood pressure from the official unions and prospered through domestic and foreign patronage from established cultural figures, influential higher officials, scientists, and diplomats.

Nonconformist artists created attention both at home and abroad in the late 1980s. Former underground artists, such as Il'ia Kabakov and Vladimir Iankilevskii, were permitted to display their works in the late 1980s, and they captured viewers' imagination with harsh criticism of the Soviet system. Paintings by such artists as Vadim Sacharov and Nikolai Belianiv, linoleum graphic works by Dshamil Mufid-Zade and Maya Tabaka, wood engravings by Dmitrii Bisti, and sculpture by Dmitrii Shilinski depicted society as gray, drab, harsh, and colorless. Their works indicted industrialization, the Great Terror (see Glossary), the annexation of Estonia, Latvia, and Lithuania, and the polluted environment.

Gorbachev based much of his policies' success on the new content of artistic expression appearing throughout the Soviet Union. By opening up cultural life and enabling mass media representatives and artists to speak more honestly, the leadership attempted to win the support of the intelligentsia for its policies. In the late 1980s, the leadership loosened the strictures of socialist realism to enrich the cultural vitality of society, although censorship laws still prevented much information from reaching the public. Although strictures were relaxed, the principle of party control remained in force.

* * *

Many works offer insights into Soviet mass media and culture. For a good overview of the mass media and descriptions of the censorship institutions, the following sources are particularly helpful: Frederick C. Barghoorn and Thomas F. Remington's *Politics in the USSR;* Jane Leftwich Curry and Joan R. Dassin's *Press Control Around the World;* Vadim Medish's *The Soviet Union;* Lilita Dzirkals, Thane Gustafson, and A. Ross Johnson's "The Media and Intra-Elite Communication in the USSR"; and Ellen Mickiewicz's *Media and the Russian Public.* More specialized works concentrating on media and culture include Maurice Friedberg's *Russian Culture in the 1980s;* Martin Ebon's *The Soviet Propaganda Machine;* Ellen

Mickiewicz's "Political Communication and the Soviet Media System"; Wilson P. Dizard and Blake S. Swensrud's *Gorbachev's Information Revolution;* Valery S. Golovskoy and John Rimberg's *Behind the Soviet Screen;* and S. Frederick Starr's *Red and Hot.* (For further information and complete citations, see Bibliography.)

Chapter 10. Foreign Policy

Ronald W. Reagan and Mikhail S. Gorbachev

ONCE A PARIAH DENIED DIPLOMATIC RECOGNITION by most countries, the Soviet Union had official relations with the majority of the nations of the world by the late 1980s. The Soviet Union also had progressed from being an outsider in international organizations and negotiations to being one of the arbiters of Europe's fate after World War II. In the 1970s, after the Soviet Union achieved rough nuclear parity with the United States, it perceived its own involvement as essential to the solution of any major international problem. The Soviet Union's effort to extend its influence or control over many states and peoples has resulted in the formation of a world socialist system (see Glossary) of states whose citizens included some one-fourth of humanity. In addition, since the early 1970s the Soviet Union has concluded friendship and cooperation treaties with a number of Third World states. For all these reasons, Soviet foreign policy is of major importance to the noncommunist world and helps determine the tenor of international relations.

Although myriad bureaucracies have been involved in the formation and execution of Soviet foreign policy, the major policy guidelines have been determined by the Politburo of the Communist Party of the Soviet Union (CPSU). The foremost objectives of Soviet foreign policy have been the maintenance and enhancement of national security and the maintenance of hegemony over Eastern Europe. Relations with the United States and Western Europe have also been of major concern to Soviet foreign policy makers, and relations with individual Third World states have been at least partly determined by the proximity of each state to the Soviet border and to Soviet estimates of its strategic significance. Despite domestic economic problems, Mikhail S. Gorbachev, who became general secretary in 1985, has emphasized increased Soviet participation in international organizations and negotiations, the pursuit of arms control and other international agreements, and the reinvigoration of diplomatic, political, cultural, and scientific initiatives in virtually every region of the world.

Ideology and Objectives

According to Soviet theorists, the basic character of Soviet foreign policy was set forth in Vladimir I. Lenin's Decree on Peace, adopted by the Second Congress of Soviets in November 1917. It set forth the dual nature of Soviet foreign policy, which encompasses both proletarian internationalism and peaceful coexistence. On the one hand, proletarian internationalism refers to the common cause of the working classes of all countries in struggling to overthrow the bourgeoisie and to establish communist regimes. Peaceful coexistence, on the other hand, refers to measures to ensure relatively peaceful government-to-government relations with capitalist states. Both policies can be pursued simultaneously: "Peaceful coexistence does not rule out but presupposes determined opposition to imperialist aggression and support for peoples defending their revolutionary gains or fighting foreign oppression."

The Soviet commitment in practice to proletarian internationalism has declined since the founding of the Soviet state, although this component of ideology still has some effect on current formulation and execution of Soviet foreign policy. Although pragmatic *raisons d'état* undoubtedly accounted for much of contemporary Soviet foreign policy, the ideology of class struggle (see Glossary) still played a role in providing a worldview and certain loose guidelines for action in the 1980s. Marxist-Leninist (see Glossary) ideology reinforces other characteristics of political culture that create an attitude of competition and conflict with other states.

The general foreign policy goals of the Soviet Union were formalized in a party program (see Glossary) ratified by delegates to the Twenty-Seventh Party Congress in February-March 1986. According to the program, "the main goals and guidelines of the CPSU's international policy" included ensuring favorable external conditions conducive to building communism in the Soviet Union; eliminating the threat of world war; disarmament; strengthening the "world socialist system"; developing "equal and friendly" relations with "liberated" [Third World] countries; peaceful coexistence with the capitalist countries; and solidarity with communist and revolutionary-democratic parties, the international workers' movement, and national liberation struggles.

Although these general foreign policy goals were apparently conceived in terms of priorities, the emphasis and ranking of the priorities have changed over time in response to domestic and international stimuli. After Gorbachev assumed power in 1985, for instance, some Western analysts discerned in the ranking of priorities a possible de-emphasis of Soviet support for national liberation movements. Although the emphasis and ranking of priorities were subject to change, two basic goals of Soviet foreign policy remained constant: national security (safeguarding CPSU rule through internal control and the maintenance of adequate military forces) and, since the late 1940s, influence over Eastern Europe.

Many Western analysts have examined the way Soviet behavior in various regions and countries supports the general goals of Soviet foreign policy. These analysts have assessed Soviet behavior in the 1970s and 1980s as placing primary emphasis on relations with the United States, which is considered the foremost threat to the national security of the Soviet Union. Second priority was given to relations with Eastern Europe (the European members of the Warsaw Pact—see Appendix B) and Western Europe (the European members of the North Atlantic Treaty Organization—NATO). Third priority was given to the littoral or propinquitous states along the southern border of the Soviet Union: Turkey (a NATO member), Iran, Afghanistan, China, Mongolia, the Democratic People's Republic of Korea (North Korea), and Japan. Regions near to, but not bordering, the Soviet Union were assigned fourth priority. These included the Middle East and North Africa, South Asia, and Southeast Asia. Last priority was given to sub-Saharan Africa, the islands in the Pacific and Indian oceans, and Latin America, except insofar as these regions either provided opportunities for strategic basing or bordered on strategic naval straits or sea lanes. In general, Soviet foreign policy was most concerned with superpower relations (and, more broadly, relations between the members of NATO and the Warsaw Pact), but during the 1980s Soviet leaders pursued improved relations with all regions of the world as part of its foreign policy objectives (see fig. 14).

Foreign Policy Making and Execution

The Foreign Policy Makers

The predominant Soviet foreign policy actor has been the general secretary of the CPSU. The dominant decision-making body has been the Politburo (see Politburo; Secretariat, ch. 7). Although the general secretary is only one of several members of the Politburo, his positions as head of the Secretariat and the Defense Council (see Glossary) gave him preeminence in the Politburo.

Other members of the Politburo also have had major foreign policy-making responsibilities, most notably the ministers of foreign affairs and defense, the chairman of the Committee for State Security (Komitet gosudarstvennoi bezopasnosti—KGB), and the chief of the CPSU's International Department. The minister of defense and the minister of foreign affairs had been full or candidate members of the Politburo intermittently since 1917. The chairman of the KGB became a candidate member of the Politburo in 1967 and has generally been a full member since then. The chief of the International Department became a candidate member of the Politburo in 1972 but from 1986 to 1988 held only Secretariat membership. Since late 1988, he has been a candidate, then full member of the Central Committee. Even when foreign policy organizations were not directly represented on the Politburo, they were nonetheless supervised by Politburo members.

It is incorrect to say that there are no policy differences within the Politburo or no policy inputs or alterations of policy by other foreign policy actors. One Western theory holds that foreign policy innovation occurs when a new general secretary consolidates his power and is able to implement his policy agenda. It is also apparent that the foreign and domestic environments affect the formulation and execution of Soviet foreign policy. According to some Western theorists, for instance, Soviet opportunism in the Third World in the 1970s owed something to American preoccupation with domestic concerns following the end of the war in Vietnam and the Watergate scandal. Similarly, the "Reagan Doctrine" of assisting anticommunist insurgencies has been suggested by some Western analysts as contributing to Soviet reassessment of the long-term viability of some Third World revolutionary democratic regimes. The extent to which human, economic, and military resources are available for diplomatic, foreign aid, and military activities also affects Soviet foreign policy. It is nevertheless true that the centralization of foreign policy decision making in the Politburo and the longevity of its members (a major factor in the Politburo's lengthy institutional memory) both have contributed to the Soviet Union's ability to plan foreign policy and guide its long-term implementation with a relative singleness of purpose lacking in pluralistic political systems.

Departments of the Central Committee

Several departments of the Central Committee had some responsibility for foreign policy in the 1980s, including the International Department and the Propaganda Department, which was absorbed by the Ideological Department in 1988. Until late 1988, when the departments were reorganized, the Liaison with Communist and Workers' Parties of Socialist Countries Department and the Cadres Abroad Department also had foreign policy responsibilities. These two departments, originally part of the International Department, were apparently reincorporated into the revamped International Department. From 1978 to 1986, there existed another department involved in foreign policy execution, the International Information Department.

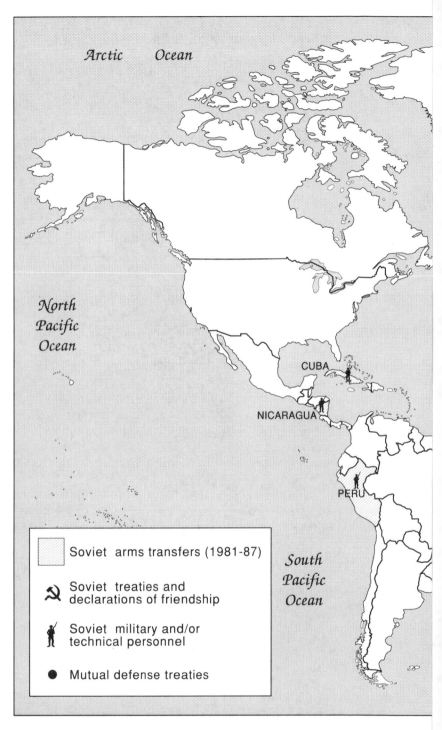

Arctic Ocean

North
Pacific
Ocean

CUBA

NICARAGUA

PERU

South
Pacific
Ocean

	Soviet arms transfers (1981-87)
☭	Soviet treaties and declarations of friendship
🪖	Soviet military and/or technical personnel
●	Mutual defense treaties

Source: Based on information from United States, Department of Defense, *Soviet Military Power*, Washin

Figure 14. Soviet Foreign Relations Worldwide, 1988

The International Department, created in 1943 essentially to carry out functions previously performed by the Third Communist International (Comintern—see Glossary), was responsible for CPSU relations with nonruling communist parties in other states. Under Boris Ponomarev, chief of the International Department from 1955 to 1986, the International Department focused mainly on CPSU relations with Third World communist and radical parties, but under Anatolii Dobrynin, appointed chief in 1986, the focus included overall party and state relations with developed Western states. In late 1988, Valentin A. Falin, an expert on Western Europe and a professional propagandist, was appointed chief.

The International Department, in focusing on party-to-party relations, had traditionally been involved in supplying various resources to the nonruling parties. These included funds, propaganda, and training. The International Department also had received international delegations from communist and leftist groups while the Soviet government was maintaining correct relations with the home government in power. Finally, the International Department acquired international support for Soviet foreign policy through extensive use of international front groups, such as the World Peace Council and the Afro-Asian People's Solidarity Organization, which were funded and controlled through Soviet parent organizations.

In late 1988, two other departments dealing with foreign policy were reincorporated into the International Department. The Liaison Department, created in 1957 as a spin-off from the International Department, had responsibility for CPSU relations with ruling communist parties in Bulgaria, Cambodia, China, Cuba, Czechoslovakia, the German Democratic Republic (East Germany), Hungary, Romania, Vietnam, and Yugoslavia. The Cadres Abroad Department, created in 1950, approved foreign travel of virtually all Soviet citizens, except for tourists visiting the Warsaw Pact states and military personnel.

The International Information Department, disestablished in 1980, had been created by Leonid I. Brezhnev to consolidate and improve upon propaganda efforts undertaken by the International Department, the Ministry of Foreign Affairs, and the Propaganda Department. It regularly held press briefings for foreign media personnel in Moscow. Its functions were reabsorbed by the International Department, Ministry of Foreign Affairs, and Propaganda Department; the Ministry of Foreign Affairs reassumed responsibility for press briefings on major policy issues.

Higher State and Government Organizations

In accordance with the 1977 Constitution and the amendments

and additions promulgated in December 1988, several organizations were involved in the formation of foreign policy, including the Congress of People's Deputies, the Supreme Soviet, the Presidium of the Supreme Soviet, and the Council of Ministers. This influence was primarily a result of the membership of high-ranking CPSU officials in these bodies, which had a limited ability to select and interpret information passed on to the party leadership.

The Congress of People's Deputies and the Supreme Soviet

The changes to the Constitution adopted in December 1988 altered the character of the Soviet legislative system (see Supreme Soviet, ch. 8). The changes invested the Congress of People's Deputies with "defining the basic guidelines" of foreign policy and expressly assigned foreign policy duties to the newly created position of chairman of the Supreme Soviet. The role of the Supreme Soviet in formulating and overseeing the execution of foreign policy was theoretically strengthened by providing for lengthy (six- to eight-month) yearly sittings of the Supreme Soviet. The duties assigned to the Supreme Soviet included forming the Defense Council, appointing the senior commanders of the armed forces, ratifying international treaties, proclaiming a state of war, and making decisions on the use of troops abroad. This latter provision was added to the list of duties of the Supreme Soviet, as explained by Gorbachev and other leaders, because of the closed nature of the decision process that led to committing troops to the invasion of Afghanistan. The Presidium of the Supreme Soviet was assigned responsibility for minor diplomatic functions and declaring war in periods when the Supreme Soviet was not in session. The chairman of the Supreme Soviet was to represent the Soviet Union in foreign relations with other states. He was also to submit reports on foreign policy to the Congress of People's Deputies and the Supreme Soviet, head the Defense Council, and negotiate and sign international treaties. A Foreign Affairs Committee was also set up and its members empowered to formulate and oversee foreign policy execution. The new legislative structures apparently provided for greater legislative oversight of foreign policy execution and even for some input into the foreign policy formulation process, with the chairman and the Presidium of the Supreme Soviet playing a guiding role in foreign policy activities.

The Council of Ministers and Its Presidium

The Presidium of the Council of Ministers also had foreign policy duties in its role as head of the executive branch of the government. The 1977 Constitution specified that the Council of Ministers be elected at a joint session of the Supreme Soviet and be constitutionally accountable to the Supreme Soviet (see Administrative Organs, ch. 8). The foreign policy duties of the Council of Ministers were not specified in the 1977 Constitution, beyond a general statement that the council was to ''provide general direction in regard to relations with other states, foreign trade, and economic, scientific, technical, and cultural cooperation of the Soviet Union with other countries; take measures to ensure fulfillment of the Soviet Union's international treaties; and ratify and repudiate international agreements.'' These duties were carried out by the various ministries and state committees involved in the execution of foreign policy. The chairman of the Presidium of the Council of Ministers, as head of government, met with foreign delegations and signed international trade and economic agreements.

In 1989 three ministries and a committee had foreign policy responsibilities: the Ministry of Foreign Affairs (diplomatic relations), the Ministry of Foreign Economic Relations (trade and arms transfers), the Ministry of Defense (military advisory assistance, use and display of military power abroad, and covert activities through the Main Intelligence Directorate—see Glossary), and the KGB (covert activities through the First Chief Directorate). Many other ministries and state committees and government agencies also had a role in foreign policy execution. These ranged from the Soviet Copyright Agency, which approved foreign requests for reproduction and translation of Soviet media materials, to the State Committee for Foreign Tourism, of which Inturist was a part.

The Ministry of Foreign Affairs

The Ministry of Foreign Affairs had responsibility for administering the diplomatic relations of the Soviet Union. Once the Council of Ministers had approved diplomatic recognition of a state, the Ministry of Foreign Affairs would establish embassies and consulates, provide the core staffs serving abroad, and serve as a conduit for formal communications between the Soviet political leadership and the host state. A Soviet ambassador serving abroad would be regarded under international law as the personal representative of the chairman of the Supreme Soviet to the head of government of the host state. In practice, the Soviet diplomatic service carried out CPSU policy as set forth by the general secretary and the Politburo.

The Bolshevik Revolution (see Glossary) of 1917 resulted in a virtually complete break in diplomatic staffing from the tsarist period because the majority of tsarist diplomatic personnel refused to work for the Bolsheviks. Another discontinuity in staffing occurred in the late 1930s, when the People's Commissariat of Foreign Affairs (known after 1946 as the Ministry of Foreign Affairs) was purged and the resulting vacancies filled by young, professionally trained and politically reliable personnel such as Andrei Gromyko. The ministry experienced continuity in personnel and structure throughout Gromyko's tenure as minister (1957–85). Eduard Shevardnadze, who succeeded Gromyko as foreign minister in 1985, reorganized the ministry and made major personnel changes among the Collegium members and ambassadors.

The Ministry of Foreign Affairs was organized into geographical and functional departments and administrations reflecting Soviet ideological and pragmatic concerns with various geographical regions or world problems. Departments and administrations of the ministry included geographical ones, dealing with the regions of Europe, Latin America, Asia, and Africa, and functional ones, dealing with such concerns as international organizations and cultural affairs. Shevardnadze restructured some of the geographical and functional departments, mainly by grouping countries into categories reflecting modern world realities. For example, he grouped communist countries into Asian and European departments, put the member states of the Association of Southeast Asian Nations into a single department, and created another African office consisting almost entirely of the "frontline states" proximal to South Africa.

Instruments of Influence

The Soviet Union interacted with other countries in a variety of ways, including diplomacy, arms transfers, state and government visits, use of communist parties abroad, front organizations, trade and aid, and educational exchanges. To achieve its general and regional foreign policy objectives, the Soviet Union made great efforts to sustain and increase relations over time. The Soviet physical and material presence in a state (which could be quantified by numbers of military and economic advisers and the amount of economic and military assistance) had traditionally been one indicator that, along with information about internal decision making, allowed Western analysts to theorize about the degree of Soviet influence on a particular state's foreign policy.

Diplomatic Relations

The Soviet Union perceived two basic forms of diplomacy: "bourgeois diplomacy" as developed by the European states, with its emphasis on state-to-state relations; and communist diplomacy of a "new type" among the ruling communist and socialist-oriented

Ministry of Foreign Affairs building, Moscow
Courtesy Jimmy Pritchard

regimes. Communist diplomacy emphasizes "equal, non-exploitative" party and state relations among the regime and "peaceful coexistence" between these regimes and the capitalist and capitalist-oriented states. Soviet diplomacy hence was multifaceted, embracing state-to-state relations with Western and Western-oriented Third World states; party-to-party ties with ruling and nonruling communist and leftist parties and national liberation groups; state representation in myriad international organizations and at international forums; and political alliances with "fraternal socialist" states and states of socialist orientation through the vehicle of treaties of friendship and cooperation (see Ideology and Objectives, this ch.).

As the prospects for world revolution faded in the first years after the establishment of Bolshevik rule in Russia, the Russian Republic began assiduously to pursue diplomatic recognition as a means of achieving legitimacy. At first, the Russian Republic had resident embassies in only a few countries. After the Soviet Union was established in December 1922—joining the Russian, Belorussian, Ukrainian, and Transcaucasian soviet socialist republics—the new state continued the policy of pursuing diplomatic recognition. The Soviet Union was particularly interested in establishing diplomatic relations with Britain and the United States. In 1924 the newly elected Labour Party government in Britain recognized the Soviet Union (in 1927 the succeeding Conservative Party government broke off relations, but they were permanently restored in 1929), and in 1933 the United States established diplomatic relations with the Soviet Union. During World War II, many Allied states recognized the Soviet Union. During the "Cold War" of the late 1940s and 1950s, many states were wary of establishing diplomatic relations with the Soviet Union, and a few states, mostly in Central America and South America, recalled their accredited representatives. Since the general improvement in East-West relations in the 1960s, however, states in all regions of the world have moved to establish diplomatic relations with the Soviet Union.

Since the 1960s, the Soviet Union has achieved diplomatic relations with states in several regions where such relations were previously unknown or uncommon—South America, Central America, islands in the Pacific, and states in the Persian Gulf region. The range and scope of the Soviet diplomatic presence has been roughly matched only by that of the United States. In the late 1980s, the Soviet Union had resident ambassadors in almost 120 states and consulates and trade offices in scores of states. The Soviet Union also tried to maintain or reestablish relations, or exchange ambassadors, with states that had exhibited hostility toward the Soviet

Union, such as China, Egypt, and Somalia. As of 1988, the Soviet Union had refused to establish relations, or had broken off relations, with only a few states, most notably Chile, Paraguay, the Republic of Korea (South Korea), Taiwan, and Israel. Soviet diplomatic recognition of the governments of the latter three states had been opposed by other regional powers with which the Soviet Union has wished to maintain or foster close relations (North Korea with respect to South Korea, China with respect to Taiwan, and the Middle Eastern Arab states with respect to Israel).

Party and State Visits Abroad

An important component of Soviet foreign relations was Soviet state and party delegation visits to states with which the Soviet Union enjoyed diplomatic relations. These visits served to improve relations with Western states by influencing elite and popular attitudes. The visits also helped cement and sustain close ties with communist states, states with a socialist orientation, and nonaligned nations. Common actions were often discussed with such states, for example, coordinated voting on United Nations (UN) resolutions. Economic, scientific, cultural, and other cooperation agreements were also signed during these visits, although such agreements were more commonly signed during visits by Third World delegations to Moscow. These visits usually concluded with the publication of joint communiqués that might reveal details of the nature of the visit and also list points of agreement on issues such as the prevention of nuclear war, nuclear-free zones, peaceful coexistence, and anti-imperialism.

Friendship and Cooperation Treaties

In the early 1970s, the Soviet Union began to formalize relations with several Third World states through the signing of friendship and cooperation treaties (see table 29, Appendix A). These treaties were aimed at regularizing economic, political, and military contacts between the Soviet Union and Third World states over extended periods (usually twenty years). Third World regimes signed these treaties to obtain help in the consolidation of their rule or to secure advantage over or protection from regional opponents. All the treaties contained military cooperation provisions or provisions calling for "mutual consultations" in case of security threats to either party. The Soviet Union proffered these treaties in order to consolidate and build on existing relations in the context of an overarching agreement. The Soviet goal has been to encourage close, long-term relations with the Soviet Union. These relations have included military cooperation and the establishment of Soviet military facilities in some Third World states.

Communist Parties Abroad

By 1984 the Soviet Union had recognized communist and workers' parties in ninety-five countries. Fifteen of these were ruling communist parties. The Soviet Union considered these most ideologically mature parties as part of the world socialist system. The select group included the ruling parties of Albania, Bulgaria, China, Cuba, Czechoslovakia, East Germany, Hungary, Laos, Mongolia, North Korea, Poland, Romania, the Soviet Union, Vietnam, and Yugoslavia. Besides these ruling parties, the Soviet Union perceived other less ideologically mature ruling parties as "Marxist-Leninist vanguard parties," a label that distinguished them from "true" communist parties. These vanguard parties existed in several Third World "revolutionary democracies," which have included Afghanistan, Angola, Congo, Ethiopia, Mozambique, and the People's Democratic Republic of Yemen (South Yemen). Nonruling communist parties (of greater or lesser ideological maturity) that existed in developed capitalist and in Third World states "on the capitalist path of development" made up another category of parties.

Lenin founded the Comintern in 1919 to guide the activities of communist parties and communist front organizations abroad. The Comintern's first act was a manifesto urging workers abroad to support the Bolshevik regime in Russia. Later, the Comintern became a tool the Soviet Union used to direct foreign communist parties to execute policies of benefit to the security of the Soviet Union. The Comintern was formally dissolved by Stalin in 1943 as a gesture of cooperation with the wartime allies, but the International Department was created to carry out its responsibilities. Another organization—the Communist Information Bureau (Cominform)—was created in 1947 to carry out liaison and propaganda duties, and it included as members the communist parties of Albania, Bulgaria, Czechoslovakia, France, Hungary, Italy, Romania, the Soviet Union, and Yugoslavia. The Cominform expelled Yugoslavia as a member in June 1948 for ideological deviation. With the thaw in relations between the Soviet Union and Yugoslavia in 1955 and 1956, the Soviet Union formally dissolved the then-moribund Cominform as a gesture to the Yugoslavs.

The Cominform conflict with Yugoslavia in 1948 signaled the breakup of what in the West was perceived as "monolithic communism" and the emergence of "polycentrism." Polycentrism (literally, many centers), a Western term, describes the relative independence from Soviet control of some nonruling and ruling communist parties. Polycentrism was further in evidence following the Sino-Soviet split that became evident in the late 1950s and early 1960s. More recently, some foreign communist parties have successfully resisted Soviet efforts to convene a conference of world communist and workers parties, the last of which occurred in 1969. The emergence in the early to mid-1970s of a broad and somewhat disparate set of ideological beliefs, termed ''Eurocommunism,'' was further evidence of polycentric tendencies. Eurocommunist beliefs were espoused by nonruling communist parties in France, Italy, Spain, and elsewhere in the West that criticized Soviet attempts to assert ideological control over foreign communist parties and even denounced Soviet foreign and domestic policies.

Despite polycentric tendencies in the world communist movement, the Soviet Union was able to influence many parties through financial and propaganda support. This influence varied over time and according to the issue involved. The influence that the Soviet Union was able to exercise through the local nonruling communist parties was seldom significant enough to affect the policies of foreign governments directly. Local communist parties have reported on the local political situation to Moscow, have engaged in subversive activities of benefit to the Soviet Union, have served as conduits for Soviet propaganda, and have attempted to rally local populations and elites to support Soviet policies. During the late 1980s, the united front (see Glossary) strategy of alliances between nonruling communist parties and other leftist, ''progressive,'' and even ''petit bourgeois'' parties received new emphasis. The goal was for communists to exercise influence through participation in electoral politics and through holding posts in legislatures and executive bodies. The global trend toward democratization was assessed by the Soviet Union as providing opportunities for the united front strategy. As was noted in *Pravda* in 1987, ''The struggle for democracy is an important way of weakening monopolistic state capitalism, and the results of this struggle can be a starting point for the preparation of socialist transformation.''

Soviet-United States Relations

A central concern of Soviet foreign and military policy since World War II, relations with the United States have gone through cycles of ''cold'' and ''warm'' periods. A crucial factor in Soviet-American relations has been the mutual nuclear threat (see The Soviet Union and Nuclear Arms Control, this ch.). A high point in Soviet-American relations occurred when the Strategic Arms Limitation Talks (SALT—see Glossary) resulted in the May 1972 signing of the Anti-Ballistic Missile Treaty and the Interim Agreement on the Limitation of Strategic Offensive Arms. This event was an early achievement of Soviet-American détente.

The Soviet Union and the United States differed over the meaning of the détente relationship. In the West, détente has usually been considered to mean a nonhostile, even harmonious, relationship. The Soviet Union, however, has preferred the terms *mirnoe sosushchestvovanie* (peaceful coexistence) or *razriadka napriazhennosti* (a discharging or easing of tensions) instead of the term détente. Brezhnev explained the Soviet perception of the détente relationship at the 1976 and 1981 CPSU party congresses, asserting that détente did not mean that the Soviet Union would cease to support Third World national liberation movements or the world class struggle. In the Soviet view, détente with the West was compatible with sponsoring Cuban intervention in the Third World. However, Soviet-sponsored intervention in the Third World met with growing protest from the United States. The détente relationship conclusively ended with the Soviet invasion of Afghanistan in December 1979.

Following the Soviet invasion, the United States instigated a number of trade sanctions against the Soviet Union, including an embargo on grain shipments to the Soviet Union, the cancellation of American participation in the 1980 Summer Olympics in Moscow, and the shelving of efforts to win ratification in the United States Senate of the second SALT agreement. In April 1981, under the new administration of President Ronald Reagan, the United States announced the lifting of the grain embargo but also moved to tighten procedures concerning the export of strategically sensitive technology to the Soviet Union. As part of this effort to limit such exports, the Reagan administration in 1982 unsuccessfully attempted to convince West European governments to block the sale of American-developed technology for the construction of Soviet natural gas pipelines. A freeze on cultural exchanges that had developed after the invasion of Afghanistan continued during Reagan's first term in office.

The Soviet Union began deploying SS-20 intermediate-range ballistic missiles equipped with nuclear warheads along its western and southeastern borders in 1977. The United States and its NATO allies regarded this deployment as destabilizing to the nuclear balance in Europe, and in December 1979 NATO decided to counter with the deployment of Pershing II intermediate-range ballistic missiles and ground-launched cruise missiles (GLCMs), both equipped with nuclear warheads. In November 1981, Reagan proposed the "zero option" as the solution to the nuclear imbalance

*Embassy of
the Soviet Union,
Washington
Courtesy
Raymond E. Zickel*

in Western Europe. Basically, the zero option included the elimination of SS–20s and other missiles targeted against Western Europe and the nondeployment of countervailing NATO weapons. The Soviet Union refused to accept the zero option and insisted that French and British nuclear forces be included in the reckoning of the balance of nuclear forces in Europe and in any agreement on reductions of nuclear forces. Feeling forced to match the Soviet nuclear threat, NATO began countervailing deployments in late 1983. As the deployment date neared, the Soviet Union threatened to deploy additional nuclear weapons targeted on Western Europe and weapons that would place the territory of the United States under threat. Also, Soviet negotiators walked out of talks on the reduction of intermediate-range nuclear forces (the INF talks) and strategic forces (the Strategic Arms Reduction Talks, or START). The refusal to come back to the negotiating table continued after General Secretary Iurii V. Andropov's death and Konstantin V. Chernenko's selection as general secretary in early 1984. The Soviet Union finally agreed to resume the INF and START talks around the time of Chernenko's death and Gorbachev's selection as general secretary in March 1985. Progress was then made on the revamped INF talks. In 1987 the Soviet Union acceded to the zero option, which involved the elimination of NATO Pershing IIs and GLCMs targeted against the Soviet Union and Eastern Europe and Soviet missiles targeted against Western Europe and

417

Asia. The Intermediate-Range Nuclear Forces Treaty (INF Treaty) was finally signed in Washington on December 8, 1987, during a summit meeting between Reagan and Gorbachev.

Between November 1982 and March 1985, the Soviet Union had four general secretaries (Brezhnev, Andropov, Chernenko, and Gorbachev) while the United States had a single chief executive. The changes of leadership in the Soviet Union had a noticeable effect on Soviet-American relations. Until Gorbachev assumed power and partially consolidated his rule by 1986, the frequent changes in Soviet leadership resulted in the continuation of policies formulated during the late Brezhnev period. Soviet foreign policy toward the United States during this period increasingly took the form of vituperative propaganda attacks on Reagan, who, it was alleged, was personally responsible for derailing Soviet-American détente and increasing the danger of nuclear war. The low point in Soviet-American relations occurred in March 1983, when Reagan described the Soviet Union as an "evil empire . . . the focus of evil in the modern world," and Soviet spokesmen responded by attacking Reagan's "bellicose, lunatic anticommunism." The Soviet shoot-down of a civilian South Korean airliner in September 1983 near the Soviet island of Sakhalin shocked world public opinion and militated against any improvement in Soviet-American relations at that time. In 1983 the United States was increasingly concerned about Soviet activities in Grenada, finally directing the military operation in October 1983 that was denounced by the Soviet Union. In November 1983, the Soviet negotiators walked out of the arms control talks.

In August 1985, Gorbachev declared a unilateral moratorium on nuclear testing. The United States, in the midst of a nuclear warhead modernization program, refused to go along with the moratorium. Some Western analysts viewed Gorbachev's unilateral moratorium as a Soviet attempt to delay weapons modernization in the United States and, in the event that the United States refused to abide by the moratorium even unofficially, an attempt to depict the United States and the Reagan administration as militaristic. The Soviet Union ended the moratorium with an underground nuclear test in February 1987.

A general improvement in Soviet-American relations began soon after Gorbachev was selected general secretary in March 1985. Annual summit meetings between Reagan and Gorbachev were held at Geneva (November 1985); Reykjavik (October 1986); Washington (December 1987); and Moscow (May 1988). At the Geneva Summit between Reagan and Gorbachev in November 1985, a new general cultural agreement was signed that involved exchanges of performing arts groups and fine arts and educational exhibits. At the Reykjavik Summit, some progress was made in strategic arms reductions negotiations, although no agreements were reached. At the Washington Summit, the INF Treaty was signed. At the Moscow Summit, an agreement increasing the level and type of educational exchanges was signed. Although no major arms control agreements were signed during the Moscow summit, the summit was significant because it demonstrated a commitment by both sides to a renewed détente.

During the mid- to late 1980s, the Soviet Union also stepped up media contacts. Soviet spokesmen appeared regularly on United States television, United States journalists were allowed unprecedented access to report on everyday life in the Soviet Union, and video conferences (termed "tele-bridges") were held between various United States groups and selected Soviet citizens.

Soviet-West European Relations

Soviet relations with Western Europe since World War II have been heavily colored by Soviet relations with Eastern Europe and by the presence of Warsaw Pact forces arrayed against NATO forces. The Soviet influence over Eastern Europe, reinforced in West European eyes by Soviet invasions of Hungary in 1956 and Czechoslovakia in 1968 and by the buildup of Soviet conventional and nuclear forces, fostered efforts in the 1980s among the West European states of NATO to bolster their defenses and discouraged closer relations between West European countries and the Soviet Union.

Since the end of World War II and the establishment of Soviet hegemony over Eastern Europe, the Soviet Union has had five goals in regard to Western Europe: preventing the rearming and nuclearization of the Federal Republic of Germany (West Germany); preventing the political, economic, and military integration of Western Europe; obtaining West European endorsement of the territorial status quo in Europe; encouraging anti-Americanism and troubled relations with the United States; and fostering neutralism, nuclear disarmament, and the creation of nuclear weapons-free zones through the encouragement of peace groups and leftist movements. The Soviet Union has succeeded in achieving some of these goals but has been unsuccessful in achieving others.

In general, Soviet leaders have stated that the proper relationship between Western Europe and the Soviet Union should be similar to the relationship between Finland and the Soviet Union. As stated by then-Politburo member Andropov in 1978, "Soviet-Finnish relations today constitute a sound and stable system of enjoyment of equal rights of cooperation in the diverse areas of political, economic, and political life. This constitutes détente, as embodied in daily contacts, détente which makes peace stronger and the life of people better and calmer.'' More broadly, neutralism is extolled by the Soviet Union as a transitional historical model for Western and Third World states to follow in their relations with the Soviet Union, typified by nonparticipation in Western military alliances and economic organizations and by political support for anti-imperialism, capitalist disarmament, national liberation, and other foreign policies favored by the Soviet Union.

During the early to mid-1980s, Soviet leaders attempted to foster a ''European détente'' separate from détente with the United States. This attempt failed, however, because of the determination of West European governments to modernize NATO and deploy countervailing nuclear systems and the failure of Soviet-cultivated peace and other groups to influence West European policy.

France

Beginning in the mid-1960s, the Soviet Union cultivated a ''privileged'' relationship with France. The high point of Soviet-French relations occurred during the administration of President Charles de Gaulle (1959–69). Following the Soviet invasion of Czechoslovakia in August 1968, Soviet-French relations cooled, although state visits continued. During the leadership of President François Mitterrand, first elected as part of a coalition government in May 1981, France pursued several policies objectionable to the Soviet Union, such as selling arms to China, militarily opposing Libya's invasion of Chad, working with West Germany to strengthen West European defense, and expelling a large number of Soviet diplomats and other personnel involved in technology theft and other forms of espionage. Gorbachev's first state visit as general secretary was to France in October 1985. The visit provided a public display of the Soviet Union's interest in maintaining a special relationship with France and also served as an attempt to exacerbate intra-European rivalries. Nevertheless, the general trend of French foreign policy in the late 1980s toward greater cooperation with NATO frustrated Soviet efforts to maintain a privileged relationship. France's refusal in 1986 and 1987 to discuss a freeze or a reduction of the French nuclear forces (*force de frappe,* or *force de dissuasion*) further strained Soviet-French relations.

West Germany

A recurrent theme in Soviet propaganda concerning West Germany has been the supposed resurgence of revanchism and militarism, indicating to some degree real Soviet fears of a rearmed and nuclearized West Germany. The Soviet Union strongly opposed the creation of multilateral nuclear forces in Europe in the 1960s and demanded that West Germany sign the Treaty on the Nonproliferation of Nuclear Weapons, which the Soviet Union had signed in July 1968. After Willy Brandt of the Social Democratic Party was elected chancellor in October 1969, he implemented a détente, termed *Ostpolitik* (literally, Eastern policy), with the Soviet Union. West Germany signed the nonproliferation treaty in November 1969. In August 1970, the Soviet Union and West Germany signed a treaty calling for the peaceful settlement of disputes, with West Germany agreeing to respect the territorial integrity of the states of Europe and the validity of the Oder-Neisse line dividing East Germany from Poland. The provisions of this bilateral treaty became multilateral with the signing of the Final Act of the Conference on Security and Cooperation in Europe (Helsinki Accords) in 1975, in which the Western signatories, including the United States, recognized the de facto hegemony of the Soviet Union over Eastern Europe and the existing territorial boundaries of the European states. The Helsinki Accords also bound the signatories to respect basic principles of human rights. In the early 1980s, the Soviet Union began a harsh propaganda campaign accusing West Germany of revanchism and militarism because of West German initiation and support of NATO efforts to counter the Soviet deployment of SS-20s targeted on Western Europe. Gorbachev remained cool toward West Germany because of its role in fostering a NATO response to SS-20 deployments and delayed scheduling his first visit until June 1989. This visit was very successful in emphasizing Gorbachev's message of the "common European home" and the peaceful intentions of the Soviet Union regarding Western Europe.

Britain

In the years immediately following the Bolshevik Revolution, the Soviet leadership assiduously pursued diplomatic relations with Britain, the archetypical "imperialist" power, as part of its efforts to win recognition as a legitimate regime. After World War II, the Soviet Union perceived Britain as an "imperialist power in decline," especially after Britain relinquished most of its colonies. Nevertheless, Britain remained an important power in Soviet eyes because of its nuclear forces, influential role as head of the British Commonwealth, and close ties with the United States.

In general, Soviet relations with Britain have never been as important a component of Soviet foreign policy toward Western Europe as have been relations with France (especially during the de Gaulle period) or with West Germany (especially during the Brandt period). Several reasons for Britain's lesser importance existed. Unlike West Germany, Britain is not subject to Soviet political pressures exerted through the instrument of a divided people. Much smaller than its French counterpart, the British Communist Party exerted less influence in electoral politics. The British economy has also been less dependent than that of other West European states on Soviet and East European trade and energy resources.

In December 1984, shortly before Gorbachev became general secretary, he made his first visit to London. Prime Minister Margaret Thatcher declared that he was a leader she could "do business with," an assessment that boosted Gorbachev's stature in the Soviet Union and abroad. This assessment was repeated upon Thatcher's visit to the Soviet Union in April 1987. Under Gorbachev's leadership, the Soviet Union renewed its attempts to persuade Britain and France to enter into strategic nuclear disarmament negotiations, which as of 1989 they had resisted.

Spain and Portugal

Soviet contacts with Spain and Portugal were almost nonexistent in the post-World War II period until the 1970s, when changes in leadership of both countries paved the way for the establishment of diplomatic relations. Portugal established diplomatic relations with the Soviet Union in June 1974, and Spain reestablished diplomatic ties in February 1977, broken in 1939 after the Nationalists defeated the Soviet-backed Republicans in the Spanish Civil War. Both countries have relatively large, long-established pro-Soviet communist parties, with the Portuguese Communist Party during the 1980s enjoying more electoral support and seats in the legislature. In March 1982, Spain joined NATO (Portugal was a founding member), a move opposed by the Soviet Union and the Communist Party of Spain. Soviet relations with Spain during the 1980s were businesslike, with King Juan Carlos visiting Moscow in May 1984 and Prime Minister Felipe González visiting in May 1986. Relations with Portugal in the early 1980s were relatively poor, with Portugal criticizing the invasion of Afghanistan and other Soviet policies. Relations improved during the late 1980s, when President Mário Soares visited Moscow in November 1987 and signed trade and other cooperation agreements; Shevardnadze paid a return visit to Lisbon in March 1988.

Scandinavia

The central factor in Scandinavian relations with the Soviet Union is the proximity of Norway, Sweden, and Finland to major

Soviet bases on the Kola Peninsula (see fig. 6). Besides Turkey, Norway is the only NATO country bordering the Soviet Union.

The interrelated Soviet objectives in Scandinavia have been to maintain freedom of navigation through the Baltic Sea into the North Sea, sustain the neutrality of Finland and Sweden, and encourage Norway, Denmark, and Iceland to withdraw from NATO. The Scandinavian states act to minimize the Soviet security threat through a mix of military preparedness and nonprovocative, accommodationist policies. Norway, Denmark, and Sweden do not allow the stationing of foreign troops, the establishment of foreign military bases, or the installation of nuclear weapons on their territory. Sweden's neutrality has been based on the concept of total national defense, which stresses involvement of the civilian population, as well as military forces, in defending territorial integrity. Since the 1970s, Sweden has been concerned about repeated Soviet submarine incursions into its territorial waters. Finland's "positive neutrality" is based on a special relationship with the Soviet Union codified in their 1948 Treaty of Mutual Assistance and Cooperation.

Soviet-East European Relations

Continued Soviet influence over the East European countries belonging to the Warsaw Pact and Council for Mutual Economic Assistance (Comecon)—Bulgaria, Czechoslovakia, East Germany, Hungary, Poland, and Romania—remained a fundamental regional priority of Soviet foreign policy in mid-1989 (see Appendix B; Appendix C). The CPSU party program ratified at the Twenty-Seventh Party Congress in 1986 designated these East European states as members of the "socialist commonwealth" (along with Cuba, Mongolia, and Vietnam) and depicted the establishment of socialism in Eastern Europe as a validation of "the general laws of socialism [communism]." By staking the validity of Marxist-Leninist ideology on the continuation of communism in Eastern Europe, the Soviet leadership in effect perceived attempts to repudiate communism as threats to the ideological validity of the Soviet system itself. The Soviet leadership expressed this sentiment in terms of the "irreversibility of the gains for socialism" in Eastern Europe. In the late 1980s, however, liberalization occurred, and the situation was tolerated by the Soviet leadership.

After the August 1968 Warsaw Pact invasion of Czechoslovakia, which ended a process of liberalization begun by the Communist Party of Czechoslovakia, the Soviet Union made clear the irreversibility of communism in Eastern Europe through statements that have come to be known in the West as the "Brezhnev Doctrine" and are termed by the Soviet Union as "socialist internationalism." In a speech delivered in Poland in November 1968, Brezhnev stated, "When external and internal forces hostile to socialism try to turn the development of a given socialist country in the direction of the restoration of the capitalist system . . . this is no longer merely a problem for that country's people, but a common problem, the concern of all socialist countries." The Brezhnev Doctrine was repeated in the 1986 party program's call for "mutual assistance in resolving the tasks of the building and defense of the new society," indicating no real change in this doctrine during the mid- to late 1980s. During his visit to Yugoslavia in March 1988, Gorbachev made statements that some Western observers termed the "repudiation of the Brezhnev Doctrine," signaling Soviet willingness to tolerate some political liberalization in Eastern Europe.

Soviet influence over Eastern Europe began with the Soviet occupation of territories during World War II. By 1948 communist regimes had come to power in all the East European states. In Yugoslavia, however, Josip Broz Tito, a nationalist communist who had played a major role in the resistance to the occupying German forces, opposed Joseph V. Stalin's attempts to assert control over Yugoslav domestic politics. Tito's actions resulted in Yugoslavia's expulsion from the Cominform in 1948 and the declaration of a trade embargo. In 1954, after Stalin's death, the Cominform ended its embargo. In May 1955, Nikita S. Khrushchev visited Belgrade and proclaimed the doctrine of "many roads to socialism," acknowledging Yugoslavia's right to a relatively independent domestic and foreign policy.

Leadership changes in the Soviet Union have often been followed by upheaval in Eastern Europe. Stalin's death created popular expectations of a relative relaxation of coercive controls. The slow pace of change contributed to domestic violence in three East European states—East Germany, Hungary, and Poland—within four years of Stalin's death in March 1953. In June 1953, the Soviet army peremptorily suppressed a wave of strikes and riots in East Germany over increased production quotas and police repression. In June 1956, four months after the Twentieth Party Congress at which Khrushchev delivered his "secret speech" denouncing Stalinist terror, anti-Soviet riots broke out in Poznań, Poland. In Hungary, anti-Soviet riots broke out in October 1956 and escalated immediately to full-scale revolt, with the Hungarians calling for full independence, the disbanding of the communist party, and withdrawal from the Warsaw Pact. The Soviet Union invaded Hungary on November 4, 1956, and Hungarian prime minister Imre Nagy was arrested and later executed. The events of the 1950s taught the Soviet Union at least three lessons: that the policy of teaching the younger generation in Eastern Europe to support Soviet-imposed communism had failed; that Soviet military power and occupation forces were the main guarantees of the continued existence of East European communism; and that some limited local control over domestic political and economic policy had to be granted, including some freedom in the selection of leading party officials.

Czechoslovakia's 1968 liberalization, or "Prague Spring" (which occurred during a period of collective leadership in the Soviet Union while Brezhnev was still consolidating power), led to a Warsaw Pact invasion in August 1968, illustrating that even gradual reforms were intolerable at that time to the Soviet Union. This lesson was illustrated again, but in a different form, during the events in Poland of 1980–81. The reforms sought by Polish workers—independent trade unions with the right to strike—were unacceptable to the Soviet Union, but for a variety of reasons the Soviet Union encouraged an "internal invasion" (use of Polish police and armed forces to quell disturbances) rather than occupation of the country by Soviet military forces. The new Polish prime minister and first secretary of the Polish United Workers' Party, Army General Wojciech Jaruzelski, declared martial law on December 13, 1981, and banned the independent trade union movement Solidarity.

Gorbachev's political report to the Twenty-Seventh Party Congress in February-March 1986 emphasized the "many roads to socialism" in Eastern Europe and called for cooperation, rather than uniformity, in Soviet-East European relations. The new party program ratified at the congress, however, reemphasized the need for tight Soviet control over Eastern Europe. Additionally, the five-year plan ratified at the congress called for integrated *perestroika* (see Glossary) among the Comecon countries, with each East European country specializing in the development and production of various high-technology goods under arrangements largely controlled by the Soviet Union.

Gorbachev's emphasis on *perestroika* and *glasnost'* (see Glossary) domestically and within Eastern Europe was supported to varying degrees by the East European leaders in the mid- to late 1980s. The leaders of Poland, Hungary, and Bulgaria apparently supported Gorbachev's reforms, while the leaders of East Germany, Czechoslovakia, and Romania resisted far-reaching reforms. Although there were varying degrees of compliance in Eastern Europe with Gorbachev's reform agenda, in the mid- to late 1980s the basic Soviet policy of maintaining a high level of influence in Eastern Europe had not been altered, although the nature of Soviet influence apparently had shifted away from coercion toward political and economic instruments of influence.

Sino-Soviet Relations

Soviet relations with China have, on the whole, been cool since the 1950s. In 1959 and 1960, the Soviet withdrawal of all economic advisers, Khrushchev's renunciation of the agreement to provide a sample nuclear weapon to China, and increasing mutual accusations of ideological deviation were all evidence of the political rift between the two countries. After Khrushchev's ouster in 1964, Brezhnev attempted to establish better relations with China, but his efforts foundered in the late 1960s. Riots by Chinese Red Guards in January-February 1967 led to the evacuation of nonessential Soviet diplomatic personnel from Beijing. In 1968 and 1969, serious Sino-Soviet border clashes occurred along the Amur and Ussuri rivers. Beginning in the late 1960s, Brezhnev proposed an "Asian collective security system," which he envisioned as a means of containing China. This proposal, repeated by successive Soviet leaders, has been rejected by most Asian countries.

During the 1970s, China began its policy of improving relations with the West to counter Soviet political and military pressure in Asia. After Mao Zedong's death in September 1976, the Soviet Union sought to improve relations with China, but by early 1977 the polemics had renewed, and by mid-1978 increasing military tensions between Cambodia (China's ally) and Vietnam (the Soviet Union's ally) contributed to a return to poor relations. At the Eleventh National Party Congress of the Chinese Communist Party (CCP), held in August 1977, CCP chairman Hua Guofeng declared that the Soviet Union represented a greater threat than the United States to world peace and Chinese national security. In keeping with this assessment, the Sino-Japanese Treaty of Peace and Friendship, signed in August 1978, contained an "anti-hegemony clause" in which the signatories renounced the pursuit of hegemony and opposed the efforts of other states—implying the Soviet Union—to gain hegemony in the Asia-Pacific region. The Sino-American joint communiqué of December 1978 contained an analogous clause.

In February 1979, China launched a limited military incursion into Vietnam in retaliation for the Vietnamese invasion of Cambodia, a Chinese ally. The Soviet Union harshly condemned this Chinese incursion and stepped up arms shipments to Vietnam.

In April 1979, China declared that it would not renew the 1950 Sino-Soviet Treaty of Friendship, Alliance, and Mutual Assistance, but it offered to begin negotiations with the Soviet Union to improve relations. These negotiations began in late September 1979 (separate border negotiations had been ongoing since 1969), with China demanding a cutback in Soviet troop strength along the border, withdrawal of Soviet troops from Mongolia, an end to Soviet aid to Vietnam, and a Vietnamese military withdrawal from Cambodia. These negotiations were cut off by the Chinese in January 1980 after the Soviet invasion of Afghanistan the previous month. The Chinese thereafter added the demand that an improvement in Sino-Soviet relations required Soviet withdrawal of troops from Afghanistan.

At the Twenty-Sixth Party Congress in February 1981, Brezhnev reported that "unfortunately, there are no grounds yet to speak of any changes for the better in Beijing's foreign policy." Relations began to improve, however, after Brezhnev delivered a conciliatory speech at Tashkent in March 1982, and in October the Sino-Soviet border "consultations"—broken off after the invasion of Afghanistan—were reopened.

After Gorbachev became general secretary in March 1985, relations with China did not improve markedly at first. Nevertheless, high-level visits and discussions were encouraging enough that Gorbachev, at the Twenty-Seventh Party Congress in February–March 1986, was able to "speak with satisfaction about a certain amount of improvement" in relations with China. In his Vladivostok speech in July 1986, Gorbachev promised to remove some of the obstacles to better Sino-Soviet relations, announcing that six Soviet regiments would be withdrawn from Afghanistan, that some troops would be withdrawn from Mongolia, that Soviet negotiators would discuss a reduction in Soviet forces along the Sino-Soviet border, and that the Soviet Union would commit itself to certain methodologies in delineating the Sino-Soviet borders. Another Soviet gesture was the removal of SS–20 missiles from the border with China as a result of the Soviet-American INF Treaty of December 1987. In April 1988, the Soviet Union signed accords calling for the total withdrawal of Soviet military forces from Afghanistan, which were a serious obstacle to better Sino-Soviet relations. During 1988 Vietnam committed itself to removing troops from Cambodia, overcoming another obstacle to improved relations and a summit. In 1987 and repeatedly in 1988, Gorbachev proposed a Sino-Soviet summit meeting, which was finally scheduled for June 1989. It was the first since the Khrushchev period.

Soviet-Japanese Relations

The poor relations between the Soviet Union and Japan can probably be said to have originated in Japan's victory over imperial

Russia in the Russo-Japanese War of 1904–05. During the Russian Civil War (1918–21), Japan (as a member of the Allied interventionist forces) occupied Vladivostok and did not leave until 1922. In the waning days of World War II, Stalin abrogated the 1941 neutrality pact between Japan and the Soviet Union, declaring war on Japan days before Japan surrendered in August 1945 in order to occupy vast areas of East Asia formerly held by the Japanese. Fifty-six islands of the Kuril chain, as well as the southern half of Sakhalin, were subsequently incorporated into the Soviet Union. The extreme southernmost islands of the Kuril chain constitute what the Japanese still term the Northern Territories—the small islands of Shikotan-tō, Kunashir, and Etorofu and the Habomai Islands. Stalin's absorption of the Northern Territories prevented the conclusion of a Soviet-Japanese World War II peace treaty and the establishment of closer relations between the two states. The Soviet Union continued to refuse to return the Northern Territories because such a return would encourage the Chinese to push their own territorial claims. Also, the Soviet Union has used the islands as part of an antisubmarine warfare network guarding the mouth of the Sea of Okhotsk.

Under Gorbachev, Soviet-Japanese relations thawed somewhat. Foreign Minister Shevardnadze visited Tokyo in January 1986 and December 1988, and a new Soviet ambassador, fluent in Japanese, was posted to Tokyo in mid-1986. As of 1989, however, political and economic relations had not shown signs of great improvement. Soviet trade with Japan remained far below its potential, given the Japanese need for energy and raw materials available from the Soviet Union and Gorbachev's desires to import technology to modernize the Soviet economy.

The Soviet Union and the Third World

Until Stalin's death in 1953, Soviet activity in the Third World was limited. Khrushchev recognized that the number of independent Third World states was increasing because of post-World War II decolonialization, and he pictured these states as moving onto the noncapitalist path of development and progressing quickly toward the achievement of Soviet-style socialism. Khrushchev divided the Third World states into three categories. The first category, capitalist-oriented states, mainly consisted of newly independent states that had not yet chosen the noncapitalist path. In the second category were the so-called national democracies, anti-Western states that were implementing some economic centralization and nationalization programs and hence had embarked on the path of noncapitalist development. In the third category were "revolutionary democracies,'' which professed Marxism-Leninism as their ideology and had set up ruling communist-style parties (termed "Marxist-Leninist vanguard parties" by the Soviet Union). Since the late 1960s, the term "socialist orientation" has been increasingly used in the Soviet Union to describe Third World states on the non-capitalist path of development, although the states with ruling vanguard parties still have been termed revolutionary democracies.

Since the late 1970s, Soviet analysts have tended to regard the nature and future of the Third World either conservatively or pragmatically. On the one hand, conservative Soviet analysts have seen the Third World as making a choice between two paths—capitalism and socialism—and have maintained that only the latter path leads to political, social, and economic development. Pragmatic analysts, on the other hand, have seen the maintenance of some elements of capitalism as essential for the economic and political development of Third World countries. Among the pragmatic analysts, though, there have been different views about the pace of the transition to socialism in the Third World, with the more pessimistic theorists even suggesting the indefinite existence of mixed economies in Third World states.

The conservative theorists have tended to advocate the establishment of Marxist-Leninist vanguard parties in Third World states, whereas the pragmatists have advocated a united front strategy in which the local communist and leftist parties ally with other "progressive" parties and groups and work to achieve change peacefully through elections and propaganda. Internal Soviet debates aside, the Soviet Union began to favor a dual policy toward the Third World in the 1970s, stressing the establishment of vanguard parties in some states and the united front policy in others. Rhetorically, and to some degree in action, though, Soviet leaders have placed greater emphasis on the united front policy in the late 1980s.

In the CPSU party program and in the political report delivered by Gorbachev in February 1986, there was a discernible de-emphasis on Soviet concern with socialist-oriented Third World states. The party program emphasized that "the practice of the Soviet Union's relations with the liberated countries has shown that there are also real grounds for cooperation with the young states that are traveling the capitalist road." According to some Western analysts, Gorbachev indicated the nature of this reorientation during his visit to India in November 1986. At that time, Gorbachev referred to Soviet relations with India as the model of the "new thinking" toward Third World states having a "capitalist orientation."

429

Reasons for this possible Soviet reorientation may have included desires to use technologies available in some of the "newly industrialized countries" for Soviet economic development, desires to foster positive trade flows and earn hard currency or access to desirable commodities, and attempts to encourage anti-Western foreign policies and closer alignment with the Soviet Union. As of the late 1980s, this possible reorientation did not include political-military abandonment of Asian communist states (Laos and Vietnam) or of "revolutionary democratic" or "progressive" regimes (such as Angola, Libya, Mozambique, or Nicaragua). The reorientation, rather, may have represented an attempt to widen the scope of Soviet interests in the Third World. As of 1989, the only case of possible Soviet "abandonment" of a so-called revolutionary democracy would be the withdrawal of military forces from Afghanistan, although the Soviet leaders hoped that they would be able to maintain some presence and influence in Kabul and in areas bordering the Soviet Union and in other enclaves.

Middle East and North Africa

Among the Third World regions, the Middle East was a central concern of Soviet foreign policy. The region borders the Soviet Union and therefore has a direct impact on national security. Also, various ethnic, religious, and language groups existing in the region are found also in Soviet border areas and thus constitute a possible threat to Soviet control. The Middle East is also of strategic concern because the Mediterranean Sea and Persian Gulf serve as waterways joining together Europe, Asia, and North Africa, and the region contains oil resources vital to Western industrial production.

In the post-World War II period, the main Soviet goal in the region has been to reduce British and, more recently, United States influence. Termination of the British colonial and protective role in the Middle East by the early 1970s created a military power vacuum in the region, which Iran sought unsuccessfully to fill with United States backing. In the late 1980s, however, the growing Soviet military presence in the region was underscored by the belated United States commitment to protect shipping in the Persian Gulf from Iranian attack, after the Soviet Union had already begun its own efforts to protect such shipping at the behest of the Kuwaitis.

Turkey

Soviet relations with Turkey were poor during the Stalin period because of Soviet territorial claims against Turkey. These claims helped induce Turkey to join NATO in 1952. Relations improved during the 1950s and 1960s to the point where Khrushchev began giving economic assistance to Turkey in the early 1960s. During the 1980s, this economic assistance represented the largest program of Soviet aid to any noncommunist Third World state. Turkish relations with the Soviet Union further improved after the United States imposed an arms embargo on Turkey to protest the 1974 invasion and occupation of northern Cyprus. During the 1980s, Turkey continued a delicate balancing act between security cooperation within NATO and good relations with the Soviet Union.

Iran and Iraq

During the 1970s, the Soviet Union attempted to consolidate a closer relationship with Iraq while also maintaining normal relations with Iran. Soviet arms transfers to Iraq started in 1959 when, after Colonel Abd al Karim Qasim overthrew the pro-Western monarchy, Iraq withdrew from the Baghdad Pact. These arms transfers continued during the 1960s and increased after the signing of the Soviet-Iraqi Treaty of Friendship and Cooperation in 1972. The Soviet Union increased arms shipments to support Iraq's counterinsurgency efforts against the Kurds (whom the Soviet Union had earlier supported). Iraqi relations with the Soviet Union became strained in the late 1970s after discovery of an Iraqi communist party plot to overthrow the leadership and because the Soviet Union was backing Ethiopian attempts to suppress the Iraqi-supported Eritrean insurgency. Nevertheless, the Iraqi policy of acquiring Soviet arms and military equipment in exchange for oil was continued by Saddam Husayn, who succeeded to the presidency of Iraq in 1979. When the Soviet Union invaded Afghanistan in December 1979, however, Saddam's government condemned the invasion, and Iraqi-Soviet relations deteriorated further. When Iraq invaded Iran in September 1980, the Soviet Union halted arms shipments to Iraq, which drove Iraq to make desperate purchases in the private arms market. Relations thus became particularly strained between the Soviet Union and Iraq. Although normal relations between the two countries were resumed after 1982 when the arms shipments were renewed, Soviet efforts to draw Iraq into its political sphere of influence were not successful during the 1980s, and Iraq remained nonaligned.

The shah of Iran, Mohammed Reza Pahlavi, responding to Iraq's military buildup and the irredentist ambitions of Iraq against Kuwait and Iran, himself concluded arms agreements with the Soviet Union in the mid- to late 1960s, while maintaining Iran's membership in the Western-oriented Central Treaty Organization (CENTO), which was formerly known as the Baghdad Pact. The

431

Soviet Union maintained cordial relations with the shah until the end of 1978, when the deteriorating security situation in Iran signaled the imminent collapse of the dynasty. The Soviet Union initially supported Ayatollah Sayyid Ruhollah Musavi Khomeini after his return to Iran in February 1979 (he had been exiled in 1963). During the initial phases of the Iran-Iraq War, the Soviet Union made overtures to Iran, but efforts to improve relations with Khomeini failed.

The hope of the Soviet Union had been to act as the broker of the Iran-Iraq conflict, much as it acted in the 1965 Indian-Pakistani conflict and as it attempted to do during the Somali-Ethiopian conflict of 1977–78. Although the cease-fire agreed to between the two belligerents in 1988 owed little to Soviet offices, the related Soviet goal of achieving close relations with both Iran and Iraq remained a component of Soviet foreign policy. The cease-fire benefited the Soviet Union in that it relieved the Soviet Union from protecting Iraq from military defeat, a defeat that would have demonstrated to the Arab world and to the Third World generally that Soviet leaders were insufficiently committed to states that had signed treaties of friendship and cooperation with the Soviet Union.

Other Middle Eastern States

Soviet relations with several Arab states improved during the mid- to late 1980s. In late 1985, Oman and the United Arab Emirates established diplomatic relations with the Soviet Union. Relations also improved with Bahrain, Kuwait, the Yemen Arab Republic (North Yemen), Jordan, Saudi Arabia, and Egypt. This Soviet policy of improving ties with Western-oriented Arab states, as well as with the radical regimes of Syria and South Yemen, indicated a shift in Soviet policy away from the forging of a radical bloc of states toward a more flexible diplomatic approach to Middle Eastern problems. A major objective of this more flexible Soviet policy was to achieve the convening of an Arab-Israeli conference in which the Soviet Union would act as the primary peace broker. The Soviet Union began pursuing this objective in the 1970s as part of its general effort to erode United States influence in the region.

Gorbachev pursued closer ties with several moderate Middle Eastern states—Kuwait, Egypt, Jordan, and Israel—while maintaining ties with radical regimes such as those in Syria, Libya, and South Yemen. In May 1987, Kuwait sought Soviet protection of its shipping in the Persian Gulf, and the Soviet Union agreed to let Kuwait charter Soviet-flagged tankers to transport oil. The Soviet Union also increased the size of its naval task force in the Persian Gulf. For the first time since the expulsion of Soviet military advisers in 1972 and the abrogation of the 1971 Soviet-Egyptian Treaty of Friendship and Cooperation in 1976, a Soviet ambassador was posted to Cairo in 1985. Also, the Soviet Union agreed to reschedule Egypt's military debts on favorable terms. The Soviet Union agreed to provide Jordan with new weaponry, and Jordan's King Hussein announced his support for the convening of an international conference on the Middle East in which the Soviet Union would participate. This improvement in relations occurred despite Jordan's arrest of local communist party leaders in the spring of 1986. Lastly, the Soviet Union made several overtures to Israel in 1985–89 regarding reestablishment of diplomatic relations— severed in June 1967 as a result of the June 1967 War—in an attempt to gain Israeli support for an international conference on the Middle East. The Soviet Union had de-emphasized its previous condition that Israel withdraw from territories occupied during the Arab-Israeli June 1967 War before the reestablishment of relations, but the Israelis insisted on restoration of relations before the convening of the international conference. In 1987–88 the Soviet Union and Israel exchanged consular missions, but as of 1989 full diplomatic relations had not been restored.

Asia

The Soviet Union had at least four regional objectives in Asia: defense of the Soviet Union's eastern borders, including border areas claimed by Japan, China, and Mongolia; maintenance of Soviet alliances, as embodied in treaties of friendship and cooperation with India, Mongolia, North Korea, Vietnam, and Afghanistan; establishment of better relations with the Western-oriented, more economically advanced states in order to obtain technology and assistance in the economic development of Siberia; and, related to the other objectives, establishment of a pro-Soviet orientation among the states of the region that would have the effect of isolating China, South Korea, and the United States. The main instrument used in pursuit of these objectives has been the large Soviet military presence in Asia. Stressing that the Soviet Union is an Asian power, Gorbachev has attempted to establish or consolidate better relations with several states in the region, mainly China, Japan, and India. In 1988 Gorbachev had also attempted to remove Afghanistan as an issue blocking the establishment or consolidation of better relations with Asian states by negotiating a timetable for the withdrawal of Soviet combat forces.

Afghanistan

Soviet involvement with Afghanistan goes back to the 1920s. In

1921, as a means to reduce British influence in the region and to get arms, Afghanistan signed a treaty of friendship with the Soviet Union. The treaty also called for Amanullah, the Afghan amir (ruler), to close his northern border. The border had been serving as a refuge for the Basmachi, Muslim insurgents opposed to the imposition of Soviet power in the khanate of Bukhara (now part of the Tadzhik, Uzbek, and Turkmen republics). In 1921 and 1931, the Soviet Union and Afghanistan signed treaties on neutrality and mutual nonaggression. Afghanistan, however, generally adhered in foreign policy to the principle of *bi-tarafi*, or a balanced relationship with great powers. In 1955 Prime Minister Mohammad Daoud Khan abandoned this policy when he signed a military agreement with Czechoslovakia. In December of that year, during a visit to Afghanistan, Khrushchev signed an economic agreement and reaffirmed the 1931 Afghan-Soviet neutrality treaty. A major reason for the shift in Afghan policy was Daoud's interest in gaining support for his goal of absorbing Pakistan's North-West Frontier Province into Afghanistan.

In April 1978, Daoud was overthrown and executed by the radical People's Democratic Party of Afghanistan (PDPA), led by Hafizullah Amin and Nur Muhammad Taraki. Later that year Taraki, then president, went to Moscow and signed a twenty-year treaty of friendship and cooperation with the Soviet Union that encompassed and revamped commitments contained in the 1921, 1926 (a trade agreement), and 1931 Soviet-Afghan treaties. In September 1979, Taraki was ousted by Amin, following an apparent attempt by Taraki himself to remove Amin. The Afghan populace became increasingly opposed to Amin's radical policies, and the security of the regime became endangered. Finding their position in Afghanistan imperiled, the Soviet leadership decided to invade the country in December 1979. Soviet troops or guards allegedly killed Amin and brought in Babrak Karmal (who had earlier fled to the Soviet Union during factional struggle within the PDPA) as the new secretary general of the PDPA. The invasion resulted in worldwide condemnation of the Soviet Union. The UN General Assembly, the Nonaligned Movement, the Organization of the Islamic Conference, NATO, and the Association of Southeast Asian Nations (ASEAN) all called for the withdrawal of "foreign" troops from Afghanistan. In June 1982, indirect talks began under UN auspices between the Afghan and Pakistani governments concerning resolution of the conflict. In May 1986, in an attempt to win Afghan support for the Soviet-installed regime, Karmal was replaced by Sayid Mohammad Najibullah as secretary general of the PDPA, and a campaign was intensified calling for "national reconciliation" between the Soviet-supported regime and the Islamic resistance, the *mujahidin* (literally, holy warriors) and their supporters.

Gorbachev repeatedly termed Afghanistan a "bleeding wound," although he did not admit that the Soviet occupation and the Soviet-supported regime were opposed by the vast majority of Afghans. According to a United States Department of State estimate made in 1987, almost 1 million Afghans had been killed and more than 5 million had fled the country since the 1979 Soviet invasion. Partly in support of the "national reconciliation" process, Gorbachev in his Vladivostok speech of July 1986 announced the withdrawal of a token number of Soviet forces from Afghanistan. Despite talk of reconciliation, a major, but eventually unsuccessful, Soviet-Afghan army offensive against the *mujahidin* was launched in Paktia Province in mid-1987. At the December 1987 Soviet-United States summit meeting in Washington, Gorbachev proposed that the Soviet Union remove the 115,000 Soviet troops in Afghanistan on the condition that the United States first cease aid to the *mujahidin*, a proposal in accord with the Soviet contention that "imperialist" interference was the main reason for the initiation and continuation of the Soviet occupation. In April 1988, Afghanistan and Pakistan signed accords, with the United States and the Soviet Union acting as "guarantors," calling for the withdrawal of Soviet military forces from Afghanistan over a nine-month period beginning on May 15, 1988. The withdrawal was completed in early 1989.

India

A cordial relationship with India that began in the 1950s represented the most successful of the Soviet attempts to foster closer relations with Third World countries. The relationship began with a visit by Indian prime minister Jawaharlal Nehru to the Soviet Union in June 1955 and Khrushchev's return trip to India in the fall of 1955. While in India, Khrushchev announced that the Soviet Union supported Indian sovereignty over the Kashmir region and over Portuguese coastal enclaves.

The Soviet relationship with India rankled the Chinese and contributed to Sino-Soviet enmity during the Khrushchev period. The Soviet Union declared its neutrality during the 1959 border dispute and the 1962 Sino-Indian war, although the Chinese strongly objected. The Soviet Union gave India substantial economic and military assistance during the Khrushchev period, and by 1960 India had received more Soviet assistance than China had. This disparity became another point of contention in Sino-Soviet relations. In 1962 the Soviet Union agreed to transfer technology to coproduce the MiG-21 jet fighter in India, which the Soviet Union had earlier denied to China.

In 1965 the Soviet Union served successfully as peace broker between India and Pakistan after an Indian-Pakistani border war. The Soviet chairman of the Council of Ministers, Aleksei N. Kosygin, met with representatives of India and Pakistan and helped them negotiate an end to the military conflict over Kashmir.

In 1971 East Pakistan initiated an effort to secede from its union with West Pakistan. India supported the secession and, as a guarantee against possible Chinese entrance into the conflict on the side of West Pakistan, signed a treaty of friendship and cooperation with the Soviet Union in August 1971. In December, India entered the conflict and ensured the victory of the secessionists and the establishment of the new state of Bangladesh.

Relations between the Soviet Union and India did not suffer much during the rightist Janata Party's coalition government in the late 1970s, although India did move to establish better economic and military relations with Western countries. To counter these efforts by India to diversify its relations, the Soviet Union proffered additional weaponry and economic assistance. During the 1980s, despite the 1984 assassination by Sikh extremists of Prime Minister Indira Gandhi, the mainstay of cordial Indian-Soviet relations, India maintained a close relationship with the Soviet Union. Indicating the high priority of relations with the Soviet Union in Indian foreign policy, the new Indian prime minister, Rajiv Gandhi, visited the Soviet Union on his first state visit abroad in May 1985 and signed two long-term economic agreements with the Soviet Union. In turn, Gorbachev's first visit to a Third World state was his meeting with Gandhi in New Delhi in late 1986. Gorbachev unsuccessfully urged Gandhi to help the Soviet Union set up an Asian collective security system. Gorbachev's advocacy of this proposal, which had also been made by Brezhnev, was an indication of continuing Soviet interest in using close relations with India as a means of containing China. With the improvement of Sino-Soviet relations in the late 1980s, containing China had less of a priority, but close relations with India remained important as an example of Gorbachev's new Third World policy.

Southeast Asia

Soviet goals in Southeast Asia included the containment of China, the introduction and maintenance of Soviet influence, and the reduction of United States influence in the region. As of 1989, the Soviet leaders had been only partially successful in attaining these somewhat contradictory goals and policies. The Soviet acquiescence, if not support, for the Vietnamese occupation of Cambodia in December 1978 resulted in the elimination of the pro-Chinese leadership of Cambodia. However, the Soviet posture regarding the occupation, along with the growing Soviet military presence in Vietnam, alarmed several ASEAN states and led to closer intra-ASEAN political, and even military, cooperation and to expanded ASEAN contacts with the United States and other Western countries. The Soviet Union also unsuccessfully urged the elimination of United States bases in the Philippines. However, the Soviet policy of improving ties with the Ferdinand Marcos regime in 1986 backfired when Marcos was forced from power.

A Soviet policy of stressing bilateral ties with individual ASEAN states, rather than multilateral relations, which would strengthen ASEAN as an organization, began to have some success in the late 1980s. After Gorbachev came to power, bilateral contacts with the ASEAN states increased as part of the Soviet leader's revised Third World policy, which emphasized relations with the newly industrialized countries, nonaligned states, and other capitalist-oriented states and improved contacts with Asian countries in general. In March 1987, Foreign Minister Shevardnadze visited Australia and Indonesia as part of this reorientation, and in late 1988 he visited the Philippines. In July 1987, Prime Minister Mahathir Bin Mohamad of Malaysia visited Moscow, and in May 1988 Prime Minister Prem Tinsulanonda of Thailand also visited.

The major Soviet success in Southeast Asia was the close political, economic, and military ties it established with Vietnam, which became a full member of Comecon in 1978. Although economic assistance to Vietnam was a heavy drain on the Soviet economy, Vietnam provided raw materials and thousands of laborers for work on Siberian development projects. Militarily, Cam Ranh Bay was the largest Soviet naval base outside the Soviet Union, allowing the Soviet Union to project increased power in the South China Sea. Politically, Vietnam aligned its foreign policy with that of the Soviet Union, and Vietnam was considered by the Soviet Union as a "fraternal party state" and as part of the "commonwealth of socialist states."

In mid-1988 Vietnam announced the withdrawal by the end of 1988 of 50,000 of the 100,000 Vietnamese troops occupying Cambodia, with all troops to be withdrawn by 1990. This withdrawal, publicly endorsed if not implemented at the urging of the Soviet Union, allowed the Soviet Union to attempt to improve relations with the ASEAN states and China.

Sub-Saharan Africa

Although the Comintern previously had made low-level contacts with local communist parties, sub-Saharan Africa was an area of limited concern to the Soviet Union until Khrushchev's reassessment of the Third World in the mid-1950s. Although Khrushchev initiated economic "show projects" in several African countries, Soviet efforts to foster socialism in Africa foundered in the Congo in the early 1960s, in Guinea in 1961, and in Kenya in 1965 partly because the Soviet Union was unable to project military power effectively into Africa.

During the first few years of the Brezhnev period, the amount of economic assistance to Africa declined from the levels of the Khrushchev period, although it increased greatly in the mid-1970s. During the Brezhnev period, the Soviet ability to project power grew, enabling it to take advantage of several opportunities in Africa during the 1970s.

Because of the deteriorating economic situation in the Soviet Union in the 1980s, economic assistance to Africa declined. Military assistance was maintained or increased in some instances in the face of insurgencies against so-called revolutionary democracies. Angola, Ethiopia, and Mozambique, all of which were fighting insurgencies, were major recipients of arms throughout the 1980s.

At the Twenty-Seventh Party Congress, Gorbachev called for a reorientation of relations with the Third World. He stressed the need to improve relations with the more developed, Western-oriented, Third World states while maintaining existing relations with other African states. In Africa the Soviet Union pursued closer relations with relatively more developed African states such as Nigeria and Zimbabwe. Gorbachev also reiterated Soviet support for the overthrow of the government of South Africa and support for the "frontline" states (states near or bordering South Africa) opposing South Africa: Angola, Botswana, Lesotho, Mozambique, Tanzania, Zambia, and Zimbabwe. As part of a Soviet attempt to coordinate Soviet policy toward southern Africa, a new office of the Ministry of Foreign Affairs was created to deal with the frontline states. In 1988-89 Soviet hostility toward the South African regime softened, and the two countries worked together diplomatically in resolving regional conflicts and issues such as negotiations over the independence of Namibia.

Angola

The Soviet Union engaged in a massive airlift of Cuban forces into Angola in 1975 to help the Popular Movement for the Liberation of Angola (Movimento Popular de Libertação de Angola—MPLA) defeat rival groups attempting to achieve power after the Portuguese colonial administration ended. The rival group, the National Union for the Total Independence of Angola (União Nacional para a Independência Total de Angola—UNITA), continued to oppose the MPLA and by the early 1980s controlled almost one-half of Angola's territory and increasingly threatened the central government. In both 1985 and 1987, massive Soviet-directed and Cuban-assisted MPLA offensives were launched against UNITA in attempts to achieve a military solution to the insurgency. Both these offensives failed. In December 1988, regional accords were signed setting a timetable for Namibian independence and the withdrawal of Cuban troops from Angola. The signatories were South Africa, Angola, and Cuba, with the United States acting as mediator and the Soviet Union as observer of the accords.

Ethiopia

In 1977 and 1978, the Soviet Union airlifted large numbers of Cuban troops into Ethiopia to help defeat an incursion by Somalia into the disputed Ogaden region. Somalia had signed a treaty of friendship and cooperation with the Soviet Union in 1974 and had received large amounts of Soviet arms. The Soviet leadership, however, ended this relationship in 1977 and switched support to Ethiopia because of Ethiopia's much greater population and economic resources and because of its location on the strait of Bab al Mandab, which links the Horn of Africa to inland Africa and the Red Sea to the Gulf of Aden. During the 1980s, the Soviet Union moved toward normalizing relations with Somalia but appeared to be waiting for a change in regime before attempting to greatly improve contacts.

Mozambique

In Mozambique the Soviet Union supplied arms to the Front for the Liberation of Mozambique (Frente da Libertação de Moçambique—Frelimo) during its 1975 effort to win power, and in 1977 the Soviet Union and Mozambique signed a treaty of friendship and cooperation. In 1977 a disaffected wing of Frelimo and other Mozambicans formed the Mozambique National Resistance Movement (Movimento Nacional da Resistência de Moçambique—Renamo), which began increasingly successful military operations against the Frelimo government. In the late 1980s, the Soviet Union stepped up military assistance to the Frelimo government in the face of the eroding security situation. The Frelimo government, because of inadequate Soviet military assistance, acted to diversify suppliers by obtaining weaponry and military advisory assistance from Britain and Portugal, among others.

Central America and South America

Latin America, like sub-Saharan Africa, had been a relatively low priority in Soviet foreign policy, although in absolute terms interactions between the Soviet Union and Latin America had increased tremendously since the early 1960s. Until the Khrushchev period, Latin America was generally regarded as in the United States sphere of influence. The Soviet Union had little interest in importing Latin American raw materials or commodities, and most Latin American governments, traditionally anticommunist, had long resisted the establishment of diplomatic relations with the Soviet Union.

A transformation of the Soviet attitude toward Latin America began in 1959 when Fidel Castro overthrew Cuba's long-time dictator, Fulgencio Batista. Castro gradually turned the island into a communist state and developed such close ties with the Soviet Union that Cuba was, by 1961, considered by the Soviet Union as its first "fraternal party state" in the Western Hemisphere.

Castro initially advocated armed revolutionary struggle in Latin America. However, after armed struggle failed to topple the government of Venezuela in 1965, the Soviet leadership stressed the "peaceful road to socialism." This path involved cooperation between communist and leftist movements in working for peaceful change and electoral victories. The "peaceful road" apparently bore fruit in 1970 with the election of Salvador Allende Gossens, the candidate of the leftist Popular Unity coalition, as president of Chile. Despite Allende's advocacy of close ties with the Soviet Union, the Soviet Union was slow in providing economic assistance essential to the survival of the regime, and in the midst of economic collapse Allende died in a bloody coup in 1973. His ouster resulted in a partial renewal of Soviet support for Castro's position that armed force is necessary for the transition to communism. Brezhnev himself conceded at the 1976 Twenty-Fifth Party Congress that a "revolution must know how to defend itself." The Soviet Union funneled weaponry and economic assistance through Cuba to various insurgent groups and leftist governments in Latin America. The Soviet Union used Cuba as a conduit for military, economic, and technical assistance to Grenada from 1979 to 1983. The United States government claimed that guerrillas operating in El Salvador received extensive assistance from Nicaragua, Cuba, Vietnam, and Libya and that Nicaragua and Cuba funneled Soviet and East European matériel to the Salvadoran guerrillas.

Direct Soviet activities in South America have mostly involved diplomacy, trade, culture, and propaganda activities. Peru was the only South American state to purchase sizable quantities of military weaponry from the Soviet Union, and for many years about 125 Soviet military advisers were stationed there. Peru's military relationship with the Soviet Union began in 1968, when General Juan Velasco Alvarado seized power. In February 1969, Peru established diplomatic relations with the Soviet Union, and one month after Allende's ouster in Chile in September 1973, the first Soviet weapons arrived in Peru. Major transfers occurred after 1976, when Peru received fighter-bombers, helicopters, jet fighters, surface-to-air missiles, and other relatively sophisticated weaponry. The Soviet Union had also been one of Peru's major trade partners, with some Peruvian exports being used to pay off Peruvian debt to the Soviet Union. Argentina in the 1980s was the Soviet Union's second largest trading partner among the noncommunist developing countries (India was the largest). In turn, the Soviet Union was a major importer of Argentine grain, meat, and wool.

Some Western analysts have posited a differentiated Soviet policy toward Latin America, which stresses military and subversive activities in Central America and diplomatic and economic (state-to-state) relations in South America. The range of instruments of influence used in Central America and South America, while varying in their mix over time, nevertheless indicated that all instruments, including support for subversive groups and arms shipments to amenable governments, had been used in Central America and South America in response to available opportunities, indicating shifting emphases but a basically undifferentiated policy toward Latin America. The main policy goal in Soviet relations with Latin America was to decrease United States influence in the region by encouraging the countries of the region either to develop close ties to the Soviet Union or to adopt a nonaligned, "anti-imperialist" foreign policy. The Soviet Union was cautious in pursuing this goal, seeking to maintain a low public profile in its relations, and was hesitant to devote major economic or military resources to countries in the region, with the exception of Cuba. As part of the reorientation of Soviet Third World policy toward better relations with Western-oriented Third World states, Gorbachev emphasized the establishment of better trade and political relations with several Latin American states. Evidence of this new emphasis was Gorbachev's visit to Cuba in April 1989 and Foreign Minister Shevardnadze's visits to Mexico, Argentina, Brazil, and Uruguay in 1986-87. While in Cuba, Gorbachev and Castro signed a friendship and cooperation treaty, indicating continued Soviet support to Cuba.

The Soviet Union and Nuclear Arms Control

The Soviet Union has championed arms control, in the guise of its extreme variant—universal and complete disarmament—since the founding of the Soviet state. Lenin stated that worldwide disarmament could occur after the victory of socialism but that before that time it would be a tactical device to foster pacifism in the capitalist world.

The Soviet Union has proposed various nuclear disarmament plans since the development of nuclear weapons during World War II. In 1946 the Soviet Union rejected the Acheson-Lilienthal-Baruch Plan proposed by the United States (calling for international control of nuclear weapons) and counterproposed that all nuclear weapons be destroyed. The United States rejected this proposal because of lack of adequate verification provisions. The Soviet Union continued to push for total nuclear disarmament, launching the worldwide "Stockholm Appeal" propaganda campaign in 1950.

The Soviet Union did not seriously contemplate nuclear disarmament or arms reductions while it was in the process of developing and deploying nuclear weapons in the 1940s, 1950s, and most of the 1960s. During the early to mid-1960s, however, the United States and the Soviet Union agreed to ban nuclear and other weapons from Antarctica and nuclear weapons tests in the atmosphere, outer space, and under water (see Objectives in Space, ch. 17). Except for these tentative measures, during the 1960s the Soviet Union built up its strategic nuclear armaments. By the late 1960s, the Soviet Union had reached a rough parity with the United States in some categories of strategic weaponry and at that time offered to negotiate limits on strategic nuclear weapons deployments. Also, the Soviet Union wished to constrain American deployment of an antiballistic missile (ABM) system and retain the ability to place multiple independently-targetable re-entry vehicles (MIRVs) on missiles (see Arms Control and Military Objectives, ch. 17).

The Soviet-American Strategic Arms Limitation Talks (SALT), initially delayed by the United States in protest of the August 1968 Warsaw Pact invasion of Czechoslovakia, began in November 1969 in Helsinki. The Interim Agreement on the Limitation of Strategic Offensive Arms, signed in Moscow in May 1972, froze existing levels of deployment of intercontinental ballistic missiles (ICBMs) and regulated the growth of submarine-launched ballistic missiles (SLBMs). As part of the SALT process, the Anti-Ballistic

*President Ronald W. Reagan and General Secretary Mikhail S. Gorbachev
signing the Intermediate-Range Nuclear Forces Treaty
in Washington, December 1987
Courtesy Bill Fitz-Patrick*

Missile Treaty was also signed, allowing two ABM deployment areas in each country (a protocol to the treaty later reduced the number of deployment areas to one).

The SALT agreements were generally considered in the West as having codified the concept of mutual assured destruction, or deterrence. Both the United States and the Soviet Union recognized their mutual vulnerability to massive destruction, no matter which state launched nuclear weapons first. A second SALT agreement was signed in June 1979 in Vienna. Among other provisions, it placed an aggregate ceiling on ICBM and SLBM launchers. The second SALT agreement was never ratified by the United States Senate, however, in large part because of the Soviet invasion of Afghanistan in December 1979. Both the Soviet Union and the United States nonetheless pledged to abide by the provisions of the agreement. Follow-on talks, termed the Strategic Arms Reduction Talks (START), began in June 1982 but as of 1989 had not resulted in agreement.

In January 1986, Gorbachev announced a three-stage proposal for nuclear disarmament. His plan called for initial strategic nuclear weapons cuts of 50 percent and the banning of space-based defenses, followed by second- and third-stage cuts that would include elimination of British and French nuclear arsenals. He also agreed to the United States position on the total elimination of intermediate-range nuclear forces (INF) in Europe and indicated a new openness to consideration of wide-ranging verification procedures. Parts of the proposal were subsequently mentioned in Gorbachev's political report to the Twenty-Seventh Party Congress in February 1986. Although the proposal as a whole was rejected by the Western nuclear powers, elements of the proposal were included in the START negotiations and in the final round of the INF negotiations, which had begun in 1981.

In November 1981, the Reagan administration proposed the elimination of intermediate (1,000 to 5,500 kilometers) and shorter range (500 to 1,000 kilometers) ballistic and cruise missiles from Europe and Asia. The Soviet Union rejected this proposal and attempted to influence public opinion in Western Europe to prevent the NATO deployment of missiles that would counter the Soviet SS–4s, SS–5s, and SS–20s targeted on Western Europe. According to some Western analysts, the Soviet Union hoped that through manipulation of European and American public opinion Western governments would be forced to cancel the deployments, a policy that the Soviet Union had successfully used in the late 1970s to force cancellation of NATO plans to deploy enhanced radiation warheads (neutron bombs). The Soviet Union walked out of the INF and other arms control negotiations in November 1983 as a result of the NATO deployment of countervailing intermediate-range nuclear forces. The Soviet Union returned to the INF negotiations around the time that Gorbachev became general secretary. Negotiations proceeded relatively quickly and resulted in the conclusion of the INF Treaty signed in Washington in December 1987. The INF Treaty called for the elimination of all American and Soviet INF and shorter-range nuclear forces from Europe and Asia within three years (see Soviet-United States Relations, this ch.). The treaty was ratified by the United States Senate and the Supreme Soviet in May 1988.

On December 7, 1988, Gorbachev made a major foreign policy speech to the UN General Assembly, announcing arms reductions that, if fully implemented, would reduce military tensions between the Soviet Union and the United States and between the Warsaw Pact and NATO. He pledged that the Soviet Union would unilaterally cut its armed forces by 500,000 troops over a two-year period and would significantly cut its deployments of conventional arms, including over 10,000 tanks. He also announced the withdrawal of six tank divisions from East Germany, Czechoslovakia, and Hungary by 1991. In early 1989, Gorbachev also announced cuts in the military budget, and several Warsaw Pact states also announced reductions in their armed forces and military budgets.

The Soviet Union and the United Nations

The Soviet Union has taken an active role in the UN and other major international and regional organizations. At the behest of the United States, the Soviet Union took a role in the establishment of the UN in 1945. The Soviet Union insisted that there be veto rights in the Security Council and that alterations in the Charter of the UN be unanimously approved by the five permanent members (Britain, China, France, the Soviet Union, and the United States). A major watershed in Soviet UN policy occurred in January 1950, when Soviet representatives boycotted UN functions in support of the seating of China as a permanent member of the Security Council. In the absence of the Soviet representatives, the UN Security Council was able to vote for the intervention of UN military forces in what would become the Korean War. The Soviet Union subsequently returned to various UN bodies in August 1950. This return marked the beginning of a new policy of active participation in international and regional organizations.

For many years, the Western powers played a guiding role in UN deliberations, but by the 1960s many former colonies had been granted independence and had joined the UN. These states, which became the majority in the General Assembly and other bodies, were increasingly receptive to Soviet "anti-imperialist" appeals. By the 1970s, the UN deliberations had generally become increasingly hostile toward the West and toward the United States in particular, as evidenced by pro-Soviet and anti-United States voting trends in the General Assembly. Although the Soviet Union benefited from and encouraged these trends, it was not mainly responsible for them. Rather, the trends were largely a result of the growing debate over the redistribution of the world's wealth between the "have" and "have-not" states.

In general, the Soviet Union used the UN as a propaganda forum and encouraged pro-Soviet positions among the nonaligned countries. The Soviet Union did not, however, achieve total support in the UN for its foreign policy positions. The Soviet Union and Third World states often agreed that "imperialism" caused and continued to maintain the disparities in the world distribution of wealth. They disagreed, however, on the proper level of Soviet aid to the Third World, with the Soviet Union refusing to grant sizable aid for development. Also, the Soviet Union encountered opposition to its occupation of Afghanistan and the Vietnamese occupation of Cambodia and got little support (as evidenced by Third World abstentions) for its 1987 proposal on the creation of a "Comprehensive System of International Peace and Security."

The Soviet Union in the late 1980s belonged to most of the specialized agencies of the UN. It resisted joining various agricultural, food, and humanitarian organizations of the UN because it eschewed multilateral food and humanitarian relief efforts. During 1986 Western media reported that East European and Asian communist countries allied with the Soviet Union received more development assistance from the UN than they and the Soviet Union contributed. This revelation belied communist states' rhetorical support in the UN for the establishment of a New International Economic Order for the transfer of wealth from the rich Northern Hemisphere to the poor Southern Hemisphere nations. Partly because of ongoing Third World criticism of the Soviet record of meager economic assistance to the Third World and of Soviet contributions to UN agencies, in September 1987 the Soviet Union announced that it would pay some portion of its arrears to the UN. This policy change also came at a time of financial hardship in the UN caused partly by the decision of the United States to withhold contributions pending cost-cutting efforts in the UN.

During the Gorbachev period, the Soviet Union made several suggestions for increasing UN involvement in the settlement of superpower and regional problems and conflicts. Although as of 1989 these suggestions had not been implemented, they constituted new initiatives in Soviet foreign policy and represented a break with the stolid, uncooperative nature of past Soviet foreign policy. While the basic character of Soviet foreign policy had not yet changed, the new flexibility in solving regional problems in Afghanistan, Angola, and Cambodia, as well as problems in the superpower relationship, indicated a pragmatic commitment to the lessening of world tensions.

* * *

Information on Soviet ideology and general foreign policy orientations can be found in Erik P. Hoffmann and Frederic J. Fleron's *The Conduct of Soviet Foreign Policy;* William Welch's *American Images of Soviet Foreign Policy;* and William A. Gamson and Andre Modigliani's *Untangling the Cold War.* Institutions and personnel involved in the formation and execution of Soviet foreign policy are discussed in Robbin F. Laird and Erik P. Hoffmann's *Soviet Foreign Policy in a Changing World;* Seweryn Bialer's *The Domestic Context of Soviet Foreign Policy;* Vernon S. Aspaturian's *Process and Power in Soviet Foreign Policy;* and Jan F. Triska and David D. Finley's

Soviet Foreign Policy. Soviet foreign policy toward various regions of the world is treated in Robbin F. Laird's *Soviet Foreign Policy;* Richard F. Staar's *USSR Foreign Policies after Detente;* Seweryn Bialer's *The Soviet Paradox;* Adam B. Ulam's *Expansion and Coexistence, The Rivals,* and *Dangerous Relations;* and Alvin Z. Rubinstein's *Soviet Foreign Policy since World War II.* Regional focuses on the Third World include Jerry F. Hough's *The Struggle for the Third World;* Andrzej Korbonski and Francis Fukuyama's *The Soviet Union and the Third World;* and Carol R. Saivetz and Sylvia Woodby's *Soviet-Third World Relations.* Soviet foreign policy focusing on specific regions is analyzed in Christopher D. Jones's *Soviet Influence in Eastern Europe;* Herbert J. Ellison's *Soviet Policy Toward Western Europe;* Donald S. Zagoria's *Soviet Policy in East Asia;* Ray S. Cline, James Arnold Miller, and Roger E. Kanet's *Asia in Soviet Global Strategy;* Ramesh Thakur and Carlyle A. Thayer's *The Soviet Union as an Asian Pacific Power;* Cole Blasier's *The Giant's Rival;* Alvin Z. Rubinstein's *Soviet Policy Toward Turkey, Iran, and Afghanistan;* and Robert O. Freedman's *Soviet Policy Toward the Middle East since 1970.* (For further information and complete citations, see Bibliography.)

because of the permafrost new bridge construction techniques had to be devised. On average, the roadbed for the BAM required moving 100,000 cubic meters of earth—either cutting or filling—for each kilometer of track.

The mean annual temperature along the BAM ranges from – 10°C to – 4°C, with extremes of – 58°C in the winter to 36°C in the summer. To operate their trains under these severe climatic conditions, the railroads used special equipment, locomotives, rolling stock, and fixed installations. Snow plows, snow-melting machines, switch heaters, and other specialized equipment were indispensable in the winter. Rails made of special steel that does not become brittle at the very low temperatures of the Siberian winters were also used.

From its western terminus at Ust'-Kut to its eastern end at Komsomol'sk-na-Amure, the BAM stretched for 3,145 kilometers, between 180 and 300 kilometers north of the Trans-Siberian Railway. It had a total of 5,000 kilometers of main line and yard track. In addition to the east-west main line, a 402-kilometer perpendicular line, the "Little BAM," ran from Bamovskaya on the Trans-Siberian Railway north to Tynda on the BAM and thence to Berkakit to serve the important mining and industrial area of Neryungri. In the late 1980s, an extension to the Yakutiya region, rich in timber and minerals, was under way.

The BAM and its feeder routes, both rail and highway, served an area of approximately 1.2 million square kilometers. Although track laying was completed in 1986, it was not yet in full operation in 1989. The projected freight traffic on the BAM was planned at 35 million tons per year, with trains of up to 9,000 tons. Moreover, the government planned for the BAM to become an important part of the Siberian land bridge from Japan, via the port of Sovetskaya Gavan', to West European destinations, saving 20 percent in time over the maritime route.

Other New Construction

Important new railroad construction was under way in the Arctic regions, Siberia, the Far East, and the Caucasus. Thus, the Urengoy-Yamburg rail line was being built to serve the Yamburg natural gas deposits north of Urengoy. In the Pechora River area, a line from the town of Synia, on the Moscow-Vorkuta road, was being extended about 120 kilometers to the Usinsk oil fields. Plans were made for a 540-kilometer spur from Labytnangi, southeast of Vorkuta, to the gas fields at Bolvanskiy Nos on the Yamal Peninsula. The project has been hampered by summer thaws. Engineers laying the rail line resolved the problem by insulating the strips increased dramatically, to approximately 19,000 long-distance and 17,000 local trains. To resolve, or at least alleviate, congestion in the summer, train lengths were increased. Thus, eighteen-car trains were extended to twenty-four cars on heavily used lines from Moscow, while in 1986 test trains of thirty-two cars were run out of Moscow and Leningrad to Simferopol' in Crimea.

The most important passenger railroads in the mid-1980s were the Moscow, October, Gor'kiy, Southern, Donetsk, Dnepr, Sverd-lovsk, and Northern Caucasus. These served the Soviet Union's most densely populated areas. The two most heavily traveled axes were the Leningrad-Moscow-Donetsk to Crimea or the Caucasus area and the Moscow to Khabarovsk (8,540 kilometers) and Vladivostok (9,300 kilometers) areas. On the latter axis, most passengers traveled distances of only 500 to 700 kilometers, rather than the full length. The seven major passenger rail centers in the European part of the Soviet Union were in Moscow, Leningrad, Tbilisi, Khar'kov, Kiev, Simferopol', and Adler; the major center in the Asian part of the country was at Novosibirsk (see fig. 18).

The Baykal-Amur Main Line

The vast Siberian region between Lake Baykal and the lower Amur River, called the Transbaykal (or Zabaykaliye), is rich in natural and mineral resources. Yet until recently, it lacked adequate transportation to the rest of the country. Its main communication artery was the overburdened Trans-Siberian Railway (see Glossary), running well south of it. Although providing the Transbaykal region with a railroad was considered in the nineteenth century, work on the Baykal-Amur Main Line (Baykalo-Amurskaya Magistral'—BAM; see Glossary) did not begin until 1974. The BAM was finally opened in 1989.

Survey and construction crews overcame formidable geological, climatic, topographic, and engineering challenges, including rivers, ground ice, unstable soil, seismic areas, mountains, and extremes of cold and heat. About two-thirds of the BAM trackage crossed areas of ground ice that caused frost heave and other unstable soil conditions. In the summer, permafrost created large bogs that hampered roadbed construction, and embankments sank into the marshy terrain during the summer thaw. To prevent such problems, engineers insulated the strip of marsh along the tracks to keep it in a continuously frozen state. Seismic activity along some 1,000 kilometers of the line also caused problems, triggering avalanches and landslides. Topographic obstacles were formidable as well. To cross the mountains, crews had to pierce over thirty kilometers of tunnels. The BAM also crossed more than 3,000 streams, and

Chapter 11. Economic Structure and Policy

Economists discussing economic plans

THE SOVIET UNION OF THE 1980s had the largest centrally directed economy in the world. The regime established its economic priorities through central planning, a system under which administrative decisions rather than the market determined resource allocation and prices.

Since the Bolshevik Revolution of 1917, the country has grown from a largely underdeveloped peasant society with minimal industry to become the second largest industrial power in the world. According to Soviet statistics, the country's share in world industrial production grew from 4 percent to 20 percent between 1913 and 1980. Although many Western analysts considered these claims to be inflated, the Soviet achievement remained remarkable. Recovering from the calamitous events of World War II, the country's economy had maintained a continuous though uneven rate of growth. Living standards, although still modest for most inhabitants by Western standards, had improved, and Soviet citizens of the late 1980s had a measure of economic security.

Although these past achievements were impressive, in the mid-1980s Soviet leaders faced many problems. Since the 1970s, the growth rate had slowed substantially. Extensive economic development (see Glossary), based on vast inputs of materials and labor, was no longer possible; yet the productivity of Soviet assets remained low compared with other major industrialized countries. Product quality needed improvement. Soviet leaders faced a fundamental dilemma: the strong central controls that had traditionally guided economic development had failed to promote the creativity and productivity urgently needed in a highly developed, modern economy.

Conceding the weaknesses of their past approaches in solving new problems, the leaders of the late 1980s were seeking to mold a program of economic reform to galvanize the economy. The *Basic Directions for the Economic and Social Development of the USSR for 1986–1990 and for the Period to the Year 2000,* a report to the Twenty-Seventh Party Congress in March 1986, spoke of a "burden of the shortcomings that had been piling up over a long period," which required "radical changes, a profound restructuring." The leadership, headed by General Secretary Mikhail S. Gorbachev, was experimenting with solutions to economic problems with an openness (*glasnost*—see Glossary) never before seen in the history of the economy. One method for improving productivity appeared to be a strengthening of the role of market forces. Yet reforms in which market forces assumed a greater role would signify a lessening of authority and control by the planning hierarchy.

Assessing developments in the economy, both past and present, remains difficult for Western observers. The country contains enormous economic and regional disparities. Yet analyzing statistical data broken down by region is a cumbersome process. Furthermore, Soviet statistics themselves may be of limited use to Western analysts because they are not directly comparable with those used in Western countries. The differing statistical concepts, valuations, and procedures used by communist and noncommunist economists make even the most basic data, such as the relative productivity of various sectors, difficult to assess. Most Western analysts, and some Soviet economists, doubt the accuracy of the published statistics, recognizing that the industrial growth figures tend to be inflated.

Economic Structure

The economy of the Soviet Union differs significantly from market economies; the country's massive and diverse economic resources are largely state owned. The central government controls directly or indirectly many aspects of the labor force, the retail and wholesale distribution system, and the financial system.

Nature of the National Economy

The Constitution of 1977 declares that the foundation of the economy is "socialist ownership of the means of production" (see The 1977 Constitution, ch. 8). The Constitution recognizes two forms of socialist ownership: state ownership, in which all members of society are said to participate, and various types of collective or cooperative ownership. According to Marxist-Leninist (see Glossary) theory, the former is more advanced, and the Constitution calls for its expansion. It is the most extensive form of ownership in the economy, incorporating all major industrial entities: the banking, transportation, and communication systems; a majority of trade and public services; and much of the agricultural sector. In the late 1980s, collective ownership was found primarily in agriculture, the small workshops of craftspeople, and some retail trade and services. In 1989 a law was passed allowing an increase in the number and kinds of cooperatives.

The Communist Party of the Soviet Union (CPSU) and, as an adjunct of it, the government set goals and chose priorities for the economy. Traditionally, the government has determined economic policy in considerable detail through its planning agencies at various levels and has issued specific instructions to individual economic units concerning quantity and type of production expected of them, wage levels and incentive funds permitted, and, to a large extent, investment policies. Control of the economy has been exerted through a hierarchy of planning agencies that interact with appropriate government and party organs to devise and implement policy to achieve these goals. Various past reform efforts have altered the specific functions and assignments of the components of the economy, but the basic hierarchical structure has remained intact since its inception during the 1920s (see Planning Process, this ch.).

All-union (see Glossary) planning and control for each major sector of the economy is handled by relevant branch ministries, subordinate to the Council of Ministers and aided by a variety of planning agencies (see Administrative Organs, ch. 8). Between the ministries and the functioning enterprises (see Glossary), a variety of bodies, such as combines (see Glossary), trusts (see Glossary), and production associations (groups of formerly separate enterprises) join together entities representing aspects of production in a given area of the economy. On this level, periodic restructurings have been attempted to achieve greater efficiency (see Reforming the Planning System, this ch.).

In 1985 industry, composed of about 45,000 enterprises and production associations, accounted for 45.6 percent of net material product (see Glossary), according to official statistics. The agricultural sector, organized into collective farms (see Glossary) and state farms (see Glossary), produced 19.4 percent of net material product. Transportation and communications accounted for 10.7 percent, and the distribution system accounted for 18.2 percent (see Retail and Wholesale Distribution System, this ch.).

The 1977 Constitution permits individuals to be self-employed, with certain restrictions. Until the late 1980s, however, the authorities strongly discouraged the practice. Citizens may own personal property, such as a dwelling or an automobile, and may sell this property as "used" merchandise or bequeath it as they choose. They may also sell products they have themselves made. Traditionally, they have not been permitted to act as middlemen for profit or to hire the labor of other citizens for personal gain, i.e., to engage in private enterprise as it is understood in the West. Nevertheless, alongside the official economy a "second economy" has long flourished, made up of private individuals offering goods and services to consumers, who have traditionally been inadequately served by the state services sector. Such activities have included those that were simply private, illegal, or of questionable legality.

453

The existence of many illicit business activities, operating outside state controls, was freely admitted and deplored by authorities and the official press of the 1980s. Upon assuming power in March 1985, Gorbachev adopted a new approach to the problem. In a major departure from past policies, on May 1, 1987, it became legal for individuals to go into a variety of business activities on their own or in cooperation with others (see The Twelfth Five-Year Plan, 1986–90, this ch.).

Labor

In 1985 the Soviet work force totaled about 130.3 million persons. According to official statistics, almost 20 percent of these employees worked in agriculture and forestry, while slightly more than 38 percent worked in industry and construction. Just under 10 percent were employed in transportation and communications. As in other industrialized countries, the percentage of the total work force employed in distribution and other services had increased. The shift had been more gradual than in Western countries, however. In 1985 just under 32 percent of the work force was employed in distribution and other service jobs. Officially, the government did not acknowledge the existence of unemployment. However, Western analysts estimated that about 2 percent of the labor force might be unemployed at a given time, most of this being short-term unemployment.

The working-age population was officially defined as males from sixteen to fifty-nine years old and females from sixteen to fifty-four years old. As in other industrialized countries, the work force was gradually aging. Precise information concerning the number of pension-age workers employed either full time or part time was not available. However, Western analysts expected such workers to account for fully 12 percent of the labor force by the year 2000. A striking feature of the work force was the prominent role played by women, who accounted for some 49 percent of the work force in the mid-1980s.

The growth rate of the labor force had declined during plan periods in the 1970s and 1980s, and this situation was expected to improve only slightly during the 1990s (see Age and Sex Structure, ch. 3). Western analysts predicted that the work force would number just over 171 million persons by the year 2000. Population growth in general had slowed markedly in the European part of the country but remained high in the more rural Central Asian areas. This fact was a source of concern to economic planners because job skills were less plentiful in the non-European areas of the country. In view of the lower birth rates of recent decades and the aging of

People lining up for scarce consumer goods in a typical Soviet scene
Courtesy Jonathan Tetzlaff

the work force, leaders called for improvements in labor productivity through automation and mechanization of work processes and through elimination of surplus workers in enterprises. Leaders also expressed concern about the deficient education and training of many in the work force. Although the education system stressed vocational and technical training, and many industrial enterprises offered additional specialized training for workers after they joined the labor force, the economy suffered from a labor shortage, particularly for skilled personnel (see Pedagogy and Planning, ch. 6).

Labor was not directly allocated. Although compulsory labor, involving the transfer of entire groups of workers, had been a significant tool of industrial development during the dictatorship of Joseph V. Stalin (the precise extent of the practice has not been determined with certainty), its use had greatly diminished in subsequent years and by the 1970s was no longer a major factor in economic activity. The inhospitable terrain and remote location of many parts of the Soviet Union impeded the flow of skilled labor to areas targeted for development outside the western and southeastern areas of the country. Wage differentials, varying according to region, industry, and occupation, were used to attract employees to the tasks and locations for which there was a labor need. In large cities, where the presence of amenities and a variety

455

of economic activities attracted workers in excess of actual employment opportunities, residence permits were used to limit the influx of additional population.

Within the labor force as a whole, trade union membership was above 90 percent nationwide in the 1980s. Labor unions had a variety of functions: administering state social funds for the sick, disabled, and elderly and for day care; sponsoring vocational training and other educational services, such as libraries and clubs; and participating in aspects of enterprise management. Unions also acted as interpreters of party policy for the workers. Union leaders were expected to work to improve discipline and morale, educate the work force, and help to raise productivity. They did not bargain with management over wages or working conditions.

Retail and Wholesale Distribution System

In the mid-1980s, about 8 percent of the labor force worked in the distribution system. For the most part, internal trade took place in state retail outlets in urban areas and in cooperatives in rural areas. Prices in state and cooperative outlets were set by the State Committee on Prices and were determined by many considerations other than supply and demand. Both rural and urban inhabitants could also use "collective farm markets," where peasants, acting both individually and in groups representing collective farms, sold their produce directly to consumers. Here prices fluctuated according to supply and demand. Similar arrangements existed for nonedible products, although in a less developed form, as could be seen in a variety of secondhand stores and flea markets. Although such enterprises specialized in used items, they also sold new products, again on a supply-and-demand basis.

With regard to many types of consumer goods, the country's economy was "taut," that is, enterprises carried low inventories and reserves. Demand for good-quality items frequently exceeded supply. In effect, some goods and services, such as housing, were rationed as a result of their scarcity. In addition, a system of special stores existed for use by privileged individuals and foreigners. These stores could be found in major population centers but were not highly publicized. They contained good-quality items, both food and nonedible goods, in scarce supply. Moreover, a second economy had long flourished to supply consumer goods and services, such as repair work and health care, for which the official retail distribution system could not meet consumer demand. Observers expected that as a result of the reforms of the 1980s, a growing variety of goods and services would be distributed through the expanding private sector of the economy (see The Twelfth Five-Year Plan, 1986–90, this ch.).

Distribution on the wholesale level took place largely through state-directed allocation, in conjunction with the planning process. Heavy industry, particularly producer goods, and the defense industry received highest priority. Reforms of the mid-1980s promised to decentralize this system somewhat, with users of materials free in many cases to make purchasing contracts with the suppliers of their choice. Western observers were uncertain as to the impact such an alteration would have on the supply system as a whole.

In 1984 per capita consumption was about one-third that of the United States. It was about half that of France and the Federal Republic of Germany (West Germany) and roughly two-thirds that of Japan. Soviet levels of consumption were below those of some of the country's allies in Eastern Europe as well.

Financial System

The ruble, consisting of 100 kopeks, is the unit of currency. In the mid-1980s, the ruble (for value of the ruble—see Glossary) was a purely internal currency unit, and the government fixed its rate of exchange with foreign currencies somewhat arbitrarily. The State Bank (Gosudarstvennyi bank—Gosbank) issued currency and established its official gold content and thus its exchange rate with foreign currencies. The real value of the ruble for purchase of domestic consumer goods in comparison with the United States dollar was very difficult to determine because the Soviet price structure, traditionally established by the State Committee on Prices, differed from that of a market economy.

The banking system was owned and managed by the government. Gosbank was the central bank of the country and also its only commercial bank. It handled all significant banking transactions, including the issuing and control of currency and credit, management of the gold reserve, and oversight of all transactions among economic enterprises. Because it held enterprise accounts, the bank could monitor their financial performance. It had main offices in each union republic (see Glossary) and many smaller branches and savings banks throughout the country. The banking system also included the Foreign Economic Activity Bank and the All-Union Capital Investment Bank. The latter bank provided capital investment funds for all branches of the economy except agriculture, which was handled by Gosbank.

Because the banking system was highly centralized, it formed an integral part of the management of the economy. The Ministry of Finance had an important role to play in the economic system, for it established financial plans to control the procurement and use of the country's financial resources. It managed the budget in accordance with the wishes of central planners. The budget had traditionally allocated most of the country's investment resources (see Tools of Control, this ch.). The reforms of the mid-1980s, however, required enterprises to rely to a greater extent on their own financial resources rather than on the central budget. These reforms also called for the creation of several new banks to finance industrial undertakings, ending the monopoly of Gosbank. Enterprises would seek and receive credit from a variety of banks.

Citizens could maintain personal savings accounts and, beginning in 1987, checking accounts. These accounts, initially limited to the Russian Republic, were offered by the newly formed Labor Savings and Consumer Credit Bank. Over the years, personal savings accounts had accumulated massive amounts of money, growing from 1.9 billion rubles in 1950 to 156.5 billion rubles in 1980. The savings represented excess purchasing power, probably the result of repressed inflation and shortages of quality consumer goods.

Economic Planning and Control

In the Soviet Union of the 1980s, the basic economic task of allocating scarce resources to competing objectives was accomplished primarily through a centrally directed planning apparatus rather than through the interplay of market forces. During the decades following the Bolshevik Revolution and especially under Stalin, a complex system of planning and control had developed, in which the state managed virtually all production activity. In the mid- and late 1980s, however, economic reforms sponsored by Gorbachev were introducing significant changes in the traditional system.

Planning Process

Economic planning, according to Marxist-Leninist doctrine, was a form of economic management by the state, indispensable both during the transition from capitalism to socialism (see Glossary) and in a socialist society. Soviet economic theorists maintained that planning was based on a profound knowledge and application of objective socialist economic laws and that it was independent of the personal will and desires of individuals. The most general of these laws, commonly referred to as the basic law of socialism, defined the aim of economic production as the fullest satisfaction of the constantly rising material and cultural requirements of the population, using advanced technology to achieve continued growth and improvement of production. Centralized planning was presented

Interior of GUM, the government department store (completed in 1893), Red Square, Moscow. The largest department store in the Soviet Union, it serves as many as 350,000 customers each day.
Courtesy Jimmy Pritchard

by its proponents as the conscious application of economic laws to benefit the people through effective use of all natural resources and productive forces.

The regime established production targets and prices and allocated resources, codifying these decisions in a comprehensive plan or set of plans. Using CPSU directives concerning major economic goals, planning authorities formulated short-term and long-term plans for meeting specific targets in virtually all spheres of economic activity. These production plans were supplemented by comprehensive plans for the supply of materials, equipment, labor, and finances to the producing sector; for the procurement of agricultural products by the government; and for the distribution of food and manufactured products to the population. Economic plans had the force of law. Traditionally, they had been worked out down to the level of the individual economic enterprise, where they were reflected in a set of output goals and performance indicators that management was expected to maintain.

Operationally, short-range planning was the most important aspect of the planning process for production and resource allocation. Annual plans underlay the basic operation of the system. They covered one calendar year and encompassed the entire economy. Targets were set at the central level for the overall rate of growth of the economy, the volume and structure of the domestic product, the use of raw materials and labor and their distribution by sector and region, and the volume and structure of exports and imports. Annual plans were broken down into quarterly and monthly plans, which served as commands and blueprints for the day-to-day operation of industrial and other economic enterprises and organizations.

The five-year plan provided continuity and direction by integrating the yearly plans into a longer time frame. Although the five-year plan was duly enacted into law, it contained a series of guidelines rather than a set of direct orders. Periods covered by the five-year plans coincided with those covered by the party congresses (see Party Congress, ch. 7; table 30, Appendix A). At each congress, the party leadership presented the targets for the next five-year plan. Thus each plan had the approval of the most authoritative body of the country's leading political institution.

Long-term planning covered fifteen years or more. It delineated principal directions of economic development and specified the way the economy could meet the desired goals.

As in other areas of leadership, so in economic policy matters it was the Central Committee of the CPSU and, more specifically, its Politburo that set basic guidelines for planning (see Central Committee; Politburo, ch. 7). The planning apparatus of the government was headed by the Council of Ministers and, under it, the State Planning Committee (Gosudarstvennyi planovyi komitet—Gosplan). This agency, made up of a large number of councils, commissions, governmental officials, and specialists, was assisted by the State Committee for Statistics (Gosudarstvennyi komitet po statistike—Goskomstat). It took plans developed by the city councils, republic legislatures, and regional conferences and incorporated them into a master plan for the nation. It also supervised the operation of all the plans. Gosplan combined the broad economic goals set forth by the Council of Ministers with data supplied by lower administrative levels regarding the current state of the economy in order to work out, through trial and error, a set of control figures. The plan stipulated the major aspects of economic activity in each economic sector and in each republic or region of the country. Gosplan was also responsible for ensuring a correct balance among the different branches of the economy, speeding the growth of the national income, and raising the level of efficiency in production.

The method used by Gosplan to achieve internally consistent plans, both in a sectoral and in a regional context, was called the system of material balances. No clear exposition of this method had been published. The system essentially consisted of preparing balance sheets in which available material, labor, and financial resources were listed as assets and plan requirements as liabilities. The task of planners was to balance resources and requirements to ensure that the necessary inputs were provided for the planned output. To reduce this task to manageable proportions, central authorities specified detailed output goals, investment projects, and supply plans for only key branches of the economy. The rest of the plan was developed only to the extent needed to ensure achievement of the main goals.

Among operational organizations participating in the planning process, a major role belonged to the State Committee for Material and Technical Supply. This agency shared with Gosplan the controls over the allocation of essential materials and equipment. Other operational agencies included the State Committee for Construction, which played an important part in industrial investment planning and housing construction; the State Committee for Labor and Social Problems; and the State Committee for Science and Technology, which prepared proposals for the introduction of new technology. Finally, the Academy of Sciences (see Glossary) helped to develop a scientific basis for optimal planning and accounting methods.

461

When the control figures had been established by Gosplan, economic ministries drafted plans within their jurisdictions and directed the planning by subordinate enterprises. The control figures were sent in disaggregated form downward through the planning hierarchy to production and industrial associations (various groupings of related enterprises) or the territorial production complex (see Glossary) for progressively more detailed elaboration. Individual enterprises at the base of the planning pyramid were called upon to develop the most detailed plans covering all aspects of their operations. In agriculture, individual collective farms and state farms worked under the supervision of local party committees. The role of the farms in planning, however, was more circumscribed.

At this point, as the individual enterprise formulated its detailed draft production plans, the flow of information was reversed. Rank-and-file workers as well as managers could participate in the planning process on the enterprise level; according to Soviet reports, approximately 110 million citizens took part in discussions of the draft guidelines for the 1986–90 period and long-term planning for the 1986–2000 period. The draft plans of the enterprises were sent back up through the planning hierarchy for review, adjustment, and integration. This process entailed intensive bargaining, with top authorities pressing for maximum and, at times, unrealizable targets and enterprises seeking assignments that they could reasonably expect to fulfill or even overfulfill. Ultimate review and revision of the draft plans by Gosplan and approval of a final all-union plan by the Council of Ministers, the CPSU, and the Supreme Soviet were followed by another downward flow of information, this time with amended and approved plans containing specific targets for each economic entity to the level of the enterprise.

A parallel system for planning existed in each union republic and each autonomous republic (see Glossary). The state planning committees in the union republics were subject to the jurisdiction of both the councils of ministers in the union republics and Gosplan. They drafted plans for all enterprises under the jurisdiction of the union republics and recommended plans for enterprises subordinated to union-republic ministries (see Glossary) and located on their territory. The regional system also included planning agencies created for several major economic regions, which were responsible either to Gosplan or to a state planning committee in a union republic. Autonomous republics had planning systems similar to those of union republics.

Advocates of the centrally planned economy (CPE) argued that it had four important advantages. First, the regime could harness the economy to serve its political and economic objectives.

Gas station between Moscow and Smolensk, Russian Republic
Courtesy Jonathan Tetzlaff

Satisfaction of consumer demand, for example, could be limited in favor of greater investment in basic industry or channeled into desired patterns, e.g., reliance on public transportation rather than on private automobiles. Centralized management could take into account long-term needs for development and disregard consumer desires for items that it considered frivolous. With a centralized system, it was possible to implement programs for the common good, such as pollution controls, construction of industrial infrastructure, and preservation of parkland. Second, in theory CPEs could make continuous, optimal use of all available resources, both human and material. Neither unemployment nor idle plant capacity would exist beyond minimal levels, and the economy would develop in a stable manner, unimpeded by inflation or recession. Industry would benefit from economies of scale and avoid duplication of capacity. Third, CPEs could serve social rather than individual ends; under such a system, the leadership could distribute rewards, whether wages or perquisites, according to the social value of the service performed, not according to the vagaries of supply and demand on an open market. Finally, proponents argued that abolition of most forms of property income, coupled with public ownership of the means of production, promoted work attitudes that enhanced team effort and conscientious attention to tasks at

463

hand; laborers could feel that they were working for their own benefit and would not need strict disciplinary supervision.

Critics of CPEs identified several characteristic problems. First, because economic processes were so complex, the plan had to be a simplification of reality. Individuals and producing units could be given directives or targets, but in executing the plan they might select courses of action that conflicted with the overall interests of society as determined by the planners. Such courses of action might include, for example, ignoring quality standards, producing an improper product mix, or using resources wastefully.

Second, critics contended that CPEs had built-in obstacles to innovation and efficiency in production. No appropriate mechanism existed to ensure the prompt, effective transfer of new technical advances to actual practice in enterprises. Managers of producing units, frequently having limited discretionary authority, saw as their first priority a strict fulfillment of the plan targets rather than the application of the insights gained through research and development or the diversification of products. Plant managers might be reluctant to shut down their production lines for modernization because the attendant delays could jeopardize the fulfillment of targets.

Third, CPEs were said to lack a system of appropriate incentives to encourage higher productivity by managers and workers. Future mandatory targets were frequently based on past performance. Planners often established targets for the next plan period by adding a certain percentage to the achieved output while reducing authorized inputs to force greater productivity (sometimes called the "ratchet" system by Western analysts). The ratchet system discouraged enterprises from revealing their full potential. Managers actually might be reluctant to report exceptional levels of output.

Fourth, the system of allocating goods and services in CPEs was inefficient. Most of the total mix of products was distributed according to the plan, with the aid of the system of material balances. But because no one could predict perfectly the actual needs of each production unit, some units received too many goods and others too few. The managers with surpluses, either in materials or in human resources, were hesitant to admit they had them, for CPEs were typically "taut." Managers preferred to hoard whatever they had and then to make informal trades for materials they needed. The scarcity of supplies resulting from a taut economy and the unpredictability of their availability were persistent problems for enterprises, forcing them to adopt erratic work schedules such as "storming." This was a phenomenon whereby many enterprises fulfilled a major portion of their monthly plan through frenzied activity during the final third of the month, by which time they had mustered the necessary supplies. The uncertainty of supply was also responsible for a general tendency among industrial ministries to become self-sufficient by developing their own internal supply bases and to give priority to the needs of enterprises under their own jurisdiction over the requirements, even though more urgent, of enterprises in other ministries (a practice sometimes referred to as "departmentalism").

Finally, detractors argued that in CPEs prices did not reflect the value of available resources, goods, or services. In market economies, prices, which are based on cost and utility considerations, permit the determination of value, even if imperfectly. In CPEs, prices were determined administratively, and the criteria the government used to establish them sometimes bore little relation to costs. The influence of consumers was weak (the exception being the Ministry of Defense, which was in a position to make explicit demands of its suppliers). Prices often varied significantly from the actual social or economic value of the products for which they had been set and were not a valid basis for comparing the relative value of two or more products. The system's almost total insulation from foreign trade competition exacerbated this problem (see Development of the State Monopoly on Foreign Trade, ch. 15).

Reforming the Planning System

Soviet economists and planners have long been aware of the alleged strengths and weaknesses of the centralized planning system. Numerous changes in the structure, scope of responsibilities, and authority of the various planning and administrative organizations have been made over the years. Nevertheless, the fundamental planning process remained virtually unchanged after the inception of full-scale central planning in 1928 until the late 1980s, when some radical changes were discussed.

In the decades that followed its introduction, the planning process became increasingly complex and detailed. Planners specified not only quantitative production of goods but also their cost, how they would be distributed, and what resources in labor, materials, and energy they would require. The complexity of the apparatus administering the plans also increased. Ministries (called people's commissariats until 1946) proliferated, reaching fifty by 1957 and reflecting the increasing variety of industrial production. By 1982 the number of ministries, state committees, and other important committees at the all-union level approached 100. Planning had become immensely complex; in the 1980s planners had to contend with more than 20 million types, varieties, and sizes of products,

465

which were produced by 45,000 industrial, 60,000 agricultural, and 33,000 construction enterprises.

Western analysts have viewed reform attempts of Soviet leaders prior to the late 1980s as mere tinkering. From 1957 to 1965, however, a radical change was made, when Nikita S. Khrushchev sponsored a shift from the predominantly sectoral approach to a regional system (see The Khrushchev Era, ch. 2). The reform abolished most industrial ministries and transferred planning and administrative authority to about 100 newly created regional economic councils. The regime hoped to end unsatisfactory coordination among the industrial ministries and ineffective regional planning. Khrushchev apparently hoped to end the traditional concentration of administrative power in Moscow, reduce departmentalism, and make more efficient use of specific economic resources of the various regions. Other changes under Khrushchev included extension of the usual five-year cycle to seven years, from 1959 to 1965, which was subsequently reduced to five years. When the regional system proved to be even less effective than the organizational structure it had replaced, and the weaknesses of the ministerial system reappeared in a regional context, Khrushchev sponsored an additional series of minor changes. But in 1965, after Leonid I. Brezhnev and Aleksei N. Kosygin had replaced Khrushchev as head of party and head of government, respectively, the regime abolished the regional economic councils and reinstituted the industrial ministerial system, although with greater participation of regional bodies in the planning process, at least in theory.

Several reforms of the mid- and late 1960s represented efforts to decentralize decision-making processes, transferring some authority from central planning authorities and ministries to lower-level entities and enterprises. A series of minor reforms in 1965 modified the incentive system by shifting emphasis from gross output to sales and profits, a reform associated with the name of the eminent economist Evsei Liberman. The reforms attempted to provide a more precise measure of labor and materials productivity. They also granted enterprise managers slightly greater latitude in making operating decisions by reducing the number of plan indicators assigned by higher authorities. In addition, the reforms introduced charges for interest and rent. Attention focused particularly on experiments with *khozraschet* (see Glossary), which, in the late 1980s, required enterprises to cover many expenses from their own revenues, thereby encouraging efficient use of resources. In the agricultural sector, state farms and collective farms received greater latitude in organizing their work activities and in establishing subsidiary industrial enterprises such as canning and food processing, timber and textile production, production of building materials, and actual construction projects.

In practice, the amount of decentralization involved in the reforms of the mid-1960s was minimal. For a variety of reasons, including uneasiness about the unrest associated with reforms in Czechoslovakia in 1967 and 1968, planning officials judged the reforms to be failures. By the early 1970s, efforts at further reforms had ceased, although the government never repealed the new regulations. As the only noteworthy, lasting change, the government began to use measures of net output rather than gross output as a success indicator for enterprises.

During the last years of Brezhnev's rule, the leadership remained relatively complacent about the system despite the economy's slowing growth rates. Increases in world oil and gold prices contributed to this attitude because they enhanced hard-currency (see Glossary) purchasing power in the early 1970s and made it possible to import increasing amounts of Western technology.

In response to the stagnation of the late Brezhnev era, a new reform attempt began under Iurii V. Andropov, who succeeded Brezhnev as general secretary in 1982. On an experimental basis, the government gave a number of enterprises greater flexibility in the use of their profits either for investment purposes or for worker incentives. The experiment was formally expanded to include all of the industrial sector on January 1, 1987, although by that time its limited nature and modest prospects for success had been widely recognized.

In the meantime, however, Gorbachev, a leading proponent of both these reforms and more extensive changes, was making his influence felt, first as adviser on economic policy under Andropov and his successor, Konstantin U. Chernenko, and then as general secretary beginning in 1985. Some of Gorbachev's early initiatives involved mere reorganization, similar to previous reform efforts. For example, from 1985 to 1987 seven industrial complexes—organs that were responsible directly to the Council of Ministers and that monitored groups of related activities—were established: agroindustrial, chemicals and timber, construction, fuel and energy, machine building, light industry, and metallurgy (see The Complexes and the Ministries, ch. 12). The ministries remained reluctant to undertake more extensive reforms that would reduce their centralized power and give greater initiative to lower-level economic units. But the conviction was growing that the centralized planning mechanism needed major changes and that simply fine-tuning the economy with minor reforms would not be sufficient.

At Gorbachev's urging, on June 30, 1987, the Supreme Soviet approved a set of measures contained in the *Basic Provisions for Fundamentally Reorganizing Economic Management.* The Supreme Soviet subsequently adopted an additional ten decrees, as well as the Law on State Enterprises (Associations). Taken as a whole, the actions of the Supreme Soviet signaled a substantial change in the system of centralized planning, with significant amounts of authority devolving upon middle and lower levels of the administrative hierarchy. Gorbachev named the economic restructuring program *perestroika* (see Glossary).

The *Basic Provisions* clearly stated that the economy would continue to function as "a unified national economic complex," carrying out the policies of the party. The regime obviously intended to retain great influence in the management and development of enterprises. The new measures also called for a redefinition and curtailment of the role of Gosplan. Beginning in 1991, Gosplan would no longer draw up annual plans. It would continue to develop five- and fifteen-year plans, specify state orders (involving about 25 percent of total output), and determine material balances for products considered to be critically important to the economy and national defense. Gosplan's development of "non-binding control figures" would suggest overall output, profit targets, and various indicators of technical and social progress. Long-term norms would regulate ongoing development, such as total wage payments and payments to various state-sponsored funds, for example, bonus funds, resources for social services, and research and development resources. Once enterprises had filled the designated state orders, however, they would have considerable freedom in deciding what to produce with the remainder of their resources and how to dispose of the products.

The new Law on State Enterprises (Associations) called for *khozraschet.* By the end of 1989, all enterprises in the economy were to make the transition to self-financing (*samofinansirovanie*—see Glossary), taking full responsibility for the financial outcome of their actions. The state budget would pay only for major investment projects. A principal criterion for judging enterprise and management performance would be the fulfillment of contracts. Enterprises would be free to reduce the size of their work force or to dismiss workers for poor performance. The law also provided for the bankruptcy and dissolution of enterprises that consistently operated at a loss. Their workers would receive severance pay and assistance in job placement from the state. In addition, the law called for the election of management personnel in enterprises, subject to approval by the next-higher authority. Finally, the law called for the election of labor councils to resolve matters of pay, discipline, training, and use of incentive funds. Only one-fourth of the membership could represent the interests of management, and the councils' decisions would be binding on the entire work force of the enterprise.

The reforms attempted to decentralize distribution. The law enabled enterprises to deal with the suppliers of their choice, either producers or wholesale outlets. Rationing would continue for only the scarcest producer goods, less than 4 percent of total industrial output in 1988. For the remainder, producers would be free to sell directly to users. Finally, the law permitted some enterprises to engage in foreign trade directly, on their own account, and to retain some of the foreign currency gains.

Tools of Control

By the 1980s, the planning system had become extremely complex. Maintaining control over plan implementation was a difficult task. The same administrative structure undertook both the planning itself and the oversight of plan fulfillment. The banking system, party units within lower-level organizations and enterprises, and any workers willing to take responsibility for bringing to light failings within their organizations provided assistance. Labor union activists also helped supervise performance at the enterprise level and solicited support for plan fulfillment.

In addition to exercising this direct control, planners and policy makers used the budget to influence the economy. The bulk of the revenues for the budget came from levies on the profits of enterprises and from an indirect tax on consumer goods. These tax levies could be readily altered to support changing plan priorities, particularly because the government produced no long-term budgets, only yearly ones. The regime distributed budget funds according to priorities that reflected the goals of the economic plans. Unlike state budgets in the West, the Soviet budget had a consolidated format for all levels of the government. Traditionally, the budget also had included most of the investment activity carried on within the economy. Reforms of the 1980s promised to alter the situation somewhat, however; the Law on State Enterprises (Associations) called upon enterprises to use their own profits as major sources of investment (see Reforming the Planning System, this ch.).

According to official Soviet sources, primary expenditures in the 1985 budget were grants for economic purposes (56 percent of the budget); funds for social and cultural services (32.5 percent); defense spending (4.9 percent); and administrative costs (0.8 percent). A small surplus remained (typical of Soviet budgets, according to published data). Western analysts considered these statistics unreliable;

most Western observers believed the defense budget's share was far greater than official figures suggested. Furthermore, Soviet definitions of various economic measurements differed markedly from Western concepts (for example, the use of net material product to measure output).

The government's pricing policy acted as another control mechanism. These prices provided a basis for calculating expenses and receipts, making possible assessment of outputs. The regime also used manipulation of prices to achieve certain social goals, such as encouragement of public transportation or dissemination of cultural values through low-priced books, journals, and recreational and cultural events.

Over the years, this centralized system had produced prices with little relationship either to the real costs of the products or to their price on the world market. For several decades, the government kept the price of basic goods, such as essential foods, housing, and transportation, artificially low, regardless of actual production costs. As agricultural costs had increased, for example, subsidies to the agricultural sector had grown, but retail prices remained stable. Only prices for luxury goods had risen, particularly during the price overhauls of 1965 and 1982.

The *Basic Provisions* passed by the Supreme Soviet called for thorough reform of the price structure by 1990, in time for use in the Thirteenth Five-Year Plan (1991–95). This price reform was more extensive than previous reforms, affecting both wholesale and retail prices. In the future, central authorities would establish far fewer prices, although all prices would still be closely monitored. Plans for reform provoked public controversy because the changes would end subsidies for many common items, such as meat, milk, fuel, and housing. Authorities promised a thorough public discussion of retail price changes and gave assurances that the living standards of workers would not decline.

Like prices, wages were a flexible tool by means of which the government influenced the economic scene. Until 1931 the regime attempted to enforce an egalitarian wage structure. Policy concerning wage differentials had fluctuated in later years, however. In some periods, ideology and egalitarianism were emphasized, whereas at other times the government used rewards and incentives. Beginning in 1956, when it established a minimum wage, the government made a concerted effort to improve the wages of those in the lower-paid categories of work and to lessen differences among workers. With the reforms of the 1980s, however, wage differentials were again increasing, with high-quality technical, executive, and professional skills being favored in the wage structure.

Modern apartment building, Frunze, Kirgiz Republic
Courtesy Jimmy Pritchard

Precise information concerning wages, including the level of the minimum wage, was not publicly available in the late 1980s. Western analysts did not agree on the size of wage differentials, although these differences were generally considered to be smaller than was the case in the West. According to Western estimates, however, important party and government personages received as much as five times the average salary. Outstanding scientists and selected intellectuals also prospered.

The average worker received fringe benefits totaling about 30 percent above and beyond his or her salary. These benefits included free education and health care, paid vacations, and other government-subsidized services. In addition to wages, the regime used other incentives, such as cash bonuses paid to both individuals and groups of workers and "socialist competitions," to spur the work force on to greater efforts.

Economic Policy

Socialist theory provides no practical guidelines or objective criteria for determining priorities for the various economic sectors and ensuring balanced growth of the entire economy. The direction of economic development depends upon decisions made by planners on the basis of their evaluation of the country's needs, taking

471

into account political, military, and other noneconomic considerations.

Past Priorities

The Bolsheviks (see Glossary), who assumed power in late 1917, sought to mold a socialist society from the ruins of old tsarist Russia. This goal was ambitious and somewhat vague; Karl Marx and Friedrich Engels, who developed Marxism (see Glossary), provided no blueprints for specific economic policies and targets. Chaotic conditions produced by World War I and subsequent struggles during the Civil War (1918–21) made pursuit of coherent policies difficult in any case. The economic policies initially adopted by the regime were a mixture of principle and expedience.

Soon after taking power, the regime published decrees nationalizing the land, most industry (all enterprises employing more than five workers), foreign trade, and banking. At the same time, for tactical reasons, the government acquiesced in the peasants' seizure of land, but the new leaders considered the resulting fragmented parcels of privately owned land to be inefficient.

Beginning in 1918, the government made vigorous but somewhat haphazard efforts to shape and control the country's economy under a policy of war communism (see Glossary). But in 1920, agricultural output had attained only half its prewar level, foreign trade had virtually ceased, and industrial production had fallen to a small fraction of its prewar quantity. Such factors as the disastrous harvest of 1920, major military actions and expenditures by the Red Army, and general wartime destruction and upheaval exacerbated the economy's problems.

In 1921 Vladimir I. Lenin called a temporary retreat from application of the ideological requirements of Marxist doctrine. His new approach, called the New Economic Policy (NEP), permitted some private enterprise, especially in agriculture, light industry, services, and internal trade, to restore prewar economic strength. The nationalization of heavy industry, transportation, foreign trade, and banking that had occurred under war communism remained in effect.

In the late 1920s, Stalin abandoned NEP in favor of centralized planning, which was modeled on a project sponsored by Lenin in the early 1920s that had greatly increased the generation of electricity. Stalin sought to rapidly transform the Soviet Union from a predominantly agricultural country into a modern industrial power. He and other leaders argued that by becoming a strong centrally planned industrial power, the country could protect itself militarily from hostile outside intervention and economically from

the booms and slumps characteristic of capitalism (see Industrialization and Collectivization, ch. 2).

The First Five-Year Plan (1928–32) focused rather narrowly upon
expansion of heavy industry and collectivization of agriculture. Stalin's decision to carry out rapid industrialization made capital-
intensive techniques necessary. International loans to build the economy were unavailable, both because the new government had
repudiated the international debts of the tsarist regime and because
industrialized countries, the potential lenders, were themselves cop-
ing with the onset of the Great Depression in the early 1930s. Stalin chose to fund the industrialization effort through internal savings
and investment. He singled out the agricultural sector in particular as a source of capital accumulation.

The First Five-Year Plan called for collectivization of agriculture to ensure the adequacy and dependability of food supplies for
the growing industrial sector and the efficient use of agricultural
labor to free labor power for the industrialization effort. The regime also expected collectivization to lead to an overall increase
in agricultural production. In fact, forced collectivization resulted
in much hardship for the rural population and lower productivity.
By 1932 about 60 percent of peasant households had joined state
farms or collective farms. During the same period, however, total
agricultural output declined by 23 percent, according to official
statistics. Heavy industry exceeded its targets in many areas during the plan period. But other industries, such as chemicals, textiles, and housing and consumer goods and services, performed
poorly. Consumption per person dropped, contrary to the planned
rates of consumption.

The Second Five-Year Plan (1933–37) continued the primary
emphasis on heavy industry. By the late 1930s, however, collectivized farms were performing somewhat better (after reaching a
nadir during the period 1931–34). In 1935 a new law permitted
individual peasants to have private plots, the produce of which they
could sell on the open market. According to official statistics, during the Second Five-Year Plan gross agricultural production increased by just under 54 percent. In contrast, gross industrial
production more than doubled.

The Third Five-Year Plan (1938–41) projected further rapid industrial growth. The government soon altered the plan, however,
in an attempt to meet the growing danger of war, devoting increasing amounts of resources to armaments. When the country
went to war with Finland (1939–40), serious disruptions occurred
in the Soviet transportation system. Nonetheless, during these years
the economy benefited from the absorption of Estonia, Latvia,

Lithuania, Bessarabia, and the eastern part of Poland and from the growing trade with Germany that resulted from the 1939 Nazi-Soviet Nonaggression Pact (see Glossary; Prelude to War, ch. 2).

After the German invasion of 1941, damage to the economy in both human and material terms was devastating. The regime virtually abandoned the Third Five-Year Plan as it sought to mobilize human and material resources for the war effort. During World War II, an increasing proportion of products and materials were allocated centrally, and Gosplan took over more of the balancing and allocation plans. Wartime economic plans did not officially replace the traditional planning process but were simply superimposed as needed to cover activities and goods essential to the war effort (see The Great Patriotic War, ch. 2).

The Fourth Five-Year Plan began in 1945. During the early years of the period, attention focused on repair and rebuilding, with minimal construction of new facilities. Repair work proceeded briskly, with spectacular results. The country received no substantial aid for postwar reconstruction, Stalin having refused to consider proposals for participation in the Marshall Plan (see Glossary) in 1947. Hungary, Bulgaria, Romania, and especially defeated Germany made reparations payments to the Soviet Union, however, consisting in large part of equipment and industrial materials. Entire German factories and their workers were brought to the Soviet Union to train Soviet citizens in specialized work processes. Although the government never published definitive statistics, an authoritative Western assessment estimated the value of reparations at an average of 5 billion rubles per year between 1945 and 1956. The exertions of the country's inhabitants, however, coupled with ambitious economic strategies, proved most crucial for the recovery.

During the war years, the government had transferred substantial numbers of industrial enterprises from threatened western areas to Asian regions of the country. After the war, these facilities remained at their new sites as part of an effort to promote economic development. These locations had the advantage of being near raw materials and energy sources. The government also deemed it strategically sound to have the important installations of the country distributed among several regions.

Like earlier plans, the Fourth Five-Year Plan stressed heavy industry and transportation. The economy met most of the targets in heavy industry. The performance of agriculture again lagged behind industry. Western observers believed that factors in agriculture's poor performance included a paucity of investment, enforcement of a strict quota system for delivery of agricultural products to the state, and tenuous linkage between wages and production, which deprived farmers of incentives. Housing construction, community services, and other consumer items also lagged noticeably. During the final years of the plan, Stalin launched several grandiose projects, including building canals and hydroelectric plants and establishing tree plantations in the Armenian, Azerbaydzhan, Georgian, and Ukrainian republics and in the Volga River area of the Russian Republic to shield land from drying winds. Collectively, these efforts were referred to as "the Stalin plan for the transformation of nature."

Throughout the Stalin era, the pace of industrial growth was forced. On those occasions when shortages developed in heavy industry and endangered plan fulfillment, the government simply shifted resources from agriculture, light industry, and other sectors. The situation of the consumer improved little during the Stalin years as a whole. Major declines in real household consumption occurred during the early 1930s and in the war years. Although living standards had rebounded after reaching a low point at the end of World War II, by 1950 real household consumption had climbed to a level only one-tenth higher than that of 1928. Judged by modern West European standards, the clothing, housing, social services, and diet of the people left much to be desired.

Although Stalin died in 1953, the Fifth Five-Year Plan (1951–55) as a whole reflected his preoccupation with heavy industry and transportation, the more so because no single leader firmly controlled policy after Stalin's death (see Collective Leadership and the Rise of Khrushchev, ch. 2). In many respects, economic performance pleased the leadership during the period. According to government statistics (considered by Western observers to be somewhat inflated), the economy met most growth targets, despite the allocation of resources to rearmament during the Korean War (1950–53). National income increased 71 percent during the plan period. As in previous plans, heavy industry received a major share of investment funds. During the final years of the Fifth Five-Year Plan, however, party leaders began to express concern about the dearth of consumer goods, housing, and services, as they reassessed traditional priorities. The new prime minister, Georgii M. Malenkov, sponsored a revision of the Fifth Five-Year Plan, reducing expenditures for heavy industry and the military somewhat in order to satisfy consumer demand. The newly appointed first secretary (see Glossary) of the party, Khrushchev, launched a program to bring under cultivation extensive tracts of virgin land in southwestern Siberia and the Kazakh Republic to bolster fodder and livestock production. Although Malenkov lost his position as prime minister in 1955, largely as a result of opposition to his economic policies, the austere approach of the Stalin era was never revived.

An ambitious Sixth Five-Year Plan was launched in 1956. After initial revision, prompted at least in part by political considerations, the regime abandoned the plan in 1957 to make way for a seven-year plan (subsequently reduced to a five-year plan) that focused particularly on coal and oil production and the chemical industry. Khrushchev, who became principal leader after 1956, took particular interest in these areas of production. The seven-year plan provided substantial investment funds—over 40 percent of the total—for the eastern areas of the country. Khrushchev also sponsored reforms to encourage production on the private plots of collective farmers.

During the seven-year plan, industrial progress was substantial, and production of consumer durables also grew. The national income increased 58 percent, according to official statistics. Gross industrial production rose by 84 percent, with producer goods up 96 percent and consumer goods up 60 percent. Growth rates slowed noticeably during the final years of the plan, however. Party leaders blamed Khrushchev's bungling efforts to reform the centralized planning system and his tendency to overemphasize programs in one economic sector (such as his favorite, the chemical industry) at the expense of other sectors (see Reforming the Planning System, this ch.). Agriculture's performance proved disappointing in the 1960s; adverse weather in 1963 and 1965, as well as Khrushchev's interference and policy reversals, which confused and discouraged the peasants' work on their private plots, were contributing factors. Khrushchev's economic policies were a significant, although not sole, reason for his dismissal in October 1964.

The Eighth Five-Year Plan (1966–70), under the leadership of Khrushchev's successor as party head, Brezhnev, chalked up respectable growth statistics: national income increased 41 percent and industrial production 50 percent, according to government statistics. Growth in producer goods (51 percent) outpaced that in consumer goods (49 percent) only slightly, reflecting planners' growing concern about the plight of consumers. During the late 1960s, Brezhnev raised procurement prices for agricultural products, while holding constant retail prices for consumers. Agriculture thus became a net burden on the rest of the economy. Although production increased, the sector's performance remained unsatisfactory. The country had to import increasing amounts of grain from the West.

In the Ninth Five-Year Plan (1971–75), a slowdown in virtually all sectors became apparent (see The Economy, ch. 2). National

income grew only 28 percent during the period, and gross industrial production increased by 43 percent. The 37 percent growth
rate for the production of consumer goods was well below the
planned target of 45.6 percent. Problems in agriculture grew more
acute during the period. The gap between supply and demand increased, especially for fodder.

Results for the Tenth Five-Year Plan (1976–80) were even more
disappointing. National income increased only 20 percent and gross
industrial production only 24 percent. The production of consumer
goods grew a meager 21 percent. Western observers rated the
growth of the country's gross national product (GNP—see Glossary) at less than 2 percent in the late 1970s.

For Soviet leaders, the modest growth rates were a perplexing
problem. The ability to maintain impressive growth rates while
providing full employment and economic security for citizens and
an equitable distribution of wealth had always been one area in
which supporters of the Soviet system had argued that it was superior. Soviet leaders could point to many achievements; by virtually any standard, the gap between the Soviet economy and the
economies of other major industrialized powers had narrowed during the years of Soviet rule. Throughout the early decades of the
economy's development, plans had emphasized large, quick additions of labor, capital, and materials to achieve rapid, "extensive"
growth.

By the 1970s, however, prospects for extensive growth were limited. During the 1960s, the Soviet Union had shown the fastest
growth in employment of all major industrial countries, and the
Soviet Union together with Japan had boasted the most rapid
growth of fixed capital stock. Yet Soviet growth rates in productivity of both labor and capital had been the lowest. In the 1970s,
the labor force grew more slowly. Drawing on surplus rural labor
was no longer possible, and the participation of women in the work
force was already extensive. Furthermore, the natural resources
required for extensive growth lay in areas increasingly difficult,
and expensive, to reach. In the less-developed eastern regions of
the country, development costs exceeded those in the European
parts by 30 percent to 100 percent. In the more developed areas
of the country, the slow rate at which fixed assets were retired was
becoming a major problem; fixed assets remained in service on
average twice as long as in Western economies, reducing overall
productivity. Nevertheless, in the late 1970s some Western analysts
estimated that the Soviet Union had the world's second largest economy, and its GNP continued to grow in the 1980s (see table 31,
Appendix A).

Serious imbalances characterized the economy, however, and the Soviet Union lagged behind most Western industrialized nations in the production of consumer goods and services. A stated goal of Soviet policy had always been to raise the material living standards of the people. Considerable progress had been made; according to Western estimates (less flattering than Soviet), from 1950 and 1980 real per capita consumption increased 300 percent. The country's leaders had devoted the bulk of the available resources to heavy industry, however, particularly to "production of the means of production." Levels of consumption remained below those of major capitalist countries and most of the socialist countries of Eastern Europe. By the late 1970s, policy makers had recognized the need to improve productivity by emphasizing quality factors, efficiency, and advanced technology and tapping "hidden production reserves" in the economy.

Concern about productivity characterized the Eleventh Five-Year Plan (1981–85). The targets were rather modest, and planners reduced even those after the first year of the period. Achievements remained below target. The plan period as a whole produced a modest growth rate of 3 to 4 percent per year, according to official statistics. National income increased only 17 percent. Total industrial output grew by 20 percent, with the production of consumer goods increasing at a marginally higher rate than producer goods. Agricultural output registered a meager 11.6 percent gain.

The Twelfth Five-Year Plan, 1986–90

When Gorbachev attained power in 1985, most Western analysts were convinced that Soviet economic performance would not improve significantly during the remainder of the 1980s. "Intensification" alone seemed unlikely to yield important immediate results. Gorbachev tackled the country's economic problems energetically, however, declaring that the economy had entered a "pre-crisis" stage. The leadership and the press acknowledged shortcomings in the economy with a new frankness.

Restating the aims of earlier intensification efforts, the *Basic Directions for the Economic and Social Development of the USSR for 1986–1990 and for the Period to the Year 2000* declared the principal tasks of the five-year plan period to be "to enhance the pace and efficiency of economic development by accelerating scientific and technical progress, retooling and adapting production, intensively using existing production potential, and improving the managerial system and accounting mechanism, and, on this basis, to further raise the standard of living of the Soviet people." A major part of the planned increase in output for the 1986–90 period was to result from the

Privately owned café, Moscow
Courtesy Irene Steckler

introduction of new machinery to replace unskilled labor. New,
advanced technologies, such as microprocessors, robots, and various computers, would automate and mechanize production. Obsolete equipment was to be retired at an accelerated rate. Industrial
operations requiring high energy inputs would be located close to
energy sources, and increasing numbers of workplaces would be
in regions with the requisite manpower resources. Economic development of Siberia and the Soviet Far East would continue to
receive special attention.

Gorbachev tackled the problem of laxness in the workplace and
low worker productivity (or, as he phrased it, the "human factor")
with great vigor. This attention to individual productivity and discipline resulted in the demotion or dismissal of influential older
officials who had proved to be corrupt or ineffective. Gorbachev
called for improved motivation among rank-and-file workers and
launched a vigorous antialcohol campaign (also a priority under
Andropov).

At the Central Committee plenum in January 1987, Gorbachev
demanded a fundamental reassessment of the role of the government in Soviet society. His economic reform program was sweeping, encompassing an array of changes. For example, it created
a new finance system through which factories would obtain loans

479

at interest, and it provided for the competitive election of managers (see Reforming the Planning System, this ch.). These changes proceeded from Gorbachev's conviction that a major weakness in the economy was the extreme centralization of economic decision making, inappropriate under modern conditions. According to Abel Aganbegian, an eminent Soviet economist and the principal scholarly spokesman for many of Gorbachev's policies, the Soviet Union was facing a critical decision: "Either we implement radical reform in management and free driving forces, or we follow an evolutionary line of slow evolution and gradual improvement. If we follow the second direction, . . . we will not achieve our goals." The country was entering "a truly new period of restructuring, a period of cardinal breakthroughs," he said, at the same time stressing the leadership's continuing commitment to socialism.

In one of his most controversial policy decisions, Gorbachev moved to encourage private economic activities and cooperative ventures. The action had clear limits, however. It established a progressive tax on profits, and regulations limited participation mainly to students, retired persons, and housewives. Full-time workers could devote only their leisure hours to private activities. Cooperatives that involved at least three people could engage in a broad range of consumer-oriented activities: using private automobiles as taxis, opening private restaurants, offering private medical care, repairing automobiles or appliances, binding books, and tailoring. In addition, the reform encouraged state enterprises to contract with private individuals for certain services. Other regulations gave official approval to the activities of profit-oriented contract brigades. These brigades consisted of groups of workers in an enterprise or collective farm who joined together to make an internal contract with management for performance of specific tasks, receiving compensation in a lump sum that the brigade itself distributed as it saw fit. Additional decrees specified types of activities that remained illegal (those involving "unearned income") and established strict penalties for violators. The new regulations legitimized major portions of the second economy and permitted their expansion. No doubt authorities hoped that the consuming public would reap immediate, tangible benefits from the changes. Authorities also expected these policies to encourage individuals who were still operating illegally to abide by the new, more lenient regulations.

In keeping with Gorbachev's ambitious reform policies, the specific targets of the Twelfth Five-Year Plan (1986–90) were challenging. The targets posited an average growth rate in national income of about 4 percent yearly. To reach this goal, increases in labor productivity were to average 4 percent annually, a rate that had not been sustained on a regular basis since the early 1970s. The ratio of expenditure on material inputs and energy to national income was to decrease by 4 to 5 percent in the plan period. Similar savings were projected for other aspects of the economy.

The plan stressed technical progress. Machine-building output was to increase by 40 to 45 percent during the five-year period. Those sectors involved in high technology were to grow faster than industry as a whole. The production of computers, for example, was to increase 2.4 times during the plan period. Growth in production of primary energy would accelerate during the period, averaging 3.6 percent per year, compared with 2.6 percent actual growth per year for 1981–85. The plan called for major growth in nuclear power capacity. (The Chernobyl' accident of 1986 did not alter these plans.)

Capital investment was to grow by 23.6 percent, whereas under the Eleventh Five-Year Plan the growth rate had been only 15.4 percent. Roughly half of the funds would be used for the retooling necessary for intensification. The previous plan had earmarked 38 percent for this purpose. Agriculture would receive large investments as well.

The plan called for a relatively modest improvement in the standard of living. The share of total investment in services was to rise only slightly, although the proportion of the labor force employed in services would continue to grow.

The regime also outlined very ambitious guidelines for the fifteen-year period beginning in 1986. The guidelines called for a 5 percent yearly growth in national income; national income was projected to double by the year 2000. Labor productivity would grow by 6.5 to 7.4 percent per year during the 1990s. Projected modernization of the workplace would release 20 million people from unskilled work by the year 2000. Plans called for increasingly efficient use of fuels, energy, raw materials, metal, and other materials. The guidelines singled out the provision of ''practically every Soviet family'' with separate housing by the beginning of the twenty-first century as a special, high-priority task.

Results of the first year of the Twelfth Five-Year Plan, 1986, were encouraging in many respects. The industrial growth rate was below target but still respectable at just above 3 percent. Agriculture made a good showing. During 1987, however, GNP grew by less than 1 percent, according to Western calculations, and industrial production grew a mere 1.5 percent. Some problems were the result of harsh weather and traditional supply bottlenecks. In addition, improvements in quality called for by Gorbachev proved difficult to realize; in 1987, when the government introduced a new inspection system for output at a number of industrial enterprises, rejection rates were high, especially for machinery.

Many of Gorbachev's reforms that immediately affected the ordinary working person—such as demands for harder work, more rigid quality controls, better discipline, and restraints on traditionally high alcohol consumption—were unlikely to please the public, particularly since the rewards and payoffs of most changes were likely to be several years away. As the Nineteenth Party Conference of 1988 demonstrated, party leaders continued to debate the pace and the degree of change. Uncertainty about the extent and permanence of reform was bound to create some disarray within the economy, at least for the short term. Western analysts did not expect Gorbachev's entire program to succeed, particularly given the lackluster performance of the economy during the second year of the Twelfth Five-Year Plan. The meager results of past reform attempts offered few grounds for optimism. But most observers believed that at least a portion of the reforms would be effective. The result was almost certain to benefit the economy.

* * *

The economic reforms of the mid-1980s have attracted the attention of many Western observers. As a result, English-language sources of information about the new measures are plentiful. An especially useful compendium of reports about the changes is *Gorbachev's Economic Plans,* produced by the United States Congress. An earlier collection of reports submitted to the United States Congress, entitled *The Soviet Economy in the 1980s,* remains useful. Valuable analyses of the "traditional," pre-reform Soviet economy, still essential for an understanding of the nature and extent of the reforms of the mid- and late 1980s, may be found in *The Soviet Economy,* edited by Abram Bergson and Herbert S. Levine, and in *Modern Soviet Economic Performance* by Trevor Buck and John Cole. For ongoing observation and commentary on the changing economic scene, the interested reader may consult current issues of the periodicals *Soviet Studies* and *Soviet Economy* as well as relevant issues of the Joint Publications Research Service. For earlier development of the Soviet economy, standard works such as Maurice Dobb's *Soviet Economic Development since 1917* and Alec Nove's *An Economic History of the U.S.S.R.* remain indispensable. (For further information and complete citations, see Bibliography.)

Chapter 12. Industry

Aspects of industry

SINCE THE BOLSHEVIK REVOLUTION of 1917, industry has been officially the most important economic activity in the Soviet Union and a critical indicator of its standing among the nations of the world. Compared with Western countries, a very high percentage of the Soviet population works in the production of material goods. The Communist Party of the Soviet Union (CPSU) considers constant growth in heavy industry vital for national security, and its policy has achieved several periods of spectacular growth. However, industrial growth has been uneven, with notable failures in light and consumer industries, and impressive statistics have often concealed failures in individual branches. And, in the late 1980s, reliable statistics continued to be unavailable in some areas and unreliable in others.

The Soviet Union is blessed with more essential industrial resources than any other nation. Using the most accessible of those materials, industries such as textiles and metallurgy have thrived since the 1600s. Large industrial centers developed almost exclusively in the European part of the country. Examples of such centers are the Donbass (see Glossary), the Moscow industrial area, and the Kursk and Magnitogorsk metallurgical centers, all of which are still in full operation. But intense industrial activity eventually exhausted the most accessible resource materials. In the late twentieth century, reserves have been tapped in the adjacent regions, especially the oil and gas fields of western Siberia. Most of the remaining reserves are outside the European sector of the country, presenting planners with the formidable task of bridging thousands of kilometers to unite raw materials, labor, energy, and centers of consumption. The urgency of industrial location decisions has grown as production quotas have risen in every new planning period. Moreover, the nature and location of the Soviet labor force presents another serious problem for planners.

Joseph V. Stalin's highly centralized industrial management system survived into the late 1980s. Numerous councils, bureaus, and committees in Moscow traditionally approved details of industrial policies. The slow reaction time of such a system was adequate for the gradual modernization of the 1950s, but the system fell behind the faster pace of high-technology advancement that began in the 1960s. Soviet policy has consistently called for "modernization" of industry and use of the most advanced automated equipment—especially because of the military significance of high technology.

Although policy programs identified automation as critical to all Soviet industry, the civilian sector generally has lagged in the modernization campaign. The priority given to the military-industrial sector, however, not only prevented the growth that planners envisioned but also caused the serious slowdown that began around 1970. In a massive effort to restructure the system under *perestroika* (see Glossary), planners have sought ways to speed decision making to meet immediate industrial needs by finding short-cuts through the ponderous industrial bureaucracy.

Another strain on the industrial system has been the commitment to improving production of consumer goods. Nikita S. Khrushchev, first secretary (see Glossary) of the CPSU in the late 1950s and early 1960s, initially tried to temper the Stalinist priority of heavy industry. Khrushchev's idea was followed with varying degrees of enthusiasm; it became more binding as consumers learned about Western standards of living and as officials began stating the goal more forcefully in the 1980s.

Development of Soviet Industry

Russian industrial activity began before 1700, although it was limited to metal-working and textile factories located on feudal estates and required some help from English and Dutch advisers. The largest industrial concerns of the seventeenth century were owned by the Stroganov trading family. In the first quarter of the eighteenth century, Peter the Great applied Western technology more widely to establish larger textile, metallurgical, and naval plants for his military ventures. This first centralized plan for Russian industrialization built some of the largest, best-equipped factories of the time, using mostly forced peasant labor. After a decline in the middle of the eighteenth century, Russian industry received another injection of Western ideas and centralized organization under Catherine the Great. Under Catherine, Russia's iron industry became the largest in the world.

Another major stage in Russian industry began with the emancipation of the serfs in 1861, creating what would eventually become a large industrial labor force. When he became tsar in 1881, Alexander III used this resource in a new, large-scale industrialization program aimed at finally changing Russia from a primarily agricultural country into a modern industrial nation. Lasting until 1914, the program depended on massive assistance from western Europe. From 1881 to 1914, the greatest expansion occurred in textiles, coal, and metallurgy, centered in the Moscow area and the present-day Ukrainian Republic (see fig. 1). But compared with the West, major industrial gaps remained throughout the prerevolutionary period.

Beginning in 1904, industry was diverted and disrupted by foreign wars, strikes, revolutions, and civil war. After the Civil War (1918–21), the victorious Bolsheviks (see Glossary) fully nationalized industry; at that point, industrial production was 13 percent of the 1913 level. To restart the economy, in 1921 Vladimir I. Lenin introduced the New Economic Policy (NEP—see Glossary), which returned light industry to private enterprise but retained government control over heavy industry. By 1927 NEP had returned many industries to their prewar levels. Under Stalin, the First Five-Year Plan began in 1928. This planning system brought spectacular industrial growth, especially in capital investment. More important, it laid the foundation for centralized industrial planning, which continued into the late 1980s. Heavy industry received much greater investment than light industry throughout the Stalin period. Although occasional plans emphasized consumer goods more strongly, considerations of national security usually militated against such changes.

Industry was again diverted and displaced by World War II, and many enterprises moved permanently eastward, into or beyond the Ural Mountains. Postwar recovery was rapid as a result of the massive application of manpower and funds. Heavy industry again grew rapidly through the 1960s, especially in fuel and energy branches. But this growth was followed by a prolonged slowdown beginning in the late 1960s. Successive five-year plans resulted in no substantial improvement in the growth rate of industrial production (see table 32, Appendix A). Policy makers began reviewing the usefulness of centralized planning in a time of advanced, fast-moving technology. By 1986 General Secretary Mikhail S. Gorbachev was making radical suggestions for restructuring the industrial system.

Industrial Resources

Although plentiful raw materials and labor are available to Soviet industrial planners, geographic factors are especially important in determining how these resources are used. Because the main resources are available in an uneven pattern, industrial policy has produced uneven results. Innovative recombination of labor, fuels, and other raw materials has had some success but has also met substantial resistance.

Raw Materials

In 1980 the Soviet Union produced about 20 percent of total world industrial output, and it led the world in producing oil, cast iron, steel, coke, mineral fertilizers, locomotives, tractors, and cement. This leadership was based on self-sufficiency in nearly all major industrial raw materials, including iron ore, most nonferrous metals, solid and liquid fuels, water power, and minerals. The country has at least some reserves of every industrially valuable nonfuel mineral, although tin, tungsten, and mercury are present only in small quantities and bauxite is imported for the aluminum industry. Despite these material advantages, the country's geography hinders exploitation. Large portions of the remaining coal, oil, natural gas, metal ores, and minerals are located in inaccessible regions with hostile climates.

Geographic Location Factors

Historically, Soviet industry has been concentrated in the European sector, where intensive development has depleted critical resources. Examples of severely reduced resources in the older industrial regions are the Krivoy Rog and Magnitogorsk iron deposits and the Donbass coal area, upon which major industrial complexes were built. Long before the German invasion of 1941, Soviet industrial policy looked eastward into Siberia and Soviet Central Asia to expand the country's material base. According to a 1977 Soviet study, 90 percent of remaining energy resources (fuels and water power) are east of the Urals; however, 80 percent of industry and nearly 80 percent of all energy requirements are in the European part of the Soviet Union. Since 1917 an official policy goal has been to bring all Soviet regions to a similar level of economic development. Periodically, leaders have proclaimed the full achievement of this goal. But in a country of extremely diverse climates, nationalities, and natural resources, such equality remains only a theoretical concept. Industrial expansion has meant finding ways to join raw materials, power, labor, and transportation at the same place and in suitable proportions. For example, many eastern regions have abundant resources, but the labor supply either is too small or is culturally disinclined to work in modern industry (see Distribution and Density, ch. 3).

The Territorial Production Complexes and Geographic Expansion

One Soviet answer to the problem of the location of industry has been the concept of the territorial production complex, which groups industries to efficiently share materials, energy, machinery, and labor. Although plans call for such complexes (see Glossary) in all parts of the Soviet Union, in the late 1980s the most fully developed examples were chiefly to the east of the Urals or in the Far North; many were in remote areas of Siberia or the Soviet Far

*Park in Moscow with a permanent exhibition praising the
economic achievements of the Soviet people*
Courtesy Irene Steckler

East. The complexes vary in size and specialization, but most are
based near cheap local fuel or a hydroelectric power source. An
example is the South Yakut complex, halfway between Lake Baykal
and the Pacific Ocean. This industrial center is based on rich
deposits of iron and coking coal, the key resources for metallurgy.
Oil and natural gas deposits exist not far to the north, and the area
is connected with the Trans-Siberian Railway and the Baikal-Amur
Main Line. An entirely new city, Neryungri, was built as an administrative center, and a number of auxiliary plants were designed
to make the complex self-sufficient and to support the iron- and
coal-mining operations. The temperature varies by 85°C from
winter to summer, the terrain is forbidding, and working conditions are hazardous. But considering that the alternative is many
separate, isolated industrial sites with the same conditions, the territorial production complex seems a rational approach to reach the
region's resources. Integrating several industries in a single complex requires cooperation among many top-level Soviet bureaucracies, but in the early 1980s the lack of such cooperation delayed
progress at centers such as the South Yakut complex.

Starting in the 1960s, the government pursued large-scale incentive programs to move workers into the three main Soviet

489

undeveloped regions: Siberia, Central Asia, and the Far East. Such programs justified bonuses for workers by saving the cost of transporting raw materials to the European sector. At the same time, some policy makers from other parts of the country had not supported redesignation of funds from their regions to the eastern projects. In 1986 the Siberian Development Program was launched for coordinated, systematic development of fuel and mineral resources through the year 2000. Despite specific plans, movement of Soviet labor to the undeveloped regions has generally fallen short of plans since the peak migration of World War II. Poor living and working conditions have caused "labor flight" from Siberian construction projects. By 1988 there were strong hints that intensified development would again be emphasized in the more accessible industrial centers west of the Urals and that more selective investment would be made in projects to the east and southeast of that boundary.

The Labor Force and Perestroika

The nature of the work force has a direct impact on industrial policy. In 1985 nearly 75 percent of the nonagricultural work force was making material goods, and that percentage was shrinking very slowly as nonmanufacturing service occupations expanded. The rate of the shift away from manufacturing actually was decreasing during the 1980s. Meanwhile, one-third of industrial workers remained in low-skilled, manual jobs through the 1980s, and slow population growth was limiting the growth of the work force. Nevertheless, significant groups of workers were better educated and more comfortable with mechanized and automated manufacturing than the previous generation. In the late 1980s, labor shortages were expected to stimulate faster automation of some industries. Official modernization plans called for eliminating 5 million manual jobs by the year 1990 and 20 million by the year 2000, and reductions were targeted for specific industries. Reductions in the labor force could not always be planned for areas where available labor was decreasing naturally. This situation meant that job elimination could bring unemployment in some places—especially since most of the jobs eliminated would be those requiring the least skill. Because unemployment theoretically cannot exist in a socialist (see Glossary) state, that prospect was a potentially traumatic repercussion of the effort at industrial streamlining.

Poor labor ethics have traditionally undermined Soviet industrial programs. Gorbachev's *perestroika* made individual productivity a major target in the drive to streamline industry in the late 1980s. But the goal met substantial resistance among ordinary workers because it called for pegging wages directly to productivity and eliminating guaranteed wage levels and bonuses.

Thus, the Soviet Union possessed a vast labor base that was very uneven in quality. In economic plans for the last decade of the twentieth century, planners placed top priority on redistributing all resources—human and material—to take advantage of their strengths. The drive for redistribution coincided with an attempt to streamline the organization of the industrial system.

Industrial Organization

Beginning with the First Five-Year Plan (1928–32), Soviet industry was directed by a complicated, centralized system that proved increasingly inflexible as its equipment base became more sophisticated. Major problems arose in allocation of resources between military and civilian sectors, centralized planning of diverse industries, and systemic changes that would make industry responsive to rapid technological developments.

The Complexes and the Ministries

In the late 1980s, industry was officially divided into seven industrial complexes, each complex (see Glossary) responsible for one or more sectors of production. The seven complexes, which were directly responsible to the Council of Ministers, were agro-industrial, chemicals and timber, construction, fuel and energy, machine building, light industry, and metallurgy. The Ministry of Light Industry was the only ministry in its complex and was intended as the foundation for a consumer industry complex, dubbed the "social complex" by the government. The remaining six complexes included several ministries to oversee one broad type of industry. For example, the fuel and energy complex included the all-union ministries of atomic power, coal, construction of petroleum and gas enterprises, the gas industry, the petroleum industry, and power and electrification. The ministry system included three types of organization: all-union (national level only), union-republic (national and republic levels), and republic (to run industry indigenous to a single republic). Ministries in the construction materials, light industry, nonferrous metallurgy, and timber complexes were in the union-republic ministry category. But machine building had all-union ministries because unified national policy and standards were considered critical in that field. Ministries with major military output fell outside this ministry structure, under the superministerial direction of the Military Industrial Commission. That body oversaw all stages of defense industry, from research

491

to production, plus the acquisition and application of foreign technology (see Military Industries and Production, ch. 18).

The Industrial Planning System

Industrial policy statements were issued by the CPSU at party congresses (see Glossary). A typical statement came from the Twenty-Seventh Party Congress in 1986: "In accelerating scientific and technical progress, a leading role is assigned to machine building, which must be raised to the highest technical level in the shortest possible time." In reaching such broad goals, the top planning level was the Council of Ministers, which represented the all-union ministries included in the seven industrial complexes. The council's decisions were passed to the State Planning Committee (Gosudarstvennyi planovyi komitet—Gosplan), which formulated specific programs to realize broad party goals. Then programs moved down through the bureaucracy to individual enterprises (see Glossary), and recommendations and changes were made along the way. The programs then reversed direction, returning to the Council of Ministers for final approval. The final planning form was the five-year plan, a concept originated by Stalin in 1928 (see The Twelfth Five-Year Plan, 1986–90, ch. 11; table 30, Appendix A).

After the First Five-Year Plan, planning was completely centralized in the all-union ministries. In day-to-day operations, this system consistently delayed interministry cooperation in such matters as equipment delivery and construction planning. An example was electric power plant construction. Planners relied on timely delivery of turbines from a machine plant, whose planners in turn relied on timely delivery of semifinished rolled and shaped metal pieces from a metallurgical combine (see Glossary). Any change in specifications or quantities required approval by all the ministries and intermediate planning bodies in the power, machine, and metallurgical industries—a formidable task under the best of circumstances.

Structural Reform of Industry

Perestroika called for wholesale revision of the industrial management system and decentralization of policy making in all industries. Elements of the management bureaucracy opposed such revision because it would place direct responsibility for poor performance and initiative on industry officials. Initial adjustment to the program was slow and uneven; in the late 1980s, tighter quality control cut production figures by eliminating substandard items. In mid-1988, eighteen months after *perestroika* had been introduced in major industries, official Soviet sources admitted that much of the program was not yet in place.

The Military-Industrial Complex

Growth in the Soviet economy slowed to 2 percent annually in the late 1970s, and it remained at about that level during the 1980s, after averaging 5 percent during the previous three decades. Because military supply remained the primary mission of industry, the military was protected from the overall slowdown. Thus, in 1988 the military share of the gross national product (GNP—see Glossary) had grown to an estimated 15 to 17 percent, up from its 12 to 14 percent share in 1970. The actual percentage of industrial resources allocated to military production has always been unclear because of Soviet secrecy about military budgets. Most military production came under the eighteen ministries of the machine-building and metal-working complex (MBMW), nine of which were primarily involved in making weapons or military matériel (see table 33, Appendix A).

Other "military-related" ministries sent a smaller percentage of their output to the military. Among their contributions were trucks (from the Ministry of Automotive and Agricultural Machine Building, under MBMW), tires and fuels (from the Ministry of Petroleum Refining and Petrochemical Industry, outside MBMW), and generators (from the Ministry of Power Machinery Building, under MBMW), plus any other items requested by the military. In overall control of this de facto structure was the Defense Council (see Glossary), which in the 1980s was chaired by the general secretary of the CPSU. Although the Council of Ministers nominally controlled all ministries, including those serving the military, military issues transcended that authority. In 1987 an estimated 450 research and development organizations were working exclusively on military projects. Among top-priority projects were a multiministerial laser program, generation of radio-frequency energy, and particle-beam research—all applicable to future battlefield weapons. In addition, about fifty major weapons design bureaus and thousands of plants were making military items exclusively. Such plants had first priority in resource allocation to ensure that production goals were met. Most defense plants were in the European part of the Soviet Union, were well dispersed, and had duplicate backup plants. Some major aircraft plants were beyond the Urals, in Irkutsk, Novosibirsk, Tashkent, Komsomol'sk-na-Amure, and Ulan-Ude.

In making military equipment, the primary goals were simplicity and reliability; parts were standardized and kept to a minimum.

New designs used as many existing parts as possible to maximize performance predictability. Because of these practices, the least experienced Soviet troops and troops of countries to which the equipment was sold could operate it. But the practices have also caused the Soviet military-industrial complex, despite having top priority, to suffer from outmoded capital equipment, much of which is left over from World War II. Western observers have suggested that the dated "keep-it-simple" philosophy has been a psychological obstacle to introducing the sophisticated production systems needed for high-technology military equipment.

Western experts have assumed that without substantial overall economic expansion, this huge military-industrial complex would remain a serious resource drain on civilian industry—although the degree of that drain has been difficult to establish. To ameliorate the situation, *perestroika* set a goal of sharply reducing the military share of MBMW allocations (estimated at 60 percent in 1987) during the Twelfth Five-Year Plan. Civilian MBMW ministries were to receive an 80 percent investment increase by 1992. And emphasis was shifting to technology sharing by military designers with their civilian counterparts—breaking down the isolation in which the two sectors have traditionally worked.

Industrial Research and Design

The Soviet Union has long recognized the importance of its domestic research and development system to make its industry competitive. Soviet research and development relies on a complex system of institutes, design bureaus, and individual plant research facilities to provide industry with advanced equipment and methodology (see Research, Development, and Production Organizations, ch. 16). A result of the system's complexity has been poor coordination both among research organizations and between research organizations and other industrial organizations. Bottlenecks existed because much research was classified and because Soviet information distribution systems, e.g., computers and copying machines, lagged far behind the West.

A barrier between theoretical and applied research also hindered the contribution of the scientific research institutes (*nauchno-issledovatel'skie instituty*—NIIs) to industry. Institutes under the Academy of Sciences (see Glossary), which emphasized theoretical research, often did not contribute their findings directly for practical application, and an institutional distrust has existed between scientists and industrial technicians. Newer organizational structures, such as scientific production associations (*nauchno-proizvodstvennye ob"edineniia*—NPOs), have combined research, design, and production facilities so that technical improvements will move into the production phase faster. This goal was an important part of *perestroika* in the late 1980s. It was especially critical in the machine-building industry, for which a central goal of the Twelfth Five-Year Plan was to shorten installation time of new industrial machines once they were designed.

Soviet industrial planning was aimed at being competitive with the West in both civilian and military industry. After years of lagging growth, by the mid-1980s authorities had recognized that the traditional Stalinist industrial system made such goals unreachable. But improvement of that system was problematic for several reasons. New emphasis on the civilian sector could not be allowed to jeopardize military production; research and development was never connected efficiently with industrial operations; the huge industrial bureaucracy contained vested interests at all levels; and personal responsibility and individual initiative were concepts alien to the Soviet Marxist-Leninist system. The most optimistic Western forecasters predicted gradual improvements in some areas, as opposed to the dramatic, irreversible changes suggested by the Soviet industrial doctrine of the late 1980s.

Machine Building and Metal Working

As the supplier of production machinery to all other branches of heavy industry, the machine-building and metal-working industry has stood at the center of modernization efforts, and its support of the military has been especially critical (see Industrial Organization, this ch.). But because of the systemic problems discussed earlier, in the late 1980s substantial inertia remained in machine building. Progress in one program was often negated by a bottleneck in another, and all industry felt the impact of this uneven performance.

The Structure and Status of the Machine-Building and Metal-Working Complex

In 1987 the machine-building industrial complex, one of the seven industrial complexes, included 300 branches and subbranches and a network of 700 research and planning organizations. Officially designated the machine-building and metal-working complex (MBMW), it was the most inclusive and varied industrial complex. Its three major types of products, were military hardware, consumer durables, and industrial machinery and equipment. In 1989 eighteen ministries were included, manufacturing a wide range of machinery; nine of the ministries chiefly produced military weapons or matériel. Ministries within MBMW often split the jurisdiction within a particular specialization. For example, although instrument manufacture fell mainly under MBMW's Ministry of Instrument Making, its Ministry of the Aviation Industry and Ministry of the Shipbuilding Industry controlled manufacture of the instruments they used in their products. The contributions of MBMW included machines for mining, agriculture, and road building; equipment for conventional and nuclear power plants; oil and gas drilling and pumping equipment; and metal-working machines for all branches, including the military. In the mid-1980s, restructuring in the machine industry was a central theme of *perestroika* because most industries needed to update their machine stock. Western studies in the 1980s showed that 40 to 60 percent of industrial production was earmarked for military uses. In the 1980s, government policy encouraged industry to buy domestic machinery to counter a frequent preference for more reliable foreign equipment. (A 1985 study by MBMW's Ministry of Heavy Machine Building said that 50 percent of that ministry's basic products did not meet operational requirements.) In the late 1970s and early 1980s, the German Democratic Republic (East Germany) sent half its machine exports to the Soviet Union. At the same time, Soviet machine exports fell behind machine imports, after exports had reached a peak in 1970.

The Planning and Investment Process of the Machine-Building and Metal-Working Complex

The Twelfth Five-Year Plan (1986–90) called for drastic production increases in the sectors producing instruments, machine tools, electrical equipment, chemicals, and agricultural machines. Fundamental investment changes were expected to raise machine production to new highs. Overall investment in the machine-building industry was to be 80 percent higher than in the Eleventh Five-Year Plan (1981–85). A crucial goal was to shorten the time between research breakthroughs and their industrial application, which had been a chronic bottleneck in the modernization of industry. Another goal of the Twelfth Five-Year Plan was to improve the quality of individual components and spare parts because their short service life was diverting too much metal to making replacement parts. In the mid-1980s, however, severe delivery delays continued for both spare parts and new machines ordered by various industries. *Perestroika* attempted to simplify the system and to fix responsibility for delays. As the largest consumer of steel in the country, MBMW had felt the impact of severe production problems in the metallurgy industry (see Metallurgy, this ch.). Automation was expected to add speed and precision to production lines. By

1987 nearly half of metal-cutting machine production was done with digital program control. New control complexes stressed microcomputers with high production capacity and low material requirements. Nevertheless, a 1987 Soviet study showed that 40 percent of the robots in machine plants were not working at all, and a 1986 study demonstrated that only 20 percent of the robots were providing the expected production advantages. A long-term (through the year 2000) cooperative program with the other members of the Council for Mutual Economic Assistance (Comecon) was expected to contribute new ideas for streamlining the Soviet machine-building industry (see Appendix B).

The Location of the Machine-Building Industry

Traditionally, the Soviet machine-building industries have been centered in the European part of the Soviet Union; large plants are located in Moscow, Leningrad, Khar'kov, Minsk, Gor'kiy, Saratov, and in cities in the Urals. In the 1980s, the industry was gradually adding major centers in the Kazakh Republic and other areas in Soviet Central Asia, Siberia, and the Soviet Far East. The instrument-building sector was more dispersed and had centers in Moscow, Leningrad, Kiev, Voronezh, Orel, Ryazan', Kazan', Gor'kiy, Riga, Minsk, Tbilisi, Chelyabinsk, Tomsk, and Frunze. Agricultural machines were produced near major crop areas. Examples of this concentration were Khar'kov in the Ukrainian Republic; Minsk in the Belorussian Republic; Lipetsk, Vladimir, Volgograd, and Chelyabinsk in the western Russian Republic; the Altai region in the eastern Russian Republic; and Pavlodar in the Kazakh Republic. Because low crop yield has been a chronic problem, the agricultural equipment industry has emphasized large mechanized tractor and harvester units that can cover vast, low-yield tracts economically.

The Automotive Industry

The Soviet automotive industry has developed on a much smaller scale than its United States counterpart. Although production grew rapidly during the 1970s and 1980s, the industry's close connection with the military made some production data inaccessible. From 1970 to 1979, automobile production grew by nearly 1 million units per year, and truck production grew by 250,000 per year. The production ratio of automobiles to trucks increased in that time from 0.7 to 1.7, indicating that more attention was being given to the consumer market.

Automobile production was concentrated in four facilities: the Volga (in Tol'yatti), Gor'kiy, Zaporozh'ye, and Likhachev

497

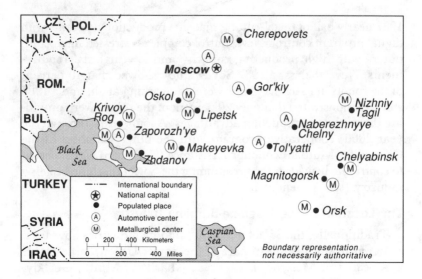

Figure 15. Automotive and Metallurgical Production Centers in the Western Soviet Union, 1988

(Moscow) plants (see fig. 15). The Volga plant was built in the late 1960s especially for passenger automobiles; by 1975 it was making half the Soviet total. The Likhachev and Gor'kiy plants, both in operation for more than fifty years, made automobiles and trucks. Truck production was less centralized, with plants in Kutaisi (Georgian Republic), the Urals, Tiraspol' (Moldavian Republic), Kremenchug (Ukrainian Republic), Minsk (Belorussian Republic), Mytishchi (Moscow area), and Naberezhnyye Chelny (eastern Russian Republic), the site of the large showpiece Kama plant built in the late 1970s. The Volga and Kama plants were located away from the established population centers; in both cases, new towns were built for transplanted workers. Long-term truck planning (through the year 2000) emphasized large capacity, fuel economy, and service life; the last two qualities were deficient in earlier models. The drive for fuel economy has encouraged the use of natural and liquefied gas. Heavy truck and trailer production was to occupy more than 40 percent of the truck industry by 1990, doubling tractor-trailer production. Vehicle parts plants were widely dispersed in the European sector of the country. Policy for the Soviet automotive industry has emphasized two divergent goals: increasing the supply of private automobiles as a symbol of attention to the consumer; and supporting heavy industry with improved equipment for heavy transport and material handling.

The Electronics Industry

Because of the drive for automation and modernization of production processes, the electronics industry increasingly supported many other industrial branches. Special emphasis was given to improving cooperation between electronics plants and the machine-building and metallurgy branches—a partnership severely hindered in many cases by the industrial bureaucracy. In official progress reports, all industries listed process automation and robotization as standards for efficiency and expansion, and conversion from manual processes has been a prime indicator of progress in heavy industry. At the same time, government policy has relied heavily on the electronics industry for televisions, recording equipment, and radios for the consumer market. None of those items came close to planned production quotas for 1987, however.

Beginning in the 1970s, the most important role of the electronics industry has been to supply lasers, optics, and computers and to perform research and development on other advanced equipment for weapons guidance, communications, and space systems. The importance of electronics for civilian industry has led to interministry research organizations that encourage the advanced military design sector to share technology with its civilian counterpart. Such an organization was called an interbranch scientific-technical complex (*mezhotraslevoi nauchno-tekhnicheskii kompleks—* MNTK). It united the research and production organizations of several ministries and had broad coordination control over the development of new technologies. Because of the military uses of Soviet electronics, the West has had incomplete specific data about it. In the early 1980s, an estimated 40 percent of Soviet electronics research projects had benefited substantially from the transfer of Western and Japanese technology. In the late 1980s, however, Soviet electronics trailed the West and Japan in most areas of applied electronics, although circuit design and systems engineering programs were comparable. The Soviet theoretical computer base was strong, but equipment and programming were below Western standards. Problems have been chronic in advanced fields such as ion implantation and microelectronics testing. The branches designated by Soviet planners as most critical in the 1980s were industrial robots and manipulators, computerized control systems for industrial machines, and semiconductors for computer circuits.

Metallurgy

Soviet industrial plans through the year 2000 have emphasized greater variety and higher quality in metals production to keep heavy industry competitive with the West. But the machinery and

499

production systems available to Soviet metallurgists in 1989 showed no signs of improving the inconsistent record the industry had established in meeting such goals. Following the Stalinist pattern, great success in some areas was hampered by breakdown in others. In the late 1980s, escape from this dilemma seemed no more likely than in earlier years.

Role of Metallurgy

Since the 1970s, the Soviet Union has led the world in the production of iron, steel, and rolled metals. In 1987 it produced about 162 million tons of steel, 114 million tons of rolled metal, and 20 million tons of steel pipe. Each of these figures was an increase of more than 2.5 times over those of 1960. Metallurgy has been the largest and fastest growing branch of Soviet industry, and metals supply remained vital to growth in virtually all other branches of industry. But yearly production increases were becoming more difficult because the cost of raw materials rose consistently in the 1980s, especially for metals such as molybdenum, nickel, magnesium, and rare earth metals, which were in increasing demand for high-quality steel alloys.

In the mid-1980s, the metallurgy industry was not meeting its goals for supplying high-quality finished metal to the manufacturing industries. Those industries were demanding higher-quality and stronger metals for new applications, such as high-pressure pipelines for oil and gas, high-capacity dump trucks and excavators, industrial buildings with large roof spans, corrosion-resistant pipe for the chemical industry, coated and treated rolled metals, and steel with high conductivity for electrical transformers. As military equipment became more sophisticated, it too required improved quality and performance from metal products. On the development side, advances in light-metal alloys using aluminum, magnesium, and titanium did provide materials for military aircraft and missiles that were among the best in the world.

Metallurgy Planning and Problems

Plans for the metallurgical industry for the 1990s stressed rebuilding older steel plants, vastly increasing the volume of continuous steel casting, and replacing open-hearth furnaces with oxygen or electric furnaces. In the period through the year 2000, a projected 52 percent of investment was to go for new equipment. This degree of investment would be a drastic turnaround because from 1981 to 1985 five times as much money was spent on equipment repair as on equipment purchase. Furthermore, to make highly pure steel, economical removal of sulfur is critical, but the scarcity of low-sulfur coking coal requires new purification technology. Although Soviet experts agreed that all these steps were necessary to enhance the variety and purity of ferrous metallurgy products, serious obstacles remained. Bottlenecks were chronic in overall administration, between research and production branches, and between the industry and its suppliers in the machine-building sector. Meanwhile, a shortage of hard currency (see Glossary) hindered the purchase of sophisticated metal-processing equipment from the West.

Bottlenecks have also affected the Donetsk metallurgical plant, where a heralded program installed new blast furnaces in the mid-1980s but where no auxiliary equipment arrived to run them as designed. In many cases, industry spokesmen have blamed the research community for neglecting practical applications in favor of theoretical projects. Whatever the causes, large-scale improvement of Soviet metallurgical technology was spotty rather than consistent during the 1980s.

Metallurgical Combine Locations and Major Producers

As production capacity has expanded, iron and steel production operations have consolidated in large-scale facilities, designated as combines. Among them was the Magnitogorsk metallurgical combine in the Urals, which in 1989 was the largest Soviet metallurgical combine. It produced nearly 16 million tons of metal annually. Long-term plans targeted Magnitogorsk for complete modernization of casting operations in the 1990s. Other important metallurgical centers in the Urals were at Chelyabinsk and Nizhniy Tagil. The Ukrainian Republic had major combines at Krivoy Rog, Zhdanov, Zaporozh'ye, and Makeyevka. The Cherepovets combine was north of Moscow, the Lipetsk and Oskol combines were south of Moscow, and the Orsk-Khalilovo combine was at the southern end of the Urals. The European sector was the traditional location of Soviet metallurgy because of available labor and materials. Newer metallurgical centers at Karaganda (in the Kazakh Republic) and the Kuzbass (see Glossary) were in the Asian part of the Soviet Union where coking coal was readily available. Nevertheless, metal-consuming industries and known iron ore reserves remained mainly west of the Urals, and major expansion of the metallurgy industry east of the Urals was considered unlikely in the near future.

Nonferrous Metals

In addition to the ferrous metal (iron and steel) centers, nonferrous metallurgy also provided vital support for heavy industry, while

501

undergoing technical innovation. The nonferrous branches had already expanded into ore-rich regions outside traditional industrial regions: copper metallurgy into the Kazakh Republic, the Caucasus, and Siberia; aluminum into the Kazakh Republic, south-central Siberia, and Soviet Central Asia; and nickel into eastern Siberia, the Urals, and the Kola Peninsula. The Soviet Union possesses abundant supplies of nonferrous metal ores, such as titanium, cobalt, chromium, nickel, and molybdenum, used in steel and iron alloys. Cobalt and nickel were specially targeted for expansion in the 1980s. Lead and zinc mining was projected to expand in the Kazakh Republic and other areas in Soviet Central Asia, Siberia, and the Soviet Far East.

Chemicals

The chemical industry received intensive investment in the five-year plans of the 1980s. The long-term goal of the chemical investment program was to increase its share of total national industrial production from the 1975 level of 6.9 percent to 8 percent by the year 2000. As defined by Soviet planners, major divisions of the industry were basic chemical products; fertilizers and pesticides; chemical fibers; plastics and synthetic resins; and detergents, paints, and synthetic rubber for making consumer products.

Plastics

A vital part of the chemical industry is polymers. The polymer industry has been centered in regions where petrochemical raw materials were processed: the Volga, Ural, and Central economic regions (see fig. 16). Among their other uses, polymers are intermediate materials in making plastics that can replace metals in machinery, construction materials, engines, and pipe. Soviet policy recognized that wider use of plastics would mean cheaper, lighter, and more durable products for many industries. Therefore, long-term plans called for nearly doubling the contribution of synthetic resins and plastics to the construction industry by the year 2000. However, the Twelfth Five-Year Plan also scheduled a 50 percent increase in consumer goods made by the chemical industry.

Petrochemicals

Major new petrochemical plants in the 1980s were located at Omsk, Tobol'sk, Urengoy, and Surgut in the West Siberia Economic Region and Ufa and Nizhnekamsk in the Volga Economic Region. New West Siberia plants were developed as joint ventures with Western companies. The huge Tobol'sk plant refined fuels and made intermediate products for synthetic rubber and plastics.

The Tomsk complex in the West Siberia Economic Region produced 75 percent of Soviet polypropylene. Refineries at Moscow, Pavlodar (Kazakh Republic), Baku, and Groznyy (the last two based on oil from the Caspian Sea) advanced their motor fuel refinement operations to enhance fuel economy (see Fuels, this ch.).

Other Branches of the Chemical Industry

Some branches of the chemical industry have been located close to their raw materials. The chemical fertilizer industry has major plants using apatite in the Kola Peninsula, phosphates in the southern Kazakhstan Economic Region, and potassium salts in the Ural, Ukraine, and Belorussia economic regions.

Synthetic rubber production increased rapidly in the 1980s, providing tires for heavy industrial vehicles and for the increasing number of passenger vehicles. Soviet mineral fertilizer production led the world in the 1970s; because of agricultural failures, the chemical industry has been under great pressure to produce more pesticides, chemical fertilizers, and feed additives. Plans called for a 70 percent increase in mineral fertilizers from 1980 to 1990. In addition, chemical fibers were a growing part of the textile industry, which was vital to expanding consumer production.

Chemical Planning Goals

Soviet industrial planners have recognized that a high-technology chemical industry is indispensable for advancement in both heavy and light industry. Although Soviet chemical engineering has advanced in such areas as composite materials, which are used to make lighter airplanes, and photochemicals, major projects have depended heavily on foreign technology.

Because of the critical role of the chemical industry in technological advancement, a major campaign in the 1980s was aimed at improving domestic technology and reducing dependence on foreign technology in the chemical and petrochemical industry. In 1984 thirty-two scientific research institutes were conducting major petrochemical research under the academies of sciences. But the technical and investment contributions of British, French, Japanese, East German, West German, Italian, and Hungarian chemical firms remained crucial during that time. Many divisions of Soviet industry failed to produce as planned through the early 1980s, and massive investment did not have the expected effect. The goal for the year 2000 remained an overall increase of 2.4 times the 1980 level and that required a doubling of investments before 1990.

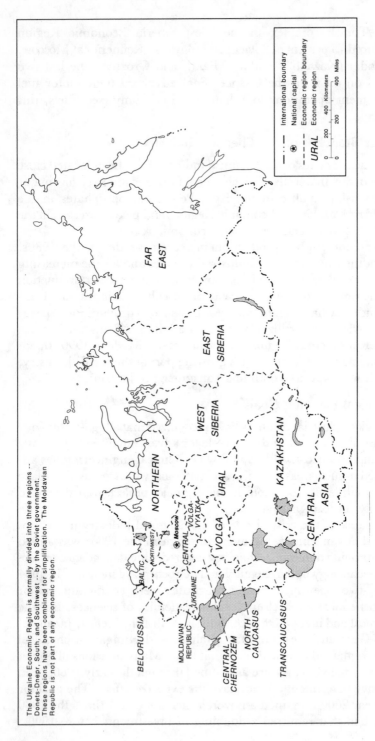

The Ukraine Economic Region is normally divided into three regions -- Donets-Dnepr, South, and Southwest -- by the Soviet government. These regions have been combined for simplification. The Moldavian Republic is not part of any economic region.

Figure 16. Economic Regions, 1985

Fuels

In the 1980s, fuels presented formidable problems for Soviet planners. Although the Soviet Union possessed enormous fuel reserves, it was difficult to balance extraction and transport costs, even as the drive continued for greater production levels. Fuel availability was a prime consideration in locating new industry. And long-term investment planning faced choices among coal, oil, and natural gas. Choices leaned strongly in the late 1980s toward gas over oil because of the greater reserves and cheaper transport of gas. Nevertheless, efforts also continued to formulate a "coal strategy" that would return coal to its former prominence. In 1988 about 28 percent of total national investment went into the Soviet fuel and energy complex, compared with nearly 12 percent in 1980.

Fuel Resource Base

The Soviet Union is self-sufficient in the three major fuels that drive its industry: coal, natural gas, and oil. It has long been a major exporter of oil and gas to its allies and to the West, and hard currency from those exports has financed the purchase of critical import commodities. In 1985 fuel and energy export provided 60 percent of Soviet hard-currency income. The question of which of the three major fuels should be emphasized has been a matter of continuous scrutiny and adjustment in government policy. The two largest users of coal are by far the metallurgy and electric power industries. Large amounts of oil products go for electric power, agriculture, transportation, and export; large amounts of natural gas go for electric power, metallurgy, the chemical industry, construction materials, and export.

Oil

After many years of occasionally spectacular growth, Soviet oil production began to level off in 1983, although the Soviet Union remained the world's largest oil producer. Since that time, Western experts have disagreed sharply about the amount and importance of production changes, especially because exact Soviet fuel reserve figures remained a state secret. It is known that at the end of the 1980s oil production did not increase significantly from year to year.

The Tyumen' reserves of western Siberia were a huge discovery of the 1960s that provided the bulk of oil production increases through the 1970s. By the end of that decade, Tyumen' had overtaken the Volga-Ural fields as the greatest Soviet oil region. The Volga-Ural fields had provided one-half the country's oil in the early 1970s but fell to a one-third share in 1977. By the mid-1980s,

Tyumen' produced 60 percent of Soviet oil, but there was already evidence that Tyumen' was approaching peak production.

Meanwhile, new policies in the early 1980s accelerated drilling rates throughout the country, especially in western Siberia, but lower yields made this drilling expensive. By 1980 the older oil reserves were already being exhausted. Substantial untapped reserves were confirmed in the Caspian, Baltic, and Black seas and above the Arctic Circle, but all of them contained natural obstacles that made exploitation expensive. Soviet planners relied on the discovery of a major new field comparable to those in western Siberia. But by 1987 no major discovery had been made for twenty-two years. In the mid-1980s, Soviet oil exploration concentrated on the farther reaches of the Tyumen' and Tomsk oblasts (see Glossary), east of the established western Siberian fields. Offshore drilling was centered on the Caspian, Barents, and Baltic seas and the Sea of Okhotsk. Several shipyards were building offshore drilling platforms, the largest being the yards at Astrakhan' and Vyborg. Foreign shipyards also provided offshore drilling equipment. In 1984 the Soviet Union had eleven semisubmersible platforms in operation.

The Soviet oil-drilling industry has relied heavily on Western equipment for difficult extraction conditions, which become more common as existing reserves dry up. The average service life of a Soviet-made drilling rig was ten years, compared with fifteen or twenty for comparable Western equipment. Centers of Soviet drilling rig production were in Volgograd, Sverdlovsk, and Verkhnyaya Pyshma, about twenty kilometers north of Sverdlovsk.

Increased distance from well to consumer was also a major concern for the oil industry. Ninety percent of oil was transported by pipeline. The Soviet oil pipeline system doubled in length between 1970 and 1983, reaching 76,200 kilometers. Before 1960 the system totaled only 15,000 kilometers of pipe (see Pipelines, ch. 14). As oil production leveled off in the 1980s, so did pipeline construction. In 1986 the Soviet Union had 81,500 kilometers of pipeline for crude and refined oil products (in 1989 the number of kilometers remained the same).

The oil boom of the 1970s in western Siberia brought rapid growth of Soviet oil-refining centers. In 1983 most of the fifty-three refineries were west of the Urals. At least five new facilities were built between 1970 and 1985. Soviet refining equipment fell below Western standards for such higher-grade fuels as gasoline, so that high-octane fuels were scarce and heavier petroleum products were in surplus.

The 2,000,000th harvester produced in Rostov-na-Donu, Russian Republic, where more than 80 percent of the country's harvesters are made
Courtesy Jimmy Pritchard

Natural Gas

Natural gas replaced oil as the ''growth fuel'' of the Soviet Union in the early 1980s. Gas is cheaper than oil to extract, and Soviet gas deposits are estimated to be three times larger than oil deposits. In 1983 an output of 536 billion cubic meters of gas put the Soviet Union ahead of the United States in gas production for the first time. In 1987 that figure rose to 727 billion cubic meters. As with oil, the majority of natural gas production (85 percent in 1965) came from the European sector until the 1970s. In that decade, the Volga-Ural and Central Asian fields dominated, but by 1983 western Siberia provided nearly 50 percent of Soviet natural gas. That area's Urengoy field was the largest in the world; its reserves were estimated at 7.8 trillion cubic meters.

Because of transport distance and harsh climate, fuel extraction in western Siberia is a monumental undertaking that becomes more formidable as the industry moves northward. Although high-power pumping stations are necessary to move gas over long distances, in the late 1980s the Soviet machine-building industry was not providing adequate equipment to maintain a steady flow through some of the major lines. The chief development target after Urengoy was the Yamburg field, directly to its north. Then, after 1990, major work was to begin in the Yamal Peninsula, for which preparations began in the late 1980s. But cost and environmental concerns delayed the Yamal project in 1989. Because growth targets were based on the timely opening of large Yamal deposits, the delay was potentially a very serious setback. The center of the older Volga-Ural fields is Orenburg; other major gas fields are located in the Uzbek, Turkmen, and Ukrainian republics.

Soviet industrial planners were replacing oil with gas widely and successfully, and proportional investment in gas increased drastically in the late 1970s and 1980s. In 1988 the shares of oil and gas in the fuel balance were equal (at 39 percent) for the first time. Gas was also a vital export product. The main instrument of gas export policy was the pipeline connecting Urengoy (and, projected for 1990, the Yamburg field) with Western Europe. This line began pumping gas to four West European countries (Austria, France, Italy, and the Federal Republic of Germany [West Germany]) in 1984, despite strong opposition from the United States. Delivery was scheduled to increase to a steady rate of 57 billion cubic meters per year by 1990. In 1988 total Soviet gas exports reached 88 billion cubic meters, after adding Greece, Turkey, and Switzerland to the customer list. Meanwhile, pipeline reliability became a serious problem; hasty construction and poor maintenance caused many accidents and breakdowns in the system.

Coal

For about 150 years, coal was the dominant fuel in Russian and later in Soviet industry, and many industrial centers were located near coal deposits. In the 1960s, oil and gas replaced coal as the dominant fuel when plentiful, accessible supplies of these fuels were discovered. But coal remained an important energy source for much of Soviet industry. Total coal reserves, estimated in 1983 at 6.8 trillion tons, were the largest in the world, and since 1980 expanded coal production has been a standard goal of industrial planners. In the mid-1980s, approximately 40 percent of coal went to power-plant boiler units (steam coal) and 20 percent to metallurgy (coking coal). The rest went for export, to other industries, and to households. Shaft mines provided 60 percent of total production, surface mines the remainder.

Historically, the most important coal region has been the Donbass, on which the metallurgical industry was centered because of the cheap, plentiful coking coal it offered. Other traditional coking-coal centers were the Kuzbass in western Siberia and the Karaganda Basin in the northern Kazakh Republic. As deeper excavation and reclamation operations raised the cost of Donbass coal, other centers challenged its position as chief producer of coking coal. The second largest coal center in the European sector of the Soviet Union was the Pechora Basin, where shaft mines were less deep and labor productivity much higher than in the Donbass. In most of the European sector, shaft mines had to be dug deeper, seams were growing thinner, and methane concentration was higher. Despite these conditions, in the late 1980s shaft mines were still providing 75 percent of high-quality coking coal.

The highest cost factor in Soviet coal production was transportation. Even when extraction was very expensive, regions such as the Donbass and the Moscow Basin remained practical because they were so close to the metallurgical centers they served. Conversely, Kuzbass coal extraction was cheap, but its high-quality coking coal had to be transported long distances to industrial centers (for example, 2,200 kilometers to the Magnitogorsk metallurgical center). Transport distance also required that new thermoelectric plants be located near the coal and water resources that fueled their steam boilers. In the late 1980s, Soviet coal experts called for gradually less reliance on the Donbass and increased emphasis on the Kuzbass. Increased investment at the Donbass had failed to maintain production levels, indicating the necessity of this step. But rail transport costs from the Kuzbass and Siberia would rise steeply with added volume. Experimental slurry lines were opened in 1988 to provide possible alternative long-distance coal transport to the west.

Future growth in coal production must come from east of the Urals, where an estimated 75 percent of the country's reserves lie. Most Siberian coal can be strip-mined, making production costs much lower and labor productivity much higher than shaft mining. Between 1977 and 1983, production in the Soviet Union's European basins fell by 32 million tons annually, and by the 1970s rail movement of coal westward across the Urals had doubled. To minimize transportation costs, major new power stations were built in the Kansko-Achinsk and Ekibastuz coal basins, whose low-quality brown coal, a cheap fuel, breaks down rapidly if transported over long distances. Coal from those mines required extensive processing before being burned in thermoelectric plants. By the year 2000, Kansko-Achinsk may be the most productive Soviet coal basin, with a planned yield of 400 million tons per year. The largest Soviet strip mine, Bogatyr, is located at Ekibastuz.

In the mid-1980s, low coal quality was still a major problem because efficient processing equipment was scarce. Huge reserves remained untapped in Siberia because of remoteness and low quality, but in the 1980s the South Yakut Basin in eastern Siberia was being developed with Japanese technical aid.

Uranium

In 1988 little was known specifically about the Soviet uranium industry. Nevertheless, foreign observers did know that the country possessed large, varied deposits that provided fuel for its fast-growing nuclear power program.

Power Engineering

Traditionally, generation and distribution of electrical power have been a high priority of Soviet industrial policy. The main generators of power, in order of importance, were thermoelectric plants burning fossil fuels (coal, oil, natural gas, and peat), nuclear power plants, and hydroelectric stations. The power industry has been one of the fastest growing branches of the economy; in 1985 power production reached 58 percent that of the United States. But the complexity and size of the country has made timely delivery of electricity a difficult problem. Huge areas of the northwestern Soviet Union, Siberia, the Soviet Far East, and Soviet Central Asia remained unconnected to the country's central power grid. Because the largest power-generating fuel reserves are located far from industrial centers, geography has limited the options of Soviet policy markers. In the early 1980s, power shortages were still frequent in the heavily industrialized European sector, where conventional fuel reserves were being fully used. Soviet policy depended heavily on large generating plants operating more hours per day than those in the West.

Energy Planning Goals

In 1986 the stated goals of Soviet energy policy were ambitious ones. The share of nuclear power was to increase drastically, and new, large-capacity nuclear plants were to be built, mainly in the European sector. Expansion of the natural gas industry was to contribute more of that fuel to power generation. More coal was to be available to thermoelectric stations from surface mining in remote fuel-and-power complexes such as Kansko-Achinsk and Ekibastuz, and larger thermoelectric stations were to be built near coal deposits. More hydroelectric plants were planned on rivers in Siberia, Soviet Central Asia, and the Soviet Far East. Ultra-high-voltage, long-distance power lines (including the longest in the world) would link thermoelectric power stations in Asia with European and Ural industrial centers and would connect Soviet nuclear plants with Warsaw Pact allies (see Appendix C). Better equipment was to limit power losses occurring over such lines. And alternative, renewable power sources such as wind and solar energy were to be exploited for small-scale local needs. Because nuclear and thermal plants were expected to increase their share of power generation, in long-term planning the industry has concentrated on making the generating units of these plants larger and more efficient. In the European sector, a primary goal has been flexible response to high- and low-demand cycles—a feature that nuclear plants do not provide.

The Balance among Energy Sources

The Twelfth Five-Year Plan called for a period of intense construction of thermal and nuclear plants. By 1990 nuclear capacity was to reach almost 1.5 times its 1985 level. By the year 2000, most large thermal stations were to be capable of burning the abundant but low-quality coal mined east of the Urals. Berezovka, the largest Soviet thermoelectric station yet built, was scheduled to open at the Kansko-Achinsk fuel and power complex by 1990. The Unified Electrical Power System (see Glossary), which is the centralized energy distribution grid and the showpiece of the Soviet energy program, was to be connected with the Central Asian Power System by 1990, bringing 95 percent of the country's power production into a single distribution network.

Despite the presence of some of the world's largest hydroelectric stations, such as Krasnoyarsk, Bratsk, Ust'-Ilimsk, and Sayano-Shushenskoye, reliance on hydroelectric power is decreasing. All large, untapped rivers are east of the Urals—in the Kazakhstan, East Siberia, and Far East economic regions—and few major hydroelectric projects are planned west of the Urals. Although hydroelectric power is renewable and flexible, water levels are subject to unpredictable climatic conditions. Plans called for ninety new hydroelectric stations to be started between 1990 and 2000. The Twelfth Five-Year Plan called for nuclear power to displace hydroelectric power by 1990 as the second largest electricity source in the Soviet Union. The planned share of nuclear power in the national power balance for 1990 was 21 percent, while hydroelectric power was already below 15 percent in 1985. By comparison, nuclear generation represented a smaller percentage—15.5 percent—of power production in the United States in 1985. An estimated sixteen nuclear plants (forty-five reactors total) were operating in 1988.

The Soviet Union has led the world in magnetohydrodynamic power generation. This highly efficient method directly converts the energy of conventional steam expansion into power, using superconductor magnetic fields. The first magnetohydrodynamic plant in the world was built at Ryazan' in the mid-1980s.

Obstacles to Power Supply

In the late 1980s, the Soviet power industry was far behind its planned expansion rate. Technology was not available for on-site burning of low-quality coal, nor for transmitting the power it would generate across the huge distances required. Moreover, the 1986 nuclear accident at Chernobyl' cast doubts on the reliability of the nuclear reactor models chosen to supply power to industrial centers in the European part of the Soviet Union. As in the case of fuels, planners faced long-term, irreversible choices among power sources.

Soviet nuclear and thermoelectric generation has relied heavily on unproven equipment and long-distance delivery systems, whose failure could slow operations in major industries. For example, the Chernobyl' incident resulted in major disruption of the industrial power supply. Although switching techniques could sometimes avoid long-term slowdowns, no permanent alternative power source existed if nuclear power failed in the European part of the Soviet Union. Meanwhile, in the late 1980s construction of new nuclear plants fell far behind schedule, and a 30 percent shortfall was expected in 1990 generation. Because hydroelectric stations fell behind in the same period, an added burden fell on thermoelectric facilities. Environmental concerns also caused local opposition to new nuclear and hydroelectric plants during this period.

Heat and Cogeneration

Although electrical energy is vital to Soviet industry, it is only about one-sixth the total energy generated in the country. Heat, which is also indispensable to industry, cannot be transported over long distances. Most heat came from central heat and power stations in urban and industrial centers, which burned coal, heavy oil, or natural gas to generate heat as well as electricity. In the 1980s, a major program developed large-scale generators to produce heat as a by-product in existing thermal and nuclear power plants. Steam from the latter can be sent as far as forty kilometers. This process, called cogeneration, centralizes the fragmented heat-generation system. In 1985 urban cogeneration plants provided 28 percent of total Soviet power.

The Consumer Industry

Soviet industry is usually divided into two major categories. Group A is "heavy industry," which includes all those branches already discussed. Group B is "consumer goods," including foods, clothing and shoes, housing, and such heavy-industry products as appliances and fuels that are used by individual consumers. From

Construction in southwest Moscow, location of the city's
newest research and education institutes
Courtesy Jimmy Pritchard

the early days of the Stalin era, Group A received top priority in economic planning and allocation. Only in 1987 was the foundation laid for a separate industrial complex for consumer industry, named the "social complex." Initially, it lacked the extensive bureaucratic structure of the other six complexes, and it contained only the Ministry of Light Industry.

Consumer Supply in the 1980s

In 1986 shortages continued in basic consumer items, even in major population centers. Such goods occasionally were rationed in major cities well into the 1980s. Besides the built-in shortages caused by planning priorities, shoddy production of consumer goods limited actual supply. According to Soviet economists, only 10 percent of Soviet finished goods could compete with their Western equivalents, and the average consumer faced long waiting periods to buy major appliances or furniture. During the 1980s, the wide availability of consumer electronics products in the West demonstrated a new phase of the Soviet Union's inability to compete, especially because Soviet consumers were becoming more aware of what they were missing. In the mid-1980s, up to 70 percent of the televisions manufactured by Ekran, a major household electronics

513

manufacturer, were rejected by quality control inspection. The television industry received special attention, and a strong drive for quality control was a response to published figures of very high rates of breakdown and repair. To improve the industry, a major cooperative color television venture was planned for the Warsaw Television Plant in 1989.

The Logic and Goals of Consumer Production

Increased availability of consumer goods was an important part of *perestroika*. A premise of that program was that workers would raise their productivity in response to incentive wages only if their money could buy a greater variety of consumer products. This idea arose when the early use of incentive wages did not have the anticipated effect on labor productivity because purchasing power had not improved. According to the theory, all Soviet industry would benefit from diversification from Group A into Group B because incentives would have real meaning. Therefore, the Twelfth Five-Year Plan called for a 5.4 percent rise in nonfood consumer goods and a 5.4 to 7 percent rise in consumer services. Both figures were well above rates in the overall economic plan.

Consumer goods targeted included radios, televisions, sewing machines, washing machines, refrigerators, printed matter, and knitwear. The highest quotas were set for the first three categories. Although in 1987 refrigerators, washing machines, televisions, tape recorders, and furniture were the consumer categories making the greatest production gains compared with the previous year, only furniture met its yearly quota. Furthermore, industrial planners have tried to use light industries to raise the industrial contributions of such economic regions as the Transcaucasus and Central Asia, which have large populations but lack the raw materials for heavy manufacturing.

Textiles and Wood Pulp

The textile and wood pulp industries are traditional branches of light industry that remain essential to the Soviet economy. The major textile center is northeast of Moscow. Because the industry receives most of its raw material from the cotton fields of the Transcaucasus and Central Asia economic regions, transport is expensive. Although large-scale cotton cultivation began in the Soviet Union only in the early 1900s, textile plant locations were established in the nineteenth century, when the country still imported most of its raw cotton. Soviet planners have tried to shift the textile industry into the Transcaucasus and Central Asia economic regions, nearer the domestic cotton fields. But textiles have been a well-established economic base for the Moscow area, and in the 1980s the bulk of the industry remained there. The Soviet wood pulp and paper industry is based on a vast supply of softwood trees. This industry is less centralized and closer to its raw material base than Soviet textiles; plants tend to be along the southern edge of forested regions, as close as possible to markets to the south and west (see Forestry, ch. 13).

After the industrial stagnation in the 1970s and early 1980s, planners expected that consumer industries would assume a more prominent role in Soviet production beginning with the Twelfth Five-Year Plan. But despite a greater emphasis on light industry and efforts to restructure the entire planning and production systems, very little upturn was visible in any sector of industry in 1989. High production quotas, particularly for some heavy industries, appeared increasingly unrealistic by the end of that plan. Although most Soviet officials agreed that *perestroika* was necessary and overdue, reforming the intricate industrial system had proved difficult.

* * *

The *USSR Energy Atlas,* prepared by the United States Central Intelligence Agency, is a detailed picture of Soviet fuels and power generation in the mid-1980s, with forecasts of future developments. It includes extensive maps, tables, and a gazetteer. Konstantin Spidchenko's *USSR: Geography of the Eleventh Five-Year Plan Period* provides an overview in English (from a Soviet perspective, which must be taken into consideration but does not mitigate its value) of the geographical distribution of industry and the rationale of expansion and location. It also describes major industrial areas and their resource bases. *Gorbachev's Challenge* by Marshall I. Goldman provides a general background for the restructuring goals of Soviet industry in the late 1980s, with emphasis on technology transfer and the domestic research and development area. William F. Scott's article, "Moscow's Military-Industrial Complex," is a comprehensive look at the system of military planning and its relation to the overall industrial system. *Siberia and the Soviet Far East,* edited by Rodger Swearingen, is a collection of articles describing in detail the economic and political factors in planning development of fuel and energy east of the Urals, with emphasis on oil and natural gas. J.P. Cole's *Geography of the Soviet Union* contains two chapters describing the geographical influence on Soviet industrial policy, including all major branches. Vadim Medish's *The Soviet Union* offers chapters on the scientific research establishment and economic planning, valuable background information in understanding Soviet industrial policy. Also, the collection of study papers for the Joint Economic Committee of the United States Congress, entitled *Gorbachev's Economic Plans,* covers Soviet economic planning and performance, industrial modernization, the role of the defense industry in the economy, and Soviet energy supply, with short articles on specific subtopics. (For further information and complete citations, see Bibliography.)

Chapter 13. Agriculture

Images of agriculture

AGRICULTURE CONTINUED TO FRUSTRATE the leaders of the Soviet Union in the 1980s. Despite immense land resources, extensive machinery and chemical support industries, a large rural work force, and two decades of massive investment in the agricultural sector, the Soviet Union continued to rely on large-scale grain and meat imports to feed its population. Persistent shortages of staples, the general unavailability of fresh meats, fruits, and vegetables in state stores, and a bland, carbohydrate-rich diet remained a fact of life for Soviet citizens and a perennial embarrassment to their government.

Although in terms of total value of output the Soviet Union was the world's second leading agricultural power and ranked first in the production of numerous commodities, agriculture was a net drain on the economy. The financial resources directed to this sector soared throughout the 1970s and by the mid-1980s accounted for nearly one-third of total investment. The ideologically motivated policy of maintaining low prices for staples created an enormous disparity between production costs and retail food prices. By 1983 the per capita food subsidy amounted to nearly 200 rubles, which the consumer had to pay in higher prices for nonfood products.

Although gross agricultural production rose by more than 50 percent between the 1950s and 1980s, outstripping population growth by 25 percent, the consumer did not see a proportionate improvement in the availability of foodstuffs (see table 34, Appendix A). This paradox indicated that the Soviet Union's inability to meet demand for agricultural commodities was only partly the result of production shortfalls and that much of the blame was attributable to other factors. Chief among these were the processing, transportation, storage, and marketing elements of the food economy, the neglect of which over the years resulted in an average wastage of about one-fourth of agricultural output. Soviet experts estimated that if waste in storage and processing were eliminated, up to 25 percent more grain, 40 percent more fruits and vegetables, and 15 percent more meat and dairy products could be brought to market.

The heavily centralized and bureaucratized system of administration, which has characterized Soviet agriculture ever since Joseph V. Stalin's campaign of forced collectivization (see Glossary), was the dominant cause of the sector's overall poor performance. Inflexible production directives from central planning

519

organs that failed to take local growing conditions into account and bureaucratic interference in the day-to-day management of individual farms fostered resentment and undermined morale in the countryside. The result was low labor productivity, the system's most intractable problem. Despite its systemic flaws, however, Soviet agriculture enjoyed certain successes. The standard of living of farm workers improved, illiteracy was reduced, incomes grew, better housing and health care were provided, and electricity was brought to virtually all villages. Farming practices were modernized, and agriculture received more machinery and became less labor intensive (see table 35, Appendix A). Ambitious irrigation and drainage projects brought millions of additional hectares under cultivation. Large livestock inventories were built up, particularly during the 1970s and 1980s. And the increased prominence accorded agriculture, coupled with wiser policies exploiting the profit motive, appeared to be paying dividends, as bumper grain harvests were reported in Mikhail S. Gorbachev's first two years in power.

Policy and Administration

Stalin's Legacy

In the 1980s, the basic structure and operation of Soviet agriculture retained many of the features of the system that became entrenched during Stalin's regime. Under Stalin agriculture was socialized, and a massive bureaucracy was created to administer policy. This bureaucracy was highly resistant to subsequent reform efforts.

Stalin's campaign of forced collectivization, begun in the autumn of 1929, confiscated the land, machinery, livestock, and grain stores of the peasantry. By 1937 approximately 99 percent of the countryside had been collectivized. Precise figures are lacking, but probably 1 million kulak (see Glossary) households with nearly 5 million members were deported and were never heard from again. About 7 million starved to death as the government confiscated grain stores. In defiance, peasants slaughtered their livestock rather than surrender it to the collectives. As a result, within five years the number of horses, cattle, and hogs in the country was halved, and the number of sheep and goats was reduced by two-thirds.

Aside from the immediate devastation wrought by forced collectivization, the experience left an enduring legacy of mutual distrust and hostility between the rural population and the Soviet authorities. The bureaucracy that evolved to administer agriculture was motivated more by political than by economic considerations. Its objectives were to industrialize agriculture, create a rural proletariat, and destroy peasant resistance to communist rule. Once entrenched, the bureaucracy relished its power, dictating policy from the top down with little regard for the opinions of individual farmers and even farm managers, who better understood local conditions. Such policies resulted in abysmally low labor productivity and massive waste of resources. This situation persisted into the 1980s, when the Soviet farmer was on average about one-tenth as productive as his American counterpart.

During Stalin's regime, virtually all farmland was assigned to the two basic agricultural production entities that still predominated in the 1980s—state farms and collective farms. The state farm (*sovetskoe khoziaistvo*—sovkhoz) was conceived in 1918 as the ideal model for socialist agriculture. It was to be a large, modern enterprise, directed and financed by the government, with a work force receiving wages and social benefits comparable to those enjoyed by industrial workers. By contrast, the collective farm (*kollektivnoe khoziaistvo*—kolkhoz) was a self-financed producer cooperative, which farmed land granted to it rent free by the state and which paid its members according to their contribution of work. Although in theory the kolkhoz was self-directed, electing its own managing committee and chairman, in reality it remained under the firm control of state planning and procurement agencies. Chairmen who did not meet ideological purity requirements were removed. Sovkhozy operated much like any other production enterprise (see Glossary) in the Soviet command economy, with production targets and operating budgets determined by distant planning organs. The entire output of sovkhozy was delivered to state procurement agencies. Kolkhozy also received procurement quotas, but they were free to sell excess production in collective farm markets, where prices were determined by supply and demand. Because kolkhozy were self-financed, they received somewhat higher prices for their products. Nevertheless, the income of the kolkhoz resident was usually lower than that of the sovkhoz resident. In general, labor productivity on the sovkhoz was higher, probably because of its access to better machinery, chemicals, and seed and because it could specialize in the crops best suited to its region. The kolkhoz was constrained to produce a variety of crops and livestock, which decreased efficiency.

Several watershed decisions by Stalin's successors reduced the differences between the two types of farms. Among these decisions were the 1958 elimination of state-operated machine tractor stations, which had given the party leverage over the kolkhoz by controlling its access to heavy farm machinery; the establishment in 1965 of a minimum wage, pension, and other benefits for kolkhoz workers; and the 1967 decision to make the sovkhoz a self-financed entity, which in theory the kolkhoz had been from the start. Not only was there a trend toward convergence of the features of the two types of farms, but there was also a pattern of official conversion of smaller, less solvent kolkhozy to sovkhozy. As a result, in 1973 the total sown area of sovkhozy surpassed that of kolkhozy for the first time. The total number of kolkhozy decreased from 235,500 in 1940 to 26,300 in 1986. But after the March 1989 Agricultural Plenum of the Central Committee of the Communist Party of the Soviet Union (CPSU), it appeared likely that the proliferation of sovkhozy would cease. Even one of the most conservative Politburo members, Egor K. Ligachev, who was named chairman of the party's Agrarian Policy Commission in September 1988, recommended gradually converting sovkhozy into cooperatives and leasing collectives.

A third production entity that survived from Stalin's era was the private plot, known in Soviet jargon as the "personal auxiliary holding." These plots were ideologically unpalatable to the bureaucrats, but they were tolerated as a means for farmers to produce their own food and supplement their incomes. The plots were small (roughly half a hectare) and were assigned one to a household. Peasants were allowed to consume whatever was grown on the plot and sell any surplus—either at the collective farm markets or to state or cooperative marketing agencies. The contribution of private plots to the nation's food supply far exceeded their size. With only 3 percent of total sown area in the 1980s, they produced over a quarter of gross agricultural output, including about 30 percent of meat and milk, 66 percent of potatoes, and 40 percent of fruits, vegetables, and eggs.

Evolution of an Integrated Food Policy

After the death of Stalin, an integrated food policy gradually evolved. Nikita S. Khrushchev was the first Soviet leader to demonstrate serious concern for the diet of the citizenry. In fact, it was his obsession with increasing the consumption of meat and dairy products that drove Khrushchev's controversial agricultural program. He switched the country's prime wheat-growing lands to the production of corn, which was supposed to feed an ever-increasing number of livestock. Khrushchev believed that the lost wheat production could be offset by extensive farming in the semi-arid virgin land of the Kazakh Republic and southwestern Siberia. However, his program, underfinanced from the start, did not produce the desired results, a major factor in his fall from power in 1964.

Agricultural tractor on road between Tallin, Estonian
Republic, and the Latvian border
Courtesy Jonathan Tetzlaff
Cornfield on a state farm south of Moscow
Courtesy Jimmy Pritchard

523

Like his predecessor, Leonid I. Brezhnev considered agriculture a top priority. Unlike Khrushchev, however, he backed his program with massive investments. During his tenure, the supply of livestock housing increased 300 percent, and similar increases in the delivery of chemical fertilizers and tractors were recorded. Brezhnev's Food Program, announced in 1982, was intended to guide agriculture throughout the 1980s. It provided for even larger investment in the agro-industrial complex (*agro-promyshlennyi kompleks*—APK), particularly in its infrastructure (see The Complexes and the Ministries, ch. 12). The program also set up regional agro-industrial associations (*regional'nye agro-promyshlennye ob''edineniia*—RAPOs) to administer all elements of the food industry on the *raion* (see Glossary), oblast (see Glossary), *krai* (see Glossary), and autonomous republic (see Glossary) levels. The program's overriding objective was improving the availability of food for the consumer. Production goals now referred to per capita consumption of meat, fruit, vegetables, and other basic foods. Unlike previous campaigns, the Food Program gave the same prominence to reducing waste as to increasing output.

In 1988 Gorbachev, who had been the Central Committee secretary for agriculture when the Food Program was announced, appeared to be pursuing a two-pronged approach to agricultural administration. On the one hand, he attempted to improve the APK's efficiency through further centralization, having merged five ministries and a state committee in late 1985 into the State Agro-Industrial Committee (Gosudarstvennyi agro-promyshlennyi komitet—Gosagroprom). Eliminated were the Ministry of Agriculture, the Ministry of the Fruit and Vegetable Industry, the Ministry of the Meat and Dairy Industry, the Ministry of the Food Industry, the Ministry of Agricultural Construction, and the State Committee for the Supply of Production Equipment for Agriculture. But, on the other hand, he called for delegation of greater decision-making authority to the farms and farmers themselves.

Gosagroprom proved to be a major disappointment to Gorbachev, and at the March 1989 Agricultural Plenum of the Central Committee, the superministerial body was eliminated. Moreover, Gorbachev complained that the RAPOs meddled excessively in the operations of individual farms, and he urged abolishing them as well. The general thrust of the reforms proposed at the plenum was to dismantle the rigid central bureaucracy, transfer authority to local governing councils, and increase the participation of farmers in decision making. Gorbachev also elected to give the individual republics greater freedom in setting food production goals that were consistent with the needs of their people.

A key objective of Gorbachev's *perestroika* (see Glossary) was to increase labor productivity by means of the proliferation of contract brigades throughout the economy. Agricultural contract brigades consisted of ten to thirty farm workers who managed a piece of land leased by the kolkhoz or sovkhoz under the terms of a contract making the brigades responsible for the entire production cycle. Because brigade members received a predetermined price for the contracted amount of output plus generous bonuses for any excess production, their income was tied to the result of their labors. After 1987 family contract brigades also became legal, and long-term leasing (up to fifteen years) was enacted—two reforms that in the opinion of some Western analysts pointed toward an eventual sanctioning of the family farm. Because contract brigades enjoyed relative autonomy, much of the administrative bureaucracy resisted them. Nevertheless, in 1984 an estimated 296,100 farm workers had already banded together in contract brigades, and the document *Basic Directions for the Economic and Social Development of the USSR for 1986–1990 and for the Period to the Year 2000* (a report presented to and subsequently adopted by the Twenty-Seventh Party Congress) called for their wider use (see Reforming the Planning System, ch. 11). The March 1989 Agricultural Plenum endorsed contract brigades and agricultural leasing, a major victory for Gorbachev's reform effort.

Soon after assuming power in 1985, Gorbachev demonstrated his intention of reforming another enduring feature of Soviet food policy—the maintenance of artificially low retail prices for staples in the state stores. In 1986 he raised prices for certain categories of bread, the first such increase in over thirty years. But much remained to be done in this critical area. For example, milk and meat prices had not been adjusted since 1962. The bill for food subsidies in 1985 came to nearly 55 billion rubles (for value of the ruble—see Glossary); of this, 35 billion rubles was for meat and milk products alone. By June 1986, the absurdity of the food subsidy policy had become a matter of open discussion in upper echelons of the party, and higher prices were expected to take effect by the end of the Twelfth Five-Year Plan (1986–90).

Land Use

Although the Soviet Union has the world's largest soil resources, climatic and hydrological conditions make farming a high-risk venture, even within the most favorable zone, the so-called fertile triangle. This tract has the general shape of an isosceles triangle, the base of which is a line between the Baltic and Black seas and the apex of which is some 5,000 kilometers to the east near Krasnoyarsk.

To the north of this triangle, the climate is generally too cold, and to the south it is too dry for farming. Because of the Soviet Union's northern latitude (most of the country lies north of 50° north latitude; all of the United States except Alaska lies south of this latitude) and the limited moderating influence of adjacent bodies of water on the climate of much of the country, growing conditions can dramatically vary from year to year. As a consequence, crop yields fluctuate greatly. Only about 27 percent of the Soviet Union is considered agricultural land, of which roughly 10 percent is arable (see fig. 17). About 15 percent of Soviet territory is too arid, 20 percent too cold, 30 percent too rugged, and 8.5 percent too marshy to permit farming. And in areas where the growing season is long enough, rainfall is frequently inadequate; only 1.1 percent of the arable land receives the optimal precipitation of at least 700 millimeters per year (compared with 60 percent of arable land in the United States and 80 percent in Canada).

North of the fertile triangle lie the treeless Arctic tundra, covering 9.3 percent of the country's territory, and an immense coniferous forest, the taiga, which occupies 31 percent of the territory. The tundra is an inhospitable region of permafrost and swampy terrain, agriculturally suitable only for reindeer herding. In the taiga zone, the climate becomes increasingly continental from the northwestern reaches of the country eastward into Siberia. East of the Yenisey River, permafrost is pervasive, and throughout the taiga vast swampy tracts and infertile podzol preclude all agricultural activity except for reindeer herding and limited cultivation of hay, rye, oats, barley, flax, potatoes, and livestock along the southern frontier of the zone. Of far greater economic importance are the forestry and fur industries of the taiga.

Along its southwestern periphery, the taiga merges with a mixed hardwood and conifer forest, which accounts for another 8.2 percent of the country's total area. This zone is shaped like a triangle with its base in the west formed by the Estonian, Latvian, Lithuanian, Belorussian, and northwestern Ukrainian republics and its apex in the east at a point beyond the Kama River. With heavy application of fertilizers, the gray-brown soils of the region can be relatively productive. Much of the land is highly marshy and requires costly drainage measures. The mixed-forest zone supports meat and milk production and the widespread cultivation of hay, oats, rye, buckwheat, sugar beets, potatoes, and flax. Wheat is also grown in the area, but with only limited success because of the shortness of the season.

A transitional forest-steppe zone stretches in a belt 250 to 500 kilometers wide from the western Ukrainian Republic to the Urals, occupying approximately 7.7 percent of Soviet territory. This area has the best agricultural land in the Soviet Union because of the richness of its chernozem (see Glossary) soil, the abundance of precipitation, and the temperateness of the climate. A wide variety of grains, sugar beets, and livestock are raised here. The most serious problem confronting agriculture in the zone is severe water and wind erosion, which has resulted from the removal of much of the forest cover.

Farther south are the vast open steppes, which extend from the Moldavian Republic in a northeasterly direction across the northern part of the Kazakh Republic as far as Krasnoyarsk, covering roughly 15 percent of the Soviet Union. It is a region of relatively low precipitation, where periodic droughts have calamitous effects on agriculture. Because the lighter soils of this region are nearly as fertile as the chernozem of the forest-steppe and because the growing season is longer, when moisture is adequate, crop yields can be large. Irrigation is widely practiced throughout the steppe, particularly in the middle and lower Volga River Valley and in the southern Ukrainian and Kazakh republics. The primary crop of the region is wheat, although barley is also widely sown. Corn is an important crop in the Donets-Dnepr region, and millet is sown along the Volga and on the Ural steppes. Sugar beets, sunflowers, fruits, and vegetables are also cultivated on a large scale.

Immediately south of the steppes is a zone of semidesert and desert that includes the northeastern edge of the Caucasus region, the Caspian Lowland and lower Volga River Valley, the central and southern Kazakh Republic, and all of Soviet Central Asia. Irrigation projects of epic proportions make agriculture in this arid region possible. Among the most noteworthy of these projects in the 1980s were the Karakum Canal (see Glossary), over 1,100 kilometers of which had been completed by 1988, designed to provide irrigation water for 1.5 million hectares in the Turkmen Republic; the Fergana Valley in the Uzbek Republic, with over 1 million hectares under irrigation; the Golodnaya Steppe, west of the Fergana Valley, where over 500,000 hectares were irrigated; and numerous other projects exploiting the limited water resources of the Vakhsh, Amu Darya, Chu, Syr Darya, Zeravshan, Kashka Darya, and other Central Asian rivers. The region specialized in such crops as cotton, alfalfa, and fruits and vegetables; the raising of sheep, goats, and cattle was widespread.

In the Caucasus region, two small subtropical areas along the Black and Caspian seas specialize in exotic crops such as citrus fruit, tea, and tobacco, as well as grapes, other fruits, early vegetables, and cotton. The mountains provide pasturage for sheep and goats.

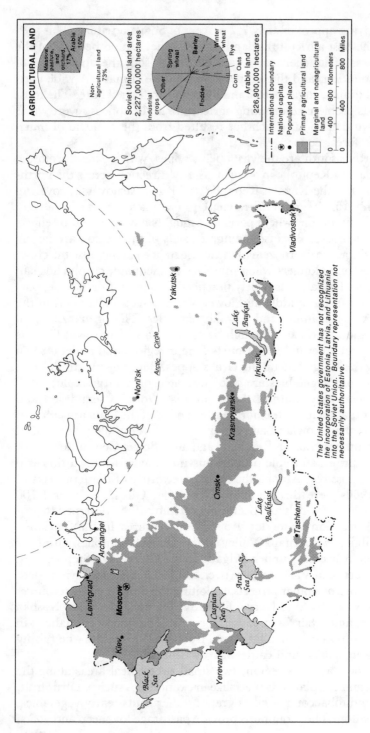

Figure 17. Land Use, 1982

Agriculture is a productive enterprise on the southern rim of eastern Siberia and the Soviet Far East, primarily in the Amur, Bureya, and Zeya river valleys; Olekminskly Raion in the central Yakut Autonomous Republic; and Primorskiy Krai on the Sea of Japan. The area is well suited for livestock, especially beef and dairy cattle, wheat, rice, sugar beets, and other crops.

Throughout the Soviet era, massive projects have been undertaken to expand the area of arable land. Drainage efforts have been concentrated in the northwest, i.e., the Belorussian, Estonian, Latvian, Lithuanian, and northwestern Russian republics. The great expense of drainage is justified by the proximity of these areas to major urban centers, where demand for farm products is highest. Between 1956 and 1986, the area of the nation's drained farmland more than doubled from 8.4 million to 19.5 million hectares. The area under irrigation increased from 10.1 million hectares in 1950 to 20.4 million hectares in 1986. Of this total, Soviet Central Asia accounted for 8.5 million, the Russian Republic for 6.1 million, and the Ukrainian Republic for 2.4 million hectares. In 1984 Gorbachev claimed that irrigated land yielded all the country's cotton and rice, three-quarters of its vegetables, half of its fruit and wine grapes, and a quarter of its feed crops. In 1986 drained or irrigated farmland accounted for almost a third of total national crop production. Irrigation has had a decidedly mixed record. On the one hand, it has transformed semiarid and arid regions into farmland, making the Soviet Union one of the world's chief producers of cotton, for example. On the other hand, excessive water withdrawal from the rivers Amu Darya and Syr Darya has practically destroyed one of the world's largest lakes, the Aral Sea, by depriving it of its major sources of water (see Environmental Concerns, ch. 3; Satellite imagery of the Aral Sea in 1987, p. 117).

Production

Agricultural self-sufficiency has been the goal of Soviet leadership since the Bolshevik Revolution (see Glossary), but it was not until the late 1940s that food supplies were adequate to prevent widespread hunger. Farm output had suffered greatly as a result of Stalin's policies of forced collectivization, low procurement prices, and underinvestment in agriculture; at the time of his death in 1953, both the quality and the quantity of the food supply were inferior to that of the precollectivization period.

Under Khrushchev and Brezhnev, improved agricultural performance became a top priority, and sown area for major crops increased (see table 36, Appendix A). By 1983 the APK accounted for more than 40 percent of the total value of the country's fixed capital assets, created 42 percent of total national income, and provided 75 percent of total retail turnover in state and cooperative trade. In spite of the massive investments of the 1970s and 1980s, however, the sector generally did not perform well. Whereas the annual growth rate of agricultural output averaged 3.9 percent between 1950 and 1970, it actually declined to 1.2 percent in the decade of the 1970s. And between 1981 and 1985, grain output averaged only 180.3 million tons, substantially below the 1976–80 average of 205 million tons and not even matching the 1971–75 average of 181.6 million tons.

In 1986 this downward trend was reversed, as the fourth best grain harvest in Soviet history was recorded—210.1 million tons. In spite of severe winter weather and a late spring, the 1987 harvest was even larger, 211.3 million tons, marking the first time in Soviet history that output exceeded 200 million tons for two consecutive years. Gorbachev's policies of increased reliance on contract-brigade farming and delegation of broader decision-making authority to local managers were given partial credit for this improvement in agricultural performance.

Another important contributing factor to the improved agricultural performance of 1986 and 1987, according to Western analysts, was the cumulative effect of nearly two decades of heavy investment in the agricultural infrastructure. Notable progress had been made in livestock housing, machinery manufacturing, and fertilizer production. Nevertheless, much remained to be done. As many as 40 percent of the nation's farms still lacked storage facilities, and the average farm was hundreds of kilometers from the nearest grain elevator or meat-packing plant. Much of the rural road network was not hard surfaced and during the rainy seasons became impassable. Although the Soviet Union had become the world's largest tractor manufacturer, surpassing the United States by 4.5 times in the 1980s, the quality of this machinery was low and spare parts were virtually nonexistent. Enormous progress had been made in the development of the agricultural chemical industry, and deliveries increased substantially (see table 37, Appendix A). The expansion of transportation, storage, and packaging capacity did not keep pace with it. Over 10 percent of the chemical fertilizer produced never reached the farms.

Grain

Grain crops have long been the foundation of agriculture in the Russian Empire and the Soviet Union. In 1986 grain was grown on 55.3 percent of the total sown area of 210.3 million hectares. The most widely cultivated grain crops continued to be wheat (48.7

Bessarabian Market, Kiev, Ukrainian Republic
Courtesy Jimmy Pritchard

million hectares, or 23.2 percent of the total sown area), followed in order by barley (30.0 million hectares), oats (13.2 million hectares), rye (8.7 million hectares), pulses (6.7 million hectares), corn for grain (4.2 million hectares), millet (2.5 million hectares), buckwheat (1.6 million hectares), and rice (600,000 hectares). The area sown with wheat declined steadily throughout the 1970s and 1980s, reaching a thirty-year low in 1987. And the total area occupied by grain fell during each year from 1981 through 1986, as more land was laid fallow or planted in fodder crops.

Although the total area allotted to grain in 1986 (116.5 million hectares) was only slightly greater than that allotted in 1960 (115.8 million hectares), total output throughout the period steadily rose, thanks to the use of more productive farming methods, improved seed, and heavier application of fertilizers. For example, average wheat yields rose from 1.34 tons per hectare between 1966 and 1970 to 1.6 tons per hectare between 1976 and 1980 (a figure slightly skewed by the record harvest of 1978), 1.45 tons per hectare from 1981 to 1985, and 1.89 tons per hectare in 1986. At the same time, rye, barley, oats, and corn yields were also gradually rising.

The Soviet Union has never had an oversupply of feed grains, and before Brezhnev's era it was customary to conduct wholesale slaughter of livestock during bad harvest years to conserve grain

531

for human consumption. Beginning in the early 1970s, however, the standard policy was to import the grain needed to sustain large livestock inventories. Thereafter, the Soviet Union appeared destined to be a permanent net importer of grains. During the Eleventh Five-Year Plan (1981–85), the country imported some 42 million tons of grain annually, almost twice as much as during the Tenth Five-Year Plan (1976–80) and three times as much as during the Ninth Five-Year Plan (1971–75). The bulk of this grain was provided by the West; in 1985, for example, 94 percent of Soviet grain imports were from the noncommunist world, with the United States supplying 14.1 million tons.

Technical Crops

So-called technical crops are widely and successfully cultivated in the Soviet Union. Among such crops are cotton, sugar beets, sunflowers and other crops producing oilseeds, flax, and hemp. In 1986 these crops were grown on 13.7 million hectares, about 6.5 percent of the total sown area. In the 1970s, the Soviet Union assumed the position of the world's largest producer of cotton, averaging more than 8 million tons of raw cotton per year. Virtually all of the country's cotton was grown on irrigated lands in Central Asia and the Azerbaydzhan Republic; the Uzbek Republic alone accounted for 62 percent of total output between 1981 and 1985.

The Soviet Union has been very successful at cultivating sunflowers, accounting for over half of world output. The crop flourishes in the low-precipitation southern zones, especially in the Donets-Dnepr and northern Caucasus regions. The area allotted to sunflower cultivation steadily decreased from a peak level of 4.8 million hectares in 1970 to 3.9 million hectares in 1987. Total output also dropped, but thanks to improved seed stock and more effective use of intensive technology, the decrease in production was not proportionate to the reduced area for cultivation. The average annual harvest between 1971 and 1975 was slightly below 6 million tons, and in 1987 it amounted to 6.1 million tons.

Since the early 1970s, sugar beets have occupied roughly the same amount of farmland as the other major technical crops—cotton and sunflowers—averaging some 3.5 million hectares. Sugar beet production, concentrated in the central and western Ukrainian Republic, the northwestern Caucasus, and the eastern areas of the Kazakh Republic and other Soviet Central Asian republics averaged 88.7 million tons per year between 1976 and 1980, well above the previous high of an average of 81.1 million tons per year in the 1966–70 period. Between 1981 and 1985, output fell to 76.3 million tons annually but rose thereafter, reaching 90 million tons in 1987. Although in the 1980s sugar beets continued to provide over 60 percent of the country's sugar production, the Soviet Union was becoming increasingly dependent on raw sugar imported primarily from Cuba, e.g., from 2.1 million tons per year between 1966 and 1970 to 4.9 million tons per year between 1981 and 1985.

Grown for fiber and as a source of linseed oil, flax has been particularly successful in the mixed-forest zone northwest of Moscow and in the Belorussian, Estonian, Latvian, Lithuanian, and northwest Ukrainian republics. Although the area sown to flax steadily decreased from 2.1 million hectares in 1940 to only 980,000 hectares in 1986, production actually rose from 349,000 tons of fiber in 1940 to a peak of 480,000 tons in 1965 and to 366,000 tons in 1986.

Hemp, the other significant fiber crop, has been grown since the eighteenth century, although its area of cultivation has steadily decreased from about 600,000 hectares in 1940 to fewer than 100,000 hectares in 1986. Used in making rope, string, and rough cloth, hemp is grown primarily in the central chernozem area south of Tula and in the northern Caucasus.

Forage Crops

Since Khrushchev's campaign to raise the consumption of meat products, the Soviet Union has been expanding the cultivation of forage crops to feed a larger number of livestock. This trend was reinforced under Brezhnev's tenure, particularly after the announcement of the Food Program in 1982. Thus the area occupied by forage crops grew dramatically from 18.1 million hectares in 1940 to 63.1 million hectares in 1960; it remained virtually unchanged throughout the 1960s and then steadily rose to reach a high of 71.4 million hectares in 1986, when it accounted for approximately one-third of the total sown area. The area occupied by perennial hay crops (alfalfa and clover) nearly doubled between 1960 and 1986, while annual grasses and corn for silage were cultivated on a gradually diminishing scale. Total nongrain feed production, including corn for silage, feed roots, and hay and green fodder, increased steadily from 427.4 million tons in 1960 to 554.6 million tons in 1986.

Potatoes and Vegetables

A staple of the Russian diet for centuries and an important animal feed source, potatoes are grown on private plots throughout the country. They are cultivated on a large scale in the Ukrainian, Belorussian, Estonian, Latvian, and Lithuanian republics and in the central European part of the Russian Republic. The area devoted to growing potatoes decreased steadily between 1960 (7.7 million hectares) and 1986 (6.4 millon hectares), although potatoes still accounted for nearly three-quarters of the total area devoted to vegetable crops. Potato harvests also declined substantially— from an average of 94.8 million tons annually between 1966 and 1970 to fewer than 78.4 million tons per year in the 1980-85 period.

Traditionally, the most widely grown vegetables in addition to potatoes have included beets, carrots, cabbages, cucumbers, tomatoes, and onions. These crops have been grown on an ever larger scale since the 1960s, and in 1986 they occupied nearly 1.7 million hectares. Yields increased proportionately, reaching a record 29.7 million tons in 1986. Thanks to the proliferation of large clusters of hothouses, it was possible to supply fresh cucumbers and tomatoes, among other produce, to the residents of major urban centers throughout the year. With private plots yielding roughly 40 percent of the vegetable harvest, much of the population, particularly the kolkhoz residents, grew a portion of their own produce.

Other Crops

Fruit cultivation in the Soviet Union is most successful in the southern, more temperate zones. The tiny Moldavian Republic, with its fertile soil and ample sunshine, produces more fruit and berries than all but the Ukrainian and Russian republics. In 1986 it harvested 1.2 million tons, as compared with 3.3 million tons in the Ukrainian Republic (which has 18 times more land area) and 2.9 million tons in the entire Russian Republic (which is 506 times the size of the Moldavian Republic). Orchards and vineyards occupied their largest area between 1971 and 1975, with a yearly average of 4.9 million hectares. However, the area allotted to non-citrus fruits decreased steadily from 3.8 million hectares in 1970 to 3.0 million hectares in 1986. Significant crops were table and wine grapes, which were widely grown in the warmer southern regions. The Azerbaydzhan and Moldavian republics accounted for over 40 percent of the total grape harvest, but the Ukrainian, Georgian, and Uzbek republics and the southern Russian Republic were also major producers. Citrus fruit growing was limited to the Black Sea coast of the Georgian Republic and a small area of the southeastern Azerbaydzhan Republic. In 1986 the Georgian Republic produced 97 percent of the total national harvest of 322,000 tons of citrus fruit.

Tea, a traditional beverage of Russians and the peoples of the Caucasus and Central Asia, is another specialty crop of the Georgian Republic, which accounted for 93.4 percent of national production in 1986. Other important centers of tea growing are the

*Azerbaydzhanis at
a central market in
Baku display produce,
including peppers,
tomatoes, cabbages,
and pomegranates.
Courtesy Jimmy Pritchard*

Azerbaydzhan Republic and Krasnodarskiy Krai in the Russian
Republic. The area reserved for tea cultivation grew significantly
between 1940 and 1986, going from 55,300 to 81,400 hectares.
Production rose steadily during the 1950s and thereafter, reaching a peak of 620,800 tons in 1985. Despite increased yields,
however, larger tea imports were necessary to meet consumer demand and reached 108,000 tons (equal to 17.4 percent of domestic production) in 1985.

Tobacco, like tea, is a fixture of Soviet life. The crop flourishes
in the warmer southern regions, particularly in the Moldavian
Republic, which produced about a third of the 1984 harvest. Other
centers of tobacco cultivation are Central Asia and the Caucasus,
which accounted for roughly 30 percent and 25 percent of the 1984
harvest, respectively. In 1940 only 72,800 tons were grown, but
by 1984 tobacco output had more than quadrupled, reaching
375,700 tons. Production, however, did not keep pace with demand,
and in 1984 about 103,000 tons (equal to more than 27 percent
of domestic output) had to be imported.

Animal Husbandry

Because it is less restricted by climatic conditions, livestock raising
is more widely distributed across the Soviet Union than is the cultivation of crops. For example, in the cooler, wetter northern regions
of the European part of the country, where few cash crops can be
grown, dairy farming is profitable because of the proximity to urban
markets and the ready availability of fodder. In the 90 percent of
the country considered nonarable, various forms of animal husbandry are practiced, such as reindeer herding in the Arctic and
sheep, goat, and cattle grazing on the grasslands of Central Asia
and Siberia. Nevertheless, it is the fertile triangle that has always
accounted for the bulk of the nation's animal products.

Animal husbandry has received special attention since the late
1950s, and a primary goal of Soviet agriculture has been to increase
the production and consumption of meat, milk, and eggs (see table
38, Appendix A). This effort has resulted in significantly larger
numbers of livestock. For example, the number of cattle more than
doubled between 1955 and 1987, rising from 56.7 million to 121.9
million head. During the same period, the number of hogs rose
even more dramatically (from 3.9 million to 80 million head), and
the number of sheep grew by half to reach 141.5 million head. The
number of goats and horses in 1987 stood at 6.5 and 5.8 million
head, slightly higher than in 1980 but well below the 1955 figures
of 14.0 and 14.2 million head, respectively. Indeed, throughout

Herder with cows on a road south of Moscow
Shepherd with his sheep, Azerbaydzhan Republic
Courtesy Jimmy Pritchard

the Soviet period, the number of horses steadily declined as agriculture became more mechanized.

Larger numbers of animals notwithstanding, food output per animal continued to lag far behind Western standards. For example, milk production per cow averaged roughly half that reported in Finland, where the climate is certainly no more favorable. And even though the Soviet Union had achieved a ratio of cattle-to-human population comparable to that of the United States, beef production per head in 1986 was 35 percent lower. Similarly, pork output per head fell some 30 percent below the figure for the United States. According to Western analysts, this low livestock productivity resulted from inadequate feed supplies in general and a deficiency of protein in feed rations in particular. Domestic producers of protein supplement from cotton and sunflower seeds and pulses were unable to meet demand, which the government did not satisfy through imports. This decision took a heavy toll on livestock productivity.

To streamline livestock raising, a new type of production entity emerged in the 1960s and became increasingly prominent—industrialized livestock enterprises outside the traditional kolkhoz and sovkhoz system. These specialized factory-like operations purchased their feed and other inputs from outside sources, to which they enjoyed priority access. In 1986 they accounted for about 20 percent of pork, 5 percent of beef and milk, and over 60 percent of poultry and egg production.

In the thirty-five years between 1950 and 1985, per capita meat and fat consumption increased some 135 percent, reaching sixty-one kilograms per year. During the same period, consumption of milk and dairy products climbed by nearly 88 percent, and egg consumption rose by an impressive 334 percent. Still, demand for these products far exceeded supply, and in the late 1980s their availability in state stores remained very limited.

Forestry

With a third of the world's forested area, the Soviet Union has long led all countries in the production of logs and sawn timber. Although Siberia and the Soviet Far East hold 75 percent of the country's total reserves, they accounted for only about 35 percent of timber output in the mid-1980s. The forests of the northern European part of the Russian Republic have supplied timber products to the major population centers for centuries, and the timber industry of the region is better organized and more efficient than that east of the Urals. In addition, the European pine and fir forests grow in denser stands and yield a generally superior product than the vast forests of the east, where the less desirable larch predominates. With the construction of some of the world's largest wood-processing centers in eastern Siberia and the Soviet Far East, and with the opening of the Baykal-Amur Main Line in 1989, the timber industry of the eastern regions was greatly advanced (see The Baykal-Amur Main Line, ch. 14).

The Soviet timber industry, which in 1986 employed roughly 454,000 workers, has had a long history of low productivity and excessive waste. Because of inadequate processing capacity, output of wood pulp, newsprint, paper, cardboard, plywood, and other wood products was scandalously low, considering the size of the Soviet Union's timber resources and its perennial position as the world leader in roundwood and sawed timber production. By the mid-1980s, the country appeared to have made substantial progress in achieving greater balance in its wood products mix. In 1986, for example, the production of pulp (9 million tons) was nearly four times the 1960 output (2.3 million tons), paper production (6.2 million tons) was almost three times higher, and cardboard output (4.6 million tons) was roughly five times the 1960 level. Nevertheless, in 1986 the Soviet Union ranked only fourth in world paper and cardboard production, with only one-sixth the output of either the United States or Japan. A high percentage of the roundwood harvest was used in the form of unprocessed logs and firewood, which remained an important fuel in the countryside.

In addition to their wood products, the north European, Siberian, and Far Eastern forests are important for their animal resources. Fur exports have long been an important source of hard currency (see Glossary). Although trapping continued to be widely practiced in the 1980s, fur farming, set up soon after the Bolshevik Revolution, accounted for most of the country's production of mink, sable, fox, and other fine furs.

One of the significant accomplishments of Soviet forestry has been the successful effort to restore and maintain production through reforestation of areas where overfelling had occurred. In 1986 alone, restoration work on 2.2 million hectares was completed, which included planting trees on 986,000 hectares. In the same year, nearly 1.7 million hectares of trees that had been planted as seedlings reached commercial maturity. In addition, some 109,000 hectares of shelterbelts were planted along gullies, ravines, sand dunes, and pastureland. This policy of conservation, in place for several decades, helped fight wind erosion and preserved soil moisture.

Fishing

Fish has always been a prominent part of the Soviet diet. Until the mid-1950s, the bulk of the Soviet catch came from inland lakes, rivers, and coastal waters. Thereafter, the Soviet Union launched an ambitious program to develop the world's largest oceangoing fishing fleet, which consisted of 4,222 ships in 1986. The Soviet Union became the world's second leading fish producer, trailing Japan by a small margin throughout the 1970s and 1980s. In 1986 Soviet production amounted to 11.4 million tons, most of which was caught in marine fisheries.

The Atlantic Ocean supplied 49.2 percent of the total catch in 1980, while the Pacific Ocean yielded 41.3 percent. The Caspian, Black, Azov, and Aral seas, suffering from lowered water levels, increased salinity, and pollution, became relatively less important fisheries in the 1970s and 1980s. Whereas Murmansk had been the one large fishing port before the expansion of the oceangoing fleet, by 1980 there were twenty-three such ports, the largest of which were Vladivostok, Nakhodka, Kaliningrad, Archangel, Klaipeda, Riga, Tallin, Sevastopol', and Kerch'. In 1982 more than 96 percent of the frozen fish, 45 percent of the canned fish, 60 percent of the fish preserve, and 94 percent of the fish meal delivered to market was processed at sea by large, modern factory ships.

Because of the worldwide trend of claiming 200-mile territorial waters, total fish production fell after 1977. The open Pacific was viewed as a promising fishery to offset reduced production in coastal waters, which had been yielding up to 60 percent of the Soviet catch. Inland fisheries also began to receive more attention, and fish farming was promoted as ponds were established close to urban centers. Between 1961 and 1980, the production of fresh fish by such enterprises increased by over 8.8 times, reaching 158,300 tons. The Eleventh Five-Year Plan called for pond fish production to be tripled.

The Twelfth Five-Year Plan, 1986–90

Following the disappointing performance of Soviet agriculture during the Eleventh Five-Year Plan, the Twelfth Five-Year Plan got off to a promising start, with larger than expected grain harvests and improved labor productivity. Nevertheless, Western analysts viewed as unrealistic most of the Twelfth Five-Year Plan production targets—both those set forth in the Food Program of 1982 and those subsequently revised downward.

According to the document *Basic Directions for the Economic and Social Development of the USSR for 1986–1990 and for the Period to the Year 2000*, the Soviet Union would significantly increase production of all agricultural commodities. The ambitious 1990 production target ranges laid out in this document called for increases over the average annual output of the Eleventh Five-Year Plan. The

Fishing boats in the port of Listvyanka, Lake Baykal, Russian Republic
Courtesy Jimmy Pritchard

target ranges for agricultural commodities were as follows: grain from 38.7 to 41.4 percent; sugar beets from 20.6 to 24.5 percent; sunflower seeds from 48.9 to 50.9 percent; potatoes from 14.9 to 17.4 percent; vegetables from 36.9 to 43.7 percent; fruits, berries, and grapes from 40.4 to 51.6 percent; raw cotton from 9.5 to 13.1 percent; meat from 10.7 to 29.4 percent; milk from 12.1 to 16.3 percent; and eggs from 7.5 to 10.2 percent. The 1990 goals for the fishing industry ranged from 4.4 to 4.6 million tons of fish food products and about 3 billion cans of fish preserve. The forestry industry was tasked with increasing the production of pulp by 15 to 18 percent, of paper by 11 to 15 percent, and of fiberboard by 17 to 20 percent. As in all sectors of the economy, conservation of raw materials and reduction of waste in transportation and storage of commodities were to be emphasized more than in any previous period.

Although grain harvests were excellent in 1986 and 1987, output fell to only 195 million tons in 1988, forcing the Soviet Union to import more than 36 million tons that year. The 1988 harvest of potatoes, other vegetables, and fruits also declined as compared with the previous two years. As a result, the availability of food products throughout the country worsened, and in mid-1989 many Western observers believed a severe shortage and possibly famine

541

were impending. Clearly the Twelfth Five-Year Plan's goals for agriculture would not be attained, a severe setback for Gorbachev's *perestroika* efforts.

* * *

An invaluable source of statistical data on the agro-industrial complex is the 1987 publication *Narodnoe khoziaistvo SSSR za 70 let,* compiled by the Soviet Union's Gosudarstvennyi komitet po statistike. *USSR Situation and Outlook Report,* published annually by the United States Department of Agriculture's Economic Research Service, presents a concise overview of recent Soviet agricultural performance. D. Gale Johnson and Karen McConnell Brooks's *Prospects for Soviet Agriculture in the 1980s* examines Soviet agricultural efficiency in light of policy and natural and climatic factors. *The Soviet Rural Economy,* edited by Robert C. Stuart, presents several highly pertinent essays on Soviet agriculture, including Michael L. Wyzan's "The Kolkhoz and the Sovkhoz," Valentin Litvin's "Agro-Industrial Complexes," and Everett M. Jacobs's "Soviet Agricultural Management and Planning and the 1982 Administrative Reforms." Two other important anthologies are *Agricultural Policies in the USSR and Eastern Europe,* edited by Ronald A. Francisco, Betty A. Laird, and Roy D. Laird, and *Soviet Agricultural and Peasant Affairs,* edited by Roy D. Laird. Paul E. Lydolph's classic *Geography of the USSR* provides a comprehensive description of Soviet agricultural resources, including forestry and fishing. The evolution of current policy is traced by Karl-Eugen Waedekin in numerous *Radio Liberty Research Bulletin* reports, including "The Private Agricultural Sector in the 1980s," " 'Contract' and 'Normless' Labor on Soviet Farms," and "What Is New about Brigades in Soviet Agriculture?" Zhores A. Medvedev's *Soviet Agriculture* and Valentin Litvin's *The Soviet Agro-Industrial Complex* provide highly detailed descriptions of the organization and functioning of Soviet agriculture. (For further information and complete citations, see Bibliography.)

Chapter 14. Transportation and Communications

Elements of the Soviet Union's transportation and communications networks

THE TRANSPORTATION AND COMMUNICATIONS systems of the Soviet Union were owned and operated by the government primarily to serve the economic needs of the country as determined by the Communist Party of the Soviet Union (CPSU). In addition to being influenced by the policies of the regime, the development of transportation and communications also has been greatly influenced by the country's vast size, geography, climate, population distribution, and location of industries and natural resources. Although the population and industrial centers were concentrated in the European part of the country, which has a more moderate climate, many of the mineral and energy resources were in sparsely inhabited, climatically inhospitable expanses of Siberia and other remote areas. Hence, the transportation and communications networks were much denser in the European part than in the Asian part of the country.

In 1989, and historically, railroads were the premier mode of transportation in the Soviet Union. Railroads played significant roles in times of war, and they accelerated industrial development. They also facilitated the normal flow of raw materials, manufactured goods, and passengers. Government policies provided for extensive trackage and large numbers of locomotives, rolling stock, and support facilities. Although railroads carried more freight and passengers over long distances, trucks and buses carried more cargo and people on short hauls. Because automotive transport was not generally used for long hauls, many roads outside of urban areas had gravel or dirt surfaces. The lack of paved roads in rural areas seriously hampered the movement of agricultural products and supplies. Privately owned automobiles, on a per capita basis, were few in number compared with those in the West and therefore were of limited importance in transportation.

Inland waterways, comprising navigable rivers, lakes, and canals, enabled a wide variety of ships, barges, and other craft to transport passengers and freight to their destinations inexpensively. Commuters in urban areas often used hydrofoils on rivers for rapid transport, while freight moved on the waterways more slowly over much greater distances. Waterways were subject to freezing in winter, although a fleet of ice breakers extended the navigable season. Most rivers in the Asian part of the country flow northward into the Arctic Ocean and thus were of little help in moving raw materials to the European part of the country. At some river ports in Siberia, raw materials were loaded onto ships for delivery to domestic and foreign ports via the Arctic to the Pacific or the Atlantic oceans.

A large, modern, and well-diversified fleet of merchant and passenger vessels conveyed not only freight and passengers to the world's maritime nations but also Soviet political influence. Many cargo vessels, often highly specialized, were designed to off-load freight and vehicles in foreign countries not having modern port facilities. Although the world's largest fleet of passenger liners belonged to the Soviet Union, the voyagers were mainly Western tourists. Extensive fishing and scientific research fleets, together with several international ferry systems, added to the already substantial worldwide maritime presence of the Soviet Union.

The civilian air fleet was primarily a fast transporter of people but was often the only mode of transport available to some areas in the Far North, Siberia, and the Soviet Far East. Using the international airports of Moscow and other major cities, Soviet airplanes flew to almost every country of the world. The air fleet also had many specialized aircraft performing various missions not associated with airlines in the West, such as agricultural spraying, medical evacuations, and energy exploration.

As a means of efficiently conveying oil, natural gas, and some other materials, pipelines played a significant part in the transportation system. Major pipelines stretched from northern and Siberian oil and gas fields to refineries and industrial users in the European part of the country. Pipelines supplied energy to Eastern Europe, which was heavily dependent on Soviet gas and oil, and to Western Europe, which exchanged hard currency (see Glossary) for Soviet natural gas.

Using a communications system that incorporated advanced satellite technologies, the government transmitted its radio and television programming throughout most of the Soviet Union. Telephones were mainly used by government or party officials or others having official responsibilities in the economy.

Railroads

Railroads were the most important component of the Soviet transportation system. They carried freight over great distances, and historically they have contributed to the economic development of the Soviet Union as efficient carriers of materials between producers and users, both domestic and foreign.

Historical Background, 1913–39

On the eve of World War I, imperial Russia had a rail network extending 58,500 kilometers. In 1913 it carried 132.4 million tons of freight over an average distance of 496 kilometers, and 184.8 million passengers boarded its trains. In 1918, following the Bolshevik Revolution (see Glossary), the new regime nationalized the railroads. During the Civil War (1918–21), the railroads played a strategic role in the Bolshevik government's struggle against both White forces and invading foreign armies but suffered serious losses and damage in tracks, locomotives, rolling stock, yards, and stations. In 1920 Vladimir I. Lenin directed the first plan for nationwide development of the economy, which created the State Commission on the Electrification of Russia (Gosudarstvennaia komissiia po elektrifikatsii Rossii—Goelro). It called for the electrification of the country over a ten- to fifteen-year period, the development of eight economic areas, and the reconstruction of the transportation network. Railroads were assigned the task of linking the economic areas and of transporting raw materials to industrial producers and finished goods to users. To that end, the regime provided for the electrification of the most important main lines and the construction of new lines.

During the 1920s and 1930s, transportation, and in particular the railroads, played a leading economic role and experienced rapid development. Feliks E. Dzerzhinskii, the chairman of the dreaded Vecheka (see Glossary) and the commissar of internal affairs, was also named the commissar of railways. Because of his first two positions, Dzerzhinskii ensured a rapid development of the railroads. New rail lines were built between the eastern regions and the industrial areas in the west. By 1925 some 4,000 kilometers of new lines had been laid in both the European and the Asian portions of the Soviet Union, including the first electrified line, an industrial spur from Baku to Surakhany completed in 1926.

During the First Five-Year Plan (1928–32), the railroad network was repaired, improved, and expanded. The plan recognized that industrial complexes (see Glossary), such as the Ural-Kuznetsk coal and iron complex, needed transportation links. Plans called for connecting the Siberian and Central Asian areas, rich in natural or agricultural resources—ores, timber, coal, cotton, and wheat—to manufacturers and consumers in the western portions of the country. Thus the Turkestan-Siberian Railway, 1,450 kilometers long, was built, along with the Central Kazakhstan and the Caucasus railroads, among other lines. The European portion of the country also saw new lines laid, connecting industrial areas with their sources of raw materials.

In the 1930s, the railroads introduced new rolling stock and locomotives that contributed to better performance. In the mid-1930s, diesel-electric locomotives began to be used. Although more costly to produce and to maintain than the electric locomotives and also less powerful and slower, diesel-electric locomotives had several advantages over the steam locomotives in use, particularly under existing operating conditions. Fuel-efficient, diesel-electric locomotives covered long distances between refuelings, required minimal maintenance between runs, sustained good speeds, damaged tracks less, used standardized spare parts, and offered operating flexibility. In contrast to the United States and Canada, two countries also employing railroads to cover vast expanses, the change from steam to diesel-electric traction in the Soviet Union was initially very slow, in large measure because of a scarcity of trained manpower, maintenance facilities, and spare parts.

During the Second Five-Year Plan (1933–37), new rolling stock, including freight cars of new design, was also produced. Although most freight cars were still of the two-axle type with a payload varying between twenty and sixty tons, specialized four-axle cars, such as hoppers and tippers of up to seventy tons, began to enter service. The new rolling stock was equipped with safety and labor saving devices, such as automatic braking and automatic couplings, which increased safety and allowed more efficient train handling at classification yards. The higher speeds and heavier train weights made possible by more modern traction and rolling stock in turn required heavier rails, improved cross ties, and ballast. The automatic block signal system and centralized traffic control increased the operating efficiency of trains.

Despite the modernization program, Soviet railroads lagged behind the performance levels set by the plans. Ineffective management, labor problems, such as poor work attitudes, and a high accident rate contributed to the failures. On the average, railcars and locomotives were idle about 71 percent and 53 percent of their operational time, respectively. Yet industrialization efforts placed increasing demands on the railroads. The military authorities were also concerned about the poor performance of the railroads, fearing their inability to support national defense requirements.

From 1928 to 1940, the length of operating lines grew from 76,900 kilometers to 106,100 kilometers and included 1,900 kilometers of electrified lines. Freight traffic more than quadrupled from 93.4 billion ton-kilometers to 420.7 billion ton-kilometers. Passenger traffic also increased in the same period, from 24.5 billion passenger-kilometers to 100.4 billion passenger-kilometers. This growth in freight and passenger traffic was made possible by track improvements, new rolling stock, locomotives, signaling and control equipment and procedures, and new and more efficient classification yards.

Passengers buying food at a stop on the Trans-Siberian Railway
Women painting a center line on the main highway
between Khar'kov and Kiev, Ukrainian Republic
Courtesy Jimmy Pritchard

549

World War II

After the Nazi-Soviet Nonaggression Pact of 1939, the Soviet Union occupied Estonia, Latvia, Lithuania, eastern Poland, and portions of Finland and Romania (see Prelude to War, ch. 2). Consequently, before Germany's 1941 attack on the Soviet Union, the size of the Soviet rail network increased by the assets located in these areas and countries. During the Soviet-Finnish War (November 1939 to March 1940), Soviet railroads supported military operations. Over 20 percent of the rolling stock was used to supply the operations against the Finnish forces. Although military cargo shipments originated in many parts of the country, they all fed into the October and Murmansk railroads in areas where few highways were able to handle motor transport. This fact and the distance that freight had to travel to the front combined to cause unloading bottlenecks at final destination stations and yards. Although delays were substantial, civilian and military railroad authorities learned important lessons from the Finnish campaign.

During World War II, railroads were of major importance in supporting military operations as well as in providing for the increased needs of the wartime economy. Because of their importance and vulnerability, trains, tracks, yards, and other facilities became the prime targets of the German air force and, in areas close to the front, of German artillery.

Railroad operations during the war corresponded to the main phases of military operations. The first phase extended from the German offensive on June 22, 1941, to the Red Army's counteroffensive, which culminated in a Soviet victory at Stalingrad in February 1943. During this phase, the railroads evacuated people, industrial plants, and their own rolling stock to the eastern areas of the country. From July to November 1941, some 1.5 million carloads of freight were moved eastward. The railroads also carried troops and military matériel from rear areas to the front. All of the operations were accomplished under threatened or actual enemy fire.

The second phase extended throughout most of 1943, when the Red Army slowly advanced against strong German resistance. The railroads coped with increasing demands for transportation services as industrial plants increased production. In addition, the Red Army relied heavily on the railroads to move personnel and supplies for major operations. Thus, during the first three months of the Kursk campaign (March to July 1943), three major rail lines averaged about 2,800 cars with military cargo per day, reaching a daily peak of 3,249 in May. Moreover, as the Soviet forces regained territories,

Metro station interior, Moscow
Passengers on the Moscow metro
Courtesy Jimmy Pritchard

military and civilian railroad construction teams restored and rebuilt trackage destroyed by the retreating enemy.

In the third phase, from early 1944 to the end of the war in May 1945, the Red Army rapidly extended the front westward, causing the distances between production facilities (in the Ural Mountains and Siberia) and military consumers to grow accordingly, thereby further straining railroad resources. The Red Army's Belorussian offensive, which was launched on June 23, 1944, required, during its buildup phase, 440,000 freight cars, or 65 percent of Soviet rolling stock. In early 1945, the Red Army pursued German forces into neighboring countries, requiring the railroads to cope with different track widths, which went from 1,520-millimeter-gauge track to 1,435-millimeter-gauge track in Romania, Bulgaria, Hungary, Poland, and eventually in Germany itself.

Despite the effort made to haul men and matériel to the front and to provide at least some service to the civilian sector, as well as to restore operations in war-damaged areas, the Soviet Union managed to build 6,700 kilometers of new lines during the war years. The new lines tapped areas rich in the mineral resources that were required for the war effort or shortened the distances between important economic regions. Of the 52,400 kilometers of Soviet main track roadway damaged during the war, 48,800 kilometers were restored by May 1945. About 166,000 freight cars were destroyed, and the number of locomotives decreased by about 1,000, although almost 2,000 were furnished by the United States as part of an agreement authorized by its Lend-Lease Law (see Glossary).

The Postwar Period, 1946–60

During the postwar recovery period, the railroads played a key role in rebuilding the national economy, in both the industrial and the agricultural sectors. To enable the railroads to carry out assignments, improvements had to be made in traction equipment, rolling stock, roadbeds, stations, yards, and traffic control equipment. New diesel-electric and electric locomotives were produced, and heavier rails allowed increased axle loads and train speeds. Automatic block signaling systems also contributed to higher speeds and better traffic control. Electrified lines were slowly extended. Although the Fourth Five-Year Plan (1945–50) provided for the restoration of damaged rolling stock and rail facilities, the Fifth Five-Year Plan (1951–55) emphasized new construction. The plan's goals were severely underfulfilled, mainly in production of freight cars, trackage, and other equipment, but freight turnover was 57 percent above plan. This achievement was made possible by increased train loads, higher operating speeds, more efficient loading and off-loading procedures, and higher labor productivity. The higher speeds and higher number of average daily runs of locomotives hauling freight were made possible by growing numbers of diesel-electric and electric locomotives coming into service.

At the urging of CPSU first secretary Nikita S. Khrushchev, in the late 1950s electrification proceeded on some high-density passenger and freight lines. Khrushchev gave priority to railroads in the Ural Mountains area and to those connecting the Urals with southeastern and central European areas and with Siberia and other eastern regions. By the end of 1960, the railroads had a network of 125,800 kilometers of lines, some 13,800 kilometers of which were electrified.

Beginning in the early 1960s, the railroads experienced a period of prosperity. Freight traffic grew rapidly, by 59 percent between 1961 and 1970, while passenger traffic increased by 50 percent. New equipment improved labor productivity. More electric and diesel-electric locomotives entering service, combined with improved tracks and roadbeds, increased net train weights and speeds. In the late 1960s, as the growth of net train weights and speeds leveled off, train density—the number of trains moving on a given track—increased, thus allowing further increases in freight carried. Nevertheless, in the early 1970s train productivity continued to grow, but at declining rates. By 1975 the railroads reached their limits in terms of traffic density and train speeds and weights. Subsequently, the railroads strained to satisfy the demands of the national economy. Between 1977 and 1982, the total tonnage of shipments stagnated, increasing only from 3.723 billion tons originated (see Glossary) to 3.725 billion tons originated. Other indicators dropped—such as the average daily distance traveled by locomotives and cars, and speeds—the result of ever increasing track congestion. Additional factors contributing to poor railroad performance in the late 1970s and early 1980s were a deteriorating labor discipline and a decline in the quality of repairs and maintenance.

In 1983 recovery from the slump started when managers reduced traffic congestion and made train and other operations more efficient. Use of electrically synchronized double and triple engines made running heavier trains possible and reduced traffic congestion.

In the late 1980s, railroads carried a larger share of freight and passengers longer distances than any other transportation system in the Soviet Union. In 1986 railroads transported 3.8 trillion tonkilometers of freight, or a 47 percent share of all freight carried by all systems (see table 39, Appendix A). At the end of 1986, the railroads reached a length of 145,600 kilometers, of which 50,600 kilometers, or almost 35 percent, were electrified.

Organization and Equipment of the Railroads

The Soviet Railroads (Sovetskie zheleznye dorogi—SZD) were managed and operated by the all-union (see Glossary) Ministry of Railways. The ministry was divided into twenty-three main administrations, each responsible for an overall segment of the railroads' operating or administrative management. Directly under the ministry were the thirty-two regional railroads, which in fact constituted the SZD. The railroads were named after republics, major cities, river basins, or larger geographic areas. The October Railroad, headquartered in Leningrad, was of course named in honor of the October (Bolshevik) Revolution. Each regional railroad, except the Moldavian, was subdivided into divisions. The divisions were generally named after their headquartered stations (see table 40, Appendix A).

In 1989 the most important lines carried heavy freight and passenger traffic and were electrified. Among them were lines linking industrial areas, maritime ports, and foreign countries. Also, major population centers were interconnected and linked to vacation areas. Lines with steep grades, as in mountainous regions, were often electrified (see table 41, Appendix A).

The railroads had about 7,000 marshaling yards, of which 100 were of major importance. Computer technology has gradually increased the efficiency and quality of train handling at the yards, many of which had centralized hump release controls and automatic rolling speed devices. Such automated procedures as checking a train's weight and composition, as well as modernized communications facilities, have sped train formation and dispatch and provided yard management with advance information on the composition of arriving trains. Nevertheless, in the mid-1980s classification yards were unable to process efficiently the required number of trains.

Automated signaling equipment and devices helped improve traffic control and train safety, although the latter remained a problem in 1989. Some 20 percent of track lines were under centralized train control. This enabled the railroads to increase track capacity substantially, particularly over long distances. In 1989 more than 60 percent of the network was equipped with the automatic block system, which regulated distances between trains, as well as with automatic cab signaling.

Electric and diesel-electric locomotives were the basic categories of traction. Within these categories were about twenty versions of of marsh along the track, thus keeping them in a continuous state of permafrost. In the Caucasus area, a new electrified line, almost 200 kilometers long, was planned from Tbilisi through the Caucasus Mountains to Ordzhonikidze. Plans called for the Caucasus Mountain Pass Railroad to shorten by 960 kilometers the distance for trains from Tbilisi to Ordzhonikidze via Armavir. Several tunnels, totaling forty-two kilometers, and numerous bridges have been planned. Originally scheduled for completion by the year 2000, the project was being stalled in 1989 by environmental groups.

A 450-kilometer rail line from Makat, in the Kazakh Republic, to Aleksandrov Gay, in Saratovskaya Oblast in the Russian Republic, was started in 1984 and was nearing completion in 1989. It was projected to cut over 1,000 kilometers from the route between Central Asia and Moscow.

Metropolitan Railways

The Ministry of Railways also operated metropolitan railway systems, or metros, in major cities. In 1987 eleven cities had one or more metro lines in operation, and ten others were either building or planning to build lines (see table 43, Appendix A). In late 1986, the length of all lines on the metro systems was 457 kilometers, and over 4.6 billion passengers rode on the combined metro systems in that year. The eleven cities' operating systems had a fleet of about 5,950 passenger railcars in 1986.

Automotive Transport

Trucks, buses, and passenger automobiles were important primarily to local transportation systems. Trucks carried freight on short hauls except in areas not served by railroads or inland waterways. Almost all freight started or finished its journey on trucks but was carried greater distances by rail, ship, airplane, or pipeline. Buses carried substantial numbers of passengers, for the most part on urban or short runs. Transportation by privately owned passenger automobiles, which were relatively few on a per capita basis, was not significant compared with public means.

Development of Automotive Transport

In 1910 a railroad car factory in Riga began producing the first passenger automobiles and trucks in imperial Russia. Under the Soviet regime, automotive transportation developed more slowly than in western Europe and the United States. As early as the 1930s, problems of poor road infrastructure, shortage of spare parts, and insufficient fueling, repair, and maintenance facilities plagued automotive transportation. Some manufacturing plants were set up with Western help.

During World War II, automotive production concentrated almost exclusively on trucks and light, jeep-like vehicles. Their chassis were also adapted for armored cars and amphibious and other types of military vehicles. During major battles and operations, automotive transportation carried needed troops and matériel to the front. While Leningrad lay besieged (1941–44), trucks, driving over the frozen surface of Lake Ladoga, brought in about 600,000 tons of supplies and brought out over 700,000 persons. During the entire war, Soviet automotive transport carried over 101 million tons of freight in support of military operations. A sizable portion of the Soviet vehicle fleet was provided by the United States as part of the lend-lease agreement.

Since 1945 Soviet authorities have continued highway construction, so that by 1987 the public road networks, which excluded roads of industrial and agricultural enterprises, amounted to 1,609,900 kilometers, of which 1,196,000 kilometers were in the hard-surfaced category—concrete, asphalt, or gravel. Nevertheless, about 40 percent of this category of roads were gravel. In addition, there were 413,900 kilometers of unsurfaced roads.

The road network varied in density according to the geographic area and the industrial concentration. Thus, the Estonian Republic had the highest road density while the Russian and Kazakh republics had the lowest. The latter republics, however, contained vast, economically underdeveloped and sparsely populated areas. Overall, the European portion, excluding the extreme northern and Arctic areas, had the densest road network, particularly in areas having concentrations of industries and population (see fig. 19).

In 1989 many roads were not all-weather roads but rather were unimproved and unstable in bad weather, especially during thaws and rains. Except for 25,000 kilometers of all-weather surfaces, all rural roads in the European and Central Asian parts of the country, as well as all roads in Siberia and the Far East, were little better than dirt tracks. Trucks, carrying light loads (fewer than four tons) and traveling at low speeds, broke down frequently. These roads caused delays in shipments, high fuel consumption, and increased tire wear. In marshy and permafrost areas, unsurfaced roads were usable only when the ground and rivers were frozen, from about November to May. Russians have coined a word, *rasputitsa*, to describe the time of year when roads are impassable. Repair and refueling facilities along rural roads were rare or nonexistent. Nevertheless, in rural areas, roads were the prime arteries for shipping farm products and bringing in the required equipment and supplies. Poor road conditions were a major factor in the Soviet Union's serious agricultural problems, particularly the one of perishables spoiling before they reached the market. Rural populations relied on bus transportation over poor roads for essential access to urban areas.

Freight Transportation by Trucks

Without a developed network of highways and service facilities, Soviet authorities have essentially relegated trucking to local and short hauls, except in remote areas not having rail or ship transport. In 1986, in terms of freight turnover, trucks ranked fourth among all transportation systems, with a 6 percent share. Nevertheless, trucking had 81 percent of the tons originated by all freight transportation systems combined (see table 44, Appendix A). This anomaly indicated that trucks were primarily used on short hauls, averaging about eighteen kilometers. Long-distance or intercity hauling was mainly by railroads and inland waterways. The agricultural sector accounted for about 80 percent of freight originated on trucks. In 1986 freight transported by trucks amounted to almost 27 billion tons originated and 488.5 billion ton-kilometers (see Glossary). Common carrier trucks accounted for 6.7 billion tons originated and 141 billion ton-kilometers. Trucking's most important customers were agriculture, industry, construction, and commerce.

Trucking enterprises were not able to meet the strong demand for their services. Among the contributing factors to the industry's failure were inadequate roads, inefficient traffic organization—some 45 percent of vehicles traveled empty—and prolonged periods of unserviceability resulting from shortages of spare parts, drivers, tires, and fuel. Even in the largest metropolitan areas, refueling and repair facilities were scarce by Western standards. In rural areas, particularly in Siberia and the Far North, such facilities were often nonexistent. Repair and maintenance of vehicles belonging to transportation enterprises (see Glossary) and collective farms (see Glossary) were performed at central facilities, which sometimes belonged to manufacturing plants. Repair was hampered by a chronic shortage of spare parts. Given the extent of poor roads, even the absence of roads, many cargo vehicles were of the rugged, cross-country type, with all-wheel traction similar to those used by the armed forces as tactical vehicles. Many vehicles were specially designed for cold weather operations.

Passenger Transportation

In the mid-1980s, buses were the primary means of passenger transportation, accounting for almost 44 percent of traffic on all

565

transportation systems in 1986 (see table 45, Appendix A). Indeed, in 1986 public transportation buses carried the most passengers—48.8 billion passengers boarded—of all means of transportation. Most passengers traveled short distances on intracity and suburban runs. In 1986 the average distance traveled by a passenger was 9.5 kilometers. In that year, taxicabs carried more than 1.4 billion fares. In the 1980s, private automobiles were rare compared with most Western nations. In 1985 the Soviet Union had 11.7 million automobiles. Some Western authorities believed that about one-third of them were owned by the CPSU or the government.

Inland Waterways

The Soviet Union used an extensive inland navigational network, both natural (rivers and lakes) and man made (canals and reservoirs). The waterways enabled a variety of general and special-purpose river craft to transport the output of mines, forests, collective farms, and factories to domestic and foreign destinations. Some Soviet ships took on cargo at river ports located well inland and delivered it directly to ports on the Arctic, Atlantic, or Pacific oceans or on the Baltic, North, or Mediterranean seas. An inland passenger fleet transported millions of commuters, as well as business and pleasure travelers. Inland waterways were of prime importance to the economic viability of remote Arctic, Siberian, and Far Eastern regions, where they constituted the main, and often the sole, means of surface transportation.

Development of Waterways

Following the Bolshevik Revolution, the new regime decided first on reconstruction and then on expansion and modernization of the inland waterway system. The plan encompassed opening to navigation, or expanding navigation on, major rivers, particularly in the Asian part of the Soviet Union, and included new infrastructure ashore.

In the 1930s, two major canals were constructed: one connecting the Baltic and White seas, 227 kilometers long, with nineteen locks; the other connecting Moscow to the Volga River, 128 kilometers long (see fig. 20). Both were built using prisoners, the first at a cost of about 225,000 lives. By 1940 about 108,900 kilometers of river and 4,200 kilometers of man-made waterways were in operation, which allowed movement of 73.9 million tons originated of freight. During World War II, most of the inland fleet was converted to landing craft for river-crossing operations. As a result of hostilities, inland navigation suffered losses in vessels, canals, and shore installations.

The Fourth Five-Year Plan provided for the restoration of navigation on major waterways in the European part of the Soviet Union after World War II. It included repair of the fleet, construction of new vessels, and rebuilding and expansion of port installations. In the 1950s, construction of the 101-kilometer canal connecting the Volga and Don rivers, also built using prisoners, brought all the major inland river ports within the reach of the Black, Baltic, Caspian, Azov, and White seas. The navigable length of the inland waterway network reached its peak of 144,500 kilometers in 1970. Thereafter, it began to decline as, on the one hand, distance-cutting reservoirs and canals were opened to navigation and, on the other hand, navigation was discontinued on rivers with a low traffic density. Thus by 1987 the length of inland waterways under navigation was reduced to 122,500 kilometers, exclusive of the Caspian Sea. Navigational channels were deepened, and canals and locks were widened. New waterways, including tributaries of major rivers, were developed in Siberia and the Far East. As part of that process, the ports of Omsk and Novosibirsk were expanded, and new ports were built at Tomsk, Surgut, and Tobol'sk. Equipment capable of handling twenty-ton containers was installed at Krasnoyarsk, Osetrovsk, and ports in the Yakutiya region. The most heavily navigated sections of Siberia's Ob', Irtysh, Yenisey, and Lena rivers were deepened to the "minimum guaranteed depth" of three meters.

Further development of navigation on smaller rivers in the Far East was begun in the early 1980s, and navigation increased on other waterways serving industrialized areas. By 1985 the Volga and Kama river locks had reached their traffic limits and required widening. To respond to increased demand and to replace obsolete vessels, 1,020 dry bulk and oil barges, 247 passenger vessels, and 945 pusher tugs, freighters, and tankers were put into service between 1981 and 1985.

The Waterway System

In 1987 the Russian Republic's Ministry of the River Fleet and the main river transportation administrations of the other republics were, among them, responsible for the 122,500 kilometers of navigable rivers and man-made waterways. Soviet inland waterways are divided into four main categories by depth: super main line, with a guaranteed depth of four meters; main line, with at least 2.6 meters of depth; local, with up to 1.4 meters of depth;

Figure 20. Major Inland Waterways, 1984

and small river, with a water depth of up to one meter. In the European part of the country, the Volga, Kama, Don, and Dnepr rivers and their reservoirs formed the 7,400-kilometer-long United Deep-Water Network. This network had thirty-six water reservoirs, ninety-two locks, and a "guaranteed depth" of four meters on 90 percent of its length. Although many tributaries of large rivers fall generally into the local and small river categories, they nevertheless contributed importantly to many regions' economies, and they represented about 55 percent of the navigable rivers in Siberia and the Far East.

The river fleet was composed of a wide variety of cargo and passenger vessels and special-purpose ships, such as tugs and icebreakers. Dry cargo river ships ranged from 150 to 5,000 tons in capacity, whereas oil barges ranged up to 9,000 tons. Barge sets, that is, motorized barges pushing one or more "dumb" barges, totaled up to 16,000 tons on Siberian rivers and up to 22,000 tons on the Volga-Kama waterways.

Among the ships, boats, and motorized and "dumb" barges were specialized vessels designed to carry fruit, grain, ore, cement, containers, automobiles, and refrigerated cargo. A variety of passenger vessels, including hydrofoils and air-cushion vehicles, had a passenger capacity from a few dozen to 1,000 people. In a special category were the river-ocean vessels, which included dry bulk carriers (2,700 to 3,000 tons) and liquid tankers (4,800 to 5,000 tons). They made possible direct shipments between domestic inland ports and some 300 maritime and river ports in twenty-six countries in Europe, North Africa, and Asia, including Iran and Japan, as well as Soviet ports on the Arctic Ocean. The fleet of tugboats, both pullers and pushers, the latter equipped with automatic couplers for barge trains, was well adapted to general and specialized operations, including towing huge timber rafts. The tugboats' engine power ranged from 110 kilowatts to 2,940 kilowatts.

All navigable rivers in the Soviet Union are affected by ice. Depending on the region, the yearly navigation season has been as short as 60 days on northern rivers and as long as 230 days on rivers in warmer climates. Icebreakers were therefore an essential component of the Soviet inland fleet in order to extend operations beyond the onset of ice. They were particularly important in the mouths of rivers flowing into the Arctic Ocean, where ice tended to accumulate because of differences between the thawing seasons of rivers and seas. Icebreakers also helped river vessels to reach their wintering ports before the end of the navigable season.

River Ports and Facilities

River ports facilitated the transfer of cargo from one mode of transportation to another. Port facilities, such as piers on free-flowing rivers, have been constructed to account for the seasonal fluctuations of water levels, which sometimes reach several meters. In 1985 the Russian Republic's inland waterway ports had 162 kilometers of mooring facilities, half of which were provided with mechanized transloading equipment. The basic portal cranes were of five-, ten- and fifteen-ton lifting capacity, while container-handling cranes, having capacities of up to 30.5 tons, were available in major ports. Floating cranes, conveyor belts, and pneumatic loading/unloading devices for grain, granular materials, and bulk cargo were in use. In 1985 river ports in the Russian Republic had 2,220 pier and floating cranes.

Passenger Transportation

Passenger transportation constituted an important function of the river fleet, although its share of the overall passenger traffic was small. In 1986 river boats carried 136 million fares. On major deep-water rivers, intercity or suburban passengers traveled on rapid—up to ninety kilometers per hour—hydrofoils. On small or shallow rivers, service was provided by surface skimmers and air-cushion vehicles.

The bulk of river travel was, however, for excursions and cruises. Big river liners, some of a catamaran type, equipped with cabins, dining rooms, and recreational facilities, took from 120 to 1,000 passengers on one-day excursions and on cruises of longer duration. On major summer holidays, the Moscow Navigation Company has transported between 80,000 and 100,000 passengers daily to and from recreational and tourist areas.

Merchant Marine

The Soviet Union has the world's most extensive coastline—along two oceans and twelve seas—which has served as a transportation link to the rest of the world. The Arctic Ocean and its seas provided international as well as domestic lines of communication to the economically emerging northern areas and constituted a water bridge between the Atlantic and Pacific oceans. The Pacific Ocean opened the Soviet Far East areas to trade with Japan and the Pacific rim countries. Although access to oceans was more restricted, the Baltic and Black seas provided the Soviet Union with outlets to the North Atlantic and South Atlantic and to the Mediterranean Sea, respectively. A fleet of modern coastal vessels provided an essential, and frequently the sole, transportation link between the extreme northern and the Far East parts of the country and the industrialized base. For foreign trade, the Soviet Union relied on a well-equipped and specialized fleet of vessels calling at the ports of practically every maritime nation in the world. Besides carrying over half of the country's export-import freight, the Merchant Fleet (Morskoi flot—Morflot) was an effective adjunct to the Soviet Naval Forces and served the country's political and military needs.

Initial Developments

Between the early 1920s, when the Soviet regime consolidated its power, and the end of the 1950s, when the merchant marine and ports had recovered from the damage of World War II, the Soviet merchant fleet ranked well below those of the major seafaring nations of the world. In the 1960s, however, new economic and political realities caused the Soviet Union to dramatically expand its merchant fleet, ports, shipyards, and related facilities. First, the regime decided to expand its foreign trade, and thus its influence, with the growing number of newly independent African and Asian nations. Second, the 1962 Cuban missile crisis, the widening conflict in Vietnam with Soviet support for Hanoi, and the relationship with China demonstrated the need for a merchant fleet ready to respond to foreign policy and military requirements. For example, in 1960 Soviet merchant ships carried 45 million tons of freight, but by 1965 they carried more than double the tonnage, almost 92 million tons, and two years later, in 1967, they transported nearly 141.5 million tons of freight. In terms of units and tonnage, the merchant fleet went from 590 ships of 3.3 million deadweight tons in 1959 to 990 vessels of 8 million deadweight tons in 1965, thereby rising from twelfth to sixth rank in merchant fleets of the world. The new freighters ranged from 9,000 to 13,500 deadweight tons and were acquired from domestic as well as East German, Polish, Yugoslav, and Finnish shipyards.

The 1970s saw a continued expansion of the merchant fleet, but the vessels put into operation were generally specialized types that had been introduced by Western shipowners in the second half of the 1960s: container carriers, roll-on/roll-off (RO/RO), lighter-aboard-ship (LASH), roll-on/float-off (RO/FLO), RO/RO-container carriers, very large crude carriers (VLCC), and very large bulk carriers (VLBC). They were put into service on expanding lines to the Americas, including the Great Lakes, and to Asia, Africa, and Australia. New Soviet ports and shore installations capable of handling these ships were built or expanded (see fig. 21). Between 1970 and 1980, the number of freight and passenger vessels grew from about 1,400 to 1,725, while their collective tonnage went from almost 12 million to almost 19 million deadweight tons.

In the 1980s, the Soviet merchant marine continued to expand, although at a less frenetic pace than before. By the end of 1985, the merchant marine had 1,741 freight-carrying vessels, of which 290 were tankers, reaching a total of about 20 million deadweight tons. The main types of cargo ships were general and bulk cargo freighters, multipurpose freighters, container ships, timber carriers and wood waste carriers, bulk carriers, ore-bulk-ore (ORO) carriers, various tankers, refrigerator ships, and RO/RO, RO–FLO, and LASH vessels.

Fleet Operations

In an effort to attain the highest labor productivity and cost efficiency, maritime authorities embarked on a policy of standardization. For vessels, this meant standardization not only by mission and areas of operation but also by major components: engines, cargo-handling equipment, and electronics. The results were higher fuel efficiency, improved and more efficient repair and maintenance, increased cargo-carrying capacity (thus decreasing the relative per ton construction and operating costs), and increased speeds (thereby ensuring faster delivery and increased vessel productivity). New ship designs allowed speedier cargo handling and better space utilization and resulted in a higher carrying capacity per ship. Automation and mechanization of shipboard operations increased labor productivity. For instance, automated control devices enabled operation of a large cargo ship's engine room by one crewman.

Most seas adjoining the Soviet coastline, particularly the Arctic Ocean, the northern Pacific Ocean, and the Baltic Sea, have short navigable seasons. To keep the sea-lanes open and prolong the navigable season, a sizable and diversified fleet of ice-breaking vessels was required. The vessels ranged from small harbor tug-icebreakers to large, nuclear-powered, oceangoing icebreakers, as well as Arctic freighters and tankers of up to 35,000 deadweight tons.

Arctic freighters were especially constructed with reinforced hulls, resembling those of icebreakers, to enable the ships to proceed through ice up to one meter thick. Arctic freighters' superstructures were protected against the severe weather to allow the crew to move from one part of the ship to another without being exposed to cold and ice. Deck de-icing equipment allowed them to operate at temperatures of as low as – 50°C.

In the late 1980s, the Soviet Union had the world's largest passenger vessel fleet. One of its major tasks was to provide transportation to the Arctic and Far Eastern coastal areas, where ships were frequently the sole means of travel. Small vessels, such as hydrofoils seating about 120 passengers and reaching speeds up to forty kilometers per hour, operated in the coastal areas of the Baltic, Black, Azov, and Caspian seas. Old passenger liners, some built prior to World War II and acquired as war reparations, catered to foreign cruise clientele, generally in contiguous waters. Modern and well-equipped cruise ships, however, either were built expressly for Morflot in foreign yards, mainly in East Germany, or were built

chiefly in the Federal Republic of Germany (West Germany) and Britain for Western cruise lines and were subsequently acquired by Morflot in the 1970s and 1980s. With cabin accommodations for 250 to 700 passengers, they catered to Western tourists and plied the world's oceans from the Norwegian fjords to the South Pacific islands. In the mid-1980s, Morflot's oceangoing passenger fleet numbered some eighty liners with a total of about 25,000 berths.

Morflot operated several major ferry lines, both international and domestic. In 1988 two important international train ferry lines were jointly operated, one with Bulgaria, the other with East Germany. The lines had been put into service to avoid transiting Romanian and Polish territory, respectively. The Soviet-Bulgarian ferry between Il'ichevsk and Varna began service in 1978. It has used two Soviet and two Bulgarian ships, each with a capacity for 108 seventy-ton freight cars on three decks. This line has shortened by six days the delivery time between the two countries.

In 1986 the Soviet-East German ferry service began between Klaipeda, in the Lithuanian Republic, and Mukran, on the island of Rügen in East Germany. When in full operation (scheduled for 1990), the line was to use six Mukran-class ferryboats, three belonging to each country. Each boat was designed to carry 103 freight cars of up to eight-four tons each that could roll on and off directly from the shore, thus reducing each boat's turnaround time to only four hours. The round trip between the two ports has taken only forty-eight hours. The annual peak capacity of the six ferries by 1990 was projected at 5 million tons. Since 1984 a Baltic automobile ferry has been operating between Leningrad and Stockholm.

Among the domestic routes were the Caspian Sea ferry lines, the Crimea-Caucasus lines, and the Sea of Japan line between Vanino and Kholmsk. Some automobile ferries in the Far East had trips lasting up to fifteen days and had cabin accommodations for 432 passengers.

The Soviet Union's freight and passenger fleets were supported in ports and at sea by a large diversified fleet of auxiliary craft. They included harbor and ocean tugs, oceangoing salvage and rescue vessels, fire boats, various service craft, and floating cranes, as well as civil engineering craft, such as dredges, used in the construction and maintenance of harbors and navigational channels.

In 1986 the Soviet Union had the world's largest oceangoing fishing fleet, comprising about 4,200 vessels under the jurisdiction of the Ministry of the Fishing Industry. Research and surveying ships numbered more than 200. They were for the most part not operated by Morflot but by various institutes of the Academy of Sciences (see Glossary) for oceanographic research and surveying, such as fisheries, marine biology, and oil and gas exploration. According to Western authorities, however, many of these ships were manned at least in part by naval crews and performed work for the Soviet Naval Forces. Usually, these were modern units outfitted with sophisticated equipment, including intelligence-gathering devices.

Most Soviet ports fell into one of three categories. General cargo ports handled a variety of break-bulk, container, RO/RO, LASH, or bulk cargo ships at the same type of pier. Specialized ports transloaded dry or liquid bulk cargo, such as ores, coal, grain, petroleum, and chemicals. They had automated transloading equipment suitable for a particular type of cargo. Major ports, and some smaller ones, had facilities and equipment to handle both types of ships.

The merchant fleet's cargo, passenger, and auxiliary vessels constituted an indispensable logistical component of the Soviet Naval Forces and provided the armed forces with strategic sealift capabilities. According to the United States Department of Defense, Morflot ships, particularly RO/RO, RO/FLO, LASH, and combination RO/RO-container ships, were fast, versatile, and capable of handling combat and combat support vehicles and equipment. Moreover, the majority were able to enter most of the world's harbors. LASH and RO/FLO ships were capable of unloading their cargo at sea and could thereby support amphibious operations. RO/ROs and container ships required minimally prepared shore facilities to discharge their cargo. Nearly half the cargo ships were equipped with cranes capable of lifting the heaviest military armor and vehicles, thereby reducing the dependence on prepared port facilities. Morflot's tankers and cargo vessels were also used for out-of-area refueling and replenishment of Soviet naval vessels operating far from home waters. Merchant ships were sometimes equipped with sophisticated communications and navigational devices, served as intelligence gatherers, and had protection against chemical, biological, and radiological hazards. According to some Western naval authorities, many Soviet merchant and fishing vessels possessed mine-laying capabilities. In the event of hostilities, the Morflot passenger fleet, with a total of about 25,000 berths in peacetime, was capable of transporting several times that number of troops into operational areas.

Civil Aviation

The civilian Air Fleet (Aero flot—Aeroflot) played a major role in transporting passengers but a minor role in transporting cargo. Civil aviation was the third most important transporter of passengers

Potemkin Steps leading to the main sea terminal, Odessa,
Ukrainian Republic
Hydrofoil on the Neva River, Leningrad, Russian Republic
Courtesy Jimmy Pritchard

577

and other scientific and exploration missions, Aeroflot used specially equipped airplanes and helicopters. Medical assistance and evacuation, especially in remote areas, was provided by aircraft such as the An-14 and An-28 and by the Ka-26 and Mi-8 helicopters, which were able to operate from most level surfaces. Various types of agricultural missions were performed by the work horse, the An-2, and its updated version, the An-3, as well as the Ka-26 helicopter.

Aeroflot was also responsible for such services as ice patrol in the Arctic Ocean and escorting of ships through frozen seas, oil exploration, power line surveillance, and transportation and heavy lifting support on construction projects. For the latter tasks, Aeroflot used, in addition to smaller helicopters, the Mi-10 flying crane, a twin-turbine aircraft with a lifting capacity of 11,000 to 14,000 kilograms, depending on the engines. Hauling of heavy cargo, including vehicles, was performed by the world's largest helicopter, the Mi-26. Its unusual eight-blade rotor enabled it to lift a maximum payload of some twenty tons.

In 1986 Aeroflot served over 3,600 population centers and had a route network, excluding overlapping routes, that extended 1,156,000 kilometers, of which 185,000 kilometers were international routes. Aeroflot's share of total freight transported by all means of transportation was only 0.01 percent, or 3,157,000 tons originated. Nevertheless, it carried 116.1 million passengers (almost 19 percent of the total passenger-kilometers), of whom 3.4 million were on international flights. The disproportion between domestic and international air travel reflected not only foreign travel restrictions imposed on Soviet citizens but underscored the importance of aircraft as an essential—sometimes the sole—link to remote cities, towns, and settlements. Thus, in 1986 Siberia, the Far North, and the Far East, although sparsely populated, accounted for 26 percent of Aeroflot's cargo and passenger transport.

Aeroflot also connected the Soviet Union with ninety-seven foreign countries; the main international hub was Moscow's Sheremetevo Airport. Other cities with international airports included Leningrad, Kiev, Minsk, Yerevan, Tashkent, Irkutsk, and Khabarovsk.

Aeroflot's domestic flights frequently have become harrowing experiences for both Western and Soviet passengers, who have complained of long waits and indifferent service at ticket offices, seemingly interminable waiting at airport terminals poorly equipped with food and toilet facilities, passengers forced to sit in hot airplane cabins without air conditioning, and indifferent cabin crews. Shortages of fuel and spare parts were among the major causes of after the highway and railroad systems in terms of passenger-kilometers. Although it transported only a small fraction of the cargo shipped on the other modes of transportation, Aeroflot was the preferred carrier where speed was essential. Aeroflot provided many services not performed by Western airlines, such as the spraying of fertilizers and pesticides over fields and forests, forest fire detection and control, pipeline inspection, medical evacuation, logistical support for oil and other exploration and extraction ventures, construction projects, and scientific expeditions to polar regions. Frequently, Aeroflot airplanes or helicopters were the sole means of reaching remote Siberian or northern settlements. Lastly, Aeroflot's crews and aircraft constituted the strategic air transport reserve of the Soviet armed forces.

Postwar Evolution of Aeroflot

During World War II, Soviet civil aviation was infused with new technology, consisting of transport airplanes, such as the American DC-3 and DC-4, supplied under the lend-lease agreement. As a result, Aeroflot experienced rapid growth in the postwar years. Between 1950 and 1955, a major route expansion occurred when the capitals of the constituent republics and major administrative centers were interconnected by air service. By 1955 the Soviet Union had established air links with neighboring communist countries in Europe and Asia.

Aeroflot entered the jet age in 1956, when it put into service the world's first jet airliner, the twin-engined Tu-104. It carried seventy passengers or twelve tons of cargo at a range of up to 4,000 kilometers. Other jet or turboprop aircraft were soon acquired by Aeroflot: the An-10, Il-18, and Tu-114 turboprops; the short-range Yak-40; the medium-range Tu-134A; the medium- to long-range Tu-154; and the long-range Il-62M jet liners.

Aeroflot Operations

In the mid- and late 1980s, Aeroflot operated a diversified fleet of both jet and turboprop aircraft, designed for either cargo or passengers and adapted to the geographic and climatic conditions of the country and to its economic needs. Many of the aircraft had raised wings to operate from unimproved airstrips, including frozen marshes or Arctic ice floes, and capable of lifting tall, wide, and heavy vehicles, including medium and heavy tanks (see table 46, Appendix A).

For tasks other than conventional passenger and cargo transportation, Aeroflot had available many types of general and special-purpose fixed and rotary-wing aircraft. For geological, weather, delayed or canceled flights. According to the head of the Ministry of Civil Aviation's Main Administration for Aviation Work and Transport Operations, a shortage of fuel was expected to keep at least 15 million people from flying on Aeroflot in 1988.

The close relationship between Aeroflot and the Soviet armed forces was underscored by the fact that the minister of civil aviation has been a high-ranking general or marshal of the Air Forces. Aeroflot pilots held reserve commissions in the Air Forces. The 1,600 medium- and long-range passenger and cargo aircraft of Aeroflot were also part of the strategic air transport reserve, ready to provide immediate airlift support to the armed forces. Indeed, many aircraft in Aeroflot's inventory were of the same basic design as military aircraft and, even when loaded with bulky cargo and vehicles, were capable of operating from unimproved fields. They were characterized by high wings, low fuselages with cargo/vehicle loading ramps, and landing gear suitable for unimproved or marshy terrain. Short-range airplanes and helicopters were available for appropriate military support missions. Civil aviation also served as a cover for military operations. According to a Western authority, military aircraft belonging to the Military Transport Aviation (Voennaia transportnaia aviatsiia) have been painted in Aeroflot colors for use as food relief and arms or personnel transports to foreign countries.

Pipelines

Although oil pipelines were first laid in Baku in 1872, the use of pipelines to move liquids and gases over long distances was essentially a post-World War II development, with most use occurring since 1970. In 1988 about 95 percent of crude oil and over 20 percent of refined petroleum products, as well as nearly 100 percent of natural gas, were shipped by pipeline. In 1986 almost 653 million tons originated of crude oil and refined petroleum products were transported by a large-diameter pipeline network of 81,500 kilometers. About 616 billion cubic meters of natural gas entered the 185,000-kilometer gas pipeline system in 1986. Other products shipped by pipelines included chemicals, petrochemicals, salts, coal, ores, and construction minerals.

The main oil pipelines were relatively new and of large diameter—1,020 and 1,220 millimeters. About 65 percent of the oil pipelines, however, were of medium diameter—530 and 820 millimeters or smaller. They linked oilfields with refineries, and in turn the refineries were linked with main user areas or export outlets, such as the port of Ventspils on the Baltic or the towns

Moscow's Central Telegraph Office, decorated for the seventy-second anniversary of the Bolshevik Revolution
Courtesy Jimmy Pritchard

of Brest (near the border with Poland) and Uzhgorod (near the borders with Czechoslovakia and Hungary).

The major gas pipelines ran from the principal natural gas producing regions of Central Asia, western Siberia (twelve large-diameter lines), and the Volga-Ural, Baku, and North Caucasus regions to major domestic and foreign industrial zones (see fig. 22). Natural gas pipelines were of 1,420 millimeter, 1,220 millimeter, 1,020 millimeter, and smaller diameters, the latter representing just over half the total length.

Among the better known pipelines were the Northern Lights line from the Komi petroleum deposit to Brest on the Polish border, the Soiuz line running from Orenburg to Uzhgorod near the Czechoslovak and Hungarian borders, and the Export pipeline from the Urengoy gas field to L'vov and thence to West European countries, including Austria, Italy, West Germany, France, Belgium, and the Netherlands. The 1,420-millimeter Export pipeline was 4,451 kilometers long. It crossed the Ural and Carpathian mountains and almost 600 rivers, including the Ob', Volga, Don, and Dnepr. It had forty-one compressor stations and a yearly capacity of 32 billion cubic meters of natural gas.

581

Communications

Communications systems were controlled by the regime and were primarily used by it to convey decisions and to facilitate the execution of directives affecting the economy, national security, and administrative governmental functions. The Ministry of Communications, a union-republic ministry (see Glossary), was responsible for radio, telegraph and telephone transmissions, communications satellites, and the postal service. Several other governmental organizations were concerned with communications, including the State Committee for Television and Radio Broadcasting, the Ministry of Defense (for military communications), the Ministry of Culture (for educational broadcasts), and others that controlled and operated electronic communications for their own needs. Communications organizations were also on the republic and lower administrative levels.

Electronic communications systems in the Soviet Union, especially radio and television broadcasting, experienced a rapid growth in the 1960s and 1970s (see Radio; Television and Video Cassette Recorders, ch. 9). Although telephone communications were also expanded in the same period, the rate was slower. By 1989 the Soviet Union had a powerful telecommunications system that sent radio, television, and telephone messages to almost any location in the world.

In 1965 the Soviet Union launched the Molniia (Lightning) satellite communications system linking Moscow to remote towns and military installations in the northern parts of the country. The Molniia system, the world's first domestic satellite communications network, retransmitted radio and television broadcasts originating in Moscow. It was used as the initial back-up teleprinter link for the "hot line" between Moscow and Washington. The system also transmitted signals to spacecraft in the Soiuz, Saliut, and other space programs. The Molniia system employed several satellites following elliptical orbits and several ground stations that exchanged signals with them as they came into range.

In 1971 the Soviet Union launched Intersputnik, an international satellite communications network, with thirteen other member nations: Afghanistan, Bulgaria, Cuba, Czechoslovakia, the Democratic People's Republic of Korea (North Korea), East Germany, Hungary, Laos, Mongolia, the People's Democratic Republic of Yemen (South Yemen), Poland, Romania, and Vietnam. Algeria, Iraq, Libya, and Syria became members subsequently, and Nicaragua and Cambodia agreed to the construction of ground stations in 1986. Headquartered in Moscow and governed by a

board representing the member nations, Intersputnik employed Molniia communications satellites to link the telephone, telegraph, television, and radio systems of member nations. Each member nation was responsible for building and operating its own ground station, and the Soviet Union had two dedicated stations—at Vladimir and Dubna. Intersputnik participants used centrally located ground stations to relay communications when they did not have direct access to the same satellite.

Communications satellites in geostationary orbits, i.e., the satellite's position remained fixed relative to a point on the earth, were first launched by the Soviet Union in 1975. In 1985 the geostationary, or Statsionar, system employed several different kinds of communications satellites, including the Raduga (Rainbow), Gorizont (Horizon), and Ekran (Screen). Since 1975 the Raduga satellites have been generally used to relay domestic message traffic between distant locations in the Soviet Union. They have also electronically transferred the daily newspapers *Pravda* and *Izvestiia* from Moscow to Khabarovsk for same-day printing in the Soviet Far East. The Gorizont satellites' main functions have been international communications with ground stations, selecting global, regional, zone, or spot beams as needed. Several Gorizont satellites have relayed electronic versions of *Pravda* and *Izvestiia* to Irkutsk and Krasnoyarsk for printing and distribution. Some Western authorities considered Gorizont satellites capable of providing Soviet television programs inexpensively to Third World countries. Ekran satellites were used to relay radio and television signals to community antenna systems in remote areas.

The Ministry of Communications operated almost 92,000 post and telegraph offices and telephone exchanges, most of which were in rural locations. In 1986 it forwarded about 8.5 billion letters, 50.3 billion newspapers and magazines, and 449 million telegrams. In addition, it processed 814 million money orders and pension payments. Despite constitutional guarantees of privacy of personal correspondence, telephone conversations, and telegraph communications, in the late 1980s the regime continued to authorize extensive eavesdropping. Domestic and international mail was subject to being opened and examined by government censors. Foreign publications ''which may cause political and economic prejudice to the Soviet Union'' were generally prohibited, and parcels from foreign addresses were routinely searched for a wide variety of prohibited articles, including consumer goods and food products, and were returned or ''lost.''

Since the 1960s, the government has tried to expand and update the telephone system, which, by Western standards of availability and service, was woefully underdeveloped. In 1988 semiautomatic and automatic telephone exchanges were coming on line within urban centers, and direct long-distance dialing was expanding. To respond to a growing demand for better telecommunications, in the 1980s the Soviet Union turned to Western communications firms to acquire digital telephone switching equipment, for which the need was rapidly growing.

At the end of 1986, an estimated 33 million telephones were connected with, or had access to, the Ministry of Communications network. However, the total number of telephone sets connected to Soviet networks was 39.5 million, which indicates that 6.5 million sets were on separate networks not belonging to the Ministry of Communications. Of the 33 million sets within the Ministry of Communications system, 27.7 million were on urban and 5.3 million on rural networks. Furthermore, of this total, 18.5 million telephone sets were classified as residential, which meant not only sets in private residences but also ones located in communal areas, such as hallways of multifamily residences or in housing projects. Indeed, according to official Soviet data, only 28 percent of urban and 9.2 percent of rural families had telephones in 1986. In early 1987, for instance, 13.3 million requests were made for installations of telephones in cities alone.

Other telecommunications systems, using both cable and microwave carriers for facsimile and data transmission systems, although under expansion by governmental authorities, still lagged behind the user demand for their services. User needs, however, determined neither the availability nor the quality of communications services in the Soviet Union. Government planners, following directives of the CPSU, allocated resources for communications and transportation with little reference to individual users. The regime gave precedence to the communications needs of decision makers and to the transportation needs of the national economy. Thus, it favored development of railroads, which served as the major long-distance transporter of freight. It also emphasized pipelines, as well as the maritime and air fleets, all of which grew substantially during the 1970s and 1980s. In contrast, the regime limited development of private automobiles and maintained a road network that primarily served areas with substantial industry and urban populations.

* * *

The overall Soviet transportation system is analyzed by Holland Hunter and Vladimir Kontorovich in "Transport Pressures and

Potentials." A detailed study of the transportation of extracted energy resources by rail, water, and pipeline can be found in Matthew J. Sagers and Milford B. Green's *The Transportation of Soviet Energy Resources.* A brief but useful transportation overview is also found in J.P. Cole's *Geography of the Soviet Union.* An insight into Soviet urban transportation services is provided in Paul M. White's *Planning of Urban Transport Systems in the Soviet Union.* Holland Hunter and Deborah Kaple's *The Soviet Railroad Situation* assesses railroad operations, and *Soviet and East European Transport Problems,* edited by John Ambler, Denis Shaw, and Leslie Symans, treats Soviet railroads within the East European context. For current reporting on Soviet railroad developments, the following trade publications may be consulted: *Rail International, Railway Gazette International,* and *International Railway Journal.* For a comprehensive summary of Soviet railroads including operating statistics, locomotives and rolling stock, trackage, new construction, and technical data and characteristics, the latest yearbook of *Jane's Railway Systems* is an excellent source. A useful evaluation of rural trucking problems is in Judith Flynn and Barbara Severin's "Soviet Agricultural Transport," as well as in Elizabeth M. Clayton's "Soviet Rural Roads." D.M. Long's *The Soviet Merchant Fleet* is a good work to consult on the state of Morflot. Useful background material on the Soviet civil airline from its inception to its maturity can be found in Hugh MacDonald's *Aeroflot.* For Aeroflot operations in the 1980s, including service, flight crew proficiency, accidents, and handling of hijackings, the two-part article by Michael York, "Flying with Aeroflot," is helpful. For information about aircraft, the latest *Jane's All the World's Aircraft* should be consulted. (For further information and complete citations, see Bibliography.)

Chapter 15. Foreign Trade

A merchant ship being loaded in a Soviet port

TRADE HAS TRADITIONALLY played only a minor role in the Soviet economy. In 1985, for example, exports and imports each accounted for only 4 percent of the Soviet gross national product. The Soviet Union maintained this low level because it could draw upon a large energy and raw material base and because it historically had pursued a policy of self-sufficiency. Other foreign economic activity included economic aid programs, which primarily benefited the less developed Council for Mutual Economic Assistance (Comecon) countries of Cuba, Mongolia, and Vietnam, and substantial borrowing from the West to supplement hard-currency (see Glossary) export earnings.

The Soviet Union conducted the bulk of its foreign economic activities with communist countries, particularly those of Eastern Europe. In 1988 Soviet trade with socialist countries amounted to 62 percent of total Soviet foreign trade. Between 1965 and 1988, trade with the Third World made up a steady 10 to 15 percent of the Soviet Union's foreign trade. Trade with the industrialized West, especially the United States, fluctuated, influenced by political relations between East and West, as well as by the Soviet Union's short-term needs. In the 1970s, during the period of détente, trade with the West gained in importance at the expense of trade with socialist countries. In the early and mid-1980s, when relations between the superpowers were poor, however, Soviet trade with the West decreased in favor of increased integration with Eastern Europe.

The manner in which the Soviet Union transacted trade varied from one trade partner to another. Soviet trade with the Western industrialized countries, except Finland, and most Third World countries was conducted with hard currency, that is, currency that was freely convertible. Because the ruble was not freely convertible, the Soviet Union could only acquire hard currency by selling Soviet goods or gold on the world market for hard currency. Therefore, the volume of imports from countries using convertible currency depended on the amount of goods the Soviet Union exported for hard currency. Alternative methods of cooperation, such as barter, counter trade, industrial cooperation, or bilateral clearing agreements were much preferred. These methods were used in transactions with Finland, members of the Comecon, China, Yugoslavia, and a number of Third World countries.

Commodity composition of Soviet trade differed by region. The Soviet Union imported manufactured, agricultural, and consumer goods from socialist countries in exchange for energy and manufactured goods. The Soviet Union earned hard currency by exporting fuels and other primary products to the industrialized West and then used this currency to buy sophisticated manufactures and agricultural products, primarily grain. Trade with the Third World usually involved exchanging machinery and armaments for tropical foodstuffs and raw materials.

Soviet aid programs expanded steadily from 1965 to 1985. In 1985 the Soviet Union provided an estimated US$6.9 billion to the Third World in the form of direct cash, credit disbursements, or trade subsidies. The communist Third World, primarily Cuba, Mongolia, and Vietnam, received 85 percent of these funds. In the late 1980s, the Soviet Union reassessed its aid programs. In light of reduced political returns and domestic economic problems, the Soviet Union could ill afford ineffective disbursements of its limited resources. Moreover, dissatisfied with Soviet economic assistance, several Soviet client states opened trade discussions with Western countries.

In the 1980s, the Soviet Union needed considerable sums of hard currency to pay for food and capital goods imports and to support client states. What the country could not earn from exports or gold sales it borrowed through its banks in London, Frankfurt, Vienna, Paris, and Luxembourg. Large grain imports pushed the Soviet debt quite high in 1981. Better harvests and lower import requirements redressed this imbalance in subsequent years. By late 1985, however, a decrease in oil revenues nearly returned the Soviet debt to its 1981 level. At the end of that same year the Soviet Union owed US$31 billion (gross) to Western creditors, mostly commercial banks and other private sources.

In the late 1980s, the Soviet Union attempted to reduce its hard-currency debt by decreasing imports from the West and increasing oil and gas exports to the West. It also sought increased participation in international markets and organizations. In 1987 the Soviet Union formally requested observer status in the General Agreement on Tariffs and Trade and in 1988 signed a normalization agreement with the European Economic Community. Structural changes in the foreign trade bureaucracy, granting direct trading rights to select enterprises, and legislation establishing joint ventures with foreigners opened up the economy to the Western technical and managerial expertise necessary to achieve the goals established by General Secretary Mikhail S. Gorbachev's program of economic restructuring (*perestroika*—see Glossary).

Development of the State Monopoly on Foreign Trade

The government of the Soviet Union has always held a monopoly on all foreign trade activity, but only after the death of Joseph V. Stalin in 1953 did the government accord importance to foreign trade activities. Before that time, the Bolsheviks' (see Glossary) ideological opposition to external economic control, their refusal to pay Russia's World War I debts, and the chaos of the Civil War (1918–21) kept trade to the minimum level required for the country's industrial development (see Revolutions and Civil War, ch. 2). Active Soviet trade operations began only in 1921, when the government established the People's Commissariat of Foreign Trade.

The commissariat's monopoly on internal and external foreign trade was loosened, beginning in 1921, when the New Economic Policy (NEP) decentralized control of the economy (see The Era of the New Economic Policy, ch. 2). Although the commissariat remained the controlling center, the regime established other organizations to deal directly with foreign partners in the buying and selling of goods. These organizations included state import and export offices, joint stock companies, specialized import and export corporations, trusts, syndicates, cooperative organizations, and mixed-ownership companies.

The end of the NEP period, the beginning of the First Five-Year Plan (1928–32), and the forced collectivization of agriculture beginning in 1929 marked the early Stalin era (see Stalin's Rise to Power, ch. 2). The government restructured foreign trade operations according to Decree Number 358, issued in February 1930, which eliminated the decentralized, essentially private, trading practices of the NEP period and established a system of monopoly specialization. The government then organized a number of foreign trade corporations under the People's Commissariat of Foreign Trade, each with a monopoly over a specific group of commodities.

Stalin's policy restricted trade as it attempted to build socialism in one country. Stalin feared the unpredictable movement and disruptive influence of such foreign market forces as demand and price fluctuations. Imports were restricted to factory equipment essential for the industrialization drive that began with the First Five-Year Plan.

World War II virtually halted Soviet trade and the activity of most foreign trade corporations. Trade was conducted primarily through Soviet trade representatives in Britain and Iran and the Soviet Buying Commission in the United States. After the war, Britain and other West European countries and the United States imposed drastic restrictions on trade with the Soviet Union. Thus, Soviet foreign trade corporations limited their efforts to Eastern Europe and China, establishing Soviet-owned companies in these countries and setting up joint-stock companies on very favorable terms. Comecon, founded in 1949, united the economies of Eastern Europe with that of the Soviet Union (see Appendix B).

Soviet trade changed considerably in the post-Stalin era. Postwar industrialization and an expansion of foreign trade resulted in the proliferation of all-union (see Glossary) foreign trade organizations (FTOs), the new name for foreign trade corporations and also known as foreign trade association. In 1946 the People's Commissariat of Foreign Trade was reorganized into the Ministry of Foreign Trade. The Ministry of Foreign Trade, through its FTOs, retained the exclusive right to negotiate and sign contracts with foreigners and to draft foreign trade plans. The State Committee for Foreign Economic Relations (Gosudarstvennyi komitet po vneshnim ekonomicheskim sviaziam—GKES), created in 1955, managed all foreign aid programs and the export of complete factories through the FTOs subordinate to it. Certain ministries, however, had the right to deal directly with foreign partners through their own FTOs.

On January 17, 1988, *Izvestiia* reported the abolition of the Ministry of Foreign Trade and GKES. These two organizations were merged into the newly created Ministry of Foreign Economic Relations, which had responsibility for administering foreign trade policy and foreign aid agreements. Other legislation provided for the establishment of joint enterprises. The government retained its monopoly on foreign trade through a streamlined version of the Soviet foreign trade bureaucracy as it existed before the January 17 decree.

Structure of the Foreign Trade Bureaucracy

In 1988 the foreign trade bureaucracy reflected the monopoly specification system created by the 1930 Decree Number 358. the authority of the Communist Party of the Soviet Union (CPSU) and the Council of Ministers, six central bodies, the Ministry of Foreign Economic Relations, and numerous FTOs together planned, regulated, monitored, and carried out all Soviet foreign economic activity (see fig. 23).

Administration

Although the CPSU had ultimate authority over all foreign economic activity, in the late 1980s administrative control was centralized in the Council of Ministers. More specifically, the council's

State Foreign Economic Commission coordinated the activities of ministries and departments in the area of economic and scientific cooperation with socialist, developing, and developed capitalist states.

Six central bodies under the Council of Ministries played important roles in foreign economic relations. The import and export of goods, services, and resources were managed by the State Planning Committee (Gosudarstvennyi planovyi komitet—Gosplan), the State Committee for Material and Technical Supply (Gosudarstvennyi komitet po material'no-tekhnicheskomu snabzheniiu—Gossnab), and the State Committee for Science and Technology (Gosudarstvennyi komitet po nauke i tekhnike—GKNT). Gosplan formulated all import and export plans, coordinated the allocation of investment and other resources, and had final authority over all decisions concerning foreign trade, including trade levels and commodity composition. Gossnab coordinated the allocation of resources not handled by Gosplan and, as the central agency responsible for matching supplies with customers, played a major role in selecting and allocating imports. GKNT negotiated technical cooperation agreements and monitored license and patent purchases and sales in order to introduce new technology into the Soviet economy.

The State Committee on Prices (Gosudarstvennyi komitet po tsenam—Goskomtsen), the Ministry of Finance, and the State Bank (Gosudarstvennyi bank—Gosbank) held jurisdiction over the financing of foreign trade. Goskomtsen established prices for all imports and some exports. The Ministry of Finance controlled the balance of payments (see Glossary) and monitored the impact of foreign trade on the state budget. Finally, Gosbank set the exchange rate for the ruble (for value of the ruble—see Glossary) and managed the system of exchange within the Soviet Union. Gosbank supervised the Foreign Economic Activity Bank (Vneshnii ekonomicheskii bank—Vneshekonombank; until January 1, 1988, known as the Foreign Trade Bank), which provided international banking services for Soviet FTOs.

Operation

Until 1988 the two operative bodies involved solely and directly in foreign economic operations were GKES and the Ministry of Foreign Trade (see fig. 24). The Ministry of Foreign Trade formulated draft import and export plans and regulated commodity trade. GKES supervised foreign aid programs and the export of complete plants. The Ministry of Foreign Trade or GKES had jurisdiction over most FTOs, which negotiated and signed commercial contracts with foreigners on behalf of individual enterprises

595

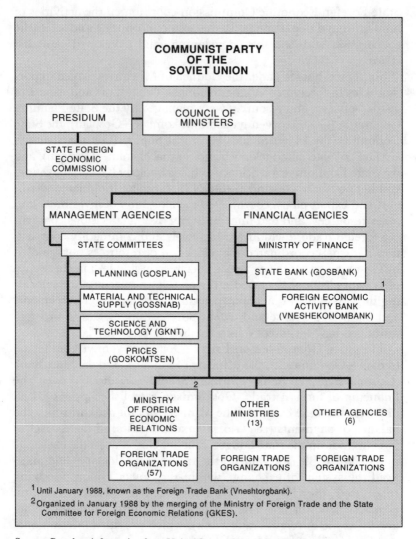

Source: Based on information from United States, Central Intelligence Agency, Directorate
of Intelligence, *Directory of Soviet Officials: National Organizations*, Washington, 1988;
and H. Stephen Gardner, *Soviet Foreign Trade*, Boston, 1983, 3.

Figure 23. Foreign Trade Bureaucracy, 1988

(see Glossary). FTOs were generally organized by product, as had
been the foreign trade corporations of the 1930s.

Some industrial ministries or other agencies, however, had their
own FTOs. As of early 1987, for example, forty-eight FTOs were
under the jurisdiction of the Ministry of Foreign Trade and nine

under the GKES, whereas the Ministry of the Maritime Fleet, the Ministry of the Fishing Industry, and the Ministry of Trade, among others, had their own FTOs. In addition, certain other agencies had their own FTOs: the Chamber of Commerce and Industry, which handled international trade exhibitions; the State Committee for Physical Culture and Sports; the Central Union of Cooperatives; the State Committee for Publishing Houses, Printing Plants, and the Book Trade; the State Committee for Cinematography; and the State Committee for Science and Technology.

Structural Reforms, 1986 to Mid-1988

The cumbersome foreign trade bureaucracy contributed to a number of problems that hindered the efficiency and effectiveness of foreign trade. The lack of direct contact between Soviet enterprises and their foreign customers or suppliers frustrated both parties by unnecessarily delaying contract negotiations and the specification of technical details. In a May 1986 interview with *Izvestiia,* the general director of the Ministry of Foreign Trade's All-Union Association for the Export and Import of Technical Equipment, Boris K. Pushkin, reported that after an enterprise submitted a request for a foreign item, two to three years were required before it was included in the import plan and funds were allocated for its purchase. In the interim, the needs of the enterprise had often changed. Pushkin stressed the need to free enterprises from unnecessary petty supervision and excessive regulation.

Taking such problems into account, the Twenty-Seventh Party Congress in February–March 1986 declared that the party anticipated a step-by-step restructuring of [the country's] foreign trade in order to make exports and imports more effective. In August of the same year, the CPSU Central Committee and the Council of Ministers adopted the decree "On Measures for Improving Management of External Economic Relations," which outlined drastic steps to change the structure of the foreign trade bureaucracy.

Also in August 1986, the Council of Ministers' State Foreign Economic Commission became a permanent body within the council, giving more authority and visibility to the commission, the domestic activities of which previously went largely unreported. The staff was augmented, and the chairman acquired a rank equivalent to that of deputy prime minister. The new charter stated that the commission's role was "to formulate and implement the country's foreign economic strategy so as to enhance its potential contributions to acceleration [*uskorenie*—see Glossary], strengthen the Soviet position in the world economy, and promote structured and

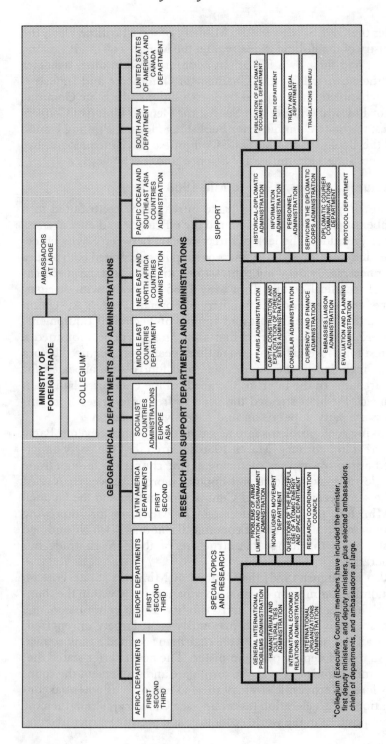

Figure 24. Organization of the Ministry of Foreign Trade, 1987

*Collegium (Executive Council) members have included the minister,
first deputy ministers, and deputy ministers, plus selected ambassadors,
chiefs of departments, and ambassadors at large.

organized development of economic cooperation with all groups of countries."

Until 1987 the forty-eight FTOs subordinate to the Ministry of Foreign Trade administered more than 90 percent of Soviet foreign trade turnover. In 1987 the ministry lost control of 20 percent of Soviet foreign trade turnover. The government granted direct foreign trade rights to twenty-one ministries and state committees, sixty-seven industrial enterprises, and eight interbranch scientific production complexes. Exporting enterprises gained the right to retain part of their hard-currency earnings. Each ministry or enterprise was to pay for its investment imports with its own hard currency, and the heads of ministries and enterprises became personally responsible for the efficient use of hard-currency funds. These measures gave enterprises more influence in import decision making.

On January 13, 1987, the Council of Ministers adopted the resolution "On Questions Concerning the Creation, on U.S.S.R. Territory, and the Activities of Joint Enterprises, International Associations, and Organizations with the Participation of Soviet and Foreign Organizations, Firms, and Management Bodies," or, more simply, a law on joint ventures. This legislation opened up enterprises inside the Soviet Union for the first time since the Bolshevik Revolution (see Glossary), to foreign participation. Joint ventures were to facilitate the acquisition and assimilation of Western technology, managerial know-how, and marketing abilities. Optimistic about the economic effects of their new undertaking, Soviet officials declared that 85 to 90 percent of "the most important types of machinery" would meet world technical standards by 1990. The Soviet Union's vast natural resources and its lucrative, previously closed, domestic market attracted Western companies. By August 1988, more than 50 joint ventures were registered in the Soviet Union, and approximately 300 were under negotiation.

Nevertheless, numerous obstacles arose in the first eighteen months after the government adopted the joint venture law. Complaints by Western partners dealt with uncertainties concerning Soviet trade regulations, problems with the supply of goods, the dilemma of the nonconvertibility of the ruble, difficulties finding qualified Soviet managers, problems in projecting production costs (as of 1989 Soviet domestic prices were administratively set and not based on market forces), and even complications finding office space in Moscow. Soviet trade officials' efforts to accommodate these complaints have included the decentralization of the foreign trade bureaucracy, the establishment of a management institute in Moscow, price reforms, and various legal reforms.

Before Western businessmen could recover from the confusion and disruption caused by this series of reforms, a second series began in early 1988. Effective January 1, 1988, the Foreign Trade Bank (Vneshnii torgovii bank—Vneshtorgbank) was renamed the Foreign Economic Activity Bank (Vneshnii ekonomicheskii bank—Vneshekonombank). The name change did not signify a major change in the bank's duties but simply more accurately reflected the nature of its operations. Vneshtorgbank had branched out from the simple management of foreign trade transactions to provide currency, credit, and accounting services as well. In a change from its previous duties, Vneshekonombank was required to administer new procedures dealing with Soviet firms that had recently acquired direct foreign trade rights.

Also on January 1, 1988, the New Enterprise Law went into effect, making enterprises economically accountable for their own business operations by 1989. According to this law, the government had the power to disband unprofitable businesses, and each ministry and its subordinate enterprises gained the responsibility for their own foreign trade activities. In addition, Gosplan, Gossnab, and GKNT relinquished some of their rights to allocate money and goods. Finally, the Ministry of Foreign Trade lost control of 15 percent more of its foreign trade turnover when fourteen additional enterprises and four other ministries acquired direct foreign trade rights.

Yet probably the most significant change in the foreign trade mechanism occurred on January 17, 1988, when *Izvestiia* announced the abolition of the Ministry of Foreign Trade and the GKES. The Ministry of Foreign Economic Relations, headed by Konstantin F. Katushev, former head of the GKES, assumed the duties of the two agencies. "Thus, the state monopoly on foreign trade and its state-wide aspects remains centralized," reported the Soviet foreign trade monthly *Vneshniaia torgovlia* (Foreign Trade), "while operational functions are continually being shifted to the business level." In March 1988, the journal reported that approximately 20 percent of foreign trade turnover was handled by the eighty-one firms that had been granted the right to deal directly with foreigners.

Other reforms followed in April 1988, when the Central Committee and the Council of Ministers agreed on a new charter for the Chamber of Commerce and Industry. In general, the chamber monitored foreign trade conducted outside the new Ministry of Foreign Economic Relations. In addition, the chamber assisted Soviet production enterprises in locating Western partners and learning foreign trade practices.

Trade with Socialist Countries

In the late 1980s, the Soviet Union traded with fourteen socialist countries. The political and economic relationships between the Soviet Union and these countries determine the four groups into which these countries can be divided: members of Comecon; Yugoslavia; China; and the developing communist countries of Cambodia, Laos, and the Democratic People's Republic of Korea (North Korea).

Business with socialist countries was conducted on a bilateral, country-by-country basis in which imports balanced exports. Soviet oil exports to these countries bought machinery and equipment and industrial consumer goods, as well as political support without the expenditure of freely convertible foreign currency. In addition, Soviet aid programs, which took the form of direct loans or trade subsidies, almost exclusively involved socialist countries.

The Council for Mutual Economic Assistance

The Soviet Union formed the Council for Mutual Economic Assistance (Comecon) in 1949, in part to discourage the countries of Eastern Europe from participating in the Marshall Plan (see Glossary) and to countereact trade boycotts imposed after World War II by the United States and by Britain and other West European countries. Ostensibly, Comecon was organized to coordinate economic and technical cooperation between the Soviet Union and the member countries. In reality, the Soviet Union's domination over Comecon activities reflected its economic, political, and military power. In 1989 Comecon comprised ten countries: the six original members—Bulgaria, Czechoslovakia, Hungary, Poland, Romania, and the Soviet Union—plus the German Democratic Republic (East Germany, which joined in 1950), Mongolia (1962), Cuba (1972), and Vietnam (1978). Albania, although it joined in February 1949, stopped participating in Comecon activities in 1961 and formally withdrew in 1987.

Since 1949 the Soviet Union has traded primarily with other Comecon members (see fig. 25). In 1960 the Soviet Union sent 56 percent of its exports to and received 58 percent of its imports from Comecon members. From that time, the volume of this trade has steadily increased, but the proportion of Soviet trade with Comecon members decreased as the Soviet Union sought to increase trade with Western industrialized countries. In contrast to 1960, trade with Comecon members accounted for only 42 percent of Soviet exports and 43 percent of Soviet imports in 1980.

The European members of Comecon have looked to the Soviet Union for oil; in turn, they have provided machinery, equipment,

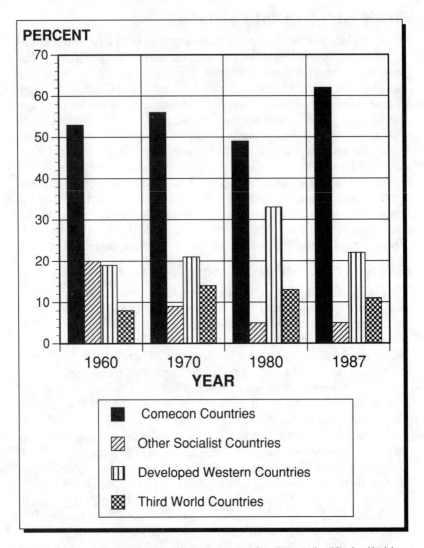

Source: Based on information from Gosudarstvennyi komitet po statistike, *Narodnoe khoziaistvo SSSR v 1987 g.*, Moscow, 1988.

Figure 25. Composition of Foreign Trade, Selected Years, 1960–87

agricultural goods, industrial goods, and consumer goods to the Soviet Union. Because of the peculiarities of the Comecon pricing system, throughout the 1970s and early 1980s Comecon prices for Soviet oil were lower than world oil prices. Western specialists have debated the political motivation of this implicit price subsidy to Comecon members. The cohesiveness within Comecon members seemed remarkable when in 1985 the fall in the world price left Comecon members paying above-market prices for Soviet oil.

The membership of Cuba, Mongolia, and Vietnam in Comecon has served Soviet foreign policy interests more than the economic welfare of Comecon members. In general, the more economically developed European members have supported the three less developed members by providing a large market for their exports, often at above-market prices. Most of Cuba's sugar and nickel and all of Mongolia's copper and molybdenum have been imported by the Soviet Union. In addition, the Soviet Union has established naval and air bases in Cuba and Vietnam.

Since 1985 Gorbachev has called for an increase in trade with Comecon members. At the Twenty-Seventh Party Congress in February–March 1986, both he and Prime Minister Nikolai I. Ryzhkov stressed the need to improve cooperation with the socialist countries on the basis of Comecon's *Comprehensive Program for Scientific and Technical Cooperation to the Year 2000*. This program stressed the self-sufficiency of Comecon countries in five key areas: electronics, automation of production, nuclear power, biotechnology, and development of new raw materials. It also called for improvement of plan coordination, joint planning, Comecon investment strategy, production specialization, and quality of machinery and equipment exported to the Soviet Union (see Appendix B).

Yugoslavia

In 1964 Yugoslavia negotiated a formal agreement of cooperation with Comecon. This relationship allowed Yugoslavia to maintain its nonaligned position while acquiring almost all the rights and privileges of a full Comecon member. In the 1980s, the Soviet Union's trade relationship with Yugoslavia resembled its relationship with full members of Comecon. The Soviet Union exported fuel, ferrous metals, plastics, and fertilizer to Yugoslavia. Yugoslavia's machine-tool, power-engineering, shipbuilding, and consumer goods industries supplied the Soviet Union with soft-currency goods (see Glossary).

In the late 1970s and early 1980s, Yugoslavia became more dependent on Soviet oil as hostilities in the Persian Gulf cut off its supply of Iraqi oil. In addition, from 1970 well into the 1980s actual trade with the Soviet Union exceeded planned trade volumes. Thus, in 1983 the Yugoslav government informed Soviet Prime Minister Nikolai A. Tikhonov of its desire to decrease trade with the Soviet Union in the mid- to late 1980s. Because of the huge foreign currency debt accumulated by Yugoslavia from 1981 to 1985, however, the Soviet Union remained its most important trade partner in the late 1980s. In fact, for some Yugoslav products, such as shoes, the Soviet Union was the sole foreign buyer.

China

In the 1950s, the Soviet Union claimed half of China's foreign trade. The political rift that developed between the two countries in the late 1950s culminated in 1960 with the withdrawal of more than 1,000 Soviet specialists from China and an official break in trade relations in 1964. Although it had been only an observer, China stopped attending Comecon sessions in 1961. Economic relations between the Soviet Union and China resumed in 1982. Primarily as a result of Soviet political concessions and pressures on the Chinese to expand trade, trade volume between the two countries increased tenfold between 1982 and 1987.

In the 1980s, the Soviet Union proved to be an ideal trade partner for China. China's exports were not competitive on the world market, and its foreign currency reserves were severely depleted by record foreign trade deficits in 1984 and 1985. Likewise, the Soviet Union, producing dated technology that was difficult to market in more industrially advanced countries and acquiring a growing hard-currency debt, eagerly pursued the Chinese market. Each country would sell the other goods it could not market elsewhere, and each could conserve scarce hard currency by bartering. The Soviet Union possessed machinery, equipment, and technical knowhow to help China develop its fuel and mineral resources and power, transportation, and metallurgical industries. China could offer a wealth of raw materials, textiles, and agricultural and industrial consumer goods.

Stepped-up economic relations reflected Soviet flexibility in overcoming various political and administrative stumbling blocks. By mid-1988 Gorbachev was speaking of reducing Soviet troops on the Chinese border, Vietnam had removed half of its troops from Cambodia, and Soviet troops had begun their withdrawal from Afghanistan (see Sino-Soviet Relations, ch. 10). Reforms of the Soviet foreign trade complex established free trade zones (see Glossary) in the Soviet Far East and Soviet Central Asia, simplifying border trade between the two countries. Soviet trade officials persuaded the Chinese to expand business ties beyond border trade into joint ventures, coproduction contracts, and the export of surplus Chinese labor to the Soviet Union. The Peking Restaurant in Moscow, specializing in Chinese cuisine, became the first joint venture between the Soviet Union and China. In April 1988, China's minister of foreign economic relations and trade, Zheng Toubin, stated that China would continue to expand trade with the Soviet Union "at a rapid pace," thus rewarding Soviet persistence in expanding trade with China.

Cambodia, Laos, and North Korea

Soviet economic relations with non-Comecon communist states have taken the form of aid and trade. In 1987 approximately 85 percent of Soviet aid went to the communist Third World. By far the largest share of these funds was absorbed by Cuba, Mongolia, and Vietnam. The rest was left to Cambodia, Laos, and North Korea. Pledges of Soviet aid increased steadily from 1985 through 1988 and were divided evenly between direct aid and trade subsidies. Commodity exchange was characterized by the Soviet Union's providing machinery, fuel, and transportation equipment in return for Laotian ores and concentrated metals, North Korean rolled ferrous metals and labor, and Cambodian rubber.

Trade with Western Industrialized Countries

The Western industrialized countries include the countries of Western Europe, as well as Australia, Canada, Japan, New Zealand, South Africa, and the United States (see table 47, Appendix A). Soviet trade with industrialized countries, except Finland, consisted of simple purchases paid for on a cash or credit basis, direct exchange of one good for another (Pepsi-Cola for Stolichnaya vodka, for example), or industrial cooperation agreements in which foreign firms participated in the construction or operation of plants in the Soviet Union. In the latter instances, payments were rendered in the form of the output of new plants. By contrast, trade with Finland, which does not have a convertible currency, was conducted through bilateral clearing agreements, much like Soviet trade with its Comecon partners.

In the 1970s and 1980s, the Soviet Union relied heavily on various kinds of fuel exports to earn hard currency, and Western partners regarded the Soviet Union as an extremely reliable supplier of oil and natural gas. In the 1980s, the Soviet Union gave domestic priority to gas, coal, and nuclear power in order to free more oil reserves for export. This was necessary because of higher production costs and losses of convertible currency resulting from the drop in world oil prices. The development of natural gas for domestic and export use was also stimulated by these factors. Between 1970 and 1986, natural gas exports rose from 1 percent to 15 percent of total Soviet exports to the West.

Because of the inferior quality of Soviet goods, the Soviet Union was unsuccessful in increasing its exports of manufactured goods. In 1987 only 18 percent of Soviet manufactured goods met world

605

technical standards. As an illustration of these problems in quality, Canadian customers who had purchased Soviet Belarus tractors often found that the tractors had to be overhauled on arrival before they could be sold on the Canadian market. In 1986 less than 5 percent of Soviet exports to the West consisted of machinery. Other Soviet nonfuel exports in the 1990s included timber, exported primarily to Japan, and chemicals, the export of which grew substantially in 1984 and 1985.

In the 1980s, Soviet imports from Western industrialized countries generally exceeded exports, although trade with the West decreased overall. One-half of Soviet agricultural imports were from developed countries, and these imports made up a considerable portion of total imports from the West. Industrial equipment formed one-quarter of Soviet imports from the West, and iron and steel products, particularly steel tubes for pipeline construction, made up most of the rest. Over the course of the 1980s, high-technology items gained in importance as well.

In the 1970s and 1980s, Soviet trade with the Western industrialized countries was more dynamic than was Soviet trade with other countries, as trade patterns fluctuated with political and economic changes. In the 1970s, the Soviet Union exchanged its energy and raw materials for Western capital goods, and growth in trade was substantial. Soviet exports jumped 55 percent, and imports jumped 207 percent. The Soviet Union ran a trade deficit with the West throughout this period.

In 1980 the Soviet Union exported slightly more to the West than it imported. After a temporary shortage of hard currency in 1981, the Soviet Union sought to improve its trade position with the industrialized countries by keeping imports at a steady level and by increasing exports. As a result, the Soviet Union began to run trade surpluses with most of its Western partners. Much of the income earned from fuel exports to Western Europe was used to pay off debts with the United States, Canada, and Australia, from which the Soviet Union had imported large quantities of grain.

In 1985 and 1986, trade with the West was suppressed because of heightened East-West political tensions, successful Soviet grain harvests, high Soviet oil production costs, a devalued United States dollar, and falling oil prices. Despite increases in oil and natural gas exports, the Soviet Union's primary hard-currency earners, the country was receiving less revenue from its exports to the West. The Soviet Union sold most of its oil and natural gas exports for United States dollars but bought most of its hard-currency imports from Western Europe. The lower value of the United States dollar meant that the purchasing power of a barrel of Soviet crude

Carpet weavers and their supervisor in Baku, Azerbaydzhan Republic. Much of the production is exported. Courtesy Jimmy Pritchard

oil, for example, was much lower than is the 1970s and early 1980s. In 1987 the purchasing power of a barrel of Soviet crude oil in exchange for West German goods had fallen to one-third of its purchasing power in 1984.

With the exception of grain, phosphates used in fertilizer production, and high-technology equipment, Soviet dependence on Western imports historically has been minimal. A growing hard-currency debt of US$31 billion in 1986 led to reductions in imports from countries with hard currencies. In 1988 Gorbachev cautioned against dependence on Western technology because it required hard currency that "we don't have." He also warned that increased borrowing to pay for imports from the West would lead to dependence on international lending institutions.

The United States

Trade between the United States and the Soviet Union averaged about 1 percent of total trade for both countries through the 1970s and 1980s. Soviet-American trade peaked in 1979 at US$4.5 billion, exactly 1 percent of total United States trade. The Soviet Union continuously ran a trade deficit with the United States in the 1970s and early 1980s, but from 1985 through 1987 the Soviet Union cut imports from the United States while maintaining its level of exports to balance trade between the two countries.

607

In 1987 total trade between the United States and the Soviet Union amounted to US$2 billion. The Soviet Union exported chemicals, metals (including gold), and petroleum products in addition to fur skins, alcoholic beverages, and fish products to the United States and received agricultural goods—mostly grain—and industrial equipment in return. The value of exports to the Soviet Union in 1987 amounted to US$1.5 billion, three-quarters of which consisted of agricultural products and one-quarter industrial equipment.

Competition from other parts of the world, improvements in Soviet grain production, and political disagreements between the two countries adversely affected American agricultural exports to the Soviet Union in the 1980s. In 1985 and 1986, trade was the lowest since 1973. The Soviet Union had turned to Canada and Western Europe for one-third of its grain supplies, as well as to Argentina, Eastern Europe, Australia, and China. United States government price subsidies helped to expand grain exports in 1987 and 1988.

The United States has long linked trade with the Soviet Union to its foreign policy toward the Soviet Union and, especially since the early 1980s, to Soviet human rights policies (see table 48, Appendix A). In 1949, for example, the Coordinating Committee for Multilateral Export Controls (CoCom—see Glossary) was established by Western governments to monitor the export of sensitive high technology that would improve military effectiveness of members of the Warsaw Pact (see Appendix C) and certain other countries. The Jackson-Vanik Amendment, which was attached to the 1974 Trade Reform Act, linked the granting of most-favored-nation status (see Glossary) to the right of Soviet Jews to emigrate.

In 1987 the United States had reason to reassess its trade policy toward the Soviet Union. The Soviet Union had restructured and decentralized authority for trade under the Ministry of Foreign Trade, made improvements in human rights policies, cooperated in arms control negotiations, and shown a willingness to experiment with joint ventures. Furthermore, the United States government recognized that restrictive trade policies were hurting its own economic interests. In April 1988, Soviet and American trade delegations met in Moscow to discuss possibilities for expanded trade. Through increased trade with the United States, the Soviet Union hoped to learn Western management, marketing, and manufacturing skills. Such skills would increase the ability of the Soviet Union to export manufactured goods, and thus earn hard currency, and would improve its competitiveness on the world market. The delegations declared that Soviet-American cooperation would be

American fast food served near Gor'kiy Park, Moscow
Courtesy Jimmy Pritchard

expanded in the areas of food processing, energy, construction equipment, medical products, and the service sector.

Western Europe

In the mid-1980s, West European exports to the Soviet Union were marginal, less than 0.5 percent of the combined gross national product (GNP—see Glossary) of countries of the Organisation for Economic Co-operation and Development (OECD—see Glossary). OECD countries provided the Soviet Union with high-technology and industrial equipment, chemicals, metals, and agricultural products. In return, Western Europe received oil and natural gas from the Soviet Union.

Although oil and gas were the primary Soviet exports to Western Europe, they represented only a small percentage of Western Europe's substantial fuel imports: Soviet oil provided 3 percent and natural gas 2 percent of the energy consumed in Western Europe. The completion of the Urengoy-Uzhgorod export pipeline project increased the importance of Soviet natural gas to Western Europe in the second half of the 1980s. In 1984 France, Austria, the Federal Republic of Germany (West Germany), and Italy began receiving natural gas from western Siberia through the pipeline, for which the Soviet Union was paid in hard currency, pumping equipment,

609

and large-diameter pipe. By 1990 the Soviet Union expected to supply 3 percent of all natural gas imported by Western Europe, including 30 percent of West Germany's gas imports.

Unlike the United States, the countries of Western Europe have not viewed trade as a tool to influence Soviet domestic and foreign policies. Western Europe rejected the trade restrictions imposed by the United States after the Soviet invasion of Afghanistan in 1979 and the declaration of martial law in Poland in 1980. From 1980 to 1982, the United States embargoed the supply of equipment for the Urengoy-Uzhgorod natural gas pipeline, but Western Europe ignored United States pleas to do the same.

Despite the poor relations between the superpowers in the early and mid-1980s, Western Europe tried to improve international relations with the Soviet Union. One major step in this direction was the normalization of relations between Comecon and the European Economic Community (EEC). After fifteen years of negotiations, the EEC approved an accord that established formal relations with Comecon effective June 25, 1988. Although it did not establish bilateral trade relations, the agreement "set the stage" for the exchange of information. This accord marked Comecon's official recognition of the EEC.

Japan

In 1985 trade with the Soviet Union accounted for 1.6 percent of Japanese exports and 1 percent of Japanese imports; Japan was the Soviet Union's fourth most important Western trading partner (see table 49, Appendix A). Japan's principal exports to the Soviet Union included steel (approximately 40 percent of Japan's exports to the Soviet Union), chemicals, and textiles. The Soviet Union exported timber, nonferrous metals, rare-earth metals, and fuel to Japan. In 1986, despite a reduction in trade between the two countries, the Soviet Union had a trade deficit with Japan. In 1987 trade dropped another 20 percent.

Numerous controversies have thwarted Soviet-Japanese trade. The Toshiba affair, in which Japan was accused of shipping equipment to the Soviet Union that was prohibited by CoCom, caused Japanese-Soviet trade to decrease in 1987. In addition, the Japanese constantly prodded the Soviet Union to return the islands off the Japanese island of Hokkaido that had come under Soviet control after World War II (see Soviet-Japanese Relations, ch. 10). For its part, the Soviet Union complained of the trade imbalance and static structure of Japanese-Soviet trade.

In the late 1980s, the Soviet Union tried to increase its exports to Japan and diversify the nature of the countries' relationship.

Soviet proposals have included establishing joint enterprises to exploit natural resources in Siberia and the Soviet Far East, specifically, coal in the southern Yakutiya of Siberia and petroleum on Sakhalin; cooperating in the monetary and credit fields; jointly surveying and studying marine resources and peaceful uses of space; and establishing joint activities in other countries. The Soviet Union also proposed branching out into joint ventures in the chemical and wood chip industries, electronics, machine tools, and fish processing. The first Japanese-Soviet joint enterprise, a wood-processing plant in the Soviet Far East, began operation in March 1988. The Soviet Union provided the raw materials, and Japan supplied the technology, equipment, and managerial expertise.

Finland

In contrast to the variable trade relationships the Soviet Union has had with other West European countries, its relationship with Finland has been somewhat stable because of five-year agreements that regulated trade between the countries. The first was established in 1947, and 1986 marked the beginning of the eighth. Accounting procedures and methods of payment were agreed upon every five years as well by the Bank of Finland and Vneshtorgbank. A steady growth in trade between the two countries occurred throughout the 1970s and 1980s.

In the late 1980s, Finland was the Soviet Union's second most important trading partner among the Western nations, after West Germany. Trade with Finland, however, was based on bilateral clearing agreements (see Glossary) rather than on exchange of hard currency used with other Western trading partners. In 1986 the Soviet Union shipped 4 percent of its exports to and received 3 percent of its imports from Finland. Finland provided the Soviet Union with ships, particularly those suited to Arctic conditions; heavy machinery; and consumer goods such as clothing, textiles, processed foodstuffs, and consumer durables. The Soviet Union exported oil, natural gas, and fuel and technology for the nuclear power industry.

The system of bilateral clearing agreements on which Soviet-Finnish trade was based required that any increase in Finnish imports from the Soviet Union be accompanied by a corresponding increase in exports to the Soviet Union in order to maintain the bilateral trade balance. At the beginning of the 1980s, Finland increased its imports of Soviet oil, which allowed it to increase its exports to the Soviet Union. This procedure accounted for the steady growth in Soviet-Finnish trade into the late 1980s. By 1988 about 90 percent of Soviet exports to Finland consisted of oil.

Because the Finns imported more oil than they could consume domestically, they reexported it to other Scandinavian and West European countries. The Finns complained in late 1987 and early 1988 of a decline in Soviet ship orders and delinquent payments. The share of Finland's exports to the Soviet Union, which had previously been as high as 25 percent, dropped to 15 percent in 1988.

Trade with Third World Countries

The Third World embraces those countries the Soviet Union terms "developing countries." This category includes those countries of socialist orientation that have some sort of privileged economic affiliation with the Soviet Union, such as Afghanistan, Angola, Iraq, and Nicaragua, but excludes the developing countries ruled by Marxist-Leninist (see Glossary) parties, such as Cambodia, Laos, and Vietnam. Soviet trade with the Third World has been marked by two characteristics. First, although the Soviet Union has generally played only a minor role in Third World trade, Soviet imports or exports have formed a large portion of the total trade of some countries. Second, the Soviet Union has concentrated its trade with the Third World in the hands of relatively few partners. For example, in 1987 India, Iran, Iraq, Syria, Argentina, Egypt, Turkey, Afghanistan, Nigeria, and Malaysia together accounted for 75 percent of Soviet imports from and 80 percent of Soviet exports to the Third World.

Although Soviet trade with the Third World increased in volume from 1965 through 1985, it remained between 13 and 15 percent of total Soviet trade for exports and 10 and 12 percent for imports. The Third World's trade with the Soviet Union, however, decreased in the 1970s and into the 1980s. These data include Cuba, since the only figures available concerning Third World trade with the Soviet Union include Cuba. As a percentage of overall Third World trade, the Soviet Union's share fell from 3.9 percent in 1970 to 2.5 percent in 1981. Deducting Soviet trade with Cuba, which has been considerable, would show an even smaller role played by the Soviet Union in Third World trade. In the late 1980s, the Soviet Union sought arrangements that would allow it to maintain a level of trade that minimized the loss of hard currency.

Balance of Trade

During the 1980s, the Soviet Union exported more to Third World countries than it imported from them. Official Soviet statistics showed a trade deficit for this period, but arms and military equipment sales, which were not reported and are thus termed "unidentifiable" exports, accounted for approximately 50 percent

Icebreaker Otto Schmidt, *used to clear the way for cargo ships*
Courtesy United States Navy

of total exports to the Third World throughout the 1980s. Thus, the Soviet Union's hard-currency balance of trade (see Glossary), including arms sales, with the Third World was positive from 1980 through 1986. In fact, the Soviet Union's positive hard-currency trade balance with the Third World exceeded its hard-currency deficit with the Western industrialized countries in 1985 and 1986. For this reason, the Soviet Union showed an overall positive hard-currency trade balance for these years.

Until the mid-1970s, bilateral clearing agreements were the primary means by which the Soviet Union settled accounts with its Third World partners. By the early 1980s, hard-currency payments had become the preferred means of settlement. Clearing agreements were used in less than half of all trade transactions. On occasion, the Soviet Union bartered arms for oil.

Composition of Trade

Not including arms sales, machinery accounted for 20 percent of total sales to the Third World in 1985. Soviet exports of machinery took up an even higher relative share of total sales to Algeria, Iran, Nigeria, Pakistan, the People's Democratic Republic of Yemen (South Yemen), and Turkey. From 1980 through 1984, fuel, mostly oil, made up approximately 33 percent of overall Soviet

613

exports to the Third World, including 50 percent of its exports to Asia and 60 to 70 percent of its exports to Latin America. Since 1985 greater competition on the world market resulting from falling world oil prices and rising Soviet extraction costs has prompted the Soviet Union to try to replace its export of oil with manufactured goods.

The Soviet Union has been the largest arms exporter to the Third World for a number of years. Major arms customers were concentrated in the belt of countries that stretches from North Africa to India, close to the Soviet Union's southern border. Some 72 percent of Soviet weapons exports went to Algeria, India, Iraq, Libya, and Syria. Other important customers included Afghanistan, Angola, Ethiopia, South Yemen, and the Yemen Arab Republic (North Yemen). The Soviet Union lost arms customers in the 1980s, however, when Brazil and Egypt began to expand their arms sales to the Third World. India, which had experienced improvements in its hard-currency balance in the 1980s, also started to buy arms from other suppliers. In an effort to retain its share of Indian arms customers, the Soviet Union continued to offer India its most sophisticated weapons at even more attractive rates.

The Soviet Union has long been an importer of Third World agricultural products. These imports increased dramatically after 1980 because of poor Soviet harvests from 1979 into the early 1980s and the United States grain embargo against the Soviet Union in 1980 and 1981. From 1980 to 1985, food and agricultural goods, half of them grain, made up 50 percent of Soviet imports from the Third World. In the first nine months of 1986, the decrease in grain purchases accounted for most of the 22 percent drop in imports from the Third World.

Africa and Latin America supplied most of the food imports other than grain. Throughout the 1980s, food imports steadily rose, but imports from individual countries fluctuated. Because of these fluctuations, the Soviet Union was often considered an unstable trade partner compared with Western customers.

Because the Soviet Union was a major producer and exporter of most of the world's minerals, its import requirements for many other commodities (nonferrous metals, in particular) were sporadic. Nonetheless, the Soviet Union was a stable importer of some minerals, particularly bauxite and phosphate rock. The Soviet Union imported up to 50 percent of its bauxite from Guinea, Guyana, India, Indonesia, and Jamaica. Phosphate rock was abundant in the Soviet Union, but because extraction costs were high most of this mineral was imported from Morocco and Syria.

A decline in Soviet imports of manufactured goods in the 1970s led Third World countries to pressure the Soviet Union to increase the import of these goods in the 1980s. In 1982 the Soviet demand for Third World manufactures began to rise. By 1984 manufactured goods, including manufactured consumer goods, made up 25 percent of Soviet imports from the Third World.

Beginning in 1973, in an effort to earn hard currency, the Soviet Union began to import oil from Third World countries for reexport to Western industrialized countries. This activity slowed from 1980 to 1982, recovered in 1983 through 1985, and continued to increase in 1986. Late that year, the Soviet Union signed an agreement with the Organization of Petroleum Exporting Countries (OPEC) that restricted the amount of oil it could buy for reexport. By 1988 this agreement had not cut total Soviet oil receipts, however, because oil was paid to the Soviet Union as compensation for arms sales.

Africa, Asia, and Latin America

During the 1980s, the geographical pattern of Soviet-Third World trade changed markedly (see table 50, Appendix A). A decrease in trade with North Africa and the Middle East balanced a substantial increase in trade with sub-Saharan Africa, South Asia, and Latin America.

In 1987 about 50 percent of the Soviet Union's total identified exports to the Third World went to Asia, and India was the Soviet Union's biggest trade partner. In exchange for Soviet oil and oil products, India supplied food, raw agricultural material, clothing, textiles, and machinery. India was also the Soviet Union's sole significant Third World supplier of equipment and advanced technology, e.g., computers and copiers, much of which was produced by Indian subsidiaries of Western multinational corporations. Malaysia, another important partner of the Soviet Union in Asia, was an important supplier of rubber, palm oil, and tin.

From 1980 to 1983, Soviet exports to Africa increased slightly to 30 percent of its Third World exports and decreased thereafter. Imports from Africa fluctuated from 1980 to 1985 but remained at about 25 percent. Nigeria was the Soviet Union's only important trade partner in sub-Saharan Africa, receiving Soviet machinery and exporting cocoa.

Exports to Latin America grew during the 1980s and reached 8 percent in 1985. Latin America's share of Soviet Third World imports was high (40 percent in 1982) because of large imports of Argentine grain. As the Soviet Union's main grain supplier, Argentina was the Soviet Union's most significant import partner in the Third World in 1980, 1981, and 1983. In 1986 the Soviet Union renewed its grain agreement with Argentina for another five years. However, because of a US$11 billion trade deficit with Argentina that the Soviet Union had amassed from 1980 through 1985 and the successful Soviet harvest of 1986, the Soviet Union cut its grain imports from Argentina drastically. In 1986 they were at a six-year low.

Countries of Socialist Orientation

The countries of socialist orientation can be categorized into two groups: those that had observer status in Comecon and those that were not observers but had privileged affiliations with Comecon member countries (see table 51, Appendix A). The Soviet Union's trade with the Third World has always been heavily skewed toward countries of socialist orientation. Soviet aid provided most of the foreign capital for these countries and influenced their domestic economic development significantly. The Soviet Union often profited more politically than economically from this trade: most Soviet surpluses were not repaid but became clearing credit, long-term cooperation credit, or short-term commercial credit.

In 1986 the countries that had formal agreements with, or observer status in, Comecon were Afghanistan, Angola, Ethiopia, Laos, and South Yemen. These countries were all characterized by political instability, low GNP, and low export potential. The share of exports to this group rose from 14 percent of total Soviet identified exports to the Third World in 1980 to 28 percent in the first nine months of 1986. Afghanistan, a recipient of Soviet machinery and military equipment, was the Soviet Union's most significant partner in this group. By contrast, trade with South Yemen was negligible.

Countries that had privileged affiliations with Comecon were Algeria, Benin, Burma, Congo, Guinea, Madagascar, Nigeria, Syria, and Tanzania and, at times, Guinea-Bissau, Mali, Seychelles, and Zimbabwe. Throughout the 1980s, Soviet exports to these countries oscillated, for example, from 27 percent in 1981 to 15 percent in 1983. This fluctuation, as well as fluctuations in imports, was primarily a result of changes in trade with Iraq, a major Soviet arms-for-oil trading partner in the Third World.

Trade with the Organization of Petroleum Exporting Countries

The Organization of Petroleum Exporting Countries (OPEC), particularly Iraq and Algeria, absorbed the largest share of the Soviet Union's "unidentified" exports (see table 52, Appendix A).

Loaded tanker Iman *at sea*
Roll-on/roll-off ship, named for composer Nikolay Rimskiy-Korsakov
Courtesy United States Navy

Although Soviet statistics usually showed a very low or negative trade balance with these countries, the balance was probably high because of arms sales. In the 1980s, some OPEC countries, particularly Iran and Iraq, together with Syria, which was not a member of OPEC, exchanged oil for Soviet arms and military equipment. Oil from these countries was resold to the West for hard currency. In the late 1980s, the Soviet Union attempted to increase its exports of nonmilitary goods to these countries. In May 1986, the Soviet Union and Iraq agreed to increase Soviet nonmilitary equipment sales, and in August 1986 an attempt was made to revive Iraqi gas sales.

Gorbachev's Economic Reforms

When Gorbachev delivered his report on the CPSU's economic policy on June 12, 1985, he noted that growth in exports, particularly machinery and equipment, was slow because the poor quality of Soviet goods prohibited them from being competitive on the world market. In the next three years, Gorbachev introduced many changes that would enable the foreign trade complex to better support his economic policy of acceleration. By May 1988, the structure of the Soviet foreign trade complex had been changed, and operations had been dramatically overhauled (see Structural Reforms, 1986 to Mid-1988, this ch.).

The price reform called for by the Twenty-Seventh Party Congress was an important step in improving Soviet international economic involvement. Soviet officials admitted that pricing was "economically unsubstantiated" and "unrealistic." They understood that although a fully convertible ruble would not be possible for some time, prices that more accurately reflected production costs, supply and demand, and world market prices were essential for developing a convertible currency. The nonconvertible ruble and the Soviet pricing system discouraged Western businessmen who could not accurately project production costs nor easily convert their ruble profits.

The new joint venture law, passed on January 13, 1987, opened up the Soviet economy to foreign participation, particularly in manufacturing. It was believed that the experience gained in such ventures would facilitate integration into the world economy. Specifically, through upgraded production processes, the Soviet Union could export more competitive manufactured goods and decrease its dependency on energy and raw materials to earn hard currency.

In August 1987, the Soviet Union formally requested observer status in the General Agreement on Tariffs and Trade (GATT— see Glossary). The Soviet Union also expressed its desire to join other international economic organizations and establish contacts with other regional groups. A major step in this direction occurred in 1988 when the Soviet Union signed a normalization agreement with the EEC. The Soviet government, however, professed no interest in joining the World Bank (see Glossary) or the International Monetary Fund (IMF—see Glossary). Although Soviet officials claimed that the international monetary system "was not managed properly," it is more likely that IMF and World Bank regulations were the obstacles: both institutions required that members' currencies be freely convertible and that members provide accurate information concerning gold sales and economic performance.

Gorbachev transformed the role of foreign trade in the Soviet economy. Whereas imports previously were regarded exclusively as a vehicle to compensate for difficulties in the short term, Soviet economists under Gorbachev declared that imports should be regarded as alternatives to domestic investment and that exports should serve to gauge the technical level of domestic production. Foreign economic ties were to support growth in production beyond the capacities of the domestic economy. The Soviet Union could thus take a place in the world market that was commensurate with its scientific and technical progress and political weight.

* * *

Numerous English-language sources cover aspects of Soviet foreign trade. The foreign economic relations section of volume two of the report submitted to the United States Congress Joint Economic Committee in November 1987 entitled *Gorbachev's Economic Plans* is particularly informative on Soviet-American trade, the Soviet Union's debt situation, and Soviet economic involvement in the Third World. H. Stephen Gardner's *Soviet Foreign Trade* very clearly lays out the institutional and political foundations for Soviet foreign economic decision making through 1980. Two chapters, one by Wilfried Czerniejewicz and another by Kazuo Ogawa, in *Siberia and the Soviet Far East* describe trade relations between the Soviet Union and Western Europe and the Soviet Union and Japan. Although it is dated, *Soviet Foreign Trade* by Glen Alden Smith is one of the best references covering all aspects of Soviet trade.

An accurate source of Soviet trade data is the Central Intelligence Agency's *Handbook of Economic Statistics*, published in September of each year. Jerry F. Hough's *Opening Up the Soviet Economy* devotes one chapter to Gorbachev's foreign trade reforms and another to the way American businessmen and government officials should view these changes. (For further information and complete citations, see Bibliography.)

Chapter 16. Science and Technology

Montage of a nuclear reactor at the Ukrainian Academy of Sciences, a cosmonaut in a space suit, a woman operating a computer, and an industrial robot

SCIENTIFIC AND TECHNOLOGICAL progress has played a crucial role in the domestic and foreign relations of the Soviet Union and other modern, industrialized nations. New domestic developments have promised to strengthen the Soviet economy, enhance military capabilities, and significantly influence Soviet relations with other countries.

The Soviet Union has placed great emphasis on science and technology. Soviet leaders since Vladimir I. Lenin have stressed that the growth of science and technology is essential to overall economic expansion of the country. They have overseen the development of a massive network of research and development organizations that in the 1980s employed more scientists, engineers, and researchers than any other nation. Their commitment also has been reflected in the annual increase in government funds allocated to science and technology and in the efforts made to incorporate science and mathematics courses in the school curriculum at all levels. In 1989 Soviet scientists were among the world's best-trained specialists in several critical fields.

The results of this commitment to science and technology have been mixed. In some areas, the Soviet Union has achieved notable success. For example, in 1964 two Soviet scientists, Nikolai Basov and Aleksandr Prokhorov, shared a Nobel Prize, together with the American Charles H. Townes, for their research in developing the laser. Soviet scientists also have excelled in space research. In 1957 they launched the first artificial earth satellite, Sputnik (see Glossary), and in 1989 they still held several records for longevity in space. Other strengths have included high-energy physics, selected areas of medicine, mathematics, and welding technologies. And in some military-related technologies the Soviet Union has equaled or even surpassed Western levels.

In other areas, the Soviet Union has been less successful. In chemistry, biology, and computers the Soviet Union in 1989 remained far behind the technological levels achieved in the West and in Japan. Research and development in industries producing consumer goods has received little attention, and the goods produced in those industries have long been considered to be of extremely low quality by Western standards.

This disparity in the achievements of Soviet technological development has resulted from a combination of historical, economic, planning, and organizational factors. All have combined to produce a system in which scientists and engineers have had little incentive to innovate because of immense bureaucratic obstacles and because of limited professional and personal rewards.

In the 1980s, the problems of science and technology received considerable attention in the Soviet Union. Cognizant of their country's serious economic shortcomings, leaders stressed the importance of scientific and technological advances to end the Soviet Union's dependence on extensive economic development (see Glossary) and to move toward intensive development. In the middle of the decade, the new leadership began examining the problems of Soviet science and technology and launched numerous programs and reforms aimed at improving the country's research, development, and production processes.

Early Development

Soviet leaders since Lenin have stated as one of their long-term goals the development of a powerful scientific and technological base. Yet at various times since the Bolshevik Revolution (see Glossary) of 1917, Soviet leaders have faced situations in which the immediate economic, military, and political demands on science and technology outweighed the long-term goals. Thus, the pursuit of short-term objectives affected scientific and technological development at some times by retarding its expansion and at other times by laying the foundation for weaknesses that emerged later. Despite this, Soviet science and technology have grown immensely in terms of organizations, personnel, funding levels, and output.

When the Bolsheviks (see Glossary) seized power in 1917, they inherited a poorly developed scientific and technological base. The major science organization at the time of the Bolshevik Revolution was the Academy of Sciences, founded by Peter the Great in 1725 in hopes of developing an indigenous science base and of eliminating his country's reliance on foreign science. Peter intended the academy to conduct research, serve as an advisory board to the tsar, and organize the empire's higher and secondary education.

In its early years, the academy struggled to resolve such issues as defining its responsibilities and reducing the extensive governmental control over academy activities. Its second charter, issued in 1803, relieved the academy of its educational responsibilities and removed some governmental controls, particularly regarding membership selection. The government continued to interfere in the work of scientists, however, particularly those who advocated progressive ideas that challenged the old order as accepted by the tsar and the Russian Orthodox Church. The academy's third charter (1836) proclaimed it the country's chief scientific body. The academy continued in this role, focusing primarily on basic research, through the end of tsarist rule. Its achievements during this time were noteworthy. Dmitrii I. Mendeleev (1843–1907) compiled the periodic table of the elements, Nobel Prize recipient Ivan P. Pavlov (1849–1936) conducted research on conditioned reflexes, and Konstantin E. Tsiolkovskii (1857–1935), a pioneer in modern rocketry, studied the theory of cosmic flight.

Another key issue that confronted the academy at the outset was the extent of foreign involvement in Russian science. Peter the Great eagerly opened Russia to the West and encouraged the participation of Western scientists in the development of Russian science. Thus, the academy initially was staffed by scientists from western Europe, principally of Germanic origin. The strong foreign influence continued well into the nineteenth century. A Russian was not elected to the academy until the 1740s, and Russians did not assume control of the academy until the late 1800s. Under the Bolsheviks, science suffered some initial setbacks but then benefited from the government's decision to expand it. In the early years, many Bolsheviks feared scientists because of ideological differences. A number of scientists were arrested or executed; others emigrated to escape from the Bolsheviks. Those who stayed worked under difficult conditions: few facilities, inadequate housing, shortages of food, little access to the West, and strict political controls.

Not long after the Bolshevik Revolution, Lenin moved to improve the situation facing scientists. In policy pronouncements, he emphasized the need to develop a Soviet scientific and technological base as the way to modernize industry. He argued that technological progress was necessary to counter the perceived threat posed by the West and to demonstrate the strength of socialism (see Glossary) to the world.

During the 1920s, Soviet science began to expand. Many new research institutes were added to the academy, which in 1925 was redesignated the Academy of Sciences of the Soviet Union. Governmental support of science increased under the New Economic Policy (NEP) introduced in 1921 (see The Era of the New Economic Policy, ch. 2). Overall, the living and working conditions of scientists improved as research potentials expanded and as opportunities for the international exchange of information resumed. Research in such fields as biology, chemistry, and physics flourished during this period.

Science and technology underwent significant changes during the years of Joseph V. Stalin's reign. The changes occurred primarily in response to three factors: Stalin's industrialization drive, his efforts to enforce strict ideological control over science, and the outbreak of World War II.

In 1928 Stalin initiated his drive to transform the Soviet Union into an industrial power, technologically independent of the West. Many new institutions were established to provide the applied research foundation needed to develop industrial technologies. Even institutes subordinate to the Academy of Sciences were directed to stop theoretical research and to focus on "practical" problems applicable to industry. In 1935 the academy adopted a charter that created the Engineering Sciences Division to oversee the academy's increased involvement in applied research.

At the same time that Stalin was encouraging the expansion of science, he also was trying to establish firmer ideological control over science. Over time, his efforts led to a significant reduction in scientific effort. In 1928 Stalin initiated a purge of scientists, engineers, and technical personnel in an effort to remove the old generation and replace them with younger scientists who supported communist ideology. In 1934 the academy was moved from Leningrad to Moscow, where political control was easier to maintain. Stalin's Great Terror (see Glossary) ravaged the ranks of scientists and engineers. Many research and development programs had to be halted simply because the leading experts were either arrested or executed. Scientific ties with the West also were severed during this time. The extent of Stalin's interference in science became evident in the post-World War II era. Stalin insisted that ideology be a part of all scientific research. In the natural sciences, he encouraged research that was compatible with the tenets of dialectical materialism (see Glossary). Such an environment opened the door for the influence of such individuals as Trofim D. Lysenko, a leading biologist and agronomist. Lysenko argued that the characteristics of a living organism could be altered by environment and that those acquired characteristics could be inherited, a theory that he tried to prove by numerous fraudulent experiments. His ideas fit nicely with Marxist emphasis on environmental influences and won him the support of Stalin. With that backing, Lysenko was able to arrange the removal and arrest of scientists who opposed his views. His influence continued well into the 1950s, when genetics research in the Soviet Union came to a virtual standstill.

Another factor affecting science and technology under Stalin was the outbreak of World War II. Soviet science and technology suffered badly during the initial period of the war. Many research institutes and industrial facilities were destroyed or seized during the German offensive. The facilities that remained were evacuated to the eastern portions of the Soviet Union. There, all efforts were directed toward developing science and technology in support of the war effort. Not surprisingly, military-related research and development thrived, while research and development in civilian sectors received little attention.

The war demonstrated to Stalin the backwardness of Soviet science and technology. After the war, he ordered the continued expansion of the research and development base, particularly in defense and heavy industries. Allocations for science increased, new research facilities opened, and salaries and perquisites for scientists were improved dramatically. All available personnel, including captured German scientists and imprisoned Soviet scientists, were employed. This effort led to some important technological successes, such as the explosion of an atomic bomb in 1949 and the design of new series of tanks, aircraft, artillery, and locomotives.

Stalin's death in 1953 led to a more relaxed environment for science and technology growth. At the Twentieth Party Congress in 1956, Nikita S. Khrushchev denounced Stalin for imprisoning thousands of the country's leading scientists, many of whom Khrushchev later rehabilitated (see Glossary). Under Khrushchev the number of research workers almost tripled, and the number of research institutes doubled. International scientific communications and cooperation resumed. Exchanges with the West were encouraged as a means of acquiring technologies that Soviet scientists could assimilate and then duplicate.

Khrushchev also initiated major changes in the organization of science and technology. In 1957 he abolished the industrial ministries in favor of regional economic councils (*sovety narodnikh khoziaistv—sovnarkhozy*). Khrushchev thought that research, development, and production facilities subordinated to the *sovnarkhozy* could cooperate on programs more easily than they could under the ministerial system. The experiment failed, partly because of excessive duplication of effort. In 1965, under the leadership of Leonid I. Brezhnev, the industrial ministries were restored. The second major organizational change occurred in 1961, when the Academy of Sciences was reorganized. Concerned that the academy had focused too much on industrial research projects, Soviet leaders transferred the industry-oriented institutes to state committees. The leadership then directed the academy to focus on fundamental research.

Under Brezhnev the Soviet Union launched another drive to modernize science and technology. Several economic and organizational reforms were instituted, but none was radical enough to cause significant improvement. Under his policy of détente, scientific contacts and exchanges with the West increased. Soviet leaders sought long-term agreements with Western firms as a means of acquiring advanced technologies. Eventually, internal disagreements over the appropriate level of technological interaction with the West, coupled with restrictions placed by the West, led to a decline in contacts. Scientific and technological policies under Iurii V. Andropov and Konstantin U. Chernenko brought little change. Of the two leaders, Andropov seemed more interested in accelerating Soviet scientific and technological growth, but neither leader lived long enough to have much impact.

The Administration of Science and Technology

The administration of civilian science and technology encompassed policy making, planning, and financing for the administration of nonmilitary science and technology. Policy making was primarily the responsibility of the Communist Party of the Soviet Union (CPSU) but also involved various all-union (see Glossary) governmental organs. At the all-union level, planning included the Council of Ministers, the State Committee for Science and Technology (Gosudarstvennyi komitet po nauke i tekhnike—GKNT), the Academy of Sciences, and the State Planning Committee (Gosudarstvennyi planovyi komitet—Gosplan). Below the all-union level, planning was handled by branch ministries and by republic or regional academies. Financing involved almost all these organizations, which worked in conjunction with the Ministry of Finance (see Administrative Organs, ch. 8).

Policy Making

The formulation of scientific and technological policy in 1989 was centered in the highest CPSU components, the Politburo and the Secretariat (see Politburo; Secretariat, ch. 7). As the party's top decision-making body, the Politburo defined priorities and the broad policies needed to meet them. Its decisions were reflected in policy deliberations and in decrees issued by the Council of Ministers. Day-to-day decisions on science and technology matters were the responsibility of the Secretariat, the party's chief executive body.

Despite their responsibilities, individual members of the Politburo and the Secretariat did not have the scientific and technical expertise needed to make policy decisions without assistance. They relied on experts working in subordinate party organs and in the governmental apparatus. The Science and Education Institutions Department was the key technical unit within the CPSU Central Committee. It functioned as a high-level advisory staff to the Politburo and as an overseer of policy implementation. The department also was responsible for monitoring the work of the Academy of

Sciences and of education institutions. Other Central Committee departments contributed to policy making for their particular branches.

Advice also was provided by personnel working in GKNT, the Academy of Sciences, and the Council of Ministers. In addition, party authorities relied on advice from special commissions composed of leading scientists and technical experts. These commissions, created by the Council of Ministers, have advised on particularly important science and technology policy matters affecting key sectors of the economy.

Planning

After formulating the nation's broad science and technology policy, the CPSU issued directives to the governmental organs responsible for planning specific programs. At the all-union level, planning involved the Council of Ministers, GKNT, the Academy of Sciences, Gosplan, and, to a much lesser extent, the Supreme Soviet.

The Council of Ministers was responsible for implementing the party's broad directives. It frequently issued decrees that reflected science and technology decisions made by the Politburo. These decrees served as the base on which science and technology plans and programs were formed. The council also confirmed the five-year plans and the annual plans for science and technology, developed measures to improve management of research and development, and resolved issues relating to authors' and inventors' rights, cadre training, and labor wages. The council operated primarily through its Presidium, whose membership included heads of many agencies concerned with science and technology.

Founded in 1965 and subordinate to the Council of Ministers, GKNT functioned as the central organ responsible for overall coordination of scientific and technological programs. GKNT met once or twice a year to decide major policy directions. Between meetings it relied on a collegium to meet weekly to examine issues. GKNT oversaw the work of a small number of research institutes.

The administrative functions of GKNT included working with the Academy of Sciences and other interested organizations to plan and coordinate the development of science and technology. GKNT contributed to the five-year planning process by drafting a list of major problems and working with relevant state committees and the Academy of Sciences to develop proposals. GKNT evaluated the level of scientific and technological development in branches of the economy and worked with science and technology policy-making bodies to develop methods to improve research and innovation.

GKNT also played an important role in coordinating and in monitoring interbranch problems, i.e., those that involved more than one industrial ministry. Proposals to conduct a project on an interbranch problem were submitted by a ministry to GKNT for approval. GKNT then oversaw the implementation of the project. GKNT also was responsible for improving the flow of information within the research and development infrastructure. Finally, GKNT was responsible for establishing and maintaining communications with foreign countries on scientific and technological cooperation and on the purchase of foreign technologies.

Another key organization was the Academy of Sciences, which both administered and performed scientific research and development. Working with GKNT and Gosplan, the academy coordinated and produced research and development plans for its subordinate research facilities and for any facility involved in a program under its jurisdiction. The academy made proposals on funding, personnel, and materials for research and development. It also worked with GKNT to develop and submit to the Council of Ministers proposals for introducing new technology and forecasting trends in the economy.

The Academy of Sciences was responsible for translating national plans into specific programs carried out by subordinate facilities. It oversaw science and technology planning for its divisions, regional branches, and the republic academies of sciences.

As the nation's chief planning organ, Gosplan was responsible for incorporating science and technology programs into the national economic plan. It worked with GKNT and the Academy of Sciences to plan the introduction of research and development results into the economy, to determine the overall volume of needed capital investment, and to decide funding levels for science and technology programs, material supplies, training, and wages. Within Gosplan, the Unified Science and Technology Department was the primary unit engaged in science and technology planning. It was aided by advisory councils and commissions organized in key economic sectors.

Below the top policy-making level, science and technology plans were implemented by the industrial ministries and the Academy of Sciences. The Soviet economy has been organized and directed by a complicated, centralized industrial system (see Industrial Organization, ch. 12). The leadership of each ministry was responsible for planning science and technology programs carried out within its specific industrial branch. The leaders based their plans on the national economic plans given to them by the higher authorities (see Economic Planning and Control, ch. 11).

*Officer on the bridge of a modern Soviet merchant ship explaining
the instruments, Murmansk, Russian Republic
Courtesy Jimmy Pritchard*

631

The science and technology planning process involved four levels of documents. The broadest plans spelled out the long-term (fifteen to twenty years), comprehensive program. These documents presented the best judgment of experts about future economic trends, probable developments in science and technology, and the resources needed to achieve those developments. The next level of documents consisted of the main directions of economic and social development, which included a section on the development of science and technology. The developmental directions provided preliminary targets for the first five years of the period covered and a very general planning framework for the remaining years (the directions can cover ten to fifteen years). The third-level document was the five-year plan and the annual plans derived from it. This has been the key document used by branch managerial organs to organize their work. The final document, the institute plan, was based on the five-year plan and described the research and development projects to be undertaken by a particular institute.

Financing

Decisions about the financing of Soviet science and technology involved many of the same high-level party and government organs involved in the policy-making and planning processes. One aspect of these processes has been the determination of resources to be allocated to specific science and technology programs. That determination has been made by the CPSU Politburo, the Council of Ministers, GKNT, and the Academy of Sciences. The Ministry of Finance has made specific science and technology allocations in accordance with approved plans. The State Bank (Gosudarstvennyi bank—Gosbank) has issued credit for science and technology development projects.

Several other organizations were involved in the administration of Soviet science and technology. The State Committee for Material and Technical Supply (Gosudarstvennyi komitet po material'no-tekhnicheskomu snabzheniiu—Gossnab) was responsible for supplying science and technology organizations with needed equipment and instruments. The State Committee for Labor and Social Problems (Gosudarstvennyi komitet po trudu i sotsial'nym voprosam—Goskomtrud) was concerned with labor and wage issues. The State Committee for Standards (Gosudarstvennyi komitet po standartam—Gosstandart) assigned and directed the development of nationwide technical and economic standards. It approved new standards and oversaw the adherence of science and technology organizations to the standards. The State Committee for Inventions and Discoveries (Gosudarstvennyi komitet po delam

Oceanographic research ship Vizir, *of the Yug class*
Courtesy United States Navy

izobretenii i otkrytii—Goskomizobretenie) maintained a state registry of inventions and discoveries, and it issued authors' certificates and patents. The All-Union Institute for Scientific and Technical Information (Vsesoiuznyi institut nauchnoi i tekhnicheskoi informatsii—VINITI) functioned as an information center containing abstracts of worldwide scientific and technical literature.

Science and Ideology

The extent to which the CPSU and communist ideology influenced Soviet science and technology has varied over time. During the Civil War (1918–21) and particularly during the Stalin era, party controls over science were extensive and oppressive. In the 1980s, party influence over science has been far less rigid but still evident.

According to one Western scholar, the CPSU controlled science in four ways. First, the CPSU maintained control by formulating the country's overall science and technology policy. Second, the party ensured that its policies were implemented at all levels of government through a network of all-union, regional, and local party organizations that oversaw the work of science and technology organs operating at comparable levels. Even in research institutes or factories, local party committees exerted their authority by requiring directors and managers to adhere to party dictates (see Primary Party Organization, ch. 7). Local party committees reported to higher authorities on plan fulfillment, labor discipline, and worker morale.

Third, the CPSU exercised full power over appointments to key positions, controlling the appointment of high-level administrators, mid-level managers, and probably institute directors and research laboratory and department heads (see Nomenklatura, ch. 7). The fourth method of control was ideological, including that exercised over both the professional and the private lives of scientists. The CPSU controlled individuals' work through its authority to dismiss personnel, to deny bonuses or fringe benefits, to restrict travel and publishing opportunities, and to impose other disciplinary actions. Control over personal lives was maintained through the Committee for State Security (Komitet gosudarstvennoi bezopasnosti—KGB) and was evident during the 1970s and early 1980s, when the government harshly treated dissident scientists accused of nonconformity with party policies. The treatment eased under General Secretary Mikhail S. Gorbachev, who, for example, permitted dissident physicist Andrei Sakharov to return to Moscow from internal exile in Gor'kiy.

Influence, though, has not been one sided. Science officials have had opportunities to affect party decisions. Since the mid-1950s, many top party officials have cultivated close ties to prominent scientists. This proximity has allowed scientists to influence decisions directly through their associations with policy makers or through appointments to policy advisory councils. Another opportunity has been appointment to top-level party organs. The number of scientists with membership in the CPSU Central Committee rose from seven in 1951 to nineteen in 1981. At the lower levels, facility managers often have used their close ties with party representatives to acquire more funds or better supplies.

Research, Development, and Production Organizations

In 1989 the Soviet scientific and technological establishment consisted of a variety of organizations engaged in the research, development, and production of new products or processes. In general, each organization specialized in one phase of the process and in one sector of industry.

Many types of organizations were involved. Western specialists placed them in three broad categories: research institutions, design organizations, and production facilities. In the first category, the most numerous organizations were the scientific research institutes (*nauchno-issledovatel'skie instituty*—NIIs), which focused on scientific research, both basic and applied. Each NII was headed by an appointed director, who oversaw a staff of researchers and technical personnel. Another type of research institution, the research laboratory (*laboratoriia*), operated independently or as a component of a larger NII or a production plant.

The second category, design organizations, included design bureaus (*konstruktorskie biuro*—KBs) and technological institutes (*tekhnologicheskie instituty*). Each of these encompassed a range of facilities with such titles as special design bureau (*spetsial'noe konstruktorskoe biuro*—SKB), central design bureau (*tsentral'noe konstruktorskoe biuro*), and project design and technology bureau (*proektno-konstruktorskoe i tekhnologicheskoe biuro*). Design bureaus planned new products and machines, although some also conducted research. Technological institutes had responsibility for designing new processes, installations, and machinery.

The third category included production facilities that manufactured the new product or applied the process developed by the research and design facilities. The output and testing of industrial prototypes, industrial innovation processes, or small-batch production prior to the stage of mass production occurred in experimental production or pilot plants (various Russian designations, e.g., *opytnye zavody, opytnye stantsii*). These functioned independently or were attached to production facilities, research institutions, or design organizations.

In addition to their categorization according to the operational phase in which they were most involved, research, development, and production facilities were characterized according to their organizational affiliation: industrial ministries, university and higher education, or the Academy of Sciences system.

Industrial ministries controlled the majority of science and technology organizations, including all types of research institutions, design organizations, and production facilities. The precise number of facilities in 1989 was not available because the Soviet press stopped publishing such statistics about a decade earlier. Western specialists, however, reported that in 1973 there were 944 independent design organizations, and in 1974 there were 2,137 industrial NIIs. The number of production facilities undoubtedly exceeded both those figures.

Industrial science and technology organizations tended to concentrate on one broad area, such as communications equipment, machine tools, or automobiles. They were directly subordinate to the industrial ministry responsible for that sector (see Industrial Research and Design, ch. 12). Science and technology work in ministries was directed by scientific-technical councils within the ministries; the councils comprised the ministry's leading scientists and engineers.

The second organizational affiliation, the higher education system, has been administered by the Ministry of Higher and Specialized Secondary Education. In addition to training scientists, the ministry's system provided a research base whose contribution to national scientific research and development has been growing. Its system included such varying scientific organizations as NIIs, design bureaus, problem laboratories (*problemnye laboratorii*), branch laboratories (*otraslevye laboratorii*), scientific sectors (*nauchnye sektory*), and such specialized institutions as computer centers, observatories, and botanical gardens. The number of organizations in the Ministry of Higher and Specialized Secondary Education and the percentage of the country's overall science budget allocated to them remained relatively small. In the late 1980s, their contribution was increasing with the expansion of contract research.

The third organizational affiliation, the Academy of Sciences, in 1989 was divided into four sections: physical sciences, engineering, and mathematics; chemistry and biology; geosciences; and social sciences. Grouped into these subject areas were approximately 300 research institutes employing more than 58,000 people. The network also included the separate academies of sciences in each of the fifteen union republics of the Soviet Union (except the Russian Republic, which was represented by the all-union academy) and regional divisions, the most prominent of which has been the Siberian Division. The academy also had responsibility for specialized schools, such as the All-Union Academy of Agricultural Sciences and the Academy of Medical Sciences.

As the most prestigious scientific establishment in the Soviet Union, the Academy of Sciences has attracted the country's best scientists. Membership has always been attained through election. In January 1988, the academy had approximately 380 academicians and 770 corresponding members. Of these, about 80 academicians and 170 corresponding members were elected in December 1987. This election was noteworthy because it was the first held since the review of academy personnel policies had begun a year earlier. The review led to a number of measures directed at removing some of the older members from active participation, such as requiring them to retire at age seventy-five. The new rules also lowered the age at which a scientist could be elected to the academy and established an age limit beyond which officials who were not academicians could hold top-level administrative positions, such as institute director. Once voted into the academy, a member held that title for life (as an example, dissident Sakharov retained his academician status even while in internal exile in Gor'kiy).

The members of the academy usually met once a year in general assembly to discuss major issues, to vote on organizational matters, and to elect new members. In October 1986, the general assembly elected Gurii Marchuk, formerly chairman of GKNT, as its president. Marchuk replaced Anatolii P. Aleksandrov, who had served as president for eleven years.

Soviet scientists and governmental officials have debated the precise role of the Academy of Sciences in the development of science and technology since the inception of the Soviet state. Such discussions continued during the 1980s. Statutes defined the academy's mission as conducting primarily basic or fundamental research. Some scientists and administrators, even within the academy, have argued that this was appropriate and that the academy should not engage in applied research. Many others, however, have argued that the academy has to be involved in applied research not only because it employs the best scientific talent in the nation but also because fundamental science drives technological development and causes technological breakthroughs. In his speech to the Nineteenth Party Conference in June 1988, academy president Marchuk stressed that "fundamental scientific research is the basis of all science and all scientific and technical progress. It defines the prospects for ten to twenty years hence, it achieves the breakthroughs both in the production sphere and in the sphere of knowledge of nature and society."

Soviet Innovation: Problems and Solutions

Central to an understanding of Soviet science and technology is an understanding of the innovation process. Innovation, which is the transfer of a scientific discovery (new product or process) into production, has long been a problem for the Soviet Union. Despite a strong scientific base, the country has had a mixed record of innovation. Although in some—particularly defense-related— industries Soviet scientists and engineers have scored major technological successes, in many other—particularly consumer— industries they have failed to implement useful innovations. In the late 1980s, the status of innovation was a key concern of the leadership, which sought new policies and institutional arrangements to facilitate the process.

In the 1980s, several key problems affected Soviet innovation. One was that factory managers had little incentive to introduce new products or processes. Innovation in a command economy differs greatly from innovation in a market economy. In the latter, the drive to introduce technological change emanates from the producers, who attempt to satisfy consumer demand before competitors do. In the Soviet economy, production of innovative products and processes has been assigned by government planners. Producers have been directed by top-level planning organs to incorporate in their plants' output a newly innovated product or process. Yet in the Soviet economy a plant's success has been measured by the gross output required by the annual plan. Factory managers have strived to fulfill the plan in terms of the quantity of goods produced. Managers have viewed introducing a new product or process, which may result in a slowdown in production, as an impediment to their goal of plan fulfillment. They generally have been unwilling to forgo certain success in exchange for potentially greater, yet unguaranteed, future capability.

Another problem concerned pricing policies. In the Soviet economy, prices of goods have been determined by central planners rather than in response to market demand. To boost innovation, planners sometimes permitted factory managers to charge higher prices for newly introduced products. These prices often were set too low to compensate for the increased cost of production and for the risk of failure. Therefore, prices have done little to encourage innovation. In fact, according to one Western specialist, this pricing mechanism often has been counterproductive. It promoted a practice whereby managers tended to exaggerate the degree of novelty of a new or improved product to central pricing authorities in an attempt to receive permission to charge higher prices and thus boost profits. Incentives given to industrial research development personnel on the basis of the expected return from a new innovation also have failed to improve the process.

Yet another problem has been the organizational separation among the various facilities engaged in research, development, and production. The separation occurred because Soviet scientific and technological facilities have tended to specialize in one phase of the research-to-production cycle. Research institutions, design organizations, testing facilities, and production facilities operated independently from one another. As a result, the transfer of a scientific discovery from the necessary development and testing phases to final production has necessitated crossing multiple organizational boundaries. To be successful, such transfers required stringent interorganizational cooperation to ensure proper timing and exchange of information. Soviet and Western observers agree that this cooperation has been generally lacking in the Soviet Union, where institutional interests have tended to override other considerations

Geological research ship Morskoi geolog, *of the Meridian class*
Courtesy United States Navy

and information exchange among scientists and engineers has been limited.

Organizational separation, however, was not limited to the successive stages of the research-to-production cycle. Soviet facilities also were separated in terms of their organizational affiliation. The results of scientific research and design work often must cross organizational boundaries to enter production. This has imposed yet another layer of bureaucracy, which has done little to encourage innovation. The most difficult barrier has been that existing between research institutions subordinate to the Academy of Sciences and production facilities subordinate to an industrial ministry. Even within the industrial ministry system, production facilities subordinate to one ministry have been hesitant to cooperate with those subordinate to a different ministry.

The ability to innovate also has been hurt by a lack of research and development equipment and of experimental testing and production facilities. Equipment has been inadequate in quality and quantity. The absence of appropriate testing facilities has affected all science and technology organizations but has been particularly evident in the Academy of Sciences organizational network. Academy scientists generally have had to rely on industry to make available testing and production facilities, but, as they often stated

639

in the 1980s, industry did not comply. As a result, academy officials, especially those in the Siberian Division and in the Ukrainian Academy of Sciences, initiated the development of the academy's own experimental facilities.

Funding has been another key factor adversely affecting innovation. In theory, one of the advantages of a command economy is the ability to concentrate resources in a given area. Over the years, the Soviet Union has repeatedly taken advantage of this ability by focusing resources on technologies and industries considered to have strategic importance, e.g., the military. Yet priority allocation, by definition, has been limited. Not all industries can receive the same attention. Indeed, the Soviet experience has been one in which selected industries and technologies were developed at the expense of others.

To some degree the innovation problems in the 1980s were a result of deliberate choices made in response to conditions arising after 1917. According to Ronald Amann, a Sovietologist affiliated with the University of Birmingham in England, some decisions made by Soviet leaders to overcome technological backwardness significantly influenced the long-range development of technology. The decisions were those that focused on replicating Western models instead of fostering Soviet innovation, that concentrated resources on industries considered by the leadership to have strategic importance, and that compensated for the shortage of skilled manpower by developing specialized and centralized research and development organizations in each branch of industry. These decisions contributed to the evolution of a system that in the 1980s was characterized by uneven technological progress and by the separation of science and production facilities.

From the mid-1960s to the mid-1980s, Soviet leaders' responses to these innovation difficulties has been a series of economic and organizational reforms. They have introduced measures aimed at improving planning and at providing greater financial incentives to organizations engaged in innovation. They also have tried to overcome the barriers separating research, development, and production facilities. The implementation of reforms accelerated under Gorbachev, who viewed the improvement of Soviet science and technology as crucial to his goal of economic restructuring (*perestroika*—see Glossary).

In September 1987, the CPSU Central Committee and the Council of Ministers issued a decree called "On the Changeover of Scientific Organizations to Full Cost Accounting and Self-Financing." Basically, the decree changed the way in which all types of scientific organizations were financed. Instead of receiving state funds allocated to finance the operation of the entire organization, scientific establishments would be financed on the basis of specific research, planning, and design projects. These would be arranged through contracts with other organizations, primarily industrial enterprises (see Glossary). The theory behind this change was to encourage scientific organizations to generate a "product" more useful to industry and to assume more responsibility for the applicability of their output. To increase the incentives for assuming greater responsibility, the decree also stipulated that the basic source of an organization's wage and incentive funds would be the profits earned by that organization. A similar decree, the Law on State Enterprises (Associations), was issued at approximately the same time. It granted to industrial enterprises greater authority to manage their own operations and established a closer link between funds for worker benefits and enterprise profits.

The organizational remedies instituted under Gorbachev expanded several arrangements to attempt to bridge the gap between scientific and production entities. The first involved the scientific production associations (*nauchno-proizvodstvennye ob''edineniia*— NPOs), which were introduced in the late 1960s. NPOs combined under one management all facilities involved in a particular research-to-production program—the research institutions, design organizations, testing facilities, and production facilities. Soviet leaders considered this arrangement more conducive to innovation because it enabled one leading component, usually the research institution, to coordinate the work of the other components engaged in the process. Although officials admitted that NPOs have had operational problems (such as poor planning and lack of an experimental base), they rated NPOs as successful overall. In 1986 they began an expansion in the number of NPOs. Whereas in 1985 there were approximately 250 NPOs (roughly the same number that existed in the early 1970s), in 1986 there were 400, with an additional 100 projected for the following year.

A similar organizational remedy was the formation of the interbranch scientific-technical complex (*mezhotraslevoi nauchno-tekhnicheskii kompleks*—MNTK). Based on so-called engineering centers established in the Ukrainian Academy of Sciences, MNTKs were initiated in 1985. MNTKs differed from NPOs in that they encompassed, as their name implies, facilities subordinate to various administrative authorities, including the Academy of Sciences. MNTKs were also larger than NPOs; in fact, some MNTKs included several NPOs and industrial production associations. In January 1988, Soviet officials reported that more than twenty MNTKs, including approximately 500 organizations and enterprises and elements of more than sixty ministries and departments, had been formed.

MNTKs were charged with coordinating and performing all the research and development work in their given area, from basic research to production. To facilitate their work, MNTKs were empowered to request resources in addition to those allocated by the plan; to receive priority in establishing pilot production bases and in ordering materials and resources; and to have the right to demand full delivery of the ordered amounts.

In an assessment of the MNTKs published in January 1988, two Soviet economists discussed the accomplishments of the "Rotor" and "Mikrokhirurgiia glaza" MNTKs. The former had expanded the production of automatic rotary and rotary conveyor lines in 1987 and expected to more than double production in 1988. The Rotor MNTK also developed a rotary conveyor line for the injection molding of items made of thermoplastic materials. The Mikrokhirugiia glaza MNTK was credited with developing a new technology for performing higher quality operations that significantly shortened overall treatment time. On the negative side, however, the economists listed several problems hindering the operation of MNTKs: lack of cooperation of superior organs, substantial lag in the development of experimental facilities, shortage of designers and manufacturing engineers, insufficient authority to obtain financing, absence of a unified plan for an MNTK, and confusion regarding the composition of MNTKs. Despite these criticisms, Soviet authorities in the late 1980s repeatedly stated their support of MNTKs and presented them as a promising link between science and production.

Technology and Information Transfer

Soviet leaders have tried to overcome technological backwardness by acquiring technology from the more advanced Western and Asian countries. Since 1917 Soviet officials have worked to obtain not only foreign equipment but also technological processes, knowhow, and information. Acquisitions have helped the Soviet Union, in some cases, to compensate for a poorly developed indigenous technology and, in other cases, to bolster or provide a missing component in an otherwise fairly well-established industry.

The transfer of foreign technology began not long after the Bolshevik Revolution and continued through the 1980s, although the official emphasis, as well as the kind and quantity of technology transferred, varied greatly over time. Lenin initially wanted to avoid any dependence on Western technological imports, but the lack of funds for indigenous development forced him to seek limited foreign investments. Stalin emphasized technological autarchy. He expended huge resources in efforts to develop indigenous science and technology, and he severely restricted contacts with Western businessmen and scientists. Nonetheless, severe backwardness in some key industries forced Stalin to engage in short-term borrowing from the West. During World War II, the Soviet regime used captured German equipment and technological experts to help develop lagging Soviet industries.

The post-Stalin era brought renewed interest in dealing with the West. Khrushchev eased restrictions on Soviet access to Western technology but found that Western governments sought political concessions in return for trade agreements. Under Brezhnev, Soviet technology acquisitions increased markedly. Many long-term agreements, as well as accords providing for foreign construction of industrial plants in the Soviet Union, were signed during the Brezhnev era. By the late 1970s, however, both Western and Soviet leaders began to question the political and economic wisdom of technology transfers. By the early 1980s, technology transfers from the United States to the Soviet Union were curtailed severely in response to political, economic, and military concerns. At the same time, however, the Soviet Union began trying to obtain Japanese technology—particularly electronics, computer science, and metallurgy—because the Japanese were much less restrictive in their exports.

In 1986 Gary K. Bertsch, a United States specialist in Soviet technology, described five means by which technology has been transferred to the Soviet Union. The most direct, and probably the most common, was the commercial sale of equipment to the Soviet Union. When the West provided opportunities, Soviet leaders increased purchases of Western equipment.

The second type of transfer included the extensive and complicated modes of industrial cooperation between Western firms and their Soviet counterparts. According to Bertsch, this cooperation has had many forms, among them: sales of equipment (sometimes for complete production systems or turnkey plants), including technical assistance; licenses of patents, copyrights, and production know-how; franchises of trademarks and production know-how; purchases and sales between partners, involving exchanges of industrial raw materials and intermediate products; subcontracts involving the provision of production services; sales of plant, equipment, and technology with payment in resulting or related products; production contracting, involving agreement for transferred production capabilities in the form of capital equipment and technology; coproduction agreements allowing partners to produce and market the same products resulting from a shared technology; and joint research and development.

Another type of transfer involved foreign travel by Soviet scientists, participation by them in academic and scholarly conferences, and screening of literature. In the early 1980s, as part of a general tightening of policies on technology export, the United States government began restricting Soviet scientists from traveling in and attending meetings in the United States to prevent their access to American science and technology. Screening of literature has been a valuable source of information for the Soviet Union. Soviet scientists have had easy access to Western and Japanese publications, and for years they have relied heavily on this literature as a primary source of foreign technology.

The fourth type of transfer was covert acquisition. This kind of transfer was the most feared because of its potential impact on Soviet and United States military development. The ways in which the Soviet Union acquired technology varied and involved more than their intelligence services. For example, some acquisitions were carried out by Soviet diplomats stationed worldwide. Other acquisitions were made by diverting controlled technology products from legitimate trade destinations to the Soviet Union. Finally, some acquisitions occurred through legitimate firms established by the Soviet Union or East European countries in Western nations.

The fifth type of transfer was intergovernmental agreements on scientific and technological cooperation. In the early 1970s, for example, the United States and the Soviet Union concluded eleven separate agreements pledging cooperation in such fields as science and technology, environmental protection, atomic energy, medicine, and energy. In some cases, these agreements led to frequent exchanges between American and Soviet scientists cooperating in specific areas. This type of arrangement, however, decreased markedly in the late 1970s as the United States responded to Soviet emigration policies and to Soviet involvement in Afghanistan and in Poland. Under Gorbachev, cooperative agreements resumed.

Using these forms of transfer, the Soviet Union obtained a range of technologies, some of which probably had significant military applications. The chemical and automotive industries relied heavily on Western imports. In the early 1980s, the Soviet Union bought equipment badly needed for the gas pipeline it was building from Urengoy to Uzhgorod. It acquired technologies applicable to the military, including complete computer systems designs, concepts, and software, plus a variety of Western general-purpose computers, minicomputers, and other hardware. It acquired low-power, low-noise, high-sensitivity receivers; optical, pulsed power source and other laser-related components; and titanium alloys, welding equipment, and furnaces for producing titanium plates applicable to submarine construction.

These acquisitions raised concerns in the West that the Soviet Union was deriving too many military and economic benefits inimical to Western interests. Some critics argued that technology transfers allowed the Soviet Union to save millions of rubles (for value of the ruble—see Glossary) in research and development costs and years of development time. They also argued that Soviet acquisitions allowed the regime to modernize critical sectors of industry without absorbing rising military production costs, to achieve greater weapons performance, and to incorporate countermeasures to Western weapons. They further argued that the West should impose stricter controls on such transfers. This position was adopted by the United States government in the early 1980s, when it began imposing strict controls and urging West European governments to follow suit.

Not everyone agreed with this position, however. Western analysts in the late 1980s pointed out that both the econometric and the case-study approaches used to assess the impact of technology transfers produced tentative results. One conclusion was that the Soviet experience in using and assimilating Western technology was a mixed success. In some cases, particularly in military-related industries, the Soviet Union was successful in incorporating Western equipment or processes. In other areas, the equipment was used inefficiently or not at all.

Many Soviet scientists and policy makers shared this negative assessment. During the 1980s, the Soviet press published many articles in which Soviet officials complained that they were wasting valuable hard currency to purchase equipment that lay idle because of industry's inability or unwillingness to install it. Other officials, including former Academy of Sciences president Aleksandrov, argued that the Soviet Union did not need to import Western technology because it had the capability to develop it domestically. In fact, too much reliance on Western imports had harmed the Soviet Union because indigenous institutions had been denied the opportunity to develop the technology and, hence, to grow technologically.

Despite these arguments, the policy under Gorbachev appeared to Western observers to increase technological trade. Soviet authorities instituted some organizational changes to facilitate and to encourage more contact with Western firms. Yet Gorbachev also expressed concern over the balance of payments issue and cautioned against too many purchases from the West.

Military Research and Development

Science and technology in defense and civilian sectors differed markedly in both organization and performance. Military research and development generally functioned more efficiently and produced more advanced technologies.

The principal organizations involved in Soviet military science and technology were subordinate to the defense industrial ministries. The ministries responsible for research, design, and production of military equipment and weapons or their components consisted of the Ministry of the Aviation Industry, the Ministry of the Communications Equipment Industry, the Ministry of the Defense Industry, the Ministry of the Electronics Industry, the Ministry of General Machine Building, the Ministry of the Machine Tool and Tool-Building Industry, the Ministry of Medium Machine Building, the Ministry of the Radio Industry, and the Ministry of the Shipbuilding Industry. These nine ministries were among the eighteen ministries of the machine-building and metal-working complex (MBMW) under the control of the Defense Council (see Machine Building and Metal Working, ch. 12). Each of the nine ministries incorporated institutes engaged in applied research and a network of bureaus responsible for designing and developing new military equipment and processes. In 1989 these ministries directed the work of thousands of plants making weapons and weapons components, at least 450 military research and development organizations, and approximately fifty major design bureaus. (Other industrial ministries contributed to military research, development, and production. For example, some military vehicles were produced by the Ministry of Automotive and Agricultural Machine Building, and fuel and chemical warfare agents were produced by the Ministry of the Chemical Industry.)

The second category consisted of the Ministry of Defense and its subordinate research facilities. Little information on these institutes has been published, but their work undoubtedly has been concentrated on those areas most relevant to military requirements. These institutes maintained close contact with the industrial research institutes and the design bureaus. Their main function appeared to be to evaluate the latest scientific achievements and to forecast the development of the Soviet armed forces.

The third category comprised the facilities considered part of civilian science. These primarily were the 300 research institutes affiliated with the Academy of Sciences. Some of the country's most important military research programs were conducted by the Academy of Sciences. Other institutes in this category included university facilities and research establishments subordinate to the civilian production ministries.

The final category consisted of the coordinating agencies. The most powerful organization was the Military Industrial Commission (Voenno-promyshlennaia komissiia—VPK), which included representatives from the defense industry ministries, the Ministry of Defense, Gosplan, and probably the CPSU Secretariat. VPK monitored and coordinated all military research and development and production. It reviewed new weapons proposals for their technical feasibility and for production requirements, approved research-to-production timetables submitted by lead organizations, and participated in planning and supervising major technological programs, apparently including those conducted by Academy of Sciences institutes.

The second important coordinating agency was GKNT. Although mandated to plan, oversee, and regulate scientific research and development, evidence on its operation suggested that it had little direct influence over the defense sector. Nevertheless, GKNT exerted some general influence over military research and development in that it formulated the basic scientific and technical problems of the country and worked out the programs needed to address them.

The various institutional components of military research and development interacted in a way that generally was far more productive than that of the civilian sector. The defense sector more often succeeded in seeing a scientific idea through the various development stages into production. Many of those ideas may not have represented a leading-edge technology (Soviet military research and development were thought to be more evolutionary than revolutionary), but at least they were carried through into production.

One of the reasons Soviet military research and development fared better has been the high priority given to it by the regime. The defense sector received not only more funds but also better resources and the best personnel. Perhaps most important in terms of priority was the level of political commitment. Maintaining a strong military capable of matching United States military strength has been a high priority for Soviet political leaders. This translated into a strong commitment to ensure that military science and technology developed and functioned to support the Soviet military. High priority was not the only factor explaining the military sector's superior performance. Another factor was that defense researchers had better access to development facilities. Research projects in the military tended not to "die" because of lack of research facilities' access to development facilities.

Another factor affecting military research and development was that the defense sector was not so rigidly bound to production quantity rather than quality. Civilian production enterprises often were reluctant to innovate because of the time needed to adjust a plant's operations to the production of the new item or use of the new process. Such adjustments have been viewed in the civilian sector as interruptions because they cut into the time needed to meet a plant's production quotas. Military production facilities, which had rigorous quality-control measures, faced less pressure to meet a specified production goal.

Finally, coordination among military research and development establishments was more effective than that in the civilian sector. Facilities involved in the various phases of the military research-to-production cycle were more inclined to interact with one another. Furthermore, design facilities in the defense establishment tended to be larger and more capable of developing a research idea further through the research-to-production cycle. Design organizations in the military also tended to generate better design documentation for production plants to implement. Some of the administrative barriers encountered in the civilian sector were overcome in the military sector, in part by giving lead institutes the power to coordinate efforts for specific programs.

The success of the defense industry has been something Soviet leaders wanted to replicate across the spectrum of scientific and technological sectors. Gorbachev patterned many of the reforms instituted during the mid-1980s after organizational arrangements and policies in the defense sector. For example, the decision to switch financing of research and development work from funding of institutes to funding of specific projects, as well as emphasizing contract work, was adapted from the military sector. Improving the long-range planning process and the quality-control process were other examples. To facilitate the reforms, Gorbachev moved several defense managers into key civilian positions. The idea was that these individuals would use skills learned in the defense sector to strive for improvements in the civilian sector.

Training

Training of scientists and engineers has been an important aspect of the country's overall scientific and technological effort. Soviet leaders since Lenin have strongly emphasized education and its contribution to the development of science and technology. The result has been the emergence of a network of education institutions that have trained some of the world's best scientists.

Training in science and engineering has generally begun in the secondary schools. The nationwide curriculum in effect during the 1980s emphasized mathematics, the natural sciences, and languages. By the time students completed their secondary education, they had taken two years of algebra, two years of geometry, and one year each of trigonometry, calculus, physics, chemistry, and biology. Beginning in the seventh grade, those with special skills in the sciences could enroll in optional science courses. Western specialists have considered Soviet science education, particularly in physics and mathematics, superior to that received in secondary schools in the United States.

Soviet institutions of higher learning (*vysshie uchebnye zavedeniia*— VUZy) included universities and institutes. The universities in the Soviet Union offered five-year programs that tended to be narrowly focused. Advanced training in many technical fields was provided in specialized institutes. The VUZy represented an additional source of research for the development of science and technology. Until 1987 that research was funded primarily through the state budget and, less frequently, through contracts with industry. The 1987 decree, which changed scientific organizations to self-financing status, charged Soviet administrators to develop a plan for transferring VUZy to the same financial arrangement.

Despite the success in education, the Soviet Union during the 1980s faced several key problems affecting its ability to train scientists and engineers and to place them where needed. Schools, especially those outside the major urban areas, suffered from a lack of qualified staff, supplies, and equipment. Efforts during the mid-1980s to launch an extensive program of computer training were hampered by the lack of computers on which to train students. Other problems included a high dropout rate and the refusal of many graduates to seek jobs in geographic locations and in specialties targeted for development by government planners. In response to these problems, Soviet officials during 1987 and 1988 initiated measures to reform the education system once again. Among the stated goals were an improvement in the overall training of scientific and technical specialists and the institution of greater cooperation between VUZy and industry.

The need to provide good training to scientists and engineers and to tear down bureaucratic impediments between the development of technology and its application in industry became especially important in the late 1980s. Gorbachev's program to reverse the country's economic decline demanded the increased application of science and technology to make industry more effective. Although much of the needed technology was available in the West, the Soviet Union could neither politically nor economically afford to neglect development of its own scientific and technological base.

* * *

Many excellent books and articles have been written about Soviet science and technology by such authors as Loren R. Graham, Philip Hanson, Bruce Parrott, Simon Kassel, and Thane Gustafson. Some of the more recent publications by these and other authors include *Science, Philosophy, and Human Behavior in the Soviet Union* by Loren R. Graham; *The Communist Party and Soviet Science* by Stephen Fortescue; and *Trade, Technology, and Soviet-American Relations,* edited by Bruce Parrott. Another excellent source on all aspects of science and technology policy is the compendium of papers submitted to the Joint Economic Committee of the United States Congress. The latest edition was released in 1987 and is titled *Gorbachev's Economic Plans.* A number of studies on particularly defense-related Soviet technologies have been published. They include *The Technological Level of Soviet Industry,* edited by Ronald Amann, Julian M. Cooper, and R.W. Davies; *Industrial Innovation in the Soviet Union,* edited by Amann and Cooper; and *Technical Progress and Soviet Economic Development,* also edited by Amann and Cooper. For information on current science and technology issues, the best sources are the Radio Free Europe/Radio Liberty research reports, the Foreign Broadcast Information Service's *Daily Report: Soviet Union,* and the Joint Publication Research Service's translations series, *USSR: Science and Technology Policy.* (For further information and complete citations, see Bibliography.)

Chapter 17. Military Doctrine and Strategic Concerns

An officer describing military strategy

UNDERSTANDING THE STANCE that the Soviet Union has adopted on military affairs requires analyzing the meaning the Soviet regime has given to concepts such as military doctrine, military policy, and military science, as well as comprehending the ideological basis of these terms. In Soviet military writings, these concepts overlapped considerably, and Soviet military theorists stressed their interdependence. Military doctrine represented the official view on the nature of future wars and on the methods of fighting them. Military policy offered practical guidelines for structuring the Soviet armed forces and for building up Soviet defenses. Military science—the study of concepts of warfare and of the weapons needed to accomplish military missions—supported the formulation of doctrine and policy. Military doctrine and military policy directed the findings of military science toward fulfillment of the political goals of the Communist Party of the Soviet Union (CPSU).

Soviet military doctrine was grounded in Marxist-Leninist (see Glossary) theory as the CPSU interpreted it. The party understood the world as a battleground of classes and social systems and predicted the "inevitable victory of socialism." Thus the party's interpretation of Marxist-Leninist doctrine provided the Soviet military with a framework for developing strategic and operational concepts for winning wars.

Soviet military doctrine was the most fundamental and the most influential of the theoretical concepts that governed the conduct of Soviet military affairs. It influenced procurement of weapons, colored threat assessments, and provided a theoretical basis for the party's military policy. It determined Soviet arms control proposals and the kinds of arms control agreements that the Soviet Union would be willing to sign. Together with the government's military policy, military doctrine shaped Soviet military-strategic initiatives abroad.

Until 1956 Soviet doctrine was based on Lenin's thesis of the "inevitability of war" between capitalism and socialism (see Glossary). Such a war would be fought in defense of the socialist motherland and end with the clear-cut victory of socialism. Thus, it would be both defensive and victory oriented. The development and deployment of nuclear weapons changed doctrinal views on war's inevitability. It soon became clear that nuclear war would cause such widespread destruction that it could not be a rational tool of policy, that victory in a nuclear war was problematic, and that a nuclear power ought to deter rather than fight such a war. Soviet civilian leaders and military theorists expressed their belief in nuclear deterrence by declaring that a world war with capitalism was no longer unavoidable. They also argued that the shift in the correlation of forces and resources (see Glossary) in favor of socialism has made war avoidable. But Soviet political and military leaders did not condemn the use of nuclear weapons for fighting a war, and they did not relinquish the requirement to win. As a result, Soviet military doctrine combined the concepts of nuclear deterrence, nuclear war, and victory.

Consequently, even in the nuclear era, Soviet military science remained, in the words of the eighteenth-century Russian commander Aleksandr Suvorov, a "science of victory" in armed conflict. The most important component of military science, military art, and the latter's highest level, military strategy, continued to aim at complete defeat of the adversary. The drive to prevail at all costs and under all circumstances directed the other two components of military art: operational art and tactics. In the late 1980s, theoretical concepts for the study and conduct of armed warfare— such as the laws of war, the laws of armed conflict, and the principles of military art—continued to emphasize victory.

Marxist-Leninist military doctrine has had considerable effect on arms control. On all levels—strategic nuclear, theater nuclear, and conventional—the doctrine's orientation toward victory has demanded capabilities for fighting and winning wars.

The Soviet Union never allowed arms control to interfere with achievement of its military objectives nor to constrain the strategic goals of the armed forces. Even in the late 1980s, in spite of General Secretary Mikhail S. Gorbachev's "new thinking" (see Glossary) and his strong emphasis on arms reductions, the military remained mistrustful of political solutions and reluctant to accept sweeping changes in doctrine and strategy.

Marxist-Leninist Theory of War

The Marxist-Leninist theory of war provided a basis for Soviet military theory and practice. Karl Marx and Friedrich Engels developed Marxism (see Glossary), which was further elaborated by Vladimir I. Lenin, the first leader of the Soviet Union. The Marxist-Leninist view of war rested on the principle that war is a continuation of politics and that the aim of war is to achieve military victory so as to hasten the political victory of socialism. Soon after the Soviet Union acquired nuclear weapons, a debate arose in Soviet leadership circles over whether a catastrophic nuclear war could be a continuation of politics. Theorists debated whether waging nuclear war was in the best interests of socialism, or whether Marxist-Leninist policy should exclude nuclear war.

Since the 1950s, two lines of argument concerning nuclear war as a tool of policy have existed in the Soviet Union. Some civilian and military leaders have maintained that because nuclear war is too destructive, one should never be fought. Conversely, the authors of a volume entitled *Marxism-Leninism on War and the Army*, which has appeared in six editions since 1957 and sets forth the Marxist-Leninist philosophy of war as well as the CPSU's official views on conducting war, have consistently upheld nuclear war as a legitimate continuation of politics and have endorsed the use of nuclear weapons.

Marxist-Leninist theory of war has not only established theoretical foundations for fighting and averting nuclear wars but also has provided practical guidelines for categorizing wars according to their "class essence" as just wars (see Glossary) and unjust (predatory) wars. It also has purportedly discovered objective "laws of war" (see fig. 26). These laws governed the conduct of war and promoted victory.

War as a Continuation of Politics

According to Marxist-Leninist theory, the essence of war is political. Lenin adopted the dictum of the nineteenth-century Prussian strategist Carl von Clausewitz that war is a continuation of politics by other, i.e., violent, means. In contrast to Clausewitz, however, who understood politics as the relationship between states, Lenin regarded politics as class struggle within states. Lenin also believed that class struggle within states dictated the kinds of preparation that these states made for war, the declarations of wars between states, the conduct of wars between states, and the outcome of wars.

Contemporary Marxist-Leninist interpretation of war derived from Lenin's understanding of war as the outcome of class struggle. According to this view, noncommunist states were ruled by classes that were hostile to the "dictatorship of the proletariat" established by the Soviet Union and other socialist states. In particular, the Marxist-Leninist understanding of war attributed to the United States, as the most powerful representative of "imperialism" (the final stage of capitalism), the goal of altering the course of world development by destroying communism (the final stage of socialism). Marxism-Leninism assigned to the Soviet armed forces the task of preventing the destruction of communism by

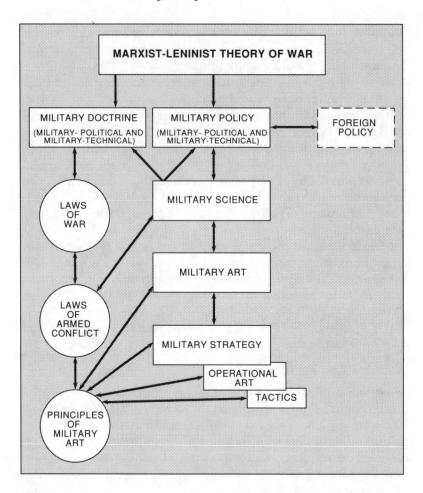

Figure 26. Soviet Military-Political Concepts, 1989

waging a defensive but victorious war with all modern weapons at their disposal.

In the 1960s, before development of the concept of limited nuclear war, Soviet strategists debated whether or not nuclear war could be a rational tool of policy because the widespread destruction it would cause could prevent it from promoting socialism's final victory. Some Soviet leaders, notably Nikita S. Khrushchev and the Soviet military theorists who shared his views, maintained that, considering the extremes of nuclear violence, nuclear war could not be a continuation of politics by means of armed force (see Evolution of Military Doctrine, this ch.). In the 1970s, Leonid I. Brezhnev claimed that whoever started a nuclear war would be committing suicide, and he asserted that the Soviet Union would never be the first to use nuclear weapons. In the 1980s, Soviet civilian and military leaders adopted a similar stance, repeatedly declaring that no victor could emerge in a general nuclear war and that it would lead to the destruction of humanity. These statements seemed to modify Lenin's dictum that war is the continuation of politics.

By contrast, the official position on war, as communicated to the military in consecutive editions of *Marxism-Leninism on War and the Army*, one of the fundamental works of Soviet military theory, has remained unchanged. The 1968 edition maintained that all wars, "even a possible thermonuclear one," are and will be "a continuation of politics by means of armed force." The most recent edition available in 1989, *Marxist-Leninist Teaching on War and the Army*, published in 1984, deemed a nuclear attack reprehensible but regarded as "just and lawful" the use of nuclear weapons either to respond to an enemy strike or to forestall an impending nuclear strike by an adversary. According to this edition, "nuclear missile war fully retains the general social essence of war" and is "a continuation of politics by other, violent means."

This apparent regarding of all weapons, no matter how destructive, as "just and lawful" means for the defense of socialism stemmed from Marxist-Leninist teaching on just and unjust wars. According to this teaching, wars waged by the Soviet Union and socialist states allied with it were a "continuation of the politics of revolution" and led to a revolutionary transformation of the world. Hence, in the Marxist-Leninist scale of values, all wars fought by socialist armies were both just and revolutionary. By contrast, all wars waged by "imperialists" were, by definition, unjust. Marxist-Leninist theory also asserted that all wars fought in defense of the socialist motherland were unconditionally just and could be fought with all modern weapons, including nuclear ones.

Laws of War

The belief that history was on the side of socialism and that Marxism-Leninism was a basis for discovering "objective" laws governing social and economic change has caused a proliferation of laws and principles in Soviet military thought. On the most general level, the laws of war were factors determining the course and outcome of wars. These laws expressed the political philosophy of the CPSU in the military sphere. These laws, however, were not immutable and could change with the emergence of new military technologies and new operational concepts.

Joseph V. Stalin, general secretary of the party between 1922 and 1953, believed in the existence of five "permanently operating factors": the stability of the rear, the morale of the army, the quantity and quality of divisions, the armaments of the armed forces, and the organizational ability of the commanders. These factors served as forerunners of the laws of war that were in force in 1989. Because Stalin's permanently operating factors did not take nuclear weapons into account, by the 1960s Soviet military political writers had largely discounted them. A new set of laws, taking into account new weapons, the new strategic environment, and the probability that future war would be mainly nuclear, did not appear until 1972, with the publication of Colonel Vasilii E. Savkin's *The Basic Principles of Operational Art and Tactics*. Savkin's four laws of war in the nuclear era specified four factors upon which the course and outcome of a war waged with unlimited use of all means of conflict depended. First, he said it depended on the correlation of available military forces; second, on the correlation of the overall military potential of each side; third, on the political content of the war; and fourth, on the correlation of the moral-political capabilities (see Glossary) and the psychological capabilities of the people and armies of the combatants.

In 1977 the *Soviet Military Encyclopedia* refined and augmented Savkin's laws and listed six laws of war that the 1984 edition of *Marxist-Leninist Teaching on War and the Army* reiterated almost verbatim. According to the most recent set of laws, the course and outcome of war depended on the following factors: the political goals of the war, which had to be just and revolutionary; and the correlation of the economic forces, scientific potentials, moral-political forces, and military forces of the warring sides. Yet another law, added in the 1984 edition of *Marxist-Leninist Teaching on War and the Army*, stressed the "dependence of the development and changes in the methods of warfare on quantitative and qualitative changes in military technology and on the moral and combat qualities of the military personnel."

Since Savkin first formulated his laws of war in 1972, a reordering of priorities has occurred. Savkin put the strictly military, primarily nuclear capabilities in first place. In 1977 and 1984, however, they occupied last place, with political goals in first place. The 1984 edition reflected the realization that new weapons and new strategies could revolutionize future warfare and that high standards of training and combat readiness of military personnel would assume more importance than before.

In addition to the laws of war just listed, which mainly influenced the course of war, Marxist-Leninist thought ostensibly has discovered the "law of objective victory," which predetermined

*Soviet and American officials observing the detonation of
a Soviet SS–12 missile in compliance with the Intermediate-Range
Nuclear Forces Treaty
Courtesy United States On-Site Inspection Agency*

the outcome of war and expressed the "historical inevitability of the
triumph of the new over the old." That is, victory would go to the
side that represented the new, more progressive socioeconomic system and that used the country's potential more effectively. Soviet
military-political writers often cited Soviet victory in World War
II as historic proof that no force in the world was capable of stop-
ping the progress of a socialist society. Soviet military theorists also
have invoked the experience of World War II to prove the superiority of a socialist economy in supplying weapons and war matériel.
They have stressed Soviet ability to produce sophisticated military
technology. "Victory will be with the countries of the world socialist
system," Soviet military writers announced confidently in 1968, because "they have the latest weapons." In 1984 Colonel General
Dmitrii A. Volkogonov, chief editor of the 1984 edition of *Marxist-
Leninist Teaching on War and the Army,* made the relationship between
weapons and victory even more specific when he wrote that "the
attainment of victory is directly dependent on the availability and
sufficient quantity of modern means of warfare."

The Party and Military Doctrine and Policy

Marxist-Leninist teaching on war and the armed forces defined

659

the essence of wars, their origins, and the laws governing the conduct of war. In developing Soviet military doctrine and policy, the CPSU relied on this teaching and on its forecasts of the nature of future wars, as well as on the concepts and weapons proposals formulated by Soviet military science. Military doctrine was the party line on military affairs. It defined the potential adversaries, the nature of future wars, the force requirements, the general direction of military development, the preparation of the country for war, and even the type of weapons needed to fight a war. The party's military policy defined the political aims of the Soviet state and proposed concrete measures for developing and strengthening the state's military might by improving the organization and the armaments of the armed forces.

Soviet military theorists asserted that military doctrine had a military-political and a military-technical component and that doctrine overlapped with military science and strategy. Marxist-Leninist teaching shaped the political aspect of doctrine, which defined the party's overriding military-political goals and was by far the more important of the two components. The technical dimension of military doctrine dealt with available means and capabilities, as well as with future technologies, and drew on the findings of Soviet military science. In its concern with capabilities, the technical aspect of doctrine also overlapped with the technical component of military policy and with military strategy. The latter coordinated technical means and methods with military concepts for the attainment of political goals.

Soviet leaders maintained that Soviet military doctrine always had been defensive, yet because it favored an offensive strategy and stressed the need to achieve victory, Western analysts have often termed Soviet military doctrine offensive. The acquisition of nuclear weapons by the Soviet armed forces not only caused disagreement over whether nuclear war could be a continuation of politics by violent means but also introduced divergence into Soviet views on the role nuclear weapons could play in deterring or fighting a war. Soviet military strategists appeared to endorse both nuclear deterrence and nuclear war-fighting (see Glossary) but placed a greater stress on war-fighting. Even the adoption of conventional options and the downgrading of the military utility of nuclear weapons by some military leaders in the 1980s did not remove the doctrinal requirement to fight and prevail in a nuclear war.

Evolution of Military Doctrine

Soviet military theorists first formulated a uniform military doctrine in the 1920s under the influence of both Lenin's teachings on the defense of the socialist homeland and the writings of Mikhail V. Frunze, a prominent Bolshevik (see Glossary) commander in the Civil War (1918–21) and a military theoretician. Frunze considered the basic conditions for the vitality of doctrine to be, first, its uniformity, i.e., doctrine should be the same for all services of the armed forces, and, second, "its conformity with the state's objectives and the resources at its disposal."

Since Frunze, Soviet doctrinal views on the nature and likelihood of future war have evolved as Soviet theorists have attempted to adapt doctrine to the changing nature of future war, to the shifting alignment of forces in the world, and to changes in the domestic economy and in the combat potential of the Soviet armed forces. The most important changes in Soviet views on the nature of war came after World War II. At that time, Stalin added the concept of the "two camps"—two mutually irreconcilable coalitions—and their impending worldwide clash to the traditional Soviet concepts of capitalist encirclement (see Glossary) and inevitability of capitalist attack. In February 1956, the Twentieth Party Congress modified the idea of inevitability when Khrushchev declared that a world war with capitalism was no longer "fatalistically inevitable."

Doctrinal views on the methods of fighting a future world war also have changed significantly since the end of World War II. Stalin, who for most of his rule did not have a nuclear arsenal, envisioned future war as a fierce combined arms struggle in Europe. As both the United States and the Soviet armed forces in Europe acquired nuclear weapons in the 1950s, Soviet views gradually changed. In 1960 and 1961, Khrushchev tried to impose the concept of nuclear deterrence on the military. Nuclear deterrence holds that the reason for having nuclear weapons is to discourage their use by a potential enemy. With each side deterred from war because of the threat of its escalation into a nuclear conflict, Khrushchev believed, "peaceful coexistence" (see Glossary) with capitalism would become permanent and allow the inherent superiority of socialism to emerge in economic and cultural competition with the West.

Khrushchev hoped that exclusive reliance on the nuclear firepower of the newly created Strategic Rocket Forces would remove the need for increased defense expenditures (see Strategic Rocket Forces, ch. 18). He also sought to use nuclear deterrence to justify his massive troop cuts; his downgrading of the Ground Forces, traditionally the "fighting arm" of the Soviet armed forces; and his plans to replace bombers with missiles and the surface fleet with nuclear missile submarines.

661

Khrushchev's attempt to introduce a nuclear doctrine limited to deterrence into Soviet military thought misfired. Discussion of nuclear war in the first authoritative Soviet monograph on strategy since the 1920s, Marshal Vasilii D. Sokolovskii's *Military Strategy* (published in 1962, 1963, and 1968) and in the 1968 edition of *Marxism-Leninism on War and the Army,* focused upon the use of nuclear weapons for fighting rather than for deterring a war. Should such a war break out, both sides would pursue the most decisive aims with the most forceful means and methods. Intercontinental ballistic missiles and aircraft would deliver massed nuclear strikes on the enemy's military and civilian objectives. The war would assume an unprecedented geographical scope, but Soviet military writers argued that the use of nuclear weapons in the initial period of the war would decide the course and outcome of the war as a whole. Both in doctrine and in strategy, the nuclear weapon reigned supreme.

After Khrushchev's ouster in 1964, Soviet doctrine began to consider the new United States concept of "flexible response," i.e., a graduated response to aggression on several levels, beginning with conventional arms. In the mid-1960s, Soviet military thinkers allowed for the possibility of a phase of conventional warfare preceding a general nuclear war. Another adjustment also occurred in the mid-1960s, as doctrine evolved to maintain that a world war need not inevitably escalate to an intercontinental nuclear exchange between the Soviet Union and the United States. Soviet doctrine allowed for the possibility of avoiding such an exchange altogether and limiting nuclear strikes to specific theaters of war. Soviet military strategists held that nuclear war could be fought in and confined to Western and Central Europe and that both United States and Soviet territory might escape nuclear devastation. Finally, after 1967, when the North Atlantic Treaty Organization (NATO) officially adopted the "flexible response" concept and began to structure its forces accordingly, Soviet doctrine began to consider the possibility of fighting an entire war with conventional arms. It did, however, allow for the likelihood of the adversary's escalating to the use of nuclear weapons.

Military Doctrine in the Late 1980s

The 1970s and 1980s were a period of questioning and transition in Soviet doctrine and strategy. Soviet military doctrine continued to assume that the Soviet Union could fight and prevail in a nuclear war and that Soviet strategic nuclear missiles could influence a war's course and outcome. Nevertheless, prominent military figures voiced concern about the military efficacy of nuclear weapons,

SS-13 intercontinental ballistic missile
Courtesy United States Department of Defense

among them the former chief of the General Staff, Marshal of the Soviet Union Nikolai V. Ogarkov; Colonel General Makhmut A. Gareev, author of a monograph on military theoretician Frunze; and Volkogonov, chief editor of *Marxist-Leninist Teaching on War and the Army*. They each expressed reservations about whether a world war of the future could be fought and won with nuclear weapons. Ogarkov, in particular, advanced the revolutionary view that a twenty-first-century battlefield might be dominated by non-nuclear, high-technology armaments and a global war could be fought with conventional weapons alone.

In the mid- to late 1980s, CPSU leaders and some military officials began to focus on the political aspects of Soviet national security and deemphasized its military aspect. They advocated a new military doctrine based on the defensive concept of "reasonable sufficiency" and on a military potential "sufficient for safeguarding the security of the country" but not adequate for launching offensives, especially surprise attacks on an adversary. In 1987 some military spokesmen also mentioned the possible reformulation of Soviet military doctrine. The chief of the General Staff, Marshal of the Soviet Union Sergei F. Akhromeev, and the minister of defense, Marshal of the Soviet Union Dmitrii T. Iazov, declared that a new Soviet military doctrine was being developed in accordance with the principles of the "new thinking" in foreign and military policy. In May 1987, the Warsaw Pact's Consultative Committee met in East Berlin and adopted a document on a defense-oriented military doctrine. In particular, the document called for reduction of conventional armaments in Europe to a level that could not support offensive operations.

When asked to explain the purportedly new concepts of war prevention and military sufficiency, however, Warsaw Pact and

Soviet spokesmen mentioned an emphasis on quality, high combat readiness, and decisive counteroperations, in short, a victory orientation that a purely defensive doctrine based on "reasonable sufficiency" could not support. The contradiction at the heart of Soviet doctrine, which claimed to be defensive but posited war scenarios calling for applying force offensively, damaged Soviet credibility in the West and led to conflicting views on Soviet intentions. Many Western analysts, among them William T. Lee and Richard F. Staar, continued to interpret Soviet intentions as "very aggressive." Others, such as Michael MccGwire and Raymond L. Garthoff, who focused on the Soviet viewpoint, saw the Soviet Union as being constrained by doctrinal requirements and threat assessments to adopt a force posture adequate for fighting a world war with both nuclear and conventional weapons.

In the late 1980s, a consensus emerged in the West on the probable Soviet doctrine. Western specialists believed that the Soviet Union would not start a nuclear war without provocation.

They also believed, however, that, should a war start, the Soviet Union would strive for victory and for protection of its territory from enemy strikes. Western specialists also held that the Soviet leadership would prefer to fight a conventional war in Europe and, should such a war escalate, would try to limit a nuclear war to Central and Western Europe. A protracted conventional conflict in the shadow of nuclear weapons, possibly worldwide, was another likely option. Many Western analysts also thought that, despite having in 1982 unilaterally forsworn the first use of nuclear weapons, the Soviet Union retained the option of a surprise first strike against the United States. They maintained that Soviet leaders would consider this option if they believed they could thereby win the war and limit damage to the homeland.

Doctrine and Weapons Programs

The relation between the military-political and military-technical aspects of Soviet doctrine and weapons programs was direct and unmistakable. A direct link existed between the military-political component of doctrine, operational requirements, weapons programs, and force deployments. Doctrinal requirements could remain unfulfilled for years, but they usually were met as technologies became available. Hence, a knowledge of the military-political component of Soviet doctrine was helpful for forecasting the direction of Soviet military technology.

The doctrine developed by the Soviet Union in the early 1960s bore little relation to actual conditions, and the Soviet Union needed fifteen years to develop the weapons described in the 1962 edition of Sokolovskii's *Military Strategy*. In October 1986, Ogarkov wrote that the Soviet Union required an industry capable of solving the most difficult defense-equipment problems and producing the sophisticated weapons needed to win a war without using nuclear weapons. He projected a future requirement to develop new equipment and weapons, a requirement that Soviet industry might not be able to fulfill for many years. And, should the party's doctrinal view of a future war differ from Ogarkov's, this requirement might never be translated into actual weapons programs.

When formulating their goals for new, important weapons systems, Soviet leaders considered both doctrinal pronouncements on the nature of future wars and estimates of the external military threat supplied by the General Staff (see General Staff, ch. 18). The services of the armed forces reviewed their missions and drew up weapons acquisition plans in cooperation with research institutes and design bureaus (see Research, Development, and Production Organizations, ch. 16). The General Staff prepared a consolidated plan, which it forwarded to the Defense Council to be recommended for the Politburo's approval (see Defense Council, ch. 18). Although the professional expertise of the military influenced the weapons request that filled a doctrinal requirement, the party made the final decision on the weapons to be produced.

Military Policy of the Communist Party of the Soviet Union

In addition to developing military doctrine, the CPSU developed military policy, which was much broader than doctrine. Whereas doctrine contains the guiding principles on the essence of future wars and on the methods and weapons for fighting them, military policy guides the development and strengthening of the state's military might through improving the organization and armaments of the armed forces so that they can be used successfully to achieve the state's political goals. Military policy is closely linked to military strategy. Policy defines the objectives of war and focuses the attention of strategy on the tasks to be performed. Strategy's dependence on policy increased with the acquisition of nuclear weapons, the use of which was controlled by the political leadership. Like military doctrine, Soviet military policy had two components: military-political and military-technical. Soviet military theorists frequently referred to these components simply as military-political policy and military-technical policy.

According to the Soviet understanding of the term, military-political policy defined the political aims of the state, evaluated the international environment and the military potentials of probable adversaries, and established guidelines for Soviet military involvement in the world. It both overlapped and supported Soviet foreign policy. Military-political policy took into account the economic, social, scientific, and specifically military capabilities of the Soviet state and was used by the party to determine the optimal directions for structuring the armed forces and for strengthening the economic-technical base of the state's defense. Concerned about the integrity and security of the state, the party could modify its military policy as the interests of the state changed. Soviet spokesmen nevertheless stressed the continuity and consistency of the party's military policy and of the military-political course of the Soviet Union.

The Soviet military-industrial complex was run according to the military-technical component of the party's military policy, which determined the cycles of military modernization. According to Soviet sources, major weapons development programs were carried out every ten to twelve years. As in doctrine, military recommendations influenced policy, but the party retained complete control over the formulation of a uniform military-technical policy and over its implementation by government organizations.

Military Science

Although the party formulated doctrine and policy, military science—the study and practice of armed conflict—was the preserve of military professionals. According to Soviet military theorists, military science was a system of knowledge dealing directly with the nature and laws of armed conflict, the preparation of the armed forces and the country for war, and the methods of waging war. It comprised both the theory of military affairs and its practical applications in combat. Military scientists studied and defined the laws of armed conflict, which were said to be objective, i.e., independent of human consciousness. They also formulated subjective interpretations of these laws, known as principles of military art. Unlike doctrine, military science permitted differing views and even debates among military professionals concerning the nature and methods of armed combat.

The principal components of military science are military art, subdivided into military strategy, operational art, and tactics; the command and control of troops; the structuring (or development) of the armed forces; training and indoctrination; military economics; military geography and history; and the increasingly important military-technical sciences, such as artillery science, naval science, cybernetics, topography, and geodesy. A main component of military science is military art, which focuses on the theory and practice of conducting military actions on land, at sea, and in the air.

Yankee-class nuclear-powered ballistic missile
submarine under way
Courtesy United States Navy

Reputedly, scientific forecasting is one of the most important functions of military science. Computer modeling and operations research are used to predict the military-technical nature of future wars and the evolution of military technology and of military affairs in general. Forecasting provides valuable input into military doctrine and can cause modification of doctrinal pronouncements on the type of war the Soviet Union may have to fight in years to come. Another key function of military science is long-term planning for development and deployment of the most effective weapons for future conflicts.

Like doctrine and policy, Soviet military science traced its origins to Lenin's teachings on the defense of the socialist motherland. Soviet military theorists credited Lenin not only with laying the foundation of Soviet military doctrine and policy but also with founding Soviet military science. Lenin also has played a prominent role in developing Soviet military strategy. Lenin's belief that political solutions would promote the spread of communism better than would military ones and that armed conflict was merely a continuation of politics by forcible means relegated military science to a subordinate role. Thus Soviet military science was not autonomous but was, in fact, a handmaiden of the party's military doctrine and policy.

667

Laws of Armed Conflict

Soviet military scientists studied and defined objective laws of armed conflict that focused on the military struggle. These laws represented the professional military consensus on the best methods of waging combat in order to achieve victory on the battlefield. Although Soviet military theorists maintained that the laws of armed conflict "express the internal, essential, necessary, stable relationships between the phenomena manifested in the course of an armed conflict," the laws were far from immutable. They retained their validity until Soviet military thinkers discovered other laws that provided better solutions to the same problems. Thus the laws of armed conflict defined in the 1970s that relied on massive strikes with nuclear weapons for the solution of most military tasks appeared outdated in the 1980s, when the Soviet military was emphasizing conventional options.

Two laws of armed conflict, however, purportedly remained unaffected by technological change. They were the law of dependence of the forms of armed combat on the material basis of the battle and operation, i.e., on people and equipment, and the law stating that the side with the greater combat power will always be favored in any battle or operation.

Principles of Military Art

The principles of military art are the basic ideas for the organization and conduct of battles, operations, and wars, and they can be applied on tactical, operational, and strategic levels. These principles evolve over time: some lose their significance, others acquire a new content, and new principles emerge. The 1978 *Soviet Military Encyclopedia* listed the following eleven principles of military art: high combat readiness; surprise and striving to seize and retain the initiative; full use of all means and methods of combat; close cooperation among the services, also known as the principle (or concept) of combined arms; concentration of essential efforts; simultaneous destruction of the enemy to the entire depth of the enemy's deployment; full use of the moral-political factor; strict and uninterrupted troop control; steadfastness and decisiveness; comprehensive security of combat activity; and timely restoration of reserves. These principles guided Soviet commanders in planning, preparing, and waging armed combat.

Military Art

Military art is the theory and practice of preparing and conducting military actions on land, at sea, and in the air. Its three components—military strategy, operational art, and tactics—are interconnected and mutually supporting. Military strategy is concerned with the conduct of the war as a whole.

Operational art deals with the preparation and conduct of military actions within geographical limits of a theater of military operations (*teatr voennykh deistvii*—TVD; see Glossary). Operational art is employed to achieve the goals set under strategy. It links strategy and tactics, in that tactical missions are assigned to support theater operations. Military tactics defines combat methods for the battlefield. Although it is subordinate to operational art and strategy, tactics can influence both the operational and the strategic levels of war.

Military Strategy

Military strategy is the most important component of military art. The study of strategy was an important part of Soviet military life, and all services of the Soviet armed forces followed the same military strategy. Strategists investigated the nature of war and its conduct, as well as the conduct of strategic operations. They defined the missions of the armed forces and specified the resources needed to accomplish them. Soviet strategists also studied the capabilities and strategies of probable adversaries and devised measures to counter them. Military strategy and military science supplied policy makers with the results of military-scientific research on the best methods for attaining a war's objectives. At the same time, the recommendations of military strategy and military science helped shape military doctrine, the principles of which then guided strategy in the conduct of war.

Nuclear Strategy in the 1950s

After the explosions of the first Soviet atomic device in 1949 and the Soviet hydrogen bomb in 1953, the Soviet armed forces acquired nuclear weapons. Also introduced in the 1950s were ballistic- and cruise-missile technologies, jet engines, and artificial earth satellites, as well as computers and automated control systems. These important events were known in the Soviet Union as the "revolution in military affairs." Of all the new developments, nuclear weapons most affected Soviet strategy. Nuclear weapons altered the nature and methods of armed struggle on the strategic level because they could accomplish the military's strategic tasks without operational art and tactics. Not until Stalin's death in 1953, however, could the Soviet military begin exploring the full strategic potential of the new weapons. Although he had pushed for the development of the "bomb," Stalin played down its importance and did

669

not encourage the military to formulate a new strategy incorporating nuclear weapons.

Transition to a nuclear strategy began in the mid-1950s, when Soviet military thinkers began recognizing the importance of surprise, of the initial period of war, and of using nuclear strikes to determine the course and outcome of a war. In February 1955, Marshal Pavel A. Rotmistrov published in the Soviet journal *Voennaia mysl'* (Military Thought) a ground-breaking article on "surprise." He stressed the importance of landing the first, "preemptive" nuclear blow to destroy the enemy's weapons when the latter was preparing a surprise attack. Since the mid-1950s, the concept of preempting an enemy's nuclear weapons has become firmly entrenched in Soviet military thought.

As the Soviet military came to view nuclear weapons as particularly suitable for general war, it needed a strategy for their use. In 1957 a series of military seminars at the highest level helped leaders develop the elements of a new nuclear strategy. A group of Soviet military strategists under the direction of Marshal Sokolovskii continued the work of the seminars. In 1962 they published *Military Strategy*, the first Soviet treatise on strategy since 1927.

The Sokolovskii Era, 1962–68

In January 1960, Khrushchev unveiled the new nuclear strategy in a speech to the Supreme Soviet. According to Khrushchev, this strategy's aim was deterring war rather than fighting it (see Evolution of Military Doctrine, this ch.). Despite Khrushchev's emphasis on deterrence and reductions in military manpower, Sokolovskii's *Military Strategy* focused on apocalyptic scenarios for fighting a world war with nuclear weapons and stressed the need for mass armies. The idea of preemption resurfaced, this time on an intercontinental basis, because the Soviet Union had acquired nuclear intercontinental ballistic missiles (ICBMs) and could threaten the territory of the United States. Sokolovskii maintained that the Soviet side had to "frustrate" an enemy coalition's attack by delivering massive nuclear strikes on the enemy's territories. These strikes would destroy not only the enemy's weapons but also the enemy's will to continue the war, thus limiting the damage from a retaliatory strike.

This view of nuclear strategy prevailed during most of the 1960s. Soon after the publication of the third edition of his *Military Strategy* in 1968, however, Sokolovskii wrote with an eye on the future: "Military affairs are entering or have already entered the next stage of their development, and apparently it is necessary to introduce essential changes into military art.'' Such changes began to occur in the 1960s and continued through the 1970s and 1980s.

New Strategic Options, 1968–89

Beginning in the mid-1960s, the Soviet military leadership tried to add new, less destructive, strategic options, not only as a response to NATO's ''flexible response'' concept but also because the leaders began to doubt the possibility of a true victory in an all-out nuclear war. Although most military writings upheld the obligatory belief in socialism's victory, doubters hinted that not only imperialism but also socialism could perish in a nuclear holocaust.

The search for options intensified in the 1970s, after the Soviet Union had achieved rough nuclear parity with the United States, thereby making a nuclear war with the West less likely. If escalation had been imminent, the Soviet Union had the capability—accurate and reliable ICBMs with multiple warheads—to limit its strikes to the adversary's weapons, thus reducing the level of violence. Other options examined in the 1970s and 1980s included a nuclear war limited to Europe, a combined arms offensive with both nuclear and conventional weapons, and a completely conventional strategic operation in Europe, where Soviet nuclear weapons deterring Western use of nuclear weapons.

In 1989 two possible future strategic options—space warfare and ballistic missile defense—had not been officially endorsed but were available to Soviet planners. Since the 1957 launching of Sputnik (see Glossary), the Soviet Union had been interested in the military use of space and had conducted research in this field. Moreover, in late 1987 Gorbachev admitted that for years the Soviet Union had been conducting basic research on a space-based defense against ballistic missiles, similar to the United States Strategic Defense Initiative (SDI).

Yet even in 1989, the addition of new strategic options did not alter the basic nuclear war scenario of the 1960s. Two monographs published in 1985 and 1986 by Gareev and Lieutenant General Pavel A. Zhilin, respectively, reaffirmed the increased importance of surprise during the initial period of a nuclear war. According to these specialists, such a ''surprise nuclear strike,'' if successful, could determine both the course and the outcome of a war. Soviet belief that the United States was acquiring nuclear missiles capable of delivering a surprise strike and was developing an antimissile shield to protect United States territory from Soviet retaliation contributed to the Soviet military's perception of the growing role of strategic surprise.

Operational Art

Operational art involves the translation of strategic goals into military objectives in TVDs by conducting decisive theater campaigns. Although a single military strategy existed for the Soviet armed forces, each of the five armed services had its own operational art and tactics. Three enduring concepts that have shaped Soviet operational art since the 1920s have been the concept of the TVD, the principle of combined arms, and the theory of deep offensive operations.

TVDs divided the world into manageable military-geographic sectors. In 1983 the Soviet *Military Encyclopedic Dictionary* defined a TVD as part of a continent or an ocean "within the boundaries of which are deployed strategic groupings of the armed forces and within which military operations are conducted." Around its periphery the Soviet military recognized five continental TVDs with their surrounding seas: the Northwestern, Western, Southwestern, Southern, and Far Eastern. Oceanic TVDs were located in the Atlantic, Pacific, Indian, and Arctic oceans (see fig. 27).

The combined arms concept is a major principle of Soviet military art. It means that all services are integrated and coordinated to achieve victory in a war, an operation, or a battle. The concept originated in the 1920s, when Marshal of the Soviet Union Mikhail N. Tukhachevskii understood combined arms primarily as the cooperation between artillery and infantry in land warfare. Since then, as the Soviet armed forces have added new weapons systems such as tanks, aircraft, submarines, and ballistic and cruise missiles, combined arms acquired a new meaning as it began to signify the interaction of all services of the armed forces to attain strategic goals.

The deep offensive operation theory evolved in the 1920s and 1930s as an outgrowth of the combined arms concept. The deep offensive operation called for the destruction of the enemy to a substantial depth of its deployment, for the use of mobile groups in the enemy's rear, for a breakthrough of tactical defense, and for encirclement and subsequent destruction of enemy troops. During World War II, Soviet commanders stressed coordination of troops, operational maneuver, and operational breakthrough, as well as the necessity of conducting an operation with combined forces on several fronts. New types of operations emerged, such as air and antiair operations, and combined operations of the Ground Forces, Air Forces, and Naval Forces. In the 1950s, the increased mobility of armor and the striking power of nuclear weapons bolstered the concept of the deep offensive operation.

Nuclear weapons produced fundamental operational changes. The scope and depth of an operational offensive grew, and its violence intensified. Soviet military thinkers believed that they could achieve a decisive victory by delivering preemptive nuclear strikes on objectives deep in the enemy's rear and, subsequently, by encircling, cutting off, and destroying the enemy's troops with nuclear and conventional munitions. Soviet military writers soon began to point out, however, that radioactive contamination, fires, and floods caused by massive nuclear strikes could interfere with the success of operations.

In the 1970s, the Soviet Union built up its conventional forces in Europe and adopted new operational concepts for the conduct of a deep offensive operation using both conventional and nuclear weapons. A conventional phase was to precede the nuclear phase. By the early 1980s, the Soviet military had developed an all-conventional option for a deep offensive operation in a TVD (see Offensive and Defensive Strategic Missions, this ch.).

Tactics

Tactics is the aspect of military art concerned with the preparation and conduct of offensive and defensive combat actions by elements of the armed forces on land, in the air, and at sea. Soviet military writers distinguish four basic tactical combat actions: offense, the meeting engagement (in which both belligerents meet while advancing), defense, and withdrawal. They view defense as a temporary action, for only offense can bring about a complete rout of the enemy and victory.

In the early 1960s, nuclear weapons became the "basic means of destruction on the field of battle." Soviet tacticians believed that nuclear strikes during an engagement would help the Soviet armed forces to seize and retain the initiative on a tactical level and achieve victory in battle. The new emphasis on nuclear weapons led to changes in tactical concepts. Instead of massive concentration of forces on the main direction of attack, theorists advocated concentration of nuclear strikes and maneuver by troops and by nuclear missiles.

Soviet military theorists came to realize that use of nuclear weapons by both belligerents could complicate offensive tactical combat by slowing down the Soviet advance while strengthening the enemy's defense. Because increased mobility and high rates of advance formed the most important Soviet operational and tactical principles, the Soviet military began to perceive nuclear weapons as problematic. Thus, in the late 1960s and the 1970s, Soviet military planners began to reorient tactics away from reliance on nuclear weapons toward reliance on new conventional weapons. Concepts such as the concentration of forces on the main

673

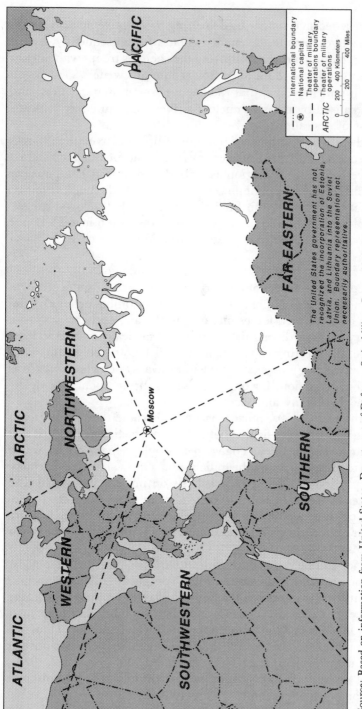

Source: Based on information from United States, Department of Defense, *Soviet Military Power, 1987*, Washington, 1987, 16.

Figure 27. Theaters of Military Operations, 1987

axis, partial victory, and economy of force again assumed their prenuclear importance.

Soviet tactics in the 1980s has experienced a resurgence, in part because improved conventional weapons with greater ranges and accuracies became available. Also, the 1979 Soviet invasion of Afghanistan provided a training ground for tactical conventional combat in mountainous and desert terrain and drew the attention of Soviet military theorists to the importance of tactics in warfare. Two revised editions of Lieutenant General Vasilii G. Reznichenko's *Tactics* were published in the 1980s: one in 1984 and a revised and augmented one in 1987. Reznichenko described tactics as the most dynamic component of contemporary military art, a component that could influence the operational and even the strategic levels of war. In the 1987 edition of *Tactics*, Reznichenko included new defensive concepts but emphasized the offensive, supported by air superiority, fire superiority, and electronic warfare. He favored conventional rather than nuclear preemption, for, if used preemptively, long-range precision-guided munitions could predetermine the outcome of a combined arms battle.

Strategic Missions of the Armed Forces

The General Staff had the responsibility for formulating the strategic missions of the five services of the Soviet armed forces. The Soviet military has defined a strategic mission as one "whose fulfillment in the course of an armed conflict leads to an abrupt change in the operational strategic situation . . . . Successful accomplishment of a strategic mission usually results in attainment of numerical superiority over the enemy, in seizure of important areas and installations on his territory . . . . Successful accomplishment of a series of strategic missions leads to the attainment of intermediate and ultimate strategic goals." Because the ultimate strategic goal of war is victory over the adversary, the successful accomplishment of strategic missions is indispensable.

The General Staff had the responsibility for assessing external threats and drawing up Soviet war plans. It reconciled its plans with Soviet military doctrine and policy. The General Staff also determined the nature of strategic missions, as well as the weapons used and the size of forces needed to accomplish these missions (see table 53, Appendix A).

Traditionally, the Soviet military has structured its armed forces offensively, on the basis of worst-case threat assessments. The primacy of offense over defense was challenged in the nuclear age, when strategic offense was often combined with strategic defense. In 1989, in spite of the new doctrinal emphasis on defense, most branches of the Soviet armed forces, such as the Strategic Rocket Forces, the Air Forces, the Naval Forces, and the Ground Forces, still had mainly offensive missions. The Ground Forces played a leading role in the combined arms strategic operation in a TVD. By contrast, the Air Defense Forces were to carry out active defense of the homeland by destroying the enemy's weapons and aircraft, whereas Civil Defense was to protect the country from nuclear devastation. In the 1980s, the Soviet military reinforced the combined arms concept on the strategic level by reorganizing and restructuring the Soviet armed forces.

Threat Assessments and Force Requirements

Since the nuclear era began, worst-case threat assessments have dominated Soviet military thinking. As a result, even during the years of détente and strategic arms control, Soviet military policy and doctrine have called for disproportionately large forces for the fulfillment of strategic missions, and Soviet military planners have drawn up plans in response to doctrinal requirements.

In the 1980s, Soviet worst-case scenarios centered on the modernization of the United States ICBMs, on United States deployment of the Trident ballistic missile submarine armed with long-range, accurate nuclear missiles, and on United States procurement of low-flying ground-, sea-, and air-launched cruise missiles. Soviet spokesmen also persisted in portraying SDI as an offensive system and claimed that it would enable the United States to launch a first strike against Soviet territory with impunity.

Dmitrii Iazov, appointed minister of defense in 1987, adopted a contradictory position on Soviet military planning and threat assessment. Implying that the Soviet Union was willing to scale down its military expenditures and would modify its military doctrine and strategy, Iazov publicly endorsed reductions in the nuclear and conventional armaments of both the United States and the Soviet Union to a level commensurate with a defense-oriented doctrine and strategy. Yet he retained the traditional worst-case scenario when he called for a robust Soviet nuclear capability that could punish an attacker "even under the most unfavorable circumstances." Although he relied on "reasonable sufficiency" rather than on superiority, Iazov also defined "reasonable sufficiency" in traditional terms as the ability to "reliably guarantee the defense of the Socialist Community" with armed forces structured and equipped for offensive action.

Offensive and Defensive Strategic Missions

Traditionally, the overall mission of the Soviet armed forces has been to deter war in peacetime and to defend the Soviet Union and the socialist states allied to it in wartime. Should war break out, the Soviet armed forces were expected to fight decisively and to achieve victory. Soviet unified military strategy, common to all services, was primarily offensive, and defense was only a temporary expedient. The primacy of strategic offense over strategic defense appeared indisputable. Since the advent of nuclear weapons, however, strategic offense and defense have become intertwined, and offensive and defensive strategic missions frequently coalesced. The combined arms concept was expressed in this growing interdependence between offense and defense in Soviet unified strategy because many strategic missions involved overlap and cooperation and would be performed by more than one service (see Military Art, this ch.). The Soviet military envisaged most strategic operations, both offensive and defensive, as mutually reinforcing components of a single strategic plan. In the 1980s, Soviet strategists believed that the synergistic effect of combined arms would maximize the armed forces' potential to achieve unambiguous victory.

To reinforce the combined arms concept on a strategic level, the Soviet military reorganized the Soviet armed forces. It centralized command and control, established theater commands in TVDs directly responsible to the Supreme High Command, and improved early warning systems (see Main Military Council, ch. 18). The new Soviet command infrastructure would enable the Soviet military to change speedily from a peacetime to a wartime footing.

Strategic Offense

The Strategic Rocket Forces, the Naval Forces, the Air Forces, and the Ground Forces have had predominantly offensive missions. Since their founding in 1959, the Strategic Rocket Forces have been charged with using their intercontinental and intermediate-range ballistic missiles to destroy military and economic targets in the United States and on the Eurasian landmass in the initial period of war. The Strategic Rocket Forces were to preempt an enemy attack by launching Soviet missiles first or to prevent the destruction of Soviet missiles by launching them soon after the enemy's missiles had left their silos. Thus the Soviet initial strike could be both offensive and defensive. In their offensive posture, the Strategic Rocket Forces could change the correlation of forces and resources and tip the nuclear balance in the Soviet Union's favor. At the same time, should the Soviet strike succeed in destroying United States missiles before launch, it would prevent a United States nuclear strike (see Military Doctrine in the Late 1980s, this ch.).

In the 1960s and 1970s, the Strategic Rocket Forces enjoyed an undisputed predominance in nuclear strategy. By the 1980s, however, the Soviet military appeared to have downgraded the Strategic Rocket Forces. Soviet spokesmen, beginning with Ogarkov in 1981, began to refer to these forces, together with the nuclear Naval Forces and the Air Forces, as an integral part of a combined arms triad of "strategic nuclear forces."

The Air Forces also have had an offensive-defensive mission similar to that of the Strategic Rocket Forces. In contrast to the Strategic Rocket Forces, however, the Air Forces' intercontinental capabilities had been very limited until the early 1980s. In addition to the Tu-26 (Backfire) bomber with a largely theater-level use, in the mid-1980s the Soviet military deployed the intercontinental Tu-160 bomber and equipped its Tu-95 bombers with air-launched cruise missiles (ALCMs). Because cruise missiles could be conventionally armed, in the late 1980s the Air Forces were beginning to acquire a significant conventional capability for strategic missions.

Of all the services, the Naval Forces experienced the most dramatic mission expansion after the 1960s. Their mission evolved from coastal defense to worldwide power projection in peacetime and to denial of the use of the seas to adversaries in wartime through the disruption of sea lines of communication. In the 1970s, the "father" of the modern Soviet Naval Forces, Admiral Sergei Gorshkov, had lobbied for independent strategic missions for the Naval Forces. Admiral Vladimir Chernavin, however, who succeeded Gorshkov as the Naval Forces commander in chief in 1986, appeared content to have a strong but less independent Naval Forces, well integrated into the traditional combined arms concept and a uniform, all-services strategy. The strategic nuclear mission was the only Naval Forces mission in which Western analysts had noted some retrenchment since the 1960s. In the 1960s, nuclear war was expected to start with a massive nuclear exchange, and strikes by submarine-launched ballistic missiles (SLBMs) were to supplement the initial strike by the Strategic Rocket Forces. In the 1970s and 1980s, when the Strategic Rocket Forces built up their counterforce capability, the primary strategic mission of the Naval Forces was to provide a secure reserve force, withheld from the initial nuclear strikes, and to protect this force from enemy antisubmarine warfare.

The strategic mission of the Ground Forces has been defense of the territorial and political integrity of the Soviet Union and its socialist allies and, in case of war, conducting combined arms operations in the TVDs with the support of air, air defense, and navy elements. In Europe the goal of the strategic combined arms mission

Tu-26 (Backfire) strike bomber
Courtesy United States Navy

has been defeating NATO as quickly as possible and occupying Western Europe without destroying its economic base.

Strategic Operation in a Theater of Military Operations

The concept of the combined arms operational offensive in a theater of military operations (*teatr voennykh deistvii*—TVD) developed in the 1920s as the theory of the deep offensive operation (see Military Art, this ch.). According to this theory, Soviet infantry, armor, and artillery would coordinate to achieve operational goals with operational breakthroughs and firepower. The deep offensive operation concept underlies the modern, expanded theater operation, which, according to Marshal Ogarkov, is ''no longer a front or group of fronts, but a strategic operation in a TVD'' and can lead directly to the achievement of strategic objectives. Since the mid-1970s, such an operation in the Western TVD, covering NATO's Central Region, was expected to be fought mainly with new, improved conventional weapons. Although primarily offensive, the modern strategic operation also incorporated defensive concepts because of changes in NATO strategy.

American military expert Phillip Petersen believed that a conventional air operation against NATO's airfields and nuclear weapons sites would substitute aviation and the fire of conventional

679

missiles for nuclear strikes. The air operation could neutralize NATO's air defense assets, destroy nuclear weapons, and disrupt command and control capabilities. Highly mobile first- and second-echelon ground forces, known as operational maneuver groups, could break through the forward defenses and penetrate deep into the enemy's rear. If NATO's nuclear weapons could be successfully destroyed, Warsaw Pact tanks and armored personnel carriers could advance rapidly across Western Europe to the North Sea coast and to the Danish Straits before NATO could mobilize fully and bring reinforcements from North America. Similar operations would take place in the Northwestern and Southwestern TVDs and would continue until Soviet troops achieved the strategic objective of victory in Europe.

Although Soviet military theorists traditionally have deemphasized defensive operations, in the 1980s they paid more attention to defensive concepts on the strategic, operational, and tactical levels and called defense "an essential form of combat action." In the 1980s, Soviet military writers also emphasized the increased depth of operational defenses in connection with the deep-strike concepts incorporated in the United States Army's AirLand Battle doctrine (see Glossary) and in NATO's Follow-on-Forces-Attack (FOFA—see Glossary) concept. The Soviet concept of defense has been distinguished by extreme "combat activeness," i.e., using massive firepower to destroy the enemy's aircraft and attacking ground forces while Soviet forces prepare a counterattack.

Strategic Defense

The Air Defense Forces, known until their 1980 reorganization as the National Air Defense Forces, was the one service whose mission was almost entirely defensive (see Air Defense Forces, ch. 18). These forces were to protect the country from nuclear attack. Formed in 1948 to counter the threat of strategic bombers, the National Air Defense Forces had no capability against ballistic missiles, which became the main threat in the 1960s. The preemptive mission of the Strategic Rocket Forces filled this gap and lightened the burden of the National Air Defense Forces.

The principal mission of the Air Defense Forces has remained practically unchanged since the 1950s. However, according to Sokolovskii's *Military Strategy,* air defense included both defense against ballistic missiles and space defense. In 1989 one antiballistic missile site around Moscow protected both the capital and the National Command Authority housed there. Extensive Soviet research on defense against ballistic missiles, however, pointed to a possible change in Soviet reliance on strategic offense.

In addition to the active defense that the mission of the Air Defense Forces has called for, the Soviet Union has invested heavily in civil defense. The declared mission of civil defense has been to provide "reliable protection for the population against weapons of mass destruction in wartime" through construction of shelters for the leadership, hardening and dispersal of industry, and evacuation of leadership and civilians from cities. Such efforts continued in the 1980s, despite civilian leaders' statements denying the viability of defense against nuclear weapons and acknowledging that nuclear war would be suicidal.

Global Strategic Concerns

Since the late 1960s, when the Soviet Union was about to achieve nuclear parity with the United States, Soviet military support for the global task of promoting Marxism-Leninism intensified. Hoping that the attainment of strategic parity with the United States would deter the latter from interfering with Soviet international activism, the Soviet Union set out to aid and abet the forces of socialism and "national liberation" worldwide.

Soviet doctrine called not only for nuclear and nonnuclear capabilities to fight a world war but also for adequate conventional forces to support the "external function" of the Soviet armed forces in defense of "socialist gains" and of the fighters for world revolution. Two components of the "internationalist duty" of the Soviet armed forces emerged: "socialist internationalism," the defense of socialist countries allied to the Soviet Union; and "proletarian internationalism," the assistance given to "wars of national liberation" in the Third World.

Soviet spokesmen have emphasized repeatedly that the Soviet Union does not believe in the "export of revolution" but opposes the export of "counterrevolution," i.e., actions by Western powers that would hinder the historic progress of socialism. In the 1970s, combating "counterrevolution" became part of the "internationalist duty" of the Soviet armed forces.

The Soviet Union has attempted, not always successfully, to reconcile Marxist-Leninist doctrine with state interests. Soviet leaders have tried to satisfy doctrinal requirements while pursuing the military and foreign policies of the Soviet state. Projected worldwide, Marxism-Leninism evolved from a purely revolutionary ideology into an ideology rationalizing the actions of a superpower. Often state interests were a more reliable guide than ideology to understanding Soviet actions.

Force Projection on the Periphery

The Soviet armed forces have exercised their "external function" mainly on the periphery of the Soviet Union. They occupied eastern Poland in 1939 and annexed Estonia, Latvia, and Lithuania in 1940 (see Prelude to War, ch. 2). Subsequently, during World War II they "liberated" Eastern Europe from German rule and then incorporated it into a bloc of socialist states (see Appendix C).

The Soviet Union managed to turn these territories into an outpost of socialism, as well as into a defensive buffer against an invasion from the West. This buffer became increasingly valuable to the Soviet Union both as an extension of Soviet air defenses to the end of the Soviet defense perimeter and as a potential springboard for an offensive against NATO.

In 1956 the Soviet Union set a precedent for military intervention "in defense of socialism" when it suppressed the uprising that threatened communist rule in Hungary. In August 1968, the Soviet Union again intervened militarily in Eastern Europe when it invaded Czechoslovakia in response to the Czechoslovak reform movement begun in the spring. The invasion later was justified on the basis of the doctrine of "limited sovereignty" of socialist states. Also known as the Brezhnev Doctrine, the doctrine was first enunciated on September 21, 1968, in a *Pravda* editorial, to justify the invasion. Because Czechoslovakia and Hungary lie on the Soviet defense perimeter, national security considerations, in addition to ideological and political concerns, undoubtedly played a part in the Soviet decision to intervene.

The December 1979 invasion of Afghanistan was another case in which doctrinal concerns and interests of state security coalesced (see Asia, ch. 10). Although nominally nonaligned, Afghanistan was, according to Soviet arguments, well on its way to socialism in 1979, and a reversal was unacceptable to the Soviet Union. In addition, because Afghanistan borders the Soviet Union, Soviet leaders sought to prevent it from aligning itself with the West or from becoming an Islamic republic allied to Ayatollah Sayyid Ruhollah Musavi Khomeini's Iran. The invasion, although "correct" according to Soviet ideological criteria, plunged the Soviet Union into one of the longest local wars (see Glossary) it had ever fought, second only to the 1939–40 Soviet-Finnish War, in which over 100,000 Soviet troops died. In 1988 the Soviet leadership declared that it would negotiate a troop withdrawal from Afghanistan and seek a political settlement. On April 14, 1988, Soviet foreign minister Eduard A. Shevardnadze signed an agreement in Geneva providing for the withdrawal of Soviet troops from Afghanistan by February 15, 1989.

Missile cruiser Slava
Courtesy United States Navy

The invasion of Afghanistan tarnished the Soviet image abroad, where the invasion was perceived and condemned as an act of aggression. Some Western analysts regarded it as an unprecedented extension of the Brezhnev Doctrine of "socialist internationalism" to a country that was nonaligned and thus not part of the world socialist system (see Glossary). A majority vote in the United Nations (UN) censured the invasion as a flagrant intervention in the internal affairs of a sovereign state. Soviet leaders hoped that the 1988 Geneva agreement, which stipulated a unilateral withdrawal of Soviet forces, would placate world opinion and repair the political damage done by the war.

The only benefit that the Soviet Union appeared to have derived from the war in Afghanistan was the use of Afghan territory to train Soviet troops to fight in mountainous terrain and to test Soviet weapons. However, Soviet concepts of offense and combined arms, and Soviet troops and weapons, fared poorly in the difficult mountain terrain. Tanks were of little use in ground combat in narrow mountain passes. The Soviet military learned that helicopters were of greater importance in the mountains because helicopters could carry out air attacks and could land troops on enemy territory. The Soviet military also found that the enemy's surface-to-air missiles posed a grave threat to attacking Soviet aircraft. Thus, the Soviet

Union probably decided to withdraw from Afghanistan not only for political but also for military reasons.

Military Presence in the Third World

The Soviet Union has sought to restructure international relations and to achieve a world socialist system largely through political influence; however, it has not reneged on the promise of military aid for revolutionary movements in the Third World under the principle of "proletarian internationalism" (see Glossary). Soviet leaders reaffirmed this principle in the 1986 party program (see Glossary) of the CPSU. Yet the Soviet Union has also sought to advance Soviet state interests by gaining a military foothold in strategically important areas of the Third World.

Because of the dual and often contradictory nature of Soviet objectives in the Third World, the Soviet military has had successes and failures in its dealings with it. Two large-scale, successful Soviet-supported interventions took place, in Angola in 1975 and in Ethiopia in 1977. In both places the Soviet Union provided arms and military advisers and used Cuban troops to help pro-Soviet elements consolidate power. By contrast, in 1976 the Soviet Union suffered a reversal in Egypt where, after years of massive military assistance, the Egyptian government asked Soviet advisers to leave, canceled access for the Soviet Naval Forces, and abrogated the Treaty of Friendship and Cooperation with the Soviet Union. Similarly, Somalia, once the most important Soviet client in sub-Saharan Africa, abrogated its friendship treaty in 1977 because of the Soviet tilt toward Ethiopia and denied use of naval facilities at Berbera to the Soviet Naval Forces. In the 1980s, combating "counterrevolution" in the Third World was not an unqualified success for the Soviet military, which, for political reasons, had shunned direct intervention in countries far from Soviet borders. In the 1980s, Soviet military aid to allied regimes in Nicaragua, Angola, Mozambique, and Cambodia was unable to rid these beleaguered Marxist regimes of "counterrevolutionary" resistance forces.

The Soviet Union has long been the world's major supplier of military advisory assistance. According to the United States government, in 1986 about 21,000 Soviet and East European military advisers (most of whom were Soviet advisers) were stationed in Third World countries, including about 8,000 in Africa, almost 6,000 in the Middle East, and about 3,000 in Afghanistan. The Soviet Union has also used military "proxies," or allied forces, to substitute for or buttress Soviet military advisers serving in Third World countries. Advisers and combatants from Cuba, Vietnam, the Democratic People's Republic of Korea (North Korea), the People's

Democratic Republic of Yemen (South Yemen), and Eastern Europe—particularly the German Democratic Republic (East Germany) and Bulgaria—have been used in various Third World countries, such as Ethiopia, Angola, and Mozambique.

Despite ideological setbacks, the Soviet Union has derived considerable military-strategic advantage by establishing bases and naval access in the Third World. In the 1980s, facilities were available to the Soviet Union at Cam Ranh Bay in Vietnam, Aden and the island of Socotra in South Yemen, Massawa and the island of Dahlak in Ethiopia, Luanda in Angola, and Maputo in Mozambique. Part of a worldwide Soviet military support structure, such installations increased Soviet influence in the Third World. American analyst Alex Alexiev has argued that Soviet arms deliveries to certain countries have actually been attempts to pre-position war matériel in case of global war. Alexiev believed such pre-positioning to have taken place in Libya, where Soviet deliveries increased the number of tanks and armored personnel carriers from 175 in 1971 to 4,400 in 1983. Similarly, South Yemen had 50 tanks and no armored personnel carriers in 1975, while in 1982, after Soviet shipments, it had 450 modern tanks and 300 armored personnel carriers.

In 1989 Soviet global military initiative appeared to be on hold. On the one hand, Gorbachev declared his "solidarity with the forces of national liberation and social emancipation" throughout the globe. On the other hand, his "new thinking" in foreign and military policy deemphasized "military-technical solutions" to the world's problems and seemed to promise fewer Soviet military forays into the Third World and less interference in the internal affairs of socialist allies. Many Western observers believed that Gorbachev wanted to replace emphasis on Soviet military power with an approach that combined economic, political, and military instruments of power.

Arms Control and Military Objectives

Since the late 1960s, the Soviet Union has made arms control an important component of its foreign and military policy. Soviet public diplomacy liberally used arms control and disarmament slogans. Arms control proposals and signed agreements, however, have been carefully coordinated with doctrinal requirements and weapons programs.

Soviet objectives in all areas of arms control—strategic, space, intermediate-range nuclear, and conventional weapons—have been, first, to help avert a world war, and, second, to prevent the erosion of Soviet capability for fighting such a war. If efforts to avert war were to fail, Soviet leaders required that their armed forces

685

be able to fulfill military missions and win all military conflicts. War was to be avoided by entering into agreements that would limit an adversary's weapons and forestall the adversary's development of a war-winning military posture. Capability for fighting and winning a war was to be continued by acquiring the necessary arsenal within the constraints of an agreement and by maintaining it against all odds.

Strategic Arms Control

Strategic arms control imposes limitations or stipulates reductions in the numbers of Soviet and United States intercontinental nuclear weapons that are capable of reaching each other's homelands. Weapons limited have included ICBMs, SLBMs, bombers armed with nuclear bombs and cruise missiles, and antiballistic missile systems. Motivated by its desire to avert a nuclear war and to be prepared to fight one, the Soviet Union has sought strategic arms control agreements that would limit United States nuclear capabilities for intercontinental attack but would permit the Soviet Union to amass a strategic arsenal for fighting and winning a nuclear war.

Averting a World War

According to the worst-case scenario, still accepted by Soviet planners in 1989, a world nuclear war could start with a disarming first strike on the Soviet Union's strategic nuclear weapons and on its strategic command and control centers (see Military Art, this ch.). An arms control agreement that is advantageous to the Soviet Union would help deter such a calamity by constraining the strategic forces of the United States and denying it the weapons needed to execute a strategic attack with impunity.

Before agreeing to limit its strategic forces, the Soviet Union wanted at least numerical equality with the United States. When arms control was first discussed in the early 1960s, under no circumstances were Soviet leaders willing to settle for a "minimum deterrent." For example, when President Lyndon B. Johnson proposed in January 1964 to freeze both Soviet and United States strategic missiles at existing levels, the Soviet Union refused because the "freeze" would have codified their strategic inferiority. Yet in 1969, after the Soviet Union began to deploy the third generation of ICBMs (the SS-9, SS-11, and SS-13) and was developing the fourth generation (the SS-17, SS-18, and SS-19), it agreed to hold the Strategic Arms Limitation Talks (SALT—see Glossary) with the United States. In 1972 the negotiations resulted in the signing of the Anti-Ballistic Missile Treaty (ABM Treaty) and of the Interim Agreement on the Limitation of Strategic Offensive Arms. Essentially, both agreements froze the deployment of strategic defensive and offensive armaments.

Because the Soviet Union wanted to continue the buildup of its strategic offensive forces, it accepted the offensive arms limitation grudgingly. Its main motive in signing the agreements resulting from the first series of SALT negotiations, known as SALT I, was to prevent the United States from deploying an effective defense against ballistic missiles. The Soviet Union clearly preferred a vulnerable adversary that would be deterred from striking by the prospect of massive Soviet retaliation on the adversary's unprotected weapons, economy, and population.

Retaining a Capability to Fight and to Win

In addition to deterring a nuclear world war, Soviet strategic forces were expected to fight it and to win it. SALT I was acceptable to the Soviet military not only because it made war less likely but also because the Soviet military would have the capability to carry out its intercontinental strike mission even in a worst-case scenario. By limiting defensive systems to one installation in each country, the ABM Treaty guaranteed that Soviet missiles could successfully penetrate United States airspace.

Because SALT I limited the number of ballistic missile launchers but not the number of warheads, the Soviet Union was able to increase its intercontinental missile arsenal. It used new technologies to equip its land- and sea-based strategic missiles with several warheads, known as multiple independently targetable reentry vehicles (MIRVs). The Soviet military also greatly improved the accuracies of its missiles, especially the SS–18 and SS–19 ICBMs.

In 1979, when President Jimmy Carter and General Secretary Leonid Brezhnev signed the second SALT agreement in Vienna, the Soviet Union had 5,000 warheads on its strategic missiles, an increase of 2,500 since 1972. By 1986 the number of Soviet strategic warheads exceeded 10,000. Thus neither of the SALT agreements significantly constrained Soviet nuclear modernization and the growth of the Soviet arsenal, whose ultimate aim was to hold at risk the vulnerable United States force of land-based Minuteman III missiles.

Soviet leaders objected to United States proposals in the Strategic Arms Reduction Talks (START), a new round of talks to reduce nuclear arsenals, that began in June 1982, because, if accepted, such proposals would have cut in half the number of Soviet ICBMs, their principal war-fighting component. In the mid-1980s, when it began deploying the fifth generation of ICBMs (the mobile

SS-24 and SS-25 missiles, to assume part of the SS-18 mission), the Soviet Union began to show interest in reducing the number of its heavy SS-18 missiles. Since their deployment in 1974, the United States had viewed the SS-18s as the most threatening and destabilizing component of the Soviet arsenal. In 1989 the Soviet leaders continued to link reduction of the SS-18s to severe restrictions on the testing of SDI. First unveiled by President Ronald W. Reagan in March 1983, SDI promised to yield advanced technologies for a North American antimissile shield. Should SDI prove feasible, it could render Soviet nuclear weapons impotent and obsolete, according to some Western specialists.

This prospect alarmed the Soviet military because such a shield could prevent it from attaining its two most important military objectives: avoiding wars and being prepared to fight them. In 1989 the Soviet Union appeared willing to agree to deep cuts in its offensive weapons in order to derail SDI or at least to force the United States to ban SDI-related tests in space for a minimum of ten years.

Objectives in Space

Soviet interest in space, both for peaceful and for military use, has been intense since the 1950s. During talks on limiting the military use of space, Soviet negotiators have tried to block development of defensive and offensive United States space systems. At the same time, the Soviet Union has conducted extensive research in military space-based technologies.

Negotiations

Attempts to limit the military use of space began soon after the Soviet Union rejected President Dwight D. Eisenhower's 1958 proposal to prohibit all military activity in space. The rejection was understandable because the Soviet Union had just launched the first artificial earth satellite, Sputnik, and was interested in deploying military reconnaissance satellites. In 1963, however, the Soviet Union signed the Limited Test Ban Treaty with the United States and Britain, prohibiting the explosion of nuclear weapons in the atmosphere, and in 1967 it became party to the Outer Space Treaty, which banned the deployment of nuclear weapons in earth orbit and on celestial bodies.

In March 1977, President Carter, concerned about Soviet resumption of antisatellite tests, called for talks about banning antisatellite (ASAT) weapons. Although the United States pressed for a comprehensive ban on such systems, the Soviet Union was unwilling to dismantle its operational ASAT in view of the heavy and still growing United States dependence on reconnaissance satellites.

After three rounds of negotiations, the talks were suspended in December 1979 after the Soviet Union invaded Afghanistan.

In international and bilateral forums, the Soviet Union tried to derail advanced space defense plans. In 1981, 1983, and 1984, the Soviet Union, anxious to prevent deployment of a United States ballistic missile defense system in space, submitted three separate draft treaties to the United Nations. Each treaty proposed to ban weapons stationed in orbit and intended to strike targets on earth, in the air, and in space. The treaties would have blocked the development of a space-based ABM system and precluded military use of vehicles like the space shuttle. In March 1985, bilateral talks on space and space weapons limitations between the United States and the Soviet Union opened in Geneva. In early 1989, the Soviet Union had not achieved its principal objective in the talks—to derail SDI.

Soviet Space Weapons Development

Since the Sputnik launch in 1957, the military potential of space has fascinated Soviet leaders. The 1962 and 1963 editions of Sokolovskii's *Military Strategy* advocated development of a military capability in space. In the late 1960s, the Soviet Union developed the fractional orbital bombardment system (FOBS)—a nuclear-armed space weapon with a depressed trajectory. The 1967 Outer Space Treaty neutralized the FOBS threat, but the Soviet Union retained an interest in undertaking offensive missions in space as part of its combined arms concept. In 1971 it acquired a ground-based orbital ASAT interceptor, the stated purpose of which was defensive but which could also attack satellites in near-earth orbit. The Soviet Union developed a variety of satellites that in 1989 were capable of reconnaissance, missile-launch detection, attack warning, command and control, and antisatellite functions. The Soviet Union also had impressive manned space programs with military implications, mostly aboard the Saliut and Mir space stations. In addition, by 1989 the Soviet Union had explored advanced space weapons, both defensive and offensive, using lasers, particle beams, radio frequencies, and kinetic energy. Although Soviet negotiators at the Geneva space talks portrayed Soviet space efforts as peaceful, in the late 1980s Soviet scientists and military strategists continued to study space in their search for new weapons and military options.

Intermediate-Range Nuclear Forces Arms Control

Intermediate-range nuclear forces (INF) are nuclear weapons systems with ranges between 500 and 5,500 kilometers. They could be used in a theater operation either at the outset of hostilities or after nuclear escalation on the battlefield. INF arms control became a Soviet concern in the 1980s, when United States nuclear missiles were deployed in Western Europe to offset new Soviet INF deployments on Soviet territory. Although the 1987 Intermediate-Range Nuclear Forces Treaty (INF Treaty) led to the dismantling of the most threatening, longer-range INF missiles, capable of hitting Soviet territory, Soviet strategists viewed complete denuclearization of Europe as the most desirable end of INF arms control.

Threat Reduction

Since the 1950s, the Soviet Union has viewed United States nuclear weapons deployed in Europe and capable of striking the Soviet Union as being particularly threatening. The Soviet military first formulated its preemptive nuclear strategy in the 1950s to neutralize the threat of United States strategic bombers armed with nuclear weapons and stationed in Europe. In 1979 NATO decided to offset Soviet deployments of the new intermediate-range SS-20 missiles by deploying new United States nuclear systems in Western Europe. These systems—108 Pershing II missiles and 464 ground-launched cruise missiles (GLCMs)—could reach Soviet territory. The Soviet military regarded both systems as a grave threat because of their high accuracy and because of the Pershing II's short flying time (under ten minutes). The Soviet Union asserted that both the Pershing IIs and the hard-to-detect GLCMs could make a surprise strike against the Soviet Union.

The Soviet Union tried both antinuclear propaganda and negotiations to forestall the NATO deployments. Formal negotiations began in November 1981, at which time the United States proposed the "global zero option," banning or eliminating all United States and Soviet longer-range intermediate nuclear forces (LRINF), including Soviet SS-4s, SS-5s, and SS-20s, and the United States Pershing IIs and GLCMs. The Soviet Union rejected the "global zero option" and insisted on including the British and French nuclear components in INF reductions.

In October 1986, at the Reykjavik Summit, the Soviet Union ceased insisting on including British and French weapons in an INF agreement. Nevertheless, it attempted to link an INF agreement to strategic arms reductions and to the renunciation of SDI. Only after Soviet negotiators abandoned all linkages and agreed to destroy all Soviet longer-range and shorter-range INF in Europe and Asia and to permit on-site inspection were they able to achieve their goal: the eventual removal of the Pershing IIs and GLCMs that are capable of reaching Soviet territory.

The INF Treaty, signed on December 8, 1987, in Washington by President Reagan and General Secretary Gorbachev, stipulated that each party would eliminate all of its intermediate-range missiles and their launchers. These missiles included Soviet SS-4, SS-5, SS-20 longer-range INF (with ranges between 1,000 and 5,500 kilometers), and SS-12 and SS-23 shorter-range missiles (with ranges between 500 and 1,000 kilometers). The treaty called for the destruction of about 2,700 United States and Soviet missiles.

Denuclearization of Europe

Since the 1950s, Soviet leaders have sought complete removal of nuclear weapons from Western Europe. Stripping Europe of nuclear weapons not only would reduce the nuclear threat on the Soviet periphery but also would make easier a Soviet conventional offensive in Europe. In 1988, even before the INF agreement had been ratified by the United States Senate, Soviet spokesmen were advocating removal of all nuclear weapons from Europe. They especially focused on NATO's tactical nuclear weapons arsenal, deployed mainly in the Federal Republic of Germany (West Germany).

In late 1987, Foreign Minister Shevardnadze asserted that on INF agreement was a step toward denuclearization and that its signing proved that "the Soviet Union and the United States have finally spoken together the first word in a nuclear-free vocabulary." Soviet and Soviet-sponsored denuclearization initiatives in Europe have included several proposals for a nuclear-weapon-free corridor in Central Europe (submitted between 1956 and 1987 by the Soviet Union, Poland, East Germany, and Czechoslovakia), as well as for nuclear-weapon-free zones in Northern Europe, the Balkans, and the Mediterranean. If such zones were established, the United States and NATO would have to withdraw nuclear weapons not only from Europe but also from the surrounding seas.

Conventional Arms Control

For many years, the Soviet Union could not reconcile conventional arms control with its military objectives of avoiding wars and being prepared to fight them. Soviet operational concepts have called for numerical superiority in conventional forces both to deter the adversary from starting a war and to destroy the adversary's forces and armaments and occupy its territory should a war break out. Yet deep reductions in Soviet armed forces have a precedent: Khrushchev reduced conventional forces by more than 2.1 million personnel between 1955 and 1958, and he announced further reductions of 1.2 million troops in 1960.

Since Khrushchev's ouster in 1964, the Soviet military has frowned on personnel reductions. In the 1960s, when United States secretary of state William Rogers suggested negotiations to reduce armed forces in Europe, the Soviet leaders resisted bitterly. They finally agreed to negotiate in exchange for United States participation in a European security conference. The Mutual Balanced Forces Reduction (MBFR) talks began in 1973 but remained stalemated for years. In the late 1960s and early 1970s, the Soviet conventional buildup in Europe progressed. Soviet leaders showed interest in the talks only in December 1975, when the Western proposal included a reduction in United States tactical nuclear weapons in Europe.

In 1987 the Soviet Union called for a new forum to discuss the balance of conventional forces in Europe "from the Atlantic to the Urals." Soviet leaders appeared to espouse the new Soviet strategic concepts of "reasonable sufficiency" and nonprovocative defense, and they maintained that reductions in conventional forces should make it impossible for either side to undertake offensive actions and launch surprise strikes. However, the Soviet military resisted a defensive concept because deep cuts in personnel and armaments such as tanks could prevent Soviet forces from pursuing their military objectives under the doctrine calling for victory.

In December 1988, Gorbachev announced unilateral reductions in Soviet armed forces. Soviet forces were to be reduced by 500,000 men by 1991. Soviet forces in the Atlantic-to-the-Urals area were to be reduced by 10,000 tanks, 8,500 artillery pieces, and 800 combat aircraft. Several Soviet tank divisions were to be withdrawn from Eastern Europe, together with assault-landing and assault-river-crossing units. Soviet and East European divisions were to be reorganized, with a major cutback in the number of tanks. During 1988 and 1989, the Non-Soviet Warsaw Pact (NSWP) countries also announced unilateral reductions in manpower and conventional armaments.

In 1989 the Soviet leadership appeared to be interested in negotiating seriously on conventional arms control in order to reduce the threat of new Western weapons and operational concepts, to create a "breathing space" for internal economic and social restructuring, and to divert manpower and resources to the country's economy. New negotiations on Conventional Forces in Europe (CFE) opened in March 1989. Both Warsaw Pact and NATO negotiators expressed interest in stabilizing the strategic situation in Europe by eliminating capabilities for initiating surprise attacks and large-scale offensive actions.

Although Gorbachev proclaimed his commitment to a doctrine that emphasized war avoidance, diplomacy, and the achievement of political goals with political means, the Soviet military continued to press for high-quality military capabilities, commensurate with perceived present and future threats to Soviet national security. Soviet military authorities endorsed Gorbachev's arms control efforts as well as the concepts of parity and "reasonable sufficiency." Nevertheless, they supported Gorbachev's pragmatic policies largely in the hope that a renewed economy would help create a modern industrial base. Such a base, they believed, would make it possible not merely to counter Western emerging technologies but also to produce fundamentally new weapons for the twenty-first century.

A transformation of NATO and of the Warsaw Pact, as proposed by Soviet leaders in 1989, would necessitate that both sides adopt a defensive, no-victory doctrine, stressing negotiations and restoration of the status quo. On the Soviet side, this would call for rejecting or circumventing Marxist-Leninist dogma and for revising political goals. Only then could the rewriting of Soviet military art yield a strategy, operational art, and tactics based on genuinely defensive principles, excluding deep offensive operations, massive counteroffensives, and the requisite capabilities. In 1989, however, Soviet military doctrine still bore the burden of Marxist-Leninist revolutionary ideology predicting the eventual worldwide ascendancy of socialism.

* * *

Most original sources on Soviet military doctrine, policy, and strategy are available only in Russian. However, a good introduction to Soviet military thought, *The Soviet Art of War,* edited by Harriet F. Scott and William F. Scott, is a judicious combination of the editors' commentaries and of excerpts from translated writings of Soviet military authorities. Paul D. Kelley's *Soviet General Doctrine for War,* a 1987 publication of the United States Army Intelligence and Threat Analysis Center (USAITAC), contains a detailed treatment of Soviet military doctrine and military science. Students of Soviet tactics should also consider William P. Baxter's *The Soviet Way of Warfare,* in which the author discusses the offensive and defensive options of Soviet tactical combat. Michael MccGwire's *Military Objectives in Soviet Foreign Policy* offers a comprehensive overview of Soviet strategic and military objectives and of Soviet operational planning. Finally, the annual Department of

Defense publication *Soviet Military Power* presents the official United States Department of Defense view of Soviet military developments.

For the reader who would like to study Soviet military thought, the United States Air Force series of translations of Soviet military monographs is invaluable. Among the most illuminating and thought-provoking in the series are the 1972 translation of the 1968 classic, *Marxism-Leninism on War and the Army,* and the controversial *Basic Principles of Operational Art and Tactics* by V.E. Savkin. Although the heavy emphasis on nuclear weapons in both works appeared outdated in the 1980s, the doctrinal tenets and many of the strategic and operational concepts remained valid. *Scientific-Technical Progress and the Revolution in Military Affairs,* edited by N.A. Lomov and published in 1973, is an important reminder that nuclear weapons were only a stage in the technological revolution and that other revolutionary developments may follow. (For further information and complete citations, see Bibliography.)

Chapter 18. Armed Forces and Defense Organization

Facets of the armed forces

IN 1988 THE ARMED FORCES of the Soviet Union celebrated their seventieth anniversary. As old as the Soviet state, they have been highly integrated into its political, economic, and social systems. The missions of the Soviet armed forces were to defend the Soviet Union and its socialist (see Glossary) allies, to ensure favorable conditions for the development of the world socialist system (see Glossary), and to assist the national liberation movements around the world. The armed forces have defended communist parties that dominated Soviet-allied socialist countries as well as the Soviet Union. They also have projected military power abroad to help pro-Soviet forces gain or maintain political power. Thus, the armed forces have provided the military might that is the basis of the Soviet Union's claim to be a superpower with global interests. To ensure that the military pursues these largely political objectives, the Communist Party of the Soviet Union (CPSU) controlled the armed forces through a combination of political indoctrination, co-optation, and party supervision at every level.

The Soviet armed forces, the world's largest military establishment, in 1989 had nearly 6 million troops in uniform. The armed forces had five armed services rather than the standard army, navy, and air force organizations found in most of the world's armed forces. In their official order of importance, the Soviet armed services were the Strategic Rocket Forces, Ground Forces, Air Forces, Air Defense Forces, and Naval Forces. The Soviet armed forces also included two paramilitary forces, the Internal Troops and the Border Troops.

The Soviet Union has always been a militarized state. One-fourth of the entire Soviet population in 1989 was engaged in military activities, whether active duty, military production, or civilian military training. Yet the sheer size of the armed forces has not translated directly into combat power. Manpower, training, logistics, equipment, and economic problems combined to limit the operational effectiveness of Soviet forces. Many servicemen were assigned nonmilitary duties that in many other countries were performed by civilians.

Organizational Development and Combat Experience

Immediately after the Bolshevik Revolution of 1917, the Bolsheviks (see Glossary) merged their 20,000-man army, the Red Guards, with 200,000 Baltic Fleet sailors and Petrograd garrison soldiers who supported the Bolsheviks. Bolshevik leader Vladimir I. Lenin decreed the establishment of the Workers' and Peasants' Red Army on January 28, 1918, and Leon Trotsky was the first commissar of war. The Bolsheviks recognized the importance of building an army under their control; without a loyal army, the Bolshevik organization itself would have been unable to hold the power it had seized.

The early Red Army was egalitarian but poorly disciplined. The Bolsheviks considered military ranks and saluting to be bourgeois customs and abolished them. Soldiers elected their own leaders and voted on which orders to follow. This arrangement was abolished, however, under pressure of the Civil War (1918–21), and ranks were reinstated (see Civil War and War Communism, ch. 2).

Because most professional officers had joined the anti-Bolshevik, or White, forces, the Red Army initially faced a shortage of experienced military leaders. To remedy this situation, the Bolsheviks recruited 50,000 former Imperial Army officers to command the Red Army. At the same time, they attached political commissars to Red Army units to monitor the actions of professional commanders and their allegiance to the Russian Communist Party (Bolshevik), the name of the Bolshevik organization as of March 1918. By 1921 the Red Army had defeated four White armies and held off five armed, foreign contingents that had intervened in the Civil War.

After the Civil War, the Red Army became an increasingly professional military organization. With most of its 5 million soldiers demobilized, the Red Army was transformed into a small regular force, and territorial militias were created for wartime mobilization. Soviet military schools, established during the Civil War, began to graduate large numbers of trained officers loyal to the party. In an effort to increase the prestige of the military profession, the party downgraded political commissars, established the principle of one-man command, and reestablished formal military ranks.

During the 1930s, Soviet leader Joseph V. Stalin's five-year plans and industrialization drive built the productive base necessary to modernize the Red Army. As the likelihood of war in Europe increased later in the decade, the Soviet Union tripled its military expenditures and doubled the size of its regular forces to match the power of its potential enemies. In 1937, however, Stalin purged the Red Army and deprived it of its best military leaders (see The Period of the Purges, ch. 2). Fearing or imagining that the military posed a challenge to his rule, Stalin jailed or executed an estimated 30,000 Red Army officers, including three of five marshals and 90 percent of all field grade officers. Stalin also restored the former dual command authority of political commissars in Red Army units. These actions were to severely impair the Red Army's capabilities in the Soviet-Finnish War of 1939–40 and in World War II.

After occupying the Baltic states and eastern Poland under the terms of the Nazi-Soviet Nonaggression Pact of 1939, the Soviet Union demanded territorial concessions from Finland in late 1939 (see Foreign Policy, 1928–39, ch. 2). When the Finnish government refused, the Red Army invaded Finland. The resulting war was a disaster for the Soviet Union. Although the Soviet Union has not published casualty statistics, about 100,000 Red Army troops are believed to have died in the process of overcoming the small, poorly equipped Finnish army.

The Red Army had little time to correct its numerous deficiencies before Adolf Hitler launched Operation Barbarossa, which began his war against the Soviet Union, on June 22, 1941. At the beginning of the Great Patriotic War (see Glossary), the Red Army was forced to retreat, trading territory for time. But it managed to halt the Wehrmacht's blitzkrieg in December 1941 at the gates of Moscow. In 1942 the Wehrmacht launched a new offensive through the Volga region aimed at seizing Soviet oil resources in the Caucasus. At this critical moment, Stalin reinstituted one-man command and gave his field commanders more operational independence. The Red Army encircled and destroyed German forces in the city of Stalingrad in a battle that ended in February 1943. In the summer of 1943, the Red Army seized the strategic initiative, and it liberated all Soviet territory from German occupation during 1944. After having driven the German army out of Eastern Europe, in May 1945 the Red Army launched the final assault on Berlin that ended the Great Patriotic War. The Red Army emerged from the war as the most powerful land army in history. (After the war, the army was known as the Soviet army.) The defeat of the Wehrmacht had come, however, at the cost of 7 million military and 13 million civilian deaths among the Soviet population.

From the late 1940s to the late 1960s, the Soviet armed forces focused on adapting to the changed nature of warfare in the era of nuclear arms and achieving parity with the United States in strategic nuclear weapons. Conventional military power showed its continued importance, however, when the Soviet Union used its troops to invade Hungary in 1956 and Czechoslovakia in 1968 to keep these countries within the Soviet alliance system (see Appendix C). In the 1970s, the Soviet Union began to modernize its conventional warfare and power projection capabilities. At the same time, it became more involved in regional conflicts or local wars (see Glossary) than ever before. The Soviet Union supplied arms and sent military advisers to a variety of Third World allies in Africa, Asia, and the Middle East. Soviet generals planned military operations against rebels in Angola and Ethiopia. Soviet troops, however, saw little combat action until the invasion of Afghanistan in December 1979. They fought a counterinsurgency against the Afghan rebels, or *mujahidin*, for nearly eight and one-half years. An estimated 15,000 Soviet soldiers had been killed and 35,000 wounded in the conflict by the time Soviet forces began to withdraw from Afghanistan in May 1988. All 110,000 Soviet troops deployed in Afghanistan had been withdrawn by February 1989, according to Soviet authorities.

Strategic Leadership of the Armed Forces

Four main organizations controlled the Soviet armed forces. The Defense Council, which included the highest party and military officials in the Soviet Union, was the supreme decision-making body on national security issues. The Main Military Council, the Ministry of Defense, and the General Staff were strictly military organizations.

Defense Council

The Soviet Constitution states that the Presidium of the Supreme Soviet forms the Defense Council. First mentioned by the Soviet press in 1976, the Defense Council has been the organ through which the CPSU Central Committee, the Supreme Soviet, and the Council of Ministers supposedly exercised supreme leadership of the armed forces and national defense. In reality, these bodies carried out the Defense Council's decisions on issues concerning the armed forces and national defense.

The general secretary of the CPSU has normally been the chairman of the Defense Council and the only member of the Defense Council identified in the Soviet media. As chairman of the Defense Council, the general secretary has also been the supreme commander in chief of the Soviet armed forces. The chairman of the Council of Ministers, the chairman of the Committee for State Security (Komitet gosudarstvennoi bezopasnosti—KGB), the minister of internal affairs, the minister of foreign affairs, and the minister of defense have also probably served as members of the Defense Council. Their official duties have enabled them to implement decisions reached in the Defense Council. The Defense Council has been described as a working group of the Politburo, and its decisions have probably been subject to ratification by a vote in a full meeting of the Politburo.

The Defense Council has made decisions on political-military and military-economic issues, using analyses and recommendations it received from the Main Military Council, the Ministry of Defense, and the General Staff. The Defense Council, according to some Western authorities, would approve changes in military doctrine and strategy, large operations, the commitment of troops abroad, and the use of nuclear weapons. It has decided on major changes in the organizational structure of the armed services and the appointment or dismissal of high-ranking officers. In addition, the Defense Council has been the highest link between the economy and the military, which were also intertwined at lower levels. The Defense Council has determined the size of the military budget. It has approved new weapons systems and coordinated the activities of the Ministry of Defense with those of ministries and state committees engaged in military research, development, and production.

Main Military Council

The Main Military Council was made up of the top leadership of the Ministry of Defense. The minister of defense was its chairman. The three first deputy ministers of defense, the eleven deputy ministers of defense, and the chief of the Main Political Directorate of the Soviet Army and Navy were members of the Main Military Council.

In peacetime the Main Military Council has been responsible for the training, readiness status, and mobilization of the armed forces. It coordinated the activities of the five armed services and resolved interservice disputes over the allocation of roles and missions, material resources, and manpower. The Main Military Council also presented the Defense Council with the economic and budgetary requirements of the armed forces, based on the force structure proposed by the General Staff and the armed services.

In wartime the Main Military Council would become the headquarters (*stavka*) of the Supreme High Command (Verkhovnoe glavnokomandovanie—VGK) of the armed forces. The Main Military Council would then report through the minister of defense to the supreme commander in chief and the Defense Council. The Supreme High Command would control military operations through the General Staff and subordinate commands.

Ministry of Defense

The Ministry of Defense, an all-union ministry (see Glossary), was technically subordinate to the Council of Ministers, as well

701

as to the Supreme Soviet and the CPSU Central Committee. In 1989 it was, however, larger than most other ministries and had special arrangements for party supervision of, and state participation in, its activities. The Ministry of Defense was made up of the General Staff, the Main Political Directorate of the Soviet Army and Navy, the Warsaw Pact, the five armed services, and the main and central directorates (see fig. 28). The minister of defense has always been either a leading CPSU civilian official or a Ground Forces general; the position has presumably been filled on the recommendation of the Defense Council with the approval of the Politburo, although the Presidium of the Supreme Soviet has made the formal announcement. The three first deputy ministers of defense were the chief of the General Staff, the commander in chief of the Warsaw Pact, and another senior officer with unspecified duties. First deputy ministers of defense have also been selected from the Ground Forces. In 1989 the eleven deputy ministers of defense included the commanders in chief of the five armed services as well as the chiefs of Civil Defense, Rear Services, Construction and Troop Billeting, Armaments, the Main Personnel Directorate, and the Main Inspectorate.

The Ministry of Defense directed the five armed services and all military activities on a daily basis. It was responsible for fielding, arming, and supplying the armed services, and in peacetime all territorial commands of the armed forces reported to it. The Ministry of Defense has been staffed almost entirely by professional military personnel, and it has had a monopoly on military information because the Soviet Union has lacked independent defense research organizations frequently found in other countries. This monopoly has given high-ranking Soviet officers undisputed influence with party and government leaders on issues, ranging from arms control to weapons development to arms sales abroad, that affect the position and prestige of the armed forces.

General Staff

The General Staff has been the center of professional military thought in the Soviet Union. Like the Ministry of Defense, the General Staff has been dominated by the Ground Forces. In 1989 the chief, two first deputy chiefs, and three deputy chiefs of the General Staff were all Ground Forces officers. The General Staff had five main directorates and four directorates. They performed strategic and operational research and planning, provided strategic military intelligence and analysis to the Defense Council, dealt with foreign military attachés, and gave occasional press briefings on political-military issues.

In wartime the General Staff would become the executive agent of the Supreme High Command, supervising the execution of military strategy and operations by subordinate commands. The General Staff would exercise direct control over the three combat arms of the armed forces that operate strategic nuclear weapons and would coordinate the activities and missions of the five armed services.

The Armed Services

The general organization of the Strategic Rocket Forces, Ground Forces, Air Forces, Air Defense Forces, and Naval Forces at the command level paralleled the organization of the Ministry of Defense. The commander in chief of an armed service was an administrative rather than an operational commander. He equipped, trained, and supplied the forces of the service, but operational control rested with the Defense Council and was exercised through the General Staff.

Each armed service had two first deputy commanders in chief, one of whom was chief of the main staff for the service (see fig. 29). The other had unspecified duties. The deputy commanders in chief were numerous. They commanded the combat arms and other branches of the service. Some deputy commanders in chief were responsible for premilitary and combat training, military education institutions, rear services, or armaments for the service as a whole. The armed services also had deputy commanders in chief with specialized duties. For example, the Strategic Rocket Forces had a deputy commander in chief for rocket engineering. Other deputy commanders in chief had responsibilities that were unknown to Western observers. The commander in chief, first deputy commanders in chief, and deputy commanders in chief, together with the chief of the service's political directorate, represented the military council or top leadership of the service.

The main staff of each service planned the operational employment of its service in coordination with the General Staff in the Ministry of Defense. In peacetime the main staff controlled the territorial commands or components of a service.

Strategic Rocket Forces

The Strategic Rocket Forces, the newest Soviet armed service, in 1989 were the preeminent armed service, based on the continued importance of their mission. Their prestige had diminished somewhat, however, because of an increasing emphasis on conventional forces.

The Strategic Rocket Forces were the main Soviet force used for attacking an enemy's offensive nuclear weapons, its military

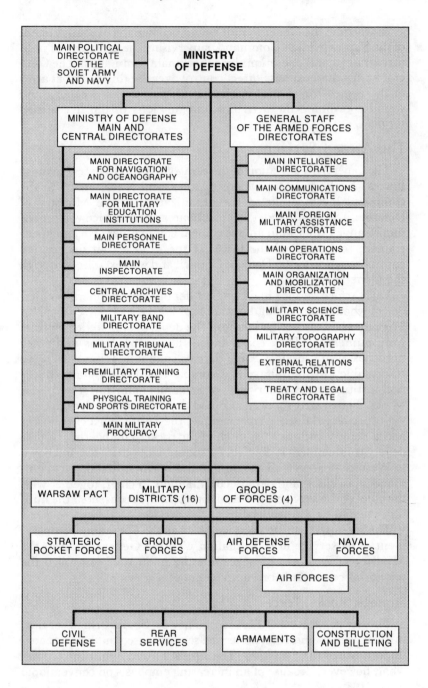

Figure 28. Organization of the Ministry of Defense, 1988

facilities, and its industrial infrastructure. They operated all Soviet ground-based intercontinental, intermediate-range, and medium-range nuclear missiles with ranges over 1,000 kilometers. The Strategic Rocket Forces also conducted all Soviet space vehicle and missile launches.

In 1989 the 300,000 Soviet soldiers in the Strategic Rocket Forces were organized into six rocket armies comprised of three to five divisions, which contained regiments of ten missile launchers each. Each missile regiment had 400 soldiers in security, transportation, and maintenance units above ground. Officers manned launch stations and command posts underground.

In 1989 the Strategic Rocket Forces had over 1,400 intercontinental ballistic missiles (ICBMs), 300 launch control centers, and twenty-eight missile bases. The Soviet Union had six types of operational ICBMs; about 50 percent were heavy SS-18 and SS-19 ICBMs, which carried 80 percent of the country's land-based ICBM warheads. In 1989 the Soviet Union was also producing new mobile, and hence survivable, ICBMs. A reported 100 road-mobile SS-25 missiles were operational, and the rail-mobile SS-24 was being deployed.

The Strategic Rocket Forces also operated SS-20 intermediate-range ballistic missiles (IRBMs) and SS-4 medium-range ballistic missiles (MRBMs). Two-thirds of the road-mobile Soviet SS-20 force was based in the western Soviet Union and was aimed at Western Europe. One-third was located east of the Ural Mountains and was targeted primarily against China. Older SS-4 missiles were deployed at fixed sites in the western Soviet Union. The Intermediate-Range Nuclear Forces Treaty (INF Treaty), signed in December 1987, called for the elimination of all 553 Soviet SS-20 and SS-4 missiles within three years (see Intermediate-Range Nuclear Forces Arms Control, ch. 17). As of mid-1989, over 50 percent of the SS-20 and SS-4 missiles had been eliminated.

Ground Forces

Despite its position as the second service in the armed forces hierarchy, the Ground Forces were the most politically influential Soviet service. Senior Ground Forces officers held all important posts within the Ministry of Defense as well as the General Staff. In 1989 the Ground Forces had 2 million men, organized into four combat arms and three supporting services.

Motorized Rifle Troops and Tank Troops

Combat elements of the Ground Forces were organized into combined arms and tank armies. A combined arms army included

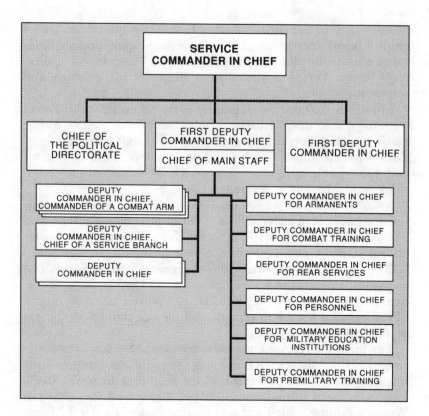

Figure 29. Typical Organization of an Armed Service, 1988

three motorized rifle divisions and a tank division. A tank army had three tank divisions and one motorized rifle division. In the late 1980s, the Ground Forces began to field corps that were more than twice the size of a single division. In 1989 the Soviet Union had 150 motorized rifle and 52 tank divisions in three states of readiness (see Glossary). A motorized rifle division had 12,000 soldiers organized into three motorized rifle regiments, a tank regiment, an artillery regiment, an air defense regiment, surface-to-surface missile and antitank battalions, and supporting chemical, engineer, signal, reconnaissance, and rear services companies. A typical tank division had 10,000 soldiers organized into three tank regiments and one motorized rifle regiment. In 1989 the Ground Forces also included eight brigades of air assault, or air-mobile, units that conducted helicopter landing operations.

The Motorized Rifle Troops have been mechanized infantry since 1957. The Soviet Union has fielded a new model of armored personnel carrier (APC) every decade since the late 1950s, and in 1967 it deployed the world's first infantry fighting vehicle (IFV). Similar to an APC, the tactically innovative IFV had much greater firepower, in the form of a 73mm main gun, an antitank missile launcher, a heavy machine gun, and firing ports that allowed troops to fire their individual weapons from inside the vehicle. In 1989 the Soviet Union had an inventory of over 65,000 APCs and IFVs, with the latter accounting for almost half of this inventory.

The Soviet Ground Forces viewed the tank as their primary weapon. In 1989 the Tank Troops had five types of main battle tanks, including the T-54/55, T-62, T-64, T-72, and T-80. The greater part of the total tank inventory of 53,000 consisted of older, although still highly potent, T-54/55 and T-62 tanks.

Rocket Troops and Artillery

The Rocket Troops and Artillery have been an important combat arm of the Ground Forces because of the Soviet belief that firepower has tremendous destructive and psychological effect on the enemy. In 1989 the Ground Forces had eighteen artillery divisions, in addition to the artillery and missile units organic to armies and divisions. Artillery and surface-to-surface missile brigades were attached to each combined arms or tank army. An artillery regiment and a surface-to-surface missile battalion were parts of each Soviet motorized rifle and tank division. In 1989 the Rocket Troops and Artillery manned 1,400 "operational-tactical" surface-to-surface missile launchers.

The December 1987 INF Treaty between the United States and the Soviet Union called for the elimination of all short-range ballistic missiles with ranges between 500 and 1,000 kilometers. The treaty required the elimination of more than 900 Soviet SS-12 and SS-23 missiles. As of mid-1989, all SS-12 missiles had been eliminated. All SS-23 missiles had to be eliminated before the end of 1989, according to the terms of the treaty. After the reductions mandated in the treaty, the Soviet battlefield missile inventory will still contain over 1,000 modern SS-21 missiles with a range of about 100 kilometers that were not covered in the treaty as well as older SS-1 missiles, a large number of unguided free rocket over ground (FROG) missiles, and Scud missiles. These tactical missiles can deliver nuclear or chemical weapons as well as conventional munitions.

In 1989 the Rocket Troops and Artillery had approximately 30,000 artillery pieces; of these, 10,000 were capable of firing conventional high-explosive, nuclear, or chemical rounds. Since the 1970s, this powerful combat arm has fielded more than 5,000 self-propelled 122mm and 152mm howitzers, 152mm and 203mm guns, and 240mm mortars. These artillery pieces, which are mounted on tank chassis, have replaced some towed artillery pieces. The Rocket Troops and Artillery also had truck-mounted multiple rocket launchers, each with forty tubes, to provide massive fire support for the Ground Forces.

Air Defense of Ground Forces

The Ground Forces relinquished control of air defense for their field formations in 1948 when the National Air Defense Forces—later renamed the Air Defense Forces—became an independent armed service. In 1958, however, Soviet air defense was decentralized again, and the Ground Forces acquired antiaircraft guns and formed tactical air defense units. In the 1960s, air defense became an integral combat arm of the Ground Forces. Since then, Air Defense of Ground Forces has been independent from the Air Defense Forces, although coordination of their respective operations remained necessary.

Air Defense of Ground Forces was equipped with a potent mix of antiaircraft artillery as well as surface-to-air missiles to defend Ground Forces units against attacking enemy aircraft. During the 1970s, the Soviet military introduced five new self-propelled air defense and radar systems into its force structure. In 1989 Air Defense of Ground Forces operated 5,000 surface-to-air missiles and 12,000 antiaircraft guns organized into brigades, regiments, and batteries. As of 1989, combined arms and tank armies had air defense brigades equipped with high-altitude SA-4 surface-to-air missiles. Motorized rifle and tank divisions had air defense regiments with the mobile SA-6 or SA-8 for medium- to low-level protection. Ground Forces regiments had SA-9, SA-13, and ZSU-23-4 antiaircraft gun batteries. Motorized rifle and tank battalions had surface-to-air missile platoons equipped with new low-altitude, shoulder-fired SA-16 and older SA-7 missiles.

Chemical Troops, Engineer Troops, and Signal Troops

The Chemical Troops, Engineer Troops, and Signal Troops were independent branches that provided support to all the military services, but principally to the Ground Forces. The chiefs of these services reported directly to the minister of defense. Units of the Chemical Troops, Engineer Troops, and Signal Troops responded to the in-branch chief regarding administrative and technical matters but were operationally subordinate to the commander of the formation to which they were attached. Chemical Troops, Engineer

708

T-72 tank
Courtesy United States Defense Intelligence Agency

Troops, and Signal Troops were organized into battalions and companies within armies and divisions.

The general mission of the supporting troops was to facilitate the advance of the Ground Forces and to eliminate obstacles blocking their path. The Signal Troops operated tactical radio and wire communications networks and intercepted enemy signals for combat intelligence purposes. They also operated strategic underground cable, microwave, and satellite communications systems. The Engineer Troops were principally combat engineers. They operated the self-propelled bridging vehicles and amphibious ferries that tanks and armored vehicles depend on to cross deep rivers. In wartime the Engineer Troops would also clear mines, antivehicle obstacles, and battlefield debris for the Ground Forces.

The mission of the Chemical Troops was to defend the armed forces against the effects of "weapons of mass destruction"— nuclear, biological, and chemical (NBC) weapons. With 50,000 soldiers in 1989, the Chemical Troops constituted the world's largest NBC defense force. The Chemical Troops would perform NBC reconnaissance; mark contaminated areas; and decontaminate personnel, weapons, and terrain during wartime. They operated 30,000 armored combat vehicles equipped for NBC reconnaissance and truck-mounted systems equipped to spray decontaminating solutions on the surface areas of tanks, combat vehicles, and aircraft. The Chemical Troops demonstrated the use of helicopters for NBC defense during the large-scale radiation cleanup operation after the Chernobyl' (see Glossary) nuclear reactor accident in April 1986. In 1989 the Chemical Troops did not operate offensive delivery systems. Yet the strength of Soviet chemical defense provided an offensive potential by enhancing the ability of Soviet forces to fight on contaminated battlefields. Thus, supported by the Chemical Troops, Soviet forces were better prepared than any other in the world for NBC operations.

Air Forces

In 1989 the Air Forces had 450,000 personnel in three combat arms and one supporting branch, the Aviation Engineering Service. The Air Forces also provided and trained prospective cosmonauts for the Soviet space program. Air Forces personnel operated all military aircraft except aircraft belonging to the Air Defense Forces and the Naval Forces. In 1989 the Air Forces were organized into air armies consisting of several air divisions. Each air division had three air regiments with three squadrons of about twelve aircraft each.

Strategic Air Armies

The Strategic Air Armies were organized in the late 1970s from elements of Long-Range Aviation. Their mission was to attack the enemy's strategic delivery systems and infrastructure, including missile and bomber bases. The Strategic Air Armies were organized into five air armies of bomber aircraft of several types. In 1989 these included Tu-95 long-range strategic bombers, a type first deployed in the late 1950s and continuously upgraded since then. Since the early 1980s, more than seventy of these bombers have been modified to carry air-launched cruise missiles (ALCMs). A new intercontinental-range bomber, the Tu-160, which also bears the North Atlantic Treaty Organization (NATO) designation Blackjack, became operational in 1989. In the late 1980s, long-range bombers carried a small, but increasing, percentage of all Soviet strategic nuclear weapons.

Although its name implies an intercontinental mission, most Strategic Air Armies aircraft were medium- and short-range bombers. In 1989 the Soviet Union had Tu-16, Tu-22, and Tu-26 medium-range bombers. The Tu-16 and Tu-22 aircraft entered service in large numbers in the early 1960s. The Tu-26, sometimes called the Tu-22M and designated the Backfire bomber, was first fielded in 1974. In 1989 the Strategic Air Armies also included Su-24 fighter-bombers, which had a combat radius of over 1,000 kilometers. Medium-range bombers and fighter-bombers would support military operations by striking the enemy's nuclear delivery systems, airfields, air defense systems, and command, control, and communications facilities in a theater of war.

Frontal Aviation

Frontal Aviation was the Soviet Union's tactical air force assigned to the military districts and the groups of forces. Its mission was to provide air support to Ground Forces units. Frontal Aviation cooperated closely with the Air Defense Aviation arm of the Air Defense Forces. Protected by the latter's fighter-interceptors, Frontal Aviation in wartime would deliver conventional, nuclear, or chemical ordnance on the enemy's supply lines and troop concentrations to interdict its combat operations. It would be under the operational control of Ground Forces field commanders. In 1989 Frontal Aviation was divided into sixteen air armies composed of fighter, fighter-bomber, tactical reconnaissance, and electronic warfare aircraft.

In 1989 Frontal Aviation operated about 5,000 fixed- and rotary-wing combat and reconnaissance aircraft, which included 270 Su-25, 650 Su-17, and 1,050 MiG-27 ground attack aircraft. It also operated 450 MiG-29 and 350 Su-24 deep interdiction fighter-bombers, in addition to the 450 that belonged to the Strategic Air Armies. The Air Forces used the heavily armed Su-25, first deployed in 1979, effectively during the early years of the war in Afghanistan when *mujahidin* forces lacked modern air defense systems.

During the 1980s, the Soviet Union doubled the size of its force of helicopters. Helicopter regiments and squadrons were attached to Frontal Aviation's air armies to provide tactical mobility for, and additional fire support to, the Ground Forces. The Mi-6, Mi-8, and Mi-26 helicopters would transport motorized rifle units and equipment into battle or land assault units behind enemy lines. The Mi-24, often referred to as the Hind, was the most heavily armed helicopter in the world. It was used extensively in both fire support and air assault roles in Afghanistan. In 1989 the Soviet Union was testing a new helicopter, the Mi-28, designed to be an antitank helicopter.

Military Transport Aviation

Military Transport Aviation provided rapid strategic mobility for the armed forces. Its missions were to transport the Airborne Troops for rapid intervention by parachute and to supply and

711

resupply Soviet forces abroad, and deliver arms and military equipment to Soviet allies around the world. In 1989 Military Transport Aviation had five air divisions, including 200 An-12, 55 An-22, 340 Il-76, and 5 An-124 transport aircraft. Having entered service only in 1987, the An-124 was the first Soviet transport that could lift outsized equipment such as main battle tanks.

In addition to these military transports, in wartime the 1,600 aircraft of Aeroflot, the national airline, would be used to augment the capabilities of Military Transport Aviation (see table 46, Appendix A). For this reason, the Ministry of Civil Aviation closely coordinated its activities with the General Staff and the Air Forces. Aeroflot flight crews, for example, were reserve officers of the Air Forces. Moreover, in 1989 the minister of civil aviation was an active-duty general officer.

Military Transport Aviation assumed a high-profile role in foreign policy in the 1970s when it airlifted weapons to such allies as Egypt, Syria, Ethiopia, and Angola. In December 1979, its transport aircraft flew 150 sorties to drop and land an Airborne Troops division and its equipment into Afghanistan. Western analysts estimated that Military Transport Aviation can lift one Airborne Troops division a distance of 4,000 kilometers. With Aeroflot transports and passenger aircraft, three divisions can be lifted at once.

Air Defense Forces

The National Air Defense Forces became a separate armed service in 1948 and were given the mission of defending the Soviet industrial, military, and administrative centers and the armed forces against strategic bombing. After Air Defense of Ground Forces was formed in 1958, the National Air Defense Forces focused on strategic aerospace and theater air defense. Around 1980 the National Air Defense Forces yielded responsibility for theater antiaircraft systems to Air Defense of Ground Forces and was renamed the Air Defense Forces. In 1989 the Air Defense Forces had more than 500,000 personnel and operated the world's most extensive strategic air defense network.

Antiaircraft Rocket Troops and Air Defense Aviation

In 1989 the Antiaircraft Rocket Troops manned 12,000 strategic surface-to-air missile launchers at 1,400 sites inside the Soviet Union. These forces were organized into brigades of launch battalions. Soviet SA-3 and SA-5 antiaircraft missiles, first produced in the 1960s, together with older SA-1 and SA-2 missiles, constituted over 90 percent of the Soviet surface-to-air missile inventory. In the late 1980s, the new SA-10 was entering service to replace

MiG-23 fighter aircraft armed with antiaircraft missiles
Courtesy United States Navy
Scud-B ballistic missile on a transporter-erector-launcher
Courtesy United States Defense Intelligence Agency

SA-1 and SA-2 missiles. The Soviet Union also had another anti-aircraft missile, the SA-12, under development. Western authorities believed the SA-10 and SA-12 had improved capabilities to destroy aircraft and missiles at low altitudes. In support of the Air Defense Forces, the Radiotechnical Troops operated 10,000 ground-based air surveillance radars for surface-to-air missile operations. In addition, the air defense systems of the Warsaw Pact countries were highly integrated into the Soviet network, effectively extending the range of Soviet early warning capabilities.

The other combat arm of the Air Defense Forces, Air Defense Aviation, had the mission of preventing aircraft and cruise missiles from entering Soviet airspace. In wartime it would strive to establish air superiority and provide air cover for Frontal Aviation's deep strike and ground attack aircraft. In 1989 Air Defense Aviation had 2,000 fighter-interceptor aircraft organized into air regiments. The Su-15, MiG-23, and MiG-25, first produced in the late 1960s and early 1970s, constituted 80 percent of Air Defense Aviation's inventory. The Soviet Union's newest interceptors, the MiG-31 and Su-27, deployed in the early 1980s, represented 10 percent of the force in 1989. The MiG-29, which first appeared in 1984, may also eventually be deployed with Air Defense Aviation. These new fighter-interceptors had "look-down, shoot-down" radars for engaging aircraft and cruise missiles penetrating Soviet airspace at low altitudes. Since the mid-1980s, the Soviet Union has built four new airborne warning and control system (AWACS) aircraft on an Il-76 airframe. These AWACS aircraft have improved Air Defense Aviation's ability to direct interceptors against enemy bombers, fighters, and cruise missiles in aerial combat.

Although equipped with numerous modern weapons systems, the Air Defense Forces have made operational errors that have raised serious questions about their command, control, and communications systems and training. In September 1983, Soviet interceptors shot down a South Korean passenger jet that strayed into Soviet airspace over Sakhalin. In May 1987, Mathias Rust, a citizen of the Federal Republic of Germany (West Germany), flew his private airplane into Soviet airspace and landed in Red Square in Moscow. As a result, the commander in chief of the Air Defense Forces, a former fighter pilot, was fired and replaced with a high-ranking Ground Forces officer who had extensive combined arms experience.

Missile and Space Defenses

Missile and space defenses have been effective arms of the Air Defense Forces since the mid-1960s. In 1989 the Soviet Union had the world's only operational antiballistic missile (ABM) and anti-satellite (ASAT) systems.

The Soviet Union deployed its first ABM defense system around Moscow in 1964. It consisted of surface-to-air missiles that could be launched to destroy incoming ballistic missiles. The Soviet leaders have continually upgraded and developed the capabilities of this initial system. A major modernization of interceptor missiles began in the late 1970s, and by 1989 the Soviet Union had up to thirty-two improved SH–04 launchers in operation and a fundamentally new SH–08 interceptor missile under development. The newest SA–10 and SA–12 surface-to-air missiles reportedly also had a limited capability to destroy cruise, tactical, and possibly even strategic ballistic missiles. Such a capability would tend to blur the distinction between missile defense and strategic air defense systems.

In 1989 the Radiotechnical Troops operated eleven ground-based radars and numerous satellites to provide strategic early warning of enemy missile launches. They also manned six large phased-array radars for ballistic missile detection. These radars could also serve as target acquisition and tracking radars to guide ABM launchers as part of a nationwide defense against ballistic missiles. In 1989 the Soviet Union was building three additional sites for phased-array radars.

The Soviet Union has had an operational ASAT interceptor system since 1966. In wartime it would launch a satellite into the same orbit as an opponent's satellite. The ASAT satellite would then maneuver nearby and detonate a conventional fragmentation or a nuclear warhead to destroy its target. Thus, the interceptor system has posed a threat to an adversary's command, control, and communications, navigation, reconnaissance, and intelligence-gathering satellites in low-earth orbits, a capability that would be critical in wartime.

By 1989 the Soviet Union was spending an estimated US$1 billion annually on scientific research into advanced technologies with potentially great ASAT and ABM applications, including ground-based laser, particle beam, radio frequency, and kinetic energy weapons. Soviet space programs also served Soviet missile and space defenses. In 1989 the Soviet effort in space was a broad-based one that included approximately 100 launches yearly, development of a reusable space shuttle and a spacecraft, and deployment of a third generation manned space station. These capabilities could also be used, for example, to conduct military operations in space, to repair and defend satellites, or to build and operate weapons platforms.

Many Western analysts have concluded that the military directs the Soviet civilian space program.

Naval Forces

Before 1962 the Soviet Naval Forces were primarily a coastal defense force. The Cuban missile crisis and United States quarantine of Cuba in 1962, however, made the importance of ocean-going naval forces clear to the Soviet Union. In 1989 the Soviet Naval Forces had nearly 500,000 servicemen organized into five combat arms and gave the Soviet Union a capability of projecting power beyond Europe and Asia.

Submarine Forces

Submarines were the most important component of the Soviet Naval Forces. In 1989 the Soviet Union had the largest number of ballistic missile submarines in the world. Most of the sixty-two ballistic missile submarines could launch their nuclear-armed missiles against intercontinental targets from Soviet home waters. The deployment of mobile land-based ICBMs in the late 1980s, however, could reduce the importance of ballistic missile submarines as the Soviet Union's most survivable strategic force.

Soviet attack submarines have had an antisubmarine warfare (ASW) mission. In wartime the attack submarine force—203 boats in 1989—would attempt to destroy the enemy's ballistic missile and attack submarines. Since 1973 the Soviet Union has deployed ten different attack submarine classes, including five new types since 1980. In 1989 the Soviet Union also had sixty-six guided missile submarines for striking the enemy's land targets, surface combatant groups, and supply convoys.

Surface Forces

Between 1962 and the early 1970s, the Soviet Union's World War II-era Naval Forces became a modern guided missile cruiser and destroyer force. In addition, in the late 1970s the Soviet Union launched its first nuclear-powered Kirov-class battle cruiser, its third class of guided missile cruisers, and two new classes of guided missile destroyers. These surface forces have had the peacetime task of supporting Soviet allies in the Third World through port visits and arms shipments as well as visibly asserting Soviet power and interests on the high seas. In wartime, they would conduct both anti-ship and antisubmarine operations.

A variety of auxiliary ships supported the Naval Forces and the armed forces in general. In 1989 the Soviet Union operated sixty-three intelligence-gathering vessels, manned by naval reservists and equipped with surface-to-air missiles. It also had the world's largest

Kiev-class helicopter carrier Baku *in the Mediterranean Sea.*
Three helicopters are parked on the flight deck.
Oscar-class nuclear cruise missile submarine
Courtesy United States Navy

fleet of oceanographic survey and marine research vessels. Over 500 ships gathered and processed data on the world's oceans that would be crucial to the Soviet Union in wartime. In 1989 eleven specially equipped vessels, including the new Marshal Nedelin class, monitored and tracked Soviet and foreign space launches. Yet Western experts have noted that the Soviet Naval Forces still lacked enough specialized underway replenishment vessels to provide adequate logistical support to naval combatants at sea.

Naval Aviation

Naval Aviation was primarily land based; its main mission was to conduct air strikes on enemy ships and fleet support infrastructure. The importance attached to its antiship mission was shown by the fact that Naval Aviation has received almost as many Tu-26 bombers as have the Strategic Air Armies. Naval Aviation also provided ASW and general reconnaissance support for naval operations.

In 1989 Naval Aviation consisted of nearly 1,000 fixed-wing aircraft and over 300 helicopters. The Naval Aviation fleet included 130 Tu-26 and 230 Tu-16 medium-range bombers armed with air-to-surface cruise missiles for carrying out antiship strikes. Naval Aviation also had 100 Su-17 and Su-24 fighter-bombers that provided close air support to Naval Infantry. Older aircraft in Naval Aviation's inventory have been converted into ASW and maritime reconnaissance platforms.

Since the 1970s, the Soviet Naval Forces have attempted to overcome their major weakness—fleet air defense beyond the range of land-based aircraft—by deploying four Kiev-class aircraft carriers. These carriers each had a squadron of Yak-38 fighters. In the late 1980s, the Soviet Union was also constructing and fitting out its first two Tbilisi-class carriers. Western observers expected that a variant of the new Su-27 or MiG-29 fighter would become the main Soviet carrier-based aircraft. Soviet carriers also operated Ka-25 and Ka-27 naval helicopters for ASW reconnaissance, targeting, and search-and-rescue missions.

Naval Infantry

In the early 1960s, Naval Infantry became a combat arm of the Soviet Naval Forces. In 1989 Naval Infantry consisted of 18,000 marine troops organized into one division and three brigades. Naval Infantry had its own amphibious versions of standard armored vehicles and tanks used by the Ground Forces. Its primary wartime missions would be to seize and hold strategic straits or islands and to make seaborne tactical landings behind enemy lines. The Soviet Naval Forces had over eighty landing ships as well as two

Ivan Rogov-class amphibious assault docks. The latter were assault ships that could transport one infantry battalion with forty armored vehicles and their amphibious landing craft. At seventy-five units, the Soviet Union had the world's largest inventory of air-cushion assault craft. In addition, many of the Soviet merchant fleet's (Morflot) 2,500 oceangoing ships could off-load weapons and supplies in an amphibious landing.

Coastal Defense Forces

Protecting the coasts of the Soviet Union from attack or invasion from the sea has remained one of the most important missions of the Naval Forces. To defend an extensive coastline along the Arctic and Pacific oceans and the Baltic, Black, and Caspian seas, the Soviet Union has deployed a sizable and diverse force. Defending naval bases from attack has been the primary focus of the Coastal Defense Forces. In 1989 the Coastal Rocket and Artillery Troops, consisting of a single division, operated coastal artillery and naval surface-to-surface missile launchers along the approaches to naval bases. A large number of surface combatants, including light frigates, missile attack boats, submarine chasers, guided missile combatants, amphibious craft, and patrol boats of many types, also participated in coastal defense.

Airborne Troops and Special Purpose Forces

The Soviet Union had substantial specialized forces having missions and subordinations distinct from those of the regular military services. The Airborne Troops, subordinated to the Supreme High Command in wartime, were closely linked to the Ground Forces and to Military Transport Aviation. The Special Purpose Forces (Voiska spetsial'nogo nazacheniia—Spetsnaz), designed to operate deep behind enemy lines, were controlled by the General Staff's Main Intelligence Directorate (see Glossary).

In 1989 the Airborne Troops were more numerous than all the other airborne forces of the world combined. The Airborne Troops consisted of seven divisions. Each division had 7,000 troops organized into three paratroop regiments and an artillery regiment. The Airborne Troops had specially designed air-transportable and, in some cases, air-droppable equipment. Their inventory included light infantry fighting vehicles for transporting and protecting airborne forces on the ground and self-propelled 85mm assault guns to provide them with firepower.

The Airborne Troops were the primary rapid intervention force of the armed forces. They spearheaded the Soviet invasions of Czechoslovakia in 1968 and Afghanistan in 1979 by seizing the airports in Prague and Kabul, respectively. The performance of the Airborne Troops in Afghanistan raised their status as an elite combat arm.

The Spetsnaz has been the subject of intense speculation among Western experts because little is known about it. In 1989 the Soviet Ground Forces had about 30,000 Spetsnaz troops organized into sixteen brigades. In 1989 the Soviet Naval Forces also had four elite naval Spetsnaz brigades trained to reconnoiter, disrupt, or sabotage enemy naval installations and coastal defenses. One Western view held that, in wartime, small Spetsnaz teams would be assigned reconnaissance missions up to several hundred kilometers behind enemy lines. Spetsnaz units would then provide Soviet forces with targeting data on important enemy rear area facilities. Another view was that Spetsnaz troops would be emplaced weeks before a war to assassinate the enemy's political and military leaders; to sabotage its airfields; to destroy its nuclear weapons facilities; and to disrupt its command, control, and communications systems. Proponents of this view asserted that Spetsnaz teams assassinated the unpopular Afghan communist leader Hafizullah Amin before the Soviet invasion of Afghanistan in December 1979.

Rear Services

In 1989 a deputy minister of defense served as chief of Rear Services for the Soviet armed forces. The Rear Services supplied the armed forces with ammunition, fuel, spare parts, food, clothing, and other matériel. In 1989 the chief of the Rear Services had nine main and central directorates and four supporting services under his command. The deputy commanders in chief for rear services of the armed services, the deputy commanders for rear services of territorial commands, and nearly 1.5 million soldiers reported to him.

The Central Military Transportation Administration was the primary traffic management organization for the armed forces, coordinating and planning supply movements by all means of transport. The Central Food Supply Administration both procured food from civilian agricultural enterprises (see Glossary) and operated a military state farm (see Glossary) system to supply troops, particularly those serving in remote areas. Similarly, the Central Clothing Supply Administration had its own clothing factories to manufacture uniforms and specialized gear. The main and central directorates operated post exchange, health care, and recreational facilities for military personnel. The Rear Services also provided financial reports on armed forces activities to party and government organs.

The chief of the Rear Services commanded the Railroad Troops, Road Troops, Pipeline Troops, and Automotive Troops. The mission of these supporting services was to construct and maintain the Soviet Union's military transport infrastructure. The Automotive Troops, for example, provided the drivers and mechanics needed to maintain and drive cargo trucks loaded with supplies from railheads to operational units in the field. After the initial airlift of Soviet forces and equipment into Afghanistan in December 1979, these troops built permanent rail lines, roads, and pipelines between the Soviet Union and Afghanistan to resupply the Soviet forces in that country.

Formerly divided among independent maintenance, medical, and motor transport companies, the provision of rear services in Soviet regiments has become the responsibility of unified matériel support units. As in most armies, these matériel support units were subordinate to operational commanders, although they worked with the next highest chief of rear services on technical matters.

Construction and Troop Billeting was an independent supporting service, similar to the Rear Services, headed by another deputy minister of defense. Construction and Troop Billeting served as a large, mobile force of cheap labor to erect military bases and troop quarters as well as civilian and government buildings. The service has been used to complete high-priority projects and to work in harsh environments. Construction and Troop Billeting has built military installations in the Soviet Far East since 1969, major airports, and the Moscow Olympics complex. The service has also worked on Siberian natural gas pipelines and the Baykal-Amur Main Line (BAM—see Glossary).

Civil Defense

Civil defense was another part of Soviet strategic defense. It originated with the large-scale relocation of defense industries from the western Soviet Union to east of the Ural Mountains in 1941. Civil defense reappeared in the late 1940s as antiaircraft units were attached to Soviet factories to defend them against strategic bombing. By the early 1970s, the emphasis on civil defense increased, and the chief of Civil Defense became a deputy minister of defense. Each union republic had a general officer as the chief of civil defense in the republic.

In 1989 the purpose of civil defense was to provide protection for leadership and population in wartime and to ensure the Soviet Union's ability to continue production of military matériel during a nuclear or a protracted conventional war. Officers from Civil Defense were attached to union republic, oblast (see Glossary), *raion*

721

(see Glossary), and municipal governments, as well as to large industrial and agricultural enterprises, and assigned to supervise civil defense work, organization, and training. These staff officers developed and implemented detailed plans for the wartime relocation of important defense industrial facilities and the evacuation of labor forces to alternative sites. They supervised the construction of blast shelters and other installations to ensure that these structures could withstand nuclear strikes. Civil Defense operated a network of 1,500 underground shelters that could protect 175,000 top party and government officials. In 1989 Civil Defense had 150,000 personnel.

After a nuclear exchange, the civil defense effort would be directed at reestablishing essential military production through decontamination, first aid, and civil engineering work to clear collapsed structures and to restore power supplies, transportation, and communications. Civil Defense trained in peacetime by conducting simulations of the aftermath of a nuclear attack and small-scale evacuation exercises. It was also called on to fight fires, conduct rescue operations, decontaminate areas affected by nuclear and chemical accidents, and provide natural disaster relief.

Specialized and Paramilitary Forces

Under Soviet law, two armed services were outside the control of the Ministry of Defense but were nonetheless part of the Soviet armed forces. These services, the Internal Troops and the Border Troops, were subordinate to the Ministry of Internal Affairs and the KGB, respectively. Although often termed "militarized police," the Internal Troops and the Border Troops were military organizations, equipped, like motorized rifle regiments, with tanks and armored personnel carriers.

Internal Troops

In 1989 the Internal Troops had a personnel strength of about 340,000 soldiers. These troops had the mission of suppressing demonstrations, revolts, riots, strikes, or other challenges to the regime that the militia (police) could not contain (see Internal Troops of the Ministry of Internal Affairs, ch. 19). The use of Internal Troops instead of the Ground Forces in these situations helped to preserve the favorable image of the latter with the population. In extreme circumstances, the Internal Troops also served as the party's counterweight to the military services.

In addition to these peacetime roles, the Internal Troops also have been assigned wartime missions. In time of war, they would support frontline operations by providing rear security against enemy sabotage, defending supply and communications lines, and operating prisoner-of-war and penal battalions. In the early days of World War II, the Internal Troops manned machine gun detachments located behind Soviet frontline units. The detachments were charged with firing on Red Army soldiers who tried to retreat or desert.

Border Troops

The mission of the Border Troops, which included 230,000 personnel in 1989, was to prevent unauthorized entry by foreigners into the Soviet Union and to keep Soviet citizens from leaving the country illegally (see Border Troops of the Committee for State Security, ch. 19). The troops patrolled clearly demarcated strips along Soviet state frontiers that contained antivehicle obstacles, fences, and barbed wire. The Border Troops used guard dogs, sophisticated electronic surveillance equipment and sensors, and helicopters to perform their duties over vast, sparsely populated frontier regions.

The Border Troops also guarded the Soviet Union's oceanic frontiers. Its Maritime Border Troops operated within the twelve-mile limit of Soviet territorial waters and were equipped with frigates, fast patrol boats, hydrofoils, helicopters, and light aircraft.

In wartime the Border Troops would become a frontline combat service. Stationed on the frontiers, Border Troops units absorbed the brunt of Nazi Germany's surprise invasion of the Soviet Union in June 1941 and fought defensive actions against the German army. The Border Troops also saw combat action in 1969 in border clashes with Chinese soldiers on islands in the Ussuri River.

In addition to the Border Troops, the KGB had other troops engaged in military-related activities that were not mentioned in legislation governing the armed forces (see Internal Security Troops, ch. 19). The KGB controlled elite units that guarded the highest party officials and stood a continuous ceremonial guard at the Lenin Mausoleum. The special KGB signal troops also operated communications linking the party with the Ministry of Defense and the major territorial commands. Another KGB armed force guarded sensitive military, scientific, and industrial installations in the Soviet Union and, until the late 1960s, controlled Soviet nuclear warhead stockpiles.

Territorial Organization of the Armed Forces

The armed forces had a peacetime territorial organization that would facilitate a rapid shift to a wartime footing. In 1989 the Soviet Union was divided into sixteen military districts and four fleets (see fig. 30). In addition, one flotilla, two naval squadrons, and six major groups of forces were stationed outside the Soviet Union.

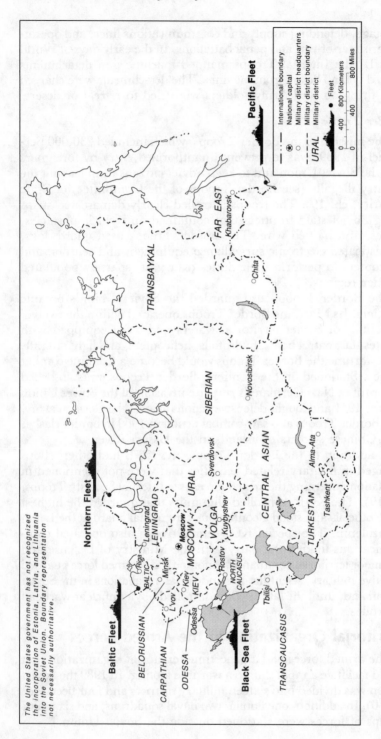

The United States government has not recognized the incorporation of Estonia, Latvia, and Lithuania into the Soviet Union. Boundary representation not necessarily authoritative.

–··–··–	International boundary
⊛	National capital
⊛	Military district headquarters
– – –	Military district boundary
URAL	Military district
	Fleet

0   400   800 Kilometers
0   400   800 Miles

Figure 30. Military Districts and Fleets, 1988

Military Districts

Military districts were the basic units of Soviet military administration. The system of sixteen military districts had evolved in response to the Soviet Union's perception of threats to its security. For example, in 1969 the Turkestan Military District was divided to create the Central Asian Military District and enable the Soviet Union to double its military forces and infrastructure along the border with China. In wartime most military districts would become fronts (see Glossary).

Senior Ground Forces officers have always commanded military districts, and experience in commanding a military district was apparently a prerequisite for promotion to most of the important Ministry of Defense positions. Commanders of military districts have deputy commanders responsible for specific military activities. Each military district had a military council, which included the commander of the district, his first deputies—one of whom was also chief of staff—the chief of the political directorate for the district, and the first secretary of the party bureau of the union republic in which the district was located.

Military districts were combined arms formations. A military district commander controlled not only the Ground Forces in the district but also the Air Forces and the Air Defense Forces (see fig. 31). The commanders of the Air Forces and the Air Defense Forces reported to the district commander on operational matters as well as to the main staffs of their services. The military district's officers worked closely with party and government officials to plan wartime mobilization and rear services, civil defense, and military training for civilians. They supervised military training in both civilian and military education establishments located in the district. Military districts coordinated activities with the Border Troops, which had a system of ten districts organized separately from the military districts.

In 1989 twelve of Frontal Aviation's sixteen air armies were stationed in the most important military districts. Western experts disagreed over the organization of the system of air defense districts. Some argued that as many as ten air defense districts, separate from military districts, still existed. It seemed more likely, however, that when the National Air Defense Forces became the Air Defense Forces after 1980, all remaining air defense districts were integrated into the military districts. At that time, commanders of the Air Defense Forces became deputy commanders of the military districts. Only the Moscow Air Defense District continued to be mentioned in the press, possibly because it operated the ABM

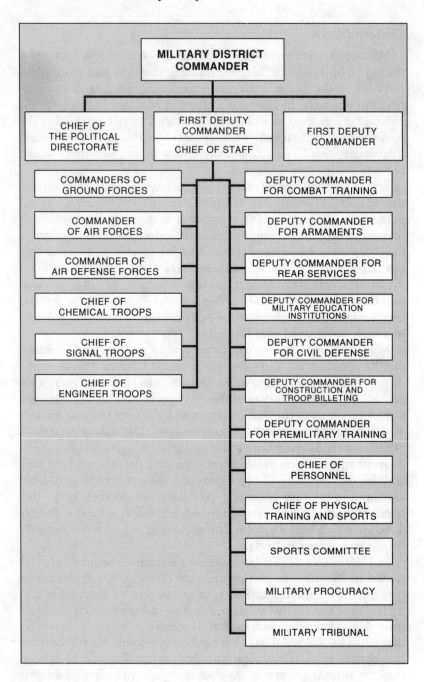

Figure 31. Organization of a Typical Military District, 1988

system that protected the capital city and the National Command Authority.

In 1989 the Ground Forces had sixty-five divisions, kept at between 50 and 75 percent of their projected wartime strengths, in the westernmost military districts of the Soviet Union. The Ground Forces also had fifty-two divisions at less than half their wartime levels in the Siberian, Transbaykal, Central Asian, and Far East military districts along the border with China and twenty-six low-readiness divisions in the Transcaucasus, North Caucasus, and Turkestan military districts.

Fleets, Flotillas, and Squadrons

The command organization of the four fleets was similar to that of the military districts. The fleet commander had a deputy for each of the combat arms of the Naval Forces, and he supervised the naval bases and ports in the fleet's area. Each fleet had a Naval Aviation air army, a naval Spetsnaz brigade, and several battalions of the Coastal Rocket and Artillery Troops. The fleets reported to the Main Staff of the Naval Forces; in wartime they would come under the operational control of the Supreme High Command and the General Staff. Although the Naval Forces operated numerous flotillas on inland seas and large lakes, only the Caspian Flotilla was operational in 1989.

The Northern Fleet, based at Murmansk-Severomorsk, was the most important Soviet fleet, having a force of over 170 submarines in 1989. The Pacific Fleet, based at Vladivostok, had the best amphibious and power projection capabilities of the Naval Forces. In 1989 it had the only Naval Infantry division, two aircraft carriers, and 120 submarines. In wartime the Northern and Pacific fleets would become components of oceanic theaters of military operations (*teatry voennykh deistvii*—TVDs; see Offensive and Defensive Strategic Missions, ch. 17). The Baltic and Black Sea fleets, as well as the Caspian Flotilla, would become maritime components of continental TVDs in wartime.

Since the mid-1960s, the Naval Forces have increasingly been deployed abroad. In 1964 the Mediterranean squadron became the first permanently forward-deployed Soviet naval force. Since its inception, it has usually had thirty-five to forty-five ships. In 1968 the Soviet Union established an Indian Ocean squadron of fifteen to twenty-five ships. Access to ports and airfields in Vietnam, Syria, Libya, Ethiopia, the People's Democratic Republic of Yemen (South Yemen), and Seychelles in the 1980s has enabled the Soviet Naval Forces to repair their ships, fly ocean reconnaissance flights, and maintain these forward deployments. In 1989 Cam Ranh Bay in Vietnam had the largest concentration of Soviet vessels outside the countries of the Warsaw Pact.

Groups of Forces Stationed Abroad

In 1989 the Soviet Union had six major groups of forces stationed abroad. The groups of Soviet forces in Eastern Europe included thirty Ground Forces divisions and four air armies in the German Democratic Republic (East Germany), Poland, Czechoslovakia, and Hungary (see Appendix C). These groups of forces have been in Eastern Europe since 1945 and have been used on several occasions to suppress anticommunist uprisings in those countries and keep them within the Soviet alliance system. They have also been the main concentration of Soviet forces against NATO. They were continuously manned and equipped at wartime levels. The Group of Soviet Forces in Germany was the most important Soviet territorial command. In 1989 it had 400,000 troops organized into nineteen divisions and five armies. Its importance was underscored by the fact that it was commanded by a commander in chief, like the five armed services.

When the cuts announced by Gorbachev in December 1988 are completed in 1991, 50,000 Soviet troops and six Soviet tank divisions will have been withdrawn from East Germany, Czechoslovakia, and Hungary (see Conventional Arms Control, ch. 17).

In addition to its forces stationed in Eastern Europe, the Soviet Union continued to maintain a large troop presence in Afghanistan throughout most of 1988. The Soviet 40th Army's four divisions and other forces—116,000 troops in all—had been fighting in Afghanistan for nearly nine years by late 1988. In mid-1988 the Soviet Union began a full-scale withdrawal from Afghanistan. The withdrawal was completed by early 1989. The Soviet Union has also had forces stationed in Mongolia since that country became an ally in 1921. Under a plan articulated in a 1986 Vladivostok speech, Gorbachev withdrew one Soviet division, leaving four in Mongolia.

The Party and the Armed Forces

The CPSU had three mechanisms of control over the country's armed forces. First, the top military leaders have been systematically integrated into the highest echelons of the CPSU and subjected to party discipline. Second, the CPSU has placed a network of political officers throughout the armed forces to influence the activities of the military. Third, the KGB, under the direction of the CPSU, has maintained a network of officers and informers in the armed forces.

Political-Military Relations

Fearing the immense popularity of the armed forces after World War II, Stalin demoted war hero Marshal Georgii K. Zhukov and took personal credit for having saved the country. After Stalin's death in 1953, Zhukov reemerged as a strong supporter of Nikita S. Khrushchev. Khrushchev rewarded Zhukov by making him minister of defense and a full Politburo member. Concern that the armed forces might become too powerful in politics, however, led to Zhukov's abrupt dismissal in the fall of 1957. But Khrushchev later alienated the armed forces by cutting defense expenditures on conventional forces in order to carry out his plans for economic reform. Leonid I. Brezhnev's years in power marked the height of party-military cooperation because he provided ample resources to the armed forces. In 1973 the minister of defense again became a full Politburo member for the first time since 1957. Yet Brezhnev evidently felt threatened by the professional military, and he sought to create an aura of military leadership around himself in an effort to establish his authority over the military.

In the early 1980s, party-military relations became strained over the issue of resource allocations to the armed forces. Despite a downturn in economic growth, the chief of the General Staff, Nikolai V. Ogarkov, argued for more resources to develop advanced conventional weapons. His outspoken stance led to his removal in September 1984. Ogarkov became commander in chief of the Western TVD, a crucial wartime command position that exists primarily on paper in peacetime. He was retired under Gorbachev and assumed a largely ceremonial post in the Main Inspectorate. His influence was considerably diminished, although he continued to publish in the military press.

Gorbachev, who became general secretary in March 1985, was a teenager during the Great Patriotic War and apparently never served in the armed forces. He has downgraded the role of the military in state ceremonies, including moving military representatives to the end of the leadership line-up atop the Lenin Mausoleum during the annual Red Square military parade on November 7. Gorbachev used the Rust incident in May 1987 as a convenient pretext for replacing Sergei Sokolov with Dmitrii T. Iazov as minister of defense (see Air Defense Forces, this ch.). Gorbachev has also emphasized civilian economic priorities and "reasonable sufficiency" in defense over the professional military's perceived requirements.

Military Representation in the Party

As of 1989, only two career military ministers of defense had become full Politburo members. Since 1984 the minister of defense has been only a candidate member. The top leaders in the Ministry of Defense, however, have been regularly elected as members or candidate members of the Central Committee. Central Committee membership apparently has come with certain important posts and major field commands. The military presence in the Central Committee has varied little over time, normally constituting between 7 and 12 percent of this influential body.

Military officers with full membership on the Central Committee have generally included the minister of defense, the first deputy ministers of defense, the deputy ministers of defense, the chief of the Main Political Directorate of the Soviet Army and Navy, the chief and one or two members of the Main Inspectorate, the commander of the Moscow Military District, and the commander in chief of the Group of Soviet Forces in Germany. At the Twenty-Seventh Party Congress in February–March 1986, full Central Committee membership was granted to the commanders of the Western and Far Eastern TVDs.

Candidate members of the Central Committee from the armed forces have included the commanders of all the military districts and fleets, the first deputy chief of the Main Political Directorate of the Soviet Army and Navy, the chiefs of the political directorates of the armed services, and the chairman of the Voluntary Society for Assistance to the Army, Air Force, and Navy (Dobrovol'noe obshchestvo sodeistviia armii, aviatsii i flotu—DOSAAF; see Glossary). All military representatives on the Central Committee were also deputies of the Supreme Soviet. Other military officials were elected to the party's Central Auditing Commission (see Central Auditing Commission, ch. 7).

Party-military interaction also occurred at lower levels, and it enabled the armed forces to coordinate their activities with local party officials and draw on them for assistance. The commanders of military districts and fleets were usually members of the party bureau and deputies of the supreme soviet of the republic in which the district or fleet was located (see Intermediate-Level Party Organizations, ch. 7). Other senior military officers sat on oblast, *raion,* or city party committees.

Party Control in the Armed Forces

The Main Political Directorate of the Soviet Army and Navy was responsible for party control over the armed forces. It organized, conducted, and reported on political and ideological indoctrination in the armed forces, supervised the military press, and monitored the ideological content of military publications.

The Main Political Directorate of the Soviet Army and Navy was subordinate to the Ministry of Defense, as well as to the CPSU Central Committee. It had the official status of a Central Committee department and reported to the Central Committee outside the military chain of command (see Secretariat, ch. 7). These reports included information on the political attitudes and reliability of armed forces personnel and high-ranking officers in particular. The Central Committee's Party Building and Cadre Work Department used the information on political reliability supplied by the Main Political Directorate of the Soviet Army and Navy to approve or deny appointments, assignments, and promotions of professionally qualified officers at the rank of colonel and above (see Nomenklatura, ch. 7).

The Main Political Directorate of the Soviet Army and Navy supervised a network of political organizations and officers within the armed forces. Every armed service, territorial command, and supporting service had a political directorate. Service branches, divisions, and military education institutions had political sections, which were smaller than directorates. Each political section had a small staff that included a chief, a deputy chief, several senior political instructors, and officers responsible for ideology and propaganda, party organizational work, and the Komsomol (see Glossary). A party commission of high-ranking personnel was attached to each political directorate and section. A deputy commander for political affairs was assigned to each unit of company, battery, and squadron size or larger (see fig. 32). Smaller military units had primary party organizations (PPOs—see Glossary). Each PPO had a secretary, and secretaries met in their regiment's or ship's party committee to elect a party bureau. About 80 percent of all companies in the Ground Forces had party organizations. They were present in half the company-sized units of the armed forces as a whole.

A deputy commander for political affairs (*zamestitel' komandira po politicheskoi chasti—zampolit*) served as a political commissar of the armed forces. A *zampolit* supervised party organizations and conducted "party political work" within a military unit. He lectured troops on Marxism-Leninism (see Glossary), the Soviet view of international issues, recent CPSU decisions and documents, and the party's tasks for the armed forces. For Soviet military personnel, political training averaged between two and four hours every week. It was usually squeezed into what might otherwise be off-duty hours and was therefore widely resented. The *zampolit* was also responsible for resolving morale, disciplinary, and interpersonal

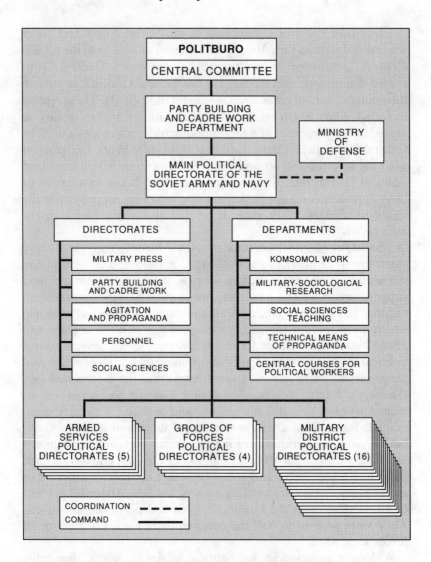

Figure 32. Apparatus of the Communist Party of the Soviet Union in the Armed Services, 1988

problems, which were chronic in military units. These problems often involved poor living conditions, conflicts among different nationalities, and poor attitudes toward training. Like the old political commissars, the modern *zampolit* remained responsible for keeping soldiers, and even entire frontline combat units, from deserting or defecting.

Since World War II, the *zampolit* has lost all command authority, although retaining the power to report to the next highest political officer or organization on the political attitudes and performance of the unit's commander. Negative reports from the *zampolit* could exert considerable influence on the course of a commander's career. Yet under the principle of one-man command, tension between professional and political officers has decreased. Commanders were fully responsible for the political state of the troops under them, and this responsibility forced them to allow adequate time for political training.

In 1989 over 20 percent of all armed forces personnel were CPSU or Komsomol members. Over 90 percent of all officers in the armed forces were CPSU or Komsomol members. The figures for party membership were even higher in such armed services as the Strategic Rocket Forces or the Border Troops, in which political reliability has been especially crucial. The Komsomol was important in the armed forces because most soldiers and young officers were in the normal age-group for Komsomol membership.

The KGB has been another instrument of party control over the armed forces. Its Third Chief Directorate had special counterintelligence sections that operated within regiments. The ''special sections'' used networks of informers inside units to monitor foreign contacts of armed forces personnel and to protect military secrets. Unknown to a commander or *zampolit,* a KGB officer could be reporting on their political attitudes, outside of military or Main Political Directorate of the Soviet Army and Navy channels.

Military Economics

With the notable exceptions of Khrushchev and possibly Gorbachev, Soviet leaders since the late 1920s have emphasized military production over investment in the civilian economy. As a result, the Soviet Union has produced some of the world's most advanced armaments, although it has been unable to produce basic consumer goods of satisfactory quality or in sufficient quantities (see Industrial Organization; The Consumer Industry, ch. 12).

Defense Spending

In 1988 military spending was a single line item in the state budget, totaling 21 billion rubles (for value of the ruble—see Glossary), or about US$33 billion. Given the size of the military establishment, however, the actual figure was at least ten times higher. Western experts have concluded that the 21 billion ruble figure reflected only operations and maintenance costs. Other military spending, including training, military construction, and arms production, was

733

possibly concealed within the budgets of all-union ministries and state committees. The amount spent on Soviet weapons research and development was an especially well-guarded state secret. Since the mid-1980s, the Soviet Union has devoted between 15 and 17 percent of its annual gross national product (GNP—see Glossary) to military spending, according to United States government sources. Until the early 1980s, Soviet defense expenditures rose between 4 and 7 percent per year. Since then, they have slowed as the yearly growth in Soviet GNP slipped to about 2 percent on average. In 1987 Gorbachev and other party officials discussed the extension of *glasnost'* to military affairs through the publication of a detailed Soviet defense budget. In early 1989, Gorbachev announced a military budget of 77.3 billion rubles, but Western authorities estimated the budget to be about twice that.

Military Industries and Production

The integration of the party, government, and military in the Soviet Union has been most evident in the area of defense-related industrial production. The Defense Council made decisions on the development and production of major weapons systems. The Defense Industry Department of the Central Committee supervised all military industries as the executive agent of the Defense Council. Within the government, the deputy chairman of the Council of Ministers headed the Military Industrial Commission. The Military Industrial Commission coordinated the activities of many industrial ministries, state committees, research and development organizations, and factories and enterprises that designed and produced arms and equipment for the armed forces.

The State Planning Committee (Gosudarstvennyi planovyi komitet—Gosplan) had an important role in directing necessary supplies and resources to military industries. The main staff and deputy commander in chief for armaments of each armed service first determined their "tactical-technical" requirements for weapons and equipment and forwarded them to the General Staff, which evaluated and altered them to conform to overall strategic and operational plans. Then the deputy minister of defense for armaments transmitted the General Staff's decisions to industrial ministries engaged in military production. He controlled several thousand senior military officers who represented the military within the industrial ministries. These military representatives supervised the entire process of military production from design through final assembly. They inspected, and had the authority to reject, all output not meeting the military's specifications and quality control standards.

In 1989 the defense industry consisted of a number of industrial ministries subordinate to the Council of Ministers. The names of most of these ministries did not indicate the types of weapons or military equipment they produced. The Ministry of Medium Machine Building manufactured nuclear warheads. The Ministry of General Machine Building produced ballistic missiles (see fig. 33; Machine Building and Metal Working, ch. 12). Other ministries, such as the Ministry of Automotive and Agricultural Machine Building, also produced military equipment and components, but to a lesser extent of their total output.

These defense industrial ministries operated 150 major arms assembly plants in addition to the more than 1,000 factories that produced components for military equipment. Each ministry had a central design office and several design bureaus attached to it. The design bureaus, named for the chief designers who headed them in the past, built competing prototypes of weapons based on the military's specifications. The central design office then selected the best design and, if the military approved it, began serial production. The aircraft design bureaus were best known because Soviet aircraft carry their designations. The Mikoian-Gurevich (MiG) and Sukhoi (Su) bureaus designed fighters; the Antonov (An), Iliushin (Il), and Tupolev (Tu) bureaus developed transport and bomber aircraft. The Mil (Mi) and Kamov (Ka) bureaus designed helicopters.

The high priority given to military production has traditionally enabled military-industrial enterprises to commandeer the best managers, labor, and materials from civilian plants. In the late 1980s, however, Gorbachev transferred some leading defense industry officials to the civilian sector of the economy in an effort to make it as efficient as its military counterpart.

Military Technology

The Soviet Union has taken an incremental approach to military research and development. The military has deployed early versions of weapons and equipment with limited capabilities and has gradually improved them. The same basic weapons system has usually been fielded over a period of years in several different variants. Arms designers have relied heavily on integrating components from earlier models into new systems in order to provide stability and compatibility in the production process. The armed forces have tended to favor weapons that were produced in mass quantities, were reliable, and were easy to use in combat over expensive, complex, and technologically superior armaments. Following this rule of simplicity, the Soviet Union has produced many

735

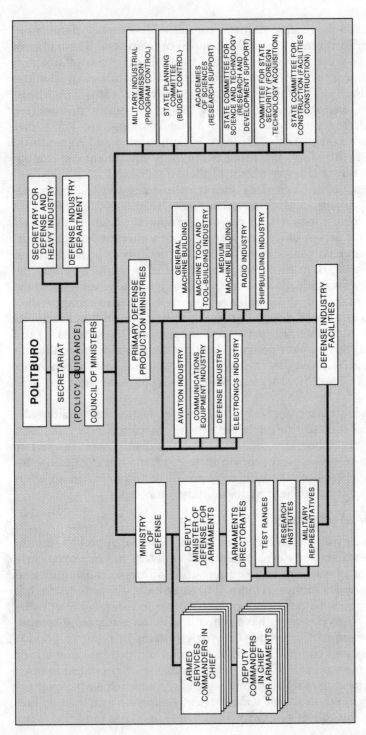

Figure 33. Management of Defense Production, 1988

outstanding and tactically innovative weapons. Nevertheless, it has had difficulties producing more sophisticated systems, such as large airframes, small nuclear reactors, and quiet submarine propellers. These problems have forced it to resort to technological espionage and to copying Western designs. The State Committee for Science and Technology has tasked KGB officers and other Soviet officials in Western countries to acquire the components or technologies needed to produce certain armaments.

Uniforms and Rank Insignia

In 1989 the uniforms and rank insignia of the Soviet armed forces were similar for all services, except the Naval Forces. Uniforms of officers and enlisted men differed only in the quality of the material used, not in their cut and style. The services could be distinguished from each other by the colors of the shoulder boards, the collar tabs, and the service hat bands. In each service, the uniforms for women generally were of the same color and fabric as those provided for men. Marshals, generals, and admirals wore double-breasted uniform coats. All services, except the Naval Forces, used full-length, medium gray, winter overcoats. Lower ranking enlisted personnel wore olive drab short overcoats. Naval personnel wore black overcoats in winter. In general, Soviet naval uniforms (in cut, color, and style) and rank insignia resembled those of foreign navies.

Each service generally had five categories of uniforms: full dress, dress, service, field, and work, with variants for winter and summer. Full dress uniforms were worn during such special military occasions as formal reviews, parades, annual service holidays, ceremonies conferring promotions or military decorations, and when taking the military oath or performing in honor guards. Dress uniforms were used for national anniversaries, such as the that of the Bolshevik Revolution; for official receptions; while attending the theater; and as otherwise ordered. Service uniforms were worn for routine duty and during off-duty hours. Field uniforms were worn during training, maneuvers, and firing exercises. Work uniforms were worn while performing equipment maintenance, fatigue detail, and construction tasks.

The colors of the uniforms varied according to the service and the category of uniform. Full dress uniforms were sea green for the Ground Forces and the Strategic Rocket Forces and nonaviation components of the Air Forces and the Air Defense Forces. Aviation components' uniforms were blue. Officers of all services wore gold belts, breeches, and boots with full dress uniforms. The dress uniforms resembled the full dress uniforms, except that long trousers and low quarter shoes were worn. The service uniforms and field uniforms for all services were olive drab. Officer field uniforms had color-suppressed insignia instead of gold, and the garrison cap or steel helmet was substituted for the service hat. The work uniform for all services was a field uniform devoid of rank insignia. It was usually an old field uniform or overalls worn as a protective garment over a field uniform.

Each of the Naval Forces four categories of uniforms (full dress, dress, service, and work) had seasonal variants. The full dress uniforms—white for summer and navy blue for the remainder of the year—were worn with dirks and white gloves. Dress uniforms were less ornate than full dress uniforms, and ribbons replaced medals. Service uniforms were the same as dress uniforms, but without dirks and white gloves. A summer service uniform variation had a blue jacket and a garrison cap instead of a service hat. Junior enlisted personnel wore service uniforms, which were white, navy blue, white top and blue bottoms or the reverse, or other variants in winter and summer. Their jumpers had broad light blue collars with three white stripes. Shipboard work uniforms were either gray or khaki. Lower ranked seamen wore visorless hats with black bands and pigtail ribbons in the back.

All services exhibited rank insignia on shoulder boards, using a system of gold stripes with gold stars on colored backgrounds and colored piping on the edges (see fig. 34; fig. 35; fig. 36). Naval officers also wore sleeve stripes. Shoulder boards of marshals, general officers, and admirals possessed large stars on broad, ornate gold stripes with piping on the edges. Shoulder boards of field grade officers displayed three longitudinal gold stripes and smaller gold stars, and those of company grade officers had two longitudinal gold stripes and even smaller stars. Shoulder boards of warrant officers had two or three gold stars superimposed on a gold checkerboard pattern. Enlisted ranks were indicated by transverse or longitudinal gold stripes on shoulder boards.

The background colors of shoulder boards, collar tabs, and service hat bands varied with the service and the branch of service. The Strategic Rocket Forces had black shoulder boards, as did the Rocket Troops and Artillery, Engineer Troops, Tank Troops, and certain other components of the Ground Forces. The Motorized Rifle Troops had red shoulder boards. The Air Forces and aviation personnel of the Air Defense Forces had light blue shoulder boards, as did the Airborne Troops. The Naval Forces had navy blue shoulder boards (see table 54, Appendix A). Metallic insignia of gold or silver were also employed to identify selected branches of the services. Personnel belonging to one service or branch but serving in another wore the background color prescribed for the latter service or branch. For example, members of an artillery battalion, which was a component of a motorized rifle division, wore the red shoulder boards and collar tabs of the Motorized Rifle Troops but displayed the crossed cannon insignia of the Rocket Troops and Artillery on their collar tabs. The Airborne Troops wore the light blue background color of the Air Forces, but with the insignia of the Airborne Troops on their collar tabs. An exception allowed the Administration Troops, Medical Troops, Military Procuracy, Quartermaster Troops, and Veterinary Troops to wear the color—magenta—prescribed for their branches regardless of assignment. The shoulder boards of enlisted personnel of the armed forces, except the Naval Forces, had large Cyrillic letters identifying the particular component. For instance, the Cyrillic "CA" signified Soviet army and was used for the five services except the Naval Forces; other letters identified the Internal Troops of the Ministry of Internal Affairs, the Border Troops of the KGB, and other elements.

Military Manpower

According to the Soviet Constitution, all citizens had a "sacred" duty to defend the Soviet Union, to enhance its power and prestige, and to serve in its armed forces. The armed forces have been manned through conscription based on the provisions of the 1967 Law on Universal Military Service. In 1989 about 75 percent of Soviet armed forces personnel were conscripts, and 5 percent were career noncommissioned officers (NCOs). The professional officer corps constituted 20 percent of the armed forces. An extensive reserve and mobilization system would augment regular forces in wartime. The Soviet Union also had a compulsory premilitary training program for the country's youth. In the late 1980s, the number of draft-age youths was stable, but fewer Russians and more non-Russians were being inducted into the armed forces.

Premilitary Training

Military and physical fitness training began at the age of ten in the Pioneers. Their activities emphasized military-patriotic indoctrination, marching, and discipline. The Pioneers also guarded Soviet war monuments and participated in military sports games held every summer since 1967. In the games, children were divided into commanders, staff, and troops for maneuvers that simulated partisan warfare behind enemy lines. Members of the Komsomol, age fourteen and older, participated in more sophisticated military games.

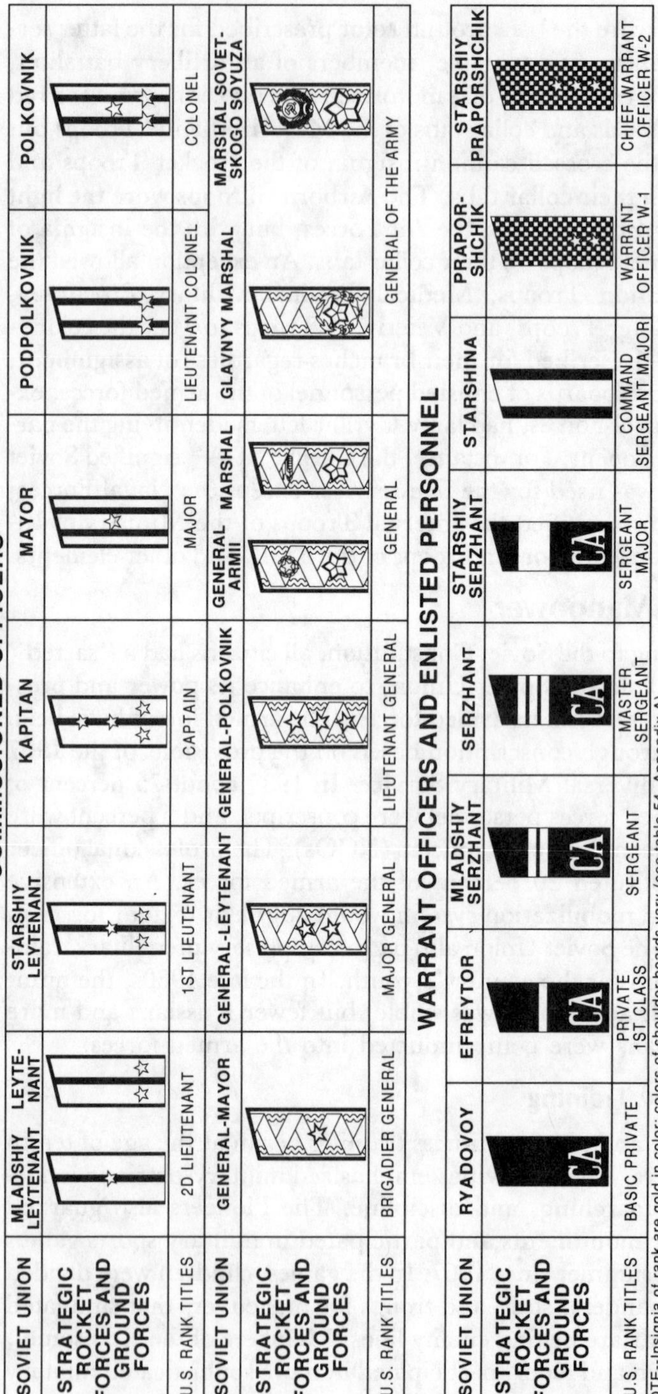

COMMISSIONED OFFICERS

SOVIET UNION	MLADSHIY LEYTENANT	LEYTE-NANT	STARSHIY LEYTENANT	KAPITAN	MAYOR	PODPOLKOVNIK	POLKOVNIK
STRATEGIC ROCKET FORCES AND GROUND FORCES							
U.S. RANK TITLES	2D LIEUTENANT	1ST LIEUTENANT	CAPTAIN	MAJOR	LIEUTENANT COLONEL	COLONEL
SOVIET UNION	GENERAL-MAYOR	GENERAL-LEYTENANT	GENERAL-POLKOVNIK	GENERAL ARMII	MARSHAL	GLAVNYY MARSHAL	MARSHAL SOVET-SKOGO SOYUZA
STRATEGIC ROCKET FORCES AND GROUND FORCES							
U.S. RANK TITLES	BRIGADIER GENERAL	MAJOR GENERAL	LIEUTENANT GENERAL	GENERAL	GENERAL OF THE ARMY

WARRANT OFFICERS AND ENLISTED PERSONNEL

SOVIET UNION	RYADOVOY	EFREYTOR	MLADSHIY SERZHANT	SERZHANT	STARSHIY SERZHANT	STARSHINA	PRAPOR-SHCHIK	STARSHIY PRAPORSHCHIK
STRATEGIC ROCKET FORCES AND GROUND FORCES								
U.S. RANK TITLES	BASIC PRIVATE	PRIVATE 1ST CLASS	SERGEANT	MASTER SERGEANT	SERGEANT MAJOR	COMMAND SERGEANT MAJOR	WARRANT OFFICER W-1	CHIEF WARRANT OFFICER W-2

NOTE—Insignia of rank are gold in color; colors of shoulder boards vary (see table 54, Appendix A).

Figure 34. Ranks and Insignia of Strategic Rocket Forces and Ground Forces, 1989

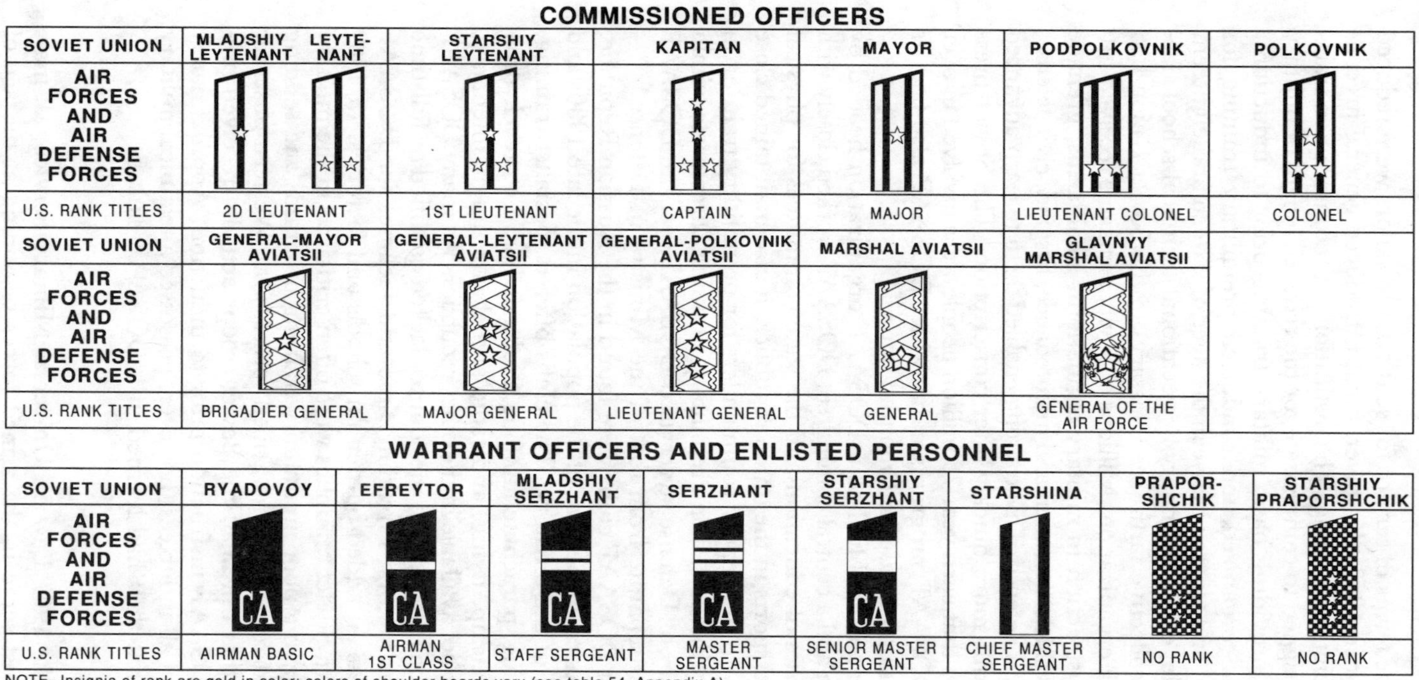

COMMISSIONED OFFICERS

SOVIET UNION	MLADSHIY LEYTENANT	LEYTENANT	STARSHIY LEYTENANT	KAPITAN	MAYOR	PODPOLKOVNIK	POLKOVNIK
AIR FORCES AND AIR DEFENSE FORCES							
U.S. RANK TITLES	2D LIEUTENANT	1ST LIEUTENANT		CAPTAIN	MAJOR	LIEUTENANT COLONEL	COLONEL

SOVIET UNION					
AIR FORCES AND AIR DEFENSE FORCES	GENERAL-MAYOR AVIATSII	GENERAL-LEYTENANT AVIATSII	GENERAL-POLKOVNIK AVIATSII	MARSHAL AVIATSII	GLAVNYY MARSHAL AVIATSII
U.S. RANK TITLES	BRIGADIER GENERAL	MAJOR GENERAL	LIEUTENANT GENERAL	GENERAL	GENERAL OF THE AIR FORCE

WARRANT OFFICERS AND ENLISTED PERSONNEL

SOVIET UNION	RYADOVOY	EFREYTOR	MLADSHIY SERZHANT	SERZHANT	STARSHIY SERZHANT	STARSHINA	PRAPORSHCHIK	STARSHIY PRAPORSHCHIK
AIR FORCES AND AIR DEFENSE FORCES	CA	CA	CA	CA	CA			
U.S. RANK TITLES	AIRMAN BASIC	AIRMAN 1ST CLASS	STAFF SERGEANT	MASTER SERGEANT	SENIOR MASTER SERGEANT	CHIEF MASTER SERGEANT	NO RANK	NO RANK

NOTE.--Insignia of rank are gold in color; colors of shoulder boards vary (see table 54, Appendix A).

Figure 35. Ranks and Insignia of Air Forces and Air Defense Forces, 1989

741

When the terms of service for soldiers and sailors were reduced by one year in 1967, the government introduced general preconscription military training. The institution of preconscription training was designed to compensate for the reduced length of military service by providing basic military training prior to induction.

DOSAAF organized and conducted premilitary training for young men and women between the ages of sixteen and eighteen. In principle, every secondary or vocational-technical school, factory, and collective farm (see Glossary) in the Soviet Union had a DOSAAF organization. Millions of Soviet teenagers received 140 hours of instruction in military regulations, small arms, grenade throwing, vehicle operation and maintenance, first aid, civil defense, and chemical defense. This training enabled them to learn advanced military skills more quickly after conscription. The Soviet press has claimed that each year 75 million people were involved in over 300,000 DOSAAF programs nationwide. DOSAAF also had its own publishing house and monthly journal.

Each union republic had a DOSAAF organization headed by a chairman and a central committee. DOSAAF worked closely with the ministries of education and the state committees for physical culture and sports in the union republics; it also maintained close relations with the deputy commanders for premilitary training in the military districts. The Premilitary Training Directorate within the Ministry of Defense supervised DOSAAF, yet the DOSAAF budget was separate from that of the Ministry of Defense.

The best DOSAAF clubs were found in the Russian Republic, which included 51 percent of the population in the late 1980s and 75 percent of the territory. The clubs offered specialist training, such as skiing, parachute jumping, scuba diving, motorcycle driving, seamanship, flying, and radio and electronics maintenance, which were not available in the other republics. Yet many DOSAAF organizations throughout the country lacked qualified or full-time military instructors. Providing time and facilities for DOSAAF training was an added burden on schools and factories. In 1989 the southern Soviet republics were often criticized in the military press for having poor premilitary training programs and sending unprepared recruits to the armed forces. One Western observer estimated that only half the Soviet troops actually received prescribed DOSAAF instruction prior to induction. Approximately one-third of all inductees, however, possessed a technical military specialty that they had learned in a DOSAAF club.

Conscripts

Under the 1967 Law on Universal Military Service, all male citizens must serve in the armed forces beginning at the age of eighteen. The conscription period for servicemen was two years except for sailors, which was three years. The 1967 law reduced the conscription period from three and four years, respectively, to provide more labor for the economy. A nationwide system of over 4,000 military commissariats (*voennye komissariaty—voenkomaty;* sing., *voenkomat*—see Glossary) at the republic, oblast, *raion,* and city levels was responsible for conscription and veterans affairs. A *voenkomat* was accountable to the commander of the military district in which it was located. All males had to report to a *voenkomat* when they turned seventeen. The induction commission of the *voenkomat* gave potential recruits a physical examination and reviewed their school and DOSAAF training records.

Each year over 2 million eighteen-year-olds have reported to *voenkomat* induction commissions. They have reported in the spring and the fall depending on whether their birthdays were in the first or second half of the year. Based on quotas assigned by the General Staff's Main Organization and Mobilization Directorate, the *voenkomat* either assigned recruits to one of the armed services or granted deferments. Assignments were based on the physical attributes, education, skills, and political background of individual conscripts. The services that required technical abilities or high reliability, therefore, received conscripts with the highest qualifications. For example, the Airborne Troops accepted only recruits that had been fully trained in parachute jumping by DOSAAF. By contrast, the Ground Forces and the Rear Services have had to take less qualified inductees. Overall, however, 90 percent of servicemen have had a secondary education.

The *voenkomaty* granted about one-quarter of eighteen-year-old men deferments from service because of ill health or family hardship. Eighteen-year-olds were also exempted from service if they were enrolled in a higher education institution. They were required, however, to participate in the reserve officer training program of that institution. Those who had participated in such training programs could serve as little as a year of active duty after graduation. In 1982 education exemptions were restricted to those enrolled in a list of institutions approved by the Ministry of Defense. Young men not conscripted into the armed forces at eighteen remained liable to induction until age twenty-seven. The number of men deferred and later conscripted was probably small, however. Deferments were reportedly obtained from some induction commissions for a bribe of 1,000 rubles. The practice has been common enough that the Law on Universal Military Service mentioned punishment for granting illegal deferments. Soviet law did not provide for a conscientious objector status. In 1987, however, a pacifist group

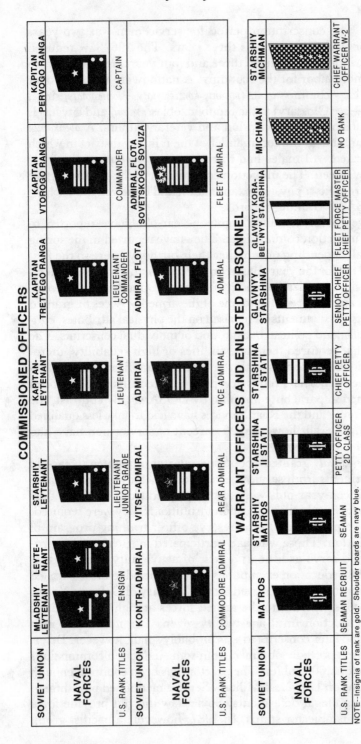

Figure 36. Ranks and Insignia of Naval Forces, 1989

called Trust took advantage of Gorbachev's policy of *glasnost'* to protest compulsory service in the armed forces.

Life in the Soviet Armed Forces

On the day before beginning to serve in the armed forces, Soviet conscripts have traditionally attended an induction ceremony in which local CPSU officials and veterans gave patriotic speeches. The next day, they were transported directly to the military unit in which they would serve their two- or three-year tours of duty. Neither the conscripts nor their families knew its location beforehand. After one month of basic training that reviewed their premilitary training, conscripts took the military oath in their regiments. In the oath, conscripts swore to guard state and military secrets, to master the craft of war, to protect state property, and to defend the homeland and government without sparing life or blood.

Soviet troops lived under harsh conditions and strict discipline. The practice of stationing troops in isolated areas outside their home republics or regions and the system of internal passports kept the desertion rate relatively low; the location of Soviet troops far from their home region also enabled them to be deployed more easily against a rebellious local population. Troops had about an hour per day of "free" time, much of which was used for additional political training and mandatory sports activities. Leave and temporary passes were not issued as a matter of course. New conscripts could also expect to be harassed by soldiers in their second year of service. Such hazing occasionally spilled over into physical abuse and theft by senior soldiers against first-year troops. Conscripts were paid between 3 and 5 rubles per month, about enough to buy cigarettes. Low pay for conscripts conserved the Ministry of Defense's resources, but soldiers often became burdens for their families, who sent them money.

The rate of alcoholism among military personnel was reported to be higher than in society as a whole, a fact that could be attributed to the boredom and isolation of life in the barracks. In addition, the expense and difficulty involved in obtaining alcohol often resulted in petty corruption and the sale of military supplies on the black market. Soldiers were confined to the stockade for minor infractions of this type. They were sent to penal battalions for more serious offenses, and time spent there did not count as time toward their discharge.

Units trained six days every week in winter and summer cycles. The majority of parade drill, tactics, weapons, chemical defense, political, and physical training took place in garrison. The armed forces have strictly limited live firings of weapons, field exercises,

745

days at sea, and flight time. The average serviceman might participate in several three-day regimental exercises and possibly one larger exercise in the military district in a two-year tour of duty. In addition to their military training, units have often been called on to help with harvesting. The semiannual turnover of conscripts, one-quarter of total conscript manpower, has meant that new inductees were constantly being assimilated into the armed services. This turnover and the two-year service term made it difficult to train and retain specialists to work on sophisticated weapons systems.

Semiannual discharge orders from the minister of defense released troops completing their active duty and automatically enlisted them in the reserves. These troops also had the option of reenlisting as extended service soldiers or applying to become noncommissioned officers. Few did so, however. On returning home, released conscripts had to register as reserves with the *voenkomat* and report to it changes in their residence, health, education, or family status until their reserve obligation ended at age fifty.

Noncommissioned Officers

The armed forces had a very low percentage of noncommissioned officers (NCOs) compared with other armies of the world and even fewer career NCOs. Soviet NCOs were essentially conscripts. At the time of induction, each *voenkomat* selected a few recruits to become NCOs. After training for from several weeks to six months, these new NCOs were assigned to units, but their authority over other conscripts was limited by their youth and inexperience. Moreover, because only 5 percent of Soviet military personnel were NCOs, junior commissioned officers had to perform many tasks assigned to sergeants in other countries' armies. The armed forces have made an effort to build a career NCO corps in order to retain needed skills, improve small unit leadership, and make a military career more attractive to conscripts. For example, in 1972 the Ministry of Defense instituted the NCO rank of warrant officer between the ranks of sergeant and junior officer. NCOs could also attend a six- to nine-month specialist course to become platoon commanders and company technicians.

National Minorities in the Armed Forces

The military tried to give the impression that soldiers of different nationalities served together harmoniously, but the number of articles in the military press devoted to relations between ethnic groups itself indicated the persistence of nationality conflict within the armed forces. Rather than contributing to nation building, service in the armed forces reportedly was more likely to increase ethnic and linguistic consciousness. In the late 1980s, the Soviet Union's non-Slavic minority groups comprised one-quarter of the conscript pool. Western experts estimated that, as Slavic birthrates declined, by the year 2000 one-third of draft-age males would be non-Slavic.

The armed forces, however, appeared to have mechanisms in place for maintaining control over national minorities in their ranks. The armed forces have been dominated by Slavs in general and Russians in particular. Russian has been the only language of command, and Slavs constituted 80 percent of all combat personnel and 95 percent of the officer corps. Although more non-Slavs will have to be drafted in the future, a pervasive inability, or unwillingness, to read or speak Russian among non-Slavic, and particularly Central Asian, recruits has impeded their training and advancement in the military. Because the Russian language was not taught to conscripts in the armed forces, non-Slavs have been limited to assignments in nontechnical and noncombat positions. Most Central Asian conscripts were assigned to Construction and Troop Billeting and served their two years in construction battalions. They received little combat training.

The military leadership viewed non-Slavs as potentially unreliable frontline troops. For example, Central Asian Muslim soldiers were deployed in Afghanistan during the early days of the war but had to be withdrawn because they sympathized with their coreligionists in that country. Moreover, non-Slavs were rarely assigned to the elite armed services. They were, however, recruited to serve with the Internal Troops in the Russian Republic because they could be counted on to suppress any disturbance in areas inhabited by ethnic Slavs.

Women in the Armed Forces

Under the Soviet Constitution, women had the same legal obligation as men for the defense of the Soviet Union and have been called on to discharge it. A women's battalion existed at the time of the Bolshevik Revolution and during the Civil War. Approximately 800,000 women served in both combat and noncombat roles during World War II. According to the 1967 Law on Universal Military Service, women with medical or other special training must register for the draft, but they have not been inducted. Women between nineteen and forty may volunteer for active duty. In wartime women would be drafted for "auxiliary or special duty." The 1967 law did not specify whether they would be used in combat. In the late 1980s, an estimated 10,000 to 30,000 women were serving in the armed forces in medical, communications, and administrative support positions. Women were not admitted to military education institutions, and few became officers. Many Western observers believe that the armed forces will have to rely more on women in the future as the number of available Slavic men declines.

Officers

The profession of officer in the armed forces has been prestigious and well respected in the Soviet Union. The number of officers was very large, in part because the armed forces have contained a large number of conscripts and relatively few NCOs. The presence of a political officer, or *zampolit,* in every company or battery also has significantly raised the total number of officers.

As of 1989, the Soviet Union had the world's largest officer training system. At the secondary level, it had eight Suvorov military schools and the Nakhimov Naval Secondary School to prepare fifteen- and sixteen-year-old cadets, who were often sons of officers, for direct admission into higher military education institutions.

In 1989 the Soviet Union had about 140 higher military schools, which trained officers for each armed service or combat arm. Young men between seventeen and twenty-one who had a secondary education could apply for admission into higher military schools. Servicemen under the age of twenty-three could also apply. Admission was based on a competitive examination in Russian language and literature, Soviet history, physics, and mathematics, as well as a thorough review of an applicant's political and educational background.

Each higher military school had over 1,000 cadets and trained either command, engineering, or political officers for a particular combat arm (see table 55, Appendix A). The four- or five-year curriculum of command schools included about 60 percent military science, weapons, and tactics instruction and 40 percent general sciences education and political training. Cadets in political or engineering schools received correspondingly more political or technical instruction. Upon graduation cadets received university diplomas and were commissioned as junior lieutenants. The higher military schools and reserve officer training programs in about 900 civilian higher education institutions produced about 60,000 new officers for the armed forces each year.

Junior officers remained in their assignments for long periods and were evaluated for promotion every four years based on their professional knowledge, performance, and moral-political capabilities (see Glossary). Some junior officer promotions were almost automatic because the time-in-grade requirement for advancement in rank was only two years. Officers' monthly pay ranged between 150 rubles for lieutenants and 2,000 rubles for generals, which was considerably more than the salary of most managers in the civilian sector.

Officers had greater opportunities to commit infractions of military law than ordinary servicemen, and their most common criminal offense was bribery. Officers inspecting units accepted bribes in return for overlooking training deficiencies, accidents, or disciplinary breaches. The misuse of state property, and vehicles in particular, was also widespread. According to the Law on Universal Military Service, however, officers could be discharged for committing acts that disgraced their titles.

Upon reaching the rank of senior lieutenant or captain, many officers began to prepare for competitive examinations to enter one of seventeen military academies. Candidates for admission were required to have held a regimental command position and received excellent ratings and to have been endorsed by the political directorate of their command or service. The two- or three-year program of a Soviet military academy was similar to command and staff training or war colleges in Western countries. Each armed service and combat arm had its own academy. The Frunze Military Academy, the most prestigious at its level, specialized in combined arms training but was attended predominantly by Ground Forces officers. Advanced study in military academies involved major military science research projects that were frequently published in books or articles. Military academies awarded diplomas equivalent to master's or doctoral degrees in the West. They also conducted correspondence courses leading to similar degrees.

Graduation from a military academy was practically a requirement for advancement to higher rank. In particular, graduation from the Voroshilov General Staff Academy, the highest-level academy, was a prerequisite for appointment to important Ministry of Defense and General Staff positions. Among its graduates have been the ministers of defense of the Warsaw Pact countries. High rank has brought a salary of as much as 2,000 rubles monthly and other perquisites that come with being part of the elite. For example, many generals had summer homes reportedly built with government construction materials and military manpower.

Officers were not under pressure to advance in rank, and higher ranking officers were not forced to retire early from the armed services. In theory, an officer could serve as a junior lieutenant until age forty. Mandatory retirement began at age forty and went up to age sixty for major generals. Above this rank, general officers could get extensions and were effectively exempt from mandatory retirement. In practice, many officers who resisted retirement were put to work in civil defense or DOSAAF organizations. High-ranking officers often moved into the Ministry of Defense's Main Inspectorate as senior inspectors or became the heads of higher military schools or academies.

Reserves and Wartime Mobilization

The Soviet Union had the world's most elaborate system of wartime mobilization, although it was not certain that the system would be as impressive in action as it was on paper. Soldiers retained a reserve obligation until age fifty. For officers, the reserve obligation extended to sixty-five. Thus, Western specialists estimated that over 50 million males were reservists. Local *voenkomaty* maintained records of residences and other data that would be important in mobilizing the reserves.

Reserves were divided into two categories of three classes based on age and the amount of refresher training they were supposed to receive after mobilization. Reserves were subject to periodic call-ups for active duty or training in the local garrison. The amount of reserve training actually conducted varied greatly.

In 1989 the Soviet Union had about 9 million servicemen who had been discharged from active duty in the preceding five years. Only 3 million of them would be needed to bring all active Ground Forces divisions to full strength in fewer than three days. Western analysts speculated that large numbers of additional divisions could be created within two to three months using civilian trucks and large stockpiles of older weapons and equipment. Such forces could be employed effectively against NATO's second echelons, as well as against less formidable opponents.

Reserves, together with additional manpower and equipment mobilized in wartime, would substantially augment the considerable strength of the peacetime Soviet military. Long favored by the political leadership, the military has received a large proportion of the human and material resources of the Soviet Union. Guided and controlled by the CPSU, the military's strategic leaders have organized, trained, and equipped the Soviet armed forces to capably fulfill their assigned missions.

* * *

The single most complete work on the Soviet armed forces is Harriet F. Scott and William F. Scott's *The Armed Forces of the USSR.* The Department of Defense's *Soviet Military Power,* the eighth edition of which was published in 1989, contains information about

Soviet forces that is not available to the public elsewhere. *The Military Balance,* issued annually by the International Institute for Strategic Studies, is a consistently accurate and independent source of information on the size of the Soviet defense effort. Coverage of current developments in Soviet weapons, tactics, strategy, and military leadership can be found in the regular columns and feature articles of many defense-oriented journals. The *Air University Library Index to Military Periodicals,* edited by Emily J. Adams, is an excellent resource for locating these articles. The *Soviet Armed Forces Review Annual,* edited by David R. Jones, provides coverage of changes in the Soviet military from year to year. Richard A. Gabriel and Ellen Jones have written extensively on the troops behind Soviet weapons and equipment. *Inside the Soviet Army,* by a Soviet officer who defected to the West and writes under the pseudonym Viktor Suvorov, also contains revealing insights into the operation of and life in the armed forces. (For further information and complete citations, see Bibliography.)

Chapter 19. Internal Security

Symbols of internal security: the crest of the Committee for State Security (KGB), border guards near a watchtower, and a member of the Ministry of Internal Affairs (MVD)

IN THE LATE 1980s, the Soviet Union continued to place great emphasis on ensuring security and internal order. Because it was governed by a monopolistic party, whose leaders were not democratically elected, the Soviet system had no legitimacy based on popular support and therefore protected itself from internal and external threats by means of a strong security system. The system included the regular police, judicial bodies, prosecuting organs, and the security police, as well as an external security and foreign intelligence apparatus. Even in the era of *perestroika* (see Glossary) and *glasnost'* (see Glossary) ushered in by General Secretary Mikhail S. Gorbachev, the organs of internal security still had a key role to play, despite the party leadership's apparent tolerance of criticism of the political system.

The Soviet security, or political, police had a long history, dating back to the prerevolutionary, tsarist period. Although the tsarist political police was ruthless and unscrupulous, the police organs established by Vladimir I. Lenin and the Bolsheviks (see Glossary) in 1917, known as the Vecheka (see Glossary), far surpassed their predecessors in terms of terror and violence. The Bolsheviks allowed the Vecheka almost unrestricted powers to persecute those who were perceived as "class enemies." This set the stage for the development of the brutal Stalinist police state, in which millions of innocent victims perished at the hands of the political police, controlled by Joseph V. Stalin.

After Stalin died, Nikita S. Khrushchev initiated legal reforms and reorganized the police apparatus. The terror ended abruptly, and the political police were brought under the control of the Communist Party of the Soviet Union (CPSU). The Committee for State Security (Komitet gosudarstvennoi bezopasnosti—KGB), established in March 1954, was tasked with security functions, and the Ministry of Internal Affairs (Ministerstvo vnutrennykh del—MVD) was charged with combating ordinary crime and maintaining the extensive network of labor camps. A new legal code was established to replace the Stalinist laws, and both the security police and the regular police were subjected to procedural norms and regulations in carrying out their functions. Nevertheless, the party leadership did not eliminate all the legal loopholes and allowed the KGB to circumvent the law when combating political dissent. The KGB also played an important role in implementing the anticorruption campaign, which resulted in the ouster of many state and party officials after General Secretary Leonid I. Brezhnev died. Among its other tasks were guarding the leadership and important government buildings; protecting Soviet state borders; and carrying out intelligence, counterintelligence, and active measures (see Glossary) abroad.

The MVD was restricted to combating ordinary crime and, unlike the KGB, was subjected to constant criticism in the Soviet press, which attacked its inefficiency and corruption. In addition to the MVD, the Procuracy (Prokuratura) and the Ministry of Justice played important roles in implementing the laws and administering justice. The Ministry of Defense's Main Military Procuracy, along with the system of military tribunals, handled crimes within the armed forces.

Both the KGB and the MVD played important roles in the succession crises that followed Brezhnev's death. The KGB, however, was more politically significant than the MVD and, after the early 1970s, had an increasing impact on Soviet domestic and foreign policy making. To reinforce their coercive role, the KGB and the MVD had special troops at their disposal, including the Border Troops, the Security Troops, and the Internal Troops.

Predecessors of the Committee for State Security and the Ministry of Internal Affairs

The KGB and the MVD had numerous predecessor organizations, dating back to the tsarist period. These organizations contributed significantly to the historical traditions of the modern Soviet police, which in several ways resembled those of its forerunners.

The Tsarist Period

The 1980s Soviet police system cannot be properly understood without considering the evolution of the tsarist police, particularly as it related to Russia's political culture and governmental institutions. By the middle of the nineteenth century, Russia was, by all accounts, a "police state," not in the modern sense of the term, which connotes all the evils of Nazi Germany and Stalinism, but in the more traditional sense as it applied to certain European states in the eighteenth and early nineteenth centuries, e.g., France and Prussia. These states, which incorporated secret political police, spying, and encroachments on individual rights with both paternalism and enlightenment, were motivated by a desire to reform and modernize.

Russia's monarchical police state was similar to those in western Europe except that it lagged far behind in its political evolution and was much less efficient. The foundations of the tsarist police state were established in 1826, when Tsar Nicholas I formed the so-called Third Section, a political police whose purpose was to protect the state from internal subversion. The staff of the Third Section was small, numbering only forty full-time employees, who were burdened with information-gathering and welfare functions that extended well beyond the realm of political surveillance. As a result, its role was vague and poorly defined, and its efforts to combat political dissent, on the whole, were ineffective.

In 1880, as part of an effort to improve the effectiveness of the political police, the much-discredited Third Section was abolished and replaced by the central State Police Department under the Ministry of the Interior. Its chief responsibility was dealing with political crimes, and, although its staff consisted of only 161 full-time employees, it had at its disposal the Corps of Gendarmes, numbering several thousand, and a large contingent of informers. In addition, the notorious "security sections" were established in several Russian cities following the assassination of Alexander II in 1881. Despite the fact that its operations were strengthened, the political police was not successful in stemming the tide of the revolutionary movement, which helped to bring down the Russian monarchy in 1917. Police operations were hampered by the low quality of personnel and grave deficiencies in training. One of the greatest impediments to an effective political police was the general reluctance on the part of the Russian state to use violence against political dissenters. Herein lies one of the crucial differences between the monarchical police state of tsarist Russia and the Soviet regime, which from the outset used violence to preserve its rule and gradually extended the violence to affect broad segments of the population.

Soviet Predecessor Organizations, 1917–54

The Bolshevik regime created a police system that proved to be far more effective than the tsarist version. It swept away the tsarist police, so despised by Russians of all political persuasions, along with other tsarist institutions, and replaced it with a political police of considerably greater dimensions, both in the scope of its authority and in the severity of its methods. However lofty their initial goals were, the Bolsheviks forcibly imposed their rule on the people. They constituted a dictatorship of a minority that had to establish a powerful political police apparatus to preserve its domination.

The first Soviet political police, created in December 1917, was the All-Russian Extraordinary Commission for Combating Counterrevolution and Sabotage (Vserossiiskaia chrezvychainaia komissiia po bor'be s kontrrevoliutsiei i sabotazhem—VChK; also known as the Vecheka or the Cheka). The Vecheka was very much an ad hoc organization whose powers gradually grew in response to various emergencies and threats to Soviet rule (see table 56, Appendix A). No formal legislation establishing the Vecheka was ever enacted. It was to serve as an organ of preliminary investigation, but the crimes it was to uncover were not defined, and the procedures for handling cases were not set forth. This situation was the result of the extralegal character of the Vecheka, which was conceived not as a permanent state institution but as a temporary organ for waging war against "class enemies." Given its militant role and supralegal status, it is not surprising that the Vecheka, which was headed by Feliks E. Dzerzhinskii, acquired powers of summary justice as the threat of counterrevolution and foreign intervention grew. After an attempt was made on Lenin's life in August 1918, the Vecheka unleashed its violence on a wide scale, the so-called Red Terror, which continued until 1920 and caused thousands to lose their lives.

The end of the Civil War (1918–21), the demobilization of the Red Army, and the introduction of the New Economic Policy (NEP) in 1921 brought about a changed atmosphere that seemed incompatible with a terrorist political police. Lenin himself spoke of the need for a reform of the political police, and in early 1922 the Vecheka was abolished and its functions transferred to the State Political Directorate (Gosudarstvennoe politicheskoe upravlenie—GPU). When the Soviet Union was formed in December 1922, the GPU was raised to the level of a federal agency, designated the Unified State Political Directorate (Ob"edinennoe gosudarstvennoe politicheskoe upravlenie—OGPU), and attached to the Council of People's Commissars. On paper it appeared that the powers of the political police had been reduced significantly. Indeed, police operations during the NEP period were considerably less violent, and the staff and budget of the political police were reduced. Initially, the OGPU was subject to definite procedural requirements regarding arrests and was not given the powers of summary justice that its predecessor had. But the legal constraints on the OGPU were gradually removed, and its authority grew throughout the 1920s. The OGPU was drawn into the intraparty struggles that ensued between Stalin and his opponents and was also enlisted in the drive to collectivize the peasantry by force, beginning in late 1929, an operation that resulted in the death of at least 5 million people.

In July 1934, the OGPU was transformed into the Main Directorate for State Security (Glavnoe upravlenie gosudarstvennoi bezopasnosti—GUGB) and integrated into the People's Commissariat of Internal Affairs (Narodnyi komissariat vnutrennykh del—NKVD), which had been given all-union (see Glossary) status earlier that year. The functions of the security police and those of the internal affairs apparatus, which controlled the regular police and the militia, were thus united in one agency. The NKVD was a powerful organization. In addition to controlling the security police and the regular police, it was in charge of border and internal troops, fire brigades, convoy troops, and, after 1934, the entire penal system, including regular prisons and forced labor camps, or the Gulag (see Glossary). During the period from 1934 to 1940, the NKVD took charge of numerous economic enterprises (see Glossary) that employed forced labor, such as gold mining, major construction projects, and other industrial activity. In addition, the Special Board, attached to the NKVD, operated outside the legal codes and was empowered to impose on persons deemed "socially dangerous" sentences of exile, deportation, or confinement in labor camps. The Special Board soon became one of the chief instruments of Stalin's purges.

Stalin's domination over the party was not absolute at this time, however. Dissatisfaction with his policies continued to be manifested by some party members, and elements existed within the leadership that might have opposed any attempt to use police terror against the party. Among Stalin's potential challengers was Sergei Kirov, chief of the Leningrad party apparatus. Conveniently for Stalin, Kirov was assassinated by a disgruntled ex-party member in December 1934. This provided Stalin with the pretext for launching an assault against the party. Although Stalin proceeded cautiously, the turning point had been reached, and the terror machinery was in place. From 1936 to 1938, the NKVD arrested and executed millions of party members, government officials, and ordinary citizens. The military also came under assault. Much of the officer corps was wiped out in 1937–38, leaving the country ill prepared for World War II. The era in which the NKVD, with Stalin's aproval, terrorized Soviet citizens became known in the West as the Great Terror (see Glossary).

The war years brought further opportunities for the political police, under the control of Lavrenty Beria, to expand its authority. The NKVD assumed a number of additional economic functions that made use of the expanding labor camp population. The NKVD also broadened its presence in the Red Army, where it conducted extensive surveillance of the troops. Toward the end of the war, the political police moved into areas formerly under German occupation to arrest those suspected of sympathy for the Nazis. They also suppressed nationalist movements in the Estonian, Latvian, Lithuanian, and western Ukrainian republics.

Beria himself steadily gained power and authority during this period. In early 1946, when he was made a full member of the Politburo and a deputy chairman of the Council of Ministers (the new name for the Council of People's Commissars), he relinquished his NKVD post, but he apparently retained some control over the police through his protégés in that organization. In March 1953, following Stalin's death, Beria became chief of the MVD, which amalgamated the regular police and the security police into one organization. Some three months later, he was viewed as a threat to the leadership and was arrested by his Kremlin colleagues, including Khrushchev.

The "Beria affair" and the shake-up in the Kremlin that followed his arrest had far-reaching consequences for the role of the police in Soviet society. The party leadership not only arrested and later executed Beria and several of his allies in the MVD but also took measures to place the political police under its firm control. Thereafter, violence was no longer to be used as a means of settling conflicts within the leadership, and widespread terror was not employed against the population.

The Security Apparatus and Kremlin Politics

The Khrushchev period was important for the development of the internal security apparatus. Legal reforms, personnel changes, and the denunciation of Stalin had a marked effect on the position of the police and the legal organs. As the successor to Khrushchev, Brezhnev did much to reverse the tide of reforms, but later, under Gorbachev, reforms progressed again. The reforms brought opposition to Gorbachev from the police apparatus because the changes curtailed police powers.

Khrushchev Period

One of the first reforms instituted by the post-Stalin leadership under Khrushchev was a reorganization of the police apparatus. On March 13, 1954 a decree of the Presidium of the Supreme Soviet established the KGB, attached to the Council of Ministers. The establishment of a state security apparatus separate from that of the regular police was designed to diminish the formidable powers that the police had wielded when its activities were concentrated in one organization. Thereafter, the functions of ensuring political security would be ascribed to a special police agency, whose powers were substantially less than they had been under Stalin.

The party leadership also instituted significant legal reforms to protect citizens from police persecution. On May 24, 1955, a new statute on procurator (see Glossary) supervision was enacted by the Presidium of the Supreme Soviet. This statute provided procedural guarantees of procuratorial power to protest illegalities committed by state agencies and to make proposals for eliminating these illegalities. Another reform that restricted the powers of the political police and protected citizens from police persecution was the enactment in December 1958 of the Fundamental Principles of Criminal Procedure, which were incorporated into the 1960 Russian Republic's Code of Criminal Procedure and were still in effect in 1989, although they had been amended several times.

The new codes, which were established according to the Russian Republic model in the other republics as well, subjected the KGB to the same procedural rules to which other investigative agencies were subject and specified precisely the types of crimes the KGB was empowered to investigate. A new law on state crimes, enacted on December 25, 1958, and incorporated into the 1960 Code of Criminal Procedure of the Russian Republic, narrowed the range of political crimes that were embodied in the Stalinist codes and made criminal sanctions less severe.

Khrushchev's policy of de-Stalinization also had significance for the role of the post-Stalin political police. His famous "secret speech," delivered at the Twentieth Party Congress in February 1956, called attention to the crimes committed by the police under Stalin. This inevitably weakened the prestige of the KGB and demoralized its cadres (see Glossary), many of whom had participated actively in the purges.

These police and legal reforms were diminished somewhat by the appointment in 1954 of two long-time police officials, Ivan Serov and Sergei Kruglov, to head the KGB and the MVD, respectively. Serov's past was heavily tainted by his participation in the Stalinist police repression, as was that of Kruglov. Both, however, had lent their support to Khrushchev when he made his move against Beria, and apparently they had to be rewarded. Although Khrushchev and the party leadership wanted to demonstrate that they were "cleansing the ranks" of the police by purging many officials, they retained others who were loyal and experienced.

In December 1958, Serov was removed from his post as KGB chief and replaced by Aleksandr Shelepin, a former Komsomol (see Glossary) official. With his higher education in humanities and his untainted record, Shelepin did much to raise the stature of the KGB and to bring renewed efficiency and legitimacy to it. By the late 1950s, efforts were under way to improve the public image of the KGB by portraying its officials in a favorable light in the media and by publishing works on the history of the Soviet political police.

In addition, changes in the legal codes in 1961 broadened the KGB's investigative powers.

Shelepin himself may have been largely responsible for the campaign to rehabilitate the security police. Although he left his post as head of the KGB in December 1961, he continued to oversee the police in his capacity as Central Committee secretary, and his successor, Vladimir Semichastnyi, was a close ally. Both Shelepin and Semichastnyi appeared to have joined the ranks of opposition to Khrushchev sometime before his ouster in October 1964 and were actively involved in the plot to overthrow the party leader. De-Stalinization, legal reforms, and various other measures promoted by Khrushchev to curtail the activities of the security police had no doubt created resentment within its ranks and aroused the displeasure of leading KGB officials.

After Khrushchev

Brezhnev evidently had learned a lesson from Khrushchev's experience and went out of his way to raise the status of the police and clamp down on political dissent. The KGB's investigative powers were extended in 1965 to include certain categories of economic crime, and it continued to be accorded favorable publicity in the Soviet press. Its growing prestige and authority accommodated those neoconservative trends that manifested themselves during the late 1960s and 1970s: curbs on cultural freedom, a crackdown on dissent, and a partial rehabilitation of Stalin.

Brezhnev and his party colleagues became worried about the ambitions of Shelepin, however, and decided to put an end to his influence over the security police. In May 1967, Semichastnyi was removed as KGB chief, and by November of that year Shelepin was out of the Central Committee Secretariat. The new KGB chairman was Iurii I. Andropov, a Central Committee secretary who had served as ambassador to Hungary and later as head of the Liaison with Communist and Workers' Parties of Socialist Countries Department of the Central Committee. He was apparently a neutral figure politically, agreed upon by all members of the collective leadership; Brezhnev, however, managed to bring in several of his own protégés to serve directly below Andropov. The most important of these was a KGB official named Semen Tsvigun, reportedly Brezhnev's brother-in-law, who was made first deputy KGB chairman in December 1967. Viktor M. Chebrikov was another official with links to Brezhnev who was brought to Moscow to serve in the KGB. The presence of his allies in the KGB leadership was a source of strength for Brezhnev, and he made certain that their careers prospered. In addition to encouraging favorable publicity for the KGB, Brezhnev was careful to ensure that employees of the KGB were well paid and enjoyed significant privileges and perquisites.

Brezhnev may have underestimated the political prowess of Andropov, however. Andropov benefited from the increased powers and prestige that the KGB gained under the Brezhnev leadership and became a powerful political leader in his own right. As Brezhnev's death became imminent in 1982, Andropov began contending for the top party post. His success in reaching his goal in November 1982 was due partly to his attack, using KGB files as weapons, on the Brezhnevites for their involvement in corruption. Not surprisingly, Andropov's short tenure as general secretary (November 1982–February 1984) was marked by a stronger KGB role. Even Andropov's illness and death did not result in a decline for the KGB. On the contrary, the extended period of political upheaval in the Kremlin following his death seemed to increase the KGB's influence. Its officials received prominent coverage in the press, and KGB representation on party and state leadership bodies grew.

Gorbachev Era

After gaining the post of general secretary in March 1985, Gorbachev moved with unprecedented speed to implement personnel changes in the party and government. His success in getting rid of so many potential political opponents in such a short time surprised Western Soviet experts, particularly because Gorbachev did not have a substantial power base or patronage network of his own when he took office. Gorbachev apparently relied on the same bases of support that Andropov had used in his ascent to the top, which included the KGB. According to Western experts, Gorbachev appealed to the KGB for help in purging the Brezhnev old guard. The main vehicle used by Gorbachev in carrying out these purges was the anticorruption campaign. By the late summer of 1985, hardly a day passed without a report in the press on cases of bribery, embezzlement, or other forms of economic crime. In addition to high-level party and state officials, MVD and Procuracy employees came under fire for their failure to uncover crimes. Even MVD chief Vitalii Fedorchuk fell victim to Gorbachev, losing his post in early 1986. Fedorchuk's replacement, Aleksandr Vlasov, was a former party apparatchik (see Glossary) with no experience in law enforcement.

Although the regular law enforcement agencies were subjected to sharp attacks for their failure to combat crime, the KGB remained unscathed, despite the fact that it was empowered by law to investigate certain types of economic crime. There was some turnover in key KGB posts, but these changes were not nearly as widespread as were the changes in the CPSU apparatus and in other state agencies.

Numerous signs pointed to the fact that the Gorbachev leadership was cultivating good relations with the KGB by maintaining its high prestige and political status. KGB chairman Chebrikov was promoted to full membership in the Politburo just a month after Gorbachev came to power. He also figured prominently in the Soviet media. At the Twenty-Seventh Party Congress in February–March 1986, for example, he delivered a speech that was an unprecedented assertion of the power and authority of the KGB.

Although Gorbachev continued to rely on the KGB in his drive to purge the party and state apparatus of corrupt officials, toward the end of 1986 signs indicated that his relations with this organization were becoming strained. The KGB cannot have been pleased about the reformist polices promoted by Gorbachev, in particular openness in the media and liberalization of cultural norms. Calls for reform of the judicial and legal systems, voiced with increasing frequency in the autumn of 1986, signified that the Gorbachev leadership was attempting to curtail arbitrary KGB actions against citizens. This attempt became even more apparent in January 1987, when Chebrikov acknowledged, on the front page of *Pravda,* that employees of the KGB had committed illegalities. Such an acknowledgment of KGB abuses was unprecedented. Even during the Khrushchev era, when the crimes of Stalin's security police were exposed, the KGB was never criticized in the press. Observers speculated that, having depended initially on KGB support to purge the Brezhnevites, Gorbachev decided by early 1987 that he was strong enough to embark on reforms that might antagonize this institution.

It was not long, however, before signs of opposition to Gorbachev's policies arose, and a "conservative backlash" occurred. Although the opposition appears to have been led by disgruntled party leaders such as Egor K. Ligachev, the second-ranking member of the Politburo, the KGB probably joined forces with these conservatives. Chebrikov's comments, in particular his strident speech delivered in September 1987, made it clear that the KGB would not allow the democratic reforms to go too far: "There must be a clear awareness that the restructuring is taking place in our state and society under the leadership of the Communist Party, within the framework of socialism and in the interests of socialism. This revolutionary process will be reliably protected against any subversive intrigues." The subsequent ouster of a leading proponent of Gorbachev's reforms, Moscow party chief Boris N. Yeltsin, was an indication of the strength of the opposition to Gorbachev.

Although he made some strategic retreats in early 1988, Gorbachev continued to pursue his policy of *perestroika,* and exposures of illegal KGB activities continued. Even more threatening for the KGB were unprecedented revelations about security police terror under Stalin. Although the role of the police in the purges had been discussed since the Khrushchev era, *glasnost'* resulted in a much more devastating critique of the role of the police during this period. Ethnic unrest of various nationalities, together with increasingly bold political demands by the Soviet intelligentsia, also presented the KGB with significant challenges. In a speech delivered in mid-April, Chebrikov expressed concern that things were going too far and that some individuals were "unleashing a wide-ranging arsenal of methods of social demagoguery and substituting bourgeois liberalism for the essence of the concept of socialist democracy." Subsequently, in October 1988 Chebrikov lost his position as chief of the KGB and was replaced by Vladimir A. Kriuchkov.

Organization of the Committee for State Security

The basic organizational structure of the KGB was created in 1954, when the reorganization of the police apparatus was carried out. In the late 1980s, the KGB remained a highly centralized institution with controls implemented by the Politburo through the KGB headquarters in Moscow.

Structure

The KGB was originally designated as a "state committee attached to the Council of Ministers." On July 5, 1978, a new law on the Council of Ministers changed the status of the KGB, along with that of several other state committees, so that its chairman was a member of the Council of Ministers by law. According to the 1977 Soviet Constitution, the Council of Ministers "coordinates and directs" the work of the ministries and state committees, including the KGB. In practice, however, the KGB had more autonomy than most other government bodies and operated with a large degree of independence from the Council of Ministers. The situation was similar with the Supreme Soviet, which had formal authority over the Council of Ministers and its agencies. In 1989 the actual powers of the Supreme Soviet, however, gave it little if any power over KGB operations.

The KGB was a union-republic state committee, controlling corresponding state committees of the same name in the fourteen non-Russian republics. (All-union ministries and state committees, by contrast, did not have corresponding branches in the republics but executed their functions directly through Moscow.) Below the republic level, there existed KGB administrations (*upravleniia*) in the *kraia* (see Glossary) and oblasts (see Glossary). In the Russian Republic, however, there was no republic-level KGB. Oblast KGB administrations in the Russian Republic were subordinated directly to the central KGB offices in Moscow. At the lower levels, autonomous *okruga* (see Glossary), cities, and *raiony* (see Glossary) had KGB departments or sections.

The KGB also had a broad network of special departments in all major government institutions, enterprises, and factories. They generally consisted of one or more KGB representatives, whose purpose was to ensure the observance of security regulations and to monitor political sentiments among employees. The special departments recruited informers to help them in their tasks. A separate and very extensive network of special departments existed within the armed forces and defense-related institutions.

Although a union-republic agency, the KGB was highly centralized and was controlled rigidly from the top. The KGB central staff kept a close watch over the operations of its branches, leaving the latter minimal autonomous authority over policy or cadre selection. Moreover, local government organs had little involvement in local KGB activities. Indeed, the high degree of centralization in the KGB was reflected in the fact that regional KGB branches were not subordinated to the local soviets (see Glossary), but only to the KGB hierarchy. Thus, they differed from local branches of most union-republic ministerial agencies, such as the MVD, which were subject to dual subordination.

The KGB was directed by a chairman—who was formally appointed by the Supreme Soviet but actually was selected by the Politburo—one or two first deputy chairmen, and several (usually four to six) deputy chairmen. Key decisions were made by the KGB Collegium, which was a collective leadership body composed of the chairman, deputy chairmen, chiefs of certain KGB directorates, and one or two chairmen of republic KGB organizations.

Functions and Internal Organization

As a state committee with ministerial status, the KGB operated on the basis of a statute (*polozhenie*), confirmed by the Council of Ministers, that set forth in legal terms the KGB's powers and duties. Unlike the majority of statutes governing ministerial agencies, the KGB's statute was not published. Nevertheless, Soviet textbooks on administrative law offered useful statements about the KGB's role and functions. The KGB's tasks were generally defined in official Soviet publications as encompassing four areas: the struggle against foreign spies and agents, the exposure and investigation of political and economic crimes by citizens, the protection of state borders, and the protection of state secrets. In addition, the KGB was charged with a wide range of preventive tasks, which were designed to eliminate the causes of both political and ordinary crimes. In other words, the KGB was tasked with ferreting out potential threats to the state and preventing the development of unorthodox political and social attitudes among the population.

Official Soviet sources did not discuss the internal structure of the KGB in detail. Nevertheless, some information on KGB organization and functions has been revealed by Soviet defectors and other sources. In 1988 the KGB had five chief directorates and three known (possibly another) directorates that were smaller in size and scope than the chief directorates, as well as various other administrative and technical support departments (see fig. 37). Western estimates of KGB manpower past ranged from 490,000 in 1973 to 700,000 in 1986.

The First Chief Directorate was responsible for all foreign operations and intelligence-gathering activities. It was divided into both functional services—training and management of covert agents, intelligence analysis, and collection of political, scientific, and technological intelligence—and geographic departments for various areas of the world.

The Second Chief Directorate was responsible for internal political control of Soviet citizens and foreigners residing within the Soviet Union, including both diplomats and tourists. The Fifth Chief Directorate also dealt with internal security. Created in the late 1960s to combat political dissent, it took up some of the tasks previously handled by the Second Chief Directorate. The Fifth Chief Directorate had special operational departments for religious dissent, national minorities, the intelligentsia and the artistic community, and censorship of literature. The Seventh Directorate handled surveillance, providing personnel and technical equipment to follow and monitor the activities of both foreigners and suspect Soviet citizens. Much of this work was centered in the Moscow and Leningrad areas, where tourists, diplomats, foreign students, and members of the Soviet intelligentsia were concentrated. The Eighth Chief Directorate was responsible for the highly sensitive area of communications. This directorate provided technical systems, including cipher systems, for other KGB departments and government agencies and also monitored and deciphered foreign communications.

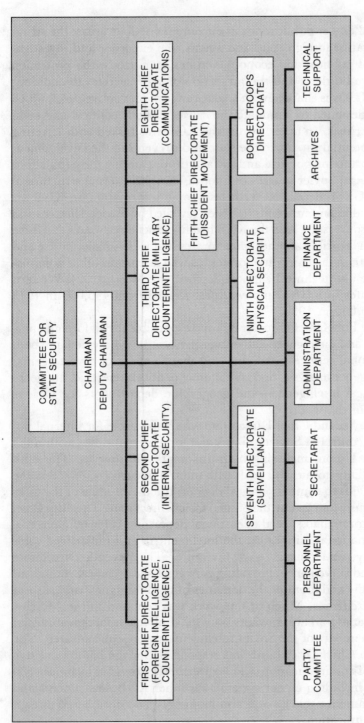

Figure 37. Organization of the Committee for State Security (KGB), 1988

The KGB had at least three additional directorates: the Third Chief Directorate, which dealt with military counterintelligence and political surveillance of the Soviet armed forces; the Border Troops Directorate, which protected Soviet land and sea borders; and the Ninth Directorate, which guarded the Kremlin and key offices of the CPSU.

In addition to the various directorates and a special network of training and education establishments, the KGB had a personnel department, a secretariat, a technical support staff, a finance department, an archives, an administration department, and a party committee. Most of these bodies had counterparts within the different directorates. Party committees, which existed in every Soviet organization, handled political indoctrination of personnel. Heads of party committees arranged regular meetings to discuss party matters and served as liaisons between the party and the KGB at various levels, although party membership was probably universal among KGB employees. At the republic level, KGB organization was probably similar to that of the central KGB, although republic KGBs did not supervise units of the Border Troops, which were administered centrally. Nor did they include functions of the Third Chief Directorate, which was organized primarily along military service lines or by military district. In addition, functions such as communications and foreign espionage may have been administered only in Moscow.

Party Control

Although the security police was always a government rather than a party institution, the party considered this agency to be its own vital arm and sought to maintain the closest supervision and control over its activities. The KGB was nominally subordinate to the Council of Ministers. But the CPSU, not the government, exercised control and direction. Aside from the Politburo, which probably issued general policy directives, another vehicle for such party control was, according to Western specialists, the State and Legal Department of the Central Committee Secretariat (see Secretariat, ch. 7). This department supervised all government agencies concerned with legal affairs, security, and defense, including the Ministry of Defense. It implemented party control by approving personnel appointments and exercising general oversight to ensure that these agencies were following party directives. From 1968 to 1988, the chief of this department, which probably had a staff of fifty to sixty employees, was Nikolai Savinkin. From the available evidence, it appears that the department did not involve itself as deeply in KGB affairs as it did in the activities of other state agencies, such as the MVD. Given the sensitive nature of KGB functions, the party leadership may have been reluctant to allocate to the State and Legal Department the most important decisions about KGB personnel and policy. Rather, the Central Committee secretaries charged with oversight responsibilities for the State and Legal Department probably made the key decisions. Such a portfolio was an important source of political power for a Central Committee secretary and was therefore a highly coveted responsibility. In January 1987, Anatolii I. Luk'ianov was brought into the Secretariat to supervise the State and Legal Department. He was, however, only a junior secretary, so Gorbachev or another senior secretary may have had the ultimate responsibility. Luk'ianov, an apparent ally of Gorbachev, had attended Moscow University's Law Faculty when Gorbachev was there in the early 1950s.

Personnel

Party personnel policy toward the KGB was designed not only to ensure that the overall security needs of the state were met by means of an efficient and well-functioning political police organization but also to prevent the police from becoming too powerful and threatening the party leadership. Achieving these two goals required the careful recruitment and promotion of KGB officials who had the appropriate education, experience, and qualifications as determined by the party. Judging from the limited biographical information on KGB employees, the Komsomol and the party were the main sources of recruitment to the KGB. Russians and Ukrainians predominated in the KGB; other nationalities were only minimally represented. In the non-Russian republics, KGB chairmen were often representatives of the indigenous nationality, as were other KGB employees. In such areas, however, KGB headquarters in Moscow appointed Russians to the post of first deputy chairman, and they monitored activities and reported back to Moscow.

Career patterns indicate that the KGB was a highly professional bureaucratic group with distinct characteristics that set it off from other Soviet elites. After the purges at the top levels of the police apparatus and the introduction of party and other cadres into the newly created KGB in 1954, the influx of outsiders was small, except at the very highest levels. Turnover rates were low in the KGB as compared with other bureaucracies, and KGB officials enjoyed security of tenure, as well as numerous material rewards. The KGB became—and in the 1980s remained—a closed bureaucracy of specialists, similar to the military. The homogeneity of their backgrounds and their sense of eliteness created a strong esprit de corps among KGB officials.

Domestic Security and the Committee for State Security

The KGB had a variety of domestic security functions. It was empowered by law to arrest and investigate individuals for certain types of political and economic crimes. It was also responsible for censorship, propaganda, and the protection of state and military secrets.

Legal Prerogatives

In carrying out its task of ensuring state security, the KGB was empowered by law to uncover and investigate certain political crimes set forth in the Russian Republic's Code of Criminal Procedure and the criminal codes of other republics. According to the Russian Republic's Code of Criminal Procedure, which came into force in 1960 and has been revised several times since then, the KGB had the authority, together with the Procuracy, to investigate the political crimes of treason, espionage, terrorism, sabotage, anti-Soviet agitation and propaganda, divulgence of state secrets, smuggling, illegal exit abroad, and illegal entry into the Soviet Union. In addition, the KGB was empowered, along with the Procuracy and the MVD, to investigate the following economic crimes: stealing of state property by appropriation or embezzlement or by abuse of official position and stealing of state property or socialist property (see Glossary) on an especially large scale.

In carrying out arrests and investigations for these crimes, the KGB was subject to specific rules that were set forth in the Code of Criminal Procedure. The Procuracy was charged with ensuring that these rules were observed. In practice, the Procuracy had little authority over the KGB, and the latter was permitted to circumvent the regulations whenever politically expedient. In 1988 closing some of these loopholes was discussed, and legal experts called for a greater role for the Procuracy in protecting Soviet citizens from abuse by the investigatory organs. As of May 1989, however, few concrete changes had been publicized.

It is important to note that the KGB frequently enlisted the MVD and the Procuracy to instigate proceedings against political nonconformists on charges that did not fall under the KGB's purview. Dissidents were often charged for defaming the Soviet state and violating public order. Sometimes the KGB arranged to have them charged for ordinary crimes, such as hooliganism or drug abuse.

771

Policy

The intensity of KGB campaigns against political crime varied considerably over the years. The Khrushchev period was marked by relative tolerance toward dissent, whereas Brezhnev reinstituted a harsh policy. The level of political arrests rose markedly from 1965 to 1973. In 1972 Brezhnev began to pursue détente, and the regime apparently tried to appease Western critics by moderating KGB operations against dissent. There was a sharp reversal after the Soviet invasion of Afghanistan in December 1979, and arrests again became more numerous. In 1986, Gorbachev's second year in power, restraint was reintroduced, and the KGB curtailed its arrests.

The forcible confinement of dissidents in psychiatric hospitals, where debilitating drugs were administered, was an alternative to straightforward arrests. This procedure avoided the unfavorable publicity that often arose with criminal trials of dissenters. Also, by labeling dissenters madmen, authorities hoped to discredit their actions and deprive them of support. The KGB often arranged for such commitments and maintained an active presence in psychiatric hospitals, despite the fact that these institutions were not under its formal authority. The Gorbachev leadership, as part of its general program of reform, introduced some reforms that were designed to prevent the abuse of psychiatric commitment by Soviet authorities, but the practical effects of these changes remained unclear in 1989.

In addition to arrests, psychiatric commitment, and other forms of coercion, the KGB also exercised a preventive function, designed to prevent political crimes and suppress deviant political attitudes. The KGB carried out this function in a variety of ways. For example, when the KGB learned that a Soviet citizen was having contact with foreigners or speaking in a negative fashion about the Soviet regime, it made efforts to set him or her straight by means of a "chat." The KGB also devoted great efforts to political indoctrination and propaganda. At local and regional levels, KGB officials regularly visited factories, schools, collective farms (see Glossary), and Komsomol organizations to deliver talks on political vigilance. National and republic-level KGB officials wrote articles and gave speeches on this theme. Their main message was that the Soviet Union was threatened by the large-scale efforts of Western intelligence agencies to penetrate the country by using cultural, scientific, and tourist exchanges to send in spies. In addition, the KGB claimed that Soviet citizens were barraged by hostile

*Headquarters of the
Committee for State
Security (KGB) and
Lubianka Prison,
Dzerzhinskii Square, Moscow
Courtesy Jimmy Pritchard*

*Plaque on KGB building,
Moscow, honoring
former KGB chairman
Iurii V. Andropov
Courtesy Jimmy Pritchard*

propaganda from the West as part of an effort to undermine the Soviet system.

Another important facet of KGB preventive work was censorship of literature and other media, which it exercised at both an informal and a formal level. The KGB censored informally by harassing writers and artists, arranging for their expulsion from professional organizations or from their jobs, and threatening them with prosecution for their unorthodox views. Such forms of intimidation forced many writers and artists to exercise self-censorship by producing only what they thought would be acceptable. The KGB maintained strong surveillance over the Union of Writers, as well as over the journalists' and artists' unions, where KGB representatives occupied top administrative posts.

The KGB played an important role in the system of formal censorship by taking part in the work of the Main Administration for Safeguarding State Secrets in the Press (Glavnoe upravlenie po okhrane gosudarstvennykh tain v pechati—Glavlit; see Administration of the Mass Media and the Arts, ch. 9). Some Western specialists believe that at least one of Glavlit's deputy chiefs was a KGB official and that the KGB assisted in Glavlit's compilation of its *Censor's Index,* a thick volume, updated frequently, listing all military, technical, statistical, and other subjects that could not be publicized without special permission from the Central Committee.

Another important internal security task of the KGB was to provide the leadership with information about the dissident movement and the political attitudes and opinions of the public as a whole. This task by its very nature gave the KGB influence over policy, particularly because Soviet leaders had no direct contact with dissidents and nonconformists and thus relied on KGB information about motives and foreign connections and on its estimates of numbers and support for various groups. The situation probably changed somewhat after Gorbachev introduced the policy of *glasnost'* in early 1987. After that the KGB no longer had a monopoly on information about the country's political mood because Soviet citizens expressed their views more freely in the press. Nevertheless, the KGB's information gathering continued to be important because direct criticism of the political system was suppressed. Computers no doubt improved KGB methods of processing information and conducting research.

The KGB was given considerable latitude in carrying out the party leadership's policy toward dissent. In other words, the Politburo decided on broad policy guidelines, but the KGB made the day-to-day decisions. Many dissidents, for example, viewed the KGB as extremely powerful and as enjoying considerable autonomy in implementing regime policy. Although the party leadership clearly determined the general policy toward dissent, it had an interest in promoting the idea that the KGB was responsible because the KGB could then be blamed for the injustices suffered by citizens. Furthermore, the image of the KGB's omnipotence no doubt helped to prevent anti-Soviet behavior. As Seweryn Bialer, a Western Sovietologist, observed of the Soviet system, "Without doubt the key to stability has been the high visibility of the coercive apparatus and policies."

Special Departments in the Armed Forces

Since the 1920s, an important internal security function of the security police has been ensuring the political reliability of the armed forces. This function was carried out through a network of so-called special departments (*osobye otdely*), which were under the supervision of the KGB's Third Chief Directorate. Officially designated as a military counterintelligence organization, the Third Chief Directorate performed tasks that extended far beyond counterintelligence to encompass extensive political surveillance of the military and other military security duties.

Special departments were responsible for security clearances of military personnel and for ensuring that security regulations and procedures were strictly observed in all branches of the armed forces. Thus they had control over (or at least immediate access to) military personnel files and information relating to the political reliability of members of the armed forces. The leadership claimed that their armed forces were continually threatened by ideological sabotage, i.e., attempts by Western governments to subvert individuals through bourgeois propaganda aimed at weakening their political convictions. Hence a key element of special department activities was political surveillance on both a formal and an informal level.

Officially, special departments were empowered to investigate armed forces personnel for the same crimes that were under KGB purview for ordinary citizens. In addition, the KGB had the authority to investigate military crimes defined in Article 259 of the Russian Republic's Code of Criminal Procedure—disclosure of a military secret or loss of a document containing a military secret. In investigating cases under their purview, special department employees were supposed to follow set rules of criminal procedure, but they did not always do so. In 1989, however, they no longer had the right to conduct trials, as they did during Stalin's time. Once an investigation was completed, the case was tried by special military tribunals under the Main Military Procuracy.

In addition to criminal investigations, the special departments had extensive informal responsibilities for ensuring the political reliability of the armed forces. Soviet authorities stated that they prevented political crimes by various preventive measures. Thus they carried on daily educational activities to increase political vigilance and communist ideological convictions among the armed forces and monitored telephone conversations and correspondence of military personnel. Special departments relied heavily on a broad network of informers, recruited from among military personnel.

The special departments were also charged with protecting all state and military secrets, including those involving nuclear weapons, a task that placed them in a position of considerable strategic importance. One Soviet official pointed out that "the reliable defense of Soviet forces from all types of espionage took on special significance when the basic defensive strength of the country came to consist of the most contemporary weapons systems, especially ballistic nuclear weapons."

According to Western sources, the KGB had custody and transport responsibilities for nuclear charges, which were separated from missiles and aircraft, until the late 1960s. At that time the KGB apparently relinquished its physical control over nuclear warheads, but it remained involved in the nuclear control process. Not only did it maintain a strategic communications network independent of the military communications system, but its responsibilities for protecting nuclear secrets presumably gave the KGB access to nuclear weapons installations as well as to military plans regarding the use of nuclear weapons.

The Foreign Intelligence Role of the Committee for State Security

The KGB played an important role in furthering Soviet foreign policy objectives abroad. In addition to straightforward intelligence collection and counterintelligence, the KGB participated in the Kremlin's program of active measures. KGB officials also contributed to foreign policy decision making.

Organization

The First Chief Directorate of the KGB was responsible for KGB operations abroad. According to John Barron, a Western authority, the First Chief Directorate was composed of three separate directorates: Directorate S, which oversaw illegal agents (those under deep cover) throughout the world; Directorate T, responsible for

Soviet intelligence collection ship at sea
Courtesy United States Navy

the collection of scientific and technological intelligence; and Directorate K, which carried out infiltration of foreign intelligence and security services and exercised surveillance over Soviet citizens abroad. In addition, the First Chief Directorate had three important services: Service I, which analyzed and distributed intelligence collected by KGB foreign intelligence officers and agents, published a daily current events summary for the Politburo, and made forecasts of future world developments; Service A, which was responsible for planning and implementing active measures; and Service R, which evaluated KGB operations abroad.

The operational core of the First Chief Directorate lay in its eleven geographical departments, which supervised KGB employees assigned to residencies abroad. These officers, or *rezidenty*, operated under legal cover, engaging in intelligence collection, espionage, and active measures. The long-time head of the First Chief Directorate, Vladimir Kriuchkov, who had served under Andropov and his successors, was named head of the KGB in 1988. The Second Chief Directorate also played a role in foreign intelligence in 1989. It recruited agents for intelligence purposes from among foreigners stationed in the Soviet Union, and it engaged in counterintelligence by uncovering attempts of foreign intelligence services to recruit Soviet citizens.

777

Intelligence and Counterintelligence

KGB intelligence gathering in the West increased markedly after the era of détente began in 1972. Détente permitted a vast influx of Soviet and East European diplomatic, cultural, and commercial officials into the United States and other Western countries. KGB officers and their East European counterparts operated under various guises, posing as diplomats, trade officials, journalists, scientists, and students. The proportion of Soviet citizens abroad who were engaged in intelligence gathering was estimated to range from 30 to 40 percent in the United States to over 50 percent in some Third World countries. In addition, many Soviet representatives who were not intelligence officers were nevertheless given some sort of assignment by the KGB.

Apparently, the First Chief Directorate had little trouble recruiting personnel for its foreign operations. The high salaries, military rank, access to foreign currency, and opportunity to live abroad offered attractive enticements to young people choosing a career. First Chief Directorate recruits were usually graduates of prestigious higher education institutions and had knowledge of one or more foreign languages. The KGB had a two-year postgraduate training course for these recruits at its Higher Intelligence School located near Moscow. The curriculum included the use of ciphers, arms and sabotage training, history and economics according to Marxist-Leninist (see Glossary) theory, CPSU history, law, and foreign languages.

The KGB was the primary agency responsible for supplying the Kremlin with foreign intelligence. According to former Soviet diplomat Arkady Shevchenko, Moscow cabled out questions on a daily basis to KGB *rezidenty* abroad to guide them in their tasks. In addition to political intelligence, KGB officers concentrated increasingly on efforts to acquire advanced Western technology. The KGB reportedly acted as a collector of militarily significant Western technology (in the form of documents and hardware) on behalf of the Military Industrial Commission of the Presidium of the Council of Ministers. This commission coordinated the development of all Soviet weapons systems, along with the program to acquire Western technology, and it levied requirements among the KGB, the Main Intelligence Directorate (see Glossary), and several other agencies, including those of East European intelligence services. The KGB and the GRU increased their technical collection efforts considerably in the early 1980s, when the number of requirements levied on them by the Military Industrial Commission rose by about 50 percent.

The Andropov era saw a greater orientation in the KGB toward electronic espionage—communications intercepts and satellites—to supplement intelligence gathered by agents. According to Robert Campbell, the Soviet Union deployed at least three satellites for intelligence collection. Some of the intelligence may have been strictly military and therefore collected by the GRU, but the KGB reportedly also made use of these satellites.

Active Measures

Active measures were clandestine operations designed to further Soviet foreign policy goals and to extend Soviet influence throughout the world. This type of activity had long been employed by the Soviet Union abroad, but it became more widespread and more effective in the late 1960s. Among these covert techniques was disinformation: leaking of false information and rumors to foreign media or planting forgeries in an attempt to deceive the public or the political elite in a given country or countries. The United States was the prime target of disinformation, in particular forgery operations, which were designed to damage foreign and defense policies of the United States in a variety of ways. Defectors reported that the Soviet Union and its allies circulated forged documents— often purporting to be speeches, letters, or policy statements by United States officials—containing false information. The use of international front (see Glossary) organizations and foreign communist parties to expand the Soviet Union's political influence and further its propaganda campaigns was another form of active measures. The World Peace Council was the largest and most important of Soviet front groups. Together with the International Department of the Central Committee, the KGB funneled money to these organizations and recruited agents of the Soviet Union to serve on their administrative bodies.

Other active measures involved support for terrorists and insurgents. As of 1989, there was no direct, public evidence that Soviet citizens had planned or orchestrated terrorist acts by groups from Western Europe or the Middle East, but there was much indirect evidence to show that the Soviet Union did support international terrorism. The Soviet Union maintained close relationships with a number of governments and organizations that were direct supporters of terrorist groups. The Soviet Union sold large quantities of arms to Libya and Syria, for example, and also maintained a close alliance with the Palestine Liberation Organization (PLO), providing it with arms, monetary assistance, and paramilitary training. Moscow's surrogate, Cuba, played a central role in Latin American terrorism by providing groups with training, arms, and sanctuary, and the Soviet Union's East European satellite states often served as middlemen or subcontractors for channeling aid to terrorist groups. Although the KGB, with some exceptions, avoided direct involvement with terrorist operations, it played an important role in diverting aid to these groups and providing the Soviet leadership with intelligence reports on their activities.

The KGB also was heavily involved in the support of "wars of national liberation" in the Third World. Together with satellite intelligence services, the KGB helped to organize military training and political indoctrination of leftist guerrillas, as well as providing arms and advisers. The manipulation of wars of national liberation enabled the Soviet Union to influence the political future of the countries in question and to make their new governments more responsive to Soviet objectives. The Soviet regime concentrated mainly on African countries until the late 1970s but then extended its support for "national liberation movements" to Central America, where it regularly employed the services of Cuba.

The KGB relied heavily on the intelligence services of satellite countries in carrying out both active measures and espionage operations. The intelligence services of the German Democratic Republic (East Germany), Czechoslovakia, Poland, Hungary, Bulgaria, and Cuba formed important adjuncts to the KGB. Although formally subordinated to their own governments, these satellite intelligence services were, according to many Western experts, heavily influenced by the KGB. A former official in the Czechoslovak intelligence service stated that Soviet intelligence was informed about every major aspect of Czechoslovak intelligence activities, and Soviet advisers (called liaison officers) participated in planning major operations and assessing the results. As far back as the 1960s, the KGB introduced a new element of coordination with the satellite intelligence services through the creation of departments for disinformation in East German, Czechoslovak, and Hungarian intelligence services and the establishment of direct lines of communication from these departments to the KGB.

Soviet active measures involved not only KGB and satellite intelligence services but also several other Soviet agencies, which all participated in a coordinated effort to further Soviet policy objectives. In addition to the KGB, the Central Committee's International Department took a leading role in directing and implementing active measures.

Influence on Foreign Policy

The KGB participated in the foreign policy decision-making process at the highest level because its chief was a member of the

Politburo. At the same time, it influenced the formulation of foreign policy at a lower level as an executor of that policy, a provider of information, and a generator of ideas, solutions, and alternatives. Thus, for example, when the Kremlin decided to invade Czechoslovakia in 1968, KGB chief Andropov, who was an expert on Eastern Europe and had a direct line of intelligence from Czechoslovakia, presumably influenced the decision-making process significantly. Furthermore, the KGB, as the main provider of intelligence to the leadership, was in a position to influence decision making by screening and interpreting the information. The KGB probably favored the invasion because of the threat posed by a possible spillover of unrest into the Soviet Union. Also, efforts by Czechoslovak reformers to reorganize their security police jeopardized KGB operations in Czechoslovakia. Considerable evidence showed that the KGB, in order to bolster the prointerventionist position, used intelligence and covert action to produce proof of counterrevolution in Czechoslovakia.

Andropov did not always favor military intervention as a solution to international problems, however. Other considerations, such as the Soviet Union's international image, no doubt affected his views on the 1979 invasion of Afghanistan (which he reportedly did not favor) and the 1980–81 Polish crisis (where he probably was among those who opposed an invasion). Both these crises occurred at a time when the KGB was trying to mobilize West European public opinion against plans by the North Atlantic Treaty Organization (NATO) to introduce intermediate-range missiles in Europe.

Chebrikov did not have Andropov's foreign policy expertise when he took over as head of the KGB in 1982, but his admission to the Politburo gave him a voice in foreign policy at the highest level. In addition, many Western experts believe that the KGB chairman served on the Defense Council, an important collegial decision-making body that provided top-level coordination for defense-related activities of the Soviet government (see Defense Council, ch. 18). Chebrikov's numerous trips to Eastern Europe after he became head of the KGB indicated that he was personally involved in KGB operations beyond Soviet borders, and his forceful advocacy of Soviet "counterpropaganda" efforts abroad implied a commitment to a strong foreign policy role for the KGB. Kriuchkov, who became head of the KGB in 1988, had been extensively involved in foreign operations as the chief of the First Chief Directorate of the KGB.

The Ministry of Internal Affairs

The MVD, which encompassed the regular, or nonpolitical, police, had a long history in the Soviet Union. It was first established as the NKVD on November 18, 1917. It has undergone several organizational and name changes since then. When the KGB was established in 1954, the security police was separated from the regular police. The MVD was originally established as a union-republic ministry (see Glossary) with headquarters in Moscow, but in 1960 the Khrushchev leadership, as part of its general downgrading of the police, abolished the central MVD, whose functions were assumed by republic ministries of internal affairs. Then, in 1962 the MVD was redesignated the Ministry for the Preservation of Public Order (Ministerstvo okhrany obshchestvennogo poriadka—MOOP). This name change implied a break with the all-powerful MVD created by Beria, as well as a narrower range of functions. The changes were accompanied by increasing criticism of the regular police in the Soviet press for its shortcomings in combating crime.

Following Khrushchev's ouster, Brezhnev did much to raise the status of the regular police. In 1966, after placing one of his protégés, Nikolai A. Shchelokov, in the post of chief, Brezhnev reinstated MOOP as a union-republic ministry. Two years later, MOOP was renamed the MVD, an apparent symbol of its increased authority. Efforts were made to raise the effectiveness of the MVD by recruiting better-qualified personnel and upgrading equipment and training. Brezhnev's death, however, left the MVD vulnerable to his opponents, Andropov in particular. Just a month after Brezhnev died, Shchelokov was ousted as its chief and replaced by the former KGB chairman, Vitalii Fedorchuk. Shchelokov was later tried on corruption charges. A similar fate befell Brezhnev's son-in-law, Iurii Churbanov, who was removed from the post of first deputy chief in 1984 and later arrested on criminal charges. After bringing several officials from the KGB and from the party apparatus into the MVD, Andropov sought to make it an effective organization for rooting out widespread corruption; Gorbachev continued these efforts.

Functions and Organization

The MVD had a wide array of duties. It was responsible for uncovering and investigating certain categories of crime, apprehending criminals, supervising the internal passport (see Glossary) system, maintaining public order, combating public intoxication, supervising parolees, managing prisons and labor camps, providing fire protection, and controlling traffic. Until early 1988, the MVD was also in charge of special psychiatric hospitals, but a law passed in January 1988 transferred all psychiatric hospitals to the authority of the Ministry of Health.

As a union-republic ministry under the Council of Ministers, the MVD had its headquarters in Moscow and branches in the republic and regional government apparatus, as well as in oblasts and cities. Unlike the KGB, the internal affairs apparatus was subject to dual subordination; local internal affairs offices reported both to the executive committees of their respective local soviets and to their superior offices in the MVD hierarchy.

The MVD headquarters in Moscow was divided into several directorates and offices (see fig. 38). The Directorate for Combating the Embezzlement of Socialist Property and Speculation was established in the late 1960s to control such white-collar crime as embezzlement and falsification of economic plan records. The Criminal Investigation Directorate assisted the Procuracy, and on occasion the KGB, in the investigation of criminal cases. There was a separate department for investigating and prosecuting minor cases, such as traffic violations, and the Maintenance of Public Order Directorate, which was responsible for ensuring order in public places and for preventing outbreaks of public unrest.

The members of the *militsiia* (uniformed police), as part of the regular police force, were distinguished by their gray uniforms with red piping. The duties of the *militsiia* included patrolling public places to ensure order and arresting persons who violated the law, including vagrants and drunks. Resisting arrest or preventing a police officer from executing his duties was a serious crime in the Soviet Union, punishable by one to five years' imprisonment. Killing a policeman was punishable by death.

The Office of Visas and Registration was charged with registering Soviet citizens and foreigners residing in each precinct of a city and with issuing internal passports to Soviet citizens. Soviet citizens wishing to emigrate from the Soviet Union and foreigners wishing to travel within the Soviet Union had to obtain visas from this office. The Office of Recruitment and Training supervised the recruitment of new members of the *militsiia,* who were recommended by work collectives and public organizations. The local party and Komsomol bodies screened candidates thoroughly to ensure their political reliability. Individuals serving in the *militsiia* were exempt from the regular military draft.

Leadership

In January 1986, when Fedorchuk was retired, Aleksandr V. Vlasov was appointed the chief of the MVD. Vlasov had no background in the police apparatus. In September 1988, Vlasov became a candidate member of the CPSU Politburo, and the following month he was replaced as chief of the MVD by Vadim V. Bakatin.

783

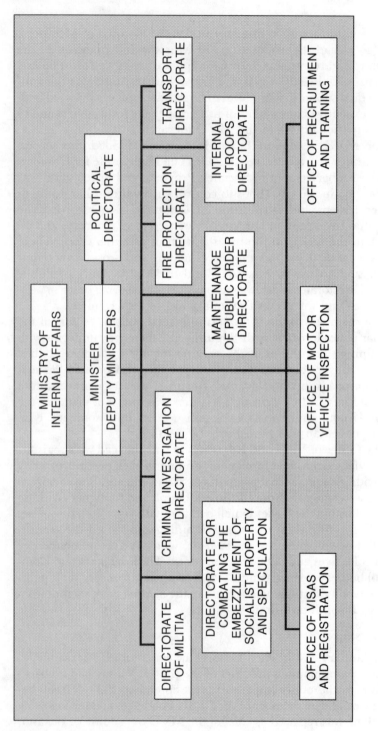

Figure 38. Organization of the Ministry of Internal Affairs (MVD), 1988

Bakatin was made a full member of the CPSU Central Committee in March 1986, but his police experience, if any, was not known in the West. In 1989 Leonid G. Sizov and Vasilii P. Trushin were first deputy ministers of the MVD. In addition, the MVD had approximately eight deputy ministers.

The MVD published a vast amount of popular literature devoted to the glorification of the MVD in order to attract well-qualified cadres to its ranks. The fact that MVD salaries were considerably lower than those for the KGB and that working conditions were generally poor (long hours and out-of-date equipment) made recruitment somewhat difficult. The MVD underwent an extensive purge in the mid-1980s as part of the party's effort to rid the organization of corruption and inefficiency. Over 170,000 police officers were fired between 1983 and 1988 for irresponsibility, lack of discipline, and violations of the law.

Control by the Party

The chief vehicle for party control over the MVD was the State and Legal Department of the Secretariat, which had a special section for supervising the MVD. This section presumably participated in the selection of MVD personnel and evaluated the MVD's work in terms of how well it carried out party directives.

Another means through which the party exercised control over the MVD was the Political Directorate of the MVD. This directorate, a network of political organs existing throughout the MVD, was established in 1983 and operated in a way similar to that of the Main Political Directorate of the Soviet Army and Navy. The Political Directorate was created because local party officials were not exercising sufficient control over the activities of internal affairs officials but rather were colluding with them in commiting economic crimes. Its chief until April 1988 was Viktor Gladyshev, a former section chief in the Administrative Organs Department (present-day State and Legal Department). Gladyshev was replaced by the former personnel chief of the MVD, Anatolii Anikiev.

The minister of internal affairs was usually a member of the Central Committee but as of 1989 had never enjoyed membership on the Politburo. Thus the regular police executed party policy but had little voice in policy formulation at the national level. At the local level, however, the police chief may have had more impact on decision making in the law enforcement realm because he was generally included on both the local soviet executive committee and the local party committee.

The Ministry of Internal Affairs, the Judicial Organs, and Nonpolitical Crime

The Soviet Union had two separate legal systems. The first maintained law and order on a daily basis, enforced the law, and adjudicated disputes that arose among the citizenry. This system was administered by the organs of justice: the MVD, the Procuracy, the Ministry of Justice, and the courts. The other legal system, administered by the KGB on behalf of the party leadership, was arbitrary and repressive and was used to suppress and punish critics of the Soviet regime. Some cases did not fall neatly into one category or another. There was a gray area in which a seemingly ordinary case took on a political character. As Western expert Gordon B. Smith pointed out, "Soviet legal policy must bridge these two systems, providing a framework for the functioning of each."

Socialist Legality

Soviet law displayed many special characteristics that derived from the socialist (see Glossary) nature of the Soviet state and reflected Marxist-Leninist ideology. Lenin accepted the Marxist conception of the law and the state as instruments of coercion in the hands of the bourgeoisie and postulated the creation of popular, informal tribunals to administer revolutionary justice. Alongside this utopian trend, a dictatorial trend developed that advocated the use of law and legal institutions to suppress all opposition to the regime. The latter trend reached its zenith under Stalin, when the administration of justice was carried out mainly by the security police in special tribunals. During the de-Stalinization of the Khrushchev era, a new trend developed, based on socialist legality (see Glossary), that stressed the need to protect the procedural and statutory rights of citizens, while still calling for obedience to the state. New legal codes, introduced in 1960, were part of the effort to establish legal norms in administering laws. Although socialist legality remained in force after 1960, the dictatorial and utopian trends continued to influence the legal process. Persecution of political and religious dissenters, in flagrant violation of their legal rights, continued, but at the same time there was a tendency to decriminalize lesser offenses by handing them over to people's courts (see Glossary) and administrative agencies and dealing with them by education rather than by incarceration.

By late 1986, the Gorbachev regime was stressing anew the importance of individual rights in relation to the state and criticizing those who violated the procedural laws in implementing Soviet justice. This signaled a resurgence of socialist legality as the dominant trend. It should be noted, however, that socialist legality itself still lacked important features associated with Western jurisprudence. In particular, the ultimate control of the legal system lay with the party leadership, which was not democratically elected by, and therefore not responsible to, the public at large.

The Procuracy

The Procuracy was the most powerful institution in the Soviet system of justice relating to nonpolitical matters. It was a hierarchical organization representing all public prosecutors, all the way down to the city or village level. As specified in the Soviet Constitution, the procurator general of the Soviet Union was appointed by the Supreme Soviet and controlled Procuracy officials throughout the system. Employees of the Procuracy were not subject to the authority of their local soviets, but they were subject to the authority of the party. The Procuracy had a wide range of functions, involving itself at all stages in the criminal process. Procurators carried out investigations of the majority of cases; supervised investigations carried out by the MVD, the KGB, and the Procuracy's own employees; authorized arrests; prosecuted offenders; and supervised prisons. In addition, procurators supervised parole and the release of prisoners and referred judicial decisions to higher courts for review. Procurators also oversaw the operation of all government bodies, enterprises, officials, and social organizations to ensure that they were observing the law. Although the Procuracy possessed the formal authority to supervise the KGB in carrying out arrests and investigations in political cases, there was little evidence that the Procuracy actually exercised this function.

Military Justice

Military justice in the Soviet Union was administered by the Main Military Procuracy, which was subordinated to the procurator general and responsible for ensuring that laws were observed within the military. It also supervised criminal investigations of armed forces personnel carried out by its employees, as well as by the KGB (in cases of political crime). Military cases were tried in military tribunals, which were under the authority of the Supreme Court.

The Judiciary and the Legal Profession

The court structure in the Soviet Union, set forth in the Constitution and governed by several all-union and republic statutes, was quite complex. In courts of first instance, one judge sat with two

787

elected people's assessors (lay judges), who were ordinary citizens, elected at general meetings of factories, offices, collective farms, or residential blocks for a term of two years. Appellate and review procedure came before a bench of three judges. Although a legal education was not required and any citizen over the age of twenty-four could in principle be elected to the post of judge, more than 95 percent of all judges had higher legal education. The party carefully screened candidates for election to the position of judge, which had a term of five years. Most judges above the local level were party members. In addition to determining innocence or guilt, judges performed an important function of socialization, often lecturing defendants for failing to uphold socialist values. Judges were part of the union-republic Ministry of Justice and the fifteen republic ministries of justice. There was no system of binding precedent, but supreme courts at all-union and republic levels gave "guiding explanations" to be followed.

Advocates, or defense attorneys, were controlled by the Ministry of Justice at the all-union and republic level and at the local level by the justice department of the local soviet. Advocates were usually law school graduates with some practical training. The Soviet Union had approximately 18,000 advocates, organized into colleges of around 150 attorneys each. These colleges maintained consultation bureaus, each with a staff of about twenty, in most towns and cities. The bureaus provided legal advice on a variety of issues, such as divorce, custody, inheritance, property rights, and housing disputes. The bureaus also offered legal defense for persons accused of criminal offenses. According to the 1977 Constitution, all defendants had the right to legal counsel. Legal fees were set by the state and were low enough for most people to afford. According to Soviet émigrés, however, many defense lawyers expected additional payments or gifts "under the table."

Legal advisers to government agencies and departments, enterprises, factories, and state farms (see Glossary) were called *iuriskonsul'ty*. Numbering approximately 29,000 in 1989, they represented their employer in court and drafted internal rules, contracts, and commercial documents.

Legal Codes and Abuses of the System

The fundamental principles of the civil and criminal branches of Soviet law were established at the all-union level and then set down in the legal codes of the republics. The Civil Code dealt with contract law, tort law, and law governing wills and inheritance. Separate codes existed for family law and labor law. The Criminal Code concerned itself with all aspects of criminal behavior.

The Criminal Code and the Code of Criminal Procedure of the Russian Republic were revised completely (along with the codes of the other republics) in 1960, incorporating the 1958 Fundamental Principles of Criminal Procedure, approved by the Supreme Soviet. These codes represented a sharp departure from the Stalinist criminal codes, which had provided a formal legal basis for the arrest and prosecution of innocent citizens on groundless charges. Under the Stalinist code, for example, an individual could be prosecuted for committing an act not specifically prohibited by the criminal code but "analogous" to such an act. The 1960 codes abolished the principle of analogy.

The 1960 codes defined political crimes in a more restricted form and made punishments considerably less severe. They also established procedural rules to govern the arrest and detention of suspected criminals. According to the law, a suspect could not be detained for more than three days without a warrant. Thereafter, permission for detention had to be obtained from the procurator or from the courts. The maximum period of pretrial detention was nine months. At the end of such detention, the accused was entitled to the services of a defense lawyer. The trial itself was supposed to be public, with the prosecution conducted by the procurator, who could recommend sentencing.

Despite the existence of formal laws to protect the rights of the accused, ample evidence indicated that these laws were not adhered to when political or other interests of the party came into play. The party was the ultimate authority in the administration of justice, and party officials frequently interfered in the judicial process to protect their own interests. Party approval was required before appointment to any important position in the legal apparatus, and this control over personnel appointments gave the party substantial power (see Nomenklatura, ch. 7). The party also exerted influence in the oversight of the legal and judicial organs.

The party sometimes interfered in the administration of justice. CPSU officials put pressure on procurators, judges, and defense attorneys in the conduct of individual cases. In some instances, party officials pressed members of the legal system to arrest and convict innocent persons who were viewed as politically unorthodox. (In these cases, the KGB was often the agency exerting such pressure on behalf of the party.) At other times, party officials arranged to have crimes covered up or ignored to protect their personal or economic interests. This situation frequently occurred with corruption and bribery offenses.

Nonpolitical Crime and Punishment

The Soviet Union did not publish comprehensive crime statistics, so it is difficult to compare its crime rates with those of other countries. According to Western observers, robberies, murders, and other violent crimes were much less prevalent than in the United States. This was explained by the large police presence, strict gun controls, and the relatively low incidence of drug abuse. By contrast, white-collar economic crime was extremely common. Bribery and covert payments for goods and services were universal, mainly because of the paucity of goods and services on the open market. Theft of state property was practiced routinely by employees, as were other forms of petty theft. In 1989 the Gorbachev leadership was making a concerted effort to curtail such white-collar crime. Revelations of corruption scandals involving high-level party employees appeared in the Soviet media on a regular basis, and there were many arrests and prosecutions.

The death penalty, carried out by shooting, was applied in the Soviet Union only in cases of treason, espionage, terrorism, sabotage, certain types of murder, and large-scale theft of state property by officials. Otherwise, the maximum punishment for a first offender was fifteen years. Parole was permitted in some cases after completion of half of the sentence, and periodic amnesties sometimes also resulted in early release.

The Soviet Union had few prisons in 1989. About 99 percent of convicted criminals served their sentences in labor camps, supervised by the Main Directorate for Corrective Labor Camps (Glavnoe upravlenie ispravitel'no-trudovykh lagerei—Gulag), which was under the MVD. The camps had four regimes of ascending severity. In the strict-regime camps, inmates worked at the most difficult jobs, usually outdoors, and received meager rations. Jobs were less demanding and rations better in the camps with milder regimes. The system of corrective labor was regarded by Soviet authorities as successful in that the rate of recidivism was quite low. Prisons and labor camps, in the views of former inmates and Western observers, however, were notorious for their harsh conditions, arbitrary and sadistic treatment of prisoners, and flagrant human rights abuses. In 1989 new legislation, which emphasized rehabilitation rather than punishment, was being drafted to "humanize" the special system. Nevertheless, in 1989 conditions for many prisoners had changed little.

Internal Security Troops

The government of the Soviet Union had several bodies of troops under its control for the purpose of ensuring internal security. These

Moscow militsiia *(uniformed police) providing security at the Kremlin for a meeting of the historic Congress of People's Deputies in May 1989*
Courtesy Jonathan Tetzlaff

troops included the Border Troops and Security Troops of the KGB and the Internal Troops of the MVD.

Border Troops of the Committee for State Security

The Border Troops were organized under the KGB's unnumbered Border Troops Directorate, which was headed in 1989 by Army General Viktor Matrosov. He was assisted by one or more first deputy chiefs, several deputy chiefs, and a chief of staff. Within the directorate, a political administration provided political indoctrination and surveillance on behalf of the party. Western specialists reported that there was an intelligence administration within the Border Troops Directorate, but this had not been confirmed by Soviet sources.

The Border Troops strength was estimated in 1989 to be in the range of 230,000 men. Although under the operational authority of the KGB, the Border Troops were conscripted as part of the biannual call-up of the Ministry of Defense, and their induction and discharge were regulated by the 1967 Law on Universal Military Service, which covered all armed forces of the Soviet Union.

The legal status, duties, and rights of the Border Troops were set forth in the Law on the State Border, confirmed by the Supreme

791

Soviet on November 24, 1982. Article 28 defined the basic duties of the Border Troops. Their duties included repulsing armed incursions into Soviet territory; preventing illegal crossings of the border or the transport of weapons, explosives, contraband, or subversive literature across the border; monitoring the observance of established procedures at border crossing points; monitoring the observance by Soviet and foreign ships of navigation procedures in Soviet territorial waters; and assisting state agencies in the preservation of natural resources and the protection of the environment from pollution. Border guards were authorized to examine documents and possessions of persons crossing the borders and to confiscate articles; to conduct inquiries in cases of violations of the state border; and to take such actions as arrest, search, and interrogation of individuals suspected of border violations.

The Border Troops Directorate administered approximately nine border districts (*pogranichnye okruga*), which covered the nearly 63,000 kilometers of the state border. Border district boundaries were distinct from civil or military district boundaries. The nine border districts were subdivided into detachments (*otriady*), covering specific sections of the border, border command posts (*pogranichnye komendatury*), passport control points (*kontrol'no-propusknye punkty*), and border outposts (*zastavy*). The border area was divided into a border zone, which included the territory of the district and settlements adjacent to the state border, and the border strip, which was approximately two kilometers in depth, running directly along the border. Only permanent residents or those who had obtained special permission from the MVD could enter the border zone. Entry into the border strip was forbidden without special permission from the Border Troops.

Soviet sources repeatedly stressed that a border guard was not only a soldier but also a defender of Soviet ideology. His mission entailed sensitive political tasks, such as detecting subversive literature, and shooting citizens attempting to escape across the border. Enlisted men were trained with their operational units, whereas officers were trained in special Border Troops schools, such as the Dzerzhinskii Higher Border Command School and the Higher Border School in Moscow. Military-political officers received training at the Voroshilov Higher Border Military-Political Academy, founded in the 1930s and located outside Leningrad. In 1972 a higher border military-political school was created in Golytsin, near Moscow. More recently, higher border command faculties were set up at the Frunze Military Academy and the Lenin Military-Political Academy. The period of instruction at the Dzerzhinskii Higher Border Command School was four years. Officer candidates, who were screened carefully by their local KGB offices before admittance, took general higher education courses along with specialized military and political studies.

To ensure a high level of discipline among personnel of the Border Troops, much attention was devoted to political training and indoctrination. For this purpose, a network of political organs, the Political Directorate of the Border Troops, was established within the Border Troops. It had political departments within all the border districts, detachments, and education institutions, and a network of full-time party political officers worked among all troop units. They conducted political study groups, gave propaganda lectures, and worked to increase the level of combat effectiveness among the troops.

Security Troops of the Committee for State Security

The KGB's Security Troops, which numbered about 40,000 in 1989, provided the KGB with a coercive potential. Although Soviet sources did not specify the functions of these special troops, Western analysts thought that one of their main tasks was to guard the top leadership in the Kremlin, as well as key government and party buildings and officials at the republic and regional levels. Such troops were presumably under the Ninth Directorate of the KGB.

The Security Troops also included several units of signal troops, which were reportedly responsible for installation, maintenance, and operation of secret communications facilities for leading party and government bodies, including the Ministry of Defense. These troops were probably under the command of the Eighth Chief Directorate. Other special KGB troops were intended for counterterrorist and counterinsurgency operations. Such troops were reportedly employed, along with the MVD's Internal Troops, to suppress public protests and disperse demonstrations, such as that of the Crimean Tatars in July 1987 and those in the republics of Armenia and Azerbaydzhan in March 1988. Special KGB troops also were trained for sabotage and diversionary missions abroad.

Internal Troops of the Ministry of Internal Affairs

Although a component of the armed forces, the Internal Troops were subordinate to the MVD. Numbering approximately 260,000 men in 1989, they were one of the largest formations of special troops in the Soviet Union. The Internal Troops were first established in 1919 under the NKVD. Later they were subordinated to the state security police, and then in 1934 they were incorporated into the expanded NKVD. They were back under the authority of the security police in the early 1950s, but when the KGB was established in 1954, control of the Internal Troops shifted to the MVD. The chief of the Internal Troops from 1954 to late 1987 was Ivan Iakovlev. Iakovlev's successor was Iurii Shatalin.

Like the regular army, the Internal Troops for the most part were composed of conscripts, who were obliged to serve for a minimum of two years. The Internal Troops accepted candidates for commission both from the ranks of the armed forces and from civilian society. The MVD had four schools for training members of the officer corps, as well as a separate school for political officers.

The Internal Troops supported MVD missions by supplementing the *militsiia* in ensuring crowd control in large cities and, in emergencies, by helping to fight fires. These troops also guarded large-scale industrial enterprises, railroad stations, certain large stockpiles of food and matériel, and certain communication centers that were strategically significant. One of their most important functions was that of preventing internal disorder that might threaten the regime's political stability. They took a direct role in suppressing anti-Soviet demonstrations in the non-Russian republics and strikes by Soviet workers. In this capacity, the Internal Troops probably worked together with the KGB Security Troops. There was little evidence to support the theory that the Internal Troops would serve as a counterweight to the armed services during a political crisis. Most Internal Troops units were composed of infantry alone and were not equipped with artillery and tanks; in 1989 there was only one operational division of the Internal Troops in Moscow. According to some Western analysts, the Internal Troops were to perform rear security functions in the event of war, just as they did in World War II.

Internal security in the Soviet Union involved numerous organizations and was guided by the party leadership. It had always served more than ordinary police functions and had covered such areas as intelligence gathering and suppression of dissent. The party and the regime as a whole depended on the internal security apparatus to ensure their own survival.

* * *

Among the sources in English on the history of Soviet internal security are Ronald Hingley's *The Russian Police;* George Leggett's *The Cheka;* Simon Wolin and Robert Slusser's *The Soviet Secret Police;* and Boris Levytsky's *The Uses of Terror.* Amy W. Knight's *The KGB* discusses the current security police. H.J. Berman and J.W. Spindler's *Soviet Criminal Law and Procedure* provides a useful background for understanding Soviet law and legality. William Fuller's "The Internal Troops of the MVD SSSR" discusses the security forces. (For further information and complete citations, see Bibliography.)

Appendix A

Table

1 Metric Conversion Coefficients and Factors
2 Rulers of Muscovy and the Russian Empire, 1462–1917
3 Comparative Population Development, Selected Years, 1850–1910
4 Historic Land Use, 1797, 1857, and 1887
5 Principal Soviet Leaders, 1917–89
6 Area, Population, and Capitals of the Republics, 1989 Census
7 Natural Resource Potential by Region, 1986
8 Vital Statistics, Selected Years, 1959–86
9 Population Distribution by Sex, Selected Years, 1913–87
10 Population Distribution by Urban-Rural Breakdown, Selected Years, 1940–87
11 Cities with Populations over One Million, 1989
12 Population Density of the Republics, 1959 and 1982
13 Nationality, Language, and Religion, 1989 Census
14 Autonomous Subdivisions, 1989
15 Republic of Residence and Population of Major Nationalities, 1989 Census
16 Russian and East Slavic Populations in the Republics, 1989 Census
17 Social Groups, 1913, 1959, and 1986
18 Average Monthly Wage by Occupation, 1986
19 Selected Low-Paid Occupations, Early 1980s
20 Urban-Rural Breakdown, Selected Years, 1917–87
21 Average Family Size by Nationality Group, 1979 Census
22 Network of Primary Party Organizations, 1977 and 1987
23 Membership in the Communist Party of the Soviet Union, Selected Years, 1971–87
24 Social Position of Members of the Communist Party of the Soviet Union, Selected Years, 1971–87
25 Education Level of Members of the Communist Party of the Soviet Union, 1967, 1977, and 1987
26 Distribution of Major Nationalities in the Communist Party of the Soviet Union and in the Soviet Population, 1981
27 Distribution of Members of the Communist Party of the Soviet Union by Sex, Selected Years, 1971–87
28 Organs and Functions of the Soviet Regime, 1988
29 Treaties of Friendship and Cooperation with Third World Countries, 1989

Table

30   Five-Year Plans, 1928–95
31   Estimated Gross National Product by Sector, Selected Years, 1970–88
32   Industrial Production, Estimated Value Added, Selected Years, 1970–88
33   Selected Ministries Producing Military Weapons and Components, 1989
34   Production of Major Farm Commodities, 1956–87
35   Farm Machinery Pool, Selected Years, 1960–86
36   Sown Area for Major Crops, Selected Years, 1940–86
37   Agricultural Chemicals Delivered, Selected Years, 1970–87
38   Selected Animal Products, Selected Years, 1940–87
39   Freight Traffic by Mode of Transport, Selected Years, 1940–86
40   Major Rail Lines, 1988
41   Principal Electrified Rail Lines, 1987
42   Passengers Boarded by Mode of Transport, Selected Years, 1940–86
43   Metropolitan Rail Systems (Metros), 1987
44   Freight Loaded by Mode of Transport, Selected Years, 1940–86
45   Passenger Traffic by Mode of Transport, Selected Years, 1940–86
46   Principal Aeroflot Aircraft, 1987
47   Hard-Currency Trading Partners, 1970–85
48   Soviet Actions Prompting United States Trade Restrictions, 1974–82
49   Major Noncommunist Trading Partners, 1980, 1985, and 1986
50   Trade with Asia, Africa, and Latin America, Selected Years, 1970–85
51   Trade with Countries of Socialist Orientation, Selected Years, 1970–85
52   Trade with the Organization of Petroleum Exporting Countries, Selected Years, 1970–85
53   Military Capabilities, 1989
54   Insignia Colors of the Armed Forces, 1989
55   Higher Military Schools and Military Academies, 1988
56   Organizational History of the Police, 1989

Table 1. Metric Conversion Coefficients and Factors

When you know	Multiply by	To find
Millimeters	0.04	inches
Centimeters	0.39	inches
Meters	3.3	feet
Kilometers	0.62	miles
Hectares (10,000 m²)	2.47	acres
Square kilometers	0.39	square miles
Cubic meters	35.3	cubic feet
Liters	0.26	gallons
Kilograms	2.2	pounds
Metric tons	0.98	long tons
....	1.1	short tons
....	2,204	pounds
Degrees Celsius	9	degrees Fahrenheit
(Centigrade)	divide by 5 and add 32	

Table 2. Rulers of Muscovy and the Russian Empire, 1462-1917

Period	Ruler
Rurikid Dynasty	
1462-1505	Ivan III
1505-33	Vasilii III
1533-84	Ivan IV (the Terrible)
1584-98	Fedor I
Time of Troubles	
1598-1605	Boris Godunov
1605	Fedor II
1605-06	First False Dmitrii
1606-10	Vasilii Shuiskii
1610-13	Second False Dmitrii
Romanov Dynasty	
1613-45	Mikhail Romanov
1645-76	Alexis I
1676-82	Fedor III
1682-89	Sofia (regent)
1682-96	Ivan V (co-tsar)
1682-1725	Peter I (the Great)
1725-27	Catherine I
1727-30	Peter II
1730-40	Anna
1740-41	Ivan VI
1741-62	Elizabeth
1762	Peter III
1762-96	Catherine II (the Great)
1796-1801	Paul
1801-25	Alexander I
1825-55	Nicholas I
1855-81	Alexander II
1881-94	Alexander III
1894-1917	Nicholas II

Source: Based on information from Marc Raeff, "History of Russia/Union of Soviet Socialist Republics," *Academic American Encyclopedia*, 16, Danbury, Connecticut, 1986, 358.

Table 3. Comparative Population Development,
Selected Years, 1850–1910
(in millions)

Country	1850	1870	1890	1910
Russia	60	75	92	140
France	36	37	38	39
Germany	35	42	49	65
Austria-Hungary	31	37	43	52
Britain	27	31	37	46
United States	23	38	63	93

Table 4. Historic Land Use, 1797, 1857, and 1887
(in percentages)

Land Use	1797	1857	1887
Fields	42.9	60.3	69.8
Forests	11.2	9.7	7.9
Gardens	1.2	2.9	6.2
Meadows	36.5	20.6	10.2
Unusable	8.2	6.5	5.9
TOTAL	100.0	100.0	100.0

801

Table 5. *Principal Soviet Leaders, 1917–89*

Period	Leader	Party Post	Government Post
1917–24	Vladimir I. Lenin	Member of Politburo	Chairman of Council of People's Commissars
1924–26	Nikolai I. Bukharin	–do–	Member of Council of People's Commissars
	Lev B. Kamenev	–do–	—
	Joseph V. Stalin	General secretary of Central Committee	—
	Leon Trotsky	Member of Politburo	Member of Council of People's Commissars
	Grigorii V. Zinov'ev	–do–	—
1926–53	Joseph V. Stalin	General secretary of Central Committee	—
1953–57	Lavrenty Beria (until June 1953)	Member of Presidium [1]	Minister of internal affairs
	Nikolai A. Bulganin	–do–	Minister of defense
	Nikita S. Khrushchev	Member of Presidium; first secretary of Central Committee [2]	—
	Georgii M. Malenkov	Member of Presidium	Chairman of Council of Ministers [3]
	Viacheslav Molotov	–do–	Member of Council of Ministers
1957–64	Nikita S. Khrushchev	Member of Presidium; first secretary of Central Committee	Chairman of Council of Ministers
1964–75	Leonid I. Brezhnev	Member of Politburo; general secretary of Central Committee	—
	Aleksei N. Kosygin	Member of Politburo	Chairman of Council of Ministers

Table 5.—Continued

Period	Leader	Party Post	Government Post
	Nikolai V. Podgornyi	Member of Politburo; secretary of Central Committee	—
1975-82	Leonid I. Brezhnev	Member of Politburo; general secretary of Central Committee	Chairman of Presidium of Supreme Soviet
1982-84	Iurii V. Andropov	-do-	—
1984-85	Konstantin U. Chernenko	-do-	Chairman of Presidium of Supreme Soviet
1985-	Mikhail S. Gorbachev	-do-	-do- [4]

—means no position in the government.

[1] The Politburo was renamed the Presidium in 1952; in 1966 the name reverted to Politburo.
[2] The title general secretary was used until Stalin's death in 1953, after which the title was changed to first secretary. In 1966 the title reverted to general secretary.
[3] In 1946 the Council of People's Commissars was renamed the Council of Ministers.
[4] In 1989 Gorbachev was named chairman of the Supreme Soviet by the Congress of People's Deputies. The newly created position superseded that of chairman of the Presidium of the Supreme Soviet.

Table 6. Area, Population, and Capitals
of the Republics, 1989 Census

Republic	Area of Republic [1] (in square kilometers)	Population of Republic [1]	Capital	Population of Capital [2]
Russian	17,075,400	145,311,000	Moscow	8,815,000
Kazakh	2,717,300	16,244,000	Alma-Ata	1,108,000
Ukrainian	603,700	51,201,000	Kiev	2,544,000
Turkmen	488,100	3,361,000	Ashkhabad	382,000
Uzbek	447,400	19,026,000	Tashkent	2,124,000
Belorussian	207,600	10,078,000	Minsk	1,543,000
Kirgiz	198,500	4,143,000	Frunze	632,000
Tadzhik	143,100	4,807,000	Dushanbe	582,000
Azerbaydzhan	86,600	6,811,000	Baku	1,115,000
Georgian	69,700	5,266,000	Tbilisi	1,194,000
Lithuanian	65,200	3,641,000	Vilnius	566,000
Latvian	64,500	2,647,000	Riga	900,000
Estonian	45,100	1,556,000	Tallin	478,000
Moldavian	33,700	4,185,000	Kishinev	663,000
Armenian	29,800	3,412,000	Yerevan	1,168,000
TOTAL	22,403,000 [3]	286,717,000 [4]		24,008,000

[1] Estimated.
[2] Estimated. Each republic's capital is also the largest city in the republic.
[3] Includes the area of the White Sea and the Sea of Azov.
[4] Soviet citizens outside the Soviet Union are included, and hence the total differs from that given on tables 13 and 15. Further, Soviet statistics sometimes have unexplained discrepancies.

Source: Based on information from *Izvestiia* [Moscow], April 29, 1989, 1-2.

Table 7. Natural Resource Potential by Region, 1986 [1]
(in percentages)

Region	Fuel and Energy	Minerals	Wood	Farmland	Total
Northern and central belt of European part	9.2	8.9	18.2	63.7	100.0
Southern European part	26.2	7.4	0.5	65.5	100.0 [2]
Volga-Ural region	39.2	4.1	5.9	50.8	100.0
Siberia and the Soviet Far East ...	66.0	6.9	11.3	15.8	100.0
Kazakh Republic	17.6	14.9	0.2	67.3	100.0
Soviet Central Asia	36.2	2.2	—	61.6	100.0
SOVIET UNION	38.5	7.5	6.0	48.0	100.0

—means negligible.
[1] The potential of a natural resource is affected by the cost effectiveness of its exploitation. Hence, some resources, although abundant, may be too costly to extract and transport to locations of refinement and use.
[2] As published.

Source: Based on information from V. Rom (ed.), *Ekonomicheskaia i sotsial'naia geografiia SSSR*, 1, Moscow, 1986, 128.

Table 8. *Vital Statistics, Selected Years, 1959–86*

Year	Population (in thousands)	Distribution by Sex (in percentages) Male	Female	Birth Rate and Death Rate (per thousand) Births	Deaths	Net	Life Expectancy (in years) Male	Female	Average
1959 ...	208,827	45	55	25.0	7.6	17.4	64	72	69
1970 ...	241,720	46	54	17.4	8.2	9.2	65	74	70
1981 ...	266,600	47	53	18.5	10.2	8.3	63	73	68
1986 ...	278,800	47	53	20.0	9.8	10.2	65	74	70

Table 9. *Population Distribution by Sex, Selected Years, 1913–87*

Year	Population (in millions) Male	Female	Total	Distribution (in percentages) Male	Female	Total
1913 [1]	79	80	159	50	50	100
1959 [2]	94	115	209	45	55	100
1970 [2]	111	131	242	46	54	100
1979 [2]	122	140	262	47	53	100
1987 [1]	133	149	282	47	53	100

[1] Estimated figures.
[2] Census figures.

Source: Based on information from J.P. Cole, *Geography of the Soviet Union,* Cambridge, 1984, 248; and Gosudarstvennyi komitet po statistike, *Narodnoe khoziaistvo SSSR v 1987 g.,* Moscow, 1988, 347.

Table 10. *Population Distribution by Urban-Rural Breakdown, Selected Years, 1940–87*

Year	Population (in millions) Urban	Rural	Total	Distribution (in percentages) Urban	Rural	Total
1940 [1]	63	131	194	33	67	100
1950 [1]	69	110	179	39	61	100
1959 [2]	100	109	209	48	52	100
1970 [2]	136	106	242	56	44	100
1975 [1]	154	100	254	61	39	100
1979 [2]	164	98	262	62	38	100
1983 [1]	174	96	270	64	36	100
1987 [1]	186	96	282	66	34	100

[1] Estimated figures.
[2] Census figures.

Table 11. Cities with Populations over One Million, 1989
(in thousands)

City	Population	City	Population
Moscow	8,769	Dnepropetrovsk	1,179
Leningrad	4,456	Baku	1,150
Kiev	2,587	Omsk	1,148
Tashkent	2,073	Chelyabinsk	1,143
Khar'kov	1,611	Alma-Ata	1,128
Minsk	1,589	Odessa	1,115
Gor'kiy	1,438	Donetsk	1,110
Novosibirsk	1,436	Kazan'	1,094
Sverdlovsk	1,367	Perm'	1,091
Tbilisi	1,260	Ufa	1,083
Kuybyshev	1,257	Rostov-na-Donu	1,020
Yerevan	1,199		

Source: Based on information from *Izvestiia* [Moscow], April 29, 1989, 2.

Table 12. Population Density of the Republics, 1959 and 1982

Republic	Number of Persons (per square kilometer) 1959 [1]	Number of Persons (per square kilometer) 1982 [2]	Percentage Change
Moldavian	85.6	119.4	39.4
Armenian	59.2	106.4	79.7
Ukrainian	69.4	83.3	20.0
Georgian	58.0	73.2	26.2
Azerbaydzhan	42.7	72.8	70.4
Lithuanian	41.6	53.3	28.1
Belorussian	38.8	46.9	20.8
Latvian	32.9	40.1	21.8
Uzbek	18.4	37.1	101.6
Estonian	26.5	33.2	25.2
Tadzhik	13.8	28.8	108.6
Kirgiz	10.4	18.8	80.7
Russian	6.9	8.2	18.8
Turkmen	3.1	6.1	96.7
Kazakh	3.4	5.6	64.7
SOVIET UNION	9.3	12.1	30.1

[1] Census figures.
[2] Estimated figures.

Source: Based on information from "Chislennost' naseleniia, ego rost i razmeshchenie," in L.M. Volodarskii (ed.), *Naselenie SSSR*, Moscow, 1983, 15.

Table 13. *Nationality, Language, and Religion, 1989 Census* [1]

Nationality and Language	Population	National Language Is Native Language	Percentage Fluent in Russian	Religion
Nationalities listed in 1979 census				
Russian	145,071,550	99.8	100.0	Orthodox
Ukrainian	44,135,989	81.1	56.2	Orthodox, Uniate
Uzbek	16,686,240	98.3	23.8	Muslim
Belorussian	10,030,441	70.9	54.7	Orthodox, Catholic
Kazakh	8,137,878	97.0	60.4	Muslim
Azerbaydzhan	6,791,106	97.6	34.4	Muslim
Tatar	6,645,588	83.2	70.8	Muslim
Armenian	4,627,227	91.6	47.1	Orthodox
Tadzhik	4,216,693	97.7	27.7	Muslim
Georgian	3,983,115	98.2	33.1	Orthodox
Moldavian	3,355,240	91.6	53.8	Orthodox
Lithuanian	3,068,296	97.7	37.9	Catholic
Turkmen	2,718,297	98.5	27.8	Muslim
Kirgiz	2,530,998	97.8	35.2	Muslim
German	2,035,807	48.7	45.0	Lutheran, Catholic
Chuvash	1,839,228	76.5	65.1	Orthodox, Muslim
Latvian	1,459,156	94.8	64.4	Lutheran
Bashkir	1,449,462	72.3	71.8	Muslim
Jewish	1,376,910	11.1	10.1	Jewish
Mordvin	1,153,516	67.0	62.5	Orthodox
Polish	1,126,137	30.4	43.9	Catholic
Estonian	1,027,255	95.5	33.8	Lutheran
Chechen	958,309	98.0	74.0	Muslim
Udmurt	746,562	69.6	61.3	Orthodox
Mari	670,277	80.8	68.8	Orthodox
Avar	604,202	96.9	60.6	Muslim
Ossetian	597,802	87.0	68.9	Muslim, Orthodox
Lezgin	466,833	91.5	53.4	Muslim
Korean	437,335	49.4	43.3	Shamanist, Confucian
Karakalpak	423,436	94.1	20.7	Muslim
Buryat	421,682	86.3	72.0	Orthodox, Shamanist, Buddhist
Kabardin	394,651	96.9	77.1	Muslim
Yakut	382,255	93.8	54.9	Orthodox
Bulgarian	378,790	67.9	60.3	Orthodox
Dargin	365,797	97.5	68.0	Muslim
Greek	357,975	44.5	39.5	Orthodox
Komi	345,007	70.4	62.1	Orthodox
Kumyk	282,178	97.4	74.5	Muslim
Uygur	262,199	86.5	58.3	Muslim
Gypsy	261,956	77.4	63.3	Orthodox, Muslim
Ingush	237,577	96.9	80.0	Muslim
Turkish	207,369	91.0	40.2	Muslim
Tuvinian	206,924	98.5	59.1	Lamaist
Gagauz	197,164	87.4	71.7	Orthodox
Kalmyk	174,528	89.9	85.1	Buddhist
Hungarian	171,941	93.7	43.3	Catholic
Karachai	156,140	96.7	79.1	Muslim
Kurdish	152,952	80.5	28.5	Muslim
Komi-Permyak	152,074	70.1	61.2	Orthodox

Table 13.—Continued

Nationality and Language	Population	National Language Is Native Language	Percentage Fluent in Russian	Religion
Romanian	145,918	60.9	50.9	Orthodox
Karelian	131,357	47.9	45.5	Orthodox
Adygy	124,941	94.7	81.7	Muslim
Lak	118,386	93.5	76.4	Muslim
Abkhazian	102,938	93.3	78.2	Muslim, Orthodox
Tabasaran	98,448	95.7	62.6	Muslim
Balkar	88,771	92.9	77.2	Muslim
Khakass	81,428	76.1	66.6	Orthodox
Nogai	75,564	89.9	79.3	Muslim
Altai	71,317	84.4	65.2	Orthodox
Dungan	69,686	94.7	70.5	Muslim
Finnish	67,318	34.7	35.4	Lutheran
Circassian	52,356	90.4	76.3	Muslim
Iranian	40,510	33.4	45.9	Muslim
Abazinian	33,801	93.4	78.1	Muslim
Tat	30,817	71.8	64.0	Muslim
Baluchi	29,091	95.7	5.0	Muslim
Assyrian	26,289	59.7	43.6	Nestorian
Rutul	20,672	94.5	63.0	Muslim
Tsakhur	20,055	95.1	23.6	Muslim
Agul	19,936	94.4	65.8	Muslim
Shor	16,572	57.7	52.8	Orthodox
Czech	16,335	36.0	37.3	Catholic
Vep	13,341	52.6	49.2	Orthodox
Slovak	10,017	42.7	51.8	Catholic
Udin	8,849	85.3	49.4	Orthodox
Mongol	4,336	90.8	74.5	Buddhist, Shamanist
Karaim	2,803	25.1	18.7	Jewish
Izhor	829	36.9	38.0	Orthodox
Peoples of the North [2] .	197,345	52.8	49.5	n.a.
Subtotal	285,200,070			
Nationalities not listed in 1979 census but listed in 1989 census				
Crimean Tatar	268,739	92.5	76.0	n.a.
Central Asian Jewish ..	36,568	64.6	50.2	n.a.
Talysh	21,914	90.1	6.1	n.a.
Mountain Jewish	19,516	73.2	53.1	n.a.
Vietnamese	16,752	98.5	25.0	n.a.
Georgian Jewish	16,123	90.7	46.4	n.a.
Arab	11,599	72.4	63.5	n.a.
Chinese	11,418	33.0	30.6	n.a.
Afghan	8,951	65.4	35.7	n.a.
Cuban	5,113	73.3	73.1	n.a.
Albanian	4,085	52.0	49.2	n.a.
Spanish	3,737	48.7	43.5	n.a.
Serbian	3,100	40.6	50.2	n.a.
Indian and Pakistani ..	2,614	77.1	40.7	n.a.
Italian	1,942	40.4	28.4	n.a.
Crimean	1,559	38.4	32.9	n.a.

Table 13.—Continued

Nationality and Language	Population	National Language Is Native Language	Percentage Fluent in Russian	Religion
Croatian	1,100	59.3	47.7	n.a.
Dutch	964	35.1	32.7	n.a.
French	798	50.3	44.4	n.a.
American	746	61.3	39.5	n.a.
Austrian	731	45.7	30.2	n.a.
Japanese	691	45.9	38.6	n.a.
British	637	70.0	50.2	n.a.
Subtotal	439,397			
TOTAL [3]	285,639,467			

n.a.—not available.

[1] The population figures given here do not include Soviet citizens abroad at the time the census was taken. Including them, the total Soviet population in 1989 was 286.7 million, which is the figure used on Table 6. It should be noted that Soviet statistics sometimes have unexplained discrepancies.

[2] In the 1979 census, twenty-three nationalities of the North were listed individually.

[3] Preliminary.

Source: Based on information from Gosudarstvennyi komitet po statistike, *Natsionalnyi sostav naseleniia, Chast' II,* Moscow, 1989, 3–5.

Table 14. Autonomous Subdivisions, 1989 *

Autonomous Republic	Autonomous Oblast	Autonomous Okrug
	Azerbaydzhan Republic	
Nakhichevan'	Nagorno-Karabakh	
	Georgian Republic	
Abkhazian	South Ossetian	
Adzhar		
	Russian Republic	
Bashkir	Adyegai	Agin-Buryat
Buryat	Gorno-Altai	Chukotskii
Chechen-Ingush	Jewish (Yevreyskaya)	Evenk
Chuvash	Karachi-Circassian	Khanty-Mansiiskii
Dagestan	Khakass	Komi-Permyak
Kabardino-Balkar		Koryak
Kalmyk		Nenet
Karelian		Taimyr
Komi		Ust'-Ordyn Buryat
Mari		Yamalo-Nenet
Mordvinian		
North Ossetian		
Tatar		
Tuva		
Udmurt		
Yakut		
	Tadzhik Republic	
	Gorno-Badakhshan	
	Uzbek Republic	
Karakalpak		

* For an explanation of the three kinds of autonomous subdivisions—see Glossary. The Armenian, Belorussian, Estonian, Kazakh, Kirgiz, Latvian, Lithuanian, Moldavian, Turkmen, and Ukrainian republics had no autonomous subdivisions.

Source: Based on information from Richard Sakwa, *Soviet Politics*, London, 1989, 298.

Table 15. *Republic of Residence and Population*
of Major Nationalities, 1989 Census

Nationality Republic of Residence	Population Number	Percentage [1]
Russians		
Russian	119,807,165	82.6
Ukrainian	11,340,250	7.8
Kazakh	6,226,400	4.3
Uzbek	1,652,179	1.1
Belorussian	1,341,055	0.9
Kirgiz	916,543	0.6
Latvian	905,515	0.6
Moldavian	560,423	0.4
Estonian	474,815	0.3
Azerbaydzhan	392,303	0.3
Tadzhik	386,630	0.3
Lithuanian	343,597	0.2
Georgian	338,645	0.2
Turkmen	334,477	0.2
Armenian	51,553	0.04
Total Russians	145,071,550	100.0
Ukrainians		
Ukrainian	37,370,368	84.7
Russian	4,363,992	9.9
Kazakh	895,964	2.0
Moldavian	599,777	1.4
Belorussian	290,368	0.7
Uzbek	154,105	0.3
Kirgiz	108,027	0.2
Latvian	92,101	0.2
Georgian	51,472	0.1
Estonian	48,273	0.1
Lithuanian	44,397	0.1
Tadzhik	40,646	0.09
Turkmen	35,814	0.08
Azerbaydzhan	32,344	0.07
Armenian	8,341	0.02
Total Ukrainians	44,135,989	100.0
Uzbeks		
Uzbek	14,123,626	84.6
Tadzhik	1,197,091	7.2
Kirgiz	550,095	3.3
Kazakh	332,016	2.0
Turkmen	317,252	1.9
Russian	127,169	0.8
Ukrainian	27,753	0.2
Belorussian	3,550	0.02
Moldavian	2,018	0.01
Lithuanian	1,452	0.01
Azerbaydzhan	1,379	0.01
Georgian	1,073	0.006
Latvian	925	0.006
Estonian	595	0.004
Armenian	246	0.001
Total Uzbeks	16,686,240	100.0

Table 15.—*Continued*

Nationality Republic of Residence	Population Number	Percentage [1]
Belorussians		
Belorussian	7,897,781	78.7
Russian	1,205,887	12.0
Ukrainian	439,858	4.4
Kazakh	182,514	1.8
Latvian	119,702	1.2
Lithuanian	63,076	0.6
Uzbek	31,737	0.3
Estonian	27,711	0.3
Moldavian	19,431	0.2
Turkmen	9,285	0.1
Kirgiz	9,187	0.1
Georgian	8,338	0.09
Azerbaydzhan	7,833	0.08
Tadzhik	7,042	0.07
Armenian	1,059	0.01
Total Belorussians	10,030,441	100.0
Kazakhs		
Kazakh	6,531,921	80.3
Uzbek	808,090	9.9
Russian	636,083	7.8
Turkmen	87,595	1.1
Kirgiz	37,318	0.5
Ukrainian	12,120	0.1
Tadzhik	11,371	0.1
Belorussian	4,530	0.06
Georgian	2,545	0.03
Moldavian	1,933	0.02
Azerbaydzhan	1,638	0.02
Latvian	1,044	0.01
Lithuanian	658	0.01
Armenian	608	0.007
Estonian	424	0.005
Total Kazakhs	8,137,878	100.0
Azerbaydzhanis		
Azerbaydzhan	5,800,994	85.4
Russian	336,908	5.0
Georgian	307,424	4.5
Kazakh	90,082	1.3
Armenian	84,860	1.2
Ukrainian	59,149	0.9
Uzbek	44,393	0.7
Turkmen	33,334	0.5
Kirgiz	15,775	0.2
Belorussian	6,634	0.1
Tadzhik	3,689	0.05
Latvian	2,765	0.04
Moldavian	2,554	0.04
Lithuanian	1,307	0.02
Estonian	1,238	0.02
Total Azerbaydzhanis	6,791,106	100.0

Table 15.—Continued

| Nationality | Population | |
Republic of Residence	Number	Percentage [1]
Tatars		
Russian	5,519,605	83.1
Uzbek	467,676	7.0
Kazakh	327,871	4.9
Ukrainian	86,789	1.3
Tadzhik	72,168	1.1
Kirgiz	70,068	1.1
Turkmen	39,243	0.6
Azerbaydzhan	28,019	0.4
Belorussian	12,352	0.2
Lithuanian	5,107	0.1
Latvian	4,828	0.1
Estonian	4,058	0.1
Georgian	3,999	0.1
Moldavian	3,335	0.05
Armenian	470	0.007
Total Tatars	6,645,588	100.0
Armenians		
Armenian	3,081,920	66.6
Russian	532,675	11.5
Georgian	436,615	9.4
Azerbaydzhan	390,495	8.4
Ukrainian	60,047	1.3
Uzbek	50,516	1.1
Turkmen	31,838	0.7
Kazakh	19,105	0.4
Tadzhik	5,630	0.1
Belorussian	5,251	0.1
Kirgiz	3,975	0.1
Latvian	3,069	0.07
Moldavian	2,774	0.06
Estonian	1,669	0.04
Lithuanian	1,648	0.04
Total Armenians	4,627,227	100.0
Tadzhiks		
Tadzhik	3,168,193	75.1
Uzbek	931,547	22.1
Russian	38,327	0.9
Kirgiz	33,842	0.8
Kazakh	25,514	0.6
Ukrainian	10,476	0.3
Turkmen	3,418	0.08
Belorussian	1,417	0.03
Georgian	1,133	0.03
Moldavian	720	0.02
Azerbaydzhan	702	0.02
Lithuanian	516	0.01
Armenian	432	0.01
Latvian	343	0.008
Estonian	113	0.003
Total Tadzhiks	4,216,693	100.0

Table 15.—Continued

Nationality	Population	
Republic of Residence	Number	Percentage [1]
Georgians		
Georgian	3,789,385	95.1
Russian	130,719	3.3
Ukrainian	23,689	0.6
Azerbaydzhan	13,986	0.4
Kazakh	9,496	0.2
Uzbek	4,726	0.1
Belorussian	2,968	0.07
Latvian	1,378	0.03
Armenian	1,364	0.03
Kirgiz	1,143	0.03
Moldavian	1,077	0.03
Tadzhik	971	0.02
Turkmen	960	0.02
Lithuanian	647	0.02
Estonian	606	0.02
Total Georgians	3,983,115	100.0
Moldavians		
Moldavian	2,790,769	83.2
Ukrainian	324,480	9.7
Russian	172,784	5.1
Kazakh	33,096	1.0
Uzbek	11,424	0.3
Belorussian	5,348	0.2
Latvian	3,223	0.1
Georgian	2,814	0.1
Turkmen	2,678	0.08
Azerbaydzhan	1,915	0.06
Kirgiz	1,875	0.06
Tadzhik	1,646	0.05
Lithuanian	1,448	0.04
Estonian	1,215	0.04
Armenian	525	0.02
Total Moldavians	3,355,240	100.0
Lithuanians		
Lithuanian	2,924,048	95.3
Russian	70,386	2.3
Latvian	34,630	1.1
Ukrainian	11,385	0.4
Kazakh	10,938	0.4
Belorussian	7,589	0.3
Estonian	2,568	0.1
Uzbek	2,234	0.07
Moldavian	1,438	0.05
Georgian	921	0.03
Azerbaydzhan	533	0.02
Tadzhik	530	0.02
Kirgiz	493	0.02
Turkmen	372	0.01
Armenian	231	0.008
Total Lithuanians	3,068,296	100.0

Table 15.—Continued

| Nationality | Population | |
Republic of Residence	Number	Percentage [1]
Turkmens		
Turkmen	2,524,138	92.9
Uzbek	122,566	4.5
Russian	39,738	1.5
Tadzhik	20,527	0.8
Kazakh	4,046	0.1
Ukrainian	3,990	0.1
Kirgiz	899	0.03
Belorussian	755	0.03
Moldavian	399	0.01
Azerbaydzhan	340	0.01
Georgian	305	0.01
Latvian	228	0.008
Lithuanian	193	0.007
Estonian	106	0.004
Armenian	67	0.002
Total Turkmens	2,718,297	100.0
Kirgiz		
Kirgiz	2,228,482	88.0
Uzbek	174,899	6.9
Tadzhik	63,831	2.5
Russian	43,083	1.7
Kazakh	14,271	0.6
Ukrainian	3,881	0.2
Turkmen	727	0.03
Belorussian	555	0.02
Armenian	271	0.01
Azerbaydzhan	224	0.01
Moldavian	216	0.01
Latvian	189	0.01
Georgian	170	0.007
Lithuanian	118	0.005
Estonian	81	0.003
Total Kirgiz	2,530,998	100.0
Germans		
Kazakh	956,235	47.0
Russian	840,980	41.3
Kirgiz	101,198	5.0
Tadzhik	32,493	1.6
Other	104,901	5.1
Total Germans	2,035,807	100.0
Chuvash		
Russian	1,771,047	93.8
Other	68,181	6.2
Total Chuvash	1,839,228	100.0
Latvians		
Latvian	1,387,646	95.1
Russian	46,818	3.2
Ukrainian	7,169	0.5
Lithuanian	4,228	0.3
Kazakh	3,370	0.2

Table 15.—Continued

Nationality	Population	
Republic of Residence	Number	Percentage [1]
Latvians—*Continued*		
Estonian	3,135	0.2
Belorussian	2,655	0.2
Uzbek	1,130	0.1
Turkmen	859	0.06
Georgian	524	0.04
Moldavian	461	0.03
Kirgiz	392	0.03
Azerbaydzhan	324	0.02
Tadzhik	300	0.02
Armenian	145	0.01
Total Latvians	1,459,156	100.0
Bashkirs		
Russian	1,345,231	92.8
Other	104,231	7.2
Total Bashkirs	1,449,462	100.0
Jews		
Russian	536,422	39.0
Ukrainian	485,975	35.3
Belorussian	111,789	8.1
Moldavian	65,668	4.8
Uzbek	65,369	4.7
Azerbaydzhan	25,190	1.8
Latvian	22,897	1.7
Kazakh	18,379	1.3
Lithuanian	12,312	0.9
Georgian	10,302	0.7
Tadzhik	9,576	0.7
Other	13,031	1.0
Total Jews	1,376,910	100.0
Mordvins		
Russian	1,072,517	93.0
Other	80,999	7.0
Total Mordvins	1,153,516	100.0
Poles		
Belorussian	417,648	37.1
Lithuanian	257,988	22.9
Ukrainian	218,891	19.4
Latvian	60,388	5.4
Other	171,222	15.2
Total Poles	1,126,137	100.0
Estonians		
Estonian	963,269	93.8
Russian	46,358	4.5
Ukrainian	4,208	0.4
Kazakh	3,397	0.3
Latvian	3,312	0.3
Georgian	2,312	0.1
Uzbek	948	0.1
Belorussian	797	0.1
Lithuanian	598	0.06

Table 15.—Continued

| Nationality | Population | |
Republic of Residence	Number	Percentage [1]
Estonians—*Continued*		
Turkmen	560	0.05
Kirgiz	430	0.04
Azerbaydzhan	324	0.03
Armenian	295	0.03
Moldavian	276	0.03
Tadzhik	171	0.02
Total Estonians	1,027,255	100.0
Other	12,173,338	
TOTAL	285,639,467 *	

[1] Figures may not add to total because of rounding.
[2] Soviet citizens outside the country are not included. Also, Soviet statistics sometimes have unexplained discrepancies.

Source: Based on information from Gosudarstvennyi komitet po statistike, *Natsionalnyi sostav naseleniia, Chast' II*, Moscow, 1989, 97–113.

Table 16. Russian and East Slavic Populations
in the Republics, 1989 Census

Republic	Native Population		Russian Population		East Slavic Population *		Total
	Number	Percentage	Number	Percentage	Number	Percentage	
Russian	119,807,165	81.5	119,807,165	81.5	125,377,044	85.2	147,001,621
Ukrainian	37,370,368	72.6	11,340,250	22.0	49,150,476	95.5	51,449,479
Uzbek	14,123,626	71.3	1,652,179	8.3	1,838,021	9.3	19,808,077
Belorussian	7,897,781	77.8	1,341,055	13.2	9,529,204	93.9	10,149,248
Kazakh	6,531,921	39.7	6,226,400	37.8	7,304,878	44.4	16,463,115
Azerbaydzhan	5,800,994	82.6	392,303	5.6	432,480	6.2	7,019,739
Georgian	3,789,385	70.2	338,645	6.3	398,455	7.4	5,395,841
Tadzhik	3,168,193	62.2	386,630	7.6	434,318	8.5	5,089,593
Armenian	3,081,920	93.3	51,553	1.6	60,953	1.8	3,304,353
Lithuanian	2,924,048	79.6	343,597	9.4	451,070	12.3	3,673,362
Moldavian	2,790,769	64.4	560,423	12.9	1,179,631	27.2	4,332,363
Turkmen	2,524,138	71.9	334,477	9.5	379,576	10.8	3,512,190
Kirgiz	2,228,482	52.3	916,543	21.5	1,033,757	24.3	4,257,755
Latvian	1,387,646	52.0	905,515	34.0	1,117,318	41.9	2,666,567
Estonian	963,269	61.5	474,815	30.3	550,799	35.2	1,565,662

* East Slavs include Russians, Ukrainians, and Belorussians.

Source: Based on information from Gosudarstvennyi komitet po statistike, *Natsionalnyi sostav naseleniia, Chast' II*, Moscow, 1989.

Table 17. Social Groups, 1913, 1959, and 1986
(in percentages)

Social Group	1913	1959	1986
Peasants	66.7	31.7	12.1
Workers	14.6	50.2	61.7
Intelligentsia [1]	2.4	18.1	26.2
Bourgeoisie [2]	16.3	n.a.	n.a.
TOTAL	100.0	100.0	100.0

n.a.—not applicable.
[1] Although officially not considered a separate class, the intelligentsia made up a considerable part of the population.
[2] After the Bolshevik Revolution, the designation *bourgeoisie* was abolished as a social class by the regime.

Source: Based on information from Tsentral'noe statisticheskoe upravlenie, *SSSR v tsifrakh v 1986 godu,* Moscow, 1987, 6.

Table 18. Average Monthly Wage by Occupation, 1986
(in rubles) [1]

Occupation	Wage [2]
Blue-collar workers	
Industrial workers	216.4
Railroad workers	220.9
Construction workers	253.2
Water transport workers	272.4
White-collar workers	
Teachers	155.7
Computer scientists	158.0
Communications workers	164.0
Government workers	176.6
Scientists	208.2
Engineers and technicians	239.0

[1] For value of the ruble—see Glossary.
[2] Nationwide average was 195.6 rubles.

Source: Based on information from Gosudarstvennyi komitet po statistike, *Narodnoe khoziaistvo SSSR za 70 let,* Moscow, 1987, 431.

Table 19. Selected Low-Paid Occupations, Early 1980s
(in rubles) ¹

Occupation	Wage ²
Librarians	100–115
Translators	95–130
Cultural administrators	90–110
Musicians	90–110
Secretaries (senior)	80–85
Cashiers	80–85
Draftsmen	80–85
Warehouse personnel	80–85
Stove keepers	80–85
Truck and bus drivers	75–90
Grounds keepers	75–85
Street cleaners	75–80
Guards	75–80
Clerks (junior)	75–80

¹ For value of the ruble—see Glossary.
² Average wage increased nearly 16 percent from 1980 to 1988.

Source: Based on information from Mervyn Matthews, ''Aspects of Poverty in the Soviet Union,'' in Horst Herlemann (ed.), *Quality of Life in the Soviet Union,* Boulder, Colorado, 1987, 48, 51.

Table 20. Urban-Rural Breakdown, Selected Years, 1917–87
(in percentages)

Year	Urban	Rural	Total
1917	17.9	82.1	100.0
1940	32.5	67.5	100.0
1959	47.9	52.1	100.0
1970	56.3	43.7	100.0
1987	66.0	34.0	100.0

Source: Based on information from Tsentral'noe statisticheskoe upravlenie, *SSSR v tsifrakh v 1986 godu,* Moscow, 1987, 5.

Table 21. Average Family Size by Nationality Group, 1979 Census *

Nationality Group	Urban	Rural	Average
Slavs			
Russians	3.2	3.2	3.2
Ukrainians	3.2	3.3	3.2
Belorussians	3.2	3.2	3.2
Baltic peoples			
Lithuanians	3.3	3.3	3.3
Latvians	3.0	3.1	3.0
Estonians	3.0	3.1	3.0
Peoples of the Caucasus			
Armenians	4.3	4.8	4.5
Georgians	3.9	4.1	4.0
Azerbaydzhanis	4.3	4.8	4.5
Central Asians			
Uzbeks	5.8	6.3	6.2
Kazakhs	5.1	5.7	5.5
Kirgiz	4.9	5.8	5.7
Tadzhiks	6.0	6.7	6.5
Turkmens	5.9	6.5	6.3
Other			
Moldavians	3.3	3.6	3.5
SOVIET UNION	3.3	3.8	3.5

* Includes only families in which all members belong to one nationality.

Source: Based on information from Tsentral'noe statisticheskoe upravlenie, *Chislennost' i sostav naseleniia SSSR*, Moscow, 1984, 284-37.

Table 22. Network of Primary Party Organizations,
1977 and 1987

Location of Primary Party Organization [1]	1977 [2]		1987 [2]	
	Number	Percentage	Number	Percentage
Industry, transportation, communications, and construction	102,720	26.1	112,866	25.5
Schools, cultural organizations, and health organizations	96,051	24.4	104,988	23.8
Rural territorial, housing sectors, and others	67,853	17.2	81,638	18.5
Institutions, organizations, and economic organs (from the central to the district, inclusive)	65,458	16.6	76,684	17.4
Collective farms	27,893	7.1	26,888	6.1
State farms	19,400	4.9	22,854	5.2
Trade and supply	14,639	3.7	15,933	3.6
TOTAL [3]	394,014	100.0	441,851	100.0

[1] Table does not include a formal designation for location of primary party organizations in the Soviet military.
[2] Figures are for January 1 of each year.
[3] Figures may not add to total because of rounding.

Source: Based on information from "KPSS v tsifrakh," *Partiinaia zhizn'* [Moscow], No. 21, November 1987, 15.

Table 23. Membership in the Communist Party of the Soviet Union,
Selected Years, 1971–87

Year	Full Members	Candidate Members	Total
1971 (Twenty-Fourth Party Congress)	13,810,089	645,232	14,455,321
1976 (Twenty-Fifth Party Congress)	15,058,017	636,170	15,694,187
1981 (Twenty-Sixth Party Congress)	16,763,009	717,759	17,480,768
1986 (Twenty-Seventh Party Congress)	18,309,693	728,253	19,037,946
1987 (As of July 1)	18,707,341	704,812	19,412,153

Source: Based on information from "KPSS v tsifrakh," *Partiinaia zhizn'* [Moscow], No. 14, July 1986, 19; and "KPSS v tsifrakh," *Partiinaia zhizn'* [Moscow], No. 21, November 1987, 6.

*Table 24. Social Position of Members of the
Communist Party of the Soviet Union,
Selected Years, 1971–87* [1]

Year [2]	Workers		Peasants		Professionals		Total	
	Number	Percentage	Number	Percentage	Number	Percentage	Number	Percentage
1971	5,759,379	40.1	2,169,437	15.1	6,443,747	44.8	14,372,563	100.0
1976	6,509,312	41.6	2,169,813	13.9	6,959,766	44.5	15,638,891	100.0
1981	7,569,261	43.4	2,223,674	12.8	7,637,478	43.8	17,430,413	100.0
1986	8,551,779	45.0	2,248,166	11.8	8,204,433	43.2	19,004,378	100.0
1987	8,722,639	45.3	2,247,432	11.6	8,297,644	43.1	19,267,715	100.0

[1] Social position refers to class affiliation of party members at the time they joined the party.
[2] Figures are for January 1 of each year.

Source: Based on information from "KPSS v tsifrakh," *Partiinaia zhizn'* [Moscow], No. 14, July 1986, 22; and "KPSS v tsifrakh," *Partiinaia zhizn'* [Moscow], No. 21, November 1987, 9.

Table 25. *Education Level of Members of the Communist Party of the Soviet Union, 1967, 1977, and 1987*

Education Level	1967 * Number	1967 * Percentage	1977 * Number	1977 * Percentage	1987 * Number	1987 * Percentage
Higher education ..	2,097,055	16.5	4,008,986	25.1	6,284,588	32.6
Incomplete higher education ..	325,985	2.6	380,349	2.4	395,581	2.0
Secondary education ..	3,993,119	31.5	6,268,336	39.2	8,633,322	44.8
Incomplete secondary education ..	3,417,251	26.9	3,154,362	19.7	2,520,697	13.1
Primary education ..	2,850,723	22.5	2,182,443	13.6	1,433,527	7.5
TOTAL	12,684,133	100.0	15,994,476	100.0	19,267,715	100.0

* Figures are for January 1 of each year.

Source: Based on information from "KPSS v tsifrakh," *Partiinaia zhizn'* [Moscow], No. 21, November 1987, 10.

Table 26. Distribution of Major Nationalities in the Communist Party of the Soviet Union and in the Soviet Population, 1981

Nationality	Party [1] Number	Party [1] Percentage	Population [2] Number	Population [2] Percentage
Russians	10,457,771	60.0	137,397,000	52.0
Ukrainians	2,794,592	16.0	42,347,000	16.0
Belorussians	651,486	3.7	9,463,000	3.0
Uzbeks	393,770	2.3	12,456,000	4.7
Kazakhs	332,821	1.9	6,556,000	2.5
Georgians	290,227	1.7	3,571,000	1.3
Azerbaydzhanis	280,498	1.6	5,477,000	2.0
Armenians	261,572	1.5	4,151,000	1.5
Lithuanians	126,704	0.7	2,851,000	1.0
Moldavians	89,680	0.5	2,968,000	1.1
Tadzhiks	74,987	0.4	2,898,000	1.1
Latvians	71,911	0.4	1,439,000	0.5
Kirgiz	62,694	0.4	1,906,000	0.7
Turkmens	61,430	0.4	2,028,000	0.7
Estonians	55,957	0.3	1,020,000	0.4
Other	1,424,313	8.2	32,760,000	11.5
TOTAL	17,430,413	100.0	269,288,000	100.0

[1] 1981 figures.
[2] 1979 estimated figures.

Source: Based on information from "KPSS v tsifrakh," *Partiinaia zhizn'* [Moscow], No. 14, July 1981, 18; and Gosudarstvennyi komitet po statistike, *Narodnoe khoziaistvo SSSR v 1985 g.*, Moscow, 1986, 24–26.

Table 27. Distribution of Members of the Communist Party of the Soviet Union by Sex, Selected Years, 1971–87

Year *	Male Number	Male Percentage	Female Number	Female Percentage	Total Number	Total Percentage
1971	11,177,007	77.8	3,195,566	22.2	14,372,563	100.0
1976	11,845,032	75.7	3,793,859	24.3	15,638,891	100.0
1981	12,814,837	73.5	4,615,576	26.5	17,430,413	100.0
1986	13,529,233	71.2	5,475,145	28.8	19,004,378	100.0
1987	13,631,686	70.7	5,636,029	29.3	19,267,715	100.0

* Figures are for January 1 of each year.

Source: Based on information from "KPSS v tsifrakh," *Partiinaia zhizn'* [Moscow], No. 14, July 1986, 24; and "KPSS v tsifrakh," *Partiinaia zhizn'* [Moscow], No. 21, November 1987, 11.

Table 28. *Organs and Functions of the Soviet Regime, 1988*

Organ	Function	Leading Official
Politburo	Makes key decisions on national policy and leadership	General secretary of the Central Committee [1]
Secretariat	Reviews and certifies government plans and policies	-do-
Defense Council	Formulates defense policy and oversees defense establishment	-do-
Congress of People's Deputies and the Supreme Soviet ..	Perform ceremonial and state functions	Chairman of the Supreme Soviet [1]
Council of Ministers	Coordinates economic administration	Chairman of the Council of Ministers
Gosplan, Ministry of Finance, and Goskomstat [2]	Perform economic and budgetary planning	Ministers and chairmen of state committees
More than twenty ministries and committees	Administer economic plans and public services	-do-
Ministry of Foreign Affairs, Ministry of Defense, and KGB [3]	Establish foreign policy	-do- [4]

[1] Function is somewhat comparable to that of United States president.
[2] Gosplan—Gosudarstvennyi planovyi komitet (State Planning Committee); Goskomstat—Gosudarstvennyi komitet po statistike (State Committee for Statistics).
[3] KGB—Komitet gosudarstvennoi bezopasnosti (Committee for State Security).
[4] Function is comparable to that of United States agency heads.

Table 29. Treaties of Friendship and Cooperation with Third World Countries, 1989 *

Country	Date
Mongolia	March 12, 1936, in Moscow (renewed February 27, 1946; another treaty was signed January 15, 1966, in Ulaanbaatar and renewed March 15, 1986)
North Korea	July 6, 1961, in Moscow
Egypt	May 27, 1971, in Cairo (abrogated March 15, 1976)
India	August 9, 1971, in New Delhi
Iraq	April 9, 1972, in Baghdad (renewed April 9, 1987)
Somalia	July 11, 1974, in Mogadishu (abrogated November 13, 1977)
Angola	October 8, 1976, in Moscow
Mozambique	March 31, 1977, in Maputo
Vietnam	November 3, 1978, in Moscow
Ethiopia	November 20, 1978, in Moscow
Afghanistan	December 5, 1978, in Moscow (previous treaties signed 1921 and 1931)
South Yemen	October 25, 1979, in Moscow
Syria	October 8, 1980, in Moscow
Congo	May 13, 1981, in Moscow
North Yemen	October 9, 1984, in Moscow
Cuba	April 4, 1989, in Havana

* In addition to these formal treaties, there have been "agreements in principle" or "declarations" of friendship and cooperation between the Soviet Union and Libya, Mali, and Benin. The Libya declaration was announced in a joint communiqué March 18, 1983, in Moscow following a visit to the Soviet Union by Abd as-Salan Jallud, member of the Revolutionary Council of the Socialist People's Libyan Arab Jamahiriyah. The Mali declaration was signed July 18, 1986, in Moscow by Andrei Gromyko and Moussa Traoré, president of Mali. The Benin declaration was signed November 25, 1986, in Moscow by Andrei Gromyko and Mathaeu Kerekou, president of Benin. Besides the Soviet Union, other Warsaw Pact countries have concluded friendship treaties with Third World countries.

Table 30. Five-Year Plans, 1928-95

Date	Plan	Date	Plan
1928-32 ...	First Five-Year Plan [1]	1966-70 ...	Eighth Five-Year Plan
1933-37 ...	Second Five-Year Plan	1971-75 ...	Ninth Five-Year Plan
1938-41 ...	Third Five-Year Plan [2]	1976-80 ...	Tenth Five-Year Plan
1945-50 ...	Fourth Five-Year Plan	1981-85 ...	Eleventh Five-Year Plan
1951-55 ...	Fifth Five-Year Plan	1986-90 ...	Twelfth Five-Year Plan
1956-60 ...	Sixth Five-Year Plan	1991-95 ...	Thirteenth Five-Year Plan [4]
1959-65 ...	Seventh Five-Year Plan [3]		

[1] Implemented October 1928, although not officially approved by Sixteenth Party Conference until April 1929.
[2] Interrupted by World War II.
[3] A seven-year plan that included last two years of Sixth Five-Year Plan.
[4] Under discussion in 1989.

Table 31. Estimated Gross National Product by Sector,
Selected Years, 1970-88
(in billions of 1982 rubles at factor cost)[1]

Sector	1970	1975	1980	1985	1986	1987	1988
Agriculture	139.6	124.7	125.6	132.9	147.5	141.8	141.0
Industry	137.9	181.3	204.2	225.1	230.7	237.8	244.7
Services	93.3	109.8	124.9	139.4	142.5	147.0	151.4
Construction	42.0	51.6	51.4	54.3	56.4	57.7	59.2
Transportation	35.9	49.3	58.8	65.5	67.5	68.2	70.0
Trade	28.5	36.1	40.9	44.6	44.5	45.2	46.7
Communications	3.1	4.2	5.3	6.4	6.8	7.2	7.6
Other [2]	11.4	12.6	13.6	14.3	14.5	14.5	14.5
TOTAL [3]	491.8	569.5	624.8	682.6	710.3	719.5	735.2

[1] For value of the ruble—see Glossary. Factor cost refers to a combination of government-administered prices of land, labor, and capital.
[2] Includes military personnel.
[3] Figures do not add to total because of rounding.

Source: Based on information from United States, Central Intelligence Agency and Defense Intelligence Agency, "The Soviet Economy Stumbles Badly in 1989," Washington, April 20, 1990, Table C-1.

Table 32. Industrial Production, Estimated Value Added, Selected Years, 1970-88 [1]
(in billions of 1982 rubles) [2]

Industry	1970	1975	1980	1985	1986	1987	1988
Machinery	44.1	62.3	72.6	80.2	82.3	85.4	88.4
Fuels	13.1	16.8	19.4	20.2	20.9	21.3	21.6
Food industry	12.0	14.7	15.7	17.2	16.4	17.0	17.7
Forest products	11.1	12.6	12.3	13.5	14.1	14.5	14.9
Light industry	11.0	12.5	14.1	15.2	15.4	15.7	16.0
Ferrous metals	9.8	11.9	12.6	13.1	13.6	13.8	14.0
Construction materials .	9.1	11.8	12.3	13.5	14.0	14.5	14.9
Chemicals	8.5	12.6	14.6	17.7	18.5	19.0	19.4
Electric power	8.1	11.4	14.2	16.5	17.1	17.8	18.2
Nonferrous metals	5.8	7.6	8.2	9.0	9.3	9.5	9.8
Other	5.5	7.2	8.1	8.9	9.2	9.4	9.7
TOTAL [3]	137.9	181.3	204.2	225.1	230.7	237.8	244.7

[1] Government-administered price of goods, less the cost of materials.
[2] For value of the ruble—see Glossary.
[3] Figures do not add to total because of rounding.

Source: Based on information from United States, Central Intelligence Agency and Defense Intelligence Agency, ''The Soviet Economy Stumbles Badly in 1989,'' Washington, April 20, 1990, Table C-2.

Table 33. Selected Ministries Producing Military
Weapons and Components, 1989 *

Ministry	Military Production Specialization
Aviation Industry	Aircraft, helicopters, and missiles
Communications Equipment Industry	Electronic warfare equipment and radar
Defense Industry	Artillery, infantry weapons, mobile ballistic missiles, and tanks
Electronics Industry	Radar and military electronics
General Machine Building	Missiles and space equipment
Machine Tool and Tool-Building Industry	Munitions and solid propellants
Medium Machine Building	Nuclear weapons and lasers
Radio Industry	Radar, radios, and guidance and control systems
Shipbuilding Industry	Ships

* Includes ministries having the largest percentage of output composed of military weapons or their components. Other ministries also produced military equipment or components, but to a lesser extent of their total output. The ministries listed here are among the eighteen ministries in the machine-building and metal-working complex (MBMW).

Source: Based on information from United States, Department of Defense, *Soviet Military Power, 1987*, Washington, March 1987, 10; and William F. Scott, "Moscow's Military-Industrial Complex," *Air Force Magazine*, 70, No. 3, March 1987, 50.

Table 34. Production of Major Farm Commodities, 1956-87
(in millions of tons)

Commodity	1956-60	1961-65	1966-70	1971-75	1976-80	1981-85	1986	1987
Grain	121.5	130.3	167.6	181.6	205.0	180.3	210.1	211.3
Potatoes	88.3	81.6	94.8	89.8	82.6	78.4	87.4	75.9
Sugar beets	45.6	59.2	81.1	76.0	88.7	76.4	79.3	90.0
Vegetables	15.1	16.9	19.5	23.0	26.3	29.2	29.7	29.1
Fruits	4.5	6.5	9.7	12.4	15.2	17.8	18.3	n.a.
Raw cotton	4.4	5.0	6.1	7.7	8.6	8.3	8.2	8.1
Sunflowers	3.7	5.1	6.4	6.0	5.3	5.0	5.3	6.1

n.a.—not available.

Source: Based on information from Gosudarstvennyi komitet po statistike, *Narodnoe khoziaistvo SSSR za 70 let*, Moscow, 1987, 209, 239; and "Zakrepit' dostignutoe, uskorit' tempy," *Izvestiia* [Moscow], No. 24, January 24, 1988, 2.

Table 35. Farm Machinery Pool, Selected Years, 1960–86
(in thousands)

Machinery	1960	1970	1980	1985	1986
Tractors	1,122	1,977	2,562	2,775	2,776
Tractor-drawn plows	813	1,053	1,103	1,167	1,148
Trucks	760	1,136	1,596	1,851	1,917
Tractor-drawn cultivators	754	1,144	1,117	1,265	1,295
Grain-harvesting combines	497	623	722	828	827
Tractor-drawn mowers (including shredders)	n.a.	546	686	702	672
Row reapers	270	335	471	521	506
Silage and fodder harvesters	121	139	269	256	254
Mineral fertilizer spreaders	n.a.	88	230	224	224
Milking machines	48	169	361	401	408
Corn pickers	35	34	52	32	30
Beet harvesters	34	57	62	53	52
Cotton pickers	11	39	55	63	63
Potato harvesters	10	36	70	63	60

n.a.—not available.
Source: Based on information from Gosudarstvennyi komitet po statistike, *Narodnoe khoziaistvo SSSR za 70 let,* Moscow, 1987, 207, 283.

Table 36. Sown Area for Major Crops, Selected Years, 1940–86
(in millions of hectares)

Crop	1940	1960	1970	1980	1985	1986
Grain	110.7	115.6	119.3	126.6	117.9	116.5
Bare fallow	28.9	17.4	18.4	13.8	21.3	32.7
Forage crops	18.1	63.1	62.8	66.9	69.8	71.4
Technical crops	11.8	13.1	14.5	14.6	13.9	13.7
Vegetables	10.0	11.2	10.1	9.2	8.7	8.7
TOTAL	179.5	220.4	225.1	231.1	231.6	243.0

Source: Based on information from Gosudarstvennyi komitet po statistike, *Narodnoe khoziaistvo SSSR za 70 let,* Moscow, 1987, 224–25.

Table 37. Agricultural Chemicals Delivered, Selected Years, 1970–87
(in thousands of tons)

Chemical	1970	1980	1985	1986	1987
Mineral fertilizers [1]					
Nitrogenous	4,605	8,262	10,950	11,475	n.a.
Potash	2,574	4,904	6,822	6,677	n.a.
Phosphatic	2,160	4,760	6,839	7,567	n.a.
Ground rock phosphate	973	830	776	787	n.a.
Total mineral fertilizers	10,312	18,756	25,387	26,506	27,400
Plant protective chemicals [2]					
Herbicides	50	127	160	172	n.a.
Other	120	152	202	174	n.a.
Total plant protective chemicals	170	279	362	346	n.a.
Chemical feed additives [1]					
Nitrogenous	n.a.	86	223	204	n.a.
Phosphatic	51	432	765	823	n.a.
Total chemical feed additives ..	51	518	988	1,027	1,100
TOTAL	10,533	19,553	26,737	27,879	28,500

n.a.—not available.
[1] Calculated at 100 percent nutritive content.
[2] Calculated at 100 percent active-ingredient content.

Source: Based on information from Gosudarstvennyi komitet po statistike, *Narodnoe khoziaistvo SSSR za 70 let,* Moscow, 1987, 284; and "Zakrepit' dostignutoe, uskorit' tempy," *Izvestiia* [Moscow], No. 24, January 24, 1988, 3.

Table 38. Selected Animal Products, Selected Years, 1940–87

Product	1940	1960	1970	1980	1985	1986	1987
Eggs [1]	12.2	27.4	40.7	67.9	77.3	80.7	82.1
Meat [2]	4.7	8.7	12.3	15.1	17.1	18.0	18.6
Milk [3]	33.6	61.7	83.0	90.9	98.6	102.2	103.4
Wool [4]	161.0	339.0	402.0	443.0	447.0	469.0	455.0

[1] In billions.
[2] In million of tons of slaughtered weight.
[3] In millions of tons.
[4] In thousands of tons.

Source: Based on information from Gosudarstvennyi komitet po statistike, *Narodnoe khoziaistvo SSSR za 70 let,* Moscow, 1987, 258; and "Zakrepit' dostignutoe, uskorit' tempy," *Izvestiia* [Moscow], No. 24, January 24, 1988, 2.

*Table 39. Freight Traffic by Mode of Transport,
Selected Years, 1940–86* [1]
(in billions of ton-kilometers)

Mode of Transport	1940	1960	1970	1980	1985	1986
Railroad	420.7	1,504.3	2,494.7	3,439.9	3,718.4	3,834.5
Inland waterway	36.1	99.6	174.0	244.9	261.5	255.6
Merchant marine	24.9	131.5	656.1	848.2	905.0	969.7
Trucks	8.9	98.5	220.8	432.1	476.4	488.5
Pipelines						
Petroleum and						
derivatives	3.8	51.2	281.7	1,216.0	1,312.5	1,401.3
Natural gas	n.a	12.6	131.4	596.9	1,130.5	1,240.0
Total pipelines	3.8	63.8	413.1	1,812.9	2,443.0	2,641.3
Civil aviation	0.0 [2]	0.6	1.9	3.1	3.4	3.4
TOTAL	494.4	1,898.3	3,960.6	6,781.1	7,807.7	8,193.0

n.a.—not applicable.
[1] Freight traffic is measured in ton-kilometers, i.e., the movement of one ton of cargo a distance of one kilometer. Ton-kilometers are computed by multiplying the weight (in tons) of each shipment transported by the distance hauled (in kilometers).
[2] Figure for 1940 is 20 million.
Source: Based on information from Gosudarstvennyi komitet po statistike, *Narodnoe khoziaistvo SSSR za 70 let,* Moscow, 1987, 341.

Table 40. Major Rail Lines, 1988

Union Republic Railroad *	English Equivalent	Headquarters
Russian Republic		
Baykalo-Amurskaya	Baykal-Amur	Tynda
Dal'nevostochnaya	Far Eastern	Khabarovsk
Gor'kovskaya	Gor'kiy	Gor'kiy
Kemerovskaya	Kemerovo	Kemerovo
Krasnoyarskaya	Krasnoyarsk	Krasnoyarsk
Kuybyshevskaya	Kuybyshev	Kuybyshev
Moskovskaya	Moscow	Moscow
Oktiabr'skaya	October	Leningrad
Privolzhskaya	Volga	Saratov
Severnaya	Northern	Yaroslavl'
Severo-Kavkazskaya	Northern Caucasus	Rostov-na-Donu
Sverdlovskaya	Sverdlovsk	Sverdlovsk
Vostochno-Sibirskaya	East Siberian	Irkutsk
Yugo-Vostochnaya	Southeastern	Voronezh
Yuzhno-Ural'skaya	South Urals	Chelyabinsk
Zabaykalskaya	Transbaykal	Chita
Zapadno-Sibirskaya	West Siberian	Novosibirsk
Ukrainian Republic		
Donetskaya	Donetsk	Donetsk
L'vovskaya	L'vov	L'vov
Odesskaya	Odessa	Odessa
Pridneprovskaya	Dnepr	Dnepropetrovsk
Yugo-Zapadnaya	Southwestern	Kiev
Yuzhnaya	Southern	Khar'kov
Other republics		
Alma-Atinskaya	Alma-Ata	Alma-Ata
Azerbaydzhanskaya	Azerbaydzhan	Baku
Belorusskaya	Belorussian	Minsk
Moldavskaya	Moldavian	Kishinev
Pribaltiyskaya	Baltic	Riga
Sredneaziatskaya	Central Asian	Tashkent
Tselinnaya	Tselina	Tselinograd
Zakavkazskaya	Transcaucasian	Tbilisi
Zapadno-Kazakhstanskaya	West Kazakhstan	Aktyubinsk

* In Russian, each railroad's name is followed by "zheleznaya doroga" (railroad), except the Baykalo-Amurskaya, which is followed by "magistral'" (main line).

NOTE—The Trans-Siberian Railway (see Glossary) is an informal term for portions of several railroads listed above that link the western part of the Soviet Union and the Soviet Far East.

Source: Based on information from "Reference Aid: Directory of the USSR Ministry of Railways," Joint Publications Research Service, *Soviet Union: Economic Affairs*, June 29, 1988, B–74.

Table 41. Principal Electrified Rail Lines, 1987

Rail Line	Principal Cities on Line	Approximate Length (in kilometers)
Moscow to Kuyenga	Moscow Kuybyshev Omsk Tayshet Karymskaya Kuyenga	7,000
Leningrad to Norashen	Leningrad Moscow Khar'kov Rostov-na-Donu Tbilisi Leninaken Norashen	3,600
Moscow to Kurgan	Moscow Gor'kiy Sverdlovsk Kurgan	2,200
Moscow to Omsk	Moscow Kirov Sverdlovsk Tyumen' Omsk	2,100
Novosibirsk to Korshunikha	Novosibirsk Novoleuznetsk Abakan Korshunikha	2,000
Magnitogorsk to Zharyk	Magnitogorsk Moscow Karanga Zharyk	1,300
Moscow to Chop	Moscow Kiev L'vov Chop	1,300
Moscow to Rostov-na-Donu	Moscow Kochetovka Rostov-na-Donu	1,200

Table 42. Passengers Boarded by Mode of
Transport, Selected Years, 1940-86
(in millions of passengers boarded)

Mode of Transport	1940	1960	1970	1980	1985	1986
Railroad	1,377.0	2,231.0	3,354.0	4,072.0	4,166.0	4,345.0
Bus	590.0	11,315.0	27,343.0	42,175.0	47,006.0	48,800.0
Inland waterway	73.4	119.0	145.0	138.0	132.0	136.0
Merchant marine	9.7	26.7	38.5	51.7	50.3	50.8
Civil aviation	0.4	16.3	71.4	103.8	112.6	116.1
TOTAL	2,050.5	13,708.0	30,951.9	46,540.5	51,466.9	53,447.9

Source: Based on information from Gosudarstvennyi komitet po statistike, *Narodnoe khozi-aistvo SSSR za 70 let,* Moscow 1987, 344-68.

Table 43. Metropolitan Rail Systems (Metros), 1987 [1]

City [2]	Number of Stations	Length [3] (in kilometers)
Moscow	132	222
Leningrad	48	90
Kiev	27	36
Tbilisi	19	26
Baku	16	25
Khar'kov	21	30
Tashkent	17	22
Yerevan	8	11
Minsk	9	11
Gor'kiy	6	8
Novosibirsk	5	9

[1] In 1987 the following cities had systems under construction: Dnepropetrovsk, Kuybyshev, and Sverd-lovsk; the following cities had systems planned: Alma-Ata, Chelyabinsk, Krasnoyarsk, Riga, Rostov-na-Donu, Odessa, and Omsk.
[2] Cities listed in order of entry into service.
[3] Approximate length of double-track line.

Source: Based on information from Gosudarstvennyi komitet po statistike, *Narodnoe khozi-aistvo SSSR za 70 let,* Moscow, 1987, 367.

Table 44. Freight Loaded by Mode of Transport, Selected Years, 1940–86 *
(in millions of tons originated)

Mode of Transport	1940	1960	1970	1980	1985	1986
Truck	858.6	8,492.7	14,622.8	24,149.3	25,878.6	26,984.8
Railroad	605.1	1,884.9	2,896.0	3,728.2	3,951.0	4,077.6
Inland waterway	73.9	210.3	357.8	568.1	632.6	648.7
Merchant marine	32.9	75.9	162.0	228.0	240.0	250.0
Pipeline						
Petroleum and derivatives	7.9	129.9	337.9	626.9	630.8	652.9
Natural gas	n.a.	21.0	143.0	323.0	482.0	515.0
Subtotal	7.9	150.9	480.9	949.9	1,112.8	1,167.9
Civil aviation	0.0584	0.697	1.844	2.989	3.183	3.157
TOTAL	1,578.5	10,815.4	18,521.3	29,626.5	31,818.2	33,132.2

n.a.—not applicable.
* Freight loaded is measured in tons originated, i.e., the weight of freight (in tons) at its original point of shipment.

Source: Based on information from Gosudarstvennyi komitet po statistike, *Narodnoe khoziaistvo SSSR za 70 let*, Moscow 1987, 340–69.

Table 45. Passenger Traffic by Mode of
Transport, Selected Years, 1940–86
(in billions of passenger-kilometers)

Mode of Transport	1940	1960	1970	1980	1985	1986
Railroad	100.4	176.0	273.5	342.2	374.0	390.2
Inland waterway	3.8	4.3	5.4	6.1	5.9	6.0
Bus	3.4	61.0	202.5	389.8	446.6	462.8
Merchant marine	0.9	1.3	1.6	2.5	2.6	2.5
Civil aviation	0.2	12.1	78.2	160.6	188.4	195.8
TOTAL	108.7	254.7	561.2	901.2	1,017.5	1,057.3

* Passenger traffic is measured in passenger-kilometers, i.e., the movement of one person a distance of one kilometer. Passenger-kilometers are computed by multiplying the number of persons transported by the distance traveled (in kilometers).

Source: Based on information from Gosudarstvennyi komitet po statistike, *Narodnoe khoziaistvo SSSR za 70 let*, Moscow, 1987, 342.

Table 46. Principal Aeroflot Aircraft, 1987

Type and Description	Manufacturer	NATO Designation [1]	Engine	Payload	Use
Long-range aircraft					
An-22	Antonov	Cock	Turboprop	80 tons plus 29 passengers	Designed for harsh Siberian and Far Eastern conditions. High wings, rear loading ramp. Accommodates tall and wide vehicles.
Il-62M	Iliushin	Classic	4 turbofan	23 tons or 195 passengers	Used primarily on domestic and international routes.
Il-76TD	–do–	Candid	–do–	48 tons	Cargo aircraft, originally developed for military aviation. Designed to operate under adverse Siberian weather conditions, using short unimproved airstrips.
Medium- to long-range aircraft					
Tu-154A	Tupolev	Careless	3 turbofan	18 tons or 152 to 168 passengers	Passenger liner.
Tu-154B	–do–	–do–	–do–	18 tons or 169 passengers	–do–
Tu-154M	–do–	–do–	–do–	18 tons or 180 passengers	–do–

Table 46.—Continued

Type and Description	Manufacturer	NATO Designation [1]	Engine	Payload	Use
Medium-range aircraft					
Tu-134A	-do-	Crusty	2 turbofan	80 passengers	Passenger liner largely replaced by the Yak-42.
Yak-42	Yakovlev	Clobber	3 turbofan	12.8 tons or 120 passengers	Designed for operations in remote areas and various climatic conditions.
Il-86	Iliushin	Camber	4 turbofan	42 tons or 350 passengers plus 8 tons of containerized cargo	Designed to operate from unpaved runways.
Short-range aircraft					
An-24	Antonov	Coke	Twin turboprop	5.5 tons or 50 passengers	Used on domestic feeder lines.
Yak-40	Yakovlev	Codling	3 turbofan	1.5 to 3 tons or 27 to 32 passengers	Designed to operate from grass runways. No longer in production.
Specialized aircraft					
An-2	Antonov	Colt	Single engine	1 to 2 tons	Performs a variety of agricultural missions.
An-3	-do-	n.a.	-do-	-do-	-do-
An-14	-do-	Clod	Twin engine	3 tons	Used for general transport and medical evacuation in remote areas.

Table 46.—Continued

Type and Description	Manufacturer	NATO Designation [1]	Engine	Payload	Use
An-26	–do–	Curl	Twin turboprop	4 tons	Presumably used for carrying cargo but can be adapted for carrying passengers.
An-28	–do–	Cash	–do–	–do–	Used for general transport and medical evacuation in remote areas.
An-32	–do–	Clive	–do–	6 tons	A STOL derived from the An-26, designed for operations from high-altitude airstrips. [2]
An-74	–do–	Coaler	Twin turboprop	10 tons or 32 passengers or 24 casualties in ambulance version	High-wing STOL designed for Arctic operations, including landings on drifting ice floes.
An-124	–do–	Condor	4 turbofan	150 tons	Modeled after, but larger than, the United States Air Force C-5A (Galaxy). Its wide cargo hold opens up fore and aft for large-sized cargo. Operates from unimproved airstrips and frozen marshes and can take off and land in relatively short distances.

Table 46.—Continued

Type and Description	Manufacturer	NATO Designation [1]	Engine	Payload	Use
Helicopters					
Ka-26	Kamov	Hoodlum	Twin engine	2 tons	Designed for cargo carrying and crop dusting. Used also for medical evacuation missions.
Mi-8	Mil	Hip	Twin turbine	4 tons	Designed for a variety of Arctic tasks.
Mi-10	–do–	Harke	Twin turbine	12 to 16 tons, depending on engine used	Used for carrying passengers and cargo and as a flying crane.
Mi-26	–do–	Halo	–do–	22 tons	World's largest helicopter. Its eight-blade main rotor and large cargo hold make its lifting capacity comparable to that of the United States C-130 (Hercules) four-engine transport aircraft. Designed for Siberian terrain and weather conditions.

n.a.—not applicable.

[1] NATO—North Atlantic Treaty Organization.

[2] STOL—short take-off and landing.

Table 47. Hard-Currency Trading Partners, 1970-85 *

Western Industrialized Countries

European Economic Community	Other European Countries	Other Countries
Belgium	Austria (since 1971)	Australia
Britain	Iceland (since 1977)	Canada
Denmark	Liechtenstein	Japan
France	Malta	New Zealand
Greece	Norway	South Africa
Ireland	Portugal	United States
Italy	Spain	
Luxembourg	Sweden	
Netherlands	Switzerland	
West Germany	Turkey (since 1983)	

Third World Countries

Africa

Algeria (since 1980)	Gambia	Mozambique
Angola	Ghana (since 1976)	Niger
Benin	Guinea (since 1980)	Nigeria
Burkina Faso	Guinea-Bissau	Rwanda
Burundi	Kenya	Senegal
Cameroon	Liberia	Sierra Leone
Cape Verde	Libya	Sudan
Central African Republic	Madagascar	Tanzania
Congo	Malawi	Togo
Côte d'Ivoire	Mali (since 1978)	Tunisia (since 1974)
Equatorial Guinea	Mauritania	Uganda
Ethiopia	Mauritius	Zaire
Gabon	Morocco (since 1982)	Zambia

Latin America

Argentina	El Salvador	Panama
Bolivia	Guatemala	Paraguay
Brazil	Guyana	Peru
Chile	Honduras	Trinidad and
Colombia	Jamaica	Tobago
Costa Rica	Mexico	Uruguay
Dominican Republic	Nicaragua	Venezuela
Ecuador		

Asia and the Middle East

Burma	Lebanon	South Yemen
Cyprus	Macao	Sri Lanka (since
Hong Kong	Malaysia	1977)
Indonesia	Nepal	Saudi Arabia
Iraq	North Yemen	Thailand
Israel	Philippines	United Arab
Jordan	Singapore	Emirates
Kuwait		

* As reported to the International Monetary Fund by partner countries. Some of the trade the Soviet Union conducts with Third World partners is on a barter basis. Likewise, those Third World countries that are considered bartering partners may conduct some trade on a hard-currency basis.

Source: Based on information from United States Congress, 100th, 1st Session, Joint Economic Committee, *Gorbachev's Economic Plans*, 2, Washington, 1987, 486-87.

Table 48. Soviet Actions Prompting United States
Trade Restrictions, 1974–82

Date	Soviet Action	United States Trade Restriction
1974	Placement of obstacles to emigration of Jews	Jackson-Vanik Amendment to Trade Reform Act of 1974 linked granting of most-favored-nation status to rights of Soviet Jews to emigrate from Soviet Union. Stevenson Amendment to Export-Import Bank Act lowered ceiling on United States credits to Soviet Union.
July–August 1978	Soviet-Cuban intervention in African affairs and internal human rights violations, specifically trials of Anatolii Sharanskii and Alexander Ginsburg	Controls placed on United States oil and gas equipment exports to Soviet Union. Sale of a Sperry-Univac computer to TASS was denied.
Early 1980	Invasion of Afghanistan by Soviet armed forces in December 1979	United States grain exports and phosphates used in fertilizer production embargoed; controls increased on high-technology exports, including oil and gas equipment.
December 1981 ...	Imposition of martial law in Poland in December 1981	Restrictions placed on granting credit to Soviet Union; more severe export-licensing procedures imposed.
June 1982	No change in situation in Poland	Foreign subsidiaries and licensees of United States firms forbidden to sell energy-related technology of United States origin to Soviet Union.

Source: Based on information from United States Congress, 100th, 1st Session, Joint Economic Committee, *Gorbachev's Economic Plans,* 2, Washington, 1987, 434, 450; Perry L. Patterson, "Foreign Trade," in James Cracraft (ed.), *The Soviet Union Today,* Chicago, 1988, 216; and Gordon B. Smith (ed.), *The Politics of East-West Trade,* Boulder, Colorado, 1984, 26–27, 176–78.

Table 49. *Major Noncommunist Trading Partners,*
1980, 1985, and 1986 [1]
(value in millions of rubles) [2]

Country	1980 Value	1980 Percentage of Trade	1985 Value	1985 Percentage of Trade	1986 Value	1986 Percentage of Trade
West Germany ..	5,780.0	6.1	7,094.6	5.0	5,577.9	4.3
France	3,752.7	4.0	3,778.7	2.7	2,670.5	2.0
Italy	3,034.3	3.2	3,796.7	2.7	3,054.3	2.3
Japan	2,722.8	2.9	3,216.0	2.3	3,185.3	2.4
Britain	1,811.8	1.9	1,903.0	1.3	1,788.6	1.4
United States ...	1,502.5	1.6	2,703.1	1.9	1,458.5	1.1
Netherlands	1,387.5	1.5	1,300.3	0.9	821.4	0.6
Belgium	1,225.3	1.3	1,440.0	1.0	1,049.2	0.8
Argentina	1,192.5	1.3	1,292.9	0.9	n.a.	n.a.
Canada	1,001.6	1.1	966.9	0.7	633.6	0.5
Austria	976.2	1.0	1,669.2	1.2	1,392.5	0.1
Switzerland	847.6	0.9	950.9	0.7	742.6	0.6
Australia	781.4	0.8	545.8	0.4	517.3	0.4
Iraq	731.7	0.8	824.2	0.6	638.6	0.5
Sweden	676.9	0.7	798.7	0.6	543.1	0.4
Greece	501.3	0.5	728.4	0.5	284.0	0.2
Libya	450.9	0.5	961.2	0.7	730.6	0.6
Spain	402.7	0.4	588.5	0.4	296.9	0.2
Denmark	341.3	0.4	n.a.	n.a.	n.a.	n.a.
Malaysia	207.5	0.2	n.a.	n.a.	n.a.	n.a.
Algeria	n.a.	n.a.	405.2	0.3	327.8	0.3
Brazil	n.a.	n.a.	450.3	0.3	266.8	0.2
Nicaragua	n.a.	n.a.	n.a.	n.a.	284.8	0.2
Other	64,768.8	68.9	106,678.1	74.9	104,669.7	80.9
TOTAL	94,097.3	100.0	142,092.7	100.0	130,934.0	100.0

n.a.—not available.
[1] Hard-currency trading partners only.
[2] For value of the ruble—see Glossary.

Source: Based on information from Ministerstvo vneshnei torgovli, *Vneshniaia torgovlia SSSR v*
1980 g., Moscow, 1981, 9–15; and Ministerstvo vneshnei torgovli, *Vneshniaia torgovlia*
SSSR v 1986 g., Moscow, 1987, 9–15.

Table 50. Trade with Asia, Africa, and Latin America,
Selected Years, 1970–85
(in percentages of trade with Third World countries) [1]

Year	Asia			Africa			Latin America		
	Exports	Imports	Balance[2]	Exports	Imports	Balance[2]	Exports	Imports	Balance[2]
1970	52.1	50.5	26.2	46.6	43.1	43.2	0.7	6.3	-70.1
1975	62.8	45.4	-179.9	29.5	29.0	-402.0	7.5	25.7	-861.0
1970	73.8	49.5	475.6	23.5	20.6	-217.3	2.7	29.9	-2,139.8
1981	74.6	44.9	461.2	23.3	15.5	-17.3	2.1	39.6	-4,051.0
1982	70.5	45.8	1,166.3	24.2	26.7	-600.3	5.3	27.5	-2,115.0
1983	66.2	46.6	355.1	29.7	24.5	-175.6	3.7	28.8	-2,438.2
1984	66.7	52.1	-408.3	27.1	26.2	-629.3	6.1	21.5	-1,567.1
1985	66.9	50.9	-339.8	25.3	25.1	-654.7	7.7	23.8	-1,663.6

[1] Percentage shares of exports and imports are computed on the basis of Soviet foreign trade yearbook statistics. Thus, arms sales are not taken into account.
[2] In millions of United States dollars.

Source: Based on information from United States Congress, 100th, 1st Session, Joint Economic Committee, Gorbachev's Economic Plans, 2, Washington, 1987, 511.

Table 51. *Trade with Countries of Socialist Orientation,*
Selected Years, 1970–85
(in percentages of trade with Third World countries) [1]

Year	First Category [2]			Second Category [3]		
	Exports	Imports	Balance [4]	Exports	Imports	Balance [4]
1970	3.7	2.8	11.3	16.1	7.4	107.9
1975	14.1	4.7	25.5	26.4	18.5	– 15.4
1980	13.6	6.1	316.9	20.6	11.1	344.4
1981	14.1	4.6	495.2	26.6	5.9	1,229.7
1982	14.1	4.7	638.6	25.6	6.3	1,366.6
1983	17.9	4.3	875.9	15.3	10.9	72.8
1984	22.4	4.5	1,857.7	16.0	14.8	– 307.2
1985	21.6	4.9	– 937.3	19.2	14.5	– 90.2

[1] Percentage shares of exports and imports are computed on the basis of Soviet foreign trade yearbook statistics. Thus, arms sales are not taken into account.
[2] Countries having observer status in the Council for Mutual Economic Assistance (Comecon): Afghanistan, Angola, Ethiopia, Laos, and South Yemen.
[3] Countries not having observer status in Comecon but having privileged affiliations with it: Algeria, Benin, Burma, Congo, Guinea, Guinea-Bissau, Madagascar, Mali, Nigeria, Seychelles, Syria, Tanzania, and Zimbabwe.
[4] In millions of United States dollars.

Source: Based on information from United States Congress, 100th, 1st Session, Joint Economic Committee, *Gorbachev's Economic Plans,* 2, Washington, 1987, 511.

Table 52. *Trade with the Organization of Petroleum Exporting*
Countries, Selected Years, 1970–85 [1]
(in percentages of trade with Third World countries) [2]

Year	Exports	Imports	Balance [3]
1970	29.9	15.1	184.4
1975	37.4	27.0	– 104.8
1980	30.0	15.0	584.5
1981	36.6	13.2	1,163.9
1982	40.9	21.6	1,126.0
1983	32.0	29.4	– 471.4
1984	18.9	34.7	1,945.5
1985	16.2	31.4	1,809.4

[1] Members included Algeria, Ecuador, Gabon, Indonesia, Iran, Iraq, Kuwait, Libya, Nigeria, Qatar, Saudi Arabia, the United Arab Emirates, and Venezuela.
[2] Percentage shares of exports and imports are computed on the basis of Soviet foreign trade yearbook statistics. Thus, arms sales are not taken into account.
[3] In millions of United States dollars.

Source: Based on information from United States Congress, 100th, 1st Session, Joint Economic Committee, *Gorbachev's Economic Plans,* 2, Washington, 1987, 511.

Table 53. Military Capabilities, 1989

Type and Description	In Inventory
Strategic offensive nuclear forces	
Intercontinental ballistic missiles	
SS-11	380
SS-17	110
SS-18	308
SS-19	320
SS-24 (MOD 1)	18 [1]
SS-24 (MOD 2)	40 [1]
SS-25	170 [1]
Sea-launched ballistic missiles	
SS-N-5	36
SS-N-6	256
SS-N-8	286
SS-N-17	12
SS-N-18	224
SS-N-20	120
SS-N-23	96
Bombers [2,3]	
Tu-16	265
Tu-22	75
Tu-26	350
Tu-95 and Tu-142	160
Tu-160	10
Strategic defensive forces	
Antiballistic missile radar	1
Interceptors [3]	2,200
Antisatellite interceptor	1
Surface-to-air missile launchers [4]	8,000
Antiballistic missile launchers	100
Intermediate- and shorter-range nuclear forces	
Intermediate-range ballistic missiles [5]	
SS-20	262
Medium-range ballistic missiles [5]	
SS-4	30
Short-range ballistic missile launchers	
SS-12	135
SS-23	102
SS-21	1,000
Scud	630
Tactical aviation	
Tactical aircraft [3]	5,170
Ground Forces	
Motorized rifle divisions	152
Tank divisions	53
Airborne divisions	7
Static defense divisions	2
Main battle tanks	53,000
Artillery pieces	49,000

Table 53.—Continued

Type and Description	In Inventory
Ground Forces—*Continued*	
Armored personnel carriers and infantry fighting vehicles	61,000
Helicopters	4,300
Naval Forces	
Aircraft carriers	4
Large principal surface combatants	116
Other combatants	445
Ballistic missile submarines	69
Attack submarines	256
Other submarines	34
Naval aircraft	1,300

[1] Estimated.
[2] Includes 160 Tu-26 (Backfire) bombers in Naval Aviation but excludes 175 Tu-16 (Badger) bombers in Naval Aviation.
[3] Excludes over 5,000 combat-capable trainers.
[4] In Soviet Union only; excludes Soviet strategic surface-to-air missiles in Mongolia or with groups of forces abroad.
[5] Deployed missiles as of May 1989.

Source: Based on information from United States, Department of Defense, *Soviet Military Power, 1989,* Washington, 1989, 14–15.

Table 54. *Insignia Colors of the Armed
Forces, 1989* [1]

Color	Armed Forces
Red	Motorized Rifle Troops
Black	Air Defense Forces (nonaviation personnel) Engineer Troops Rocket Troops and Artillery Strategic Rocket Forces Tank Troops
Light blue	Airborne Troops Air Defense Forces (aviation personnel) Air Forces Naval Aviation
Magenta	Administration Troops Medical Troops Military Procuracy Quartermaster Troops Veterinary Troops
Navy blue	Naval Forces [2]
Deep crimson	Internal Troops (MVD) [3]
Green	Border Troops (KGB) [4]
Royal blue	Security Troops (KGB)

[1] The Ground Forces, as an entity, has no insignia color because it consists of the Motorized Rifle Troops, Tank Troops, Rocket Troops and Artillery, and other components, which have specific insignia colors.
[2] Support and staff components of the Naval Forces have insignia of colors other than navy blue.
[3] MVD—Ministerstvo vnutrennykh del (Ministry of Internal Affairs).
[4] KGB—Komitet gosudarstvennoi bezopasnosti (Committee for State Security).

Table 55. Higher Military Schools and Military Academies, 1988

| Armed Service | Higher Military Schools | | | Military |
Component	Command	Engineering	Political	Academies
Strategic Rocket Forces	4 [1]	0	1	1
Ground Forces				
Motorized Rifle Troops	9	0	2	3 [2]
Tank Troops	6	2	1 [3]	1
Rocket Troops and Artillery	7	3	0	1
Air Defense of Ground Forces	3	2	0	1
Air Forces	15	13	1	2
Air Defense Forces	10	3	1	2
Naval Forces	7	3	1	2
Airborne Troops	1	0	0	0
Special troops				
Chemical Troops	2	1	0	1
Engineer Troops	2	1	1 [4]	1
Signal Troops	7	3	0	1
Rear Services	13	4	2	1
Border Troops (KGB) [5]	2	0	1	0
Internal Troops (MVD) [6]	4	0	1	0
TOTAL	92	35	12	17

[1] Joint school for command and engineering.
[2] Includes Voroshilov General Staff Academy and Lenin Military-Political Academy.
[3] Joint school for Tank Troops and Rocket Troops and Artillery.
[4] Joint school for Engineer Troops and Signal Troops.
[5] KGB—Komitet gosudarstvennoi bezopasnosti (Committee for State Security).
[6] MVD—Ministerstvo vnutrennykh del (Ministry of Internal Affairs).

Table 56. Organizational History of the Police, 1989

Period	Organization Name
Security police	
1917-22	All-Russian Extraordinary Commission for Combating Counterrevolution and Sabotage (Vserossiiskaia chrezvychainaia komissiia po bor'be s kontrrevoliutsiei i sabotazhem—Vecheka; also known as VChK or Cheka)
1922-23	State Political Directorate (Gosudarstvennoe politicheskoe upravlenie—GPU)
1923-34	Unified State Political Directorate (Ob''edinennoe gosudarstvennoe politicheskoe upravlenie—OGPU)
1934-41	Main Directorate for State Security (Glavnoe upravlenie gosudarstvennoi bezopasnosti—GUGB)
1941	People's Commissariat of State Security (Narodnyi komissariat gosudarstvennoi bezopasnosti—NKGB)
1941-43	GUGB
1943-46	NKGB
1946-53	Ministry of State Security (Ministerstvo gosudarstvennoi bezopasnosti—MGB)
1953-54	GUGB *
1954-	Committee for State Security (Komitet gosudarstvennoi bezopasnosti—KGB)
Regular police	
1917-46	People's Commissariat of Internal Affairs (Narodnyi komissariat vnutrennykh del—NKVD)
1946-62	Ministry of Internal Affairs (Ministerstvo vnutrennykh del—MVD)
1962-68	Ministry for the Preservation of Public Order (Ministerstvo okhrany obshchestvennogo poriadka—MOOP)
1968-	MVD

* Subordinate to MVD during this period.

Appendix B

The Council for Mutual Economic Assistance

THE FOUNDING of the Council for Mutual Economic Assistance (Comecon, also referred to as CMEA or CEMA) dates from a 1949 communiqué agreed upon by Bulgaria, Czechoslovakia, Hungary, Poland, Romania, and the Soviet Union. The reasons for the creation of Comecon in the aftermath of World War II are complicated, given the political and economic turmoil of that time. The primary factor in Comecon's formation, however, was Joseph V. Stalin's desire to enforce Soviet domination of the small countries of Eastern Europe and to deter some states that had expressed interest in the Marshall Plan (see Glossary). The stated purpose of the organization was to enable member states "to exchange economic experiences, extend technical aid to one another, and to render mutual assistance with respect to raw materials, foodstuffs, machines, equipment, etc." Although in the late 1960s "cooperation" was the official term used to describe its activities, improved economic integration was always Comecon's goal.

Soviet domination of Comecon was a function of its economic, political, and military power. The Soviet Union possessed 90 percent of total Comecon land and energy resources, 70 percent of its population, 65 percent of its total national income, and industrial and military capacities second in the world only to those of the United States. The location of many Comecon committee headquarters in Moscow and the large number of Soviet citizens in positions of authority also testified to the power of the Soviet Union within the organization.

Soviet efforts to exercise political power over its Comecon partners sometimes were met with determined opposition, however. The "sovereign equality" of members prescribed in the Comecon Charter assured members that they could abstain from a given project if they did not wish to participate. East European members frequently invoked this principle when they feared that economic interdependence would further reduce their political sovereignty. Thus, neither Comecon nor the Soviet Union as a major force within Comecon had supranational authority. Although this arrangement provided the lesser members some degree of freedom from Soviet economic domination, it also deprived Comecon of the necessary power to achieve maximum economic efficiency.

In 1989 the full members in Comecon consisted of Bulgaria, Cuba, Czechoslovakia, the German Democratic Republic (East Germany), Hungary, Mongolia, Poland, Romania, the Soviet Union, and Vietnam. (For the purposes of this appendix, the phrases the "six European members" or the "European members of Comecon" are used interchangeably to signify Bulgaria, Czechoslovakia, East Germany, Hungary, Poland, and Romania.) The primary documents governing the objectives, organization, and functions of Comecon were the Charter (first adopted in 1959 and subsequently amended; all references herein are to the amended 1974 text); the *Comprehensive Program for the Further Extension and Improvement of Cooperation and the Further Development of Socialist Economic Integration by the Comecon Member Countries,* adopted in 1971; and the *Comprehensive Program for Scientific and Technical Cooperation to the Year 2000,* adopted in December 1985. Adoption of the 1985 *Comprehensive Program* and the rise to power of Soviet general secretary Mikhail S. Gorbachev increased Soviet influence in Comecon operations and led to attempts to give Comecon some degree of supranational authority. The 1985 *Comprehensive Program* sought to improve economic cooperation through the development of a more efficient and interconnected scientific and technical base.

Membership, Structure, Nature, and Scope

Membership

In a January 1949 meeting in Moscow, representatives of Bulgaria, Czechoslovakia, Hungary, Poland, Romania, and the Soviet Union reached the formal decision to establish the Council for Mutual Economic Assistance. The communiqué announcing the event cited the refusal of these countries to "subordinate themselves to the dictates of the Marshall Plan" and their intention to resist the trade boycott imposed by "the United States, Britain, and certain other countries of Western Europe" as the major factors contributing to the decision "to organize a more broadly based economic cooperation among the countries of the people's democracy and the USSR."

Albania joined the six original members in February 1949, and East Germany entered Comecon in 1950. (Although it did not formally revoke its membership until 1987, Albania stopped participating in Comecon activities in 1961.) Mongolia acceded to membership in 1962, and in the 1970s Comecon expanded its membership to include Cuba (1972) and Vietnam (1978). As of 1987, the ten full members consisted of the Soviet Union, the six East European countries, and the three extraregional members (see table A, this Appendix).

Table A. *National Participation in the Council for Mutual Economic Assistance (Comecon), 1989*

Member Countries *

Bulgaria (1949)	Soviet Union (1949)
Czechoslovakia (1949)	East Germany (1950)
Hungary (1949)	Mongolia (1962)
Poland (1949)	Cuba (1972)
Romania (1949)	Vietnam (1978)

Nonmember Countries with Close Ties to Comecon

Countries that have concluded formal agreements of cooperation with Comecon:

Countries that have attended Comecon sessions as observers:

Yugoslavia (1964)	Afghanistan
Finland (1973)	Angola
Iraq (1975)	Ethiopia
Mexico (1975)	Laos
Nicaragua (1983)	South Yemen
Mozambique (1985)	

Countries that have had, at various times, other affiliations with Comecon:

Algeria	Mali
Benin	Nigeria
Burma	Seychelles
Congo	Syria
Guinea	Tanzania
Guinea-Bissau	Zimbabwe
Madagascar	

* Dates of accession are in parentheses. Albania joined Comecon in February 1949, one month after the organization was formed by the original six members. Albania stopped participating in Comecon activities in 1961 and formally revoked its membership in 1987.

There were four kinds of relationships a country could have had with Comecon: full membership, associate membership, nonsocialist "cooperant" status, and "observer country" status. Yugoslavia was the only country considered to have associate member status. Finland, Iraq, Mexico, Mozambique, and Nicaragua, had a nonsocialist cooperant status with Comecon and, together with Yugoslavia, had concluded formal agreements of cooperation with Comecon. Since 1957 Comecon has allowed certain countries with communist or pro-Soviet governments to attend sessions as observers. Delegations from Afghanistan, Angola, Ethiopia, Laos, and the People's Democratic Republic of Yemen (South Yemen) have attended Comecon sessions as observers.

Structure

Although not formally part of the organization's hierarchy, the Conference of First Secretaries of Communist and Workers' Parties and of the Heads of Government of the Comecon Member Countries was, in fact, Comecon's most important organ. These party and government leaders met regularly to discuss topics of mutual interest. Decisions made in these meetings had considerable influence on the actions taken by Comecon and its organs.

The official hierarchy of Comecon consisted of the Council Session, the Executive Committee, the Secretariat, four council committees, twenty-four standing commissions, six interstate conferences, two scientific institutes, and several associated organizations.

The Council Session, officially the highest Comecon organ, examined fundamental problems of socialist economic integration and directed the activities of the Secretariat and other subordinate organizations. Delegations from each Comecon member country, usually headed by prime ministers, met in the second quarter of each year in a member country's capital. Each country appointed one permanent representative to maintain relations between members and Comecon between annual meetings. Extraordinary sessions were held with the consent of at least one-third of the members. Such meetings usually took place in Moscow.

The highest executive organ in Comecon, the Executive Committee, elaborated policy recommendations and supervised policy implementation between sessions. It also supervised plan coordination and scientific-technical cooperation. Composed of one representative from each member country, usually a deputy chairman of the country's Council of Ministers, the Executive Committee met quarterly, usually in Moscow. In 1971 and 1974, the Executive Committee acquired economic departments that ranked above the standing commissions. These economic departments considerably strengthened the authority and importance of the Executive Committee.

Four council committees were operational in 1987: the Council Committee for Cooperation in Planning, the Council Committee for Cooperation in Science and Technology, the Council Committee for Cooperation in Material and Technical Supply, and the Council Committee for Cooperation in Machine Building. Their mission was "to ensure the comprehensive examination and a multilateral settlement of the major problems of cooperation among member countries in the economy, science, and technology." All four committees were headquartered in Moscow and usually met there.

These committees advised the standing commissions, the Secretariat, the interstate conferences, and the scientific institutes in their areas of specialization. Their jurisdiction was generally wider than that of the standing commissions because they were empowered to make policy recommendations to other Comecon organizations.

The Council Committee for Cooperation in Planning was the most important of the four because it coordinated the national economic plans of Comecon members. As such, it ranked in importance only below the Council Session and the Executive Committee. Made up of the chairmen of the Comecon members' national central planning offices, the Council Committee for Cooperation in Planning drew up draft agreements for joint projects, adopted resolutions approving these projects, and recommended approval to the concerned parties.

The Secretariat, Comecon's only permanent body, was the primary economic research and administrative organ. The secretary, who was always a Soviet official, was the official Comecon representative to Comecon member states, other states, and international organizations. Subordinate to the secretary were his deputy and the various departments of the Secretariat, which generally corresponded to the standing commissions. The Secretariat's responsibilities included preparation and organization of Comecon sessions and other meetings conducted under the auspices of Comecon; compilation of digests on Comecon activities; economic and other research for Comecon members; and preparation of recommendations on various issues concerning Comecon operations.

In 1987 there were twenty-four standing commissions, set up to help Comecon make recommendations pertaining to specific economic sectors. The Secretariat supervised the actual operations of the commissions, which had authority only to make recommendations, subject to the approval by the Executive Committee and ratification by the member countries involved. Commissions usually met twice a year in Moscow.

The six interstate conferences (on water management, internal trade, legal matters, inventions and patents, pricing, and labor affairs) served as forums for discussing shared issues and experiences. They were purely consultative and generally acted in an advisory capacity to the Executive Committee or its specialized committees.

The scientific institutes on standardization and on economic problems of the world socialist system (see Glossary) concerned themselves with theoretical problems of international cooperation. Both were headquartered in Moscow and were staffed by experts from various member countries.

Several affiliated agencies functioned outside the official Comecon hierarchy and served to develop "direct links between appropriate bodies and organizations of Comecon member countries." These affiliated agencies were divided into two categories: intergovernmental economic organizations (which worked on a higher level in the member countries and generally dealt with a wider range of managerial and coordinative activities) and international economic organizations (which worked closer to the operational level of research, production, or trade).

Nature of Operation

Comecon was an interstate organization through which members attempted to coordinate economic activities of mutual interest and to develop multilateral economic, scientific, and technical cooperation. The Charter stated that "the sovereign equality of all members" was fundamental to the organization and procedures of Comecon. The 1971 *Comprehensive Program* emphasized that the processes of integration of members' economies were "completely voluntary and [did] not involve the creation of supranational bodies." Hence, under the Charter each country had the right to equal representation and one vote in all organs of Comecon, regardless of the country's economic stature or its contribution to Comecon's budget.

The "interestedness" provisions of the Charter reinforced the principle of "sovereign equality." Comecon's recommendations and decisions could be adopted only upon agreement among the interested members, each of which had the right to declare its "interest" in any matter under consideration. Furthermore, in the words of the Charter, "recommendations and decisions shall not apply to countries that have declared that they have no interest in a particular matter."

Although Comecon recognized the principle of unanimity, disinterested parties did not have a veto but rather the right to abstain from participation. A declaration of disinterest could not block a project unless the disinterested party's participation was vital. Otherwise, the Charter implied that the interested parties could proceed without the abstaining member, and the abstaining country could "subsequently adhere to the recommendations and decision adopted by the remaining members of the Council."

Evolution

Early Years

During Comecon's early years (through 1955), its sessions were convened on an ad hoc basis. The organization lacked clear

Comecon headquarters,
Moscow

structure and operated without a charter until a decade after its founding. From 1949 to 1953, Comecon's function consisted primarily of redirecting trade of member countries toward each other and introducing import-replacement industries, thus making members economically more self-sufficient. Little was done to solve economic problems through a regional policy. Because of Stalin's distrust of multilateral bodies, bilateral ties with the Soviet Union dominated the East European members' external relations. Each country dealt with the Soviet Union on a one-to-one basis. Although reparations transfers (extracted by the Soviet Union in the immediate postwar years from those East European states it regarded as former World War II enemies) had been replaced by more normal trade relations, outstanding reparations obligations were not halted until 1956. In these circumstances, there was scarcely the need nor the scope for multilateral policies or institutions.

Rediscovery of Comecon after Stalin's Death

After Stalin's death in 1953, the more industrialized and more trade dependent East European countries (Czechoslovakia, East Germany, and Poland) sought relief from their economic isolation in new forms of regional cooperation. For countries with small, centrally planned economies, this meant the need to develop a mechanism through which to coordinate investment and trade policies.

859

In the 1950s, instability in Eastern Europe and integration in Western Europe increased the desirability of regularizing relations among the Soviet Union and Eastern Europe in a more elaborate institutional framework. The 1955 Treaty of Friendship, Cooperation, and Mutual Assistance, which established the Warsaw Pact, and its implementing machinery reinforced political-military links (see Appendix C). On the economic front, Comecon was rediscovered.

Rapid Growth in Comecon Activity, 1956–63

The years 1956 to 1963 witnessed the rapid growth of Comecon institutions and activities. Comecon, for example, launched a program to unify the electrical power systems of its member states and in 1962 created the Central Dispatching Board to manage the unified system. The organization took similar steps to coordinate railroad and river transport. In 1963 a special bank, the International Bank for Economic Cooperation, was created to facilitate financial settlements among members. In this period, Comecon also undertook a number of bilateral and multilateral investment projects. The most notable project led to the coordinated construction of the Friendship (Druzhba) oil pipeline for the transport and distribution of crude oil from the Soviet Union to Eastern Europe. The joint Institute for Nuclear Research, established in 1956, initiated cooperation in another area of long-term importance.

Parallel to these developments, the Soviet Union led efforts to coordinate the investment strategies of the members in the interest of a more rational pattern of regional specialization, increased productivity, and a more rapid overtaking of the capitalist economies. These efforts culminated in 1962 with the adoption at the Fifteenth Council Session of the *Basic Principles of the International Socialist Division of Labor,* which called for increased economic interdependence. Furthermore, Soviet party leader Nikita S. Khrushchev proposed a central Comecon planning organ to implement the *Basic Principles* and to pave the way for a "socialist commonwealth" based on a unified regional economy.

These proposals provoked strong objection from Romania, which charged that they violated the principle of the "sovereign equality" of members. Romania's opposition (combined with the more passive resistance of some other members) deterred supranational planning and reinforced the interested-party provisions of the Charter. The institutional compromise was the creation of the Bureau for Integrated Planning, which was attached to the Executive Committee and limited to an advisory role on the coordination of members' development plans. The *Basic Principles* were super-seded several years later by the 1971 *Comprehensive Program.*

Inactivity and Subsequent Revitalization in the Late 1960s

After the fall of Khrushchev in 1964, a comparative lull in Come-con activities ensued, which lasted until well after the 1968 Soviet-led intervention in Czechoslovakia. By the end of the 1960s, Eastern Europe, shaken by the 1968 events, recognized the need to revitalize programs that would strengthen regional cohesion. Disillusioned by traditional methods and concerned with the need to decentral-ize planning and management in their domestic economies, reform-ers argued for strengthening market relations among Comecon states. Conservatives, however, continued to advocate planned ap-proaches that would involve supranational planning of major aspects of members' economies and the inevitable loss of national control over domestic investment policy.

The 1971 Comprehensive Program

The controversy over supranational planning led to a compromise in the form of the 1971 *Comprehensive Program,* which laid the guide-lines for Comecon activity through 1990. The program incorpo-rated elements of both market and planned approaches. From the former, the program advocated a stronger role for money, prices, and exchange rates in intra-Comecon relations and incentives for direct contacts among lower level economic entities. From the lat-ter, the program called for more joint planning on a sectoral basis through interstate coordinating bodies for activities in a given sec-tor. In addition, international associations would engage in actual operations in a designated sector on behalf of the participating coun-tries. Finally, the program emphasized the need for multilateral projects to develop new regional sources of fuels, energy, and raw materials. Such projects were to be jointly planned, financed, and executed.

The 1971 *Comprehensive Program* introduced a new concept in rela-tions among members: "socialist economic integration," whose aim was "to intensify and improve" cooperation among members. The program avoided, however, the suggestion of ultimate fusion of members' economies that had been contained in the 1962 *Basic Principles.* It set limits on the integrative process in the following terms: "Socialist economic integration is completely voluntary and does not involve the creation of supranational bodies."

Comecon members adopted the 1971 *Comprehensive Program* at a time when they were actively developing economic relations with the rest of the world, especially with the industrialized Western economies. The program viewed the two sets of policies as complementary and affirmed that "because the international socialist division of labor is effected with due account taken of the world division of labor, the Comecon member countries shall continue to develop economic, scientific, and technological ties with other countries, irrespective of their social and political system."

In the years following the adoption of the 1971 *Comprehensive Program,* Comecon made some progress toward strengthening market relations among its members. The objectives of the program proved somewhat inconsistent with the predominant trends within members' economies in the 1970s, which was a period of recentralization—rather than decentralization—of domestic systems of planning and management. The major exception to this lack of progress lay in the area of intra-Comecon pricing and payment, where the expansion of relations with the West contributed to the adoption of prices and extra-plan settlements closer to international norms.

A number of projects formulated in the years immediately following the adoption of the 1971 *Comprehensive Program* were assembled in a document signed at the Twenty-Ninth Council Session in 1975. Entitled the *Concerted Plan for Multilateral Integration Measures,* the document covered the 1976–80 five-year-plan period and was proclaimed as the first general plan for the Comecon economies. The joint projects included in the plan were largely completed in the course of the plan period.

By the end of the 1970s, with the exception of Poland's agricultural sector, the economic sectors of all Comecon countries had converted to the socialist system. Member states had restructured their economies to emphasize industry, transportation, communications, material, and technical supply, and they had decreased the share of resources devoted to agricultural development. Within industry, member states devoted additional funds to machine building and the production of chemicals. Socialist economic integration resulted in the production of goods capable of competing on the world market.

The 1980s

Most Comecon countries ended their 1981–85 five-year plans with decreased extensive economic development (see Glossary), increased expenses for fuel and raw materials, and decreased dependency on the West for both credit and hard-currency (see Glossary) imports. The sharp rise in interest rates in the West resulted in a liquidity shortage (see Glossary) in all Comecon countries in the early 1980s and forced them to reduce hard-currency imports. High interest rates and the increased value of the United States dollar on international markets made debt servicing more expensive. Thus, reducing indebtedness to the West also became a top priority within Comecon. From 1981 to 1985, the European members of Comecon attempted to promote the faster growth of exports over imports and sought to strengthen intraregional trade, build up an increased trade surplus, and decrease indebtedness to Western countries.

In the 1980s, Comecon sessions were held on their regular annual schedule. The two most notable meetings were the special sessions called in June 1984 and December 1985. The first summit-level meeting of Comecon member states in fifteen years was held with much fanfare June 12–14, 1984, in Moscow. The two fundamental objectives of the meeting were to strengthen unity among members and to establish a closer connection between the production base, scientific and technological progress, and capital construction. Despite the introduction of proposals for improving efficiency and cooperation in six key areas, analysts from East and West considered the meeting a failure.

The ideas and results of the June 14 session were elaborated at a special session held December 17–18, 1985, in Moscow. This special session featured the culmination of several years of work on the new *Comprehensive Program for Scientific and Technical Cooperation to the Year 2000*. It aimed to create ''a firm base for working out an agreed and, in some areas, unified scientific and technical policy and the practical implementation, in the common interest, of higher achievements in science and technology.''

The 1985 *Comprehensive Program* laid out sizable tasks in five key areas: electronics, automation systems, nuclear energy, development of new materials, and biotechnology. It sought to restructure and modernize the member states' economies to counteract constraints on labor and material supplies. The need to move to intensive production techniques within Comecon was evident from the fact that from 1961 to 1984 the overall material intensiveness of production did not improve substantially.

Cooperation under the 1971 Comprehensive Program

The distinction between ''market'' relations and ''planned'' relations made in the discussions within Comecon prior to the adoption of the 1971 *Comprehensive Program* remained important in subsequent Comecon activities. Comecon was in fact a mixed system, combining elements of both planned and market economies. Although official rhetoric emphasized regional planning, intra-Comecon relations were conducted among national entities not governed by any supranational authority. They thus interacted on a decentralized basis according to terms negotiated in bilateral and multilateral agreements on trade and cooperation.

Market Relations and Instruments

The size of the Soviet economy determined that intra-Comecon trade was dominated by exchanges between the Soviet Union and the other members. Exchanges of Soviet fuels and raw materials for capital goods and consumer manufactures characterized trade, particularly among the original members. The liquidity shortage in the early 1980s forced the European members of Comecon to work to strengthen intraregional trade. In the early 1980s, intraregional trade rose to 60 percent of foreign trade of Comecon countries as a whole; for individual members it ranged from 45 to 50 percent in the case of Hungary, Romania, and the Soviet Union, to 83 percent for Cuba, and to 96 percent for Mongolia.

Trade among the members was negotiated on an annual basis and in considerable detail at the governmental level and was then followed up by contracts between enterprises (see Glossary). Early Comecon efforts to facilitate trade among members concentrated on the development of uniform technical, legal, and statistical standards and on the encouragement of long-term trade agreements. The 1971 *Comprehensive Program* sought to liberalize the system somewhat by recommending broad limits on ''fixed-quota'' trade among members (trade subject to quantitative or value targets set by bilateral trade agreements). There is no evidence, however, to indicate that quota-free trade grew in importance under the program.

Prices

The 1971 *Comprehensive Program* also called for improvement in the Comecon system of foreign trade prices. Administratively set prices, such as those used in intra-Comecon trade, did not reflect costs or relative scarcities of inputs and outputs. For this reason, intra-Comecon trade was based on world market prices. By 1971 a price system governing exchanges among members had developed, under which prices agreed on through negotiation were fixed for five-year periods. These contract prices were based on adjusted world market prices averaged over the immediately preceding five years. Under this system, therefore, intra-Comecon prices could and did depart substantially from relative prices on world markets.

Although the possibility of breaking this tenuous link with world prices and developing an indigenous system of prices for the Comecon market had been discussed in the 1960s, Comecon prices evolved in the opposite direction after 1971. Far from a technical or academic matter, the question of prices underlay vital issues of the terms and gains of intra-Comecon trade. In particular, relative to actual world prices, intra-Comecon prices in the early 1970s penalized exporters of raw materials and benefited exporters of manufactures. After the oil price explosion of 1973, Comecon foreign trade prices swung further away from world prices to the disadvantage of Comecon suppliers of raw materials, in particular the Soviet Union. In view of the extraregional opportunities opened up by the expansion of East-West trade, this yawning gap between Comecon and world prices could no longer be ignored. Hence in 1975, at Soviet instigation, the system of intra-Comecon pricing was reformed.

The reform involved a substantial modification of existing procedures (known as the ''Bucharest formula''), but not their abandonment. Under the modified Bucharest formula, prices were fixed every year and were based on a moving average of world prices for the preceding five years. The world-price base of the Bucharest formula was thus retained and still represented an average of adjusted world prices for the preceding five years. For 1975 alone, however, the average was for the preceding three years. Under these arrangements, intra-Comecon prices were more closely linked with world prices than before, and throughout the remainder of the 1970s they rose with world prices, although lagging behind them. Until the early 1980s, this new system benefited both the Soviet Union and the other Comecon countries since Soviet oil, priced with the lagged formula, was considerably cheaper than oil from the Organization of Petroleum Exporting Countries (OPEC), which charged drastically higher prices in the 1970s. By 1983–84 this system turned to the Soviet Union's advantage because world market oil prices began to fall, whereas the lagged Soviet oil prices continued to rise.

Exchange Rates and Currencies

Basic features of the state trading systems of the Comecon countries were multiple exchange rates and comprehensive exchange controls that severely restricted the convertibility of members' currencies. These features were rooted in the planned character of the members' economies and their systems of administered prices. Currency inconvertibility in turn dictated bilateral balancing of accounts, one of the basic objectives of intergovernmental trade agreements among members. As of mid-1989, the transferable ruble remained an artificial currency functioning as an accounting unit and was not a common instrument for multilateral settlement. For this reason, this currency continued to be termed "transferable" and not "convertible."

The member countries recognized that the multiplicity and inconsistency of their administered exchange rates, the separation of their domestic prices from foreign prices, and the inconvertibility of their currencies were significant obstacles to multilateral trade and cooperation. In 1989 Comecon lacked not only a flexible means of payment but also a meaningful, standard unit of account. Both problems vastly complicated the already complex multilateral projects and programs envisaged by the 1971 *Comprehensive Program.* The creation in 1971 of the International Investment Bank provided a mechanism for joint investment financing, but, like the International Bank for Economic Cooperation, this institution could not by itself resolve these fundamental monetary problems.

Recognizing that money and credit should play a more active role in the Comecon system, the 1971 *Comprehensive Program* established a timetable for the improvement of monetary relations. According to the timetable, measures would be taken "to strengthen and extend" the functions of the "collective currency" (the transferable ruble) and "to make the transferable ruble convertible into national currencies and to make national currencies mutually convertible." To this end, steps would be taken to introduce "economically well-founded and mutually coordinated" rates of exchange between members' currencies and between 1976 and 1979 to prepare the groundwork for the introduction by 1980 of a "single rate of exchange for the national currency of every country." This timetable was not met. Only in Hungary were the conditions for convertibility gradually being introduced by reforms intended to link domestic prices more directly to world prices.

Cooperation in Planning

Since the early 1960s, official Comecon documents have stressed the need for a more cost-effective pattern of specialization in production. Especially in the manufacturing sector, this "international socialist division of labor" would involve specialization within major branches of industry. In the absence of significant, decentralized allocation of resources within these economies, however, production specialization could be achieved only through the mechanism of the national plan and the investment decisions incorporated in it. In the absence at the regional level of supranational planning bodies, a rational pattern of production specialization among members' economies required coordination of national economic plans, a process that posed inescapable political problems.

The coordination of national five-year economic plans was the most traditional form of cooperation among the members in the area of planning. Although the process of consultation underlying plan coordination remained essentially bilateral, Comecon organs were indirectly involved. The standing commissions drew up proposals for consideration by competent, national planning bodies; the Secretariat assembled information on the results of bilateral consultations; and the Council Committee for Cooperation in Planning (created by Comecon in 1971 at the same session at which the *Comprehensive Program* was adopted) reviewed the progress of plan coordination by members.

In principle, plan coordination covered all economic sectors. Effective and comprehensive plan coordination was significantly impeded, however, by the continued momentum of earlier parallel development strategies and the desire of members to minimize the risks of mutual dependence (especially given the uncertainties of supply that were characteristic of the members' economies). Plan coordination in practice, therefore, remained for the most part limited to mutual adjustment, through bilateral consultation, of the foreign trade sectors of national five-year plans. Under the 1971 *Comprehensive Program,* there were renewed efforts to extend plan coordination beyond foreign trade to the spheres of production, investment, science, and technology.

Plan Coordination

According to the 1971 *Comprehensive Program,* joint planning— multilateral or bilateral—was to be limited to "interested countries" and was "not to interfere with the autonomy of internal planning." Participating countries were to retain, moreover, national ownership of the productive capacities and resources jointly planned.

The *Comprehensive Program* did not clearly assign responsibility for joint planning to any single agency. On the one hand, "coordination of work concerned with joint planning [was to] be carried out by the central planning bodies of Comecon member countries or their authorized representatives." On the other hand, "decisions on joint, multilateral planning of chosen branches and lines of production by interested countries [were to] be based on proposals by countries or Comecon agencies and [were to] be made by the Comecon Executive Committee, which also [was to determine] the Comecon agencies responsible for the organization of such work." Finally, mutual commitments resulting from joint planning and other aspects of cooperation were to be incorporated in agreements signed by the interested parties.

It is extremely difficult to gauge the implementation of plan coordination or joint planning under the 1971 *Comprehensive Program* or to assess the activities of the diverse international economic organizations. There is no single, adequate measure of such cooperation. The results were inconclusive, at best.

Joint Projects

The clearest area of achievement under the 1971 *Comprehensive Program* was the joint exploitation and development of natural resources for the economies of the member countries. Particular attention was given to energy and fuels, forest industries, and iron and steel and various other metals and minerals. Most of this activity was carried out in the Soviet Union, the great storehouse of natural resources within Comecon.

Joint development projects were usually organized on a "compensation" basis, a form of investment "in kind." Participating members advanced materials, equipment, and manpower and were repaid through scheduled deliveries of the output resulting from, or distributed through, the new facility. Repayment included a modest "fraternal" rate of interest, but the real financial return to the participating countries depended on the value of the output at the time of delivery. Deliveries at contract prices below world prices provided an important extra return. No doubt the most important advantage from participation in joint projects, however, was the guarantee of long-term access to basic fuels and raw materials in a world of increasing uncertainty about the supply of such products.

The Concerted Plan

The multilateral development projects concluded under the 1971 *Comprehensive Program* formed the backbone of Comecon's *Concerted Plan* for the 1976–80 period. The program allotted 9 billion rubles (nearly US$12 billion at the official 1975 exchange rate of US$1.30 per ruble) for joint investments. The Orenburg project was the largest project under the *Comprehensive Program*. It was undertaken by all East European Comecon countries and the Soviet Union at an estimated cost ranging from the equivalent of US$5 billion to US$6 billion, or about half the cost of all Comecon projects under the *Concerted Plan*. It consisted of a natural gas production facility at Orenburg in western Siberia and the 2,677-kilometer Union (Soiuz) natural gas pipeline, completed in 1978, linking the Orenburg facility to the western border of the Soviet Union. Construction of a pulp mill in Ust' Ilimsk (in eastern Siberia) was the other major project under this program.

Appendix B

These two projects differed from other joint Comecon investment projects in that they were jointly planned and jointly built in the host country (the Soviet Union in both cases). Although the other projects were jointly planned, each country was responsible only for construction within its own borders. Western technology, equipment, and financing played a considerable role.

The early 1980s were characterized by more bilateral investment specialization but on a much smaller scale than required for the Orenburg and Ust' Ilimsk projects. In these latter projects, Eastern Europe provided machinery and equipment for Soviet multilateral resource development.

Cooperation in Science and Technology

To supplement national efforts to upgrade indigenous technology, the 1971 *Comprehensive Program* emphasized cooperation in science and technology. The development of new technology was envisioned as a major object of cooperation; collaboration in resource development and specialization in production were to be facilitated by transfers of technology between members. The 1971 Comecon session, which adopted the *Comprehensive Program,* decided to establish the Council Committee for Cooperation in Science and Technology to ensure the organization and fulfillment of the provisions of the program in this area. Jointly planned and coordinated research programs extended to the creation of joint research institutes and centers. In terms of the number of patents, documents, and other scientific and technical information exchanges, the available data indicate that the Soviet Union has been the dominant source of technology within Comecon. On the whole, it provided more technology to its East European partners than it received from them. Soviet science also formed the base for several high-technology programs for regional specialization and cooperation, such as nuclear power and computers.

The 1985 *Comprehensive Program,* adopted in December, was intended to boost cooperation in science and technology. Under this program, enterprises and research institutes were established throughout the East European member countries and assigned particular research and development tasks. Each project was headed, however, by a Soviet organization, which awarded contracts to other Comecon member organizations. The Soviet project heads, who were not responsible to domestic planners, were given extensive executive powers of their own and closely supervised all activities. The program represented a fundamentally new approach to multilateral collaboration and a first step toward investing Comecon with some supranational authority. Genuine economic benefits of this program were marginal, however, since prices and exchange rates were artificially set and currencies remained mutually inconvertible.

Labor Resources

Just as the 1971 *Comprehensive Program* stimulated investment flows and technology transfers among members, it also increased intra-Comecon flows of another important factor of production: labor. Most of the transfers occurred in connection with joint resource development projects, such as Bulgarian workers aiding in the exploitation of Siberian forest resources or Vietnamese workers helping on the Friendship pipeline in the Soviet Union. Labor was also transferred in response to labor imbalances in member countries. Hungarian workers, for example, were sent to work in East Germany under a bilateral agreement between the two countries. Such transfers, however, were restricted by the universal scarcity of labor that emerged with the industrialization of the less developed Comecon countries. Moreover, the presence of foreign workers raised practical and ideological issues in socialist planned economies.

Power Configurations Within Comecon

The Soviet Union and Eastern Europe

Between Comecon's creation in 1949 and the anticommunist revolutions in 1989, the relationship between the Soviet Union and the six East European countries generally remained stable. The Soviet Union provided fuel, nonfood raw materials, and semi-finished (hard) goods to Eastern Europe, which in turn supplied the Soviet Union with finished machinery and industrial consumer (soft) goods.

This kind of economic relationship stemmed from a genuine need by the Comecon members in the 1950s. Eastern Europe has poor energy and mineral resources, a problem exacerbated by the low energy efficiency of East European industry. As of mid-1985, factories in Eastern Europe still used 40 percent more fuel than those in the West. As a result of these factors, East European countries have always relied heavily on the Soviet Union for oil. For its part, in the 1950s Eastern Europe supplied the Soviet Union with goods otherwise unavailable because of Western embargoes. Thus, from the early 1950s to the early 1970s, during the time when there was no world shortage of energy and raw materials, the Soviet Union inexpensively supplied its East European clients with hard goods in exchange for finished machinery and equipment. In addition, Soviet economic policies bought political and military support. During these years, the Soviet Union could be assured of relative political tranquillity within Eastern Europe, obedience in international strategy as laid down by the Soviet Union, and military support of Soviet aims. By the 1980s, the members of Comecon were accustomed to this arrangement. The Soviet Union was particularly happy with the arrangement because it still could expand its energy and raw materials sector quickly and relatively cheaply.

Mongolia, Cuba, and Vietnam

Soviet-initiated Comecon support for Comecon's three least-developed members—Cuba, Mongolia, and Vietnam—clearly benefited them, but the burden on the six East European Comecon members was most unwelcome. Comecon was structured in such a way that the more economically developed members provided support for the less developed members in their major economic sectors. Initially, the addition of Mongolia in 1962 brought no great added burden. The population of Mongolia was relatively small (1 million), and the country's subsidies came primarily from the Soviet Union. The addition of Cuba (9 million people) in 1972 and Vietnam (40 million people) in 1978, however, quickly escalated the burden. In 1987 three-fourths of Comecon's overseas economic aid went to Cuba, Mongolia, and Vietnam.

Comecon had invested heavily in Mongolia, Cuba, and Vietnam; and the three countries benefited substantially from these resources. In 1984 increases in capital investments within Comecon were highest for Vietnam and Cuba (26.9 percent for Vietnam and 14 percent for Cuba, compared with 3.3 percent and less for the others, except Poland and Romania). Increased investments in Mongolia lagged behind those in Poland and Romania but were nevertheless substantial (5.8 percent). In 1984 the economies of the three developing countries registered the fastest industrial growth of all the Comecon members.

Given their locations, Comecon membership for Mongolia, Cuba, and Vietnam served principally to advance Soviet foreign policy interests. Among the Comecon members, the Soviet Union contributed the most to the development of the three poorer Comecon members, and it also reaped most of the benefits. The Soviet Union imported most of Cuba's sugar and nickel and all of Mongolia's copper and molybdenum (widely used in the construction of aircraft, automobiles, machine tools, gas turbines, and in the field of electronics). In return, Cuba provided bases for the Soviet Naval Forces and military support to Soviet allies in Africa. Vietnam made its naval and air bases, as well as some 100,000 guest workers, available to the Soviet Union.

Support for Developing Countries

Comecon provided economic and technical support to 34 developing countries in 1960, 62 developing countries in 1970, and over 100 developing countries in 1985. As of 1987, Comecon had assisted in the construction or preparation of over 4,000 projects (mostly industrial) in Asia, Latin America, and Africa. A monetary figure for this assistance is difficult to estimate, although a June 1986 Czechoslovak source valued the exchange between Comecon and developing countries at 34 billion rubles per year (US$48.3 billion at the official June 1986 exchange rate of US$1.42 per ruble). The precise nature of this aid was unclear, and Western observers believe the data to be inflated.

From the 1960s to the mid-1980s, Comecon sought to encourage the development of industry, energy, transportation, mineral resources, and agriculture of Third World countries. Comecon countries also provided technical and economic training for personnel in Asia, Africa, and Latin America. When Comecon initially lent support to developing countries, it generally concentrated on developing those products that would support the domestic economies of the Third World, including replacements for imports. In the 1970s and 1980s, assistance from Comecon was directed toward export-oriented industries. Third World countries paid for this support with products made by the project for which Comecon rendered help. This policy gave Comecon a stable source of necessary deliveries in addition to political influence in these strategically important areas.

Trends and Prospects

Comecon served for more than three decades as a framework for cooperation among the planned economies of the Soviet Union, its allies in Eastern Europe, and Soviet allies in the Third World. Over the years, the Comecon system grew steadily in scope and experience.

This institutional evolution reflected changing and expanding goals. Initial, modest objectives of ''exchanging experience'' and providing ''technical assistance'' and other forms of ''mutual aid'' were extended to the development of an integrated set of economies based on a coordinated international pattern of production and investment. These ambitious goals were pursued through a broad spectrum of cooperative measures extending from monetary to technological relations.

At the same time, the extraregional goals of the organization also expanded; other countries, both geographically distant and systemically different, were encouraged to participate in Comecon activities. Parallel efforts sought to develop Comecon as a mechanism through which to coordinate the foreign economic policies of the members as well as their actual relations with nonmember countries and with such organizations as the European Economic Community (EEC) and the United Nations.

Asymmetries of size and differences in levels of development among Comecon members deeply affected the institutional character and evolution of the organization. The overwhelming dominance of the Soviet economy necessarily meant that the bulk of intra-Comecon relations took the form of bilateral relations between the Soviet Union and the smaller members of Comecon.

The planned nature of the members' economies and the lack of effective market-price mechanisms to facilitate integration hindered progress toward Comecon goals. Without the automatic workings of market forces, progress depended upon conscious acts of policy. This fact tended to politicize the processes of integration to a greater degree than was the case in countries with market economies.

By 1987 Comecon's 1971 *Comprehensive Program* had undergone considerable change. Multilateral planning faded into traditional bilateral cooperation, and the Bucharest formula for prices assumed a revised form. The 1985 *Comprehensive Program* or, as some Western analysts call it, the "Gorbachev Charter," became Comecon's new blueprint for taking a firm grip on its future. The purpose of the 1985 program was to offset centrifugal forces and reduce Comecon's vulnerability to "technological blackmail" through better mutual cooperation, increased efficiency of cooperation, and improved quality of output.

Additional progress in this direction was made at the Forty-First Council Session held in Moscow in October 1987 and the Forty-Fourth Council Session held in Prague in July 1988. As a result of these sessions, all Comecon members, with the exception of Romania, reached an agreement on the necessity within Comecon of a "unified market," which would lead to the "free movement of goods, services, and other production factors." They also agreed to work toward a genuine multilateral convertibility of their currencies, recognizing, nevertheless, that achievement of such a goal was some ten to fifteen years in the future.

Members attending the Forty-Third Council Session also agreed to changes in Comecon's organizational structure. Some Comecon bodies were abolished, others were reorganized or merged, and new bodies were created. The aim of these changes was to streamline and improve their performance. At the same time, however, as meaningful changes were being made within Comecon, the

873

rapidly changing political climate of Eastern Europe and the pressure for economic reforms within each of the Comecon member states were not only threatening the unity of Comecon but also raising serious doubts about any further need for its existence.

* * *

Although the selection is still rather sparse, several English-language works on Comecon appeared in the early 1980s. *Socialist Economic Integration* by Jozef M. van Brabant discusses in great detail the mechanisms and operations of socialist economic integration in general and Comecon in particular. It is perhaps the most comprehensive English-language work on the subject. Analysis of Comecon's operations and development in the modern economic and political arena is provided in Paul Marer's "The Political Economy of Soviet Relations with Eastern Europe." The best sources for up-to-date political and economic analysis are the Radio Free Europe background reports. Articles by Vladimir Sobell, in particular, provide useful information about the 1985 *Comprehensive Program*.

Russian-language sources provide useful information on Comecon procedures and structure in addition to insight into the Soviet and East European view of Comecon's goals and shortcomings. Articles in this vein can be found in *Voprosy ekonomiki* and in *Ekonomika*. Translations of selected articles from these publications can be found in the Joint Publications Research Service's *USSR Report on Economic Affairs*. The Comecon Secretariat publishes a bimonthly bulletin (*Ekonomicheskoe sotrudnichestvo stran-chlenov SEV*), which has a table of contents and a summary in English; the annual *Statisticheskii ezhegodnik stran-chlenov SEV;* and various handbooks. (For further information and complete citations, see Bibliography.)

The Warsaw Pact

THE POLITICAL AND MILITARY ALLIANCE of the Soviet Union and East European socialist states, known as the Warsaw Pact, was formed in 1955 as a counterweight to the North Atlantic Treaty Organization (NATO), created in 1949. During much of its early existence, the Warsaw Pact essentially functioned as part of the Soviet Ministry of Defense. In fact, in the early years of its existence the Warsaw Pact served as one of the Soviet Union's primary mechanisms for keeping its East European allies under its political and military control. The Soviet Union used the Warsaw Pact to erect a facade of collective decisions and actions around the reality of its political domination and military intervention in the internal affairs of its allies. At the same time, the Soviet Union also used the Warsaw Pact to develop East European socialist armies and harness them to its military strategy and security policy.

Since its inception, the Warsaw Pact reflected the changing pattern of Soviet-East European relations and manifested problems that affect all alliances. The Warsaw Pact evolved into something other than the mechanism of control the Soviet Union originally intended it to be and, since the 1960s, became less dominated by the Soviet Union. Thus, in 1962 Albania stopped participating in Warsaw Pact activities and formally withdrew from the alliance in 1968. The organizational structure of the Warsaw Pact also provided a forum for greater intra-alliance debate, bargaining, and conflict between the Soviet Union and its allies over the issues of national independence, policy autonomy, and East European participation in alliance decision making. At the same time that the Warsaw Pact retained its internal function in Soviet-East European relations, its non-Soviet members developed sufficient military capabilities to become useful adjuncts of Soviet power against NATO in Europe (see fig. A, this Appendix).

The Soviet Alliance System, 1943–55

Long before the establishment of the Warsaw Pact in 1955, the Soviet Union had molded the East European states into an alliance serving its security interests. While liberating Eastern Europe from Nazi Germany in World War II, the Red Army (see Glossary) established political and military control over that region. The Soviet Union intended to use Eastern Europe as a buffer zone for

Figure A. The Warsaw Pact Member States, 1989

the forward defense of its western borders and to keep threatening ideological influences at bay. Continued control of Eastern Europe became second only to defense of the homeland in the hierarchy of Soviet security priorities.

The Red Army began to form, train, and arm Polish and Czechoslovak national units on Soviet territory in 1943. These units fought with the Red Army as it carried its offensive westward into German-occupied Poland and Czechoslovakia and then into Germany itself. By 1943 the Red Army had destroyed the Bulgarian, Hungarian, and Romanian forces fighting alongside the German armed forces. Shortly thereafter it began the process of transforming the remnants of their armies into allied units that could re-enter the war on the side of the Soviet Union. Red Army political officers (*zampoliti*—see Glossary) organized extensive indoctrination programs in the allied units under Soviet control and purged any politically suspect personnel. In all, the Soviet Union formed and armed more than twenty-nine divisions and thirty-seven brigades and regiments, which included more than 500,000 East European troops.

The allied national formations were directly subordinate to the headquarters of the Soviet Union's Supreme High Command and its executive body, the General Staff of the Armed Forces. Although the Soviet Union directly commanded all allied units, the Supreme High Command included one representative from each of the East European forces. Lacking authority, these representatives simply relayed directives from the Supreme High Command and General Staff to the commanders of East European units. While all national units had so-called Soviet advisers, some Red Army officers openly discharged command and staff responsibilities in the East European armies. Even when commanded by East European officers, non-Soviet contingents participated in operations against the German armed forces only as part of Soviet fronts.

By the end of World War I?, the Red Army (renamed the Soviet army after the war) occupied Bulgaria, Romania, Hungary, Poland, significant portions of Czechoslovakia, and eastern Germany, and Soviet front commanders headed the Allied Control Commission in each of these occupied countries. The Soviet Union gave its most important occupation forces a garrison status when it established the Northern Group of Forces in 1947 and the Group of Soviet Forces in Germany in 1949. By 1949 the Soviet Union had concluded twenty-year bilateral treaties of friendship, cooperation, and mutual assistance with Bulgaria, Czechoslovakia, Hungary, Poland, and Romania, which granted the Soviet Union rights to a continued military presence on their territory. The continued presence of

Soviet armed forces guaranteed Soviet control of these countries. The East European satellite regimes depended entirely on Soviet military power—and the continued deployment of 1 million Soviet soldiers—to stay in power. In return, the new East European political and military elites were obliged to respect Soviet political and security interests in the region. By contrast, the Soviet Union did not occupy either Albania or Yugoslavia during or after the war, and both countries remained outside direct Soviet control.

In the late 1940s and the 1950s, the Soviet Union was more concerned about cultivating and monitoring political loyalty in its East European military allies than increasing their utility as combat forces. The Soviet Union assigned trusted communist party leaders of the East European nations to the most important military command positions despite their lack of military qualifications. It forced its East European allies to emulate Soviet military ranks and uniforms and abandon all distinctive national military customs and practices; these allied armies used all Soviet-made weapons and equipment. The Soviet Union accepted many of the most promising and eager East European officers into Soviet mid-career military institutions and academies for the advanced study essential to their promotion within the national armed forces command structures. Furthermore, the East European ministries of defense established political departments on the model of the Soviet Union's Main Political Directorate of the Soviet Army and Navy.

The Formation of the Warsaw Pact, 1955–70

On May 14, 1955, the Soviet Union institutionalized its East European alliance system, henceforth known as the Warsaw Pact, when it met with representatives from Albania, Bulgaria, Czechoslovakia, Hungary, Poland, and Romania in Warsaw to sign the multilateral Treaty of Friendship, Cooperation, and Mutual Assistance, which was identical to their existing bilateral treaties with the Soviet Union. The Soviet Union claimed that the creation of the Warsaw Pact was in direct response to the inclusion of the Federal Republic of Germany (West Germany) in NATO in 1955. At the same time, the formation of a legally defined, multilateral alliance reinforced the Soviet Union's claim to be leader of the world socialist system (see Glossary), enhanced its prestige, and legitimized its presence and influence in Eastern Europe. The new alliance system also gave the Soviet Union a structure for dealing with its East European allies more efficiently when it superimposed the multilateral Warsaw Pact on their existing bilateral treaty ties. Finally, as a formal organization the Warsaw Pact provided the Soviet Union an official counterweight to NATO in East-West diplomacy.

The 1955 treaty establishing the Warsaw Pact stated that relations among the signatories were based on total equality, mutual noninterference in internal affairs, and respect for national sovereignty and independence. It declared that the Warsaw Pact's function was collective self-defense of the member states against external aggression, as provided for in Article 51 of the United Nations Charter. The terms of the alliance specified the Political Consultative Committee (PCC) as the highest alliance organ. The founding document formed the Joint Command to organize the actual defense of the Warsaw Pact member states, declared that the national deputy ministers of defense would act as the deputies of the Warsaw Pact commander in chief, and established the Joint Staff, which included the representatives of the general (main) staffs of all its member states. The treaty set the Warsaw Pact's duration at twenty years with an automatic ten-year extension, provided that none of the member states renounced it before its expiration. The treaty also included a standing offer to disband simultaneously with other military alliances, i.e., NATO, contingent on East-West agreement about a general treaty on collective security in Europe. This provision indicated that the Soviet Union either did not expect that such an accord could be negotiated or did not consider its new multilateral alliance structure very important.

Until the early 1960s, the Soviet Union used the Warsaw Pact more as a tool in East-West diplomacy than as a functioning political-military alliance. Under the leadership of Nikita S. Khrushchev, the Soviet Union sought to project a more flexible and less threatening image abroad and, toward this end, used the alliance's PCC to publicize its foreign policy initiatives and peace offensives, including frequent calls for the formation of an all-European collective security system to replace the continent's existing military alliances. In 1956 the Warsaw Pact member states admitted East Germany to the Joint Command and sanctioned the transformation of East Germany's Garrisoned People's Police into a full-fledged army. But the Soviet Union took no steps to integrate the allied armies into a multinational force.

In his 1956 "secret speech" at the Twentieth Party Congress of the Communist Party of the Soviet Union (CPSU), Khrushchev denounced the arbitrariness, excesses, and terror of the Joseph V. Stalin era. Khrushchev sought to achieve greater legitimacy for his authoritarian rule on the basis of the party's ability to meet the material needs of the Soviet population. His de-Stalinization campaign quickly influenced developments in Eastern Europe. Responding to East European demands for greater political autonomy, Khrushchev accepted the replacement of Stalinist Polish and Hungarian leaders with newly rehabilitated (see Glossary) communist party figures, who were able to generate genuine popular support for their regimes. He sought to turn Soviet-controlled East European satellites into at least semiautonomous countries and to make Soviet domination of the Warsaw Pact less obvious. He allowed the East European armies to restore their distinctive national practices and to reemphasize professional military opinions over political considerations in most areas. Military training supplanted political indoctrination as the primary task of the East European military establishments. Most important, the Soviet Ministry of Defense recalled many Soviet army officers and advisers from their positions within the East European armies.

In October 1956, the Polish and Hungarian communist parties lost control of the de-Stalinization process in their countries. The ensuing crises threatened the integrity of the entire Soviet alliance system in Eastern Europe and led to a significant change in the role of the Warsaw Pact as an element of Soviet security.

The Polish October

The Polish government's handling of the workers' riots in Poland in October 1956 defined the boundaries of national communism acceptable to the Soviet Union. The Polish United Workers' Party found that the grievances that inspired the riots could be ameliorated without presenting a challenge to its monopoly on political power or its strict adherence to Soviet foreign policy and security interests. Poland's new communist party leader, Wladyslaw Gomulka, and the Polish People's Army's top commanders indicated to Khrushchev and the other Soviet leaders that any Soviet intervention in the internal affairs of Poland would meet united, massive resistance. While insisting on Poland's right to exercise greater autonomy in domestic matters, Gomulka also pointed out that the Polish United Workers' Party remained in firm control of the country and expressed his intention to continue to accept Soviet direction in external affairs. Gomulka's position permitted the Soviet Union to redefine the minimum requirements for its East European allies: upholding the leading role of the communist party in society and remaining a member of the Warsaw Pact. These two conditions ensured that the Soviet Union's most vital interests would be protected and that Eastern Europe would remain a buffer zone for the Soviet Union.

The Hungarian Revolution

By contrast, the full-scale revolution in Hungary, which began in late October with public demonstrations in support of the rioting

Polish workers, openly flouted these Soviet stipulations. Initial domestic liberalization acceptable to the Soviet Union quickly escalated to nonnegotiable issues like challenging the communist party's exclusive hold on political power and establishing genuine national independence. Imre Nagy, the new communist party leader, withdrew Hungary from the Warsaw Pact and ended Hungary's alliance with the Soviet Union. The Soviet army invaded with 200,000 troops, crushed the Hungarian Revolution, and brought Hungary back within limits tolerable to the Soviet Union. The five days of pitched battles left 25,000 Hungarians dead.

After 1956 the Soviet Union practically disbanded the Hungarian People's Army and reinstituted a program of political indoctrination in the units that remained. In May 1957, unable to rely on Hungarian forces to maintain order, the Soviet Union increased its troop level in Hungary from two to four divisions and forced Hungary to sign a status-of-forces agreement, placing the Soviet military presence on a solid and permanent legal basis. The Soviet forces stationed in Hungary officially became the Southern Group of Forces.

The events of 1956 in Poland and Hungary forced a Soviet reevaluation of the reliability and roles of the Non-Soviet Warsaw Pact (NSWP) countries in its alliance system. Before 1956 the Soviet leadership believed that the Stalinist policy of heavy political indoctrination and enforced Sovietization had transformed the national armies into reliable instruments of the Soviet Union. After 1956 the Soviet Union increasingly suspected that the East European armies were likely to remain loyal to national causes.

A Shift Toward Greater Cohesion

After the very foundation of the Soviet alliance system in Eastern Europe was shaken in 1956, Khrushchev sought to shore up the Soviet Union's position. Although Khrushchev had invoked the terms of the Warsaw Pact as a justification for the Soviet invasion of Hungary, the action was in no sense a cooperative allied effort. In the early 1960s, however, the Soviet Union took steps to turn the alliance's armed forces into a multinational intervention force. In the future, an appeal to the Warsaw Pact's collective self-defense provisions and the participation of allied forces would put a multilateral cover over unilateral Soviet interventions to keep errant member states in the alliance and their communist parties in power. By presenting future policing actions as the product of joint Warsaw Pact decisions, the Soviet Union hoped to deflect the kind of direct international criticism the Soviet Union was subjected to after the invasion of Hungary. Such internal deployments, however, were clearly contrary to the Warsaw Pact's rule of mutual noninterference in domestic affairs and conflicted with the alliance's declared purpose of collective self-defense against external aggression. To circumvent this semantic difficulty, the Soviet Union merely redefined external aggression to include any spontaneous anti-Soviet, anticommunist uprising in an allied state.

In the late 1950s, the Soviet Union began to take a series of steps to transform the Warsaw Pact into its intra-alliance intervention force. Although it had previously worked with the East European military establishments on a bilateral basis, the Soviet Union started to integrate the national armies under the Warsaw Pact framework. Military exercises with Soviet forces and the allied national armies became the primary focus of Warsaw Pact military activities.

The Soviet Union planned these joint exercises to prevent any NSWP member state from fully controlling its national army and to reduce the possibility that an East European regime could successfully resist Soviet domination and pursue independent policies. A series of joint Warsaw Pact exercises, organized and controlled by the Soviet Union, was intended to prevent other East European national command authorities from following the example of Yugoslavia and Albania and adopting a territorial defense strategy.

The Prague Spring

In 1968 an acute crisis in the Soviet alliance system suddenly occurred. The domestic liberalization program of the Czechoslovak communist regime led by Alexander Dubček threatened to generate popular demands for similar changes in the other East European countries and even parts of the Soviet Union. Domestic change in Czechoslovakia also began to affect defense and foreign policy, just as it had in Hungary in 1956, despite Dubček's declared intention to keep Czechoslovakia within the Warsaw Pact. Once again, the Soviet Union felt it necessary to forestall the spread of liberalization and to assert its right to enforce the boundaries of ideological permissibility in Eastern Europe. This concern was the major factor in the Soviet Union's decision to invade Czechoslovakia in 1968. The Soviet decision in favor of intervention focused, in large measure, on ensuring its ability to maintain physical control of its wayward ally in the future.

In contrast to its rapid, bloody suppression of the 1956 Hungarian Revolution, the Soviet Union engaged in a lengthy campaign of military coercion against Czechoslovakia. In 1968 the Soviet Union conducted more joint Warsaw Pact exercises than in any other year since the maneuvers began in the early 1960s. The Soviet Union used these exercises to mask preparations for, and threaten, a Warsaw Pact invasion of Czechoslovakia that would occur unless Dubček complied with Soviet demands and abandoned his political liberalization program. Massive Warsaw Pact rear services and communications exercises in July and August enabled the Soviet Union's General Staff to execute its plan for the invasion without alerting Western governments. Under the pretext of conducting exercises, Soviet and NSWP divisions were brought up to full strength, reservists were called up, and civilian transportation resources were requisitioned. The cover that these exercises provided allowed the Soviet Union to deploy forces along Czechoslovakia's borders with Poland and East Germany and to demonstrate to the Czechoslovak leadership its readiness to intervene.

On August 20, a force consisting of twenty-three Soviet divisions invaded Czechoslovakia. Token NSWP contingents, including one Hungarian, two East German, and two Polish divisions, along with one Bulgarian brigade, also took part in the invasion. In the wake of the invasion, the Soviet Union installed a more compliant communist party leadership and concluded a status-of-forces agreement with Czechoslovakia, which established a permanent Soviet presence in that country for the first time. Five Soviet divisions remained in Czechoslovakia to protect the country from future "imperialist threats." These troops became the Central Group of Forces and added to Soviet strength directly bordering NATO member states. The Czechoslovak People's Army, having failed to oppose the Soviet intervention and defend the country's sovereignty, suffered a tremendous loss of prestige after 1968. At Soviet direction, reliable Czechoslovak authorities conducted a purge and political reeducation campaign in the Czechoslovak People's Army and cut its size. With its one-time closest partner now proven unreliable, the Soviet Union turned to Poland as its principal East European ally.

The Warsaw Pact invasion of Czechoslovakia showed the hollowness of the Soviet alliance system in Eastern Europe in both its political and its military aspects. The Soviet Union did not convene the PCC to invoke Warsaw Pact action during the 1968 crisis because a formal session would have revealed a deep rift in the Warsaw Pact alliance and given Czechoslovakia an international platform from which it could have defended its reform program.

While the participation of four NSWP armies in the Soviet-led invasion of Czechoslovakia ostensibly demonstrated considerable Warsaw Pact cohesion, the invasion also served to erode it. The invasion of Czechoslovakia proved that the Warsaw Pact's mission of keeping orthodox East European communist party regimes in power—and less orthodox ones in line—was more important than the mission of defending its member states against external aggression. The Soviet Union was unable to conceal the fact that the alliance served as the ultimate mechanism for its control of Eastern Europe. Formulated in response to the crisis in Czechoslovakia, the Brezhnev Doctrine (see Glossary) declared that the East European countries had "limited" sovereignty, to be exercised only as long as it did not damage the interests of the "socialist commonwealth" as a whole.

The Romanian leader, Nicolae Ceauşescu, after refusing to contribute troops to the Soviet intervention force as the other East European countries had done, denounced the invasion of Czechoslovakia as a violation of international law and the Warsaw Pact's cardinal principle of mutual noninterference in internal affairs. Ceauşescu insisted that collective self-defense against external aggression was the only valid mission of the Warsaw Pact. Albania also objected to the Soviet invasion and indicated its disapproval by withdrawing formally from the Warsaw Pact after six years of inactive membership.

In 1968, following the Warsaw Pact's invasion of Czechoslovakia, Romania demanded the withdrawal from its territory of all Soviet troops, advisers, and the Soviet resident representative. Reducing its participation in Warsaw Pact activities considerably, Romania also refused to allow Soviet or NSWP forces, which could serve as Warsaw Pact intervention forces, to cross or conduct exercises on its territory. Following the lead of Yugoslavia and Albania, Romania reasserted full national control over its armed forces and military policies by adopting a territorial defense strategy called "War of the Entire People," whose aim was to end Soviet domination and to guard against Soviet encroachments.

Organization and Strategy of the Warsaw Pact

The Warsaw Pact administered both the political and the military activities of the Soviet alliance system in Eastern Europe. A series of changes that began in 1969 gave the Warsaw Pact the structure it retained through the late 1980s.

Political Organization

The general (or first) secretaries of the communist and workers' parties and heads of state of the Warsaw Pact member states met in the PCC. The PCC provided a formal point of contact for the Soviet and East European leaders in addition to less formal bilateral meetings and visits. As the highest decision-making body of the Warsaw Pact, the PCC was charged with assessing international developments that affected the security of the allied states and warranted the execution of the Warsaw Pact's collective self-defense provisions. In practice, however, the Soviet Union was unwilling to rely on the PCC to perform this function, fearing that Hungary, Czechoslovakia, and Romania would use PCC meetings to oppose Soviet plans and policies. The PCC was also the main center for coordinating the foreign policy activities of the Warsaw Pact countries. After the late 1960s, when several member states began to use the alliance structure to confront Soviet domination and assert more independent foreign policies, the Soviet Union had to negotiate to gain support for its foreign policy within Warsaw Pact councils.

In 1976 the PCC established the permanent Committee of Ministers of Foreign Affairs (CMFA) to regularize the previously ad hoc meetings of Soviet and East European representatives to the Warsaw Pact. Given the official task of preparing recommendations for and executing the decisions of the PCC, the CMFA and its permanent Joint Secretariat provided the Soviet Union an additional point of contact to establish a consensus among its allies on contentious issues. Less formal meetings of the deputy ministers of foreign affairs of the Warsaw Pact member states represented another layer of alliance coordination. The ministers were tasked with resolving alliance problems at these working levels so that they would not erupt into embarrassing disputes between the Soviet and East European leaders at PCC meetings.

Military Organization

The Warsaw Pact's military organization was larger and more active than the alliance's political bodies. Several different organizations were responsible for implementing PCC directives on defense matters and developing the capabilities of the national armies that constituted the Warsaw Pact's armed forces. The principal task, however, of the military organizations was to link the East European armies to the Soviet armed forces. The alliance's military agencies coordinated the training and mobilization of the East European national forces assigned to the Warsaw Pact. In turn, these forces could be deployed in accordance with Soviet military strategy against an NSWP country or NATO.

Soviet control of the Warsaw Pact as a military alliance was scarcely veiled. The Warsaw Pact's armed forces had no command structure, logistics network, air defense system, or operations directorate separate from the Soviet Ministry of Defense. The 1968 invasion of Czechoslovakia demonstrated how easily control of the Warsaw Pact's armed forces could be transferred in wartime to the Soviet General Staff and to Soviet field commanders. The dual roles of the Warsaw Pact commander in chief, who was a first deputy Soviet minister of defense, and the Warsaw Pact chief of staff, who was a first deputy chief of the Soviet General Staff, facilitated the transfer of Warsaw Pact forces to Soviet control. The subordination of the Warsaw Pact to the Soviet General Staff was also shown clearly in the Soviet military hierarchy. In the Soviet order of precedence, the chief of the Soviet General Staff was listed above the Warsaw Pact commander in chief even though both positions also were designated first deputy ministers of defense.

Ironically, the first innovations in the Warsaw Pact's structure after 1955 came after the invasion of Czechoslovakia, which had clearly underlined Soviet control of the alliance. At the 1969 PCC session in Budapest, the Soviet Union agreed to cosmetic alterations in the Warsaw Pact designed to address East European complaints that the Soviet Union dominated the alliance. These changes included the establishment of the formal Committee of Ministers of Defense (CMD) and the Military Council, as well as the addition of more non-Soviet officers to the Joint Command and the Joint Staff.

Headed by the Warsaw Pact's commander in chief, the Joint Command was divided into distinct Soviet and East European tiers. The deputy commanders in chief included Soviet and East European officers. The Soviet officers serving as deputy commanders in chief were specifically responsible for coordinating the East European navies and air forces with the corresponding Soviet service branches. The East European deputy commanders in chief were the deputy ministers of defense of the NSWP countries. While providing formal NSWP representation in the Joint Command, the East European deputies also assisted in the coordination of Soviet and non-Soviet forces. The commander in chief, deputy commanders in chief, and chief of staff of the Warsaw Pact's armed forces gathered in the Military Council on a semiannual basis to plan and evaluate operational and combat training. With the Warsaw Pact's commander in chief acting as chairman, the sessions of the Military Council rotated among the capitals of the Warsaw Pact countries.

The Joint Staff was the only standing Warsaw Pact military body and the official executive organ of the CMD, commander in chief, and Military Council. As such, it performed the bulk of the Warsaw Pact's work in the military realm. Like the Joint Command, the Joint Staff had both Soviet and East European officers. The non-Soviet officers also served as the principal link between the Soviet and East European armed forces. The Joint Staff organized all joint exercises and arranged multilateral meetings and contacts of Warsaw Pact military personnel at all levels.

The 1969 PCC meeting also approved the formation of two more Warsaw Pact military bodies, the Military Scientific-Technical Council and the Technical Committee. These innovations in the Warsaw Pact structure represented a Soviet attempt to harness NSWP weapons and military equipment production, which had greatly increased during the 1960s. After 1969 the Soviet Union insisted on tighter Warsaw Pact military integration as the price for greater NSWP participation in alliance decision making.

Soviet Military Strategy and the Warsaw Pact

The Soviet armed forces constituted the bulk of the Warsaw Pact's military manpower. In the 1980s, the Soviet Union provided 73 of the 126 Warsaw Pact tank and motorized rifle divisions. Located in the groups of Soviet forces and the four westernmost military districts of the Soviet Union, these divisions comprised the majority of the Warsaw Pact's combat-ready, full-strength units. Looking at the numbers of Soviet troops stationed in or near Eastern Europe, and the historical record, one could conclude that the Warsaw Pact was only a Soviet mechanism for organizing intra-alliance interventions or maintaining control of Eastern Europe and did not significantly augment Soviet offensive power vis-à-vis NATO. Essentially a peacetime structure for NSWP training and mobilization, the Warsaw Pact had no independent role in wartime nor a military strategy distinct from Soviet military strategy. The individual NSWP armies, however, played important roles in the Soviet strategy for war outside the formal context of the Warsaw Pact.

The goal of Soviet military strategy in Europe was a quick victory over NATO in a nonnuclear war. Soviet miliary strategists planned to defeat NATO decisively before its political and military command structure could consult and decide how to respond to an attack. Under this strategy, success would hinge on inflicting a rapid succession of defeats on NATO to break its will to fight, knock some of its member states out of the war, and cause the collapse of the Western alliance. In this plan, the Warsaw Pact countries would provide forward bases, staging areas, and interior lines of communication for the Soviet Union against NATO. A quick victory would be needed to keep the United States from escalating the conflict to the nuclear level by making retaliation against the Soviet Union futile. A rapid defeat of NATO would preempt the mobilization of the West's superior industrial and economic resources, as well as reinforcement from the United States, which

887

would enable NATO to prevail in a longer war. Most significant, in a strictly conventional war the Soviet Union could have conceivably captured its objective, the economic potential of Western Europe, relatively intact. This plan for winning a conventional war quickly to preclude the possibility of a nuclear response by NATO and the United States was based on the deep offensive operation concept that Soviet military theoreticians first proposed in the 1930s.

Continuing Soviet concern over the combat reliability of its East European allies influenced, to a great extent, the deployment of NSWP forces under the Soviet military strategy. Soviet leaders believed that the Warsaw Pact allies would be most likely to remain loyal if the Soviet armed forces engaged in a short, successful offensive operation against NATO while deploying NSWP forces defensively. Soviet concern over the reliability of its Warsaw Pact allies was reflected in the alliance's military-technical policy, which was under Soviet control. The Soviet Union gave the East European allies less modern, though still effective, weapons and equipment to keep their armies less capable than the Soviet armed forces. Thus the Soviet Union could keep the East European armies somewhat modernized while not substantially increasing their capability to resist Soviet intervention.

The Weakening of the Alliance's Cohesion, 1970-85

Beginning in the early 1970s, the East European allies formed intra-alliance coalitions in Warsaw Pact meetings to oppose the Soviet Union, defuse its pressure on any one NSWP member state, and delay or obstruct Soviet policies. The Soviet Union could no longer use the alliance to transmit its positions to, and receive automatic endorsements from, the subordinate NSWP countries. While still far from genuine consultation, Warsaw Pact policy coordination between the Soviet Union and the East European countries in the 1970s was a step away from the blatant Soviet control of the alliance that had characterized the 1950s. East European opposition forced the Soviet Union to treat the Warsaw Pact as a forum for managing relations with its allies and bidding for their support on issues like détente, the Third World, the Solidarity movement in Poland, alliance burden-sharing, and relations with NATO.

Détente

In the late 1960s, the Soviet Union abandoned its earlier efforts to achieve the simultaneous dissolution of NATO and the Warsaw Pact and concentrated instead on legitimating the territorial status quo in Europe. The Soviet Union asserted that the official East-West agreements reached during the détente era ''legally secured the most important political-territorial results of World War II.'' Under these arrangements, the Soviet Union allowed its East European allies to recognize West Germany's existence as a separate state. In return the West, and West Germany in particular, explicitly accepted the inviolability of postwar borders in Eastern Europe and tacitly recognized Soviet control of the eastern portion of both Germany and Europe. The Soviet Union claimed the 1975 Helsinki Accords (see Glossary), which ratified the existing political division of Europe, as a major victory for Soviet diplomacy and the realization of long-standing Soviet calls, issued through the PCC, for a general European conference on collective security.

The consequences of détente, however, also posed a significant challenge to Soviet control of Eastern Europe. First, détente caused a crisis in Soviet-East German relations. East Germany's leader, Walter Ulbricht, opposed improved relations with West Germany and, following Ceauşescu's tactics, used Warsaw Pact councils to attack the Soviet détente policy openly. In the end, the Soviet Union removed Ulbricht from power and subsequently proceeded unhindered into détente with the West. Second, détente blurred the strict bipolarity of the Cold War era, opened Eastern Europe to greater Western influence, and loosened Soviet control over its allies. The relaxation of East-West tensions in the 1970s reduced the level of threat perceived by the NSWP countries, along with their perceived need for Soviet protection, and eroded Warsaw Pact alliance cohesion. After the West formally accepted the territorial status quo in Europe, the Soviet Union was unable to point to the danger of "imperialist" attempts to overturn East European communist party regimes to justify its demand for strict Warsaw Pact unity behind its leadership, as it had in earlier years. The Soviet Union resorted to occasional propaganda offensives, accusing West Germany of revanchism and aggressive intentions in Eastern Europe, to remind its allies of their ultimate dependence on Soviet protection and to reinforce the Warsaw Pact's cohesion against the attraction of good relations with the West.

Despite these problems, the détente period witnessed relatively stable Soviet-East European relations within the Warsaw Pact. In the early 1970s, the Soviet Union greatly expanded military cooperation with the NSWP countries. Joint Warsaw Pact exercises conducted in the 1970s gave the Soviet allies their first real capability for offensive operations other than policing actions within the alliance. The East European countries also began to take an active part in Soviet strategy in the Third World.

With Eastern Europe in a relatively quiescent phase, the Soviet Union began to build an informal alliance system in the Third

World during the 1970s. It employed its Warsaw Pact allies as surrogates primarily because their activities minimized the need for
direct Soviet involvement and obviated possible international criticism of Soviet actions in the Third World. East European allies
followed the lead of Soviet diplomacy and signed treaties of friendship, cooperation, and mutual assistance with most of the important Soviet Third World allies. These treaties established a "socialist
division of labor" among the East European countries in which
each specialized in the provision of certain aspects of military or
economic assistance to different Soviet Third World allies.

In the 1970s and 1980s, Bulgaria, Czechoslovakia, and East Germany were the principal Soviet proxies for arms transfers to the Third
World. These NSWP countries supplied Soviet-manufactured
equipment, spare parts, and training personnel to various Third
World armies. During this period, the Soviet Union also relied on
its East European allies to provide the bulk of the economic aid
and credits given by the Soviet Union and Eastern Europe to the
countries of the Third World. Beginning in the late 1970s, mounting
economic problems sharply curtailed the contribution of the East
European allies to the Soviet Union's Third World activities. In
the early 1980s, when turmoil in Poland reminded the Soviet Union
that Eastern Europe remained its most valuable asset, the Third
World became a somewhat less important object of Soviet attention.

The rise of the independent trade union movement Solidarity
shook the foundation of communist party rule in Poland and, consequently, Soviet control of a country the Soviet Union considered
critical to its security and alliance system. Given Poland's central
geographic position, this unrest threatened to isolate East Germany,
sever vital lines of communication to Soviet forces deployed against
NATO, and disrupt Soviet control in the rest of Eastern Europe.

As it did in Czechoslovakia in 1968, the Soviet Union used the
Warsaw Pact to carry out a campaign of military coercion against
the Polish leadership. In 1980 and 1981, the Soviet Union conducted joint Warsaw Pact exercises with a higher frequency than
at any time since 1968 to exert pressure on the Polish regime to
solve the Solidarity problem. Under the cover that the exercises
afforded, the Soviet Union mobilized and deployed its reserve and
regular troops in the Belorussian Military District as a potential
invasion force (see fig. 30). Faced with the threat of Soviet military intervention, the Polish government instituted martial law and
suppressed Solidarity. From the Soviet perspective, the imposition
of martial law by Polish internal security forces was the best possible outcome. Martial law made the suppression of Solidarity a

strictly domestic affair and spared the Soviet Union the international criticism that an invasion would have generated.

Although the Polish People's Army had previously played an important role in Soviet strategy for a coalition war against NATO, the Soviet Union had to revise its plans and estimates of Poland's reliability after 1981, and it turned to East Germany as its most reliable ally. In the early 1980s, because of its eager promotion of Soviet interests in the Third World and its importance in Soviet military strategy, East Germany completed its transformation from defeated enemy and dependent ally into the principal junior partner of the Soviet Union.

The End of Détente

In the late 1970s, the West grew disenchanted with détente, which had failed to prevent Soviet advances in the Third World, the deployment of SS-20 intermediate-range ballistic missiles (IRBMs) aimed at West European targets, the invasion of Afghanistan, or the suppression of Solidarity. The Soviet Union used the renewal of East-West tension as a justification for forcing its allies to close ranks within the Warsaw Pact. But restoring the alliance's cohesion and renewing its confrontation with Western Europe proved difficult after several years of good East-West relations. In the early 1980s, internal Warsaw Pact disputes centered on relations with the West after détente, NSWP contributions to alliance defense spending, and the alliance's reaction to IRBM deployments in NATO. The resolution of these disputes produced significant changes in the Warsaw Pact as, for the first time, two or more NSWP countries simultaneously challenged Soviet military and foreign policy preferences within the alliance.

In the PCC meetings of the late 1970s and early 1980s, Soviet and East European leaders of the Warsaw Pact debated the threat that they perceived emanated from NATO. Discussions of the "NATO threat" also played a large part in Warsaw Pact debates about an appropriate level of NSWP military expenditure. The issue of an appropriate Warsaw Pact response to NATO's 1983 deployment of American Pershing II and cruise missiles, matching the Soviet SS-20s, proved to be the most divisive one for the Soviet Union and its East European allies in the early and mid-1980s. After joining in a vociferous Soviet propaganda campaign against the deployment, the East European countries split with the Soviet Union over how to react when their "peace offensive" failed to forestall it. The refusal of the NSWP countries to meet their Warsaw Pact financial obligations in the 1980s further indicated diminished alliance cohesion.

The Renewal of the Alliance, 1985-89

After becoming general secretary of the CPSU in March 1985, Mikhail S. Gorbachev organized a meeting of the East European leaders to renew the Warsaw Pact, which was due to expire that May. Few people doubted that the Warsaw Pact member states would renew the alliance. Some Western analysts speculated, however, that the Soviet Union might unilaterally dismantle its formal alliance structure to improve the Soviet image and to put pressure on the West to disband NATO. The Soviet Union could still have relied on the network of bilateral treaties in Eastern Europe, which predated the formation of the Warsaw Pact and had been renewed regularly. Combined with later status-of-forces agreements, these treaties assured the Soviet Union that the essence of its alliance system and buffer zone in Eastern Europe would remain intact, regardless of the Warsaw Pact's status. But despite their utility, the bilateral treaties could not fully substitute for the Warsaw Pact. Without a formal alliance, the Soviet Union would have to coordinate foreign policy and military integration with its East European allies through cumbersome bilateral arrangements. Although the Soviet and East European leaders debated the terms of the Warsaw Pact's renewal at their April 1985 meeting, they did not change the original 1955 treaty, nor the alliance's structure, in any way.

In the mid- to late 1980s, the future of the Warsaw Pact hinged on Gorbachev's developing policy toward Eastern Europe. At the Twenty-Seventh Party Congress in 1986, Gorbachev acknowledged that differences existed among the Soviet allies and that it would be unrealistic to expect them to have identical views on all issues. He demonstrated a greater sensitivity to East European concerns than previous Soviet leaders by briefing the NSWP leaders in their own capitals after the 1985 Geneva and 1986 Reykjavik superpower summit meetings. In 1987 the Warsaw Pact, under Soviet tutelage, adopted a defense-oriented military doctrine. And, following Gorbachev's announced unilateral reduction in the Soviet armed forces, the NSWP countries also announced unilateral military reductions during 1988 and 1989. In the late 1980s, however, mounting economic difficulties and the advanced age of trusted, long-time communist party leaders, like Gustáv Husák in Czechoslovakia, Todor Zhivkov in Bulgaria, and János Kádár in Hungary, intensified the danger of domestic turmoil and internal power struggles in the NSWP countries and threatened the alliance's cohesion.

* * *

The 1980s have witnessed a dramatic increase in the amount of secondary source material published about the Warsaw Pact. The works of Alex Alexiev, Andrzej Korbonski, and Condoleezza Rice, as well as those of various Soviet writers, provide a complete picture of the Soviet alliance system and the East European military establishments before the formation of the Warsaw Pact. William J. Lewis's *The Warsaw Pact* is a very useful reference work with considerable information on the establishment of the Warsaw Pact and the armies of its member states. The works of Malcolm Mackintosh, a long-time observer of the Warsaw Pact, cover the changes in the Warsaw Pact's organizational structure and functions through the years. Christopher D. Jones's *Soviet Influence in Eastern Europe* and subsequent articles provide a coherent interpretation of the Soviet Union's use of the Warsaw Pact to control its East European allies. In "The Warsaw Pact at 25," Dale R. Herspring examines intra-alliance politics in the PCC and East European attempts to reduce Soviet domination of the Warsaw Pact. Soviet military journals are the best source for insights into the East European role in Soviet military strategy. Daniel N. Nelson and Ivan Volgyes analyze East European reliability in the Warsaw Pact. Nelson takes a quantitative approach to this perennial topic. By contrast, Volgyes uses a historical and political framework to draw his conclusions on the reliability issue. The works of Richard C. Martin and Daniel S. Papp present thorough discussions of Soviet policies on arming and equipping the NSWP allies. (For further information and complete citations, see Bibliography.)

Bibliography

Chapter 1

Auty, Robert, and Dmitry Obolensky (eds.). *An Introduction to Russian History, 1: Companion to Russian Studies.* Cambridge: Cambridge University Press, 1976.

Avrich, Paul. *Russian Rebels, 1600–1800.* New York: Schocken, 1972.

Baron, Samuel Haskell. *Plekhanov: The Father of Russian Marxism.* Stanford: Stanford University Press, 1963.

Billington, James H. *The Icon and the Axe: An Interpretive History of Russian Culture.* New York: Knopf, 1966.

Blackwell, William L. *The Beginnings of Russian Industrialization, 1800–1860.* Princeton: Princeton University Press, 1968.

Blum, Jerome. *Lord and Peasant in Russia from the Ninth to the Nineteenth Century.* Princeton: Princeton University Press, 1961.

Cherniavsky, Michael. *Tsar and People: Studies in Russian Myths.* New York: Random House, 1969.

Chew, Allen F. *An Atlas of Russian History: Eleven Centuries of Changing Borders.* New Haven: Yale University Press, 1970.

Crummey, Robert O. *The Formation of Muscovy, 1304–1613.* London: Longman, 1987.

Curtiss, John Shelton. *The Russian Army under Nicholas I, 1825–1855.* Durham: Duke University Press, 1965.

De Madariagha, Isabel. *Russia in the Age of Catherine the Great.* New Haven: Yale University Press, 1981.

Dmytryshyn, Basil. *A History of Russia.* Englewood Cliffs, New Jersey: Prentice-Hall, 1977.

Emmons, Terrance. *The Russian Landed Gentry and the Peasant Emancipation of 1861.* London: Cambridge University Press, 1968.

Fedotov, Georgii Petrovich. *The Russian Religious Mind.* (2 vols.) Cambridge: Harvard University Press, 1946–66.

Fennell, John Lister Illingsworth. *Ivan the Great of Moscow.* London: Macmillan, 1961.

Florinsky, Michael T. *Russia: A History and Interpretation.* (2 vols.) New York: Macmillan, 1953.

Gershchenkron, Alexander. *Europe in the Russian Mirror: Four Lectures on Economic History.* London: Cambridge University Press, 1970.

Geyer, Dietrich. *Russian Imperialism: The Interaction of Domestic and Foreign Policy, 1860–1914.* (Trans., Bruce Little.) New Haven: Yale University Press, 1987.

Grekov, Boris Dmitreevich. *Kievan Rus.* (Trans., Y. Sdobnikov.) Moscow: Foreign Languages, 1959.

Gurko, Vladimir Iosifovich. *Features and Figures of the Past: Government and Opinion in the Reign of Nicholas II.* Stanford: Stanford University Press, 1939.

Hittle, J.M. *The Service City: State and Townsmen in Russia, 1600–1800.* Cambridge: Harvard University Press, 1979.

Hosking, Geoffrey A. *The Russian Constitutional Experiment: Government and Duma, 1907–1914.* Cambridge: Cambridge University Press, 1973.

Hrushevsky, Mykhailo. *A History of the Ukraine.* (Trans. and condensed, O.J. Fredericksen.) New Haven: Yale University Press, 1941.

Jelavich, Barbara Brightfield. *A Century of Russian Foreign Policy.* Philadelphia: Lippincott, 1964.

Keep, John L.H. *The Rise of Social Democracy in Russia.* Oxford: Clarendon, 1963.

Kliuchevsky, Vasily. *A Course in Russian History, 3: The Seventeenth Century.* (Trans., N. Duddington.) Chicago: University of Chicago Press, 1968.

————. *A Course in Russian History, 4: Peter the Great.* (Trans., Liliana Archibald.) New York: Knopf, 1959.

————. *Course of Russian History.* (5 vols.) (Trans., C.J. Hogarth.) New York: Dutton, 1911–31.

Kohut, Zenon E. *Russian Centralism and Ukrainian Autonomy: Imperial Absorption of the Hetmanate, 1760s–1830s.* Cambridge: Harvard Ukrainian Research Institute and Harvard University Press, 1988.

Lang, David Marshall. *A Modern History of Soviet Georgia.* New York: Grove Press, 1962.

Liashchenko, P.I. *A History of the National Economy of Russia to the 1917 Revolution.* (Trans., L.M. Herman.) New York: Macmillan, 1949. Reprint. New York: Octagon, 1970.

Lincoln, Bruce D. *Nicholas I: Emperor and Autocrat of all the Russians.* Bloomington: Indiana University Press, 1978.

MacKenzie, David, and Michael W. Curran. *A History of Russia and the Soviet Union.* Chicago: Dorsey Press, 1987.

Malia, Martin Edward. *Alexander Herzen and the Birth of Russian Socialism, 1812–1855.* Cambridge: Harvard University Press, 1961.

Malozemoff, Andrew. *Russian Far Eastern Policy, 1881–1904.* Berkeley: University of California Press, 1958. Reprint. New York: Octagon, 1977.

Masaryk, Thomaš Garrigue. *The Spirit of Russia: Studies in History, Literature, and Philosophy.* (3 vols.) (Trans., Eden and Cedar Paul.) New York: Macmillan, 1961–67.

Miliukov, Pavel Nikolaevich. *Outlines of Russian Culture.* (Ed., Michael Karpovich; trans., Eleanor Davis and Valentine Ughert.) Philadelphia: University of Pennsylvania Press, 1942.

Nichols, Robert L., and Theofanis George Stavrous (eds.). *Russian Orthodoxy under the Old Regime.* Minneapolis: University of Minnesota Press, 1978.

Norretranders, Bjarne. *The Shaping of Czardom under Ivan Groznnyi.* Copenhagen: 1964. Reprint. London: Variorum, 1971.

Oberländer, Edwin (ed.). *Russia Enters the Twentieth Century.* New York: Schocken, 1971.

Orlovsky, Daniel T. *The Limits of Reforms: The Ministry of Internal Affairs in Imperial Russia, 1807–1881.* Cambridge: Harvard University Press, 1981.

Pares, Bernard. *The Fall of the Russian Monarchy: A Study of Evidence.* New York: Knopf, 1939.

Pelenski, Jaroslav. *Russia and Kazan: Conquest and Imperial Ideology, 1438–1560s.* The Hague: Mouton, 1974.

Pierce, Richard A. *Russian Central Asia, 1867–1917: A Study in Colonial Rule.* Berkeley: University of California Press, 1960.

Pintner, Walter McKenzie, and Don Karl Rowney (eds.). *Russian Officialdom: The Bureaucratization of Russian Society from the Seventeenth to the Twentieth Century.* Chapel Hill: University of North Carolina Press, 1980.

Pipes, Richard. *Russia under the Old Regime.* New York: Scribner's, 1974.

Platonov, Sergei Fedorovich. *The Time of Troubles: A Historical Study of the Internal Crisis and Social Struggle in Sixteenth and Seventeenth Century Muscovy.* (Trans., J.T. Alexander.) Lawrence: University Press of Kansas, 1970.

Raeff, Marc. "History of Russia/Union of Soviet Socialist Republics." Page 358 in *Academic American Encyclopedia,* 16. Danbury, Connecticut: Grolier, 1986.

————. *Michael Speransky: Statesman of Imperial Russia, 1772–1839.* The Hague: Martinus Nijhoff, 1969.

————. *Russian Intellectual History: An Anthology.* New York: Humanities Press, 1978.

Riasanovsky, Nicholas. *A History of Russia.* (4th ed.) New York: Oxford University Press, 1984.

Rieber, Alfred J. *Merchants and Entrepreneurs in Imperial Russia.* Chapel Hill: University of North Carolina Press, 1982.

————. *Nicholas I and Official Nationality in Russia, 1825–1855.* Berkeley: University of California Press, 1959.

Rogger, Hans. *National Consciousness in Eighteenth-Century Russia.* Cambridge: Harvard University Press, 1960.

_____. *Russia in the Age of Modernization and Reform, 1881–1917.* London: Longman, 1987.

Rurad, C.A. *Fighting Words: Imperial Censorship and the Russian Press, 1804–1906.* Toronto: University of Toronto Press, 1982.

"Russia and the Soviet Union, History of." *New Encyclopaedia Britannica,* Macropaedia, 16. (15th ed.) Chicago: Encyclopaedia Britannica, 1975.

Schwartz, Solomon H. *The Russian Revolution of 1905: The Workers' Movement and the Formation of Bolshevism and Menshevism.* Chicago: University Press, 1967.

Seton-Watson, Hugh. *The Russian Empire, 1801–1917.* Oxford: Clarendon, 1967.

Smith, Clarence J. *The Russian Struggle for World Power, 1914–1917: A Study of Russian Foreign Policy During World War I.* New York: Philosophical Society, 1946.

Stites, Richard. *The Women's Liberation Movement in Russia: Feminism, Nihilism, and Bolshevism, 1890–1930.* Princeton: Princeton University Press, 1978.

Subtelny, Orest. *Ukraine: A History.* Toronto: University of Toronto Press, 1988.

Sumner, Benedict Humphrey. *Russia and the Balkans, 1870–1880.* Oxford: Clarendon, 1947.

Thaden, Edward C. *Conservative Nationalism in Nineteenth-Century Russia.* Seattle: University of Washington Press, 1964.

Thaden, Edward C. (ed.). *Russification of the Baltic Provinces and Finland, 1855–1914.* Princeton: Princeton University Press, 1981.

Treadgold, Donald W. *The West in Russia and China: Religious and Secular Thought in Modern Times.* (2 vols.) Cambridge: Cambridge University Press, 1973.

Venturi, Franco. *Roots of Revolution: A History of the Populist and Socialist Movements in Nineteenth-Century Russia.* (Trans., Francis Haskill.) New York: Knopf, 1960.

Vernadsky, George. *The Mongols and Russia.* New Haven: Yale University Press, 1954.

Von Laue, Theodore. *Sergei Witte and the Industrialization of Russia.* New York: Columbia University Press, 1963.

Walicki, Andrzej. *A History of Russian Thought from the Enlightenment to Marxism.* Stanford: Stanford University Press, 1979.

Wortman, Richard. *The Development of a Russian Legal Consciousness.* Chicago: University of Chicago Press, 1976.

Zaionchkovsky, Peter Andreevich. *The Russian Autocracy under Alexander III.* (Trans., David R. Jones.) Gulf Breeze, Florida: Academic International Press, 1976.

Zenkovsky, Serge A. *Pan-Turkism and Islam in Russia*. Cambridge: Harvard University Press, 1960.

Chapter 2

Antonov-Ovseyenko, Anton. *The Time of Stalin*. New York: Harper and Row, 1981.

Bialer, Seweryn. *Stalin's Successors: Leadership, Stability, and Change in the Soviet Union*. Cambridge: Cambridge University Press, 1980.

Black, Cyril E. (ed.). *The Transformation of Russian Society*. Cambridge: Harvard University Press, 1960.

Bradley, J.F.N. *Civil War in Russia, 1917–1920*. London: Batsford, 1975.

Brown, Archie, and Michael Kaser (eds.). *The Soviet Union since the Fall of Khrushchev*. New York: Macmillan, 1978.

Burant, Stephen R. "The Influence of Russian Tradition on the Political Style of the Soviet Elite," *Political Science Quarterly*, 102, No. 2, Summer 1987, 273–93.

Burdzhalov, E.N. *Russia's Second Revolution: The February 1917 Uprising in Petrograd*. Bloomington: Indiana University Press, 1987.

Chamberlin, William H. *The Russian Revolution, 1917–1921*. (2 vols.) New York: Macmillan, 1972.

Cohen, Stephen F. *Rethinking the Soviet Experience: Politics and History since 1917*. New York: Oxford University Press, 1985.

Conquest, Robert. *The Great Terror: Stalin's Purge of the Thirties*. New York: Macmillan, 1968.

_____. *Harvest of Sorrow*. New York: Oxford University Press, 1986.

Daniels, Robert V. *Red October: The Bolshevik Revolution of 1917*. Boston: Beacon Press, 1984.

_____. *Russia: The Roots of Confrontation*. Cambridge: Harvard University Press, 1985.

Fitzpatrick, Sheila. *The Russian Revolution*. New York: Oxford University Press, 1982.

Florinsky, Michael T. *The End of the Russian Empire*. New York: Fertig, 1973.

Gelman, Harry. *The Brezhnev Politburo and the Decline of Detente*. Ithaca: Cornell University Press, 1985.

Haimson, Leopold H. "The Parties and the State: The Evolution of Political Attitudes." Pages 110–44 in Cyril E. Black (ed.), *The Transformation of Russian Society*. Cambridge: Harvard University Press, 1960.

Hasegawa, Tsuyoshi. *The February Revolution: Petrograd, 1917.* Seattle: University of Washington Press, 1981.

Heller, Mikhail, and Aleksandr Nekrich. *Utopia in Power.* New York: Summit Books, 1986.

Hosking, Geoffrey A. *The First Socialist Society.* London: Fontana Press/Collins, 1985.

Khrushchev, Nikita S. *Khrushchev Remembers.* (Ed. and trans., Strobe Talbott.) Boston: Little, Brown, 1970.

_____. *Khrushchev Remembers: The Last Testament.* Boston: Little, Brown, 1974.

Lewin, Moshe. *Russian Peasants and Soviet Power.* Evanston: Northwestern University Press, 1968.

Linden, Carl A. *Khrushchev and the Soviet Leadership, 1957–1964.* Baltimore: Johns Hopkins Press, 1966.

MacKenzie, David, and Michael W. Curran. *A History of Russia and the Soviet Union.* Chicago: Dorsey Press, 1987.

Medvedev, Roy A. *Khrushchev.* Garden City, New York: Anchor Press, 1983.

_____. *Let History Judge.* New York: Knopf, 1971.

Pares, Bernard. *The Fall of the Russian Monarchy: A Study of Evidence.* New York: Knopf, 1939.

Pipes, Richard. *The Formation of the Soviet Union.* Cambridge: Harvard University Press, 1954.

Rabinowich, Alexander. *The Bolsheviks Come to Power.* New York: Norton, 1976.

Remington, Thomas. *Building Socialism in Bolshevik Russia.* Pittsburgh: University of Pittsburgh Press, 1984.

Riasanovsky, Nicholas. *A History of Russia.* (4th ed.) New York: Oxford University Press, 1984.

Schapiro, Leonard B. *The Communist Party of the Soviet Union.* New York: Vintage Books, 1960.

_____. *The Russian Revolutions of 1917.* New York: Basic Books, 1984.

Treadgold, Donald W. *Twentieth Century Russia.* Boulder, Colorado: Westview Press, 1987.

Tucker, Robert C. *Stalin as Revolutionary, 1879–1929.* New York: Norton, 1977.

Tucker, Robert C. (ed.). *Stalinism: Essays in Historical Interpretation.* New York: Norton, 1977.

Ulam, Adam B. *Expansion and Coexistence: Soviet Foreign Policy, 1917–1973.* (2d ed.) New York: Praeger, 1974.

_____. *A History of Soviet Russia.* New York: Praeger, 1976.

_____. *Stalin: The Man and His Era.* New York: Viking Press, 1973.

Chapter 3

Alexiev, Alexander R., and S. Enders Wimbush (eds.). *Ethnic Minorities in the Red Army: Asset or Liability?* (Rand Corporation Research Study.) Boulder, Colorado: Westview Press, 1988.

Bestuzhev-Lada, Igor'. "SSSR 2017," *Nedelia* [Moscow], Nos. 45–46, November 1987, 12–14.

Borisov, V.A., G.P. Kiseleva, Iu. M. Lukashuk, and A.B. Sinel'-nikov. *Vosproizvodstvo naseleniia i demograficheskaia politika v SSSR.* Moscow: Nauka, 1987.

"Chislennost' naseleniia, ego rost i razmeshchenie." Pages 7–18 in L.M. Volodarskii (ed.), *Naselenie SSSR.* Moscow: Politizdat, 1983.

Cole, J.P. *Geography of the Soviet Union.* Cambridge: Cambridge University Press, 1984.

Dienes, Leslie. *Soviet Asia: Economic Development and National Policy Choices.* Boulder, Colorado: Westview Press, 1987.

Feshbach, Murray. *The Soviet Population Policy Debate: Actors and Issues.* (Project Air Force, No. N–2472–AF.) Santa Monica, California: Rand, 1986.

_____. "Trends in the Soviet Muslim Population—Demographic Aspects." Pages 297–322 in United States Congress, 97th, 2d Session, Joint Economic Committee, *Soviet Economy in the 1980's: Problems and Prospects.* Washington: GPO, 1983.

Gel'fand, Vladimir. "Skol'ko nas? Kakie my?" *Nedelia* [Moscow], No. 37, 1987, 21.

Gosudarstvennyi komitet po statistike. *Narodnoe khoziaistvo SSSR v 1987 g.* Moscow: Finansy i statistika, 1988.

_____. *Narodnoe khoziaistvo SSSR za 70 let.* Moscow: Finansy i statistika, 1987.

_____. *Naselenie SSSR, 1987: Statisticheskii sbornik.* Moscow: Finansy i statistika, 1988.

Gur'ev, V.I. "436 stranits o nas," *Nedelia* [Moscow], No. 44, November 1988, 12–13.

Hooson, David. *The Soviet Union: People and Regions.* London: University of London Press, 1966.

Howe, G. Melvyn (ed.). *The Soviet Union: A Geographical Survey.* (World's Landscapes Series.) Plymouth: Macdonald and Evans, 1983.

Izvestiia [Moscow], April 29, 1989, 1–2.

Khorev, B.S. "On Basic Directions of Environmental Policy in the USSR," *Soviet Geography,* No. 9, September 1987.

Kingkade, W. Ward. "Demographic Trends in the Soviet Union." Pages 166–86 in United States Congress, 100th, 1st Session, Joint

Economic Committee, *Gorbachev's Economic Plans.* (2 vols.) Washington: GPO, 1987.

_____. "Recent and Prospective Population Growth in the U.S.S.R., 1979–2025," *Soviet Geography,* No. 4, April 1988, 394–412.

Kotlyakov, V.M. "Geography and Ecological Problems," *Soviet Geography,* No. 6, June 1988, 569–76.

Kravchenko, M. "Kakaia sem'ia nam nuzhna," *Nedelia* [Moscow], No. 47, November 1987, 17–18.

Kvasha, A.Ia. *Demograficheskaia politika v SSSR.* Moscow: Finansy i statistika.

Lydolph, Paul E. *Geography of the U.S.S.R.* Elkhart Lake, Wisconsin: Misty Valley, 1979.

Medish, Vadim. *The Soviet Union.* (3d ed.) Englewood Cliffs, New Jersey: Prentice-Hall, 1987.

Micklin, Philip. "The Status of the Soviet Union's North-South Water Transfer Projects Before Their Abandonment in 1985–86," *Soviet Geography,* No. 5, May 1986, 287–329.

"Naselenie SSSR," *Ekonomicheskaia gazeta* [Moscow], No. 43, October 1986, 6–7.

"Naselenie SSSR," *Vestnik statistiki* [Moscow], No. 12, December 1987, 44–53.

"O predvaritel'nykh itogakh vsesoiuznoi perepisi naseleniia 1989 goda," *Sovetskaia Rossiia* [Moscow], No. 99, April 29, 1989, 1–2.

"Osnovnyye itogi vyborochnogo sotsial'no-demograficheskogo obsledovaniia naseleniia SSSR 1985 goda," *Vestnik statistiki,* No. 6, June 1986, 53–55.

Parker, William Henry. *The Soviet Union.* (World's Landscapes Series.) New York: Longman Group, 1983.

Petrunia, V. "Skol'ko nas, kakie my?" *Sovetskaia Litva* [Vilnius], No. 7, January 9, 1988, 3.

Pryde, Philip. "The Future Environmental Agenda of the USSR," *Soviet Geography,* No. 6, June 1988, 555–67.

Rapawy, Stephen, and Godfrey Baldwin. "Demographic Trends in the Soviet Union: 1950–2000." Pages 265–96 in United States Congress, 97th, 2d Session, Joint Economic Committee, *Soviet Economy in the 1980's: Problems and Prospects.* Washington: GPO, 1983.

Riabushkin, T.V. (ed.). *Sovetskaia demografiia za 70 let.* Moscow: Nauka, 1987.

Rom, V. (ed.). *Ekonomicheskaia i sotsial'naia geografiia SSSR,* 1. Moscow: Prosveshchenie, 1986.

Rybakovskii, L.L. *Migratsiia naseleniia: prognozy, faktory, politika.* Moscow: Nauka, 1987.

Shabad, Theodore. "Geographic Aspects of the New Soviet Five-Year Plan, 1986-90," *Soviet Geography*, 27, No. 1, January 1986, 1-16.

_____. "Population Trends of Soviet Cities, 1970-1984," *Soviet Geography*, No. 2, February 1985.

Shabad, Theodore (panel chairman). "Panel on the Soviet Union in the Year 2000," *Soviet Geography*, No. 6, June 1987, 388-408.

Solov'ev, E. "Emigratsiia: novaia volna?" *Nedelia* [Moscow], No. 22, May 29-June 4, 1989, 12.

Tochenov, V.V. (ed.). *Atlas SSSR*. Moscow: GUGK, 1983.

Topilin, A. "Osnovnye napravleniia mezhrespublikanskoi migratsii naseleniia," *Planovoe khoziaistvo* [Moscow], No. 1, January 1988, 86-91.

Trehub, Aaron. "New Figures on Infant Mortality in the USSR," Radio Free Europe/Radio Liberty, *Radio Liberty Research Bulletin* [Munich], No. 438, October 29, 1987, 1-3.

United States. Central Intelligence Agency. *USSR Energy Atlas*. Washington: GPO, 1985.

_____. Congress. 97th, 2d Session. Joint Economic Committee. *Soviet Economy in the 1980's: Problems and Prospects*. Washington: GPO, 1983.

_____. Congress. 100th, 1st Session. Joint Economic Committee. *Gorbachev's Economic Plans*. (2 vols.) Washington: GPO, 1987.

Vasil'eva, E.K., I.I. Yeliseeva, O.N. Kashira, and V.I. Laptev. *Dinamika naseleniia SSSR 1960-1980 godov*. Moscow: Finansy i statistika, 1985.

Vedeneeva, I. "Shag poslednii," *Ogonek* [Moscow], No. 3, January 1989, 14-17.

Vishnevskii, A.G. (ed.). *Brachnost', rozhdaemost', smertnost' v Rossii i v SSSR*. Moscow: Statistika, 1977.

Yelizarov, Valerii. "150,000,000," *Nedelia* [Moscow], No. 37, 1987, 20.

Zvidrin'sh, P.P., and M.A. Zvidrinia. *Naselenie i ekonomika*. (Populiarnaia demografiia.) Moscow: Mysl', 1987.

Chapter 4

"Activists Call for 'German Autonomy'," *Pravda* [Moscow], April 2, 1989. Foreign Broadcast Information Service, *Daily Report: Soviet Union*. (FBIS-SOV-89-063.) April 4, 1989, 55.

Akiner, Shirin. *Islamic Peoples of the Soviet Union*. (2d ed.) London: KPI, 1986.

Alexiev, Alexander R. *Dissent and Nationalism in the Soviet Baltic.* Santa Monica, California: Rand, 1983.

Alexiev, Alexander R., and S. Enders Wimbush. *The Ethnic Factor in the Soviet Armed Forces.* Santa Monica, California: Rand, 1983.

Allworth, Edward (ed.). *Nationality Group Survival in Multi-Ethnic States: Shifting Support Patterns in the Soviet Baltic Region.* New York: Praeger, 1977.

_____. *Soviet Nationality Problems.* New York: Columbia University Press, 1971.

_____. *Tatars of the Crimea: Their Struggle for Survival.* Durham: Duke University Press, 1988.

Altshuler, Mordechai. *Soviet Jewry since the Second World War: Population and Social Structure.* New York: Greenwood Press, 1987.

Altstadt, Audrey L. "Nagorno-Karabakh: 'Apple of Discord' in the Azerbaydzhan SSR," *Central Asian Survey* [Oxford], 7, No. 4, 1988, 63–78.

Anderson, John. *Religion and the Soviet State: A Report on Religious Repression in the USSR on the Occasion of the Christian Millennium.* Washington: Puebla Institute, 1988.

Antic, Oxana. "First Publication of Official Statistics on Churches in the USSR," Radio Free Europe/Radio Liberty, *Radio Liberty Research Bulletin* [Munich], January, 11, 1988, 1–5.

_____. "Kharchev Replaced as Chairman of Council for Religious Affairs," Radio Free Europe/Radio Liberty, *Report on the USSR* [Munich], 1, No. 31, August 4, 1989, 1–6.

_____. "No Respite for Pentecostals in Chuguevka," Radio Free Europe/Radio Liberty, *Radio Liberty Research Bulletin* [Munich], January 18, 1988, 1–4.

_____. "Policy Towards Unofficial Religious Groups under Gorbachev," Radio Free Europe/Radio Liberty, *Radio Liberty Research Bulletin* [Munich], March 31, 1988, 1–8.

_____. "Religion in Lithuania during 1987," Radio Free Europe/ Radio Liberty, *Radio Liberty Research Bulletin* [Munich], August 25, 1988, 1–5.

_____. "Religious Policy under Gorbachev," Radio Free Europe/Radio Liberty, *Radio Liberty Research Bulletin* [Munich], September 28, 1987, 1–5.

_____. "Soviet Law and the Religious Upbringing of Children," Radio Free Europe/Radio Liberty, *Radio Liberty Research Bulletin* [Munich], September 19, 1986, 1–4.

"An Appeal for Religious in the Soviet Union," *This World,* Fall 1988, 50–65.

Aron, Leon. "Gorbachev's Mounting Nationalities Crisis," *Heritage Foundation Backgrounder,* No. 695, March 1989, 1–12.

Azrael, Jeremy R. (ed.). *Soviet Nationality Policies and Practices.* New York: Praeger, 1978.

Bagramov, Eduard. *One Hundred Nationalities: One People.* Moscow: Progress, 1982.

Balzer, Marjorie M. "Ethnicity Without Power: The Siberian Khauty in Soviet Society," *Slavic Review,* 42, No. 4, Winter 1983, 633–48.

Bennigsen, Alexandre. "Marxism or Pan-Islamism: Russian Bolsheviks and Tatar National Communists at the Beginning of the Civil War, July 1918," *Central Asian Survey* [Oxford], 6, No. 2, 1987, 55–66.

_____. "Unrest in the World of Soviet Islam," *Third World Quarterly* [London], 10, April 1988, 770–86.

Bennigsen, Alexandre, and S. Enders Wimbush. *Muslims of the Soviet Empire: The Guide.* Bloomington: Indiana University Press, 1986.

_____. *Mystics and Commissars: Sufism in the Soviet Union.* Berkeley: University of California Press, 1985.

Besançon, Alain. "The Nationalities Issue in the USSR," *Survey* [London], 30, June 1989, 113–30.

Bialer, Seweryn (ed.). *Politics, Society, and Nationality: Inside Gorbachev's Russia.* Boulder, Colorado: Westview Press, 1988.

Bilinsky, Yaroslaw. "Nationality Policy in Gorbachev's First Year," *Orbis,* 30, Summer 1986, 331–42.

Bilocerkowycz, Jaroslaw. *Soviet Ukrainian Dissent: A Study of Political Alienation.* Boulder, Colorado: Westview Press, 1988.

Birch, Julian. "Border Disputes and Disputed Borders in the Soviet Federal System," *Nationalities Papers,* 15, Spring 1987, 43–70.

_____. "The 1986 Party Program and the National Minorities in the USSR," *Nationalities Papers,* 15, Fall 1987, 147–57.

Bociurkiw, Bohdan R. "Religion and Nationalism in the Contemporary Ukraine." Pages 81–93 in George W. Simmonds (ed.), *Nationalism in the USSR and Eastern Europe.* Detroit: Detroit University Press, 1977.

_____. "The Ukrainian Autocephalous Orthodox Church." Pages 309–19 in Pedro Ramet (ed.), *Eastern Christianity and Politics in the Twentieth Century.* Durham: Duke University Press, 1988.

_____. *Ukrainian Churches under Soviet Rule: Two Case Studies.* (Millennium of Christianity in Rus'-Ukraine Series.) Cambridge: Harvard University Ukrainian Studies Fund, 1984.

Bohr, Annette. "A Belated Step in the Repatriation of the Chechen and Ingush," Radio Free Europe/Radio Liberty, *Radio Liberty Research Bulletin* [Munich], April 19, 1988, 1–5.

_____. "Breaking the Silence: The Mass Deportation of Koreans under Stalin," Radio Free Europe/Radio Liberty, *Radio Liberty Research Bulletin* [Munich], September 1, 1988, 1–4.

Brown, Bess. "Religion in Tajikistan: A Tough Nut for the Ideologists," Radio Free Europe/Radio Liberty, *Radio Liberty Research Bulletin* [Munich], January 13, 1988, 1–7.

————. "Tajik Survey Reveals Extent of Religious Belief," Radio Free Europe/Radio Liberty, *Radio Liberty Research Bulletin* [Munich], March 31, 1988, 1–3.

Bruchis, Michael. "The Language Policy of the Soviet Communist Party: Comments and Observations," *East European Quarterly,* 21, June 1987, 231–57.

Bungs, Dzintra. "The Deportation of Balts to the USSR: Still a Touchy Subject," Radio Free Europe/Radio Liberty, *Radio Free Europe Research* [Munich], 13, No. 23, June 10, 1988, 1–6.

Burg, Steven L. "The Soviet Union's Nationalities Question," *Current History,* 88, No. 540, October 1989, 341–44, 359–62.

"Chislennost' naseleniia, ego rost i razmeshchenie." Pages 7–18 in L.M. Volodarskii (ed.), *Naselenie SSSR.* Moscow: Politizdat, 1983.

Clem, Ralph S. "Recent Demographic Trends among Soviet Nationalities and Their Implications." Pages 37–44 in George W. Simmonds (ed.), *Nationalism in the USSR and Eastern Europe.* Detroit: Detroit University Press, 1977.

————. *The Soviet West: Interplay Between Nationality and Social Organization.* (Studies in International Politics and Government Series.) New York: Praeger, 1975.

Conquest, Robert (ed.). *The Last Empire: Nationality and the Soviet Future.* Stanford, California: Hoover Institution Press, 1986.

————. *Soviet Nationalities Policy in Practice.* London: Bodley Head, 1967.

Critchlow, James. "Islam and Nationalism in Soviet Central Asia." Pages 104–20 in Pedro Ramet (ed.), *Religion and Nationalism in Soviet and East European Politics.* Durham: Duke Press Policy Studies, 1984.

————. "Nationalism in Uzbekistan in the Brezhnev Era." Pages 306–15 in George W. Simmonds (ed.), *Nationalism in the USSR and Eastern Europe.* Detroit: Detroit University Press, 1977.

Dadrian, Vahakn N. "Nationalism in Soviet Armenia: A Case Study of Ethnocentrism." Pages 202–58 in George W. Simmonds (ed.), *Nationalism in the USSR and Eastern Europe.* Detroit: Detroit University Press, 1977.

de Lageard, Helene A. "The Revolt of the Basmachi According to Red Army Journals (1920–1922)," *Central Asian Survey* [Oxford], 6, No. 3, 1987, 1–35.

D'Encansse, Helene C. *Islam and the Russian Empire: Reform and Revolution in Central Asia.* Berkeley: University of California Press, 1966.

Dreifelds, Juris. "Latvian National Demands and Group Consciousness since 1959." Pages 136–56 in George W. Simmonds (ed.), *Nationalism in the USSR and Eastern Europe*. Detroit: Detroit University Press, 1977.

Duncan, Peter J. "The Fate of Russian Nationalism: the Samizdat Journal *Veche* Revisited," *Religion in Communist Lands* [Chislehurst, United Kingdom], 16, Spring 1988, 36–53.

Dunlop, John B. "The Contemporary Russian Nationalist Spectrum," Radio Free Europe/Radio Liberty, *Radio Liberty Research Bulletin* [Munich], Special Edition, December 19, 1988, 1–10.

_____. *The Faces of Contemporary Russian Nationalism*. Princeton: Princeton University Press, 1983.

Dzyuba, Ivan. *Internationalism or Russification? A Study in the Soviet Nationalities Problem*. New York: Monad Press, 1974.

Ellis, Jane. "New Soviet Thinking on Religion," *Religion in Communist Lands* [Chislehurst, United Kingdom], 17, Summer 1989, 100–11.

_____. *The Russian Orthodox Church: A Contemporary History*. Bloomington: Indiana University Press, 1986.

"The Events in Kazakhstan: An Eyewitness Report," *Central Asian Survey* [Oxford], 6, No. 3, 1987, 73–75.

Fedoseyev, P.N. *Leninism and the National Question*. Moscow: Progress, 1977.

Fraser, Glenda. "Basmachi—I," *Central Asian Survey* [Oxford], 6, No. 1, 1987, 1–73.

_____. "Basmachi—II," *Central Asian Survey* [Oxford], 6, No. 2, 1987, 7–42.

Germroth, David S. "The Soviet Republics and Nationalism," *Global Affairs*, 4, Spring 1989, 140–57.

Gililov, S. *The Nationalities Question: Lenin's Approach (Theory and Practice in the USSR)*. Moscow: Progress, 1983.

Girnius, Kestutis K. "Nationalism and the Catholic Church in Lithuania." Pages 82–103 in Pedro Ramet (ed.), *Religion and Nationalism in Soviet and East European Politics*. Durham: Duke Press Policy Studies, 1984.

Gitelman, Zvi Y. "The Jewish Question in the USSR since 1964." Pages 324–34 in George W. Simmonds (ed.), *Nationalism in the USSR and Eastern Europe*. Detroit: Detroit University Press, 1977.

Goldhagen, Erich (ed.). *Ethnic Minorities in the Soviet Union*. New York: Praeger, 1968.

Goldman, Marshall I. "The USSR's New Class Struggle," *World Monitor*, 2, February 1989, 46–50.

Gosudarstvennyi komitet po statistike. *Natsionalnyi sostav naseleniia, Chast' II*. Moscow: Finansy i statistika, 1989.

Hammer, Darrell P. "'Glasnost' and 'The Russian Idea'," Radio Free Europe/Radio Liberty, *Radio Liberty Research Bulletin* [Munich], Special Edition, December 19, 1988, 11–24.

Hegaard, Steven E. "Nationalism in Azerbaydzhan in the Era of Brezhnev." Pages 188–99 in George W. Simmonds (ed.), *Nationalism in the USSR and Eastern Europe.* Detroit: Detroit University Press, 1977.

Hetmanek, Allen. "National Renascence in Soviet Kazakhstan: The Brezhnev Era." Pages 295–305 in George W. Simmonds (ed.), *Nationalism in the USSR and Eastern Europe.* Detroit: Detroit University Press, 1977.

Hill, Kent R. *The Puzzle of the Soviet Church: An Inside Look at Christianity and Glasnost.* Portland, Oregon: Multnomah Press, 1989.

Hvat, Ivan. "The Ukrainian Catholic Church, the Vatican, and the Soviet Union During the Pontificate of Pope John Paul II," *Religion in Communist Lands* [Chislehurst, United Kingdom], 11, No. 3, Winter 1983, 264–80.

Isajiw, Wsewolod, W. "Social Bases of Change in the Ukraine since 1964." Pages 58–62 in George W. Simmonds (ed.), *Nationalism in the USSR and Eastern Europe.* Detroit: Detroit University Press, 1977.

Karklins, Rasma. *Ethnic Relations in the USSR: The Perspective from Below.* Boston: Allen and Unwin, 1986.

Katz, Zev (ed.). *Handbook of Major Soviet Nationalities.* New York: Free Press, 1975.

Kingkade, W. Ward. "USSR: Estimates and Projections of the Population by Major Nationality, 1979 to 2050." (Center for International Research Staff Paper No. 41.) Washington: Department of the Interior, Bureau of the Census, Center for International Research, May 1988.

Kipel, Vitaut. "Some Demographic and Industrial Aspects of Soviet Belorussia during 1965–1975." Pages 96–104 in George W. Simmonds (ed.), *Nationalism in the USSR and Eastern Europe.* Detroit: Detroit University Press, 1977.

Klier, John Doyle. *Russia Gathers Her Jews: The Origins of the 'Jewish Question' in Russia, 1772–1825.* Dekalb: Northern Illinois University Press, 1986.

Koropeckyj, I.S. "Soviet Statistics on Ukraine: Selective Omissions," *Problems of Communism,* May–August 1988, 95–100.

Kreindler, Isabelle. *The Mordvinians: A Doomed Soviet Nationality?* (Soviet and East European Research Centre Series.) Jerusalem: Soviet and East European Research Centre, 1984.

Kudryavtsev, V.N. (ed.). *The Soviet Constitution: A Dictionary.* Moscow: Progress, 1986.

Kuzio, Taras. "Nationalist Ferment in Western Ukraine," *Soviet Analyst* [Richmond, Surrey, United Kingdom], 17, No. 15, August 3, 1988, 4–5.

_____. "Nationalist Riots in Kazakhstan," *Central Asian Survey* [Oxford], 7, No. 4, 1988, 79–100.

Landsbergis, Algirdas. "The Organic and the Synthetic: A Dialectical Dance." Pages 181–86 in George W. Simmonds (ed.), *Nationalism in the USSR and Eastern Europe.* Detroit: Detroit University Press, 1977.

Lapidus, Gail Warshosky. "Gorbachev's Nationalities Problem," *Foreign Affairs,* 68, No. 4, Fall 1989, 92–108.

Lenin, Vladimir I. *Questions of National Policy and Proletarian Internationalism.* Moscow: Progress, 1970.

Levin, Nora. *The Jews in the Soviet Union since 1917.* (2 vols.) New York: New York University Press, 1988.

Lubin, Nancy. *Labour and Nationality in Soviet Central Asia.* Princeton: Princeton University Press, 1984.

Mandel, William M. *Soviet But Not Russian: The 'Other' Peoples of the Soviet Union.* Palo Alto, California: Ramparts Press, 1984.

Markus, Vasyl. "Religion and Nationalism in Ukraine." Pages 59–80 in Pedro Ramet (ed.), *Religion and Nationalism in Soviet and East European Politics.* Durham: Duke Press Policy Studies, 1984.

Meerson, Michael A. "The Doctrinal Foundations of Orthodoxy." Pages 20–36 in Pedro Ramet (ed.), *Eastern Christianity and Politics in the Twentieth Century.* Durham: Duke University Press, 1988.

Mihalisko, Kathleen. "Belorussian Activists Charged with Violating Law of Assembly," Radio Free Europe/Radio Liberty, *Radio Liberty Research Bulletin* [Munich], September 28, 1988, 1–3.

_____. "Historian Outlines Revisionist View of Belorussia's Past," Radio Free Europe/Radio Liberty, *Radio Liberty Research Bulletin* [Munich], September 28, 1988, 1–5.

_____. "A Profile of Informal Patriotic Youth Groups in Belorussia," Radio Free Europe/Radio Liberty, *Radio Liberty Research Bulletin* [Munich], July 27, 1988, 1–6.

Miller, Jack. *Jews in Soviet Culture.* London: Institute of Jewish Affairs, 1984.

Miller, Marshall L. "Between Moscow and Mecca: Ethnic Minorities in the Soviet Union," *Armed Forces Journal International,* 124, March 1987, 26–27.

Motyl, Alexander J. "The Sobering of Gorbachev: Nationality, Restructuring, and the West." Pages 149–73 in Seweryn Bialer (ed.), *Politics, Society, and Nationality: Inside Gorbachev's Russia.* Boulder, Colorado: Westview Press, 1988.

Mouradian, Claire Seda. "The Armenian Apostolic Church." Pages 353-74 in Pedro Ramet (ed.), *Eastern Christianity and Politics in the Twentieth Century.* Durham: Duke University Press, 1988.

Murat, Aman B., and George W. Simmonds. "Nationalism in Turkmenistan since 1964." Pages 316-21 in George W. Simmonds (ed.), *Nationalism in the USSR and Eastern Europe.* Detroit: Detroit University Press, 1977.

Nahaylo, Bohdan. "Concern Voiced about Six Million Ukrainians Condemned to 'Denationalization'," Radio Free Europe/Radio Liberty, *Radio Liberty Research Bulletin* [Munich], February 27, 1988, 1-7.

_____. "Four Decades of Resistance: An Interview with Danylo Shumuk," Radio Free Europe/Radio Liberty, *Radio Liberty Research Bulletin* [Munich], August 25, 1987, 1-25.

_____. "Independent Groups in the Ukraine under Attack," Radio Free Europe/Radio Liberty, *Radio Liberty Research Bulletin* [Munich], September 28, 1988, 1-5.

_____. "Initiative Group for Restoration of Ukrainian Autocephalous Orthodox Church Founded," Radio Free Europe/Radio Liberty, *Report on the USSR* [Munich], 1, No. 9, March 3, 1989, 24-27.

_____. "National Ferment in Moldavia," Radio Free Europe/Radio Liberty, *Radio Liberty Research Bulletin* [Munich], January 24, 1988, 1-10.

_____. "Political Demonstration in Minsk Attests to Belorussian National Assertiveness," Radio Free Europe/Radio Liberty, *Radio Liberty Research Bulletin* [Munich], November 26, 1987, 1-5.

_____. "Representatives of Non-Russian National Movements Establish Coordinating Committee," Radio Free Europe/Radio Liberty, *Radio Liberty Research Bulletin* [Munich], June 22, 1988, 1-7.

_____. "Ukrainian Writers' Plenum Reveals Growing Frustration and Radicalization," Radio Free Europe/Radio Liberty, *Radio Liberty Research Bulletin* [Munich], August 10, 1988, 1-8.

Nahaylo, Bohdan, and C.J. Peters. *The Ukrainians and Georgians.* London: Minority Rights Group, 1981.

Newman, Sally. "Soviet Scholars Advocate Fostering Cultures of National Minorities," Radio Free Europe/Radio Liberty, *Radio Liberty Research Bulletin* [Munich], June 29, 1988, 1-3.

Nichol, James P. "Political Selection and Life History Types in the Central Committee of the Communist Party of the Soviet Union." (Ph.D. dissertation, University of Washington, March 1982.) Ann Arbor: University Microfilms International, 1982.

Nichols, Mary F. *Problems and Prospects of Soviet Nationalities.* Meerut: Anu Prakashan, 1982.

Novak, Michael. "Toward an Open Soviet Union," *Freedom at Issue,* No. 96, May–June 1987, 9–12.

Olcott, Martha Brill. *The Kazakhs.* Stanford, California: Hoover Institution Press, 1987.

_____. "Yuri Andropov and the 'National Question'," *Soviet Studies,* 37, No. 1, January 1985, 103–17.

Orr, Michael. "Soviet Armed Forces and the Nationalities Problem," *Soviet Analyst* [Howe, Sussex, United Kingdom], 18, April 5, 1989, 5–7.

Parming, Tönu. "Nationalism in Soviet Estonia since 1964." Pages 116–34 in George W. Simmonds (ed.), *Nationalism in the USSR and Eastern Europe.* Detroit: Detroit University Press, 1977.

Parsons, Howard L. *Christianity Today in the USSR.* New York: International, 1987.

Penikis, Janis J. "Latvian Nationalism: Preface to a Dissenting View." Pages 157–61 in George W. Simmonds (ed.), *Nationalism in the USSR and Eastern Europe.* Detroit: Detroit University Press, 1977.

Perfecky, George A. "The Status of the Ukrainian Language in the Ukrainian SSR," *East European Quarterly,* 21, No. 2, June 1987, 207–30.

Peters, C.J. "The Georgian Orthodox Church." Pages 286–308 in Pedro Ramet (ed.), *Eastern Christianity and Politics in the Twentieth Century.* Durham: Duke University Press, 1988.

Pinkus, Benjamin. *The Jews of the Soviet Union: The History of a National Minority.* Cambridge: Cambridge University Press, 1988.

Pirzada, Shaziae. "Federalism in the USSR: The Central Asian Context," *Strategic Studies* [Islamabad], 10, Winter 1987, 67–94.

Popp, Gary E., and Syed T. Anwar. "From Perestroika to Ethnic Nationalism," *International Perspectives* [Ottawa], 18, March–April 1989, 21–23.

Pospielovsky, Dmitry V. *A History of Marxist-Leninist Atheism and Soviet Antireligious Policies.* (History of Soviet Atheism in Theory and Practice, and the Believer Series.) New York: St. Martin's Press, 1987.

_____. "The Neo-Slavophile Trend and Its Relation to the Contemporary Religious Revival in the USSR." Pages 41–58 in Pedro Ramet (ed.), *Religion and Nationalism in Soviet and East European Politics.* Durham: Duke Press Policy Studies, 1984.

_____. *Soviet Antireligious Campaigns and Persecutions,* 2. (History of Soviet Atheism in Theory and Practice, and the Believer Series.) New York: St. Martin's Press, 1988.

Preobrazhensky, Alexander (ed.). *The Russian Orthodox Church: 10th to 20th Centuries.* Moscow: Progress, 1988.

Pushkarev, Sergei, Vladimir Rusak, and Gleb Yakunin. *Christianity and Government in Russia and the Soviet Union: Reflections on the Millennium.* (Change in Contemporary Soviet Society Series.) Boulder, Colorado: Westview Press, 1989.

Pyle, Emily. "Calls for Legalization of Ukrainian Catholic Church," Radio Free Europe/Radio Liberty, *Report on the USSR* [Munich], 1, No. 29, July 21, 1988, 24-27.

Rakowska-Harmstone, Teresa. "Nationalism in Soviet Central Asia since 1964." Pages 272-94 in George W. Simmonds (ed.), *Nationalism in the USSR and Eastern Europe.* Detroit: Detroit University Press, 1977.

―――. "The Study of Ethnic Politics in the USSR." Pages 20-36 in George W. Simmonds (ed.), *Nationalism in the USSR and Eastern Europe.* Detroit: Detroit University Press, 1977.

Ramet, Pedro. "Autocephaly and National Identity in Church-State Relations in Eastern Christianity: An Introduction." Pages 3-19 in Pedro Ramet (ed.), *Eastern Christianity and Politics in the Twentieth Century.* Durham: Duke University Press, 1988.

―――. *Cross and Commissar: The Politics of Religion in Eastern Europe and the USSR.* Bloomington: Indiana University Press, 1987.

―――. "The Interplay of Religious Policy and Nationalities Policy in the Soviet Union and Eastern Europe." Pages 3-30 in Pedro Ramet (ed.), *Religion and Nationalism in Soviet and East European Politics.* Durham: Duke Press Policy Studies, 1984.

Ramet, Pedro (ed.). *Eastern Christianity and Politics in the Twentieth Century.* Durham: Duke University Press, 1988.

―――. *Religion and Nationalism in Soviet and East European Politics.* Durham: Duke Press Policy Studies, 1984.

Rapawy, Stephen. "Census Data on Nationality Composition and Language Characteristics of the Soviet Population: 1959, 1970, and 1979." (Research paper.) Washington: Department of the Interior, Bureau of the Census, Foreign Demographic Analysis Division, January 1982.

Raun, Toivo U. *Estonia and the Estonians.* Stanford, California: Hoover Institution Press, 1987.

Remeikis, Thomas. "Political Developments in Lithuania During the Brezhnev Era." Pages 164-80 in George W. Simmonds (ed.), *Nationalism in the USSR and Eastern Europe.* Detroit: Detroit University Press, 1977.

Remnick, David. "Key Soviet Official Urges New Rights for Religious Believers," *Washington Post,* December 23, 1988, A12.

Rorlich, Azade-Ayse. *The Volga Tatars: A Profile in National Resilience.* Stanford, California: Hoover Institution Press, 1986.

Rozitis, Ojars. "The Rise of Latvian Nationalism," *Swiss Review of World Affairs* [Zurich], 38, February 1989, 24–26.

Rubenstein, Joshua. *Soviet Dissidents: Their Struggle for Human Rights.* (2d ed.) Boston: Beacon Press, 1985.

Rywkin, Michael. "Islam and the New Soviet Man: 70 Years of Evolution," *Central Asian Survey* [Oxford], 6, No. 4, 1987, 23–32.

Rywkin, Michael (ed.). *Russian Colonial Expansion to 1917.* London: Mansell, 1988.

Sakwa, Richard. *Soviet Politics: An Introduction.* London: Routledge, 1989.

Sallnow, John. "Belorussia: The Demographic Transition and the Settlement Network in the 1980s," *Soviet Geography,* 28, January 1987, 25–33.

Sawczuk, Konstantyn. "Resistance Against Russification in the Ukraine since 1964: A Profile of Three Ukrainians in Opposition." Pages 63–71 in George W. Simmonds (ed.), *Nationalism in the USSR and Eastern Europe.* Detroit: Detroit University Press, 1977.

Sheehy, Ann. "Interethnic Relations in the Soviet Armed Forces," Radio Free Europe/Radio Liberty, *Radio Liberty Research Bulletin* [Munich], June 29, 1988, 1–5.

_____. "Kazakh Minister Defends Territorial Integrity of Kazakhstan," Radio Free Europe/Radio Liberty, *Radio Liberty Research Bulletin* [Munich], June 29, 1988, 1–3.

_____. "Migration to RSFSR and Baltic Republics Continues," Radio Free Europe/Radio Liberty, *Radio Liberty Research Bulletin* [Munich], November 30, 1987, 1–9.

_____. "Moldavians Gain Some Language Concessions," Radio Free Europe/Radio Liberty, *Radio Liberty Research Bulletin* [Munich], August 27, 1987, 1–5.

Shtromas, Alex. "Soviet Occupation of the Baltic States and Their Incorporation into the USSR: Political and Legal Aspects," *East European Quarterly,* 19, September 1985, 289–304.

Sieff, Martin, and Boris Shragin. "Will the Soviet Union Survive until 1994?," *National Review,* 41, April 7, 1989, 24, 26–28, 30.

Simmonds, George W. (ed.). *Nationalism in the USSR and Eastern Europe.* Detroit: Detroit University Press, 1977.

Sinyawsky, Andrei. "Russian Nationalism," Radio Free Europe/Radio Liberty, *Radio Liberty Research Bulletin* [Munich], Special Edition, December 19, 1988, 25–36.

Solchanyk, Roman. "Belorussian Informal Groups Criticized for Nationalism," Radio Free Europe/Radio Liberty, *Radio Liberty Research Bulletin* [Munich], November 16, 1988, 1–4.

_____. "Belorussian Ministry of Education Accused of Sabotaging the Native Language," Radio Free Europe/Radio Liberty, *Radio Liberty Research Bulletin* [Munich], November 10, 1986, 1–3.

_____. "Catastrophic Language Situation in Major Ukrainian Cities," Radio Free Europe/Radio Liberty, *Radio Liberty Research Bulletin* [Munich], July 15, 1987, 1–5.

_____. "Letters to Belorussian Weekly Evidence Strong Support for Native Language," Radio Free Europe/Radio Liberty, *Radio Liberty Research Bulletin* [Munich], November 9, 1989, 1–5.

_____. "Shcherbitsky on Nationalism and Religion," Radio Free Europe/Radio Liberty, *Radio Liberty Research Bulletin* [Munich], April 6, 1987, 1–5.

_____. "A Strong Center and Strong Republics: The CPSU's Draft 'Platform' on Nationalities Policy," Radio Free Europe/Radio Liberty, *Report on the USSR,* No. 35, September 1, 1989, 1–4.

_____. "Ukrainians and Belorussians Focus on Language and Ecology," Radio Free Europe/Radio Liberty, *Radio Liberty Research Bulletin* [Munich], April 6, 1988, 1–5.

_____. "Ukrainians in Moscow and Leningrad Organize," Radio Free Europe/Radio Liberty, *Radio Liberty Research Bulletin* [Munich], September 5, 1988, 1–4.

Soper, John. "Classical Central Asian Language to be Taught in Uzbek Schools?," Radio Free Europe/Radio Liberty, *Radio Liberty Research Bulletin* [Munich], June 29, 1988, 1–4.

_____. "Kirgiz Intelligentsia Seeking to Lessen Russian Influence on Native Language," Radio Free Europe/Radio Liberty, *Radio Liberty Research Bulletin* [Munich], September 24, 1987, 1–5.

_____. "Nationality Issues under Review in Kirgizia," Radio Free Europe/Radio Liberty, *Radio Liberty Research Bulletin* [Munich], January 29, 1988, 1–10.

"Soviet Police Break Up Minsk Rally," *Guardian* [London], November 3, 1988. Foreign Broadcast Information Service: *Daily Report: Soviet Union.* (FBIS–SOV–88–218.) November 10, 1988, 5–6.

Spector, Sherman David. "The Moldavian S.S.R. 1964–74." Pages 260–69 in George W. Simmonds (ed.), *Nationalism in the USSR and Eastern Europe.* Detroit: Detroit University Press, 1977.

Stepanenko, Mykola. "Ukrainian Culture in the Brezhnev-Kosygin Era: Some Observations." Pages 72–80 in George W. Simmonds (ed.), *Nationalism in the USSR and Eastern Europe.* Detroit: Detroit University Press, 1977.

Subtelny, Orest. *Ukraine: A History.* Toronto: University of Toronto Press, 1988.

Suny, Ronald G. "Russian Nationalism in the Era of Glasnost' and Perestroika," Radio Free Europe/Radio Liberty, *Radio Liberty Research Bulletin* [Munich], Special Edition, December 19, 1988, 37–42.

Sysyn, Frank E. *The Ukrainian Orthodox Question in the USSR.* (Millennium of Christianity in Rus'-Ukraine Series.) Cambridge: Harvard University Ukrainian Studies Fund, 1987.

United States. Congress. 100th, 2d Session. House of Representatives. Commission on Security and Cooperation in Europe. *Reform and Human Rights: The Gorbachev Record.* Washington: GPO, 1988.

_____. Department of State. Bureau of Public Affairs. "Soviet Repression of the Ukrainian Catholic Church." (Paper prepared by Bureau of Human Rights and Humanitarian Affairs, Special Report No. 159.) Washington: GPO, January 1987.

Wimbush, S. Enders (ed.). *Soviet Nationalities in Strategic Perspective.* New York: St. Martin's Press, 1985.

Wishnevsky, Julia. "The Origins of Pamyat," *Survey* [London], 30, No. 3 (130), October 1988, 79–91.

_____. "A Tribute to the Crimean Tatar Movement," Radio Free Europe/Radio Liberty, *Radio Liberty Research Bulletin* [Munich], July 29, 1987, 1–3.

Yanov, Alexander. "Russian Nationalism as the Ideology of Counterreform," Radio Free Europe/Radio Liberty, *Radio Liberty Research Bulletin* [Munich], Special Edition, December 19, 1988, 43–52.

Zaprudnik, Jan. "Developments in Belorussia since 1964." Pages 105–14 in George W. Simmonds (ed.), *Nationalism in the USSR and Eastern Europe.* Detroit: Detroit University Press, 1977.

Zaslavsky, Viktor, and Robert Brym. *Soviet-Jewish Emigration and Soviet Nationality Policy.* New York: St. Martin's Press, 1983.

Chapter 5

Abramkin, Vitaliy. "Health Care under the Reforms," *Soviet Analyst* [Richmond, Surrey, United Kingdom], 18, No. 2, January 25, 1989, 7–8.

Aleksandrova, Ekaterina. "Why Soviet Women Want to Get Married." Pages 31–50 in Tat'yana Mamonova (ed.), *Women and Russia.* Boston: Beacon Press, 1984.

Bohr, Annette. "Abortion Is Still Number One Method of Birth Control in Soviet Union," Radio Free Europe/Radio Liberty, *Radio Liberty Research Bulletin* [Munich], September 13, 1988, 1–4.

Browning, Genia R. *Women and Politics in the USSR: Consciousness Raising and Soviet Women's Groups.* Sussex: Wheatsheaf Books, 1987.

Byrnes, Robert F. (ed.). *After Brezhnev: Sources of Soviet Conduct in the 1980s.* Bloomington: Indiana University Press, 1983.

Cambridge Encyclopedia of Russia and the Soviet Union. Cambridge: Cambridge University Press, 1982.

Clem, Ralph S. "The Ethnic Dimension of the Soviet Union, Part I." Pages 11–31 in Jerry G. Pankhurst and Michael Paul Sacks (eds.), *Contemporary Soviet Society: Sociological Perspectives.* New York: Praeger, 1980.

_____. "The Ethnic Dimension of the Soviet Union, Part II." Pages 32–62 in Jerry G. Pankhurst and Michael Paul Sacks (eds.), *Contemporary Soviet Society: Sociological Perspectives.* New York: Praeger, 1980.

Dmytryshyn, Basil. *USSR: A Concise History.* New York: Scribner's, 1965.

Dobson, Richard R. "Socialism and Social Stratification." Pages 88–114 in Jerry G. Pankhurst and Michael Paul Sacks (eds.), *Contemporary Soviet Society: Sociological Perspectives.* New York: Praeger, 1980.

Field, Mark G. "The Contemporary Soviet Family: Problems, Issues, Perspectives." Pages 3–29 in Maurice Friedberg and Heyward Isham (eds.), *Soviet Society under Gorbachev: Current Trends and the Prospects for Reform.* Armonk, New York: Sharpe, 1987.

Friedberg, Maurice, and Heyward Isham (eds.). *Soviet Society under Gorbachev: Current Trends and the Prospects for Reform.* Armonk, New York: Sharpe, 1987.

Gosudarstvennyi komitet po statistike. *Narodnoe khoziaistvo SSSR za 70 let.* Moscow: Finansy i statistika, 1987.

Hazard, John N. *The Soviet System of Government.* (5th ed.) Chicago: University of Chicago Press, 1980.

Herlemann, Horst (ed.). *Quality of Life in the Soviet Union.* Boulder, Colorado: Westview Press, 1987.

Jones, Ellen, and Fred W. Grupp. *Modernization, Value Change, and Fertility in the Soviet Union.* Cambridge: Cambridge University Press, 1987.

Juviler, Peter H. "Cell Mutation in the Soviet Society: The Family." Pages 39–57 in Terry L. Thompson and Richard Sheldon (eds.), *Soviet Society and Culture: Essays in Honor of Vera Dunham.* Boulder, Colorado: Westview Press, 1988.

Kerblay, Basile. *Modern Soviet Society.* New York: Pantheon, 1983.

Lane, David. *Soviet Economy and Society.* New York: New York University Press, 1985.

Lapidus, Gail Warshofsky. "Social Trends." Pages 186–249 in Robert F. Byrnes (ed.), *After Brezhnev: Sources of Soviet Conduct in the 1980s*. Bloomington: Indiana University Press, 1983.

Mamonova, Tat'yana (ed.). *Women and Russia*. Boston: Beacon Press, 1984.

Matthews, Mervyn. "Aspects of Poverty in the Soviet Union." Pages 43–63 in Horst Herlemann (ed.), *Quality of Life in the Soviet Union*. Boulder, Colorado: Westview Press, 1987.

_____. *Poverty in the Soviet Union: The Life-Styles of the Underprivileged in Recent Years*. Cambridge: Cambridge University Press, 1986.

_____. *Privilege in the Soviet Union: A Study of Elite Life-Styles under Communism*. London: Allen and Unwin, 1978.

Medish, Vadim. *The Soviet Union*. (3d ed.) Englewood Cliffs, New Jersey: Prentice-Hall, 1987.

Ordena SSSR. (Bol'shaia sovetskaia entsiklopediia.) Moscow: Sovetskaia entsiklopediia, 1973.

Pankhurst, Jerry G., and Michael Paul Sacks (eds.). *Contemporary Soviet Society: Sociological Perspectives*. New York: Praeger, 1980.

"Professional'nye soiuzy SSSR." Pages 17–18 in *Ezhegodnik Bol'shoi sovetskoi entsiklopedii*. Moscow: Sovetskaia entsiklopediia, 1984.

Remnick, David. "Soviet Editor Reveals Gorbachev's Pay and Perks," *Washington Post*, February 1, 1989, D1, D11.

Rimashevskaia, N., and A. Milovidov. "O sovershenstvovanii gosudarstvennoi pomoshchi sem'iam, imeiushchim detei," *Planovoe khoziaistvo*, No. 1, January 1988, 82–85.

Sacks, Michael Paul. "The Place of Women." Pages 227–50 in Jerry G. Pankhurst and Michael Paul Sacks (eds.), *Contemporary Soviet Society: Sociological Perspectives*. New York: Praeger, 1980.

Sheehy, Ann. "Opposition to Family Planning in Uzbekistan and Tadzhikistan," Radio Free Europe/Radio Liberty, *Radio Liberty Research Bulletin* [Munich], April 5, 1988, 1–7.

Smith, Gordon B. *Soviet Politics: Continuity and Contradiction*. New York: St. Martin's Press, 1988.

"Table of Ranks." Pages 152–55 in Joseph L. Wieczynski (ed.), *The Modern Encyclopedia of Russian and Soviet History*. Gulf Breeze, Florida: Academic International Press, 1984.

Thaden, Edward C. *Russia since 1801: The Making of a New Society*. New York: Wiley Interscience, 1971.

Thompson, Terry L., and Richard Sheldon (eds.). *Soviet Society and Culture: Essays in Honor of Vera Dunham*. Boulder, Colorado: Westview Press, 1988.

Trehub, Aaron. "Children in the Soviet Union," Radio Free Europe/Radio Liberty, *Radio Liberty Research Bulletin* [Munich], December 23, 1987, 1–9.

Tsentral'noe statisticheskoe upravlenie. *Chislennost' i sostav naseleniia SSSR: Po dannym Vsesoiuznoi perepisi naseleniia 1979 goda.* Moscow: Finansy i statistika, 1984.

———. *SSSR v tsifrakh v 1986 godu: Kratkii statisticheskii sbornik.* Moscow: Finansy i statistika, 1987.

Wieczynski Joseph L. (ed.). *The Modern Encyclopedia of Russian and Soviet History.* Gulf Breeze, Florida: Academic International Press, 1984.

Zaslavskaya, Tat'yana. "Socioeconomic Aspects of *Perestroyka,*" *Soviet Studies,* 4, No. 3, October–December 1987, 313–31.

Chapter 6

Avis, George (ed.). *The Making of the Soviet Citizen: Character Formation and Civic Training in Soviet Education.* London: Croom Helm, 1987.

Balzer, Harley D. "Education, Science, and Technology." Pages 245–57 in James Cracraft (ed.), *The Soviet Union Today: An Interpretive Guide.* Chicago: University of Chicago Press, 1988.

———. "Recent Soviet Education Reforms (Summary of Talk Presented October 19, 1986)," Kennan Institute for Advanced Russian Studies, *Meeting Report,* 1.

Barringer, Felicity. "Top Soviet Aide Calls for Change for the Schools," *New York Times,* February 18, 1988, A1, A6.

Bednyi, M.S. *Sem'ia, zdorov'e i obshchestvo.* Moscow: Mysl', 1986.

Bloch, Sidney, and Peter Reddaway. *Soviet Psychiatric Abuse: The Shadow over World Psychiatry.* London: Victor Gollancz, 1984.

"Bol'she voprosov, chem otvetov," *Moskovskaia pravda* [Moscow], July 17, 1987, 3.

Brine, Jenny, Maureen Perrie, and Andrew Sutton (eds.). *Home, School and Leisure in the Soviet Union.* London: Allen and Unwin, 1980.

Bronfenbrenner, Urie. *Two Worlds of Childhood: U.S. and U.S.S.R.* New York: Russell Sage Foundation, 1970.

"Colleges in Soviet Union Overhauled to Spur Gorbachev Changes," *New York Times,* March 22, 1987, 18.

Cracraft, James (ed.). *The Soviet Union Today: An Interpretive Guide.* Chicago: University of Chicago Press, 1988.

Crisostomo, R. McDonald. *Soviet Language Policy and Education in the Southern Tier, 1950 to 1982.* Washington: Department of the Interior, Bureau of the Census, Center for International Research, 1984.

Davis, Christopher. *The Medical and Pharmaceutical Sectors of the Soviet Economy.* Washington: Wharton Econometric Forecasting Associates, 1984.

"Education, Science, and Culture in the USSR." Pages 189–94 in *The Soviet Union.* Moscow: Progress, 1986.

Feshbach, Murray. "'Glasnost' and Health Issues in the USSR," *KIARS Meeting Report,* October 5, 1987.

Field, Mark G. "Medical Care in the Soviet Union: Promises and Realities." Pages 65–82 in Horst Herlemann (ed.), *Quality of Life in the Soviet Union.* Boulder, Colorado: Westview Press, 1987.

_____. "Soviet Infant Mortality," *KIARS Meeting Report,* October 9, 1987.

Fuller, Elizabeth. "Problems in Higher Education in Georgia," Radio Free Europe/Radio Liberty, *Radio Liberty Research Bulletin* [Munich], October 20, 1987, 1–6.

_____. "USSR Minister of Health Cites Data on Infant Mortality and Infectious Diseases in Two Transcaucasian Republics," Radio Free Europe/Radio Liberty, *Radio Liberty Research Bulletin* [Munich], October 16, 1987, 1–5.

Golyakhovsky, Vladimir. *Russian Doctor.* (Trans., Michael Sylvester and Eugene Ostrovsky.) New York: St. Martin's Press, 1984.

Gosudarstvennyi komitet po statistike. *Narodnoe khoziaistvo SSSR za 70 let.* Moscow: Finansy i statistika, 1987.

"Health Care." Pages 174–75 in *The Soviet Union.* Washington: Congressional Quarterly, 1986.

"Health Care and Physical Education." Pages 194–99 in *The Soviet Union.* Moscow: Progress, 1986.

Hechinger, Fred M. "Education: Triumphs and Doubts." Pages 131–65 in Harrison E. Salisbury (ed.), *The Soviet Union: The Fifty Years.* New York: Harcourt, Brace, and World, 1967.

Herlemann, Horst (ed.). *Quality of Life in the Soviet Union.* Boulder, Colorado: Westview Press, 1987.

Holland, Barry. "Education: Reforming the Reforms," *Soviet Analyst,* 17, No. 5, 3–5.

Holmes, Brian. "Soviet Education: Travellers' Tales." Pages 30–56 in J.J. Tomiak (ed.), *Western Perspectives on Soviet Education in the 1980s.* New York: St. Martin's Press, 1986.

"Increased Smoking Among Population," *Planovoe khoziaistvo* [Moscow], No. 3, March 1988, 124.

Jacoby, Susan. *Inside Soviet Schools.* New York: Hill and Wang, 1974.

Keubart, Friedrich. "Aspects of Soviet Secondary Education: School Performance and Teacher Accountability." Pages 83–94 in Horst Herlemann (ed.), *Quality of Life in the Soviet Union.* Boulder, Colorado: Westview Press, 1987.

"Khotim otkryt' shkolu na kooperativnykh nachalakh," *Literaturnaia gazeta* [Moscow], July 15, 1987, 10.

Khvalynskaia, M.S. "Economic Geography of Higher Education in the USSR," *Soviet Geography*, 25, June 1984, 381–89.

_____. "Some Aspects of the Spatial Organization of Higher Education in the USSR," *Soviet Geography*, 27, September 1986, 461–68.

Knaus, William A. *Inside Russian Medicine: An American Doctor's First-Hand Report.* New York: Everest House, 1981.

Konovalev, Valerii. "Transmission of AIDS Is Made a Criminal Offense," Radio Free Europe/Radio Liberty, *Radio Liberty Research Bulletin* [Munich], September 21, 1987, 1–4.

Koriagina, T.I., and Iu. E. Sheviakhov. *Obshchestvennye fondy potrebleniia*, 3. (Novoe v zhizni, nauke, tekhnike. Seriia "Ekonomika," No. 3.) Moscow: Znanie, 1988.

"Krik boli," *Literaturnaia gazeta* [Moscow], October 14, 1987, 12.

Lane, David. *Soviet Economy and Society.* New York: New York University Press, 1985.

"Lechenie? Ili—nakazanie?," *Literaturnaia gazeta* [Moscow], June 17, 1987, 2.

Lee, Gary. "Soviets Pass Strict Law to Stem Spread of AIDS," *Washington Post,* August 26, 1987, 1.

Liegle, Ludwig. "Education in the Family and Family Policy in the Soviet Union." Pages 57–74 in J.J. Tomiak (ed.), *Western Perspectives on Soviet Education in the 1980s.* New York: St. Martin's Press, 1986.

Long, Delbert H. "Soviet Education and the Development of Communist Ethics." Pages 327–35 in Frank M. Sorrentino and Frances R. Curcio (eds.), *Soviet Politics and Education.* Lanham, Maryland: University Press of America, 1986.

McAuley, Alastair. *Economic Welfare in the Soviet Union.* Madison: University of Wisconsin Press, 1979.

Matthews, Mervyn. "Aspects of Poverty in the Soviet Union." Pages 43–63 in Horst Herlemann (ed.), *Quality of Life in the Soviet Union.* Boulder, Colorado: Westview Press, 1987.

_____. *Poverty in the Soviet Union: The Life-Styles of the Underprivileged in Recent Years.* Cambridge: Cambridge University Press, 1986.

Medish, Vadim. *The Soviet Union.* (3d ed.) Englewood Cliffs, New Jersey: Prentice-Hall, 1987.

Morison, John. "Recent Development in Political Education in the Soviet Union." Pages 23–49 in George Avis (ed.), *The Making of the Soviet Citizen: Character Formation and Civic Training in Soviet Education.* London: Croom Helm, 1987.

Muller-Dietz, Heinz. "Die Diskussion um die Entwinklung des sowjetischen Gesundheitswesens," *Osteuropa* [Stuttgart], 1, January 1988, 35–44.

"My sebe ne proshchaem," *Pravda* [Moscow], August 17, 1987, 3.

"Nastavnik pokoleniia: Uchitel'—vazhneishee deistvuiushchee litso perestroiki," *Pravda* [Moscow], March 2, 1988, 1.

"Nastupat' na alkogol'," *Pravda* [Moscow], November 15, 1987, 3.

"Ne mogu prostit'," *Literaturnaia gazeta* [Moscow], June 17, 1987, 12.

"Obrazovanie—nepreryvnoe," *Literaturnaia gazeta* [Moscow], December 2, 1987, 10.

"Odinochestvo," *Literaturnaia gazeta* [Moscow], November 11, 1987, 12.

"O khode perestroiki srednei i vysshei shkoly i zadachakh partii po ee osushchestvleniiu," *Pravda* [Moscow], February 18, 1988, 1–4.

"O studentakh, prepodavateliakh i ne tol'ko o nikh," *Ogonek* [Moscow], No. 35, August 1987, 14–15.

"Otsenku daet patsient," *Trud* [Moscow], May 21, 1987, 2.

"Ozhidanie: Kak gotovitsia novyi zakon o pensiiakh," *Ogonek* [Moscow], 7, No. 7, July 1989, 31–33.

"Perestroika dlia shkoly," *Pravda* [Moscow], January 2, 1988, 2.

Petrovskiy, B.V. *Novyi etap v razvitii narodnogo zdravookhraneniia SSSR.* Moscow: Meditsina, 1981.

"Pochemu osechka," *Pravda* [Moscow], September 20, 1987, 2.

"Pomogaiut mnogodetnym materiam," *Sovetskaia Rossiia* [Moscow], October 26, 1987, 4.

"Pomoshch' sem'e," *Trud* [Moscow], June 16, 1987, 2.

Popkewitz, Thomas S., and Robert B. Tabachnik. *Themes in Current Soviet Curriculum Reform.* Lanham, Maryland: University Press of America, 1986.

"Posle poludnia," *Pravda* [Moscow], July 21, 1987, 3.

Powell, David E. "A Troubled Society." Pages 349–63 in James Cracraft (ed.), *The Soviet Union Today: An Interpretive Guide.* Chicago: University of Chicago Press, 1988.

"Pregrady dlia SPIDa," *Pravda* [Moscow], June 29, 1987, 4.

"Prophylaktisches AIDS-Zentrum in Moskau," *Die Wirtschaft des Ostblocks* [Moscow], No. 33, March 31, 1987, 3.

"Rebenok bez osmotra," *Pravda* [Moscow], August 10, 1987, 4.

Reddaway, Peter. "Soviet Psychiatry: An End to Political Abuse?," *Survey* [London], 30, No. 130, October 1988, 25–38.

Redl, Helen B. (ed.). *Soviet Educators on Soviet Education.* London: Free Press of Glencoe Collier-MacMillan, 1964.

Remnick, David. "Painful Topic Confronts Soviets: Homelessness at Home," *Washington Post,* February 21, 1988, A1, A24.

_____. "Soviets Cancel History Tests over Texts," *Washington Post,* June 11, 1988, A1, A21.

Ryan, Michael, and Richard Prentice. *Social Trends in the Soviet Union from 1950.* New York: St. Martin's Press, 1987.

Salisbury, Harrison (ed.). *The Soviet Union: The Fifty Years.* New York: Harcourt, Brace, and World, 1967.

"Serdtse shkoly—uchitel'," *Pravda* [Moscow], January 20, 1988, 3.

"Seventy Years after Lenin," *U.S. News and World Report,* October 19, 1987, 30–55.

Sheehy, Ann. "Steps to Combat Infant Mortality in Central Asian Republics," Radio Free Europe/Radio Liberty, *Radio Liberty Research Bulletin* [Munich], July 14, 1987, 1–3.

"Shkola s uklonem v budushchee," *Literaturnaia gazeta* [Moscow], May 27, 1987, 10.

Shuval, Judith T. *Newcomers and Colleagues: Soviet Immigrant Physicians in Israel.* Houston: Cap and Gown Press, 1983.

Soper, John. "Problems in the Kazakh Educational System," Radio Free Europe/Radio Liberty, *Radio Liberty Research Bulletin* [Munich], December 2, 1987, 1–4.

Sorrentino, Frank M., and Frances R. Curcio (eds.). *Soviet Politics and Education.* Lanham, Maryland: University Press of America, 1986.

"Soviet Authorities Worry That Shortage of Syringes May Abet Spread of AIDS," Radio Free Europe/Radio Liberty, *Radio Free Europe Research* [Munich], May 20, 1989, 1.

"Soviet Health Ministry Issues Brochure about AIDS," Radio Free Europe/Radio Liberty, *Radio Liberty Research Bulletin* [Munich], September 2, 1987, 2.

"SPID—Opasnosti real'nye i mnimye," *Trud* [Moscow], July 6, 1987, 4.

"SPID—O pol'ze azbuchnykh istin," *Literaturnaia gazeta* [Moscow], September 16, 1987, 10.

"SPID—Zaslon smertonosnoi 'chume'," *Literaturnaia gazeta* [Moscow], September 2, 1987, 1.

Stepanov, V.K. *Spetsializirovannye uchebno-lechebnye tsentry.* Moscow: Stroizdat, 1987.

Sternheimer, Stephen. "The Vanishing *Babushka*: A Roleless Role for Older Soviet Women?" Pages 133–49 in Horst Herlemann (ed.), *Quality of Life in the Soviet Union.* Boulder, Colorado: Westview Press, 1987.

Tomiak, J.J. (ed.). *Western Perspectives on Soviet Education in the 1980s.* New York: St. Martin's Press, 1986.

"Tragediia, kotoroi moglo ne byt'," *Nedelia* [Moscow], No. 27, July 4–10, 1988, 18.

Trehub, Aaron. "Children in the Soviet Union," Radio Free Europe/Radio Liberty, *Radio Liberty Research Bulletin* [Munich], December 15, 1987, 1–7.

_____. "First Fee-for-Service Hospital in USSR to Open in Moscow," Radio Free Europe/Radio Liberty, *Radio Liberty Research Bulletin* [Munich], September 14, 1987, 1–3.

_____. "More Glasnost' on Soviet Health Issues," Radio Free Europe/Radio Liberty, *Radio Liberty Research Bulletin* [Munich], October 12, 1987, 1–4.

_____. "New Figures on Infant Mortality in the USSR," Radio Free Europe/Radio Liberty, *Radio Liberty Research Bulletin* [Munich], October 29, 1987, 1–3.

_____. "Poverty in the Soviet Union," Radio Free Europe/Radio Liberty, *Radio Liberty Research Bulletin* [Munich], June 20, 1988, 1–7.

_____. "Quality of Soviet Health Care under Attack," Radio Free Europe/Radio Liberty, *Radio Liberty Research Bulletin* [Munich], July 28, 1986, 1–7.

Treml, Vladimir. "Alcohol Abuse and the Quality of Life in the Soviet Union." Pages 151–61 in Horst Herlemann (ed.), *Quality of Life in the Soviet Union*. Boulder, Colorado: Westview Press, 1987.

"Tsifry i fakty," *Pravda* [Moscow], October 3, 1987, 3.

"Tsifry vmesto bol'nykh," *Pravda* [Moscow], September 2, 1987, 3.

"Uchebniki novogo pokolenia: Kogda oni budut?," *Pravda* [Moscow], September 26, 1987, 3.

"Vnimanie: Deti v bede!" *Nedelia* [Moscow], No. 26, June 27–July 3, 1988, 12.

Voronitsyn, Sergei. "The Less Well-off Sector and the Pending Price Reform," Radio Free Europe/Radio Liberty, *Radio Liberty Research Bulletin* [Munich], September 24, 1987, 1–5.

_____. "Restructuring of Higher Education: Plans and Contradictions," Radio Free Europe/Radio Liberty, *Radio Liberty Research Bulletin* [Munich], April 15, 1987, 1–4.

_____. "Why Has the All-Union Congress of Teachers Been Postponed?" Radio Free Europe/Radio Liberty, *Radio Liberty Research Bulletin* [Munich], July 7, 1987, 1–4.

"V put', uchebnyi god. Segodnia—Den' znanii," *Pravda* [Moscow], September 1, 1987, 1.

"Vysokaia tsena besplatnogo lecheniia," *Literaturnaia gazeta* [Moscow], September 16, 1987, 2.

"Vzroslye igry: Razmyshleniia po povodu vyborov direktora shkoly," *Ekonomicheskaia gazeta* [Moscow], No. 6, February 1988, 13.

Weaver, Kitty D. *Russia's Future: The Communist Education of Soviet Youth.* New York: Praeger, 1981.

Winter, Sonia. "An Interview with Vladimir Treml on Alcoholism in the USSR," Radio Free Europe/Radio Liberty, *Radio Liberty Research Bulletin* [Munich], August 3, 1987, 1–6.

"Zabota o mnogodetnykh sem'iakh," *Pravda* [Moscow], October 9, 1987, 2.

Chapter 7

Armstrong, John A. *Ideology, Politics, and Government in the Soviet Union.* New York: Praeger, 1978.

Barghoorn, Frederick C., and Thomas F. Remington. *Politics in the USSR.* (3d ed.) Boston: Little, Brown, 1987.

Bialer, Seweryn. *The Soviet Paradox: External Expansion, Internal Decline.* New York: Vintage Books, 1986.

_____. *Stalin's Successors: Leadership, Stability, and Change in the Soviet Union.* Cambridge: Cambridge University Press, 1980.

Bialer, Seweryn (ed.). *Inside Gorbachev's Russia.* Boulder, Colorado: Westview Press, 1989.

Bialer, Seweryn, and Thane Gustafson (eds.). *Russia at the Crossroads.* London: Allen and Unwin, 1982.

Breslauer, George. *Khrushchev and Brezhnev as Leaders: Building Authority in Soviet Politics.* London: Allen and Unwin, 1982.

_____. "Power and Authority in Soviet Politics." Pages 15–33 in Joseph L. Nogee (ed.), *Soviet Politics: Russia after Brezhnev.* New York: Praeger, 1985.

_____. "Provincial Party Leaders Demand Articulation and the Nature of Center-Periphery Relations in the USSR," *Slavic Review,* 45, No. 4, Winter 1986, 650–72.

Brown, Archie, and Michael Kaser (eds.). *Soviet Policy for the 1980s.* Bloomington: Indiana University Press, 1982.

Burant, Stephen R. "The Influence of Russian Tradition on the Political Style of the Soviet Elite," *Political Science Quarterly,* 102, No. 2, Summer 1987, 273–93.

_____. "Soviet Political Culture." (Paper presented at Midwest Slavic Conference, University of Wisconsin, April 18–19, 1986.) Madison: 1986.

D'Agostino, Anthony. *Soviet Succession Struggles.* Winchester, Massachusetts: Allen and Unwin, 1987.

"Departments 'May Be Halved'," Moscow World Service [Moscow], September 29, 1988. Foreign Broadcast Information Service, *Daily Report: Soviet Union.* (FBIS-SOV-88-190.) September 30, 1988, 33.

Deputaty verkhovnogo soveta SSSR. Moscow: Izvestiia, 1984.

Fainsod, Merle. *How Russia Is Ruled.* Cambridge: Harvard University Press, 1965.

Fehér, Ferenc, and Andrew Arato (eds.). *Gorbachev: The Debate.* Atlantic Highlands, New Jersey: Humanities Press International, 1989.

Gosudarstvennyi komitet po statistike. *Narodnoe khoziaistvo SSSR v 1985 g.* Moscow: Finansy i statistika, 1986.

_____. *Narodnoe khoziaistvo SSSR za 70 let.* Moscow: Finansy i statistika, 1987.

Hahn, Jeffrey W. *Soviet Grassroots: Citizen Participation in Local Soviet Government.* Princeton: Princeton University Press, 1987.

Hahn, Werner. "Electoral 'Choice' in the Soviet Bloc," *Problems of Communism,* 36, No. 2, March–April 1987, 29–39.

Harasymiw, Bohdan. *Political Elite Recruitment in the Soviet Union.* New York: St. Martin's Press, 1984.

Hazard, John N. *The Soviet System of Government.* (5th ed.) Chicago: University of Chicago Press, 1980.

Heller, Mikhail. *Cogs in the Wheel.* New York: Knopf, 1988.

Hill, Ronald J., and Peter Frank. *The Soviet Communist Party.* London: Allen and Unwin, 1983.

Holmes, Leslie. *Politics in the Communist World.* Oxford: Clarendon Press, 1986.

Hough, Jerry F. "Changes in Soviet Elite Composition." Pages 39–64 in Seweryn Bialer and Thane Gustafson (eds.), *Russia at the Crossroads.* London: Allen and Unwin, 1982.

_____. *Russia and the West: Gorbachev and the Politics of Reform.* New York: Simon and Schuster, 1988.

_____. *The Soviet Union and Social Science Theory.* Cambridge: Harvard University Press, 1977.

Jozsza, Gyula. "Bureaucracy in Party and State." Pages 312–23 in Hans-Joachim Veen (ed.), *From Brezhnev to Gorbachev.* New York: BERG, 1987.

_____. "Political Seilschaften in the USSR." Pages 139–73 in T.H. Rigby and Bohdan Harasymiw (eds.), *Leadership Selection and Patron-Client Relations in the USSR and Yugoslavia.* London: Allen and Unwin, 1983.

Konstitutsiia SSSR i razvitie sovetskogo zakonodatel'stva. Moscow: Iuridicheskaia literatura, 1981.

KPSS i razvitie sovetskoi politicheskoi sistemy. Moscow: Mysl', 1987.

"KPSS v tsifrakh," *Partiinaia zhizn'* [Moscow], No. 14, July 1981, 13–26.

"KPSS v tsifrakh," *Partiinaia zhizn'* [Moscow], No. 14, July 1986, 19–32.

"KPSS v tsifrakh," *Partiinaia zhizn'* [Moscow], No. 21, November 1987, 6–20.

Kratkii politicheskii slovar'. Moscow: Izdatel'stvo politicheskoi literatury, 1980.

Laqueur, Walter. *The Long Road to Freedom: Russia and Glasnost.* New York: Scribner's, 1989.

Lewis, Moshe. *The Gorbachev Phenomenon.* Berkeley: University of California Press, 1988.

Linden, Carl. *The Soviet Party-State: The Politics of Ideocratic Despotism.* New York: Praeger, 1983.

Mandel, Ernst. *Beyond Perestroika: The Future of Gorbachev's USSR.* London: Verso, 1989.

Mann, Dawn. "The Party Conference Resolution on Democratization and Political Reform," Radio Free Europe/Radio Liberty, *Radio Free Liberty Research Bulletin* [Munich], July 6, 1988, 1–8.

Medish, Vadim. *The Soviet Union.* (3d ed.) Englewood Cliffs, New Jersey: Prentice-Hall, 1987.

"Medvedev Answers Journalists Questions," Moscow TASS [Moscow], September 30, 1988. Foreign Broadcast Information Service, *Daily Report: Soviet Union.* (FBIS-SOV-88-191.) October 3, 1988, 42.

Meissner, Boris. "Social Change in the Soviet Union and Social Structure of the CPSU." Pages 299–311 in Hans-Joachim Veen (ed.), *From Brezhnev to Gorbachev.* New York: BERG, 1987.

Meyer, Alfred G. *Leninism.* New York: Praeger, 1963.

Michnik, Adam. *Letters from Prison and Other Essays.* Berkeley: University of California Press, 1985.

Miller, John H. "The Communist Party: Trends and Problems." Pages 1–34 in Archie Brown and Michael Kaser (eds.), *Soviet Policy for the 1980s.* Bloomington: Indiana University Press, 1982.

Moore, Barrington, Jr. *Soviet Politics: The Dilemma of Power.* New York: Harper and Row, 1965.

Moses, Joel C. "Functional Career Specialization in Soviet Regional Elite Recruitment." Pages 15–63 in T.H. Rigby and Bohdan Harasymiw (eds.), *Leadership Selection and Patron-Client Relations in the USSR and Yugoslavia.* London: Allen and Unwin, 1983.

Nogee, Joseph L. (ed.). *Soviet Politics: Russia after Brezhnev.* New York: Praeger, 1985.

Nor-Mesek, Nikolaij, and Wolfgang Rieper. *Politburo: Leading Organs of the Central Committee of the Communist Party of the Soviet*

Union and Leading Organs of the Republics. Frankfurt: Institut für Sowjet-Studien, 1987.

"O demokratizatsii sovetskogo obshchestva i reforme politicheskoi sistemy," *Pravda* [Moscow], July 5, 1988, 2.

Rahr, Alexander. "Gorbachev's Personal Staff," Radio Free Europe/Radio Liberty, *Radio Liberty Research Bulletin* [Munich], May 30, 1988, 1-5.

————. "Restructuring the Kremlin Leadership," Radio Free Europe/Radio Liberty, *Radio Liberty Research Bulletin* [Munich], October 4, 1988, 1-6.

————. "Turnover in the Central Party Apparatus," Radio Free Europe/Radio Liberty, *Radio Liberty Research Bulletin* [Munich], July 9, 1987, 1-10.

————. "Turnover in the Soviet *nomenklatura?*," Radio Free Europe/Radio Liberty, *Radio Liberty Research Bulletin* [Munich], June 5, 1988, 1-4.

————. "Who Is in Charge of the Party Apparatus?," Radio Free Europe/Radio Liberty, *Report on the USSR* [Munich], 1, No. 15, April 14, 1989, 19-24.

Remington, Thomas F. *The Truth of Authority*. Pittsburgh: University of Pittsburgh Press, 1988.

Rigby, T.H., and Bohdan Harasymiw (eds.). *Leadership Selection and Patron-Client Relations in the USSR and Yugoslavia*. London: Allen and Unwin, 1983.

Ross, Cameron. *Local Government in the Soviet Union*. London: Croom Helm, 1987.

Smith, Gordon B. *Soviet Politics: Continuity and Contradiction*. New York: St. Martin's Press, 1988.

Tatu, Michel. *Gorbatchev: l'URSS va-t-elle changer?* Paris: Le Centurion, 1987.

————. "19th Party Conference," *Problems of Communism*, 37, Nos. 3-4, May-August 1988, 1-15.

Teague, Elizabeth. "Central Committee Resolution Fudges Issue of Party Elections," Radio Free Europe/Radio Liberty, *Radio Liberty Research Bulletin* [Munich], January 29, 1987, 1-3.

————. "Conference Preparations Run into Trouble," Radio Free Europe/Radio Liberty, *Radio Liberty Research Bulletin* [Munich], May 7, 1988, 1-6.

————. "Fall in Representation of Party Apparatus in CPSU Central Committee," Radio Free Europe/Radio Liberty, *Report on the USSR* [Munich], May 12, 1989, 3-5.

"Text of the Resolution 'On Reorganisation and The Party's Personnel Policy' Adopted by the Plenary Meeting of the CPSU Central Committee," *Soviet Review*, 24, No. 5, February 5, 1987, 65-81.

Tumarkin, Nina. *Lenin Lives* Cambridge: Harvard University Press, 1983.

United States. Central Intelligence Agency. *CPSU Central Committee and Central Auditing Commission: Members Elected at the 27th Party Congress.* (LDA 86–10123.) Washington: 1986.

Ustav Kommunisticheskoi Partii Sovetskogo Soiuza. Moscow: Politizdat, 1986.

Veen, Hans-Joachim (ed.). *From Brezhnev to Gorbachev.* New York: BERG, 1987.

Voslensky, Michael. *Nomenklatura.* Garden City, New York: Doubleday, 1984.

White, Stephen, and Alex Pravda (eds.). *Ideology and Soviet Politics.* New York: St. Martin's Press, 1988.

Willerton, John P., Jr. "Patronage Networks and Coalition Building in the Brezhnev Era," *Soviet Studies,* 39, No. 2, April 1987, 175–204.

Yanov, Alexander. *The Drama of the Soviet 1960s.* Berkeley: University of California, Institute of International Studies, 1984.

Zemtsov, Ilya, and John Farrar. *Gorbachev: The Man and the System.* New Brunswick, New Jersey: Transaction Books, 1988.

Chapter 8

Bahry, Donna. *Outside Moscow: Power, Politics, and Budgetary Policy in the Soviet Republics.* New York: Columbia University Press, 1987.

Friedgut, Theodore. *Political Participation in the USSR.* Princeton: Princeton University Press, 1979.

"Gorbachev Chairs Councils of Elders," Moscow TASS International Service [Moscow], June 3, 1989. Foreign Broadcast Information Service, *Daily Report: Soviet Union.* (FBIS–SOV–89–106–S.) June 5, 1989, 45.

Hammer, Darrell P. *The USSR: The Politics of Oligarchy.* Boulder, Colorado: Westview Press, 1986.

Hough, Jerry F. "Gorbachev Consolidating Power," *Problems of Communism,* 36, No. 4, July–August 1987, 21–43.

_____. *The Soviet Prefects.* Durham: Duke University Press, 1969.

Hough, Jerry F., and Merle Fainsod. *How the Soviet Union Is Governed.* Cambridge: Harvard University Press, 1979.

Jacobs, Everett M. (ed.). *Soviet Local Government and Politics.* London: Allen and Unwin, 1983.

Khrushchev, Nikita S. *Khrushchev Remembers.* (Ed. and trans., Strobe Talbott.) Boston: Little, Brown, 1970.

Konstitutsiia SSSR i razvitie sovetskogo zakonodatel'stva. Moscow: Iuridicheskaia literatura, 1981.

Laird, Roy D., and Betty A. Laird. *A Soviet Lexicon.* Lexington, Massachusetts: Heath, 1988.

Medish, Vadim. *The Soviet Union.* (3d ed.) Englewood Cliffs, New Jersey: Prentice-Hall, 1987.

Pavlovskii, R. *Sovetskoe administrativnoe pravo.* Kiev: Vyshcha shkola, 1986.

Potichnyj, Peter J., and Jane Shapiro Zacek (eds.). *Politics and Participation under Communist Rule.* New York: Praeger, 1983.

Proskurin, Alexander. *Fraternal Alliance.* Moscow: Novosti, 1986.

"Report of the Congress of USSR People's Deputies Credentials Commission, Delivered by Deputy Z.V. Gidaspov at May 25 Evening Session of the Congress of USSR People's Deputies," *Pravda* [Moscow], May 26, 1989, 2, 4.

Rodionov, R.A. *Kollektivnost'—vysshii printsip partiinogo rukovodstva.* Moscow: Politizdat, 1967.

Shchetinin, B.V., and A.N. Gorshenev. *Kurs sovetskogo gosudarstvennogo prava.* Moscow: Vyshaia shkola, 1971.

Shevchenko, Arkady. *Breaking with Moscow.* New York: Knopf, 1985.

Shtromas, Alex. "The Legal Position of Nationalities in the 1977 Constitution," *Russian Review,* No. 37, 1978, 265–72.

Siegler, R.W. *The Standing Committees of the Supreme Soviet.* New York: Praeger, 1982.

"Soobshchenie ob itogakh vyborov v mestnykh sovetakh narodnykh deputatov," *Pravda* [Moscow], June 27, 1978, 4.

Stalin, Joseph. *Problems of Leninism.* (11th ed.) Moscow: Foreign Languages, 1953.

Tolkunov, Lev. *How the Supreme Soviet Functions.* Moscow: Novosti, 1987.

Toporin, Boris. *The New Constitution of the USSR.* Moscow: Progress, 1980.

Towster, Julian. *Political Power in the USSR, 1917–1947.* Oxford: Oxford University Press, 1948.

United States. Central Intelligence Agency. *Deputaty Verkhovnogo Soveta.* Washington: 1984.

_____. Central Intelligence Agency. Directorate of Intelligence. *Directory of Soviet Officials: National Organizations.* Washington: 1987.

_____. Central Intelligence Agency. Directorate of Intelligence. *Directory of Soviet Officials: Republic Organizations Update.* Washington: 1987.

_____. Department of State. "The Soviet Constitution: Myth and Reality," *Department of State Bulletin.* Washington: 1987.

"USSR SS Resolution 'On the Organization of Work to Fulfill the Instructions Given to the USSR SS by the Congress of USSR People's Deputies'," *Pravda* [Moscow], July 27, 1989, 1.

Vanneman, P. *The Supreme Soviet: Politics and Legislative Process.* Durham: Duke University Press, 1977.

Verkhovnyi Sovet SSSR, odinnadtsatogo sozyva. Moscow: Politizdat, 1984.

Yurkin, G. "Letter to the Editor and Response," *Argumenty i fakty* [Moscow], No. 1, January 6–12, 1989, 2.

Chapter 9

Barghoorn, Frederick C., and Thomas F. Remington. *Politics in the USSR.* (3d ed.) Boston: Little, Brown, 1986.

Barringer, Felicity. "Pasternak House to Be a Museum," *New York Times,* May 17, 1988, 8.

Christie, Ian. "The Cinema." Pages 284–92 in James Cracraft (ed.), *The Soviet Union Today: An Interpretive Guide.* Chicago: University of Chicago Press, 1988.

Cracraft, James (ed.). *The Soviet Today: An Interpretive Guide.* Chicago: University of Chicago Press, 1988.

Curry, Jane Leftwich, and Joan R. Dassin. *Press Control Around the World.* New York: Praeger, 1982.

Dizard, Wilson P., and Blake S. Swensrud. *Gorbachev's Information Revolution: Controlling Glasnost in a New Electronic Era.* Washington: Center for Strategic and International Studies, 1987.

Dunham, Vera S. *In Stalin's Time: Middle-Class Values in Soviet Fiction.* Cambridge: Cambridge University Press, 1976.

Dunlop, John B. "Soviet Cultural Politics," *Problems of Communism,* 36, No. 6, November–December 1987, 34–56.

———. "Soviet Film under Gorbachev," Kennan Institute for Advanced Russian Studies, *Meeting Report,* May 6, 1987.

Dzirkals, Lilita, Thane Gustafson, and A. Ross Johnson. "The Media and Intra-Elite Communication in the USSR," *Rand Report,* No. R–2869, September 1982, 1–61.

Ebon, Martin. *The Soviet Propaganda Machine.* New York: McGraw-Hill, 1987.

Fein, Esther B. "Impressario Is Back in Moscow, for Now," *New York Times,* May 10, 1988, A1, A3.

Friedberg, Maurice. *Russian Culture in the 1980s.* (Significant Issues Series.) Washington: Center for Strategic and International Studies, 1985.

Glazov, Yuri. *The Russian Mind since Stalin's Death.* Boston: Reidel, 1985.

Golovskoy, Valery S. "Is There Censorship in the Soviet Union?," Kennan Institute for Advanced Russian Studies, *Meeting Report,* 1986, 1–16.

Golovskoy, Valery S., and John Rimberg. *Behind the Soviet Screen: The Motion-Picture Industry in the USSR, 1972–1982.* Ann Arbor: Ardis, 1986.

Goscilo, Helena. "Tatiana Tolstaia's 'Dome of Many-Colored Glass': The World Refracted Through Multiple Perspectives," *Slavic Review,* 47, No. 2, Summer 1988, 280–90.

Hosking, Geoffrey A. "The Politics of Literature." Pages 272–83 in James Cracraft (ed.), *The Soviet Union Today: An Interpretive Guide.* Chicago: University of Chicago Press, 1988.

Howe, Irving. "At the Mercy of Apparatchiks," *New York Times Book Review,* May 22, 1988.

Jacobs, George, and Associates. "The Rapid Expansion in Soviet Satellite TV Broadcasting," *United States Information Agency Contract Report,* No. R–6–85, February 1985, 1–28.

Judy, Richard W., and Jane M. Lommel. "The New Computer Literacy Campaign," *Educational Communication and Technology: A Journal of Theory,* 34, No. 2, Summer 1986, 108–23.

Keller, Bill. "Lenin Faulted on State Terror, and a Soviet Taboo Is Broken," *New York Times,* June 8, 1988, A1, A12.

Lee, Andrea. *Russian Journal.* New York: Random House, 1981.

Lee, Gary. "Our Only Rule: Live Outside Society—Leningrad Emerging as Center of Youth Protest Movement," *Washington Post,* May 16, 1988, A1.

McGulgan, Cathleen. "Art in from the Cold," *Newsweek,* May 23, 1988, 16–17.

Medish, Vadim. *The Soviet Union.* (3d ed.) Englewood Cliffs, New Jersey: Prentice-Hall, 1987.

Medvedev, Roy. "Liquidating Stalin: Behind Gorbachev's Speech Was a Surge of Popular Outrage," *Washington Post,* November 2, 1987, C5.

Mickiewicz, Ellen. "The Mass Media." Pages 293–300 in James Cracraft (ed.), *The Soviet Union Today: An Interpretive Guide.* Chicago: University of Chicago Press, 1988.

_____. *Media and the Russian Public.* New York: Praeger, 1981.

_____. "Political Communication and the Soviet Media System." Pages 34–65 in Joseph L. Nogee (ed.), *Soviet Politics: Russia after Brezhnev.* New York: Praeger, 1985.

Nogee, Joseph L. (ed.). *Soviet Politics: Russia after Brezhnev.* New York: Praeger, 1985.

Petrosyan, Gavrill. *Cultural Life.* Moscow: Novosti Press Agency, 1983.

Remnick, David. "Lyubimov: Return of the Exile: In Moscow, a Director's Hope for a New Era," *Washington Post,* May 11, 1988, C1, C11.

_____. "Soviet Union Relaxing Ban on Forbidden Books," *Washington Post,* March 23, 1988, A15.

Romanov, Andre. "The Press We Choose," *Moscow News,* No. 8, February 21, 1988, 2.

Shlapentokh, Vladimir. *Soviet Public Opinion and Ideology: Mythology and Pragmatism in Interaction.* New York: Praeger, 1986.

Starr, S. Frederick. *Red and Hot: The Fate of Jazz in the Soviet Union, 1917-1980.* New York: Oxford University Press, 1983.

Swed, Mark. "Schnittke: At the Summit of Soviet Music," *Wall Street Journal,* June 7, 1988, 24.

Szamuely, Tibor. *The Russian Tradition.* New York: McGraw-Hill, 1974.

Walicki, Andrzej. *Russian Social Thought: An Introduction to the Intellectual History of Nineteenth-Century Russia.* Goleta, California: Kimberly Press, 1977.

Weil, Irwin. "A Survey of the Cultural Scene." Pages 261-72 in James Cracraft (ed.), *The Soviet Union Today: A Interpretive Guide.* Chicago: University of Chicago Press, 1988.

White, Stephen. "Propagating Communist Values in the USSR," *Problems of Communism,* 34, No. 6, November–December 1985, 1-17.

Wishnevsky, Julia. "Gumilev and Nabokov Published in Soviet Journals," Radio Free Europe/Radio Liberty, *Radio Liberty Research Bulletin* [Munich], September 24, 1986, 1-5.

Chapter 10

Allison, Roy. *Finland's Relations with the Soviet Union, 1944-1984.* New York: St. Martin's Press, 1985.

Aspaturian, Vernon S. *Process and Power in Soviet Foreign Policy.* Boston: Little, Brown, 1971.

_____. "Soviet Foreign Policy." Pages 170-245 in Roy C. MaCridis (ed.), *Foreign Policy in World Politics.* Englewood Cliffs, New Jersey: Prentice-Hall, 1985.

Baxter, William P. *The Soviet Way of Warfare.* London: Brassey's Defense, 1986.

Becker, Abraham S. "Soviet Union and the Third World: The Economic Dimension," *Soviet Economy,* 2, No. 3, July–September, 1986, 233-60.

Bialer, Seweryn. *The Soviet Paradox: External Expansion, Internal Decline.* New York: Knopf, 1986.

Bialer, Seweryn (ed.). *The Domestic Context of Soviet Foreign Policy.* London: Croom Helm, 1981.

Blasier, Cole. *The Giant's Rival: The USSR and Latin America.* Pittsburgh: University of Pittsburgh Press, 1982.

Buszynski, Leszek. *Soviet Foreign Policy and Southeast Asia.* New York: St. Martin's Press, 1986.

_____. "Soviet Foreign Policy and Southeast Asia: Prospects for the Gorbachev Era," *Asian Survey*, 26, No. 5, May 1986, 559–609.

Bykov, O., V. Razmerov, and D. Tomashevsky. *The Priorities of Soviet Foreign Policy Today.* Moscow: Progress, 1981.

Caldwell, Dan (ed.). *Soviet International Behavior and U.S. Policy Options.* Lexington, Massachusetts: Heath, 1985.

Campbell, Kurt M. *Southern Africa in Soviet Foreign Policy.* (Adelphi Papers.) London: International Institute for Strategic Studies, 1987.

Cheng, Joseph Y.S. "Sino-Soviet Relations in the 1980s," *Asia Pacific Community*, 27, Winter 1985, 44–62.

Chernyakov, Yu. "The Development of Diplomatic Services and Today's World," *International Affairs* [Moscow], 9, September 1986, 106–15.

Chirkin, V., and Yu Yudin. *A Socialist Oriented State.* Moscow: Progress, 1983.

Clement, Peter. "Moscow and Southern Africa," *Problems of Communism*, 34, No. 2, March–April 1985, 29–50.

Cline, Ray S., James Arnold Miller, and Roger E. Kanet (eds.). *Asia in Soviet Global Strategy.* Boulder, Colorado: Westview Press, 1987.

Cracraft, James (ed.). *The Soviet Union Today: An Interpretive Guide.* Chicago: University of Chicago Press, 1988.

Currie, Kenneth M., and Gregory Varhall (eds.). *The Soviet Union: What Lies Ahead? Military-Political Affairs in the 1980s.* (Studies in Communist Affairs Series, No. 6.) Washington: GPO for United States Air Force, 1985.

Dawisha, Karen. "Gorbachev and Eastern Europe: A New Challenge for the West," *World Policy Journal*, 3, Spring 1986, 277–99.

de Carmay, Guy, and Jonathan Story. *Western Europe in World Affairs.* New York: Praeger, 1986.

Dismukes, Bradford, and James M. McConnell (eds.). *Soviet Naval Diplomacy.* New York: Pergamon Press, 1979.

Dupree, Louis. "Afghanistan under the Khalq," *Problems of Communism*, 28, No. 4, July–August 1979, 34–50.

_____. "The Soviet Union and Afghanistan in 1987," *Current History,* 86, October 1987, 333–35.

Dyker, David A. (ed.). *The Soviet Union under Gorbachev: Prospects for Reform.* London: Croom Helm, 1987.

Edelman, Marc. "The Other Super Powers: The Soviet Union and Latin America, 1917–1987," *Report on the Americas,* 21, No. 1, January–February 1987.

Ellison, Herbert J. "Changing Sino-Soviet Relations," *Problems of Communism,* 36, No. 3, May–June 1987, 17–29.

Ellison, Herbert J. (ed.). *Soviet Policy Toward Western Europe.* Seattle: University of Washington Press, 1983.

Fedoseyev, P.N. (ed.). *Disastrous Effects of Nuclear War: Socio-Economic Aspects.* (International Peace and Disarmament Series.) Moscow: Nauka, 1985.

Fitzgerald, Mary C. "Marshal Ogarkov on the Modern Theater Operation," *Naval War College Review,* 39, No. 4/Sequence 316, Autumn 1986, 6–25.

Fitzmaurice, John. *Security and Politics in the Nordic Area.* Aldershot, United Kingdom: Avebury, 1987.

Freedman, Lawrence. *Atlas of Global Strategy.* New York: Facts on File, 1985.

Freedman, Robert O. *Soviet Policy Toward the Middle East since 1970.* (3d ed.) New York: Praeger, 1982.

Fukuyama, Francis. "Patterns of Soviet Third World Policy," *Problems of Communism,* 36, September–October 1987, 1–13.

_____. *Soviet Civil-Military Relations and the Power Projection Mission.* (Project Air Force Series.) Santa Monica, California: Rand, 1987.

Gamson, William A., and Andre Modigliani. *Untangling the Cold War.* Boston: Little, Brown, 1971.

Gareev, M.A. *M.V. Frunze, voennii teoretik.* Moscow: Voenizdat, 1985.

Garthoff, Raymond L. *Soviet Military Policy: A Historical Analysis.* New York: Praeger, 1966.

_____. "Soviet Views on the Interrelations of Diplomacy and Military Strategy," *Political Science Quarterly,* 94, No. 3, Fall 1979, 391–405.

Gelman, Harry. *Gorbachev's Policies Toward Western Europe: A Balance Sheet.* Santa Monica, California: Rand, October 1987.

George, James L. (ed.). *The Soviet and Other Communist Navies: The View from the Mid-1980s.* Annapolis: Naval Institute Press, 1986.

Ginsburgs, George, and Alvin Z. Rubinstein (eds). *Soviet Policy Toward Western Europe.* New York: Praeger, 1978.

Golan, Galia. "Gorbachev's Middle East Strategy," *Foreign Affairs,* 65, No. 1, Fall 1987, 41-57.

_____. "The 'Vanguard Party' Controversy," *Soviet Studies,* 39, No. 4, October 1987, 599-609.

Gorman, Robert F. "Soviet Perspectives on the Prospects for Socialist Development in Africa," *African Affairs,* 83, April 1984, 163-87.

Gorshkov, S.G. *Morskaia moshch' gosudarstva.* Moscow: Voenizdat, 1979.

Grechko, A.A. *The Armed Forces of the Soviet Union.* Moscow: Progress 1977.

Gromyko, A.A., and B.N. Ponomarev (eds.). *Soviet Foreign Policy: Vol. I: 1917-1945, Vol. II: 1945-80.* (4th ed.) Moscow: Progress, 1981.

Hoffmann, Erik P., and Frederic J. Fleron, Jr. (eds.). *The Conduct of Soviet Foreign Policy.* New York: Aldine, 1980.

Holloway, David. "Arms Control." Pages 126-34 in James Cracraft (ed.), *The Soviet Union Today: An Interpretive Guide.* Chicago: University of Chicago Press, 1988.

Hough, Jerry F. *Soviet Leadership in Transition.* Washington: Brookings Institution, 1980.

_____. *The Struggle for the Third World: Soviet Debates and American Options.* Washington: Brookings Institution, 1985.

Jones, Christopher D. *Soviet Influence in Eastern Europe.* New York: Praeger, 1981.

Jones, David R. (ed.). *Soviet Armed Forces Review* (annuals 1977 through 1985). Gulf Breeze, Florida: Academic International Press, 1977-85.

Kanet, Roger E. (ed.). *Soviet Foreign Policy in the 1980s.* New York: Praeger, 1982.

Kaplan, Stephen S., Michel F. Tatu, Thomas W. Robinson, et al. *Diplomacy of Power: Soviet Armed Forces as a Political Instrument.* Washington: Brookings Institution, 1981.

Katz, Mark N. *The Third World in Soviet Military Thought.* London: Croom Helm, 1983.

Kavan, Zdeněk. "Gorbachev and the World: The Political Side." Pages 164-204 in David A. Dyker (ed.), *The Soviet Union under Gorbachev: Prospects for Reform.* London: Croom Helm, 1987.

Kelley, Paul D. *Soviet General Doctrine for War,* 1. (Soviet Battlefield Development Plan.) Washington: United States Army Intelligence and Threat Analysis Center, 1987.

Kitrinos, Robert W. "The CPSU Central Committee's International Department," *Problems of Communism,* 33, No. 5, September-October 1984, 47-65.

Klintworth, Gary. *Mr. Gorbachev's China Diplomacy*. (Working Paper No. 111.) Canberra: Australian National University, Strategic and Defense Studies Centre, Research School of Pacific Studies, October 1986.

Korbonski, Andrzej, and Francis Fukuyama (eds.). *The Soviet Union and the Third World: The Last Three Decades*. Ithaca: Cornell University Press, 1987.

Kozlov, S.N. (ed.). *The Officer's Handbook*. (Trans., Translation Bureau, Secretary of State Department, Ottawa, Canada.) (Soviet Military Thought Series.) Washington: United States Air Force, 1977.

Kozlov, S.N., D. Volkogonov, and S. Tyushkevich, et al. *Marxism-Leninism on War and the Army: A Soviet View*. (Trans., Progress, Moscow.) (Soviet Military Thought Series, 2.) Washington: United States Air Force, 1973.

Krakowski, Elie. "Afghanistan and Beyond: The Strategy of Dismemberment," *National Interest*, 37, No. 2, Spring 1987, 28–38.

Laird, Robbin F. (ed.). *Soviet Foreign Policy*. Montpelier, Vermont: Capital City Press for Academy of Political Science, 1987.

Laird, Robbin F., and Erik P. Hoffmann (eds.). *Soviet Foreign Policy in a Changing World*. Berlin: W. de Gruyter, 1986.

Lederer, Ivo. J. (ed.). *Russian Foreign Policy*. New Haven: Yale University Press, 1962.

Lee, William T., and Richard F. Staar. *Soviet Military Policy since World War II*. Stanford, California: Hoover Institution Press, 1986.

Leites, Nathan. *Soviet Style in War*. (Rand Publication Series.) Santa Monica, California: Rand, 1982.

Lomov, N.A. (ed.). *Scientific-Technical Progress and the Revolution in Military Affairs: A Soviet View*. (Trans., United States Air Force.) (Soviet Military Thought Series.) Washington: United States Air Force, 1973.

Lynch, Allen. *The Soviet Study of International Relations*. Cambridge: Cambridge University Press, 1987.

Lyne, Roderic. "Making Waves: Mr. Gorbachev's Public Diplomacy 1985-6," *International Affairs* [London], 63, No. 2, Spring 1987, 205-24.

Mccgwire, Michael. *Military Objectives in Soviet Foreign Policy*. Washington: Brookings Institution, 1987.

Macridis, Roy C. (ed.). *Foreign Policy in World Politics*. Englewood Cliffs, New Jersey: Prentice-Hall, 1985.

Malik, M. (ed.). *Soviet-American Relations with Pakistan, Iran, and Afghanistan*. Basingstoke, Hampshire, United Kingdom: Macmillan, 1986.

Mediansky, F.A., and Dianne Court. *The Soviet Union in Southeast Asia.* Canberra: Australian National University, Strategic and Defense Studies Centre, Research School of Pacific Studies, 1984.

Meissner, Boris. "The Foreign Ministry and Foreign Service of the USSR," *Aussenpolitik* [Hamburg], English edition, 28, No. 1, 1977, 49–64.

Menon, Rajan. *Soviet Power and the Third World.* New Haven: Yale University Press, 1986.

Milovidov, A.S., and V.G. Kozlov (eds.). *The Philosophical Heritage of V.I. Lenin and Problems of Contemporary War: A Soviet View.* (Trans., United States Air Force.) (Soviet Military Thought Series.) Washington: United States Air Force, 1977.

Moser, Charles (ed.). *Combat on Communist Territory.* Lake Bluff, Illinois: Regnery Gateway, 1985.

Nelsen, Harvey. "Strategic Weapons and the Sino-Soviet Dispute: An Overview," *Issues and Studies* [Taipei], 21, November 1985, 103–18.

Odom, William E. "Soviet Force Posture: Dilemmas and Directions," *Problems of Communism,* 34, No. 4, July–August 1985, 1–14.

Ogarkov, N.V. *Istoriia uchit bditel'nosti.* Moscow: Voenizdat, 1985.

_____. "Strategiia voennaia," *Sovetskaia Voennaia Entsiklopediia,* 7. Moscow: Voenizdat, 1979.

_____. *Vsegda v gotovnosti k zashchite otechestva.* Moscow: Voenizdat, 1982.

Osgood, Eugenia V. "Military Strategy in the Nuclear Age." Pages 114–25 in James Cracraft (ed.), *The Soviet Union Today: An Interpretive Guide.* Chicago: University of Chicago Press, 1988.

Petersen, Phillip, and John G. Hines. "The Conventional Offensive in Soviet Theater Strategy," *Orbis,* Fall 1983, 695–739.

Popov, V.I., I.D. Ovsyany, and V.P. Nikhamin (eds.). *A Study of Soviet Foreign Policy.* Moscow: Progress, 1975.

Ra'anan, Uri, and Charles M. Perry (eds.). *The USSR Today and Tomorrow.* Lexington, Massachusetts: Heath, 1987.

Ra'anan, Uri, Francis Fukuyama, Mark Falcoff, Sam C. Sarkesian, and Richard H. Shultz, Jr. *Third World Marxist-Leninist Regimes: Strengths, Vulnerabilities, and U.S. Policy.* Washington: Pergamon-Brassey, 1985.

Radzievskii, A.I. (ed.). *Dictionary of Basic Military Terms.* (Trans., Translation Bureau, Secretary of State Department, Ottawa, Canada.) (Soviet Military Thought Series.) Washington: United States Air Force, 1976.

Reznichenko, V.G., I.N. Vorob'ev, et al. *Taktika.* (Biblioteka ofitsera.) Moscow: Voenizdat, 1987.

Rubinstein, Alvin Z. *Soviet Foreign Policy since World War II: Imperial and Global.* (2d ed.) Boston: Little, Brown, 1985.

————. "Soviet Policy in the Third World in Perspective," *Military Review*, 58, No. 7, July 1978, 2-8.

————. *Soviet Policy Toward Turkey, Iran, and Afghanistan: The Dynamics of Influence.* New York: Praeger, 1982.

Saivetz, Carol R., and Sylvia Woodby. *Soviet-Third World Relations.* Boulder, Colorado: Westview Press, 1985.

Savkin, V.E. *The Basic Principles of Operational Art and Tactics.* (Trans., United States Air Force.) (Soviet Military Thought Series.) Washington: United States Air Force, 1972.

Scott, Harriet F., and William F. Scott. *The Soviet Art of War: Doctrine, Strategy, and Tactics.* Boulder, Colorado: Westview Press, 1982.

Scott, William F. *Soviet Sources of Military Doctrine and Strategy.* New York: Crane, Russak, 1975.

Selected Readings from Military Thought, 1963-1973, 5, Pts. 1-2. (Comp., Joseph D. Douglas and Amoretta M. Heeber.) (Studies in Communist Affairs.) Washington: United States Air Force, 1982.

Selected Soviet Military Writings, 1970-1975: A Soviet View. (Trans., United States Air Force.) (Soviet Military Thought Series.) Washington: United States Air Force, 1976.

Shansab, Nasir. "The Struggle for Afghanistan." Pages 106-27 in Charles Moser (ed.), *Combat on Communist Territory.* Lake Bluff, Illinois: Regnery Gateway, 1985.

Shenfield, Stephen. *The Nuclear Predicament: Explorations in Soviet Ideology*, 37. (Chatham House Papers, Royal Institute of International Affairs.) London: Routledge and Kegan Paul, 1987.

Sidorenko, A.A. *The Offensive.* (Trans., United States Air Force.) (Soviet Military Thought Series.) Washington: United States Air Force, 1973.

Slusser, Robert. "The Role of the Foreign Ministry." Pages 197-239 in Ivo. J. Lederer (ed.), *Russian Foreign Policy.* New Haven: Yale University Press, 1962.

Snyder, Jed C. "Turkey's Critical Role." Pages 45-52 in Jed C. Snyder (ed.), *Defending the Fringe: NATO, the Mediterranean, and the Persian Gulf.* Boulder, Colorado: Westview Press, 1987.

Snyder, Jed C. (ed.). *Defending the Fringe: NATO, the Mediterranean, and the Persian Gulf.* Boulder, Colorado: Westview Press, 1987.

Sokolovskiy, V.D. (ed.). *Soviet Military Strategy.* (Trans. and ed., Harriet F. Scott.) New York: Crane, Russak, 1975.

Sovetskaia voennaia entsiklopediia. (8 vols.) Moscow: Voenizdat, 1976-80.

"Soviet Calculus of Nuclear War," *Soviet Union,* Special Issue, 10, Pts. 2–3, 1983.

Staar, Richard F. *USSR: Foreign Policies after Detente.* Stanford, California: Hoover Institution Press, 1985.

Thakur, Ramesh, and Carlyle A. Thayer (eds.). *The Soviet Union as an Asian Pacific Power.* Boulder, Colorado: Westview Press, 1987.

Thom, Francoise. *Moscow's New Thinking as an Instrument of Foreign Policy.* Toronto: Mackenzie Institute, 1987.

Triska, Jan F., and David D. Finley. *Soviet Foreign Policy.* New York: Macmillan, 1968.

Ulam, Adam B. *Dangerous Relations: The Soviet Union in World Politics, 1970–1982.* New York: Oxford University Press, 1983.

———. *Expansion and Coexistence: Soviet Foreign Policy, 1917–1973.* (2d ed.). New York: Praeger, 1974.

———. *The Rivals: America and Russia since World War II.* New York: Viking, 1971.

———. "United States-Soviet Relations: Current Trends." Pages 121–29 in Uri Ra'anan and Charles M. Perry (eds.), *The USSR Today and Tomorrow.* Lexington, Massachusetts: Heath, 1987.

United States. Department of Defense. *Soviet Military Power: An Assessment of the Threat, 1988.* (7th ed.) Washington: 1988.

Vigor, Peter H. *The Soviet View of War, Peace, and Neutrality.* London: Routledge and Kegan Paul, 1975.

Voennii entsiklopedicheskii slovar'. Moscow: Voenizdat, 1983.

Volgyes, Ivan. "Troubled Friendship or Mutual Dependence? Eastern Europe and the USSR in the Gorbachev Era," *Orbis,* September 1986, 343–53.

Volkogonov, D.A. (ed.). *Marksistsko-Leninskoe uchenie o voine i armii.* (Biblioteka ofitsera.) Moscow: Voenizdat, 1984.

von Beyme, Klaus. *The Soviet Union in World Politics.* New York: St. Martin's Press, 1987.

Welch, William. *American Images of Soviet Foreign Policy.* New Haven: Yale University Press, 1970.

Wettig, Gerhard. "Eastern Europe in East-West Relations," *Aussenpolitik* [Hamburg], English edition, 37, No. 1, 1986, 3–23.

Wilson, Edward. *Russia and Black Africa Before World War II.* New York: Holmes and Meier, 1974.

Wolfe, Thomas W. *Soviet Strategy at the Crossroads.* Cambridge: Harvard University Press, 1964.

Zagoria, Donald S. (ed.). *Soviet Policy in East Asia.* New Haven: Yale University Press, 1982.

Zamostny, Thomas J. "Moscow and the Third World: Recent Trends in Soviet Thinking," *Soviet Studies,* 36, No. 2, April 1984, 223–35.

Zhilin, P.A. (ed.). *Istoriia voennogo iskusstva*. (Biblioteka ofitsera.) Moscow: Voenizdat, 1986.

(Various issues of the following publications were also used in the preparation of this chapter: Foreign Broadcast Information Service, *Daily Report: Soviet Union,* 1985–89; *Izvestiia* [Moscow], 1985–89; and *Pravda* [Moscow], 1985–89.)

Chapter 11

Becker, Abraham S. *Sitting on Bayonets: The Soviet Defense Burden and the Slowdown of Soviet Defense Spending*. Santa Monica, California: Rand, 1985.

_____. *Soviet Central Decisionmaking and Economic Growth: A Summing Up*. (Project Air Force, No. R–3349–AF.) Santa Monica, California: Rand, 1986.

Bergson, Abram. *The Economics of Soviet Planning*. Westport, Connecticut: Greenwood Press, 1980.

Bergson, Abram, and Herbert S. Levine (eds.). *The Soviet Economy: Toward the Year 2000*. London: Allen and Unwin, 1983.

Birman, Igor. "The Imbalance of the Soviet Economy," *Soviet Studies* [Glasgow], 60, No. 2, April 1988, 210–21.

_____. "The Soviet Economy: Alternative Views," *Atlantic Community Quarterly*, 24, No. 4, Winter 1986–87, 345–55.

Bohlen, Celestine. "Soviet Party Leadership Endorses Sweeping Economic Restructuring," *Washington Post*, June 27, 1987, A24.

Bornstein, Morris. "Soviet Price Policies," *Soviet Economy*, 3, No. 2, April–June 1987, 96–134.

Bornstein, Morris (ed.). *The Soviet Economy: Continuity and Change*. Boulder, Colorado: Westview Press, 1981.

Brown, Archie. "Gorbachev: New Man in the Kremlin," *Problems of Communism*, 34, No. 3, May–June 1985, 1–12.

Buck, Trevor, and John Cole. *Modern Soviet Economic Performance*. Oxford: Basil Blackwell, 1987.

Campbell, Robert Wellington. *Soviet Economic Power*. Boston: Houghton Mifflin, 1974.

Clarke, Roger A., and Dubravko J.I. Matko. *Soviet Economic Facts, 1917–1981*. (2d ed.) New York: St. Martin's Press, 1983.

Countries of the World and Their Leaders: Yearbook, 1986. Detroit: Gale Research, 1986.

Country Profile USSR, 1987–88. London: Economist Intelligence Unit, 1988.

Crane, Keith. *The Soviet Economic Dilemma of Eastern Europe.* (Project Air Force, No. R–3368–AF.) Santa Monica, California: Rand, 1986.

Dobb, Maurice. *Soviet Economic Development since 1917.* (Rev. ed.) New York: International, 1966.

Dyker, David A. (ed.). *The Soviet Union under Gorbachev.* Beckenham, Kent, United Kingdom: Croom Helm, 1987.

Elek, Peter S. "Soviet Capital Strategy and Performance During the Eleventh Five-Year Plan: Past, Present, and Prospective." Pages 139–69 in Philip Joseph (ed.), *The Soviet Economy after Brezhnev.* Brussels: North Atlantic Treaty Organization, 1984.

Europa Year Book, 1987, 2. London: Europa, 1987.

Fewtrell, David. *The Soviet Economic Crisis: Prospects for the Military and the Consumer.* (Adelphi Papers, No. 186.) London: International Institute for Strategic Studies, 1983.

Freidzon, Sergei. *Top-Level Administration of the Soviet Economy: A Partial View.* (Rand Paper Series, No. P–7178.) Santa Monica, California: Rand, 1986.

Galuszka, Peter, and Bill Javetski. "Reforming the Soviet Economy," *Business Week,* No. 3029, December 7, 1987, 76–80, 84, 88.

Gorbachev, Mikhail. *Restructuring: A Vital Concern of the People.* (Speech at 18th Congress of the Trade Unions of the USSR, February 25, 1987.) Moscow: Novosti Press Agency, 1987.

Gregory, Paul R., and Robert C. Stuart. *Soviet Economic Structure and Performance.* (3d ed.) New York: Harper and Row, 1986.

Guidelines for the Economic and Social Development of the USSR for 1986–1990 and the Period to the Year 2000. Moscow: Novosti Press Agency, 1986.

Gustafson, Thane. *The Soviet Economy in the 1980s.* (Rand Paper Series, No. P6755.) Santa Monica, California: Rand, 1982.

Gustafson, Thane, and Dawn Mann. "Gorbachev's First Year: Building Power and Authority," *Problems of Communism,* 35, No. 3, May–June 1986, 1–19.

Hanson, Philip. "The Soviet Economy after Seventy Years," Radio Free Europe/Radio Liberty, *Radio Liberty Research Bulletin* [Munich], October 19, 1987, 1–7.

Hewett, Ed A. *Reforming the Soviet Economy: Equality Versus Efficiency.* Washington: Brookings Institution, 1988.

Hofheinz, Paul. "Gorbachev's Double Burden: Economic Reform and Growth Acceleration," *Millennium,* 16, No. 1, Spring 1987, 21–53.

Hough, Jerry F. *Opening Up the Soviet Economy.* Washington: Brookings Institution, 1988.

Hutchings, Raymond. *The Soviet Budget.* Albany: State University of New York Press, 1983.

_____. *Soviet Economic Development.* (2d ed.) New York: New York University Press, 1982.

Joseph, Philip (ed.). *The Soviet Economy after Brezhnev.* Brussels: North Atlantic Treaty Organization, 1984.

Kennan, George F. "The Gorbachev Prospect," *New York Review of Books,* 34, Nos. 21-22, January 21, 1988, 3, 6-7.

Lee, Gary. "Gorbachev's Reforms Become Law," *Washington Post,* July 1, 1987, A1, A27.

_____. "Reforms Entering Crucial Phase," *Washington Post,* May 22, 1988, A1, A34.

_____. "Three Gorbachev Backers Put on Politburo," *Washington Post,* June 27, 1987, A1, A24.

Levine, Herbert S. "Gorbachev's Economic Reform: A Soviet Economy Roundtable," *Soviet Economy,* 3, No. 1, January–March 1987, 40-53.

Linden, Carl A. *Khrushchev and the Soviet Leadership, 1957-1964.* Baltimore: Johns Hopkins Press, 1966.

Linz, Susan J. "Managerial Autonomy in Soviet Firms," *Soviet Studies* [Glasgow], 40, No. 2, April 1988, 175-95.

McCauley, Martin. "The Soviet Union Seventy Years after the Revolution," Radio Free Europe/Radio Liberty, *Radio Liberty Research Bulletin* [Munich], October 21, 1987, 1-5.

McNeill, Terry. "Gorbachev's First Three Years in Power," Radio Free Europe/Radio Liberty, *Radio Liberty Research Bulletin* [Munich], February 29, 1988, 1-8.

_____. "The USSR and Communism: The Twilight Years," Radio Free Europe/Radio Liberty, *Radio Liberty Research Bulletin* [Munich], October 29, 1987, 1-5.

Medish, Vadim. *The Soviet Union.* (3d ed.) Englewood Cliffs, New Jersey: Prentice-Hall, 1987.

Miller, Robert F. "Will the Next Seventy Years Be 'Even Better'?" Radio Free Europe/Radio Liberty, *Radio Liberty Research Bulletin* [Munich], October 30, 1987, 1-5.

Moore, Barrington, Jr. *Authority and Inequality under Capitalism and Socialism.* Oxford: Oxford University Press, 1987.

Nove, Alec. *An Economic History of the U.S.S.R.* New York: Penguin Press, 1969.

Remnick, David. "Gorbachev Goals Seem Far from Fruition," *Washington Post,* December 3, 1987, A26.

Roucek, Tibor. "Private Enterprise in Soviet Political Debates," *Soviet Studies* [Glasgow], 40, No. 1, January 1988, 46–63.

Rumer, Boris. "Realities of Gorbachev's Economic Program," *Problems of Communism*, 35, No. 3, May–June 1986, 20–31.

Scherer, John L. (ed.). *USSR Facts and Figures Annual.* Gulf Breeze, Florida: Academic International Press, 1986.

Schoepflin, George (ed.). *The Soviet Union and Eastern Europe.* (Handbooks to the Modern World.) New York: Facts on File, 1986.

Schroeder, Gertrude E. "Anatomy of Gorbachev's Economic Reform," *Soviet Economy*, 3, No. 3, July–September 1987, 219–41.

Scott, William F. "Moscow's Military-Industrial Complex," *Air Force Magazine*, 70, No. 3, March 1987, 47–51.

Scrivener, Ronald. *USSR Economic Handbook.* London: Euromonitor, 1986.

Sestanovich, Stephen. "Gorbachev's Secret Foe: The Workers," *Washington Post,* November 1, 1987, C1, C2.

Sherman, Howard J. *The Soviet Economy.* Boston: Little, Brown, 1969.

Shoup, Paul. *The East European and Soviet Data Handbook: Political, Social, and Developmental Indicators, 1945–1975.* Stanford, California: Hoover Institution Press, 1981.

Slider, Darrell. "The Brigade System in Soviet Industry: An Effort to Restructure the Labour Force," *Soviet Studies* [Glasgow], 39, No. 3, July 1987, 388–405.

Tatu, Michel. "Seventy Years after the Revolution: What Next?," Radio Free Europe/Radio Liberty, *Radio Liberty Research Bulletin* [Munich], October 26, 1987, 1–5.

Teague, Elizabeth. "Gorbachev Tells Plenum Soviet Economy Has Stopped Growing," Radio Free Europe/Radio Liberty, *Radio Liberty Research Bulletin* [Munich], February 22, 1988, 1–4.

Thompson, John M. *Russia and the Soviet Union: An Historical Introduction.* New York: Scribner's, 1986.

United States. Central Intelligence Agency and Defense Intelligence Agency. "The Soviet Economy Stumbles Badly in 1989." (Report presented to United States Congress, 102d, 1st Session, Joint Economic Committee, Subcommittee on Technology and National Security.) Washington: April 20, 1990.

————. Congress. 97th, 2d Session. Joint Economic Committee. *Soviet Economy in the 1980's: Problems and Prospects.* Washington: GPO, 1983.

————. Congress. 100th, 1st Session. Joint Economic Committee. *Gorbachev's Economic Plans.* (2 vols.) Washington: GPO, 1987.

Weickhardt, George G. "The Soviet Military-Industrial Complex and Economic Reform," *Soviet Economy*, 2, No. 3, 1986, 193–220.

Zaleski, Eugene. *Stalinist Planning for Economic Growth, 1933–1952.* (Trans., Marie-Christine MacAndrew and John H. Moore.) Chapel Hill: University of North Carolina Press, 1980.

(Various issues of the following publications were also used in the preparation of this chapter: Joint Publications Research Service, *USSR Report: National Economy* and *Soviet Union: Economic Affairs,* 1983–87.)

Chapter 12

Babak, Ye. "Robot trebuet rabotu," *Ekonomicheskaia gazeta* [Moscow], No. 44, November 1987, 12.

Bairam, Erkin. *Technical Progress and Industrial Growth in the USSR and Eastern Europe.* Aldershot, United Kingdom: Avebury, 1988.

Bergson, A.S. *Technical Progress and Soviet Economic Development.* New York: Basil Blackwell, 1986.

Berliner, Joseph S. *Soviet Industry from Stalin to Gorbachev.* Ithaca: Cornell University Press, 1988.

Brucan, Silviu. *World Socialism at the Crossroads: An Insider's View.* New York: Praeger, 1987.

Cochrane, Nancy. "The Classification of the Branch and Ministerial System of the Machine Building and Metal Working Branch of Soviet Industry." (Library of Congress, Federal Research Division, Research Report.) Washington: July 1985.

Cole, J.P. *Geography of the Soviet Union.* Cambridge: Cambridge University Press, 1984.

Cook, Linda J. "Gorbachev's Reforms, Workers, and Welfare: The Threat to Employment Security and Its Political Implications." (Paper presented at American Association for the Advancement of Slavic Studies Meeting, Boston, November 5–8, 1987.) Boston: 1987.

Dellenbrant, Jan Ake. *The Soviet Regional Dilemma: Planning, People, and Natural Resources.* Armonk, New York: Sharpe, 1986.

Dienes, Leslie. "The Soviet Oil Industry in the Twelfth Five-Year Plan," *Soviet Geography,* 28, No. 11, November 1987, 617–55.

Fadeev, V.T. "Effektivnost' gazotransportnoi sistemy: Sovremennaia taktika tekhnicheskogo obnovleniia," *Gazovaia promyshlennost'* [Moscow], 11, November 1987, 28.

Freris, Andrew. *The Soviet Industrial Enterprise.* London: Croom Helm, 1984.

Goldman, Marshall I. *Gorbachev's Challenge: Economic Reform in the Age of High Technology.* New York: Norton, 1987.

Gosudarstvennyi komitet po statistike. *Narodnoe khoziaistvo SSSR za 70 let.* Moscow: Finansy i statistika, 1987.

Kelly, William J., Hugh L. Shaffer, and J. Kenneth Thompson. *Energy Research and Development in the USSR: Preparations for the Twenty-First Century.* Durham: Duke University Press, 1986.

Khrushchev, A.T. *Geografiia promyshlennosti SSSR.* Moscow: Mysl', 1986.

Kirichenko, Vadim Nikitovich (ed.). *Uskoreniie sotsial'no-ekonomicheskogo razvitiia i perspektivnoe planirovaniie.* Moscow: Ekonomika, 1987.

Koropeckyj, I.S., and Gertrude E. Schroeder. *Economics of Soviet Regions.* New York: Praeger, 1981.

Kostakov, Vladimir G. "Labor Problems in Light of Perestroika," *Soviet Economy,* 4, No. 1, January–March 1988, 95–101.

Kuleshov, M.V. "How the Branches Should Produce Consumer Goods," *Ekonomika i organizatsiia promyshlennogo proizvodstva* [Novosibirsk], No. 2, February 1987. Joint Publications Research Service, *USSR Report: National Economy.* (JPRS–UEA–87–003L.) May 19, 1987, 39–47.

Kuromiya, Hiroaki. *Stalin's Industrial Revolution.* Cambridge: Cambridge University Press, 1988.

Liubomirov, P.G. *Ocherk po istorii russkoi promyshlennosti XVII, XVIII i nachalo XIX veka.* Moscow: Gosudarstvennoe izdatel'stvo politicheskoi literatury, 1947.

Matosich, Andrew J. "Machine Building: Perestroika's Sputtering Engine," *Soviet Economy,* 4, No. 2, April–June 1988, 144–78.

Medish, Vadim. *The Soviet Union.* (3d ed.) Englewood Cliffs, New Jersey: Prentice-Hall, 1987.

"Ob itogakh vypolneniia Gosudarstvennogo plana ekonomicheskogo i sotsial'nogo razvitiia SSSR v pervom polugodii 1987 goda," *Ekonomicheskaia gazeta* [Moscow], No. 31, June 1987, 2.

Pares, Bernard. *A History of Russia.* New York: Knopf, 1953.

Planirovanie razvitiia mezhotraslevykh kompleksov. Moscow: Moskovskii Universitet, 1982.

"Pora budit' printsessu," *Pravda* [Moscow], No. 189, July 8, 1987, 3.

Sagers, Matthew J. "New Notes: Soviet Energy Industries," *Soviet Geography,* 30, No. 4, April 1989, 306–35.

Sagers, Matthew J., and Milford E. Green. "Coal Movements in the USSR," *Soviet Geography,* 25, No. 12, December 1984, 713–32.

Scott, William F. "Moscow's Military-Industrial Complex," *Air Force Magazine,* 70, No. 3, March 1987, 46–51.

945

Sestanovich, Stephen. "Gorbachev's Secret Foe: The Workers," *Washington Post,* January 11, 1987, C1, C2.

Seton-Watson, Hugh. *The Russian Empire, 1801–1917.* Oxford: Clarendon Press, 1967.

Shabad, Theodore. "Geographic Aspects of the New Soviet Five-Year Plan, 1986–90," *Soviet Geography,* 27, No. 1, January 1986, 1–16.

The Soviet Union. (2d ed.) Washington: Congressional Quarterly, 1986.

Spidchenko, Konstantin. *USSR: Geography of the Eleventh Five-Year Plan Period.* Moscow: Progress, 1984.

Stal' [Moscow], No. 4, April 1987, 1–6.

Swearingen, Rodger (ed.). *Siberia and the Soviet Far East: Strategic Dimensions in Multinational Perspective.* Stanford, California: Hoover Institution Press, 1987.

Trofimuk, Andrei. "Siberia Unfreezes Its Assets," *New Science,* 113, No. 1566, June 25, 1987, 52–54.

Trubchanin, V.I. "Gorno-prokhodcheskaia tekhnika Yasinovat-skogo mashinostroitel'nogo zavoda im. 60-letiia SSSR," *Ugol' Ukrainy* [Kiev], No. 5, May 1987, 16.

United States. Central Intelligence Agency. *USSR Energy Atlas.* Washington: GPO, 1985.

_____. Central Intelligence Agency and Defense Intelligence Agency. "The Soviet Economy Stumbles Badly in 1989." Washington: April 20, 1990.

_____. Congress. 97th, 2d Session. Joint Economic Committee. *Soviet Economy in the 1980's: Problems and Prospects.* Washington: GPO, 1983.

_____. Congress. 100th, 1st Session. Joint Economic Committee. *Gorbachev's Economic Plans.* (2 vols.) Washington: GPO, 1987.

_____. Department of Defense. *Soviet Military Power: An Assessment of the Threat, 1988.* (7th ed.) Washington: 1988.

_____. Department of Defense. *Soviet Military Power, 1987.* Washington: GPO, March 1987.

Wood, Alan (ed.). *Siberia: Problems and Prospects.* London: Croom Helm, 1987.

Yershov, A.P. "Automation of the Work of Employees: Experience of Developed Capitalist Countries," *Ekonomika i organizatsiia promyshlennogo proizvodstva* [Novosibirsk], No. 2, February 1987. Joint Publications Research Service, *USSR Report: National Economy.* (JPRS-UNE-87-038.) May 19, 1987, 187–98.

"Zakrepit' dostignutoe, uskorit' tempy," *Izvestiia* [Moscow], No. 24, January 24, 1988, 3.

Beaucourt, Chantal. "The Crop Policy of the Soviet Union: Present Characteristics and Future Perspectives." Pages 49–69 in Ronald A. Francisco, Betty A. Laird, and Roy D. Laird (eds.), *Agricultural Policies in the USSR and Eastern Europe.* (Westview Special Studies on the Soviet Union and Eastern Europe.) Boulder, Colorado: Westview Press, 1980.

Bohlen, Celestine. "From Russia, with Hope and Skepticism," *Washington Post,* August 16, 1987, A1, A20.

_____. "Gorbachev Stirs Consumer Fears That Food Subsidies Are Target," *Washington Post,* October 23, 1987, A25, A34.

Buck, Trevor, and John Cole. *Modern Soviet Economic Performance.* Oxford: Basil Blackwell, 1987.

Communist Party of the Soviet Union. *Basic Directions for the Economic and Social Development of the USSR for 1986–1990 and for the Period to the Year 2000.* Moscow: Novosti Press Agency, 1985.

Conolly, Violet. "Siberia: Yesterday, Today, and Tomorrow." Pages 3–39 in Rodger Swearingen (ed.), *Siberia and the Soviet Far East: Strategic Dimensions in Multinational Perspective.* Stanford, California: Hoover Institution Press, 1987.

Dovring, Folke. "Soviet Agriculture: A State Secret," *Current History,* 83, October 1984, 323–26, 338–39.

Evans, Alfred, Jr. "Changes in the Soviet Model of Rural Transformation." Pages 143–58 in Robert C. Stuart (ed.), *The Soviet Rural Economy.* Totowa, New Jersey: Rowman and Allanheld, 1983.

Francisco, Ronald A., Betty A. Laird, and Roy D. Laird (eds.). *Agricultural Policies in the USSR and Eastern Europe.* (Westview Special Studies on the Soviet Union and Eastern Europe.) Boulder, Colorado: Westview Press, 1980.

Gagnon, V.P., Jr. "Gorbachev and the Collective Contract Brigade," *Soviet Studies,* 39, No. 1, January 1987, 26–40.

Goldman, Marshall I. *Gorbachev's Challenge: Economic Reform in the Age of High Technology.* New York: Norton, 1987.

Gosudarstvennyi komitet po statistike. *Narodnoe khoziaistvo SSSR za 70 let.* Moscow: Finansy i statistika, 1987.

Jacobs, Everett M. "Soviet Agricultural Management and Planning and the 1982 Administrative Reforms." Pages 273–95 in Robert C. Stuart (ed.), *The Soviet Rural Economy.* Totowa, New Jersey: Rowman and Allanheld, 1983.

Johnson, D. Gale, and Karen McConnell Brooks. *Prospects for Soviet Agriculture in the 1980s.* (CSIS Publication Series on the Soviet Union in the 1980s.) Bloomington: Indiana University Press, 1983.

Joseph, Philip (ed.). *The Soviet Economy after Brezhnev.* Brussels: North Atlantic Treaty Organizations, 1984.

Kahan, Arcadius. "Shifts to Off-Farm Agricultural Inputs in the Tenth Economic Plan: The Economic and Institutional Implications." Pages 9–25 in Roy D. Laird, Joseph Hajda, and Betty A. Laird (eds.), *The Future of Agriculture in the Soviet Union and Eastern Europe.* (Westview Special Studies on the Soviet Union and Eastern Europe.) Boulder, Colorado: Westview Press, 1977.

Kerblay, Basile. *Modern Soviet Society.* New York: Pantheon, 1983.

Kirichenko, V.N. *Piatiletka dvenadtsataia: Piatiletka kachestvennykh sdvigov.* Moscow: Izdatel'stvo politicheskoi literatury, 1986.

Laird, Roy D. (ed.). *Soviet Agricultural and Peasant Affairs.* (Slavic Studies Series, 1.) Westport, Connecticut: Greenwood Press, 1982.

Laird, Roy D., and Betty A. Laird. "The Widening Soviet Grain Gap and Prospects for 1980 and 1990." Pages 27–47 in Roy D. Laird, Joseph Hajda, and Betty A. Laird (eds.), *The Future of Agriculture in the Soviet Union and Eastern Europe.* (Westview Special Studies on the Soviet Union and Eastern Europe.) Boulder, Colorado: Westview Press, 1977.

Laird, Roy D., Joseph Hajda, and Betty A. Laird (eds.). *The Future of Agriculture in the Soviet Union and Eastern Europe.* (Westview Special Studies on the Soviet Union and Eastern Europe.) Boulder, Colorado: Westview Press, 1977.

Lane, David. *Soviet Economy and Society.* New York: New York University Press, 1985.

Litvin, Valentin. "Agro-Industrial Complexes: Recent Structural Reform in the Rural Economy of the USSR." Pages 258–72 in Robert C. Stuart (ed.), *The Soviet Rural Economy.* Totowa, New Jersey: Rowman and Allanheld, 1983.

_____. *The Soviet Agro-Industrial Complex: Structure and Performance.* Boulder, Colorado: Westview Press, 1987.

Lydolph, Paul E. *Geography of the USSR.* Elkhart Lake, Wisconsin: Misty Valley, 1979.

Manucharova, E. "Otstupit' nekuda: Beseda s ivestnym sovetskim ekonomistom akademikom A. Aganbegianom," *Izvestiia* [Moscow], No. 237, August 25, 1987, 2.

Medish, Vadim. *The Soviet Union.* (3d ed.) Englewood Cliffs, New Jersey: Prentice Hall, 1987.

Medvedev, Zhores A. *Soviet Agriculture.* New York: Norton, 1987.

Mikheyev, Dmitry. "The Woes of Farmer Andropov," *Worldview,* 27, February 1984, 5–8.

"New Phenomena in the Private Subsidiary Farm," *Voprosy ekonomiki* [Moscow], July 1987. Joint Publications Research

Service, *Soviet Union: Economic Affairs*. (JPRS-UEA-87-017-L.) November 20, 1987, 12-24.

"Perestroika nabiraet silu," *Izvestiia* [Moscow], No. 19, January 19, 1988, 1-3.

Sergeyev, Valentin. *The Breadwinners*. Moscow: Progress, 1984.

Severin, Keith. "An Assessment of the Soviet Food Program." Pages 85-112 in Philip Joseph (ed.), *The Soviet Economy after Brezhnev*. Brussels: North Atlantic Treaty Organization, 1984.

_____. "Soviet Policies on Agriculture, Trade, and the Consumer." Pages 37-48 in Ronald A. Francisco, Betty A. Laird, and Roy D. Laird (eds.), *Agricultural Policies in the USSR and Eastern Europe*. (Westview Special Studies on the Soviet Union and Eastern Europe.) Boulder, Colorado: Westview Press, 1980.

Shatkhan, A.S., V.D. Filippov, S.A. Avakov, and A.P. Kuznetsova (eds.). *Razmeshchenie pishchevoi promyshlennosti SSSR*. Moscow: Legkaia i pishchevaia promyshlennost', 1983.

Spidchenko, Konstantin. *USSR: Geography of the Eleventh Five-Year Plan Period*. Moscow: Progress, 1984.

Stanglin, Douglas, and Jeff Trimble. "For Moscow, a Harvest of Good News," *U.S. News and World Report*, September 28, 1987, 79.

Stuart, Robert C. "Introduction: Perspectives on the Russian and Soviet Rural Economy." Pages 1-17 in Robert C. Stuart (ed.), *The Soviet Rural Economy*. Totowa, New Jersey: Rowman and Allanheld, 1983.

Stuart, Robert C. (ed.). *The Soviet Rural Economy*. Totowa, New Jersey: Rowman and Allanheld, 1983.

Swearer, Howard R. "Agricultural Administration under Khrushchev." Pages 9-40 in Roy D. Laird (ed.), *Soviet Agricultural and Peasant Affairs*. (Slavic Studies Series, 1.) Westport, Connecticut: Greenwood Press, 1982.

Swearingen, Rodger. "The Soviet Far East, East Asia, and the Pacific—Strategic Dimensions." Pages 226-72 in Rodger Swearingen (ed.), *Siberia and the Soviet Far East: Strategic Dimensions in Multinational Perspective*. Stanford, California: Hoover Institution Press, 1987.

Swearingen, Rodger (ed.). *Siberia and the Soviet Far East: Strategic Dimensions in Multinational Perspective*. Stanford, California: Hoover Institution Press, 1987. ·

Sysoev, N.P. "Rybnaia promyshlennost'." Pages 65-74 in A.S. Shatkhan, V.D. Filippov, S.A. Avakov, and A.P. Kuznestsova (eds.), *Razmeshchenie pishchevoi promyshlennosti SSSR*. Moscow: Legkaia i pishchevaia promyshlennost', 1983.

Treadgold, Donald W. "Soviet Agriculture in the Light of History." Pages 3-8 in Roy D. Laird (ed.), *Soviet Agricultural and Peasant Affairs.* (Slavic Studies Series, 1.) Westport, Connecticut: Greenwood Press, 1982.

United States. Department of Agriculture. Economic Research Service. *USSR Situation and Outlook Report.* (Regional Report Series, No. RS-86-3.) Washington: GPO, 1986.

―――. Department of Agriculture. Economic Research Service. *USSR Situation and Outlook Report.* (Regional Report Series, No. RS-87-4.) Washington: GPO, 1987.

"V protsesse perestroiki," *Izvestiia* [Moscow], No. 200, July 19, 1987, 1-3.

Waedekin, Karl-Eugen. "Agroindustrial Associations Take Root Across the USSR," Radio Free Europe/Radio Liberty, *Radio Liberty Research Bulletin* [Munich], February 13, 1984, 1-5.

―――. "'Contract' and 'Normless' Labor on Soviet Farms: An Interpretation and Prognosis," Radio Free Europe/Radio Liberty, *Radio Liberty Research Bulletin* [Munich], February 8, 1984, 1-6.

―――. "The New Kolkhoz Statute: A Codification of Restructuring on the Farm," Radio Free Europe/Radio Liberty, *Radio Liberty Research Bulletin* [Munich], January 28, 1988, 1-4.

―――. "The Private Agricultural Sector in the 1980s," Radio Free Europe/Radio Liberty, *Radio Liberty Research Bulletin* [Munich], August 2, 1985, 1-6.

―――. "Soviet Agriculture in 1987 and the Private Sector," Radio Free Europe/Radio Liberty, *Radio Liberty Research Bulletin* [Munich], March 15, 1988, 1-6.

―――. "Two Agricultural Decrees of September, 1987," Radio Free Europe/Radio Liberty, *Radio Liberty Research Bulletin* [Munich], October 16, 1987, 1-6.

―――. "What Is New about Brigades in Soviet Agriculture?," Radio Free Europe/Radio Liberty, *Radio Liberty Research Bulletin* [Munich], February 18, 1985, 1-7.

Wyzan, Michael L. "The Kolkhoz and the Sovkhoz: Relative Performance as Measured by Productive Technology." Pages 173-98 in Robert C. Stuart (ed.), *The Soviet Rural Economy.* Totowa, New Jersey: Rowman and Allanheld, 1983.

"Zakrepit' dostignutoe, uskorit' tempy," *Izvestiia* [Moscow], No. 24, January 24, 1988, 1-4.

Chapter 14

Ambler, John, Denis Shaw, and Leslie Symans (eds.). *Soviet and East European Transport Problems.* New York: St. Martin's Press, 1985.

Bagrov, L.V. *Rechnoi transport Rossii na puti intensifikatsii.* Moscow: Transport, 1986.

Belov, I.V. (ed.). *Transport strany sovetov.* Moscow: Transport, 1987.

B(oblet), D(ominique). "Le R200 en service commercial," *La Vie du rail* [Paris], August 1986, 14.

Bock, Bruno, and Klaus Bock. *Soviet Bloc Merchant Ships.* Annapolis: Naval Institute Press, 1981.

Carr, William. "The Soviet Merchant Fleet: Its Economic Role and Its Impact on Western Shipping." Pages 663–77 in United States Congress, 86th, 1st Session, Joint Economic Committee, *Soviet Economy in a Time of Change.* Washington: GPO, 1979.

Clayton, Elizabeth M. "Soviet Rural Roads: Problems and Prospects," *Studies in Comparative Communism* [Guildford, United Kingdom], 20, No. 2, Summer 1987, 163–73.

Cole, J.P. *Geography of the Soviet Union.* Cambridge: Cambridge University Press, 1984.

Communist Party of the Soviet Union. *The Great Patriotic War of the Soviet Union, 1941–1945.* Moscow: Progress, 1974.

Coutou-Bégarie, Hervé. *La puissance maritime soviétique.* Paris: Economica, 1983.

"Dritte Strecke der SZD jenseits des Polarkreises," *Eisenbahnpraxis* [East Berlin], No. 3, 1987, 120.

Ekonomika morskogo transporta. Moscow: Transport, 1987.

Ermolaev, V. "Zamerli samolety," *Pravda* [Moscow], 329, November 25, 1987, 6.

Flynn, Judith, and Barbara Severin. "Soviet Agricultural Transport: Bottlenecks to Continue." Pages 62–78 in United States Congress, 100th, 1st Session. Joint Economic Committee, *Gorbachev's Economic Plans.* (2 vols.) Washington: GPO, 1987.

"Fuel Shortage Stops 15 Million Passengers Flying Aeroflot," Radio Free Europe/Radio Liberty, *Radio Liberty Research Bulletin* [Munich], February 5, 1988, 9.

Gold, Philip. "A Merchant Fleet That Serves More Than Trade Purposes," *Insight,* March 7, 1988, 30–31.

Gosudarstvennyi komitet po statistike. *Narodnoe khoziaistvo SSSR za 70 let.* Moscow: Finansy i statistika, 1987.

Gromov, Panchenko, Chudnovskiy. *Edinaia transportnaia sistema.* Moscow: Transport, 1987.

Guzhenko, T.B. (ed.). *Morskoi transport SSSR: K 60-letiiu otrasli.* Moscow: Transport, 1984.

Hunter, Holland. *Soviet Transportation Policy.* Cambridge: Harvard University Press, 1957.

Hunter, Holland, and Deborah Kaple. *The Soviet Railroad Situation.* Washington: Wharton Econometric Forecasting Association, 1983.

Hunter, Holland, and Vladimir Kontorovich. "Transport Pressures and Potentials." Pages 382–96 in United States Congress, 100th, 1st Session, Joint Economic Committee, *Gorbachev's Economic Plans.* (2 vols.) Washington: GPO, 1987.

Jane's All the World's Aircraft, 1985–86. (Comp. and ed., John W.R. Taylor.) New York: Jane's, 1985.

Jane's Military Vehicles and Ground Support Equipment. (Eds., Christopher F. Foss and Terry J. Gander.) London: Jane's, 1985.

Jane's World Railways, 1986–87. (Ed., Jeoffrey Freeman Allen.) London: Jane's, 1986.

Katz, Zev. *The Communications System in the USSR.* Cambridge: Center for International Studies, Massachusetts Institute of Technology, 1987.

Kazanskii, N.N. (ed.). *Geografiia putei soobshcheniia.* Moscow: Transport, 1987.

Kerezhin, M. "Poezda poidut morskim putem," *Ekonomicheskaia gazeta* [Moscow], No. 40, October 1986, 20.

Kontorovich, Vladimir. "Discipline and Growth in the Soviet Economy," *Problems of Communism,* 34, No. 6, November–December 1985, 18–31.

Long, D.M. *The Soviet Merchant Fleet.* London: Lloyd's of London Press, 1986.

MacDonald, Hugh. *Aeroflot: Soviet Air Transport since 1923.* London: Putnam, 1975.

Moguchii, A. "Shipy i rozy," *Moskovskaia pravda* [Moscow], July 16, 1987, 3.

Mote, Victor L. "The Communications Infrastructure." Pages 61–64 in Rodger Swearingen (ed.), *Siberia and the Soviet Far East: Strategic Dimensions in Multinational Perspective.* Stanford, California: Hoover Institution Press, 1987.

Mushrub, A.G. (ed.). *Razvitie sovetskogo zheleznodorozhnogo transporta.* Moscow: Transport, 1984.

Nooijer, C.C.M. de. "Countering the Mine Threat," *Naval Forces* [Farnborough, Hampshire, United Kingdom], No. 4, 1985, 67.

"Reference Aid: Directory of the USSR Ministry of Railways." Joint Publications Research Service, *Soviet Union: Economic Affairs.* (JPRS-UEA-88-025.) June 29, 1988, B–74.

Sagers, Matthew J., and Milford B. Green. *The Transportation of Soviet Energy Resources.* Totowa, New Jersey: Rowman and Littlefield, 1986.

"Samyi dlinnyi poezd," *Trud* [Moscow], April 19, 1986, 4.

Shabad, Theodore, and Victor L. Mote. *Gateway to Siberian Resources (The BAM).* New York: John Wiley and Sons, 1977.

Shafirkin, B.I. *Edinaia transportnaia sistema SSSR i vzaimodeistvie.* Moscow: Vysshaia shkola, 1983.

Solzhenitsyn, Aleksandr. *The Gulag Archipelago,* 3-4. New York: Harper and Row, 1975.

Swearingen, Rodger (ed.). *Siberia and the Soviet Far East: Strategic Dimensions in Multilateral Perspective.* Stanford, California: Hoover Institution Press, 1987.

Teeter, Lorie. "Alcatel: Big Soviet Deal," *MIS Week,* 10, No. 11, March 13, 1989, 1, 5.

United States. Central Intelligence Agency. Directorate of Intelligence. *Directory of Soviet Officials: National Organizations.* Washington: GPO, August 1983.

_____. Central Intelligence Agency. Directorate of Intelligence. *Handbook of Economic Statistics, 1987.* Washington: GPO, 1987.

_____. Central Intelligence Agency. Directorate of Intelligence. *USSR Energy Atlas.* Washington: GPO, 1985.

_____. Congress. 86th, 1st Session. Joint Economic Committee. *Soviet Economy in a Time of Change.* Washington: GPO, 1979.

_____. Congress. 100th, 1st Session. Joint Economic Committee. *Gorbachev's Economic Plans.* (2 vols.) Washington: GPO, 1987.

_____. Department of Commerce. *Statistical Abstract of the United States, 1988.* Washington: GPO, 1989.

_____. Department of Defense. *Soviet Military Power, 1987.* Washington: GPO, March 1987.

White, Paul M. *Planning of Urban Transport Systems in the Soviet Union.* Birmingham, United Kingdom: Centre for Urban and Regional Studies, University of Birmingham, 1978.

York, Michael. "Flying with Aeroflot," *Washington Post,* Pts. 1-2, December 11-12, 1988.

(Various issues of the following publications were also used in the preparation of this chapter: *International Railway Journal,* 1985-88; *Rail International* [Brussels], 1985-88; and *Railway Gazette International* [Surrey, United Kingdom], 1985-88.)

Chapter 15

"And All Siberia Still Between," *Economist* [London], November 21, 1987, 44.

Assetto, Valerie J. "The Soviet Union at Bretton Woods." Pages 53-68 in *The Soviet Bloc in the IMF and the IBRD.* Boulder, Colorado: Westview Press, 1988.

Becker, Abraham S. "Soviet Union and the Third World: The Economic Dimension," *Soviet Economy*, 2, No. 3, July–September 1986, 233–60.

Bergson, Abram, and Herbert S. Levine (eds.). *The Soviet Economy: Toward the Year 2000.* London: Allen and Unwin, 1983.

Brown, Archie, John Fennell, and Michael Kaser (eds.). *The Cambridge Encyclopedia of Russia and the Soviet Union.* Cambridge: Cambridge University Press, 1982.

Cracraft, James (ed.). *The Soviet Union Today: An Interpretive Guide.* Chicago: University of Chicago Press, 1988.

Czerniejewicz, Wilfried. "Linkage with Europe." Pages 135–57 in Rodger Swearingen (ed.), *Siberia and the Soviet Far East: Strategic Dimensions in Multinational Perspective.* Stanford, California: Hoover Institution Press, 1987.

Delfs, Robert. "Three Obstacles, Two Leaders, and One Problem," *Far East Economic Review*, March 24, 1988, 56–57.

Diamond-Kim, Deborah. "Partners in Austerity," *China Business Review*, 14, No. 3, May–June 1987, 12–17.

Dyker, David A. (ed.). *The Soviet Union under Gorbachev: Prospects for Reform.* London: Croom Helm, 1987.

Ericson, Richard E. "The New Enterprise Law," *Harriman Institute FORUM*, 1, No. 2, February 1988, 1–8.

"Foreign Economic Relations." Pages 367–70 in Archie Brown, John Fennell, and Michael Kaser (eds.), *The Cambridge Encyclopedia of Russia and the Soviet Union.* Cambridge: Cambridge University Press, 1982.

Galuszka, Peter, and Bill Javetski. "Reforming the Soviet Economy," *Business Week*, No. 3029, December 7, 1987, 76–80, 84, 88.

Gardner, H. Stephen. *Soviet Foreign Trade: The Decision Process.* Boston: Kluwer-Nijhoff, 1983.

Gorbachev, Mikhail S. "Korennoi vopros ekonomicheskoi politiki partii: Doklad tovarishcha m.s. Gorbacheva," *Pravda* [Moscow], No. 163, June 12, 1985, 1.

"Gorbachev's Speech at ASTEC Reception." British Broadcasting Corporation, *Summary of World Broadcasts* [Reading, United Kingdom], No. SU/0126, April 15, 1988, A1–A4.

Gosudarstvennyi komitet po statistike. *Narodnoe khoziaistvo SSSR v 1987 g.* Moscow: Finansy i statistika, 1988.

_____. *Narodnoe khoziaistvo SSSR za 70 let.* Moscow: Finansy i statistika, 1987.

Haberl, Othmar Nikola. "Yugoslavia and the USSR in the Post-Tito Era." Pages 276–306 in Pedro Ramet (ed.), *Yugoslavia in the 1980s.* Boulder, Colorado: Westview Press, 1985.

Hanson, Philip. "Soviet Imports from the West Continue to Fall," Radio Free Europe/Radio Liberty, *Radio Liberty Research Bulletin* [Munich], No. 129, March 21, 1988, 1-2.

Hardt, John P., and Jean F. Boone. "Soviet Agriculture: US-USSR Grain Sales and Prospects for Expanded Agricultural Trade." (Library of Congress, Congressional Research Service, Major Issues System, IB86019.) Washington: May 18, 1988, 1-16.

_____. "US-Soviet Commercial Relations in a Period of Negotiation." (Library of Congress, Congressional Research Service, Major Issues System, IB88065.) Washington: May 31, 1988, 1-16.

Hewett, Ed A. "Foreign Economic Relations." Pages 269-310 in Abram Bergson and Herbert S. Levine (eds.), *The Soviet Economy: Toward the Year 2000.* London: Allen and Unwin, 1983.

Hough, Jerry F. *Opening Up the Soviet Economy.* Washington: Brookings Institution, 1988.

Ivanov, I. "Gosudarstvennaia monopoliia vneshnei torgovli: Formy i problemy na 70-letnem rubezhe," *Vneshniaia torgovlia* [Moscow], No. 4, April 1988, 2-4.

Ivanov, Iu. "Vneshtorgbank SSSR i perestroika mekhanizma vneshneekonomicheskoi deiatel'nosti," *Vneshniaia torgovlia* [Moscow], No. 11, November 1987, 12-16.

Ivanov, Ivan D. "Restructuring the Mechanism of Foreign Economic Relations in the USSR," *Soviet Economy,* 3, No. 3, July-September 1987, 192-218.

Kanet, Roger E. "Economic Aspects of Soviet Policy in the Third World: A Comment," *Soviet Economy,* 2, No. 3, July-September 1986, 261-68.

Lawson, Colin W. "Soviet Economic Aid: Volume, Function, and Importance," *Development Policy Review* [London], 5, September 1987, 257-76.

"A Littler List," *Economist* [London], February 6, 1988, 67.

Medish, Vadim. "Foreign Trade." Pages 167-71 in Vadim Medish (ed.), *The Soviet Union.* (3d ed.) Englewood Cliffs, New Jersey: Prentice-Hall, 1987.

Medish, Vadim (ed.). *The Soviet Union.* (3d ed.) Englewood Cliffs, New Jersey: Prentice-Hall, 1987.

Miasoedov, S. "Tikhookeanskii bassein: Problemy sotrudnichestva," *Ekonomicheskaia gazeta* [Moscow], No. 43, October 1987, 21.

Ministerstvo vneshnei torgovli. *Vneshniaia torgovlia SSSR v 1980 g.* Moscow: Finansy i statistika, 1981.

_____. *Vneshniaia torgovlia SSSR v 1986 g.* Moscow: Finansy i statistika, 1987.

Neu, C.R., and John Lund. *Toward a Profile of Soviet Behavior in International Financial Markets.* Santa Monica, California: Rand, August 1987.

Ogawa, Kazuo. "Economic Relations with Japan." Pages 158–78 in Rodger Swearingen (ed.), *Siberia and the Soviet Far East: Strategic Dimensions in Multinational Perspective.* Stanford, California: Hoover Institution Press, 1987.

Papp, Daniel S. "Economic Assistance and Trade." Pages 89–117 in Daniel S. Papp (ed.), *Soviet Policies Toward the Developing World During the 1980s: The Dilemmas of Power.* Maxwell Air Force Base, Alabama: Air University Press, December 1986.

Papp, Daniel S. (ed.). *Soviet Policies Toward the Developing World During the 1980s: The Dilemmas of Power.* Maxwell Air Force Base, Alabama: Air University Press, December 1986.

Patterson, Perry L. "Foreign Trade." Pages 210–19 in James Cracraft (ed.), *The Soviet Union Today: An Interpretive Guide.* Chicago: University of Chicago Press, 1988.

Rowen, Hobart. "Soviet Economic Envoy Spurns IMF, World Bank Membership," *Washington Post,* February 4, 1988, E1, E4.

Singleton, Fred. "Finnish-Soviet Trade; Project Exports." Pages 82–93 in Fred Singleton (ed.), *The Economy of Finland in the Twentieth Century.* Bradford, United Kingdom: University of Bradford, 1987.

Singleton, Fred (ed.). *The Economy of Finland in the Twentieth Century.* Bradford, United Kingdom: University of Bradford, 1987.

Smith, Alan H. "Gorbachev and the World—the Economic Side." Pages 126–63 in David A. Dyker (ed.), *The Soviet Union under Gorbachev: Prospects for Reform.* London: Croom Helm, 1987.

Smith, Glen Alden. *Soviet Foreign Trade: Organization, Operations, and Policy, 1918–1971.* New York: Praeger, 1973.

Smith, Gordon B. (ed.). *The Politics of East-West Trade.* Boulder, Colorado: Westview Press, 1984.

Sobell, Vladimir. "Oil Prices and the Nature of CEMA Cohesion," Radio Free Europe/Radio Liberty, *Radio Free Europe Research Bulletin* [Munich], No. 21, February 19, 1988, 1–6.

———. "Soviet and CMEA Foreign Aid in the Age of 'New Thinking'," Radio Free Europe/Radio Liberty, *Radio Free Europe Research Bulletin* [Munich], No. 174, September 30, 1987, 1–6.

United States. Central Intelligence Agency. Directorate of Intelligence. *Directory of Soviet Officials: National Organizations.* Washington: GPO, 1988.

———. Central Intelligence Agency. Directorate of Intelligence. *Directory of Soviet Officials: Republic Organizations Update.* Washington: GPO, 1987.

_____. Central Intelligence Agency. Directorate of Intelligence. *Directory of USSR Foreign Trade Organizations and Officials.* Washington: GPO, May 1986.

_____. Central Intelligence Agency. Directorate of Intelligence. *Handbook of Economic Statistics, 1985.* Washington: GPO, September 1985.

_____. Central Intelligence Agency. Directorate of Intelligence. *Handbook of Economic Statistics, 1987.* Washington: GPO, September 1987.

_____. Central Intelligence Agency. Directorate of Intelligence. "The USSR Confronts the Information Revolution: A Conference Report." (Proceedings of Conference held at Airlie House, Virginia, November 12–13, 1986.) May 1987, 1–16.

_____. Central Intelligence Agency and Defense Intelligence Agency. *Gorbachev's Economic Program: Problems Emerge.* Washington: GPO, June 1988.

_____. Congress. 100th, 1st Session. Joint Economic Committee. *Gorbachev's Economic Plans.* (2 vols.) Washington: GPO, 1987.

_____. Department of State. Bureau of Public Affairs. "Controlling Transfer of Strategic Technology," *Gist,* May 1988, 1–2.

Vernet, Daniel. "Eté finlandais," *Le Monde* [Paris], July 9, 1988, 1, 4.

"V prezidiume verkhovnogo soveta SSSR," *Izvestiia* [Moscow], No. 17, January 17, 1988, 1.

Wharton Econometric Forecasting Associates Group. "Yugoslavia," *Centrally Planned Economic Outlook,* 9, No. 1, April 1988, 3.65–74.

Wolf, Charles Jr., K.C. Yeh, Edmund Brunner, Jr., Aaron Gurwitz, and Marilee Lawrence. *The Costs of the Soviet Empire.* Santa Monica, California: Rand, September 1983.

(Various issues of the following publications were also used in the preparation of this chapter: *Business Eastern Europe; Current Digest of the Soviet Press;* Foreign Broadcast Information Service, *Daily Report: Soviet Union; Izvestiia* [Moscow]; *New York Times; Soviet Business and Trade;* and *Vneshniaia torgovlia* [Moscow].)

Chapter 16

Alexander, Arthur J. *Soviet Science and Weapons Acquisition.* Santa Monica, California: Rand, 1982.

Amann, Ronald. "Industrial Innovation in the Soviet Union: Methodological Perspectives and Conclusions." Pages 1–37 in

Ronald Amann and Julian M. Cooper (eds.), *Industrial Innovation in the Soviet Union.* New Haven: Yale University Press, 1982.

Amann, Ronald, and Julian M. Cooper (eds.). *Industrial Innovation in the Soviet Union.* New Haven: Yale University Press, 1982.

_____. *Technical Progress and Soviet Economic Development.* New York: Basil Blackwell, 1986.

Amann, Ronald, Julian M. Cooper, and R.W. Davies (eds.). *The Technological Level of Soviet Industry.* New Haven: Yale University Press, 1977.

Balzer, Harley D. "Education, Science, and Technology." Pages 245–57 in James Cracraft (ed.), *The Soviet Union Today: An Interpretive Guide.* Chicago: University of Chicago Press, 1988.

Bertsch, Gary K. "Technology Transfers and Technology Controls: A Synthesis of the Western-Soviet Relationship." Pages 115–34 in Ronald Amann and Julian M. Cooper (eds.), *Technical Progress and Soviet Economic Development.* New York: Basil Blackwell, 1986.

Cocks, Paul. *Science Policy: USA/USSR,* 2. Washington: GPO, 1980.

_____. "Soviet Science and Technology Strategy: Borrowing from the Defense Sector." Pages 145–60 in United States, Congress, 100th, 1st Session, Joint Economic Committee, *Gorbachev's Economic Plans.* (2 vols.) Washington: GPO, 1987.

Cracraft, James (ed.). *The Soviet Union Today: An Interpretive Guide.* Chicago: University of Chicago Press, 1988.

Deutch, Shelley. "The Soviet Weapons Industry: An Overview." Pages 405–30 in United States, Congress, 100th, 1st Session, Joint Economic Committee, *Gorbachev's Economic Plans.* (2 vols.) Washington: GPO, 1987.

Fortescue, Stephen. *The Communist Party and Soviet Science.* Baltimore: John Hopkins University Press, 1986.

Graham, Loren R. "Science and Computers in Soviet Society." Pages 347–60 in Frank M. Sorrentino and Frances R. Curcio (eds.), *Soviet Politics and Education.* Lanham, Maryland: University Press of America, 1986.

_____. *Science, Philosophy, and Human Behavior in the Soviet Union.* New York: Columbia University Press, 1987.

_____. "Science Policy and Organization." Pages 223–33 in James Cracraft (ed.), *The Soviet Union Today: An Interpretive Guide.* Chicago: University of Chicago Press, 1988.

Gustafson, Thane. *Selling the Russians the Rope? Soviet Technology Policy and United States Export Controls.* Santa Monica, California: Rand, 1982.

Hanson, Philip. "Soviet Imports from the West Continue to Fall," Radio Free Europe/Radio Liberty, *Radio Liberty Research Bulletin* [Munich], No. 129, March 21, 1988, 1–2.

Hanson, Philip, and Keith Pavitt. *The Comparative Economics of Research, Development and Innovation in East and West: A Survey.* Switzerland: Harwood Academic Press, 1987.

Holloway, David. "Innovation in the Defense Sector." Pages 276–367 in Ronald Amann and Julian M. Cooper (eds.), *Industrial Innovation in the Soviet Union.* New Haven: Yale University Press, 1982.

Joint Publications Research Service—JPRS (Washington). The following items are from the JPRS series:
USSR: Science and Technology Policy.
"Academy of Sciences Election Problems Viewed." (JPRS-UST-88-008, May 20, 1988, 51–53.)
"Decree on Changeover of Science to Cost Accounting, Self-Financing." (JPRS-UST-88-007, May 2, 1988, 29–35.)
"Elections, Functions of Academy Members." (JPRS-UST-88-009, July 18, 1988, 84–86.)
"Experience, Problems of Establishing Interbranch Complexes." (JPRS-UST-88-007, May 2, 1988, 1–8.)
"Marchuk on Scope of Academy Restructuring." (JPRS-UST-88-009, July 18, 1988, 79–84.)
"USSR Law on State Enterprise (Associations)." (JPRS-UST-88-001, February 8, 1988, 1–4.)

Kassel, Simon, and Cathleen A. Campbell. *The Soviet Academy of Sciences and Technological Development.* Santa Monica, California: Rand, 1980.

Kelly, William J., Hugh L. Shaffer, and J. Kenneth Thompson. *Energy Research and Development in the USSR: Preparation for the Twenty-First Century.* Durham: Duke University Press, 1986.

Kruse-Vaucienne, Ursula M., and John Logsdon. *Science and Technology in the Soviet Union: A Profile.* Washington: GWLL, 1979.

Lewis, Robert. *Science and Industrialization in the USSR.* New York: Holmes and Meier, 1979.

"Marchuk Speech." Foreign Broadcast Information Service, *Daily Report: Soviet Union.* (FBIS-SOV-88-127.) July 1, 1988, 57.

Medish, Vadim (ed.). *The Soviet Union.* (3d ed.) Englewood Cliffs, New Jersey: Prentice-Hall, 1987.

Nolting, Louvan E. *The Financing of Research, Development, and Innovation in the USSR, by Type of Performer.* Washington: GPO, 1976.

Nolting, Louvan E., and Murray Feshback. *Statistics on Research and Development Employment in the USSR.* Washington: GPO, 1981.

Parrott, Bruce. *Politics and Technology in the Soviet Union.* Cambridge: MIT Press, 1983.

Parrott, Bruce (ed.). *Trade, Technology, and Soviet-American Relations.* Bloomington: Indiana University Press, 1985.

Protopopov, V.A. (ed.). *Upravlenie sotsialisticheskoi ekonomikoi.* Moscow: Moskovskii rabochii, 1986.

"Siberian Scientific Department Roundtable." Foreign Broadcast Information Service, *Daily Report: Soviet Union.* (FBIS-SOV-88-017.) January 27, 1988, 1-13.

Smith, Gordon B. *Soviet Politics: Continuity and Contradiction.* New York: St. Martin's Press, 1988.

United States. Congress. 100th, 1st Session. Joint Economic Committee. *Gorbachev's Economic Plans.* (2 vols.) Washington: GPO, 1987.

"V avangarde tekhnicheskogo progressa," *Pravda* [Moscow], October 24, 1986, 1.

Voronitsyn, Sergei. "Educational Reform on the Eve of the Central Committee Plenum," Radio Free Europe/Radio Liberty, *Radio Liberty Research Bulletin* [Munich], December 23, 1987, 1-4.

Zaleski, E., J.P. Kozlowski, H. Wienert, R.W. Davies, M.J. Berry, and R. Amann. *Science Policy in the USSR.* Paris: Organization for Economic Cooperation and Development, 1969.

(Various issues of the following publications were also used in the preparation of this chapter: Foreign Broadcast Information Service, *Daily Report: Soviet Union;* Joint Publications Research Service, *USSR: Science and Technology Policy;* and Radio Free Europe/Radio Liberty, *Radio Liberty Research Bulletin* [Munich].)

Chapter 17

Alexiev, Alexander R. *The New Soviet Strategy in the Third World.* Santa Monica, California: Rand, 1983.

Baxter, William P. *The Soviet Way of Warfare.* London: Brassey's Defense, 1986.

Cracraft, James (ed.). *The Soviet Union Today: An Interpretive Guide.* Chicago: University of Chicago Press, 1987.

Currie, Kenneth M., and Gregory Varhall (eds.). *The Soviet Union: What Lies Ahead? Military-Political Affairs in the 1980s.* (Studies in Communist Affairs Series, No. 6.) Washington: GPO for United States Air Force, 1985.

Dismukes, Bradford, and James M. McConnell (eds.). *Soviet Naval Diplomacy.* New York: Pergamon Press, 1979.

Fedoseyev, P.N. (ed.). *Disastrous Effects of Nuclear War: Socio-Economic Aspects.* (International Peace and Disarmament Series.) Moscow: Navka, 1985.

Fitzgerald, Mary C. "Marshal Ogarkov on the Modern Theater Operation," *Naval War College Review,* 39, No. 4/Sequence 316, Autumn 1986, 6-25.

Freedman, Lawrence. *Atlas of Global Strategy.* New York: Facts on File, 1985.

Fukuyama, Francis. *Soviet Civil-Military Relations and the Power Projection Mission.* (Project Air Force Series.) Santa Monica, California: Rand, 1987.

Gareev, M.A. *M.V. Frunze, voennii teoretik.* Moscow: Voenizdat, 1985.

Garthoff, Raymond L. *Soviet Military Policy: A Historical Analysis.* New York: Praeger, 1966.

George, James L. (ed.). *The Soviet and Other Communist Navies: The View from the Mid-1980s.* Annapolis: Naval Institute Press, 1986.

Gorshkov, S.G. *Morskaia moshch' gosudarstva.* Moscow: Voenizdat, 1979.

Grechko, A.A. *The Armed Forces of the Soviet Union.* Moscow: Progress, 1977.

Jones, David R. (ed.). *Soviet Armed Forces Review* (annuals 1977 through 1985). Gulf Breeze, Florida: Academic International Press, 1977-1986.

Kaplan, Stephen S., Michel Tatu, Thomas W. Robinson, et al. *Diplomacy of Power: Soviet Armed Forces as a Political Instrument.* Washington: Brookings Institution, 1981.

Kelley, Paul D. *Soviet General Doctrine for War,* 1. (Soviet Battlefield Development Plan.) Washington: United States Army Intelligence and Threat Analysis Center, 1987.

Kozlov, S.N. (ed.). *The Officer's Handbook.* (Trans., Translation Bureau, Secretary of State Department, Ottawa, Canada.) Washington: United States Air Force, 1977.

Kozlov, S.N., D. Volkogonov, and S. Tyushkevich, et al. *Marxism-Leninism on War and the Army: A Soviet View.* (Trans., Progress, Moscow.) (Soviet Military Thought Series, 2.) Washington: United States Air Force, 1973.

Lee, William T., and Richard F. Staar. *Soviet Military Policy since World War II.* Stanford, California: Hoover Institution Press, 1986.

Leites, Nathan. *Soviet Style in War.* Santa Monica, California: Rand, 1982.

Lomov, N.A. (ed.). *Scientific-Technical Progress and the Revolution in Military Affairs: A Soviet View.* (Trans., United States Air Force.) (Soviet Military Thought Series.) Washington: United States Air Force, 1973.

MccGwire, Michael. *Military Objectives in Soviet Foreign Policy.* Washington: Brookings Institution, 1986.

Menon, Rajan. *Soviet Power and the Third World.* New Haven: Yale University Press, 1986.

Milovidov, A.S., and V.G. Kozlov (eds.). *The Philosophical Heritage of V.I. Lenin and Problems of Contemporary War: A Soviet View.* (Trans., United States Air Force.) (Soviet Military Thought Series.) Washington: United States Air Force, 1977.

Odom, William E. "Soviet Force Posture: Dilemmas and Directions," *Problems of Communism,* 34, No. 4, July–August 1985, 4.

Ogarkov, N.V. *Istoriia uchit bditel'nosti.* Moscow: Voenizdat, 1985.

———. "Strategiia voennaia." Pages 555–65 in *Sovetskaia voennaia entsiklopediia,* 7. Moscow: Voenizdat, 1979.

———. *Vsegda v gotovnosti k zashchite otechestva.* Moscow: Voenizdat, 1982.

Osgood, Eugenia V. "Military Strategy in the Nuclear Age." Pages 114–25 in James Cracraft (ed.), *The Soviet Union Today: An Interpretive Guide.* Chicago: University of Chicago Press, 1987.

Petersen, Phillip, and John G. Hines. "The Conventional Offensive in Soviet Theater Strategy," *Orbis,* Fall 1983, 695–739.

Radzievskii, A.I. (ed.). *Dictionary of Basic Military Terms.* (Trans., Translation Bureau, Secretary of State Department, Ottawa, Canada.) (Soviet Military Thought Series.) Washington: United States Air Force, 1976.

Reznichenko, V.G., I.N. Vorob'ev, et al. *Taktika.* (Biblioteka ofitsera.) Moscow: Voenizdat, 1984.

Savkin, V.E. *The Basic Principles of Operational Art and Tactics.* (Soviet Military Thought Series.) Washington: United States Air Force, 1972.

Scott, Harriet F., and William F. Scott. *The Soviet Art of War: Doctrine, Strategy and Tactics.* Boulder, Colorado: Westview Press, 1982.

Scott, William F. *Soviet Sources of Military Doctrine and Strategy,* 5. (Comp., Joseph D. Douglass and Amoretta M. Herber.) New York: Crane, Russak, 1975.

Selected Soviet Military Writings, 1970–1975: A Soviet View. (Trans., United States Air Force.) (Soviet Military Thought Series.) Washington: United States Air Force, 1976.

Sidorenko, A.A. *The Offensive.* (Soviet Military Thought Series.) Washington: United States Air Force, 1973.

Sokolovskiy, V.D. (ed.). *Soviet Military Strategy.* (Trans. and ed., Harriet F. Scott.) New York: Crane, Russak, 1980.

Sovetskaia voennaia entsiklopediia. (8 vols.) Moscow: Voenizdat, 1976–1980.

"Soviet Calculus of Nuclear War," *Soviet Union,* Special Issue, 10, Pts. 2–3, 1983.

United States. Department of Defense. *Soviet Military Power, 1987.* Washington: GPO, 1987.

_____. Department of Defense. *Soviet Military Power, 1989.* Washington: GPO, 1989.

Vigor, Peter H. *The Soviet View of War, Peace, and Neutrality.* London: Routledge and Kegan Paul, 1975.

Voennyi entsiklopedicheskii slovar'. Moscow: Voenizdat, 1983.

Volkogonov, Dmitrii Antonovich (ed.). *Marksistsko-Leninskoe uchenie o voine i armii.* (Biblioteka ofitsera.) Moscow: Voenizdat, 1984.

Wolfe, Thomas W. *Soviet Strategy at the Crossroads.* Cambridge: Harvard University Press, 1964.

Zhilin, P.A. (ed.). *Istoriia voennogo iskusstva.* (Biblioteka ofitsera.) Moscow: Voenizdat, 1986.

Chapter 18

Adams, Emily J. (ed.). *Air University Library Index to Military Periodicals.* Maxwell Air Force Base, Alabama: Air University Library, January–December 1987.

Adelman, Jonathan R. "The Soviet Army." Pages 1–14 in Jonathan R. Adelman (ed.), *Communist Armies in Politics.* Boulder, Colorado: Westview Press, 1982.

Adelman, Jonathan R. (ed.). *Communist Armies in Politics.* Boulder, Colorado: Westview Press, 1982.

Alexeev, Michael. "Military Expenditures and the Soviet Economy," Radio Free Europe/Radio Liberty, *Radio Liberty Research Bulletin* [Munich], April 22, 1985, 1–14.

Alexiev, Alexander R., and S. Enders Wimbush (eds.). *Ethnic Minorities in the Red Army: Asset or Liability?* (Rand Corporation Research Study.) Boulder, Colorado: Westview Press, 1988.

Alford, Jonathon. *The Soviet Union: Security Policies and Constraints.* New York: St. Martin's Press, 1985.

Azrael, Jeremy R. "The Soviet Civilian Leadership and the Military High Command, 1976–1986." (Project Air Force Series, R–3521–AF.) Santa Monica, California: Rand, 1987.

Baxter, William P. *Soviet Airland Battle Tactics.* Novato, California: Presidio Press, 1986.

Bellamy, Chris. *Red God of War: Soviet Artillery and Rocket Forces.* London: Brassey's, 1986.

Berman, Robert P., and John C. Baker. *Soviet Strategic Forces: Requirements and Responses.* Washington: Brookings Institution, 1982.

Blacker, Coit D. "Military Forces." Pages 125–85 in Robert F. Byrnes (ed.), *After Brezhnev: Sources of Soviet Conduct in the 1980s.* Bloomington: Indiana University Press, 1983.

Bonds, Ray (ed.). *The Illustrated Directory of Modern Soviet Weapons.* New York: Prentice-Hall, 1986.

Breyer, Siegfried. "The Soviet Submarine Force Today," *International Defense Review,* 20, No. 9, 1987, 1155–59.

Bridge, T.D. "Gorbachev Reforms: Soviet Army Views," *Army Quarterly and Defence Journal,* 117, No. 4, April 1987, 188–93.

Byrnes, Robert F. (ed.). *After Brezhnev: Sources of Soviet Conduct in the 1980s.* Bloomington: Indiana University Press, 1983.

Capaccio, Tony. "Killers or Infiltrators: Pentagon Analysts Differ on Wartime Role of New Soviet Forces," *Defense Week,* 8, No. 34, August 24, 1987, 1, 10–11.

Chitty, David A. "Carrier-Based Aviation in the Soviet Navy," *Armed Forces,* 6, No. 5, May 1987, 221–22.

Clancy, Tom. "Why Moscow Is No Match for America's Military," *Washington Post,* January 24, 1988, C1–C2.

Clawson, Robert W., and Lawrence S. Kaplan (eds.). *The Warsaw Pact: Political Purpose and Military Means.* Wilmington, Delaware: Scholarly Resources, 1982.

Cockburn, Andrew. *The Threat: Inside the Soviet Military Machine.* New York: Vintage Books, 1984.

Collins, John M. *U.S.-Soviet Military Balance, 1980–1985.* Washington: Pergamon-Brassey's 1985.

Collins, Robert F. "Soviet Weaknesses and Problems," *Military Review,* 63, August 1983, 60–72.

Colton, Timothy J. *Commissars, Commanders, and Civilian Authority: Structure of Soviet Military Politics.* Cambridge: Harvard University Press, 1979.

Currie, Kenneth M., and Gregory Varhall (eds.). *The Soviet Union: What Lies Ahead: Military-Political Affairs in the 1980s.* (Studies in Communist Affairs Series, No. 6.) Washington: GPO for United States Air Force, 1985.

Davis, Robert B. "Alcohol Abuse and the Soviet Military," *Armed Forces and Society,* 11, No. 3, Spring 1985, 399–411.

Dibb, Paul. *The Soviet Union: The Incomplete Superpower.* Urbana: University of Illinois Press, 1986.

Donnelly, Christopher N. *The Soviet Military under Gorbachev.* Sandhurst, United Kingdom: Soviet Studies Research Center RMA, December 1986.

Erickson, John, Lynn Hansen, and William Schneider. *Soviet Ground Forces: An Operational Assessment.* Boulder, Colorado: Westview Press, 1986.

Everett-Heath, John. *Soviet Helicopters: Design, Development, and Tactics*. London: Jane's, 1983.

Gabriel, Richard A. *The Antagonists: A Comparative Combat Assessment of the Soviet and American Soldier*. Westport, Connecticut: Greenwood Press, 1984.

George, James L. (ed.). *The Soviet and Other Communist Navies: The View from the Mid-1980s*. Annapolis: Naval Institute Press, 1986.

Gervasi, Tom. *The Myth of Soviet Military Supremacy*. New York: Harper and Row, 1986.

Gouré, Leon. *Civil Defense in the Soviet Union*. Westport, Connecticut: Greenwood Press, 1986.

Gustafson, Thane. "The Chances of a Military Takeover in the Soviet Union," Radio Free Europe/Radio Liberty, *Radio Liberty Research Bulletin* [Munich], June 27, 1985, 1–3.

Herspring, Dale R. "Gorbachev, Yazov, and the Military," *Problems of Communism*, 36, July–August 1987, 99–107.

Herspring, Dale R., and Ivan Volgyes (eds.). *Civil-Military Relations in Communist Systems*. Boulder, Colorado: Westview Press, 1978.

Isby, David C. *Weapons and Tactics of the Soviet Army*. London: Jane's, 1981.

Jones, David R. (ed.). *Soviet Armed Forces Review Annual (1984–85)*, 9. Gulf Breeze, Florida: Academic International Press, 1986.

Jones, Ellen. *Red Army and Society: A Sociology of the Soviet Military*. Boston: Allen and Unwin, 1985.

Keltner, Kenneth M., and Graham H. Turbiville, Jr. "Soviet Reinforcement in Europe," *Military Review*, 67, No. 4, April 1987, 34–43.

Kruzhin, Peter. "Are Military Farms Meeting Their Targets?," Radio Free Europe/Radio Liberty, *Radio Liberty Research Bulletin* [Munich], April 19, 1985, 1–4.

_____. "Bribery and Corruption in the Soviet Armed Forces," Radio Free Europe/Radio Liberty, *Radio Liberty Research Bulletin* [Munich], August 2, 1983, New York, 1–3.

_____. "Draftees, Parents, and Recruiting Offices," Radio Free Europe/Radio Liberty, *Radio Liberty Research Bulletin* [Munich], August 11, 1983, 1–3.

_____. "Fiftieth Anniversary of the General Staff Academy," Radio Free Europe/Radio Liberty, *Radio Liberty Research Bulletin* [Munich], November 17, 1986, 1–3.

_____. "Health Problems in the Soviet Army and Navy," Radio Free Europe/Radio Liberty, *Radio Liberty Research Bulletin* [Munich], April 3, 1986, 1–4.

_____. "Military Representation in the Leading Organs of the CPSU Following the Twenty-Sixth Congress," Radio Free Europe/Radio Liberty, *Radio Liberty Research Bulletin* [Munich], March 16, 1986, 1–9.

_____. "Military Representation in the Leading Organs of the CPSU Following the Twenty-Seventh Congress," Radio Free Europe/Radio Liberty, *Radio Liberty Research Bulletin* [Munich], March 27, 1986, 1–9.

_____. "Pulling Rank in the Soviet Army," Radio Free Europe/ Radio Liberty, *Radio Liberty Research Bulletin* [Munich], August 8, 1983, New York, 1–3.

_____. "The Soviet Military Air Transport Force," Radio Free Europe/Radio Liberty, *Radio Liberty Research Bulletin* [Munich], September 25, 1981, 1–4.

_____. "Soviet Military Officers to Undergo Next Round of Regular Four-Year Evaluations," Radio Free Europe/Radio Liberty, *Radio Liberty Research Bulletin* [Munich], February 26, 1985, 1–2.

_____. "Soviet Officers and 'Communist Morality'," Radio Free Europe/Radio Liberty, *Radio Liberty Research Bulletin* [Munich], September 21, 1983, New York, 1–3.

_____. "*Veshchizm,* a Profitable Sideline for Soviet Officers," Radio Free Europe/Radio Liberty, *Radio Liberty Research Bulletin* [Munich], September 22, 1983, New York, 1–3.

Lewis, William J. *The Warsaw Pact: Arms, Doctrine, and Strategy.* New York: McGraw-Hill, 1982.

Mackintosh, Malcolm. "Power in the Kremlin: Politics and the Military," *RUSI: Journal of the Royal United Services Institute for Defence Studies* [London], 129, December 1984, 9–13.

Maddock, Roland Thomas. *The Political Economy of Soviet Defense Spending.* New York: St. Martin's Press, 1988.

The Military Balance, 1987–1988. London: International Institute for Strategic Studies, 1987.

Moffett, Julie. "Women in the Soviet Armed Forces," Radio Free Europe/Radio Liberty, *Radio Liberty Research Bulletin* [Munich], March 13, 1986, 1–6.

Mullinex, Klaus M. "The Soviet Military: Its Power in Soviet Politics," *Military Review,* 65, April 1985, 66–76.

Murphy, Bill. "Political-Military Relations in the USSR," Radio Free Europe/Radio Liberty, *Radio Liberty Reserach Bulletin* [Munich], October 23, 1984, 1–16.

Murphy, Paul J. (ed.). *The Soviet Air Forces.* Jefferson, North Carolina: McFarland, 1984.

Odom, William E. "Soviet Force Posture: Dilemmas and Directions," *Problems of Communism,* 34, No. 4, July–August 1985, 1–14.

Petersen, Charles C. "Aircraft Carrier Development in Soviet Naval Theory," *Naval War College Review,* 37, January–February 1984, 4–13.

Plummer, R.C.F. "The Soviet Army—A View from Inside the Soviet Union," *Army Quarterly and Defense Journal,* 117, No. 1, January 1987, 7–13.

Polmar, Norman. *Guide to the Soviet Navy.* Annapolis: Naval Institute Press, 1986.

Reitz, James T. "The Soviet Armed Forces: Perceptions over Twenty Years." Pages 111–36 in Robert W. Clawson and Lawrence S. Kaplan (eds.), *The Warsaw Pact: Political Purpose and Military Means.* Wilmington, Delaware: Scholarly Resources, 1982.

Scott, Harriet F., and William F. Scott. *The Armed Forces of the USSR.* Boulder, Colorado: Westview Press, 1984.

Scott, William F. "Moscow's Military-Industrial Complex," *Air Force Magazine,* 70, No. 3, March 1987, 46–51.

Seaton, Albert. *The Soviet Army: 1918 to the Present.* New York: New American Library, 1986.

Sheehy, Ann. "Concern about Preparedness of Central Asians for Military Service," Radio Free Europe/Radio Liberty, *Radio Liberty Research Bulletin* [Munich], May 30, 1986, 1–2.

Solomon, Richard H., and Masataka Kosaka (eds.). *The Soviet Far East Military Buildup: Nuclear Dilemmas and Asian Security.* Dover, Massachusetts: Auburn House, 1986.

Strode, Dan L., and Rebecca V. Strode. "Diplomacy and Defense in Soviet National Security Policy," *International Security,* 8, Fall 1983, 91–116.

Suvorov, Viktor. *Inside the Soviet Army.* New York: Macmillan, 1982.

Tarasulo, Yitzhak. "A Profile of the Soviet Soldier," *Armed Forces and Society,* 11, Winter 1985, 221–34.

Taylor, John W.R., and R.A. Mason. *Aircraft, Strategy, and Operations of the Soviet Air Force.* London: Jane's, 1986.

Thompson, Graham N. "Tactical Air Defence for Soviet Ground Forces," *Armed Forces,* 6, No. 5, May 1987, 213–17.

Thompson, Graham N., James Kinnear, and Alaric Searle. "Fighting in a Toxic Environment: Chemical Defence Capability in the Soviet Ground Forces," *Armed Forces,* 6, September 1987, 400–404.

United States. Defense Intelligence Agency. "Soviet Chemical Weapons Threat 1985." (DST–1620F–051–85.) Washington: 1985.

_____. Department of Defense. *Soviet Military Power, 1989.* Washington: GPO, March 1989.

_____. Department of Defense. *The Soviet Space Challenge.* Washington: GPO, November 1987.

_____. Department of Defense and Department of State. *Soviet Strategic Defense Programs.* Washington: GPO, October 1985.

Warner, Edward L., III, Josephine J. Bonan, and Erma F. Packman. *Key Personnel and Organizations of the Soviet Military High Command.* (Rand Note, N-2567-AF.) Santa Monica, California: Rand, 1987.

Weickhardt, George G. "The Soviet Military-Industrial Complex and Economic Reform," *Soviet Economy,* 2, No. 3, 1986, 193-220.

Weinstein, John M. "Soviet Offensive Strategic Nuclear Forces: Evolution and Prospects," *Parameters: Journal of the U.S. Army War College,* 15, Winter 1985, 29-40.

Wettig, Gerhard. "Sufficiency in Defense—A New Guideline for the Soviet Military Posture," Radio Free Europe/Radio Liberty, *Radio Liberty Research Bulletin* [Munich], September 23, 1987, 1-5.

Whiting, Kenneth R. *The Development of the Soviet Armed Forces, 1917-1977.* Maxwell Air Force Base, Alabama: Air University Press, 1977.

_____. "Soviet Air Power." Maxwell Air Force Base, Alabama: Air University Press, 1985.

Williams, E.S. "'Restructuring' and the SRF," *Armed Forces,* 6, No. 4, April 1987, 175.

_____. *The Soviet Military: Political Education, Training, and Morale.* New York: St. Martin's Press, 1986.

Williams, John Allen. "The U.S. and Soviet Navies: Missions and Forces," *Armed Forces and Society,* 10, Summer 1984, 507-28.

Zamascikov, Sergei. "The Role of the Military in the Social Integration of Ethnic Muslims in the USSR," Radio Free Europe/Radio Liberty, *Radio Liberty Research Bulletin* [Munich], December 23, 1983, 1-21.

Chapter 19

Barghoorn, Frederick C. "The Security Police." Pages 33-51 in H. Gordon Skilling and Franklyn Griffiths (eds.), *Interest Groups in Soviet Politics.* Princeton: Princeton University Press, 1971.

Barron, John. *KGB: Secret Work of Soviet Secret Agents.* New York: Readers Digest Press, 1974.

_____. *KGB Today: The Hidden Hand.* New York: Readers Digest Press, 1983.

_____. *Soviet Criminal Law and Procedure.* Cambridge: Harvard University Press, 1972.

Barry, Donald, George Ginsburgs, and Peter Maggs (eds.). *Soviet Law after Stalin, Pt. 2: Social Engineering Through Law.* The Hague: Sijthoff and Noordhoff, 1978.

Berman, H.J. "Soviet Law Reform—Dateline Moscow," *Yale Law Journal,* 8, 1957, 1192–98.

Berman, H.J., and J.W. Spindler. *Soviet Criminal Law and Procedure.* Cambridge: Harvard University Press, 1972.

Bialer, Seweryn. *The Soviet Paradox: External Expansion, Internal Decline.* New York: Knopf, 1986.

Bittman, Ladislav. *The KGB and Soviet Disinformation: An Insider's View.* Washington: Pergamon-Brassey's, 1985.

Brzezinski, Zbigniew K. *The Permanent Purge: Politics in Soviet Totalitarianism.* Cambridge: Harvard University Press, 1964.

Butler, William. *Soviet Law.* London: Butterworths, 1983.

Campbell, Robert W. "Satellite Communications in the USSR," *Soviet Economy,* 1, No. 4, October–December 1985, 330–39.

Conquest, Robert. *The Great Terror: Stalin's Purge of the Thirties.* New York: Collier, 1973.

_____. *Inside Stalin's Secret Police: NKVD Politics, 1936–39.* Stanford, California: Hoover Institution Press, 1985.

Deriabin, Peter, with T.H. Bagley. "Fedorchuk, the KGB, and the Soviet Succession," *Orbis,* 26, No. 3, Fall 1982, 611–36.

Dziak, John. "Soviet Intelligence and Security Services in the Eighties: The Paramilitary Dimension," *Orbis,* No. 4, Winter 1982, 771–86.

Fuller, William. "The Internal Troops of the MVD SSSR." (College Station Papers, No. 6.) College Station, Texas: 1983.

Hingley, Ronald. *The Russian Police: Muscovite, Imperial Russian, and Soviet Security Operations, 1565–1970.* London: Hutchinson, 1970.

Huskey, Eugene. "The Politics of the Soviet Criminal Process: Expanding the Right to Counsel in Pre-Trial Proceeding," *American Journal of Comparative Law,* 35, No. 1, Winter 1986, 93–112.

Jones, David (ed.). *Soviet Armed Forces Review Annual.* Gulf Breeze, Florida: Academic International Press, 1982.

Knight, Amy W. *The KGB: Police and Politics in the Soviet Union.* Boston: Unwin-Hyman, 1988.

_____. "The KGB's Special Departments in the Soviet Armed Forces," *Orbis,* 28, No. 2, Summer 1984, 257–80.

Kotkov, V., and V. Zhuravlev. "Iz istorii vnutrennikh voisk," *Voenno-istoricheskii zhurnal* [Moscow], No. 11, 1972, 90–95.

Lampert, Nick. "Law and Order in the USSR: The Case of Economic and Official Crime," *Soviet Studies,* 34, No. 3, July 1984, 366–85.

Leggett, George. *The Cheka: Lenin's Political Police.* Oxford: Clarendon, 1986.

Levytsky, Boris. *The Uses of Terror: The Soviet Secret Police, 1917–1970.* New York: Coward, McCann, and Geoghegan, 1972.

Medvedev, Zhores. *Andropov.* New York: Norton, 1983.

Reddaway, Peter. "Dissent in the Soviet Union," *Problems of Communism,* 33, No. 6, November–December 1983, 1–15.

Reitz, James T. "The Soviet Security Troops—The Kremlin's Other Armies." Pages 243–72 in David Jones (ed.), *Soviet Armed Forces Review Annual.* Gulf Breeze, Florida: Academic International Press, 1982.

Richelson, Jeffrey T. *Sword and Shield: Soviet Intelligence and Security Apparatus.* Cambridge: Ballinger, 1986.

Schultz, Richard H., and Roy Godson. *Dezinformatsia: Active Measures in Soviet Strategy.* Washington: Pergamon-Brassey's, 1984.

Sharlet, Robert. "Dissent and Repression in the Soviet Union," *Current History,* 73, No. 430, October 1977, 112–30.

_____. "Legal Policy under Khrushchev and Brezhnev: Continuity and Change." Pages 319–30 in Donald Barry, George Ginsburghs, and Peter Maggs (eds.), *Soviet Law after Stalin, Pt. 2: Social Engineering Through Law.* The Hague: Sijthoff and Noordhoff, 1978.

Shevchenko, Arkady. *Breaking with Moscow.* New York: Ballantine, 1985.

Skilling, Gordon, and Franklyn Griffiths (eds.). *Interest Groups in Soviet Politics.* Princeton: Princeton University Press, 1971.

Smith, Gordon B. *Soviet Politics: Continuity and Contradiction.* New York: St. Martin's Press, 1988.

Solovyov, Vladimir. "Knowing the KGB," *Partisan Review,* 99, No. 2, 1982, 167–83.

Van den Berg, Ger P. "The Council of Ministers of the Soviet Union," *Review of Socialist Law* [Leiden], 6, No. 3, September 1980, 292–323.

Voslensky, Michael. *Nomenklatura: Anatomy of the Soviet Ruling Class.* London: Bodley Head, 1984.

Wolin, Simon, and Robert Slusser (eds.). *The Soviet Secret Police.* New York: Praeger, 1957.

(Various issues of the following publications were also used in the preparation of this chapter: Foreign Broadcast Information Service, *Daily Report: Soviet Union; Izvestiia* [Moscow]; *Pravda* [Moscow]; and Radio Free Europe/Radio Liberty, *Radio Liberty Research Bulletin* [Munich].)

Appendix B

Ausch, Sandor. *Theory and Practice of CMEA Cooperation.* Budapest: Akadémiai Kiadó, 1972.

Chukanov, O.A. (ed.). *Nauchno-tekhnicheskoe sotrudnichestvo stran SEV.* Moscow: Ekonomika, 1986.

de Weydenthal, J.B. "The Realities of Economic Integration," Radio Free Europe, *RAD Background Report* [Munich], 160 November 7, 1986.

Diehl, Jackson. "Bloc Tries to Reconcile Imports, Home Industry," *Washington Post,* October 20, 1986, A1, A18.

_____. "Pursuit of Technology Risks Upheaval in Political System," *Washington Post,* October 21, 1986, A1, A24.

East European Economic Handbook. London: Euromonitor, 1985.

Hannigan, John, and Carl McMillan. "Joint Investment in Resource Development: Sectoral Approaches to Socialist Integration." Pages 259–95 in United States, Congress, 97th, 1st Session, Joint Economic Committee, *East European Economic Assessment.* Washington: GPO, 1981.

Hewett, Edward A. "The Impact of the World Economic Crisis on Intra-CMEA Trade." Pages 323–48 in Egon Neuberger and Laura D'Andrea Tyson (eds.), *The Impact of International Economic Disturbances on the Soviet Union and Eastern Europe.* New York: Pergamon Press, 1980.

Holzman, Franklyn D. "CMEA's Hard Currency Deficits and Ruble Convertibility." Pages 144–63 in Nita G.M. Watts (ed.), *Economic Relations Between East and West.* London: Macmillan, 1978.

Karavaev, V.P. *Integratsiia i investitsii: Problemy sotrudnichestva stran SEV.* Moscow: Nauka, 1979.

Katushev, K. "Sotrudnichestvo vo imia velikih tselei sotsializma i kommunizma," *Ekonomicheskoe sotrudnichestvo stran-chlenov SEV* [Moscow], No. 1, January 1979, 4–11.

Kohn, M.J., and N.R. Lang. "The Intra-CMEA Foreign Trade System: Major Price Changes, Little Reform." Pages 135–51 in United States, Congress, 95th, 1st Session, Joint Economic Committee, *East European Economies Post-Helsinki.* Washington: 1977.

"A Little Late in Learning the Facts of Life," *Economist* [London], 295, No. 7390, April 20, 1985.

Marer, Paul. "The Political Economy of Soviet Relations with Eastern Europe." Pages 155–88 in S.M. Terry (ed.), *Soviet Policy in Eastern Europe.* New Haven: Yale University Press, 1984.

Marer, Paul, and John Michael Montias (eds.). *East European Integration and East-West Trade.* Bloomington: Indiana University Press, 1980.

Medvedev, Boris. "Sovershenstvovanie struktury ekonomiki," *Ekonomicheskoe sotrudnichestvo stran-chlenov SEV* [Moscow], No. 2, 1986, 70–75.

Mellor, Roy E.H. "The Genesis of Comecon and the Sovietization of Eastern Europe." Pages 221–48 in Roy E.H. Mellor (ed.), *Eastern Europe: A Geography of the Comecon Countries.* New York: Columbia University Press, 1975.

Mellor, Roy E.H. (ed.). *Eastern Europe: A Geography of the Comecon Countries.* New York: Columbia University Press, 1975.

The Multilateral Economic Cooperation of Socialist States: A Collection of Documents. Moscow: Progress, 1977.

Neuberger, Egon, and Laura D'Andrea Tyson (eds.). *The Impact of International Economic Disturbances on the Soviet Union and Eastern Europe.* New York: Pergamon Press, 1980.

Nicolae, Petre. *CMEA in Theory and Practice.* Falls Church, Virginia: Delphic, 1984.

Pecsi, K. "Nekotorye problemy ustanovleniia tsen vo vzaimnoi torgovle stran SEV," *Mirovaia ekonomika i mezhdunarodnye otnosheniia* [Moscow], No. 9, September 1979, 93–101.

Prybyla, Jan S. "The Dawn of Real Communism: Problems of Comecon," *Conflict Quarterly* [New Brunswick, Canada], 29, No. 2, Summer 1985, 387–402.

Schiavone, Giuseppe. *The Institutions of Comecon.* London: Macmillan, 1981.

SEV: Real'nosti i perspektivy sotrudnichestva. Moscow: Sekretariat SEV, 1985.

SEV: Tsifry, fakty, argumenty. Moscow: Sekretariat SEV, 1982.

SEV: Voprosy i otvety. Moscow: Sekretariat SEV, 1985.

Shastitko, V.M. (ed.). *Vneshniaia torgovlia SSSR so stranami SEV.* Moscow: Nauka, 1986.

Shiriaev, Iu.S, and N.N. Khmelevskii. "SEV: Uglublenie sotsialisticheskoi ekonomicheskoi integratsii," *Ekonomika* [Moscow], No. 1, 1986, 16.

Sobell, Vladimir. "The CMEA Scientific Program Gets More (Soviet) Teeth," Radio Free Europe, *RAD Background Report* [Munich], 49, April 8, 1986.

_____. "Mikhail Gorbachev Takes Charge of the CMEA," Radio Free Europe, *RAD Background Report* [Munich], 146, December 20, 1985.

_____. "The Shifting Focus of CMEA Integration," Radio Free Europe, *RAD Background Report* [Munich], 159, November 7, 1986.

Statisticheskii ezhegodnik stran-chlenov SEV. Moscow: Finansy i statistika, 1985.

Tarasov, L. "Ekonomika stran-chlenov SEV v 1981–1985 gg," *Voprosy ekonomiki* [Moscow], July 1986.

Terry, S.M. (ed.). *Soviet Policy in Eastern Europe.* New Haven: Yale University Press, 1984.

United States. Congress. 95th, 1st Session. Joint Economic Committee. *East European Economies Post-Helsinki.* Washington: GPO, 1977.

_____. Congress. 97th, 1st Session. Joint Economic Committee. *East European Economic Assessment.* Washington: GPO, 1981.

van Brabant, Jozef M. *East European Cooperation: The Role of Money and Finance.* (Studies in International Business, Finance, and Trade.) New York: Praeger, 1977.

_____. *Socialist Economic Integration.* Cambridge: Cambridge University Press, 1980.

Vanous, Jan. "Eastern European and Soviet Fuel Trade, 1970–1985." Pages 541–60 in United States, Congress, 97th, 1st Session, Joint Economic Committee, *East European Economic Assessment.* Washington: GPO, 1981.

Watts, Nita G.M. (ed.). *Economic Relations Between East and West.* London: Macmillan, 1978.

(Various issues of the following publication were also used in the preparation of this appendix: Joint Publications Research Service, *USSR Report on Economic Affairs.*)

Appendix C

Adelman, Jonathan R. (ed.). *Communist Armies in Politics.* Boulder, Colorado: Westview Press, 1982.

_____. *Superpowers and Revolution.* New York: Praeger, 1986.

Alexiev, Alex. "The Romanian Army." Pages 149–66 in Jonathan R. Adelman (ed.), *Communist Armies in Politics.* Boulder, Colorado: Westview Press, 1982.

Alexiev, Alexander, and A. Ross Johnson. *East European Military Reliability: An Emigré-Based Assessment.* Santa Moncia, California: Rand, 1986.

Alford, Jonathan (ed.). *The Soviet Union: Security Policies and Constraints.* New York: St. Martin's Press, 1985.

Atkeson, Edward B. "The 'Fault Line' in the Warsaw Pact: Implications for NATO Strategy," *Orbis,* 30, No. 1, Spring 1986, 111–32.

Broadhurst, Arlene Idol (ed.). *The Future of European Alliance Systems: NATO and the Warswaw Pact.* Boulder, Colorado: Westveiw Press, 1982.

Byrnes, Robert F. (ed.). *After Brezhnev: Sources of Soviet Conduct in the 1980s.* Bloomington: Indiana University Press, 1983.

Caravelli, John M. "Soviet and Joint Warsaw Pact Exercises: Functions and Utility," *Armed Forces and Society,* 9, Spring 1983, 393–426.

Checinski, Michael. "Warsaw Pact/CMEA Military-Economic Trends," *Problems of Communism,* 36, No. 2, March–April 1987, 15–28.

Clawson, Robert W., and Lawrence S. Kaplan (eds.). *The Warsaw Pact: Political Purpose and Military Means.* Wilmington, Delaware: Scholarly Resources, 1982.

Copper, John F., and Daniel S. Papp (eds.). *Communist Nations' Military Assistance.* Boulder, Colorado: Westview Press, 1983.

Crane, Keith. *Military Spending in Eastern Europe.* Santa Monica, California: Rand, 1987.

Donnelly, Christopher. "The Military Significance of the Polish Crisis." Pages 10–13 in *RUSI and Brassey's Defence Yearbook, 1983.* London: Brassey's, 1983.

Erickson, John. "The Warsaw Pact: From Here to Eternity," *Current History,* 84, No. 505, November 1985, 357–60, 387.

Getman, I.P. *30-letie Varshavskogo dogovora, ukazatel' literatury 1970–1984 gg.* Moscow: MISON, 1985.

Grechko, A.A., et al. (eds.). *Sovetskaia voennaia entsiklopediia.* Moscow: Voenizdat, 1976.

Herspring, Dale R. "The Warsaw Pact at 25," *Problems of Communism,* 29, No. 5, September–October 1980, 1–15.

Holloway, David, and Jane M.O. Sharp (eds.). *The Warsaw Pact: Alliance in Transition?* Ithaca: Cornell University Press, 1984.

Hutchings, Robert L. *Foreign and Security Policy Coordination in the Warsaw Pact.* (Berichte 15–1985.) Cologne: Bundesinstitut für Ostwissenschaftliche und Internationale Studien, 1985.

Jones, Christopher D. *Soviet Influence in Eastern Europe: Political Autonomy and the Warsaw Pact.* (Studies of Influence in International Relations.) New York: Praeger, 1981.

———. "The USSR, the Warsaw Pact, and NATO." Pages 15–36 in Ingmar Oldberg (ed.), *Proceedings of a Symposium on Unity and Conflict in the Warsaw Pact.* Stockholm: Swedish National Defence Research Institute, 1984.

———. "Warsaw Pact Exercises: The Genesis of a Greater Socialist Army?" Pages 429–50 in David R. Jones (ed.), *Soviet Armed Forces Review Annual.* Gulf Breeze, Florida: Academic International Press, 1984.

Jones, David R. (ed.). *Soviet Armed Forces Review Annual.* Gulf Breeze, Florida: Academic International Press, 1984.

Kaplan, Stephen S. (ed.). *Diplomacy of Power: Soviet Armed Forces as a Political Instrument.* Washington: Brookings Institution, 1981.

Korbonski, Andrzej. "Eastern Europe." Pages 290–344 in Robert F. Byrnes (ed.), *After Brezhnev: Sources of Soviet Conduct in the 1980s.* Bloomington: Indiana University Press, 1983.

Korbonski, Andrzej, and Lubov Fajfer. "The Soviet Union and Two Crises in Poland." Pages 241–65 in Jonathan R. Adelman (ed.), *Superpowers and Revolution.* New York: Praeger, 1986.

Lewis, William J. *The Warsaw Pact: Arms, Doctrine, and Strategy.* Cambridge: Institute for Foreign Policy Analysis, 1982.

McGregor, Douglas A. "Uncertain Allies? East European Forces in the Warsaw Pact," *Soviet Studies,* 38, No. 2, April 1986, 227–47.

Mackintosh, Malcolm. "Developments in Alliance Politics: The Warsaw Pact." Pages 147–64 in *RUSI and Brassey's Defence Yearbook, 1986.* London: Brassey's 1986.

Maltsev, V.F., et al. (eds.). *Organizatsiia Varshavskogo dogovora, 1955–1985: Dokumenty i materialy.* Moscow: Politizdat, 1986.

Martin, Richard C. "Warsaw Pact Force Modernization: A Closer Look," *Parameters,* 15, No. 2, Summer 1985, 3–11.

Nelson, Daniel N. *Alliance Behavior in the Warsaw Pact.* (Westview Special Studies on the Soviet Union and Eastern Europe.) Boulder, Colorado: Westview Press, 1986.

Nelson, Daniel N. (ed.). *Soviet Allies: The Warsaw Pact and the Issue of Reliability.* Boulder, Colorado: Westview Press, 1984.

Nelson, Daniel N., and Joseph Lepgold. "Alliances and Burden-sharing: A NATO-Warsaw Pact Comparison," *Defense Analysis,* 2, September 1986, 205–24.

Oldberg, Ingmar (ed.). *Proceedings of a Symposium on Unity and Conflict in the Warsaw Pact.* Stockholm: Swedish National Defence Research Institute, 1984.

Orlik, I.I. *Vneshniaia politika stran Varshavskogo dogovora, pervaya polovina 80-kh godov.* Moscow: Nauka, 1986.

Papp, Daniel S. "Soviet Military Assistance to Eastern Europe." Pages 13–38 in John F. Copper and Daniel S. Papp (eds.), *Communist Nations' Military Assistance.* Boulder, Colorado: Westview Press, 1983.

Petrovskii, V.F. *Sovetskaia kontseptsiia bezopastnosti.* Moscow: Nauka, 1986.

Radzievskii, S. "Voennoe sotrudnichestvo i soglasovanie usilii stran antigitlerovskoi koalitsii," *Voenno-istoricheskii zhurnal* [Moscow], June 1982, 39–47.

Rakowska-Harmstone, Teresa. *The Warsaw Pact: The Question of Cohesion.* (ORAE Extra-Mural Papers, Nos. 29, 33, and 39.) Ottawa: Department of National Defence, 1984.

Remington, Robin Alison. "Western Images of the Warsaw Pact," *Problems of Communism,* 36, No. 2, March–April 1987, 69–80.

Rice, Condoleezza. "Warsaw Pact Reliability: The Czechoslovak People's Army." Pages 125–42 in Daniel N. Nelson (ed.), *Soviet Allies: The Warsaw Pact and the Issue of Reliability.* Boulder, Colorado: Westview Press, 1984.

Rice, Condoleezza, and Michael Fry. "The Hungarian Crisis of 1956: The Soviet Decision." Pages 181–99 in Jonathan R. Adelman (ed.), *Superpowers and Revolution.* New York: Praeger, 1986.

RUSI and Brassey's Defence Yearbook, 1983. London: Brassey's, 1983.

Savinov, K.I. *Varshavskii dogovor—faktor mira, shchit sotsialisma.* Moscow: Mezhdunarodnye otnosheniia, 1986.

Shtemenko, S.M. "Varshavskii dogovor." Pages 20–22 in A.A. Grechko et al. (eds.), *Sovetskaia voennaia entsiklopediia.* Moscow: Voenizdat, 1976.

Simon, Jeffrey. *Warsaw Pact Forces: Problems of Command and Control.* Boulder, Colorado: Westview Press, 1985.

Simon, Jeffrey, and Trono Gilberg (eds.). *Security Implications of Nationalism in Eastern Europe.* Boulder, Colorado: Westview Press, 1986.

Skorodenko, P.P. *Vo glave boevogo soiuza: Kommunisticheskie partii—sozdateli i rukovoditeli organizatsii Varshavskogo dogovora.* Moscow: Voenizdat, 1985.

Staar, Richard F. "Soviet Relations with East Europe," *Current History,* 83, No. 496, November 1984, 353–56, 386–87.

Tatu, Michel. "Intervention in Eastern Europe." Pages 205–64 in Stephen S. Kaplan (ed.), *Diplomacy of Power: Soviet Armed Forces as a Political Instrument.* Washington: Brookings Institution, 1981.

Valenta, Jiri. "Perspectives on Soviet Intervention: Soviet Use of Surprise and Deception." Pages 157–68 in Jonathan Alford (ed.), *The Soviet Union: Security Policies and Constraints.* New York: St. Martin's Press, 1985.

Volgyes, Ivan. *The Political Reliability of the Warsaw Pact Armies: The Southern Tier.* (Duke Press Policy Studies.) Durham: Duke University Press, 1982.

―――. "The Reliability of the Warsaw Pact Armies." Pages 350–77 in Kenneth M. Currie and Gregory Varhall (eds.), *The Soviet Union: What Lies Ahead? Military-Political Affairs in the 1980s.* Washington: GPO, 1985.

Volkogonov, D.A., et al. *Armii stran Varshavskogo dogovora: Spravochnik.* Moscow: Voenizdat, 1985.

Zhilin, P.A., et al. *Stroitelstvo armii evropeiskhikh stran sotsialisticheskogo sodruzhestva 1949–1980.* Moscow: Nauka, 1984.

(Various issues of the following publication were also used in the preparation of this appendix: Joint Publications Research Service, *Soviet Union: Military Affairs.*)

Glossary

Academy of Sciences (Akademiia nauk)—The Soviet Union's most prestigious scholarly institute, which conducted basic research in the physical, natural, mathematical, and social sciences. Established in 1725 by Peter the Great, it carried out long-range research and developed new technology. Union republics (*q.v.*) also had academies of sciences. The Academy of Sciences was under the direction of the Council of Ministers.

active measures (*aktivnye meropriiatiia*)—Covert or deceptive operations (including the creation and dissemination of disinformation) conducted in support of Soviet foreign policy and designed to influence the opinions or actions of the general public, particular individuals, or foreign governments.

Agitprop (Otdel agitatsii i propagandy)—Agitation and Propaganda Department, established by the Central Committee of the party in 1920. Absorbed by the Ideological Department in 1988. The term *agitprop* means the use of mass media to mobilize the public to accomplish the regime's demands.

AirLand Battle doctrine—A United States Army doctrine, adopted in the early 1980s, for generating combat power by using air and land assets on an extended and integrated battlefield.

all-union—National, with purview throughout the entire territory of the Soviet Union.

all-union ministries—Ministries of the Soviet central government that did not have counterpart ministries at the republic level. Other ministries were termed union-republic ministries (*q.v.*).

apparatchik—Russian colloquial expression for a person of the party apparatus, i.e., an individual who has been engaged full time in the work of the CPSU (*q.v.*). Sometimes used in a derogatory sense.

army—In general usage, the armed forces of the Soviet Union except the navy. In military usage, an army in the Ground Forces usually consisted of two to five divisions.

autocephalous—Independent or self-governing; an Orthodox church that was headed by its own patriarch (*q.v.*).

autonomous oblast—A territorial and administrative subdivision of a union republic (*q.v.*), or of a *krai* (*q.v.*) in the Russian Republic, created to grant a degree of autonomy to a national minority within that *krai* or union republic. In 1989 the Soviet Union had eight autonomous oblasts, five of which were in the Russian Republic.

autonomous *okrug*—A territorial and administrative subdivision of a *krai* (*q.v.*) or oblast (*q.v.*) in the Russian Republic that granted a degree of administrative autonomy to a nationality; usually found in large, remote areas of sparse population. In 1989 the Soviet Union had ten autonomous *okruga,* all of which were in the Russian Republic.

autonomous republic (autonomous soviet socialist republic—ASSR)—A territorial and administrative subdivision of some union republics (*q.v.*), created to grant a degree of administrative autonomy to some major minority groups. Directly subordinate to its union republic. In 1989 the Soviet Union had twenty autonomous republics, sixteen of which were in the Russian Republic.

babushka—Literally, grandmother. Generally, any old woman.

balance of payments—The international transactions of a country, including commodity and service transactions, capital transactions, and gold movements.

balance of trade—The relationship between a country's exports and imports.

BAM (Baykalo-Amurskaya Magistral'—Baykal-Amur Main Line)—A second trans-Siberian railroad, running 100 to 500 kilometers north of the original Trans-Siberian Railway (*q.v.*) and extending 3,145 kilometers from the western terminus at Ust'-Kut to the eastern terminus at Komsomol'sk-na-Amure. Opened in 1989, the BAM was designed and built to relieve traffic on the Trans-Siberian Railway, lessen rail traffic's vulnerability to Chinese military incursion, and facilitate transport of natural resources from huge, unexploited deposits in eastern Siberia.

Basmachi Rebellion—A sporadic and protracted revolt by Muslims of Central Asia against Soviet rule beginning in 1918 and continuing in some parts of Central Asia until 1931.

bilateral clearing agreements—The basis of the Soviet Union's trade with most socialist countries and some market economies (Finland and India). Trade imbalances were not normally cleared by convertible currency payments. Instead, the value of exports equaled the value of imports (for each country) over a specified period of time.

blat—Profitable connections, influence, pull, or illegal dealings, usually for personal gain.

Bolshevik—A member of the radical group within the Russian Social Democratic Labor Party (*q.v.*), which, under Vladimir I. Lenin's leadership, staged the Bolshevik Revolution (*q.v.*). The term *bol'shevik* means a member of the majority (*bol'shenstvo*) and was applied to the radical members of the Russian Social Democratic Labor Party after they won a majority of votes cast at a party congress (*q.v.*) in 1903. In March 1918, the Bolsheviks formed the Russian Communist Party (Bolshevik) and began calling themselves Communists. That party was the precursor of the Communist Party of the Soviet Union (CPSU—*q.v.*).

Bolshevik Revolution—The coup organized by Lenin and carried out by the Bolsheviks (*q.v.*) that overthrew the Provisional Government in November 1917 (October 1917, according to the Julian calendar—*q.v.*). Also known as the October Revolution.

boyar—A hereditary nobleman in Muscovy (*q.v.*) and the early Russian Empire (*q.v.*).

Brezhnev Doctrine—The Soviet Union's declared right to intervene militarily to prevent other states from eliminating the leading role of the communist party and returning to capitalism once they have achieved socialism. First expressed after Czechoslovakia's Prague Spring in 1968 and used as justification for the Soviet Union's invasion of Czechoslovakia in August 1968. In the late 1980s, Mikhail S. Gorbachev made statements interpreted by some in the West as repudiating the Brezhnev Doctrine.

cadre—Organized group of party activists. A party member who holds a responsible position (usually administrative) in either the party or the government apparatus. In a more restricted sense, a person who has been fully indoctrinated in party ideology and methods and uses this training in his or her work.

capitalist encirclement—A term coined by Joseph V. Stalin to indicate that the Soviet Union was surrounded by capitalist states pursuing political, military, and economic policies aimed at weakening and destroying the Soviet regime.

Carpatho-Ukraine (before October 1938 known as Subcarpathian Ruthenia)—An area historically belonging to Hungary but attached to Czechoslovakia from 1918 to October 1938. In October 1938, Carpatho-Ukraine became autonomous, and in March 1939, it became independent. But Hungary occupied it nine days later and, after World War II, ceded the area to the Soviet Union. Populated mostly by Ukrainians, who, prior to World War II, were sometimes referred to as Ruthenians.

Charter to the Nobility—An edict, granted by Catherine the Great, that increased and confirmed the personal and class privileges of the nobility.

Cheka—*See* Vecheka.

Chernobyl'—A town in the Ukrainian Republic, site of the world's most catastropic nuclear accident. On April 26, 1986, a reactor at the Chernobyl' nuclear power plant exploded and irradiated areas as far away as Sweden. Most radioactivity contaminated large sections of rich farmland in the Ukrainian, Russian, and Belorussian republics and affected millions of their inhabitants. Soviet and Western experts believe that damage to the people's health, to the economy, and to the environment will be felt for decades. As of 1989, the accident had cost hundreds of lives and billions of rubles, caused a major slowdown in what had been an ambitious nuclear energy program, and provided an impetus to the fledgling environmental movement in the Soviet Union. Although the accident was caused by a combination of human error and faulty reactor design, the remaining three reactors at the Chernobyl' power plant and reactors of this type remained operational elsewhere in the Soviet Union in 1989.

chernozem—Literally, black earth. The zone of rich, black soil that extends across the southwestern Soviet Union.

class struggle—In Marxist terms, every nonsocialist society has been characterized by conflict between the classes of which it has been composed. The struggle has pitted the workers against the privileged, oppressive, and property-owning ruling class.

CoCom (Coordinating Committee for Multilateral Export Controls)—Formed by Western governments in 1949 to prevent the transfer of military-related technology from the West to the Soviet Union and Eastern Europe. In 1989 members of CoCom included Belgium, Britain, Canada, Denmark, the Federal Republic of Germany (West Germany), France, Greece, Italy, Japan, Luxembourg, the Netherlands, Norway, Portugal, Spain, Turkey, and the United States. With no formal relationship to the North Atlantic Treaty Organization (NATO), CoCom operated on informal agreements on items having military applications and those with nuclear uses.

collective farm (*kollektivnoe khoziaistvo*—kolkhoz)—An agricultural "cooperative" where peasants, under the direction of party-approved plans and leaders, are paid wages based, in part, on the success of their harvest.

collectivization—Stalin's policy of confiscating privately owned agricultural lands and facilities and consolidating them, the farmers, and their families into large collective farms (*q.v.*) and state farms (*q.v.*). Forced collectivization took place from 1929 to 1937.

combat readiness—The availability of equipment and qualified personnel in military organizations capable of conducting combat operations. Motorized rifle and tank divisions of the Soviet Ground Forces were maintained in three general categories of combat readiness: those divisions with sufficient personnel and equipment to begin combat operations after brief preparation; those with the necessary equipment but with less than 50 percent of wartime manpower; and those that were inactive and essentially unmanned equipment sets.

combine (*kombinat*)—An economic entity of an industrial or service nature that consists of several specialized, technologically related enterprises (*q.v.*).

Comecon (Council for Mutual Economic Assistance)—A multilateral economic alliance headquartered in Moscow. Members in 1989 were Bulgaria, Cuba, Czechoslovakia, the German Democratic Republic (East Germany), Hungary, Mongolia, Poland, Romania, the Soviet Union, and Vietnam. Comecon was created in January 1949, ostensibly to promote economic development of member states through cooperation and specialization, but actually to enforce Soviet economic domination of Eastern Europe and to provide a counterweight to the Marshall Plan (*q.v.*). Also referred to as CEMA or CMEA.

Cominform (Communist Information Bureau)—An international organization of communist parties, founded and controlled by the Soviet Union in 1947 and dissolved in 1956. The Cominform published propaganda touting international communist solidarity but was primarily a tool of Soviet foreign policy.

Comintern (Communist International)—An international organization of communist parties founded by Lenin in 1919. Initially, it attempted to control the international socialist (*q.v.*) movement and to foment world revolution; later, it also became an instrument of Soviet foreign policy. Dissolved by Stalin in 1943 as a conciliatory measure toward his Western allies.

communism/communist—A doctrine, based on revolutionary Marxian socialism (*q.v.*) and Marxism-Leninism (*q.v.*), and the official ideology of the Soviet Union. The doctrine provided for a system of authoritarian government in which the communist party alone controlled state-owned means of production. It sought to establish a society in which the state withers away and goods and services are distributed equitably. A communist is an adherent or advocate of communism.

complex (*kompleks*)—An aggregate of entities constituting a whole. Sometimes applied to groupings of industries.

Congress of People's Deputies—The highest organ of legislative and executive authority, according to the Soviet Constitution. Existed in the early Soviet period as the Congress of Soviets (*q.v.*) and was resurrected in 1988 by constitutional amendment.

Congress of Soviets—First met in June 1917 and elected the All-Russian Central Committee of over 250 members dominated by the leaders of the Petrograd Soviet. The Second Congress of Soviets met on October 25, 1917, one day after the start of the Bolshevik Revolution (*q.v.*). Dominated by Bolshevik delegates, the Second Congress of Soviets approved the Bolshevik coup d'état and the decrees on peace and land issued by Lenin. It also confirmed the Council of People's Commissars, drawn exclusively from Bolshevik ranks, as the new government and elected the All-Russian Central Executive Committee. It adjourned on October 27 and was not reconvened.

correlation of forces and resources (*sootnosheniie sil i sredstv*)—A Soviet term meaning the aggregate of indexes permitting evaluation of the relative strength of friendly and hostile troops, by comparative analysis of the quantitative and qualitative characteristics of troop organization, performance data on armament and combat matériel, and other indexes that define combat readiness (*q.v.*) and combat capability.

cossacks—Originally peasants, primarily Ukrainian and Russian, who fled from bondage to the lower Dnepr and Don river regions to settle in the frontier areas separating fifteenth-century Muscovy (*q.v.*), Poland, and the lands occupied by Tatars. The cossacks, engaged in hunting, fishing, and cattle raising, established permanent settlements and later organized themselves into military formations to resist Tatar raids. Renowned as horsemen, they were absorbed into the Russian army as light cavalry or irregular troops by the late eighteenth century.

Council of Ministers—The highest executive and administrative body of the Soviet Union, according to the Constitution. In practice, its members directed most day-to-day state activities.

CPSU (Communist Party of the Soviet Union)—The official name of the communist party in the Soviet Union since 1952. Originally the Bolshevik (*q.v.*) faction of the Russian Social Democratic Labor Party (*q.v.*), the party was named the Russian Communist Party (Bolshevik) from March 1918 to December 1925, the All-Union Communist Party (Bolshevik) from December 1925 to October 1952, and the CPSU thereafter.

cult of personality—A term coined by Nikita S. Khrushchev at the Twentieth Party Congress of the CPSU in 1956 to describe the rule of Stalin, in which the Soviet people were compelled to deify the dictator. Leonid I. Brezhnev also established a cult of personality around himself, although to a lesser extent than Stalin. Similar cults of saints, heroes, and the just tsar formed a historical basis for the cult of personality.

Cyrillic—An alphabet based on Greek characters that was created in the ninth century to serve as a medium for translating Eastern Orthodox texts into Old Church Slavonic (*q.v.*). Named for Cyril, the leader of the first religious mission from Byzantium to the Slavic people, Cyrillic is used in modern Russian and several other Slavic languages.

Defense Council—The chief decision-making organ of the Soviet national security apparatus, composed of selected members of the Politburo (*q.v.*) and headed by the general secretary (*q.v.*) of the CPSU (*q.v.*) and the chairman of the Presidium (*q.v.*) of the CPSU Central Committee.

democratic centralism—A Leninist doctrine requiring discussion of issues until a decision is reached by the party. After a decision is made, discussion concerns only planning and execution. This method of decision making directed lower bodies unconditionally to implement the decisions of higher bodies.

demokratizatsiia (democratization)—Campaign initiated by Gorbachev to enable different interest groups to participate in political processes to a greater extent than previously allowed.

dialectical materialism—A Marxist (*q.v.*) tenet describing the process by which the class struggle between bourgeois capitalist society and the exploited workers produces the dictatorship of the proletariat (*q.v.*) and evolves into socialism (*q.v.*) and, finally, communism (*q.v.*).

dictatorship of the proletariat—According to Marxism-Leninism (*q.v.*), the early stage of societal organization under socialism (*q.v.*) after the overthrow of capitalism. It involves workers' dominance in suppressing the counterrevolutionary resistance of the bourgeois "exploiting classes."

Donbass (Donetskiy basseyn)—Donets Basin. A major coal-mining and industrial area located in the southeastern Ukrainian Republic and the adjacent Russian Republic.

DOSAAF (Dobrovol'noe obshchestvo sodeistviia armii, aviatsii i flotu)—Voluntary Society for Assistance to the Army, Air Force, and Navy. Responsible for premilitary training of Soviet youth.

duma—An advisory council to the princes of Kievan Rus' (*q.v.*) and the tsars of the Russian Empire (*q.v.*).

Duma—Lower chamber of the legislature, established by Nicholas II after the Revolution of 1905.

East Slavs—A subdivision of Slavic peoples, who evolved into Russians, Ukrainians, and Belorussians and speak languages belonging to the East Slavic branch of the Indo-European family of languages.

enterprise—A production establishment, such as a plant or a factory; not to be confused with a privately owned, Western-style business.

extensive economic development—Expansion of production by adding resources rather than by improving the efficiency of resource use, as in intensive economic development.

False Dmitrii—Name applied to three pretenders to the Muscovite throne during the Time of Troubles (*q.v.*). These pretenders claimed to be Dmitrii (who died as a child), the son of Tsar Ivan IV.

February Revolution—The popular uprising that overthrew the government of the Russian Empire (*q.v.*) under Tsar Nicholas II in February 1917 (according to the Julian calendar—*q.v.*), thus ending 300 years of rule by the Romanov Dynasty.

first secretary—The title of the head of the CPSU (*q.v.*) Secretariat that was adopted after Stalin's death in 1953; used by Khrushchev, and by Brezhnev until 1966, before the title was changed back to general secretary (*q.v.*).

fiscal year—A one-year period for financial accounting purposes, which can coincide with the calendar year (as it did in the Soviet Union).

five-year plan—A comprehensive plan that sets the economic goals for a five-year period. Once the Soviet regime stipulated the plan figures, all levels of the economy, from individual enterprises to the national level, were obligated to meet those goals.

FOFA (Follow-on-Forces-Attack)—A North Atlantic Treaty Organization (NATO) military concept emphasizing deep offensive operations against the enemy's second-echelon (follow-on) forces.

free trade zones—Areas where autonomy is allowed in conducting direct trade with foreigners.

front—In military usage, a front consists of two or more armies (*q.v.*). Two or more fronts constitute a theater of military operations (TVD—*q.v.*). In political usage, an organization controlled by the Soviet regime (through funding links and Soviet officials in leading positions) to support Soviet policies through lobbying and propaganda.

GATT (General Agreement on Tariffs and Trade)—An integrated set of bilateral trade agreements among more than 100 contracting nations. Originally drawn up in 1947, GATT aimed at abolishing quotas and reducing tariffs among members. The Soviet Union eschewed joining GATT until 1987, when it applied for membership. As of May 1989, its application had not been approved.

GDP (gross domestic product)—A measure of the total value of goods and services produced by the domestic economy during a given period, usually one year. Obtained by adding the value contributed by each sector of the economy in the form of profits, compensation to employees, and depreciation (consumption of capital). Only domestic production is included, not income arising from investments and possessions owned abroad, hence the use of the word *domestic* to distinguish GDP from gross national product (GNP—*q.v.*). Real GDP is the value of GDP when inflation has been taken into account.

general secretary—The title of the head of the CPSU (*q.v.*) Secretariat, who presides over the Politburo (*q.v.*) and has been the Soviet Union's de facto supreme leader. Stalin became general secretary of the Russian Communist Party (Bolshevik) in 1922 and employed the position to amass personal power. After Stalin's death in 1953, the title was changed to first secretary (*q.v.*), which was used by Khrushchev and by Brezhnev until 1966, when the title of general secretary was reinstituted. Brezhnev's successors—Iurii Andropov, Konstantin Chernenko, and Mikhail S. Gorbachev—were all general secretaries.

glasnost'—Public discussion of issues; accessibility of information so that the public can become familiar with it and discuss it. Gorbachev's policy of using the media to make information available on some controversial issues, in order to provoke public discussion, challenge government and party bureaucrats, and mobilize greater support for his policy of *perestroika* (*q.v.*).

Glavlit—The official censorship organ, established in 1922 as the Main Administration for Literary and Publishing Affairs (Glavnoe upravlenie po delam literatury i izdatv—Glavlit). Although the formal name of that organization has since been changed to the Main Administration for Safeguarding State Secrets in the Press (Glavnoe upravlenie po okhrane gosudarstvennykh tain v pechati), the acronym *Glavlit* continued to be used in the late 1980s.

Glavrepertkom (Glavnyi komitet po kontroliu za zrelishchami i repertuarom)—Main Committee for Control of Entertainment and Repertory. The governmental organization that directed theatrical, film, and other cultural productions and sanctioned their release for public viewing. The acronym, Glavrepertkom, continued in use although the organization was changed from a committee (*komitet*) to an administration (*upravelenie*) under the Ministry of Culture.

GNP (gross national product)—The total market value of final goods and services produced by an economy during a year. Obtained by adding the gross domestic product (GDP—*q.v.*) and the income received from abroad by residents and subtracting payments remitted abroad to nonresidents. Real GNP is the value of GNP when inflation has been taken into account.

Golden Horde—A federative Mongol state that extended from western Siberia to the Carpathian Mountains, encompassing much of eastern Europe. It ravaged Kievan Rus' (*q.v.*), subjugated Muscovy (*q.v.*) to the Mongol "yoke" (*q.v.*), and was a major political force from the mid-thirteenth century to the end of the fifteenth century. Generally, it exacted tribute and controlled external relations but allowed local authorities to decide internal affairs. The term is derived from the Mongol *altan ordo* or the Tatar *altun ordu,* literally meaning golden palace or camp, apparently based on the color of the tent used by Batu Khan (died 1255), the leader or ruler, during the Golden Horde's conquest of the region. Also known as the khanate of Kipchak.

Gosbank (Gosudarstvennyi bank)—State Bank. The main bank in the Soviet Union, which acted as a combination central bank, commercial bank, and settlement bank. It issued and regulated currency and credit and handled payments between enterprises (*q.v.*) and organizations. It received all taxes and payments to the state and paid out budgetary appropriations.

Goskino (Gosudarstvennyi komitet po kinematografii)—State Committee for Cinematography. Absorbed by the Ministry of Culture in 1953, it became an independent organization again in 1963.

Goskomizdat (Gosudarstvennyi komitet po delam izdatel'stv, poligrafii i knizhoy torgovli)—State Committee for Publishing Houses, Printing Plants, and the Book Trade. Supervises the publishing and printing industry and exercises all-union (*q.v.*) control over the thematic trend and content of literature.

Goskompriroda (Gosudarstvennyi komitet po okhrane prirody)—State Committee for the Protection of Nature. Formed in 1988, the government agency charged with responsibility for overseeing environmental protection in the Soviet Union.

Goskomtsen (Gosudarstvennyi komitet po tsenam)—State Committee on Prices. The government body that established, under party guidance, the official prices of virtually everything produced in the Soviet Union, including agricultural produce, natural resources, manufactured products, and consumer goods and services.

Gosplan (Gosudarstvennyi planovyi komitet)—State Planning Committee. Under party guidance, it was primarily responsible for creating and monitoring five-year plans (*q.v.*) and annual plans. The name was changed from State Planning Commission in 1948, but the acronym was retained.

Gostelradio (Gosudarstvennyi komitet po televideniyu i radioveshchaniyu)—State Committee for Television and Radio Broadcasting. Established in 1957 as the Committee for Radio Broadcasting and Television. Upgraded to a state committee in 1970.

GPU (Gosudarstvennoe politicheskoe upravlenie)—State Political Directorate. The security police successor to the Vecheka (*q.v.*) from 1922 to 1923.

Great Patriotic War—The Soviet name for the part of World War II in which the Soviet people fought against fascism from June 1941 to May 1945. Considered one of the just wars (*q.v.*) by the CPSU (*q.v.*).

Great Terror—A period, from about 1934 to 1939, of intense fear among Soviet citizens, millions of whom were arrested, interrogated, tortured, imprisoned, deported from their native lands, and executed by Stalin's secret police for political or economic crimes that were spurious. The Great Terror encompassed the general population and peaked in 1937 and 1938, when it included extensive purges of party members, many of whom held high positions in the government, economy, armed forces, party, and secret police itself.

GRU—*See* Main Intelligence Directorate.

GUGB (Glavnoe upravlenie gosudarstvennoi bezopasnosti)—Main Directorate for State Security. The security police, successor to the OGPU (*q.v.*), subordinate to the NKVD (*q.v.*). Existed from 1934 to 1941, 1941 to 1943, and 1953 to 1954.

Gulag (Glavnoe upravlenie ispravitel'no-trudovykh lagerei)—Main Directorate for Corrective Labor Camps. The penal system of the Soviet Union, consisting of a network of harsh labor camps where criminals and political prisoners were forced to serve sentences.

hard currency—Currency that was freely convertible and traded on international currency markets.

Helsinki Accords—Signed in August by all the countries of Europe (except Albania) plus Canada and the United States at the conclusion of the Conference on Security and Cooperation in Europe, the Helsinki Accords endorsed general principles of international behavior and measures to enhance security and addressed selected economic, environmental, and humnitarian issues. In essence, the Helsinki Accords confirmed existing, post-World War II national boundaries and obligated signatories to respect basic principles of human rights. Helsinki watch groups (*q.v.*) were formed in 1976 to monitor compliance. The term Helsinki Accords is the short form for the Final Act of the Conference on Security and Cooperation in Europe and is also known as the Final Act.

Helsinki watch groups—Informal, unofficial organizations of citizens monitoring their regimes' adherence to the human rights provisions of the 1975 Helsinki Accords (*q.v.*).

horde—A Mongol military force of about 30,000 to 40,000 troops mounted on horseback that was roughly equivalent in size to a modern army corps. A territory conquered by a horde (*ordo* in Mongol) was organized into a khanate (*q.v.*). Troops of the horde were accompanied by their families, and their descendants were gradually assimilated into the peoples that they conquered.

IMF (International Monetary Fund)—Established along with the World Bank (*q.v.*) in 1945, the IMF is a specialized agency affiliated with the United Nations and responsible for stabilizing international exchange rates and payments. Its main function is to provide loans to its members (including industrialized and developing countries) when they experience balance of payments (*q.v.*) difficulties. These loans frequently have conditions that require substantial internal economic adjustments by the recipients, most of which are developing countries.

intelligentsia—Intellectuals constituting the cultural, academic, social, and political elite.

internal passport—Government-issued document, presented to officials on demand, identifying citizens, their nationality, and their authorized residence. Used in both the Russian Empire (*q.v.*) and the Soviet Union to restrict the movement of people.

Izvestiia (News)—Daily, nationwide newspaper published by the Presidium (*q.v.*) of the Supreme Soviet of the Soviet Union.

Julian calendar—A calendar, named for Gaius Julius Caesar and introduced in Rome in 46 B.C., that established the twelve-month year of 365 days. It was adopted throughout much of the Western world, including Kievan Rus' (*q.v.*) and Muscovy (*q.v.*). The Julian calendar's year, however, was over eleven minutes too long compared with the solar year, i.e., the time the earth requires to make one revolution around the sun. Because of this discrepancy, Pope Gregory XIII introduced a revised calendar in 1582 that had a shortened year and then omitted the ten excess days that had accumulated since A.D. 325, the year of the Council of Nicea, which was chosen as the base year. Although most of the Western world adopted the Gregorian calendar, Russian regimes retained the Julian calendar (termed old style or O.S.) until after the Bolshevik Revolution (*q.v.*). On February 1, 1918 O.S., the Bolsheviks introduced the Gregorian calendar and omitted the thirteen excess days that had accumulated since A.D. 325, thus making that day February 14, 1918 (new style or N.S.). The Russian Orthodox Church and other Eastern Christian churches continue to use the Julian calendar.

just wars—According to Marxism-Leninism (*q.v.*), just wars are those waged to protect the interests of the working class and the toiling masses, to liquidate social and national oppression, and to protect national sovereignty against imperialist aggression. The most just wars are those waged in defense of the socialist fatherland. In contrast, unjust wars are reactionary or predatory wars waged by imperialist countries.

Karakum Canal—An irrigation and water supply canal, which is navigable, in the Turkmen Republic. Under construction since 1954, the 1,100 kilometers completed by 1988 diverted a significant amount of the Amu Darya's waters west through and into the Kara Desert and Ashkhabad, the republic's capital, and beyond. The canal opened up expansive new tracts of land to agriculture, while contributing to a major environmental disaster, the drying up of the Aral Sea. The primitive construction of the canal allows almost 50 percent of the water to escape en route.

Kazakhstan—Literally, land of the Kazakhs. A vast region in Central Asia settled by the Golden Horde (*q.v.*) in the thirteenth century that the Russian Empire (*q.v.*) acquired during the eighteenth and nineteenth centuries. In 1924 the Soviet regime began dividing Kazakhstan into its major nationality groups, the Kazakhs and the Kirgiz. Subsequently, both of these groups were given union republic (*q.v.*) status in the Soviet Union.

KGB (Komitet gosudarstvennoi bezopasnosti)—Committee for State Security. The predominant security police organization since its establishment in 1954.

khanate—Dominion or territorial jurisdiction of a Mongol khan (ruler).

khozraschet—A system of "self-supporting operations," applied to such individual enterprises (*q.v.*) as factories, encompassing a wide range of activities, including *samofinansirovanie* (*q.v.*), and a management process involving a large number of individuals.

Kievan Rus'—An East Slavic state, centered on Kiev, established by Oleg ca. 880. Disintegrated by the thirteenth century.

kolkhoz (pl., kolkhozy)—*See* collective farm.

Komsomol (Vsesoiuznyi Leninskii kommunisticheskii soiuz molo-dezhi)—All-Union Lenin Communist Youth League. An organization administered by the CPSU (*q.v.*) for youth between ages fourteen and twenty-eight. Since its establishment in 1918, the Komsomol has helped the party prepare new generations for an elite role in Soviet society. It has instilled in young people the principles of Marxism-Leninism (*q.v.*) and involved them in large-scale industrial projects, such as factory construction and the virgin land campaign (*q.v.*). Members were expected to be politically conscious, vigilant, and loyal to the communist cause. Membership privileges included better opportunities for higher education and preferential consideration for career advancement. In 1982 the Komsomol had 41.7 million members.

krai (pl., *kraia*)—A large territorial and administrative subdivision found only in the Russian Republic, where there are six, all of which are thinly populated. The boundaries of a *krai* are laid out primarily for ease of administration but may also contain lesser political subdivisions based on nationality groups—autonomous oblast (*q.v.*), or autonomous *okrug* (*q.v.*), or both. Directly subordinate to its union republic (*q.v.*).

kremlin (*kreml'*)—Central citadel in many medieval Russian towns, usually located at a strategic spot along a river. Moscow's Kremlin is now the seat of the CPSU (*q.v.*) and the government of the Soviet Union.

kulak—A successful, independent farmer of the period of Soviet history before collectivization (*q.v.*). According to the Bolsheviks (*q.v.*), any peasant who hired labor. The term eventually was applied to any peasant who opposed collectivization.

Kuzbass (Kuznetskiy basseyn)—Kuznetsk Basin. A major coal-mining and industrial area located in southern Siberia, east and southeast of Novosibirsk.

League of Nations—An organization for international cooperation, established by the victorious Allied Powers at the end of World War I. The Soviet Union joined in 1934 but was expelled in 1939.

Lend-Lease Law—A foreign aid program initiated by the United States in March 1941 that authorized the transfer of substantial quantities of war matériel, such as tanks, munitions, locomotives, and ships, to countries opposing the military aggression of the Axis Powers (Germany, Italy, and Japan) while the United States mobilized for war. In November 1941, the Soviet Union was added to the list of recipients and, during the course of World War II, received supplies and equipment worth billions of dollars.

liquidity shortage—A lack of assets that can be readily converted to cash.

local war—Armed conflict short of general war, usually waged with limited forces and in a limited area. In Soviet usage, local war usually referred to a war waged by capitalist countries against "wars of national liberation."

Main Intelligence Directorate (Glavnoe razvedyvatel'noe upravlenie—GRU)—A military organization, subordinate to the General Staff of the armed forces, that collected and processed strategic, technical, and tactical information of value to the armed forces. It may also have included special units for engaging in active measures (*q.v.*), guerrilla warfare, and sabotage.

Main Political Directorate of the Soviet Army and Navy—The organ the CPSU (*q.v.*) used to control the armed forces of the Soviet Union and other Warsaw Pact (*q.v.*) countries. An organ of the CPSU in the Ministry of Defense, it was responsible for conducting ideological indoctrination and propaganda activities to prepare the armed forces for their role in national security.

Marshall Plan—A plan announced in June 1947 by United States secretary of state George C. Marshall for the reconstruction of Europe after World War II. The plan involved a considerable amount of United States aid to Western Europe, but the Soviet Union refused the offer of aid and forbade the East European countries it dominated from taking part in the Marshall Plan. As a counterweight, the Soviet Union created the Council for Mutual Economic Assistance (Comecon—*q.v.*).

Marxism/Marxist—The economic, political, and social theories of Karl Marx, a nineteenth-century German philosopher and socialist, especially his concept of socialism (*q.v.*), which includes the labor theory of value, dialectical materialism (*q.v.*), class struggle (*q.v.*), and the dictatorship of the proletariat (*q.v.*) until a classless society can be established. Another German socialist, Friederich Engels, collaborated with Marx and was a major contributor to the development of Marxism.

993

Marxism-Leninism/Marxist-Leninist—The ideology of communism (*q.v.*), developed by Karl Marx and refined and adapted
to social and economic conditions in Russia by Lenin, that has
guided the party and the Soviet Union. Marx talked of the establishment of the dictatorship of the proletariat (*q.v.*), after
the overthrow of the bourgeoisie, as a transitional socialist (*q.v.*)
phase before the achievement of communism. Lenin added the
idea of a communist party as the vanguard or leading force
in promoting the proletarian revolution and building communism. Stalin and subsequent leaders contributed their own
interpretations of the ideology.

Menshevik—A member of a wing of the Russian Social Democratic
Labor Party (*q.v.*) before and during the Russian revolutions
of 1905 and 1917. Unlike the Bolsheviks (*q.v.*), the Mensheviks believed in the gradual achievement of socialism (*q.v.*) by
parliamentary methods. The term Menshevik is derived from
the word *menshenstvo* (minority).

metropolitan—The primate of an ecclesiastical province of the Orthodox Church.

MGB (Ministerstvo gosudarstvennoi bezopasnosti)—Ministry of
State Security. The paramount security police organization
from 1946 to 1953.

military commissariat (*voennyi komissariat—voenkomat*)—A local military administrative agency that prepares and executes plans
for military mobilization, maintains records on military manpower and economic resources available to the armed forces,
provides premilitary training, drafts men for military service,
organizes reserves for training, and performs other military
functions at the local level.

mir—A peasant commune established at the village level in tsarist
Russia. It controlled the redistribution of farmland and was
held responsible for collecting taxes and levying recruits for military service. In Russian, mir also means "world" and "peace."

Mongol "yoke"—Period of Mongol domination of much of eastern
Europe by the Golden Horde (*q.v.*) from the mid-thirteenth
century to the end of the fifteenth century.

MOOP (Ministerstvo okhrany obshchestvennogo poriadka)—
Ministry for the Preservation of Public Order. Functioned between 1962 and 1968.

moral-political capabilities—The ability of the people and the armed
forces to assume a positive attitude toward a war fought by the
Soviet Union and to support the political goals of the war under
trying circumstances.

most-favored-nation status—Under the provisions of the General Agreement on Tariffs and Trade (GATT—*q.v.*), when one country accords another most-favored-nation status it agrees to extend that country the same trade concessions, e.g., lower tariffs or reduced nontariff barriers, that it grants to any other recipients having most-favored-nation status. As of May 1989, the Soviet Union had not been a member of GATT and had not received most-favored-nation status from the United States.

mujahidin (sing., *mujahid*)—Derived from the word *jihad,* the term means holy warriors and is used by and applied to the Afghan resistance or freedom fighters.

mullah—Muslim man trained in Islamic law and doctrine.

Muscovy—The state that emerged around Moscow after the decline of Kievan Rus' (*q.v.*) in the thirteenth century. Predecessor to the Russian Empire (*q.v.*), which was proclaimed in 1721 by Peter the Great.

MVD (Ministerstvo vnutrennykh del)—Ministry of Internal Affairs. Existed from 1946 to 1962 and since 1968 began to exercise regular police functions.

nationality—A people linked by a common language, culture, history, and territory who may have developed a common economic and political life; an individual's ethnic background. Not to be confused with an individual's country of citizenship.

Nazi-Soviet Nonaggression Pact—Agreement signed by Nazi Germany and the Soviet Union on August 23, 1939, immediately preceding the German invasion of Poland, which began World War II. A secret protocol divided Poland between the two powers and gave Bessarabia, Latvia, Lithuania, Estonia, and the eastern part of Poland to the Soviet Union. The pact also delayed the Soviet Union's entry into World War II. Also known as the Molotov-Ribbentrop Pact.

NEP (Novaia ekonomicheskaia politika)—New Economic Policy. Instituted in 1921, it let peasants sell produce on an open market and permitted small enterprises (*q.v.*) to be privately owned and operated. Cultural restrictions were also relaxed during this period. NEP declined with the forced collectivization (*q.v.*) of farms and was officially ended by Stalin in December 1929.

net material product—The official measure of the value of goods and services produced in the Soviet Union, and in other countries having a planned economy, during a given period, usually a year. It approximates the term gross national product (GNP—*q.v.*) used by economists in the United States and in other countries having a market economy. The Soviet measure has been

based on constant prices, which do not fully account for inflation, and has excluded depreciation.

"new Soviet man"—A theoretical goal of several Soviet regimes
to transform the culturally, ethnically, and linguistically diverse
peoples of the Soviet Union into a single Soviet people, be-
having according to the ideology of Marxism-Leninism (*q.v.*).

"new thinking"—Gorbachev's view that international politics
should be based on common moral and ethical norms rather
than military force, including nuclear war; an integral part of
perestroika (*q.v.*).

NKGB (Narodnyi komissariat gosudarstvennoi bezopasnosti)—
People's Commissariat of State Security. Functioned in 1941
and again from 1943 to 1946.

NKVD (Narodnyi komissariat vnutrennykh del)—People's Commissariat of Internal· Affairs. The commissariat that administered regular police organizations from 1917 to 1946.
When the OGPU (*q.v.*) was abolished in 1934, the NKVD incorporated the security police organization until 1946.

nomenklatura—The CPSU's (*q.v.*) system of appointing key personnel
in the government and other important organizations, based
on lists of critical positions and people in political favor. Also
refers to the individuals included on these lists.

nonchernozem (*nechernozem'e*)—A large agricultural and industrial
region in the European part of the Soviet Union, extending
approximately 2,300 kilometers from Kaliningrad in the northwest to Sverdlovsk in the east with a north-south expanse of
more than 1,000 kilometers in places. The region does not have
the black earth of the chernozem (*q.v.*) zone.

Novosti (Agentstvo pechati novosti)—News Press Agency. The
news agency responsible for disseminating Soviet information
abroad. (The word *novost'* means news or something new.)

nuclear war-fighting—The capability to use nuclear weapons to
fight a war.

oblast (pl., oblasts)—A territorial and administrative subdivision
in ten of the fifteen union republics (*q.v.*). Directly subordinate
to its union republic. *See also* autonomous oblast.

OECD (Organisation for Economic Co-operation and Development)—Founded by Western nations in 1961 to stimulate economic progress and world trade. It also coordinated economic
aid to less developed countries. In 1989 members included Australia, Austria, Belgium, Britain, Canada, Denmark, Finland,
France, Greece, Iceland, Ireland, Italy, Japan, Luxembourg,
the Netherlands, New Zealand, Norway, Portugal, Spain,

Sweden, Switzerland, Turkey, the United States, and West Germany.

OGPU (Ob''edinennoe gosudarstvennoe politicheskoe upravlenie)—Unified State Political Directorate. The security police from 1923 to 1934; successor to the GPU.

Okhrana—The security police under Alexander III (1881–94). Covert operations (using nonuniformed agents and informers) were used to uncover and collect evidence against revolutionary groups.

okrug (pl., *okruga*)—*See* autonomous *okrug*.

Old Believers—A sect of the Russian Orthodox Church that rejected the changes made by Patriarch Nikon in the mid-seventeenth century.

Old Church Slavonic (also known as Church Slavonic)—The first Slavic literary language. Influenced development of modern Slavic languages, especially literary Russian. Used in liturgies of the Russian Orthodox Church and other Slavic churches.

opportunity cost—The value of goods or services in terms of what had to be sacrificed to obtain them.

oprichnina—The era in the 1550s during which Ivan IV (the Terrible) brutally punished and decimated the boyar (*q.v.*) class.

Pale of Settlement—A district created by Catherine II in 1792 for the Jewish population of the Russian Empire. By the nineteenth century, it encompassed all of Russian Poland, the Baltic provinces, Belorussia, most of Ukraine, Crimea, and Bessarabia. Jews were prohibited from living or traveling beyond the Pale of Settlement. Although eventually some Jews were allowed to settle in other parts of the empire, the Russian census of 1897 indicated that nearly 5 million Jews remained in the Pale of Settlement and only about 200,000 lived outside its boundaries.

party congress—In theory, the ruling body of the communist party. Party congresses, which usually met every five years, were largely ceremonial and legitimizing events at which several thousand "elected" delegates convened to approve new party programs (*q.v.*) and *Party Rules* (*q.v.*).

party program—A comprehensive statement adopted by a party congress (*q.v.*) that states the goals and principles of the party. The 1986 party program, the fourth since 1918, was adopted by the Twenty-Seventh Party Congress. It was notable in that it did not set definite dates for the attainment of goals, unlike its predecessor, the 1961 party program.

Party Rules (*Ustav kommunisticheskoi partii Sovetskogo Soiuza*)—CPSU document containing regulations for admission of individuals into the CPSU (*q.v.*); the organizational structure of the party; the principles of democratic centralism (*q.v.*); the role of the primary party organization (*q.v.*); the party's relations with the Komsomol (*q.v.*); party organizations in the armed forces; and membership dues. It can be altered by the party congress (*q.v.*). Also called *Party Statute*.

passenger-kilometer—The movement of one person a distance of one kilometer.

patriarch—Head of an independent Orthodox Church, such as the Russian Orthodox Church, or one of the Eastern Rite Catholic churches.

peaceful coexistence—According to Marxism-Leninism (*q.v.*), the doctrine of maintaining proper state-to-state relations between socialist (*q.v.*) and capitalist states, while simultaneously encouraging friction and strife within and among capitalist countries by every means, short of all-out war, and pursuing expansionist aims in the Third World.

people's court—An official tribunal having jurisdiction in most civil and criminal cases originating in a (*raion*) (*q.v.*). The court was presided over by a professional judge, assisted by two people's assessors (*narodnye zasedateli*), or lay judges. Cases were decided by a majority vote. Professional judges were elected for five-year terms and were members of the CPSU (*q.v.*); most had some legal training. People's assessors, who had no legal training, were elected for two and one-half years but sat only for a few weeks; they corresponded somewhat to jurors in United States courts.

perestroika (restructuring)—Gorbachev's campaign to revitalize the economy, party, and society by adjusting economic, political, and social mechanisms. Announced at Twenty-Seventh Party Congress in August 1986.

permafrost—Ground permanently frozen except for the surface soils that thaw when temperatures rise above freezing. Thawing and refreezing cause instability of the soil, which greatly complicates the construction and maintenance of roads, railroads, and buildings. Permafrost covers roughly the northern one-third of the Soviet landmass.

permanent revolution—A theory, developed by Leon Trotsky, that in a backward society, such as that of Russia in the early 1900s, a bourgeois revolution would evolve into a proletarian, socialist (*q.v.*) revolution and would inspire the continuous or permanent outbreak of socialist revolutions internationally. Continuing world revolution remained a doctrine of the CPSU (*q.v.*) in the late 1980s.

Pioneer (Pioner)—A member of the All-Union Pioneer Organization named for Lenin. Founded in 1922, and open to children ages ten to fifteen, the main purpose of the organization has been the rudimentary political indoctrination of Soviet youth. At age fourteen, a Pioneer can enter the Komsomol (*q.v.*). In 1980 about 20 million children were members of the Pioneer organization.

Politburo—Political Bureau of the Central Committee of the CPSU (*q.v.*); the foremost policy-making body of the Soviet Union. In February 1989, the Politburo had twelve members and eight candidate members. From 1952 to 1966, the Politburo was called the Presidium.

popular front—A device of Soviet foreign policy, implemented with the assistance of the Comintern (*q.v.*), that attempted to gain allies, principally the Western democracies, against the fascists in Spain, Germany, and elsewhere, from 1939 through World War II.

Pravda (Truth)—Daily, nationwide newspaper published by the Central Committee of the CPSU (*q.v.*).

Presidium (of the Central Committee of the CPSU)—The CPSU Politburo (*q.v.*) was called the Presidium between 1952 and 1966.

Presidium (of the Council of Ministers)—The executive committee of the national executive branch of the government.

Presidium (of the Supreme Soviet)—The executive committee of the national legislative branch of the government.

primary party organization—The basic unit of the party, known as a party cell until 1934; comprised of three or more party members. Each party member is a member of a primary party organization.

procurator—A member of the Procuracy whose responsibilities can include conducting investigations, supervising investigations carried out by the MVD (*q.v.*) and the KGB (*q.v.*), prosecuting criminal and civil offenders, referring judicial decisions to higher courts for review, supervising prisons, administering parole and release of prisoners, and overseeing the legality of operations of all government bodies. Procurators, who were appointed by the procurator general and served throughout the Soviet Union, were generally members of the CPSU (*q.v.*) and subject to party discipline. During the tsarist period, Peter the Great appointed a chief procurator as head of the Holy Synod.

proletarian internationalism—The Marxist belief that workers around the world are linked together by a bond that transcends nationalism; the commitment of communists to do all they can to convert the world to communism (*q.v.*).

raion (pl., *raiony*)—A low-level territorial and administrative subdivision for rural and municipal administration. A rural *raion* was a county-sized district in a *krai* (*q.v.*), oblast (*q.v.*), autonomous republic (*q.v.*), autonomous *okrug* (*q.v.*), or union republic (*q.v.*). A city *raion* was similar to a borough in some large cities in the United States.

readiness—The ability of military units to deploy to achieve a wartime objective without delay. According to Western authorities, divisions of the Soviet Ground Forces varied greatly in their readiness and could be placed in three states of readiness. About 40 percent of the divisions were in a high state of readiness with trained manpower at more than 50 percent of wartime authorization and with late-model weapons and equipment. About 50 percent of the divisions were in a lower state of readiness with trained personnel at less than 50 percent authorization and with older weapons and equipment. (These divisions would require mobilization and training of reservists before being committed to combat.) About 10 percent of the divisions were essentially unmanned, inactive equipment sets that would require extensive time for mobilization and training before deployment.

Red Army—The name for the Soviet army from 1918 until 1945.

Red Terror—Initiated by the Bolsheviks (*q.v.*) after an August 1918 attempt on Lenin's life. The bloody reign of the Vecheka (*q.v.*), during which the nation was ruthlessly subjugated to the Bolshevik will. The Red Terror continued until 1920.

rehabilitation/rehabilitated—Official restoration of a person or group of people sentenced and imprisoned or exiled for political crimes.

repressed inflation—An economic situation in which government price controls restrict increases in prices but do not substantially decrease underlying causes of inflation.

RSFSR (Rossiiskaia Sovetskaia Federativnaia Sotsialisticheskaia Respublika)—Russian Soviet Federated Socialist Republic; the Russian Republic. The largest of the fifteen union republics (*q.v.*), inhabited predominantly by Russians. It comprised approximately 75 percent of the area of the Soviet Union, about 62 percent of its population, and over 60 percent of its economic output.

ruble—The monetary unit of the Soviet Union; divided into 100 kopeks. The official Soviet exchange rate was 0.61 ruble per US$1 (1988 average). The black market rate varied from 4 to

6 rubles per US$1 in 1988. The ruble has historically not been considered hard currency (*q.v.*).

Rus'—*See* Kievan Rus'.

Russian Empire—Successor state to Muscovy (*q.v.*). Formally proclaimed by Tsar Peter the Great in 1721 and significantly expanded during the reign of Catherine II, becoming a major multinational state. It collapsed during the revolutions of 1917.

Russianization—The policy of several Soviet regimes promoting Russian as the national language of the Soviet Union. Russian was given equal and official status with local languages in all non-Russian republics; it was made the official language of state and diplomatic affairs, in the armed forces, and on postage stamps, currency, and military and civilian decorations. A prerequisite for Russification (*q.v.*).

Russian Social Democratic Labor Party (Rossiiskaia sotsial-demokraticheskaia rabochaia partiia)—A Marxist party founded in 1898 that split into Bolshevik (majority) and Menshevik (minority) factions in 1903. The Bolsheviks changed the name of the party in March 1918 to the Russian Communist Party (Bolshevik) and began calling themselves Communists. *See also* CPSU.

Russification—A process of changing the national identity of non-Russians to an identity culturally similar to that of the Russians. Although not the official policy of any Soviet regime, such assimilation often resulted from the policy of Russianization (*q.v.*), particularly in the case of Ukrainians, Belorussians, and non-Russian educated elites.

SALT (Strategic Arms Limitation Talks)—A series of negotiations between the Soviet Union and the United States that attempted to place limits and restraints on some of their central and most important armaments. The first series began in November 1969 and culminated on May 26, 1972, when General Secretary Leonid Brezhnev and President Richard M. Nixon signed a treaty on the limitation of anti-ballistic missile systems (the ABM Treaty) and an interim agreement limiting strategic offensive arms. The second series began in November 1972 and resulted in a completed agreement, signed by General Secretary Brezhnev and President Jimmy Carter on June 18, 1979. Neither country, however, ratified the agreement.

samizdat—Literally, self-publication. Russian word for the printing and circulating of literary, political, and other written manuscripts without passing them through the official censor, thus making them unauthorized and illegal. If published abroad, such publications are called *tamizdat* (*q.v.*).

samofinansirovanie—Literally, self-financing. A practice of some ministries enabling selected enterprises (*q.v.*) to recover production costs and sufficient profits for investment. Without such financial autonomy, enterprises had to rely on funds allocated by central economic planners.

sblizhenie—Literally, drawing together. A Soviet policy of bringing the diverse nationalities into a close socialist community by gradually reducing ethnic differences of individual nationalities. The policy was included in the 1961 party program (*q.v.*).

serf—A peasant legally bound to the land. Serfs were emancipated by Tsar Alexander II in 1861.

Shia (or Shiite)—A member of the smaller of the two great divisions of Islam. The Shias supported the claims of Ali and his line to presumptive right to the caliphate and leadership of the world Muslim community, and on this issue they divided from the Sunnis (*q.v.*) in the first great schism of Islam. Later schisms have produced further divisions among the Shias. In 1989 about 10 percent of the Soviet Union's Muslims were Shias.

Slavophiles—Members of the Russian intelligentsia (*q.v.*) in the mid-nineteenth century who advocated Slavic, and specifically Russian, culture over western European culture, as opposed to Westernizers (*q.v.*).

sliianie—Literally, blending, merging. A theory that all Soviet nationalities could be merged into one by eliminating ethnic identity and national consciousness. Adopted by Stalin and included in the 1930 party program (*q.v.*), its intent was to achieve a single Russian-speaking, Soviet nationality.

socialism/socialist—According to Marxism-Leninism (*q.v.*), the first phase of communism (*q.v.*). A transition from capitalism in which the means of production are state owned and whose guiding principle was "from each according to his abilities, to each according to his work." Soviet socialism bore scant resemblance to the democratic socialism of, for example, some West European countries.

socialist countries—As defined by the CPSU (*q.v.*), those countries governed by a Marxist ideology. In May 1989, these included Bulgaria, Cambodia, China, Cuba, Czechoslovakia, the Democratic People's Republic of Korea (North Korea), East Germany, Hungary, Laos, Madagascar, Mongolia, Nicaragua, Poland, the Soviet Union, and Vietnam.

socialist internationalism—The linking of all socialist (*q.v.*) countries. *See* Brezhnev Doctrine; proletarian internationalism.

socialist legality—A legal doctrine that ensured that the law and the legal system served the interests of the state and the regime rather than protecting individuals' rights vis-à-vis the state. Under Stalin, the doctrine was interpreted narrowly, with emphasis on facilitating fulfillment of the economic five-year plans (*q.v.*). Under Khrushchev, and particularly under Gorbachev, emphasis was placed on codifying criminal and civil laws, establishing and strengthening legal institutions, and adhering to laws and legal procedures.

socialist property—According to a basic precept of socialism (*q.v.*), the state owns all land, resources, and the means of production in industry, construction, and agriculture, as well as the transportation and communication systems, banks, and trade enterprises (*q.v.*). In the Soviet Union, the CPSU (*q.v.*) controlled socialist property.

socialist realism—An aesthetic doctrine that measured artistic and literary merit by the degree to which a work contributed to the building of socialism (*q.v.*) among the masses.

soft-currency goods—Items that could be bought without the expenditure of hard currency (*q.v.*).

soviet (*sovet*)—Literally, advice, counsel, or council. The basic governmental organ at all levels of the Soviet Union.

sovkhoz (pl., sovkhozy)—*See* state farm.

Spetsnaz (Voiska spetsial'nogo naznacheniia)—Special Purpose Forces of the Soviet armed forces or KGB (*q.v.*), trained to attack important command, communications, and weapons centers behind enemy lines.

sputnik—Literally, fellow traveler. A man-made spacecraft that orbited the earth. In the West, the term Sputnik (capitalized) was used to refer to the first man-made earth satellite, which was launched by the Soviet Union in 1957 to the surprise of the Western scientific and defense communities.

SSR (*sovetskaia sotsialisticheskaia respublika*)— Soviet socialist republic. A soviet union republic (*q.v.*).

Stakhanovite—A worker whose output was said to be well beyond production norms. Named for Aleksandr Stakhanov, an outstanding worker. The Stakhanovite movement began in August 1935.

state farm (*sovetskoe khoziaistvo*—sovkhoz)—A government-owned and government-managed agricultural enterprise (*q.v.*) where workers are paid salaries.

steppe—The vast, semiarid, grass-covered plain in the southeastern portion of the European part of the Soviet Union. One of the five primary natural zones of the Soviet Union.

Sufism—An Islamic movement that emphasizes a personal and mystical approach in the search for "divine truth." Sufism consists of semisecret Sufi brotherhoods, each pursuing a different school or "path" of mystic discipline but having a common goal.

Sunni—A member of the larger of the two great divisions of Islam. The Sunnis, who rejected the claim of Ali's line, believe that they are the true followers of the sunna, the guide to proper behavior composed of the Quran and *hadith,* the precedent of Muhammad's words that serves as one of the sources of Islamic law. In 1989 about 90 percent of the Soviet Union's Muslims were Sunnis.

Table of Ranks—A system of ranks for nobles based on service to the tsar rather than on birth or seniority. Created by Peter the Great in 1722.

taiga—The extensive, sub-Arctic evergreen forest of the Soviet Union. The taiga, the largest of the five primary natural zones, lies south of the tundra (*q.v.*).

tamizdat—Literally, published there (abroad). Russian word for samizdat (*q.v.*) manuscripts surreptitiously sent abroad for publication.

TASS (Telegrafnoe agentstvo Sovetskogo Soiuza)—Telegraph Agency of the Soviet Union. The news agency that had a monopoly on collecting and distributing news within the Soviet Union.

territorial production complex (*territorial'no proizvodstvennyi kompleks*)—An economic entity consisting of various economically related industrial and agricultural enterprises (*q.v.*) in a particular geographic area.

Time of Troubles—Period of civil war in Muscovy between boyar (*q.v.*) factions from 1598 to 1613, with heavy Polish involvement.

ton-kilometer—The movement of one ton of cargo a distance of one kilometer. Ton-kilometers are computed by multiplying the weight (in tons) of each shipment transported by the distance hauled (in kilometers).

tons originated—The weight of freight (in tons) at its original point of shipment.

transmission belt—An organization, not formally part of the CPSU (*q.v.*) apparatus, used by the party to convey its party program (*q.v.*) and propaganda to the population at large, for example, Soviet trade unions.

Trans-Siberian Railway—The 7,000-kilometer railroad line, stretching from its western terminus at Chelyabinsk on the eastern slopes of the Ural Mountains to Vladivostok on the

Pacific Ocean, was built between 1891 and 1916 to link the European part of Russia with Siberia and the Far East. In the late 1980s, the Trans-Siberian Railway informally consisted of several Soviet railroads that remained the only rail link between the western part of the Soviet Union and the Soviet Far East until the BAM (*q.v.*) was opened in 1989.

trust (*trest*)—An economic entity that consists of several industrial enterprises (*q.v.*) of the same type, e.g., construction trust, assembly trust.

tundra—The treeless plain within the Arctic Circle that has low-growing vegetation and permanently frozen subsoil (permafrost—*q.v.*). The northernmost of the five primary natural zones of the Soviet Union.

Turkestan—Literally, the land of the Turks. An immense, ancient territory in Central Asia stretching from the Caspian Sea in the west and extending into China's present-day Xinjiang Autonomous Region and northern Afghanistan in the east. Includes a large part of Kazakhstan (*q.v.*).

turnover tax—A sales tax levied primarily on consumer goods.

TVD (*teatr voennykh deistvii*)—Theater of military operations. A Soviet term meaning part of a continent or ocean within which are deployed strategic groupings of armed forces and within which military operations are conducted.

Uniate Church—A branch of the Catholic Church that preserved the Eastern Rite and discipline but submitted to papal authority. Established in 1596 at the Union of Brest. In the Soviet Union, the Uniate Church is found primarily in the western Ukrainian Republic, where it has been referred to as the Ukrainian Catholic Church. Also known as the Greek Catholic Church or the Byzantine Rite Church. It is one of the Eastern Rite Catholic churches.

Unified Electrical Power System (Ob''edinennaia elektroenergeticheskaia sistema)—The national electric power generating and transmission network of the Soviet Union. The system includes over 90 percent of the country's generating capacity and is divided into regional power networks, each serving a single administrative or industrial area. It is linked to systems in Bulgaria, Finland, Norway, Poland, Romania, and Turkey.

union republic—One of the fifteen primary administrative subdivisions of the Soviet Union. Except for some of the smaller ones, the union republics were divided into oblasts (*q.v.*), autonomous oblasts (*q.v.*), *kraia* (*q.v.*), and autonomous republics (*q.v.*) as major subdivisions. Also known as Soviet socialist republic (SSR—*q.v.*).

union-republic ministries—Ministries that had counterpart ministries in each of the republics. Other ministries of the central
government were termed all-union ministries (*q.v.*).

united front—A Leninist tactic used by the Soviet regime to authorize communist parties in other countries to collaborate
temporarily with noncommunist parties. The purpose was theoretically to promote democratic institutions and workers'
rights, but in reality it provided opportunities for communists
to secure political gains and to seize power without resorting
to revolution.

uskorenie (acceleration)—Under Gorbachev, an on-going effort to
speed up the rate of growth and modernization of the economy.

USSR—Union of Soviet Socialist Republics. The Soviet Union.

Varangians—A group of Norsemen who assumed control over communities of East Slavs (*q.v.*) ca. A.D. 860 and who founded
the Rurikid Dynasty, which ruled for over 700 years.

Vecheka (Vserossiiskaia chrezvychainaia komissiia po bor'be s
kontrrevoliutsiei i sabotazhem—VChK)—All-Russian Extraordinary Commission for Combating Counterrevolution and
Sabotage. The political police created by the Bolsheviks (*q.v.*)
in 1917; supposed to be dissolved when the new regime, under
Lenin, had defeated its enemies and secured its power. But
the Vecheka, also known as the Cheka, continued until 1922,
becoming the leading instrument of terror and oppression as
well as the predecessor of other secret police organizations.
Members of successor security organizations continued to be
referred to as "Chekisty" in the late 1980s.

virgin land campaign—An intensive but ultimately unsuccessful
agricultural project directed by Nikita S. Khrushchev to raise
crops in the vast grasslands of the Kazakh Republic and some
neighboring areas of the Russian Republic that had never been
farmed before.

voenkomat—*See* military commissariat.

Volga Germans—Ethnic Germans who had lived in the Volga River
area for several centuries and who were moved eastward, mostly
to the Kazakh Republic, en masse by Stalin on the suspicion
of collaborating with the Germans during World War II. Rehabilitated (*q.v.*) in August 1965.

war communism—Policy of the Bolshevik (*q.v.*) regime during the
Civil War (1918–21), in which the country's economy was
almost totally directed toward equipping and maintaining the
Red Army (*q.v.*).

Warsaw Pact—Political-military alliance founded by the Soviet
Union in 1955 as a counterweight to NATO. Members in 1989

included Bulgaria, Czechoslovakia, East Germany, Hungary, Poland, Romania, and the Soviet Union. Served as the Soviet Union's primary mechanism for keeping political and military control over Eastern Europe.

Westernizers—Russian intellectuals in the mid-nineteenth century who emphasized Russia's cultural ties with the West, as opposed to the Slavophiles (*q.v.*).

White armies—Various military forces that attempted to overthrow the Bolshevik (*q.v.*) regime during the Civil War (1918–21). The principal leaders of the White armies were former tsarist officers, including generals Anton Denikin, Nikolai Yudenich, Petr Wrangel, and Evgenii Miller and former tsarist admiral Aleksandr Kolchak. They operated with no unified command, no clear political goal, and no supplies from the Russian heartland and thus were defeated piecemeal by the Red Army (*q.v.*).

World Bank—Informal name used to designate a group of three affiliated international institutions—the International Bank for Reconstruction and Development (IBRD), the International Development Association (IDA), and the International Finance Corporation (IFC). The IBRD, established in 1945, has the primary purpose of providing loans to developing countries for productive projects. The IDA, a legally separate loan fund but administered by the staff of the IBRD, was set up in 1960 to furnish credits to the poorest developing countries on much easier terms than those of conventional IBRD loans. The IFC, founded in 1956, supplements the activities of the IBRD through loans and assistance designed specifically to encourage the growth of productive private enterprises in the less developed countries. The president and certain senior officers of the IBRD hold the same positions in the IFC. The three institutions are owned by the governments of the countries that subscribe their capital. To participate in the World Bank group, member states must first belong to the International Monetary Fund (IMF—*q.v.*).

world socialist system—In the Soviet view, a commonwealth of advanced socialist states that accept the Soviet model of government and interpretation of Marxism-Leninism (*q.v.*).

Yalta Conference—Meeting of Stalin, Winston Churchill, and Franklin D. Roosevelt in February 1945 that redrew post-World War II national borders and established spheres of influence in Europe.

Young Octobrists (Oktiabriata)—Literally, "Children of October." An organization that has prepared Soviet schoolchildren ages six to nine for membership in the Pioneer (*q.v.*) organization.

Established in 1923, the first Young Octobrists were contemporaries of the October Revolution of 1917 (Bolshevik Revolution—*q.v.*), hence the name "Children of October."

zampolit (*zamestitel' komandira po politicheskoi chasti*)—Deputy commander for political affairs. Found in each unit of the armed forces; responsible for overseeing the political reliability in the armed forces.

zemskii sobor—A national assembly consisting of members of the duma (*q.v.*) of the boyars (*q.v.*), high church dignitaries, elected representatives of the nobility, the townspeople, and sometimes the peasants. Originally a consultative body in the mid-sixteenth century, this organization shared some minor governing functions with the tsars by the mid-seventeenth century but was not convened in the eighteenth century or subsequently.

zemstvo—A rural, self-governing institution with jurisdiction over schools, public health, food supply, roads, insurance, relief for the poor, maintenance of prisons, and other local concerns. Existed from about 1864 until the Bolshevik Revolution (*q.v.*) in 1917.

Zhdanovshchina—Literally, era of Zhdanov. A period from 1946 to 1948 when Andrei Zhdanov, with Stalin's permission, led attacks on writers, musicians, and scientists for deviance from concepts approved by the CPSU (*q.v.*). Many attacks were made against persons of Jewish nationality (*q.v.*), who were termed "rootless cosmopolitans." Zhdanov died in 1948, but the purge continued.

Index

Abkhazian Autonomous Republic, 156

abortion, lxvi; abolition of, 71; attitudes of non-Russian nationalities toward, 231; availability of, 266; as chief form of contraception, 234; cost of, 234, 266; death from, 271; factors contributing to rate of, 212; legality of, 234, 235; in NEP era, 68; rates, 125, 234

Abu Bakr, 194

Abuladze, Tengiz, 392

Academy of Fine Arts, 23

Academy of Medical Sciences, 636

Academy of Pedagogical Sciences, 253; facilities of, 248; mission of, 248-49; research and development in education by, 248

Academy of Sciences, 645; absence of appropriate testing facilities, 639-40; achievements of, 625; advice of, on policy, 335, 629; under Brezhnev, 627; censorship in, 376; charters of, 624-65, 626; Engineering Sciences Division of, 626; financial decision by, 632; founded by Peter the Great, 22, 624; meetings of, 637; membership of, 636; military research and development under, 646-47; monitored by Science and Education Institutions Department, 628-29; in NEP era, 625; personnel policies, 636; purge of, 626; research of, 625, 630, 635; research institutes under, 503, 636, 639; research vessels of, 575-76; role of, 248, 345, 461, 637; sections of, 636; under Stalin, 625-26; Western scientists in, 625

Academy of Social Sciences, 321

Acheson-Lilienthal-Baruch Plan, 442

acquired immune deficiency syndrome (AIDS). See AIDS

active measures: defined, 779; international front groups, 779; support for terrorists, 779

Aden, Gulf of, 439

Aden: Soviet military base in, 685

Adler, 557

Administration of Affairs Department (CPSU), 300, 301

Administrative Organs Department (CPSU), 785

Adzhar Autonomous Republic, 156

Aeroflot. See civil aviation

Afghanistan, 37, 38, 48, 101, 108, 160, 170, 171, 414, 433-35, 446; bi-tarafi (balanced relationship) principle, 434; emigration of Kazakhs to, 164; emigration of Kirgiz to, 167; history of Soviet involvement in, 433-34; land of, appropriated by Soviet Union, 434; military advisers in, 684; military agreement of, with Czechoslovakia, 434; Soviet arms bought by, 614; Soviet forces stationed in, 728; Soviet occupation of, 434-35; Soviet support for, lx; Soviet trade with, 612; ties to Comecon, 616, 855; treaty of, with Pakistan; treaties of, with Soviet Union; withdrawal of Soviet troops from, lxxvi, 430, 435, 604, 682, 684, 700

Afghanistan, Soviet invasion of (1979), 56, 92, 682-84, 700, 772, 781, 891; Airborne Troops in, 719; arguments for, 682; background of, 434; condemned by Iraq, 431; decision for, 408, 434; international response to, 91, 416, 422, 427, 434, 443, 609, 683, 689; military airlifts into, 712, 721; as training for tactical conventional combat, 675, 683-84; United Nations condemnation of, 434, 445, 683

Afghanistan, war in, 384; Afghan deaths from, 435; Afghan refugees from, 435; helicopters in, 683; Muslims in, 747; Soviet weapons used in, 711

Afghan-Soviet neutrality treaty (1931), 434

Africa, 410; food imported from, 614; military advisers in, 684, 700; Soviet influence in, 291, 872; Soviet trade with, 571, 615-16

Africa, North, 569, 615

Africa, sub-Saharan, 438-40, 684; economic assistance to, under Brezhnev, 438; Khrushchev's efforts in, 438; military assistance to, 438; Soviet trade with, 615

Afro-Asian People's Solidarity Organization, 407

After the Storm (Zalygin), 388-89

Aganbegian, Abel, 480

Age of Realism (literature), 38-40; "thick journal" as outlet for literary opinion in, 39

agitation and propaganda departments, 311

agitprop, 377

Agoniia (Klimov), 392

Agrarian Policy Commission, 300, 522

agricultural administration: bureaucracy of, dismantling of, 524; Gorbachev's approach to, 524; motivations of, 520; objectives of, 520-21; under Stalin, 520

Agricultural Construction, Ministry of, 524

agricultural enterprises, 720

Agricultural Plenum, 522, 524, 525

agricultural policy: under Khrushchev, 522; results of, 521; under Stalin, 520

agricultural production, 529-42; economic performance, 529-30; food production goals, 524; growth of, 519, 530; improvement in, under Gorbachev, 530; problems with, under Gorbachev, lxii agricultural products: causes of shortages of, 519; cotton, 532; flax, 532; forage crops, 533; fruit, 534; grain harvests, 520; hemp, 532; import of, 602, 606, 608, 614; potatoes and vegetables, 533–34; shortages of, 519, 541; sugar beets, 532–33; sunflowers, 532; tea, 534–36; technical crops, 532–33; tobacco, 536; transportation of, hampered by poor roads, 545, 565; vegetables, 534, 541; wheat, 531

agricultural sector, 452; collective farms in, 453, 466–67; collectivization as dominant cause of poor performance of, 519–20; factors in poor performance of, 474–75; materials imported for, 615; planning in, 462; output of, 453, 476; as source of capital accumulation, 473; state farms in, 453, 466–67

agricultural workers, 211; categories of, 217, 226; children of, in higher education, 258; educational level of, 217; living standards of, 520; income of, 217, 220, 520; increased participation of, in decision making, 524, 530; position of children of, 211; women as, 217

agriculture, 457; agricultural land, 526; arable land, 526, 529; decrease in output during World War II, 77–78; forced collectivization of, lviii, 473, 520, 593, 758; grain as foundation of, 530–31; industrialization of, 226–27, 472; innovations in, 87–88; investments in, under Twelfth Five-Year Plan, 481; Khrushchev's reforms in, 56, 87–88; as a net drain on the economy, 519; party influence in, lxix; problems in, under Brezhnev, 93, 477; problems in, under Khrushchev, 93; problems in, under Stalin, 70; production in, 473, 476, 478, 481; reform of, 524; reform of, resistance to, 520; underinvestment in, under Stalin, 529

Agriculture, Ministry of, 524
agro-industrial complex (APK), 524, 529–30
Aguls, 159
AIDS (SPID): accidental infection with, 272; advice regarding, 271; anti-AIDS Law, 272; compulsory testing for, 272; *glasnost'* regarding, 271; laws regarding, 272; number of cases, 272; public education about, 272; testing centers, 271–72; threat of the spread of, 272

Aigun, Treaty of (1858), 37
Airborne Troops, lxxvi, 711, 712, 719–20; conscripts in, 743; control of, 719; missions of, 719–20; number of, 719; uniforms and rank insignia of, 738–39
aircraft plants, 493; locations of, 493
Air Defense Aviation, 711, 714; aircraft of, 714; mission of, 714
Air Defense Forces (*see also* under name of branch), lxxvi, 676, 697, 712–16, 725; Air Defense Aviation, 714; Antiaircraft Rocket

Troops, 712–14; background of, 712; general organization of, 703; missile and space defenses of, 714–16; mission of, 680–81; uniforms and rank insignia of, 737–39
Air Defense of Ground Forces, 708, 712; background of, 708; equipment of, 708
air fleet (Aeroflot), lxiii; civilian, 546; missions of, 546
Air Forces (*see also* under name of branch), lxxvi, 672, 676, 677, 697, 725; Aeroflot work for, 580; in Afghan war, 711; aircraft of, 678; Frontal Aviation, 711; general organization of, 703; Military Transport Aviation, 711–12; mission of, 678; as part of strategic nuclear forces, 678; role of, 678; Strategic Air Armies, 710–11; uniforms and rank insignia of, 737–39; weapons of, 678
AirLand Battle doctrine (United States), 680
airports, 574
Aitmatov, Chingiz, 388
Akhmadulina, Bella, 389
Akhmatova, Anna, 382
Akhromeev, Sergei F., 663
Aksionov, Vasilii, lxxii, 381
Alaska, 29; Russian acquisition of, 27
Albania, 86, 414; as member of Comecon, 601, 854; as member of Warsaw Pact, 875, 884
alcohol, availability of, 93, 121
alcoholism (*see also* antialcohol campaign), lxvi; as contributor to death rate, 93, 100, 269; effect of, on divorce, 130, 270; incidence of, 269; among Slavs, 269; treatment for, 270
Aleksandra, 50, 57; execution of, 63
Aleksandrov, Anatolii P., 637, 645
Aleksandrov Gay, 561
Alexander I, 27; acquisition of territory by, 28; alliance of, with Napoleon, 28; ascension to throne, 28; changes in government structure under, 28; defeat of Napoleon by, 29; focus of, on foreign affairs, 28; as monarch of Finland, 29; as monarch of Poland, 29; revolutionary movements under, 29–30
Alexander II, 33–36, 179, 757; assassination of, 34, 36, 41; cultural reform under, 35; educational reform under, 35; emancipation of serfs by, 34; expansion of empire under, 36–37; financial reform under, 35; foreign affairs of, after the Crimean War, 36–38; foreign policy goals in East under, 38; foreign policy goals in Europe under, 37–38; judicial reform under, 34–35; military reform under, 35; Ottoman war under, 37–38; reform of local government system by, 34; rise of Marxism under, 40–41; rise of revolutionary populism under, 40–41
Alexander III, 34; attempted assassination of, 41; industrialization under, 486; political reaction under, 36
Alexander the Great, 160

Alexiev, Alex, 685
Alexis, 22
Algeria, 582; privileged affiliation of, with Comecon, 616; Soviet trade with, 613, 614, 616
Ali, 194
Allende Gossens, Salvador, 440, 441
Allied Control Commission, 877
Allied Powers (World War I), 60; involvement of, in Russian Civil War, 61, 63
Allied Powers (World War II), 80
All-Russian Congress of Soviets, 332
All-Union Academy of Agricultural Sciences, 636
All-Union Association for the Export and Import of Technical Equipment, 597
All-Union Capital Investment Bank, 457
All-Union Central Council of Trade Unions, 228, 247, 276
All-Union Communist Party (Bolshevik) (*see also* Russian Communist Party (Bolshevik), Communist Party of the Soviet Union), 66, 81
All-Union Council of Evangelical Christian Baptists, 200
All-Union Institute for Scientific and Technical Information, 633
Alma-Ata, 108, 166
Alsace-Lorraine, 50
Altai region, 497
Alvarado, Juan Velasco, 441
Amann, Ronald, 640
Amanullah, 434
Amin, Hafizullah, 434, 720
Amu Darya, 527, 529
Amur River, 37, 109, 426, 558
Amur River Valley, 18, 37, 107, 529
Andropov, Iurii V., lix, 304, 352, 417, 628; career of, 762; détente defined by, 419–20; economic reform under, lix, 467; as KGB chief, 95, 762, 777, 781, 782; KGB under, 762–63; and letters to the editor, 379; loosening of party strictures on media and the arts, lxxii, 372–73, 378, 383–84, 388
Andrusovo, Treaty of (1667), 18
Angola, 414, 430, 438–39, 446, 712; military advisers in, 684; Soviet arms bought by, 614; Soviet military aid to, 438–39, 684; Soviet military base in, 685; Soviet support for Cuban troops in, 684, 700; Soviet trade with, 612; ties to Comecon, 616, 855; withdrawal by Soviet Union of support for Cuban military operation in, lx
Anikiev, Anatolii, 785
animal husbandry, 536–38; consumption of food from, 538; dairy farming, 536; distribution of, 536; food output per animal, 538; kinds of livestock, 536–38; reindeer herding, 536
Anna Karenina (Tolstoy), 40

Antarctica, 442
Anthem of the Soviet Union, 340
Antiaircraft Rocket Troops, 712–14; organization of, 712; weapons of, 712
antialcohol campaign, 272, 304, 479; reaction to, 270; reasons for, 121, 263, 270; results of, 270
antiballistic missiles, 689
Anti-Ballistic Missile Treaty (ABM Treaty), 416, 442–43, 686
anti-Catholic campaign, 199–200
Anti-Comintern Pact (1936), 73
anticorruption campaign, 763
anti-imperialism, 413
anti-Jewish regulations, 179
"anti-party group," 84
antisatellite weapons (ASAT), 688–89
anti-Semitism, 178, 180, 201; tolerated under Brezhnev, 90
antismoking campaign, 270, 272
antisubmarine warfare (ASW), 718
apparatchiks, 297, 763
"April Days," 58
April Theses (Lenin), 58; popular response to, 58, 59
Arab Empire, 169
Arabian Peninsula, 192
Arabic, 166, 172
Arab-Israeli conference, 432
Arab-Israeli conflict, 91
Arabs, 155, 160
Aral region: as ecological disaster area, 115, 117
Aral Sea, lxxiii, 113; diversion project, 113–15, 529
Archangel, 540
Arctic Circle, 102, 506, 558
Arctic Ocean, 101, 102, 104, 108, 109, 546, 566, 569, 570, 572, 719
Arctic region, 566
Argentina, 441, 608; Soviet trade with, 612, 615–16
arid zone, 104, 110; agriculture in, 527; as center for space exploration, 107; described, 107; irrigation in, 527
Armaments, 702
Armavir, 561
armed forces, Soviet (*see also* under name of branch): combat experience of, 697–700; CPSU members in, 733; design bureaus of, 735; external function of, 681, 682; Komsomol members in, 733; lack of preparation of, for World War II, 74; life in, 745–46; limited effectiveness of, 697; loyalty of, to party lxxv; military districts, 725–27; minorities in, lxxvi, 746–47; missions of, troops in, lxxv, 697; number of, 697; occupation of Eastern Europe by, 79; organizational development of, 697–700; organization of, territorial, 723–28; organization of, typical

armed service, 706; overall mission of, 676; and the party, 728-33; party apparatus in, 732; party control of, lxxv, 35-36; party influence in, lxix, lxxiv, 24, 35; political directorates in, 731; political indoctrination in lxxv; political sections in, lxxv, 731; political training in, 731; problems in, 731-32; reaction of, to coup of 1991, lxxix; reorganization of, 677; reserves, 750; role of, in coup of 1991, lxxx; special departments in, 775-76; stationed abroad, 728; strategic leadership in, 700-703; strategic missions of, 675-81; unilateral reductions in, 692; theoretical basis for, lxxvi; victory requirement, 685-86; women in, 747-48

armed forces, uniforms and rank insignia, 737-39; categories of, 737; coats, 737; colors of, 737, 738; components of, 737-38; shoulder boards, 738-39

Armenia, 50, 61

Armenian Apostolic Church, 189

Armenian Republic, lxx, 102, 115, 308; area of, 153; earthquake in, 384; establishment of, 61, 154, 362; legal age for marriage in, 232; life expectancy in, 116; major cities in, 154; nationalist demonstrations in, 202, 793; nationalities in, 154; population density, 124; territory of, 153; tree farms in, 475

Armenians, lxvi, 27, 124, 153-55, 156, 158; alphabet of, 154; distribution of, 154; in higher education, 154; history of, 153; as members of CPSU, 155, 324; language of, 154; national assertiveness by, 153, 154, 201-2; persecution of, 153; population of, 154; as scientific workers, 154; early socialist parties among, 42-43, 45; urbanization of, 154

arms control (*see also* nuclear disarmament), 401, 608, 654; conventional, 691-93; for Lenin, 442; in foreign policy, 685; intermediate-range nuclear forces, 689-91; and military objectives, 685-93; in military policy, 685; nuclear, 442-45; objectives in, 685-86; proposals for, by Gorbachev, 444; threat reduction, 690-91

arms control, strategic, 676, 686-88; to avert world war, 686-87; defined, 686; motive for, 687; to retain victory capability, 687-88

art, 396-97; avant-garde, 397; censorship of, 774; during NEP era, 67-68; under Nicholas I, 31; schools of, 247, 257; socialist realism and, 397; survivalist, 397

Artillery. See Rocket Troops and Artillery

arts, the (*see also* under individual arts), 93-94, 385-97; administration of, 373-77; under Brezhnev, 94; control of, 385, 388; control of, hindered by technological revolution, 369; critical realism in, 370; films, 370; history of party control of, 369; Leninist principles

for, 371-72; literature, 370, 385; music, 370, 394-96; party control of, 71-72, 370, 373-74; politicization of, lxxii, 370-73; protest in, 369, 370, 397; revolution in, lxxii; role of, in influencing the population, 385; theater, 370; themes of, 370, 373

asbestos, 112

Ashkhabad, 172

Asia, 410, 430, 433-37, 569, 700; destruction of targets in, 677; imperialism in, 44-45; Russian influence in, 44; Soviet goals in Southeast, 436-37; Soviet influence in, 291, 872; Soviet objectives in, 433; Soviet trade with, 571, 615-16

Asian collective security system, 426, 436

Association of Southeast Asian Nations (ASEAN), 410, 437; Soviet ties with, 437; condemnation by, of Soviet invasion of Afghanistan, 434

Astrakhan', 506

Astrakhan' horde, 175

Astrakhan' Khanate, 14, 175

atheism, 184; in Marxism-Leninism, 198; number of Soviets professing, 184

Atlantic Ocean, 102, 540, 546, 566, 570

atomic bomb, 627

Austerlitz: Russian defeat by Napoleon at, 28

Australia, 437, 571; Soviet trade with, 605, 606, 608

Austria (*see also* Austria-Hungary), 24, 32, 36; as importer of Soviet gas, 508, 581, 609; as member of Quadruple Alliance, 29; permanent neutrality for, 85; Russian alliance with, 23; Russian alliance with, against Napoleon, 28

Austria-Hungary, 37, 42, 47, 142; ambitions of, in Balkans, 37, 38, 48; annexation of Bosnia and Hercegovina by, 48-49; territory gained from, by Russia, 50; western Ukraine incorporated into, 141, 190; in World War I, 49

"autocracy, Orthodoxy, and nationality" principle, 30

autocracy, Russian, 15, 27; defined, 3; efforts at restricting, 15; and inability to develop constitutional government, 47; legacy of, lvii; Marxism adapted to, 282, 283, 284; under Nicholas I, 30; origins of, 3; Radishchev's attack on, 26; subordination of people to, 17

autocrat, defined, 13

automation, 455; importance of, in industry, 485, 499; in metallurgy industry, 496-97; self-sufficiency in, for Comecon, 603; workers' ability to deal with, 490

automobiles, 545, 561; importance of, to local transportation systems, 561; number of, lxiii, 566

Automotive and Agricultural Machine Building, Ministry of, 493, 646, 735 automotive industry, 497–98; facilities in, 497–98; goals of, 498; growth of, 498; production ratio of automobiles to trucks, 497; technology transfer to, 644; truck planning in, 498

automotive transportation (*see also* roads and under individual means of transport), 545, 561–66; automobiles, 545, 561; buses, 545, 561; development of, 561–65; origins of, 561; problems in, 561–62; trucks, 545, 561

Automotive Troops, 721

autonomous oblasts, 102, 137, 139, 153, 156, 184, 195, 311, 353, 364, 374; defined, 361–62

autonomous *okruga*, 102, 137, 139, 153, 184, 195, 353, 364, 374; defined, 361–62

autonomous republics, 102, 137, 139, 153, 156, 184, 293, 353, 364, 374; defined, 361–62; food program in, 524; planning in, 464

Avars, 5, 159, 194

Aviation Industry, Ministry of the, 496, 646

Avvakum, 19

Azerbaydzhan, 61, 157; influx of Slavs into, 157

Azerbaydzhanis, lxvi, 153, 156–59; alphabet of, 158; characteristics of, 158; distribution of, 158; in higher education, 159; history of, 156–58; Iranian, 158; Islamic faction, 157–58, 194; language of, 158–59; and literacy, 158; Marxist faction, 157; as members of CPSU, 159; national resurgence of, 157–58; population of, 158; repression of, 158; as scientific workers, 159; urbanization of, 159

Azerbaydzhan Republic, 61, 102, 154, 362; agriculture in, 534–36; cities in, 159; cotton grown in, 532; mosques in, 200–201; nationalist demonstrations in, 793; rate of premarital pregnancy in, 234; tree farms in, 475

Azov, Port of, 20, 21, 23

Azov, Sea of, 20, 113, 567, 572

Bab al Mandab, Strait of, 439

backwardness, 3–4, 27, 41; innovation as reaction to, 640; manifested in Crimean War, 34; of military, 34, 35–36; Peter the Great's efforts to reverse, 22; technology acquisition to overcome, 642

Baghdad Pact (*see also* CENTO), 431

Bahrain, 432

Bakatin, Vadim V., lxxx, 783–85

Baku, 157, 158, 159, 201, 503, 547; oil pipelines in, 580, 581; Russian acquisition of, 29, 157

Bakunin, Mikhail, 40

balance of payments, 595, 645

Balkan policy, 48–49

Balkans, 74; crisis in, 36, 49; international alliances regarding, 49; nuclear-free zone, 691;

revolutionary movements in, 42; rivalry between Austria-Hungary and Russia in, 48; Russian ambitions in, 37, 45; Russian influence over, 24, 32; after Treaty of San Stefano, 38

ballet: under Nicholas I, 31; schools of, 247, 257

Baltic Fleet, 697, 727

Baltic nationalities, 138, 146–52, 156; characteristics and experiences of, 146–47; German and Polish influences on, 147; national assertiveness by, 201–2

Baltic Sea, 5, 8, 10, 12, 14, 21, 50, 139, 150, 423, 525, 566, 566, 570, 571, 580, 719; automobile ferry on, 575; oil reserves in, 506

Baltic states, 25, 61, 178; climate of, 110; establishment of independence, 61; industrialization of agriculture in, 227; nationalist demonstrations in, 201–2; Soviet occupation of, 699

Baltic tribes, 145

Baltic-White Sea canal, 566

Baluchi, 194

Bamovskaya, 558

Bangladesh, 436

banking, 469; checking accounts, 458; industry, 452; nationalization of, 472; personal savings accounts, 458

Baptists, 184, 191

Barannikov, Viktor, lxxx

barges, 545

Barghorn, Frederick C., 322

Bashkir Autonomous Republic, 176, 181, 182

Bashkirs, 152, 176, 182–83; alphabet of, 182; history of, 182; language of, 182; nationalist movement, 182; population of, 182; urbanization of, 182–83

Basic Directions for the Economic and Social Development of the USSR for 1986–1990 and for the Period to the Year 2000, 451, 478, 525, 540

Basic Principles of Operational Art and Tactics (Savkin), 658

Basic Principles of the International Socialist Division of Labor, 860, 861

Basic Provisions for Fundamentally Reorganizing Economic Management, 468; described, 468; reform of price structure in, 470

Basmachi, 170, 434

Basmachi Rebellion, 162, 168, 170, 171, 172

Basov, Nikolai, 623

Batista, Fulgencio, 440

Battle of Stalingrad, 56

Baykal, Lake, 107, 109, 113, 489, 557

Baykal-Amur Main Line (BAM), 124, 489, 539, 557–58, 721; area serviced by, 558; construction challenges, 557–58; extension of, 558; freight traffic on, 558; Little BAM, 558; mean annual temperature along, 558; opening of, 557

Beijing, Treaty of (1860), 37

Belarus tractors, 606
Belgium, 49, 581
Belianiv, Nikolai, 397
Belinskii, Vissarion, 38, 371
Belorussia, 5, 10, 12, 24, 30, 42, 145, 178; economic region, 503; Polish influence in, 145; Soviet republic established in, 61
Belorussian Autocephalous Orthodox Church, 199
Belorussian Democratic Republic, 145
Belorussian Military District, 890
Belorussian offensive, 552
Belorussian Republic, 5, 64, 102, 123, 147, 154, 188, 254, 412, 526; agriculture in, 533; candidates for Congress of People's Deputies, 347; depopulation in, 127; drainage projects in, 529; establishment of, 145; families in, 236; Jewish community in, 178, 180; major cities in, 146; nationalities in, 146; party apparatus in, 307, 308; Roman Catholic community in, 190
Belorussians, 3, 5, 8, 24, 27, 138, 144-46; alphabet of, 145; higher education of, 146; history of, 144-45; independence movement, 145; language of, 145-46; as members of Central Committee, 146; as members of CPSU, 146, 323, 324; nationalist movement among, 205; persecution of, 145; Polonization of, 145; population, 145; as scientific workers, 146; urbanization of, 146
benefits, 222-23, 471; allocation of housing, 222-23; maternity, 234, 243, 276; perquisites, 222; of social position, 219-24
Benin: priviliged affiliation of, with Comecon, 616
Berbera, 684
Berezovka, 511
Beria, Lavrenty, 81, 156, 392, 761; coup plotted by, 82; execution of, 82, 760; expansion of police authority under, 759; power of, 760
Bering Strait, 101, 102, 104
Berkakit, 558
Berlin, 88; airlift, 80; blockade, 80; building of Wall in, 87; division of, 80; East, 663; Soviet invasion of, 75, 699
Bertsch, Gary K., 643
Bessarabia, 179; annexation of, lviii, 74, 474; ceded to Russia, 174; seized by Russia, 28, 36, 363; Russification of, 174
Bialer, Seweryn, 289, 305, 775
Big Diomede Island (Ratmanova Island), 101
bilateral trade agreements: described, 611; with Finland, 605, 611; with the Third World, 613
Biriukova, Aleksandra P., 346
Birmingham, University of, 640
birth rates, 122, 123, 125, 127; and population problems, 125
Bismarck, Otto von, 32, 38; dismissal of, 38

Bisti, Dmitrii, 397
Black Repartition, 41
Black Sea, 5, 7, 12, 24, 26, 36, 50, 100, 107, 139, 178, 525, 527, 534, 567, 570, 719; oil reserves in, 506; remilitarization of, 37
Black Sea Fleet, 727
blat (influence), lvi, 222
"Bloody Sunday," 45
Bogoliubskii, Prince Andrei, 8-9
Bolshevik Central Committee, 59, 60, 371
Bolshevik Revolution (1917), 55, 59-61, 147, 392, 554, 737; economic change following, 213; impact of, on diplomatic affairs, 409; impact of, on population, 118; initial phase of, 59; social change following, 213; solidification of power after, 60; taught for political indoctrination, 253; women in, 747
Bolsheviks (*see also* Communists), 43, 44, 55, 58, 63, 135, 139, 162, 176, 179, 182, 188, 189, 369, 624, 661; Belorussian, 145; critical realism used by, 370, 371; as constitutional rulers of Russia, 332; coup by, in Georgia, 155; increase in power of, 59; nationalization of industry under, 487; outlawed by Provisional Government, 59; overthrow of Provisional Government by, lvii; popular uprisings in support of, 58, 59, 60; and World War I, 60
Bolshoi Theater, 393
Bolvanskiy Nos, 558
Border Troops, lxxvi, 697, 722, 733, 756, 791-93; administration of, 769; conscription of, 791; Dzerzhinskii Higher Border Command School, 792; equipment of, 723; Higher Border School, 792; Maritime, 723; mission of, 723, 791-92; number of, 723, 791; organization of, 725; Political Directorate of, 793; political training and indoctrination, 793; schools, 792; training, 792-93; uniforms and rank insignia of, 739; Voroshilov Higher Border Military-Political Academy, 792; in World War II, 723
Border Troops Directorate, 769, 791; intelligence administration, 791; organization of, 792
border zone, 792
Boris Godunov (Liubimov), 394
Bosnia, 37
Bosporus, 28, 32, 48, 50
botanical gardens, 636
Botswana, 438
bourgeoisie: increase in, 42
Boxer Rebellion, 44
boyars, 13, 14
Brandenburg, 20
Brandt, Willy, 421
Bratsk, 511
Brazil, 441, 614
Brecht, Berthold, 394

Breslauer, George, 303, 304
Brest, 581
Brest-Litovsk, Treaty of, 61, 150; repudiated, 61
Brezhnev, Leonid I., 56, 88, 91, 299, 305, 315, 352, 372, 394, 407, 436, 440, 476, 531, 756; agriculture under, 93, 524, 529, 533; assistance to Africa under, 438; attempt by, to improve Sino-Soviet relations, 426, 427; background of, 89; as chairman of Presidium, 89–90; conservative policies under, 89, 371; consolidation of power by, 89, 425, 762; cult of, 94, 291; death of, 56, 94–95; détente under, lix; economy under, lix, 466, 467; as first secretary, 89; Food Program of, 524; ill health of, 94–95; KGB under, 762-63, 772; and letters to the editor, 379; literature under, 388; military-political relations under, 729; nationalities under, 197; nuclear war viewed by, 656-57; patronage systems under, 219, 315–16; police under, 782; religion under, 200; SALT II signed by, 687; science and technology under, 627–28; standard of living under, 93; status of KGB under, 762; treaties signed by, 92
Brezhnev Doctrine, 423–24, 682, 683, 884; defined, 90; repudiated by Gorbachev, 424
Britain, 20, 44, 50, 56, 73, 78, 87, 172, 593; acquiescence of, to Hitler's demands, 73; assistance of, to Soviet Union in World War II, 75; concerns of, regarding Russian expansionism, 38, 44, 49; contributions of, to Soviet chemical industry, 503; after Crimean War, 36; in Crimean War, 32; declaration of war on Germany, 73; diplomatic recognition by, of Soviet Union, 67, 412, 421; diplomatic support of, for Iran, 79; establishing relations with Japan, 37; Gorbachev's 1984 visit to, 357, 42; influence of, in Middle East, 430, 434; involvement of, in Russian Civil War, 61, 63; Limited Test Ban Treaty signed, 688; as member of Quadruple Alliance, 29; as member of United Nations, 445; nuclear forces of, 417, 421, 444, 690; percentage of GNP spent on health care in, 273; relations of, with Soviet Union, 421–22; Russian alliance against, with Napoleon, 28; Russian dealings with, 48; ships acquired from, 575; Soviet alliance with, in World War II, 76–77; trade boycott of Soviet Union by, 601
British Broadcasting Corporation, 382
British Communist Party, 422
Brodsky, Joseph, lxxii
Brothers Karamazov, The (Dostoevskii), 40
Bucharest formula, 865
Buddhism, 184
budget: for influencing the economy, 469; kinds of, 469; method of distributing funds from,

469; for 1985, primary expenditures in, 469
Bug River, 5
Bukhara, 160, 161, 169, 170, 434
Bukharin, Nikolai I., 44, 65, 66, 70; demotion of, by Stalin, 68; in show trials, 70; support of, for Stalin, 66
Bukovina, Soviet invasion of, 74
Bulgakov, Mikhail, 394
Bulganin, Nikolai A., 82, 84
Bulgaria, 38, 49, 407, 414, 423, 425, 474, 552, 575, 877, 883, 890; intelligence gathering by, 780; labor transfers from, 870; as member of Comecon, 601, 854; military advisers in, 684; occupation of, by Red Army, 877; satellite communications hookup to, 582; Soviet treaty with, 877
Bulgarians, 138, 146
Bulgars, 175, 181
Bund (Jewish socialist party), 42
burany (blizzards), 110
Bure, R., 253
Bureya River Valley, 529
burghers: legal status of, 17
Burma, 616
Buryats, 184
buses, 545, 561, 565–66; average distance traveled, 566; importance of, to local transportation systems, 561, 565; passengers on, 561, 566
Bush, George H.W., lx
Byzantine culture, 3, 4, 7, 10
Byzantine Empire, 3, 5, 186; influence of, 13

Cabinet of Ministers, lxxii
cadres, 89, 260, 296, 307, 629; specialist, 308-9
Cadres Abroad Department (CPSU), 404, 407
Cambodia, 407, 426, 427, 446; satellite communications hookup to, 582; Soviet economic relations with, 601, 605, 612; Soviet military aid to, 684; Vietnamese occupation of, 437, 445–46; withdrawal of Vietnamese troops from, 604
Campbell, Robert, 779
Cam Ranh Bay, 437; Soviet military base in, 685, 727-28
Canada, 526, 548, 606; Soviet trade with, 605, 606, 608
canals: amount of freight carried on, 566; construction of, using prisoners, 566, 567; kilometers of, 566
capitalist-oriented states, 428
cardiovascular disease, 269, 271
Carpathian Mountains, 5, 107, 108, 581
Carter, Jimmy, 92, 687
Caspian Flotilla, 727
Caspian Sea, 10, 99, 107, 109, 113, 160, 502, 527, 567, 572, 719; ferry line on, 575; oil reserves in, 506

Castro, Fidel, 440
Catherine I, 23
Catherine II (the Great), 24–27, 28; Charter of Nobility issued by, 26; Charter to the Towns issued by, 26; death of, 27; expansion of Russian Empire under, 24–25; government reforms under, 25; "Greek project" of, 24; legacy of, 26; organization of society into estates by, 26, 27; overthrow of Peter III by, 23; Poland partitioned by, 24, 141; reorganization of provincial administration by, 26; Ukrainians enserfed by, 141
Catholic Church, Soviet policies toward, 199–200
Catholicism, 145, 147, 178, 184
Catholics, 149, 189–90; Lithuanian, 199–200, 202; Roman, 190; persecution of, 148; Ukrainian, 190, 199–200
cattle, 536
Caucasus Mountain Pass Railroad, 561
Caucasus Mountains, 99, 107–8, 153, 159, 561
Caucasus Railroad, 547
Caucasus region, 5, 12, 29, 61, 102, 108, 110, 124, 534; agriculture in, 532, 536; climate of, 112; family in, 230, 236, 238; famine in, 196; gender relations in, 230; increase of infectious diseases in, 270; industrialization of agriculture in, 227; introduction of Islam into, 192; metal industry in, 502; motherhood medals in, 236; nationalities in, 138, 152–59; oil pipelines in, 581; patronage systems in, 219; railroad construction in, 558, 561; unofficial income in, 221–22
Ceaușescu, Nicolae, 884, 889
censorship, 369, 370, 372, 373, 382, 397; abolished, lxxiv; of art, 397; by Glavlit, 373, 774; by Glavrepertkom, 391; government institutions involved in, 373; government role in, 374–76; hierarchy, 375; by KGB, 376, 774; loosening of, 390; of military and scientific information, 376; of music, 396; of periodicals, 381; policies, 375; topics of, 376
Censor's Index: contents of, 374–75; KGB work on, 774; size of, 374
census, 115–16; 1940, 119; 1959, 119; 1979, 127; 1989, 116
CENTO. *See* Central Treaty Organization
Central Asia, 14, 121, 124, 171, 172; Muslims in, 194; nationalities in, 138, 159–60; patronage systems in, 219
Central Asian Military District, 725
Central Asian Power System, 511
Central Auditing Commission, 292, 298, 730
Central Committee (CPSU), 65, 84, 88, 95, 276, 281, 296, 299, 301, 303, 309, 315, 340, 346, 348, 392, 404, 479, 522, 597, 600, 640; apparatchiks in, 297; armed forces under,

700; authority of, delegated, 296; censorship under, 774; criticism in, 319; departments of, responsible for foreign policy, 404–7; described, 292; duties of, 296; election of members of, 295; functions of, 298; history of, 296–98; KGB under, 770; meetings of, 296; members of, 297, 634, 730, 785; membership of, 298; membership of, selection process for, 297; military representation in, 297; Ministry of Defense and, 702; planning function of, 460–61; as policy maker, 628–29; role of, in education, 247; stability in, under Brezhnev, 89; turnover in, 297, 303; turnover in, under Gorbachev, 297–98; *uchraspredy* of, 314; worker and peasant representation in, 297
Central Europe, 664, 691
Central Executive Committee, 332; presidium of, 333; soviets of, 333
Central Group of Forces, 883
centralized planning (*see also* under types of planning), lix: advantages of, 462–64; committees involved in, 461; defined, 451, 458–60; in metallurgy, 500; problems in, 491; reasons for, 472–73; reassessment of, 487; for science and technology, 630
Central Kazakhstan Railroad, 547
Central Siberian Plain, 104
Central Treaty Organization (CENTO) (*see also* Baghdad Pact), 431
Chad, 420
Chamber of Commerce and Industry, 597, 600
Chardzhou, 172
Charles XII, 20
Charter of Nobility, 26
Charter to the Towns, 26
Chazov, Evgenii, 269, 273
Cheboksary, 181
Chebrikov, Viktor M., 346, 762, 764, 781; acknowledgment of KGB abuses, 764, 765; ouster of, from KGB, 765
Chechen-Ingush, 184
Chekhov, Anton, 40
Chelyabinsk, 124, 497, 501
chemical industry, 476, 502–3; long-term goals of, 502, 503; major divisions of, 502; petrochemicals, 502–3; planning goals of, 503; plastics, 502; role of, in technological advancement, 503; technology transfer to, 644
Chemical Industry, Ministry of the, 646
Chemical Troops, 708–10; equipment of, 709–10; mission of, 709; number of, 709; organization of, 708–9
Cherepovets, 124
Chernavin, Vladimir, 678
Chernenko, Konstantin U., lix, 94–95, 290, 305, 417, 467, 627; literature under, 388–89; loosening of party strictures on media and the arts, 372–73, 379

Chernichenko, Iurii, 389
Chernobyl' nuclear accident, lxxiii, 115, 262, 384, 481, 512, 710
chernozem soil, 107, 526, 527, 533
Chernyshevskii, Nikolai, 40, 371
Cherry Orchard, The (Chekhov), 40
Chiang Kai-shek, 67
Chicherin, Georgii, 67
children: care of, 251; custody of, 235; deaths of, due to medical negligence, 271; health care of, 265, 266; illegitimate, 235
Children of the Arbat (Rybakov), 390
Chile, 413, 440, 441; Soviet assistance to, 440
China (*see also* Sino-Soviet relations), 50, 56, 88, 99, 101, 108, 109, 116, 160, 164, 167, 176, 194, 413, 414, 428, 433, 436, 705; Boxer Rebellion in, 44; Communist victory over Nationalists in, 80–81; discontent of, with Soviet leadership, 86; exports of, 604; foreign currency reserves of, 604; foreign trade deficits of, 604; French arms sold to, 420; incursion into Vietnam, 426; involvement of, in Korean War, 81; Japanese victory over, 44; as member of United Nations, 445; Soviet attempt to undermine influence of, 90, 436; Soviet foreign policy toward, under Khrushchev, 56; Soviet foreign policy toward, under Lenin, 67; Soviet trade with, 591, 54, 601, 604–5, 608; Soviet troops on border with, 604, 725; summit of, proposed with Soviet Union, 427; withdrawal of, from Comecon, 604
Chinese Communist Party, 67, 86, 426
Chinese Empire, 18, 41
Chinggis Khan, 155
Christianity, 3, 149, 151, 179; introduction of, to Kievan Rus', 7, 138, 205
Christians, 153, 159
Chronicle of the Catholic Church in Lithuania, 190
Chu River, 527
Churbanov, Iurii, 782
Churchill, Winston, 77
Church Slavonic. *See* Old Church Slavonic
Chuvash, 152, 181, 182; alphabet of, 181; history of, 181; language of, 181; population of, 181; religion of, 181; urbanization of, 181
Chuvash Autonomous Oblast, 181
Chuvash Autonomous Republic, 181
citizenship, 339; duties of, 339
civil aviation (Aeroflot), 576–80; adaptation of aircraft in, 578–579; cargo transportation, 576; domestic flights, 578–80; evolution of, 579; fuel shortage, 578–80; helicopters in, 578; jets in, 579; kinds of aircraft operated by, 579; number of passengers served, 578; operations of, 579–80; passenger transportation, 576–79; rapid growth of, 579; technology in, 579; unusual services performed by, 578–579; work of, for Soviet armed

forces, 580, 712; in World War II, 579
Civil Aviation, Ministry of, 580, 712
civil defense, 676, 702, 721–22; mission of, 681; number of personnel, 722; origin of, 721; purpose of, 721–22
Civil War, lvii, 55, 61–64, 100, 139, 147, 164, 179, 182, 290, 472, 487, 661, 758; Allied Powers' involvement in, 61, 63; armed forces in, 698; Communist triumph in, 62; effect of, on family, 235; foreign trade during, 593; non-Russian nationalities during, 64; origins of, 61; party controls over science during, 633; relations with Japan during, 428; repression of opponents in, 63; role of railroads in, 547; women in, 747
Civil War in France, 1848-1850, The (Marx), 332
class conflict, 214–15
class struggle, 402
Clausewitz, Carl von, lxxvi, 655
clergy: persecution of, under Stalin, 72
climate, 109–12, 122; cold weather, effects of, 109–12; diversity of, 112; dominance of winter, 110; influence of, on agriculture, 526; monsoonal, 112; precipitation levels, 112, 526; of Soviet Asia, 489; temperate zone, 110; temperatures, 110, 489; in Transbaykal area, 558; weather patterns, 110
clinics (*see also* health care, hospitals, polyclinic complexes), 263
coal, lxxvii, 112, 476, 486, 489, 508–9, 510; export of, 508; location of, 508; mining, 509, 611; obstacles to access to, 488; production growth, 509; quality, 50; reserves of, 509; source of, 508; transportation of, 509; uses of, 505, 508; yield, 509
Coastal Defense Forces, 719; focus of, 719
Coastal Rocket and Artillery Troops, 719, 727
Cold War, 56, 78–81, 382; declaration of, lvii; defined, 79; end of, lx; establishment of diplomatic relations during, 412; as reaction to Stalin, 79; Soviet contribution to end of, lx
collective enterprises, 71
collective farms (kolkhozy), lxii, 76, 118, 473, 538, 565; changes to, 521–22; control of, by state agencies, 521; conversion of, to state farms, 522; defined, 521; DOSAAF clubs in, 742; KGB lectures to, 772–74; income in, 521; labor productivity of, 521; markets, 456; number of, 522; output of, 521; planning reform in, 466–67; preschools in, 251; quota for deputies to Congress of People's Deputies, 348; resistance to, 69
collective ownership: defined, 452; kinds of, 452
collectivization, forced, lviii, 295; of agriculture, 473, 519–20, 529, 593; described, 520; effect of, 529; of peasantry, 69, 148, 154; regimentation and, 71; resistance to, 69, 520; results of, 473, 520
combined arms operational offensive, 679

combined arms strategic operation, 676, 678-79
combines, 453, 492
Come and See (Klimov), 392
Comecon. *See* Council for Mutual Economic Assistance
Comecon Council Session, 856; function of, 856
Comecon Executive Committee, 856-57; Bureau for Integrated Planning and, 860; council committees of, 856-57; economic departments in, 856; function of, 856
Comecon planning, 866-70; coordination of national plans under, 867-68; political problems in, 866
Comecon Secretariat, 856, 857; function of, 857
Commission on Research and Exploitation of Cosmic Space, 376
commissions, party, 292, 301-2, 351, 355-57; assignments to, 355; deputies on, 355; drafting legislation, 356; economic planning in, 357, 358; formation of, factors in, 301; functions of, 355-56; influence of CPSU over, 356; membership of, 355, 356; oversight of government by, 356; as party bureaucracy administrators, 292; as policy implementers, 292; purpose of, 301; role of, 350-51; significance of, 301-2
Committee for State Security (KGB) (*see also* intelligence; *see also* under names of directorates), 95, 301, 307, 346, 700, 756, 761, 783; acknowledgment of abuses by, 764; in armed forces, 728; authority of, lxxx; autonomy, 765; Border Troops, 791-93; branches of, 765-66; cadres demoralized by "secret speech," 761; cadre selection, 766; campaigns against dissidents, 772; campaigns against political crime, 772; career patterns, 770; censorship by, 373,774; centralization of, 766; Collegium, 766; control by, of scientists, 634; control in, 766; creation of, 755, 782; directed, 766; dissidents monitored by, 774; and domestic security, 771-76; economic crimes investigated by, 771; efforts to improve image of, 761; Eighth Chief Directorate, 767; electronic espionage, 779; Fifth Chief Directorate, 767; First Chief Directorate, 767; foreign intelligence role of, 776-81; foreign policy responsibilities of, 409; functions of, 766-69, 771; Glavlit controlled by, 374; under Gorbachev, 763-64; influence of, on foreign policy, 780-81; informers recruited by, 766; interference of, in legal system, 789; investigations by, 787; local administration of, 766; manpower, 767; mission of, 755; nationalities in, 770; nuclear weapons charged to, 776; organization of, 766-69, 768; party control of, lxxiv, 769-70; party influence in, lxix; as party members,

769; personnel, 770-71; political crimes investigated by, 771; political police powers of, restricted, 760-71; political vigilance lectures, 772-74; predecessors of, 756-60; preventive tasks, 767, 772; in purges by Gorbachev, 763-64; purges of, 770; recruitment sources, 770; restrictions on, 761, 762, 771; role of, in coup of 1991, lxxx; role of, in making foreign policy, 403; role of, in leadership succession, 756; rules governing, 771; Russians as bureau chiefs of, 140; Second Chief Directorate, 767; security troops of, 793, 794; Seventh Directorate, 767; signal troops of, 723; special departments of, 733, 775, 766; statute of, 766; structure of, 765-66; supervision of, 360; support of, for terrorism, 779-80; tasks of, 766-67; technological espionage by, 737; Third Chief Directorate, 733; turnover rate, 770
Committee of People's Control, 335, 344, 351, 360
Committee of Soviet Women: quota for deputies to Congress of People's Deputies, 348
committees, party, 351, 355-57; assignments to, 355; deputies on, 355; drafting legislation, 356; economic planning in, 358; functions of, 355-56; influence of CPSU over, 356; membership of, 355, 356; oversight of government by, 356
communications industry (*see also* mass media and under form of communication), 452, 582-86; density of, 545; government control of, 582; government use of, 582; growth in, 582; influences on development of, 545; output of, as percentage of net material product, 453; party influence in, lxix; products of, 499; radio, 546, 582; satellite system of, 582; telephone, 546, 582; television, 546, 582
Communications, Ministry of, 582, 586; responsibilities of, 582, 585
Communications Equipment Industry, Ministry of the, 646
communism, 655; full, 290; Marx's definition of, 281
Communism, Mount, 108
communist ethics, 249
Communist Information Bureau (Cominform), 80; conflict over, with Yugoslavia, 414, 424; dissolved, 414; members of, 414
Communist International (Comintern), 80, 407; contacts by, in sub-Saharan Africa, 438; dissolution of, by Stalin, 414; founded by Lenin, 62, 414; as means of controlling foreign communists, 62; support of, for Nazi Party, 72; Yugoslavia expelled from, 424
Communist Manifesto, The (Marx and Engels), 339
communist parties abroad, 410, 414-15; activities of, 415; ideological maturity of, 414;

nonruling, 407, 414; recognition of, 414; Soviet influence on, 415

Communist Party of Czechoslovakia, 90, 423

Communist Party of Spain, 422

Communist Party of the Soviet Union (CPSU) (*see also* party control, party membership), 81, 90, 137, 228, 311, 330, 331, 344, 347, 493, 522, 553, 594, 731, 750, 764, 783; agitprop of, 377; appointments, criteria for, 314; and armed forces, 697, 728–33, 732; arts and media used by, to support communism, 371, 377; atheists in, 184; banned, lxxx; bifurcation of apparatus, 88, 89; bureaucracy of, 281; central institutions in, 292–306; control by, of security police, lxxiv; controls, 358; criticism of, lxxii, lxxiv, 30, 33; demographics of, 289; demographics of, as source of legitimacy, 289; discipline, 319; economic planning by, 452–53, 632; effect of membership in, 211; as elite body, 289; endorsement for university admission, 258; enforcement of authority, 281, 282; ethnic composition of, 323–24; exchange of party documents, 319; factions proscribed by, 286–88; foreign policy of, 409; functions of government, as performed by, 329; general secretary of, 302–6; Georgians as members of, 140, 323; goals of, 281; and government, distinctions between, 292, 329; guarded by Ninth Directorate, 769; hierarchy of, 306; importance of, lxxvii; importance to, of growth in heavy industry, 485; industrial policy statements by, 492; influence of, on military-industrial complex, lxxv; influence of, over commissions and committees, 356; influence of, over science, 633; interference of, in legal system, 789; intermediate-level organizations in, 306–13; Jews as members of, 140; journalists as members of, 378; judges screened by, 788; KGB created by, 755; KGB as members, 769; KGB under, 769; as leader of world communist movement, 290–91, 320; legitimacy of, 282, 288–91, 329; membership of, lxviii–lxix, 313, 346, 348, 733; military doctrine of, 653, 659–66; military policy of, 659–66; military representation in, 729–30; *nomenklatura* authority of, 313; organization of, 294; origins of, 282; pensions for administrative elite, 275; people's dissatisfaction with, lxxv; planning function of, 462; as policy maker, 292, 329, 628; power of, lxix; power of, under Stalin, 71; primary party organizations (PPOs), 281, 292, 312–13; purges, 319; purpose of rule of, 290; quota for deputies to Congress of People's Deputies, 348; reasons for joining, 319–20; recruitment for KGB from, 770; reform in, 309; resignation of prominent members of, lxviii; role of, lxvii–lxviii; role of, in Constitution of 1977, 334; role of, in education, 244–45, 247–48;

in rural society, 225; Russian tradition incorporated into, 289, 291; Russians as members of, 140; salaries in, 220; social composition of, 322–25; as sole interpreter of Marxist ideology, 281, 282, 284, 289; training, 282, 320–22; as vehicle for upward mobility, 289–90; youth organizations used by, 229–30

Communists (*see also* Bolshevik government, Bolsheviks, Communist Party of the Soviet Union), 55; central Soviet government administered by, 64; execution of imperial family by, 63; policies of left-wing, 66; policies of right-wing, 66

Comprehensive Program for Scientific and Technical Cooperation to the Year 2000 (1985) (Comecon), 603, 854, 873; areas of self-sufficiency under, 603; benefits of, 869–70; economic restructuring under, 863; purposes of, 854, 863, 869

Comprehensive Program for the Further Extension and Improvement of Cooperation and the Further Development of Socialist Economic Integration by the Comecon Member Countries (1971), 854, 858, 861, 867, 873; described, 861; function of, 861–62; joint projects under, 868; joint planning under, 867–68; market relations under, 862; monetary problems under, 866; prices under, 864–65; socialist economic integration in, 861

Comprehensive System of International Peace and Security, 446

computer centers, 636

computers, 384–85, 479, 499, 623, 869; developed by Soviet Union, 385; lack of, 649; literacy requirement, 385; planned production of, 481

Concerted Plan for Multilateral Integration Measures (Comecon), 862, 867–68; projects under, 868

Conference of First Secretaries of Communist and Workers' Parties and of the Heads of Government of the Comecon Member Countries, 856

Congo, 414, 438; priviliged affiliation of, with Comecon, 616

Congress of Berlin, 38

Congress of People's Deputies, lxviii, lxxiv, 296, 304, 329, 335, 341, 342, 346–50, 352, 353, 355, 358, 408; activities of, 340; antecedent of, 334; candidates for, 347; categories of deputies, 348; demographics of deputies, 3; dissolution of, lxxxi; elections to, 347, 348–50; eligibility for election to, 348; foreign policy responsibilities of, 408; origin of, 346–47; quotas for deputies, 348; responsibilities of, 347; role of, 330; voters in elections to, 347, 348

Congress of Soviets, 332, 334; Central Executive Committee of, 332; eliminated, 333; power of, 332; Second, 60, 401

Congress of Vienna, 29

Constantine Alexandrovich, 30
Constantinople, 3, 5, 7, 8, 19, 186; fall of, 13
Constituent Assembly, 60
Constitutional Democratic Party, 46
Constitutional Oversight Committee, 330, 334, 335, 342, 347, 353; powers of, 334–35
constitutional rights, 335–38; lack of protection for, 338; limits on, 338
constitution of 1905, 4
constitution of 1918, 332–33; party as ruler of Russia under, 332; power granted under, 332; provisions of, 332; rights in, 332; Sovnarkom in, 332–33
constitution of 1924, 333
constitution of 1936, 71, 333
Constitution of 1977, lxi, 89, 284, 304, 329, 331, 333–40, 343, 346, 355; amendments to, 334–35, 340, 347, 352; changes in, lxxi; content of, 329–30; councils of elder members in, 354; Defense Council in, 700; duties in, 331, 339; equal rights for women under, 212, 230–31; federal system in, 361; foreign policy under, 407–8, 408–9; free education guaranteed in, 243; free medical care guaranteed in, 243; judiciary under, 787; KGB under, 765; military service under, 739, 747; ministries under, 345; ownership of means of production under, 452; political theory underlying, 331; Presidium's authority in, 352; Presidium's chairman in, 352; principles established in, 334; Procuracy under, 787; provisions of, 331; rights in, 331, 335–38; Supreme Court in, 359; Supreme Soviet in, 354; system of soviets in, 332
constitutions: Marx's understanding of role of, 332
constitutions, Soviet, 331–32; amendment process, 335; political theory underlying, 331; provisions of, 331–32; rights under, 335–38; role of, 332
Construction and Troop Billeting, 702, 721, 747
Consultative Committee (Warsaw Pact), 663
consumer goods, 475, 476, 495; availability of, 513–14; commitment to improving production of, 486; defined, 512; electronic, availability of, 513–14; import of, 602, 611, 615; lack of priority in producing, 513; poor quality of, 513; produced by the chemical industry, 502; and private enterprise, 480; rationing of, 513; role of electronics industry in producing, 499; shortages in, 513; waiting periods for, 513
consumer industry, 512–25; production goals of, 514
consumption, per capita, 457, 478
contraception (*see also* abortion): abortion as chief form of, 234; to control family size in Central Asia, 236; lack of artificial methods,

234; method, by social category, 234; number of unwanted pregnancies resulting from lack of, 234
contract brigades, agricultural: autonomy of, 525; bonuses under, 525; described, 525; family, 525; and improvement in agricultural performance, 530; number of, 525
control: agencies for, 453; defined, 358–59; economic, 472; figures, 461, 462; figures, nonbinding, 468; justification for, 284; of society by party, 281, 282
control organs, 358–61
conventional forces: modernization of, 699; reduced by Khrushchev, 691
Conventional Forces in Europe (CFE), 692
cooperative ownership, defined, 452
cooperatives, 456
Coordinating Committee for Multilateral Export Controls (CoCom), 608, 610
Corps of Gendarmes, 757
corruption, campaign against, 304
cossacks, 14, 107, 141
Cossacks, Ukrainian, 141; defined, 18; role of, in Ukrainian uprising (1648), 18
Council Committee for Cooperation in Planning, 856, 867; function of, 857, 867
Council for Mutual Economic Assistance (Comecon), 344, 437, 497, 853–74; agencies affiliated with, 858; Charter of, 854, 858; China's withdrawal from, 604; *Comprehensive Program* (1971), 861–62, 863–64; concern of, with world socialist system, 857; *Concerted Plan* of, 868–69; coordinated activities of, 860; council committees of, 856–57, 867; Council Session of, 856; dissolution of, lx; economic cooperation in, 854, 856, 870–71; economic restructuring under, 862, 863; and the EEC, 610, 873; evolution of, 858–64, 872–73; exchange rates in, 865–66; Executive Committee of, 856–57, 860, 867; formal cooperation of Yugoslavia with, 603; founding of, 853, 854; frequency of meetings of, 858, 863; function of, 859; goals of, 853; interstate conferences in, 857; joint projects in, 868; under Khrushchev, 859–61; kinds of relationships with, 855; labor resources of, 870; liquidity shortages in, 862, 864; market relations and investments of, 864–66; meetings of, 863, 873; members of, 423, 601, 854; membership, 854–55; military support in, 870–71; mixed economic system of, 863; national participation in, 855; in the 1980s, 862–63; observer countires in, 616, 855; operation of, 858; planning and, 866– 70, 872; power configurations within, 870; pricing system of, 602, 864–65; problems in, 873; purpose of, 594, 601, 853, 854; resistance to Soviet domination of, 853; right to refrain from participation in, 858; science and technology

cooperation among, 856, 869-70; scientific institutes in, 857; Secretariat of, 856, 857; Soviet domination of, 853, 854; Soviet economic aid to, 591, 871; Soviet trade with, 591, 601-3, 605; standing commissions in, 873-74; 857; structure of, 856-58; support of, for developing countries, 872; trade, intraregional, in, 864, 865-66; trade, multilateral, in, 866; and the United Nations, 873
Council of Chalcedon, 189
Council of Ministers, lxxii, 82, 247, 276, 292, 295, 316, 330, 332, 333, 335, 340, 341'-42, 353, 354, 356, 436, 493, 594, 595, 597, 600, 640, 734, 735, 760; activities of, 340; advice of, on policy, 629; armed forces under, 700; authority of, 330, 341; diplomatic recognition by, 409; duties of, 341; economic planning by, 357-58, 453, 632; elected, 333; foreign policy role of, 408-9; Glavlit's role under, 374; industrial complexes under, 467, 491-92; KGB under, 760, 765, 769; Law on, 335; meetings of, 342; members of, 342, 346; membership in, 341-42; Ministry of Defense and, 701; planning function of, 461, 462, 492; policies of, 628; as policy implementer, 629; powers of, 342; Presidium of, 341, 408-9; responsibilities of, 332-33; role of, 330; structure of, 341
Council of Ministers chairman, 342-43; appointed by Supreme Soviet, 350; as head of government, 329, 342; as head of party, 342; Khrushchev as, 342; Lenin as, 342; as member of Politburo, 330; power of, 343; role of, in economic administration, 342-43; Stalin as, 342
Council of Ministers Presidium, 343-44; as economic bureau, 344; members of, 343-44; power of, 343
Council of Nationalities, 195
Council of People's Commissars (Sovnarkom) (*see also* Council of Ministers), 60, 82, 760
Council of the Federation, lxxii; formed, lxxi
Counterrevolution (1905-07), 45-46
counterrevolution, combating, 684
coup d'état of August 1991, lxxviii-lxxxi; civil reaction to, lxxix; civilian casualties in resisting, lxxix; collapse of, lxxx; decrees under, lxxix; international reaction to, lxxix; plotters, lxxviii-lxxix; support for, lxxix
Courland, Duchy of, 150
court system, 359, 360-61; appeals under, 361; role of judge, 360-61; structure of court cases, 360
CPSU. *See* Communist Party of the Soviet Union
Credentials Commission, 350
Crimea, lxxviii, lxxx, 75, 88, 100, 110, 557; annexed by Catherine II, 24; climate of, 112; European attack on, 27; nationalist demon-

strations in, 793; Tatar population in, 176
Crimean Autonomous Republic, 176
crime and punishment: amnesty, 790; in armed forces, 749; death penalty, 790; economic, 763, 790; under Gorbachev, 790; labor camps, 790; nonpolitical, 790; parole, 790; penalties for, 790; violent, 790
Crime and Punishment (Dostoevskii), 40, 394
Crimean Khanate, 175
Crimean Mountains, 108
Crimean War, 32; backwardness manifested in, 34; foreign affairs after, 36-38
critical realism: defined, 370; as artistic protest, 370, 371; used by Bolsheviks to control culture, 370
criticism, 318-19
Croatians, 138
crusades, 8
Cuba, 86, 407, 414, 416, 423, 439, 441, 716; as burden on Comecon, 871; Comecon aid to, 871; communist revolution in, 440; Gorbachev's visit to, 441; as member of Comecon, 601, 603, 854, 871; military advisers in, 684; military forces of, airlifted to Angola, 438-39; power of, in Comecon, 871; role of, in Latin American terrorism, 779-80; satellite communications hookup to, 582; Soviet economic aid to, 591, 592, 605; Soviet military bases in, 603, 871; Soviet support for, lx; Soviet trade with, 612; Soviet treaty with, 441; troops of, in Third World, 684; withdrawal of, from Angola, 439
Cuban missile crisis, lix, 87, 88, 571, 716
cult of personality, 291; Brezhnev's, 94, 291; history of, 291; Khrushchev's, 291; Lenin's, 291; Stalin's, 84, 88, 291
cult of the just tsar, 291
cultural exchanges, 416, 418-19
cultural purges, 78
cultural revolution, 281, 283
cultural thaw, 84, 385, 392
culture (*see also* arts, literature, music), 93-94; restrictions on, under Brezhnev, 94
Culture, Ministry of, 247, 257, 391, 582
currency of Comecon members, 865-66
Cyprus, 431
Cyrillic: Eastern Orthodox liturgy written in, 7
Czechoslovakia, 101, 414, 423, 425, 467, 581, 885, 890; army of, under Soviet control; Hitler's demands for, 73; intelligence gathering by, 780; liberalization in, 882; as member of Comecon, 601, 854, 859; military agreement of, with Afghanistan, 434; nuclear-free zone proposed by, 691; occupation of, by Red Army, 877; revolution of 1989, lix; satellite communications hookup to, 582; Soviet forces stationed in, 728; Soviet military alliance with, 73; Soviet relations with, 407;

Soviet treaty with, 877; Soviet withdrawal of forces from, 444; Warsaw Pact invasion of (1968), 90, 419, 420, 423, 425, 442, 682, 699, 719, 781, 861, 882-83, 885
Czechoslovak People's Army, 883; purge of, 883
Czechs, 138, 146

Dagestan Autonomous Republic, 159
Dahlak, Soviet military base in, 685
dairy farming, 536
Dalmatia, 50
Danes, 151
Daniel, Iulii, 381
Daniil (Prince), 9
Daniil Aleksandrovich, 12
Danish Straits, 680
Danube River, 36
Danzig, Gulf of, 101
Daoud Khan, Mohammad, 434
Dardanelles, 28, 32, 48, 50
Day Lasts More Than a Hundred Years, The (Aitmatov), 388
death: causes of, 269, 271; rates, 269
Decembrists: origins of, 30; revolt of, 291
Decembrists' revolt, 30
decentralization, 608
Decree Number 358: 593, 594
Decree of the Press, 371
Decree on Peace, 401-2
Defense, Ministry of, lxxvi, 582, 700, 701-2, 723, 725, 731, 745, 746, 749, 756, 791, 793, 880, 885; foreign policy responsibilities of, 409; KGB control by, 769; in Main Military Council, 701; members of, 702, 730; military research and development under, 646, 647; minister of, 702; organization of, 704; Premilitary Training Directorate of, 742; responsibilities of, 702; salaries in, 220; as strong consumer, 465; supervision of, 701-2
Defense Council, 303, 350, 665, 700-701, 702, 703, 781; decisions of, 701, 734; chairman of, 353, 403, 408, 700; membership of, 700; military research and development under, 493, 646
Defense Industry, Ministry of the, 646
Defense Industry Department (CPSU Central Committee), 734
defense spending, 469-70, 733-34; budget items, 733-34; *glasnost'* in, 734; on research and development, 734; as percentage of GNP, 734; total for 1988, 733
de Gaulle, Charles, 420
Delianov, Ivan, 36
democratic centralism, lxxv, 65, 228, 284-88, 309, 312, 313, 329, 340, 346; accountability in, 286; contradictions in principles of,

286; decision making in, 286; defined, 281, 282-83; in Presidium, 358; principles of, 284-86; Western view of, 286
Democratic People's Republic of Korea (North Korea), 81, 101, 413, 414, 433; military advisers in, 684; satellite communications hookup to, 582; Soviet economic relations with, 601, 605
demographic literacy, 130
demography. *See* population
demokratizatsiia (democratization), lvii, 262; defined, lxvii; effects of, lix; problems with, lvii
Denmark, 14, 423
deserts, 107, 112, 527
design organizations, 635; design bureaus, 635, 636, 665; organizational separation and, 638-39, 640; planning by, 635; responsibilities of, 635; technological institutions in, 635
de-Stalinization, 88, 255, 762, 879-80; effect of, on Eastern Europe, 86; effect of, on security police, 761; halted under Brezhnev, 89; initiated by "secret speech," 84, 761
détente, 92, 416, 418, 421, 772; under Brezhnev, lix; consequences of, for Warsaw Pact, 889; end of, 891; meaning of, 416, 420; military strategy during, 676; new, 419; science under, 627-28; Warsaw Pact under, 888-91
Deutsche Welle, 382
development, 624; expansion of, 627; organizational separation and, 638-39, 640; organizations, 634-37
Dewey, John, 249
dialectical materialism, 626
Dictatorship of Conscience (Shatrov), 394
dictatorship of the proletariat, 60, 65, 284, 332, 655; fulfilled, 334
diet, 519; fish in, 539; Khrushchev's concern for, 522; per capita consumption of meat and dairy products, 538
diplomacy, 345, 357, 408, 409, 410-13; bourgeois, 410; communist, 410-13; described, 412
diplomatic recognition: establishment of, 412; pursuit of, 412
disease: causes of, 270; increases in, 269, 270; kinds of, 269
disinformation: defined, 779; United States as prime target for, 779
dissidents: confinement of, in psychiatric hospitals, 772; KGB attacks on, 771; party policy toward, 774-75; repression of, by Brezhnev, 90; scientists as, 634
distribution system, 456-57, 460; agricultural, 460; collective farm markets, 456; cooperatives, 456; decentralization of, 457, 468-69; output of, as percentage of net material product, 453; percentage of labor force in, 456; rationing in, 469; retail outlets, 456; sales by individuals, 453; wholesale, 457

divorce, lxvi, 100, 125-27, 233; attitudes of non-Russian nationalities toward, 231; child custody after, 233; cost of, 233; effect of alcoholism on, 130, 270; factors contributing to rate of, 212; housing shortage as cause of, 233; in NEP era, 68; obtaining, 233; rates of, 233; rates of, and population problems, 125; reasons for, 233; restriction of, 71

Dmitrii, First False, 15

Dmitrii, Second False, 15

Dnepropetrovsk, 315-16

Dnepropetrovskaya Oblast, 316

Dnepropetrovsk College of Metallurgy, 316

Dnepr Railroad, 557

Dnepr River, 7, 18, 24, 25, 33, 101, 138, 568, 581; hydroelectric system on, 108; Ukraine split along, 141

Dnepr River Valley, 3, 5, 8, 12, 527, 532

Dnestr River, 5, 24; hydroelectric system on, 108

Dnestr River Valley, 125

Dobroliubov, Nikolai, 371

Dobrynin, Anatolii, 407

doctor of science degree, 260

"doctors' plot," 81

Doctor Zhivago (Pasternak), 382, 398

Donbass industrial area: coal industry in, 508-9; coal reserves in, 508; reduction of resources in, 488

Donetsk metallurgical plant, 501

Donetsk Railroad, 557

Donets River basin, 12, 527, 532

Don River, 18, 33, 568, 581; hydroelectric system on, 108

DOSAAF. *See* Voluntary Society for Assistance to the Army, Air Force, and Navy

Dostoevskii, Fedor, 39-40, 394

drug abuse, 99; increase in, 271

Druzhba (Friendship) oil pipeline, 860

dual subordination, 346

Dubček, Alexander, 882, 883

Dubna, 585

Duma, lvii, 47, 50; defined, 46; dissolution of, 46; elections in, 46; Executive Committee formed, 57; First, 46, 176; Fourth, 47; Second, 46-47, 176; Third, 47

dumas, 7, 34, 36, 283

Dushanbe, 170

dvorianstvo (nobility), 17

Dzerzhinskii, Feliks E., 547; expansion of railroad system under, 547; Vecheka under, 758

Eastern Europe, 56; consumption levels of, 478; as defensive buffer, 682, 875-77, 892; energy pipeline to, 546; military advisers in, 684; reaction of, to changes in Soviet leadership, 424; revolutions of 1989, lix-lx; Soviet armed forces withdrawn from, 692; Soviet control of, 877; Soviet demands for supplies from, 78; Soviet economic activity with, 591, 594; Soviet forces stationed in, 728; Soviet hegemony in, lviii; Soviet hegemony in, as foreign policy, 401, 419; Soviet influence over, 419, 424; Soviet military intervention in, 682; Soviet occupation of, lviii, 77, 79, 699; Soviet trade with, lxiii, 594; Soviet troops stationed in, 883, 884-87; and Soviet Union, power of, in Comecon, 870; terrorist aid channeled through, 780; withdrawal of Soviet troops from, lx

Eastern Front (World War I), 50

Eastern Orthodox Church (*see also* Belorussian Autocephalous Orthodox Church, Georgian Orthodox Church, Russian Orthodox Church, Ukrainian Autocephalous Orthodox Church), 4, 8, 9, 10, 12, 13, 145, 181, 183, 184-89; administration of, 185-86; beliefs, 184-85; clergy, 185; denominations in, 185; in Kievan Rus', 9; reasons for dominance of, 7; teachings, 184-85; worship, 185

"Eastern Question," 31-32

East European Plain, 4, 104

East Germany. *See* German Democratic Republic

East Siberian Economic Region, 511

East Slavic region, 5

East Slavs (*see also* Belorussians, Russians, Ukrainians, Kievan Rus', Muscovy, Russian Empire), 3, 4, 7, 10, 141, 144; dominance of, lvii, 138; isolation of, 7; major pre-Soviet political formations of, 3; as members of CPSU, 324; origins of, 5

economic aid, 601; amount of, 592; to Comecon members, 591; expansion of, 592; under GKES, 594; reassessment of, 592; to Third World, 605

economic control, 458-71; figures, 461, 462; pricing policy as, 470

economic councils, 466, 627

economic development, 451, 488, 624; for Siberia, 479; of the Soviet Far East, 479

economic laws of socialism, 458

economic measurements: net output, 467; Soviet-style, 452, 467, 470

economic plan, 315, 357; distribution of funds to reflect goals of, 469; elaboration of successive, 462

economic planning, 458-71; advantages of, 462-64; basis of, 458; centralized, defined, 458-60; Marxist-Leninist definition of, 458; ratchet system of, 464; socialist laws for, 458

economic policies, 471-82; and Comecon, 603; Marxist blueprint for, 472; past priorities of, 472-78; problems caused by, 472

economic production, 458

economic reform: under Andropov, 467; description of, 458; effect of, on wages,

470-71; under Gorbachev, 314, 456-57, 458, 467, 618-19; under Khrushchev, 84, 92, 310, 466, 467; under Kosygin, 92, 466, 467
economic regions, 504
economic structure, 452-58; centralization of, under Stalin, 458
economy, centrally planned (CPE): advantages of, 462-64; under Brezhnev, 466, 467; problems in, 464-65, 472; production storming in, 464-65; science and technology plans under, 630; as taut economy, 464
economy, official, 92-93, 452-54, 456; before World War II, 55; centralized under Kosygin, 92-93; centralized under Stalin, 69; debt, 592, 606; expansion of, after World War II, 56; growth of, 467, 476, 477, 478, 480-81, 493; health care in, 456; impact of low population growth on, 119; impact of surplus of women on, 119; industrialized under Stalin, lviii, 69-70; management of, by Council of Ministers, 341, 343, 345; opening of, 592; priorities for, 452-53; private sector in, 457, 480; problems in, under Khrushchev, 88; problems in, under Gorbachev, lx-lxi, lxiv; reform efforts in, 453; role of Ministry of Finance in, 457-58; size of, 477; socialist ownership of means of production in, 452; supply and demand in, 456; "taut," 456, 464
economy, unofficial: defined, 211; description of, 453-54; illegal activities in, 480; legitimized, 480
education, 244-62; access to, in Russian Empire, 243; access to, in Soviet Union, 218, 223; under Alexander II, 35; for artistically gifted students, 257; under Brezhnev, 93-94; characteristics of, 244-45; creation of "new school," 245, 250; engineering training in, 649; exchanges, 410; free, guaranteed by Constitution, 243; for handicapped students, 257; for intellectually gifted students, 257; under Khrushchev, 243-44; level of, 93-94, 250; literacy rate, 243; under Lunacharskii, 68; Marxist-Leninist philosophical underpinnings of, 244; medical, of women, 35; military, 257; *obrazovanie* (formal), 245; obstacles to reform of, 262; and occupation, 217-18; orthodox Marxist interpretation of, 72; overbureaucratization in, 248; party influence in, lxix; party's role in, 247-48; of peasants, 35; perpetuation of elite in, 94, 218, 223; under Peter the Great, 22; political indoctrination in, 243, 244, 248, 249, 253; polytechnical, 244; providing workers, 248-49; purpose of, lxv; reforms in, under *perestroika*, 245, 649; research and development in, 248; responsibility of, for socialization, 245; rote learning in, 243; science training in, 649; under

Stalin, 243-44; and *vospitanie* (upbringing), 245
education, higher, lxix-lxv; access to, restricted, 214; backgrounds of students in, 258; engineering training in, 649; graduate training in, 260; jobs assigned to graduates of, 260; kinds of, 257-58; length of study, 259; locations of, 258; management of, 247-48; nationalities represented in, 140; programs of, 259; reform of, 262, 649; science training in, 636, 649; tuition and fees, 259-60; universities, 258; women in, 258
Education, Ministry of, 35, 247, 248
Education, Ministry of Higher and Specialized, 247
education, secondary, 253-56; class time, 254; computer training in, 254, 256; enrollment, 253; entry of six-year-olds into, 254; final examinations in, 255; foreign language study in, 254; grades in, 255; intermediate and upper curriculum, 254-55; kinds of, 253; length of compulsory, 253; number of facilities, 253; phases in, 254; primary curriculum in, 254; reform of (1984), 254; rural and urban, 254; school year, 254; "socially beneficial" labor in, 255; specialized (technicums), 256, 262; study of Russian language in, 254; vocational counseling in, 254; vocational-technical, 256
education system, structure of, 252
egalitarianism, repudiated by Stalin, 214
Egypt, 43, 86, 614, 712; abrogation of treaty with Soviet Union, 684; expulsion of Soviet advisers from, 91, 413, 684; improvement in Soviet relations with, 432, 433; Soviet trade with, 612
Egyptian army, 91
Eighth Chief Directorate: responsibility of, 767; Security Troops under, 793
Eighth Five-Year Plan (1966-70), 476
Eisenhower, Dwight D., 85, 86, 87, 688
Eisenstein, Sergei, 68, 390
Ekibastuz, 509, 510
Ekran, 513-14
Ekran satellite system, 585; uses of, 585
El'brus, Mount, 108
elections, 365-66; campaigning, 365; effect of, lxix; efforts to democratize, 365-66; as forum for requesting services, 365; multicandidate, 365; party control over, 365; right to campaign for, 350; right to stand for, 348; selection of candidates for, 365
electricity: generation and distribution of, 510; in rural areas, 520; sources of, 510
electrification, 472; Lenin's program for, 547; of railroads, 547
electronics industry, 499; chronic problems in, 499; consumer goods produced by, 499; cooperation of, with machine building, 499;

critical branches in, 499; joint ventures in, 611; most important role of, 499; self-sufficiency of Comecon in, 603; technology transfer to, 499

Electronics Industry, Ministry of the, 646

Eleventh Five-Year Plan (1981–85), 478, 481, 496, 532, 540

elite, lxv–lxvi; allocation of housing to, 223; defined, 216; health care of, 268–69; income and benefits of, 216, 220, 471; intelligentsia as, 216; KGB as, 216; Muslim, 176; party membership of, 298; pensions of, 275; perpetuated by education system, 218; position of children of, 211; Soviet, 211

Elizabeth I, 23

El Salvador, 440

emigration, lxxiv, 124

employment: full, 477; growth in, 477

energy (*see also* coal, electricity, fuel, gas, nuclear power, oil), 487; acceleration in production of, 481; cogeneration, 512; efficiency in use of, 481; generators of, 510; growth of, 510; heat generation, 512; network, integration of, 510; obstacles to supply of, 512; policy goals, 510; renewable, 510–11; requirements, 488; resources, 488

Engels, Friedrich, 44, 339, 472, 654

engineering: curriculum for, 649; problems in training, 649; training in, 648–50

Engineer Troops, 708–10; equipment of, 709–10; mission of, 709; organization of, 708–9; uniforms and rank insignia of, 738–39

enterprise, individual, 453, 492; production plans for, 462

enterprise, industrial: transfer of, to Asian areas, 474

enterprise, private, 454, 480; activities in, 480; regulations for, 480

enterprise, state: election of management personnel in, 468, 480; election of labor councils in, 468–69; fulfillment of contracts by, 468; government power to disband unprofitable, 600; responsibility of, for foreign trade, 600; self-financing requirement, 468

environment, 113–15, 121, 397; air pollution, 115, 122; Aral region as ecological disaster area, 115; degradation of, lxxiii, 100; green movement, lxxiii, 113, 130; and opposition to construction of electrical plants, 512; protection of neglected, 113

Ermak, 14

Estonia, 21, 73, 147, 363; annexation of, lviii, 397, 473, 682; ceded to Russia, 151; controlled by Sweden, 151; establishment of independence, 61; German control of, 151; independence of, lxxxi; Russification in, 151; Soviet invasion of, in 1939, 74, 550

Estonian Republic, lxx–lxxi, lxxix, 102, 123, 127, 151, 188, 308, 526; agriculture in, 533;

autonomy sought by, 362; candidates for Congress of People's Deputies, 347; drainage projects in, 529; families in, 236; legal age for marriage in, 232; minorities in, 152; nationalist movement suppressed in, 759; population of, 152; rate of premarital pregnancy in, 234; religion in, 191; roads in, 562

Estonians, lxvi, 27, 150, 151–52; distribution of, 152; divorce of, 233; education of, 152; Germanization of, 151; history of, 151; independence movement, 151; language of, 152; as members of CPSU, 152; oppression of, 151–52; population of, 152; as scientific workers, 152; secession by, lxxix; urbanization of, 152

Ethiopia, 90, 431, 438, 439, 684, 712; Eritrean insurgency, 431; military access to, 727; military advisers in, 684; Soviet arms bought by, 614; Soviet military base in, 685; Soviet support for Cuban troops in, 684, 700; ties to Comecon, 616, 855

ethnic diversity (*see also* minorities, nationalities), 99

ethnic groups. *See* nationalities

Etorofu Island, 428

Eurocommunism, 90, 415

Europe, 44, 410, 430, 561, 569; arms buildup in, 692; denuclearization of, 690, 691; destruction of targets in, 677; nuclear-free zone, 691

European Community, lxxxi

European Economic Community (EEC), 592, 610; normalization agreement with, 619

Evtushenko, Evgenii, 388, 389, 390, 392

Executive Committee of the Duma, 57

exploiting classes; description of, 214; official discrimination against, 214

Export pipeline, 581

exports: of arms, 614; attempt to increase, 610, 618; of chemicals, 606, 608; of fuel, 592, 603, 605, 606, 608, 609, 610, 611–12, 615; of manufactured goods, 605–6; of metals, 610; as source of hard currency, 592, 605; of timber, 606, 610; of tractors, 606; unidentified, 616

Ezhov, Nikolai, 70

Ezhovshchina, 70

factories: DOSAAF units in, 742; KGB lectures to, 772–74; preschools in, 251

factory workers: in nineteenth-century Russia, 33

Falin, Valentin A., 300, 407

family, 125–27, 234–38; decline of, 100, 235; evolution of, 235–36; extended, 238; function of, 238; government as surrogate, 238; law on, 234, 235; Muslim, 232–33; in NEP era, 68; number of children in, 235; role of,

in child-rearing, 246; size of, 127, 212, 236; strengthening of, under Stalin, 235; structures, 238; subsidies for poor, 235-36, 243; typical, 127, 236
farming. *See* agriculture
Fathers and Sons (Turgenev), 39
Federal Republic of Germany (West Germany), 87, 419, 420, 457, 714; as importer of Soviet gas, 508, 581, 609, 610; percentage of GNP spent on health care in, 273; relations of, with Soviet Union, 420-21; ships acquired from, 575; trade with, 607
Fedor I, reign of, 14-15
Fedor II, 15
Fedor III, 20
Fedorchuk, Vitalii, 763, 782, 783
Fel'tsman, Vladimir, 395
Fergana Valley, 527
ferry lines: Crimea-Caucasus, 575; Klaipeda-Mukran, 575; Leningrad-Stockholm, 575; Vanino-Kholmsk, 575
fertile triangle, 525
fertility, 121, 130
Fifth Chief Directorate (KGB), 767
Fifth Five-Year Plan (1951-55), 475, 552; investment in heavy industry under, 475
film, 390-92; industry, liberalizing trends in, 390-91; as propaganda, 384; under Stalin, 385-88; themes in, dictated by the party, 390
Final Act of the Conference on Security and Cooperation in Europe. *See* Helsinki Accords
Finance, Ministry of, 35, 345, 357; functions of, 595, 632; role of, in economic system, 457-58
financial system, 457-58
Finland, 47, 61, 79, 101; army of, 699; Bank of, 611; bilateral clearing agreements with, 611; independence of, 61; land concessions of, to Soviet Union, 77, 362; reexport by, of Soviet oil, 612; resistance of, to Soviet invasion, 74; Russian acquisition of, 28; Soviet invasion of, 550, 699; Soviet relations with, 422; Soviet trade with, 591, 605, 611-12; ties to Comecon, 855
Finland, Gulf of, 22
Finnish Civil War, 61
Finnish Russians, 27, 36, 42, 45
Finnish-Soviet war. *See* Soviet-Finnish war
Finno-Ugric tribes, 8, 138, 149, 151, 181, 182, 183
Finns, 151
First Chief Directorate (KGB), 781; composed of, 776-77; Directorate K, 777; Directorate S, 776; Directorate T, 776; recruitment for, 778; responsibility of, 767; *rezidenty*, 777; Service A, 777; Service I, 777; Service R, 777
First Five-Year Plan (1928-32), 68-69, 295, 487; agriculture under, 55, 473; centraliza-

tion under, 491; collectivization of peasantry under, 69, 473; failure of, 69; focus of, 473; industry under, 55; political controls over cultural activity under, 372; problems under, 69, 492; railroads under, 547; rapid industrialization under, 69; starvation under, 55
First Party Congress, 293, 296
first secretary (*see also* general secretary), 342
fish: sources of, 539-40; in Soviet diet, 539; Soviet Union as producer of, 540
fishing, 539-40; factory ships used in, 540; fleet, 540, 575; production, 540; source of catch, 539-40
Fishing Industry, Ministry of the, 575, 595
five-year plans (*see also* under individual plans), 492; for science and technology, 632
flexible response: adopted by NATO, 662; defined, 662; Soviet response to, 671
Follow-on-Forces-Attack (FOFA) (United States), 680
Food Industry, Ministry of the, 524
food policy, 522-25
food production: problems with, under Gorbachev, lxii
Food Program of Brezhnev, 524, 533; objective of, 524
food subsidies, 519, 525
food supply: output from animal husbandry, 536-38; problems with, 93, 529; pre-World War II, 529
Foreign Affairs, Ministry of, 345, 407, 409, 410, 438; diplomatic service in, 409; organization of, 410; responsibilities of, 409-10
Foreign Affairs Commission, 356, 357, 408
Foreign Affairs Committee, 356, 357
foreign aid, 410; economic, 410, 415, 431, 438, 601; military, 410, 438; propaganda, 415
foreign economic activity: administration of, 594-95; amount of, 591; borrowing of hard currency, 591; centralization of, 594-95; with communist countries, 591; economic aid programs, 591, 605; with Third World, 591; with Western industrialized countries, 591
Foreign Economic Activity Bank, 457, 600; expansion of activities of, 600
Foreign Economic Relations, Ministry of, 409, 594, 600
foreign policy: assistance to national liberation movements, 402; basic character of, 401-2; under Brezhnev, 90-92; Central Committee departments responsible for, 404-7; change in priorities in, 402; and Comecon, 603; Congress of People's Deputies responsibilities for, 408; Council of Ministers Presidium responsibilities for, 408-9; diplomatic isolation under Stalin, 72; in Eastern Europe, 84, 402; environment for innovation in, 404; ideology of, 401-3; under Khrushchev, 84, 85-87; in

Latin America, 440–41; national security as goal of, 402; in the 1920s, 66–67; in the 1930s, 72–73; objectives of, 401–2; organizations responsible for, 408; Politburo as maker of, 403–4; Presidium responsibilities for, 408; priorities in, 402; in sub-Saharan Africa, 438–40; Supreme Soviet responsibilities for, 408; toward non-Western world, 67; toward Western world, 66–67, 91–92

foreign relations: 406; with bordering states, 403; after the Crimean War, 36–38; with Eastern Europe, 403; East-West, 412; state visits for, 413; with Third World, 403; with United States, 403; with Western Europe, 403

foreign trade, 410, 452, 469, 472, 570; amount of exports and imports, 591, 607; balance of, 612–13, 618; bureaucracy, 594–600; bureaucracy, decentralization of, 599, 600; bureaucracy, problems caused by, 597; with Cambodia, 605; changes in, 594; with China, 604–5; with Comecon, 601–3; commodity composition of, 592; composition of, 613–15; conduct of, 593, 601; deficit in, 606, 607, 610; with Eastern Europe, lxiii; expansion of, 571, 608; exports, 595, 601–2, 603, 605–6; with Finland, 611; fluctuation of trade patterns, 606; free trade zones, 604; imports, 595, 601–2, 603, 606; with Japan, 610–11; with Laos, 605; manner of transactions, 591; methods of, 591; nationalization of, 472; under NEP, 593; with North Korea, 605; operation of, 595–97; organizations (FTOs), 594, 595, 596; origins of, 593; *perestroika* in, 597, 608; restrictions on, by Western nations, 593–94; role of, 591, 619; and self-sufficiency policy, 591, 607; with socialist countries, 601–5; state monopoly on, 593–94; with Third World, lxiii, 592, 612–18; turnover, 599; with United States, lxiii, 607–9; unnecessary delays in, 597; with West, lxiii; with Western industrialized countries, 592, 601, 605–12; with Yugoslavia, 603–4

Foreign Trade, Ministry of, 594, 597, 608; abolition of, 600; FTOs under, 596, 599; functions of, 595; organization of, 598

Foreign Trade Bank, 595, 600

forestry, 538–39; accomplishments of, 539; animal resources in, 539; employment in, 539; industry, 526; product of, 538–39; production, 538, 539; region, 538

forest-steppe zone, 526–27; agriculture in, 527; chernozem soil in, 527; climate of, 527

Fourth Five-Year Plan (1945–50), 474, 552, 566

fractional orbital bombardment system, 689

France, 44, 47, 49, 50, 73, 457; acquiescence of, to Hitler's demands, 73; contributions of, to Soviet chemical industry, 503; in Crimean War, 32; declaration of war on Germany, 73; establishing relations with Japan, 37; as

importer of Soviet gas, 508, 581, 609; involvement of, in Russian Civil War, 61, 63; as member of Cominform, 414; as member of United Nations, 445; nuclear forces of, 417, 420, 444, 690; Russian relations with, 36, 37; Russian wars with, 27, 28; Soviet military alliance with, 73; Soviet relations with, 420, 421–22; state visit by Gorbachev to, 420

Franco-Prussian War, 35

Frank, Peter, 297

Frederick the Great, 23

French Revolution, 26, 27

Friedland, Russian defeat by Napoleon at, 28

Frontal Aviation, 711, 714, 725; aircraft of, 711; helicopters of, 711; mission of, 711; organization of, 711

Front for the Liberation of Mozambique (Frelimo), 439

Fruit and Vegetable Industry, Ministry of the, 524

fruit cultivation, 534–36; harvest, 541; kinds of, 534; volume of, 534

Frunze, 169, 497

Frunze, Mikhail V., 661, 663

fuel, 505–10; availability of, 505; coal, 505; domestic uses of, 505; economy, 490, 503; exports of, 505, 605, 613–14; exchanges, in Comecon, 864; fossil, 112, 510; gas, 505; oil, 505–6; and planning, 505; problems with, 505; reserves of, 505; resource base of, 505; as source of hard-currency income, 505

Fundamental Principles of Criminal Procedure, 761

fur industry, 526, 539

Further . . . Further, and Further! (Shatrov), 394

Galicia, 49, 50, 141, 174

Galicia-Volhynia, 141; as a successor to Kievan Rus', 9

Gandhi, Indira, 436

Gandhi, Rajiv, 436

Gapon, Georgii (Fr.), 45

Gareev, Makhmut A., 663, 671

Garthoff, Raymond L., 664

gas, liquefied, 498

gas, natural, lxxvii, 485, 498, 505, 507–8, 510; deposits of, 489; development of, 605; exports of, lxiv, 508, 592, 605, 606, 609, 618; exports of, amount, 609; obstacles to access to, 488; pipeline, 508, 581; problems with, 507–8; production of, 507; as replacement for oil, 507, 508; reserves of, 507; uses of, 505

gender roles (*see also* women), 230–34

General Agreement on Tariffs and Trade (GATT), 592; observer status requested, 618

General Machine Building, Ministry of, 646, 735

general practitioner, 264
general secretary, 293, 302–6, 342, 344, 348, 409; base of authority and power of, 303; as chairman of Defense Council, 700; client turnover under, 303, 305; cult of leader of, 304; description of, 293; high government offices acquired by, 304; importance of, 302–3; increase of authority by, 303–4; as maker of foreign policy, 403; potential successors to, 305; powers of, 303, 304–5, 343; rights and duties of, 304–5, 702; transfer of authority to, 305
General Staff, lxxvi, 700, 701, 702–3, 705, 712, 719, 743, 749, 877, 883, 885–86; domination of Ground Forces in, 702; and Ministry of Defense, 702; and military production, 665, 734; making war plans, 675
genetics research, 626
Geneva Summit (1985), 418–19, 892
Georgia, 61; early commitment to Marxism in, 155
Georgian language, 180
Georgian Orthodox Church, 188, 199
Georgian Republic, lxx, 61, 102, 154, 254, 362; citrus fruit grown in, 534; drug abuse in, 271; Helsinki watch group established in, 197; major cities of, 156; nationalities in, 156; party apparatus in, 308; Russian language in, 198; sexually transmitted diseases in, 271; tea grown in, 534; tree farms in, 475
Georgians, lxvi, 27, 42, 45, 139, 153, 155–56, 158; distribution of, 155; in higher education, 156; history of, 155; language of, 156; as members of CPSU, 156, 323; national resurgence of, 155, 205; population of, 155; prominent, 156; as scientific workers, 156; urbanization of, 156
German, Aleksei, 392
German army, 74, 75, 145, 148, 150, 877
German Democratic Republic (East Germany), 414, 424, 425, 496, 572, 575, 883, 890; contributions of, to Soviet chemical industry, 503; formation of, 80; Garrisoned People's Police of, 879; intelligence gathering by, 780; labor transfers from, 870; as member of Comecon, 601, 859; military advisers in, 684; nuclear-free zone proposed by, 691; revolution of 1989, lix; satellite communications hookup to, 582; Soviet forces stationed in, 728; Soviet influence over, 423; Soviet relations with, 407; Soviet withdrawal of forces from, 444
Germanic Order of the Brethren of the Sword, 149
German Russians, 27, 124
Germans (Soviet), 149, 151, 152, 164, 166, 168; language of, 183; population of, 183
Germany, 37, 42, 44, 44, 48, 56, 60, 474, 552, 756; Anti-Comintern Pact signed by, 73; in Balkans, 38; contributions of, to Soviet chemical industry, 503; control of Eastern Europe by, 682; declaration of war by, on Soviet Union, 74; division of, 80; influence of, on Baltic nationalities, 147; interests of, in Ottoman Empire, 48; invasion of Soviet Union by, in World War II, lviii, 55–56, 142, 180, 474, 488, 550, 723; occupation of, by Red Army, 877; occupation of Soviet Union by, in World War II, 75–76, 189, 759; as power under Bismarck, 32; as source of Cold War conflict, 80; Soviet military operations against, in World War II, 76; Soviet relations with, 67; trade with, 474; in World War I, 49
Germany (united), lx; emigration to, lxxiv
Gladyshev, Viktor, 785
glasnost' (public discussion), 100, 113, 296, 356, 745, 765, 774; discussion of nationality questions under, 201; East European reaction to, 425; effects of, lix, lxxii–lxxiv; exposure of inadequacies of social services, 244; under Gorbachev, lix, lxxii; in health care, 269; internal security under, 755; journalism under, 379; literature under, 389; loss of control of, lxxiii; opposition to, 389–90; political freedom under, 338; poverty under, 277
Glinka, Mikhail, 31
global zero option, 690
Godunov, Boris, 14; proclaimed tsar, 15
Gogol, Nikolai, 31, 39
Golden Horde, 9, 160, 175, 182, 192; defeated by Russian army, 10
Golodnaya Steppe, 527
Golytsn, 792
Gomulka, Wladyslaw, 880
Goncharov, Ivan, 39
González, Felipe, 422
Good Woman of Szechuan, The (Brecht), 394
Gorbachev, Mikhail S., lx, 125, 205, 255, 209, 301, 304, 305, 311, 348, 366, 417, 446, 693, 735; agriculture under, 520, 524, 529; anti-alcohol campaign of, 270; arms control efforts, 692, 693; arms reductions proposal, 444; assessment of nationalities question, 135; attempt by, to retain power, lxxii; Brezhnev Doctrine repudiated by, 424; call of, for promotion of women and minorities in party, 325; "common European home" speech of, 421; concessions to nationalities by, 202–4; conservative backlash against, 764; crime and punishment under, 790; cultural thaw under, 369, 370, 372–73, 383–84, 389, 392, 394, 397; cuts by, in military budget, 445, 734; *demokratizatsiia* under, lvii, lix, 262, 303, 370; dissidents under, 634; dissolution of Soviet Union under, lxxxi; economic reform under, 314, 467, 479–80, 607, 618–19; economy under, lxiv; efforts to

reduce mortality rate under, 121; environmental concerns under, 113; foreign policy under, 401, 402, 433; formation of commissions by, 301; *glasnost'* under, lix, lxxii, 100, 113, 201, 244, 295, 303, 370, 745, 755; as head of State Council, lxxxi; and independence of republics, lxx–lxxi; individual rights under, 786–87; internal security under, 760; KGB under, 763, 770, 772; lack of support for, lxxviii; and letters to the editor, 379; loosening of party strictures on media and the arts, lxxii; loss of power of, after coup, lxxx; military cuts announced by, 728; military-political relations under, 729; military research and development under, 648, 671; moratorium declared by, on nuclear testing, 418; "new thinking" of, lx, 373, 429, 654; in Nineteenth Party Conference, 296; Nobel Prize for Peace awarded to, lx; nuclear disarmament proposal of, 443–44; overthrow of, lxxviii–lxxix; patronage systems under, 219; *perestroika* under, lvii, lix, lxxviii, 244, 295, 303, 360, 370, 451, 525, 592, 755; and polytechnical education, 246; popularity of, lxviii; post-coup personnel changes by, lxxviii; as president, lxxi; as Presidium chairman, 352, 354; as Presidium member-at-large, 351; purge of old guard by, 763; reduction of armed forces by, lxxvi; reform efforts of, 360, 764; reinstatement of, lxxx; relations with Japanese under, 428; relations with Latin America under, 441; relations with Middle East under, 432; religion under, lxvii, 20–21; restrictions on KGB, 764; salary of, 220; science and technology under, 640, 649–50; Sino-Soviet relations under, 427; socialist legality under, 786; state visits of, 420, 421, 436, 441; summits of, with Reagan, 418–19; technology transfer under, 644, 649–50; Third World policy of, 437; ties with ASEAN under, 437; trade with Comecon under, 603; turnover by, in Central Committee, 297–98; welfare under, 277; and Yeltsin, lxviii

Gorizont satellite system, 585; uses of, 585
Gor'kiy, lxxiv, 108, 497–98, 634, 637
Gor'kiy Railroad, 557
gorkom (city committee): bureau of, 310; composition of, 310–11; economic administration in, 311–12; first secretary of, 311; meetings of, 311; members of, 310; secretariat of, 311; structure of, 310
Gorky, Maksim, 67, 389, 394
Gorno-Badakhshan Autonomous Oblast, 170
gorodskie raiony (urban districts), 361
Gorshkov, Sergei, 678
Gosbank: described, 457; functions of, 595, 632; monopoly of, ended, 458
Goskino, 375, 390–91, 597

Goskomizdat, 375, 597
Goskomizobretenie, 632–33
Goskompriroda, 115
Goskomstat, 461; planning function of, 461
Goskomtrud, 632
Gosplan, 260, 344, 357, 595, 600; control figures established by, 462; described, 461; First Five-Year Plan of, 68; functions of, 595; health care programs of, 263; manpower problems caused by, 250; military research and development under, 647, 734; output quotas of, 69; planning methods of, 461–62, 492; responsibilities of, 461, 630; role of, curtailed, 468; role of, in World War II, 474; training and distribution of specialists by, 250
Gossnab, 595, 600; functions of, 595, 632
Gosstandart, 632
Gostelradio, 375, 582
Goths, 5
government, Bolshevik, lvii, 414; armed forces organized under, 697–98; arts and media controlled by, 372; arts and media used by, to support communism, 371, 377; economy under, 63; effect of, on marriage, 235; newspapers closed by, 371; opposition of, to external economic control, 593; press controlled by, 371; refusal of, to pay World War I debts, 593; repression by, of opponents, 63; revolutionary decrees of, 60; role of railroads under, 547; science setbacks under, 625; socialist society imposed on tsarist Russia by, 472; Vecheka under, 755, 757–58; war communism under, 63; and World War I, 60
government, Soviet: agencies, 345; branches of, 329; constitutional authority of, 331–40; criticism of, lxxii; disengagement from World War I by, 60; functions of, performed by party, 329; head of, 329; hierarchy of, 329; as implementer of policy, 292, 329; leaders of, 340; legislative authority in, 340; party control over, 340–41; and party, distinction between, 292; planning apparatus of, 460–61; as source of party legitimacy, 329; structure of, 340
government, transitional, lxxxi
Grachev, Pavel, lxxix
grain, 530–32; decrease in area allotted to, 531; embargo, 92, 416, 614; feed, 531; as foundation of agriculture, 530–31; harvest, 541; importing of, lxii, lxiv, 532, 592, 606, 615–16; kinds of, 530–31; output, 530; slaughter of livestock to conserve, 531; yields, 531
graphic arts, 397
Great Depression, 473
Great Northern War, 21
Great Patriotic War. *See* World War II
Great Terror, lviii, 71, 139, 392, 397, 759; end of, 755; effect of, on non-Russian nationalities, 164, 172, 196; and technology, 626

Grebenshchikov, Boris, 396
Greece, 49, 80; as importer of Soviet gas, 508
Greek philosophy, 7
Greek Russians, 27
Grenada, 418, 440
Gribachev, Nikolai, 389
Grishin, Viktor V., 305
Gromyko, Andrei, 410
Grossman, Vasilii, 390
gross national product (GNP), 47, 273, 477, 481, 609; military share of, 493
Ground Forces (*see also* under name of service), lxxvi, 661, 672, 676, 677, 697, 705–10, 702, 714, 718, 719, 725, 731, 750; Air Defense of Ground Forces, 708; Chemical Troops, 708–10; combined arms army, 705–6; conscripts in, 743; deployment of, 727; Engineer Troops, 708–9; Frontal Aviation under, 711; general organization of, 703; in General Staff, 705; in Ministry of Defense, 702, 705; mission of, 678–79; motorized rifle division, 706; Motorized Rifle Troops, 706–7; political influence of, 705; Rocket Troops and Artillery, 707–8; Signal Troops, 708–9; stationed in Eastern Europe, 728; tank army, 706; Tank Troops, 707; uniforms and rank insignia of, 737–39
Group of Soviet Forces in Germany, 728, 730, 877
Groznyy, 503
GRU. *See* Main Intelligence Directorate
"Guidelines for the Stabilization of the Economy and Transition to a Market Economy": description of, lxi–lxii; phases of, lxi; reform under, lxi
Guinea, 438, 614; priviliged affiliation of, with Comecon, 616
Guinea-Bissau, 616
Gulag. *See* Main Directorate for Corrective Labor Camps
Gulf Stream, 102
Gumilev, Nikolai S., 381
Guyana, 614

Habomai Island, 428
Habsburgs, 31
hajj, 193
Hanseatic League, 8
Harbin, 44
hard currency, 501, 546, 591, 613; acquisition of, lxiii–lxiv; balance of trade, 613, 614; Comecon dependence on, 862; debt, lxiv; debt, attempt to reduce, 592, 604, 607; defined, 591; earnings, of exporting enterprises, 599; fuel exports to earn, 605, 606–7, 609, 615, 618; loans for, 592; methods of acquisition, 591, 592; need for, 592, 606; responsibility of heads of ministries and enterprises for, 599

Health, Ministry of, 263; emergency first-aid facilities operated by, 266; "fourth department" of, 268; psychiatric hospitals operated by, 268, 782; quotas and standards developed by, 263
health care, 121, 262–73; access to, in Russian Empire, 243; access to, in Soviet Union, 243; alcoholism treatment in, 270; annual budget for, 264; bribes for, 269, 271; of cancer patients, 271; centralization of, 263; of children, 266; death, causes of, 269; death rates, 269; of elite, 268–69; emergency, 266–67; expansion of fee-for-service, 273; facilities, 263, 264; and family size, 125; free, guaranteed by Constitution, 243; hospitalization, 265–66; influence of party on, 263; inpatient, 265–66; under Khrushchev, 243–44; negative trends in, causes of, 270–71; negligence in, 271; in the 1970s and 1980s, 269–73; overbureaucratization, 263–64, 271; payment for routine, 269, 271; percentage of GNP spent on, 273; polyclinics, 263, 264; provision of, 263–69; psychiatric, 263; quality of, lxv; quantitative expansion of, 262, 263, 273; quotas and standards for treatment, 263; of railroad workers' union, 264; reform of, 263, 272–73; in rural areas, 269, 273, 520; as service in unofficial economy, 456; sick leave, 264–65, 276; and social position, 223; socialized, in practice, 268; socialized, principles of, 262–63, 268; staff, 264, 273; statistics on, 268, 269; in urban areas, 269; under Stalin, 243–44, 262; of women, 266; workplace clinic, 264
health care professionals: training of, lxv
Heavy Machine Building, Ministry of, 496
Hebrew, 201, 205
Helsinki Accords, 90, 92, 338, 421; as source of Warsaw Pact erosion, 889
Helsinki watch groups, 197
Hercegovina, 37
Hermitage Museum, 396
Heroine Mother medal, 236
Higher and Specialized Secondary Education, Ministry of, 636
Higher Intelligence School, 778; curriculum, 778
Higher Party School, 321
Hill, Ronald J., 297
Himalaya Mountains, 108
Hindu Kush, 161
Hitler, Adolf, 55, 392, 699; Comintern support for, 72
Holiday of Learning, 254
Holland, 20
Holy Alliance, 29
Holy Roman Empire, 20
Holy Synod, 22, 36, 186
Horn of Africa, 439

Horowitz, Vladimir, 395
hospitals (*see also* clinics, health care, polyclinic complexes), 263; inefficiency of, 266; inpatient care, 265–66; lack of emergency facilities in, 266–67; number of, 265; official specifications for length of stay in, 265–66; psychiatric, 267, 268, 782; shortage of modern medical equipment in, 271; urban complexes, 265
"hot line," 87
Hough, Jerry F., 343
housing supply: allocation of, 222–23; effect of, on family size, 125; planned increase in, 481; problems with, 93; rationing of, 456; in rural areas, 223, 520; shared, 223; shortage, 122; in urban areas, 223
Hua Guofeng, 426
Hungarian People's Army, 881
Hungarian Revolution, 86, 880–81
Hungarians, 8
Hungary, 9, 31, 101, 414, 425, 474, 552, 581, 762, 877, 882, 885; anti-Soviet uprising of 1956, 86, 424–25, 682; contributions of, to Soviet chemical industry, 503; convertibility of currency of, 866; de-Stalinization in, 879–80; labor transfers from, 870; as member of Comecon, 601, 854; Mongol invasion of, 9; occupation of, by Red Army, 877; revolution of 1956–57, 880–81, 882; revolution of 1989, lix; satellite communications hookup to, 582; Soviet forces stationed in, 728; Soviet influence over, 423; Soviet invasion of, 419, 682, 699; Soviet relations with, 407; Soviet treaty with, 877; Soviet withdrawal of forces from, 444
Huns, 5, 160
Hunter's Sketches (Turgenev), 39
Husák, Gustáv, 892
hydroelectric generation, 510; location of plants for, 510, 511
hydrofoils, 545, 570, 572

Iakovlev, Aleksandr N., 299, 300; resignation by, from CPSU, lxviii
Iakovlev, Ivan, 794
Ianaev, Gennadii I., lxxi, lxxix
Iankilevskii, Vladimir, 397
Iaroslav the Wise (Prince); accomplishments of, 7
Iazov, Dmitrii T., lxxix, 663, 729
Ibero-Caucasian language, 156
Iceland, 423
Ideological Department (CPSU), 247, 300, 374; censorship regulated by, 374; function of, 373–74; role of Glavlit under, 374
ideology, 307, 731; role of, 281–82; and science, 633–34; as source of legitimacy, 288
Il'ichevsk, 575

Imperial Army, 698; backwardness of, 35–36
imperialism, 655
imports: of agricultural products, 609; attempts to reduce, 592, 607; of chemicals, 608, 610; of consumer goods, 611, 615; of food, 614; of grain, 608; of high technology, 609, 615; of industrial equipment, 608, 609, 611; of machinery, 615; of metals, 608, 610; of minerals, 614; restrictions on, 593; of ships, 611; from socialist countries, 592; of textiles, 610, 611, 615; of Western technology, 467, 592, 606; from Yugoslavia, 603–4
incentive system, 466
income, 220–21, 471; hierarchy, 220; highest salaries, 220; lowest salaries, 220–21; and prestige, 224; salary ratio, 220; and social position, 219–22; unofficial, 221–22; wage differentiation, 213
India, 37, 86, 99, 116, 435–36, 441; Soviet arms bought by, 614; Soviet economic and military assistance to, 435; Soviet relations with, 429, 433, 435; Soviet technology transfer to, 435–46; Soviet trade with, 612, 614, 615; state visit by Gorbachev to, 436
Indian Ocean squadron, 727
Indian-Pakistani war, 432, 436
individual enterprises, 92; *khozraschet* under, 466, 468
Indochina, 81
Indonesia, 437, 614
industrial centers, 485, 488–90; Donbass, 485; geographic expansion of, 488–90; Kursk, 485; locating, 485; Magnitogorsk, 485; Moscow, 485
industrial complexes, 467, 488–90, 491–92; agro-industrial, 491; chemical and timber, 491; construction, 491; description of, 489, 491; fuel and energy, 491; light industry, 491; location of, 488–89; machine building, 491; metallurgy, 491
industrial cooperation agreements, 605
industrial development, lxxvii, 42
industrial enterprises, 641
industrialization, 125, 127, 397; under Alexander III, 486; of animal husbandry, 538; and gender roles, 230; regimentation and, 71
industrial ministries: abolished by Khrushchev's economic reform, 466; reinstituted by Brezhnev, 466, 627
industrial planning, 492; for metallurgy, 499
industrial production, 472; examples of, 487–88; gross, under Second Five-Year Plan, 473; growth of, 481; problems with, under Gorbachev, lxii; Soviet share of world, 451, 487
industrial research and design system: concentrations of, 635–36; design bureaus in, 494; improvement of, problems with, 495; institutes in, 494; problems with, 494; research facilities in, 494

industry: under Catherine the Great, 486; centralized plans in, 93, 485, 486; decrease in output during World War II, 77–78; development of, 486–87; defense, 457; equipment and machinery for, 495, 602, 606, 608; expansion of, 488; growth in, 475, 481; heavy, 478, 486, 487, 501-2, 627; history of, 486, 488; impact of emancipation of serfs on, 486; importance of, 485; Khrushchev's reforms in, 88, 486; kinds of, 452; location of, 488–89; modernization in, 485; nationalization of, 472, 487; number of enterprises and production associations, 453; output of, 453; party policy statements on, 492; under Peter the Great, 486; priority of, for allocation of materials, 457; raw materials for, 487–88; reform of, 492–93; resources for, 487–91
industry, heavy, lviii, lxxvii
infant mortality, 93, 99, 116–18; distribution of, 116–18; increases in, 244, 269, 270; reasons for, 118
information transfer, 642–45
Ingria, 21
inheritance of property, 235
inland waterways, 545, 566–70; amount of cargo carried on, 566; canals, 545, 566; categories of, by depth, 567–68; development of, 566–67; lakes, 545, 566; length of, in operation, 566; major, 568; passenger transportation on, 566, 570; planning for, 566; reconstruction of, after World War II, 567; reservoirs, 566; river ports and facilities, 569–70; rivers, 545, 566; system of, 567-69
innovation, 637–42; defined, 637; funding for, 640; in a market economy, 637–38; organizational separation and, 638–39, 640; pricing policies and, 638; problems in, 637–40; as reaction to backwardness, 640; response to problems with, 640; in the Soviet economy, 638
In Search of Melancholy Baby (Aksionov), 381
Institute for Nuclear Research, 860
Instrument Making, Ministry of, 496
intelligence gathering, 778–81; active measures, 779–80; under détente, 778; by Eastern European countries, 780; electronic espionage, 779; influence of, on foreign policy, 780–81; *rezidenty* engaged in, 778; on Western technology, 778
intelligentsia, lxv, 39, 211, 216, 370; and the arts, 397; Bolshevik, 213; description of, 212; income of, 214, 220; as nonmanual laborers, 215; perpetuated by education system, 218; position of children of, 211
interbranch scientific-technical complex (MNTK), 499; components of, 641; defined, 641–42; Mikrokhirurgiia glaza, 642; mission of, 642; number of, 641; problems with, 642; Rotor, 642

Interim Agreement on the Limitation of Strategic Offensive Arms, 92, 416, 442, 687
Interior, Ministry of the (tsarist), 35; State Police Department under, 757
intermediate-range nuclear forces: control of, 689–91; defined, 689–90; reductions, 690
Intermediate-Range Nuclear Forces (INF) talks, 417, 444
Intermediate-Range Nuclear Forces Treaty (INF Treaty), 418, 419, 427, 690; contents of, 444, 705, 707; signing of, 444; stipulations of, 691
Internal Affairs, Ministry of (MVD), 267, 268, 301, 760, 761, 766, 781–94; Administrative Organs Department, 785; under Andropov, 782; censorship by, 373; Criminal Investigation Directorate, 783; criticism of, 756; Directorate for Combating the Embezzlement of Socialist Property and Speculation, 783; directorates, 783; functions of, 782–83; history of, 781–82; internal passport, 782; Internal Troops of, 722, 793; judicial system and, 786–90; KGB in, 782; labor camps under, 755, 790; leadership of, 783–85; local branches of, 783; Maintenance of Public Order Directorate, 783; mission of, 755, 771; Office of Recruitment and Training, 783; Office of Visas and Registration, 783; organization of, 783, 784; party control of, lxxiv–lxxv, 785; party influence in, lxix; Political Directorate, 785; predecessors of, 756–60; psychiatric hospitals under, 782; purge of, 763, 785; recruitment for, 785; role of, in coup of 1991, lxxx; role of, in leadership succession, 756; successor to NKVD, 782
internal passport, 782
internal security police (*see also* Committee for State Security) 284; under Andropov, 762–63; under Brezhnev, 762–63, 786; components of, 755; under Gorbachev, 763–65; under Khrushchev, 760–62
internal security troops, 790–93
Internal Troops, lxxvi, 697, 722–23, 794, 747, 756, 793; composition of units, 794; conscripts in, 794; established, 793; mission of, 722, 794; number of, 722; training, 794; uniforms and rank insignia of, 739; wartime missions of, 722–23, 794
International Bank for Economic Cooperation, 869
International Department (CPSU), 35, 403, 404, 404, 414, 779; active measures by, 780; focus of, 407; responsibilities of, 407; support of, for nonruling Communist parties abroad, 407
international front groups, 407, 410, 779
International Information Department (CPSU), 374, 404; functions of, 407

International Investment Bank, 866
International Monetary Fund (IMF), 619
international strategic concerns, 681–85; military, 684–85
Interrepublican Economic Committee, lxxxi
Intersputnik, 582–85
Inturist. *See* State Committee for Foreign Tourism
Iran, 29, 37, 38, 48, 50, 101, 153, 155, 157, 171, 176, 431–32, 569, 593; American and British diplomatic support for, 79–80; invasion of, by Iraq, 431; role of, as military power, 430; Soviet arms agreements with, 431; Soviet relations with, 431–32; Soviet trade with, 612, 613, 618
Iranians, 5, 155, 156, 171
Iran-Iraq War, 432; Soviet goals in, 432
Iraq, 171, 431–32, 582, 603; invasion of Iran by, 431; invasion of Kuwait by, lx; Soviet arms transfers to, 431, 614, 616; Soviet trade with, 612, 616; ties to Comecon, 616, 855; withdrawal of, from Baghdad Pact, 431
Irkutsk, 493, 578, 585
iron ore, 112, 489
irrigation projects, 529; effects of, 529
Irtysh River, 14, 109, 567
Iskra (Spark), 43
Islam: beliefs, 193–94; conversion of Central Asians to, 192; defined, 193; duties in, 193; mullahs, 193–94, 195; number of believers, 184, 191; official recognition of, in Russia, 175; origins of, 192; Quran, 192; *shahada*, 193; Shia, 157, 159, 194; Soviet policy toward, 200–201; "spiritual directorates," 192; Sufi, 195; Sunni, 157, 159, 181, 182, 184, 194
ispolkom (executive committee); defined, 364; size of, 364–65
Israel, 413, 433; emigration to, lxxiv
Istanbul, 186
Italy, 50; contributions of, to Soviet chemical industry, 503; as importer of Soviet gas, 508, 581, 609; as member of Cominform, 414; Russian military campaign in, 28
Ivan I: cooperation of, with Mongols, 12
Ivan III, 13, 139; expansion of Russia by, 12; use of title tsar by, 12
Ivan IV ("the Terrible"), 13–14; break with boyars, 14; division of Muscovy by, 14; psychological profile of, 13; series of reforms begun by, 13
Ivan V, 20, 23
Ivan VI, 23
Izvestiia (News), 585, 597, 600; circulation of, 380; focus of, 380
Izvol'skii, Aleksandr P., 48

Jackson-Vanik Amendment, 608

Jamaica, 614
Janata Party, 436
Japan, 41, 50, 433, 457, 477, 509, 539, 569, 623; Anti-Comintern Pact signed by, 73; contributions of, to Soviet chemical industry, 503; involvement of, in Russian Civil War, 61, 63; Northern Territories (Kuril Islands) ceded to Soviet Union by, 77, 428; as power under Meiji Restoration, 32; rail service to, 558; role of, in putting down Boxer Rebellion, 44; Russian dealings with, 48; in Russo-Japanese War, 44–45; Soviet trade with, 605, 610–11; victory of, over China, 44
Japan, Sea of, 529, 570; ferry on, 575
Jaruzelski, Wojciech, 425
Jassy, Treaty of, 24
Jehovah's Witnesses, 191
Jewish (Yevreyskaya) Autonomous Oblast, 180
Jews, 152, 159, 164, 173, 174, 177–81; as Bolsheviks, 322; Bund founded by, 42; discrimination against, 48, 78, 179, 212, 219; distribution of, 180; effect of German invasion on, 180; emigration of, 124, 608; expulsion of, from Russia, 178; in higher education, 181; history of, 177–78; killing of, 179; language of, 180; as members of CPSU, 180, 181, 323–24; migration of, to Poland, 178; national dissent movement of, 197, 205; Nazi genocide of, in Soviet Union, 76; occupations of, 178; opportunities for, in early Soviet state, 179–80; oppression of, 178; Pale of Settlement and, 24, 178–79; pogroms against, 46, 179; population of, 179, 180; in Russian Empire, 24, 36; as scientific workers, 181; social position of, 219; Soviet concessions to, 205; urbanization of, 139, 180–81
Johnson, Lyndon B., 686
joint enterprises, 594; with Japan, 611
joint ventures, 502, 608; with China, 604; law on, 599, 618; number of, 599; obstacles to, 599; purpose of, 599; Western interest in, 599
Jordan, 432, 433
journalists: number of, 378; party membership of, 378; training of, 378
journals, 381–82; circulation of, 381; controversial articles in, 381; party control of, 381; rehabilitation of writers in, 381–82; "thick," 39
Journey from St. Petersburg to Moscow (Radishchev), 26
Juan Carlos (King), 422
Judaism (*see also* Jews), 184; Soviet hostility toward, 201
judicial system: abuses of, 789; party influence in, lxix
judiciary, 330, 359, 787–88; lay assessors, 359, 788; elected judges, 359, 787–88

"July Days," 58, 59
June 1967 War, 91, 433
Justice, Ministry of, 756, 788

Kabakov, Il'ia, 397
Kabardian-Balkars, 184
Kabul, 430, 720
Kádár, János, 892
Kadets, 46
Kaganovich, Lazar M., 84, 180, 315
KAL 007 shoot-down, 384, 418, 714
Kaliningrad, 101, 540
Kalita (Ivan I), 12
Kalmyk Autonomous Republic, 272
Kalmyks, 164, 167, 184
Kama automotive plant, 498
Kama River, 122, 181, 182, 567, 568
Kamchatka Peninsula, 104, 139
Kamenev, Lev B., 65, 66, 180; accused of murdering Kirov, 70; in show trials, 70
Kansko-Achinsk, 509, 510, 511
Kapto, Aleksandr S., 300
Karaganda, 166, 501; coal reserves in, 508
Karakalpak Autonomous Oblast, 162
Karakalpaks, 162, 163
Kara-Kirgiz Autonomous Republic, 167
Karakum Canal, 527
Karelian Autonomous Republic, 362, 363
Karelians, 184
Karelo-Finnish Republic, 362
Karmal, Babrak, 434
Karpov, Vladimir, 389
Kashka Darya, 527
Kashmir, 435, 436
Katushev, Konstantin F., 600
Kazakh Autonomous Republic, 164, 167
Kazakh Republic, 87, 102, 107, 110, 145, 159, 160, 166, 527, 561; agriculture in, 532; coal reserves in, 508; industry in, 497, 501; legal age for marriage in, 232; metal industry in, 502; nationalist movement in, 204; nationalities in, 164–66, 177, 362; party apparatus in, 307, 308; roads in, 562; virgin land campaign in, 475, 522
Kazakhs, lxvi, 137, 160, 162, 163–67; alphabet of, 166; distribution of, 164–66; emigration of, 164; grievances of, 204; in higher education, 166; history of, 163–64; language of, 166; as members of CPSU, 166–67; as minorities in Kazakh Republic, 197, 362; national resurgence of, 164; population of, 164; rebellions of, against Russian rulers, 164; Russian control over, 163–64; as scientific workers, 166; under Soviet rule, 164; urbanization of, 166
Kazakhstan, 161, 164, 362; economic region, 503, 511
Kazakh Upland, 104
Kazan', 108, 497

Kazan' Horde, 181, 183
Kennan, George F., lxxviii
Kennedy, John F., 86
Kenya, 438
Kerblay, Basile, 220, 224
Kerch', 540
Kerensky, Aleksandr, 58, 59; countercoup attempted by, 60
KGB. *See* Committee for State Security
Khabarovsk, 557, 578, 585
Khar'kov, 497, 557
Khazan' Khanate, 14, 175
Khazars, 5; converted to Judaism, 178; expelled by Oleg, 5
Kherson, 124
Khiva (*see also* Khorzem), 160, 161, 162
Khmel'nyts'kyi, Bohdan, 18
Kholmsk, 575
Khomeini, Sayyid Ruhollah Musavi (Ayatollah), 432, 682
Khorzem (*see also* Khiva), 162
khozraschet (self-supporting operating operations), 466, 468
Khrushchev, Nikita S., 56, 89, 306, 315, 342, 379, 392, 760; agricultural problems under, 93, 522; agricultural reform under, lviii, 87–88, 522, 529, 533; antireligions campaign under, 199, 201; authority of, 84–85; avoidability of war, 661; background of, 82; Comecon under, 860; consolidation of power by, lviii, 84, 288; cult of, 291; cultural thaw under, 372; economic agreement signed with Afghanistan, 434; economic assistance of, to Turkey, 431; economic policies of, 476; economic reforms under, 84, 92, 310, 312, 466, 729; education programs established under, 243–44; elected first secretary, 82; foreign policy under, 85–87; health care programs established under, 243–44; industrial reform under, 476, 486; internal security under, 755, 762; involvement of, in Africa, 438; KGB under, 772; meeting of, with Eisenhower, 86; meeting of, with Kennedy, 86; merger-of-nationalities policy, 196, 197; military force reductions by, 691; military-political relations under, 729; nationalities policies under, 196–97; nuclear war viewed by, 656, 670; ouster of, 56, 88, 476, 662, 782, 861; and peaceful coexistence, 85, 86, 303; and polytechnic education, 246; Presidium's attempt to remove from office in 1957, 84; railroads under, 553; relations with India under, 435; reorganization of security police under, 760; rivalry of, with Malenkov, 82; "secret speech" of, 82–84, 295, 305, 627, 765, 879; science reforms under, 627; virgin land campaign of, 87, 303, 475; visit of, to Yugoslavia, 424; welfare programs established under, 243–44

Kiev, 5, 9, 18, 122, 138, 497, 557; domination of Kievan Rus' by, 6–8; international airport, 578; invasion by Mongols, 9; Orthodox church in, 188–89; Jewish community in, 178, 180

Kievan Rus', 5, 7, 9, 12, 138, 139, 141, 144–45, 147, 174; achievements of, 4; anniversary of adoption of Christianity by, 205; Christianized under Vladimir, 7; decline of, 8; destruction of, 3, 4–5, 8–9; domination of, by Kiev, 6–8; founding of, 5, 6; Jewish community in, 178; legacy of, 5, 10; Mongol invasion of, 9, 10, 12; Muscovy as heir of, 3; organization of, 7; origins of, 3, 4; principalities of, 6; Russian Orthodox Church in, 186; society of, 7–8; successors to, 8–9; Varangians in, 5

Kipchak tribes, 175

Kirgiz, lxvi, 160, 161, 162, 163, 166, 167–69, 174; alphabet of, 168; collectivization of, 168; distribution of, 168; emigration of, 167; etymology of, 167; grievances of, 204; in higher education, 169; history of, 167; language of, 168–69; legal age for marriage in, 232; as members of CPSU, 168, 169, 324; as minorities in Kirgiz Republic, 197; national resurgence of, 168; population of, 168; rebellion of, against Soviet rule, 168; Russian conquest of, 167; as scientific workers, 169; under Soviets, 167; urbanization of, 169

Kirgiz Autonomous Oblast, 167

Kirgiz Autonomous Republic, 162, 164, 167, 168

Kirgizia, 167, 362

Kirgiz Republic, 102, 121, 159, 160, 162, 169, 388; families in, 236; major cities in, 169; nationalist movement in, 204; nationalities in, 168, 183; party apparatus in, 308

Kirilenko, Andrei P., 94, 315

Kirishi, 115

Kirov, Sergei, 759; assassination of, 70, 759

Kirovabad, 159

Kirovakan, 108, 154

Kirov Theater, 393

Kishinev, 175

Klaipeda, 540, 575

Klimov, Elem, 390, 392

Kokand, 160, 161

Kokand Khanate, 167

Kokovtsev, Vladimir N., 47

Kola Peninsula, 104, 423; chemical industry in, 503; metal industry in, 502

Kolbin, Gennadii, 307

kolkhozy. *See* collective farms

Komi, 184, 581

Komsomol, 229–30, 246, 248, 308, 310, 358, 731, 761, 783; endorsement for university admission, 258; KGB lectures to, 772–74; members in armed forces, 733; military training of, 739; quota for deputies to Congress of People's Deputies, 348; recruitment for KGB from, 770; schools administered by, 320

Komsomol'skaia pravda (Komsomol Truth), 380

Komsomol'sk-na-Amure, 493, 557

Korea, 41, 42, 44, 48

Korean War, 81, 475

Kornilov, Lavr, 59

Kornilov revolt, 59

Kosygin, Aleksei N., 88, 436; economic reform program of, 92, 466; as prime minister, 88–89

Kozlov, Aleksei, 396

kraia (territorial divisions), 102, 293, 308, 361, 364, 374; Brezhnev's Food Program in, 524; KGB administrations in, 766

Krasnaia zvezda (Red Star), 380

Krasnoyarsk, 525, 527, 567, 585

Krasnoyarskiy Krai, 536

Kremenchug, 498

Kremlin, 15, 769

Kriuchkov, Georgii, 309

Kriuchkov, Vladimir A., lxxv, lxxix, 765, 777, 781

Krivoy Rog, 488, 501; reduction of resources in, 488

Krokodil (Crocodile), 381

Kronshtadt Rebellion, 63, 286; and war communism, 64

Kruglov, Sergei, 761

Kuchuk-Kainarji, Treaty of (1774), 24; nullified by Treaty of Paris, 36

kulaks: deported to Siberia, 69, 520; described, 69; Stalin's attempt to liquidate, 69, 213

Kulikovo, 10

Kunashir Island, 428

Kurds, 194, 431

Kuril Islands (Northern Territories), 77, 428, 610

Kursk campaign of World War II, 550

Kushka, 101

Kutaisi, 156, 498

Kuwait, 430, 431, 432; invasion of, by Iraq, lx

Kuybyshev, 108, 124

Kuzbass, 501, 509; coal reserves in, 508

Kuznetsov, Vasilii, 352

labor, 454–56; compulsory, under Stalin, 455; nonmanual strata, 215; resources, in Comecon, 870; strikes by, lxxiv

laboratories: branch, 636; problem, 636

labor camps (Gulag): administered by MVD, 755, 790; administered by NKVD, 759

labor force. *See* work force

Labor Savings and Consumer Credit Bank, 458

labor unions, 456

Labytnangi, 558

Ladoga, Lake, 5, 562
Lamaism, 184
land: agricultural, 526; arable, 526, 529; nationalization of, 472; redistribution of, 58; use, 525-29
Land and Liberty (Zemlia i volia), 41
Lane, David, 232, 233
language: Russian as dominant, 197-98; as tool of nationality policy, 197
Laos, 414, 430; satellite communications hookup to, 582; Soviet economic relations with, 601, 605, 612; ties to Comecon, 616, 855
laser equipment, 499, 623
Latin America, 410, 412, 440-41, 571; food imported from, 614; KGB activities in, 780; under Khrushchev, 440; low priority of, under Stalin, 440; Soviet activities in, 441; Soviet influence in, 291, 441, 872; Soviet policy toward, 441; Soviet support for leftist groups in, 440; Soviet trade with, 613, 615-16
Latvia, 73, 147, 179, 363; annexation of, lviii, 397, 473, 682; establishment of independence, 61; incorporation of, into Soviet Union, 150; independence of, lxxxi; Soviet invasion of, in 1939, 74, 550; uprisings in, 45
Latvian Republic, lxx-lxxi, 102, 121, 123, 127, 145, 188, 308, 526; agriculture in, 533; candidates for Congress of People's Deputies, 347; drainage projects in, 529; families in, 236; legal age for marriage in, 232; migration to cities in, 226; nationalist demonstrations in, 201; nationalities in, 146, 150; nationalist movement suppressed in, 759; party apparatus in, 307; religion in, 190, 191; Russification of, 150-51
Latvians, lxvi, 27, 36, 42, 149-51; in higher education of, 151; history of, 149-50; independence movement of, 150; language of, 150; major cities of, 150; as members of CPSU, 151; population of, 150; rebellion of, against Soviet rule, 150; as scientific workers, 151; urbanization of, 150
Lavrov, Petr, 41
Law on People's Control, 360
Law on State Enterprises (Associations), 468, 459; described, 468-69, 641; *khozraschet* under, 468
Law on the State Border, 791
Law on Universal Military Service (1967), 739, 742-43, 749, 791
League of Nations: joined by Soviet Union, 73
League of the Militant Godless, 198
League of the Three Emperors, 37, 38
Lee, William T., 664
"Left Opposition," 66
legal codes, 788-89; civil, 788; criminal, 788-89; principle of analogy in, 789; of 1649, 17; Stalinist, 789

legal profession, 788; advocates, 788; fees, 788; legal advisers (*iuriskonsul'ty*), 788; organization of, 788
legal system: party control of, 787; party influence in, lxix; party interference in, 789; pretrial detention, 789; trials under, 788, 789
Legislative Commission, 25
legitimacy, political, 288-91; defined, 288; diplomatic recognition as source of, 412; election as source of, 288; ideology as source of, 288; party saturation as source of, 289; party schools as source of, 322; patriotism as source of, 289, 290-91; sources of, in communist party, 288-89; sources of, in democratic countries, 288; tradition as source of, 288, 289; well-being as source of, 288
Lena River, 18, 109, 567
lend-lease agreement, 562, 577
Lend-Lease Law (United States), 552
Lenin, Vladimir I. (*see also* Bolsheviks, Communist Party of the Soviet Union), lvii, 71, 303, 320, 623, 624, 648; *April Theses* of, 58; arts and media used by, to support communism, 371, 377; assassination attempt against, 63; background of, 58; as Bolshevik leader, 44, 55, 281, 697; call by, for overthrow of Provisional Government, 58; as chairman of Council of People's Commissars, 60; conception by, of communist party, 282-88; constitution, understanding of role of, 332; control by, of arts and mass media, 369, 370; control justified by, 281; criteria of, for party appointments, 314; criticism of, under *glasnost'*, lxxii, 370, 382; cult of, 291; death of, 65, 66; Decree on Peace of, 401; differences of, with Marxism, 283; dislike of Stalin, 65; and education as political indoctrination, 244, 245; electrification program of, 547; ethos of political thought of, 284; factions denounced by, 65; flight of, to Finland, 59; founding by, of Comintern, 62, 414; founding by, of Russian Communist Party (Bolshevik), 281; and inevitability of war, 653; and international relations, 66-67; interpretation of Marxism, 65; as leader of Bolshevik Revolution, 281; as leader of Soviet state, 65; legacy of, 65, 394; and letters to the editor, 379; merger of nationalities, 196, 197; military theories of, 667; New Economic Policy (NEP) proposed by, 64, 213, 472, 487; position of, in Bolshevik government, 60; science and technology under, 625; social system revolutionized by, 213; stories about, used for political indoctrination, 253; succession to, 288, 304; and Treaty of Brest-Litovsk, 61; Vecheka under, 755, 758
Leninabad, 170
Leninakan, 108, 154

Leningrad (*see also* Petrograd, St. Petersburg), 74, 112, 122, 124, 181, 257, 348, 554, 557, 575, 626,767; apartment sharing in, 223, 233; art in, 396; divorce rate in, 233; emergency health care in, 267; German siege of, 75; industry in, 497; international airport, 578; Kirov Theater, 393; music in, 395, 396; rate of premarital pregnancy in, 234; Russian nationalism in, 205; in World War II, 562

Lenin Mausoleum, 729; ceremonial guard, 723; Stalin's body removed from, 84

Lenin's birthday (holiday), 246

Lermontov, Mikhail, 38

Lesotho, 438

Letters Department (CPSU), 379

letters to the editor, 381; departments for, 380; as influence on public opinion, 380; purpose of, 379; responses to, 380

Liaison with Communist and Workers' Parties of Socialist Countries Department (CPSU), 356, 404; Andropov as head of, 762; responsibilities of, 407

Liaotung Peninsula, 44

liberal arts: orthodox Marxist interpretation of, 72; party control of, during 1930s, 71–72

Liberman, Evsei, 92, 466

Libya, 420, 430, 440, 582; military access to, 727; Soviet arms bought by, 614, 779; Soviet arms deliveries to, 685

Life and Fate (Grossman), 390

life expectancy, 93, 99, 116; declines in, 244, 269; low, causes of, 271

Ligachev, Egor K., 300, 301, 522, 764

Light Industry, Ministry of, 491

Likhachev automotive plant, 497–98

limited sovereignty. *See* Brezhnev Doctrine

Limited Test Ban Treaty (1963), 87, 688

Lipetsk, 497, 501

literature, 388–90; age of realism in, 38–40; under Andropov, 388; under Brezhnev, 94, 388; censorship of, 774; control of, 388; critical realism in, 370; under Gorbachev, 388–89; literary thaw, 388; as model for politicization of arts and mass media, 370; during NEP era, 67–68; under Nicholas I, 31; party control of, 71–72, 370; qualities of, 38; socialist realism in, 388; as source of protest, 369; taboo subjects, 389

Literaturnaia gazeta (Literary Gazette), 380

Lithuania, 3, 9, 10, 12, 14, 42, 73, 147, 179, 308, 363; annexation of, lviii, 397, 474, 682; establishment of independence, 61; families in, 236; incorporation of, into Russian Empire, 147; incorporation of, into Soviet Union, 148; independence of, lxxi; as potential successor to Kievan Rus', 10; Soviet invasion of, in 1939, 74, 550

Lithuania, Grand Duchy of, 141, 145

Lithuania Minor, 147

Lithuanian Republic, lxx–lxxi, lxxix, 102, 121, 123, 127, 254, 526, 575; agriculture in, 533; autonomy sought by, 362; candidates for Congress of People's Deputies, 347; Catholics in, 199–200, 202; drainage projects in, 529; Helsinki watch group established in, 197; infant mortality in, 116; Jewish community in, 178; major cities in, 148; migration to cities in, 226; nationalities in, 146, 148; nationalist movement suppressed in, 759; party apparatus in, 307; Roman Catholic community in, 190; secession by, lxxix

Lithuanians, lxvi, 36, 147–49, 150, 151; distribution of, 148; education of, 148; history of, 147; independence movement, 147–48; language of, 148; as members of Central Committee, 148; as members of CPSU, 148; national dissent movement of, 197; Polonization of, 147; population of, 148; rebellion of, against Russian rule, 147; rebellion of, against Soviet rule, 148; as scientific workers, 148; urbanization of, 148

Litvonov, Maksim M., 73, 180

Liubimov, Iurii, 394

Living Church, 68

living conditions, lxiv

living standards, 451, 478; and availability of consumer goods, 486; effect of economic reform on, 470; of farm workers, 320; planned improvement in, 481

Livonia, 14, 21

Livonian Confederation, 149

Livonian Order of the Teutonic Knights, 149

local wars, 682, 700

Lomonosov, Mikhail V., 23

London, 592

London Straits Convention (1841), 32

Long-Range Aviation, 710

Luanda, Soviet military base in, 685

Luk'ianov, Anatolii I., lxxix, 770

Lunacharskii, Anatolii, 68, 72

Lutheranism, 151, 191

Luxembourg, 592

L'vov, 581

L'vov University, 258

Lysenko, Trofim D., 78, 626

MccGwire, Michael, 664

machine-building and metal-working complex (MBMW), 493, 494, 495, 495–502, 496; contributions of, 496; cooperation of, with electronics industry, 499; locations of, 497; military production under, 493, 646; ministries in, 495–96; *perestroika* in, 496; planning and investment in, 496–97; status of, 495–96; structure of, 495–96; types of products in, 495

machinery: export of, 613; import of, 611, 615
Machine Tool and Tool-Building Industry, Ministry of the, 646
Madagascar, 616
magazines, 381–82; circulation of, 381; controversial articles in, 381; party control of, 381; rehabilitation of writers in, 381–82
magnetohydrodynamic power generation, 511
Magnitogorsk, 509; metallurgical combines in, 501; reduction of resources in, 488
Magyars, 5
Maiakovskii, Vladimir, 67
Main Administration for Aviation Work and Transport Operations, 580
Main Administration for Safeguarding State Secrets in the Press (Glavlit), 373; censorship coordinated for, 375, 774; distribution of representatives, 374; role of, 374; role of, in censorship process, 376
Main Administration for State Insurance, 275
Main Directorate for Corrective Labor Camps (Gulag), 790
Main Directorate for State Security, 758
Main Inspectorate, 702, 730
Main Intelligence Directorate (GRU), 409, 719, 778
Main Military Council, 700, 701; members of, 701; responsibilities of, 701
Main Military Procuracy, 756, 775, 787
Main Organization and Mobilization Directorate, 743
Main Personnel Directorate, 702
Main Political Directorate of the Soviet Army and Navy, 376, 701, 730, 731, 785, 878; and Ministry of Defense, 702; and party control over the armed forces, 730–31, 733
Main Repertory Administration (Glavrepertkom), 391
Makarenko, Anton S., 249
Makat, 561
Makeyevka, 501
Malaia Gruzinskaia street, 397
Malaya, 81
Malaysia, 437; Soviet trade with, 612, 615
Malenkov, Georgii M., 81, 82, 84, 85; economic policies of, 475; as general secretary, 82; as prime minister, 82; resignation of, as prime minister, 82, 475–76; rivalry of, with Khrushchev, 82
Mali, 616
Malta Summit (1989), lx
management: academy in Moscow, 599; skills, acquired from Western trading partners, 608–9
Manchuria, 42, 44, 48
Manchus, 167
manganese, 112
manual laborers (*see also* workers, blue-collar), 217

manufactured goods: exports of, 605–6; imports of, 615
Mao Zedong, 80, 86, 90, 426
Marchuk, Gurii, 637
Marcos, Ferdinand, 437
marine transportation (*see also* under individual means of transport): barges, 545; hydrofoils, 545; ships, 545
Maritime Border Troops, 723
Maritime Fleet, Ministry of the, 597
maritime ports, 574
Markov, Georgii, 389
marriage, 125–27, 231–32; attitudes of non-Russian nationalities toward, 231; common-law, 235; and housing shortage, 232; legal age for, 231–32; of Muslim families, 232–33; pregnancy as cause of, 232; reasons for, 232; roles in, 232–33; roles in, of elite, 232; sharing of housework in, 232
Marshall Plan, 80; Comecon formed as response to, 601; Soviet refusal of assistance from, 78, 474
Marx, Karl, 44, 71, 332, 339, 472, 654
Marxism, 44, 472; advocates of, 40; in Georgia, 155; as intellectually demanding theory, 284; Lenin's alterations of, 283–84; Lenin's attempt to apply, to Russia, 282; rise of, 40–41; summary of, 283
Marxism-Leninism, lxv, lxxv, lxxvi–lxxvii, 86, 90, 291, 304, 423, 693; atheism in, 198; and constitution, 330, 335; defined, 65; characterized as outdated, by Gorbachev, lxxvii; as educational philosophy, 244, 245, 248; effect of, on foreign policy, 402; history interpreted by, 72; inculcation of ideals of, 262; international promotion of, 681; knowledge of, required for candidate degree, 260; law under, 786; lectures on, to armed forces, 731; means of production in, 214; military doctrine of, 653, 654; modifications of, 290; ownership of means of production in, 452; party as sole interpreter of, 284, 289; renunciation of, by former CPSU members, lxviii; as social science, 289, 290; socialist realism and, 369, 372; as source of party legitimacy, 290; in teacher education, 261; training in, 312, 320–22; values of, spread by mass media, 377; war theory of, 654–59, 659–60
Marxism-Leninism on War and the Army: nuclear war as legitimate continuation of politics, 655, 657; nuclear weapons for fighting, 662
Marxist-Leninist Teaching on War and the Army, 657, 663; laws of war in, 658; relationship between weapons and victory, 659
Marxist-Leninist vanguard parties, 414, 429
Masliunikov, Iurii D., 346
mass media (*see also* under individual media): administration of, 373–77; computers, 384–85; contacts by, with West, 419; control of,

hindered by technological revolution, 369, 384, 385; history of party control of, 369; investigative reports by, lxxii; journals, 370, 381–82; Leninist principles for, 371–72; loss of control of, lxxiii; magazines, 370, 381–82; necessity of, to socialist system, 369–70; newspapers, 370, 377–81; party control of, 373–74; party influence in, lxix; politicization of, lxxii, 370–73; radio, lxxii, 370, 382; restrictions on, lxxiii; revolution in, lxxii; television, 370, 382–84; themes in, 370, 373; video cassette recorders, 382–84

Massawa, Soviet military base in, 685

Master and Margarita, The (Bulgakov), 394

maternity benefits, 243, 276

maternity leave, 130, 276

mathematics, 623

Matrosov, Viktor, 791

Matthews, Mervyn, 221, 222

May Day, 246

Mazepa, 141

means of production: advantages of public ownership of, 463–64; and social class, 214; socialist ownership of, lxi, 452

Meat and Dairy Industry, Ministry of the, 524

Mecca, 192

mechanization, 455, 479; workers' ability to deal with, 490

Medical Troops, 739

medicine, Soviet research in, 623

Medina, 192

Medish, Vadim, 260

Mediterranean Sea, 430, 566, 570; nuclear-free zone, 691

Mediterranean squadron, 727

Medium Machine Building, Ministry of, 646, 735

Medvedev, Vadim A., 300

Mendeleev, Dmitrii I., 625

Mennonites, 191

Mensheviks, 43, 58, 60; exile of, 65; in Georgia, 155

merchant fleet (Morflot), 570–76; cruise ships of, 575; expansion of, 571; ferry lines, 575; freighters, Arctic, 572; freighters in, 571; growth of, 571; icebreakers, 572; initial developments, 571–72; intelligence-gathering by, 576; operations, 572–76; size of, before 1960, 671; standardization in, 572

Mesopotamia, 153

metallurgical industry, 22, 94, 492, 499–502, 509; applications in, 500; automation in, 496–97; bottlenecks, in, 501; equipment in, 500; imports for, 606; inconsistent record of, 500; locations of combines, 501; military equipment produced by, 500; in nineteenth-century Russia, 33; nonferrous metals in, 501–2; origins of, 486; plans for, 499, 500–501; problems in, 496–97, 501; products of, 500;

resources for, 489; serious obstacles in, 501; shortage of hard currency in, 501; support of, for heavy industry, 501–2; in twentieth-century Russia, 47

Mexico, 441; ties to Comecon, 855

Meyer, Alfred G., 286

Michael, Grand Duke, 57

microprocessors, 479

Middle East, 50, 171; KGB-sponsored terrorism in, 779; main Soviet goal in, 430; military advisers in, 684, 700; Soviet diplomatic relations in, 413, 432; Soviet influence in, 90–91; Soviet trade with, 615; strategic importance of, to Soviet Union, 430

midwives, medical training for, 268

migration, 130; and birth rate, 123; control over, 122; emigration, 124; impediments to, 122; incentives, 123; influence of climate on, 123; of peasants, 213; profile of migrants, 122–23; rate of, 122–23

Mikhalkov, Sergei, 389

militarized police. *See* Border Troops, Internal Troops

military (*see also* armed forces, Ministry of Defense): budgets, 493, 733–34; design, 735; force requirements, 676; profession, 698; protection of, from economic slowdown, 493; research, 627; role of, downgraded in state ceremonies, 729; schools, 698; share of gross national product, 493; threat assessments, 676

military, minorities in, 746–47; control over, 747; language and, 747; nationality conflict, 746–47; as potentially unreliable, 747

military, women in, 747–48; number of, 747; positions in, 747–48; volunteers, 747; in World War II, 747

military academies: admission, 749; diplomas, 749; examinations for, 749; Frunze Military Academy, 792; Lenin Military-Political Academy, 792; necessity of, for promotion, 749; program, 749; research projects, 749

military advisers to Third World: countries in, 684–85; number of, 684

military art, 668–675; combined arms concept, 672, 677; components of, 654, 668–69; deep offensive operation theory, 672, 673, 888; defined, 666, 668–69; focus of, 666; principles of, 666, 668; revision of, 693; tactics in, 673–75

military boarding schools, 748; cadets in, 748; enrollments, 257; purpose of, 257

military commissariat. *See* voenkomat

military conscripts, 742–48; alcoholism among, 745; assignment of, 743; basic training, 745; bribes for deferment, 743; conscientious objector status, 43–45; conscription period for, 743; daily training of, 745–46; deferment, 743; harvesting by, 746; hazing of, 745; induction of, 743, 745; number of, 739; pay, 745; reenlistment rate of, 746; reserve officer

training program for deferred, 743; turnover, 746
military districts, 724, 725–27; as combined
arms formations, 725; command of, 725;
deployment of, 726; duties of, 725; organization of typical, 726; personnel of, 725; as
response to perceived threats, 725
military doctrine (*see also* military science, military strategy): avoidability of war, 653–54, 661;
basis of, in Frunze, 661; basis of, in Lenin,
660–61; capitalist encirclement, 661; defense-
oriented, lxxvii, 660, 675, 676; defined, 653;
effect of, on arms control, 654; evolution of,
660–62; on fighting a future world war, 661,
663, 681; foundation of, in Marxism-Leninism,
653; and inevitability of war between capitalism and socialism, 653, 661; influence of, 653;
in the late 1980s, 662–64; large forces in, 676;
and military policy, difference between, 665;
military-political component, 660, 664; military-technical component, 660; new concepts
in, 663–64, 693; of nuclear war, 653–54, 662;
and nuclear weapons, 643–54; as offensive, 660,
675; offense-oriented, lxxvii; as party line on
military affairs, 660; of reasonable sufficiency,
663, 664, 676; in support of world socialism,
681; two-camps concepts of, 661; victory orientation of, 660, 664, 673; war plans and, 675;
and weapons programs, 664–65; Western consensus on, 664
military equipment, 495; armored personnel
carriers (APCs), 706–7; infantry fighting vehicle (IFV), 707; inventory of, 707; manufacturing goals, 493–94; tanks, 707; weapons
guidance systems, 499
Military Industrial Commission (VPK), 491–
92, 647, 734, 778
military-industrial complex, 303, 493–94; design in, 735; high technology in, 485; influence of military-technical concepts on,
666; keep-it-simple philosophy of, 494, 735–
37; party influence on, lxxv; priority of, for
resource allocation, 493; as resource drain,
494; top-priority projects in, 493
military industries, 734–35
military insignia, 737–39; of Air Forces, 741;
of Air Defense Forces, 741; of Ground Forces,
740; of Naval Forces, 744; of Strategic Rocket
Forces, 740
military justice, 787
military life: conditions, 745; discipline, 745;
hazing in, 745
military oath, 745
military officers, 212, 748–50; assignment, 748;
criminal offenses, 749; number of, 739, 748;
pay, 749; perquisites, 749; prestige of, 748;
promotion, 748–49; retirement, 749–50;
training system, 748
military operational art, 672–73; concepts shap-

ing, 672; deep offensive operation in, 673,
679, 692; defined, 669, 672
military policy: arms control in, 685, 691; continuity and consistency of, 666; defined, 653,
665; large forces in, 676; influence of, 643;
influence of nuclear weapons on, 665; and
military doctrine, difference between, 665;
military-political component, 665; and military strategy, connection between, 665; military-technical component, 665; modification
of, 666; as political aim of the Soviet state,
660; war plans and, 675
military-political concepts, 656, 665–66; continuity and consistency of, 666; and direction of military technology, 664; influence
of Marxism-Leninism on, 660
military-political relations, 729–730; under
Brezhnev, 729; under Khrushchev, 729; under
Stalin, 729; and resource allocations, 729
Military Procuracy, 739
military production (*see also* military-industrial
complex, Military Industrial Commission),
734–35; management of, 736
military research and development, 646–48; access of, to development facilities, 647; bureaucracy reduced in, 648; civilian facilities
involved in, 646–47; coordinating agencies'
function in, 647; Ministry of Defense facilities' function in, 646; design bureaus in, 735;
effectiveness of coordination in, 648; efficiency of, 646; high priority assigned to, 647;
incremental approach to, 735; keep-it-simple
philosophy of, 494, 735–37; machine-building and metal-working ministries responsible for, 646; political commitment to, 647;
principal organizations involved in, 646–48;
production goals in, 648; productivity of,
647; quality control in, 648; technological espionage for, 737
military reserves, 750
military schools, higher (*see also* military academies): admission, 748; cadets in, 748; curriculum, 748; women in, 748
military science, 660, 666–75; defined, 653,
666; and military doctrine, 669; origins of,
667; principal components of, 666; scientific
forecasting in, 667; theoretical basis for,
lxxvi–lxxvii
military service, 339
military spending. See defense spending
military strategic missions, 675; defensive,
676–77, 680–81; defined, 675; formulation
of, 675; interdependence between defensive
and offensive, 67; offensive, 676–79; overall, 676–77; Soviet vision of, 677
military strategy, 660; against NATO, 887–88;
ballistic missile defense, 671; based on worst-
case scenario, 675, 676; conventional air

operation, 679–80; defense-oriented, 676; defined, 665, 669; deterrence, 670; influence of nuclear weapons on, 665, 669, 675, 677; investigations of, 669; and military doctrine, 669; and military policy, connection between, 665; missions under, 676; new options for, 671; nuclear deterrence as, 660, 670; nuclear war-fighting as, 660; preemptive nuclear strikes as, 673; response to flexible response, 671; space warfare, 671; under Stalin, 669; subordinate role of, 667; unified, 677; victory as goal of, lxxvi, 675; and the Warsaw Pact, 887–88

Military Strategy (Sokolovskii), 662, 665, 670, 680, 689

military tactics, 666, 672, 673–75; basic combat actions, 673; defined, 669, 673; invasion of Afghanistan as test of, 675; nuclear weapons and, 673; orientation of, toward conventional weapons, 673–74; resurgence of, 675; Soviet principles of, 673

military-technical concepts: influence of, on military-industrial complex, 666; prediction of, 667

military-technical sciences, 666

military technology, 623, 735–37

military theater. *See* theater of military operations

military training: of conscripts, 742–48; preinduction, 739–42

Military Transport Aviation, 580, 711–12, 719; airlift capabilities of, 712; missions of, 711–12; organization of, 712

military uniforms, 737–39

Mindaugas (King), 147

ministerial system, 344–46; all-union ministries in, 344–45, 491; internal structures of, 345; party control of, 346; powers of ministries in, 345; republic, 491; union-republic ministries in, 344–45, 491

ministries: military, 491, 493; reaction of, to economic reform, 467

Minsk, 497, 578

mir (commune), 34, 213

Mir space station, 689

missile defenses, 714–16; ABM system around Moscow, 715, 725–27; modernization of, 715

missiles, 891

Mitterrand, François, 420

modernization: in civilian industry, 485; in defense industry, 486; in industry, 485; progress of, 4; under Stalin, 72

Mohamad, Mahathir bin, 437

Mohila (Metropolitan), 19

Moldavian Autonomous Republic, lxx, 174, 363

Moldavian Railroad, 554

Moldavian Republic, lxx, 74, 102, 122, 124, 174, 188, 308, 363, 527; agriculture in, 534, 536; autonomy sought by, 362; families in, 236; legal age for marriage in, 232; major cities in, 175; nationalities in, 146, 174; party apparatus in, 307; population density, 124; Roman Catholic community in, 190

Moldavians, lxvi, 173–75; alphabet of, 174, 205; distribution of, 174; as ethnic Romanians, 173, 174; in higher education, 175; history of, 173–74; as members of CPSU, 175, 324; language of, 174; national resurgence of, 174, 205; population of, 174; as scientific workers, 175; urbanization of, 174–75

Molniia satellite system, 582; as "hot line" backup, 582; as spacecraft transmission system, 582

Molotov, Viacheslav, 73, 81, 84

Monastery of the Caves, 7

Mongol Empire, 3, 160, 175

Mongolia, 101, 414, 423, 427, 433; as burden on Comecon, 871; as member of Comecon, 601, 603; power of, in Comecon, 871; satellite communications hookup to, 582; Soviet economic aid to, 591, 592, 605; Soviet forces stationed in, 728

Mongol invasion, 9, 12, 145, 160, 171; and destruction of Galicia-Volhynia, 9; and destruction of Kievan Rus', 9, 10, 138; impact of, 9–10

Mongols, 181; Golden Horde, 9, 10; role of, in development of Muscovy, 10

Montenegro, 49

Moore, Barrington, 290

Mordvinian Autonomous Oblast, 183

Mordvinian Autonomous Republic, 183

Mordvins, 183; alphabet of, 183; language of, 183; population of, 183; religion of, 183

Morocco, 614

Morozov, Boris, 17

mortality rate, 120–21; among males, 120; efforts to reduce, 121; impact of alcoholism on, 130; increases in, 120; major determinants of, 121

Moscow, 9–10, 12, 122, 124, 140, 180, 186, 257, 314, 557, 561, 585, 626, 767, 792; art in, 396; Bolshevik control of, 60; Bolshevik government moved to, 61; Bolshoi Theater, 393; emergency health care in, 267; as industrial region, 33, 486, 497, 503, 514, 515; management institute established in, 599; missile site around, 680; music in, 395, 396; Napoleon's occupation of, 29; office space in, 599; Russian nationalism in, 205; Sheremetevo Airport, 546; uprisings in, 45

Moscow Air Defense District, 725–27

Moscow Military District, 730

Moscow Navigation Company, 570

Moscow Railroad, 557

Moscow Soviet, 59
Moscow Summit: of 1972, 92; of 1988, 418, 419
Moscow University, 23, 258–59, 770; School of Journalism, 378
Moscow-Volga canal, 566
Moscow-Vorkuta road, 558
Mosfilm studios, 392
Moskovskaya Oblast, 124
Moskovskie novosti (Moscow News), 380–81
mosques, 200–201
most-favored-nation status, 608
Mother (Gorky), 394
Motherhood Medal, Second Class, 236
Motorized Rifle Troops, 705–7; equipment of, 706–7; organization of, 706–7; uniforms and rank insignia of, 738–39
mountain zone, 104; described, 107–8; location, 107–8
Mozambique, 414, 430, 438, 439–40; military advisers in, 684; Soviet military aid to, 439–40, 684; Soviet military base in, 685; Soviet treaty with, 439; ties to Comecon, 616, 855
Mozambique National Resistance Movement (Renamo), 439
Mufid-Zade, Dshamil, 397
Muhammad, 192
mujahidin (Afghan resistance), 435, 700, 711
Mukden, 44
Mukran, 575
Munich, 73
municipal government: civil defense in, 722
Murmansk, 102, 122, 540
Murmansk Railroad, 550
Murmansk-Severomorsk, 727
Muscovy, 10–19, 139, 186; development of, 10–19; eastward expansion of, 18; expansion of, 14, 18–19, 101; as heir of Kievan Rus', 3; historical characteristics that emerged in, 3; influence of, on Russian and Soviet society, 10; influence of, on Soviet Union, lvii; as origin of Russian Empire, 3, 21; rise of, 12; role of Mongols in developing, 10; Russian lands annexed to, 12; war of, with Poland, 18, 141; war of with Sweden, 141; Westernization of, 18–19; territorial expansion of, 16; westward expansion of, 18–19
music, 388, 394–96; classical, 395–96; control of, 395; critical realism in, 370; jazz, 396; *metallisti* (heavy-metal fans), 396; *punki* (punk rock fans), 396; rock and roll, 396; schools of, 247, 257
Muslims (*see also* Islam), 168, 191–95; in Afghan war, 747; Azerbaydzhani, 153, 157; Central Asian, 159; Chuvash, 181; congregations of, 195; cultures of, 194; defined, 193; differences between Shia and Sunni, 194; discrimination against, 212; distribution of, 194–95; divorce of, 233; duties of,

193; ethnic differences, 194; execution of duties in Soviet Union, 193; exemption of, from military service, 162; families of, 212; languages of, 194; marriages of, 232–33; as members of CPSU, 324; mosques, 191–92; number of, 191; rate of abortion among, 234; Russian, 43; Shia, 157, 159; Soviet policy toward, 200–201; "spiritual directorates," 192; Sufi, 195; Sunni, 157, 159, 181, 182, 184; Tatars as elite, 176
Mussolini, Benito, 392
Mustafa-Zadek, Vadim, 396
Mutual Balanced Forces Reduction (MBFR) talks, 692
My Friend Ivan Lapshin (German), 392

Naberezhnyye Chelny, 122, 498
Nagorno-Karabakh Autonomous Oblast, 158, 202
Nagy, Imre, 86, 424, 881
Najibullah, Sayid Mohammad, 434
Nakhichevan' Autonomous Republic, 158
Nakhimov Naval School, 257, 748
Nakhodka, 540
Namibia, 438, 439
Napoleon: defeat of Russians at Austerlitz and Friedland by, 28; defeat of, by Russians, 29; invasion of Russia by, 28–29; Russian alliance with, 28; Russian wars against, 27, 28
Narva, 20
nation, Stalin's definition of, 195
National Air Defense Forces. *See* Air Defense Forces
national assertiveness, 201–5; by Armenians, 202; by Baltic nationalities, 201–2; by Central Asian nationalities, 204; by Russians, 205; by Ukrainians, 202–4
National Command Authority, 680
national élan, 304
Nationalist Party (China), 67
nationalities, 102; under Brezhnev, 197; cultural concessions granted to, 196; dissent movement of 1970s, 197; factors influencing position of, 137; impact of, on Soviet Union, 137–38; importance of language in, lxvii, 197; imposition of Russian language on, lxvii, 196, 197–98; intermarriage among, 219; under Khrushchev, 196–97; major, in Soviet Union, 102; merger-of-nationalities policy, 196, 197; and nationality groups, 135; patronage systems among, 219; position of, after coup of 1991, lxxxi; religion identified with, 198, 199–200; resistance of, to Russian language, 198; resistance of, to Soviet rule, lxvii; rights of, under Constitution, 195; Russification of, 196; self-government, 195; and social position, 218–19; Soviet policy on, 195–98; Stalin's definition

of, 195; under Stalin, 196; struggle of, for independence, lxviii; union republics of, 196
nationalities question: background of, 135; Gorbachev's assessment of, 135; increased animosity under Soviet rule, 135–37
nationality problems, lvii, 3, 27; ethnic diversity and, 27; in union republics, lxx
nationalization: by Lenin, 213, 472
national liberation movements, 697
national security: and foreign policy, 401, 402; importance of heavy industry to, 487; political and military aspects of, 663; Soviet military intervention in Eastern Europe for, 682
National Socialist German Workers' Party (Nazi Party): Comintern support for, 72
National Union for the Total Independence of Angola (UNITA), 439
natural resources (*see also* raw materials), 112–13; exploration and development of, 112; joint exploitation and development of, by Comecon, 868; major mineral deposits, 114; fossil fuels, 112; Soviet imports of, 871
Naval Aviation, 718, 727; aircraft carriers, 718; antisubmarine warfare by, 718; kinds of aircraft, 718; mission of, 718; as support for Naval Infantry, 718
naval fleets (*see also* under individual fleets): composition of, 727; force of, 727; organization of, 727
Naval Forces (*see also* under individual branches), lxxvi, 570, 576, 672, 676, 677, 684, 697, 716–19, 720; Coastal Defense Forces, 719; fleets, 727–28; flotillas, 727; general organization of, 703; Main Staff of, 727; mission of, 678; Morflot as component of, 576; Naval Aviation, 718; Naval Infantry, 718–19; as part of strategic nuclear forces, 678; role of, 678; squadrons, 727–28; submarine forces, 716–18; uniforms and rank insignia of, 737–39; weapons of, 678
Naval Infantry, 718–19, 727; components of, 718; missions of, 718; ships and equipment of, 718–19
naval squadrons (*see also* under individual squadrons), 727–28; forward deployments of, 727–28
Nazi-Soviet Nonaggression Pact (1939), lviii, 55, 73, 74, 77, 142, 148, 474, 550, 699
Nechaev, Sergei, 40
Nedelia (Week), 381
Nehru, Jawaharlal, 435
NEP era: art and literature during, 67–68; description of, 67–68; elite class developed in, 213; end of, 66; family under, 68; religion in, 68; security police under, 758
Nerchinsk, Treaty of, 18
Neryungri, 489, 558
Netherlands, 581

neutralism, 419, 420
neutrality, 423; positive, 423
neutron bomb, 444
Neva River Basin, 5
New Economic Policy (NEP), 65; abandoned, 472; defined, 64; described, 472, 487; foreign trade under, 593; introduced, 758; NEP man, 64; proposed by Lenin, 64, 472
New Enterprise Law, 600
New International Economic Order, 446
newly industrialized countries, 430
new Soviet man, 245, 281; as goal of party, 290
newspapers (*see also* under name of individual paper), 377–81; all-union, 377–78, 379; circulation of, 378, 380; closed by Bolshevik government, 371; controlled by Bolshevik government, 371–72; focus of local, 379; letters to the editor in, 379–80; new formats and issues in, 378–79; number of, 377; proscribed topics, 379; style of reading, and party membership, 378; regional, 378, 379
new thinking, 373, 654; and military policy, 663
New Zealand, 605
Nicaragua, 90, 430, 440, 582; Soviet military aid to, 684; Soviet trade with, 612; ties to Comecon, 616, 855
Nicholas I, 30–32, 33, 179; censorship under, 30; death of, 32; emphasis of, on Russian nationalism, 30; foreign policy under, 31; suppression of revolutions by, 31; Third Section (secret police) under, 30, 757
Nicholas II, 44, 46, 50, 392; abdication of, lvii, 57; conduct of government handed to Aleksandra, 57; duma formed by, 283; execution of, 63; involvement of, in World War I, 57
Nigeria, 438; privileged affiliation of, with Comecon, 616; Soviet trade with, 612, 613, 615
Nikon, 19
Nikonov, Viktor P., 300
Nineteenth Party Congress, 81, 637
Ninth Chief Directorate (KGB): responsibility of, 767; Security Troops under, 793
Ninth Five-Year Plan (1971–75), 476–77, 532
Nixon, Richard M., 92
Nizhnekamsk, 502
Nizhniy Tagil, 501
Nizovtseva, Alla A., 298
NKVD, 758–59, 782; economic functions of, 759; labor camps administered by, 759; powers of, 759; role of, in Stalin's purges, 70, 759; role of, in Trotsky's murder, 70
Nobel Prize for Literature, lxxii
Nobel Prize for Peace, lx, lxxiv
nobility, 212
Nobles' Land Bank, 35
nomenklatura (appointment authority), lxxiv, 301, 307, 311, 313–16, 348; Council of

Ministers' authority of, 346; Council of Ministers selected by, 341; criteria of, 314; defined, 218, 313; economic, reduced under Gorbachev, 314; editorial staff selected under, 374; history of, 314; lists for, 314; of party, 340; and patron-client relations, 313–14; for procuracy, 359; province-level, 308; as source of party power, 282, 329; for science, 634; supervised by CPSU general secretary, 303; for Supreme Soviet, 358

Nonaligned Movement, 434

noncommissioned officers, 746; lack of, lxxvi; number of, 739; as percentage of armed forces, 746; training of, 746

non-Russian nationalities: attitudes of, toward abortion, divorce, and marriage, 231; discrimination against, 212; urbanization of, 219

Noril'sk, 104

North Africa, 430

North America, 571, 680

North Atlantic Treaty Organization (NATO), lx, 420, 421, 422, 423, 430, 431, 444, 693, 710, 750, 781, 891; arms reductions, 692; condemnation by, of Soviet invasion of Afghanistan, 434; Eastern Europe as buffer against, 728; flexible response concept adopted by, 662; formation of, 80; military strategy of, 679, 680; military strategy against, 679; nuclear weapons of, 680, 690, 691; offensive against, 682; relations of, with Warsaw Pact, 403, 419; as target of war, 679; threat of, to Warsaw Pact, 891; Warsaw Pact as counterweight to, 875

North Caucasus Military District, 727

Northern Caucasus Railroad, 557

Northern Fleet, 727

Northern Group of Forces, 877

Northern Lights pipeline, 581

Northern Territories (Kuril Islands), 77, 428, 610

North Korea. *See* Democratic People's Republic of Korea

North Sea, 423, 566, 680

North Yemen. *See* Yemen Arab Republic

Norway, 101, 422–23, 575

Novgorod, 5, 8, 12; ascendancy of, 8; character of, 8; and Mongol invasion, 9

Novosibirsk, 265, 493, 557, 567

Novosti, 373; focus of, 375–76

Novyi mir (New World), 381–82, 388, 389, 390

nuclear deterrence: defined, 661; to justify Khrushchev's troop cuts, 661

nuclear disarmament (*see also* arms control), 419; proposal for, by Gorbachev, 443–44; proposal for, by Reagan, 444; proposed by Soviet Union, 442, 691; proposed by United States, 442; rejected by Soviet Union, 442

nuclear forces: of Britain, 417, 421, 444, 690;

of France, 417, 420, 444, 690; of West Germany, Soviet fears of, 421

nuclear-free zones, 413, 419, 691

nuclear parity, 92, 401, 442, 671, 681, 693, 699

nuclear power, 481, 510, 511, 512, 869; export of technology for, 611; self-sufficiency in, for Comecon, 603

nuclear testing, moratorium on, 418

nuclear war, 86, 392, 413, 418; as beyond politics, 656–57; civil defense after, 721; as continuation of politics, 655–56; deterring, 687; devastation of, 670, 681; effect of preemptive strike in, 673; importance of preemptive strike in, 670, 671, 673; Khrushchev's view of, 85; limited, 662, 664, 671; Malenkov's view of, 85; possibility of, 671; scenarios, 670, 671, 678, 686, 687; Soviet military doctrine on, 653–54, 662; Soviet victory in, 662; strategy for, in 1950s, 669–70; transition to strategy for, 670; unprovoked not likely, 664; victory in, 671, 673

nuclear weapons, 423, 442–43, 671, 699; deep offensive operation using, 673; defense against, 681; development of, 627, 669; effect of, on operations, 672–73; effect of, on strategy, 669, 677; fractional orbital bombardment system, 689; in general war, 670; and inevitability of war, 653; limits on strategic, 442; manufacture of, 735; as means of destruction, 673; as means of deterrence, 443, 670; military efficacy of, 662–63; missiles, 676, 687–88, 690, 710–11, 716; NATO's, 416, 417, 444, 680; reductions in, 676, 690, 692; Soviet, 416, 417, 421, 427, 444; Soviet refusal to provide, to China, 426; United States, 690

nurses, 268, 273

Nystad, Treaty of, 21

Ob' River, 14, 18, 109, 567, 581

obkom (oblast committee), 297; bureau of, 308; bureau membership, 308–9, 324; effect of party reform on, 309; first secretary of, 309–10; members of, 308; positions in, 308–9; secretaries, 310

oblasts, 293, 361, 364, 374; Brezhnev's Food Program in, 524; civil defense in, 721; defined, 102, 308; described, 102–4; KGB administrations in, 766; number of, 308; *obkom*, 308; party conference of, 308

Oblomov (Goncharov), 39

obrazovanie (formal education), 245

occupation (*see also* socio-occupational categories): manual labor, 223; prestige of, 223–24; professional and technical, 223; role of earning in, 224

October Manifesto, 46

October Railroad, 550, 554, 557

October Revolution. *See* Bolshevik Revolution

Octobrists, 46, 47
Oder-Neisse line, 421
Odessa, 26, 122, 181
Ogaden region, 439
Ogarkov, Nikolai V., 663, 665, 678, 679, 729
Ogonek (Little Fire), 381
oil, lxiv, lxxvii, 112, 430, 431, 476, 485, 487, 505–6; arms traded for, 613, 615, 618; drilling, 506, 611; drilling equipment, 506; export of, lxiv, 592, 601, 605, 606, 609, 615; exports of, amount, 609; replaced by gas, 508; pipeline system, 506, 580–81, 860; prices for, 602–3, 865; production level, 505; refining centers, 506; reserves of, 505–6, 584; reexports of, 615, 618; uses of, 505
Oka River, 124
Okhotsk, Sea of, 428, 505
Okhrana, 36, 47
okrug (territorial subdivision), 361, 766
Oktiabr' (October), 382, 390
Okudzhava, Bulat, 389
Old Believers, 19; discrimination against, 48
Old Bolsheviks, 70
Old Church Slavonic, 190, 199
Oleg, 5, 7
Olekminskly Raion, 529
Olympics: boycott of Moscow, 92, 416; Moscow complex, 721
Oman, 432; obstacles to access to, 488
Omsk, 502, 567
One Day in the Life of Ivan Denisovich (Solzhenitsyn), 392
"On Measures for Improving Management of External Economic Relations," 597
"On Questions Concerning the Creation, on U.S.S.R. Territory, and the Activities of Joint Enterprises, International Associations, and Organizations with the Participation of Soviet and Foreign Organizations, Firms, and Management Bodies," 599
"On the Changeover of Scientific Organizations to Full Cost Accounting and Self-Financing," 640–41
operational art and tactics. *See* military operational art, military tactics
Operation Barbarossa, 699
Opium War, Second, 37
oprichnina, 14
optics, 499
Ordzhonikidze, 561
Ordzhonikidze, Sergo, 156
Orel, 497
Orenburg, 508, 581
Orenburg natural gas project, 868–69
Organisation for Economic Co-operation and Development (OECD), 609
Organization of Petroleum Exporting Countries (OPEC), 615, 865; Soviet trade with, 616–18

Organization of the Islamic Conference; condemnation by, of Soviet invasion of Afghanistan, 434
Orguz Turks, 171
Orlov, Aleksei, 24
Orsk-Khalilovo, 501
Orthodox Church. *See* Eastern Orthodox Church, Russian Orthodox Church
Osetrovsk, 567
Osh, 169
Oskol, 501
Ossetians, 184, 194
Ostpolitik (Eastern Policy), 421
Ostrovskii, Aleksandr, 39
Ottoman Empire, 32, 36, 43, 49, 50, 153; fall of Constantinople to, 13; German interests in, 48; as inspiration for Armenian revolutionaries, 42–43; wars of, with Russia, 20, 21, 23, 24, 25, 32, 37–38
Ottoman Turks, 20, 153
Outer Mongolia, 48
Outer Space Treaty, 688, 689
overbureaucratization, 277; in education, 248; of medical services, 263–64, 271; in schools, 262

Pacific Fleet, 727
Pacific Ocean, 3, 101, 102, 109, 112, 139, 489, 540, 546, 566, 570, 571, 575, 719
Pacific region, 412
Pacific rim, 570
Pahlavi, Mohammed Reza (Shah), 431
Pakistan, 108, 434, 435; secession of East from West, 436; Soviet trade with, 613
Pale of Settlement, 24, 178–79
Paleologue, Sophia, 13
Palestine, 91
Palestine Liberation Organization, 779
Pamiat, 205
Pamir Mountains, 108, 139
pan-Islamic movement, 43
pan-Turkic movement, 43
Paraguay, 413
paramedics, 264; medical training for, 268
Paris, 592
Paris, Treaty of (1856), 36, 37
Party Building and Cadre Work Department (CPSU), 301, 314, 731
party commission, 731
party committees: indoctrination of personnel by, 769
Party Conference: Eighteenth, 295; Nineteenth, 295, 296, 304, 311, 482
party conferences, 295–96; goals of Nineteenth, 296; importance of, 295–96; meetings of, 295; province-level, 308; resolutions of Nineteenth, 296

party congresses (*see also* under individual congresses), 71, 292, 293–95; attendance at, 293; defined, 293; delegates, 293; economic plans presented at, 460; events, 295; frequency of, 293–95; industrial policy statements at, 492; notable, 295; turnover rate at Twenty-Seventh, 297; turnover rate at Twenty-Sixth, 297

party control: in the armed forces, 697, 730–33; of art, 369, 371, 372; of film, 390; of government, 340–41; hindered by technological revolution, 369; of journalists, 378; justification for, 370; of legislative system, 347–48; of mass media, 369; of military-technical policy, 666; of Ministry of Internal Affairs, 785; of music, 395; of science, 633–34; of society, 281, 282; of society justified, 281

Party Control Committee, lxxxi, 292, 298

party members: candidate, 317–18, 321; demographics of, 289; disciplinary action against, 319; educational level of, 323; full, 318, 321; number of, 322; obligations for, 318; occupations of, 281; peasant, 323; professional, 323; rights of, 318–19; training of (*see also* party schools), 316, 320–22; white-collar, 323; working-class, 323

party membership, 316–22; benefits of, 218, 319–20; dues and fees of, 317–18; ethnic groups in, 322, 323–24; necessary for advancement, 218, 316; occupational status of, 322–23; and political power, 211, 218; professionals in, 322; proportional representation in, 322; requirements for, 316; selection procedures for, 317–20; social composition of, 322–25; standards for admission, 317; of teachers, 248; women in, 322

party-organizational work, 307, 731

party organizations, city- and district-level, 310–12; composition of, 310–11; economic administration in, 311–12; first secretary of, 311; members of, 310; science and technology under, 633–34; secretariat of, 311; structure of, 310

party organizations, republic-level, 306–7; first secretaries of, 307; members of, 307; second secretaries of, 307; secretariats of, 307; structure of, 306–7

party political work, 731

party program, 295; 1986, proletarian internationalism in, 684

Party Rules, 295, 299, 379; Central Committee described in, 296; factions banned by, 288; on members' obligations, 318; on members' rights, 318; on party congresses, 295; on party hierarchy, 292, 308; on party membership, 297; on primary party organizations, 312

party schools: higher, 321; intermediate-level, 320–21; primary, 320; purposes, 321–22

Pasternak, Boris, 382, 390

patron-client relations, 313–14, 315–16; Brezhnev's as example, 315–16; factors in, 315; loyalty in, 315; and *nomenklatura* 313–14, 315–16; policy-making implications of, 316; replacement of patron by client, 315

Paul, 27; assassination of, 28; reign of, 27–28

Pavlodar, 497, 503

Pavlov, Ivan P., 625

Pavlov, Valentin, lxxix

peaceful coexistence, 85, 86, 303, 412, 413, 416; defined, 402; as foreign policy goal, 402; nuclear deterrence as cause of, 661

peaceful road to socialism, 440

Peasant Land Bank, 35

peasants, lxv, 26, 33, 51, 93, 211; collectivization of, 148, 150, 151, 758; education of, 35; enserfment of, 149, 151; legal status of, 17; as party members, 323; and Populist movement, 40; private plots of, 473, 476, 522; reform of court system for, 47; resistance of, to collectivization, 69; seizure of land by, 472; social position of, in Russian Empire, 212–13; starvation of, by Stalin, 69, 520

Pechora Basin, 558; coal reserves in, 508–9

pedagogy, 249–50

pensioners: continuing to work, 274; income of, 221, 274; number of, 274

pension system, 274–75; eligibility, 274; new law for, 275; long-service pensions, 275; personal pensions, 275

Pentecostals, 191

People's Commissariat of Foreign Affairs, 410

People's Commissariat of Foreign Trade, 593, 594

People's Commissariat of Internal Affairs. *See* NKVD

people's court, 359

People's Democratic Party of Afghanistan (PDPA), 434

People's Democratic Republic of Yemen (South Yemen), 414, 432; military advisers in, 684; military access to, 727; observer status of, in Comecon, 616; satellite communications hookup to, 582; Soviet arms bought by, 614; Soviet arms deliveries to, 685; Soviet military base in, 685; Soviet trade with, 613; ties to Comecon, 855

People's Will, 41, 44

perestroika (restructuring), lvii, lxi, 115, 451, 480, 515, 542, 764, 765; changes in economy under, 592; contract brigades under, 525; demands of, for industry, 492–93; East European reaction to, 425; effects of, lix, lxiv; in foreign trade, 597; of health care, 263; individual productivity as target under, 490; in industry, 486, 495, 496; internal security under, 755; in military industry,

494; problems with, lvii, lxxviii; reaction to, lix; resistance to, 490–91, 492; of science and technology, 640; of schools, 244, 246–47, 256, 262; of trade, 608

Perm', 124

permafrost, 104

permanent revolution, 66

Persian, 172

Persian Achaemenid Empire, 160, 169

Persian Armenia, 153

Persian Empire. *See* Persian Achaemenid Empire, Persian Savafid Empire

Persian Gulf, 412, 430, 603

Persian Savafid Empire, 153

Peru, 441; Soviet aid to, 441

Peter I (the Great), 4, 19, 26, 28, 30, 139, 150, 161, 171; Academy of Sciences founded by, 624; annexation of Azerbaydzhan by, 157; ascension of, to throne, 20; drive for Westernization by, 22, 625; governmental structure under, 21–22; Grand Embassy of, 20; industries developed under, 22, 486; military accomplishments of, 20; reign of, 20–22; Russian Orthodox Church under, 186; succession to, 22–23; Table of Ranks of, 21, 212; taxes levied under, 22; youth of, 20

Peter II, 23

Peter III, 23; deposed by Catherine II, 23; murdered, 23–24; reign of, 23

Petersen, Phillip, 679

petrochemical industry, 502–3; joint ventures in, 502; plants in, 502–3; products of, 502–3

Petrograd (*see also* Leningrad, St. Petersburg), 51, 697

Petrograd Soviet of Workers' and Soldiers' Deputies, 57; Bolshevik domination of, 59; contravention of Provisional Government by, 57–58; joint rule of, with Provisional Government, 57–59; "Order No. 1," 58; reaction of, to "July Days," 58

Petroleum Refining and Petrochemical Industry, Ministry of the, 493

Philippines, 437

physicians, 264; medical training for, 268, 272–73; improvement in quality of medical training for, 273; poor quality of training for, 271; prestige of, 224; research by, 268, 273; salaries of, 217, 224; women as, 221, 268; work load of, 263–64

physicians' assistants, 264; medical training for, 268, 273

physics, 623

Pioneers, 230, 246; military training of, 739

pipelines, 546, 580–81, 584; amount transported, 580; first, 580; gas, 581, 609, 721; materials for, 606; oil, 580; technology transfer for, 644–45

Pipeline Troops, 721

planning: agencies for, 453, 629; allocation of resources under, 460; bargaining in, 462; complexity of, 465–66; among Comecon members, 866–70; difficulty of maintaining control over, 469; for machine-building and metal-working complex, 496, 500–501; prices established by, 460; reform of, 465–69; reform of, under Khrushchev, 466; for science and technology, 629–32; targets in, 460, 500; worker participation in, 462

Planning, Budgeting, and Finance Commission, 357

planning, economic, 357

planning, long-range: for end of the twentieth century, 481; norms of, 468; period covered by, 460

planning, short-range: kinds of, 460; period covered by, 460

plans: annual, 460, 638; coordination of Comecon, 867–68; five-year, described, 460; production, 460, 462; review and revision of draft, 462

plastics industry, 502

Plekhanov, Georgii, 41

Pobedonostsev, Konstantin, 36

Podgornyi, Nikolai, 88; as chairman of Presidium, 89

podmena (substitution), 292

pogroms, anti-Jewish, 46

Poland, 3, 9, 14, 15, 17, 18, 24, 42, 61, 62, 86, 101, 141, 151, 179, 414, 424, 425, 552, 575, 581, 862, 883, 890; army of, under Soviet control, 877; Belorussia ceded to, 145; de-Stalinization in, 879–80; Hitler's invasion of, 73; influence of, on Baltic nationalities, 147; influence of, on Muscovy, 19; intelligence gathering by, 780; Jewish migration to, 178; Latvia ceded to, 149; martial law imposed in, 610; as member of Comecon, 601, 854, 859, 871; Mongol invasion of, 9; nuclear-free zone proposed by, 691; occupation of, by Red Army, 877; October 1956 riots in, 880; partition of, by Catherine II, 24, 145, 190; partition of, by Hitler and Stalin, 73, 474; revolution of 1989, lix; satellite communications hookup to, 582; Solidarity trade union movement in, 90, 229, 425; Soviet forces stationed in, 728; Soviet influence over, 423; Soviet invasion of, in 1939, lviii, 74, 550, 682, 699; Soviet treaty with, 877; Stalin's desire for influence in, 77; Ukraine ruled by, 141; uprisings in, 45, 424; war of, with Muscovy, 18, 141; in World War I, 49

Poland, Russian, 29, 42; anti-Russian uprising in, 31; constitution granted to, 29; as industrial area, 33; partition of, 24; reduced to province, 31; in World War I, 49

Poles, 8, 24, 36, 45, 124, 138, 146, 148, 152, 178; as Bolsheviks, 322; discrimination against, 48; rebellion of, against Russia, 147; rebellion of, against Russification, 42

police (*see also* Committee for State Security, internal security police): under Brezhnev, 782; criticism of, 782; *militsiia* (uniformed police), 783, 794; separated from security police, 782

police state, tsarist: defined, 756; foundations of, 756–57; impediments to, 757

policy: formation, 292–93, 633–34; implementation, 292–93

Polish Counter-Reformation, 18

Polish-Lithuanian Commonwealth, 145, 147, 178

Polish People's Army, 880, 891

Polish Socialist Party, 42

Polish-Soviet War (1920–21), 62

Polish Succession, War of, 23

Polish United Workers' Party, 425, 880

Politburo (*see also* Presidium), 65, 88, 292, 298–300, 303, 305, 315, 330, 341, 343, 346, 347, 358, 629, 665, 702, 729, 764, 764, 781; authority of, 330; Central Committee's authorities delegated to, 296; defense minister as member of, 729–30; as determiner of foreign policy, 401; financial planning by, 632; formation of, 298; KGB control by, 769; as maker of foreign policy, 403–4, 409; members of, 299, 324, 783, 785; membership in, accession to, 299; membership of, in Secretariat, 300; nationalities represented on, 140; newspaper reports on, 379; *nomenklatura* authority of, 313; as policy maker, 292, 628; power of, 299; purpose of, 298–99; role of Defense Council in, 700; salaries in, 220; under Stalin, 71, 81; trends characterizing, 299–300

political action groups: conservative, lxix–lxx; liberal, lxix–lxx

Political Consultative Committee (Warsaw Pact), 879, 884–85, 889, 891; Committee of Minister of Foreign Affairs, 885; functions of, 884–85; Joint Secretariat, 885; organization of, 884–85

political indoctrination, 880; in armed forces, 697, 877, 880; defined, 244; in education, 243, 244, 250, 262; in Hungary, 881; in preschool, 253; reinforcements of, 245

political rights, lxxiv

Polonization: of Belorussians, 145; of Lithuanians, 147

Polovtsians, 8

Poltava, 20, 21

polycentrism, 414–15

polyclinic complexes (*see also* clinics, health care, hospitals), 263

polymers, 502

polytechnical education, 244; components of, 246; as creator of classless society, 247; focus

of, 258; importance of, 246–47; practical training in, 246, 250

Ponomarev, Boris, 407

Popular Movement for the Liberation of Angola (MPLA), 439

Popular Unity (Chile), 440

population, 99, 115–30; able-bodied, 119; age, 119–20, 123; birth rates, 118, 119; causes of death, 120; censuses, 115–16; "center of gravity" of, 124; density, 124–25, 126; disasters decreasing, 99–100, 118–19; distribution of, 101, 108, 124–25; divorce, 125– 27; and economy, 119; family, 125–27; fertility, 121; government reaction to problems of, 130; growth, 116, 118, 119, 125; importance of demographic issues, 100; infant mortality, 116–18, 244; life expectancy, 116; marriage, 119, 125–27; migration, 122–24; mortality, 120–21; in 1940, 119; in 1959, 119; in 1989, 116; policies, 127–30; problems, 127–30; rural, 224; of Russians, 127; in Russian Republic, 102; sex ratio, 118, 119–20; sex structure, 119–20, 123; urban, 224; urbanization, 121–22, 224; vital statistics, 116–19

Populist movement, 43; goals of, 40; leaders of, 40; terrorism in, 41

Populists (Narodniki), 40

Port Arthur, 44

ports, categories of, 576

Portugal, 422, 435, 439

Portuguese Communist Party, 422

Postnikov, Mikhail M., 250

post offices, 585; censors in, 585; inspection of incoming parcels in, 585

potatoes, 533–34; area occupied by, 533–34; cultivation of, 533; harvest, 541

Potsdam Conference, 80

poverty, 221; benefits, 276–77; among pensioners, 274; number of Soviet citizens living in, lxiv

Power Machinery Building, Ministry of, 493

Poznań, 424

Prague, 720

Prague Spring, 425, 882–84; international reaction to, 884; outcome of, 883–84; Warsaw Pact exercises in preparation for, 882–83

Pravda (Truth), 311, 371, 378–79, 390, 415, 585, 682, 764; circulation of, 380; focus of, 380

preemptive nuclear strike, 690, 692

Premilitary Training Directorate, 742

preschool, 251–53; academic preparation in, 251–53; enrollment, 251; extended day care, 251; kindergartens, 251; locations of, 251; number of institutions, 251; nurseries, 251; political indoctrination in, 253; problems in, 253

Preservation of Public Order, Ministry for the (MOOP) (*see also* Ministry of Internal Affairs), 782
presidency: creation of, lxxi; effect of, lxxi; powers of, lxxi
Presidential Council: dissolved, lxxii; formed, lxxi
Presidium chairman (of Supreme Soviet), 352–53; duties of, 352; power of, 352; responsibilities of, 352–53; status of, 352
Presidium of the Supreme Soviet, 81, 82, 84, 88, 268, 292, 333, 335, 339, 340, 347–48, 350, 351–52, 358, 702, 761; chairman of, 352–53; composition of, 330; decrees by, 351, 760; as creator of Defense Council, 700; first deputy chairman, 352; foreign policy responsibilities of, 408; KGB established by, 760; and law, 359; as leading legislative organ, 351; members of, 351, 629; powers of, 351–52; as steering committee for Supreme Soviet, 351
price reform, lxi
prices: under Comecon 1978 *Comprehensive Program*, 864–65; effect of subsidies on, lxiv, 470; government policy for setting, lxiv, 470; increase of food, 525; manipulation of, 470, 476; reform of structure of, 470, 599, 618
prikazi (government departments), 17, 21
primary party organizations (PPOs), 281, 292, 298, 310, 311, 312–13, 341, 346, 731; authority of, 282; and economic plan, 313; decisions of, on applications for party membership, 317; number of, 312; party meeting of, 312; secretary of, 213; stimulation by, of production, 313; tasks of, 312
Primorskiy Krai, 529
Principles of Legislation on Marriage and the Family of the USSR and the Union Republics, 234
Private Life (Raizman), 391
private plot: defined, 522; output of, 522
Procuracy, 301, 335, 359–60, 756, 783, 787; description of, 787; functioning of, 359, 787; purge of, 763; responsibilities of, 360, 771
procurator: defined, 359; general, 359; role of, 330, 787; supervision, 760–61
production, 624; organizations, 634–37; organizational separation and, 638–39, 640
production associations, 453
production facilities, 635; functions of, 635; organizational separation and, 638–39, 640; pilot plants in, 635
productivity: method for improving, 451–52; need for improving, 478; under *perestroika*, 490
professional revolutionaries: necessity for, 283–84; party as, 281, 282
Progressive Bloc, 50
Prokhanov, Aleksandr, 390

Prokhorov, Aleksandr, 623
proletarian internationalism: defined, 402; effect of, on current foreign policy, 402; and Soviet intervention in Third World, 684
proletarian populism, 389
pronatalist policy, 125
Propaganda Department (CPSU), 404, 407; power of, 374
property, personal ownership of, 453
prostitution, 234
Protestants, 184, 191; growth in number of, 200
Provisional Government, 59; downfall of, 59–60; formation of, 55, 58; joint rule of, with Petrograd Soviet, 57–59; Lenin's call for overthrow of, 58; loss of popular support for, 59; membership of, 57, 58; overthrow of, by Bolsheviks, lvii; Petrograd Soviet's contravention of, 57–58; popular uprising against, 58; prosecution of World War I by, 58; reforms under, 58; right-wing challenge to, 59
Prussia, 24, 31, 32, 147; end of Russian alliance with, 38; as member of Quadruple Alliance, 29; Russian alliance with, 23, 37; Russian invasion of, 23, 49; Russian relations with, 36
Pskov, 57
psychiatry, 263; abuses of, 267; hospital-prisons, 267; number of hospital beds for, 268; outdated, 267; possible reform of, 268; statistics, 268; as treatment for political dissenters, 267
Pugachev, Emelian, 25
Pugachev Uprising, 25–26
Pugo, Boris K., lxxv, lxxix, 298
purges by Stalin (*see also* Great Terror), 55, 70–71, 78, 382, 761; of diplomats, 410; of East European leaders, 80; effect of, on elite, 213; initiated, 70; of Kirgiz members of CPSU, 168; of military, 698–99; of party members, lviii; reasons for, 70–71; revealed in "secret speech," 84; role of police in, 765; of scientists, 626
Pushkin, Aleksandr, 31, 38
Pushkin, Boris, 597

Qasim, Abd al Karim
Quadruple Alliance, 29
Quartermaster Troops, 739
Quran, 192

radio, 546; audience, 382; growth of, 582; international, 382; jamming of broadcasts, 382; Soviet, 382
Radio Free Europe/Radio Liberty, 382
Radio Industry, Ministry of the, 646

radios, 499
Radiotechnical Troops, 714, 715
Radishchev, Aleksandr, 26
Raduga satellite system, 585; uses of, 585
Rahr, Alexander, 300
raikom (*raion* committee): bureau of, 210; composition of, 310–11; economic administration in, 311–12; first secretary of, 311; meetings of, 311; members of, 310; secretariat of, 311; structure of, 310
railroads, 545; automated signaling equipment, 554; Baykal-Amur Main Line, 557–58; cargo on, 546–47; centralized train control, 554; classification yards, 554; computerization in, 554; electrification of, 547, 552, 554; equipment of, 554–56; expansion of, 547, 553, 554; freight traffic, 548, 553; heavily traveled axes, 557; history of (1913–39), 546–48; improvements, 552, 553; length of operating lines, 548; lessons learned from Soviet-Finnish war, 550; limits of, 553; major, 560; marshaling yards, 554; mission of, under Lenin, 547; in nineteenth-century Russia, 33; names of, 554; nationalization of, 547; network of, 546, 553; organization of, 554–56; passengers on, 547; passenger traffic, 548, 553, 556–57; in postwar period, 552–54; problems, 548, 552, 553; purpose of, lxiii; in Soviet-Finnish War, 550; in World War II, 550–52
Railroad Troops, 721
railways, metropolitan (metros), 561
Railways, Ministry of, 554
raion (territorial subdivision), 104, 225, 310, 361, 364, 766; Brezhnev's Food Program in, 524; civil defense in, 721–22
Raizman, Iulii, 391–92
Ramadan, 193
Rapallo, Treaty of, 67
rapid medical assistance system, 266–67
Rasputin, 50; assassination of, 51
Rasputin (Klimov), 392
Ratmanova Island (Big Diomede Island), 101
Razumovskii, 300
Reagan, Ronald W.: "Reagan Doctrine" of, 404; Soviet-United States relations under, 416; summits of, with Gorbachev, 418–19
Rear Services, lxxvi, 702, 720–21; conscripts in, 743; mission of, 720–21; number of, 720; organizations in, 720–21
reasonable sufficiency, lxxvii, 663, 692, 693, 729
recording equipment, 499
Red Army (*see also* armed forces, Soviet), 55, 142, 148, 150, 154, 155, 158, 170, 171, 176, 472, 723, 758, 875, 876; in Civil War, 698; control of non-Russian Soviet republics by, 64; egalitarianism of early, 698; formation of, 697–98; Kronshtadt Rebellion put down by, 63; modernization of, 698; NKVD in,

759; occupation of Eastern Europe by, 877–78; organized by Trotsky, 61; professionalization of, 698; under Stalin, 698; in World War II, lviii, 75, 550–52
Red Guard, 426, 697
Red Sea, 439
Red Square, 291, 714, 729
Red Terror, 63, 758
reform, 452, 624; in research and development, 640
reform, economic. *See* economic reform
Reformation, 186
rehabilitation: of banned artists and writers, 370; of scientists, 627; of Stalin's victims, 84
regional agro-industrial associations (RAPOs), 524
Reinsurance Treaty (1887), 38
religion (*see also* under individual religions): diversity in, 27; under Gorbachev, lxvii; identified with nationality, 198, 199–200; under Khrushchev, 199; under NEP, 68; number of believers, 184; repression of, lxvii; repression of, under Stalin, 72; resurgence in, under Brezhnev, 94; Soviet attempts to control, 198–99; Soviet attempts to eliminate, 198; Soviet attempts to exploit, 198–99; Soviet policy on, 195, 198–201; Soviet repression of, 198, 199–201; under Stalin, 198–99
religious groups (*see also* under individual denominations), 184–95
Remington, Thomas F., 322
Renaissance, 186
Repentance (Abuladze), 392
Republic of Korea (South Korea), 81, 413, 433, 714
republics (*see also* under individual republics): government of, 363–64; legal status of, 362–63; new union, 362–63; original, 362; planning in, 464; requirements for status as, 362
"Requiem" (Akhmatova), 382
research, 624; applied, 626; and development, 641; equipment, inadequacy of, 639–40; expansion of, 627; genetics, 626; institutions, 638–39, 640, 665; laboratory, 635; in NEP era, 625; organizational separation and, 638–39, 640; organizations, 634–37; vessels, 575–76
reserve officer training programs, 748
residence permits, 456
resources (*see also* natural resources), 547; allocation of, problems in, 491; exhaustion of, 485, 488; industrial, 487–91; restricted availability of, 99, 488; uneven distribution of, 99
retail outlets, 456
revolutionary democracies, 428–29, 438
revolutionary tribunals, 372
revolution of 1905, 4, 45–46, 147, 176; causes of, 45

revolution of February 1917, 55, 56–57, 145, 147, 164, 171, 174, 176, 179; description of uprising, 57; economic change following, 213; social change following, 213
Reykjavik Summit (1986), 418, 419, 690, 892
rezidenty (KGB employees abroad), 777, 778; guidelines for, 778
Reznichenko, Vasilii G., 675
Riga, 150, 201, 497, 540, 561
river fleet: air-cushion vehicles, 569, 570; barges, 569; cargo vessels, 569; hydrofoils, 569; icebreakers, 569; passenger vessels, 569; specialized vessels, 569; special-purpose ships, 569; tugboats, 569
River Fleet, Ministry of the, 567
rivers, 108–9, 122; cargo transportation on, 545–46, 566; cargo vessels, 546; facilities on, 569–70; international ferries, 546; kilometers of, 566; passenger liners, 546; ports on, 569–70, 571; research ships, 546
roads, lxiii; density, 562; networks, 562, 565; poor condition of, 530, 545, 562–65; problems caused by unpaved, 545; surfaces of, 562; unsurfaced, 562
Road Troops, 721
robots, 479; importance of, to industry, 499
Rocket Troops and Artillery, 707–8; artillery pieces, 707–8; missiles, 707; organization of, 707; uniforms and rank insignia of, 738–39
Rogers, William, 692
Roman Empire, 173
Romania, 49, 50, 73, 86, 90, 101, 174, 363, 414, 425, 474, 552, 575, 877, 885; as member of Comecon, 601, 854, 860, 871; occupation of, by Red Army, 877; reaction of, to Soviet invasion of Czechoslovakia, 884; revolution of 1989, lix; satellite communications hookup to, 582; Soviet influence over, 423; Soviet invasion of, in 1939, 550; Soviet relations with, 407; Soviet treaty with, 877
Romanians, Moldavians as, 173, 174
Roman Mstislavich (Prince), 9
Romanov, Alexis, 17, 20
Romanov, Filaret, 17
Romanov, Grigorii V., 305
Romanov, Mikhail, 17
Romanov Dynasty, 15–18, 139; overthrown, 51, 139
Romans, 155
Roosevelt, Franklin D., 77
Rostov, 8, 12
Rostov-na-Donu, 124, 265
Rostropovich, Mstislav, 395
Rotmistrov, Pavel A., 670
ruble, 591, 599; convertibility of, 618, 866; defined, 457; function of, 865–66; under price reform, lxi
Rügen, 575

rural society, 224–26; agriculture as major employer in, 225; agricultural machinery specialists in, 226; collective farm markets in, 456; cooperatives in, 456; culture, 224; demographics of, 226; divorce rate in, 233; economy, 224; *golovki* in, 225; housing conditions, 224; influx of urbanites, 227; migration to the city, 226; nonpolitical elite, 226; role of party in, 225; structure of, 225–26; teachers, 226; tractor drivers in, 226; travel, 225; and urban society, differences between, 224–25; urbanization of, 226; white-collar workers in, 226; women in, 226
Rurik, 5, 8
Rurikid Dynasty, 5, 10, 12; end of, 15; organization of Kievan Rus' under, 7; succession in, 7
Ruska Pravda (Russian Truth), 7
Russia: territorial expansion of, 16; war of, with Sweden, 141
Russian autocracy, evolution of, 12–13
Russian Central Asia (*see also* Central Asia, Soviet Central Asia), 161, 162, 167, 171
Russian Communist Party (Bolshevik) (*see also* All-Union Communist Party (Bolshevik), Communist Party of the Soviet Union, Russian Social Democratic Labor Party), 55, 61, 64, 698; composition of, 322; consolidation of authority by, 64–65; as constitutional rulers of Russia, 332; control of non- Russian nationalities by, 64; as engine of proletarian revolution, 283; founding of, by Lenin; intellectuals as professional revolutionaries, 283–84; Lenin's conception of, 282–88; as professional revolutionaries, 281, 282; as sole interpreter of Marxist ideology, 281, 282
Russian culture, 196; influence of Western culture on, 4; special status of, 140
Russian Empire, 101, 138, 139, 142, 153, 167, 182; agriculture in, 33, 530; alliances of, 23, 37–38; annexation of Georgian lands by, 155; attempted reforms in, 47–48; automotive transportation in, 561; dismantled, lvii, 61, 150; education in, 249; economy of, 27, 33, 47, 50; expanding role of, in Europe, 23; expansion of, 29, 36–37, 41; foreign affairs of, 41; foreign policy goals of, under Alexander II, 37–38; genesis of, under Peter the Great, 21; impact of military victories of, 21; incompetence of, in World War I, 50; incorporation of Lithuania into, 147; industry in, 33; influence of, on Soviet Union, lvii; literacy rate in, 243; as member of Quadruple Alliance, 29; Napoleonic wars of, 27, 28; nationalities problems origins in, 135; origins of, in Muscovy, 3, 10–19, 21; as police state, 756; population growth in, 33; power of, 27; problems of, 26–27; railroads in, 546–47; role of, in putting down Boxer

Rebellion, 44; social categories in, 212; territorial expansion of, 16; territory gained by, in World War I, 50

Russian Far East, 41

Russianization, 137

Russian language, 127, 219; in armed forces, 747, 748; in Georgian Republic, 198; in school curriculum, 254; special status of, 140, 197; as tool of national unification, 196, 197–98

Russian nationalism: emphasis of Nicholas I on, 30; in literature, 389; after World War II, 78

Russian navy, creation of, 20

Russian Orthodox Church (*see also* Holy Synod), 17, 30, 36, 68, 184, 190, 291, 624; autonomy denied to, 48; characteristics of medieval, 186; convents of, 188; number of active churches, 188; establishment of, 15; incorporation of, into government structure, 22, 186–88; infiltration of, by KGB, 199; as instrument of Russification, 199, 200; under Khrushchev, 199; as manifestation of Russian nationalism, 205; monasteries of, 186, 188; number of believers, 188; origins of, 186; under Peter the Great, 186–88; schism in, 19, 186; Soviet attempts to eliminate, 198; Soviet cooperation with, 198–99; Soviet repression of, 198; under Stalin, 198–99; in World War II, 75, 198–99

Russian Republic, lviii, lxviii, 64, 87, 121, 123, 125, 139, 154, 162, 164, 166, 183, 184, 293, 361, 389, 412, 497, 561, 567; agriculture in, 533, 534, 536; alcoholism in, 270; area of, 102, 139; autonomous republics in, 176, 181; Code of Criminal Procedure, 761, 771, 775, 789; death following abortion or childbirth in, 271; DOSAAF clubs in, 734; drainage projects in, 529; families in, 236; fertility in, 121; forestry in, 538; infant mortality in, 116; irrigation projects in, 529; Jewish community in, 180; KGB in, 766; migration to and from, 123; minorities in, 137, 145; party apparatus of, 140, 306, 308; population of, 102, 127; roads in, 562; Roman Catholic community in, 190; tree farms in, 475

Russians, 3, 5, 8, 135, 138, 151, 158, 162, 163, 164, 174, 182; declining birth rates among, 125, 127; distribution of, 139; divorce of, 233; dominance of, lxvi, 138–39, 747; dominance of, in high positions, 140; education of, 218; in higher education, 140; history of, 139; membership of, in CPSU, 140, 219, 323, 324; membership of, in Politburo, 140; nationalist movement among, 205; and non-Russians, tensions between, 388; population, lxvi; as republic party first secretaries, 307; as percentage of Soviet population, 102; population of, 137, 139; social advantage of,

218; urbanization of, 139–40

Russian Social Democratic Labor Party (*see also* Russian Communist Party (Bolshevik)), 42, 43, 61, 296–97; Bolshevik faction of, 57; Menshevik faction of, 57; politburo formed by, 298–99

Russian Soviet Federated Socialist Republic (*see also* Russian Republic), 332, 333, 362

Russian Turkestan, 167

Russification, 4; under Alexander III, 36; Central Asians' resistance to, 159; presaged by Catherine II, 25; rebellion against, 42; Russian Orthodox Church as instrument of, 199; under Stalin, 154, 154

Russo-Japanese War, 4, 44–45, 428; acceleration by, of political movements, 45

Rust, Mathias, 714, 729

Ruthenian language, 10

Ryazan', 12, 497, 511

Rybakov, Anatolii, 390

Ryzhkov, Nikolai I., 341, 356, 603

Sacharov, Vadim, 397

Saddam Husayn, 431

St. Petersburg (*see also* Leningrad, Petrograd), 22, 23; "Bloody Sunday" in, 45; as industrial region, 33

St. Petersburg Soviet, 57

St. Sofia Cathedral (Kiev), 7

St. Sofia Cathedral (Novgorod), 7

Sakhalin, 45, 418, 611, 714

Sakharov, Andrei, lxxiv, 634, 637

Saliut space program, 582, 689

samizdat, 197, 389

sanatoriums, 267

San Stefano, Treaty of (1878), 38

Sarai, 9

Saratov, 497

Saratovskaya Oblast, 561

Sardinia, in Crimean War, 32

Saudi Arabia, 432

savings accounts, 458; amounts in, 458

Savinkin, Nikolai, 769

Savkin, Vasilii E., 658

Sayano-Shushenskoye, 511

Scandinavia, 3, 612; Soviet objectives in, 423; Soviet relations with, 422–23

Schnittke, Alfred, 395

schools: abuses in, 261; administration of, 247; centralization of, 243, 247; differences between rural and urban, 251; excessive bureaucracy in, 262; failure of, to meet labor needs, 261; formal academic education in, 246; higher education, 257–60; KGB lectures to, 772–74; kinds of, 250; preschool, 251–53; problems in, 261; reform of, 262; secondary education, 253–56, 742; special education, 257; upgrading vocational education and labor training in, 249

schools, specialized secondary, 742; enrollment, 256; major fields of study, 256; school reform in, 256, 262
Schools for Young Communists, 321
Schools of the Fundamentals of Marxism-Leninism, 320
school system: administration of, 247; administrative organs of, 247–48; structure of, 252
science: administration of, 628–33; under Brezhnev, 94; Comecon cooperation in, 869–70; commitment to, 623; curriculum for, 649; directions of, 632; financing of, 632–33, 640–41; and ideology, 633–34; implementation of plans for, 630; influence of, on party decisions, 634; Khrushchev's reforms in, 627; literature abstracts, 633; long-term goals and, 624, 632; mixed results of commitment to, 623–24; necessity of growth in, 623; orthodox Marxist interpretation of, 72; party control of, during 1930s, 71–72; planning for, 629–32; policy making for, 628–29, 633–34; problems in training, 649; problems of, 624; and production, connection between, 641; severance of ties with West, 626; short-term goals and, 624; spending on, 715; under Stalin, 625–26; training in, 648–50
Science and Education Institutions Department (CPSU): educational policies instituted by, 247; as monitor of Academy of Sciences, 628–29
scientific production associations (NPOs), 494–95; defined, 641; number of, 641; problems in, 641
scientific research institutes (NIIs), 494, 503, 636; focus of, 634–35; number of, 635; research laboratories under, 635
"Segodnia v mire," 383; audience, 383; format, 383
sculpture, 396–97
Scythia, 173
Scythians, 5
sea lines of communication, 678
sea routes, 574
Second Chief Directorate (KGB): foreign intelligence role of, 777; responsibility of, 767
Second Five-Year Plan (1933–37), 69, 473, 548
secondhand stores, 456
Secretariat (CPSU), 88, 292, 300–301, 314, 403, 404, 762; Central Committee's authorities delegated to, 296; departments of, 301; lines of authority in, 300–301; military research and production under, 647; as party bureaucracy administration, 292; as policy implementer, 292; as policy maker, 292–93, 628; political weight of, 300; power of, 300; role of, 300; State and Legal Department, 769; supervision of arts and mass media by, 373
"secret speech," 82–84, 305, 424, 627, 760
Security Council, lxxii

security sections, 757
Security Troops, 756; number of, 793; organization of, 793; tasks of, 793
self-employment, under 1977 Constitution, 453
self-sufficiency: in agricultural production, 529; in industrial raw materials, lxxvii, 488, 603; as reason for low level of foreign trade, 591; as socialist goal
Seljuk Turks, 155
sel'sovet (village soviet), 225
Semichastnyi, Vladimir, 762
Senate, 35
Serbia, 49, 50
Serbo-Ottoman war, 37
Serbs, 138, 146
serfdom, 26, 27; abolition of, 212; Radishchev's attack on, 26; sanction of, by government, 17
serfs, 33; dissatisfaction of, with outcome of emancipation, 34; emancipation of, 4, 34, 35, 486; Ukrainians as, 141
Serov, Ivan, 761
Sevastopol', 32, 540
Seventeenth Party Congress, 295
Seventh Chief Directorate (KGB): responsibility of, 767
Seventh-Day Adventists, 191
Seven Years' War, 23
sexually transmitted diseases, 269, 271
Seychelles, 616, 727
shamanism, 184
Shaposhnikov, Eugenii, lxxix, lxxx
Shatalin, Iurii, 794
Shatrov, Mikhail, 394
Shchelokov, Nikolai, 316, 782
Shcherbyts'kyy, Volodymyr, 299, 316
Shchetinin, M., 250
Shelepin, Aleksandr, 761, 762
Shevardnadze, Eduard A., 156, 346, 410, 422, 428, 437, 441, 682; resignation by, from CPSU, lxviii
Shevchenko, Arkady, 778
Shikotan-to Island, 428
Shilinski, Dmitrii, 397
Shipbuilding Industry, Ministry of the, 496, 646
ships, 545; freighters, 571–72; import of, 611; passenger fleet, 572
Shostakovich, Dmitrii, 395
show trials, 70
Shubkin, Vladimir N., 250
Shuiskii, Vasilii, 15
Siberia, 99, 101, 102, 108, 110, 125, 139, 176, 194, 433, 546, 550, 553, 566, 567, 581, 727; age-sex structure in, 123; agriculture in, 529; Aeroflot service to, 578; climate and terrain of, 100, 110, 112; coal reserves in, 508; Decembrists exiled to, 30; deportation of purged party members to, 70; economic development of, 479; electric generation in, 510;

exploitation of resources of, 41, 488, 611; forestry in, 538–39; gas in, 609; kulaks deported to, 69; lack of electricity in, 510; lack of road service facilities in, 565; location of industry in, 488, 497; metal industry in, 502; migration to and from, 122, 123; mountains of, 107; natural resources in, 113, 485; obtained by Muscovy, 18; oil reserves in, 506; railroad construction in, 558; railroads in, 547; relocation of workers to, 490; roads in, 562; virgin land campaign in, 475, 522; water resources in, 108; winter in, 558
Siberian Development Program, 490
Siberian Division (Academy of Sciences), 636, 640
Siberian Khanate, 14, 175
Signal Troops, 708–10; equipment of, 709; mission of, 709; organization of, 708–9
Sikhs, 436
Simferopol', 557
Sino-Indian war, 435; Soviet neutrality during, 435
Sino-Japanese Treaty of Peace and Friendship, 426
Sino-Soviet relations, 80–81, 407, 426–27, 571; border clashes, 426; breakup of, 415, 426, 604; Brezhnev's attempt to reconcile, 426, 427; decline in, 90; under Gorbachev, 427; mutual defense treaty, 81; negotiations to improve, 426–27; resumption of, 604; and Soviet relationship with India, 435–36; Soviet withdrawal of troops from Chinese border, 604; trade, 604
Sino-Soviet Treaty of Friendship, Alliance, and Mutual Assistance, 426
Sixth Five-Year Plan, 476
Sizov, Leonid G., 785
Slavic culture, 3, 4, 10
Slavic nationalities (*see also* under name of nationality), 138–46
Slavophiles, 30–31
Slavs (*see also* East Slavs, South Slavs, West Slavs), 127, 138, 168; birth rates of, 118; dominance of, 138, 218, 747; influence of, in development of Kievan Rus', 6; origins of, 5
Sliun'kov, 299
Slovaks, 138, 146
Slovenes, 138
smoking: campaign against, 270; efforts to reduce, 121, 270; health problems of, 270; number of smokers, 270
Smolensk, 17
Soares, Mário, 422
socialism, 40, 331, 480
"socialism in one country," 66, 593
socialist competitions, 228–29, 471
socialist internationalism, 683
socialist legality, 786–87; under Gorbachev,

786–87; under Stalin, 786
socialist morality (*see also* communist ethics): defined, 246, 262; schools as molders of, 246
socialist orientation, countries of, 429
socialist ownership, lxi; environments of, 452; forms of, 452
socialist parties, 42
socialist property, 331, 339, 771
socialist realism, lxxii, 71–72, 370–71, 372–73; defined, 369, 372; demands of, 372; interpretation of, under *glasnost'*, 371, 397; in literature, 389–90; as official party doctrine, 372; under Stalin, 372
Socialist Revolutionary Party, 45, 57, 60, 63; exile of members of, 65
socialist virtues: examples of, 245
social mobility, 226, 227–28; under Brezhnev, 227–28; and cronyism and nepotism, 227; downward, 227–28; effect of *perestroika* on, 227; and geographic mobility, 227; Russian language necessary for, 227, 228; slow progress of, 227, 228; as source of party legitimacy, 289–90; under Stalin, 227
social organizations, 228–30; examples of, 212; sports organizations as, 230; trade unions as, 228–29; youth organizations as, 229–30
social position: and allocation of housing, 222–23; benefits of, 219–24; determiners of, 211; and income, 211; and nationality, 218–19; and party membership, 218; role of education in, 217–18
social sciences: institutes for, 257; orthodox Marxist interpretation of, 72; party control of, during 1930s, 71–72
social structure: changes in, in industrializing economy, 213; male-female relationships, 231–34; self-perpetuation of, 211–12
society (*see also* under individual categories): classes in, 214; cleavages in, 215; formation of, 212–15; socio-occupational categories in, 211; stratification of, 214, 215–27
socio-occupational categories, lxv, 211; agricultural workers, 217; blue-collar workers, 217; elite, 216; manual laborers, 217; white-collar workers, 216–17
Socotra: Soviet military base in, 685
Sofia, 20
soft-currency goods, 603
Soiuz pipeline, 581
Soiuz space program, 582
Sokolov, Sergei, 729
Sokolovskii, Vasilii D., 662, 665, 670–71, 680, 689
Solidarity (Polish trade union movement), 90, 229, 425, 888, 890; consequences of, for Soviet hegemony, 890; suppression of, 890–91
Solov'ev, Iurii, 348

Solzhenitsyn, Aleksandr, lxxii, 392
Somalia, 413, 439, 684
Somali-Ethiopian war, 432
Sotsialisticheskaia industriia (Socialist Industry), 381
South Africa, 438, 439, 605
Southern Group of Forces, 881
Southern Railroad, 557
South Korea. *See* Republic of Korea
South Ossetian Autonomous Oblast, 156
South Slavs, 7, 138, 146
South Yakut industrial complex, 489
South Yemen. *See* People's Democratic Republic of Yemen
Sovetskaia kul'tura (Soviet Culture), 382
Sovetskaia Rossiia (Soviet Russia), 380
Sovetskaya Gavan', 558
Soviet alliance system, 875–78
Soviet anthem, 339–40
Soviet army. *See* armed forces, Red Army
Soviet Asians, 127
Soviet-Bulgarian ferry line, 575
Soviet Central Asia, 100, 102, 107, 108, 123, 124, 130, 161, 162, 164, 168, 388, 514, 534, 561, 581, 727; agriculture in, 532, 536; area, 159; birth rates in, 118; climate of, 112; cotton grown in, 532; divorce rate in, 233; educational quality in, 261; electric generation in, 510; families in, 236, 238; fertility in, 121, 139; free trade zones in, 604; gas reserves in, 507; increase in infectious diseases in, 270; industrialization of agriculture in, 227; industry in, 497; infant mortality in, 116; irrigation projects in, 529; lack of electricity in, 510; metal industry in, 502; migration to cities in, 226; mosques in, 200–201; motherhood medals in, 236; nationalities in, 159–72; natural resources in, 488; population of, 159, 226; railroads in, 547; relocation of workers to, 490; resistance of residents of, to party membership, 324; rivers in, 527; steppes of, 110; Tatars in, 177; unofficial income in, 221–22
Soviet Copyright Agency, 409
Soviet-East European relations, 423–26
Soviet-East German ferry line, 575
Soviet-Egyptian Treaty of Friendship and Cooperation, 433
Soviet Europeans, 127
Soviet expansion: to create buffer zone, 79; prevention of, by Western allies, 79–80
Soviet Far East, 73, 108, 110, 125, 180, 546, 566, 567, 570, 572, 585, 721,725; Aeroflot service to, 578; agriculture in, 529; climate of, 112; economic development of, 479; electric generation in, 510, 511; exploitation of resources in, 611; forestry in, 538–39; free trade zones in, 604; lack of electricity in, 510; location of industry in, 488–89, 497; migra-

tion to and from, 122; poverty benefits in, 277; railroad construction in, 558; relocation of workers to, 490; rivers in, 567; roads in, 562
Soviet Far North, 124, 546; Aeroflot service to, 578; lack of road service facilities in, 565; location of industry in, 488
Soviet-Finnish relations, 419–20, 422–23
Soviet-Finnish War, 74, 473, 682, 699; role of railroads in, 550; Soviet casualties in, 699
Soviet flag, 339
Soviet-Indian relations, 429, 433, 435–36; Chinese antipathy to, 435; genesis of, 435; Soviet economic and military assistance, 435; Soviet technology transfer, 435–36; state visits between, 436
Soviet-Iraqi Treaty of Friendship and Cooperation (1972), 431
Soviet-Japanese relations, 427–28; origins of poor, 427–28
Soviet-Middle East relations, 430–33; with Iran, 431–32; with Iraq, 431–32; with Turkey, 430–31
Soviet Military Encyclopedia, 658, 668
Soviet of Nationalities, 333, 351; legislation passed by, 351; members of, 353; powers of, 353; purposes of, 353–54; status of, 353
Soviet of the Union, 333, 351, 356, 357; legislation passed by, 351; members of, 353; powers of, 353; purposes of, 353–54; status of, 353
Soviet Railroads (SZD), 554
Soviets, 213; sessions of provincial and district, 365
Soviet-Spanish relations, 422
Soviet-United States relations, 415–19; cold, 419; détente in, 416; effect on, of changes in Soviet leadership, 418; under Gorbachev, 418; nuclear threat as factor in, 415; under Reagan, 416; trade, 607–9
Soviet-West European relations, 419–23; with Britain, 421–22; with France, 420; goals in, 419; proper relationship between, 419–20; with Portugal, 422; with Scandinavia, 422–23; since World War II, 419; with Spain, 422; with West Germany, 420–21
sovkhozy. *See* state farms
Sovnarkom. *See* Council of People's Commissars
space, 611, 715; ban on nuclear weapons in, 442, 688; defenses, 715–16; objectives in, 688–89; race to the moon, 94; research, 623, 624; systems, 499; talks, 689; treaties proposed, 689; weapons development, 689
Spanish Civil War: Soviet support for, 73, 422
special departments (KGB), 775–76; criminal investigations, 775; duties of, 775; organization of, 775; political surveillance by, 775, 776; protecting state secrets, 776; under Stalin, 775

Special Purpose Forces (Spetsnaz), 719–20, 727; in Afghan war, 720; mission of, 720; number of, 720
Speranskii, Mikhail, 28
Spitak, 108
sports organizations, 230
Sputnik, 623, 689
SRs. *See* Socialist Revolutionary Party
Staar, Richard F., 664
Stalin, Joseph V., 44, 55, 67, 74, 82, 85, 139, 154, 183, 293, 295, 305, 342, 379, 385, 394, 522, 756; Academy of Sciences under, 625; *Anthem of the Soviet Union* composed under, 340; assigned to post of general secretary, 65; body of, removed from Lenin Mausoleum, 84; centralized planning under, 495; change of domestic policies by, in World War II, 75; Comecon under, 859; Comintern dissolved by, 414; compulsory labor under, 455; consolidation of power of, lviii, 66, 68, 759; control by, of Politburo, 299; control over science under, 633; cult of, 84, 88, 291, 295; death of, 81–82; denunciation of, by Khrushchev, 760; education under, 249; education programs established under, 243–44; elimination of NEP by, 68; environmental damage by, 113; family, strengthening of, under, 235; First Five-Year Plan, 68–69, 487; five-year plans of, 492; forced collectivization under, lviii, 213, 473, 519, 593, 758; forced industrialization under, lviii; foreign policy under, 72; Great Terror of, 392; health care programs established under, 243–44; industrial management system of, 485; instigation of Great Terror by, lviii; labor camps under, 389; legacy of, 82; Lenin's dislike of, 65; Marshall Plan aid refused by, 474; military-political relations under, 729; nation defined by, 195; nationalities policy under, 243; opposition of, to Nazi Germany, 73; opposition of, to social democrats, 72; opposition of, to Trotsky, 65; original name of, 156; partial rehabilitation of, 762; patronage system built by, 314; political police under, 755; position of, in Bolshevik government, 60; power of, 71; program of intensive construction under, 68; purges by, 55, 56, 78, 84, 213, 382, 626, 698, 759, 765; purges of party members by, lviii; religion under, 198–99, 200, 201; repression justified by, 78; reverence accorded, 71; "revolution from above," 68; Red Army under, 698; rise to power of, 66; Russification under, 196; science and technology under, 625–27; security police under, 786; "socialism in one country" proposed by, 66; socialist realism implemented under, lviii, 369, 371, 372; and Soviet constitution, 332, 362; Soviet expansion into Eastern Europe by, 79; special departments under, 775; territorial claims against Turkey by, 430; titles appropriated by, 291; war philosophy of, 658, 661; welfare programs established under, 243–44; Yugoslavia expelled from Cominform by, 414, 424
"Stalin Constitution" (of 1936), 333
Stalingrad (*see also* Volgograd): Soviet victory at, in World War II, 75, 550, 699
Stalin Prize, 214
State Agro-Industrial Committee, 524
State and Legal Department, 301, 769, 770, 785
State Bank, 35
State Commission on the Electrification of Russia, 547
State Committee for Cinematography. *See* Goskino
State Committee for Construction, 461; role of, in planning process, 461
State Committee for Foreign Economic Relations (GKES), 594, 600; functions of, 595, 596
State Committee for Foreign Tourism (Inturist), 409
State Committee for Labor and Social Problems, 275; role of, in planning process, 461
State Committee for Material and Technical Supply: role of, in planning process, 461
State Committee for Physical Culture and Sports, 230, 597
State Committee for Publishing Houses, Printing Plants, and the Book Trade. *See* Goskomizdat
State Committee for Science and Technology (GKNT), 597, 737, 600, 629, 637; functions of, 595, 629–30, 632; military research and development under, 647; role of, in planning process, 461
State Committee for Television and Radio Broadcasting (see Gostelradio)
State Committee for the Protection of Nature. *See* Goskompriroda
State Committee for the State of Emergency, lxxviii; decrees under, lxxviii–lxxix
State Committee for the Supply of Production Equipment for Agriculture, 524
State Committee for the Utilization of Atomic Energy, 376
State Committee on Prices, 595
State Council, lxxxi
State Examination Committee, 259
state farms (sovkhozy), lxii, 69, 118, 538; changes to, 521–22; conversion of collective farms to, 522; conversion of, to cooperatives, 522; defined, 521; income of, 521; labor productivity of, 521; military, 720; output of, 521; planning reform in, 466–67; self-financing of, 522
State Foreign Economic Commission, 595; role of, 597–99; upgrading of, 597

State Planning Commission. *See* Gosplan
State Police Department, 757
State Political Directorate (GPU); formed, 758; powers of, 758, 758
state secrets, censorship of, 374
Statsionar satellite system, 585
steppes, 104, 110; agriculture in, 527; chernozem soil of, 527; climate of, 527; described, 107; irrigation in, 527
Stockholm, 575
Stolypin, Petr, 46, 48; assassination of, 47; peasant reform program of, 47
Strategic Air Armies, 710-11; bombers of, 710-11; mission of, 710; organization of, 710
Strategic Arms Limitation Talks (SALT I), 91-92, 415, 442, 443, 686-87
Strategic Arms Limitation Talks (SALT II), 92, 416, 443
strategic arms reductions, 690
Strategic Arms Reduction Talks (START), lx, 417, 443, 687
Strategic Arms Reduction Treaty: described, lx; signing of, lx
Strategic Defense Initiative (SDI), 671, 688; Soviet reaction to, 688, 689
Strategic Rocket Forces, lxxvi, 661, 676, 697, 703-5, 733; downgraded, 678; general organization of, 703, 705; locations of, 705; mission of, 677, 703-5; as part of strategic nuclear forces, 678; purpose of, lxxvi; role of, 678, 703-5; uniforms and rank insignia of, 737-39; weapons of, 705
strategy. *See* military strategy
Stroganov family, 14, 486
Submarine Forces, 716-18; incursions into Scandinavia, 423; intelligence-gathering by, 716; kinds of vessels, 716-18; mission of, 716; number of vessels, 716
subtropical zone, agriculture in, 527
succession, leadership, 288, 304; stages in struggle for, 305-06
Sumgait, 202
Supreme Court, 329, 330, 335, 359
Supreme High Command (VGK), 677, 701, 703, 719, 727
Supreme Soviet, 195, 204, 272, 296, 304, 329, 330, 333, 334, 335, 338, 339, 341, 345, 350-58, 409, 670, 730, 765, 791-92; armed forces under, 700; authority of, 330, 350; authority of chairman of, 330; chairman of, 334, 352-53; chambers of, 333; commissions and committees, 355-57; delegation of powers by, 350; election to, 330; foreign policy responsibilities of, 408; function of, 350; and independence of republics, lxxi; legislative process in, 357-58; meetings of, 354; Ministry of Defense and, 702; new, after coup of 1991, lxxxi; new republics created by, 362; party controls, 358; party membership in,

358; planning function of, 462; powers of chairman of, 334; Presidium of, 351-52; procedures in sessions of, 354; selection of delegates to, 358; sequence of events in sessions of, 354; sessions of, 354-55; Soviet of Nationalities, 353-54; Soviet of the Union, 353-54; term of, 354
Surakhany, 547
Surgut, 502, 567
Suslov, Mikhail A., 94, 95, 299
Suvorov, Aleksandr, 28; science of victory, 654
Suvorov military schools, 257, 748
Suzdal' (*see also* Vladimir-Suzdal'), 8
Sverdlovsk, 506
Sverdlovsk Railroad, 557
Sweden, 14, 15, 21, 28, 78, 141, 149; attack by Peter the Great on, 20; Estonia controlled by, 151; Soviet relations with, 422; war between Russia and, 141
Switzerland: as importer of Soviet gas, 508; Russian military campaign in, 28
Synia, 558
Syr Darya, 527, 529
Syria, 91, 153, 432, 582, 712; privileged affiliation of, with Comecon, 616; military access to, 727; Soviet arms bought by, 614, 616, 779; Soviet trade with, 612, 614
Syrian army, 91
system of material balances, 461

Tabaka, Maya, 397
Tabasarans, 194
Table of Ranks, 21, 212
tactics. *See* military tactics
Tactics (Reznichenko), 675
Tadzhik Autonomous Republic, 162, 170
Tadzhikistan, 362; Afghan conquest of, 169-70; Russian conquest of, 170
Tadzhik language, 180
Tadzhik Republic, 102, 121-22, 159, 160, 434; families in, 236; major cities of, 170; nationalist movement in, 204; opposition to family planning in, 236; party apparatus in, 308
Tadzhiks, lxvi, 160-61, 162, 169-71, 194; distribution of, 170; etymology of, 169; grievances of, 204; in higher education, 170-71; history of, 169-70; language of, 170; as members of Central Committee, 171; as members of CPSU, 171, 324; Pamiri, 170; of the plain, 170; population of, 170; as scientific workers, 171; urbanization of, 170
Taganka Theater, 394
taiga zone, 104, 110, 526; agriculture in, 526; climate in, 526; described, 104-7, 526; forestry and fur industries in, 526
Taiwan, 86, 413
Tallin, 152, 540
Tamerlane, 155

tamizdat (underground literature published abroad), 389
Tank Troops, 707; uniforms and rank insignia of, 738–39
Tanzania, 438, 616
Taraki, Nur Muhammad, 434
Tartu, 152
Tashauz, 172
Tashkent, 162, 163, 427, 493, 578
TASS, 345, 373; operations of, 375
Tatar Autonomous Republic, 176, 177, 181
Tatar lands, 18
Tatar language, 166, 182
Tatars, 20, 24, 152, 162, 168, 173, 174, 175–77, 182; attempts to create independent state, 176; conversion of, to Islam, 192; distribution of, 176–77; in higher education, 177; history of, 175–76; languages of, 177; as members of Central Committee, 177; as members of CPSU, 177; as Muslims, 176, 194; population of, 176; urbanization of, 177
Tatars, Crimean, 175; attempt to establish independent state, 176; conquered by Russia, 175; emigration of, 176; exile of, during World War II, 176; national dissent movement of, 197; Russian repression of, 176
Tatars, Siberian, 175; conquered by Russia, 175; employment, 176; language, 177; population, 176
Tatars, Volga, 175; attempt to establish independent state, 176; conquered by Russia, 175; conversion to Christianity, 175; language of, 177; revolts against Russian rulers, 175
taxes: under Peter the Great, 22; to support economic plans, 469
Taymyr Peninsula, 101
Tbilisi, 156, 198, 497, 557, 561
teachers, 226, 251; education level of, 261; elite, 261; respect for, 260; salaries of, 217, 226, 261; women as, 261
teacher training, 260–61; focus of, 261; level of, 261
technicums, 256
technology (*see also* innovation): administration of, 628–33; for Comecon, 854, 863, 869; Comecon cooperation in, 869–70; commitment to, 623; directions of, 632; financing of, 632–33; high, 479, 608; implementation of plans for, 630; Khrushchev's reforms in, 627; literature abstracts, 633; long-term goals and, 624, 632; mixed results of commitment to, 623–24; planning for, 629–32; policy making for, 628–29; problems of, 624; short-term goals and, 624; under Stalin, 643
technology transfers: under Brezhnev, 643; by commercial sale, 643; by covert acquisition, 644; under Gorbachev, 644; impact of, 645; by industrial cooperation, 643–44; industries

using, 644–45; by intergovernmental agreement, 644; from Japan, 643; under Khrushchev, 643; under Lenin, 642–43; means of, 643–44; to overcome backwardness, 642; problems with, 645; by scholarly exchange, 644; from the United States, 643, 644, 645
telecommunications systems, 586
telegraph offices, 585
telephone, 546; exchanges, 585; government eavesdropping, 585; system, 585–86; underdeveloped, 586
telephones: number of, 586; requests for installation of, 586
television, 382–84, 546; audience, 382–83; coverage, 383–84; growth of, 582; ideological themes of, 384; industry, 514; programs on, 384; "Segodnia v mire," 383; "Vremia," 383
televisions, 499, 514
Tenth Five-Year Plan (1976–80), 477–78, 532
Tenth Party Congress, 64, 286, 293
Tereshkova, Valentina, 351
territorial administration, 361–66; administrative subdivisions, 361; district level, 364–65; of economy, 361; government, 363–64, 365; provincial level, 364–65; republic level, 362–64; of security, 361
territorial expansion, origins of, 3
testing facilities (scientific and technological): lack of, 639–40; organizational separation and, 638–39, 640
textile industry, 22, 503, 514–15; in nineteenth-century Russia, 33; origins of, 486
textiles, 615
Thailand, 437
Thatcher, Margaret, 422
theater, 388, 393–94; avant-garde, 393–94; conventional, 393; liberalization of, 394; performers, 393
theater of military operations (TVD), 669, 674, 678, 727, 729, 730; combined arms strategic operation in, 676, 677; continental, 672; deep offensive operation in, 673; defined, 672; oceanic, 672; strategic operation in, 679–80
thermonuclear fusion, 94
thermonuclear plants, 510, 511, 512
Third Chief Directorate (KGB), 733; responsibility of, 768, 775
Third Five-Year Plan (1938–41), 69, 473–74
Third Section, 30, 757
Third World (*see also* under individual countries), 585; agreements with, 413; arms transfers to, 890; characteristics of Soviet trade with, 612; Chinese attempt to influence, 90; deemphasis on Soviet influence in, 429; division of, between China and Soviet Union, 86; expansion of Soviet influence in, 90–91, 404, 416; Khrushchev's categories of, 428–29; Soviet aid to, 431, 446; Soviet arms and

military sales to, 612–13; Soviet conservative view of, 429; Soviet diplomacy in, 412; Soviet disagreements with, in United Nations, 445; Soviet influence in, 401, 407, 413, 429, 684, 889–90; Soviet military interventions in, 684; Soviet military presence in, 684–85; Soviet objectives in, 684; Soviet policy toward, 85–86, 428, 441; Soviet pragmatist view of, 429; Soviet reorientation of relations in, under Gorbachev, 438; Soviet support for, lx; Soviet trade with, lxiii, 591, 592, 612–18
Thirteenth Five-Year Plan (1991–95), 470
Tibet, 48
Tien Shan Mountains, 108
Tikhonov, Nikolai A., 316, 603
Tilsit, Treaty of, 28
Time of Troubles, 14–15, 17, 18; events in, 15; origins of, 14
Time of Wishes, A (Raizman), 391–92
Tinsulanonda, Prem, 437
Tiraspol', 498
Titarenko, Sergei M., 307
Tithe Church (Kiev), 7
Tito, Josip Broz, 80, 424
Tkachev, Petr, 40, 43
Tobol River, 182
Tobol'sk, 502, 567
Tolstaia, Tat'iana, 390
Tolstoi, Aleksei, 389, 390
Tolstoy, Lev, 39–40
Tol'yatti, 122, 497
Tomsk, 497, 503, 506, 567
topography and drainage, 104–9, 105–6
Toshiba scandal, 610
Townes, Charles H., 623
Trade, Ministry of, 597
Trade Reform Act of 1974 (United States), 608
trade unions: aim of, 228–29; membership, 456; operation of, 228; quota for deputies to Congress of People's Deputies, 348; socialist competitions organized by, 228–29; system, 228; and workers' interests, 229
trains: diesel-electric, 547–48, 554–56; electric, 554–56; freight cars, 548, 556; inventory, 556; maximum axle loads, 556; maximum speeds, 556; number of, 556; operating efficiency of, 548; passenger capacity, 556; passenger operations, 556–57; short-haul, 556; suburban, 556
Transbaykal (Zabaykaliye), 557, 727
Transcaucasian Federated Republic (1918), 153–54
Transcaucasian Soviet Federated Socialist Republic (1922–36), 64, 154, 155, 333, 412
Transcaucasus, 153, 514
Transcaucasus Military District, 727
transportation (*see also* transportation system), lxii, lxiii; automobiles, lxiii; party influence in, lxix; purpose of, lxiii; railroads, lxiii; trucks, lxiii

transportation enterprises, 565
transportation system: air, 546; automotive, 545; density of, 545; disruptions of, in Soviet-Finnish War, 473; expansion of, 530; freight, 565; local, 561; inadequacy of, 530; influences on development of, 545; output of, as percentage of net material product, 453; passenger, 565–66, 570, 572, 545; water, 545–46
Trans-Siberian Railway, 41, 42, 44, 124, 489, 557, 558
treaties, 412, 413–14; with Egypt, 684; military, 414; purposes of, 413; with Third World, 413
Treaty of Mutual Assistance and Cooperation (Finnish-Soviet), 423
Treaty on the Nonproliferation of Nuclear Weapons (1968), 91, 421
Tret'iakov Gallery, 396
Trifonov, Iurii, 94
Triple Entente, 48, 50
troika of Kamenev, Stalin, and Zinov'ev, 65–66
Trotsky, Leon, 65, 67, 68, 180; as chairman of Petrograd Soviet, 59; as commissar of war, 61, 698; exiled by Stalin, 66; jailed after "July Days," 59; Kronshtadt Rebellion put down by, 63; murder of, 70; position of, in Bolshevik government, 60; Red Army organized by, 61; troika's opposition to, 65, 66
trucks, 545, 561; failure of, factors contributing to, 565; freight on, 561; importance of, to local transportation systems, 561; local and short hauls, 565; most important customers of, 565; use of, lxiii
Trud (Labor); circulation of, 380; focus of, 380
Truman Doctrine, 80
Trushin, Vasilii P., 785
Trust, 743–45
"Trust in Cadres," 89
trusts, 453
tsars (*see also* under individual names), 4; end of rule of, 57; Ivan III as first, 12, 13
Tsiolkovskii, Konstantin E., 625
Tsushima Straits, 44
Tsvigun, Semen, 762
tuberculosis, 269
Tukhachevskii, Mikhail N., 672
Tula, 533
tundra zone, 104, 526; agriculture in, 526; area of, 526; climate of, 526; described, 104, 526; employers in, 104; frost weathering in, 104; percentage of Soviet population in, 104; reindeer herding in, 526; vegetation of, 104
Turan Lowland, 104
Turgenev, Ivan, 31, 39, 40
Turkestan, 160, 161, 168, 176
Turkestan Autonomous Republic, 162, 167, 170; Soviet organization of, 162
Turkestan Military District, 725, 727
Turkestan-Siberian Railway, 547

Turkey, 28, 61, 80, 101, 153, 155, 157, 171, 174, 423, 430–31; as importer of Soviet gas, 508; Soviet economic assistance to, 431; Soviet territorial claims against, 430–31; Soviet trade with, 612, 613; United States arms embargo against, 431
Turkic languages, 168, 182
Turkic tribes, 156–57, 160, 176
Turkish army, 158
Turkmenia, 171, 172, 362
Turkmenistan, 171, 362
Turkmen lands, 38
Turkmen Republic, 102, 121, 159, 160, 162, 434, 527; gas reserves in, 507; infant mortality in, 116; life expectancy in, 116; major cities in, 172; nationalist movement in, 204; party apparatus in, 307, 308
Turkmens, lxx, 160, 162, 166, 171–72; distribution of, 172; forced collectivization of, 172; grievances of, 204; in higher education, 172; history of, 171; as members of CPSU, 172, 324; language of, 172; national resurgence of, 172; population of, 172; opposition of, to Russian rule, 171; Russian conquest of, 171; as scientific workers, 172; urbanization of, 172; Uzbek conquest of, 171
Tuvinians, 184
Tver', 12
Twelfth Five-Year Plan (1986–90), 478–82, 492, 494, 515, 540–42; agricultural targets, 541–42; computerization goals, 384–85; conservation emphasized in, 541; consumer goods in, 502, 514; energy goals under, 511; first-year results of, 482–81; goals of, 495, 496; increase in food prices in, 525; increase in preschool facilities in, 251; principal tasks of, 478; second-year results of, 482; targets for, 480–81, 540; technical progress in, 481; telecommunications goals, 384–85
Twentieth Party Congress, 82–84, 295, 424, 661; Khrushchev's "secret speech," 627, 761
Twenty-Fifth Party Congress, 125, 440
Twenty-First Party Congress, 84
Twenty-Fourth Party Congress, 197
Twenty-Second Party Congress, 84
Twenty-Seventh Party Congress, 427, 444, 730; Chebrikov's KGB speech to, 764; Comecon as "socialist commonwealth," 423, 425; delegates to, 293; discussion of Warsaw Pact in, 892; foreign policy goals, 402; Gorbachev's call for *glasnost'* and *perestroika*, 295, 451, 525, 597; price reform under, 618; member turnover at, 297; pronatalist policy, 125; technology policy, 492, 603; Third World relations, 438; women elected at, 324
Twenty-Sixth Party Congress, 125, 297, 427
Twenty-Third Party Congress, 88
Tynda, 558
Tyuman oil fields, 505–6

Tyumenskaya Oblast, 102

U-2 shoot-down, 87
Ufa, 182–83, 201, 502
Ukraine, 5, 10, 12, 24, 25, 30, 42, 61, 145, 178; economic region, 503; partition of, 142; Soviet republic established in, 61; split between Muscovy and Poland, 18, 141; western, incorporated by Soviet Union in 1939, lviii, 200
Ukrainian Academy of Sciences, 640, 641
Ukrainian Autocephalous Orthodox Church, 188–89, 199; Soviet government's hostility toward, 189, 200; origins of, 188–89
Ukrainian party organization: Khrushchev as head of, 82
Ukrainian Republic, 5, 64, 74, 102, 107, 123, 125, 138, 141, 145, 147, 154, 188, 307, 333, 362, 412, 526, 527; agriculture in, 532–34; alcoholism in, 270; Catholics in, 199–200; establishment of, 142; families in, 236; famine in, 196; forced collectivization of, 142; gas reserves in, 507; Helsinki watch group established in, 197; industry in, 486; irrigation projects in, 529; Jewish community in, 178, 180; legal age for marriage in, 232; major cities in, 144; nationalities in, 146; nationalist demonstrations in, 202–4; nationalist movement suppressed in, 759; occupation of, by German army, 74–75, 142; party apparatus in, 308; population decline, 127; population density, 124; Roman Catholic community in, 190. 204; Russification in, 204; starvation of peasants in, 69, 142; tree farms in, 475
Ukrainians, 3, 5, 8, 24, 27, 36, 138, 141–44, 164, 166, 168, 174; deportation of, by Nazis, 76; discrimination against, 48, 142; distribution of, 144; enserfed by Polish rulers, 141; in higher education, 144; history of, 141; influence of, on Muscovy, 18–19; influence of Polish rule on, 141; language of, 35, 204; language of, prohibited, 35; as members of CPSU, 144, 324; as members of Central Committee, 144; national assertiveness by, 141, 142, 202–4; oppression of, by Polish nobility, 141; oppression of, by Russian government, 141–42; persecution of Catholic, 200; population of, 144; as scientific workers, 144; struggle of, for independence, 143, 144; urbanization of, 144
Ukrainization, 142
Ulan-Ude, 493
Ulbricht, Walter, 889
Ulianov, Aleksandr, 41
Ulianov, Vladimir (*see also* Lenin, Vladimir I.), 41; exiled, 43; influence of Chernyshevskii on, 41
underprovisioning, 221, 274, 277
unemployment, 490

Uniate Church, 190; suppression of, 30, 145
Unified Electrical Power System, 511
Unified Science and Technology Department, 630
union agreement of 1991, lxx; republics refusing to join, lxx
Union of Brest, 190
Union of Cinematographers, 390; Disputes Committee of, 390
Union of Journalists, 378
Union of Liberation, 45
Union of Unions, 45–46
Union of Writers, 370, 372, 382, 385, 774; conservative views in, 389–90; Eighth Congress of, 389–90; liberal changes in, 389
union republics (*see also* republics and under individual republics): civil defense in, 721; defined, 102; desire of, for autonomy, lxx; determinants for status as, 102, 196; independence declared by, lxx–lxxi; minority nationalities in, lxx; nationalities in, 135–36, 137; proclamations of independence by, lxx; status as, lxvi
union treaty, lxx–lxxi, lxxix
United Arab Emirates, 432
United Deep-Water Network, 568
united front, 415, 429
United Nations, 445–46; condemnation by, of Soviet invasion of Afghanistan, 434, 445; condemnation by, of Vietnamese occupation of Cambodia, 445; Gorbachev's arms reductions announcement in, 444; involvement of, in Korean War, 81, 445; permanent members, 445; Soviet boycott of, 445; Soviet financial contributions to, 446; Soviet role in establishing, 445; United States contributions withheld from, 446; voting in, 413, 445
United Socialist Revolutionary Party, 43
United States, 45, 56, 121, 433, 435, 439, 457, 497, 526, 539, 548, 561, 562, 671; agricultural exports to Soviet Union, 608; Army, strategy of, 680; assistance of, to Soviet Union in World War II, 75, 550; and Cold War, 79; debt payments to, 606; destruction of targets in, 677; diplomatic recognition by, of Soviet Union, 412; diplomatic recognition withheld from Soviet Union, 67; diplomatic support of, for Iran, 79; emigration to, lxxiv; establishing relations with Japan, 37; influence of, in Middle East, 430, 432; involvement of, in Korean War, 81; involvement of, in Civil War (Russia's), 61; Limited Test Ban Treaty signed by, 87, 688; Marxist-Leninist view of, 655; as member of United Nations, 445–46; nuclear parity of, with Soviet Union, 401, 681, 699; nuclear weapons of, 691; recognition by, of independence of Baltic states, lxxxi; relations of, with Egypt, 91; relations of, with Soviet Union,

91–92, 401; role of, in putting down Boxer Rebellion, 44; Russian relations with, 36; Soviet support from, in World War II, 76–77; Soviet attempts to limit influence of, 441; Soviet Buying Commission in, 593; Soviet trade with, lxiii, 605, 607–9; START talks, 687; technology transfers from, 645; trade boycott of Soviet Union by, 601, 609; trade policy of, 608; as world power, 32
universities, lxiv–lxv; competition for entrance to, 258; enrollment, 258; graduate training in, 260; mission of, 258; restricted under Alexander II, 35
Unkiar-Skelessi, Treaty of, 32
Ural-Kuznetsk industrial complex, 547
Ural Mountains, 33, 45, 99, 101, 104, 107, 124, 139, 487, 550, 581, 705, 721; coal reserves in, 508; forestry in, 538; location of industry in, 488, 490, 493, 497, 501, 503; metal industry in, 502; natural resources in, 112–13, 506; railroads in, 553
Ural River, 182
uranium, 510
urbanization, 121–22, 125, 127, 130, 224; and control over migration, 122; distribution of, among regions and nationalities, 121–22; and gender roles, 230; rates of, 121–22; of rural life, 224
urban society: culture, 224; economy, 224; housing conditions, 224; and rural society, differences between, 224–25; state retail outlets in, 456; travel, 225; workers with peasant backgrounds in, 227
Urengoy, 502, 558; gas reserves in, 507, 581
Urengoy-Uzhgorod pipeline, 609, 610; foreign technology acquired for, 644–45
Urengoy-Yamburg rail line, 558
Uruguay, 441
Usinsk, 558
uskorenie (acceleration), 597
Ussuri River, 37, 90, 426, 723
Ust'-Ilimsk, 511
Ust'-Kut, 558
Uvarov, Sergei, 30
Uygurs, 194
Uzbekistan, 362
Uzbek Khan, 160
Uzbek Republic, 102, 121, 159, 160, 162, 166, 170, 177, 362, 434, 527; agriculture in, 534; cities in, 163; cotton grown in, 532; families in, 238; gas reserves in, 507; infant mortality in, 116; nationalities in, 168; party apparatus in, 308; population of, 162; opposition to family planning in, 236
Uzbeks, lxvi, 168, 170; alphabet of, 163; ancient history of, 160; conquest by, of Turkmens, 171; distribution of, 162; divorce of, 233; in higher education, 163; language of, 163, 166; medieval history of, 160–61; as

members of the Central Committee, 163; as members of CPSU, 163; modern history of, 161–62; as Muslims, 194; population of, 162; as scientific workers, 163; urbanization of, 163

Uzhgorod, 581

Vanino, 575

Varangians, 138; described, 5; Oleg, 5; role of, in establishing Kievan Rus', 5–6; Rurik, 5

Varna, 575

Vasilii III, 12

veche (popular assembly), 8

Vecheka, 60, 547; abolished, 758; described, 755; growth of, 757–58

Venezuela, 440

Ventspils, 580

Verdun, 49

Verkhnyaya Pyshma, 506

Verkhoyansk Range, 107

Vernyy, 108

Veterinary Troops, 739

victory, 692; combined arms for, 677; objective, 659; and weapons, relationship between, 659

video cassette recorders, 384, 385, 499

Vienna, 592

Vietnam, 90, 407, 414, 423, 426, 427, 430, 433, 440, 612; as burden on Comecon, 871; Chinese incursion into, 426; Comecon aid to, 871; labor transfers from, 870; as member of Comecon, 601, 603, 854, 871; military access to, 727–28; Soviet and East European military advisers in, 684; occupation by, of Cambodia, 437; power of, in Comecon, 871; satellite communications hookup to, 582; Soviet economic aid to, 591, 592, 605; Soviet economic relations with, 612; Soviet military bases in, 603, 685; Soviet support for, lx; Soviet ties with, 437; war, 91, 404, 571; withdrawal of troops from Cambodia, 604

village, defined, 224

Vilnius, 147, 148

Vinnitsa district, 311

virgin land campaign, 87, 303, 475, 522

Vladimir (*see also* Vladimir-Suzdal'), 8, 9, 186, 497, 585

Vladimir (Prince): accomplishments of, 7; Christianization of Kievan Rus' under, 7, 186

Vladimir-Suzdal', 8, 9, 10, 12

Vladivostok, 122, 540, 727; building of Russian naval base at, 37; Gorbachev's speech in, 435, 728

Vlasov, Aleksandr V., 763, 783

Vneshniaia torgovlia (Foreign Trade), 600

Vneshtorgbank, 611

vocational-technical schools, 256

vodka, 93

voenkomat (military commissariat), 743, 746, 750

Voennaia mysl' (Military Thought), 670

Voice of America, 382

Voinovich, Vladimir, lxxii

Volga automotive plant, 497–98

Volga-Don canal, 567

Volga Economic Region, 502

Volga-Kama waterways, 569

Volga River, 5, 8, 9, 14, 18, 108, 122, 124, 181, 182, 183, 567, 568, 581; hydroelectric system on, 108

Volga River Valley, 18, 113, 475, 527, 699

Volga-Ural region, 175, 176, 581; gas reserves in, 507; oil fields in, 505

Volgograd (*see also* Stalingrad), 75, 124, 497, 506

Volhynia, 141

Volkogonov, Dmitrii A., 659, 663

Vologda, 124

Voluntary Society for Assistance to the Army, Air Force, and Navy (DOSAAF), 730; organization of, 742; premilitary training by, 739; specialist training in, 742

Vorkuta, 558

Voronezh, 497

Voroshilov General Staff Academy, 749

Voslensky, Michael, 315

vospitanie (upbringing), 245

voting, 333; as duty, 348; for deputies in Congress of People's Deputies, 347, 348

Voznesenskii, Andrei, 388, 389, 390

"Vremia," 383; audience, 383; format, 383

VUZy. *See* education, higher

Vyborg, 506

Vysotskii, Vladimir, 94, 393–94; grave of, 395

wages: effect of reform on, 470–71; egalitarian, 470; minimum, 470, 471; as tool of economic control, 470

war (*see also* nuclear war): arms control to avoid, 686, 691; avoidability of, 654, 661; combined arms offensive in, 671, 675, 676; as continuation of politics, lxxvi, 654, 655–57, 667; fought with conventional weapons, 663, 671, 673; guidelines for categorizing, 655; inevitability of, 653, 661; just, 655, 657; Marxist-Leninist theory of, 654–59; mobilization for, 750; of national liberation, 681, 780; as outcome of class struggle, 655; unjust, 655; world, doctrine of fighting, 661, 681

war, laws of, 657–69, 668; combat power, 668; with conventional weapons, 668; defined, 657; dependence of the forms of war on people and equipment, 668; Marxism-Leninism as basis for discovering, 657; mutability of,

657, 668; with nuclear weapons, 668; objective victory, 658–59; permanently operating factors in, 658; as political philosophy of CPSU, 657; and principles of military art, 666; reordering of, 658; Savkin's, 658

War and Peace (Tolstoy), 40

war communism, 68, 472; defined, 63; economy under, 63; and Kronshtadt Rebellion, 63, 64; results of, 63

War Industries Committee, 50, 51

Warsaw, Grand Duchy of, 28

Warsaw Pact, 90, 424, 444, 510, 608, 693, 714, 727, 749, 875–92; arms reductions by, 663, 692; arms transfers by, 890; cohesion in, 881–82, 888–91; Committee of Ministers of Defense, 886; as counterweight to NATO, 875, 878; cuts by, in military budget, 445; in deep offensive operation, 680, 888; defense-oriented military doctrine of, 663, 892; defined, 86; détente and, 888–91; dissolution of, lx; East European participation in, 875; and end of détente, 891; formation of, 860, 878–80; function of, 875; under Gorbachev, 892; invasion of Czechoslovakia by, 425, 442, 882–83; Joint Command of, 879, 886; Joint Staff of, 886–87; under Khrushchev, 879–80, 881–82; leadership of, 886; as legitimation of status quo, 888–89; meetings of, 885, 886; members of, 423, 692, 876; Military Council, 886; military exercises of, 882–83, 889, 890; military organization of, 882, 885–87; Military Scientific- Technical Council, 887; military tasks of, 885; and Ministry of Defense, 702; NATO as threat to, 891; policy coordination in, 888; political Consultative Committee of, 879, 884–85; problems in, 875; relations of, with NATO, 403, 419; Soviet control of, 885–86; 887; and Soviet military strategy, 885, 887–88; Soviet reevaluation of, after 1956 revolutions, 881–82, 888; Technical Committee, 887; as tool in East-West diplomacy, 879; treaty establishing, 879; structural changes in, 886

Warsaw Television Plant, 514

Washington Summit: of 1987, 418, 419; of 1990, lx

Watergate scandal, 404

water resources, 108–9; inland bodies, 109

weapons, 339; antisatellite (ASAT), 688–89; buildup of conventional, 692; conventional, improved, 675; customers for, 614, 618; development programs, 666; export of, 613–14, 615; limited by treaty, 686; nuclear, biological, and chemical (NBC), 709–10; prepositioning of, 685; Soviet strategic, 687; transfers, 410; United States strategic, 687; and victory, relationship between, 659

Wehrmacht, 699

welding technology, 623

welfare programs: family subsidies, 276–77; under Khrushchev, 243–44; maternity benefits, 276; pension system, 274–75; under Stalin, 243–44; total-care facilities, 275; types of, 243; workers' compensation, 276

Western culture, lxvii; defined, 4; influence of, on Russian culture, 4, 19; progress of modernization in, 4

Western Europe, 121, 581, 664, 781; fuel exports to, 606, 612; grain imports from, 608; KGB-sponsored terrorism in, 779; missiles aimed at, 705; Soviet relations with, 401; Soviet trade with, 609–10; trade boycott of Soviet Union by, 601; war scenario in, 680

Western Front (World War I), 49

Westernization: under Alexander I, 29; under Catherine II, 25, 26; under Elizabeth I, 23; Peter the Great's drive for, 22

Westernizers, 30

Western technology, lvii, 623; imports of, 592; interest of tsars in, 19; military, 36; Soviet import of, lxiii

West Germany. *See* Federal Republic of Germany

West Siberia Economic Region, 502, 503

West Siberian Plain, 104

West Slavs, 138, 146

West Turkic-Kipchak languages, 177

What Is to Be Done? (Chernyshevskii), 40

What Is to Be Done? (Lenin), 43, 283

White armies, 142, 167, 171, 176; defeat of, 62–63; professional officers in, 698; rights of, denied under constitution, 332; supported by Allied Powers, 61

White Sea, 10, 567

Wilhelm II (Kaiser), 38

Winter War. *See* Soviet-Finnish War

Witte, Sergei, 46, 47, 48; dismissal of, 42, 46; economic programs of, 41; and evacuation of Manchuria, 44; results of policies of, 42; Russo-Chinese Bank established by, 44

women, 391–92; as agricultural workers, lxii, 217; in armed forces, 747–48; burdens of, lxvi; child care by, 265; death following abortion or childbirth, 271; equal rights of, lxvi, 212, 230–31; health care of, 266; in the labor force, 477; in higher education, 258; low status of, 231; maternity benefits for, 234, 243, 276; maternity leave for, lxvi, 130, 231, 276; medals and payments to mothers with large families, 235, 236; medical care of, 231; medical education of, 35; as members of Central Committee, 324; as members of CPSU, 231, 322, 324; occupations of, 212, 221, 231; percentage of, in work force, 119, 120; as physicians, 221, 268; protection of, in workplace, 231; reasons of, for not joining party, 324; salaries of, 221, 231; social status of, 212; status of, lxvi; subsidies to, with more than two children, 276; surplus of, 119; as teachers, 261; time spent on housework by, 232

wood industries, 514–15, 539, 611

workers, 48, 51, 214; blue-collar, lxv, 211; motivation of, 479; number of, 454; pay of, lxv; productivity of, 479; white-collar, lxv

workers, agricultural: children of, in higher education, 258; defined, 217; as party members, 217, 323; as percentage of population, 217; position of children of, 211; wages and benefits of, 217, 220

workers, white-collar, 211, 216–17; children of, in higher education, 258; income of, 216, 220; as members of CPSU, 216, 323; number of, 216; position of children of, 211; privileges of, 216; in rural areas, 226

Workers' and Peasants' Red Army, 698

workers' compensation: maternity leave, 276; sick leave, 276

workers' insurance organizations, 47

work force: distribution of, 455–56, 485, 490; health care to guarantee, 262–63; laxness of, 479; and *perestroika*, 490–91; redistribution of, 489–90; shift in nature of, 490

working-age population, 454

working class, 42, 48, 331

World Bank, 619

World Peace Council, 407, 779

world revolution, 412, 681

world socialist system, lxxvi, 401, 414, 683, 697; and Comecon, 857; and Soviet political influence, 684; Soviet Union as leader of, 878

World War I, 4, 61, 147, 179, 472; Bolshevik refusal to pay debts from, 593; disengagement by Soviet government from, 60; impact of, on Russia, 56–57; initial phase of, 49, 50; land ceded by Russia in, 61; Russia's offensives in, 49; Russian casualties in, 50; strains of, 50–51

World War II, 82, 101, 139, 145, 150, 183, 200, 290, 291, 342, 401, 415, 421, 422, 424, 474, 475, 494, 571, 572, 580, 610, 626, 659, 661, 699, 733, 875, 877; Allied assistance in, to Soviet Union, 75, 77; automotive production during, 562; automotive transportation during, 562; beginning of, 73; church used in, to arouse patriotism, 198–99; Crimean Tatars exiled during, 176; depletion of male population in, 226; deportation of nationalities during, 196; diplomatic recognition of Soviet Union during, 412; domestic policies changed to increase support for, 75, 198–99; early Soviet losses in, 74; effect of, on population, 118–19; effect of Stalin's purges on success in, 84, 699, 759; friction among Allies in, 77; German victories in, 75; inland navigation in, 566–67; Internal Troops in,

794; maritime fleet in, 566–67; military political relations after, 729; patriotic films on, 384; recovery from, 451; Red Army in, lviii; role of Internal Troops in, 723; role of railroad in, 550–52; science and technology during, 626–27; Soviet deaths in, lviii, 77, 699; Soviet civil aviation in, 577; Soviet lack of preparation for, 74; Soviet material losses in, 77–78; Soviet strategy in, 672; Soviet trade during, 593; Soviet victory at Stalingrad, 75; Soviet victory in, 75; use of German technology during, 643; trade boycott of Soviet Union after, 601; and transfer of industry to Asian part of Soviet Union, 487, 490

Yakut Autonomous Republic, 529
Yakut Basin, 509
Yakutiya, 558, 567, 611
Yakuts, 184
Yakutsk, 110, 112
Yalta Conference, 77
Yamal Peninsula, 507, 558
Yamburg, 507, 558
Yanov, Alexander, 310
Yaroslavl', 12
Yeltsin, Boris N.: action by, after coup of 1991, lxxx; career of, lxviii; opposition by, to coup, lxxix; ouster of, as Moscow party chief, 764–65; political agenda of, lxviii; popularity of, lxviii; resignation by, from CPSU, lxviii
Yemen Arab Republic (North Yemen), 432; Soviet arms bought by, 614
Yenisey River, 18, 104, 109, 122, 167, 526, 567
Yerevan, 115, 154, 202
Yiddish, 180, 201
Young Octobrists, 229, 230, 246
Young Turks, 157
youth organizations: activities of, 246; description of, 229–30; Komsomol, 229, 230, 246; Pioneers, 229, 230, 246; purpose of, 246; Young Octobrists, 229, 230, 246
Yugoslavia, 80, 86, 407, 414, 424, 878, 884; Soviet trade with, 591, 603–4; ties to Comecon, 603, 855

Zalygin, Sergei, 388
Zambia, 438
zampolit (deputy commander for political affairs), 748, 877; power of, 733; responsibilities of, 731–32
Zankov, Leonid V., 249
Zaporozh'ye, 497, 501
Za rubezhom (Abroad), 381
zemskii sobor (national assembly), 15
zemstvos, 34, 35, 36, 45, 46, 50
Zeravshan River, 527
zero option, 416–17
Zeya River Valley, 529

Zhdanov, 501
Zhdanov, Andrei, 78, 81
Zhdanovshchina, 78
Zheng Toubin, 604
Zhilin, Pavel A., 617
Zhivkov, Todor, 892

Zhukov (Marshal), 82, 84
Zimbabwe, 438, 616
Zinov'ev, Grigorii V., 65, 66, 180; accused of
 murdering Kirov, 70; in show trials, 70
Zionism, 201
Zukov, Georgii K., 729

Published Country Studies

(Area Handbook Series)

550–65	Afghanistan	550–87	Greece
550–98	Albania	550–78	Guatemala
550–44	Algeria	550–174	Guinea
550–59	Angola	550–82	Guyana and Belize
550–73	Argentina	550–151	Honduras
550–169	Australia	550–165	Hungary
550–176	Austria	550–21	India
550–175	Bangladesh	550–154	Indian Ocean
550–170	Belgium	550–39	Indonesia
550–66	Bolivia	550–68	Iran
550–20	Brazil	550–31	Iraq
550–168	Bulgaria	550–25	Israel
550–61	Burma	550–182	Italy
550–50	Cambodia	550–30	Japan
550–166	Cameroon	550–34	Jordan
550–159	Chad	550–56	Kenya
550–77	Chile	550–81	Korea, North
550–60	China	550–41	Korea, South
550–26	Colombia	550–58	Laos
550–33	Commonwealth Caribbean, Islands of the	550–24	Lebanon
550–91	Congo	550–38	Liberia
550–90	Costa Rica	550–85	Libya
550–69	Côte d'Ivoire (Ivory Coast)	550–172	Malawi
550–152	Cuba	550–45	Malaysia
550–22	Cyprus	550–161	Mauritania
550–158	Czechoslovakia	550–79	Mexico
550–36	Dominican Republic and Haiti	550–76	Mongolia
550–52	Ecuador	550–49	Morocco
550–43	Egypt	550–64	Mozambique
550–150	El Salvador	550–35	Nepal and Bhutan
550–28	Ethiopia	550–88	Nicaragua
550–167	Finland	550–157	Nigeria
550–155	Germany, East	550–94	Oceania
550–173	Germany, Fed. Rep. of	550–48	Pakistan
550–153	Ghana	550–46	Panama

550–156	Paraguay	550–53	Thailand
550–185	Persian Gulf States	550–89	Tunisia
550–42	Peru	550–80	Turkey
550–72	Philippines	550–74	Uganda
550–162	Poland	550–97	Uruguay
550–181	Portugal	550–71	Venezuela
550–160	Romania	550–32	Vietnam
550–37	Rwanda and Burundi	550–183	Yemens, The
550–51	Saudi Arabia	550–99	Yugoslavia
550–70	Senegal	550–67	Zaire
550–180	Sierra Leone	550–75	Zambia
550–184	Singapore	550–171	Zimbabwe
550–86	Somalia		
550–93	South Africa		
550–95	Soviet Union		
550–179	Spain		
550–96	Sri Lanka		
550–27	Sudan		
550–47	Syria		
550–62	Tanzania